routard

Provence & the Côte d'Azur

**The ultimate
food, drink and
accommodation guide**

HACHETTE

Contents

Provence
& the
Côte d'Azur

routard

Managing editor: Liz Coghill
English translation: Jane Moseley,
Vanessa Dowell
Editorial: Jane Franklin, Hilary Hughes

Additional research and assistance: Sofi
Mogensen, Jane Moseley, Kate Williams
Index: Dorothy Frame

Series director: Philippe Gloaguen
Series creators: Philippe Gloaguen, Michel
Duval
Chief editor: Pierre Josse
Assistant chief editor: Benoît Lucchini
Coordination director: Florence
Charmetant

Editorial team: Yves Couprie, Olivier Page,
Véronique de Chardon, Amanda Keravel,
Isabelle Al Subaihi, Anne-Caroline Dumas,
Carole Bordes, Bénédicte Bazaille, André
Poncelet, Jérôme de Gubernatis, Marie
Burin des Roziers and Thierry Brouard.

Our guides provide independent advice. The authors and compilers do not accept any remuneration for the inclusion of addresses in this guide. Please note that we cannot accept any responsibility for any loss, injury or inconvenience sustained by anyone as a result of any information or advice contained in this guide.

Feedback

We have done our best to ensure the accuracy of the information contained in this guide. However, addresses, phone numbers, opening times etc. do invariably change from time to time, so if you find a discrepancy please do let us know and help us update the guides. As prices may change so may other circumstances – a restaurant may change hands or the standard of service at a hotel may deteriorate since our researchers made their visit. Again, we do our best to ensure information is accurate, but if you notice any discrepancy, please let us know. You can contact us at: hachetteuk@orionbooks.co.uk or write to us at Cassell & Co, address below.

Price guide

Because of rapid inflation in many countries, it is impossible to give an accurate indication of prices in hotels and restaurants. Prices can change enormously from one year to the next. As a result we have adopted a system of categories for the prices in the guides: 'Budget', 'Moderate', 'Chic' and 'Très Chic' (in the guides to France), otherwise 'Expensive' and 'Splash out' in the others.

First published in the United Kingdom in 2002 by Cassell & Co
© English Translation Cassell & Co 2002
© Hachette Livre (Hachette Tourisme) 2001
© Cartography Hachette Tourisme

Distributed in the United States of America by Sterling Publishing Co., Inc.
387 Park Avenue South, New York, NY 10016-8810.

A CIP catalogue for this book is available from the British Library.

ISBN 1 84202 019 6

Typeset at The Spartan Press Ltd, Lymington, Hants.
Printed and bound by Aubin, France. E-mail: sales@aubin-imprimeur.fr

Cover design by Emmanuel Le Vallois (Hachette Livre) and Paul Cooper.
Cover photo © Hachette Tourisme. Back cover photo © Hachette Tourisme.

Cassell & Co, Wellington House, 125 Strand, London WC2R 0BB

THE RHÔNE VALLEY AND HAUTE-PROVENCE 219

THE ALPES-DE-HAUTE-PROVENCE 344

THE CÔTE D'AZUR 405–732

PROVENCE-BY-THE-SEA 405

THE GULF OF ST-TROPEZ AND THE PAYS DES MAURES 459

THE HINTERLAND OF THE VAR REGION 504

THE COASTLINE FROM ST-RAPHAËL TO NICE AND THE HINTERLAND 536

Just Exactly Who or What is a Routard?

You are. Yes, you! The fact that you are reading this book means that you are a Routard. You are probably still none the wiser, so to explain we will take you back to the origin of the guides. Routard was the brainchild of a Frenchman named Philippe Gloaguen, who compiled the first guide some 25 years ago with his friend Michel Duval. They simply could not find the kind of guide book they wanted and so the solution was clear – they would just have to write it themselves. When it came to naming the guide, Philippe came up with the term Routard, which at the time did not exist as a bona fide word – at least, not in conventional dictionary terms. Today, if you look the word up in a French-English dictionary you will find that it means 'traveller' or 'globetrotter' – so there you have it, that's what you are!

From this humble beginning has grown a vast collection of some 100 titles to destinations all over the world. Routard is now the bestselling guide book series in France. The guides have been translated into five different languages, so keep an eye out for fellow Routard readers on your travels.

What exactly do the guides do?
The short answer is that they provide all the information you need to enable you to have a successful holiday or trip. Routards' great strength however, lies in their listings. The guides provide comprehensive listings for accommodation, eating and drinking – ranging from campsites and youth hostels through to four star hotels – and from bars, clubs and greasy spoons to tearooms, cafés and restaurants. Each entry is accompanied by a detailed and frank appraisal of the address, rather like a friend coming back from holiday who is recommending all the good places to go (or even the places to avoid!). The guides aim to help you find the best addresses and the best value for money within your price range, whilst giving you invaluable insider advice at the same time.

Anything else?
Routard also provides oceans of practical advice on how to get along in the country or city you are visiting plus an insight into the character and customs of the people. How do you negotiate your way around the transport system? Will you offend if you bare your knees in the temple? And so on. In addition, you will find plenty of sightseeing information, backed up by historical and cultural detail, interesting facts and figures, addresses and opening times. The humanitarian aspect is also of great importance, with the guides commenting freely and often pithily, and most titles contain a section on human rights.

Routard are truly useful guides that are convivial, irreverent, down-to-earth and honest. We very much hope you enjoy them and that they will serve you well during your stay.

Happy travelling.

Note: all place names in bold are covered in this guide.

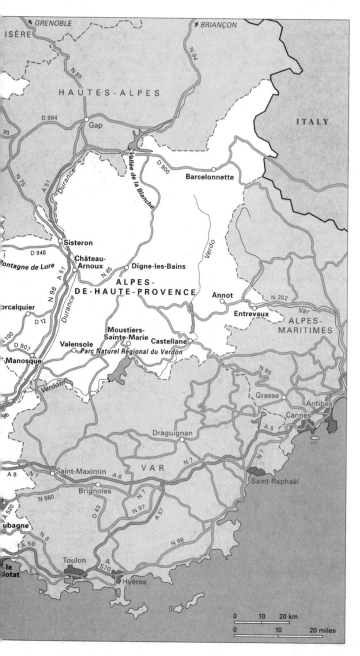

PROVENCE

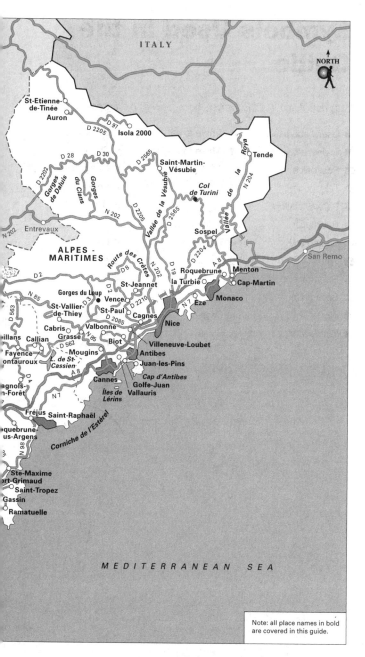

Note: all place names in bold
are covered in this guide.

THE CÔTE D'AZUR

Symbols Used in the Guide

Please note that not all the symbols below appear in every guide.

- Useful addresses
- Tourist office
- Post office
- Telephone
- Railway station
- Bus station
- Shared taxi
- Tram
- River transport
- Sea transport
- Airport
- Where to stay

- Where to eat
- Where to go for a drink
- Where to listen to music
- Where to go for an ice-cream
- To see
- Shopping
- 'Other'
- Parking
- Castle
- Ruins

- Diving site
- Shelter
- Camp site
- Peak
- Site
- Town
- Hill
- Abbey, chapel
- Lookout
- Beach
- Lighthouse
- Facilities for the disabled

Getting There

By Air

FROM BRITAIN

There are frequent flights to Nice and Marseille-Provence from Heathrow and Gatwick and regular services from regional airports. **Air France** provides 20 daily flights between London and Nice during peak season and up to 10 flights to Marseille-Provence. **British Airways** fly regularly to Nice and Marseille-Provence.

Travellers may find the best deals on flights to Nice. Promotions on **bmi British Midland** and ticketless airlines such as **Virgin Express**, **easyJet** and **buzz** can provide excellent deals, although your airport of departure will be limited. British Midland fly from the widest range of regional airports, although some of these flights will involve a change or an extended stop to pick up further passengers at Heathrow.

Prices vary between airlines and according to season. If booking in advance, expect to pay between £90 and £180 for a return flight to Marseille and between £100 and £210 to Nice. Anticipate a supplement of £10 to £30 if departing from a regional airport or travelling over a weekend.

Many travellers pay less than the quoted full fare thanks to the intense competition within the UK airline industry. Many excellent deals are offered outside of the peak months of July, August and December by airlines and travel agents. The travel pages of the weekend broadsheet newspapers and websites such as www.cheapflights.com, www.expedia.com and www.last minute.com are also good hunting grounds for flight bargains. Always ensure that any company is ABTA endorsed. Contact the Air Travel Advisory Bureau for advice and information on airlines and prices (*see below*). The advent of the Eurostar service has increased the competition between airlines, lowering prices from the north of England, Northern Ireland and Scotland in particular.

• **The Air Travel Advisory Bureau Ltd**: Columbus House, 28 Charles Square, London N1 6HT. ☎ (020) 7636 5000. Website: www.atab.co.uk

• **Air France**: 10 Warwick Street, First Floor, London WR1 5RA. ☎ (0845) 084 5111. Website: www.airfrance.com

• **British Airways**: Waterside, PO Box 365, Harmondsworth UB7 0GB. ☎ (0845) 773 3377. Website: www.britishairways.co.uk

• **bmi British Midland**: Donington Hall, Castle Donington, Derby DE74 2SB. ☎ (0870) 607 0555. Website: www.iflybmi.com

• **buzz**: Endeavour House, Stansted Airport, Essex CM24 1RS. ☎ (0870) 240 7070. Website: www.buzzaway.com

• **easyJet**: easyLand, Luton Airport LU2 9LS. ☎ (0870) 600 0000. Website: www.easyjet.com

- **Virgin Express**: Brussels Airport, Building 116, B-1820, Belgium. ☎ (020) 7744 0004. Website: www.virgin-express.com

TRAVEL AGENTS IN BRITAIN

- **Airline Network**: (discount flights by phone only). ☎ (0870) 241 0019.

- **Bridge the World**: (discount flights and packages). 47 Chalk Farm Road, London NW1 8AJ. ☎ (0870) 444 7474. Website: www.bridgetheworld.com

- **Council Travel**: (discount flights). 28a Poland Street, London W1V 3DB. ☎ (020) 7287 9410. Website: www.counciltravel.com

- **Flightbookers**: (discount flights and packages). 177–178 Tottenham Court Road, London W1P 0LX. ☎ (0870) 010 7000. Website: www.flightbookers.com

- **STA Travel**: (students and those under 26; 37 branches nationwide). 86 Old Brompton Road, London SW7 3LQ. ☎ (0870) 160 0599. Website: www.statravel.co.uk

- **Thomas Cook**: (flights and packages; branches nationwide). ☎ (0990) 666 222. Website: www.thomascook.com

- **Trailfinders**: (discounts and specialist itineraries; six branches nationwide). 42–50 Earl's Court Road, London W8 6FT. ☎ (020) 7938 3366. Website: www.trailfinders.com

- **USIT Campus Travel**: (students and those under 26; 51 branches nationwide). 52 Grosvenor Gardens, London SW1W 0AG. ☎ (0870) 240 1010. Website: www.usitcampus.co.uk

Specialist Travel Agents

The travel sections of the Sunday broadsheets are particularly good sources of information on travel agents providing specialist packages to Provence and the Côte d'Azur. Many offer villas and country houses for rent.

- **Balfour Travel**: (country houses to rent in Provence). ☎ (01189) 402620. Website: www.balfourtravel.com

- **Destination Provence**: (special interest tours, accommodation and packages). The Travel Centre, 5 Bishopthorpe Road, York YO23 1NA. ☎ (01904) 622220. Website: www.destinationprovence.co.uk

- **Quality Villas**: (villas with pools, domestic services available). ☎ (01442) 870055. Website: www.quality-villas.co.uk

- **VFB Holidays**: (cottage holidays, packages and villas). Normandy House, High Street, Cheltenham, Gloucestershire GL50 3FB. ☎ (01242) 240340. Website: www.vfbholidays.co.uk

FROM IRELAND

Air France, **Aer Lingus** and **bmi British Midland** fly direct from the Republic of Ireland to Nice and Marseilles-Provence. **British Airways** flights from Ireland connect through Heathrow.

British Airways and bmi British Midland fly regularly from Belfast International Airport to Paris. From Paris, travellers can transfer for flights to the South of France. Several airlines offer good deals on flights to London from Belfast including **easyJet** and **British European Airlines** (from Belfast City).

Travellers from Ireland may find that their cheapest option is to take advantage of the frequent special deals on flights to Paris and then catch a connecting flight to Marseille-Provence or Nice or travel overland. **Ryanair** often discounts fares on its four times daily service to Beauvais-Tille airport, just outside Paris. Dublin is the busiest airport for overseas flights, but travellers from Shannon and Cork can often find good deals. Always ensure that any company is ABTA endorsed.

- **Aer Lingus**: 40–41 Upper O'Connell Street, Dublin 1. ☎ (01) 886 8888. Website: www.aerlingus.com

- **Air France**: ☎ (01) 844 5633. Website: www.airfrance.com

- **British Airways**: 13 St Stephen's Green, Dublin 1. ☎ 1-800-626-6747. Website: www.britishairways.co.uk

- **bmi British Midland**: Donington Hall, Castle Donington, Derby DE74 2SB. ☎ (0870) 607 0555. Website: www.iflybmi.com

- **British European Airlines**: Exeter Airport, Exeter CX5 2BD. ☎ (1890) 925532. Website: www.british-european.com

- **easyJet**: easyLand, Luton Airport LU2 9LS. ☎ (0870) 600 0000. Website: www.easyjet.com

- **Ryanair**: Dublin Airport, County Dublin. ☎ (01) 609 7800. Website: www.ryanair.ie

- **Virgin Express**: Virgin House, Shannon, County Clare. ☎ (061) 704 4470. Website: www.virgin-express.com

TRAVEL AGENTS IN IRELAND

- **American Express Travel**: 116 Grafton Street, Dublin 2. ☎ (01) 677 2784.

- **Budget Travel**: 134 Lower Baggot Street, Dublin 2. ☎ (01) 661 3122.

- **Budget Travel Shops**: 63 Main Street, Finglas 11, Dublin. ☎ (01) 834 0637.

- **Hello France**: The Mill, Crosses Green, Cork. ☎ (021) 378 404.

- **Thomas Cook**: 11 Donegal Place, Belfast BT1 6ET. ☎ (028) 9088 3900. Website: www.thomascook.com

- **Trailfinders**: 4–5 Dawson Street, Dublin 2. ☎ (01) 677 7888. Website: www.trailfinders.com
- **USIT Now**: 19–21 Aston Quay, O'Connell Bridge, Dublin 2. ☎ (01) 677 8117. 13B Fountain Centre, College Street, Belfast BT61 6ET. ☎ (0870) 240 1010. Website: www.usitcampus.co.uk

FROM THE UNITED STATES

Air France flies direct from New York and Nice once daily (6 hours). Air France, in partnership with **Continental** and **Delta Airlines**, also provides frequent connecting services between Los Angeles, Boston, Chicago and New York, and Nice or Marseille-Provence.

If booking in advance, expect a return ticket from New York and Nice to cost from $600. Flights between the east coast of the United States and Europe are among the most competitive in the world, and those travelling outside of peak months especially, should be able to find excellent deals on flights to Provence and the Côte d'Azur.

An alternative option is flying to another European airport before proceeding to Provence and the Côte d'Azur. Flights between London and New York, in particular, can often be exceptionally good value during 'price wars' or promotions. US airlines also offer low-price flights to Brussels, Amsterdam and Frankfurt on a regular basis.

Discount travel agents sell tickets offloaded by airlines, often on an 'open jaw' basis that will enable you to fly into one European city and fly out of another. Such travel agencies are often the most useful for students and those under 26, as they also sell railcards and tours. Travel clubs can also be worthwhile if you're planning to do a bit of travelling. The travel sections of Sunday broadsheets are good for bargain hunting. Internet travel sites such as www.lowestfare.com, www.priceline.com and www.previewtravel.com can find you excellent deals. Always ensure that your travel agent is endorsed by ASTA. Airlines themselves can often be as competitive as agencies, especially if booking APEX (Advanced Purchase Excursion) tickets or winter Super APEX tickets.

- **Air France**: 125 West 55th Street, New York, New York 10019. ☎1-800-237-2747. Website: www.airfrance.com
- **American Airlines**: 4200 Amon Carter, PD 2400, Fort Worth, Texas. ☎ 1-800-443-7300. Website: www.aa.com
- **Continental Airlines**: 2929 Alan Parkway, PO Box 4607, Houston, Texas. ☎ 1-800-525-0280. Website: www.continental.com
- **Delta Airlines**: Hartsfield, Atlanta International Airport, Atlanta, Georgia 30320. ☎ 1-800-221-1212. Website: www.delta-air.com
- **Northwest/KLM**: Northwest Airlines, Central Airline Terminal, 100 East 42nd Street, Second Floor, New York, New York 10017. ☎ 1-800-225-2525. Websites: www.nwa.com or www.klm.com
- **TWA**: 650 Anton Boulevard, Suite F, Costa Mesa, California 91364. ☎ 1-800-892-4141. Website: www.twa.com

- **United Airlines**: ☎ 1-800-241-6522. Website: www.ual.com

- **US Airways**: 10 Eyck Plaza, 40 North Pearl Street, Albany, New York 12207. ☎ 1-800-428-4322. Website: www.usairways.com

TRAVEL AGENTS IN THE UNITED STATES

- **Last Minute Travel Club**: (travel club for standby deals). 132 Brookline Avenue, Boston, Massachusetts 02215. ☎ 1-800-LAST-MIN.

- **STA Travel**: (students and those under 26; branches nationwide). 48 East 11th Street, New York, New York 10003. ☎ 1-800-781-4040. Website: www.statravel.com

- **USIT (Council Travel) USA**: (students and those under 26; over 60 offices nationwide). 931 Westwood Boulevard, Westwood, Los Angeles, California 90024. ☎ 1-800-226-8624. Website: www.counciltravel.com

Specialist Travel Agents

- **A Taste of Provence**: (cookery courses). 925 Vernal Avenue, Mill Valley, California 94941. ☎ (415) 383-9439. Website: www.tasteofprovence.com

- **French Dirt Cycling Tours**: (specialist cycling tours to Provence). PO Box 94, Richmond, Vermont 05477. ☎ (802) 434-8150. Website: www.frenchdirt.com

- **French Foto Tours**: (photography and landscape tours of Provence). 626 C. Admiral Drive, Box 153, Annapolis, Maryland 21401. Website: www.atprovence.com

- **Pleasure in Provence**: (specialist food and wine tours). 8103 Bay Drive, Tampa, Florida 33635. ☎ (813) 854-1201. Website: www.pleasureinprovence.com

- **The French Experience**: (tours, packages and accommodation across France). 370 Lexington Avenue, New York, New York 10017. ☎ 1-800-28-FRANCE. Website: www.frenchexperience.com

- **Tours of Provence**: (Avignon-based tours). 1700 Glen Bar Square, Denver, Colorado 80215. ☎ (302) 275-9899. Website: www.toursofprovence.com

FROM CANADA

There are no direct flights to either Nice or Marseille-Provence from any Canadian city. **Air France** flies daily from both Montreal and Toronto directly to Paris, where travellers can pick up one of the regular flights to Nice or Marseille-Provence. **Air Canada**, **British Airways** and **KLM** also make daily flights to Paris from either Montreal or Toronto. **Air Canada** and **Canadian Airlines** operate linking services to Montreal and Toronto from regional cities in Canada. Flight time to Paris is 6 hours 30 minutes from Montreal, 7 hours 30 minutes from Toronto and 12 hours 30 minutes from Vancouver. Expect to pay around CAN$800 for a return from Montreal or Toronto during July, August and December and CAN$700 at other times.

Travellers with a flexible itinerary may find it cheaper to travel first to the United States and then proceed to Paris or Marseille-Provence and Nice. The best deals are usually available on flights from the East Coast, particularly New York, where return flights to Paris can cost as little as US$350. An alternative option is to fly from Canada to another city in Europe, and then transfer to Marseille-Provence or Nice. Air Canada and Canadian Airlines fly daily from Toronto to London and British Airways flies twice daily.

- **Air Canada**: 979 de Maisonneuve Boulevard West, Montreal H4A 3T2. ☎ 1-800-361-3000. Website: www.aircanada.ca
- **Air France**: Suite 810, 151 Bloor Street West, Toronto. ☎ 1-800-667-2747. Website: www.airfrance.com
- **British Airways**: 4120 Yonge Street, Suite 100, Toronto, Ontario M2P 2B8. ☎ 1-800-AIRWAYS. Website: www.britishairways.com
- **Canadian Airlines**: 165–168 Street SE, Calgary T2E 6J5. ☎ 1-800-466-7000. Website: www.cdnair.ca
- **Northwest/KLM**: Toronto Pearson International Airport, Toronto. ☎ 1-800-374-7747. Website: www.klm.com

TRAVEL AGENTS IN CANADA

- **Collacutt Travel**: (comprehensive services). The Bayview Village Centre, 2901 Bayview Avenue, Toronto, Ontario M2K 1E6. ☎ 1-888-225-9811. Website: www.collacutt-travel.com
- **New Frontiers/Nouvelles Frontières**: 1001 Sherbrook East, Suite 720, Montreal, Quebec H2L 1L3. ☎ (514) 526-8444.
- **Sears Travel**: (general services; 81 branches nationwide). ☎ 1-888-884-2359. Website: www.sears.ca
- **Travel Cuts**: (student and youth travel; branches nationwide). 187 College St, Toronto, Ontario M5T 1P7. ☎ 1-800-667-2887.
- **Travel House**: (tours, packages, discounted travel). 1491 Younge Street, Suite 401, Toronto M4T 1ZR. ☎ (416) 925-6322. Website: www.travel-house.com

Canadian travellers can also use many of the travel agents listed in 'Travel Agents in the United States'.

FROM AUSTRALIA AND NEW ZEALAND

There are no direct flights from cities in Australia and New Zealand to Nice or Marseille-Provence. However, there are frequent flights to Paris and other cities in Europe from the major cities in Australia and New Zealand. These flights nearly always include a stopover in an Asian city. Because flight times vary from 19 to 25 hours, many travellers extend their stop-over for one or two nights. This must be arranged in advance with the airline and can usually be done for a minimal charge.

The cheapest fares tend to be on Asian airlines such as **Garuda Air** and **Malaysia Airlines**. **British Airways** and **Qantas** are usually more expensive, although they fly more regularly. Travellers should expect to pay between AUS$1,500 and AUS$2,000 for a return flight to Paris in low season and about AUS$2,000 to AUS$2,500 in high season. Sydney is the most competitive airport from which to travel, although travellers from Australia and New Zealand should find more promotions on round-the-world or extended itinerary tickets than on direct flights. The exceptions to this rule are flights to London, which can be cheaper than those to other European cities. Check with travel agents, the travel sections of the broadsheets and with the airlines direct.

Travellers could include Provence and the Côte d'Azur on a round-the-world itinerary. For example, the Qantas 'Global Explorer' Pass allows 15 stopovers in all continents flown to by the airline and its partners within a mileage of 27,000 miles. The Global Explorer costs from AUS$2,500 in low season, plus airport taxes and from AUS$3,000 in high season, plus airport taxes. Check the website at www.qantas.com or contact your local travel agent or one of the offices below:

• **Air France**: 64 York Street, Sydney 2000. ☎ (02) 932-1000; 2nd Floor, Dataset House, 143 Nelson Street, Auckland. ☎ (09) 303-3521. Website: www.airfrance.com

• **British Airways**: Chifley Square, 70 Hunter Street, Sydney 2000. ☎ (02) 8904-8800. ☎ (09) 356-8690. Website: www.britishairways.com

• **Cathay Pacific**: 3/F International Term, Sydney International Airport, Mascot NSW 2020. ☎ (13)1747; 11th Floor, Arthur Andersen Tower, National Bank Centre, 205–209 Queen Street, PO Box 313, Auckland. ☎ (0508) 800-454. Website: www.cathaypacific.com

• **Malaysia Airlines**: MAS, 16th Spring Street, Sydney NSW. ☎ (02) 913-2627; MAS, 12th Floor, The Swanson Centre, 12–16 Swanson Street, PO Box 3729, Auckland. ☎ (09) 373-2741. Website: www.malaysiaairlines.com

• **Qantas**: Qantas Centre, 203 Coward Street, Mascot, Sydney, NSW 2020. ☎ (13) 1313/(13) 1211; 191 Queen Street, Auckland 1. ☎ (0800) 808-767. Website: www.qantas.com

• **Singapore Airlines**: Singapore Airlines House, 17–19 Bridge Street, Sydney NSW 2000. ☎ (02) 9350-0100; 10th Floor, West Plaza Building, Corner Albert and Fanshawe Streets, Auckland 1. ☎ (0800) 808-909. Website: www.singaporeair.com

TRAVEL AGENTS IN AUSTRALIA AND NEW ZEALAND

• **Flight Centres**: Level 13, 33 Berry Street, North Sydney 2060. ☎ (02) 9241-2422; 205 Queen Street, Auckland. ☎ (09) 309-6171. ☎1-1300-131-600 for your nearest branch.

• **STA Travel**: 855 George Street, Sydney 2000. ☎ (02) 9212-1255 (72 branches); 90 Cashel Street, Christchurch, New Zealand. ☎ (03) 0379-9098 (13 branches). Website: www.statravel.com.au

- **Thomas Cook**: 175 Pitt Street, Sydney 2000. ☎ (1300) 728 748 (branches nationwide). Website: www.thomascook.com.au; 96 Anzac Avenue, Auckland, New Zealand. ☎ (0800) 500-600 (branches nationwide). Website: www.thomascook.com.nz

- **Trailfinders**: 91 Elizabeth Street, Brisbane, Queensland 4000. ☎ (07) 3229-0887 (branches in Sydney and Cairns). Website: www.trailfinders. com/australia

FROM SOUTH AFRICA

There are no direct flights from South Africa to Marseille-Provence or Nice. Travellers from South Africa would need to fly to Paris and then fly to one of the airports in the Provence or on the Côte d'Azur. **Air France** and **South African Airways** fly regularly to Paris from Johannesburg and Cape Town. Travellers can book onward flights from Paris in South Africa. Transfers can also be arranged from other cities in South Africa to Johannesburg and Cape Town.

Travellers may find particularly good deals on flights from South Africa to London. Promotional offers can result in flights from London to Nice being considerably cheaper than flights within France or travelling overland. **Virgin Atlantic**, **British Airways** and South African Airways tend to be the best value.

- **Air France**: 196 Oxford Road, Oxford Manor, Illovo, Johannesburg 2196. ☎ (011) 880-8040. Website: www.airfrance.com

- **British Airways**: Grosvenor Court, 196 Grosvenor Corner, Rosebank, Johannesburg 2196. ☎ (011) 441-8600. Website: www.britishairways.com

- **South African Airways**: Airways Park, Jones Road, Johannesburg International Airport, Johannesburg 1627. ☎ (011) 978-1762. Website: www. as.co.za

- **Virgin Atlantic**: Olivetti House, 17 Lower Long Street, Cape Town 8001. ☎ (011) 340-3400. Website: www.virginatlantic.com

TRAVEL AGENTS IN SOUTH AFRICA

- **STA Travel South Africa**: Level 3, Leslie Social Sciences Building, University of Cape Town, Rondebosch 7700, Cape Town. ☎ (021) 685-1808. Website: www.sta-travel.co.za

- **USIT Adventures**: Rondebosch Shopping Centre, Rondebosch Main Road, Rondebosch, Cape Town. ☎ (021) 685-2226.

By Train

FROM BRITAIN

Travellers to Provence and the Côte d'Azur can now travel all the way through to Marseille in 6 hours 50 minutes from London Waterloo. **Eurostar/ TGV** sells connecting tickets allowing you to travel by Eurostar to Paris or Lille and then join a high-speed TGV service to Marseille.

Standard return fares to Marseille from Waterloo begin at about £130 with advance booking and can go up to over £250. Reduced fares are available for students, senior citizens, advance bookings and group travel. Eurostar often offers promotions that can really lower the price of a return ticket, although these are not always at the most convenient times for travelling. It is usually best to book tickets and promotions with Eurostar directly as high street travel agents will usually charge a booking fee.

Travellers on the Eurostar/TGV service should consider changing at Lille rather than Paris. The change at Lille involves crossing to another platform, whereas the Paris change entails crossing the city to join the train at Gare du Lyon.

Travellers from other parts of the UK can buy connecting tickets on regional train operators to London Waterloo. Alternatively, you can pick up the Eurostar service at Ashford in Kent. Ensure that you arrive at Waterloo/ Ashford at least 25 minutes before the time of departure.

For those who prefer to journey to Paris and organize their own onward travel, there are 20 Eurostar trains Monday to Saturday (15 on Sundays) from London Waterloo to Paris Gare du Nord. Prices range from £70 to £270 for a standard second-class return from London to Paris whilst a first-class return can cost up to £450. Tickets for SNCF services can be bought at Paris stations, but travellers with access to the Internet can book on their website. The website allows you to specify the price and the speed of the train you require. Fares vary according to the time of travel and the speed of train. As well as Marseille, regular SNCF trains run from Paris Gare de Lyon to Avignon (3 hours 30 minutes), Nice (6 hours 30 minutes) and Toulon (5 hours 30 minutes).

Travellers may find an Inter-Rail pass for travel around France good value. 22 days of travel in France begins at £160 for students and those under 26. The Inter-Rail pass entitles you to half-price travel in Britain and free passage on some cross-channel ferries. You do have to pay supplements for travel on high-speed services. Contact travel agents specializing in student travel such as STA travel or USIT Campus Travel (see 'Travel Agents in Britain').

Eurostar: (London Waterloo–Paris Gare du Nord, London Waterloo– Marseille), Waterloo International Terminal, London SE1. Also: Eurostar Ticket Office, 102–104 Victoria Street, London SW1 5JL. ☎ (0990) 186186 (7am to 10pm). Website: www.eurostar.co.uk

SNCF: Rail Europe Ltd, French Railways House, 179 Piccadilly, London W1V 0B8. ☎ (0870) 584 8848. Websites: www.sncf.com or www.raileurope.com

FROM IRELAND

The quickest way to travel to Paris from the Republic of Ireland by train and sea is to catch an **Irish Ferries** service from Dublin Port or **Stena Sealink** ferry from Dun Laoghaire to Holyhead in Anglesey (*see* 'By Sea from Ireland' *below*).

The Continental Rail Desk of **Iarnrod Éireann** in Dublin can arrange the entire Dublin–Paris journey. Iarnrod Éireann links cities throughout Ireland to Dublin. Once in Dublin train station, travellers can catch the DART train to Dun Laoghaire (20 minutes) or a bus to Dublin Port (about 15 minutes). The ferry service to Holyhead is about 3 hours 30 minutes long. Once in Holyhead, travellers can catch the direct **Virgin** train to London Euston which takes 3 hours 30 minutes (leaves about three times daily). From Euston, the southbound Northern line tube connects to Waterloo, the departure station for the **Eurostar** service to Paris and the **Eurostar/TGV** service to Marseille (*see* 'Getting There by Train from Britain' for more details). SNCF trains can either be booked in person at the Gare de Lyon in Paris or bought in advance from the SNCF office or through their website.

SNCF: Britrail Ltd, Third Floor, 123 Lower Baggot Street, Dublin 2. ☎ (01) 661 2866. Website: www.sncf.com

Iarnrod Éireann (Continental Rail Desk): 35 Lower Abbey Street, Dublin 1. ☎ (01) 677 1871. Website: www.irishrail.ie

Virgin Trains: (Holyhead–London Euston). ☎ (0345) 222333. Website: www.virgintrains.co.uk

By Sea

FROM BRITAIN

The Dover–Calais route is the shortest (90 minutes) and most popular. Portsmouth and Southampton are the main ports of departure to Caen and Le Havre (crossing time about 6 hours). Expect to pay from £40 to £100 for a car and two passengers between Dover and Calais and from £70 to £200 for the longer crossings. Prices vary according to the season. The foot passenger fare starts at about £20. Contact your local travel agent or the ferry service direct for more information and watch the national press for promotions.

The **SeaCat** travels from Dover to Calais in 45 minutes and from Newhaven to Dieppe in 4 hours, although bad weather can lengthen journey times or delay departure. Prices begin at £100 for a single fare and vary according to season and time of departure. Foot passengers can also travel on coaches through the Eurotunnel, although this can prove more costly.

⚓ **Brittany Ferries**: (Portsmouth–Caen/Poole–Cherbourg). Wharf Road, Portsmouth PO2 8RU. ☎ (0990) 360360. Website: www.brittanyferries.com

⚓ **P&O Stena Line**: (Dover–Calais). Channel House, Channel View Road, Dover CT17 9TJ. ☎ (0870) 600 0600. Website: www.posl.com

⚓ **P&O Portsmouth**: (Portsmouth–Le Havre/Cherbourg). Peninsula House, Wharf Road, Portsmouth PO2 8TA. ☎ (0990) 980555. Website: www.poef.com

⚓ **Sea France**: (Dover–Calais). Eastern Docks, Kent CT16 1JA. ☎ (08705) 711711. Website: www.seafrance.co.uk

⚓ **SeaCat**: (Folkestone–Boulogne, Dover–Calais and Newhaven–Dieppe). International Hoverport, Dover CT17 9TG. ☎ (0870) 240 8070/(0870) 524 0241. Website: www.hoverspeed.co.uk

FROM IRELAND

Travellers from Ireland heading overland to Provence and the Côte d'Azur frequently take a route through Britain, but it can be cheaper to sail directly from Rosslare to Cherbourg or Le Havre. However, the journey time (16 to 22 hours) and the infrequency of the service (three times weekly in peak season and once fortnightly in off-peak) can be daunting. Expect to pay about IR£200–300 for a standard single. Many prefer to take the ferry from Rosslare to Fishguard and then drive to Dover. Journey times are about 3 hours 30 minutes on the ferry and 1 hour 40 minutes on the catamaran. Expect to pay upwards of IR£80–240 for a standard single for car and passengers, with a supplement if travelling by catamaran.

The Dublin–Holyhead route is the quickest for travellers from the Dublin area. **Stena Line** and **Irish Ferries** sail the crossing from Dublin to Holyhead. Stena Line also run a 'Superferry' from Dublin Port to Holyhead. Expect to pay upwards of IR£100–£250 for a standard single for car and passengers, more for the Superferry and for peak times. Foot passenger fares begin at IR£30. Foot passengers can pick up a Virgin train at Holyhead to London Euston and then trains from London to south-coast ports. The drive from Holyhead to the south coast of England takes at least 7 hours. Stena Line also run a direct service from Belfast to London Euston via Liverpool six times daily on weekdays and three times daily on Sundays. The SeaCat sails daily (twice daily in peak season) from Dublin to Liverpool in 2 hours 30 minutes and daily (twice daily in peak season) from Belfast to Heysham in 2 hours 30 minutes.

⚓ **Irish Ferries**: (Dublin–Holyhead, Rosslare–Cherbourg/Le Havre). Reliance House, Water Street, Liverpool L2 8TP. Dublin ☎ (01) 638 3333. Rosslare ☎ (053) 33158. Website: www.irishferries.ie

⚓ **SeaCat**: SeaCat Terminal, West Pier, Stranraer DG9 7RE. ☎ (0870) 552 3523. Website: www.seacat.co.uk

⚓ **Stena Line**: (Dun Loaghaire/Dublin Port–Holyhead, Rosslare–Fishguard). Charter House, Park Street, Ashford TN24 8EX. Dun Loaghaire ☎ (01) 204 7700. Rosslare ☎ (053) 331 115. Website: www.stenaline.co.uk

By Car

FROM BRITAIN

UK driving licences are valid in France and you will need at least third party insurance to drive on French roads. Petrol in France is usually cheaper than in Britain, but tolls and parking charges can prove expensive. The speed limit on French motorways is 130 kph (80 mph).

Travellers wishing to take their car to Provence and the Côte d'Azur can either take the **Eurotunnel** and **Motorail**, or travel by hovercraft/catamaran or ferry across the Channel to Calais. The journey from Calais to the South Coast of France should take about ten hours.

The Eurotunnel's auto-train service from Folkestone (accessible via Junction 11a on the M20) to Calais–Coquelles carries cars and their passengers under the Channel in about 35 minutes. The auto-trains run 24 hours a day and depart twice an hour during the day and once an hour during the night. Expect to pay from £200 upwards for a return ticket for car and passengers from Folkestone to Calais. Tickets are usually cheaper with advance booking and seasonal promotions are sometimes available. It is a good idea to arrive at least 30 minutes before departure.

Instead of driving, travellers can put the car on the Motorail service at Calais and travel overnight in sleeping accommodation. The Motorail service is convenient but can be expensive. At the time of writing, all services to the South of France except the Lille–Nice route were running in summer only. Check the website for special deals.

The cheapest option for cross-channel travel with a car is the ferry. *See* 'Getting There by Sea from the UK' and 'Getting There by Sea from Ireland' for more details on ferry crossings and companies serving the UK and Ireland.

🚉 **Eurotunnel**: (Folkestone–Calais). Customer Service Centre, PO Box 300, Folkestone CT19 4DQ. ☎ (08705) 353353. Website: www.eurotunnel.co.uk

🚉 **Motorail**: (Calais–Avignon–Nice, Lille–Nice). ☎ (0870) 744221. Website: www.eurodestination.com/rail/motorail

By Coach

FROM BRITAIN

Travelling to Provence and the Côte d'Azur by coach from the UK is not the quickest option but can be the cheapest. **Eurolines** run regular services to and from London to Aix-en-Provence and Marseilles (five times a week in summer, twice a week in winter). There are nine services per week in summer to Avignon and five services per week in winter. There are also special summer services to Cannes, Frejus, Marseilles, Nice, St-Raphaël and Toulon. There are regular services to Paris throughout the year.

Eurolines leave from London Victoria Coach Station (a 10-minute walk from Victoria railway station). National Express buses link cities throughout Britain and Northern Ireland to London. The journey from London Victoria to Aix-en-Provence takes about 20 hours. Return fares from London to Paris begin at about £35. Return fares to destinations in Provence and the Côte d'Azur begin at around £50. Reductions are available for senior citizens, those under 26 and on advance purchases.

Travellers wishing to see more of Europe may find the Eurolines Pass good value. Prices start at £200 for 30 days travel in over 21 European countries. Contact Eurolines or your travel agent for more details.

Eurolines: Victoria Coach Station, 52 Grosvenor Gardens (opposite Victoria Rail/Underground Station), London SW1. ☎ (0870) 808080. Website: www.eurolines.co.uk

FROM IRELAND

Eurolines is affiliated to the **Bus Éireann** system that serves every destination in Ireland. There is a twice-daily service from Dublin to Paris (via London). Services leave in the early morning or evening and take 22 hours, with an hour's stop in London Victoria. Adult return fares in high season cost from IR£90–110 and youth fares from IR£50–70. There is no direct bus service from Belfast to Paris.

Eurolines with **Stena Line** runs a direct service twice daily from Belfast to London Victoria (13 hours 50 minutes) and travellers can change to one of the frequent services from London to the south of France.

Bus Éireann: Booking Office, Central Bus Station (Busaras), Store Street, Dublin 1. ☎ (01) 830 2222. Website: www.buseirann.ie

Eurolines: See details above.

Introduction

Provence

For a long time, Provence sold itself as a place of delightful idleness and self-indulgent *farniente*. By the 1990s, the mission statement had become rather less poetic – 'efficiency and profitability' – but, with the dawn of the new century, the old image is back.

Visitors come from all over the world to discover this photogenic region, captured so beautifully on canvas by Van Gogh and Renoir, and described so humorously by English ex-patriot Peter Mayle. This is the land of white horses and black bulls, of sun-ripened olives and relaxing pastis, of stunning ochre cliffs in the Roussillon and bright white rocks in the Alpilles, of ancient towns with rounded, red roof-tiles and frothing fountains. There is no better time to discover it (or rediscover it), just when it seems to be rediscovering itself.

Almost every image of Provence shows the utter charm of this part of France. The colours are so vivid, with traditional, age-old markets and festivals, olive oils in every shade of green and good quaffing wines, all set against an azure sky. And everywhere there is the summer sound of crickets.

Where exactly is Provence? Those who know the region's wines from its famous 'Côtes' are well aware that the wine trail take visitors way beyond the hills to the east, as far as Fréjus. Historians, on the other hand, would say that the Côte d'Azur does not really begin until well after that, and that St-Tropez is a quintessentially Provençal *village* (although those who have been there in the summer might not agree!). The Rhône to the west, the watershed in the east and the Mediterranean coast mark the boundaries of Provence. This is the delineation used in this guide, although it does provoke differences of opinion with regard to the southern limits, after Marseille, as well as for the northern extremities, beyond Avignon. Marseille was the gateway to the Orient, and is now the 'window' on the West. In Avignon, all you have to do is cross the bridge to find yourself in another land, blessed by the gods and by the popes. And between the two cities there is a whole world, or perhaps several different worlds.

Just a short distance from touristy Provence, with its blue skies, busy beaches, crowded festivals – and a twanging accent that sounds like the metallic clash of *pétanque* balls – lies the other Provence, of craftsmen, fishermen, shepherds and agricultural workers. Explore these two Provences in one according to your mood or tastes, but don't miss the chance to follow in the footsteps of Mistral or Cézanne, wander through olive groves or visit local *santonnier* craftsmen. In all these places, the Provençal *art de vivre* remains unspoiled.

To see all this, follow the holiday route, the RN (Route Nationale) 7; it may no longer bear any resemblance to the road that Trenet used to sing about, but remains preferable to the *autoroute*. For more lavender-scented adventure, branch off from the RN7, to pass through Salon and Aix-en-Provence. If you have time, detours to the Alpilles and the Luberon are essential, as is the Camargue (better out of season, when there are no mosquitoes and far fewer tourists). Other places to explore are the Provençal part of the Drôme, bounded to the north by Montélimar (famous for its **nougat**), and the Alpes-de-Haute-Provence, from the area around Forcalquier to the Valensole Plateau and from the Verdon Gorges to the alpine valleys, such as the Ubaye and the Blanche.

You may well hear the Marseillais accent at an altitude of 3,000m in this beautiful landscape – the **autoroute** provides fast access. After a spring walk under an astonishingly clear sky, or a run down the ski slopes, don't be surprised to find the Provençal dishes of **pieds et paquets** or **daube** (beef stew) on the lunchtime menu alongside **raclette** and other mountain food. Instead of a pastis, though, order a Génépi aperitif, made from Alpine Yarrow. It will make your hosts happy – and won't do you any harm, either!

The Côte d'Azur

It's become something of a truism to say that the Côte d'Azur has been badly damaged by the effects of tourism, disfigured by property developers and transformed into a mixture of huge car park and showy playground for holiday-makers. Admittedly, there's some truth in this description, but, despite this, the Côte d'Azur retains its faithful followers, who wouldn't think of spending their holiday anywhere else. It also has its fair share of detractors, who won't subject themselves to the extreme heat, exorbitant prices and unfriendly welcome.

Try to visit outside the very busy summer months and explore the less obvious parts (or arrive in the early morning in St-Tropez when the party-goers are still in bed!). You'll still find a touch of paradise, places that have been miraculously preserved, and charming villages where the locals will greet visitors with a smile, but without dollar (or franc) signs in their eyes. Small restaurants that have served the same tasty and generous dishes for centuries stand alongside hotels where the prices won't break the bank. The almost impossibly blue sky and extraordinary quality of light have hardly changed since they drew Renoir, Van Gogh, Bonnard, Cézanne and others to the area.

This is a land of geographic contrasts, teeming with different landscapes and charming routes. Those in search of places off the beaten track won't be disappointed. The Côte d'Azur still has its secret, aromatic forests, peaceful roads where you may encounter the odd postman, and little else, and picturesque hilltop villages.

General Information

ACCOMMODATION

The medieval villages and ports of Provence and the Côte d'Azur have been offering shelter to travellers since the crusades of the Middle Ages. Today, the region offers a range of accommodation that's as diverse as the area itself. The choice varies widely in terms of facilities and prices, from glitzy and glamorous palaces via one-to four-star hotels to simple but adequate bed and breakfasts, self-catering gîtes and inexpensive youth hostels. There's something to suit all budgets. Those included here have been selected using the criteria of value for money, central position, charm and attractiveness. Some have all of these qualities, or most of them.

The best source for information on accommodation in France is the **French Government Tourist Office**. *See* 'Tourist Offices' for details.

HOTELS

Booking

One word of advice: it's best to make a reservation if you plan to stay in a hotel. In high season, in July and August, you must book well in advance, particularly for popular places on the coast. When you're sure of your dates, phone first to make the booking and then send a letter to confirm your reservation details, along with the required guarantee. Ring before you arrive to double-check everything is confirmed. It's worth checking whether the establishment accepts your preferred method of payment. Some proprietors may demand a cheque/money order rather than a credit card number. Tourist offices have accommodation lists in their given areas or even *département* and many will call around and book a room for you for free, or for a nominal fee.

Some hotels close from two weeks to up to five months of the year, reopening for Easter. If you are travelling out of season you may be able to turn up on the day and find a room, but it's worth ringing ahead to check the hotel or establishment is open.

Tariffs

Prices and facilities vary greatly from hotel to hotel and within the establishments themselves, depending on the quality of the room. For example, a balcony, sea-view or en-suite facilities with bath, rather than a shower, will add to the tariff. The proprietor is obliged to display a list of the various tariffs, and the room facilities. Single occupancy rates are only marginally cheaper than double occupancy, since prices are normally per room rather than per person. Triple or quad rooms are often available, with extra beds added to a double room, and this is usually cheaper than staying in two rooms. Double beds are usually available, but you should specify *un grand lit* if that's what you'd prefer.

During festivals, many establishments add a premium to their prices, so watch out for these dates. In low season (October–March), prices drop considerably and discount packages may be available.

Breakfast (usually coffee, a croissant, bread and jam) is almost always optional (at a cost of around 20–35F). Remember to stipulate whether you want it or not; it can often be cheaper to go to a nearby bar or café. Tax and service are included in the price except if you are staying on a half board (*demi-pension*) or full board (*pension*) basis. Half board includes breakfast and a set lunch or dinner and can be compulsory in some hotels with restaurants in the busy season (holidays and summer or in the winter in ski resorts). Full board includes all meals. These options can be good value, particularly if the hotel has the only restaurant in the village!

Facilities and Ratings

It's also worth thinking about the facilities you're looking for. Many three-star hotels have swimming pools (as do some bed and breakfast establishments), in which to relax after a hot day on the road or beach. Parking is usually readily available in country hotels, but it's worth checking in advance. Some city hotels offer underground or lock-up garages (increasingly important in some of the larger cities where car crime is on the rise).

The French tourist authorities classify hotels into five categories, ranging from one to four stars, plus a four-star deluxe rating. They indicate the level of facilities but not always the warmth, friendliness and charm of the establishments. For many readers, the family-run hotels found in most villages will be a good option. Relaxed and friendly, they often have a dining room that is open to both residents and non-residents.

LOGIS DE FRANCE, AUBERGES AND *RELAIS*

Personal callers to the Maison de la France (*see above*) can pick up a free copy of the *Logis de France* guide, which details one- and two-star establishments with restaurants (*auberges*). These establishments are usually found in smaller towns and villages.

Relais are usually located on the roadside outside built-up areas (the word actually means posting house, and the *relais* was the place where horses were changed). Independently run, they provide good (and frequently excellent) accommodation and offer regional cuisine, often in rustic surroundings. The free *Relais du Silence* guide features hotels in chateaux or characterful houses, located in peaceful surroundings. Website: www.silencehotel.com

Historic independent hotels and chateaux in all price ranges are detailed in the *Châteaux & Hotels de France* guide. The *Relais et Châteaux* guide, listing some of the best hotels in France, is also available free of charge from the Maison de la France. To have it sent within the UK (charge for postage and packing), call ☎ (020) 7630 7667. Freephone information is available on ☎ (00) 800 2000 0002. Website: www.relaischateaux.com

GENERAL INFORMATION

CHAMBRES D'HÔTE

In rural areas there are plenty of opportunities to stay in a private home or farm in what are known as *chambres d'hôte* (the nearest equivalent to British bed and breakfast). Mostly situated in farmhouses or villages, they range in size from one to several bedrooms and some will provide dinner (*table d'hôte*) on request. Listed separately in tourist office brochures, many are inspected and registered by the *gîtes de France* organization. Look out for the distinctive *chambre d'hôte* road signs. Prices vary but they are often an opportunity to enjoy traditional home cooking, French company and local information.

GÎTES

If self-catering is an option, there are a number of companies that rent different types of accommodation, ranging from rural farm cottages to beach apartments. The *gîtes de France* organization provides brochures and detailed lists of accommodation. Contact the Maison de Gites de France, 59 rue St-Lazare, 75439 Paris Cedex 09, ☎ (01) 49-70-75-75. Fax: (01) 42-81-28-53. Website: www.gites-de-France.fr. Reservations should be made with the gîtes de France office in each département.

The owners of the *gîte* often live near by and are usually very welcoming, although rarely in English! The standard of facilities does vary, but it is a great way to experience Provençal life.

Gîtes d'Étape

A gîte d'étape is a simple walking shelter with bunk beds (minus bedding) and a basic self-catering kitchen, established by the local village or municipality along GR (Grande Randonnée) walking paths or scenic bike routes. These are attractively priced (usually from 40F to 50F per night) and are listed in the individual Topoguides.

YOUTH HOSTELS

The good news is that there's no age limit for staying in a youth hostel in France. The non-profit-making French youth hostel federation, FUAJ, produces a free guide listing the addresses of all hostels in France.

Services include reservations for a maximum number of 6 nights, as much as 6 months in advance in certain youth hostels. Hostels are often very busy (or even full), but the organization can make a booking for you (in a dormitory only) well ahead of your trip. You pay for the bed, plus a reservation fee of about 17F. In return, you receive a voucher confirming your reservation, which you present at the youth hostel on arrival. You may cancel (the cancellation period varies from one hostel to another), for a charge of about 33F.

FUAJ membership cards are 70F for under-26s and 100F for over-26s. A family card, valid for families with 2 adults and one or more children under 14, costs 150F. You will need to prove your family's identity with some form of documentation.

To obtain a membership card, contact the FUAJ National Office in Paris. For on-the-spot purchases you will need to show some ID such as a passport. By post, send a photocopy of your passport together with a cheque/money order for the above amounts plus 5F handling charge.

Information is available in all youth hostels and at all FUAJ centres in France.

Fédération Unie des Auberges de Jeunesse (FUAJ). National Office: 27 rue Pajol, 75018 Paris. ☎ 01-44-89-87-27. Fax: 01-44-89-87-49. Recorded information: ☎ 08-36-68-36-93 (2.23F per min). Website: www.fuaj.org

Joining in Britain

For information about joining before you leave, contact the **Youth Hostels Association (YHA)** for membership details and other information. An international YHA card costs £12 for adults for a year and is valid worldwide. The **International Youth Hostel Federation (IYHF)** will issue the card. They also produce guidebooks to hostels overseas and run an international booking network from the same number.

■ **YHA**: Trevelyan House, Matlock, Derbyshire DE4 3YH. ☎ (0870) 870 8808. Fax: (01727) 844126. Email: customerservices@yha.org.uk. Website: www.yha.org.uk

■ **IYHF**: First Floor, Fountain House, Parkway, Welwyn Garden City, Herts AL1 6JH. ☎ (01707) 324170. Email: iyhf@iyhf.org. Website: www.iyhf.org

■ International booking site: www.hostelbooking.com

■ Irish website: www.irelandyha.org

■ French website: www.fuaj.org

■ Scottish website: www.syha.org.uk

CAMPING

Camping is an extremely popular pastime in Provence, almost a passion, and nearly every village and town has at least one campsite. There are more than 11,000 campsites in France, officially graded by the Fédération Française de Camping-Caravanning. ☎ 01-42-72-84-08. Fax: 01-42-72-70-21. There are four grades of sites, with facilities varying from a (deliberately) basic one- and two-star farm or vineyard site for back-to-nature campers to three- or four-star superior categories of site, equipped with hot showers, bar, restaurant, grocery shop, washing machines and swimming pool. Some also have permanently sited, fully furnished mobile homes for six to eight people. The Côte d'Azur has luxury camping metropolises offering water fun parks and even satellite TV.

Camping à la ferme (camping on a private farm) is generally without facilities but is an invitingly cheap and atmospheric way of seeing the region. The *camping municipal*, run by the local council, is another cheap option. They are generally clean and have plenty of hot water, and often occupy a prime position in the locality.

In the busy months it's advisable to book your pitch ahead as sites become very crowded.

Don't be tempted to camp rough (*camping sauvage*) on land without asking permission, or you'll risk a furious farmer, his dog or perhaps the police. Check the addresses listed under 'Tourist Offices' in this section, or use a tourist offices' listing. Also look out for *Le Guide Officiel Camping/Caravanning*, available in bookshops in France.

BUDGET

ACCOMMODATION

The visitor's daily budget will depend largely on the location and standard of accommodation chosen, and on modes of transport (*see* 'Car Hire', below). Hotels in the larger, more fashionable coastal resorts tend inevitably to be expensive, and heading inland can be more affordable. Self-catering is obviously a good way of keeping costs down and half or full board in a hotel can be a good-value option.

This guide lists a wide selection of accommodation in four price categories:

Budget

Moderate

Chic

Très Chic

FOOD AND DRINK

Good-quality, inexpensive food is available in many local restaurants (this is France, after all) and most offer fixed-price (*prix fixe*) menus that are generally better value than à la carte. Lunch can be very reasonable – often a couple of courses with wine for under 70F. Inland you can dine well in the evening for less than 200F a head, while on the coast competition tends to keep restaurant prices reasonably low. For picnics and self-catering, head to the local markets where you'll find fresh, delicious and tempting produce. Other good sources for picnic food include the *charcutier* for cold meats, or *traiteur*, which offers pre-prepared dishes sold by weight in cartons or tubs. The local specialities of *pissaladière*, *socca* and *pan bagnat* are perfect for the hamper.

If your hotel tariff doesn't include breakfast, it is often better value to venture out for your coffee and croissant. Hotel breakfasts charged separately tend to be rather pricey.

Wine and beer are generally very cheap in supermarkets, but mark-up on wine in restaurants is high, so go for the house wine or *vin de pays*, which is usually excellent and much cheaper. Drinks in cafés and bars can make a big hole in your pocket, and prices may take your breath – and cash – away in some of the smarter spots on the Côte. Black coffee, wine and draught lager (*un demi*) are the safest options.

CLIMATE

The lovely Mediterranean climate and mild winters have attracted visitors since the earliest days of tourism, when royals, aristocrats, playboys, consumptives and painters all came to this sun-kissed area. Provence has high mountains as well as a Mediterranean coastline and does experience regional variations in its climate, but, generally speaking, the summer months are hot. During these months, it can be uncomfortable during the day, but the evenings are cool and perfect for sitting and dining outside. Sea breezes can lower temperatures dramatically.

May and June are the best months to visit, with bright and sunny days, and gorgeous floral displays. July and August are hot and busy. The weather is still warm in September in Provence and on the Côte d'Azur, when the summer crowds have left, and can remain pleasant into October. The first snow falls in the Alps in October. The winter months can be bright and cool, too, but November and December are Provence's potentially rainy months. In November, some museums, restaurants and hotels are closed. December brings Christmas holiday tourists and the first skiers.

The Mistral wind (*see* page 86) blows down from the north along the Rhône Valley and roars over Provence to clear away the clouds. It generally spares the Côte d'Azur and rarely gets as far as Nice, but it does affect the area in and around Marseille. It is more prevalent in winter and spring but you might be unlucky enough to encounter it in early May. A cloudless sky and dry and cold atmosphere are good indications of its imminent arrival.

If you fancy a dip in the Mediterranean, the sea is usually warm enough for the first swim of the year in April and May.

CLOTHING

Even during the warmer months, a sweater or light jacket is useful for the evenings, when temperatures can drop dramatically. The sea breeze can cause it to be quite chilly at night, even at the height of summer. Take a pair of comfortable walking shoes if you want to enjoy some of the region's spectacular walking routes. In the winter months, you'll need warm clothing. It may be sunny, but the Mistral or rain clouds might be lying in wait. The French are generally quite smartly dressed, particularly in the evenings. If you're planning to visit an upmarket restaurant or enjoy a drink in a chic café in St Tropez, Cannes or Nice (or some star-spotting in a nightclub), you won't feel out of place if you make a bit of an effort.

GENERAL INFORMATION

COMMUNICATIONS

POST

Stamps are available at post offices (*la poste*, closed after 12 noon Saturday and all day Sunday), at newsagents (*tabacs*) and sometimes in souvenir or postcard shops. Postcards and letters up to 20g to the UK cost 3F. Post offices are listed in this guide where relevant; last pick-up is around 6pm or 7pm. Outgoing post can usually be left at the reception desk of larger hotels.

You can receive mail at the central post offices of most towns through the *Poste Restante* system. Letters should be addressed to you (preferably with the surname first and in capitals) at 'Poste Restante, Poste Centrale', followed by the name of the town and its postcode, if possible (detailed in this guide for all the main cities). Remember to ask for the staff to check the sorting boxed under the initial of your first name as well as your surname. To collect your mail you will need a passport or other identification. There may be a charge of a couple of francs.

French post-boxes are yellow and often have three slots – one for the town you are in, one for the surrounding *département* and one for other destinations. Each town has its own postcode, this is indicated in brackets next to the town name in the guide e.g.: SALON-DE-PROVENCE (13330).

TELEPHONE

Phone calls in France cost roughly the same as in the US and UK. As in all countries, phoning from a hotel is expensive. Few public phones accept coins, with phone cards (*télécartes*) being far more widely used. The cards are good value for money, and are available from *tabacs* or from post offices.

For all calls within France – both local and long-distance – dial all 10 digits of the phone number. For calls from outside France, dial the country code (*see below*), then drop the first zero of the 10-digit number and dial the remaining nine digits.

Phone numbers are broken up into five sets of two, and each set is spoken as a whole number, unless you ask for them to be given *chiffre par chiffre* (singly). The number 02-25-30-55-68, for example, would be said 'zero-two, twenty-five, thirty, fifty-five, sixty-eight'.

Area codes

France is divided into five telephone regions, using the area codes 1 to 5. The regions have been allocated as follows:

01 Paris (and environs)

02 North West France (Nantes, Rouen, and including Brittany)

03 North East France (Lille, Strasbourg, and so on)

04 South East France (Lyon, Marseille, and so on)

05 South West France (Bordeaux, Toulouse, and so on)

Dialling codes to France

From United Kingdom: 00 33

From Republic of Ireland: 00 33

From United States: 011 33

From Canada: 011 33

From Australia: 0011 33

From New Zealand: 00 33

From South Africa: 09 33

Dialling codes from France

United Kingdom: 00 44

Republic of Ireland: 00 353

United States: 00 1

Canada: 00 1

Australia: 00 61

New Zealand: 00 64

South Africa: 00 27

GENERAL INFORMATION

Mobile Phones

A large proportion of the French population seems to live by and through its mobile phones. Many British-registered mobile phones can be used in Provence and Côte d'Azur, but most US mobile phones don't work in Europe, so check with your supplier before you leave.

INTERNET

The French are mad about technology – indeed, they have had access to online information for more than 15 years, with France Telecom's Minitel service. Tourist offices should be able to provide details of local Internet cafés, which provide computer terminals by the hour where you can pick up and send emails and surf the Web. Many serve coffee and other drinks, and sometimes sandwiches and snacks. Some of the larger post offices and libraries also have terminals for public use.

To set up a free Web-based email account to use while you are away, visit the websites at www.hotmail.com or www.yahoo.com and follow instructions.

This guide also lists email addresses of hotels where available, and this is a useful way of booking a room in advance.

CONVERSION TABLES

Men's sizes

Shirts

UK	USA	EUROPE
14	14	36
14½	14½	37
15	15	38
15½	15½	39
16	16	41
16½	16½	42
17	17	43
17½	17½	44
18	18	46

Suits

UK	USA	EUROPE
36	36	46
38	38	48
40	40	50
42	42	52
44	44	54
46	46	56

Shoes

UK	USA	EUROPE
6	8	39
7	9	40
8	10	41
9	10.5	42
10	11	43
11	12	44
12	13	45

Women's sizes

Shirts/dresses

UK	USA	EUROPE
8	6	36
10	8	38
12	10	40
14	12	42
16	14	44
18	16	46

Sweaters

UK	USA	EUROPE
8	6	44
10	8	46
12	10	48
14	12	50
16	14	52

Shoes

UK	USA	EUROPE
3	5	36
4	6	37
5	7	38
6	8	39
7	9	40
8	10	41

Temperature

- To convert °C to °F, multiply by 1.8 and add 32.
- To convert °F to °C, subtract 32 and multiply by 5/9 (0.55). 0° C = 32° F

US weights and measures

1 centimetre	0.39 inches	1 inch	2.54 centimetres
1 metre	3.28 feet	1 foot	0.30 metres
1 metre	1.09 yards	1 yard	0.91 metres
1 kilometre	0.62 miles	1 mile	1.61 kilometres
1 hectare	2.47 acres	1 acre	0.40 hectares
1 litre	2.11 pints	1 pint	0.47 litres
1 litre	0.26 gallons	1 gallon	3.79 litres
1 gram	0.035 ounces	1 ounce	28.35 grams
1 kilogram	2.2 pounds	1 pound	0.45 kilograms

TRAVELLERS WITH DISABILITIES

The ♿ logo is used in this guide to indicate those establishments that have disabled access or offer rooms that are suitable for guests with disabilities. Some places are fully equipped in this respect and meet the latest requirements. Others are older or less sophisticated and, as a result, unable to fulfill the most recent requirements. However, they still welcome all travellers and manage to provide access to bedrooms or to the restaurant. As always, it is advisable to check in advance if a hotel or restaurant is able to cater to your personal mobility needs.

A number of groups and associations continue to try to integrate people with disabilities into everyday life in France and in Europe in general.

Useful information on access and facilities for the disabled is available from the **Comité National Français de Liaison pour la Réadaptation des Handicapés** (CNRH), 236 *bis* rue de Tolbiac, 75013 Paris. ☎ 01-53-80-66-44. They will send you a catalogue of publications.

Other helpful information can be found at the following websites:

www.access-able.com

www.handitel.org

EATING OUT

For more on food and drink in the region, *see* page 90.

The choice of places to eat in Provence and on the Côte d'Azur is as varied as the landscape of the region. The coast is known for its seafood restaurants (some of which are quite pricey), while in the larger towns a wide selection of excellent establishments includes some of the best eating places outside Paris. Italian cooking is popular in the area, and it's not hard to find North African, Vietnamese, Chinese, Cambodian or Thai food. Visitors head inland to the smaller villages of the Var for more traditional Provençal fare.

In every chapter, this guide lists a wide range of places to eat, to suit various budgets and tastes.

Restaurants generally serve lunch from noon until 2pm, with dinner from 7pm to 10pm. Cafés and bars in towns stay open later and brasseries in the cities tend to offer continuous service. Meals are important daily events in the south of France and some villages or small towns come to a virtual standstill during lunch or dinner.

Many hotel restaurants serve non-residents, too, and can be a good choice. The prices are generally reasonable and the atmosphere friendly and interesting. If you are staying in a *chambre d'hôte*, take up the option of a meal with your hosts; it will usually be prepared from fresh, home-grown or local produce, and will be inexpensive. In rural areas, you'll find bars and cafés at the centre of village life, sometimes with tables outside or even a garden. A café lunch will usually include a *plat du jour* (daily special) and a dessert plus a quarter-litre of wine for around 50F, or sandwiches, omelettes and salads. In some rural areas, the local café may serve dinner too. Bars tend to serve sandwiches or a *croque monsieur* (toasted ham and cheese sandwich) rather than a full meal.

There's also a wide selection of portable and picnic food in the shops of Provençal villages and towns. Snack-food opportunities include outdoor kiosks selling crêpes, pizza slices and sandwiches, not forgetting *frites* (chips), of course. In Nice and Antibes, the popular snack is *socca*, a pancake made from chickpea flour and cooked before your eyes.

PRICES AND *MENUS*

Prices, and what they include, are usually posted outside. If prices are not listed, they may be quite high, so do check. There's often more than one set-price menu (*menu fixe*), with a specified number of courses and a relatively limited choice. Eating your main meal at midday can be a good way of saving money, since many places offer great-value lunch menus. The *menu fixe* often includes a glass or half-carafe of house wine (*vin compris*). At the cheaper end, menus tend to focus on standard dishes, including *steak-frites* (steak and chips). The more expensive ones offer a good way of enjoying up to five courses of regional dishes, while a set-price gourmet *menu dégustation* can be a great treat, with a range of the chef's specialities. If you just want one course, go for the *plat du jour*, often served in bars and brasseries. The other alternative is the no-choice *formule* menu, where what you read is what you get.

If you decide to go à la carte, you'll enjoy a much greater choice, unlimited access to the chef's specialities and suffer a larger bill! At least you can opt to go for just one course, choose several starters (*entrées*), or share dishes, and it's a good option for vegetarians.

If service is included, it will say *service compris* (*s.c.*) on the menu; if it is not included, you'll see the words *service non compris* (*s.n.c.* or *servis en sus*), meaning that a tip should be added.

DRINKS

Wine (*vin*) or a drink (*boisson*) is occasionally included in the cost of a *menu fixe*. When ordering house wine (*cuvée du patron*), the cheapest option and usually produced locally, ask for *un quart* or *un pichet* (a quarter-litre), *un demi-litre* (0.5 litre) or *une carafe* (1 litre). This is a good and inexpensive way of sampling the region's wines. For just one glass, ask for *un verre de rouge* (red), *blanc* (white) or *rosé* (pink). If you're anxious about cost, ask for *vin ordinaire* or *vin de table*. *Brut* is very dry, *sec* dry, *demi-sec* and *moelleux* sweetish, *doux* sweet, and *méthode champenoise* sparkling.

Mineral water (*eau minérale*) comes either sparkling (*gazeuse* or *pétillante*) or still (*non-gazeuse* or *plate*). If you would prefer tap water ask for *une carafe d'eau* or *eau du robinet*, which will be brought free to your table. Beer (*bière*) is usually one of the big brands from Alsace, Germany and Belgium, and draft beer (*à la pression*) is cheaper than bottled varieties. Ask for *une pression* or *un demi* (0.33 litre). Pastis is the strong spirit of the Midi and the national drink of the south (for more on local drinks, *see* 'Drinking', p.94).

COURSES IN A FRENCH MEAL

You don't have to 'do as the French do' (generally only on Sunday afternoon) and indulge in a full-scale meal, but, in case you're tempted, it can consist of some or all of the following:

Apéritif: a pre-meal drink, such as Kir (white wine with a dash of Cassis blackcurrant liqueur; Kir Royale uses sparkling white wine). Pastis is celebrated for its appetite-stimulating properties

Hors d'oeuvres: usually soup, pâté or charcuterie. *Tapenade* (a purée of olives, anchovies, olive oil and capers served on toast) is a popular hors d'oeuvres in the region

Entrée: starter or first course, usually fish, salad (often *salade niçoise* here) or an omelette

Plat principal (main course): usually meat, poultry, game or offal, *garni de* (accompanied by) vegetables, rice or potatoes

Salade verte (green salad): to refresh the stomach

Fromage (cheese)

Dessert (also known as *entremets*)

Café, chocolats ou mignardises (coffee, chocolates or petit-fours)

Digestif: an after-dinner drink, such as brandy. Some *digestifs* from the Alps are made with walnuts, cherries, pears and herbs

L'addition (the bill): also known as *la douleureuse* (literally translated as 'the painful one', which it can sometimes be)

WITH THE KIDS (OR THE DOG)

The French welcome children in most places – meals in Provence are very much a family affair. You may find special facilities such as high chairs and baby seats hard to come by, and specific children's menus are rare. However, many establishments will be happy to provide smaller dishes at a reduced price.

It is not uncommon to discover a dog hidden under a neighbouring table or even on its own chair, partly concealed in a smart handbag.

ELECTRICITY

Voltage in France is 220V and sockets accept plugs with two round pins. Adaptors can be bought at the airport before you leave but you can also buy them at most department stores. Some of the more expensive hotels have built-in adaptors, for shavers only.

EMBASSIES AND CONSULATES

FRENCH EMBASSIES AND CONSULATES ABROAD

United Kingdom: French Embassy, 58 Knightsbridge, London SW1X 7JT. ☎ (020) 7201 1000. Website: www.ambafrance.org.uk
French Consulate-General (visas) 6 Cromwell Place, London SW7 7EN. ☎ (020) 7838 2050. 24-hour visa information ☎ (0891) 600215 (premium rate).

Scotland: French Consulate, 11 Randolph Crescent, Edinburgh EH3 7TT. ☎ (0131) 220 6324. 24-hour visa information ☎ (0891) 600215.

Republic of Ireland: French Embassy, 36 Ailesbury Road, Dublin 4. ☎ (01) 260 1666.

United States: French Embassy, 4101 Reservoir Road NW, Washington, DC 20007. ☎ (202) 944-6000 or 6212. Website: www.info-france-usa.org. There are also consulates in Atlanta, Boston, Chicago, Houston, Los Angeles, Miami, New Orleans, New York, San Francisco and Washington, DC.

Canada: French Embassy, 42 Sussex Drive, Ottawa, Ontario K1M 2C9. ☎ (613) 789-1795. Fax: (613) 562-3704. Website: www.amba-ottawa.fr. There are consulates-general in Moncton, Quebec, Toronto and Vancouver.

Australia: French Embassy, 6 Perth Avenue, Yarralumla, ACT 2600. ☎ (43) 2216-0100. Fax: (43) 2216-0156. Email: embassy@france.net.au. Website: www.france.net.au. There are also consulates-general in Sydney and Melbourne.

New Zealand: French Embassy, 34-42 Manners Street, POB 11-343, Wellington. ☎ (04) 384-2555 or 2577. Website: www.ambafrance.net.nz. There is a consulate in Auckland.

South Africa: French Embassy, 807 George Avenue, Arcadia, Pretoria, 0083, Gauteng. ☎ (12) 429-7000 or 7029. Website: www.france.co.za. There are consulates in Johannesburg and Cape Town.

CONSULATES IN PROVENCE AND THE CÔTE D'AZUR

Marseille: UK Consulate: 24 avenue du Prado. ☎ 04-91-15-72-10. Fax: 04-91-37-47-06. Website: www.amb-grandebretagne.fr

US Consulate: 12 boulevard Peytral. Tel 04-91-54-92-00. Website: www.amb-usa.fr

Nice: UK Consulate: 8 rue Alphonse Karr. ☎ 04-93-82-32-04. Fax: 04-93-82-48-24.

US Consulate: 31 rue Maréchal Joffre. ☎ 04-93-88-89-55.

Canadian Consulate: 64 avenue Jean Médecin. ☎ 04-93-92-93-22. Website: www.amba-canada.fr

GENERAL INFORMATION

Antibes: Irish Consulate: boulevard John Kennedy. ☎ 04-93-61-50-63. Fax: 04-93-67-96-08.

Australian citizens can visit the website: www.austgov.fr

EMERGENCIES

Police (Gendarmerie): ☎ 17

Fire (Sapeurs Pompiers): ☎ 18

Emergency medical advice Ambulance service (SAMU), information on nearest hospital, doctor or pharmacy: ☎ 15

SOS Médecins (emergency doctors) and **SOS Dentistes** (emergency dentists): call the local number in the phone book or call ☎ 12 for directory enquiries.

ENTRY FORMALITIES

PASSPORTS AND VISAS

France signed an international agreement in 1985, since which time a visa issued by a French Embassy has included entry not only to France, but also to Austria, Belgium, Germany, Italy, Luxembourg, The Netherlands, Portugal and Spain. There is no longer any formal border between many of these countries, and flights between them now take off and land from domestic terminals.

The UK did not sign this agreement and as a consequence has maintained inter-EU immigration control. However, many UK ports of entry have a separate passenger exit, marked by a blue sign with yellow stars, where EU members can simply wave their passport at an immigration officer.

Citizens of the UK and any other EU country, who hold a valid passport, may remain in France for as long as they wish without a visa and may also be employed while abroad.

Citizens of the United States, **Australia** and **New Zealand** do not require a visa for short stays (up to three months), but they must apply to their nearest consulate or embassy for long-stay visas or a Carte de Commerçant, which permits employment in France.

Canadian citizens do not need a visa to visit France; they are at liberty to remain in the country for a period of up to three months providing they are in possession of a passport valid up to six months after the end of the intended visit. For longer (and working) stays a visa will be required and may be obtained at the French embassy or consulate.

Citizens of South Africa need a visa to enter France and must apply at least three weeks before leaving South Africa. Out of season, visas can be obtained relatively quickly at the nearest consulate or embassy, but queues can be long in summer. Applicants must have a passport that is valid for at least three months after the expiry date of the visa. Short-stay visas are valid for 90 days from the day of issue, and can be used for multiple entries. Transit visas are valid for two months, and long-stay visas are valid for continuous periods of up to 90 days for three years, but are only issued after consideration of each individual case. Students, diplomats or those who have business interests in France should contact their nearest French embassy before departure.

CUSTOMS AND DUTY-FREE

No matter where you are travelling from, the importing of narcotics, copyright infringements, fakes and counterfeit goods is strictly prohibited for anyone travelling to France. Firearms and ammunition are also forbidden unless accompanied by specific authorization from the appropriate Ministry in Paris.

When returning to the UK, obscene material and offensive weapons are prohibited in addition to those items listed by French customs.

UK (EU) citizens: any goods that are for personal use are free from both French and UK customs duty. To meet the criteria of 'personal use' there is a set of guidelines that are used by all EU customs officers. These allow up to 800 cigarettes or 1kg of loose tobacco, 10 litres of spirits, 90 litres of wine and 110 litres of beer. Despite the liberalized restrictions on importing and exporting tobacco and alcohol, the removal of duty-free allowances for EU visitors means that prices in France now include duty, which cannot be recuperated.

At any port of entry, those with nothing to declare should use the 'Green Channel' and those with goods in excess of their allowance should use the 'Red Channel', both marked clearly after passport control. There is a separate 'Blue Channel' for EU residents (*see* 'Passports and Visas').

For further information and clarification, in the UK contact the Excise and Inland Customs Advice Centre ☎ (020) 7202 4227, or visit their website at www.hmce.gov.uk. The UK Customs Office (☎ (020) 7919 6700) publishes a leaflet called *A Guide for Travellers*, detailing regulations and duty-free allowances. In France, call the customs information centre in Paris: ☎ 01-40-01-02-06.

Non-EU citizens: the limitations on import and export outside the EU are far more stringent than within it, but visitors from outside the EU may take home goods free of duty or tax. To qualify, you must spend more than 1,200F at a single store; the retailer will supply a Retail Export Form, called a *bordereau de détaxe*, which must be endorsed by customs and will be returned by them to the retailer, who will in turn refund the tax portion (20.6 per cent) of your purchase.

Visitors over 15 may take up to 1,200F worth of articles back home with them free of duty or tax. In addition they may leave France with 200 cigarettes or 250g of smoking tobacco, 2 litres of wine, 1 litre of spirits and 50g of perfume. Those under 17 may not export tobacco or alcohol from France.

The US Customs Service (PO Box 7407, Washington, DC 20044; ☎ (202) 927-5580) publishes a free leaflet entitled *Know Before You Go*.

GETTING A JOB

See 'Working in France' *below.*

FESTIVALS AND EVENTS

The south of France offers a huge range of festivals and events, ranging from the celebrated and star-spangled Cannes Film Festival to village processions that trace their origins back to the fourteenth century. The following calendar includes some (but by no means all) of the events in the region. Dates change from year to year, so do seek precise information from local tourist offices before travelling.

January
Mid-January: Fête de la St-Marcel, Barjols. Folk-dancing, singing and an ox roast every four years

15–21 January: Rallye de Monte-Carlo. Monte Carlo car rally

February
8–27 February: Fête du Citron, Menton. Lemon festival, with lemon-decorated floats and partying

Week before Ash Wednesday (6 weeks before Easter): Carnaval de Nice. Famous pre-Lenten festivities in the city, including a battle of the flowers and costumed processions

10 February: Corso du Mimosa, Bormes-les-Mimosas, Mandelieu-la-Napoule, St Raphael. Traditional processions

March
End March to early April: Exposition Internationale de la Fleur, Cagnes-sur-Mer. International flower festival

Last Sunday: Festin des Courgourdons, Nice. Festival of folklore and special sculpted local gourds

April
Throughout the month: international tennis, Monaco and Nice

Throughout the month: Jazz Festival, Juan-les-Pins and Antibes

Good Friday: Procession aux Limaces, Roquebrune-Cap-Martin. Traditional Easter procession

Easter: Féria Pascale, Arles. Costumed processions and parties to mark the beginning of the bullfighting season

End April/beginning of May: Fête des Gardians, Arles. Festival of Camargue horsemen

May
Third Sunday after Easter: Bravade St-François, Fréjus. Traditional southern merry-making

May: Jazz en Pays d'Apt. Jazz festival

1 May: Labour Day, throughout the region. Processions and marches, and gifts of lily-of-the-valley

9–20 May: Festival International du Film, Cannes. Annual film festival, with celebs, screenings, prizes and high-powered deals

16–18 May: Bravade de St-Torpes, St-Tropez. Traditional southern merry-making

24–25 May: Gypsy pilgrimage, Stes-Maries-de-la-Mer

27 May: Grand Prix Automobile de Formula 1, Monaco. Grand Prix action

Late May to mid-July: Festival International de Musique, Toulon. International summer music festival

June

Throughout the month: Festival International d'Aix, Aix-en-Provence. Prestigious festival of classical music and opera

Early June, biennial: Fête de la Faïence, Moustiers-Ste-Marie. Pottery festival

15 June: Bravade des Espagnols, St-Tropez. Traditional Spanish-style merry-making

Around 21 June: Fête de la Musique, throughout France. Mid-summer celebration of music in all its forms, with professionals and amateurs performing in all sorts of venues

22 June to 14 August: Chorégies d'Orange, Orange. Choral and opera concerts, in the Roman theatre

23–24 June: Fête de la St-Jean, Arles and other locations. Mid-summer parties and bonfires

July

Chorégies d'Orange, Orange (*see above*)

Throughout the month: Avignon Festival. Wide-ranging arts festival, with its own fringe, known as Le Festival 'Off'

Throughout the month and in August: Riches Heures Musicales, Rotunda, Simiane-la-Rotonde. Medieval, Renaissance and Baroque music

July weekends: International Fireworks Festival, Monaco

First two weeks: Rencontres Internationales de la Photographie, Arles. Photography exhibitions, workshops and seminars

Second week: Jazz à Juan, Juan-les-Pins. Long-running internationally renowned jazz festival

14 July: Bastille Day, throughout the region. Fireworks, parties and big celebrations, including a Grand Banquet on Nice's Promenade des Anglais

Mid-July: Festival de Jazz, Toulon and Nice. Internationally renowned jazz festivals

Mid-July to mid-August: Les Nuits du Sud, Vence. Festival of southern music

Mid-July to early August: Nuits de la Citadelle (Citadel Nights), Sisteron. Programme of music and theatre

August

Throughout the month: Festival de Musique, Menton. Chamber music in the square

August weekends: International Fireworks Festival, Monaco and Cannes

First weekend: Corso de la Lavande, Digne-les-Bains. Traditional procession in celebration of the local crop of lavender

First weekend: Fête du Jasmin, Grasse. Jasmine festival, with floats, music and dancing in the 'capital of perfume'

Around 15 August: Festival of Mexican Folklore, Barcelonnette. Exhibitions and events celebrating Barcelonnette's Mexican connections, including concerts and dance performances, and food

September

Early September: Feria des Prémices du Riz, Arles. Festival celebrating the rice harvest

Mid-September: Journées de la Patrimoine. Heritage days, with national treasures open to the public, free entry to museums

Last week September and first week October: Nioulargue, St-Tropez. Popular yacht race

October

Throughout the month: Fête de la Châtaigne (chestnut festival); St-Paul-de-Vence, Collobrières and other villages in the Maures

November

Throughout the month and into December: Foires aux Santons, Marseille, Digne-les-Bains, and other locations. Fairs and exhibitions showcasing the local speciality of traditional terracotta figurines known as *santons*

19 November: Jour National, Monaco. National day with fireworks

Late November or early December (biennial): Festival International de la Danse, Cannes. Festival of contemporary dance and ballet

December

Throughout the month: Foires aux Santons (*see above*)

Early December: Fête du Vin, Bandol. Wine festival

24 December: Fête des Bergers, Les Baux-de-Provence. Shepherds' festival, with processions and traditional activities, followed by midnight mass

FOREST FIRES

Extensive areas in Provence are forested, largely made up of white or green oak, and pine trees with bushy undergrowth where the famous *herbes de Provence* are found. Every summer, several thousands (and sometimes several tens of thousands) of hectares go up in smoke. Vandals may make the headlines, but they are responsible for only 10 to 20 per cent of the fires, the vast majority of which are caused by careless behaviour.

To avoid the risk of forest fires, follow the basic rules: do not light barbecues, do not use camping gas for campfires, and do not throw cigarette ends away.

The authorities of the Bouches-du-Rhône have had to put draconian measures in place. Cars and pedestrians are forbidden in certain forested areas from 1 July until the second Saturday in September and out of season whenever the wind speed is over 40km/h (25mph). During these periods, exploration of the Mont Sainte-Victoire, the cliff-tops or the Alpilles is not possible. In reality, the rules of the Bouches-du-Rhône are so strict that they are extremely difficult to enforce. In other departments, the approach is more relaxed, with pathways being closed at specific times. Read the signs before setting off down any track.

HEALTH AND INSURANCE

France has a very good public health service, and standards are comparable with those found in other western European countries and the US. For minor ailments, go in the first instance to a pharmacy (look out for the green cross), where highly qualified pharmacists should be able to give you valuable advice. Many medicines are available over the counter in France. There are no compulsory inoculations for visitors to France.

In an emergency, doctors' and dentists' services are available at the end of the phone (see 'Emergencies'). Hospitalized visitors will be expected to make immediate payment for any treatment, but hospital staff will help with arrangements with insurance companies.

Statistically speaking, you are far more likely to encounter accidents or fall victim to some form of crime when abroad than at home. Travel insurance is therefore highly recommended. It is available through credit card companies, travel agents and student and senior-affiliated organisations (such as STA and SAGA). Insurance may be included in the price of your ticket or package, or you may be covered by your credit card company (particularly American Express) if your ticket was purchased with that card.

For South Africans coming to France, the French Embassy will insist on proof of insurance before issuing a visa.

HOSPITALS IN THE REGION

Avignon:
Hôpital de la Durance, 305 rue Raoul Follereau. ☎ 04-90-80-33-33.

Marseille:
La Conception, 147 boulevard Baille. ☎ 04-91-38-30-00.

SOS Médecins (emergency doctor) ☎ 04-91-52-91-52.

Nice:

Hôpital St-Roch, 5 rue Pierre-Devoluy. ☎ 04-92-03-33-75.

Nice Médecins (24-hour doctor service) ☎ 04 93 52 42 42.

Hospitalized visitors will be expected to make immediate payment for any treatment, but hospital staff will help with arrangements with insurance companies.

IF YOU NEED TREATMENT

Local hospitals are the place to go in an emergency (*urgence*). Even French citizens have to pay for ambulances. Doctors take turns being on duty at night and on holidays, even in rural areas. Their telephone numbers normally carry a recorded message with instructions on what to do, so try to get a French speaker to help you understand these. It's worth carrying a phone card with you for just such an occasion. You can ask for a doctor's details at a pharmacy (*pharmacie*) or look them up under '*Médecins qualifiés*'. *See also* 'Emergencies'.

British and Irish visitors: Form E111 entitles the holder to free or reduced-cost medical treatment when in France. Available at any main post office, the E111 must be filled out and stamped by the post office before departure; it is issued free of charge and is valid indefinitely, or until used to claim treatment.

North American visitors: whereas Canada's public health service will pay a proportion of its citizens' medical costs while abroad, the US Medicare/Medicaid programme does not cover health expenses outside the USA, and US medical insurance is not always valid in France. It is advisable to check the nature and extent of foreign coverage with individual insurance companies; often, the visitor will have to pay first and claim reimbursement later.

Australians, New Zealanders and South African visitors: citizens of these countries are on their own if they need treatment and do not have health insurance. French hospitals demand on-the-spot payment for medical care, so insurance is vital.

If it isn't an emergency, visit a pharmacy. There's a rota of pharmacies in cities and information is available in the local newspaper or in the windows of the pharmacies themselves.

GENERAL INFORMATION

LANGUAGE

French is the official language of the region, but 'Provençal,' the tongue of the medieval troubadours, survives. It's known as *langue d'oc* (as opposed to the *langue d'oïl* of northern France, *oc* and *oïl* meaning 'yes' in the south and north respectively). It is spoken only by a very few local people nowadays but is officially being encouraged and appears sometimes on dual-language road signs. It differs from standard French because of the richness of its vowels, which are distinctly voiced, resulting in a rounder and more musical language.

Visitors need not worry too much about mastering Provençal, but it is worth trying to get to grips with some French. Just a few words or sentences will be appreciated by the locals.

A selection of very basic French vocabulary follows, with apologies if the word you need is missing. For those struggling with French menus, there is more help at the back of this guide in the detailed menu decoder.

Finally, if you do not know the correct French word, try using the English one with a French accent – it is surprising how often this works.

BASIC GRAMMAR

The French language is closely linked to its grammar and a grasp of the basics is useful.

Nouns and Adjectives

All French nouns are either masculine or feminine and gender is denoted as follows: 'the' singular is translated by le (m), la (f) or l' (used only before a word beginning with a vowel or a mute 'h'; 'the' plural = les (whatever gender and in front of a vowel or mute 'h'). 'A' = un (m), une (f) (there are no exceptions for vowels or mute 'h').

Adjectives agree with the gender of the accompanying noun. A singular masculine noun uses the adjective with no change; for a singular feminine noun, an 'e' is added. In the plural, in either case, add an 's' to whatever you had in the singular. Don't worry too much about gender agreement when talking, although if you wish to perfect your pronunciation, remember that as 'e' or 'es' usually makes the final consonant hard. The 's' in the plural is not pronounced. When you are in a hurry, worrying about the correct gender can complicate things – just say 'le' or 'la', whichever comes into your head first. Sometimes you will get it right and you'll usually be understood.

In the listings that follow, the feminine versions of nouns and adjectives, where applicable, are given simply to help you to understand written French. The words are either written out in full or shown as '(e)'.

Pronouns

There are two forms of the word 'you' – tu is 'you' in the singular, very informal and used with people you know, vous is 'you' in the singular but is used in formal situations and when you don't know the person, vous is also the plural form. Young people often address each other as 'tu' automatically, but when in doubt and to avoid offence, always use 'vous'.

Verbs

Just three verbs are the foundation of all verb forms in French: the verbs 'être' ('to be'), 'avoir' ('to have') and 'aller' ('to go'). However sketchy your knowledge of French may be, you can get a long way by just knowing these. The past tenses of verbs are constructed using the verb 'to have' (a small number of exceptions use the verb 'to be') and the future tense is built using the verb 'to go' (as 'I am going to . . .'). Be familiar with them and you're halfway there!

The verb 'to be' ('être'):

I am	je suis
you are (informal/sing.)	tu es
he/it is	il(m)/elle(f)/il est
we are	nous sommes
you are (formal/plural)	vous êtes
they are	ils(m)/elles(f) sont

To say 'it is'/'that is'/'this is' use 'c'est'; the plural is 'ce sont'. It is not gender-specific.

The verb 'to have' ('avoir'):

I have	j'ai
you have (informal/sing.)	tu as
he/she/it has	il(m)/elle(f)/il a
we have	nous avons
you have (formal/plural)	vous avez
they have	ils(m)/elles(f) ont

The verb 'to go' ('aller'):

I go	je vais
you go (informal/sing.)	tu vas
he/she/it goes	il(m)/elle(f)/il va
we go	nous allons
you go (formal/plural)	vous allez
they go	ils(m)/elles(f) vont

ESSENTIAL VOCABULARY

Yes/No	Oui/Non
OK	D'accord
That's fine	C'est bon
Please	S'il vous plaît
Thank you	Merci
Good morning/Hello (during the day)	Bonjour
Good evening/night/Hello (during the evening)	Bonsoir
Hello/Goodbye (very informal)	Salut
Goodbye	Au revoir
See you soon	A bientôt
Excuse me	Excusez-moi
I am sorry	Je suis désolé(m)/désolée(f)
Pardon?	Comment?

GENERAL INFORMATION

Handy Phrases

Do you speak English?	Parlez-vous anglais?
I don't speak French	Je ne parle pas français
I don't understand	Je ne comprends pas
Could you speak more slowly please?	Pouvez-vous parler moins vite, s'il vous plaît?
Could you repeat that, please?	Pouvez-vous répéter, s'il vous plaît?
again/once again	encore/encore une fois
I am English/Scottish/ Welsh/Irish/American/ Canadian/Australian/ a New Zealander	Je suis anglais(e)/écossaise)/ gallois(e)/irlandais(e)/américain(e)/ canadien(ne)/australien(ne)/ néo-zélandais(e)
My name is . . .	Je m'appelle . . .
What is your name?	Comment vous appelez-vous?
How are you?	Comment allez-vous?
Very well, thank you	Très bien, merci
Pleased to meet you	Enchanté(e).
Mr/Mrs	Monsieur/Madame
Miss/Ms	Mademoiselle/Madame
How?	Comment?
What?	Quel (m)/Quelle (f)?
When?	Quand?
Where (is/are)?	Où (est/sont)?
Which?	Quel (m)/Quelle (f)?
Who?	Qui?
Why?	Pourquoi?

Essential Words

good	bon/bonne
bad	mauvais/mauvaise
big	grand/grande
small	petit/petite
hot	chaud/chaude
cold	froid/froide
open	ouvert/ouverte
closed	fermé/fermée
toilets	les toilettes/les W.C.
women	dames
men	hommes
free (unoccupied)	libre
occupied	occupé/occupée
free (no charge)	gratuit/gratuite
entrance	l'entrée
exit	la sortie
prohibited	interdit/interdite
no smoking	défense de fumer

TIME AND SPACE

Periods of Time

a minute	une minute
half an hour	une demie-heure
an hour	une heure
week	une semaine
fortnight	une quinzaine
month	un mois
year	un an/une année
today	aujourd'hui
yesterday/tomorrow	hier/demain
morning	le matin
afternoon	l'après-midi
evening/night	le soir/la nuit
during (the night)	pendant (la nuit)
early/late	tôt/tard

Telling the Time

What time is it?	Quelle heure est-il?
At what time?	À quelle heure?
(at) 1 o'clock/2 o'clock etc.	(à) une heure/deux heures etc.
half past one	une heure et demie
quarter past two	deux heures et quart
quarter to three	trois heures moins le quart
(at) midday	à midi
(at) midnight	à minuit

See also 'Numbers'

GETTING AROUND

by bicycle	à bicyclette/en vélo
by bus	en bus
by car	en voiture
by coach	en car
on foot	à pied
by plane	en avion
by taxi	en taxi
by train	en train

In Town

map of the city	un plan de la ville
I am going to . . .	Je vais à . . .
I want to go to . . .	Je voudrais aller à . . .
I want to get off at . . .	Je voudrais descendre à . . .
platform	le quai
return ticket	un aller-retour
single ticket	un aller simple
ticket	le billet

timetable	l'horaire
airport	l'aéroport
bus/coach station	la gare routière
bus stop	l'arrêt de bus
district	le quartier/l'arrondissement
street	la rue
taxi rank	la station de taxi
tourist information office	l'office du tourisme
train station	la gare
underground	le métro
underground station	la station de métro
bag/handbag	le sac/le sac-à-main
case	la valise
left luggage	la consigne
luggage	les bagages

Directions

Is it far?	Est-ce que c'est loin?
How far is it (from here) to . . . ?	Combien de kilomètres (d'ici) à . . . ?
Is it near?	Est-ce que c'est près d'ici?
here/there	ici/là
near/far	près/loin
left/right	gauche/droite
on the left/right	à gauche/à droite
straight on	tout droit
at the end of	au bout de
up	en haut
down	en bas
above (the shop)	au-dessus (du magasin)
below (the bed)	au-dessous (du lit)
opposite (the bank)	en face (de la banque)
next to (the window)	à côté (de la fenêtre)

DRIVING

Please fill the tank (car)	Le plein, s'il vous plaît
car hire	la location de voitures
driver's licence	le permis de conduire
petrol	l'essence
to rent/hire a car	louer une voiture
unleaded	sans plomb

IN THE HOTEL

I have a reservation	J'ai une réservation
for 2 nights	pour 2 nuits
I leave . . .	Je pars . . .
I'd like a room.	Je voudrais une chambre.
Is breakfast included?	le petit-déjeuner est inclus/compris?
single room	une chambre à un lit/une chambre simple

room with double bed	une chambre à lit double/ Une chambre à grand lit
twin room	une chambre à deux lits
room with bathroom and toilet	une chambre avec salle de bains et toilette/W.C.
a quiet room	une chambre calme
bath	le bain
shower	la douche
with air conditioning	avec climatisation
1st/2nd floor etc	premier/deuxième étage
breakfast	le petit-déjeuner
dining room	la salle à manger
ground floor	le rez-de-chaussée (RC)
key	la clef
lift/elevator	l'ascenseur

Paying

How much?	C'est combien, s'il vous plaît?/ Quel est le prix?
Do you accept credit cards?	Est-ce que vous acceptez les cartes de crédit?
Do you have any change?	Avez-vous de la monnaie?
(in) cash	(en) espèces
coin	la pièce de monnaie
money	l'argent
notes	les billets
price	le prix
travellers' cheques	les chèques de voyage

EATING OUT

See also 'Understanding the Menu' at the end of the book.

General

Do you have a table?	Avez-vous une table libre?
I would like to reserve a table.	Je voudrais réserver une table.
I would like to eat.	Je voudrais manger.
I would like something to drink.	Je voudrais boire quelque-chose.
I would like to order, please.	Je voudrais commander, s'il vous plaît.
The bill, please.	L'addition, s'il vous plaît.
I am a vegetarian.	Je suis végétarien (ne).

Meals and Mealtimes

breakfast	le petit-déjeuner
cover charge	le couvert
dessert	le dessert
dinner	le dîner
dish of the day	le plat du jour

fixed price menu	la formule/le menu à prix fixe
fork	la fourchette
knife	le couteau
lunch	le déjeuner
main course	le plat principal
menu	le menu/la carte
(Is the) service included?	Est-ce que le service est compris?
soup	la soupe/le potage
spoon	la cuillère
starter	l'entrée/le hors-d'oeuvre
waiter	Monsieur
waitress	Madame, Mademoiselle
wine list	la carte des vins

Cooking Styles

baked	cuit/cuite au four
boiled	bouilli/bouillie
fried	à la poêle
grilled	grillé/grillée
medium	cuit/cuite à point
poached	poché/pochée
rare	saignant
steamed	à la vapeur
very rare	bleu
well done	bien cuit/cuite

Meat, Poultry, Game and Offal

bacon	le bacon
beef	le boeuf
chicken	le poulet
duck	le canard
frogs' legs	les cuisses de grenouilles
game	le gibier
ham	le jambon
kidneys	les rognons
lamb	l'agneau
meat	la viande
pork	le porc
rabbit	le lapin
salami style sausage (dry)	le saucisson-sec
sausage	la saucisse
snails	les escargots
steak	l'entrecôte/le steak/le bifteck
veal	le veau

Fish and Seafood

cod	le cabillaud/la morue
Dublin bay prawn/scampi	la langoustine
fish	le poisson

herring	le hareng
lobster	le homard
mullet	le rouget
mussels	les moules
oysters	les huîtres
pike	le brochet
prawns	les crevettes
salmon (smoked)	le saumon (fumé)
sea bass	le bar
seafood	les fruits de mer
shellfish	les crustacés
skate	le raie
squid	le calmar
trout	la truite
tuna	le thon

Vegetables, Pasta and Rice

cabbage	le chou
cauliflower	le chou-fleur
chips/french fries	les frites
garlic	l'ail
green beans	les haricots verts
leeks	les poireaux
onions	les oignons
pasta	les pâtes
peas	les petits pois
potatoes	les pommes-de-terre
rice	le riz
sauerkraut	la choucroute
spinach	les épinards
vegetables	les légumes

Salad Items

beetroot	la betterave
cucumber	le concombre
curly endive	la salade frisée
egg	un oeuf
green pepper/red pepper	le poivron/poivron rouge
green salad	la salade verte
lettuce	la laitue
tomato	la tomate

Fruit

apple	la pomme
banana	la banane
blackberries	les mûres
blackcurrants	les cassis
cherries	les cerises
fresh fruit	le fruit frais

grapefruit	le pamplemousse
grapes	les raisins
lemon/lime	le citron/le citron vert
orange	l'orange
peach	la pêche
pear	la poire
plums	les prunes/les mirabelles (type of plum)
raspberries	les framboises
red/whitecurrants	les groseilles
strawberries	les fraises

Desserts and Cheese

apple tart	la tarte aux pommes
cake	le gâteau
cheese	le fromage
cream	la crème fraîche
goat's cheese	le fromage de chèvre
ice cream	la glace

Sundries

ashtray	un cendrier
bread	le pain
bread roll	le petit pain
butter	le beurre
crisps	les chips
mustard	la moutarde
napkin	la serviette
oil	l'huile
peanuts	les cacahuètes
salt/pepper	le sel/le poivre
toast	le toast
vinegar	le vinaigre

DRINKS

beer	la bière
a bottle of . . .	une bouteille de . . .
black coffee	un café noir
coffee	un café
with cream	un café-crème
with milk	un café au lait
a cup of . . .	une tasse de . . .
decaffeinated coffee	un café/décaféiné/un déca
espresso coffee	un express
freshly-squeezed lemon/orange juice	un citron pressé/une orange pressée
a glass of . . .	un verre de . . .
herbal tea	une tisane/infusion
with lime/verbena	au tilleul/à la verveine

with mint	à la menthe
with milk/lemon	au lait/au citron
milk	le lait
(some) mineral water	de l'eau minérale
orange juice	un jus d'orange
(some) tap water	de l'eau du robinet
(some) sugar	du sucre
tea	un thé
wine (red/white)	le vin (rouge/blanc)

SHOPPING

See also 'Paying'

Useful Shopping Vocabulary

I'd like to buy . . .	Je voudrais acheter . . .
Do you have . . . ?	Avez-vous . . . ?
How much, please?	C'est combien, s'il vous plaît?
I'm just looking, thank you.	Je regarde, merci.
It's for a gift.	C'est pour un cadeau/C'est pour offrir.

Shops

antique shop	le magasin d'antiquités
baker	la boulangerie
bank	la banque
book shop	la librairie
cake shop	la pâtisserie
cheese shop	la fromagerie
chemist/drugstore	la pharmacie
clothes shop	le magasin de vêtements
delicatessen	la charcuterie
department store	le grand magasin
gift shop	le magasin de cadeaux
the market	le marché
newsagent	le magasin de journaux
post office	la poste/le PTT
shoe shop	le magasin de chaussures
the shops	les boutiques/magasins
tobacconist	le tabac
travel agent	l'agence de voyages
expensive	cher
cheap	pas cher, bon marché
sales	les soldes
size (in clothes)	la taille
size (in shoes)	la pointure
too expensive	trop cher

TELEPHONING

telephone/phone booth	le téléphone/la cabine téléphonique
phone card	la carte téléphonique
post card	la carte postale
stamps	les timbres

DAYS OF THE WEEK

Monday	lundi
Tuesday	mardi
Wednesday	mercredi
Thursday	jeudi
Friday	vendredi
Saturday	samedi
Sunday	dimanche

COLOURS

black	noir/noire
blue	bleu/bleue
brown	brun/brune
green	vert/verte
orange	orange
pink	rose
red	rouge
white	blanc/blanche
yellow	jaune

NUMBERS

enough	assez
zero	zéro
one; first	un/une; premier/première
two/second	deux/deuxième
three/third	trois/troisième
four/fourth	quatre/quatrième
five/fifth	cinq/cinquième
six/sixth	six/sixième
seven/seventh	sept/septième
eight/eighth	huit/huitième
nine/nineth	neuf/neuvième
ten/tenth etc	dix/dixième etc
eleven	onze
twelve	douze
thirteen	treize
fourteen	quatorze
fifteen	quinze
sixteen	seize
seventeen	dix-sept
eighteen	dix-huit

nineteen	dix-neuf
twenty	vingt
twenty-one	vingt-et-un
twenty-two/three etc	vingt-deux/vingt-trois etc
thirty	trente
forty	quarante
fifty	cinquante
sixty	soixante
seventy	soixante-dix
eighty	quatre-vingts
ninety	quatre-vingt-dix
hundred	cent
thousand	mille

MEDIA

NEWSPAPERS AND MAGAZINES

For those of you who want to keep in touch, English-language newspapers (British and American) are on sale on the day after publication in most large cities and resorts. If you fancy reading a French newspaper, *Le Monde* is the most widely respected, but it is rather highbrow, with few photos! It is also available online (in French), at www.lemonde.fr. *Le Figaro* is also quite conservative whereas *Libération* (known as *Libé*) is more left-wing. The top-selling national is *L'Équipe* ('The Team'), which is dedicated to sports coverage.

Numerous magazines, covering every subject from health, nature and cycling, to travel and gossip, are sold in shops and *tabacs*, and from traditional *kiosques* (newsstands) on the streets.

Regional dailies enjoy a wide circulation and are useful to visitors for their listings of current events. You'll see *La Marseillaise*, *Le Provençal* and *Le Méridional* at the local kiosks. Many cities and resorts publish their own free magazine – for example, *Taktik* in Marseille – with local information and events listings. They are usually available from tourist offices, hotels, and some restaurants and bars.

RADIO AND TV

France has four television channels in the public sector (France 2, France 3, Arte and La 5ème), together with three private channels (TF1, M6 and Canal Plus). Viewing reaches its peak at 8pm when the French gather round their sets to watch the news either on TF1 or France 2. There are 250 channels available on cable or via satellite and some hotels offer these facilities, as do a few of the more luxurious campsites. Cable networks include CNN, BBC World Service, BBC Prime, MTV and Paris Première, with its selection of original-language (*VO*, or *version originale*) films, which are subtitled rather than dubbed into French.

On the radio, you can tune into the English-language news on the BBC World Service on 648kHz AM or 198kHz LW from midnight to 5am and

Radio 4 during the day. You can listen to Voice of America on 90.5, 98.8 and 102.4 FM. For radio news in French, listen to France Inter on 87.8 FM, Europe 1 on 104.7 FM or France Infos, the national rolling-news station, on 105.5 FM. Riviera Radio broadcasts in English throughout the south of France on 106.3 FM and 106.5 FM stereo from Monte-Carlo. Their programmes include news in English from the BBC, 24-hour music and current affairs.

French and international news is accessible online at www.afp.com

MONEY

THE EURO

TIP Euro coins and notes are due to be introduced in January 2002 and the euro will be the sole currency in France (and Monaco) from 17 February 2002. At the time of writing we were unable to include the equivalent euro prices alongside prices in francs, however those readers familiar with the French franc should find the franc prices a useful guide.

To convert franc prices into euros, divide the amount in francs by 6.56; so for example, 1,000F = 152.43€. The official euro/franc conversion rate has been fixed at 6.56 French francs to one euro. The euro/£ conversion rate stands at about 63 pence to one euro. Check the currency website **www.oanda.com** for up-to-date Sterling/euro conversion rates.

1 euro = 6.56 FF

1 euro = circa 63 pence

CHANGING MONEY

Foreign currency or travellers' cheques can be exchanged at banks displaying a *Change* sign (closed Saturday and Sunday) or at Bureaux de Change at all French airports, in train stations of big cities and in town centres. They are likely to stay open on Sundays in popular tourist areas, but their rates are less favourable than at the bank. American Express travellers cheques are widely accepted in France and if they are exchanged at an Amex office, you won't pay commission. You can also obtain travellers cheques from Thomas Cook or your bank.

Bureaux de Change

Cannes: Office Provençal, 17 avenue Maréchal Foch. ☎ 04-93-39-34-37.

Marseille: Change de la Canebière, 39 La Canabière. ☎ 04-91-13-71-26.

Monaco: Compagnie Monégasque de Change, avenue Quarantaine. ☎ 00-377-93-25-02-50.

Nice: Office Provençal, 64 avenue Jean Médecin. ☎ 04-93-13-45-44.

CREDIT CARDS

Credit cards are widely accepted in France, but check window stickers in hotels, shops or restaurants to make sure that yours is there. Visa (Carte Bleue in France) is almost universally recognized, with Access, Mastercard (also known as Eurocard), Diners Club and American Express also commonly accepted. Some Provençal businesses don't accept American Express, and smaller hotels and restaurant often take payment in cash only.

Credit cards may be used for cash advances at banks and in automatic teller machines (ATMs), with instructions in French or English. The PIN number should be the same as the one you use at home but do check before you leave. Since all French credit cards are now smart cards (containing a microchip capable of storing data, known as a *puce*), your request may be denied. Try another machine if so. If your card is denied in a restaurant or hotel, explain that it is a foreign card with a magnetic strip (*piste magnétique*). You may have to tap in your PIN code and press the green key (*validez*) on a keypad or the staff may make a call to clear it.

When paying by credit card, check the amount that appears on the slip or on the machine – there's no decimal point between 'francs' and 'centimes', but there may be a comma.

Most French banks and other establishments no longer accept Euro-cheques, not to be confused with cheques in euros.

Lost or Stolen Cards

If your card is lost or stolen, cancel it as soon as possible by calling the number in your own country; make sure you have the 24-hour contact number with you. Visa and Barclaycard holders can freephone from France for assistance:

Barclaycard (24-hour) ☎ (01604) 234234.

Visa (24-hour) ☎ (01383) 621166.

Numbers in France are as follows:

Visa ☎ 01-45-67-84-84.

American Express (cards) ☎ 01-47-77-72-00.

American Express (travellers' cheques) ☎ 08-00-90-86-00 (free call from France only).

Diners Club ☎ 01-49-06-17-50.

MUSEUMS

A museum pass from the *Centre des Monuments Nationaux* (Centre for National Monuments) is valid for one year and gives entry to 107 historic sites throughout France. Benefits include free access to temporary exhibitions in the listed locations and no queueing.

In Provence, the card is valid for the Hôtel de Sade, the Glanum archaeological site in St-Rémy-de-Provence, Château d'If in Marseille, Abbaye de Montmajour and Château de Tarascon. On the Côte d'Azur, the card is valid for the Roman Trophy of the Alps at La Turbie, the monastery in Saorge, the cloister of Fréjus Cathedral, the Abbaye du Thoronet and the archaeological site of Olbia, near Hyères.

The pass costs 280F and can be purchased at the sites mentioned or by post from the *Centre des Monuments Nationaux,* Centre d'Information, 62 rue St-Antoine, 75186 Paris Cedex 04. ☎ 01-44-61-21-50.

Guid'Arts: this excellent guide (in French) to contemporary art in Provence-Alpes-Côte d'Azur lists all the museums, galleries and exhibition spaces, and gives lots of useful addresses.

POLICE

If you're unlucky enough to be the victim of a theft, head to the nearest police station or *gendarmerie* with your identity (and vehicle papers). You need a police statement for insurance purposes. You may need to be patient, and it is also helpful to speak some French. In the event of losing your passport, inform both the police and the nearest consulate.

By law, the French police can stop anyone and demand to see their ID; the French are obliged to carry their identity cards with them at all times. The police don't often pick on respectable-looking tourists, but be polite and patient if they do choose to stop you.

In the Alps you may come across specialized mountaineering sections of the police force. They supply rescue services and guidance, and are usually friendly and approachable.

The emergency number to call for police is ☎ 17.

PUBLIC HOLIDAYS

Banks, shops and museums will be closed on the following public holidays, but most restaurants will stay open:

1 January (New Year's Day – *le jour de l'An*); Easter Monday – *le lundi de Pâques* (March or April); 1 May (Labour Day – *la fête du Travail*); 8 May (VE Day); last Thursday in May (Ascension Day – *l'Ascension*); Whit Sunday (*Pentecôte*) and Whit Monday (May or early June); 14 July, National Day (Bastille Day); 15 August (Assumption – *l'Assomption*); 1 November (All Saints' Day – *la Toussaint*); 11 November (Armistice Day – *l'Armistice*); 25 December (Christmas Day – *le jour de Noël*).

When a national holiday falls on a Sunday, the next day is taken as a holiday instead. If a national holiday falls on a Thursday, the French often take the Thursday and the Friday off, making a four-day weekend. This is known as *faire le pont*, 'to make the bridge' over the Friday.

SAFETY

Provence is generally safe for visitors, but it's always wise to take precautions, particularly in the larger cities. You need to be extra vigilant along the Côte d'Azur, particularly in Nice and Marseille, where juvenile pickpockets practise their skills from time to time. Bands of gipsy children may try to distract you while heading for your wallet. Always keep car doors locked when driving; bag-snatching by scooter riders is something of a speciality, particularly in and around Antibes and Vallauris. Rental cars are easily identified from their non-local number plates and a foreign number plate makes a tempting target.

When parking, don't leave valuables in the vehicle. Car theft is becoming more common and the main car parks near the beaches in Les Calanques are notorious for theft. In towns and cities, try to park your car in underground or covered parking if possible. Avoid leaving your car in a remote spot. Don't take your valuables to the beach or leave them unattended, should you have them with you.

Insure your belongings and carry travellers cheques rather than cash. Make copies of your passport and driving licence and leave one copy at home with someone, in case of an emergency.

SHOPPING

If you enjoy shopping, Provence is the place for you.

OPENING HOURS

Opening hours are usually 10am to 6.30pm or 7pm, with a couple of hours' break for lunch. Food shops are open from around 7am to noon and then from after lunch to 7pm, sometimes later in larger towns. Small shops close on Sunday afternoons and on Mondays. Bakers are open until around 1pm or later. Supermarkets and hypermarkets stay open through lunchtime. Department stores stay open late once a week and on Sundays for a few weeks before Christmas.

If you don't have cash, you can usually pay by credit card. Few shops accept Eurocheques or travellers cheques, although the larger department stores probably will.

FROM HYPERMARKETS TO SPECIALIST FOOD STORES

Hypermakets (*hypermarchés*) such as Casino, Carrefour, LeClerc and Auchan are usually located in the *Centre Commercial* on the outskirts of a sizeable town. Buying petrol from their stations will save you money.

Department stores such as Monoprix, Prisunic and the more upmarket Galeries Lafayette are usually found in the town centre. However, if you buy all your provisions in larger stores, you will miss out on one of the delights of shopping in Provence – the specialist food outlets. The *boulangerie* and *pâtisserie* sell delicious bread and pastries, the *fromagerie* offers an impossible choice of cheeses, and the *charcuteries* and *traiteurs* have done all the work by preparing and selling dishes by weight – all perfect for picnics.

MARKETS

Provence's produce markets (*marchés*) are legendary. They take place daily in larger cities, often in more than one location, and weekly in smaller communities (market day is given in this guide with the information for each town or village). They are wonderfully colourful and fragrant places to explore, with stallholders selling tempting regional produce, from flowers and super-fresh vegetables and fruit, to olives, apricots, almonds and *herbes de Provence*. If you are in the Var region, try to get to a truffle market, which is quite an experience. The markets are a vital part of the social fabric of Provence and it's well worth taking time out in a nearby bar or café to watch the world go by, once you've made all your purchases. Most markets finish around noon.

Many villages and towns have small, individually run shops on every corner, where you'll find local handicrafts such as *santons* (*see* page 88); the vividly coloured local fabrics known as *indiennes* (*see* page 89), sold by the metre or made up into a variety of objects; dried lavender, sachets of *herbes de Provence* and perfumed olive oil soap (*savon de Marseille*); honey, dried-flower arrangements, and scented oils and perfumes from Grasse. Provence is also known for its ceramics, particularly in Vallauris, as well as items made from olive wood, rich in colour and texture.

Locally grown olives and locally produced olive oil make lovely and useful gifts to take home. Sweet-toothed friends will also enjoy the *fruits confits* (candied fruits) from Apt, *marrons glacés* (crystallized chestnuts) from Collobrières, or the sugar and almond, or marzipan, sweets (*calissons*) from Aix-en-Provence.

In the *villages perchés* (hilltop villages) you'll be spoilt for choice in the artists' and artisans' studios. Cogolin is the place to go for pipes and carpets and in Biot you can watch glass being blown and buy some of the finished product.

If the catwalk is more your style, the boutiques of top French and Italian designers in Cannes, Monaco and Nice lie in wait.

SMOKING

Cigarettes are still relatively inexpensive in France, and the French remain inveterate smokers. Smoking is quite common in business meetings, for example, and you will often come across that familiar image of the archetypal Frenchman, Gauloise stuck to his bottom lip, eyes screwed up against the blue smoke. Some restaurants offer non-smoking (*non fumeur*) areas, but the rules are not always observed. If you need an ashtray, ask for a *cendrier*, and if you need a light, simply say '*Vous avez du feu?*'

SPORT AND LEISURE ACTIVITIES

BULLFIGHTING

In and around the Camargue, this is the number-one sport. For more on the *course Camargue*, *see* 'Traditions' in the Background section.

Spanish-style bullfights, in which the bull is put to death, can be seen at the arena in Arles or Nîmes.

CANOEING AND KAYAKING

The Verdon gorges offer wonderful opportunities for more adventurous watersports, such as canoeing and white-water rafting. The trip requires experience and supervision, as the powerful water flow can change and the river isn't always navigable. For more information, contact the Fédération Française de Canoë-Kayak, 87 quai de la Marne, 94340 Joinville le Pont. ☎ 01-45-11-08-50. Fax: 01-48-86-13-25.

An international canoeing even is held in the Verdon canyon in July.

With its constant levels, the Sorgue river is ideal for kayaking between the end of April and the end of December. Find out more at www.canoefrance.com and *see* Pays des Sorgues, page 283.

CAVING

The many caves gouged out by the waters of the Sorgue river make Fontaine-de-Vaucluse (*see* page 281) a caving centre.

CYCLING

Cycling is a great way to discover Provence. Bicycles (*vélos*) may be hired at a number of train stations, taken on some trains (check timetables for the bike symbol), and then dropped off at another station (having arranged this beforehand). Rental shops are also common (see the listings in this guide) and mountain bikes (*VTT*) are also available. You'll be asked to leave a deposit or a credit card number and you should insure your bicycle (whether it's rented or owned), as theft is common along the Côte d'Azur.

Despite the enthusiasm of the French for the sport of cycling, the number of cycle lanes in towns is disappointing. Arles, Avignon and Nîmes are some of the exceptions. The French generally respect cyclists, both on and off the road, and you will find that most hotels and restaurants are happy to look after a bike.

Consider wearing a cycling helmet and, in summer, set off early and avoid heat stroke by resting during the hottest part of the day. Make sure you take plenty of drinking water with you.

For more information on bicycle touring, contact the Fédération Française de Cyclotourisme, 8 rue Jean-Marie Jégo, 75013 Paris, ☎ 01-44-16-88-89. Fax: 01-44-16-88-89.

If you like the idea of cycling, but aren't particularly energetic, British company Cycling for Softies operates trips to most regions of France, including Provence. The tours include accommodation in family-run hotels, a bike, and emergency back-up. ☎ 0161 248 8282. Website: www.cycling-for-softies.co.uk

Based in the USA, CBT Bicycle Tours organizes cycling tours through-out France from $110 to $125 per day. ☎ 1-800-736–2453. Websites: www.francetourism.com or www.cbttours.com

DIVING

While exploring the coastal areas, why not take the opportunity to try diving? You will need to be more than 8 years old and in good health. It is not essential to be very sporty or a very good swimmer, but participants should not be pregnant or on certain medication, and should check the health of their teeth. First-timers will have to provide a medical certificate. Children should be introduced to the sport in a registered place, in calm waters, with no current, and using appropriate equipment.

For the wary, diving does not hurt the ears and you do not need to force the breath into the mouthpiece. It is, however, essential to follow the safety rules that are explained as you progress, and to observe the 12- to 24-hour gap before taking a plane (which can interfere with the process of desaturation).

Introductory dives

When choosing a diving club in France, look for affiliation to the Fédération Française d'Etudes et de Sports Sous-Marins (FFESSM) (French federation of underwater sports) or the Fédération Sportive Gymnique du Travail (FSGT). Others are linked to the Association Nationale des Moniteurs de Plongée (ANMP) or the Syndicat National des Moniteurs de Plongée (SNMP) (national associations of diving instructors). Instructors' diplomas should be on display.

Dive sites are monitored by instructors who are licensed by the state; they manage the environment of the dives and know everything about their area. A good diving centre respects every single safety rule without forgetting about enjoyment. An instructor should not take a diver out before asking questions about their level of ability. Check whether the centre is well maintained and clean (look for rust on the equipment), and whether the compulsory safety equipment (oxygen, first-aid kit, radio) is carried on board.

Prices for an introductory dive, hand-in-hand with an instructor, will vary from 150 to 250F on average, plus the cost of an annual licence, which is about 250F. The equipment may feel cumbersome at first, but it is completely forgotten once you are in the water. You should go no deeper than 5m (16ft) and your suit should be as closely adjusted as possible to avoid trapping water pockets that could make you cold.

PADI

To experience diving before arriving in France, contact your local diving association, or PADI (Professional Association of Diving Instructors), the world's largest recreational diving membership organization. It has more than 4,300 dive centres and resorts in more than 175 countries. Translations of PADI materials are available in more than 20 languages.

PADI runs courses to teach you to dive but also trains instructors. Certi-fication progresses from entry-level 'Open Water Diver' to 'Advanced Open Water', 'Specialty' and 'Rescue Diver'. To become a dive leader, enthusiasts can follow the 'Divemaster' and 'Assistant Instructor' courses.

UK PADI International Ltd, Unit 7, St Philips Central, Albert Road, St Philips, Bristol BS2 0PD. ☎ 0117 3007234.

USA PADI Americas, 30151 Tomas Street, Rancho, Santa Margarita, CA 92688 USA. ☎ 001 949 858 7234.

Australia PADI Asia-Pacific, Unit 3, 4 Skyline Place, French's Forest, NSW 2086 Australia. ☎ 02 9451 2300.

PADI's comprehensive website – www.padi.com – has links to other diving sites.

Training levels

Training courses in clubs are graded as follows: at Level I – from 1,500F – you go down to 20m (66ft) accompanied by an instructor; at Level II – from 1,800F – you go on your own down to 20m (66ft), and accompanied down to a maximum depth of 40m (131ft); at Level III – from 1,500F – you are entirely on your own on a limited range of dives. Level IV and V are for training future instructors to accompany divers. Passing through the different levels should be done over time in order to gain the necessary experience. Ask your instructor's advice.

All schools or clubs in France should provide a *Carnet de Plongée* (diver's logbook), which sets out each diver's experience, as well as a 'passport' listing the tests passed.

In Provence

Bathed in a velvet-soft climate, and with warm clear waters, the Mediterra-nean is perfect for diving. There are a number of wrecks that are well known to divers and, in certain places, a wealth of sub-marine life.

Be aware that this enclosed sea has a delicate ecological balance, and is constantly being damaged by human activity. The most deplorable example was the accidental introduction about a decade ago of *Caulerpa taxifolia*, a mutating algae of tropical origin that stifles other species (particularly *posidonia*) and takes over. Some magnificent diving sites have been trans-formed into fluorescent green carpets. It is possible to control the spread of the algae, but urgent measures are essential.

– **Weather forecasts**: the best time to dive is between June and November, when the temperature is very comfortable on the surface (although the water remains cooler the deeper you go). The biting Mistral or east wind can prevent a dive from taking place, but there are usually some areas where there are sheltered spots.

– **Depth**: diving around rocks, you can generally keep to fairly shallow waters (still taking great care). Exploring wrecks – at between 40 and 60m (131–197ft) – is only for divers who are experienced at significant depths.

– **Visibility**: excellent, with an average visibility of around 20m (66ft). The water is crystal-clear around the islands, but often murky around the wrecks.

GENERAL INFORMATION

– **Currents**: highly localized but can be very strong and lead to a dive being cancelled. Take great care.

– **Recommended equipment**: a 5mm-thick *wetsuit* with a hood; *gloves* to protect hands from the sharp metal on wrecks; a *lamp* to see the colours, to explore in tunnels and to be spotted by team-mates.

– **Underwater life**: in some concentrated areas, the marine life is very rich. Ask your instructor to point out interesting species. You may see *posidonia*, gorgons, anemones, sponges, conger or moray eels, sardines, sea bream, sea bass, scorpion fish. Shoals of *mérou*, a protected species, are currently returning in abundance in all parts of the Mediterranean. Respect the fragile environment. Never feed the fish (some creatures may even turn on you), never remove anything and be careful where you put your flippers.

– **Safety**: keep in constant visual contact with team-mates. Take care not to get caught in nets that may have been left on the rocks or in the wrecks. Dive boats must carry oxygen cylinders and first-aid treatment (for burns or cuts), and there are de-compression chambers in Marseille and Toulon.

FISHING

Head for the local tourist office for information on how to become a member of an authorized fishing club in order to obtain freshwater fishing rights. You can fish in the sea without a permit as long as your catch is for local consumption. Along the coast, boat captains will often offer visitors a place on fishing trips, to fish tuna and other deep-sea species. Ask around.

GOLF

There are golf courses near most of the major Côte d'Azur resorts, with many more being planned. Cannes offers the widest choice, with courses in Mandelieu and Le Cannet. Monaco has a spectacular course. Contact the Ligue de Golf Provence-Alpes-Côte d'Azur on ☎ 04-42-39-86-83. A Var Golf Pass covers 10 of the finest courses in the area.

HORSE-RIDING

Local tourist offices will be able to supply you with a list of equestrian centres (*centres hippique* or *centres equestres*) in the region, which hire out horses and organize trails. The Camargue, with its cowboy traditions and open spaces, is a very popular area for the sport. Contact the Association Camarguaise de Tourisme Équestre ☎ 04-90-97-86-32.

PÉTANQUE

Pétanque (sometimes referred to as *boules*) is the most popular game in the south of France. The name comes from the local language: *pé* or *pied* (meaning 'foot') and *tanco* (meaning 'fixed to the ground'). Until the early 1900s it was played according to Provençal rules, with players taking three steps before throwing the ball. A certain Jules Le Noir, who suffered from rheumatism, suggested that the player's feet should remain planted to the ground within the throwing circle – and this was adopted.

The game is played in teams of either two or three participants (in a *doublette* or *triplette*). The object is to get your metal ball closest to the wooden marker ball (*cochonnet*, or 'piglet'); generally speaking, the feet remain still and the ball is thrown an average distance of 10m (30ft). In Provence, the distance can be greater and players are allowed to move; this is known as the *longue*.

If one player has aimed (*pointé*) well and come very close to the *cochonnet*, opponents have to *tirer* or aim for the ball, to remove it. Great players manage to take their adversary's ball out while leaving their own successfully in place. This tactic is called *un carreau*.

SKIING

The biggest ski resorts in the Alpes Maritimes are Isola 2000, Auron and Valberg. The organization for the sport in France is the Fédération Française de Ski, 50 rue des Marquisats, 74011 Annecy. ☎ 04-50-51-40-34. Fax: 04-50-51-75-90. Visit their website at www.ffs.fr, or the individual websites on those resorts included in this guide: www.isola-2000.com, www.valberg.com and www.french-ski.com/alpeazur/auron

WALKING

There is a network of long-distance marked paths (*Grandes Randonnées* or GRs for short) throughout France and 5,000km (about 3,000 miles) in the Alpes Maritimes alone. They are fully signposted (with red and white signs) and cover some of the finest scenery in the south of the country.

Each GR path is described in a *topoguide*, with maps and details about campsites, refuge huts and sources of provisions. These are available in bookshops in the region, or in the UK from Stanfords, 12–14 Long Acre, London WC2E 9LP. ☎ 020 7836 1321. Fax: 020 7836 0189 Website: www.stanfords.co.uk. The *topoguides* are published by the principal French walkers' organization, the Fédération Française de Randonnée Pédestre, 14 rue Riquet, 75019 Paris. ☎ 01-44-89-93-93. Fax: 01-40-35-85-67. Stanfords also stocks *Walks in Provence*, an English translation covering several GRs.

In France, most tourist information centres will be able to supply maps and leaflets on walks in their area and many of the GRs are detailed in this guide.

The Fédération des Parcs Naturels Régionaux de France looks after the country's nature parks, guiding visitors around the spectacular scenery and fascinating flora and fauna. Visit their website at www.parcs-naturels-regionaux.tm.fr

WATERSPORTS

Pack your bikini and shorts to make the most of the many fine, sandy beaches in the region, but be prepared to pay for the pleasure in some places, such as Menton, Nice and Monte-Carlo. Their beaches are usually well maintained and have good sports facilities, but some beachcombers or sunbathers may prefer the quieter spots that are free to visitors. Some of the best of these are found in Les Calanques, the coves below the Esterel and the Maures and on the Hyères Islands. A number of beaches in the region are reserved for nudists (*naturistes*); indeed, the Île du Levant was home to France's first (and continuing) nudist colony. If star-spotting and people-watching are on your agenda, Cannes and St-Tropez are some of the best hunting grounds.

Check out the information given on beaches in each section of the guide.

Boards and sails are available for rent at most beaches along the coast. Keen windsurfers usually head to 'Brutal Beach' at Six-Fours, near Cap Sicié, west of Toulon, where an international windsurfing competition is held. The frequent and variable winds at Marseille, Carro and Les Stes-Maries-de-la-Mer make these very popular areas for the sport.

Sailing courses are increasingly popular and France Station Voile links six Provençal resorts, offering week-long courses. Contact them at 91 avenue Kléber, 7516 Paris. ☎ 01-44-05-96-55. Fax: 01-44-05-02-20. Sailing boats can be rented from most towns.

The Golfe d'Hyères offers great sailing opportunities and is the venue for a world sailing competition in April ('Les Semaines Olympiques de Voile'). The Bandol sailing centre has a 1,500-berth marina and offers many water-based activities. Martigues has become something of a sailing centre due to the diversity and quality of the watersports activities on offer.

Water-skiing can be pricey in the area, so check before launching yourself. Nice offers watersports fanatics a chance to indulge in a spot of jet-skiing and parasailing.

There are lots of opportunities for snorkelling in the region. There are also many impressive dive sites; see the listings in this guide for information on sites and clubs. With its many wrecks, Marseille is a world diving centre and some of the best diving in the Mediterranean is found off Île de Port-Cros in the Var. (*See also* 'Diving', page 68.)

Swimming pools (*piscines*) are well signposted in most French towns and are reasonably priced. Ask at the tourist office for the address. Municipal pools sometimes insist on swimmers wearing a bathing cap, so take one along just in case.

TIME

France is one hour ahead of GMT (Greenwich Mean Time) and changes its clock in spring and autumn. In France, 'am' and 'pm' are not used – the 24-hour clock is widely applied.

TIPPING

There are no strict rules for tipping in France, as there are in the USA, for example. In **bars**, it's quite common to leave the smallest bits of change for the waiter, but not necessarily expected. Waiting at restaurant tables in France is a respected profession, with special colleges and exams, and waiting staff are paid properly, and do not have to rely on tips (not always the case in some countries). Unscrupulous waiters may, however, return your change to you on a saucer with the coins hidden on the bottom, then the bill, then the notes. Remember to check underneath, or you could be leaving a very generous tip indeed.

In **restaurants**, a 15 per cent service charge is already included in the price, but it is customary to tip the waiter or waitress, especially if the food or service was exceptional (up to 10F in a bistrot, more in a nice restaurant). It's a similar situation in hotels, where standard service is included, according to law, and a tip is proffered only for special service.

Taxi drivers do expect a tip of 10 per cent.

Until recently, there was a long-held tradition in France of tipping **cinema** ushers or usherettes 1 or 2F after they had shown you to your seat, but this is no longer the case.

TOILETS

The infamous French *toilettes à la Turque* – two footprints, a hole in the ground and a ferocious flushing system that always splashes your shoes – is less common these days in most of France, although you'll still find them in the dark basements of some bars and cafés. These days you're likely to find a more conventional and familiar arrangement, although this doesn't always apply to segregation of the sexes. It's very common for a bar or restaurant to have only one toilet, which is used by everyone. Female readers might like to know that you often have to walk past a urinal to get to the sit-down.

It's rather impolite to use an establishment's toilets without being a customer. If you're desperate, leave 1F on the counter as you leave, with a smiling '*Merci, Monsieur*'. Otherwise, the facilities in museums or department stores might be a better bet.

If you're travelling on main roads, it's advisable to use the free facilities at service stations and roadside stopping places (*aires de repos*). Watch out for the occasional public toilets where you have to pay to enter – or exit! And it's normal to leave a small tip for the caretaker of the toilets if you see that there is one.

TOURIST OFFICES

The best source for information on accommodation in France is the **French Government Tourist Office** (known as **Maison de la France**), 178 Piccadilly, London W1V OAL. ☎ (020) 7399 3500. Information line ☎ (0906) 824 4123 (calls charged at 60 pence per minute). E-mail: info@mdlf.co.uk

Alternatively, visit the French tourist office website at www.franceguide.com for useful listings.

Tourist Offices Abroad

United States: ☎ (410) 286-8310 and ☎ (312) 751-7800.

Canada: ☎ (514) 288-4264.

Australia: ☎ (02) 9231-5244.

GENERAL INFORMATION

Tourist Information in Provence and the Côte d'Azur

☐ *Comité régional du tourisme Provence-Alpes-Côte d'Azur* (regional tourism commission): 10 place Joliette, BP 46214, 13567 Marseille Cedex 02. ☎ 04-91-56-47-00. Fax: 04-91-56-47-01. Email: information @crt-paca.fr, Website: www.crt-paca.fr

☐ *Comité régional du tourisme Rhône-Alpes* (regional tourism commission): 104 route de Paris, 69260 Charbonnières-les-Bains. ☎ 04-72-59-21-59. Fax: 04-72-59-21-60. Website: www.cr-rhone-alpes.fr

☐ *Comité régional du tourisme Riviera-Côte d'Azur* (regional tourism commission): 55 promenade des Anglais, 06000 Nice. ☎ 04-93-37-78-78. Fax: 04-93-86-01-06. Email: crt06@crt-riviera.fr

☐ *Comité départemental de tourisme du Var* (departmental tourism commission for the Var district): 1 boulevard Foch, 83003 Draguignan. ☎ 04-94-50-55-50. Fax: 04-94-50-55-51. Email: info@cdtvar.com

☐ *Comités départementaux du tourisme* (departmental tourist commission): *see* relevant chapters.

TRANSPORTATION

Local information on train and bus connections is provided in this guide. The SNCF (online at www.sncf.com) runs an efficient network of trains through the major cities of the south. Trains are generally fast, clean and frequent and the staff are (usually) friendly and helpful. A useful additional service is the Métrazur, linking all the resorts on the Côte d'Azur from Menton to St-Raphaël. In high season there are generally departures every half-hour.

Don't forget to *composter votre billet* (stamp your ticket) in the little orange machines by the entrance to the platforms, to date and validate it. After a break of more than 24 hours, you must *composter* your ticket again.

Buses are run by the SNCF (replacing discontinued rail routes) or private firms. They can be useful for local and some cross-country journeys. However, it would not be wise to depend on buses as they rarely serve the regions outside the SNCF network. The timetable in rural areas is designed to suit working, market and school hours. Buses often leave very early and return in the afternoon. Private bus firms tend to charge more than trains. Some towns have a coach station (*gare routière*), which is usually located near the train station, but often the line will start near the main square. Check with the local tourist office for departure points.

CAR HIRE

Hiring a car in France is a relatively expensive proposition, but driving in Provence can be a delight, with stunning coastal routes and charming hilly lanes. Petrol prices can be high; service stations on the motorways charge more than those in towns and villages, but the lowest prices are found at the big supermarket chains. For a trip into the hinterland, make sure you fill up, as petrol can be difficult to find in rural areas. Petrol stations throughout the region keep shop hours and most close on Sunday and/or Monday.

In high season the motorways and coastal roads can get very busy and driving around the large cities and major seaside resorts is not advisable in these periods. Park away from the centre and walk.

Don't forget that there's a charge for use of *autoroutes* (motorways), payable at the *péages* (toll gates). The A8 from Marseille to Menton is one of the most expensive stretches of toll motorway in France. The RNs and Ds (Routes Nationales and Départmentales) are good alternatives.

There are several car hire companies in France, but pre-booking cars may get you a more competitive price; check local agents before you leave. Car rental in France costs between 300F and 700F a day, and the big firms – Hertz, Avis, Europcar and Budget – are represented at most airports and in most big cities. Local firms can be cheaper but check the small print and confirm where you can drop off the car.

All drivers must be over 21 with one year's experience, and most rental firms will only deal with people over 25 (without a hefty extra insurance premium). Most cars are manual, so if you really want to drive an automatic transmission vehicle, book well ahead.

Speed limits are 130km/h (80mph) on motorways, 110km/h (68mph) on dual carriageways and 50km/h (30mph) in towns. On other roads, keep to 90km/h (56mph). Instant and hefty fines are issued for speeding and driving under the influence of alcohol. The police must issue a receipt showing the amount paid.

Useful websites and telephone numbers include:

www.iti.fr (route planner)

www.autoroutes.fr (motorway information)

www.bison-fute.equipment.gouv.fr (road conditions info)

Traffic and road conditions ☎ 08-36-68-20-00 (outside Paris and Île de France).

WORKING IN FRANCE

Working in France is theoretically possible for all EU nationals, who are also allowed to claim the French Jobseeker's Allowance, and are entitled to the minimum French wage. In practice, high unemployment levels mean that finding a job can be difficult, and foreigners employed at the lower end of the scale (as nannies, bar staff or fruit pickers, for example) are likely to be poorly paid. Non-EU citizens must obtain a work permit, which is given instantly to students with at least one term left to complete in France, on application.

If you are planning to work in France you need to bear a few things in mind. Anyone staying in France for over three months must have a *carte de séjour*, or residency permit. EU citizens are automatically entitled to one.

Despite the high unemployment levels, you may find jobs in the cities doing bar or club work, freelance translating, teaching English, fixing software or data processing or as an au-pair. In more rural areas, seasonal fruit picking, teaching English or working on a farm (*see below*) are other options.

GENERAL INFORMATION

If you speak good French, the travel industry is a possibility – working on bus tours or in summer campsites. Write to tour operators in early spring and keep an eye out in travel magazines.

Eurocamp recruits staff for its holidays and campsites. To contact them in the UK ☎ (01606) 787522, or visit their website: www.eurocamp.co.uk

If you are already in France, check the job section of local newspapers and of *Le Monde*, *Le Figaro* and *International Herald Tribune*, and keep an eye on the notice boards in English-language bookshops.

Also try **CIDJ** (Centre d'Information et de Documentation Jeunesse), 101 quai Branly, 75740 Paris, Cedex 15. ☎ 01-44-49-12-00. Email: cidj@cidj. asso.fr. Website: www.cidj.asso.fr. Alternatively, contact **CRIJ** (Centre Régional Information Jeunesse): CRIJ Côte d'Azur, 19 rue Gioffrédo, 06000 Nice. ☎ 04-93-80-93-93. Email: CRIJ.COTE.DAZUR@wanadoo.fr. Website: www.crij.org/nice

For those who want to find out more about rural life, there are opportunities to work on **organic farms** as working guests. For more information, send a stamped addressed envelope to Organic Farms at:

WWOOF UK, Fran Whittle, PO Box 2675, Lewes BN7 1RB.

WWOOF Canada, RR 2, S.18, C.9, Nelson, British Columbia VIL 5P5.

WWOOF Australia, RSD, Buchan, VIC 3885.

WWOOF New Zealand, Jane and Andrew Strange, PO Box 1172, Nelson.

Also check out their website at: www.wwoof.org

If you are looking for something more secure, you should do some research and plan in advance. The following books, telephone numbers and websites may help.

TEACHING

British Council: www.britcoun.org/english/engvacs has listings of English-teaching vacancies.

Teaching English Abroad: published by Vacation Work, 9 Park End St, Oxford OX1 1HJ. ☎ (01865) 241978. Fax: (01865) 790885.

WORKING AS AN AU-PAIR

UK: Avalon Au Pairs ☎ (01344) 778246).

United States: American Institute for Foreign Study. ☎ (203) 869-9090.

France: Accueil Familial des Jeunes Etrangers ☎ 01-42-22-50-34.

VOLUNTARY WORK

If you're interested in history and archaeology and are over 18, there's a range of restoration projects and archaeological digs in which to get involved. In exchange for your labour, you get board and lodging. Contact:

Cotravaux, 11 rue de Clichy, 75009 Paris. ☎ 01-48-74-79-20. Fax: 01-48-74-14-01 or **CHAM**, 5 and 7 rue Guilleminot, 75014 Paris. ☎ 01-43-35-15-51. Fax: 01-43-20-46-82.

Another organization to contact for voluntary work is **Concordia**, 1 rue de Metz, 75010 Paris. ☎ 01-45-23-00-23.

Useful Reading

Emplois d'Été en France (Summer Jobs in France): Vac-Job, 46 avenue Rénée Coty, 75014 Paris. ☎ 01-43-20-70-51.

Living and Working in France by Victoria Pybus, published by Vacation Work (*see above*).

Background

DATES

– **27 000 BC** : Ice Age worshippers cover the walls of a cave near Cassis with paintings. The sea covers the entrance to the Grotte de Cosquer, a cave that is now accessible only to divers.

– **1,800 BC** : Ligurian hunters use flint to carve magic symbols on the sacred slopes of Mont Bégo.

– **Sixth century BC** : *Massalia* (Marseille) is founded by the Phocaeans. The town goes on to found Nice, Hyères, Antibes and Agde.

– **124 BC** : the Romans come to defend Marseille again and stay this time. *Provincia* (Provence) is born, soon becoming 'another Italy', according to Pliny.

– **1 BC** : the Romans establish a more permanent presence in Provence, building towns, ports and roads. Arles takes over from Marseille.

– **413** : Barbarian invasion.

– **536** : falling into the hands of the Francs, the region loses its status and becomes a far-off appendage of the northern empire.

– **Ninth century** : establishment of the first Kingdom of Provence.

– **883** : the Saracens turn the Maures mountains into a military base.

– **13th century** : Nice and Grasse attached once more to Provence.

– **14th century** : the popes establish themselves in Avignon for 70 years.

– **1388** : Nice and the Alpes-Maritimes come under the protection of the Counts of Savoy until 1860, when they are ceded to France.

– **End of the 14th century** : plague, famine and fighting halve the Provençal population.

– **1481** : Provence, excluding Savoy, Monaco and the County of Venaissin, becomes part of France.

– **17th century** : first Richelieu then Louis XIV strengthen central power. Toulon becomes a military port of war, slave ships dock at Marseille, the coast of Provence becomes a major base for Royal power.

– **1660** : Louis IX puts down a rebellion and takes Marseille. The French steamroller begins its inexorable progress.

– **1720** : a terrible epidemic of plague decimates the population. Half the inhabitants of Marseille are lost.

– **1789** : led by Mirabeau, the province is one of the first to become involved in the Revolution. With the establishment of the French departments the old Provence disappears.

– **1793**: the proud Provençals are on red alert in the Revolution (*The Marseillaise*), then support different factions. Marseille supports the 'Whites', Toulon allies itself with the English. Toulon is recaptured by Bonaparte, and re-named Port-la-Montagne; Marseille becomes – the supreme outrage – 'Ville-sans-nom' ('No-name-town').

– **Late 18th century**: Provence reaches the pinnacle in the world of pictorial arts with Honoré Fragonard and Joseph Vernet.

– **1815**: Napoleon lands from Elba and proceeds north, following the now legendary 'Route Napoléon', through Grasse, Digne and Gap.

– **1848** and **1851**: many Provençal towns exhibit deep republican sympathies, first at the time of the Revolution and then during Napoleon III's *coup d'état*.

– **1854**: foundation of the Félibrige, the regionalist, cultural movement (*see* page 80)

– **1860**: the counties of Nice and Savoy are attached to France in repayment for Napoleon III's support of the Italians in their struggle for unification against the Austrians. In the following year, Menton and Roquebrune are joined to the Principality of Monaco.

– **1947**: establishment of the Avignon arts festival.

THE ENGLISH ON THE CÔTE D'AZUR

When English novelist Tobias Smollett crossed the Var river on the back of a fellow traveller in 1763, his 'porter', a local from Nice, could hardly have imagined that his 'luggage' was to be the founder of tourism on the Côte d'Azur. Swimming in the sea off Nice in 1765, Smollett began a trend. Seduced by the town, he published an account of his travels, amazing his English readers with the fact that the almond trees on the Côte d'Azur were in flower in January.

It wasn't unusual in the eighteenth century to find a mature English gentlewoman travelling alone up the Nile. Entire English families would visit the Middle East and retired colonels were often spotted studying African wildlife. Following in the footsteps of Smollett, hordes of British tourists virtually annexed the Côte d'Azur – frequently going 'out in the midday sun'. The Provençal locals were less adventurous travellers and somewhat surprised at the arrival of the empire-builders, but they welcomed them none the less. Certainly, the invaders brought both wealth and renown to the region.

By 1820, the town of **Nice** was home to more than 100 British families and an Anglican church had been built. In 1851, Alexandre Dumas described Nice as an English town where one could still meet the odd Niçois. In the seven years up to her death, Queen Victoria wintered in Nice in a house on the Cimiez hill. Her frequent strolls, surrounded by an entourage of Hindu servants and Scottish guards, left locals rather confused about British fashion!

Nice's early 'guests' are remembered today in the Promenade des Anglais and rue Smollett, among others.

Menton was so famous for its mild climate that English doctors would prescribe a holiday under its clear skies for even the most minor cough. One resident was author Augustus Hare, a strict Protestant. After staying with him in Menton, Somerset Maugham recounted how Hare would read from the scriptures to his staff, in an attempt to convert the local Catholics.

English visitors largely ignored the French side of the river Var until 1834, when Lord Henry Brougham, one of the politicians involved in the abolition of slavery arrived in the region. On his way to Nice, he was turned back by Italian frontier guards, due to an outbreak of cholera, and forced to spend the night in a small fishing village called **Cannes**. Less than a week later, he abandoned his plans to travel to Nice. He bought some land near Cannes and built his Villa Eleonora, amazing the locals by constructing a garden that contained no vegetables and consumed incredible amounts of water in its cultivation of English roses. Many other English travellers soon followed Brougham, building palatial homes. The English lord even obtained permission from King Louis-Philippe to develop the port, for the sole purposes of importing lawns!

In 1868, Monaco was linked by railway to Paris and, by consequence, to London. In February 1869, the Prince of Monaco announced to his delighted citizens that taxes were to be abolished. Thanks to the railway and the casino (and the delights offered by swimming in the sea), the principality was able to support and finance its own development. Before the building of the railway, the journey from the north had been long and arduous, with many visitors opting to come by sea instead.

With easier access, the Côte d'Azur began to attract visitors who were interested less in sport and more in parties. The future King Edward VII of England caused a scandal in Cannes high society when he asked French singer Yvette Guilbert to entertain him with a few coarse songs. He was evidently forgiven, since his statue now stands in Cannes. During the Roaring Twenties, the Côte d'Azur was *the* place to be seen. People from all over the world came to the 'French Riviera', and the French themselves began to discover the delights of the region.

With the arrival of paid holidays and the end of colonial rents in the 1950s, the English presence began to diminish. In 1975, the British Consul in Nice closed its doors, marking the conclusion of this page of Anglo-Provençal history.

FÉLIBRIGE MOVEMENT

In the 19th century, the regionalist Félibrige movement was set up to fight against the cultural and linguistic domination of the French and to promote Provençal culture and language. Local people were outraged at the attitude that 'Northerners' and teachers had towards the local *patois* – children were whacked with rulers if they spoke in Provençal.

Frédéric Mistral, the great poet, led the movement. To begin with it gained a certain amount of credit, especially when Mistral was awarded the Nobel Prize, in 1904, but it lost popularity when it refused to become involved with local economic and social problems. In 1907, it made the mistake of not supporting a significant union of local wine-growers.

The Félibrige does still exist, but it is now made up of dozens of associations from all over the territory of the Langue d'Oc (*see* 'Language', page 49). At Whitsun every year, a great gathering of *félibres* – the *Santo Estello* – takes place in the Pays d'Oc.

PROVENÇAL PEOPLE

– **Pierre Boulle** (1912–94): this native of Avignon used his adventurous life as a rubber planter in Malaysia, then as a soldier in Burma, as the subject matter for his most famous novel, *Bridge on the River Kwai* (1959). It was made into a film in 1957 by British director David Lean, and won seven Oscars. Boulle's *Planet of the Apes* was also successfully adapted for the screen.

– **César** (1921–99): the most famous of French contemporary sculptors was born César Baldiccini, into a family of Italian immigrants in the Belle de Mai, a working-class district in Marseille. His best-known works are his rather difficult *Compressions*, but he was also very talented at making figurative pieces, such as *Pouce*, a bronze giant.

– **Paul Cézanne** (1839–1906): one of the most important painters of the *avant garde* of the first half of the 20th century, Cézanne was born and died in Aix-en-Provence, the town has none of his pictures! Through his life, he divided his time between Paris, L'Estaque and Aix. He was a schoolfriend of Émile Zola and sought him out when he first went to Paris to become a painter. (They fell out for ever after the writer described him as a failed painter in *l'œuvre*.) Cézanne was faithful to certain principles of Impressionism, such as painting in the open air or using coloured shadows, but he was particularly interested in light and the way it changes the colours of an object. He would paint some objects from two or three points of view. He first exhibited in Paris in 1895, selling a large number of canvases. Following his success, he continued to go deeper into his art and his compositions became increasingly opaque. After his death, his work had a considerable influence on the Fauvistes and the Cubists.

– **Alphonse Daudet** (1840–97): born in Nîmes, Daudet quickly moved to Paris where he dedicated himself to writing. He found fame after the publication of his *Lettres de Mon Moulin*, in 1866, which paint a genuine, fresh image of Provence. Other works inspired by the region include *Tartarin de Tarascon*, *Tartarin dans les Alpes*, *Port Tarascon*. In 1869, Daudet published *L'Arlésienne* which later inspired the composer Bizet to create *L'Arlésienne*. Daudet spent long periods of time at Fontvieille in the Alpilles, living as a guest with friends at the Château of Montauban.

– **Honoré Daumier** (1808–79): born in Marseille in 1808, Daumier followed his father to Paris to seek his fortune in 1816. His skill lay in caricaturing politicians and the *bourgeoisie* in *Charivari* magazine, a precursor of the present-day satirical paper *Le Canard Enchaîné*. He knew Corot and Delacroix and also left some beautiful paintings which did not make his name at the time. He died penniless and practically blind.

– **Alexandra David-Néel** (1868–1969): a backpacker before her time, the first woman to reach the forbidden city of Lhasa spent the end of her

BACKGROUND

wandering life in a tiny house at the foot of the Pré-Alpes. To her, the area was 'a miniature Tibet for Lilliputians' (*see* 'Digne-les-Bains', page 349).

– **Jean Giono** (1895–1970): with Pagnol and Daudet, Giono is one of the best known of the Provençal writers, intimately linked with and inspired by the region of his birth (he lived in Manosque all his life). His first novels, *Colline* and *Regain* evoke a return to nature. He became very famous following *Que ma joie demeure* and *Le Chant du monde*, published in the 1930s. In 1939, he preached an anti-war message and his pacifist writings led to him being imprisoned after the Liberation for sympathizing with the Vichy régime. He was profoundly affected by the experience and his subsequent writings, including *Un Roi sans divertissement*, expressed a new anxiety. *Le Hussard sur le toit* was recently adapted for the cinema by French director Rappeneau.

– **Christian Lacroix**: born in 1951 in Arles, this most Provençal of the great couturiers trained at Hermès then with Patou. His roots were clear in his first collection, presented in 1987, which met with great success. His distinctive style reinterprets opulence, with Provençal, gypsy or Hispanic influences, and dazzling colours. He has been awarded two *Dés d'Or* (Golden Thimbles), the highest accolade of his profession.

– **Peter Mayle**: this Englishman gave up advertising and life in London to settle in the Luberon. His book *A Year in Provence*, published in 1994, in which he humorously describes (though sometimes with a trace of condescension) his daily life in Ménerbes met with unimaginable success. Responsible for a tourist invasion and apparently a little upset by some of the locals, Mayle fled the area. The word is, though, that he has returned incognito.

– **Frédéric Mistral** (1830–1914): born into a family of prosperous farmers, Mistral was described by Lamartine as the new Homer. He spent his childhood in Maillane and was obliged to abandon his brilliant studies to help his poorly father on the farm. He began to write, and fame came with the publication of *Mireio*, a dramatic poem about Provence. He took an active role in the *Félibrige* (*see* page 80), contributed a great deal in widening its reputation by publishing articles in the *Armana provençau* and *Le Trésor du Félibrige*, a Provençal-French dictionary and an encyclopedia of the Langue d'Oc. He received the Nobel Prize for Literature in 1904.

– **Nostradamus**: the star from Salon-de-Provence, whose real name was Michel de Nostradame, settled in the town in 1547. An impressive series of literature has been produced over the centuries to discuss his famous *Centuries* and his prophecies.

– **Marcel Pagnol** (1895–1974): born in Aubagne, Pagnol spent his childhood in Marseille. From 1922–27, he was a literature teacher at the Lycée Condorcet in Paris. His stories, *La Gloire de mon Père*, *Le Château de ma Mère*, *Le Temps des Secrets*, published at the end of the 1950s, recount his youth and evoke his love for the region of his birth. He is equally famous in France for his plays, including *Marius* (1929) and *Fanny* (1930), and for numerous films, including *Angèle* (1934), *César* (1936), and *Regain* (1937), which he began to make in 1932 in his own studios, near Aubagne. The cards scene in *Regain* remains one of the great cult moments of French cinema, but the Marseillais still bear a grudge against Pagnol for creating what they see as a caricature of their city.

– **Petrarch** (1304–74): born in Arezzo, the Italian poet fled Italy and the Guelphs. A great admirer of ancient texts and of the poets of his time, he studied law at Montpellier before going to live in Avignon, where he became secretary to a cardinal at the papal court. In 1327, he met the love of his life, Laura de Noves, whom he praises in the poems of his *Canzoniere* collection. In 1341, he was honoured with the distinction of 'Poet of Poets', which he received in Rome. Having taken an active part in the renaissance of literature and in the discovery of many forgotten texts, he was an inspiration for the humanists. He journeyed throughout Europe and also wrote *Lives of Famous Men*. Seeking open spaces, he retired to Fontaine-de-Vaucluse, but died in Italy at Arque.

– **Raimbaud d'Orange**: the Count of Orange is one of the best known of the Provençal troubadours from the Middle Ages, along with Raimbaud de Vacqueyras, the son of a poor knight of Provence and Fouguet de Marseille, who, having tried his hand at composing love songs, withdrew to take orders. Their work introduced the Provençal language, the Langue d'Oc, to the rest of Europe.

– **King René**: the son of Louis II of Sicily and Yolande of Aragon did not spend much time in Provence, although he ruled it. During his seven years in his palace in Aix-en-Provence he gained a reputation as a good king, and his court attracted many artists. His successor and nephew joined Provence to France in 1482.

– **Edmond Rostand** (1868–1918): born in Marseille into a family of prosperous merchants, Rostand achieved glory in 1897 with his play *Cyrano de Bergerac*. His other plays included *L'Aiglon*, which starred Sarah Bernhardt.

– **Sade** (1740–1814): born a Marquis, Donatien-Albert-François de Sade arrived in Provence aged 4, to be placed in the care of his uncle, an erudite abbot and a libertine, at the Château of Saumane. In 1771, Sade, who had already been imprisoned for immoral behaviour, moved into the Château de Lacoste in the Luberon. A first sexual scandal occurred in Arcueuil. He left the chateau for Italy after the notorious Affair of Marseille (June 1772). He was sentenced to death in his absence and effigies of him and his valet were executed on the square in Aix. None the less, he returned to Aix from 1774 to 1778. Imprisoned in the Bastille, freed a number of times and imprisoned again, he was to finish his days in exile in Charenton. The Château de Lacoste was pillaged in 1792 and was sold in 1796.

– **Van Gogh** (1853–90): born in Holland, the tormented painter experienced his most productive period in Provence (supported emotionally by his brother Theo). In 1888, Van Gogh moved to Arles and, in May, rented the famous Maison Jaune. Between crises of raving exaltation and the attempted murder of his guest Gauguin, he painted and drew harvests, gipsy caravans, cafés, evening scenes, and the world-famous sunflowers. He mutilated himself (producing self-portraits with his ear cut off), and begged to be hospitalized in the Hospice of St-Rémy-de-Provence in May 1889. During periods of intensive work, which alternated with terrifying crises, he painted several of his most famous canvases, including *Bedroom at Arles*. In May 1890, he decided to return to Paris but committed suicide at Auvers-sur-Oise on 27 July.

– **Émile Zola** (1840–1902): the son of an Italian engineer, writer Zola spent his adolescence in Aix-en-Provence where he was at school with the painter

Cézanne. His youth is described in *l'œuvre*, in which the character of Claude Lantier is undoubtedly inspired by Cézanne. The portrait of the failed painter caused an irreconcilable rift between the two.

GEOGRAPHY

CABANONS AND *CALANQUES*

Marseille is a city of contrasts – between the sumptuous villas on the Corniche and the cabanons, or beach huts, near the water; between those who see it as the boom town of the Mediterranean Basin and those who dream of nothing more than *pétanque* and siestas; between Marseille's seedy criminal reputation and the delights of its unique location. Beaches and boats are just a step away from the offices, and there is nothing better than meandering through the creeks – at least until winter comes.

According to a 19th-century official, 'There is no town where country excursions happen more frequently than in Marseille.' As a result, one of the distinctive features of the city are its little huts, or *cabanons*, scene of many a family outing. The *cabanons* in the countryside were torn down for the construction of the city suburbs, but many by the seashore have stood the test of time. These simple little cabins, built (often without any planning permission) right on the water's edge, always have a sun-shade, sometimes benefit from electricity but almost never boast a television set.

Just as there are genuine *cabanons* and there are 'cabins', so there are proper Marseillais *calanques* and there are other rocky inlets. Here, white cliffs tower over a sea of azure blue, covered by scraps of vegetation and colourful old fishing huts (fishing was once the main activity). The real *calanques* belong to Marseille's eighth *arrondissement*. How many city-dwellers can take a short bus ride to arrive at such a gorgeous landscape, where waves lap gently (or *calancher*, as they say in French – which is how the *calanques* got their name).

This 5,000-hectare site, protected for more than 20 years, may only be explored on foot or by boat. The breathtaking sight is well worth the long walk in the sun, along scented paths and some more difficult tracks.

THE CAMARGUE

By the time the Rhône river reaches Arles it's no longer a 'raging bull' but rather a 'quiet cousin.' It divides into two branches, the Grand Rhône to the east and the Petit Rhône to the west. Between them sit the marshes of the Vaccarès lake, known as the *Grand Mar* (*grand mer*, or 'open sea'). This extensive area of salt marsh, lakes, pastures and sand dunes is the Camargue, It is one of the major wetland regions in Europe, but it also incorporates a very arid and stony area, known as La Crau, the former delta of the River Durance.

The Camargue is a wonderful environment for wildlife. Native white horses feed in the pastures, ridden by the *gardians*, the local herdsman who round up the black bulls. Arles merinos also roam the area, perfectly adapted to the conditions and climate, fertile and harsh at one and the same time. The Mistral wind and the mosquitoes (happily, decreasing in number) can make the area challenging, but adventurous tourists will find rich flora and fauna and extraordinary skies.

The Camargue represents an unusual symbiosis between man and his environment. The soil is fertile, enriched by the huge alluvial deposits. The hay grown in La Crau infuses the meat of the sheep that eat it with such a delicate perfume that it has been awarded its own *appellation contrôlée*. One of the greatest problems in the past used to be the unpredictable and damaging floods, but drainage, canal maintenance and regulation of the Rhône and Durance rivers have led to greater control over water levels. Rice and fruit trees are now cultivated, and marsh reeds (used in the roofing of the local houses) are strategically planted to protect the land and hamlets from the wild winds. A network of roads leads to isolated farmhouses in the wet pastures, where the black bulls reign. The creation of the Regional Nature Park of the Camargue has ensured the area's protection from the dangers of mass tourism.

Native horses in the Camargue are small and robust, well adapted to the wetlands and able to protect themselves from the Mistral. They are intelligent creatures and easy to train, making them the perfect companion of the *gardian*. A procession of these white horses in the streets of Arles is a sight to behold.

The black bulls of the Camargue are equally small and delicate, resembling the animals that decorate Cretan vases. Contrary to popular belief, the majority of them are destined for the abattoir rather than the bullfighting arena. Only ten per cent of the bulls from the area are considered good enough to face the matadors, but some have proved themselves legendary. The meat of the other bulls is dignified by a Camargue *appellation contrôlée*; it is considered most tasty served pink and with a hint of parsley. Sausages are also made from the meat, but with a mixture of pork as a preservative, since bulls' meat perishes quickly.

The merino sheep from Arles is a small animal with thick, rust-coloured wool that mosquitoes cannot penetrate. Less than 30 years ago, the flocks of merino sheep would leave the Camargue in April to spend time in the mountain pastures of the Haute-Savoie. Bred more often today for its wool than for its meat, the merino is gradually disappearing.

Birdlife here is prolific. The greater flamingo is the most famous species in the Camargue, but there are also heron, egret, lapwing, curlew and sandpiper, as well as many thousands of varieties of duck.

The Vaccarès lake is brimming with fish, but fishing is strictly controlled. In the local restaurants, quickly cooked fresh fish, and small grey prawns, fished only in winter, are delicious culinary highlights.

BACKGROUND

HILLTOP VILLAGES (*villages perchés*)

Hilltop villages – *villages perchés* or *nids d'aigle* (eagle's nests) – are found both in inland Provence and in the area around Nice, where the mountains tumble down into the sea. The little villages are perched on hilltops, slopes, outcrops, ridges and terraces. Typical, picturesque examples include Éze-village, La Colle-sur-Loup, L'Escarène, Peille, Peillon and Saorge. Many are ancient border villages, including Saorge, which guards the Vallée de la Roya and overlooks the ruins of the fort. Most are magnificent, with slate-roofed houses and narrow, stepped streets.

MAS OR *BASTIDE*?

How do you tell a *mas* from a *bastide*? A *mas* in Provence means a small family-run farm. A *bastide*, in this region, means a secondary residence abutted by farm buildings.

The *mas* would have been the home of a comfortably-off farmer. Those on the plains are generally built on two floors, with the ground floor generally comprising a living room, the *salle*, and the farm buildings. The first floor houses the bedrooms and the granary. In the mountains, a *mas* is more often built on three floors. The ground floor houses the sheep-pen, the cellar and the stable. On the first floor you find the living room, and the bedrooms are on the second floor. The roof of the *mas* is either like that of a lean-to (in one single section) or saddle-back style (in two sections). The materials used – stone, lime, clay, sand – come from the region. The current fashion is for exposed stone walls, but in the past the stonework would have been hidden by a render made from lime and coloured sand. The house would face south and the side walls would have had no windows, making it easy to add new buildings. A *mas* was a dwelling that could develop according to need.

Bastides were generally built not too far from a town (particularly coastal towns, and Aix) as secondary residences for the well-off urban middle class. At the beginning of the 19th century, there were as many as 5,000 *bastides* in the Marseille area. They are huge, with façades decorated with balconies and sculptures and, generally, symmetrically placed windows. The walls are in hewn stone. Next to the *bastide* there are usually farm buildings.

THE MISTRAL

The notorious Mistral is a cold, dry north wind caused by high pressure that sits above the Massif Central or the east of France. Blowing down the Rhône corridor to fill the depressions over the Mediterranean, it is refreshing in summer but in winter it seems to penetrate deeply, everywhere. It frequently blows at 80–100km/h (50–63mph); the record is 270km/h (167mph), measured at the summit of the Mont Ventoux. It blows 120 days a year in Orange, and 90 days a year in Marseille. If you get caught in it, console yourself with the thought that, without it, the Rhône valley would be a damp, boggy place to be.

TRADITIONS

BULL RACING (*course Camargue*)

The spectacle of the *course Camargue* (Camargue races), the Provençal version of bullfighting, is probably the closest to the sport's ancient origins. The bulls are tested in the arena for their bravery, intelligence and capacity to combat man. Successful beasts travel from one arena to the next until they end up in Arles, hoping to achieve the same status as the legendary retired bull *Goya*.

In this form of bullfighting, the bull is released into the arena, with a rosette attached to its horns with tasselled strips of yarn. Men known as *razetteurs* then provoke and dodge the bull, aiming to grab the rosette from its horns. Once the rosette has been removed, the *razetteurs* try to do the same with the tassels, which are smaller and more difficult to get hold of. The most skilled *razetteur* removes not only the tassels but also the strips of wool. Points are allocated at each stage in the procedure, and there are sometimes financial rewards from sponsors or the public.

The *razetteur* needs skill, speed and courage – an arm's length is virtually the same as that of the horns – as well as an understanding of the bull, which may be lured and tricked into surrendering its trophies. There's a palpable relationship between bull and *razetteur*, who may come face to face more than once in a season. *Razetteurs* also sometimes work in teams.

The *course Camargue* may be bloodless, but there's no lack of danger or injury. The bulls are treated with respect, and tradition and rituals are important. The bulls are led into the arena for the *abrivado*, at the centre of a triangle formed by mounted *gardians*. Experts scrutinize each *gardian*, and verify that the *manade* (the herding of horses and bulls) is controlled and harmonious, with no chance for escape. The *manades* sometimes move into the streets, where the *gardians* are judged for the elegance of their handling and their control.

After the competition the bulls return to their pasture where a *bandito* is held. This is less formal than the *abrivado* – the animals are often tired and outfits are crumpled – but both the *bandito* and *abrivado* are highlights of local *ferias* (festivals) and a must if you are in the area at the time.

Following the Spanish tradition, more and more *encierros* now take place in the region. For the *encierro*, the bulls are released into the streets of a town and young people run ahead of them. The tips of the bull's horns are covered by balls and the bulls are significantly smaller than those in Pamplona, for example, so the risk of injury is diminished, but the runners can fall and be trampled. Beware: most accidents happen to tourists.

CARD GAMES

Banned by the Church, card games first arrived in France in 'pious' Provence. Today, players of *belote* or *manille* are as intrinsic to the region as players of *pétanque* (*see* 'Sport and Leisure Activities' in General

Information) or drinkers of *pastis*. Fortune-tellers reading tarot cards first came to popularity in Marseille and later captivated huge audiences with their divinations.

CHRISTMAS IN PROVENCE

Santons

On the weekends leading up to Christmas Eve, *foires aux santons* are held in Marseille, Aix-en-Provence, Aubagne, Chateaurenard, Martigues and Vitrolles. The fairs celebrate the local tradition of making terracotta figures (*santons*), usually dressed in 19th-century Provençal costume, and using them to decorate Christmas nativity scenes.

Provence has a long tradition of Christmas cribs and nativity scenes in its churches, sometimes using live actors. The *santons* tradition really took off in Provence during the French Revolution, when Christmas Mass and cribs were banned. A Marseillais manufacturer of statues had the inspirational idea of making a series of cheap *santons* for people to buy for their own cribs at home. The more commercially aware created cribs and invited the public to see them, at a cost of two *sols*, or *sous*. The *foires aux santons* tradition began in Marseille, in 1802 on the Allées de Meilhan (the largest *foire* is still held in the city today). The art of *santon*-making reached its climax in the first half of the 19th century, which is why the costumes mostly date from this period.

Santons – the word comes from *santoun*, a Provençal word meaning 'little saint' – are sculpted from clay. The figures are made throughout the year by craftsmen known as *santonniers*, to be sold at Christmas time. There are classic figures (the Holy Family, shepherds and the Magi), as well as figures from local life (farmers, knife-grinders, butchers, bakers, fishermen and, often, a woman with a black hen, whose soup was meant to be good for newborn babies). Some *santonniers* seek to represent the ideal village, with all its members. Nowadays, media celebrities and other contemporary figures also feature.

The first *santonniers* were rural craftsmen who drew upon the characters around them, inspired by folklore and tradition. The designs today again show some of that original naïvety. A number of *santonniers* are still at work today in Provence and it is possible to visit a workshop, to find out more about the manufacture and importance of these traditional clay figures.

After Christmas and throughout the month of January, live performances of pastorals take place. Dressed as *santons*, the participants re-enact scenes from the nativity with singing and acting in the local dialect.

Christmas Night

Christmas in Provence remains very much an intimate family affair, celebrated in simple but beautiful style, as described by 19th-century son of Provence Frédéric Mistral. In his recollection of Christmas supper, *Le Gros Souper*, eaten in the farmhouses of his childhood village of Maillane, the writer mentions snails removed from their shell with a new nail, fried salt cod, grey mullet with olives, dried fruit, nougat and, of course, the *pain de Noël*, the Christmas bread that must be shared with the first poor man who passes by the house.

The Christmas log, or *bûche de Noël* (Christmas log, referring to a piece of olive or cherry wood and not a cake), is set alight in a ritual known as the *cache-fio*. Traditionally, liqueur is poured over the log and it is then placed in the hearth, where it is lit. This usually takes place in the presence of the oldest and the youngest member of the household, before everyone sits down to eat.

Le Gros Souper starts at around 5 or 6pm and is in fact quite a meagre meal. However, it involves elaborate preparations, with three tablecloths placed one on top of the other, holly branches, three bowls and a wheat sheaf placed in water (its ability to flourish predicting a plentiful or poor harvest). The food normally consists of snails, salt cod, celeriac and plenty of sauce with which to eat the large quantities of bread.

Supper must be over in time for midnight Mass, where a live nativity scene is enacted, together with shepherds and sheep. The best-known traditional *Fête des Bergers* (or feast of the shepherds) is held before Mass in the escarpment town of Les Baux, where the locals crowd into the church to get a good view. In years gone by, it was considered that the greatest miracle of midnight Mass was 'getting the women's choir to sing in tune, since they were never in accord for the rest of the year'.

After Mass, the locals return home to place the baby Jesus in his crib, and then eat 13 desserts, representing Christ and the Apostles. This custom seems to have been introduced around 1920; the list includes nougat, grapes, honey, apples, pears, dates, *fruits confits* (dried fruits) and figs.

BACKGROUND

INDIENNES

Provence has been fashionable for many years, with its painters, antiques dealers, artisans and craftsmen, and its colourful, patterned cotton fabrics, known as *indiennes*.

The origins of Provençal fabric design and manufacture date back to the middle of the 17th century. With the creation in 1664 of the East India Company, vividly printed cotton cloths began to arrive by sea at the port of Marseille. These *indienne* fabrics proved to be a great success in Provence and local entrepreneurs quickly established their own workshops, in order to undercut the high prices of the imported fabric.

Provence has maintained its own textile industry and traditions by working inventively and imaginatively with the fabric. Today, the cotton is printed by hand on huge copper rolls. The designs are based on sketches done by artisans over 200 years ago or inspired by different motifs found in ancient documents.

Among the traditional fabrics are *boutis*, quilted pieces decorated with stitched motifs, which would have been created by local women over many long months. Originally intended for upholstery, the embroidered cotton was also used to make 'Sunday-best' dresses. Despite industrialization and the gradual decline of the manufacturing industry, these cotton fabrics are still made using the original techniques.

To find out about the Provençal textile industry, and the fascinating history of hand-printing, visit the Musée Charles-Demery in Tarascon. All over the region (and elsewhere in France), you'll see the shops of the *Souleiado* company (*souleiado* means 'the sun passing through the clouds'), which has had much success in making and selling brightly coloured traditional fabrics and cotton items.

LAVENDER

Lavender is indisputably linked with Provence. Most people have seen photos of lavender-blue fields in the Luberon or have lavender sachets in their wardrobes, reminding them of long, hot Provençal days.

The Romans grew lavender and used it to perfume their linen and their baths. Extensive cultivation developed in the 19th century and reached a peak in the 1920s, when the perfumeries near Grasse used the essential oils. (In the past, only violets and lavender were considered acceptable for use in male toiletries.) Today, with the use of synthesized lavender scents in washing powders, real lavender is disappearing from the mountains.

There is a difference between 'real' fine lavender, which grows at between 600–1,600m (1,970–5,250ft) and *lavandin*, a hybrid (French lavender crossed with *Lavandula officinalis*) that is cultivated at below 600m (1,970ft). Lavandin is most widely grown, being easier to cultivate and producing a greater quantity of natural oil; however, the essence is of a lesser quality and not so beautifully scented. Picking takes place in summer, when the heat encourages the essential oils to rise up the secreting glands of the plant.

It is rare to find farms nowadays that distill their own 'real' lavender but in some of the more remote mountains in the Drôme or the Vaucluse, stills are occasionally heaved into the lavender fields, which teem with red- or blue-winged grasshoppers. In Provence, production of lavender is centred on the Albion plateau, the Lure mountain, the Val de Sault and has only been mechanized since the 1970s. Lavender is distilled in a steam still, which permits the essential oils of the plant to be extracted.

To find out more, visit the Lavender Museum in Coustellet, in the Vaucluse.

FOOD AND DRINK

Provence and the Côte d'Azur have enjoyed 26 centuries of gastronomy. Six hundred years before Christ, a Greek sailor was offered the chance to marry the most beautiful maiden in the tribe in exchange for a few jars of wine and olive oil. Well, that's how the Marseillais spin the yarn of the birth of their city, anyway. Today in Marseille there's nothing to touch a plate of lamb's tripe and trotters (*pieds-paquets*) enjoyed sitting at a bar, *aïoli* served on the terrace of a café or by the old waterfront huts, or a good pizza, a meal that has become genuinely Marseillais.

Other dishes have arrived in Provence with the continuing influx of refugees – look out for couscous, oriental pastries and Armenian specialities. You'll find fast food, too. Who knows? Maybe the modern burger is a descendant of the good old local *pans bagnats* . . .

REGIONAL SPECIALITIES

The cuisine of this region is rich and delicious. Liberal use of olive oil, fragrant herbs, garlic and various spices is the essence of Provençal cooking. Among the most tasty specialities are the following:

– **Agneau de Provence** or Provençal lamb: the star dish in any little Provençal eaterie as well at the best restaurants in the area – lamb cutlets cooked with herbs that grow in the hills from the Durance as far as Les Baux. The sheep here graze on particularly flavoursome grass (the hay of La Crau even has an *appellation contrôlée*!). For many years, the lamb from Sisteron was considered to be the best, but it has recently lost some credibility.

– **Aïgo Bouido**: garlic and sage soup – with bread (or eggs and cheese).

– **Aïgo saou**: fish soup (no *rascasse* – scorpion fish) with *rouille*.

– **Ail rouge** (red garlic): aromatic garlic grown around Nice and used to flavour anchovy purée and *pissaladière*.

– **Aïoli** (*ailloli*): mayonnaise with garlic (but without mustard), thick and strongly flavoured and made exclusively with olive oil. (This is Provence, after all.)

– **Anchoïade**: anchovy purée mixed with olive oil and capers, thick and creamy.

– **Banon**: a soft cheese made with goat's milk in the shape of a small disk. Usually wrapped in chestnut leaves; sometimes *au poivre* (covered with black pepper).

– **Berlingueto**: chopped spinach and hard-boiled eggs.

– **Boeuf en daube**: pieces of beef cooked in olive oil with smoked bacon and onions, garlic and spices, served with a red wine sauce.

– **Bouillabaisse**: a noble dish – a seasoned soup with at least 12 different kinds of fish. Originally a dish for the poor, it is now enjoyed by the more affluent, and you should expect to pay at least 150F for a decent one. A cheaper *bouillabaisse* may have a good flavour but it won't really deserve the name because it will be made of very few rock fish and many frozen ones. Rare species (scorpion fish, sea bass, red mullet, and so on) are part of the basic composition of the *bouillabaisse* and the limited quantities available justify the high prices. The fish must be very fresh and the saffron for the broth must be of good quality. To accompany the *bouillabaisse*, *rouille*, an oily spiced sauce, is served with toasted croutons that have been generously rubbed with garlic.

– **Bourride**: a type of *bouillabaisse*, a little less pricey, made with white fish (mullet, angler fish, whiting) and flavoured with crawfish, served mainly with *aïoli*. Apart from the fish in *bouillabaisse* and its local variants, the fish that you will eat here will not come from the Mediterranean, but this does not mean that it won't be well prepared.

– **Brandade (de morue) à l'huile d'olive**: a mousse of salt cod with cream, olive oil and garlic.

– **Brousse de la Vésubie**: a mild creamy cheese made with ewe's milk, preserved in olive oil and eaten as it is or in a vinaigrette with garlic and spices. From the Vésubie Valley, north of Nice.

– **Brousse du Rove**: creamy and mild-flavoured cheese made with ewe's milk; best in the winter.

– **Cachat**: also known as **Tomme du Mont Ventoux**: A very soft, sweet and creamy flavoured cheese made with ewe's milk; available in the summer.

– **Cade**: a Toulon pancake made with chickpea flour, cousin of the *Socca* found in Nice. You can still find this in the markets of Toulon although it is not as popular as it once was.

– **Capoum**: a large pink *rascasse* (scorpion fish).

– **Citrons de Menton** (Menton lemons): lemon trees in Menton boast flowers and fruit all year round, making Menton one of the major suppliers of lemons in Europe. It is a key part of the local tourist programme with its own festival.

– **Farcis niçois**: delicious stuffed vegetables, usually aubergines, sweet peppers, tomatoes and courgette flowers.

– **Gnocchi**: potato dumplings, served with a béchamel sauce, covered in grated cheese and then cooked in the oven. Gnocchi are of Niçois origin, via Italy.

– **Les grenouilles à la provençale**: frog's legs coated in flour and fried with olive oil and garlic.

– **Lapin à la provençale**: rabbit cooked in white wine, on a very low fire, with garlic, mustard, spices and tomatoes.

– **Loup au fenouil**: this is one of the highlights of Provençal cuisine, known as '*bar*' in other regions. The sea bass is grilled over fennel stalks or stuffed.

– **Olives and Huile d'olive**: Nice (the 'Big Olive') is home to the *cailletier*, a delicious black olive used in many local recipes. The local olive oil is famous throughout the south of France for its aroma and smoothness.

– **Pan bagnat**: a typically Niçois speciality, a substantial bread roll stuffed with anchovies, olives, tomatoes and capers, and brushed with olive oil.

– **Picodon de Valréas**: soft, nutty-tasting, small disk of goat's cheese.

– **Pieds-paquets** (lamb tripe and trotters): small parcels of tripe prepared Marseille-style (served with lamb's trotters), stuffed and cooked on a low fire in white wine with onions, carrots and bacon. There are numerous variations in the area; *pieds-paquets* in Barcelonnette or in the Luberon bear no resemblance to their Marseillais cousins.

– **Pissaladière**: onion tart garnished with anchovies and olives.

– **Poivre-d'Ane**: a goat's cheese flavoured with rosemary or the herb savory (*sarriette*). Aromatic taste and perfume.

– **Pollo pépitora**: Provençal chicken *fricassée* thickened with lemon-flavoured mayonnaise.

– **Pommade**: a thick paste of garlic, basil, cheese and olive oil.

– **Porchetta niçoise**: suckling pig, stuffed with all sorts of goodies, including garlic, onion and herbs.

– **Poutines**: another speciality of Nice, alevins or young fish are served in omelettes, and only in spring, due to fishing regulations.

– **Ratatouille niçoise**: a healthy, light, aromatic and economic dish made with courgettes (zucchini), aubergines (eggplant), tomatoes, sweet peppers (optional), garlic, onions and *herbes de Provence*. The vegetables have to be cooked separately to preserve their individual flavour before being mixed together in olive oil. The courgettes (zucchini) grown around Nice are smaller and more bulbous than other varieties, and their flavour gives locally made ratatouille its unique quality. The dish is just as delicious eaten cold.

– **Raviolis**: another Niçois speciality, but of Italian origin, large squares of pasta stuffed with meat or vegetables and cooked in boiling water. Certain specialist shops make and sell home-made fresh *raviolis*.

– **Rouille**: the unmissable sauce accompaniment for *bouillabaisse*. Fresh red chilli, crushed with garlic, mixed with olive oil, a few bread crumbs and some broth.

– **Salade niçoise**: a refreshing summer-time favourite for those hot days when you want a light and flavourful dish. The salad contains green peppers, tomatoes (in quarters), anchovies, radishes, eggs, lettuce, black olives and olive oil. Sometimes tuna fish.

– **Socca**: a pancake made with chickpea flour, water and olive oil, cooked over a wood-fired oven.

– **Soupe au pistou**: a classic of Provençal cooking, a *pesto*, or vegetable soup flavoured with a paste made of garlic and basil crushed in olive oil.

– **Stockfish** or **Estocaficada**: dried salt cod soaked for a while and then cooked in white wine with tomatoes, onions and, of course, garlic.

– **Supions**: small cuttlefish rolled in flour and then fried in oil.

– **Tapenade**: a purée of olives, anchovies, olive oil and capers, served on toast as an hors d'oeuvres.

– **Tarte (Tourte) aux blettes**: open-crust pastry with filling of Swiss chard (not unlike Chinese cabbage) and pine nuts.

– **Tian**: Provençal earthenware dish.

– **Tomme du Mont Ventoux**: *see Cachat*.

– **Truffes du Tricastin** (*Truffles from Tricastin*): although two out of three truffles grown in France come from around Valréas, the 'black diamond' was curiously absent from local cooking for a long time. Nowadays, people will travel miles to buy truffles from the markets or to indulge in them in country inns. In the winter, the markets at Valréas, Richerenches, Apt, Vaison or Carpentras sell truffles – for a relatively reasonable price – with which to make a truffle purée or to flavour *tournedos*.

WHAT TO DRINK

Wine

For a long time, the wine from Provence has been seen as suitable only for swigging, well-chilled, with a pizza. In fact, Provençal wines have been well known and appreciated since ancient times and over the last few years the quality of the wines has begun to catch up with the quantity.

The best-quality wines are from the Côtes-du-Rhône. Even though the greatest (Côte-Rôtie, Hermitage, St-Joseph) come from the Rhône-Alpes, on the high valley of the river, Provence also has its Côtes-du-Rhône *Villages* and some other interesting cultures. Châteauneuf-du-Pape is a well-structured, full-bodied wine with a powerful, complex bouquet – the perfect accompaniment for red meats, game and strong cheeses. Vacqueyras and Gigondas, produced near Vaison-la-Romaine, are noble ruby-coloured wines; a strong flavour of plums and cherries develops with age, until they somewhat resemble their Papal neighbour.

The sun helps to produce large crops, and Provence produces the majority of the Côtes-du-Rhône wines on the market. They are light and fruity (the grape varieties used are Cinsault and Mourèdre) rather than sophisticated, but they offer good, easy drinking. The wines from the slopes tend to be better than those produced on the plains; try, for example, the reds from Tricastin (north-east of Orange), labelled as either Coteaux-du-Tricastin or Côtes-du-Rhône. For a more thorough investigation, pay a visit to the Caves Coopératives de Rousset-les-Vignes or the cellars in St-Pantaléon in the Provençal part of the Drôme, near Valréas. In Vinsobres, the village name (which means 'sober wine') is totally inappropriate.

Lovers of naturally sweet wines, *vins doux naturels*, will fall for the very famous, aromatic and fruity Muscat de Beaumes-de-Venise, produced on the curious soil type found around the Dentelles de Montmirail.

Finally, there are the Côtes-de-Provence, known mainly for their *rosés* in characteristic bottles. There are no great wines here, but some really deserve to be discovered. The white wine from Cassis, Vin Blanc de Cassis is the perfect accompaniment for fish and *bouillabaisse*, while a good red Côtes-de-Provence will go perfectly with pasta and game. Bandol, rarely seen on tables in France, is an excellent AOC that is worth a try, although it does need to age.

Throughout the region, there is a whole panoply of country wines, or *vins de pays*, such as Côtes-du-Ventoux, Côtes-du-Luberon, and so on.

Pastis

The taking of this aniseed-based aperitif – the *pastaga* – is a real ritual at lunch-time and after work. The ingredients are about 50g of green aniseed, half a vanilla pod, some cinnamon and a litre of alcohol at 90 degrees proof.

A *momie* is a thimble-sized Pastis glass, which allows drinkers to carry on longer. Try Pastis with different mixers. With mint syrup it is called a *perroquet* (or parrot), with grenadine it is a *tomate* (or tomato) and with barley water it's known as a *mauresque*.

Bouches-du-Rhône

The Mediterranean Coast and the Hinterland

MARSEILLE

Marseille is considered to be France's second city after Paris. Although the name evokes a number of clichés, from *pastis* and *pétanque* to soap and siestas, many people think of the city as a concrete jungle choked with traffic and riddled with crime.

This is a reputation to which the Marseillais have to some extent contributed. Natural-born actors on a metropolitan stage, which none the less maintains a provincial scale and a local dialect, they quite enjoyed being caricatured by actors and writers such as Pagnol in the 1930s. Typical operettas, plays and films set in Marseille mixed sunny tunes about seaside holidays with darker songs of gangsters, con-men and pimps. Decades later, the songs and stories have become a reality with gangsters settling scores amid political and financial scandals. The media's best efforts turned Marseille into the capital of vice and danger – hardly an obvious destination for tourists.

Few French people bother to visit Marseille, unless they are on a business trip or staying with family. With its reputation for filthy streets and big-city tensions, it would appear to be the least Provençal of places. In fact, it is well worth spending more than just a few hours here, to find out more about Marseille's complex character and its remarkable museums, and to enjoy the unique atmosphere of some of its districts. After a short walk, you'll find that this is one of the most beautiful towns in the south or, indeed, in the whole of France.

Visit Callelongue, take a tour of the corniche or stroll around the Jardins du Pharo (the palace built by Napoleon III for his Empress), and you'll understand why the locals love their home to the point of reverence. Watch the sun rise or set over the Vieux-Port and you'll appreciate why the Marseillais are reluctant to let 'non-locals' (that is, people who live as far away as Aix-en-Provence and Hyères) in on their secret. This ancient city is very beautiful, with something in the air – a real *je ne sais quoi* – that just isn't to be found anywhere else.

2,600 Years of History

The history of this great sea port has been shaped by waves of immigrants, all bringing their own culture to the melting pot. Marseille has absorbed more people from more diverse origins than any other town in France.

Around 600 BC, the Greek Phocaeans landed from their galleys at the foot of a cliff, at what is now the Vieux-Port. They were particularly struck by the bubbling spring, the Lacydon, that reminded them so much of their native land, in Asia Minor. A few months later (according to legend), Protis, the leader of the Greek expedition, married Guptis, the daughter of the local king and founded Massalia (later called 'Massilia' by the Romans).

The kingdom developed its own trading posts and colonies, including Nice, Antibes, Olbia (near present-day Hyères), St-Tropez, La Ciotat and Agde. It was allied to Rome, which helped it to fend off the greedy ambitions of the Celts and Ligurians, and it maintained a statute as an independent republic when the rest of Provence was under direct Roman rule. In 49 BC, Caesar imposed a maritime blockade and seized the town, when it showed allegiance to Pompey. From that time it was an integral part of the Roman Empire and became renowned as a city of science and culture. In AD 18, Strabon wrote in his *Geography* that, 'The town was able to persuade even the most illustrious of Romans to study within its walls in preference to Athens, if they were intent on learning.' As the centuries went by, universities were built: today, Marseille is internationally recognized in the sciences, notably in the field of medicine.

In the Middle Ages, Marseille went through alternating phases of prosperity and poverty. It established itself as the 'Gate to the Orient' in the time of the French kings, but it also suffered a number of barbarian invasions and was hit by the first epidemics of the plague. The port regained its importance after the departure of the Third Crusade, but there were new difficulties in the 14th and 15th centuries, from the Black Death in 1348 to pillage by the Catalans in 1423. It only recovered its earlier splendour when Louis XIV made it the base for his navy. In spite of the Great Plague of 1720, Marseille, under the strictures of the French Revolution, became the largest trading port in the Mediterranean. Marseille embraced the Revolution and was the first city to call for the abolition of the monarchy. It played an important role in the insurrection against the Convention Montagnarde, and as a result suffered repression under the Terror, including being deprived of its name.

Under the Second Empire, with the conquest of Algeria, the building of the Suez Canal and the rise in trade with the colony in Indochina, Marseille became established as a colonial port. Until World War II, this was the main source of its wealth. The city profited enormously and decolonization inevitably dealt a severe blow. The vast steelworks at Fos-sur-Mer were built, in the belief that they would save the city, but the steel crisis a few years later brought Marseille to the brink of ruin.

Despite the ups and downs of the past, Marseille is still, after 26 centuries, France's most important port. During its long trading history, it has created some marvels alongside many sordid horrors – in this city, the ugly sits side by side with the beautiful. It's hard to see why it might appeal to visitors, but Marseille is an exceptional place to visit and, with a little understanding, everyone can appreciate its unique atmosphere.

BOUCHES-DU-RHÔNE

Marseille's Immigrants

Marseille has always been a place of asylum and assimilation. It has been, in turn, under the control of the Greeks, the Romans, the Visigoths (in 480 under King Euric), and the Ostrogoths (a few years later under Theodoricus). Jews, Armenians, hordes of Italians, Corsicans and Spaniards, 'Pieds-Noirs'

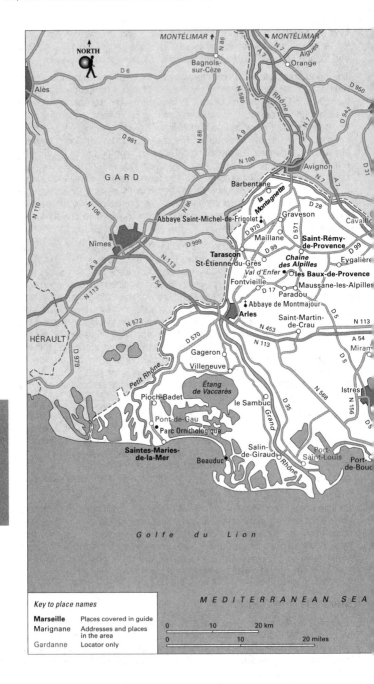

BOUCHES-DU-RHÔNE

Key to place names

Marseille	Places covered in guide
Marignane	Addresses and places in the area
Gardanne	Locator only

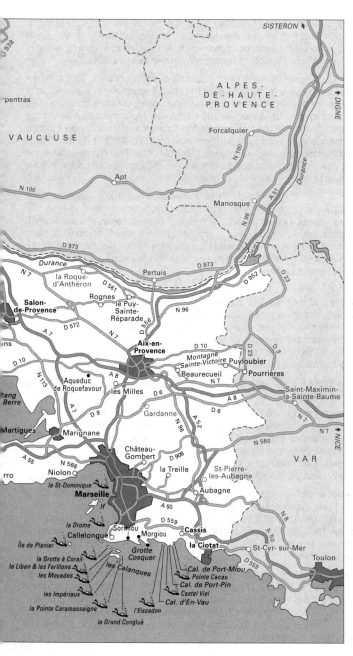

(Algerian-born French) and other North Africans, Vietnamese, Cambodians, French West Indians, and islanders from Réunion and the Comores have all sought refuge in Marseille at some stage. All of which adds up to a turbulent history with a multiplicity of people contributing to a Marseillais unity.

In 1822, Greeks fleeing Turkish massacre become cobblers, tailors, fishermen and merchants. Italians ruined by crop failures arrived in a great wave at the end of the 19th century. They were paid peanuts by the factory owners who sometimes used them as strike-breakers. Nicknamed 'Babbis' by the French, they were seen as competition for work in the docks, the tobacco factories and on building sites. There were racist incidents in 1885 and 1886 and several were killed in organized 'Babbi hunts'. Towards the end of the 19th century, tensions subsided thanks to the commercial boom and the growth of the unions.

The Armenian genocide in 1915 followed by the 1922 Turkish War of Independence brought thousands of Armenians and Greeks to Marseille. Many stayed. One Armenian called Hagop Malakian opened a sweet shop and his son, Achod, became a cinematographer, under the name of Henri Verneuil and is now a celebrated film director in France. Another family had a son called Charles Aznavourian, who was later to become one of France's most famous singers.

In 1925, a wave of Italian anti-fascists started to arrive, including the Livi family and their son Ivo. Brought up on the streets, Ivo worked in a soap factory from the age of 11 before becoming a docker. In 1938, he launched his career as a singer, making his debut at the Alcazar. He took his stage name from the memory of his mother shouting down to him from the balcony, 'Ivo monta!' ('Ivo, come on up!'). Ivo Livi became the legendary French star Yves Montand.

The Spanish Civil War contributed to the population of Marseille with the arrival of Spanish Republicans defeated by Franco's forces.

Early in the 20th century, many North Africans, principally Algerians, were brought in en masse to work in Marseille's oil and sugar refineries, and in the Fos steelworks. The majority settled in the district of the Porte d'Aix. With the economic crisis and the war in Algeria, racial tension mounted. The war had a deep psychological impact on the Pied-Noir community, and on the French, and there is still much bitterness, as former enemies live side by side.

Racial tension undoubtedly exists in Marseille but no more so than in cities like Paris, Lyons or Lille. The city seems to mould its 'foreigners' to its own image. Today, the children and grandchildren of the 'Babbis', so detested in the 19th century and the 1920s, are great defenders of their Marseillais identity; perhaps the descendants of the original Pieds-Noirs will feel the same in time.

Famous French footballer, Zinedine Zidane, is a powerful symbol of Arab integration in France. Despite being born in the underprivileged northern ghettos of Marseille, he has achieved worldwide fame and is seen as a hero, not only among Marseille's Arab community, but throughout France. Zizou (as he is known) is a symbol of hope, not only for disadvantaged children but also for racial integration.

Country Cooking

It's impossible to really understand Marseille, without getting to grips with the concept of the *cabanons*, the holiday huts described by a popular French song as 'no bigger than a pocket handkerchief' and adored by the locals. Generations of Marseillais have perfected the art of doing nothing very much, except playing a game of *boules*, taking a dip in the sea, relaxing with an *apéritif* and savouring a *bouillabaisse*. In the community of the *cabanons*, everyone knows everyone else, and the night air is heavy with the scent of *aïoli*, sardines and fish soup.

■ Useful Addresses

- **🏠 1** Office du tourisme (tourist office)
- **🏠 2** Comité départemental du tourisme (departmental tourist office)
- **✉** Post office
- **🚌** Coach station
- **🚆** Train station (SNCF)
- **🚢** Naval station (SNCM)
- **3** Police station

■ Where to Stay

- **10** AJ de Bois-Luzy
- **11** AJ de Bonne-Veine
- **12** Hôtel du Coq
- **13** Hôtel Beaulieu-Glaris
- **14** Hôtel Hermes
- **15** Hôtel Rome et St Pierre
- **17** Hôtel Azur
- **18** Chambres d'hôte Schaufelberger (guest rooms)
- **19** St-Ferréol's Hôtel
- **20** Hôtel Mercure Marseille Prado
- **21** Hôtel Edmond Rostand
- **22** Hôtel Mistral
- **23** New Hôtel Vieux-Port
- **24** La Résidence du Vieux-Port
- **26** Hôtel Le Richelieu
- **27** Hôtel Peron
- **28** New Hotel Bompard
- **29** La Cigale et la Fourmi
- **30** Hôtel Alizé
- **31** Hôtel Béarn
- **32** La Maison du Petit Canard
- **33** Hôtel Beauvau
- **34** Sofitel Vieux-Port
- **35** Chambre chez Mme Conte-Champigny
- **36** La Petite Maison à Marseille

✗ Where to Eat

- **40** Chez Angèle
- **41** Les Menus Plaisirs
- **42** Le Chalet
- **43** L'Art et les Thés
- **44** Chez Madie-Les Galinettes
- **45** Au Vieux Panier
- **46** Pâtes Fraîches et Raviolis
- **47** Pizzeria Au Feu de Bois
- **49** Le Miramar
- **50** Le Mas
- **51** Le Fémina
- **52** Le Quinze
- **53** Le Panier des Arts
- **54** L'Orient Exploré
- **56** Le Sud du Haut
- **57** La Kahéna
- **58** L'Infidèle
- **59** Pizzeria Chez Jeannot
- **60** Pizzeria des Catalans
- **62** L'Ambassade des Vignobles
- **63** Chez Vincent
- **64** O'Stop
- **65** Grancafé
- **66** Le Café Parisien
- **67** L'Oliveraie
- **68** Le Dock de Suez
- **69** Le Milano des Docks

♀ Where to Go for a Drink

- **71** Aux Caprices de Marianne
- **73** Les Colonies
- **74** Caffe Milano
- **75** La Part des Anges
- **76** L'Assiette Lyonnaise
- **77** Toinou
- **78** Le Café des Arts
- **79** Les Trois Forts
- **80** Chez Fonfon

BOUCHES-DU-RHÔNE

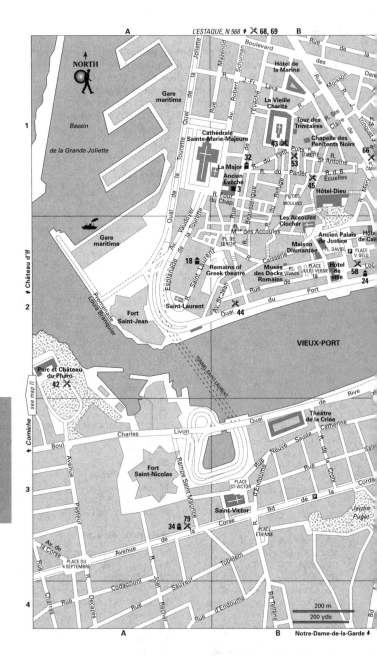

L'ESTAQUE, N 568 ↑ ✕ 68, 69

A   B

NORTH

Bassin

de la Grande Joliette

Boulevard

Rue   de   Rue   des

Gare
maritime

Hôtel de
la Marine

La Vieille
Charité

Tour des
Trinitaires

Chapelle des
Pénitents Noirs

66

Cathédrale
Sainte-Marie-Majeure

43 ✕

32

53

R. St Antoine

La Major

Ancien
Évêché

3

45

R. d. B.
Ecuelles

Hôtel-Dieu

1

← Château d'If

Gare
maritime

Les Accoules
Clocher

Ancien Palais
de Justice

Hôt
de Ca

Maison
Diamantée

PLACE
V. GELU

18

Remains of
Greek theatre

Saint-Laurent

Musée
des Docks
Romains

Hôtel
de
Ville

58

24

Fort
Saint-Jean

Saint-Laurent

44

2

← Corniche   see map II

Parc et Château
du Pharo

42 ✕

VIEUX-PORT

Rive

Théâtre
de la Criée

Charles   Livon   Quai

Fort
Saint-Nicolas

Rampe Saint-Maurice

PLACE
ST-VICTOR

Saint-Victor

Jardin
Puget

34   79

PLACE
ETIENNE

3

Av. de
la Corse

Avenue

de   Corse

PLACE DU
4 SEPTEMBRE

Codaccioni

200 m

200 yds

4

A   B   Notre-Dame-de-la-Garde ↓

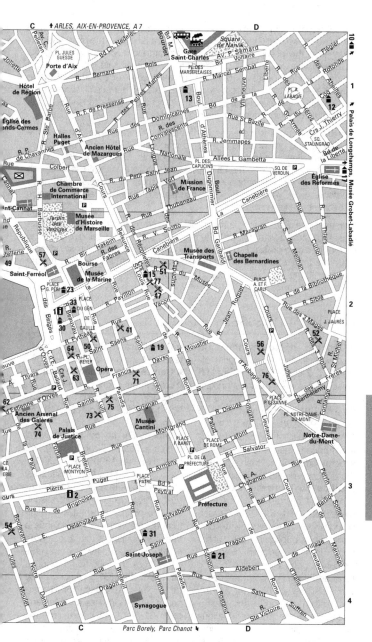

Marseille's colourful gastronomic past dates back to the time – in the sixth century BC – when a Greek sailor was offered the hand of the most beautiful daughter of the tribe in exchange for several amphorae of olive oil and casks of wine. Today, try *pieds et paquets* (tripe) in a small café, enjoy a bowl of *soupe au pistou* (pesto soup) under a pine tree or a delicious *aïoli* (garlic mayonnaise, served with fish) on a sun-drenched terrace. Delicious and simple dishes are devoured and digested rather than just tasted in the former fishing huts or on the stunning seafront.

One dish that used to be eaten by the poor and was never served in the country houses or mansions of the ship-owners is the famous *bouillabaisse* (mixed fish stew). Today, a decent version of this poor man's dish costs a small fortune. The fishermen's wives used to make it with leftover fish cooked in stock with potatoes, *aïoli*, *rouille* (spicy mayonnaise) and garlic croutons. Now, relatively rare and expensive fish have replaced simple leftovers as the key ingredients.

Marseille's best 'fast food' is the traditional *pan bagnat* ('soaked bread'), a crusty roll stuffed with tuna, olives, peppers, onions and salad, steeped in olive oil and then pressed so that the flavours blend together. It may be more elaborate than a burger, but the principle is the same. Another fast treat in Marseille is the *pizze* (pronounced here without an 'a'); grab a slice when you're on the run.

USEFUL ADDRESSES

◘ Comité départemental du tourisme (departmental tourist office) (C3, **2** on map I): 'Le Montesquieu', 13 rue Roux-de-Brignoles, 13006. ☎ 04-91-13-84-13. Fax: 04-91-33-01-82. Open Monday to Friday 9–12.30pm and 1.40–5.30pm. Excellent themed information (monuments, leisure, festivals, accommodation) in Marseille and the Bouches-du-Rhône region.

◘ Office du tourisme (tourist office) (C2, **1** on map I): 4 La Canebière. ☎ 04-91-13-89-00. Open Monday to Saturday 9am–7pm; Sunday and public holidays 10am–5pm (6pm in summer). Excellent welcome, good information on the town and things to do, hotel reservation service (on the spot and no commission charged), and organized guided visits. There are various offices, located at the station, in Le Panier and on the Prado beaches.

■ Gîtes ruraux (country cottages): reservations on ☎ 04-90-59-49-39.

■ Centre Information Jeunesse (Youth Information Centre): 96 La Canebière, 13001. ☎ 04-91-24-33-50. Open Monday to Friday 10am–6pm.

■ Office de la culture (cultural events office) (C2 on map I): 42 La Canebière, 13001. ☎ 04-96-11-04-60. Open Monday to Saturday 10am–7pm (afternoons only in August). This association, established in 1901 to provide information on cultural events in the city, publishes a free monthly listings magazine called *In Situ*. Book seats for various events on the spot or through other offices.

✉ Post office (C1 on map I): Place de l'Hôtel-des-Postes, 13001 (corner of Henri-Barbusse and Colbert). ☎ 04-91-33-50-47. Next to the Bourse commercial centre. Poste restante open 8am–7pm (Saturday 8am–noon).

■ **SOS Médecins** (emergency doctor): ☎ 04-91-52-91-52.

■ **SAMU** (fire brigade): ☎ 15.

■ **Timone Hospital:** boulevard Jean-Moulin, 13005. ☎ 04-91-38-60-00.

■ **Pharmacy:** 154 boulevard National (near the train station), 13003. Open 8am–9pm except Sunday. For the on-duty pharmacy, call the police.

■ **SOS Voyageurs** (travellers' helpline): ☎ 04-91-62-12-80.

■ **Police** (B1, **3** on map I): rue du Commissaire-Becker, 13002. ☎ 04-91-39-80-00. Annexe: 29 rue Nationale, 13001.

– **Météo** (weather forecast): ☎ 08-36-68-02-13.

– **Météo marine** (maritime forecast): ☎ 08-36-68-08-13.

Changing money

■ **Comptoir Marseillais de Bourse**: 22 La Canebière, 13001. ☎ 04-91-54-93-04. Open 9am–7pm except Sunday from June to September and 9am–6pm except Sunday the rest of the year.

■ **Change de la Bourse** (C2 on map I): 3 place du Général-de-Gaulle (at the bottom of La Canebière). ☎ 04-91-13-09-00. Open 8.30am–6.30pm except Sunday.

TRANSPORT

– **Métro** (underground train network): very useful, with two lines running 5am–9pm (tickets sold 6.30am–7.30pm). The same price as the bus. Information: RTM ☎ 04-91-91-92-10.

– **Bus** (C2 on map I): information, maps and tickets from the information desks at the RTM, 6 rue des Fabres, 13001. ☎ 04-91-91-92-10. A day pass costs 25F and a rechargeable magnetic card is 50F or 100F; both are valid for the whole network (metro, bus and tram). Individual tickets are 9F, valid for 1 hour, and for changes from bus to metro and vice versa. Passes and tickets are sold from machines in metro stations and from some shops licensed by the RTM. The Fluobus provides a service at night.

✈ **Marseille-Provence Airport**: at Marignane, 25 kilometres (15.5 miles) west. ☎ 04-42-14-14-14 for flight information and confirmation. This international airport has services to all the major towns in France and the major destinations in Europe and the rest of the world.

✈ **Représentation commerciale d'AOM** (commercial representation): ☎ 04-91-14-22-25.

– **Bus for the airport**: St-Charles station for Marseille-Provence. Every 20 minutes 5am–9.30pm. Takes 45 minutes and costs 45F.

🚌 **Bus station**: place Victor-Hugo (next to the SNCF St-Charles train station), 13003. Information: ☎ 04-91-08-16-40.

🚆 **SNCF Gare St-Charles** (train station) (D1 on map I): ☎ 08-36-35-35-35 (2,23F per minute) or 04-91-54-42-61. The St-Charles train station is a terminus at the end of the Rhône valley. The TGV (high-speed train) serves Paris (3 hours), Lyon (3 hours), and the Côte d'Azur. The SNCF office in town is at 17 rue Grignan.

⚓ **Maritime transport** (information on boat departure times): ☎ 04-91-39-42-42. The SNCM company (A2 on map I) sails to Corsica and Tunisia from the port of La Joliette: 61 boulevard des Dames. ☎ 08-36-67-95-00.

■ **Taxis**: ☎ 04-91-03-60-03 or 04-91-02-20-20 or 04-91-05-80-80. There are taxi ranks at the Vieux-Port and the station, among other places. Confirm the price of your journey before setting off. There have been an increasing number of complaints about meter swindling, so be careful.

■ **Bicycles and scooters**: hire a bike for the day from Cycles Do, 76 cours Lieutard, 13006. ☎ 04-91-33-65-57. To hire a scooter, Point 124, 44 avenue des Chartreux, 13003. ☎ 04-91-49-59-89.

WHERE TO STAY

Marseille has never been specifically geared towards tourism, and in the past has lacked good hotel facilities. Today, the choice is better. The following suggestions are based on various criteria, such as peace and quiet, good views, warm welcome and lively atmosphere, as well as basic practicalities. There are few really charming hotels, but you'll find pleasant places to stay with lovely views of the sea, the Vieux-Port or the corniche, as long as you aren't too fussy about facilities or noise. Some hotels in the city centre are still a bit shabby.

☼ Budget

🛏 **Auberge de jeunesse de Bois-Luzy** (youth hostel) (D1, **10** off map I): Château de Bois-Luzy, allée des Primevères, 13012. ☎ and fax: 04-91-49-06-18. In the northeast of the town about 5 kilometres (3 miles) from the centre, with a view of the sea, in the distance. Take bus No. 6 through the Montolivet district, getting off at Marius-Richard. From St-Charles station, take the metro in the direction of La Rose (line No. 1) and get off at Réformés-Canebière. From there, take bus No. 6 to Marius-Richard. Like all official youth hostels, this one is closed from noon to 5pm, but it does operate all year round. 90 beds in rooms of four or six beds for 45F. Expect to pay 55F per person sharing a double (not including city tax). Sheet hire is 7F, breakfast is 18F and there is a set menu for 43F. The hostel is located in a magnificent *bastide* built in 1850, with an impressive entrance hall. Washing and kitchen facilities are available free of charge and visitors can pitch their tents on a neighbouring sports field, and use the facilities. Free parking.

🛏 **Auberge de jeunesse de Bonne-Veine** (youth hostel) (C3, **11** on map II): 47 avenue J.-Vidal, 13008 (in the Dr-Bonfils cul-de-sac). ☎ 04-91-73-21-81. Fax: 04-91-73-97-23. Take bus No. 44 to Place Bonnefon. You need a youth hostel card to stay here. There are 150 beds at 70F per night in a five-bed dorm or 90F for a double room including breakfast. There are facilities for left luggage and a night-watchman. Sheets for hire and snacks to buy for around 40F. This modern hostel has no particular charm, but it is in a quiet district near the beach.

Vieux-port and Le Panier

🛏 **Hôtel Alizé** (C2, **30** on map II): 35 quai des Belges. ☎ 04-91-33-66-97. Fax: 04-91-54-80-06. Email: alize-hotel@wanadoo.fr. Double rooms from 335F to 395F, not including breakfast (40F). Probably the best value for money of all the hotels overlooking the Vieux-Port, offering a warm welcome, good facilities and a lively atmosphere. Early birds can watch the fishermen return with their catches and then stroll through the markets. The rooms are quite small but they are air-conditioned and soundproofed, and some even have their own patio.

≜ La Maison du Petit Canard (B1, **32** on map I): 2 impasse St-François, 13002. ☎ 04-91-91-40-31. B&B in the heart of Le Panier, a stone's throw from Vieille-Charité. Double room 250F, including breakfast; single occupancy 150F. There are two guest rooms, an oriental-style drawing room and an interesting 50F menu.

≜ Hôtel Hermes (C2, **14** on map I): 2 rue Bonneterie, 13002. ☎ 04-91-90-34-51. Fax: 04-91-91-14-44. Double rooms from 300 to 380F. A recent renovation has helped this wonderfully located little hotel (between Le Panier and the Vieux-Port) to become really popular. Ask for one of the rooms with a terrace overlooking the quayside. The best rooms are on the top floor, but they are much in demand and often pre-booked.

☆☆ Moderate

≜ Chambres d'hôte Schaufelberger (A2, **18** on map I): 2 rue St-Laurent. ☎ and fax: 04-91-90-29-02. Email: schauf@wanadoo.fr. ✗ Open all year round; booking necessary. Double room 300F including breakfast. A great place to stay – on the 14th floor of a block of flats of questionable taste, built by the Vieux-Port at the foot of Le Panier to house homeless victims of the bombing in the World War II. The spectacular view from the balcony makes up for the ugliness of the building. The two pleasant rooms share a bathroom. Credit cards not accepted.

≜ New Hotel Vieux-Port (C2, **23** on map I): 3a rue Reine-élisabeth, 13001. ☎ 04-91-90-51-42. Fax: 04-

91-90-76-24. Email: marseillevieux-port@new-hotel.com. Metro: Vieux-Port. In the pedestrian area, conveniently located close to Vieux-Port. Double room with shower or bath 480F; buffet-style breakfast 55F. The modern building has been totally renovated but is already showing signs of wear and tear. The service could do with a bit of improvement too. The rooms are pleasant; those with numbers ending in 1, 2, 3 and 4 have the best views on all four floors.

≜ La Résidence du Vieux-Port (B2, **24** on map I): 18 quai du Port, 13002. ☎ 04-91-91-91-22. Fax: 04-91-56-60-88. Email: hotel-residence@wanadoo.fr. ✗ Metro: Vieux-Port-Hôtel-de-Ville. The hotel is in Vieux-Port, on the same side side as the town hall, overlooking Notre-Dame. Double room 590F. Wide balconies with comfortable chairs give views of the boats. The rooms, with all the mod-cons you would expect from a three-star establishment, are spacious, light and pleasantly furnished; the bathrooms, however, are small and gloomy. Rooms on the seventh floor have bright *provençal* furnishings. Ideally located for exploration of the town (or a night out on it!), offering a warm welcome and a good breakfast. Parking is in the Jules-Verne car park behind the Hôtel de Ville.

☆☆☆☆ Très Chic

≜ Mercure Beauvau Vieux-Port (C2, **33** on map I): 4 rue Beauvau, 13001. ☎ 04-91-54-91-00. Fax: 04-91-54-15-76. Next door to the tourist office; double rooms from 660F to 780F. One of the oldest hotels in Marseille, occupying the best location in the city and offering charm, an authentic atmosphere and Louis-Philippe furniture. Many famous people have had drinks in the bar and enjoyed the view over Vieux-Port from the *privilège* rooms.

⚓ **Sofitel Vieux Port** (A3, **34** on map I): 36 boulevard Charles-Livon, 13007. ☎ 04-91-15-59-00. Fax: 04-91-15-59-50. Double rooms from 900F; rooms with a terrace overlooking the Vieux-Port 1,200F. A particularly attractive hotel in a lovely location near the Jardins du Pharo. Recently renovated, it has been decorated in local style. Some rooms have charming terraces on which guests can enjoy breakfast overlooking the Vieux-Port, or watch the sun set with a relaxing drink. Facilities include a solarium and swimming pool with bar. The service is excellent, and the view of the port from the breakfast room is unbeatable.

In the Centre

☆ – ☆☆ Budget to Moderate

⚓ **Hôtel du Coq** (D1, **12** on map I): 26 rue du Coq, 13001. ☎ 04-91-62-61-29. Fax: 04-91-64-02-05. This hotel, open all year, is in a small street, just a five-minute walk from St-Charles station; the owners will even come and collect you if you would like. Double rooms from 165F to 195F, depending on facilities and whether or not breakfast is included. A warm welcome, recently refurbished rooms and attractive prices. Ask for a room at the back of the building.

⚓ **Hôtel Beaulieu-Glaris** (D1, **13** on map I): 1 place des Marseillaises, 13001. ☎ 04-91-90-70-59. Fax: 04-91-56-14-04. Closed between Christmas and New Year. At the foot of a monumental stairway leading to St-Charles station, making it convenient for guests arriving by train. Rooms from 160F to 250F, depending on facilities. A travellers' hotel with fairly unimaginative decor and clean, well-maintained (if not luxurious) rooms. Those at the back are spacious, quiet and sunny, but those at the front can be very noisy.

⚓ **Hôtel Edmond Rostand** (D3, **21** on map I): 31 rue Dragon, 13006 (at the corner of rue Edmond-Rostand). ☎ 04-91-37-74-95. Fax: 04-91-57-19-04. Metro: Castellane or Estrangin-Préfecture. Double rooms with bath, toilet, telephone and TV cost 290F; rooms large enough for four cost 450F. Dinner is 70F, and breakfasts are excellent, particularly the homemade jams. There's also a limited lunchtime menu every day except Sunday. The clientele includes travelling salesmen, business executives and families. This charming hotel is in a quiet street between Place Castellane and the Préfecture, not far from the house in which Edmond Rostand, author of *Cyrano de Bergerac*, was born in 1868 (hence the name). The rooms are soundproofed, modern and functional, and some overlook the garden. The very reasonable meals are taken in a small restaurant under the veranda.

⚓ **Hôtel Rome et St-Pierre** (C2, **15** on map I): 7 cours St-Louis, 13001. ☎ 04-91-54-19-52. Fax: 04-91-54-34-56. Double rooms from 330F to 430F in a comfortable hotel that is better for business rather than for romance. The Vieux-Port-Noailles station is very close and rue d'Aubagne is a stone's throw away. Service is good. Some rooms have antique Provençal wardrobes.

⚓ **Hôtel Béarn** (C3, **31** on map I): 63 rue Sylvabelle. ☎ 04-91-37-75-83. Fax: 04-91-81-54-98. Rooms from 148F to 218F; five-bed family rooms are 266F. Located in the Préfecture, this hotel has been completely renovated. The owners do all they can to help guests, even organizing additional activities such as introductory dives or expeditions for more experienced sub-aqua enthusiasts.

BOUCHES-DU-RHÔNE

♠ **Hôtel Azur** (D1, **17** off map I): 24 cours Franklin-Roosevelt, 13001. ☎ 04-91-42-74-38. Fax: 04-91-47-27-91. Metro: Réformés-Canebière. Website: www.azur-hotel.fr. Open all year, this hotel has renovated air-conditioned rooms. Double room with shower 290F, double rooms with bath, toilet, telephone and TV 450F. Other, simpler rooms are very cheap. Behind the Eglise des Réformés, the hotel is housed in an attractive building in a relatively quiet, steep road in La Canebière. The owners extend a warm welcome; ask for one of the rooms overlooking the garden. Breakfast is excellent, particularly the home-made pastries.

☆☆☆ Chic

♠ **St-Ferréol's Hôtel** (C2, **19** on map I): 19 rue Pisançon, 13001. ☎ 04-91-33-12-21. Fax: 04-91-54-29-97. Website: www.chateaudon.com/stferreol. This hotel is conveniently located near the Vieux-Port, on the corner of pedestrianized rue St-Ferréol, one of the busiest shopping areas in Marseille with both Galeries Lafayette and a Virgin Megastore. Comfortable double rooms from 440F to 580F; children under four stay free of charge. The rooms are named after artists such as Van Gogh, Picasso, Monet, Cézanne and Signac and reproductions of their pictures hang on the walls. Ten of the rooms are equipped with TV and double-glazing. The staff offer a warm welcome.

♠ **Hôtel Mercure Marseille Prado** (D2, **20** on map II): 11 avenue de Mazargues, 13008. ☎ 04-96-20-37-37. Fax: 04-96-20-37-99. From the motorway coming from the coast, from the north or the east, and the Prado Carénage tunnel, follow signs to Boulevard du Prado and the Parc des Exhibitions. Rooms cost 550F, suites 670F;

buffet breakfast 65F. Entirely renovated hotel near the Parc Borély. Reasonable prices, bright and cheerful decor and a sea view from the fourth floor.

On the Corniche, near the Beaches and Close to the Coastal Creeks

☆ – ☆☆ Budget to Moderate

♠ **La Cigale et la Fourmi Guesthouse des Calanques** (D2, **29** off map II): 19–21 rue Théophile-Boudier, in Mazargues, 13009. ☎ and fax: 04-91-40-05-12. Metro: Stade Vélodrome. A 15-minute drive from the *calanques* (rocky coastal inlets, *see* page 84), or accessible on bus No. 22 to Mazargues. Open from early June to end September; in low season, phone ahead. Guestrooms and studios equipped with kitchenette and bathroom start at 60F per person (for a minimum of two people). This guesthouse, named 'The Cricket and the Ant', is in a quiet street in Mazargues, a 'village' district of Marseille. Quite a way from the centre, it's not by the sea, but is one of closest places to stay if you want to visit the *calanques*. The owner's inspiration came from the Philippines and his guesthouse is made up of two Provençal houses with a network of narrow staircases, half-landings and small terraces – it is therefore not ideal for small children. The Mediterranean-style decor is attractive. Facilities include a laundry room and telephone point, and the owner Jean knows the *calanques* like the back of his hand and will take guests on a boating picnic, if time allows. There's also a good restaurant in the neighbourhood, *La Coussoussière* ☎ 04-91-40-60-90.

♠ **Hôtel Le Richelieu** (B1, **26** on map II): 52 corniche Kennedy,

BOUCHES-DU-RHÔNE

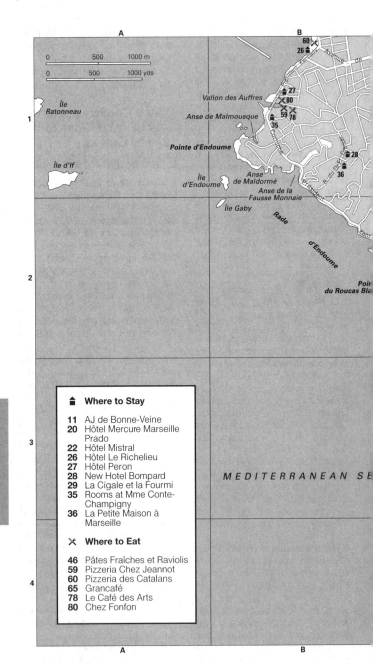

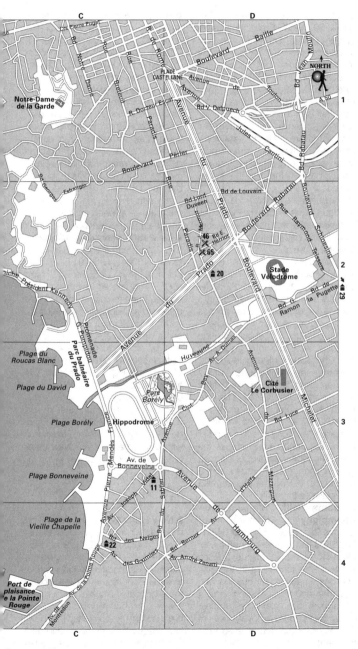

MARSEILLE – THE BEACHES (MAP II)

13007. ☎ 04-91-31-01-92. Fax: 04-91-59-38-09. Email: hotelmer@club-internet.fr. Bus No. 83 from Vieux-Port to Catalans. Double rooms with sea view, shower and toilet from 235F to 260F; with bath, toilet and TV, 290F and 340F. Good value for money. Very close to the sea, this well-renovated hotel's exterior isn't particularly enticing, but the rooms are pleasant. Ask for a room with a sea view and, if possible, a balcony, for breathtaking panoramas of the Îles du Frioul. Breakfast can be taken on the shared terrace, which is partly shaded. The little beach, Plage des Catalans, is a few steps away, but you have to pay to use it.

⌂ **Hôtel Mistral** (C4, **22** on map II): 31 avenue de la Pointe-Rouge, 13008. ☎ 04-91-73-44-69. Fax: 04-91-25-02-19. Bus No. 83 as far as Pointe-Rouge. Escape the city's concrete, and take one of this hotel's small, reasonably priced rooms (180F, doubles around 280F). It isn't luxurious and you'll hear the sound of engines rather than the lapping of waves, but it's an ideal spot for divers and other watersports enthusiasts. The entrance is through the brightly coloured bar and there's a small snack bar and *crêperie* in the other room. The beach is just across the road. The rooms are air-conditioned but not soundproofed; some of the rooms overlooking the sea are also very close to the traffic.

⌂ **Rooms with Mme Conte-Champigny** (B1, **35** on map II): 12 rue des Pêcheurs, 13007. ☎ 04-91-59-20-73. An increasing number of pleasant rooms in private houses are available to visitors in the city. This one, in a pleasant building with a garden and terrace, clinging to a hill above the Vallon des Auffes, costs 300F. Enjoy a lovely view of the bay from the bed or even from the bath!

⌂ **Hôtel Peron** (B1, **27** on map II): 119 corniche Kennedy. ☎ 04-91-31-01-41. Fax: 04-91-59-42-01. Email: marseillehotelperon@minitel.net. Bus No. 83 to Corniche-Frégier. Double rooms from 320F. Hotel right on the seafront, offering spectacular, uninterrupted views from its balconies. In the 1960s, each room was decorated in the style of a particular area or region in France, with moulded plaster murals, dressed dolls and ceramic fish (in the bathrooms). It's incredibly kitsch, but the owners extend a warm welcome. The rooms overlooking the sea (and the road) have been soundproofed, and there is free parking.

⌂ **La Petite Maison à Marseille** (B1, **36** on map II): 5 rue des Flots-Bleus, 13001. ☎ 04-91-31-74-63. Open all year. Doubles 350F and 400F. This hotel, in the picturesquely named 'ocean blue road', stands in a residential area, high up on the coastal road, offering a wonderful view over the sea. The family are extremely friendly and serve tasty meals to order from 95F to 150F, including fresh sea urchins and oysters, fruit and vegetables grown by neighbours and family, and local game. Breakfasts, served on the terrace, overlooking the garden, are generous and delicious, with homemade jams and other delicacies. And it's all just five minutes from the sea.

☆☆☆ Chic

⌂ **New Hotel Bompard** (B1, **28** on map II): 2 rue des Flots-Bleus, 13007. ☎ 04-91-52-10-93. Fax: 04-91-31-02-14. ✗ Drive along the corniche Kennedy, turn left just before *Le Ruhl* restaurant and follow the signposts. Double rooms with shower or bathroom cost 500F. High up on the corniche, this hotel comprises a mixture of old and new buildings, standing in a large garden of acacia and palm trees. Peace and quiet are guaranteed, except in the rooms overlooking the (free) car park. There's a lovely swimming pool, and meals are served too. Part of the same chain as the New Hotel Vieux-Port. The func-tional rooms, with terrace or balcony, are not especially charming, but a leisurely breakfast in the flower garden makes up for any lack of architectural appeal. Bungalows and studios with kitchenettes are also available for rent.

WHERE TO EAT

Marseille doesn't have a reputation as a centre of gastronomy, but you will find some good places to eat, a few restaurants offering good value and a couple of specialities that are worth a detour.

Bouillabaisse is frequently on the menu, but you'll also find fish prepared in a variety of other delicious ways, particularly sea bass, known either as *loup* or *bar*. Beware those who offer you a 'real' *bouillabaisse* for under 100F in the restaurants in the Vieux-Port. You may find that you have a disturbed night.

Accept the fact that real Provençal cusine will only be found further inland, and take advantage instead of the cosmopolitan nature of the food that Marseille has to offer. Avoid Marseille's tourist traps, and seek the delights of small restaurants on street corners or near the port. Enjoy a tasty *grillade aux herbes de Provence*, a *daube* or a pizza, which, despite its Italian origins, is very much at home in Marseille. For a small *pastis*, an authentic wood-fired *moitié-moitié pizze* (half with anchovy, half with cheese), and an inexpensive Provençal wine, you'll pay around 50F, or 100F if you add dessert and coffee.

Near Quai du Port-le Panier-République

☒ Budget

✗ **Chez Angèle** (B2, **40** on map I): 50 rue Caisserie, 13002. ☎ 04-91-90-63-35. In Le Panier, near the Maison Diamantée. Closed on Saturday, Sunday lunchtime and during August. 'Small' (but generously sized) pizzas from 45F to 65F – choose from a wide selection of toppings. There's also a menu at 100F. One of the oldest pizzerias in town, with an antique wood-fired oven, it serves crispy pizzas to a mixed clientele in *trattoria*-style surroundings.

–In the same area, another shrine to the pizza has no telephone, doesn't take bookings and doesn't even have a menu. **Étienne**, at 2 rue Lorette, is an institution in Marseille, always full of regulars. It's closed on Sunday and from mid-July to early September.

✗ **L'Art et les Thés** (B1, **43** on map I): Centre de la Vieille-Charité, 2 rue de la Charité, 13002. ☎ 04-91-14-58-71. Open 9am–7pm; closed on public holidays. A small tearoom tucked inside the Vieille-Charité, one of Marseille's most beautiful monuments. The simple of menus, mainly salads and savoury tarts, is not cheap – expect to pay 75F. The dining room is a little dreary, but you can eat outside on the terrace from springtime, right at the water's edge in the courtyard of this historic spot.

✗ **Au Vieux Panier** (B1, **45** on map I): 13 rue du Panier, 13002. ☎ 04-91-91-52-94. Metro: Vieux-Port-Hôtel-de-Ville. Open 9am–8pm ex-

BOUCHES-DU-RHÔNE

cept Sunday and in September. Expect to pay between 35F and 60F per dish. This grocery shop with its blue facade manages to be traditional and contemporary at the same time. Taste products from Provence and Corsica on the spot, or have a platter of mixed *charcuterie*, cheeses or *crudités*, leaning on the tiled counter. A good pre-theatre spot, run by friendly young people. Breakfast also served.

✗ There's a different type of place at No.18 in the same street. **Chez Nénette** (☎ 04-91-90-75-72) ♿ is a genuine local restaurant run by a Corsican woman. Closed Sunday. Expect to pay 60F to 100F for a meal. Best to book at aperitif time; try their fish specialities.

✗ **L'Infidèle** (B2, **58** on map I): 18 rue Coutellerie, 13002. ☎ 04-91-90-91-16. A stone's throw from the port, behind the town hall. Closed in the evening and at the weekend. You'll pay around 40F for large, reasonably priced dishes of ossobucco, fresh ravioli, pork in lemon, and much more. There's a quiet sunny terrace and a very pleasant air-conditioned room upstairs.

☆☆ Moderate

✗ **Le Panier des Arts** (B1, **53** on map I): 3 rue du Petit-Puits, 13002. ☎ 04-91-56-02-32. Open every evening (except Sunday and between 15 and 30 August). There's a menu at 98F at this bistrot, a highlight of Le Panier, with its old zinc bar and tables with waxed tablecloths. Both tourists and locals enjoy the lively atmosphere. The menu may include *brochettes de lotte ou langoustines* (monkfish and prawn kebabs), delicious accompanied by a glass of chilled rosé.

✗ **La Kahéna** (C2, **57** on map I): 2 rue de la République, 13002. ☎ 04-91-90-61-93. Popular Tunisian restaurant near Vieux-Port, open all year. Dinner served at 8pm and 9.30pm, for around 120F. Delicious fish couscous on Thursdays and Fridays. Try the *brick à l'oeuf* (egg fritter) to start and a Tunisian cake to finish. The dining room can be noisy, but the service is faultless. Take a walk around the port or along the cours Julien afterwards.

✗ **Le Café Parisien** (B1, **66** on map I): 1 place Sadi-Carnot, 13002. ☎ and fax 04-91-90-05-77. Open 4–10pm. Superb and generous dishes for 55F; a meal will cost you around 100–120F. This is Marseille's last café with nostalgic turn-of-the-century decor and atmosphere. Locals come to read their newspapers at breakfast-time, to meet friends for a good lunch and to have a drink and tapas in the evening.

☆☆☆ Chic

✗ **Le Dock de Suez** (B1, **68** off map I): 10 place de la Joliette. ☎ 04-91-56-07-56. Fax: 04-91-56-10-01. A few hundred metres from the La Major cathedrals and opposite the Port Autonome, with a terrace on the Quai du Lazaret. Open for lunch from Monday to Friday. This smart brasserie has a lunch menu at 145F, including wine – and service with a smile. À la carte will set you back around 150F, and the daily special costs around 80F. This is trendy Marseille, in the renovated Joliette dock area, where fashion industry and marketing professionals meet young executives from radio and TV. Not really the place to come for peace and quiet.

✗ **Le Milano des Docks** (B1, **69** on map I): 10 place de la Joliette, Atrium 10.4, 13002. ☎ and fax: 04-91-91-27-10. Dishes cost between 50F and 85F at this popular and lively restaurant, a stone's throw from the Dock de Suez (*see above*). The food is mainly Italian, with no real surprises, except perhaps the duck with honey and the pigeon.

✕ **Chez Madie Les Galinettes** (B2, **44** on map I): 138 quai du Port, 13002. ☎ 04-91-90-40-87 or 04-91-53-48-48. Closed on Sunday. Menus at 80F, including starter and daily special for lunch, and between 110F and 150F for dinner. À la carte will set you back 180F. Hidden at the end of the quay, towards the northwest end of the Vieux-Port, Chez Madie serves tasty Provençal fare. Madie's granddaughter is now in charge; her speciality is meat (her father is a wholesale butcher). The cooking is simple and tasty, particularly the *pieds et paquets* (trotters) and the *palourdes au thym* (clams in fresh thyme).

☆☆☆☆ Très Chic

✕ **Le Miramar** (C2, **49** on map I): 12 quai du Port, 13002. ☎ 04-91-91-10-40. Fax: 04-91-56-64-31. Closed on Sunday. This Vieux-Port restaurant has many regulars, all prepared to pay at least 300F for a seafood platter or wonderful fresh fish served by the well-respected Minguella brothers. The brasserie has a 1960s decor and is very much an institution. Try the raw sardines marinated in olive oil and lemon, followed by Niçoise-style grilled fish with *pisala* butter, and perhaps one of their imaginative desserts. The service is an ideal combination of relaxed professionalism.

Quai de Rive-Neuve, Cours d'Estienne-d'Orves and near the Opera House

☆ Budget

✕ **Les Menus Plaisirs** (C2, **41** on map I): 1 rue Haxo, 13001. ☎ 04-91-54-94-38. Metro: Vieux-Port-

Hôtel-de-Ville. Open for lunch only, except on Friday and Saturday, when dinner is served from 7pm to 10pm. The *formule* menu costs 62F. A pleasant spot, with a lively and warm atmosphere and a terrace. The excellent prices mean that it can be very busy at lunchtime. The menu changes daily and includes such dishes as chickpea or feta cheese salads, skate, lasagne, and pork with red beans. The desserts are very tasty, particularly the fig tart.

✕ **Chez Vincent** (C2, **63** on map I): 25 rue Glandeves, 13001. ☎ 04-91-33-96-78. Open on Sunday evening, but closed on Monday. À la carte around 120F. The prices are very reasonable, for tasty pizzas, cannelloni, lasagne, grilled peppers and other dishes, all served in a Sicilian atmosphere. The customers include opera singers who come here to relax after a performance.

✕ **Aux Caprices de Marianne** (C2, **71** on map I): 25 rue Francis-Davso, 13001. ☎ 04-91-55-67-71. Open Tuesday to Saturday from 8am to 6pm. A meal here will cost between 60F and 100F. A stone's throw from the Opéra, and popular with older ladies and couples who come here to reminisce. The lunch buffet includes vegetable dishes, quiches and seafood. On the way out, go downstairs and buy some delicious Puyricard chocolates, and then have a coffee at **Maison Debout**, a few doors away at No.46 (☎ 04-91-33-00-12), where there's also a terrace. For those who are still hungry, the fresh pasta at the deli opposite, **La Casertane**, is delicious. Get there early for lunch (no service in the evening; ☎ 04-91-54-98-51).

✕ **Le Mas de Lully** (C2, **50** on map I): 4 rue Lulli, 13001. ☎ 04-91-33-25-90. Closed during the last two weeks in August. Three-course à la carte meals at 120F. Nightowls enjoy this spot (which is open until

6am), just behind the Opéra in the trendy district of Marseille, and it won't break the bank either. The pasta is very good and reasonably priced. The lively atmosphere makes it a good place for a night out.

✗ **O'Stop** (C2, **64** on map I): 16 rue St-Saëns, 13001. ☎ 04-91-33-85-34. Metro: Vieux-Port-Hôtel-de-Ville. It's non-stop at O'Stop (except between 7 and 8am), a Marseillais institution opposite the Opéra. The menu costs 55F, and à la carte will set you back 100F. This well-known place is enjoyed by all sorts of people, including singers and sound technicians from the opera, who pop in before the performance to enjoy a quick *alouette* (meatball) or a bowl of pasta with pesto sauce. The sandwiches are good, too.

☆☆ Moderate

✗ **L'Oliveraie** (B-C3, **67** on map I): 10 place aux Huiles. ☎ 04-91-33-34-41. Fax: 04-91-33-34-67. Metro: Vieux-Port. Closed for lunch on Saturday and all day Sunday. Superb lunch menu at 100F and dinner with wine for 140F; around 220F for à la carte. This fashionable Provençal bistrot is much frequented by busy executives. The welcome is warm and the food sun-drenched.

✗ **Caffe Milano** (C3, **74** on map I): 43 rue Sainte, 13001. ☎ 04-91-33-14-33. This restaurant is closed for lunch on Saturday and all day Sunday, and a meal will cost you around 120F. The decor has a Chinese feel but the food has a definite Italian flavour. It's a trendy but unpretentious spot serving very acceptable dishes including *carpaccio* of beef and *penne all arrabiata*. You should book at the weekend.

✗ **Les Colonies** (C2, **73** on map I): 26 rue Lulli, 13001. ☎ 04-91-54-11-17. Open Monday to Saturday from 8am to 7pm. A friendly and welcoming, non-smoking (it's too small)

restaurant with a warm atmosphere. It also sells tea, preserves, chocolates and delicious 'Le Petit Duc' biscuits (visit the shop in St-Rémy-de-Provence, if you're heading there). At lunchtime, customers come to snack on cannelloni or gingerbread.

✗ **La Part des Anges** (C3, **75** on map I): 33 rue Sainte, 13001. ☎ 04-91-33-55-70. Open every day from 9am to 2am; closed only on Sunday, between 1 and 6pm. Count on spending around 80–120F at this wine bar, where you can also buy wine in bulk or by the bottle if you're looking for something special. After a night at the opera, enjoy a salad at 45F or a *brochette de viande* (kebab) with rice and courgettes and a glass of wine, for the same price. The atmosphere is friendly and lively. It's generally a bit quieter in the small room at the back.

☆☆☆ Chic

✗ **L'Ambassade des Vignobles** (C3, **62** on map I): 42 place aux Huiles, 13001. ☎ 04-91-33-00-25. Closed for lunch on Saturday, all day Sunday and throughout August. The menu costs 210F and there's also a *formule* menu offering a seasonal daily special with a glass of wine chosen by Paul Léonard, owner of the most impressive moustache in Marseille. His wine list is also impressive. If he can't fit you in here, he'll find you a table next door in **La Côte de Boeuf** (☎ 04-91-54-89-08), a favourite with meat lovers. The amazing wine cellar is shared by both restaurants.

In the Centre

✗ **Le Fémina** (C2, **51** on map I): 1 rue du Musée, 13001. ☎ 04-91-54-03-56. Metro: Noailles. Closed on Sunday and Monday. Huge high-ceilinged restaurant, decorated with naive murals of rural scenes from Kabylia, offering *formule* menus from 50F to 110F. The couscous is particularly tasty. Be adventurous and health-conscious, and try the barley semolina couscous, typical of the Kabyle region. It's easy on the digestion but a bit heavy on the wallet.

✕ **Pizzeria Au Feu de Bois** (C2, **47** on map I): 10 rue d'Aubagne, 13001. ☎ 04-91-54-33-96. Metro: Noailles. Closed on Sunday. Pizzas from 55F to 70F, *pieds-paquets* (tripe) at 65F and lasagne at 60F. Famous for many years as 'Sauveur', this popular pizzeria is now owned by a former baker. The excellent pizzas are cooked in a wood-fired oven, and can incorporate a selection of toppings: *royale* has mushrooms, garlic, sausage and cheese, *orientale* has cottage cheese with herbs, egg and tomato. A great place with friendly efficient service. Also does take-away dishes.

✕ **Toinou** (C2, **77** on map I): 3 cours St-Louis, 13001. ☎ 04-91-33-14-94. Opens at noon Tuesday to Saturday and in the evenings on Thursday, Friday and Saturday. Expect to pay around 100–120F. This used to be just a kiosk on the square selling shellfish at low prices. Thirty years later, the shellfish is now sold against a rather un-Provençal background of wood and steel. Often very noisy, Toinou serves three shellfish *formule* menus at 80–110F and the well-trained staff can open oysters in a flash.

☆☆ Moderate

✕ **L'Assiette Lyonnaise** (D2, **76** on map I): 102 cours Julien, 1306. ☎ 04-91-42-37-21. Closed for lunch on Saturday and all day Sunday. *Menu lyonnais* for 100F (lunch and dinner); à la carte will set you back around 150F. Leave your car in a car park and head up cours Julien on foot to enjoy classic regional dishes accompanied by a wide selection of beverages. The food is fresh and tasty in the summer and warming in the winter, and it's great value for money.

✕ **Le Quinze** (D2, **52** on map I): 15 rue des Trois-Rois, 13006. ☎ 04-91-92-00-52. Open only in the evening, from 7.30pm. Menus 89F and 109F. With the cours Julien, the rue des Trois-Rois is one of the best areas for restaurants. Recently extended, Le Quinze is a fun, popular place serving simple, honest cooking. Highlights include *daube* and tasty curries.

✕ **L'Orient Exploré** (C3, **54** map I): 9 rue Dejean, 13006. ☎ 04-91-33-54-15. Metro: Estrangin-Préfecture. Open every day but closed for lunch on Saturday, all day Sunday and Monday lunchtime. Menu at 84F, and à la carte. Good Egyptian restaurant on the edge of the Notre-Dame district. One menu includes Middle Eastern food such as hummus and kofta. For the same price, excellent Egyptian couscous comes with four different meats. The dining room downstairs is not as nice as the one upstairs, with its frescoes and rugs. If you're feeling agile, take a seat on one of the huge pouffes and enjoy the huge platters of excellent food and the friendly service.

☆☆☆ Chic

✕ **Le Sud du Haut** (D2, **56** on map I): 80 cours Julien, 13006. ☎ 04-91-92-66-64. Closed on Sunday and Monday, lunchtime from Tuesday to Saturday and evenings on Thursday, Friday and Saturday, and between 15 August and 6 September. Expect to pay 70–90F for lunch and 150–180F for dinner in a rather elegant setting with 'world' music playing in the background. The terrace overlooks the amazing fountain

BOUCHES-DU-RHÔNE

on cours Julien, and the service is efficient but relaxed. The chef re-invents age-old recipes, adding a touch of flair and a dash of originality to such dishes as *petits farcis* and chicken with basil.

The Pharo District, along the Corniche and on the Beaches

☆ Budget

✗ **Le Chalet** (A2, **42** on map I): Jardin Émile-Duclaux (Palais du Pharo, entrance on boulevard Charles-Livon), 13007. ☎ 04-91-52-80-11. Open March to October from noon to 6pm. Daily specials at 74F and 84F and full meals for 90F to 150F. Large salads for about 50F. This is more of an open-air drinking place than a 'chalet', sheltering under the trees in the garden of the palace built by Napoleon III for Empress Eugénie. The kitchen, virtually outside, serves traditional dishes such as stuffed squid and tuna Catalan-style. A light sea breeze blows across the shady terrace and there is a fine view over the Vieux-Port.

✗ **Grancafé** (D2, **65** on map II): ☎ 158 rue Jean-Mermoz, 13008. 04-91-22-70-84. Metro: Rond-Point-du-Prado. Closed in the evening and at the weekend, a pleasant spot to meet friends for lunch. For fine weather, there is a peaceful (if small) garden. The buffet-style *formule* menu costs 67F and includes a selection of hot or cold starters. Finish off with a delicious home-made dessert, such as *tarte au citron* (lemon tart).

☆☆ Moderate

✗ **Pâtes Fraîches et Raviolis** (D2, **46** on map II): 150 rue Jean-Mermoz, 13008. ☎ 04-91-76-18-

85. Metro: Rond-Point-du-Prado. Open for lunch only and closed on Sunday, public holidays and for three weeks in August. Expect to pay around 100F. Walk through the kitchens belonging to the shop, which specializes in Italian products, to reach the veranda with all its windows open on to a peaceful little street. Writer Marcel Pagnol used to come here from his nearby studio and the actor Raimu was another frequent visitor. Try the San Daniele ham or a mozzarella kebab to start before getting down to the more serious business of fresh pasta or ravioli.

✗ **Pizzeria des Catalans** (B1, **60** on map II): 3 rue des Catalans, 13007. ☎ 04-91-52-37-82. Open all year. Lunch only from Tuesday to Sunday between 14 January and 23 December; open for lunch and dinner every day (except Sunday) between 1 May to 15 September. Closed Sunday evening all year. Located on the nearest private beach to the city, this pizzeria is very popular. In warm weather, young locals crowd the sheltered terrace, keeping one eye on their swimsuited contemporaries and the other on the volleyball match near by. À la carte menu, pizzas or dishes such as a plate of squid. Prices are similar to Pâtes Fraîches et Raviolis (*see above*); it's probably a good idea to stick to the pizza.

☆☆☆ Chic

✗ **Pizzeria Chez Jeannot** (B1, **59** on map II): in the Vallon des Auffes, 13007. ☎ 04-91-52-11-28. Fax: 04-91-31-66-24. ✗ Closed on Monday and during the New Year holiday. Pizzeria deep in the picturesque Auffes valley (which has a memorial archway to those lost in the Far East). Expect to pay about 120F à la carte, depending on how hungry you are. The large restaurant has a long-standing reputation and serves delicious pizzas, fresh pasta and tripe (except in summer). Everything is fresh, and the *brochettes de moules panées* (mussel kebabs), particularly, are delicious. There are several terraces, including one by the water in the small fishing port, sadly rather spoiled during the building boom of the 1960s.

✗ **Le Café des Arts** (B1, **78** on map II): 122 rue du Vallon-des-Auffes, 13007. ☎ 04-91-31-51-64. Open noon–2.30pm and 7.30–11pm. Closed on Sunday and for lunch on Monday in August. A menu at 125F, and à la carte will cost you 170F. More 'St-Trop' than 'Marseille', with a delightful patio planted with olive trees and a Mediterranean menu that also includes an Argentinian meat dish.

✗ **Chez Fonfon** (B1, **80** on map II): 140 rue du Vallon-des-Auffes, 13007. ☎ 04-91-52-14-38. Open noon–2pm and 7–10pm. Closed on Sunday evening and for three weeks in January. A meal will cost you around 300F, and the excellent *bouillabaisse* costs a princely 250F. The restaurant's glory days were in the 1980s, when Fonfon himself ran it, but it's still a great place to come, with a great view of the boats coming back to port. You can also select your own fresh fish before it's prepared.

☆☆☆☆ Très Chic

✗ **Les Trois Forts** (A3, **79** on map I): 36 boulevard Charles-Livon, 13007. ☎ 04-91-15-59-56. Menus from 195F to 235F; à la carte at least 300F. Spectacular view over the Vieux-Port, tiptop cuisine (and prices) and smartly dressed locals. The best time to enjoy the sunny dining room is at midday, when a good *petit menu* is served. In the evening the atmosphere is rather more subdued. Dominique Frérard's menu is original and inventive, simple, but full of sun-drenched Provençal flavours.

Near the *Calanques*

☆–☆☆ Budget to Moderate

✗ **Nautic Bar** (C4 off map II): Calanque de Morgiou, 13009. ☎ 04-91-40-06-37 or 04-91-40-17-71. Open every day (but phone to check in low season). Metro: Rond-Point-du-Prado. Bus No. 23 to Morgiou-Beauvallon and then a (rewarding) one-hour walk. The road is closed to traffic in summer due to the fire risk, but the restaurant has an allowance of 15 car passes for its guests, so do phone. Enjoy whitebait or fish soup at 60F, fried *girelles* (a brightly coloured local fish) for 85F or a set menu at 140F. Known locally as 'Chez Sylvie', the Nautic Bar has a lovely terrace on which to enjoy your fishy snack and a glass of chilled wine in the sea breeze. Credit cards not accepted.

✗ **Chez le Belge** (C4 off map II): Calanque de Marseilleveyre, 13009. No phone. Open during the weekend in low season and every day in summer. A meal will set you back around 100F. Follow the GR98 marked footpath and enjoy a one-hour walk from Callelongue. In case you were wondering, the Belgian in the name of the restaurant came to the area 30 years ago and never left. The view makes the walk worthwhile but the food, which includes salads or spaghetti, is less spectacular. Supplies are brought in by boat. A refreshing swim is almost compulsory.

✗ **Chez Aldo** (off map II): 28 rue Audemar-Tibido, 13008. ☎ 04-91-73-31-55. Follow signs to Port de la Madrague de Montredon. Open all year. À la carte between 150F and 180F. Don't be put off by the rather unprepossessing exterior; inside, you can enjoy pizza or delicious fresh fish, locally caught and lightly grilled. No pretensions here – you'll share platters of prawns, mussels and squid with your neighbouring diners. The welcome is warm, the terrace large and the whole experience a delight.

☆☆☆ Chic

✕ **La Maronaise** (off map II): route de la Maronaise, Les Goudes, 13008. ☎ 04-91-73-25-21. Open only for Friday, Saturday and Sunday lunch in winter; daily except Sunday evening in summer. Almost at the end of the road that hugs the shore, on a private beach facing the rather austere Île de Maïre. The decor in the restaurant is a bit fussy but the cooking is typically Marseillais: pizzas around 50F, fish (about 40F per 100g for sea bass). After dinner, there's a nightclub that is popular with the city's gilded youth. The setting is superb and entrance strictly controlled. One surefire way of getting past the bouncers is to eat in the restaurant first. It is best to get there early on the weekend.

✕ **L'Escale** (off map II, beyond Pointe-Rouge): Les Goudes, 2 boulevard Alexandre-Delabre, 13008. ☎ 04-91-73-16-78. Fax: 04-91-73-52-12. ♿ Closed Sunday evening and Monday. Around 200F for à la carte. This restaurant, at the entrance to the fishing village, is run by a former fishmonger. Unsurprisingly, the fish is top quality and its preparation is faultless. The *bouillabaisse* and seafood paella are delicious and generous, or you can choose your own fish before it's superbly grilled. The setting is enchanting, even though it's just off the road, and a large terrace overlooks the sea and the small fishing port.

✕ **La Grotte** (off map II, at the end of the route des Goudes): Calanque de Callelongue, 13008. ☎ 04-91-73-17-79. Open every day all year for lunch and dinner. Metro to Castellane, then bus No. 19 to La Madrague and from there bus No. 20 to Callelongue, the starting point for the walk along the *calanques* to Cassis. Around 120–250F per person. By a miniature port with the occasional boat, La Grotte is popular with lunching Marseillais because of its terrace, sheltered by an awning. Book a table on the superb flower-filled patio for dinner (the sun is too hot at lunchtime). The pizzas are excellent, as is the grilled fish, although it's inevitably more expensive. The restaurant is large and feels a bit like a factory (orders are taken electronically, and it can seat 200), but it has managed to maintain its friendliness. Protect yourself from mosquitoes at night.

✕ **Chez Dédé** (off map II): 32 boulevard Bonne-Brise, 13008. ☎ 04-91-73-01-03. Open every day between April and October; closed Sunday evening to Wednesday evening in winter. Drive along the corniche to La Madrague, beyond Pointe-Rouge, and follow the signposts to Chez Dédé, further down on a sandy beach surrounded by the *cabanons* (beach huts). No menu; around 150F for a meal (about average for the area). The terrace hangs right over the waves; the body-boarders love windy conditions, but it doesn't make eating very easy. Settle for the dining room, which is decorated with model boats. The food is simple, including pizzas, pasta and grilled fish, and grilled sardines, which are not found in many places.

✕ **Le Lunch** (off map II): Calanque de Sormiou, 13009. ☎ 04-91-25-05-37. Open for lunch and dinner from mid-March to the end of October. Metro: Rond-Point-du-Prado. About 200F or more, excluding wine. Because of the risk of fire, the road is closed to vehicles from 23 June to 8 September, except for access and, sometimes, for people dining at Le Lunch. Booking is essential; give your registration number and they will open the barrier, for a fee of 18F. On the way down, there is a magnificent view of the sea, a magical blue flecked with turquoise. Settled on the terrace, you'll hardly notice the time pass, with the help of a glass of cool white Cassis wine, and the fish of the day – sea bream or red snapper. Beware: the fish are priced by weight, so costs can climb quickly.

BARS AND NIGHTCLUBS

You'll have to make quite an effort to get to know the Marseille music and bar scene, where things can be rather showy. As in every big city, the nightlife is focused on several different areas: for live rock music and blues, and the trendiest bars, look in the La Plaine quarter and around the cours Julien; the more well-heeled usually head for the promenade de la Plage and Escale Borély; for a more laid-back atmosphere and live jazz; around the Îlot Thiars and the quai de Rive-Neuve, it's more of a pick'n'mix. Going out elsewhere at night is not easy – the cinemas and theatres are scattered all over the place.

The city has its codes and standards. For example, if you're heading for some of the smarter nightclubs on the corniche, towards Borély and beyond, dress up in your finest (designer labels and glitzy jewellery go down well), adopt a confident air and, above all, telephone ahead to book a table, like the regulars do.

If all you want is a terrace, make for the Vieux-Port. The Bar de la Marine, on quai de Rive-Neuve, is a replica of the bar made famous by the writer Marcel Pagnol.

For listings of what's on, pick up the free weekly magazine *Taktik* in bars or in the tourist office.

– La Plaine and **cours Julien** (D2, **70** on map I): if you like rock or blues, head for the place Jean-Jaurès, in the heart of the La Plaine district. On the square and in adjacent roads (particularly the cours Julien, rue des Trois-Mages, rue des Trois-Rois and rue Poggioli), you'll find plenty of bars and restaurants, as well as a few concert venues and show spaces, like the **Espace Julien** or the **Chocolat-Théâtre** (at 39 and 59 cours Julien, respectively). The population round here is made up ageing rockers and punks, bikers and intellectuals, second-generation North Africans and a few locals, some junkies, mostly living peaceably side by side.

♥ **L'Intermédiaire**: 63 place Jean-Jaurès, 13006. ☎ 04-91-47-01-25. Open 7pm–2am all year round. Closed Sunday and Monday. Local bands Wednesday to Saturday evening around 10pm. Jam sessions every Tuesday. All types of music.

♥ **Le Poste à Galène**: 103 rue Ferrari, 13005. ☎ 04-91-47-57-99. Closed in August. Rock concerts, themed music nights (rock, disco, techno), and a mostly friendly atmosphere. Beer drinkers will appreciate the lengthy menu that lists beers from all over the world.

♥ **Le May Be Blues**: 2 rue André-Poggioli, 13006. ☎ 04-91-42-41-00. Open 8pm–2am except Sunday and Monday. Blues and rock concerts of a reasonable standard from Thursday to Saturday (occasional entrance fee). Attractive room with a mezzanine floor.

♟ Even if they don't have live music any more (after complaints from the neighbours), try to get to **La Maison Hantée**: 10 rue Vian, 13006. ☎ 04-91-92-09-40. Open 7pm–2am; closed on Sunday and 15 July to 15 August. About 100F for a meal à la carte. This used to be *the* rock venue in Marseille. Now a bar, it's also a restaurant at night, serving traditional family cooking.

♟ **La Passerelle**: 26 rue des Trois-Mages, 13006. ☎ 04-91-48-46-40. Fax: 04 91 42 54 95. Also worth a visit, this bar-restaurant-bookshop is open from midday to midnight (and a bit later for the bar), except on Sunday. Lunchtime menu 50F; evening menu 60F. Specialities include Dublin Bay prawns with aniseed, chitterlings, sausage in pastry, duck with preserved onion and ginger. The atmosphere is rather 'trendy intellectual'.

– **Promenade de la Plage** and **Escale Borély** (near A3 off map I): if you prefer the atmosphere of cocktail bars, Brazilian music and karaoke, head for the promenade de la Plage, alongside the sea. The newly built Escale Borély is an esplanade that has been reclaimed from the sea, where bars, restaurants and American-style nightspots jostle for space. The Marseillais architect of the Escale also recently designed Coconut Grove in Miami in similar style.

– **Îlot Thiars** and **quai de Rive-Neuve** (B2, **72** on map I): the main meeting place of Marseille's young and not-so-young (place Thiars is immediately on the left as you go down La Canebière). Bars, night-clubs, restaurants and 'private' clubs – there's something for all tastes, and it's usually easy to get in.

♟ On the small place aux Huiles, **Le Pelle Mèle** (☎ 04-91-54-85-26), open at 6pm from Tuesday to Saturday, is a jazz bistrot for those in the know. Concerts take place on Tuesday, Wednesday and Thursday at 9pm, except in summer. Jazz fans will also enjoy the **Jazz Club**, 19 rue Venture (not far from the Virgin store). ☎ 04-91-33-49-49. If you're hungry, treat yourself to an *assiette musicale* while you enjoy the music.

♟ **Le Trolleybus**: 24 quai de Rive-Neuve, 13007. ☎ 04-91-54-30-45. Open from Thursday to Saturday, entrance charge on the weekend. Just off the Îlot Thiars, 100 metres along the quai de Rive-Neuve. A reliable place to find 'swingin' Marseille' for a chat, a drink and to dance, if you feel like it, because Le Trolleybus is a discotheque – in fact one of the biggest in town. There are several beautiful vaulted cellars leading into each other with different styles (techno, a variety, rock), including one for playing *pétanque*!

♟ There are loads of other nightclubs around: **Metal Café** (20 rue Fortia) has seen better days; the three rooms of **Le Club 116** (5 rue du Chantier; ☎ 04-91-33-77-22) are popular with students and teenagers, and oddly connected to a restaurant with a transvestite cabaret. Different styles (salsa, rock, techno) are catered for.

CULTURE

Besides the opera, Marseille has a very rich cultural life, with three officially recognized national theatres (La Criée, Le Merlan and Lieux Publics), cinemas, rock cafés and other types of music venue dotted all over the city. The different places are quite spread out, so getting around is easiest by car, even though the night-time Fluobus (about 20 routes) does run until around midnight (RTM information: ☎ 04-91-91-92-10).

Marseille has experienced its own mini Madrid-style *movida* in the last few years, with something of a renaissance in the arts. Painters, sculptors, rap groups, dance groups, bars and restaurants are all beginning to invest in old commercial buildings like **La Belle de Mai** (41 rue Jobin, 13003; ☎ 04-91-11-45-65).

There is an increasing number of arts festivals, from the Fictions du réel (a festival of documentary film-making) in June, to the Festival Marseille, in various districts in the town in July, and the Festival des Îles at the Port Autonome (Dock J4), also in July.

To find out more about Marseille's busy cultural programme, pick up a copy of the indispensable free weekly *Taktik*, in any one of 600 strategically placed outlets. Information: ☎ 04-91-08-80-80. Information also available from the Office de la Culture (☎ 04-91-33-33-79); *see* 'Useful Addresses' on page 104.

WHAT TO SEE

To see the town, turn left outside the St-Charles train station and go down the monumental staircase. If you're travelling by car, take the Marseille-Vieux-Port exit to enter Marseille via the working-class districts and the docks.

Marseille is a group of neighbouring villages that have gradually been absorbed into the urban sprawl. The city is characterized by its often breathtaking centre and seafront, but equally significant are the suburban micro-towns, which all have a measure of independence: **St-Barnabé**, already occupied in Roman times; **Mazargues**, with its obelisk, on the road to Cassis; **Les Camoins** with its thermal springs; the fishing village of **Les Goudes;** the rural idyll of **Château-Gombert; La Treille**, Pagnol country; and **L'Estaque**, immortalized by more than one painter.

But Marseille's most extraordinary feature is its *calanques*, the rocky inlets that lie between the town and the spectacular sea, just a 20-minute drive from the centre.

In the Centre

★ **Vieux-Port**: the loyal Marseillais claim that their port is the most beautiful in the world. Today, pleasure boats are tied up close together in the inlet where the Phoenicians first disembarked all those years ago. Two fortresses guard the harbour entrance. On the right bank, the buildings that make up the Fort St-Jean date from the 15th, 16th and 17th centuries. On the left bank, the Fort St-Nicolas was built on the orders of Louis XIV – not to defend the city but to control unrest within it.

The appearance of the *quais*, built at the time of Louis XIII, was changed considerably by the Nazis. They considered Marseille to be terribly degenerate, particularly along the quai du Port, and in early 1943, Hitler himself ordered nearly 2,000 houses to be blown up; 20,000 people were thrown out. Only a handful of monuments escaped, including the 17th-century town hall, with its Genoese-inspired architecture. Just behind it, the Pavillon Daviel, the old courthouse, still has its elegant wrought-iron balcony and the Maison Diamantée its mural decoration, dating from the end of the 16th century.

On the corner of the Grande-Rue and the rue de la Bonneterie is the Hôtel de Cabre (1535), the oldest house in Marseille and an example of elaborate French Renaissance style. When the district was rebuilt the house was lifted and turned through 90 degrees, so that it would be in alignment with the new buildings.

On the other bank, take a walk through the Thiars district behind the quai de Rive-Neuve, former site of the Galères arsenal, refurbished at the end of the 18th century. The architecture around here is the most harmonious in the town. In the place Thiars you might imagine yourself in a Venetian *campo*, while the cours d'Estienne-d'Orves looks rather like one of those elongated piazzas found in Rome. In the past, there was an L-shaped canal on the current site of the cours and the place aux Huiles, and the whole district was enclosed, imprisoning the galley-slaves who lived there. In the 18th century, the canal was filled in; recent revitalization of the district included demolition of a monstrous car park that was built in the 1960s. Signs in the Porche des Arsenaulx, between the restaurant and the Soeurs Lafitte bookshop, explain the history.

At the very end of the quai de Rive-Neuve, the entrance to the Vieux-Port car tunnel spoils the view. To avoid it, climb up to the Pharo, the palace built by Napoleon III for his empress. Carry on to the top of the promontory for a remarkable view that takes in the lively Vieux-Port on one side and the Mediterranean on the other, with the Château d'If and Frioul islands in the distance.

All around the Vieux-Port there are countless terraces, cafés and restaurants. Cross from one bank to the other on the famous old ferry described by Pagnol; the return journey from the town hall to the place aux Huiles costs just a few francs.

On the quai des Belges, where La Canebière meets the port, the famous fish market opens at 8am every morning. The catch – scorpion fish, conger eels, girella (a brilliantly coloured local fish), sea bream, octopus – is sold by auction. Go there for the lively local atmosphere more than for the prices.

★ **Le Panier**: this lively area, between the quai du Port, the place de la Major and the rue de la République, behind the town hall, is the real Marseille and one of the last districts with a genuine atmosphere. Thousands of immigrants settled in this district on arriving in Marseille – perhaps this was the reason behind Hitler's destruction of it. Past the towers (rebuilt in post-war haste), you will find typically Mediterranean streets, staircases and narrow passageways.

To see Le Panier, start from the place Daviel, behind the Vieux-Port by the arcades of the Second Empire Hôtel-Dieu hospital. A few steps will take you to the Montée des Accoules and its solitary bell-tower, all that remains of the 11th-century church. Turn into the ruelle des Moulins and then look for the adorable place des Moulins (there are three, so look carefully). The Maison du Refuge (1 rue des Honneurs) used to be a convent-prison for fallen women, who would go in through the door on this road (which used to be called the rue du Déshonneur – the street of dishonour) and would emerge on to the rue des Repenties (the street of the penitent women)! After crossing the rue du Panier, take the main artery of the district, the rue des Pistoles, which will lead you to the majestic group of buildings known as the Vieille-Charité (see 'Museums', page 131).

– Weight watchers with a sweet tooth should carry on to the rue du Petit-Puits, where the tiny **Chocolaterie du Panier** (4 place des Treize-Cantons, ☎ 04-91-91-67-66; open 8am–1pm and 2.30–6pm, closed Sunday and Monday) sells chocolate made without butter or cream. The recipe is a family secret.

Continue south towards the sea along the rue de l'évêché (past the police headquarters), emerging on the village-like place de Lenche. This was probably the site of the *agora*, or market, in Roman times. At the very end of the rue St-Laurent, the square in front of a pretty little Romanesque church offers a lovely view of the Vieux-Port. Continue along the Esplanade de la Tourette. The walk finishes at the foot of the La Major cathedrals, sadly inundated by traffic.

There is a walk organized by the tourist office, which follows red markings on the ground.

★ **La Major cathedrals**: the old cathedral, La Vieille-Major, is purported to have been erected on the site where the first Christians, Lazarus, Marie-Salomé and Marie-Madeleine, are said to have landed. It is overshadowed today by the neo-Byzantine birthday cake of La Nouvelle-Major. La Vieille is a fine example of Provençal Romanesque, with an octagonal cupola, but it was cut off from its cloister and baptistery when its monstrous neighbour was built in the 19th century. A petition prevented it from being totally destroyed and work is still going on. Join the queue to see the interesting altars and bas-reliefs in white ceramic by Della Robbia. Chapels date from the 13th and 15th centuries.

★ **Joliette docks**: entrance at 10 place de la Joliette, 13002. ☎ 04-91-91-17-70. Open 7.30am–8pm every day except Sunday. A few hundred metres from La Major, opposite the Port Autonome. A vast group of buildings (more than 400 metres of forbidding facades), built in the middle of the 19th century. To get the measure of it, go into the interior courtyards, surrounded by high walls. Recently, the complex has been successfully renovated, with wooden gangways over the docks, huge atriums and windows, and it now houses bars, restaurants and a local radio station, as well as international companies in new, attractive offices.

★ From the place de la Joliette, find your way back to La Canebière along Haussmann's impressive conduit, the **rue de la République**. On the corner of boulevard des Dames, a pretty stained-glass window is a reminder of the Perroquet Bleu (the Blue Parrot), the hottest American bar of the post-war years. On place Sadi-Carnot are two ancient palaces and another bar, the Café Parisien, with its elegant 1900s decor. The passage de Lorette, just before the large square, is an impressive enclosed courtyard leading into Le Panier.

BOUCHES-DU-RHÔNE

★ **La Canebière**: the most famous avenue in Marseille runs at right-angles to the Vieux-Port. A kind of symbol of the town, it was popularized in a well-known French song by Vincent Scotto but today, in spite of new plans to rehabilitate it (part of the Law Faculty was supposed to come back here), there's nothing much to see. The name comes from the Provençal word *canebe*, meaning 'hemp', which was used to make the ropes for the boats.

At the bottom of La Canebière, before you arrive at the port, you will see the **Bourse** (Stock Exchange), a fine example of Second Empire architecture. Inside is France's oldest Chamber of Commerce, set up under Henri IV. King Alexander of Yugoslavia was assassinated in front of the building in 1934.

The area on and around La Canebière is the heart of multi-ethnic Marseille, particularly in the **Belsunce district**. Bordered by the cours Belsunce, rue d'Aix, boulevard d'Athènes and La Canebière, this very old area is mostly inhabited by immigrants. This is unusual in that it is right in the centre of town and its decrepit buildings and shabby streets are on display for all the world to see.

Along with Le Panier, the Belsunce district has always welcomed immigrants (*see* 'Marseille's Immigrants', page 97). In fact, it is one of Marseille's economic lungs, with different races, ethnic and religious groups living and shopping side by side. In the northeast of the district, there are Jewish wholesalers downstairs with African workers in the upstairs workshops, in the southwest are the North African retailers, in the north, Lebanese business-men organize imports and exports, while Armenians trade in leather.

The pulsating energy of the streets changes as the day goes by. When the shops close, the streets belong again to the locals, curious visitors, prostitutes, pimps, dealers and petty criminals. There are lots of cheap little restaurants and, under the grime, examples of beautiful 17th-century architecture, with carved porticoes and wrought-iron balconies. The beautiful buildings in the rue d'Aix have been renovated. Rue Thubaneau is one of the hottest streets in Marseille; No. 25 used to resonate to the strains of the French national anthem, *La Marseillaise* (see the dilapidated plaque on the building).

Among the few old churches is St-Théodore, at the beginning of rue des Dominicaines. The triumphal archway at the Porte d'Aix was built in 1825, with sculptures and bas-reliefs by David d'Aners, and a superb vaulted roof. It's best admired from a distance as it's pretty much impossible to cross the roundabout.

There are more lively, attractive little places on the other side of the Belsunce district. Everything to the right of La Canebière (looking away from the port) used to be considered smart and clean-living, but La Canebière is no longer the symbolic divide between rich and poor. Before Belsunce began to be renovated, many shopkeepers and businesses moved to this side. Stop off at the famous Torréfaction Noailles, at No. 56 (closed Sunday), for a quick cup of Brazilian coffee before carrying on.

★ In the **Noailles** district, the rumbling underbelly of Marseille, take rue des Feuillants as far as place du Marché-des-Capucins. Breathe in the smells of the street market, which is brought to life by the brilliant colours of Africa and the East. Arrax at 24 rue d'Aubagne is one of the finest Armenian grocers.

Further up, around the popular cours Julien and the rue des Trois-Rois you'll find places to eat and drink at almost any time of the day or night. Streets of shops run in straight lines at right-angles off La Canebière. The long rues de Paradis and de Rome – which come out at the place Castellane, where you find the allegorical Cantini fountain – are equally fashionable. On the corner of the rue de Rome and rue de la Palud, is the house that the architect Pierre Puget built for himself in 1680.

At 33 rue Vacon, the **Boulangerie Michel** (☎ 04-91-33-79-43, closed on Sunday) is one bakery that still makes the *pompe à huile*, one of the 13 desserts traditionally eaten in Provence at Christmas, as well as its own delicious bread. Have some to give you the strength to walk up the semi-pedestrian rue St-Ferréol, which is just as long, to the prefecture of the Bouches-du-Rhône department, built in the 19th century. The neo-Renaissance facade has no space for statues to the glory of Marseille. Monsignor Belsunce and the Chevalier Roze, heroes of the 1720 plague, have been relegated to the garden side.

Join the locals and treat yourself to an ice-cream at the **Belle Époque**, an art nouveau café (perhaps not entirely authentic) on the square. Alternatively, pick up a book or a CD at **Virgin**, housed in a former bank on rue St-Ferréol.

The neighbouring streets are packed with 18th- and 19th-century mansions. The Hôtel Mongrand at No. 13 of the street of the same name is a narrow semi-detached house with lavish sculpted decoration, and the Hôtel de la Compagnie du Cap-Nègre at 19 rue Grignan houses the Musée Cantini. The rue Sainte leads to the basilica of St Victor.

At 47 rue Neuve-Ste-Catherine, in the workshop of **Marcel Carbonel** (☎ 04-91-54-26-58. Website: www.carbonel.com), traditional *santons* have been made for several generations. The terracotta figures sell for anything between 60F and 800F, depending on size. The small museum at No. 49 is open daily, except Sunday; the workshop is open from Monday to Thursday, 8am–1pm and 2–5.15pm; closed on Friday. Guided tours take place on Tuesday and Thursday at 2.30pm. Both Aubagne and Marseille claim to be the *santon* capital of Provence. For the record, it was a Marseillais called Lagnel who invented the little figures, in the 18th century (*see* 'Christmas in Provence' page 88).

★ **Abbaye de St-Victor**: open 9am–7pm; entrance fee 10F. The abbey stands on a site thought to have been occupied by one of the first Gallic monasteries, founded at the beginning of the fifth century in honour of third-century martyr St Victor. It was destroyed by the Saracens, rebuilt in the 11th century, then fortified in the 14th century by Pope Urban V and again in the 18th. The basilica is the only thing left; visit the crypt (entrance charge) to understand its history. The ruins are apparently the remains of the fifth-century church, which was covered by the abbey in the 11th century.

In the square hall, only the columns have changed. In the 19th century a town official thought it might be good idea to erect the original ones around the town. From the central St-André's chapel, you can see part of the old cemetery on which the first monastery was built. The crypt also contains a remarkable group of ancient Christian and pagan sarcophagi (look for the child's tomb decorated by Éros Forgerons, of the Companions of St-Ursula)

BOUCHES-DU-RHÔNE

and epitaphs. Note the colour of the candles – St Victor was given the privilege of using green wax, normally reserved for royalty.

A Black Virgin has been venerated here since the 13th century. Every year on 2 February, for Candlemas, she is taken in procession as far as the bakery at 136 rue Sainte (the Four des Navettes, ☎ 04-91-33-32-12, open every day). An institution since 1781, the bakery makes curious *navettes*, boat-shaped biscuits, recalling St Lazarus's arrival by sea in Marseille. They are usually eaten warm, and cost around 40F for a packet of twelve.

Outside the Centre

★ **Notre-Dame-de-la-Garde**: to get there by car, follow the signs to Notre-Dame-de-la-Garde from the Vieux-Port. By bus, take No. 60 from the Vieux-Port. It's very hard work on foot, even without chickpeas inside your shoes (traditionally recommended for serious pilgrims), taking about half an hour via the cours Puget and the jardin de la Colline. The basilica and crypt are open 7am–7.30pm (until 9pm in July and August).

If you're short of time in Marseille, don't miss the Bonne Mère (as it's known locally). Perched 160 metres (525 feet) up on a limestone peak, it's the perfect place from which to see the whole town in one sweeping view. The first chapel was built in 1214 by the hermit Pierre, with the permission of the abbot of St Victor. When Pierre died, the chapel became a priory, was rebuilt in the 15th century and enlarged in the 16th. After François I visited it, on 22 January 1516, a fortress was added to the site. In 1853, the old chapel was pulled down and replaced by a more substantial basilica, capable of accommodating the increasing numbers of pilgrims who flocked here after the first cholera epidemics, believing it to be a place of miracles. At one time, it was receiving more than 1.5 million visitors a year.

There is an extraordinary collection of votive offerings (naively drawn pictures, and models of boats and aeroplanes hanging in the nave or on show in the corridors), which express a particularly Mediterranean kind of faith. In the crypt, countless hands have deepened the wounds of Christ on the cross. The Bonne Mère uses marbles and mosaics in Romano-Byzantine-style and is crowned by a glittering 10-metre (33-foot) statue of the Virgin.

To hear the odd *Ave Maria* and prolong your visit, have a bite to eat at the Eau Vive, the peaceful and friendly café attached to the basilica (closed on Monday). Menus range from 60F to 120F.

★ **Palais Longchamp**: Metro: Line 1, Cinq-Avenues-Longchamp. This water tower, a sumptuous building, is unique in France. It was built at the end of the 19th century, in honour of the waters of the Durance, which supplied Marseille. Inside is the Musée des Beaux-Arts et d'Histoire Naturelle (Fine Arts and Natural History Museum, *see* page 132).

★ **Église des Chartreux**: church in the Chartreux district, not far from the Palais Longchamp. Metro: Line 1, Chartreux. A convent from the 17th century, and now a parish church, particularly famous for its Christmas nativity scenes.

★ **Vélodrome Stadium**: Metro: Line 2, Rond-Point-du-Prado. A mecca for fans of the beautiful game and, more accurately, of the local football team,

Olympique de Marseille (OM), the first French team to become European champions. The stadium was renovated for the 1998 World Cup and is now the largest in country after the Stade de France in Paris. With its new stands, which look a bit like Mickey Mouse ears, it can hold 60,000. The refurbishment was a good birthday present for OM, which celebrated its centenary in the same year; a small museum and a restaurant were also set up. Unless you really hate football, try to go to a game. All self-respecting Marseillais are OM fans and their behaviour is something to see – and you might learn some new French phrases!

★ **Cité Radieuse**: boulevard Michelet (extension of rue de Rome and avenue du Prado). From place Castellane, take bus No. 21 or 22 to Le Corbusier. When this new residential quarter ('radiant city', was built, in 1945, it caused a furore. Students of urban architecture come here to see the Maison du Fada, one of Le Corbusier's most famous buildings. Le Corbusier's project aimed to bring together every essential in one place, including shops, schools, crêches, sports facilities and social clubs. There are 350 duplex flats and, on the third floor, a hotel-restaurant with a few very basic rooms that have apparently become popular with the Japanese. Despite its imposing size, there is an extraordinary sense of space and light. Today, many of the flats are occupied by architects' firms. There's no 'show home' as such, but if you're interested, ask at the tourist office.

★ **Borély Park**: in the south of the town, near the promenade de la Plage. Bus Nos. 83, 19 or 72, to Borély. This park was used as a backdrop in the film of Pagnol's book *Le Château de ma Mère*. There's a little lake with ducks, a rose garden and, at the east gate, a botanical garden (entrance charge) and a tropical greenhouse. In the middle of the park there is a classical-style chateau, which was intended to house the museum of decorative arts. In July, the park becomes the venue for an international *pétanque* competition, with games being won and lost to the sound of *La Marseillaise*. Keen followers of the game and its traditions will enjoy La Boule Bleue, the last remaining workshop where *boules* are made. It's hidden in the industrial estate ZI La Valentine, 130011 Marseille (☎ 04-91-43-27-20). With several weeks' warning, they will even make personalized *boules*, engraved with the player's name.

MUSEUMS

After Paris, Marseille has France's most important range of museums, with collections of antiquities, ethnic artefacts, classical, modern, contemporary and folk art, and fashion. A new museum pass (50F; students and under-10s, 25F; on sale in the tourist office and at the Vieille-Charité) gives entry to all permanent exhibitions in all municipal museums for 15 days from the date of purchase.

In the Centre

★ **Musée de la Marine et de l'Économie** (maritime and commercial museum) (C2 on map I): Palais de la Bourse (stock exchange building), Chambre de Commerce et d'Industrie, 7 La Canebière. ☎ 04-91-39-33-33. Metro: Vieux-Port. Open 10am–6pm. Entrance fee: 12F (half-price for concessions). This wonderful Second Empire building houses collections that tell the history of the port and its trading past, including numerous paintings and superb models. Temporary exhibitions, often focusing on old and restored posters from the Belle Époque.

★ **L'Espace Mode** (fashion museum) (C2 on map I): 11 La Canebière. ☎ 04-91-56-59-57. Metro: Vieux-Port. Open noon–7pm. Closed Monday and public holidays. Entrance fee: 18F (concession for students). Housed in a 'Haussmannian' building, designed by the architect Jean-Michel Wilmotte, this museum covers fashion, from the 1930s to the present day. Interesting temporary exhibitions are based on different themes (for example, men's clothing, fashions in sport, and so on), or focus on the work of one particular designer, from Paco Rabanne to Jean-Paul Gaultier. The permanent collection of the museum has 6,000 outfits and accessories, including a superb collection that once belonged to Coco Chanel. An important fashion archive.

★ **Jardin des Vestiges** and **Musée d'Histoire de Marseille** (C2 on map I): on the ground floor of the unattractive Centre Bourse shopping centre. ☎ 04-91-90-42-22. Metro: Vieux-Port. Open noon–7pm. Closed Sunday. Entrance fee to museum and garden: 12F. Guided tour (16F) Monday 3pm. During regeneration works in the Bourse district in 1967, workers were amazed to discover the remains of the ancient Greek port of Massalia. Until then, historians had known nothing about this period of Marseille's history. For centuries, the Marseillais had been walking on the evidence without knowing it. Today, you can see the extraordinary hewn stone walls of the quay, which were rebuilt by the Romans using material taken from local Greek monuments, as well as a rampart, a paved street and a necropolis. The most significant find was a magnificent boat from the third century AD, unearthed in 1974. More recent archaeological digs have brought to light an enormous number of objects from the era (seventh century BC) when Marseille was founded. Among them is an amazing example of a fishing boat 'stitched' together with ligatures.

The original discoveries led to the establishment, just next door, of the **Musée d'Histoire de Marseille** (Marseille history museum). Temporary exhibitions and informative displays tell the history of Marseille in a modern, airy setting. A model of the original Greek city of Massalia was made using references in Aristotle and information gleaned from the excavations. Exhibits from the Roman era include milestones and mosaics, as well as a reconstructed potters' kiln, amphorae, and copper and pewter ingots. An exhibition on the wreck of the third-century boat that was found in the port also includes information on a fishing boat from the fourth century BC, which was unearthed during digs in the shipping lane north of the Lacydon.

New displays lead the visitor through to the 18th century, where finds from recent digs are exhibited, including a fine collection of medieval ceramics, as well as potters' moulds and a Louis XIV room. Plans are afoot to expand the museum to house items from the 19th century.

The Vieux-Port and le Panier Districts

★ **Musée des Docks Romains** (museum of the Roman docks) (B2 on map I): place de Vivaux (at the bottom of Le Panier). ☎ 04-91-91-24-62. Metro: Vieux-Port. Early October to end May, open 10am–5pm; early June to end September, open 11am–6pm. Closed on Monday. Entrance: 12F (concessions: free to over-65s and under-10s, and to all on Sunday morning). Post-war building work started in Vieux-Port in 1947 uncovered the remains of a Roman commercial warehouse. A collection of *dolias*, large storage urns for wine, grain and oil, is displayed on the original site. Also on display are numerous archaeological exhibits discovered in the sea, illustrating the history of trade in Marseille and its links in ancient times with the rest of the Mediterranean.

★ **Centre de la Vieille-Charité** (Vieille-Charité centre): 2 rue de la Charité. ☎ 04-91-14-58-80. Metro: Joliette. Exhibition centre open every day (except Monday) 11am–6pm (1 June to 30 September) and 10am–5pm (1 October to 31 May). Entrance: 18F for temporary exhibitions (often excellent). A superb example of 17th-century urban architecture, the Vieille-Charité is one of Pierre Puget's finest buildings and also one of the very few to have survived. Its central chapel is one of the most beautiful baroque structures in the country. Originally built to house rural migrants, the architectural masterpiece served as a barracks in the 19th century, but was then left to rot. It was on the brink of ruin when Le Corbusier brought it to the attention of the local authorities. It was classified as a historic monument and a 15-year programme of renovation began. During exhibitions, visitors can now admire the luminous pink stone and beautiful proportions of the building. In summer, it becomes a concert venue and there's also a pleasant tearoom (*see* 'Where to Eat').

★ **Musées de la Vieille-Charité** (Vieille-Charité museums): same address and opening hours as above. Entrance: 25F. Two museums tucked under the arcades of La Vieille-Charité.

– **Musée d'Archéologie Méditerranéenne** (museum of Mediterranean archaeology). Three substantial collections: classical, protohistoric and Egyptian.

The classical collection presents an almost complete overview of the ancient Mediterranean civilizations, with a multitude of Greek, Etruscan and Roman exhibits (bronzes, pottery, glass), as well as pieces from the Near East. The jewel of the collection is a Cretan *œnoche* (wine jug) from the 15th century BC.

The protohistoric collection displays exhibits from local digs, including *Hermes with a double head* (third century BC), unearthed during the excavations of the sanctuary at Roquepertuse.

Finally, the impressive Egyptian collection (the second most important in France after the Louvre's) has no fewer than 2,000 objects used in daily life or funeral rites from the beginning of the Ancient Empire (2700 BC) to the Coptic period (fourth century AD). The pieces include amulets, sarcophagi, human and animal mummies, vases, containers for kohl make-up, the rare offertory table from Kenhi Hopchef with 34 royal cartouches, an altar with the head of King Tet, and four unique steles, which protected the tomb of General Kasa.

– **Musée d'Arts Africains, Océaniens et Amérindiens** (MAAOA) (museum of African, Oceanian and Amerindian arts). An interesting display of ritual objects from Africa (including a reliquary figure of Fang, a Marqua mask in *repoussé* metal), and Oceania (including a totem pole from Kanaka), and the impressive Gastaut collection, which has a human head as its centre-

BOUCHES-DU-RHÔNE

piece and comprises shrunken heads from the Amazon and carved skulls from Vanuatu. It's quite creepy – and not the sort of place you want to visit on your own!

La Canebière

★ **La Galerie des Transports** (transport museum): place du Marché-des-Capucins (in the Noailles metro station), 13001. ☎ 04-91-54-15-15. Metro: Noailles. Open every day except Sunday, Monday and Tuesday, 10am–6pm in high season and 10am–5pm in low season (but advisable to phone beforehand). Free entrance. Horse-drawn omnibuses, the town's first tram, a steam train from l'Estque, as well as photographs and old postcards, all displayed in the old tram garage.

★ **Musée Cantini**: 19 rue Grignan, 13006. (Rue Grignan is the little road between rue St-Ferréol and rue Paradis.) ☎ 04-91-54-77-75. Metro: Estrangin-Préfecture. Open every day except Monday and public holidays, 10am–5pm (11am–6pm in summer). Entrance fee: 18F for the museum and temporary exhibitions. Modern art museum housed in a 17th-century private mansion. Broadly speaking, the collection covers the development of modern art from 1900, from fauvism to abstraction, via cubism, geometric abstraction, figurative art and surrealism, with sections on photography. There are works by Signac, Matisse, Dufy, Léger, Le Corbusier, Kandinsky, Laszlo Moholy-Nagy, Eugen Batz, Kisling, Max Ernst, André Masson, Picabia and Tapiés. The museum also has the second-largest publicly owned collection in France of drawings by Antonin Artaud, as well as Jean Dubuffet's *Vénus du trottoir* (1946), and Francis Bacon's *Self portrait* (1976).

Sometimes, temporary exhibitions either totally or partially replace the museum's permanent collection, but there will still be plenty to see.

Outside the Centre

★ **Musée des Beaux-Arts** (fine arts museum): in the left wing of the imposing Palais Longchamp. Metro: Cinq-Avenues-Longchamp. ☎ 04-91-14-59-30. Open daily except Monday, 10am–5pm from 1 October to 31 May; 11am–6pm 1 June to 30 September. Entrance fee: 12F. Opened in 1869, one section of this slightly over-the-top building is supposed to symbolize the River Durance and its tributaries, surrounded by vines and corn. The few highlights of the museum itself include a few works by Nattier, Dufy, Vuillard and Ziem and Paul Signac's *L'Entrée du port de Marseille* (*Entrance to the port of Marseille*), an interesting collection of Daumier bronzes (36 busts of Louis-Philippe parliamentarians) and some attractive marbles by Pierre Puget.

– The right wing of the Palais Longchamp houses the **Muséum d'Histoire Naturelle** (natural history museum): open every day (except Monday and public holidays) 10am–5pm. ☎ 04-91-14-59-50. Entrance fee: 10F. This museum has an old-fashioned feel about it, with a substantial collection of stuffed birds in the superb Salle de Provence. Temporary exhibitions cover a variety of themes, not just natural history. There's a pleasant garden behind the palace.

★ **Musée Grobet-Labadié**: 140 boulevard Longchamp, 13001. ☎ 04-91-62-21-82. Metro: Cinq-Avenues-Longchamp. Bus No. 81 from Vieux-Port. Open 11am–6pm in summer and from 10am to 5pm in winter. Closed on Monday and public holidays. Entrance fee: 6F (concessions available). Opposite the Palais Longchamp. Museum housed in the private 19th-century mansion where bourgeois couple Louis Grobet and Marie-Louise Labadié amassed an impressive and eclectic collection of paintings and *objets d'art* from the 15th- to 19th-century French and European schools.

★ **St-Pierre cemetery**: at the terminus of the No. 68 tram, which departs from Noailles station. This is one of the biggest cemeteries in France. The interesting tombs of the great 19th-century Marseille families lie on both sides of the Grande Allée. The oriental-style tomb of Camille Olive has multicoloured ceramic features reminiscent of Notre-Dame-de-la-Garde. Dr Clot-Bley's tomb is in the shape of a minaret, and bell-towers and gargoyles decorate the family tombs of Burel de Barbaria and Gazanvillar. Look out for the Italianate statuary among the pines.

★ **Musée des Arts et Traditions Populaires de Château-Gombert** (Chateau-Gombert museum of rural arts and traditions): 5 place des Héros. Entrance fee: 20F (concessions available). ☎ 04-91-68-14-38. Open every day (except Tuesday) 2.30–6.30pm. Bus: Line 1 to La Rose terminus, and then No. 5 to Château-Gombert. The charming village of Château-Gombert is known mostly for its techno-park, but it remains fiercely protective of its Provençal identity. On Place des Héros, across from the bubbling fountain, there's a pretty little 17th-century church with a bell-tower, and this unusual museum, founded in 1928 by Jean-Baptiste Julien-Pignol, a passionate member of the Félibrige group. Beautiful Provençal artefacts are displayed in a dozen rooms, together with permanent and temporary exhibitions of Provençal costumes, crafts and traditions.

In June, the **festival of St Eloi** is celebrated in Château-Gombert. Patron of silversmiths and blacksmiths, the saint is commemorated with processions of *Carreto Ramado*, during which horses harnessed to carts Saracen-style parade through the streets to the sound of tambourines and fifes.

As you leave Château-Gombert, head to Allauch, where you'll find the traditional pâtisserie, **Le Moulin Bleu**, 7 cours du 11-Novembre, ☎ 04-91-68-19-06, which sells *bonbons* made by Les Nougats Brémond (☎ 04-91-68-17-86), official suppliers to the Vatican no less.

Near the Beaches

★ **Galeries Contemporaines des Musées de Marseille (Le MAC)** (modern art galleries of the museums of Marseille): 69 avenue de Haïfa, 13008. ☎ 04-91-25-01-07. Open every day 11am–6pm except Monday and public holidays; 10am–5pm between October and the end of May. Bus Nos. 23 or 45 from the rond-point (roundabout) du Prado, getting off at Marie-Louise or Hambourg-Haïfa. Sculptures by French artist Buren and a gigantic *Pouce* ('Thumb') by César, line the path. The gallery is light and airy. The permanent collection features contemporary artists, from new realists (Tinguely) to Rauschenberg and Richard Baquié via the Support-Surface group and Arte Povera. First-rate temporary exhibitions have included the

BOUCHES-DU-RHÔNE

first retrospective of contemporary artist Ben. Films and videos are shown in the Cinémac (the cinema of the Musées de Marseille).

★ **Musée de la Faïence** (ceramics museum): Château Pastré, 157 avenue de Montredon, 13008. ☎ 04-91-72-43-47. Bus No. 19, from the rond-point (roundabout) du Prado, to Montredon-Pastré. Open 11am–6pm (10am–5pm in winter). Closed Monday and public holidays. Entrance fee: 12F. This vast and elegant *bastide* was the scene of some of the wildest parties of the Second Empire. Today, it houses a collection of more than 1,200 historic pieces dating from the neolithic era to the present day. In the 18th century, Marseille was one of the most famous porcelain-making centres in France. This museum displays remarkable table services from the factory of Joseph Fauchier and ceramic floral decorations by La Veuve (widow) Perrin. Ceramics factories from the provinces (Moustiers, Apt and Castellet) are also repre-sented. The extraordinary mottled effects on the pots come from the mixing of the soils of the Luberon. There are beautiful portrait plates by Théodore Deck, from Alsace, director of manufacturing at Sèvres in 1887, and an important influence on the development of art nouveau. On the top floor, the contemporary pieces include creations by Starck, Garouste and Bonetti.

Surrounding the *bastide*, a magnificent park climbs from the road up to the crest of the hill. The canal that crosses it provides irrigation and general watering here, and then carries on to other properties. At the time when the great families lived in this area, the gates between the *bastides* were opened by a waterman whose role was to maintain the canals. Today, in spite of the efforts of Pagnol and of other traditionalists, almost all of the gates have been condemned.

– Don't miss **Faïenceries Figuières et fils** (Figuières and Sons Ceramics), 10 avenue Lauzier, 13008. ☎ 04-91-73-06-79. Open Monday to Friday 8.30am–noon and 1–6.30pm; Saturday 8.30am–noon. Closed mid-August to mid-September. Opened in 1952, this workshop creates wonderful *trompe-l'oeil* and hand-painted pieces.

THE COAST

★ **The islands**: from Vieux-Port, take the GACM shuttle service; check the timetable for your return trip if you're planning to head back to Marseille in the evening. ☎ 04-91-55-50-09.

– The Château d'If was built on the Île d'If by François I and was fortified in the 16th century. Visits to the castle are possible from April to September (except public holidays), 9am–7pm; closed on Monday in low season. Check timetables by calling ☎ 04-91-59-02-30 or 04-91-13-89-00 (tourist office). It was here that Alexandre Dumas imprisoned his hero Edmond Dantès in the novel *The Count of Monte-Cristo*. Today you can visit the 'cell of Dantès', and see the story re-created in the film made by French TV channel TF1, starring Gérard Depardieu.

– The islands of **Frioul**, **Pomègues** and **Ratonneau** became districts of Marseille in the 1970s, during a residential building boom that was much disputed at the time and, indeed, never completed. On the Île Ratonneau stand the ruins of the Hôpital Caroline, an isolation hospital deliberately exposed to the elements in order to 'blow away' the patients' diseases during their (supposed) recuperation. The Île de Pomègues also served as a quarantine port. Here, you can still swim in small, practically deserted inlets.

★ **Port Autonome** (A1 on map I): 23 place de la Joliette. The largest port on the Mediterranean and in France, and the biggest industrialized zone in southern Europe, embracing all the harbours up to St-Louis-du-Rhône and the industrial zones of Fos and Lavéra. Information: ☎ 04-91-39-40-00. The tourist office organizes a 2-hour tour of the Bassin Est (east dock).

★ **Corniche Kennedy**: with the longest bench in the world (according to the *Guinness Book of Records*), the corniche offers spectacular views of Marseille, the Mediterranean and the islands. From Vieux-Port, take bus No. 83, or drive along the quai de Rive-Neuve, passing in front of the Théâtre National de la Criée, and continue until you arrive at Les Catalans, the start of the corniche. The corniche is also the favoured route of local joggers.

★ After the imposing **war memorial** to the fallen of the wars in the Far East, you arrive at a picture-postcard fishing port, above the Vallon des Auffes, which has been encroached upon by the modern city. Looking straight down, the picturesque district of **Endoume** has a network of narrow streets and staircases, hanging gardens and houses surprisingly decorated with sculpted cement (particularly No. 11 rue Pierre-Mouren and 365 rue d'Endoume).

After this, the corniche is lined by sumptuous 19th-century villas, sometimes of dubious taste. **Château Berger** would not look out of place in the Loire Valley, **Villa Valmer** has a pleasant public park, **Castel Alléluia** has a miniature medieval tower, while **Château Talabot**, with its starkly contrasting verdigris roof and red-brick walls, is splendidly dominant. Behind this part of the corniche is the very smart area of **Roucas Blanc**.

At the end of the promenade de la Plage, the continuation of the corniche, a copy of Michaelangelo's *David* gazes at a publicity mural by modern artist César. Towards the beaches there's a modern sculpture to the memory of poet Arthur Rimbaud who 'arrived at the end of his earthly adventure' in Marseille.

★ **Beaches:** bus No. 83, from the Vieux-Port, travels to all the beaches, stopping at Catalans, Prophète, Plage-Roucas-Blanc, La Plage-Gaston-Defferre (better known as the Plage du Prado), La Plage, then Escale Borély (a beach complex with restaurants and bars, built over the sea) and Pointe-Rouge.

– The **plage des Catalans** is very lively and the closest to the centre. There is a charge to use it, but it has an agreeable 1960s feel and a beach volleyball area.

– Further along, tucked under the corniche, the **plage du Prophète** is similar, but free of charge.

– Stretching out at the end of the avenue du Prado, the five **Gaston-Deferre** beaches – some sand, some small pebbles – have 45 hectares (112 acres) of grass for Sunday footballers and kite-fliers, and a noisy family atmosphere.

– For windsurfers, **Epluchures Beach** is one of the most popular spots on the French Mediterranean coast.

BOUCHES-DU-RHÔNE

– Beyond Epluchures, following the coast to Goudes, little beaches like **Bonne Brise** or **plage des Phocéens** nestle in the coves. After this stretch of coastline, you come to the *calanques*.

★ **The *calanques***: according to a Marseillais, the famous *calanques* (*see* page 84) belong not to Cassis, as some guides would have you believe, but to Marseille. A few may be geographically closer to Cassis, but they are officially within the commune of Marseille. The best known (En-Vau, Port-Miou and Port-Pin) may be more easily accessed from Cassis, but the ones closer to Marseille are still attractive.

The *calanques* are part of the life and soul of Marseille. Callelongue even features in the lyrics of local ragga band Massilia Sound System: '*Et pour être au bout du monde, je m'en vais à Callelongue,*' ('To get to the ends of the earth, I go to Callelongue'). This secret spot is familiar to every courting Marseillais couple; even under a watery winter sun, love is frequently in the air. Just a dozen kilometres from the Vieux-Port, a few fishermen's huts and beach huts tucked in this rocky inlet, and a suprisingly good pizzeria, make it the perfect place to discover the spirit of the Mediterranean, to forget the strains and stresses of everyday life and escape from 'civilization'.

The GR98 long-distance coastal footpath route from Marseille to Cassis passes through Samena, Callelongue, La Mounine, Marseilleveyre, Podestat, Cortiou, Sormiou, Morgiou, Sugiton, Devenson, L'Oule, En-Vau, Port-Pin, Port-Miou. *Note*: the route is not always easy to find. It is forbidden to take mountain bikes to the *calanques*, to camp in the area or to light fires. Seek all the information you might need from the tourist office before setting off. If it's within your budget, one of the best ways of making the trip is by boat, with departures from both Marseille and Cassis.

– To get to **Callelongue**: by car, go along the promenade de la Plage to the south and then follow the coast road; at Goudes, go straight on. By bus, take the No. 19 from Castellane to the end of the line, then line 20 to its terminus.

– Less than an hour's walk from Callelongue, the **Marseilleveyre** inlet, with its little beach, has a pleasant bar with a terrace.

– For **Sormiou**: by car take the promenade de la Plage heading south, and turn left at the rounabout after the Hippodrome onto the avenue de Bonneveine. At the next big roundabout take the second major exit into the avenue de Hamborg carrying on to the chemin du Lancier. Follow the signs to a little road at the end of the chemin du Roi-d'Espagne which leads to the inlet; it is closed from June to September, but a shuttle takes visitors to the *calenque* and back. By bus, take No. 23 from the rond-point du Prado, get off at La Cayolle.

The inlet at Sormiou is simply superb. At one edge, divers discovered the Grotte de Cosquer (otherwise known as the 'Underwater Lascaux', *see* page 148), accessible only from below water level. It is not open to the public as Sourmiou is privately owned, although the its beaches are public. There have been holiday huts, or *cabanons*, here and at Morgiou since the beginning of the 20th century.

– **Morgiou** is reached by car via the D559 out of town to the south towards Cassis; take the right turn for Mazargues and then first left signed for

Morgiou. There is no direct vehicle access from mid-June to mid-September and, generally, no shuttle. By bus, take No. 22, at Baumettes or No. 23 as far as the Morgiou-Beauvallon terminus.

– To get to **Sugiton** and **Les Pierres Tombées** ('fallen rocks') by car, take the same route as for Morgiou. Alternatively, take bus No. 21 from Castellane to the end of the line at Luminy; the *calanques* are reached by a 30-minute walk from there.

DIVING

Lovers of the sea can go swimming around here, of course (*see* 'Beaches', page 135), but it is also possible to go fishing, sailing, kayaking, to visit the *calanques* and to dive. Pick up the detailed guide *Marseille sur mer* ('Marseille by the Sea') from the tourist office for information on all the activities.

In a way, Marseille saw the birth of diving when, in the 1930s, Commander Le Prieur invented the precursor to modern-day breathing equipment. For many years, Vieux Plongeur was *the* diving shop in the town, selling bubble masks and rubber suits to the first intrepid underwater adventurers. After World War II, Marseille was fascinated by the work of a bunch of pioneers – Philippe Taillez, Frédéric Dumas, and a young naval officer called Jacques-Yves Cousteau – who called themselves the 'Musketeers'. Diving from their famous boat *Calypso*, they used the 'Cousteau-Gagnan diving bell', and made the first underwater films by putting their cameras in jam jars! As they explored the many ancient wrecks around Marseille, they began to define the basis of modern deep-sea diving.

Since those times, 'Marseille la Bleue' has become a mecca for the French sub-aqua federation (the Fédération Française des Activités Subaquatiques, or FFESSM). The centre of professional diving is the city's Comex d'Henri-Germain Delauze, and Marseille is also home to the headquarters of French underwater archaeology (DRASSM). Marine biologists from all over the world work at the oceanographic centre (the Centre Océanologique de Marseille), and many manufacturers and importers of diving equipment are also based in the area.

For all divers, or future divers, Marseille is a must. Its crystal-clear seas teem with curious wrecks and fabulous fauna and flora. The best dives can be done when the mistral (*see* page 86) blows; with an east wind, the choice is more limited.

Dive Schools

■ **Les Plaisirs de la Mer**: 82 rue Denis Magdelon, 13009. ☎ 04-91-48-37-83 and 04-91-48-79-48. Website: www.vieuxplongeur.com. Open all year at weekends, Thursday and Friday; every day in summer. Meet at quai Marcel-Pagnol on the Vieux-Port (at the foot of fort St-Nicolas) to board one of the boats belonging to the school (which is FFESSM- and FSGT-licensed). All are equipped with cylinders (no bottles to carry) and the school also has a passenger boat. The instructors are all state-registered, and can organize trial dives as well as training up to instructor level. They keep an eye on all the best spots in the area and friendly boss Jean-Michel Icard is happy to take customers on dives off the beaten track, too. There are courses specializing in wrecks or ecology, and introductory courses for children (from aged 8). Booking essential. Costs go down for more than 10 dives. Reduced-price hotel accommodation is also available. The school is popular with local students.

■ **Atoll Club Evasion**: 31 traverse Prat, 13008. ☎ 04-91-72-18-14 and 06-11-54-71-40. Open every day from mid-March to mid-November. Dives à la carte or in small groups (maximum 19 people) in two sailings organized by this well-equipped school (FFESSM-licensed). Friendly owner Frédéric Ciavaldini and his state-registered instructors offer trial dives as well as courses up to Level IV, memorable exploratory dives and classes for children over 8. Complete equipment is provided (two valves per diver). Booking essential. Costs go down for more than 10 dives.

■ **No Limit Plongée**: 109 avenue Madrague-Mondredon, 13008. ☎ 04-91-25-32-77 and 06-09-57-24-89. Open all year; every day in summer. Another school (licensed by FFESSM, ANMP and PADI), which emphasizes diving in a small group (maximum 19 people). With two fast boats, Pascal Perino and his state-registered instructors oversee first dives, training up to Level IV and PADI licences, as well as exploration of the wreck and the sea bed for which Marseille is so famous. Full equipment is supplied. Booking essential. Costs go down for more than 10 dives. Reduced-price hotel accommodation is also available.

Dive Sites

Around the Île de Riou

〜 **Les Impériaux**: the diving highlight of this part of the Mediterranean, around three impressive rocks that stand 15–60 metres (50–200 feet) high to the southeast of the Île de Riou. Masses of flora and fauna, all flourishing in a wild and unspoilt underwater environment. In the grottoes, chimneys, vaults, faults and arches, magnificent red and yellow corals grow in the crystal-clear water. You'll see anthias, sea bream, mantis shrimps and other curious prawn-like creatures. From a distance, you can watch morays with monstrous heads, John Dory and masses of playful local fish. Under the vaults there is a forest of red coral and banks of shy barracuda. This is a great dive, with lots of interest. The site is somewhat exposed but suitable for Level I.

〜 **La Grotte à Corail** (coral cave): on the southern side of Île Maïre, this fabulous (Level I) dive takes you into the territory of 'red gold', as old Marseillais divers used to call it. Only 15 metres (50 feet) down, the red coral on the arch looks like fire in the light of a diver's torch. Don't touch anything and be careful not to kick your fins too vigorously.

〜 **Le Liban** and **Les Farillons**: southeast of the Île Maïre, this dive (24–37 metres/80–120 feet) begins with an exploration of the cruise liner *Le Liban*, sunk in 1903, and now liveried in sumptuous red and yellow corals (don't forget your torch). Expect to see conger eels, morays, curious crayfish and pomfrets weaving around the bronze propellers and majestic bow of the liner. The nearby wreck of *Les Farillons* has three amazing cathedral-like arches, decorated with red coral and inhabited by masses of fish. Under no circumstances should you go into the wreck. This exposed site is suitable for experienced Level II divers.

⚒ **Les Moyades**: off the western point of Rio, this dive (Level II) is very popular with photographers. The descent (to 20–40 metres/65–130 feet) is superb – brilliant tree corals hide crayfish (identify them by their feelers), scorpion fish, mantis shrimps and big-daddy conger eels (take a torch). You should also see shoals of pomfret and blue-striped *mendoles* as well as a fair number of octopus, sardines, *saupes*, *corbs*, and sea bream.

⚒ **La Pointe Caramassaigne**: east of the Île de Riou, this is a 'typical' Marseillais dive (experienced Level II). The colourful wreck (at 40 metres/130 feet maximum) is literally covered with red tree coral, yellow anemones and sponges in bright pinks and oranges. Living in this underwater Marseillais garden are sparkling sea bream, sardines, *dentis*, as well as many morays and some beautiful conger eels. *Note*: the current is often strong here. Just near by lies the wreck of the *Grand Conglué* (at 43 metres/140 feet; Level II). Cousteau made a number of interesting finds in and around these old wrecks in the 1950s.

Around the Île de Planier
⚒ One of the best dive sites in this area that is particularly famous for its wrecks lies just out to sea from the town. At 3–26 metres (10–85 feet), the wreck of the cargo ship *Chaouen*, which sank in 1970, is an ideal site for beginners (experienced Level I), with charming and non-threatening creatures (conger eels, scorpion fish, and so on).

– The same fish hide in tree coral that grows on another cargo ship, the *Dalàn*, which sank in 1928 (at 15–32 metres/50–105 feet; Level II). The site starred in the film *épaves* ('wrecks'), made by Cousteau in the 1950s.

– Even hardened divers will be amazed by the sight of morays, congers and lobsters swimming through the cockpit of a complete World War II *Messerschmitt 109* plane, which lies at 45 metres/150 feet (suitable for experienced divers only).

The crystal-clear waters around the island have other remarkable places with large populations of octopus, sea bass, *dentis*, sea bream, and pomfret.

St-Dominique
⚒ This seductive dive (at 33 metres/108 feet; Level II) explores an intact three-masted yacht that foundered in 1897 off the Port Autonome. Its straight, clean metallic hull still evokes the elegance of sailing. Around the bow, shoals of pomfret dance like synchronized swimmers in front of conger eels, morays and scorpion fish. Keep an eye out for the nets.

La Drome
⚒ Only very experienced divers (experienced Level III) are permitted to dive the wreck of this munitions ship, which has lain 51 metres (167 feet) below the sea, right in the middle of the shipping lane into Marseille, since 1918. The boat, which is cut in two, has a particularly attractive outline and an astonishing gun at the rear. It is inhabited by conger eels and crayfish. Divers must *not* venture inside and, for their own safety, should not spend more than 15 minutes on this hazardous dive.

Along the Côte Bleue – Marseille to Martigues

The coastal route from Marseille to Martigues is no longer the romantic, unspoiled experience that it once was. Cézanne, Braque, Dufy and Derain all immortalized the little port of Estaque in their paintings. They would have great difficulty in recognizing it today, although people still queue in the port to enjoy a traditional *chichi-fregi*, a deep-fried doughnut snack sprinkled with sugar. There remain a few enjoyable places to visit, however, and if you don't have a car, the trip on the small local train from Marseille, which follows the Côte Bleue, very close to the sea, is delightful.

NIOLON

Niolon (18 kilometres/11 miles from Marseille) is a tiny fishing harbour full of charm and character. The fresh-fish and seafood restaurants all have terraces, of course. *Rove* goats are reared in the surrounding hills, their milk being used to make a local cottage cheese known as *brousse*.

WHERE TO EAT

✕ **Le Mange-Tout**: calanque de Mejean, 8 chemin Tire-Ceul, 13820 Ensuès-la-Redonne. ☎ 04-42-45-91-68. Open every day from 1 May to 15 September; closed out of season in the evening and on Wednesday. Annual closure from December to February. Enjoy a simple meal of fried fish or fish soup for around 150F, on the terrace of a real *cabanon* (holiday hut), located on a port that's not much bigger than the cabin itself.

CARRY-LE-ROUET AND SAUSSET-LES-PINS

Carry-le-Rouet and Sausset-les-Pins are both pretty little resorts in attractive surroundings with lovely views. The underwater environment is protected here. Between January and March, picturesque festivals take place along the Côte Bleue, to the sound of drums and flutes, celebrating the sea-urchin. Restaurants and cafés create special dishes and menus for the events.

CARRO

The fishing port of Carro has a colourful fish market. Try to arrive early, to see the boats coming in with their catch.

WHERE TO EAT

✕ **Le Chalut**: Place Joseph-Fasciola. ☎ 04-42-80-70-61. Open every day (except Monday). Menus from 88F to 150F. À la carte around 200F. Enjoy tasty grilled fish or delicious fish soup with garlic croutons and *rouille* in a pleasant setting, with a view over the port. If you feel like a treat, order ahead for an authentic *bouillabaisse*.

★ At the very end of the D9 road, the *Plage Populaire de la Couronne* is a favourite beach with the Marseillais. It is often very busy, so you need to pick your moment. The small, pleasant beach next to it, among the rocks, is called *Plage de Ste-Croix*.

MARTIGUES (13500)

This little Provençal port is literally being suffocated by industrial advance – with a motorway viaduct and an oil terminal right on its doorstep – but it has none the less managed to retain some of its charm. In the middle, an island is linked to the rest of the town by two bridges. The small church of Ste-Madeleine-de-l'Île has a façade of Corinthian columns and pretty decoration inside. A stretch of water lined with brightly painted fishermen's cottages is known locally as the Miroir aux Oiseaux ('birds' looking glass'), and is a favourite subject for Sunday artists (following in the footsteps of Corot and Ziem, among others). Occasionally, you might see the suspension bridge open to let a *citerna* (oil-tanker) through. The local gastronomic speciality is the famous *poutargue* (caviar). For food-lovers, there are *sardinades* every evening in July and August. From 6pm, locals and visitors gather along the banks of the canal to grill and eat sardines and drink local wine.

USEFUL ADDRESS

🛈 **Tourist office**: 2 quai Paul-Doumer. ☎ 04-42-42-31-10.

WHERE TO STAY AND EAT

🛏 **Hôtel Le Cigalon**: 37 boulevard du 14-Juillet, near the pond. ☎ 04-42-80-49-16. Fax: 04-42-49-26-71. Rooms cost from 280F to 380F in this charming hotel, which offers a warm welcome and excellent food.

✗ **Le Miroir**: 4 rue Marcel-Galdy. ☎ and fax: 04-42-80-50-45. Restaurant on the island in the middle of the town. ✗ Closed for lunch on Saturday, dinner on Sunday and all day Monday, on the public holidays of All Saints and Christmas and for a week in April. Menus 118–175F (125F on Sunday). Decorated in pastel shades and with a sunny terrace, Le Miroir serves excellent food at reasonable prices.

✗ **Délices en Provence**: 1 boulevard Richaud. ☎ 04-42-07-17-87. Enjoy coffee or tea with a selection of pastries in this charming little spot, open 8.30am–7pm. Daily specials and *formule* menus at lunchtime.

✗ **Excalibur**: quai des Girondins. ☎ 04-42-80-46-15. A favourite with locals, this place has daily specials for 45F and a menu at 60F. The food is full of flavour, particularly the *daube provençale*, and the staff offer a pleasant welcome.

WHAT TO SEE

– **Musée du Vieux-Martigues** (or Musée Ziem): ☎ 04-42-80-66-06. Small museum open every day during July and August (except public holidays) 10am–noon and 2.30–6.30pm. In low season, open from Wednesday to Sunday from 2.30–6.30pm (except public holidays). Entrance free. On display are some works by the Oriental and landscape painter Félix Ziem (1821–1911), together with others of the Provençal School, as well as contemporary works and items on local archaeology and folklore. Temporary exhibitions are held throughout the year.

BOUCHES-DU-RHÔNE

WHAT TO SEE IN THE AREA

– **Musée Charles Morales**: route de Fos, 13110 Port-de-Bouc. ☎ 04-42-06-26-29. Open every day (except Tuesday) 9am–noon and 2–4pm. Entrance fee: 25F. A bit of a surprise in an otherwise uninviting industrial town, this museum was once the studio of a sculptor who spent his artistic life creating metallic works of all sizes. Pieces range from the fantastic and grotesque, to the humorous and simply aesthetic.

★ **Istres**: 15 kilometres/9 miles from Martigues. ☎ 04-42-55-50-08. Istres' museum (open every day 2–6pm) has a substantial submarine archaeology section, displaying numerous *amphorae* and other pieces recovered from the Fos Gulf.

Pagnol Country

The reputation of the quintessentially Provençal writer Marcel Pagnol is somewhat tarnished around here. His work may have made the Marseille accent familiar in far-flung corners of the world – first in print, and then on the big screen – but some find it hard to forgive him for creating an image of the Marseillais as arrogant, cheating and lazy. However, in lovely weather, even the resentful Marseillais will take themselves off across the scented *garrigue* to the places inhabited by Pagnol's characters, to look down on their city from the hills, and to explore the countryside made famous by the Pagnol films.

East of Marseille, there's a lovely walk to La Treille, a small hilltop village 7 kilometres (4 miles) from Marseille (but in its 11th *arrondissement*), where Pagnol was buried after his death in 1974, and Aubagne, where he was born in 1895.

LA TREILLE

Take tram No. 68 from Noailles station to the end of the line and then bus No. 12 S to La Treille. Pagnol grew up here and is buried in its small cemetery in the lower part of the village. His holiday home, the Bastide Neuve, is higher up. Marked routes start from there, heading across the herb-scented valleys. Walkers familiar with his works will certainly recognize the countryside.

References to the author are ubiquitous but, even if you're not a Pagnol fan, you can still enjoy the adorable Provençal village of La Treille. Stroll through the narrow streets to the small square, with its tiny fountain. The *garrigue*, typically Provençal scrubland, around the village is wonderfully unspoilt. The Cigalon, the café-restaurant where Pagnol's film of the same name was set, has barely changed since the 1930s. There's a lovely view from the terrace.

★ **Suggested walk around the Taoumé** (a 12-kilometre/7.5-mile loop north of Allauch, 11 kilometres/7 miles northeast of Marseille; 3-hour round trip of medium difficulty; yellow, green and blue markings): this route follows the limestone crests in the hinterland behind Marseille and the Garlaban hills. All along the route, you feel Pagnol's presence, as the landscapes and place-names recall his life and work.

– From the Canteperdrix pass, reached from Allauch or by the D4A, take the yellow-marked track, dominated by the towering Tête Rouge cliffs. At the crossing, follow the blue markings up towards Les Escaouprés. Opposite, the west side of the Taoumé is typical Pagnol countryside. A track by the base of the Taoumé leads straight to the easily visited Grosibou Grotto, where, as children, Pagnol and his pal Lili had many an adventure. Pagnol later described their exploits in *Le Château de ma Mère* (1958).

– Coming back on the left, you arrive at the top of the Taoumé (670 metres/ 2200 feet high), with views to the Garlaban, Marseille and the sea, Ste-Baume and Ste-Victoire. Walk along the crest for more magnificent views. The descent through the shady passes at Baume-Sourne and Canteperdrix, past the yellow signs followed on the way up, can be tricky.

AUBAGNE (13400)

This market town has a tradition of making ceramics and *santons* (see page 88), as well as focusing its activity on the life and work of Pagnol. There are a number of studios run by potters, ceramic artists and *santonniers*. Every two years, in August, Aubagne hosts Argilla, the largest pottery market in France. The **Festival du Rire** (laughter festival) takes place in July. The local produce market is held on Tuesday and Saturday.

USEFUL ADDRESS

fl Tourist office: esplanade Charles-de-Gaulle. ☎ 04-42-03-49-98. Organizes guided tours of the town, giving information about the life of Pagnol and on the colourful flora and fauna of the region.

WHERE TO STAY AND EAT

♠ ✕ Hostellerie de la Source: St-Pierre-les-Aubagne. ☎ 04-42-04-09-19. Fax: 04-42-04-58-72. Closed on Sunday evening and on Monday. This fine hotel, in an attractive building with a lovely garden, has a good reputation. Pleasant rooms at 450–1,000F. An à la carte meal will set you back between 220F and 280F. Enjoy an intimate dinner on the quiet shady terrace.

♠ ✕ Chambres d'hôte Les Quatre Vents (B&B): with Brigitte and Michel Arlès, route de Lascours. ☎ 04-42-03-76-35. Fax: 04-42-18-98-58. Rooms cost 450F, including breakfast, and dinner with the hosts (bookable in advance) is 140F. This beautiful house, at the foot of the hills of 'Pagnol country', has exposed beams, Provençal-style furniture, terracotta-tiled floors and a swimming pool. Delicious and plentiful breakfasts include pastries with jam.

✕ Snack El Madrid: 7 rue Mireille-Lauze. ☎ 04-42-82-05-49. In the kingdom of the tortilla, choose a *plato combinado* for 28F, including Serrano cured ham and spicy chorizo sausage. Alternatively, single dishes cost between 20F and 30F. Unsurprisingly, the décor is Spanish.

BOUCHES-DU-RHÔNE

WHAT TO SEE

Have a look at the 'Petit Monde de Marcel Pagnol' on display in the tourist information office, where characters and sites from his life are re-constructed by the local *santonniers*.

From the Maison de l'Argile on the Chemin des Ateliers Thérèse-Neveu take a stroll around the old part of town and through its narrow streets. You'll see houses with red tiled rooftops and small squares, set against the lovely backdrop of Pagnol's hill, known as the Garlaban.

CASSIS (13260)   Population: 8,070

Cassis (the final 's' is silent, unlike the blackcurrant liqueur *cassis*) is a lovely little port surrounded by tall cliffs. The town is generally quite peaceful except in high season, when it can get busy with pale-faced Parisians seeking the warmth of the Mediterranean climate; parking is always difficult. To enjoy it to the full, try to visit in the cooler months. The Cassis *calanques* are always relatively quiet, even in summer. To see them you will need to be prepared to walk a little way, unless you want to treat yourself to a boat trip.

Try the local white wine, which has a bouquet of the rosemary, heather and myrtle that grow wild on the surrounding hills. This is one of the oldest *appellation d'origine contrôlée* (AOC) areas in France and the quality standard applies also to its reds and rosé wines.

Note: there have been problems with thefts from cars left in the main car parks for Les Calanques beaches, and in the town itself, so be vigilant.

GETTING THERE

– **Coach travel**: travelling by coach is a good idea, because Cassis' train station is over 3 kilometres/2 miles from the port. Coach travel information: ☎ 04-42-73-29-29. There are five departures a day from the Gare St-Charles. Train travel information: ☎ 08-36-35-35-35 (2.23F per minute).

USEFUL ADDRESS

🛈 Tourist office: place P.-Baragnon. ☎ 04-42-01-71-17. Open Monday to Friday 9am–12.30pm and 1.30–5.30pm in winter. Open on Saturday 10am–12.30pm and 1.30–5pm, and on Sunday 10am–12.30pm. Between 15 June and 15 September, open 9am–6pm, and in July and August, open every day 9am–8pm. Lots of useful information, including a helpful leaflet on walks in and around the inlets.

WHERE TO STAY

⚓ Auberge de jeunesse La Fontasse (youth hostel): ☎ 04-42-01-02-72. Superbly located in the Calanques hills. To get there (by car or bike) from Marseille, after about 15 kilometres (9 miles), turn right for the Gardiole pass (3 kilometres/1.8 miles of good road, then 2 kilometres/1.25 miles of stony road). On foot, walk down from the cross-roads for La Gardiole. To come from Cassis via the *calanques* (about an hour's walk), take avenue de l'Amiral-Ganteaume, then avenue des Calanques as far as the Port-Miou *calanque* and climb up to the youth hostel. Open all year (except 5 January to 5 March), 8–10am and 5–11pm. In July and August, check in as early as possible; it gets very busy, but walkers and cyclists won't be turned away. 65 beds in 10-bed rooms, 50F per night. Youth hostel association membership card essential (on sale here).

This pleasant Provençal house, in an exceptional setting, is ideal for those who want to get right back to nature. It has kitchen facilities (bring your own food), a reservoir for rainwater and solar-powered electricity. The manager is friendly, and knowledge-able about the region. There's lots to do, with walks (particularly the nearby GR98 long-distance foot-path), climbing, swimming, masses of interesting flora (450 different species) in the area, and *pétanque*.

‎☖ **Le Provençal**: 7 rue Victor-Hugo, in Cassis port. ☎ 04-42-01-72-13. Open all year. Double rooms cost around 190F (in low season) and 280–360F (in high season). Can be noisy in summer but the rooms are really lovely, with air-conditioning and TV. The welcome is warm and the decor is attractive and sunny, with tasteful wrought-iron features. Breakfast is served in the rooms.

‎☖ **Hôtel de France Maguy**: avenue du Revestel. ☎ 04-42-01-72-21. Fax: 04-42-01-96-50. Closed from December to February, this hotel has double rooms with TV, shower and toilet (some with kitch-enette), at 300–400F. Parking costs 35F per day. This hotel is in a secluded spot slightly above the town, the furthest from the port,

but still only a 10-minute walk. The welcome is warm.

‎☖ **Hôtel Liautaud**: on the port. ☎ 04-42-01-75-37. Fax: 04-42-01-12-08. Closed from 1 December to 1 February, this hotel has rooms from 390F to 410F. In the late 19th century, Cassis was no more than a simple fishing port, with one hotel overlooking the sea. Built in 1875, the Liautaud has been redecorated since then, but the decor remains very 1960s. It's well-maintained, and the rooms have double-glazing, terraces, views of the port and fairly modern bathrooms.

‎☖ **La Bastidaine** (B&B): 6a ave-nue des Alibizi. ☎ 04-42-98-83-09. Email: bastiden@club-internet.fr. Four rooms (330F) in a *bastide* 2 kilometres from the centre, on the edge of a huge pine forest and surrounded by vineyards. Peace and quiet guaranteed. This is a great starting point for walks and the owners also have mountain bikes available.

☆☆☆ Chic

‎☖ **Hôtel de la Rade**: 1 avenue des Dardanelles. ☎ 04-42-01-02-97. Fax: 04-42-01-01-32. Email: larade @hotel-cassis.com. Open all year. Double rooms 495–595F, break-fast 48F, lock-up garage 70F; half-board available. Redecorated throughout, this very comfortable hotel has a panoramic terrace and a swimming pool. Just near by, on the port, is the **Restaurant Romano** (15 quai Barthémely), popular for its lovely terrace and good food.

‎☖ **Le Jardin d'Émile**: plage du Bes-touan. ☎ 04-42-01-80-55. Fax: 04-42-01-80-70. Closed for two weeks in January and November. Rooms 400–700F, according to season. Menus from 180F (weekday lunch) to 295F. The seven soundproofed rooms (one reserved for honeymooners) are superb; two nestle under the eaves and are particularly charming. This is the place to enjoy life and lovely views. The chic but relaxed restaurant serves creative and delicious Mediterranean food, such as Marseille-style tripe, fresh cod and garlic potatoes. The garden is wonderful, with ancient pines, and olive, fig and cypress trees.

Campsite

🛖 **Camping Les Cigales**: avenue de la Marne, route de Marseille. On the way out of town. ☎ 04-42-01-07-34. Fax: 04-42-01-34-18. Campsite open from 15 March to 15 November, less than 1 kilometre from the sea. Try to get a pitch far away from the road, or you may have a sleepless night, particularly at the weekend. Booking ahead is not possible.

WHERE TO EAT

✖ **Restaurant Chez César**: 21 quai des Baux. ☎ 04-42-01-75-47. Café-restaurant open every evening in high season and closed on Monday and on Sunday evening in low season. Annual closure in January. Menus 98–172F; daily specials for 80F. The decor is typical of the region and could easily serve as the setting for a Pagnol film. Even though it's in a prime position right on the port, Chez César offers a proper welcome and good value for money. Try the fish couscous or bass cooked on a skewer.

✖ **Le Dauphin**: 3 rue Séverin-Icard. ☎ 04-42-01-10-00. Fax: 04-42-01-10-00. Closed on Wednesday and for lunch on Thursday. Open every evening in high season. Simple but tasty menus 65–102F. Located in a pedestrianized street that runs parallel with the port, Le Dauphin serves regional specialities such as rockfish soup and mussels *à la provençale*. The prices are reasonable. It does get very busy in summer and booking is highly recommended.

✖ **Le Bonaparte**: 14 rue Bonaparte. ☎ 04-42-01-80-84. Closed on Sunday evening, Monday and during November. Menus from 65F to 110F. Located very near the port, Le Bonaparte serves *bouillabaisse* at 170F per person, and other specialities such as *lotte à la provençale*

(Provençal-style monkfish) and *cuisse de canard à la niçoise* (duck). With delicious cooking and a dynamic owner, it's very popular with those in the know.

☆☆☆ Chic

✖ **Le Clos des Arômes**: 10 rue Paul-Mouton. ☎ 04-42-01-71-84. Fax: 04-42-01-31-76. Less than two minutes from the centre. Closed Monday, Tuesday and Wednesday lunchtime except public holidays. Menus 115 and 160F and eight rooms at 400–500F. Just outside the centre of town, this is a haven of peace from the noise of the port. The restaurant is really pretty, serving refined Provençal cooking. As soon as the warm weather arrives, customers can move outside to a large, shady flower-filled courtyard.

✖ **Le Bistrot d'Hugo**: 39 avenue Victor-Hugo. ☎ 04-42-01-78-61. 150 metres from the port. Closed Wednesday except in season; annual holiday in November. Menus at 42F, 79F and 95F. A pleasant and elegant restaurant, producing gourmet cooking at attractive prices, and with a lovely Provençal, family spirit.

✖ **Nino**: 1 quai Barthélemy. ☎ and fax: 04-42-01-74-32. Closed on Monday and on Sunday evening in low season and from 15 December to 10 February. Menus from 100F (weekday and lunch) to 185F, and à la carte dishes. Customers come to this brasserie for fish soup, mussels in cream, *bouillabaisse* with anchovies, and a friendly welcome. It has a unique atmosphere and a view across the port to the Château de Cassis. Interestingly, the fishermen's tribunal, which resolves conflicts and concerns to do with fishing, is housed in the same building.

WHERE TO GO FOR A DRINK

♥ **La Marine**: 5 quai des Baux. Closed in January. Daily specials for 55F. A local woman called Yette owned this bistrot for many years, and the walls are still adorned with signed black-and-white photographs of her many devoted celebrity customers. Marcel Pagnol and, later, actress Brigitte Bardot used to come here for a *pastis* or a glass of local wine.

WHAT TO SEE AND DO

– **Market**: every Wednesday and Friday morning.

– **Fête des Vins**: the wine festival is held on the first Sunday in September. The blessing of the vines is followed by a tasting and a lively programme of events, both in town and by the sea, including a Provençal folklore procession of old carts.

★ **Musée d'Art et Traditions Populaires**: rue Xavier-d'Authier. ☎ 04-42-01-88-66. Between April and end September, open on Wednesday, Thursday and Saturday 3.30–6.30pm. Open 2.30–5.30pm October to March. Entrance free. The museum of local arts and culture displays some archaeological remains, including some Greek finds, as well as works by local painters and archive material about the town.

IN THE AREA

★ **Plage du Bestouan**: towards the *calanques*. The water is very clear but the beach is pebbly. There's another beach, the **plage de la Grande-Mer**, near the promenade des Lombards, at the foot of the chateau.

★ **The *calanques***: the picturesque rocky inlets along the coast between Cassis and Marseille are a highlight of the region. See them by taking one of the boat trips from the port at Cassis (departures all day 9am–5pm; 50F to visit three, 70F for five or 90F for eight). They can also be explored on foot in the space of a day, but you should allow 6 hours to get to Morgiou and 12 hours to La Madrague de Montredon. There's no fresh water along the way and you must take care close to any edges, as the limestone rocks are often very slippery.

In 1975, the *calanques* were officially protected as a natural site of interest, but this has not saved them from being ravaged several times by forest fires. Between 1 July and the second Saturday in September, walkers must not stray from the GR marked route, and even this closes in very dry conditions.

Visits during this period are by boat and only partly on foot, hugging the shore. Smoking is absolutely forbidden.

– **Port-Miou**: the closest inlet to Cassis, about a 30-minute walk, and also accessible by car. For a longer walk, go on to the end of the Cap Cable peninsula, where there's a wide view of the sea. The big quarry closed down about six years ago.

– **Port-Pin** and **Pointe Cacau**: about 2 hours walk from Cassis, there and back, mostly along the marked route of the GR98 B. There's a little beach and, from Pointe Cacau, a lovely view of the cliffs and the En-Vau inlet.

– **En-Vau**: beyond question, this is the most beautiful of the three *calanques*, with rocky needles and cliffs that plummet into the sea, as well as its own little beach. To get to the car park at the col de la Gardiole (where there have been thefts from cars), turn on to the route de la Gardiole (5 kilometres/3 miles before you get to Cassis on the Marseille–Cassis road). From the car park, a superb walk along the GR98 B footpath leads to the inlet, passing a forester's hut, and the valleys of La Gardiole and En-Vau.

★ **Grotte de Cosquer**: also known as the 'underwater Lascaux', this cave among the inlets may not be visited by the public. In 1991, diver Henri Cosquer discovered prehistoric representations of animals on the walls here. They were believed to date back at least 27,000 years, and were therefore even older than the world-famous 16,000-year-old paintings in the caves at Lascaux. Since then, the discovery of 32,000-year-old engravings in the Grotte de Chauvet, in the Ardèche, also in France, have beaten the record.

DIVING

The azure Mediterranean depths around here, surrounded by tall, forbidding cliffs, are colonized by rich, luxuriant sea-life. For some, this is the most spectacular part of the French Mediterranean, particularly when the crystal-clear water is lit up by the intense rays of sun. Lucky divers may even be escorted by dolphins.

Dive Schools

■ **Cassidain de Plongée**: 3 rue Michel-Armand, BP 65, 13714 Cassis. ☎ 04-42-01-89-16. Fax: 04-42-01-23-76. Website: www.cassis-services-plongee.fr. Open from 15 March to 15 November. Henri Cosquer, the bearded owner of this FFESSM- and ANMP-affiliated school, was the diver who discovered the underwater cave that now bears his name (*see above*). Unsurprisingly, one of his diving boats is called the *Cro-Magnon*. The state-registered instructors take novice divers on first dives, teach others up to Level III and also organize special daily dives, depending on the weather. Full equipment is supplied. Costs go down for more than 6 or 10 dives. Booking advisable.

Dive Sites

⚓ **Castel Viel**: at the foot of the cliffs, this colourful dive (Level I) plunges to 40 metres (130 feet) with a short platform at 17 metres (56 feet). Dazzling sea bass, mérou, sardines, squid, peacock girella and pomfret dart in and out of the spreading branches of bright tree coral and red coral. Just near by, at 12–24 metres (40–80 feet), you can see the ledges of the renowned *Grotte à Corail*, or Coral Cave.

La Pointe Cacau: at the foot of the plummeting cliffs, this is a dive (Level I) around a cascade of rocky debris, then a magnificent drop (43 metres/140 feet maximum), blooming with tree coral and red coral and home to spiny lobsters, mérou, peacock girella, anthias, pomfret and, occasionally, brilliantly coloured moon fish and John Dory.

Phare de la Cassidaigne: to the south of the *calanques*, this huge rocky plateau, encircled by ledges (from 6 metres/20 feet), offers several magnificent dives (Level I). The clear water in this rather exposed site supports a particularly unspoilt environment, with congers, morays and many other huge fish, and entertaining 'lièvres de mer' which waddle across the sand.

L'Eissadon: off the point of the little island, this fault has a criss-cross pattern of tunnels that are safe to explore one after the other, down to 15 metres (50 feet) (Level I). Dive in the afternoon, when the sun lights up the rocks and shoals of young grouper.

The Route des Crêtes: Cassis to La Ciotat

The Route des Crêtes, with its fabulous views, is a must. All along the D141 towards La Ciotat there are marked viewpoints. The road climbs up to **Cap Canaille** and then snakes up to the summit of the **Falaises Subeyranes**, the highest cliffs in France, reaching a height of 416 metres (1,364 feet). After another 13 kilometres (8 miles) you'll reach the signal station (*sémaphore*) on the right; from here, the view along the entire coastline is spectacular. Sufferers of vertigo may feel a bit dizzy.

If you're on foot, walk along the Route des Crêtes until 100 metres after the Pas-de-la-Bécasse and Saoupe crossroads. The GR footpath heading off to the right will take you past the Grotte des Espagnols (cave) to the top of the cliff. Follow the path to get to the signal station, then take a left turn down to the bottom of the valley. Beyond here is the chapel of Notre-Dame-de-la-Garde and La Ciotat. The walk takes about 2 hours 30 minutes, and you can get back to Cassis on the bus at 6.15pm.

LA CIOTAT (13600)   Population: 31,923

Don't dismiss La Ciotat out of hand. In spite of the huge cranes in the naval docks, it has a certain appeal. The old houses in the harbour have changed little since the town's most famous son Louis Lumière invented cinematography. This is the place where the Lumière brothers filmed *L'Arrivée d'un train en gare de La Ciotat* ('Train arriving at La Ciotat station'), first shown here on 21 September 1895, more than two months before its legendary showing in Paris. Contrary to popular belief, this wasn't the first piece of cinematic film ever; *La sortie de l'usine Lumière* ('Leaving the Lumière factory') had been made in March 1895. Jules Le Noir was another La

Ciotat local who invented a great French tradition – *pétanque* – and you can still see the old 'boulodrome'.

USEFUL ADDRESS

⊞ Tourist office : boulevard Anatole-France, facing the sea. ☎ 04-42-08-61-32. Open Monday to Saturday, 1 June to 30 September, 9am–8pm and Sunday 10am–1pm; from 1 October, 9am–noon and 2.30–6pm.

WHERE TO STAY AND EAT

≜ ✕ Chez Tania-RIF (République Indépendante de Figuerolles) (the Independent Republic of Figuerolles): calanque de Figuerolles. ☎ 04-42-08-41-71. Fax: 04-42-71-93-39. Website: www.figuerolles.com. Open every day 1 May to 31 October but closed for lunch on Tuesday and for the month of November. Double rooms from 240F to 440F and bungalows up to 590F, excluding breakfast. A meal will set you back about 160F. Just a few minutes from the port of La Ciotat, the rocks and cliffs of this bizarre protected site create strange silhouettes and human shapes against the sky. Painted by Braque in 1909, and much visited by American writer Ernest Hemingway, the declared 'Independent Republic' has a Mediterranean restaurant serving Provençal, Greek and Lebanese specialities, and also does B&B. The restaurant gets pretty full in high season. In summer, the rooms can be rather noisy, but the more adventurous can also rent bungalows nestled in the inlet, close to the pebble beach and crystal-clear water.

≜ ✕ Le Revestel : corniche du Liouquet, route des Lecques. ☎ 04-42-83-11-06. Fax: 04-42-83-29-50. At the exit to La Ciotat, heading towards St-Cyr-sur-Mer. Closed for lunch on Wednesday (and for dinner in low season), on Sunday evening, and during January and the first two weeks of February. This pleasant traditional hotel offers rooms for 330F without breakfast and menus for 180F and 220F. Classic dishes are served on the terrace on sunny days, overlooking the sea.

✕ La Fleur de Thym : 17 avenue F.-Roosevelt. ☎ 04-42-08-32-44. Closed on Sunday evening and on Wednesday out of season. Menus from 155F to 198F. Regional dishes (from the Landes as well as Provence) are served in the dining room and a limited menu, with a selection of salads and grilled meats, is also offered on the terrace (expect to pay around 100F) which has a view of the sea.

WHAT TO SEE AND DO

In summer, there are three trips per day to the *calanques* by catamaran. Information is available from the tourist office.

The Pays d'Aix (Aix Country)

AIX-EN-PROVENCE (13100)   Population: 137,067

Aix, dating back to 122 BC, was the first Roman settlement in Gaul, founded as a garrison by one Caius Sextus Calvinus. The town, with its thermal springs, gained the name Aquae Sextiae ('waters of Sextus'), and the conquering hero is still remembered today in the cours Sextius. The Romans left their mark and it's hardly surprising that Aix, the birthplace of Impressionist painter Paul Cézanne, has a northern Italian charm about it. Its delightful architecture features warm-toned limestone, simple red round-tiled roofs without attics, and harmonious lines of facades influenced by Italian baroque style.

The town may have a reputation for being charming, but it's not an easy place to visit – certainly not by car. It takes ages to get into the centre, there's no way of avoiding the traffic jams on the ring road and it's totally unrealistic to expect to find a parking space. The only way to travel around the town centre is on foot. Wander through the labyrinth of alleys and passageways, past luxury shops, antique dealers and brilliantly coloured, intensely perfumed markets. Follow the footsteps of Cézanne, from the golden cobbles of the cours Mirabeau, past café terraces thronging with people of all ages, as far as the Ste-Victoire.

Aix is famous for its many fountains. The wines of the Coteaux d'Aix are equally numerous. Loved by novelist Colette, they provide what she described as a 'true flavour of the region'.

Aix is so proud of its local products that it has been seeking an *appellation d'origine contrôlée* (AOC) to protect them. The first candidate is the *calisson*, an unusual little boat-shaped almond-flavoured sweet treat that smells and tastes of all the flavours found around Aix. Its texture and taste come from melons and oranges preserved in syrup and mixed into the almond paste. According to Provençal poet Frédéric Mistral, the word *calisson* was a corruption of the Provençal word *canissoun*, referring to a small rack made of reeds and used by local pastry-cooks to carry their wares. A few years ago, the *calisson*-makers revived the tradition of the *Bénédiction des Calissons d'Aix* (blessing of Aix *calissons*), which dates back to 1630 when a church Mass delivered Provence from the plague. On the first Sunday in September, *calissons* are distributed to the congregation after Mass, to the accompaniment of dancing and song.

BOUCHES-DU-RHÔNE

USEFUL ADDRESSES

🛈 Tourist office (A2 on the map): 2 place du Général-de-Gaulle. ☎ 04-42-16-11-61. Open 8.30am–7pm. On Sunday and public holidays, open 10am–1pm and 2–6pm. Opening times extended in high season. **➊ Marseille–Provence Airport**: ☎ 04-42-14-14-14.

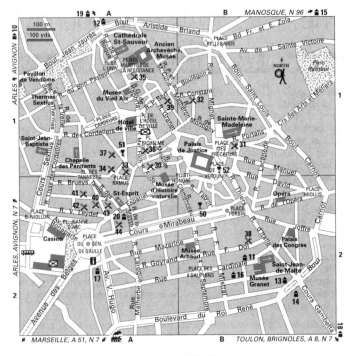

AIX-EN-PROVENCE

■ **Useful Addresses**

- 🅸 Office du tourisme (tourist office)
- 🚌 Coach station
- 🚆 Train station (SNCF)

🛏 **Where to Stay**

- 10 Youth hostel
- 11 Hôtel Cardinal
- 12 Hôtel Paul
- 13 Hôtel La Caravelle
- 14 Hôtel Le Concorde
- 15 Hôtel Le Prieuré
- 16 Les Quatre Dauphins
- 17 Hôtel St-Christophe
- 18 La Bastide du Roy René
- 19 Mas d'Entremont
- 20 Hôtel des Augustins

✕ **Where to Eat**

- 30 La Tasca

- 31 Le Carillon
- 32 Le Dernier Bistrot
- 33 Chex Maxime
- 34 Jacquou le Croquant
- 35 Le Démodé
- 36 Le Pain Quotidien
- 37 Antioche
- 38 La Brocherie
- 39 Chez Féraud
- 40 Le Poivre d'Ane
- 41 Chez Charlotte
- 42 Laurane et sa maison
- 43 Les Bacchanales
- 44 L'Amphytrion

🍷 **Where to Go for a Drink**

- 50 Les Deux Garçons
- 51 Le Scat-Club
- 52 Le Verdun

Train station (A2, off the map): Reservations: ☎ 08-36-35-35-35 (2.23F per minute).

Coach station (A2 on the map): rue de l'Europe. ☎ 04-42-91-26-80. Persevere!

Guided Tours : information available at the tourist office.
– **Aix-en-Provence Festival** : in July. Information: ☎ 04-42-17-34-00. Reservations: ☎ 04-42-17-34-34.

WHERE TO STAY

There are some lovely (and expensive) places to stay, with many people coming back year after year in the warm months. Advance booking is strongly recommended. You may not encounter many smiling faces in Aix, but that just seems to be the way things are here. For a warmer welcome, venture further afield, as there are some delightful places to stay in the surrounding area.

☆ Budget

Auberge de jeunesse/CIRS (youth hostel) (A1, **10**, off the map): 3 avenue Marcel-Pagnol, quartier Jas-de-Bouffan, 13090. Near the Fondation Vasarely, 2 kilometres (1.5 miles) from the town centre. Closed from 20 December to 31 January. ☎ 04-42-20-15-99. Fax: 04-42-59-36-12. Accommodation for 100 guests at a cost of 85F for the first night, including breakfast, and 72F for subsequent nights. Meals available between April and November, with *formule* menus at 50F and packed lunches and dinners at 38F. Facilities include a garden, tennis courts and a games area.

☆☆ Moderate

Hôtel Paul (A1, **12** on the map): 10 avenue Pasteur. ☎ 04-42-23-23-89. Fax: 04-42-63-17-80. Email: hotel.paul@wanadoo.fr. *Note*: on Sunday between noon and 6pm there's no one on duty to meet guests. Double rooms cost from 190F to 250F in this old-style hotel, recommended by regulars and locals for its warm welcome, clean rooms and reasonable prices. It's well located near to the cathedral

and the cafés on one of the squares in Aix's old town. Some rooms overlook the garden, and it's perfect for a bit of peace and quiet. Direct access for bikes and cars.

Hôtel La Caravelle (B2, **13** on the map): 19-31, boulevard du Roi-René. ☎ 04-42-21-53-05. Fax: 04-42-96-55-46. With 30 double rooms from 290F to 420F, this hotel is almost always full, even in low season. The rooms overlooking the garden are the most spacious, the quietest and the most expensive.

Hôtel Le Concorde (B2, **14** on the map): 68 boulevard du Roi-René, opposite La Caravelle. ☎ 04-42-26-03-95. Fax: 04-42-27-38-90. Open all year. Double rooms from 215F to 260F, some looking on to the small and pleasant courtyard, which has a garden for relaxing or picnicking. The welcome is always warm, and there are garage facilities.

☆☆☆ Chic

Hôtel Le Prieuré (B1, **15**, off the map): route des Alpes (on the RN96 towards Manosque-Sisteron, exit 12. 2 kilometres (1.25 miles) from Aix-en-Provence. ☎ 04-42-21-05-23. Fax: 04-42-21-60-56. Double rooms 190F with a basin and 300–

400F with a bathroom. This former archbishop's priory has been converted into a hotel with 21 rooms, all overlooking the French-style park of Le Nôtre's neighbouring Pavillon Lenfant. Sadly, it isn't possible to visit the *pavillon*, which is the property of the University of Aix, but at least you can enjoy it from the outside. The hotel rooms are very cosy and the welcome is warm. Free parking.

⚓ **Hôtel Cardinal** (B2, **11** on the map): 24 rue Cardinal. ☎ 04-42-38-32-30. Fax: 04-42-26-39-05. Rooms from 260–350F; those in the annexe are better and more spacious, for 400–450F. Atmospheric hotel offering peace and comfort near the Musée Granet. Some rooms are in the process of being redecorated. The welcome is typical of Aix (rather unsmiling).

⚓ **Les Quatre Dauphins** (B2, **16** on the map): 54 rue Roux-Alphéran. ☎ 04-42-38-16-39. Fax: 04-42-38-60-19. Quaint Aix hotel with rooms with shower for around 375F and rooms with bathroom for 395F. Guests have to accept the rather indifferent welcome if they want to enjoy the adorable rooms of this *bourgeois* townhouse. Even more quaint, there's no lift.

⚓ **Hôtel St-Christophe** (A2, **17** on the map): 2 avenue Victor-Hugo. ☎ 04-42-26-01-24. Fax: 04-42-38-53-17. ⚓ Ideally located near the cours Mirabeau in the centre of Aix, one of *the* places to stay in town. Rooms in art-deco style for 420–460F, with air-conditioning and excellent facilities, including terraces (in some cases). Suites for 600F. Menus at 120F and 180F. The **Brasserie Léopold** on the ground floor (closed on Monday) is a local institution, with closely packed tables, starched tablecloths and waiters in long white aprons. Try a tasty steak *tartare* or *farcis provençaux*.

☆☆☆☆ Très Chic

⚓ **Bastide du Roy René** (B2, **18**, off the map): Chemin des Infirmeries. ☎ 04-42-37-83-00. Fax: 04-42-27-54-40. Email: bastide.roy. rene@wanadoo.fr. Open all year. Superb studios for 290–420F in a beautifully restored country house and duplex apartments for 480–650F. Kitchenettes available and free parking. Surely the scene of many a party in the past, this house was then turned into a hospital for victims of 17th-century epidemics and is now the perfect place for a peaceful break in the Aix area.

⚓ **Mas d'Entremont** (A1, **19**, off the map): 3 kilometres (2 miles) to the north of the RN7, Montée d'Avignon. ☎ 04-42-17-42-42. Fax: 04-42-21-15-83. Email: entremont @wanadoo.fr. Closed from 1 November to 15 March. Double room without breakfast from 680F to 1,030F. Breakfast is 85F. This peaceful and luxurious Provençal country house is set in a terraced park overlooking Aix, with a pool and tennis courts. The restaurant (closed on Sunday from 1 November to 15 March) offers menus at 210F and 250F. The excellence of the cooking justifies the high prices. Free car park.

⚓ **Hôtel des Augustins** (A2, **20**, off the map): 3 rue de la Masse, in the town centre. ☎ 04-42-27-28-59. Fax: 04-42-26-74-87. Double rooms, with bathroom, toilet and TV, from 600F to 1,500F in high season. Housed in a former 12th-century Grands-Augustins convent, the hotel has some very comfortable rooms furnished in Louis XIII style, and Gothic-style arches, stained glass and exposed stone walls. The rooms do vary – some are very spacious and have large bathrooms with jacuzzis, while others are quite ordinary. It may be expensive, but it is just round the corner from the cours Mirabeau.

Campsites

☎ **Arc-en-ciel** : pont des Trois-Sautets, route de Nice (RN7). ☎ 04-42-26-14-28. 2 kilometres from the town centre. Open from mid-March to mid-October. The site has a pool, tennis courts and all mod cons, but it is quite expensive.

☎ **Chantecler** : avenue du Val-St-André, 2 kilometres from the centre. Take the Val-St-André exit from the motorway, heading towards Nice. Bus No. 3. ☎ 04-42-26-12-98. Fax: 04-42-27-33-53. This shady and terraced site, which also has a swimming pool, is open all year, with meals available from June to end September. Booking is advisable from Easter to September.

WHERE TO EAT

✩ Budget

✗ **La Tasca** (A1, **30** on the map): 12 rue de la Glacière. ☎ 04-42-26-07-26. Closed all day Sunday. Menus at 88F (slightly more expensive for paella), a *menu espagnol* (Spanish menu) at 125F and a tapas menu at 110F. Rather touristy Spanish restaurant in the centre of Aix's old town.

✗ **Le Carillon** (B1, **31** on the map): 10 rue Portalis, near the law courts. No phone, so no booking. Closed Saturday evening, Sunday, the whole of August and a week in February. Menus for 60F and 80F. Try to arrive early if you want to secure a seat alongside the regulars, many of whom are local retirees, who come here for the unpretentious regional cooking. It's become something of a classic in the area and is an ideal spot for lunch.

✗ **Le Dernier Bistrot** (B1, **32** on the map): 15 rue Constantin. ☎ 04-42-21-13-02. Closed on Sunday in winter and Sunday lunchtime in summer as well as during the February school holidays. Menus cost 52F (weekday lunch) 95F, 125F and 140F. Rather tucked away, this bistrot is a bit easier to find when its tables are put outside in the summer months. It serves a mixture of Provençal and traditional bistrot dishes,

which means that if you don't fancy *pieds-paquets* (tripe) you can have *blanquette de veau à l'ancienne* (fillet of veal) instead.

✗ **Chez Maxime** (B2, **33** on the map): 12 place Ramus. ☎ 04-42-26-28-51. Fax: 04-42-26-74-70. Closed on Sunday and Monday lunchtime in summer and for the last two weeks in January. Menus cost 78F (weekday lunch) and 135–270F. This very well-known restaurant has tables under the plane trees in the very heart of Aix and offers inventive Provençal dishes and top-quality meat.

✗ **Jacquou Le Croquant** (A1, **34** on the map): 2 rue de l'Aumône-Vieille. ☎ 04-42-27-37-19. ✗ Closed on Sunday and Monday in winter but open on Sunday evening between May and mid-August. Menus cost 59F (lunch), 79F and 99F. Regulars come here for the friendly welcome as much as for the food, which is inspired by the traditions of southwest France. The highlight of the menu is *tourtou*, a buckwheat pancake stuffed with meat and vegetables. There's lots of duck on the menu, served in different ways, and in winter you can enjoy a warming casserole (*cassoulet*). There are tables in the courtyard in summer.

✗ **Le Démodé** (A1, **35** on the map): 5 rue Campra. ☎ and fax 04-

42-23-30-66. Turn right off rue Gaston-de-Saporta; rue Campra is the continuation of rue Littera. Closed on Sunday and Monday as well as during the month of August and for a week at Christmas. Menus at 85F, 102F and 122F. Located between the cathedral and the town hall, this restaurant-*crêperie* concerns itself more with its customers than with redecorating. It still boasts a decor straight out of the 1930s and 40s (plus air-conditioning), but it offers a pleasant, relaxing atmosphere, modest prices, and a warm welcome.

✗ **Le Pain Quotidien** (A1, **36** on the map): 5 place Richelme. ☎ 04-42-23-48-57. This bakery/cake shop/tearoom is in a perfect spot with tables outside (even on market days). Sandwiches range from 25F to 52F and large mixed salads are from 60F.

✗ **Antioche** (A1, **37** on the map): 18 rue Félibre-Gaut. ☎ 04-42-33-11-88. Menus at 60F and 80F. Locals come here for Turkish and Lebanese specialities, a warm welcome and great prices.

☆☆☆ Chic

✗ **La Brocherie** (B2, **38** on the map): 5 rue Fernand-Dol. ☎ 04-42-38-53-21. Fax: 04-42-26-11-38. Closed for lunch on Saturday, all day Sunday, on public holidays and for the month of August. Menus at 119F and 148F and *formule* menus at 75F (lunch only) and 87F. Restaurant in a pleasant rustic-style setting, just around the corner from cours Mirabeau. Chickens are roasted on an ancient spit in the Renaissance fireplace, but the grilled fish and Provençal specialities are just as popular. There's a pleasant patio for the summer months.

✗ **Chez Féraud** (A1, **39** on the map): 8 rue du Puits-Juif. ☎ 04-42-63-07-27. Closed on Sunday, Mon-

day and during August. Menus at 120F and 150F. Right in the centre of Aix, and guaranteed to give you a real feel of Provence. The father of the family prepares the tasty food – soup with pesto, and *daube* (casserole) – which is served by the son under the watchful eye of the mother. If it's not too busy, ask to see the cellar.

✗ **Le Poivre d'âne** (B2, **40** on the map): 7 rue de la Couronne. ☎ 04-42-93-45-56. Closed on Sunday and Monday. Weekday lunch menu at 95F and à la carte on average around 145F. Atmosphere, a colourful setting and delicious food – unsurprisingly, this place is rarely empty. The menu changes every two months, and the cuisine is inventive, original and based on a wide range of top-quality produce – the chef denies having any 'specialities'. The wine list is very reasonably priced. Incidentally, the name *poivre d'âne* comes from the Provençal *pèbre d'aï*, which means the herb savory.

✗ **Chez Charlotte** (B2, **41** on the map): 32 rue des Bernardines. ☎ 04-42-26-77-56 (phone ahead to book). Closed on Sunday, Monday and during August. Small menu at 90F, and another at 100F, not including drinks. Five minutes from cours Mirabeau, this restaurant is always full, they do provide chess sets and a piano to pass the time while you're waiting for your table. The atmosphere is young, and the delicious terrines and savoury tarts are reasonably priced. Credit cards not accepted.

✗ **Laurane et sa maison** (B2, **42** on the map): 16 rue Victor-Leydet. ☎ 04-42-93-02-03. Around 150F for a meal. You'll be tempted to linger in this pleasant and comforting, sunny setting. The cooking has a light, fresh touch.

☆☆☆☆ Très Chic

✕ **Les Bacchanales** (B2, **43** on the map): 10 rue de la Couronne. ☎ 04-42-27-21-06. Near place de la Rotonde. Closed on Tuesday and for lunch on Wednesday. The *menu Manou* is 145F, and others are 165F and 195F, but the best value is the excellent 'gastronomic' lunch menu at 95F. This popular and intimate restaurant offers comfort, calm and imaginative Provençal cooking using quality produce. The quality of its food is high, even by Aix standards.

✕ **L'Amphytrion** (B2, **44** on the map): 2 rue Paul-Doumer. ☎ 04-42-26-54-10. Menus at 100F (lunch) and 175F. The chef shows his love for his native Provence with imaginative interpretations of regional dishes, offering a delicious *menu du marché* (using ingredients 'fresh from the market'). Take a table in the courtyard and enjoy some excellent local wine as you watch the world go by.

WHERE TO GO FOR A DRINK

♟ **Les Deux Garçons** (B2, **50** on the map): cours Mirabeau. This bar gets its name from the two waiters who bought it in the 19th century. The decor – in late 18th-century style, all ivory and gold – is more memorable than the welcome. Cézanne, Zola and, more recently, Mauriac, Cocteau and Mistinguett were regular customers.

♟ **Le Scat-Club** (A1, **51** on the map): 11 rue de la Verrerie. ☎ 04-42-23-00-23. Jazz club open from Tuesday to Saturday from 11pm. No entry charge and drinks cost between 30F and 60F. More than 10 years old, the club is something of an institution and gets very busy on some evenings. Perfect for those who like listening to jazz music or dancing.

♟ **Le Verdun** (B1, **52** on the map): 20 place de Verdun. ☎ 04-42-27-03-24. Enjoy good food for around 100F or just a drink at a table under the plane trees, in a young friendly atmosphere.

WHAT TO SEE AND DO

★ **Old facades**: there are delightful old facades everywhere in Aix, a town with about 190 17th- and 18th-century private mansions. Also charming are the wide, straight roads of the Mazarin district, which are very often quite deserted. (The Mazarin who designed the district was an architect and brother of the more famous cardinal.) Take a look at **rue Roux-Alphéran** near the Granet museum and wander along **rues Mazarine, Gayrand, Cardinalel**. You're unlikely to come across many other tourists, but you'll be amazed at how much this area is like a forgotten corner of Italy.

★ **Fountains**: numerous fountains add to the charm of Aix, particularly those in the **forum des Cardeurs**, in **place des Chapeliers**, the **Fontaine Cézanne** and the **Fontaine des Quatre-Dauphins** (where the dolphins have scales), and the extremely elegant example in the **place d'Albertas**. Cocteau was very struck by their appeal, writing in one of his poems of 'cent fontaines bleues' ('a hundred blue fountains').

★ **Parcours Paul Cézanne** (Cézanne route): Aix failed to commemorate its world-famous artist for many years, but they're making up for it now. The route through the painter's life is marked in the town with brass studs. (A map and leaflet are available at the tourist office; you don't really need them, but they will take you to spots that other tourists don't always reach.) From rue d'Italie to rue de l'Opéra, lined with private mansions from the 17th and 18th centuries, follow in the artist's childhood footsteps until you reach 55 cours Mirabeau, where the sign for Paul's father's hat shop has been partially erased. Also on cours Mirabeau is his favourite watering hole, the Café des Deux Garçons (*see above*).

The hatter's son attended Bourbon college, now Lycée Mignet, before studying law to please his father, who had become a banker in the mean time. The family moved to the Mas de Bouffan, a lovely property (closed to the public) set in a large park, where Cézanne wrote poetry and painted. (The town has plans to buy the building and convert it into a museum of the artist's life and works.) In 1861, Paul gained permission from his father to study art in Paris, where, thanks to his fellow Bourbon student, Émile Zola, he met members of the Impressionist movement. Cézanne spent 15 unsuccessful years exhibiting in Paris but always felt more at home in Aix and the surrounding countryside. From 1876, he was to return to the region again and again.

Cézanne was not a natural bohemian. For many years, he hid from his father his relationship with Hortense Fiquet, one of his models and mother of his son (also Paul). When his father died, in 1886, Cézanne inherited an enormous fortune and he was then able to marry Hortense in Aix and live with his family at the foot of St-Victoire.

Art-lovers can walk from the house in which Cézanne was born to the St-Pierre cemetery where he is buried, via 23 rue Boulegon, where he died at the age of 67 on 23 October 1906. The Café des Deux Garçons on cours Mirabeau is an important stage on the journey, the place where the penniless artist would give paintings away to friends. Those escaping without a cumbersome canvas would pay for his food instead. Those unable to desist would take the pictures home and put them in the attic. Since then, generations of people in Aix have feverishly searched their attics in the vain hope of finding a lost masterpiece (and a fortune).

★ **Cours Mirabeau**: this lovely avenue, lined with plane trees and cafés, was laid out in the 17th century and gives Aix a relaxed feeling, reminiscent of northern Italy. Of the three fountains, one spouts warm water, and another commemorates King René, showing the good king holding a bunch of the Muscat grapes that he introduced to the region.

★ **Cathédrale St-Sauveur**: open to the public 8am–noon and 2–6pm (2–6pm only on Sunday). The various styles in this cathedral range from the 12th- to the 16th-centuries. The unusual organ chest is worth seeing, although not an original. The famous triptych of *The Burning Bush* by Nicolas Froment (1476) hangs high in the nave, which is currently being restored. Commissioned by King René, it came from the Carmelite convent, now destroyed, which opened just once a year to mark the anniversary of the king's death. There's also a fine pre-Roman baptistry and tiled Romanesque cloisters.

★ **Musée des Tapisseries** (tapestry museum): place de l'Ancien-Arche-vêché. ☎ 04-42-23-09-91. Open 10am–noon and 2–6pm. Closed Tuesday. Entrance fee: 10F, free for under-25s. In a beautiful private mansion, built between the 12th and 18th centuries, the museum has a fine setting and some wonderful tapestries of the same period. A separate section shows the latest in avant-garde textile art. There's also a display of theatre costumes and stage-set models, celebrating the Festival International d'Aix, which takes place in June and is based in the courtyard theatre of the Archbishop's Palace.

★ Look for the **place de l'Université** and then take the **rue Gaston-de-Saporta** down to the centre. On the way, take a look at the famous clock on the place de l'Hôtel-de-Ville. The squares around this area are very lively on market days.

★ **Église Ste-Marie-Madeleine**: known as 'La Madeleine', this church has an unusual structure and, inside, the famous tryptich of the Annunciation, of which only the central section has survived. The baby Paul Cézanne was baptized here in 1839.

★ **Passage Agard**: an interesting little passageway between the law courts and cours Mirabeau.

★ **Musée Granet**: place St-Jean-de-Malte. ☎ 04-42-38-14-70. Open every day except Tuesday, 10am–noon and 2–6pm. Entrance fee: 10F. Housed in the former priory of the Knights of Malta, this museum has a number of splendid paintings by Cézanne, Ingres, David and Géricault, and other interesting views of the region by Granet himself, who was from Aix. In the other rooms hang interesting pictures from the 17th and 18th centuries, including portraits of the Gueidan family, a Largillierre, a Philippe de Champaigne, a Le Nain and a Mignard, as well as works from the Northern School. The archaeological collection on the lower ground floor has some interesting pieces – mosaics, urns, tombstones and olive-oil presses – dating mainly from the Roman era.

★ **Paul Cézanne's studio**: 9 avenue Paul-Cézanne. Take avenue Pasteur to north Aix. ☎ 04-42-21-06-53. Open 10am–noon and 2.30–6pm, 1 April to 30 September. Open 10am–noon and 2–5pm, 1 October to 31 March. Closed at Christmas, on New Year's Day and 1 May. Entrance fee: 25F (students 10F). Guided tours on Wednesday and Saturday at 10am and 3pm, 35F (concessions 25F). Cézanne's studio, bathed in sunlight and surrounded by greenery, stands on the hill known as the Colline des Louves. It was designed by the artist himself, to have an inspirational view of Montagne Ste-Victoire, a favourite subject. Visitors come from all over the world and wait patiently in the garden before entering the studio in small groups. It's 53 square metres (174 square feet) in size, and is much as he left it when he died, full of memorabilia – pots, bottles and jars, skulls that he used for still life paintings, and the huge ladder he needed when working on larger canvases. Only its flooring has been refurbished, in order to cope with the crowds. The surroundings have changed much more than the studio itself, and trees and buildings now obscure the mountain view. Sadly, there's no longer a donkey or cart to transport you, like Cézanne, from the studio to Château Noir, at the foot of Montagne Ste-Victoire, where the artist rented two rooms for his materials and spent much time during the last years of his life. There's a shop under the museum.

BOUCHES-DU-RHÔNE

WHAT ELSE TO SEE AND DO

★ **Pavillon de Vendome**: 32 rue Célony. ☎ 04-42-21-05-78. Open every day (except Tuesday and public holidays) 10am–noon and 2–6pm. Two huge figures embellish the facade of this grand house, built for Cardinal de Vendôme, and overlooking a huge, remarkably restored, French-style garden. The rooms are full of beautiful paintings and furniture from the 17th and 18th centuries. Makes a good stop on any tour of the country around Aix.

★ **Thermes Sextius**: 55 cours Sextius. ☎ 04-42-23-81-81. An ideal spot for recuperation, built on the site of the ancient Roman baths of Sextius, of which you can still see the remains in the hall. The modern establishment uses the healing and relaxing qualities of the natural springwater, which has a temperature of 34°C (93°F), in spa baths, massages, water jets. There's also a pretty garden. Pampering is complete with a night at the Aquabella hotel next door – expensive and chic, but relaxation guaranteed.

★ **Les Santons Fouque**: 65 cours Gambetta. ☎ 04-42-26-33-38. Website: www.santonsfouque.com. Opened in 1934, this shop has a collection of about 1,800 models of terracotta *santons* (*see* page 88), all made on the premises, as well as a pretty Provençal garden.

★ **Fondation Vasarely**: 1 avenue Marcel-Pagnol. ☎ 04-42-20-01-09. Fax: 04-42-59-14-65. Website: www.netprovence.com/fondationvasarely. Open Monday to Friday, 10am–1pm and 2–7pm; Saturday and Sunday, 10am–7pm. Entrance fee: 35F. This art foundation is housed in a series of black-and-white hexagons designed by Victor Vasarely, a devoted exponent of abstract geometric art, and successful in decorative art and advertising. Forty-two pieces, called *intégrations monumentales*, stand in a great space, visible from quite a long way off. Throughout the year, there are also temporary exhibitions of works by great contemporary artists.

– There are a couple of interesting sites near by:

★ **Memorial to the Armenian massacres**: place d'Arménie. Note the unusual Armenian alphabet.

★ **Monument donated by Joseph Sec**: near 6 boulevard Pasteur. Dating from 26 February 1792, the monument is dedicated to the observance of the law by the people (*à la municipalité observatrice de la loi*). This is one of the few structures remaining from the French Revolution.

SHOPPING

🔒 **Confiserie d'Entrecasteaux**: 2 rue Entrecasteaux. ☎ 04-42-27-15-02. Fax: 04-42-38-37-78. Closed Sunday and public holidays. This pretty sweet shop sells the traditional almond-flavoured *calissons d'Aix*.

🔒 **Les Chocolats de Puyricard**: 7 rue Rifle-Rafle. ☎ 04-42-21-13-26. At Puyricard, in the countryside out-side Aix where the chocolates of the same name were first made in 1967. You can visit the factory (by appointment), or just go to the shop in Aix for *clous de Cézanne*, ('Cézanne's nails'), made from figs and Garlaban (old *marc*) and dipped in chocolate, splendid *calissons*, and 80 varieties of homemade chocolates.

Markets

The markets of Aix are an institution and play an important role in the 'branding' of the town. Groups of tourists are constantly amazed by the fruit and vegetable market on place Richelme and the flower market on place des Prêcheurs.

– The **fruit and vegetable market** on place Richelme takes place every day, even Sunday. It is said to have been going since the time of Good King René.

Other food markets are set up on the place des Prêcheurs and place de la Madeleine on Tuesday, Thursday and Saturday.

– **Flower markets** enliven the place de l'Hôtel-de-Ville on Tuesday, Thursday and Saturday and place des Prêcheurs on Monday, Wednesday, Friday and Saturday.

Note: don't even think about trying to park near by on market days. Any cars parked the night before in spaces reserved for the market, will be towed away.

– **Antique book market**: first Sunday of the month on the place de l'Hôtel de Ville, 9am–6pm.

Excursions around Aix

ROQUEFAVOUR AQUEDUCT

Situated 12 kilometres (7.5 miles) west of Aix via the D64. Until 1973, this 90-kilometre (56-mile) aqueduct, built in the middle of the 19th century, provided the town's water supply. It is almost twice the height of the more famous Pont du Gard. Around the area there are pleasant walks in the Gorges de l'Arc. Ventabren is a typical Provençal village with stepped streets, old houses and mills.

WHERE TO STAY AND EAT

⬥ ✕ **Le Mistral**: 8 rue Frédéric-Mistral, Ventabren. ☎ 04-42-28-87-27. Fax: 04-42-28-87-37. 16 kilometres (10 miles) west of Aix via the D10, then the D64A, in the centre of the village. Phone ahead to check opening times – the restaurant is usually closed in low season on Wednesday, for lunch on Saturday and for dinner on Sunday. Rooms for 380F and menus at 85F (lunch) and 130F. Visitors regularly fall in love with the typically Provençal hilltop village of Ventabren . . . when they finally get there (it's easy to get lost between Les Milles and the Étang de Berre). The hotel has a magnificent view and offers a warm welcome. Have lunch or dinner at *La Table de Ventabren* close by, either in the dining room or on the lovely little terrace with its view over Berre. The food is delicious. Make the trip for the food and the view, even if there are no rooms available in the hotel.

⬥ ✕ **Chambres d'hote Campagne Jeanne** (B&B): 670 chemin des Loups, Les Milles, 13290 Aix-en-Provence. ☎ 04-42-60-83-10. Email: martine@campagne-jeanne.com. Rooms for 290–340F, including breakfast. Dinner for 120F, including wine. This stone house, restored in keeping with local traditions and the environment, is surrounded by fields, but just 4 kilometres (2.5 miles) from the town centre. Private double rooms have terrace, bathroom and toilet. The food makes the most of the flavours of the region.

Around Montagne Ste-Victoire

★ **In the footsteps of Cézanne around Montagne Ste-Victoire**: Leave Aix on boulevard des Poilus and then take the D17. If you have a car, you can drive around the Montagne Ste-Victoire, immortalized by the great artist in more than 60 paintings. The road to Tholonet has changed substantially since Cézanne's time, but you should still recognize his wonderful scenes. The route is about 60 kilometres (38 miles) long; the scenery is magnificent, despite a devastating forest fire around Ste-Victoire in 1989. The fire may have been a terrible disaster, but if anything it has made the Aixois more aware of the importance of the natural heritage that lies on their doorstep.

Cross the route de Beaurecueil and carry on to the village of Puyloubier, which clings to the side of the mountain. In summer, walking in the area is prohibited, due to the fire risk, but you can continue your Cézanne route by making a detour over the Trois-Sautets bridge, which features in a well-known Cézanne watercolour. Make your way back via Picasso's village of Vauvenargues, and St-Marc-Jaumegarde, to discover the northern face of the Ste-Victoire. Here, the landscape is quite different, flourishing as a result of the Zola and Bimont dams.

By bus: on weekdays, there are four buses a day to Vauvenargues, three to Puyloubier and 12 to Le Tholonet.

There are a number of footpaths marked on and around the Montagne Ste-Victoire:

– 9 kilometres (5.5 miles) from Aix, the **Ferme de l'Hubac** is the starting point for a two-hour walk (medium difficulty) to the 'croix de Provence'. Fossilized dinosaur eggs have been found to the north, in the Roques-Hautes.

– 12 kilometres (7.5 miles) from Aix, at **St-Antonin-sur-Bayon**, the difficult route to the 'croix de Provence' begins. The path can be quite dangerous.

– 20 kilometres (12.5 miles) from Aix, **Puyloubier** is the starting point for a four-hour walk giving access to the mountain and climbing up to the Pic des Mouches, at 1011 metres (3317 feet), following the blue markings. The red markings lead to the hermitage at St-Ser.

– 12 kilometres (7.5 miles) from Aix, at Cabassols, there is access to the priory of Ste-Victoire, which can be reached in 1 hour 30 minutes.

WHERE TO STAY AND EAT AROUND STE-VICTOIRE

⚑ **Camping 'Ste-Victoire'**: in the Paradou district of Beaurecueil (13100). ☎ 04-42-66-91-31. Fax: 04-42-66-96-43. 43F per person or 60F for two. The campsite site is 10 kilometres (6 miles) east of Aix, at the foot of Montagne Ste-Victoire, in quiet countryside. Much cheaper and more pleasant than those closer to town, and open all year. Activities include treks, horse riding, mountain-biking, rock-climbing and archery.

🛏 ✕ **Relais Ste-Victoire**: Beaurecueil. ☎ 04-42-66-94-98. Fax: 04-42-66-85-96. Email: relais-ste-victoire@wanadoo.fr. Closed Monday, Friday lunch, Sunday evening, first week in January, a fortnight in February and at All Saints. *Formule* menus 160–400F. Rooms overlooking the grounds or the surrounding countryside for 600F. Standing at the foot of the mountain, the Jugy-Bergès family home has been extended, without losing its ambience. This lively family-run business offers one of the best places to eat in the area, with a bright and colourful interior and an unusual collection of ceramic mosaics. René Bergès' sun-drenched cooking (a little expensive for the average budget) includes poached eggs with truffle cream, sun-dried tomato tart served with grilled sardines and rack of lamb glazed with local honey.

✕ **Les Sarments**: 4 rue Qui-Monte, 13114 Puyloubier. ☎ 04-42-66-31-58. After a wonderful walk (20 kilometres/12.5 miles) along the D17, you reach the foot of Montagne Ste-Victoire. Climb up the main street of the picturesque village of Puyloubier and then the aptly named rue Qui-Monte ('climbing street'). The restaurant is open all year for lunch on Saturday, Sunday and public holidays, as well as for dinner on Friday between June and end August. There's just one menu at 160F, including local wine. The restaurant is now in the hands of René Bergès, son-in-law of the former owner, the legendary Mamie Gabrielle. René's brother serves the

food with great professionalism. The dining room, refurbished in Provençal style, is air-conditioned. The locals from Aix come for the fish soup, the *pieds-paquets maison* (tripe), *souris d'agneau confit* (lamb) and rabbit with cream and ceps (mushrooms).

🛏 **Chambres d'hôte** (B&B): Domaine Genty, route de St-Antonin, 13114 Puyloubier. ☎ 04-42-66-32-44. Rooms from 400F to 450F. This place, full of charm and style and with a pool, is hard to beat in the area.

🛏 **Gîte l'Oustaou de Garagaï**: Puyloubier. ☎ 04-42-66-35-05. Fax: 04-42-66-35-80. Located in a small road that opens on to the main street, this establishment has beds in three- or eight-bed dormitories at 40 to 50F. Half-board available by the day at 150F. The manager designed the accommodation as a mountain shelter, and many reach it by walking along winding routes for 25 kilometres (16 miles). He is also a guide and can give information on all the various footpaths.

🛏 **La Maison des Minimes**: 80 rue des Cèdres, 83910 Pourrières. ☎ 04-94-78-40-98. 24 kilometres (15 miles) east of Aix and just five minutes from Puyloubier on the D17A, towards the Var. Double rooms are 280F, with a view of Cézanne's mountain, or 320F if you prefer a view of the chapel. The hotel sits in the heart of a typical village, which has vineyards and a view of the Montagne Ste-Victoire. The owners, farmers and winegrowers, offer a very pleasant welcome. Their melon jam is particularly delicious and the rooms are quiet.

TOUR OF THE *BASTIDES* AROUND AIX

★ **Circuit des bastides: from Aix to Puy-Ste-Réparade**. This little-known tour of 18th-century *bastides*, or country houses is stunning, especially if you manage to get inside some of them. Usually, the *bastide* owners allow visits only from those on the official route organized by the tourist office (for information, contact the office at 2 place du Général-de-Gaulle, 13100 Aix-en-Provence). However, if you're buying wine, you might be able to see more of the houses, since many stand in flourishing vineyards.

On the outskirts of Aix (2 kilometres from the centre), your first stop is at the *pavillon* (the name used to describe a *bastide* very close to the town) of the Lenfant family. The original Lenfant was formerly the general paymaster; today, his house is the home of the university's faculty of law. If you want to enjoy the view of the grounds (laid out in the 18th century) outside official visiting times, book a room in the adjoining Hôtel du Prieuré.

From Aix, head to Venelles on the route des Pinchinats (the D63). The name derives from the word *peignage* (combing), the activity of the local work-shops, which manufactured sheets in the 15th and 16th centuries. There are two unmissable country houses: **La Mignarde**, former residence of Pauline Bonaparte, and its neighbour **La Gaude** (4 kilometres/2.5 miles north of Aix). At La Mignarde, take time to appreciate the workmanship of the stone dogs, magnificently carved in the studios of Toulon and exchange glances with the many expressive statues. Imagine the harvest festivals that used to take place here, or the peasants bringing the ass milk that Pauline insisted on having when she came here from Gréoux-les-Bains.

La Gaude is the ideal place to unwind and understand the history of the gardens of Provence, a delicate balance of French symmetry and Italianate fantasy. Two centuries ago, the Aixois bourgeoisie, with their servants and belongings, would de-camp en masse from their townhouses to the country, to escape the unbearable heat of the summer months. Family carriages, brimming with trunks full of the family silver and treasures, furniture and carpets, would have passed through the monumental entrance and made their way down the chestnut-lined avenue at La Gaude. The poorer inhabitants of Aix, who would make do with a *cabanon*, or small country hut, would find good employment in helping the wealthy to make their escape.

The *bastide* offered the privileged few a chance to get back to nature for the summer, to enjoy a simple and healthy life, and lovely family parties, away from the public gaze. For those who preferred not to hide themselves away, the warmer months meant a succession of social occasions, from Easter get-togethers to harvest festivals and autumn hunting parties, inviting family and friends to the *bastide* until the advent of the first frosts. The relationship between master and servant was more relaxed, while children and dogs would play freely together in the gardens, where classical-style statues stood alongside simple water features and beautifully coiffed boxwood hedges.

The Provençal *bastide* owners threw themselves into rural life. They were proud to serve their guests with produce from their own gardens and fields, and wine from their own vineyards (no *grand cru* here, just a tasty drop that family and friends would enjoy). Eggs, milk, poultry, fruit and vegetables would be delivered from the local farm.

The reality of the present day is that many *bastide* owners, fearful of burglary and burdened by maintenance costs, are less than keen to open their doors to impromptu visitors. Fortunately, some do still welcome visitors who arrive unannounced, particularly if they are interested in tasting and buying wine.

WHERE TO STAY AND EAT

⚑ **La Pauline**: chemin de la Fontaine-des-Tuiles, just as you leave Aix-en-Provence. ☎ 04-42-17-02-60. Rooms from 750F to 850F. Napoleon's sister, an infamous seductress, had this pretty and secluded house built in large grounds. It has been well renovated and is now a stylish mix of nostalgia and contemporary decor. The swimming pool is in the former pond. Worth splashing out . . .

⚑ **Chambres d'hôte Le Château de la Brillane** (B&B): 8 kilometres (5 miles) from the centre of Aix, on the route de Couteron. ☎ and fax 04-42-54-12-78. Spacious and pretty rooms, full of character and with stylish bathrooms, cost between 350F and 500F in this wonderful, grand house. You can play pool, tinkle on the piano, enjoy a game of *pétanque* or fish for a snack in the pond. If this all sounds too active, the large grounds have lots of quiet spots for some peace and quiet.

⚑ **Chambres d'hôte L'Our du Château** (B&B): 22 kilometres (14 miles) northwest of Aix on the RN7 in the direction of St-Cannat and then the D543 to Rognes (13840). ☎ 04-42-50-21-15. Closed in August. Double rooms 280F including breakfast. Expect a warm, genuine welcome from the Régnaults, the organic farmers who own and run the place. The rooms are decorated with pastoral prettiness and there's a huge pond fed by a spring and the Verdon river for very hot days. No restaurant but there are a few close by. Free parking. Credit cards not accepted.

⚑ **Chambres d'hôte La Châineraie** (B&B): 22 kilometres (14 miles) northwest of Aix on the RN7 in the direction of St-Cannat and then the D543 to Rognes (13840). ☎ 04-42-50-19-01. The house is 3.5 kilometres (2 miles) from the village, via the RD543. Rooms 450F. The atmospheric 18th-century *bastide du plan* is a delight, with large grounds, vines, a swimming pool, a barbecue area, a terrace and a lovely lawn on which to take a siesta.

⚑ ✕ **Le Mas des Olivades**: in La Taillade district, Puy-Ste-Réparade. ☎ 04-42-61-89-39. Fax: 04-42-50-07-25. Located 20 kilometres (12.5 miles) north of Aix, on the D556 and then the D561, the farmhouse is well signposted. Head into the hill for about 1 kilometre after the *tabac*. Restaurant closed on Sunday evening and on Monday, as well as from mid-February to mid-March. Double rooms in the chalet 420F. Menus from 80F to 140F. This popular and well-reputed venue has small, peaceful wooden chalets with air-conditioning and terraces, and a pool. There is a dining room for large parties, so it may be noisy. Free parking.

WINE TASTING AND BUYING AROUND AIX

– **Château de la Gaude**: route des Pinchinats, 13100 Aix-en-Provence. ☎ 04-42-21-64-19. Open all year on weekdays 9am–7pm. This beautiful 18th-century building (*see above*) is well known for its gardens and its wine.

– **Château du Seuil**: 13540 Puyricard. ☎ 04-42-92-15-99. Open all year on weekdays 9am–noon and 2–7pm. This is a 'real' *château*, since its original owner had land rights. Almond trees and vines were grown here. The Italianate mansion and the gardens remain largely unchanged, on the edge of one of the last remaining pretty little country roads.

– **Château de Beaupré**: Les Plantades, 13760 St-Cannat (9 kilometres/6 miles to the north of Aix on the N7). ☎ 04-42-57-33-59. This is one of the loveliest 18th-century country houses in the area. Its fountain, of traditional design, portrays four dolphins spouting water. The owners offer *gîte* accommodation among the pine trees, and welcome wine-lovers to their ancient cellars, with their traditional oak barrels.

– **Commanderie de la Bargemone**: RN7, 13760 St-Cannat. ☎ 04-42-57-22-44. Open Monday to Friday 8am–noon and 2–6pm. This impressive property gives a good idea of what life was like two centuries ago. The surroundings are pleasant and the wine is remarkable.

– **Château de Fonscolombe**: route de St-Canadet, 13160 Le Puy-Ste-Réparade. ☎ 04-42-61-89-62. Open all year during the week. You should be able to take a guided visit to the cellars, although the gardens and grounds are likely to be closed.

SALON-DE-PROVENCE (13330)
Population: 38,137

'God himself knows how good it is to live between
the sea, the Rhône and the Durance.'
Frédéric Mistral

Best known as the headquarters for the French aerobatic team and for a famous flying school, and the birthplace of Nostradamus, Salon-de-Provence is also a good base for visitors wishing to explore Provence. Close to Arles, Avignon, the Luberon and Marseille, in the 19th century it was an important trading centre. It established a solid reputation for the production of olive oil, traditional Marseille soap, and coffee too. Today, its trade is more likely to be in souvenirs of the esoteric doctor, but Salon is still a provincial town on a human scale, and an agreeable place to stay. Take a look at the extraordinary 18th-century fountain, known as the Fontaine Moussue ('mossy fountain'); over the last 250 years, moss has totally covered the stone. In the cool of the evening, enjoy a glass of something or other in one of the cafés on place Crousillat. Every Wednesday morning, there's a farmers' market on and around place Morgan in the town centre.

USEFUL ADDRESSES

🛈 **Tourist office**: 56 cours Gimon. ☎ 04-90-56-27-60. Fax: 04-90-56-77-09. Open in the week, out of season 9am–noon and 2–6.30pm; in season 9am–1pm and 2–9pm. Open Sunday, in July and August only, 10am–noon.

🚆 SNCF train station: ☎ 08-36-35-35-35 (higher call tariff 2.23F per minute).

🚌 Several **coach** companies run services to different towns in the region. Contact the **Direction des Transports et des Ports** on ☎ 08-00-19-94-13 for timetables for the whole *département*.

WHERE TO STAY

☆☆ Moderate

⚓ **Hôtel d'Angleterre**: 98 cours Carnot. ☎ 04-90-56-01-10. Fax: 04-90-56-71-75. Very close to the centre. Closed from 22 December to 4 January. 27 comfortable double rooms from 270F to 310F, with modern facilities, excellent bath-rooms, Cable TV and electric fans. The rooms overlooking the court-yard are less noisy. There is a gar-age, for a fee.

⚓ **Hôtel du Midi**: 518 allées Cra-ponne. ☎ 04-90-53-34-67. Fax: 04-90-53-37-41. Spotless rooms from 310F to 340F, with soundproofing and direct-dial telephone. A stone's throw from the centre, this hotel offers a warm welcome, renovated facilites and a Provençal menu.

⚓ **Hôtel Vendôme**: 34 rue du Maréchal-Joffre. ☎ 04-90-56-01-96. Fax: 04-90-56-48-78. Email: hotelvendome@ifrance.com. Open all year round. Double rooms from 280F to 300F. The rooms overlook-ing the cool, charming patio are particularly nice, painted in Proven-çal colours. All the rooms have cable TV, excellent bedding and huge, slightly retro, bathrooms. The wel-come is kind and old-fashioned in the best sense.

⚓ **Grand Hôtel de la Poste**: 1 rue des Frères-Kennedy. ☎ 04-90-56-01-94. Fax: 04-90-56-20-77. Right at the top of cours Carnot. Rooms 190–260F. It may be less well known than the mossy fountain that cools the little square outside the main entrance, but the Grand Hôtel de la Poste has its own place in Salon's history. The present owners have a great sense of hospitality and are happy to give all sorts of infor-mation about the area. Their hotel is a very good town-centre stop.

Campsite

⚓ **Camping Nostradamus**: route d'Eyguières. ☎ 04-90-56-08-36. Fax: 04-90-56-65-05. ☒ Email: gilles.nostra@wanadoo.fr. 5 kilo-metres (3 miles) north of Salon on the CD17. Closed between 1 No-vember and 28 February. 80F per night for two people on the camp-site; studios or chalets also available for 240F for a double room with shower and toilet, plus breakfast. The large-capacity campsite is in a shady spot near the canal and has a swimming pool. There's a regular bus service (six a day) between Arles and Salon. Free car park.

WHERE TO EAT

☆☆ Moderate

✕ **Regain**: 13 place Neuve. ☎ 04-90-56-11-04. Closed Sunday even-ing and Monday. Menus cost 100F and 175F. 'Aïoli special' for 130F, including wine, dessert and coffee, available on Friday lunchtime (order in advance between September and May). Little restaurant sitting quietly at the foot of the steps leading to Château de l'Empéri, with a terrace for sunny days, serving Provençal cooking in the old tradition.

✕ **La Salle à Manger**: 6 rue du Maréchal-Joffre. ☎ 04-90-56-28-01. Closed Sunday evening and Monday. Two *formule* menus for 89F and 135F; the second including a starter and a main course. A lovely choice of desserts (about 45F). At this restaurant, the Miège family offer a new slant on rococo with an amazing transformation of the 19th-

BOUCHES-DU-RHÔNE

century mansion, using very contemporary colours, successful richly flavoured cooking and unbelievable prices.

✕ **La Brocherie des Cordeliers**: 20 rue d'Hozier. Near place du Général-de-Gaulle. ☎ 04-90-56-53-42. Closed Sunday evening and Monday as well as in early May. Menus from 70F to 120F and a well-priced grill *formule* menu at 60F. Housed in the 13th-century chapel where Nostradamus was once buried, this restaurant's speciality is *noisette d'agneau au beurre d'herbes* (lamb noisettes with herb butter). It's best in winter or in the evening, when customers really let go.

✕ **Le Vincennes**: route de Pélissannes. ☎ 04-90-42-08-67. On the way out of town. Closed Tuesday and Saturday lunch. Menus for 75F (weekday lunch), from 98F to 175F with an *assiette de gargantua* for 150F. This is *the* place for meat-eaters, serving the best and largest portions of steak *tartare* in the whole of Aix and its surrounding area (or so they claim). The owner was a driver in trotting races, hence the name, which refers to a racecourse. Some customers come from miles away to enjoy homemade charcuterie, tasty carpaccio and tender, pan-fried meat dishes served with sauces. Loads of people and loads of space both indoors and out on the terrace under the trees.

WHERE TO STAY IN THE AREA

🛏 **Chambres d'hôte**: B&B with Alain and Marie-Jehanne Martini, 12 rue des Moulins, in Grans. 5 kilometres (3 miles) southwest. ☎ 04-90-55-86-46. Take the little road that runs along the side of the village post office; turn left at the end; the house is on the steep part of the road. Closed in December and January. 300F for two, including breakfast. Two attractive rooms in a delightful old olive mill, with an odd little swimming pool on the terrace and a warm welcome. No meals, but there are restaurants in the village. Car park.

🛏 **La Magnanerie**: montée de la Glacière, à Grans. ☎ 04-90-55-98-96. B&B from 350F to 500F in a white-stone, vine-covered country house in the heart of the town, with a jasmine- and honeysuckle-scented garden. This unusual place has beautiful rooms, and serves delicious breakfasts to the calming sound of classical music.

🛏 **Chambres d'hôte Mas de Raiponce**: in the Adane district of La Barben, 8 kilometres (5 miles) away. ☎ 04-90-55-31-70. Double room around 280F including breakfast. This Provençal farmhouse, lost in the meadows and surrounded by crops, offers three country-style rooms. On sunny days you can take breakfast outside under the plane trees. This is a good place to stay with children (the owners have seven of their own), but animals are not allowed. Families will enjoy nearby La Barben zoo.

WHAT TO SEE

★ **Château-Musée de l'Empéri**: ☎ 04-90-56-22-36. Open 10am–noon and 2–6pm between 1 October and 31 March, and non-stop from June to September. Closed on Tuesday, 1 May, at Christmas and on New Year's Day. Entrance fee: 20F (concessions 15F). The oldest and most substantial medieval fortress in Provence houses a museum of French military history, second in importance only to the museum at Les Invalides, in Paris. The rich collection covers the period from the reign of Louis XIV to the end of World War I, and includes rooms of exhibits from the First and Second Empires.

★ **Musée de Salon et de La Crau**: avenue R.-Donnadieu. ☎ 04-90-56-28-37. ♿ (partially). Open during the week 10am–noon and 2–6pm (until 6.30pm in July and August), and at the weekend from 2–6pm only. Entrance fee: 20F (concessions 15F). This museum covers the late 19th-century history of the manufacture of traditional Marseille soap and olive oil. A working model shows the history of Salon and La Crau. There's a collection of local stuffed birds from what was the last desert area in France and exhibitions of works by local landscape painters. The only museum focusing on Marseille soap, it is very 'local' but interesting.

★ **Nostradamus's house**: rue Nostradamus. ☎ 04-90-56-64-31. Open 9am–noon and 2–6pm, September to end May; 9.30am–noon and 2–6.30pm, 1 July to end August. Closed on some public holidays. Michel de Nostredame (Nostradamus) settled in Salon in 1547. He was a physician and astrologer and his growing fame was enhanced when Catherine de Médici came to have a horoscope drawn up for her baby Charles IX, who became king of France. Nostradamus wrote his famous book of predictions, *Les Centuries*, in Salon; for centuries, people all over the world have been trying to decipher them. According to some interpretations, he foretold that the end of the 20th century would be marked by a succession of wars, revolutions and upheavals, heralding the predicted reign of the Antichrist.

Salon has become 'Nostradamus Land', with sweets and statues in his likeness on sale in all the tourist shops, and even a clothes shop claiming to be 'By appointment to Michel de Nostradamus'. A wax museum dedicated to him, and retracing his life, is housed in a building in which he is alleged to have lived.

★ **Musée Grévin de la Provence**: place des Centuries. ☎ 04-90-56-56-30. Same opening hours as Nostradamus's house (combined tickets available). Closed on Saturday morning and Sunday morning. The history of Provence (using mythical and real historical characters), recounted in 17 waxwork scenes – very kitsch.

★ **Marius Fabre soap factory**: 148 avenue Paul-Bourret. ☎ 04-90-53-24-77. Open for visits on Monday and Thursday at 10.30am (except between Christmas and New Year's Day and on public holidays). In the 19th century, Salon developed an important market in olive oil, and in the Marseille soap manufactured from the oil. This factory was built in 1900 and is typical of the era. You can also see the remains of pseudo-baroque villas built during this successful period by a number of wealthy soap magnates.

★ **St-Laurent collegiate church**: Nostradamus is buried in this Gothic church.

★ **Porte de l'Horloge** (clock gate): the remains of the ramparts built in the 18th century.

BOUCHES-DU-RHÔNE

FESTIVALS

– **Festival de Jazz Off** (fringe jazz festival): held in the streets at the beginning of August. Information from the Café des Arts: ☎ 04-90-56-00-07.

– **Festival d'Orgue de Barbarie** (organ festival): held every two years, either in May or September. Information available from the tourist office.

– **Évolution et entraînement de la patrouille de France** (development and training of the French aerobatic team): for more information, call the air base: ☎ 04-90-53-90-90 or just look up at regular intervals!

In the Surrounding Area towards St-Martin-de-Crau

The 55,000-hectare (212-square-mile) Crau plain stretches out to the west of Salon-de-Provence (known until recently as Salon-de-Crau). Some claim that it was created by the River Rhône and its alluvial deposits, but others believe it's the natural delta of the Durance river. The name comes from *craou*, a local word meaning 'stony terrain'.

This unique natural environment is traversed by large flocks of sheep and (in smaller groups) tourists. In the 16th century, following irrigation work undertaken by Adam de Craponne, the area began to be transformed into a larger, much greener environment, expanding towards the south. Gone was the dry terrain for which the area had become famous.

Today, 11,500 hectares (44 square miles) remain, covered with round pebbles of all shapes and sizes, offering refuge to several species of birds.

Learn from the story of one of Mistral's characters, Mireille, who crossed the plain and ended up dying on the steps of the church of Les Saintes-Maries-de-la-Mer! Wear a hat in the summer, to ward off the fierce sun.

ST-MARTIN-DE-CRAU

USEFUL ADDRESS

🛈 **Tourist office**: St-Martin-de-Crau ☎ 04-90-47-38-88.

WHERE TO STAY AND EAT

🛏 **Château de Vergières**: on the D24, follow signs for Vergières. ☎ 04-90-47-17-16. Fax: 04-990-47-38-30. Email: vergieres@vergieres.com. Excellent rooms from 850F to 1,200F in an incredible building in large and peaceful grounds dotted with ancient trees. Drive along the narrow road until the pebbles run out, when you will see the avenue that leads to the chateau. It's one way of entering a different world, but at a price.

✖ **Mas de la Closière**: route de Moules Caphan. ☎ 04-90-47-31-09. Closed on Wednesday. Menus at 60F (lunchtime), 90F and 160F for dinner. This pleasant little farmhouse-inn has country-style decor and serves classic fare, such as *boeuf gardian* (beef in local style). There's a terrace in the garden and free parking.

WHAT TO SEE

★ **Écomusée de la Crau**: boulevard de Provence. ☎ 04-90-47-02-01. Housed in a former sheepfold, near the church, this museum is open all year 9am–noon and 2–6pm. Entrance free. Find out more about the conservation of the flora and fauna of La Crau, its famous hay and the farming traditions of the area, with an exhibition of antique tools. For bird-watchers, there is access to the observatory of the Peau de Meau reserve. Regional produce and books are on sale in the shop.

FESTIVAL

– **Musique aux Aulnes**: festival of symphony music held at the end of July.

The Camargue

The Camargue is an 'island', hovering between Arles to the north and the Mediterranean to the south, separated from the rest of France by the two branches of the Rhône river. This flat, sparsely inhabited land, created by centuries of alluvial deposits and shored up at the end of the 19th century, became a protected zone in 1967.

There are plenty of bridges and viewing points over the marshland and the dunes, but it's not easy for the visitor to get to grips with the Camargue. The people do not demean themselves with superficial celebrations of their 'folklore'. Their unusual customs remain vivid and visible as a part of everyday life. You may no longer see traditionally costumed gypsies in caravans with guitars, but the native white horses and black bulls – the symbols of the region – are still herded and tended by *gardians*. These 'cowboys', in their black felt hats, flowered shirts, black velvet waistcoats, moleskin trousers, leather boots and knotted scarves, are a common enough sight, but they don't go out of their way to welcome tourists. The Camargue locals have a real fear that their extensive woods, saltmarshes, lakes, pastures and sand dunes will be ruined by visitors, before being overwhelmed by rising water levels.

The king of the Camargue is not the white horse or the greater flamingo, but the black bull. Different from the Spanish bull, it is destined not for death in a bullfight but bred to run free in the popular *courses Camargue* (*see* page 87). From the road between Arles and Les Saintes you may well be able to see the bulls being herded.

The economic activity in the Camargue varies throughout the region, depending on the salinity of the soil. The lowest land, around the Étang du Vaccarès, is dedicated to rice-growing and cattle-rearing. Fishing is done from flat-bottomed boats, propelled by a pole on the lakes and in the wide canals. Eel and mullet seem to appear on every menu, but the real speciality of the area is the *telline*, a small shellfish, cooked with a little garlic and parsley or a touch of *aïoli* (garlic mayonnaise). The cooking of the Camargue reflects the region: hearty, wholesome dishes, intended as nourishment for people who have spent a long time in the saddle – a good portion of grilled

BOUCHES-DU-RHÔNE

sea bass, for example – are more common than the *bouillabaisse* or *bourride* enjoyed on the other side of the river.

ARLES (13200)   Population: 51,614

Battered by the mistral, scorched by the sun and watered by the Rhône, Arles is a town of ancient stones. The soft-coloured blocks used for the belfry of the town hall and the neat 17th-century houses, and the St-Trophime cloister, a fine example of high Romanesque style, are reminiscent of Rome. But Arles is far more than a museum of a town. Standing at a crossroads, it has played a significant role in history, but today bullfighting and photography add to the liveliness of the town. Fashion has been important here, too, since flamboyant French designer Christian Lacroix began to look to his Arles roots for colour and inspiration.

Wander along Arles' narrow streets, through its squares and past the noble facades of the buildings. On the place du Forum, you can't avoid the bronze statue of Frédéric Mistral. Here, every year at the festival (*see* page 183, 'Festivals'), the 'Queen of Arles' makes a bow to the winner of the 1904 Nobel Prize for Literature. But don't linger too long when the town's delightful bistrots are open. Between Easter and September, the season of *corridas* and fairs, the town and its eateries are alive with hoards of noisy locals and visitors.

Parking: you can leave your car overnight in place Lamartine or on the boulevards, but be careful on market days, as cars parked in traders' spaces will not be there in the morning.

History

Arles was originally a small Gaulish settlement on the Rhône, before the river expanded into an uncrossable delta. The town's strategic location, between Provence and Narbonne, tempted Roman general Marius to install himself in Arles, which quickly became a major Roman city. The impressive amphitheatre bears witness to the importance and prosperity of Arles at the time when the Visigoth Euric made it his capital. It stood at the gateway to the Rhône valley and held the key to Provence and Languedoc.

St Trophime, a friend of St Paul, is thought to have been the first bishop of Arles, and the council sat in Arles to decide upon the crusade against the Albigensians (another instance of the rivalry between Provence and Languedoc). As a result of the crusades, many churches were built in the town.

At the end of the 18th century, Charles d'Anjou incorporated Arles into Provence, and the town became a commercial centre controlling east–west trade. Competition with Avignon and other towns, together with the difficult conditions in the hinterland, led to a decline, but Provençal promoters Frédéric Mistral and Alphonse Daudet helped to revive Arles' fortunes at the end of the 19th century. The town's strategic importance came to the fore once more at the end of World War II, when the Allied airforce destroyed the Trinquetaille district and its noble homes in order to incapacitate key bridges and stop the advancing army.

USEFUL ADDRESSES

🛈 Tourist office (C4, **1** on the map): esplanade Charles-de-Gaulle, on boulevard des Lices. ☎ 04-90-18-41-20. Open daily 9am–5pm in summer, 9am–6pm in winter, and 10am–noon on Sunday. 'Arles and Van Gogh' guided tours meet at the station.

■ **Espace Van Gogh** (B3, **2** on the map): ☎ 04-90-49-39-39. Complicated opening hours! It's closed on Thursday and Sunday and is housed in the former Hôtel-Dieu, now beautifully restored, in which Van Gogh lived. The library and media centre are a great success.

🚆 **Train station** (D1 on the map): ☎ 08-36-35-35-35 (2.23F per minute).

🚌 **Coach station** (D1, off the map): ☎ 04-90-49-38-01.

➕ **Nîmes–Arles–Camargues airport**: in Garons (23 kilometres/14 miles from Arles). ☎ 04-66-70-49-49. Shuttle bus run by STD Gard and Autocars Ginoux: ☎ 04-66-29-17-27.

📖 **Actes Sud bookshop**: place Nina-Berberova, on the banks of the Rhône. ☎ 04-90-49-56-77. Open Monday 2–8pm and Tuesday to Saturday 9am–8pm (7pm on Thursday); closed on Sunday. The bookshop sells regional publications from local company Actes Sud and also has an unremarkable restaurant, and a cinema.

📖 **Forum Harmonia Mundi**: 3–5 rue de la République. ☎ 04-90-93-38-00. This record shop is a temple to baroque music as well as a bookshop.

■ **Useful Addresses**

  🛈 **1** Office du tourisme (tourist office)
  🛈 **2** Espace Van Gogh

🛏 **Where to Stay**

  10 Auberge de jeunesse (youth hostel)
  11 Hôtel Gauguin
  12 Hôtel de l'Amphithéâtre
  13 Hôtel Constantin
  14 Hôtel de la Muette
  15 Hôtel de la Poste
  16 Hôtel Calenda
  17 Hôtel du Musée
  18 Hôtel Le Cloître
  19 Hôtel du Forum
  20 Hôtel Mireille
  21 Hôtel Nord Pinus

✖ **Where to Eat**

  30 Le Grillon
  31 L'Arlaten
  32 Vitamine
  33 L'Escaladou
  34 La Charcuterie
  35 Le Poisson Banane
  36 L'Acqua Café
  37 Provincia Romana
  38 Plain Sud
  39 La Gueule du Loup
  40 Le Jardin de Manon
  41 Côté Courr
  42 L'Olivier

🍸 **Where to Go for a Drink**

  50 Le Tropical
  51 Cargo de Nuit

BOUCHES-DU-RHÔNE

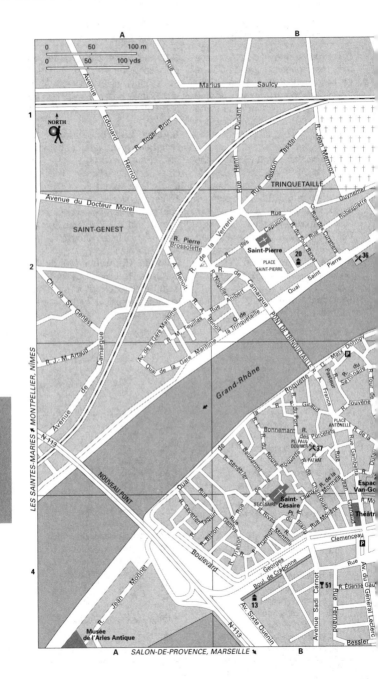

BOUCHES-DU-RHÔNE

LES SAINTES-MARIES ↗ MONTPELLIER, NÎMES

0 50 100 m
0 50 100 yds

NORTH

Marius Saufcy

Rue

Avenue Edouard Herriot

R. Roger Brun

Rue Henri Dunant

Rue Gaston Tessier

Rue Jean Mermoz

TRINQUETAILLE

Guynemar

Robespierre

Avenue du Docteur Morel

SAINT-GENEST

R. de la Verrerie

Rue Capucins

Rue des Curatees

R. Pierre Brossolette

R. A. Benoit

Saint-Pierre

PLACE SAINT-PIERRE

20

36

R. Noguier

R. de Camargue

Quai Saint Pierre

Ch. de St-Genest

R. Anibert

R. M. Feuillas

Rue Benoit

O de la Trinquetaille

Av. de la Gare Maritime

Quai de la Gare Maritime

PONT DE TRINQUETAILLE

R. J.-M. Artaud

Camargue de Avenue

N-113

NOUVEAU PONT

Quai

Grand-Rhône

Marx Dormoy

P

R. du Séminaire

R. Tour de

Pasteur France

R. Roquette

R. Giraud

Jouvène

R. la

Bonnemant

R. des Porcelets

PLACE ANTONELLE

PL. PAUL DOUMER

37

PL. PATRAT

R. Balechou

R. Rouge

R. Gambetta

R. de la Roquette

Espace Van-Gogh

R. Sénébier

Saint-Césaire

PL. ST-CÉSAIRE

R. de la Monnaie

Jean Granaud

Théâtre

R. Mo

R. Saverien Taquin

R. Gallye

R. Rivès

R. du

R. de la Charfouse

Rue Molière

R. Bihlon

R. Trinon

R. Promon

R. Monille

Clemenceau

P

R. Jean Monnet

Boulevard Georges

Boul. de Craponne

Av. Sixte Quenin

Rue

Av. du Général Leclerc

R. Fernand

51

R. Etienne Gau

N-113

Avenue Sadi Carnot

13

Bessier

Musée de l'Arles Antique

A SALON-DE-PROVENCE, MARSEILLE ↘ B

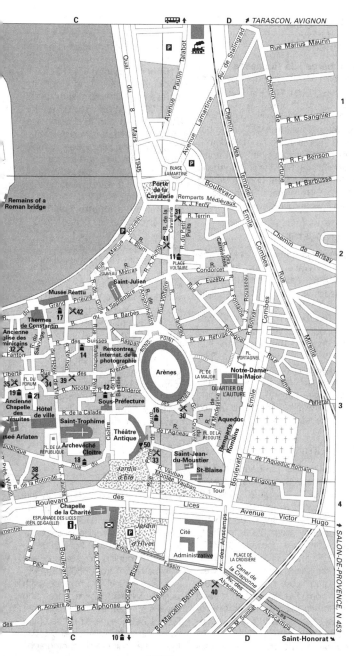

Rue Marius Maurin

Av. de Stalingrad

Chemin de

R. M. Sangnier

1

R. Fr. Benson

R. H. Barbusse

PLACE
LAMARTINE

Boulevard

Émile

Chemin de Brisay

**Porte
de la
Cavalerie**

Remparts Médiévaux

R. J. Ferry

31

R. Terrin

41

11

R. du Petit Puits

PLACE
VOLTAIRE

Combes

R.
Condorcet

2

Chemin des Templiers

Mireille

Rue

**Remains of a
Roman bridge**

Quai du 8 Mars 1945

Avenue Paulin Talabot

Avenue Lamartine

R. de la Cavalerie

Musée Réattu

17 42

**Thermes
de Constantin**

**Ancienne
Église des
Dominicains**

32
Fanton

Liberté

PL. DU
FORUM

35

19 21

**Ancienne
Chapelle
des
Jésuites**

**Hôtel
de ville**

Saint-Trophime

Muséeé Arlaten

République

38

R. de la Rotonde

R. Wilson

Boulevard des Lices

**Chapelle
de la Charité**

ESPLANADE DES LICES
(GÉN. DE GAULLE)

1

Jardin
d'Été

Jardin
d'Hiver

**Cité
Administrative**

Saint-Julien

Grand Prieuré

4 Septembre

R. du Grille

R. de l'Amphithéâtre

R. Barbès

R. Voltaire

Rue du Refuge

POINT

ROND

Arènes

PL. DE
LA MAJOR

R. des
Arènes

12
Diderot

Sous-Préfecture

39

R. Nicolaï

16

R. de l'Agneau

50

33

**Théâtre
Antique**

Archevéché

Cloître

18

**Notre-Dame-
la-Major**

30

QUARTIER DE
L'AUTURE

Aqueduc

PL. DE LA
REDOUTE

R. du Convent

**Saint-Jean-
du-Moustier**

St-Blaise

R. Vauban

Montée Vauban

Tour

Remparts Romains

Boulevard

R. de l'Aqueduc Romain

R. Férigoule

Lices

Avenue Victor Hugo

4

PLACE DE
LA CROISIÈRE

Canal de
la Craponne

R. des Alyscamps

40

Av. des Alyscamps

Boulevard

Paix

R. Ampère

Bd Alphonse Daudet

R. Marcelin Berthelot

Émile Zola

Bd Georges Bizet

Rue Émile Fassin

Ch.-M. Sembat

Alyscamps

Les

Alyscamps

BOUCHES-DU-RHÔNE

SALON-DE-PROVENCE, N 453

WHERE TO STAY

☆ Budget

♠ **Auberge de jeunesse** (youth hostel) (C4, **10**, off the map): 20 avenue Foch. ☎ 04-90-96-18-25. Fax: 04-90-96-31-26. A 10-minute walk from the town centre, this hostel is closed from 20 December to 10 February and has 100 dormitory beds (membership card compulsory), at 80F for the first night and 68F for subsequent ones, including sheets and breakfast. There's also a restaurant serving meals at 50F.

☆☆ Moderate

♠ **Hôtel Gauguin** (D2, **11** on the map): 5 place Voltaire. ☎ 04-90-96-14-35. Fax: 04-90-18-98-87. Closed in November. Double rooms from 180F to 210F, without breakfast. The rooms are simple but well equipped and very close to the amphitheatre. The six rooms that look on to the square have their own balcony and a view over place Voltaire, but the post-war district lacks any real charm. Every morning the local weather forecast is pinned up in the reception area.

☆☆☆ Chic

♠ **Hôtel de l'Amphithéâtre** (C3, **12** on the map): 5 rue Diderot. ☎ 04-90-96-10-30. Fax: 04-90-93-98-69. Email: contact@hotelamphitheatre. fr. Closed in January. Double rooms with shower from 290F to 350F, and with bathroom from 345F to 420F. Internet connection possible in every room. This well-renovated hotel, just a two-minute walk from the amphitheatre and the Roman theatre, has small Provençal-style rooms that are air-conditioned and equipped with safes and hair-dryers. The owner is very

friendly and the breakfast is generous.

♠ **Hôtel Constantin** (B4, **13** on the map): 59 boulevard de Craponne (parallel to boulevard Clemenceau). ☎ 04-90-96-04-05. Fax: 04-90-96-84-07. Closed from 15 November to 15 March (except between Christmas and New Year's Day). Simple but comfortable double rooms from 130F to 280F in a pleasant hotel, which offers a warm welcome and has a private car park.

♠ **Hôtel de la Muette** (C3, **14** on the map): 15 rue des Suisses. ☎ 04-90-96-15-39. Fax: 04-90-49-73-16. Email: jotel.muette@wanadoo.fr. Rooms from 400F to 450F in a 12th- and 15th-century building, entirely renovated in typically Provençal style. Close to the amphitheatre, it has comfortable rooms and a pleasant atmosphere.

♠ **Hôtel de la Poste** (C4, **15** on the map): 2 rue Molière ☎ 04-90-52-05-76. ☎ 04-90-49-80-28. Spotless rooms from 270F to 420F in this renovated (but still not luxury) hotel, just a stone's throw from all the action in rue Molière. Enjoy breakfast on the terrace or in the typically Arlesian dining room, with its pretty frescoes.

☆☆☆☆ Très Chic

♠ **Hôtel Calendal** (C3, **16** on the map): 5 rue Porte-de-Laure. ☎ 04-90-96-11-89. Fax: 04-90-96-75-84. Email: contact@lecalendal.com. ✂ Rooms with shower from 280F to 320F, depending on season, and with bathroom from 380F to 480F. This is the heart of Provence, with brightly coloured fabrics, vases and flowers. Legendary photographer Robert Doisneau used to stay here when he came to Arles and today there are numerous photographs displayed up the stairs. Since his day, the hotel has been renovated and turned into a haven of peace, with a little, shady garden. A few simple dishes and salads are served at tables under ancient trees. There's also a tearoom serving homemade pastries (closed on Tuesday). The bedrooms are air-conditioned, a necessary luxury on hot and humid days. Private and secure parking in the recent extension is an even greater luxury in the centre of town. Highly recommended.

≜ Hôtel du Musée (C2, **17** on the map): 11 rue du Grand-Prieuré. ☎ 04-90-93-88-88. Fax: 04-90-49-98-15. Closed in January. Double rooms from 300F to 400F, and breakfast on a pretty patio at 38F. This town-centre hotel is in a lovely 17th-century house, opposite the Musée Réattu and a stone's throw from the river. A good hotel in a great location, with a warm welcome guaranteed.

≜ Hôtel Le Cloître (C3, **18** on the map): 16 rue du Cloître. ☎ 04-90-96-29-50. Fax: 04-90-96-02-88. Email: hotel-cloitre@hotmail.com. Closed between 1 November and 1 March. Rooms at 250F with basin and toilet and 295F with bath and toilet. The larger rooms on the first floor, with exposed beams and handmade tiling, are more expensive, at 360–390F. This charming provincial-style hotel, built over eight 13th-century vaults, is tucked away on a small and gently sloping street. It's a gem, completely renovated by its owner, with stripped walls and redone floors in the larger rooms. A friendly welcome awaits you and the peace is only broken by the bells of the neighbouring church.

≜ Hôtel du Forum (C3, **19** on the map): 10 place du Forum. ☎ 04-90-93-48-95. Fax: 04-90-93-90-00. Email: info@hotelduforum.com. ✕ Closed from 15 November to 1

March. Rooms from 300F to 700F. This very central but peaceful hotel, a former private mansion, has huge rooms of a certain charm. There's a lift and a pleasant sheltered swimming pool. Picasso is said to have preferred room No. 2.

≜ Hôtel Mireille (B2, **20** on the map): 2 place St-Pierre. ☎ 04-90-93-70-74. Fax: 04-90-93-87-28. On the other side of the Rhône, in the Trinquetaille district, but still close to the town centre. Closed between November and March. Double rooms with a view of the garden and pool from 399F to 630F (depending on the season); half-board compulsory during Easter holiday. Menus cost 110F and 170F. Parking is free, or there is a secure garage, for a charge. Delicious fresh fish and seafood, including *bouillabaisse provençale*, and local meat dishes are served in the large and pleasant dining room. The swimming pool is sheltered behind trees and the welcome is friendly and warm.

≜ Hôtel Nord Pinus (C3, **21** on the map): place du Forum. ☎ 04-90-93-44-44. Fax: 04-90-93-34-00. Email: info@nord-pinus.com. Open all year. Double rooms from 840F to 990F, with breakfast for 75F. According to fashion designer Christian Lacroix (quoted in the hotel), 'This hotel is a part of the collective memory of the inhabitants of Arles. When I was a child, I saw it as a temple to provincial traditions, to worldliness and, above all, to bull-fighting.' Opened in 1865 by a certain Monsieur Pinus, the hotel has had new owners since 1989, but the ghosts of legendary guests still walk the corridors, from Jean Cocteau, Pablo Picasso and F. Scott Fitzgerald to Winston Churchill, King Farouk, and generations of matadors. Their names are inscribed on a glass pane, opposite the lift. Each room is decorated in a different style, and there's also a garage. For a special treat or a romantic tryst, it's perfect. At least have a drink in the bar, which is full of memorabilia about local matadors and images taken by one of the world's greatest photographers, Peter Lindbergh.

Campsite

☎ **Camping City**: 67 route de Crau. ☎ 04-90-93-08-86. Fax: 04-90-93-91-07. One kilometre out of town on the road towards Raphèle-lès-Arles.

From the motorway, take Exit 7, signposted '*Centre-ville*'. Closed from 30 October to 1 March. The site is quite shady but pretty noisy, and there are a few mosquitoes due to its proximity to the marshes. Facilities include a pool, food shop and take-away meals. Mobile homes are also welcome. The facilities have been recently renovated, and a number of activities are organized in the summer.

WHERE TO EAT

☆ Budget

✕ **Le Grillon** (D3, **30** on the map): 36 rond-point des Arènes. ☎ 04-90-96-70-97. Closed Sunday evening and Wednesday. Annual holiday between 15 January and end February. Menus cost 59F (lunchtime) and 85F. À la carte around 120F for a three-course meal. This restaurant-cum-brasserie-cum-*crêperie*-cum-ice-cream parlour may not look much but it has outdoor tables with a lovely view of the amphitheatre and serves lots of tasty little dishes. Booking advisable in summer.

✕ **L'Arlaten** (D2, **31** on the map): 7 rue de la Cavalerie. ☎ 04-90-96-24-85. Closed on Wednesday. Menus from 69F to 129F. In among some fairly uninteresting cafés, this little family restaurant serves well-presented regional dishes that are good for the digestion and for the wallet.

✕ **Vitamine** (C3, **32** on the map): 16 rue du Docteur-Fanton, behind place du Forum. ☎ 04-90-93-77-36. Closed Saturday evening and Sunday, except during the Féria and the month-long photography festival. The menu lists 50 different salads from 50F, 15 pâté specialities from 35F to 48F and a selection of dishes from 40F to 70F. Pleasantly decorated dining room (with tem-porary photo exhibitions), a relaxed welcome and tables outside.

✕ **L'Escaladou** (C3, **33** on the map): 23 rue Porte-de-Laure. ☎ 04-90-96-70-43. Open all year. Menus at 85F, 105F and 140F. The locals love it here, and the owner – a local character who specializes in dressing the women of Arles in their traditional costumes for the festivals – serves a mean fresh fish soup and a serious *bouillabaisse*. The restaurant is full of atmosphere.

✕ **La Charcuterie** (C3, **34** on the map): 51 rue des Arènes. ☎ 04-90-96-56-96. Closed Sunday and Monday. About 90F for lunch and 130F for dinner. A real Lyons *bouchon* (typical Lyonnais bar-brasserie), but in the middle of Arles! Every week, the *patron* goes to Lyons to source products, like the essential *andouillette de Bobosse* (chitterling sausage). The restaurant is in an old 1940s charcuterie (the marble slab and the butcher's hooks have survived). The food is prepared in front of the customers on an old marble counter and the specialities are very tasty. The boss is also a painter and displays some of his work on the walls. In summer, the menu includes salads, grills and tapas and there is room for about a dozen customers outside.

✗ **Le Poisson Banane** (C3, **35** on the map): 6 rue du Forum. ☎ 04-90-96-02-58. ♨ Open in the evening only but closed on Sunday out of season. Menus at 120F and 135F. This little restaurant, behind place du Forum, has a large terrace and serves imaginative 'sweet and sour' cooking and the Caribbean speciality *poisson banane*, daily until 9pm.

✗ **L'Acqua Café** (B2, **36** on the map): on the quai St-Pierre, in the Trinquetaille district. ☎ 06-08-45-91-66 (mobile). Closed on Sunday, lunchtime on Monday and from 15 December to 15 January. *Formule* menu (main course and dessert) for 89F, and an average three-course meal for around 170F. Service until midnight. This trendy place is a sort of floating wine bar/café, on a barge moored in the Rhône. (Remember, Arles was once a river port.) It has a pleasant interior and simple tables, and offers a selection of original salads. Some tables have a view over the old town.

✗ **Provincia Romana** (B3, **37** on the map): 13 rue des Porcelets. ☎ 04-90-49-85-49. Closed on Monday and for dinner on Sunday. Part-deli and part-restaurant, serving Provençal and Italian cuisine, this pleasant place has a tiny dining room and a few tables outside. Enjoy a plate of gnocchi, cheese and a couple of glasses of wine for just 60F.

✗ **Plein Sud** (C3, **38** on the map): 8 rue de la Rotonde. ☎ 04-90-96-94-76. Closed on Wednesday, this pretty restaurant overlooking the street serves dishes at around 70F. It has wooden tables and tablemats made of old press cuttings. The food is imaginative and classic, including dishes such as *andouillette vieux garçon* (chitterling sausage), *lotte à la vanille* (monkfish with vanilla) and *dorade à la citronelle* (gilt-head fish with pumpkin). The

welcome is warm and welcoming. You may prefer to eat inside on hot and humid evenings.

✗ **La Gueule du Loup** (C3, **39** on the map): 39 rue des Arènes. ☎ 04-90-96-96-69. Enter from the street via a small door and go upstairs to the tiny dining room. *Menu gastronomique* at 140F and a special Féria menu at 150F. The owner, an ex-magician, has posters on the walls featuring magic and sorcery, and displays his skills on Friday evening in winter. The menus might include such dishes as Roquefort quiche with dried figs or *gigot d'agneau à la provençale* (Provençal-style lamb). Book ahead, as there are only a few tables.

☆☆ Moderate

✗ **Le Jardin de Manon** (D4, **14** on the map): 14 avenue des Alyscamps. ☎ 04-90-93-38-68. Fax: 04-90-49-62-03. Just outside the town centre, at the lower end of boulevard des Lices, past the police station. Closed on Wednesday throughout the year and on Sunday evening from 15 October until Easter as well as in February and for All Saints. Lunch menu at 85F and others ranging from 98F to 200F, which change with the seasons. This pleasant little restaurant has a friendly owner and a small garden and is good value for money. The food is imaginative and excellent, and the wine list is enormous.

✗ **Côté Cour** (D2, **41** on the map): 65 rue Amédée-Pichot. ☎ 04-90-49-77-76. Closed on Wednesday and for 10 days in January. Menus at 105F, 135F and 198F, all including cheese and dessert. The air-conditioned dining room is superb, with its stonework, beams, traditional tablecloths and red floor tiles. The cooking is classic, portions are generous and the dessert menu is

BOUCHES-DU-RHÔNE

tempting. The welcome from the relatively new young team is charming, if a little restrained.

☆☆☆ Chic

✕ **L'Olivier** (C2, **42** on the map): 1a rue Reattu. ☎ 04-90-49-64-88. Menus at 158F and 248F and a Féria menu at 218F. The huge rooms are painted white, furnished with antiques and reproduction medieval tapestries. The cooking is traditional, with a modern touch, using local produce. The gastronomic menus might include *spirale de saumon et dorade* (salmon and gilt-head) or *filet de taureau* (fillet of beef) served with a black pepper sauce and *tapenade*. It's a favourite with key local figures, but the welcome remains unpretentious, warming up the slightly 'cool' setting.

WHERE TO GO FOR A DRINK

❢ **Le Tropical** (C3, **50** on the map): 28 rue Porte-de-Laure. ☎ and fax: 04-90-96-94-16. ✗ Open daily 10am–12.30am (2am in high season). Closed in January. This bar, between the *jardin d'été* (summer garden) and the amphitheatre, is a beer-drinkers' paradise, with an exotic sheltered terrace. Small meals – mussels or paella, for example – are also available. Credit cards not accepted.

❢ **Cargo de Nuit** (B4, **51** on the map): 7 avenue Sadi-Carnot. ☎ 04-90-49-55-99. Open 8pm–dawn. Closed Sunday and Monday. Music café, tapas bar and wine bar, all open until the early hours, with marine-theme decor, and serving cocktails and beers at good prices. At weekends, gigs (blues, salsa, world music; entrance fee from 30F to 110F) are held in a large room which also serves as an occasional exhibition space.

WHAT TO SEE

BOUCHES-DU-RHÔNE

★ **Arlésiennes**: today, women in traditional Arles costume, complete with lace shawl, ribbons and head-dress, are really only seen during festivals. The costume dates from the beginning of the 10th century and takes ages to put on, with dozens of ribbons to be pinned in place. To find out more, visit Maryse Mincarelli's shop, where you'll find *gardian* costumes, Arlesian skirts and traditional wedding clothes: L'Arlésienne, 12 rue du Président-Wilson. ☎ 04-90-93-28-05.

★ The old streets in the centre, between the town hall, the St-Trophime church and the arena, are delightful for wandering.

★ **Musée de l'Arles Antique** (museum of ancient Arles): Cirque-Romain peninsula . ☎ 04-90-18-88-88. Fax: 04-90-18-88-93. Outside the town, about 20 minutes' walk from the centre. Open 9am–7pm every day, 1 March to 31 October; 10 am–5pm between 1 November and 28 February. Entrance fee: 35F (concessions 25F). A 65F (50F concessions) ticket gives permits entry to the museum and to all the historic sites in the town.

The rather surprising architecture of this large and very successful museum is the work of Henri Ciriani. Many of the displays are worth the visit, from the carved sarcophagi depicting the olive harvest, and a reconstruction of the Barbegal flour mill, the biggest hydraulic mill of the Roman world (see the remains of the original on the road to Fontvieille), to numerous models, such as the place du Forum in the time of Astérix. Daily life in ancient times is brought to life, with a multitude of sarcophagi, statues, artefacts and mosaics, and you can also follow routes on the themes of water, perfume, navigation, commerce or agriculture.

The excavations opposite the museum are in the process of unearthing a Roman circus built in the second century. This is Arles' third (and largest) arena, after the theatre and the amphitheatre, and has been listed by UNESCO as a world heritage site.

★ **Cryptoporticus**: rue Bazé. Entrance fee: 15F. These huge subterranean galleries, ventilated by air shafts, provide a memorable experience. Constructed in 30 BC and probably used for storing grain, they formed part of the forum's structure. Drainage systems are also visible and the lighting is quite dramatic. Claustrophobics may not enjoy the visit.

★ **St-Trophime church and cloister**: next to the town hall, this old cathedral is one of the most interesting Romanesque churches in Provence. The portal is particularly rich, in contrast to the plain interior, which is shown to its best advantage after recent restoration work. The cloister is very beautiful. Built between the 12th and 14th centuries, it comprises two Romanesque and two Gothic galleries. Unfortunately, the sculptures on the capitals are badly damaged. There's a good view of the whole ensemble from the upper gallery. The lovely halls where the monks stored the crops they grew are now used as a venue for temporary exhibitions (often very interesting).

★ **Les Arènes** (amphitheatre): located right in the middle of the old quarter of Arles, this first-century amphitheatre is a little larger than the one at Nîmes. After the Romans left, it was used as a fortress, and village houses and two churches were built inside. In its days as an amphitheatre, it could hold more than 20,000 spectators. It is still used today for shows and performances, which explains the presence of the miles of wiring that somewhat spoil the grandeur of the setting. The external walls are still impressive, however.

★ **Roman theatre**: dating from the first years of the reign of Augustus, a time when Arles enjoyed great prosperity, because of its geographical situation at the crossroads of the Roman roads that connected the Rhône valley to Italy and Spain. It could seat nearly 12,000 spectators on tiers that have been partly restored. The paving on the floor of the orchestra is original and just two majestic Corinthian columns remain in the stage area. The Vénus d'Arles, now housed in the Louvre in Paris, was found in the ruins of the stage and given to Louis XIV in 1683 for the gardens of Versailles. The theatre is still used as a venue for summer events.

★ **Musée Arlaten**: rue de la République, in the Hôtel de Laval-Castellane. Closed Monday, except July and August. Seen as the 'pantheon of Provence' by Frédéric Mistral, who set up this museum in 1896, with the money from his Nobel Prize. Its aim is to show what life was like in the Arles area in the 19th century, with costumes and head-dresses, furniture, and information on crafts and professions. Displays tell the story of the three most important Mediterranean staples: the olive, the vine and wheat. The staff are dressed in traditional Arlesian costume.

★ **Musée Réattu**: ☎ 04-90-96-37-68. On the banks of the Rhône, in the old priory of the Knights of Malta. Open from March to November 10am–12.15pm and 2–6.30pm; July and August, 9am–12.15pm and 2–7.30pm; and from November 10am to 12.15pm and 2–5.30pm. Entrance fee: 15F for adults, 19F for children. An essential stop for anyone who is interested in contemporary art. Displayed alongside old paintings, including one depicting Tintoretto's studio, there are also numerous sculptures and drawings from artists as varied as Prassinos, Bezombes, André Marchand and Alechinsky. At the core of the collection are 57 drawings by Picasso, done in January 1971 and donated by the artist to the town. Even at the age of 90, 'The Spaniard', as Matisse used to call him, was still able to produce as many as eight drawings in a single day. In his creative frenzy, he would often draw on both sides of the paper. There are a couple of very beautiful portraits of the artist's mother, donated by Jacqueline Picasso, and of Lee Miller, an Arlésienne. There is a photographic section in the room on the ground floor.

★ **Les Alyscamps**: the word comes from *Elysii Campi* ('Elysian fields'). This peaceful avenue, lined with tombs under shady cypress trees, leads to a ruined church, the remains of an immense necropolis where, for 15 centuries, many thousands of Christians were buried. Their tombs covered an area almost 2 kilometres long. In the 19th century, the cemetery was cut in two to make way for a railway line. Entrance charge.

★ **Fondation Van Gogh** (Van Gogh Foundation): ☎ 04-90-49-94-04. Fax: 04-90-49-61-32. Email: fondwga@wanadoo.fr. Housed in the Palais de Luppé, built in the 18th and 19th centuries, opposite the amphitheatre. Entrance fee: 30F. Open daily 10am–7pm. Van Gogh stayed in Arles in 1888, living in a four-roomed house at 2 place Lamartine. A version of his famous *La Chambre* (The Room), painted here on a day when the mistral was blowing so strongly that it was impossible to paint outside, hangs today in the Musée d'Orsay in Paris. The light of the south was a revelation to Van Gogh, who completed more than 200 paintings and 200 drawings in Arles alone. The foundation concentrates on the work of contemporary artists (Bacon, César, Botero, Arman, David Hockney, Di Rosa, among others), produced in homage to the painter, and reflects his wish to create a 'studio of the Midi', in Arles. It's a fitting tribute to a painter whose works now fetch the highest prices in the world, but who sold just one picture during his life.

WHAT TO SEE IN THE AREA

★ **Abbaye de Montmajour**: 6 kilometres (4 miles) from Arles. Tours every day 10am–1pm and 2–5pm (non-stop in summer, until 7pm). ☎ 04-90-54-64-17. Closed 1 January, 1 May, 1 and 11 November, and 25 December. Entrance fee: 35F; free on the first Sunday in the month between October and May; concessions 23F; free for under-18s. This exceptional place, where nature and architecture are in perfect harmony, offers a marvellous viewpoint. To begin with there were only a few hermits at the site. Later, in the 12th century, monks drained the marshland and began building the abbey. It was never really completed. In the 18th century, the buildings had partly fallen down, but they were rebuilt more sumptuously for Cardinal de Rohan and the laity, which, little by little, had replaced the Benedictines. The abbey was closed, on the orders of the king.

During the Revolution, the abbey was sold to a rag-picker who, not having the money, pillaged all its treasurers. A property dealer then bought it and rented it out to share-croppers. Eventually, the painter Réattu and others from Arles saved and restored it before it was bought by the state.

The abbey is entered via the St-Maur building, completed by Pierre Mignard in 1713. The Romanesque part of the complex is very rich architecturally, comprising the unfinished higher church, of which only two of the five bays were built, the lower church, and the cloister, probably one of the most affecting in Provence. The writing room and the refectory are still intact. The final stage of the visit is to the Chapel of St-Pierre, part of which is underground. The whole thing is dominated by the imposing mass of the square turret. Van Gogh was overwhelmed by the abbey's grandeur and beauty and often came here to draw.

SHOPPING FOR FOOD

Charcuterie La Farandole: 11 rue des Porcelets. ☎ 04-90-96-01-12. **Au vrai saucisson d'Arles**, chez Pierre Milhau: 11 rue Réattu. ☎ 04-90-96-16-05. Two fine food emporia where you can stock up with *saucisson d'Arles* and other specialities.

Pâtisserie du Forum: 4 rue de la Liberté. ☎ 04-90-96-03-72. Lovely 'retro' tearoom.

Le Mas de Rey: at Trinquetaille. ☎ 04-90-96-11-84. 3 kilometres (2 miles) from Arles, in the rice fields. This typically Provençal 17th-century estate is really worth a visit. The Mazzoleni family cultivate rice, still the most important crop in the 'north' of the Camargue, and produce original and authentic wines. After much research, they use three grape varieties (Caladoc and Marsalan to make red wines and Chasan for white), which are naturally rich and good for the health but also produce good wines on soil that is not well adapted to vine-growing.

Caves du Domaine de l'Île St-Pierre: on St-Pierre island, towards Mas Thibert and Port-St-Louis. Follow the signposts. ☎ 04-90-98-70-30. Phone ahead. Excellent and well-balanced wines produced by Patrick and Marie-Cécile Henry, the third generation of a wine-making family.

Markets: try not to miss the Wednesday market, held on boulevard Emile-Ceombes, and the large Saturday market on boulevard des Lices, which is 3 kilometres (2 miles) long with 600 stalls.

FESTIVALS

– **Fête des Gardians**: held on 1 May, the festival of the *gardians* (the 'cowboys' who herd the famous black Camargue bulls) commemorates the establishment in 1512 of the Brotherhood of St George. After the official salute to the statue of Frédéric Mistral, on the place du Forum, the whole day is dedicated to bull and horse events in the amphitheatre. Mass is held for the *gardians* on the church square of Notre-Dame-La-Major. Every three years, a Queen of Arles is crowned.

– **Fête de la St-Jean**: at the end of June on place de l'Hôtel-de-Ville, with Arlesian dances around a bonfire and blessed bread distributed to the sounds of the fife and drum.

– **Les Suds à Arles**: this huge festival of music from the Mediterranean and Africa takes place in mid-July, with concerts and many workshops. For more information, contact the tourist office.

– **Prémices du Riz** (rice harvest festival): held in Arles in September, this celebration is much enjoyed by the locals. Bullfights are held in the amphitheatre, and there is a huge procession of floats in the streets.

– **Foire aux Potiers** (potters' fair): held during the last weekend in May on the boulevard des Lices. There's also a second-hand market in the same place on the first Wednesday of the month.

– **Pegoulado**: large procession held in early July, celebrating local culture.

– **Fête du Costume** (costume festival): on the Sunday after Pegoulado. The most beautiful traditional costumes and ribbons are fished out of the attic for this event, which involves a delightful parade and culminates in a gathering at the Roman theatre.

– **Les Rencontres Internationales de la Photographie** (international photography seminars). For information: 10 rond-point des Arènes. ☎ 04-90-96-76-06. Fax: 04-90-49-94-39. Seminars over five or six days during the first fortnight of July. Exhibitions carry on throughout the summer, usually until the end of August. Established in 1970, by Arlesian photographer Lucien Clergue and writer Michel Tournier, the RIPs, as they are known locally, attract photographers from all over the world. There are numerous exhibitions of photographs, an *off* (fringe) festival that spills into all sorts of venues, and evening shows in the Roman theatre. Amateur photographers will delight in wandering around the place du Forum or the gardens of the Hôtel de l'Arlatan or the Hôtel du Forum, spotting the great photographers of today and the stars of tomorrow.

THE FÉRIA

The Easter Féria in Arles traditionally heralds the start of the bull season, *temporada*, in France. Thousands of bull-deprived enthusiasts descend on Arles to enjoy the events. The old part of town becomes a pedestrianized zone, and all the hotels are teeming. The restaurants offer special festival menus and orchestras invade the streets, along with kebab and *churros* stalls . . . and, sadly, pickpockets.

Accommodation

If you haven't booked a room at least two months ahead, go to the tourist office, which has a list of available accommodation (including rooms in private homes). If all else fails, you might be lucky in the surrounding area, up to 20 or 30 kilometres (10 or 20 miles) away.

Cars and Parking

Cars are banned from all streets, except boulevard des Lices, where the car park is difficult to get to. There's a free shuttle bus from the car park in the commercial centre (signposted 'Parking Casino') to the centre of town. The tourist office produces a map showing alternative car parks and shuttle buses. Try parking in the Trinquetaille district and crossing the pedestrian bridge. Don't leave valuables in your vehicle.

Dangers and Nuisances

Watch out for pickpockets in the crowds and for thieves on skateboards. Keep your money and valuables well hidden and keep cash withdrawals to a minimum, as thefts often occur at cashpoints. Things can sometimes get a bit ugly after midnight, so be careful and polite, particularly when approached by anyone who has had a drink or two.

What to Eat during the Féria

Many bars and restaurants are happy to serve paella at prohibitive prices (up to 70F for a small plateful), reheated throughout the day. They are an insult to the Camargue rice they contain and a danger to health. Try to go for a *menu spécial Féria*, which can be reasonably priced and still delicious, despite the numbers of people being served.

Another trap is laid in bars serving so-called *champagne* at high prices that is in fact the cheaper (but still enjoyable) Spanish bubbly, *cava*.

Bodegas

For the Féria, temporary food outlets and bars are set up (with permission) under awnings, outside bistrots or in various buildings around the town. They serve drinks until 3am, and close on the dot of 4am. The atmosphere around them is lively and interesting. The following are some of the best among the many:

♈ Le Tambourin: rue du Palais, at the corner of place du Forum. The the social headquarters of the Club Taurin (bullfighting club) of Luc Jalabert (the owner of the Arles amphitheatre). The whole world jostles to buy a drink here.

♈ Peña Richard Millian: behind the tourist office, in the Bourse du Travail. Highly recommended, this is a large and lively spot, never too busy. There's a long wooden counter where you can order a cool glass of *fino* (dry sherry) at 10F and watch local women performing traditional dances.

♈ La Muleta: 2a rue Vauban (behind the tourist office). This is one of Arles' oldest *clubs taurins* (bullfighting clubs), where the events of the day are debated long into the night, with the aid of videos. It gets very technical and passionate. Walk around the building to find the entrance to the *bodega*, housed in the courtyard and in a large vaulted room (the doorway is opposite the Crédit Agricole). Things may start off quietly but they usually hot up during the course of the evening.

♈ Bodega du Vaccarès: 10 rue de la Liberté. A small room and a courtyard, with large counters, owned by Paquito Léal, a bullfighter from Arles. There's a great atmosphere and it's less noisy than elsewhere.

♥ Bigouden Blues: rue Gambetta, next to the *crêperie*. Young Arlesians gather here to enjoy music, sangria and cider in an overheated atmosphere. Opening times depend on the mood of the owner, but he does manage to open up most Saturdays.

♥ Bodega des Étudiants en BTS: on the lower end of rue Wilson, under an awning. Owned and run by students.

Events, Exhibitions and Shows

There's no shortage of exhibitions and events focusing on the local events, and if you really want to talk *toro* (bull!) there are even conferences. Buy a local paper to check what's on, or ask at the tourist office. Every night, in place de la Mairie, there is a public screening of the events of the afternoon.

– **L'Été Dangereux**: excellent bookshop on rue de la Muette, on the corner with rue Raspail, stocking second-hand books, posters and engravings about bullfights. Closed during the bullfights themselves.

– **Les Arènes** (Roman amphitheatre): the bullfights in the magnificent amphitheatre can be seen by as many as 14,000 spectators. If you want to examine all the detail, try to get hold of *Tribunes* (500F), *Premières* and *Toril bas* (400F) tickets, otherwise, you'll find yourself too high up. The seats at the top (still 200F) do afford panoramic views (which you might prefer). Book in writing: Arènes d'Arles BP 42, 13633 Cedex. ☎ 04-90-96-03-70. Fax: 04-90-96-64-31.

A wonderful orchestra, known as **Chicuelo**, plays during the event. The crowds tend to be serious and attentive and noisily supportive of their favourite bullfighters. Take a jumper, as it can get windy.

The smart set like to be seen in the **Village des Arènes**, where sponsors and the town council serve cocktails. You may be able to slip past the friendly doormen and enjoy a free glass.

Where to See the Féria

The focus of the Féria is the place du Forum and adjacent streets. Around the amphitheatre and in boulevard des Lices there are too many stalls selling spicy *merguez* sausages for the areas to be very attractive. Have a look around place Voltaire and nearby streets and in rue de la Cavalerie, where the *encierros* (bull runs) take place.

Around Arles towards Salin-de-Giraud

The *commune* of Arles is an extensive one, made up of the five hamlets of Albaron, Gimeaux, Saliers, Salin-de-Giraud and Sambuc. This is the heart of deepest Camargue at its most authentic.

SALIN-DE-GIRAUD

USEFUL ADDRESS

fl Tourist office: next to the town hall. ☎ 04-42-86-80-87. Open 1 April to 30 September 9am–noon and 4–7pm; Saturday and Sunday 9am–noon. Closed the rest of the year.

WHERE TO STAY AND EAT

fl ✕ Hôtel-Restaurant La Camargue: ☎ 04-42-86-88-52. Double rooms 220F (250F with bathroom). Menu 85F. This lovely building, owned by a director of the saltworks in the 19th century, is entered via a large foyer. An impressive stone staircase leads to the 20 rooms, which are being renovated. Some are already brand new (No. 4 overlooks the square from an enormous balcony). The chef is a fish fanatic, producing wonderful *bourrides* and *bouillabaisse*, but meat-lovers are also catered for with a delicious beef dish, *gardianne de taureau*, served in a wine sauce.

✕ Chez Bob: Mas du Petit Antonelle, route du Sambuc, Villeneuve-Gageron. ☎ 04-90-97-00-29. Fax: 04-90-97-01-15. Closed Monday evening and all day Tuesday. One menu at 180F, for lunch and dinner. Booking essential. This pleasant restaurant, in a country farmhouse, is easy to miss for first-timers, so keep your eyes open. Bob serves comforting food – rib of beef, grilled duck breast – in a welcoming dining room, which has an open fire and a convivial atmosphere.

fl ✕ La Grand Mar: in Gageron, 13200 Arles. ☎ 04-90-97-00-64. Fax: 04-90-97-01-79. Meal with wine around 150F. This former farmhouse was converted 20 years ago by a native Camarguais. Freshly caught fish and meat (usually *taureau*, or bull, in a variety of forms) are cooked in the fireplace in the main room. The airy, light-filled room is decorated with sculptures of birds from the Camargue and most of the guests also come from this area. Dishes are plentiful, and the owner enjoys talking about his region. He has also built a few *maisons de gardians* (traditional herdsmen's homes) next door, which he rents out by the weekend or the week. Each sleeps four to six people and costs 3,300F for a week in July and August, 3,000F in the spring and autumn and 2,500F in winter. Linen costs a little extra.

fl ✕ Longo Mai: in Le Sambuc, a hamlet half-way between Arles and the coast. ☎ 04-90-97-21-91. Fax: 04-90-97-22-92. Closed between 1 November and 14 March. Menus from 100F to 180F. The owner, who has been here for 16 years, was formerly a cancan dancer at the Moulin Rouge, the Folies-Bergère and in Las Vegas. His modern building has pleasant rooms (Nos. 16, 17 and 18 have a little terrace overlooking the Camargue). The menu includes classic dishes such as lamb cutlets with herbs. You can also enjoy horse rides along the Étang du Vaccarès at 80F per hour or 290F per day.

fl ✕ Chambres d'hôte Mas St-Germain (B&B): ☎ 04-90-97-00-60. Follow the route du Vaccarès. At the Villeneuve junction, continue straight on for about 300 metres and take the first road on the right. This pretty farmhouse with green shutters has one room at 280F for two, including breakfast, taken in the large dining room. The family cats will keep you company during dinner with your hosts (95F), which may include *daube de taureau* (beef stew). The owners are farmers and you can join them for a horse ride (extra cost), to help them move the bulls from one field to another for the night.

WHAT TO SEE

★ **Les salines** (salt deposits): the unusual architecture of this village of just 3,000 inhabitants makes it look more like a mining town. Salin-de-Giraud developed at the end of the 19th century to meet the needs of the salt and chemical industries, and was also the site for a factory making Marseille soap. Salt has been extracted since Roman times, and today the salt pans are the most extensive in Europe. From March to September, seawater is pumped into the drying pans through 50 kilometres (30 miles) of canals. When a concentration level of 260g per litre (5ozs per pint) is attained, salt deposits build up through evaporation. The salt is harvested and piled into pyramids called *camelles*. They are the only features that rise above ground level on the Rhône delta. To visit the salt pans, ask for information at the tourist office or call ☎ 04-90-18-41-20. In summer, a small train takes visitors on a tour of the salt pans at night. Even if you choose not to visit, there is a wonderful view towards Piémanson beach.

★ **Musée du Riz** (rice museum): in Le Petit Manusclat rice-processing factory, Le Sambuc, 13200 Arles ☎ 04-90-97-20-29. Open 8.30am–12.30pm and 1.30–5.30pm; at weekends, by prior arrangement only. Entrance fee: 25F. The museum, the creation of energetic rice-grower Robert Bon, traces the history of rice and its cultivation, with displays of implements, machines and documents. There's also a shop selling local products.

★ **Domaine de la Palissade**: route de la Mer (D36), Salin-de-Giraud. ☎ 04-42-86-81-28. ☖ Open every day except public holidays, 9am–5pm. Entrance fee: 15F. This estate offers a number of ways to discover the Camargue. A one-hour horse ride, organized by local herdsman Jean-Marie Reissi, costs 80F, including 15 minutes of guided bird-spotting from a hide. The price is 150F for two hours and 350F for the whole day, not including your picnic. The horses are all in very good condition, and the rides take place on the estate, which is within the protected reserve, so there are no cars or tourists, just peace and quiet, birds and fascinating flora.

★ **Arles beach** or **Piémanson beach**: from Salin-de-Giraud, take the D36. There are great views of the salt pans, flamingoes and all the other wildlife that inhabits the banks of the canals and the Grande-Palun lake. On the beach (be careful, swimming is dangerous), Arlésiens' caravans vie for space with naturists. It's worth seeing, but Beauduc (*see below*) is much nicer.

LA POINTE DE BEAUDUC

La pointe de Beauduc is 17 kilometres (10.5 miles) from Salin, along a not very clearly signposted road, or mud track. The drive takes about an hour. To be safe, park at the back of the beach, near the pumping station.

The Étang du Fangassier (lake) is a haven of peace and beauty just behind the last *cabane des gardes flamants* (flamingo wardens' cabin). From April to mid-July, the warders watch over 10,000 pairs of flamingoes, which breed on the vast expanse of water. They will be only too pleased to give you the benefit of their knowledge of the Camargue and these extraordinary waders. Push on a bit further to get to the plage de Beauduc. In the extreme south of the Camargue, this beach used to be known as the 'end of the world'. The lick of land is brightened up by a small village with a muddle of trucks and buses among the houses, built out of corrugated iron and weathered, wooden planks.

WHERE TO EAT

✕ **Chez Juju**: plage de Beauduc. ☎ 04-42-86-83-86. Closed on Thursday (except in July and August) and from October to April. A meal will cost between 150F and 200F. Juju is a permanent fixture here, along with his huge turtle, caught in the waters around here. There are tables outside, or a small heated dining room for windy days.

Meat-lovers will be disappointed: sole, sea bream, sea bass, turbot and other Mediterranean fish dominate the menu here.

✕ **Marc et Mireille**: plage de Beauduc, next door to Chez Juju. ☎ 04-42-48-80-08. Open in season. Closed Wednesday. Menu 95F. Same fish as Chez Juju and pizzas. They also organize horse rides.

GETTING TO LES SAINTES-MARIES-DE-LA-MER

Take time to enjoy the smaller roads, with their beautiful views of the surrounding countryside.

– The D36B runs parallel to the Arles–Salin-de-Giraud road to the west and is spectacular as it hugs the Vaccarès lake to Villeneuve. The D37 allows you to rejoin the Arles–Les Saintes road.

– Known as the route de Cacharel, the D85A goes from Pioch-Badet to Les Saintes-Maries and is the ideal route to take to get to Les Saintes out of season.

LES SAINTES-MARIES-DE-LA-MER (13460)
Population: 2,509

Les Saintes-Maries is most famous for its gypsy festival, which can be traced back to 12th-century documents, and still takes place on 24 and 25 May. Some say that it has been spoilt by the annual influx of tourists, but the fact is that it has managed to preserve some of its mystery.

The gypsy travellers, or pilgrims, come from all over Europe to Les Saintes-Maries to venerate St Sarah and to carry her statue to the sea. Sarah was the servant of the village's two leading ladies, Marie Jacobé and Marie Salomé, who were forced to flee from Palestine after the crucifixion of Christ. Provençal tradition has it that they arrived here in a boat that had neither sails nor oars. On the second day of the festival, the two Maries are transported to the water's edge, to the place where they are reputed to have landed. A great gypsy festival follows the procession. The *gardians'* pilgrimage in October is a part of the same ritual.

The whole of the Camargue around Les Saintes-Maries is protected. The creation of the natural park, in 1967, ensured that Saintes has not suffered the same fate as the Grau-du-Roi.

Avoid the hotels along the road from Arles, from the north, most of which are very ordinary. There are others that are much more pleasant and peaceful (*see below*), but you will need to book during school holidays.

USEFUL ADDRESS

🛈 **Tourist office**: 5 avenue Van-Gogh. ☎ 04-90-97-82-55. Fax: 04-90-97-71-15. Email: saintes-maries@enprovence.com. Open 9am–9pm April to end June; open until 8pm in July and August, until 7pm in September and until 6pm during the rest of the year.

WHERE TO STAY

As you might expect, accommodation around here is relatively expensive. Prices are at their highest in July and August, so avoid those months. On the other hand, the hotels are not at their best in the winter.

☆☆ Moderate

⚓ **Le Mirage**: 14 rue Camille-Pelletan. ☎ 04-90-97-80-43. Fax: 04-90-97-72-22. ♨ Closed October to end March. Double rooms from 280F to 320F, with half-board at 265F. Restaurant open every evening (except on Sunday). Menus from 110F to 170F. This pleasant modern hotel, in a building that housed a cinema from 1953 to 1963, has an attractive sitting room on the first floor. The ground-floor rooms are rather sombre, but there's a pretty indoor garden and a good restaurant called **Au Fond du Jardin** ('At the bottom of the garden'). The wall-paintings are by Juan Benito, a name that is worth something in this region. The welcome is warm, but the cooking smells do tend to float up to the hotel, even though the restaurant is on the other side.

⚓ **Hôtel Méditerranée**: 4 rue Frédéric-Mistral. In the town centre, near the amphitheatre. ☎ 04-90-97-82-09. Fax: 04-90-97-76-31. There are 14 rooms costing between 230F and 280F. Three are on the ground floor, with doors on to a pretty courtyard.

⚓ **Chambres d'hôte Le Mas des Colverts** (B&B): 1.5 kilometres (1 mile) from Les Saintes, on the Arles road. Coming from Arles on the D570, the *mas* is after Hôtel Le Boumian but before Auberge Cavalière. ☎ 04-90-97-83-73. Fax: 04-90-97-74-28. Simple but excellent accommodation and breakfast on the water's edge, surrounded by ducks, coots, moorhens and herons. Studios or apartments can be rented by the week (from 1,500F to 3,000F) or by the night (from 190F to 250F) and the owner also offers activities such as fishing, mountain-biking and, best of all, advice on discovering the unknown areas of the Camargue.

⚑ Le Mas des Salicornes: on the route d'Arles. ☎ 04-90-97-83-41 or 04-90-97-83-73. Fax: 04-90-97-74-28. Email: lessalicornes@wanadoo.fr. Closed mid-November to end March. Comfortable double rooms, with whitewashed walls, from 250F to 300F. Dinner menu, prepared using olive oil as a main ingredient, for 90F and flamenco evenings on the beach for 150F. Horse riding is one of the many activities on offer, which also include impromptu evenings in the local tradition – traditional food (with a contemporary touch) served with invigorating drinks and story-telling. They can also organize a visit to the wine producers who supply the *mas*, at the Mas de Rey and the Domaine de l'Île St-Pierre (*see* page 183), for a tasting. Lunches are not served, but there are cookery classes for those who are interested. The pool is lovely and there's free parking.

⚑ Le Bleu Marine: 1 avenue du Dr-Cambon. ☎ 04-90-97-77-00. Fax: 04-90-97-76-00. Email: lebleumar@aol.com. ☒ Closed from November to end March (except for New Year). Rooms from 350F to 390F. Very close to the thalassotherapy (seawater) spa and tennis courts, this hotel has 26 tastefully decorated rooms, all by the pool. The welcome is warm.

⚑ Le Mazet du Maréchal-Ferrant: on the D85. ☎ 04-90-97-84-60. 4 kilometres (2.5 miles) from the town centre. Bright rooms for around 320F, including a substantial breakfast. The atmosphere is relaxed.

★★★ Chic

⚑ Mas des Rièges: route de Cacharel. ☎ 04-90-97-85-07. Fax: 04-90-97-72-26. Access via a dyke, reached along route de Cacharel,

on the way into Les Saintes. Closed from 5 January to 15 February. Rooms from 350F to 420F. No restaurant, but snacks are served near the pool at lunchtime. Peace is guaranteed here, although it's close to the town centre. The small rooms, with their pretty furniture, overlook an attractive and neat walled garden. The sitting room has been decorated with great care and had magnificent seats and sofas covered in beautiful fabrics. The bathrooms are a little over the top. Free parking.

⚑ Le Mangio Fango: route d'Arles (D 570). 800 metres from the town centre. ☎ 04-90-97-80-56. Fax: 04-90-97-83-60. ☒ Restaurant closed on Tuesday, lunchtime on Thursday and Wednesday (except in high season and for half-board residents), and between 5 January and 5 February. Spacious double rooms for 350F to 630F (half-board compulsory on long weekends and in August). Menus from 150F to 290F. The rooms in this modern farmhouse overlook marshland and lakes and there are private terraces and a swimming pool in the grounds. The cooking is typically Provençal and there's also a local Camarguais menu based on fish dishes and grilled meat.

⚑ Le Galoubet: route de Cacharel, at the entrance to the village, near the water. ☎ 04-90-97-82-17. Fax: 04-90-97-71-20. Closed 5 January to 15 February. Rooms from 320F to 420F in high season. Located at the start of the track that leads to Mas des Rièges, this is an adequate alternative if the *mas* is fully booked. Although modern and well equipped, with a swimming pool and secure parking, it lacks character.

⚑ Hostellerie du Mas de Cacharel: route de Cacharel, around 5 kilometres (3 miles) from the centre on the D85A. ☎ 04-90-97-95-

44. Fax: 04-90-97-87-97. ✗ Open all year round. Double rooms cost 610F, some with a view over the lake. *Assiettes campagnardes* (platters of cold meats or cheeses) cost 90F and are served from noon until 8pm. A potholed track leads to this very quiet spot, far from the crowds and the main road. The former farm building has been decorated in attractive rustic style, and the sitting rooms are so comfortable you won't want to leave. The dining room has a lovely view over the Camargue and the lakes, attractive tablecloths and an impressive fireplace. There's a swimming pool, free car parking and horses available for hire. Best to book well in advance.

Campsites

⚓ **La Brise**: rue Marcel-Carrière. ☎ 04-90-97-84-67. Fax: 04-90-97-72-01. Email: sainte-maries@enprovence.com. Open all year round, this site is popular with families and has tennis courts near by and a swimming pool. It's near the beach and its prices are reasonable, but there are problems with mosquitoes at certain times. Snacks are available.

⚓ **Le Clos du Rhône**: 2 kilometres along the D38, the road for Aigues-Mortes. ☎ 04-90-97-85-99. Fax: 04-90-97-78-85. Open from mid-April to 30 September. Located between the Petit Rhône and the sea, this comfortable site is more expensive than others, costing from 50F to 70F per person plus tent. It has a swimming pool and bungalows and mobile homes for hire, but lacks shade. Booking is essential in January or February and in July and August.

WHERE TO STAY IN THE AREA

⚓ **Le Mas de Pioch**: route d'Arles, in Pioch-Badet (about 10 kilometres/6.25 miles north of Les Saintes-Maries). ☎ 04-90-97-50-06. Fax: 04-90-97-55-51. Open all year round. Rooms from 270F to 295F. Breakfast extra at 29F. In attractive relaxing surroundings, guests are woken by birdsong. There's some shade on the swimming pool. The 18 spacious rooms are tastefully decorated and you can enjoy a relaxing meal in the garden, as well as horse-riding. Free parking. Booking essential.

⚓ **Mas de Sylvereal**: on the road for Aigues-Mortes, on the edge of the Gard region. ☎ 04-66-73-51-54. Rooms for 170F to 350F. Menu for 110F. This enormous, pleasant farmhouse property is run by friendly owners. Although the main building is on the roadside, it remains a haven of peace and cool, its thick walls built by canny Cistercian monks. The food is tasty, with dishes such as local lamb dishes and fig tart. The Petit Rhône is just near by, perfect for kayaking.

WHERE TO EAT

Generally speaking, menus are pretty similar all around this area. You may find eel and grey mullet offered in the better restaurants but the speciality of Les Saintes is still *telline*, a shellfish that's cooked with a little garlic and parsley or served with *aïoli* (garlic mayonnaise). On the list of starters, you will usually find mussels and fish soup. For main courses, you will inevitably find *boeuf gardian* (locally reared beef) or sea bream.

✗ **Le Delta**: 1 place Mireille. ☎ 04-90-97-81-12. Fax: 04-90-97-72-85. On the way into town, near the church. Closed on Wednesday (except during school holidays) and from 10 January to 15 February. Several menus from 89F to 170F and double rooms from 205F to 260F. Half-board compulsory in August. Local specialities include *bourride*, *bouillabaisse* and *aïoli*. Good family-style cooking served on warms days on the rather touristy covered terrace.

✗ **Le Sauvageon**: route du Bac. ☎ 04-90-97-89-43. 5 kilometres (3 miles) from Les Saintes, near the Sauvage ferry. Menus, from 110F to 150F, include colourful and flavourful local dishes. A huge selection of starters is followed by meat or fish caught by the son of the house and prepared by his father. There's a gypsy atmosphere on Saturday evening (230F per person).

✗ **Mas des Baumelles**: cabanes de Cambon. ☎ 04-90-97-88-24. The complete experience costs 150F, and includes aperitif, wine and a tour of the estate. A cart takes visitors to join the herdsmen for a drink near the former stables, now restored. Then there's a meal eaten at a large table inside, or on the terrace, with a selection of Provençal starters, such as tomato tart or Arles sausage, followed by *toro* or grey mullet and a large dessert.

☆☆☆ Chic

✗ **L'Hippocampe**: rue Camille-Pelletan. ☎ 04-90-97-80-91. Fax: 04-90-97-73-05. Closed Tuesday out of season and from November to mid-March. Menus 128–200F. The restaurant overlooks an enclosed garden and offers a good meal at an attractive price. The classic regional menu includes dishes such as *petite marmite du pêcheur* (fish casserole) or *bourride de lotte* (monkfish stew). Credit cards are accepted, except Diners Club.

✗ **L'Impérial**: 1 place des Impériaux. ☎ 04-90-97-81-84. Closed on Tuesday out of season and from All Saints Day until Palm Sunday. Menus 135–185F. A big notice on the wall declares: 'Former prizewinner at the École Hôtelière, Cointreau Cup 1979 . . . and now selected to appear in the venerable Routard guide.' Choose from *tellines* (small shellfish served in garlic), Provençal fish soup, beef fillet with an African groundnut sauce or the fish dish *capitaine à la vanille*. There's a small sheltered terrace.

WHAT TO SEE AND DO

★ **Église des Saintes-Maries** this is a typical village church from the outside, but the rough seas made fortifications necessary. The very lovely interior is Romanesque in style, in stone of different shades of green. Put money in the slot to switch on the time-controlled lighting. Follow in the footsteps of countless pilgrims and go down to the crypt, which contains the relics of St Sarah and a strange jewel-covered statue of her. The upper chapel, which contains shrines to the saints, is in the process of being restored. Climb up to the roof (for a charge) for a splendid view of the vast plain surrounding the town, and of the old town itself, the port, the sea and the whole of the Camargue. The scene is particularly splendid at sunset.

★ **Parc Ornithologique du Pont de Gau** (Pont de Gau bird sanctuary): 4 kilometres (2.5 miles) before Les Saintes, going north on the road from

Arles. Near the information centre at Ginès. ☎ 04-90-97-82-62. Open all year from 9am (10am in winter) to sunset. Entrance: 35F. The sanctuary gives visitors the chance to see the birdlife of the Camargue, either in aviaries or flying free. In summer, go early in the morning or at the end of the afternoon, because there are no trees and it does get really hot.

★ **Château d'Avignon**: ☎ 04-90-97-58-58. Open from 1 April to 31 October (closed 1 May). This splendid group of buildings is a lovely place to visit. In the grounds, a botanical trail winds its way past around 30 species of plants, some rare in the Camargue.

– **Boat trips**: several companies offer excursions, mostly departing from the port in the town centre or from the road along the sea, to the west of Les Saintes. Ask at the tourist office for details. Four boats, one a paddle-boat, operate from mid-March to mid-September, travelling up the Petit Rhône to the Petit Sauvage ferry.

– **The Camargue by flat-bottomed boat**: ☎ 04-90-97-94-59. An alternative way of exploring this fascinating area, for keen fishermen or sun-worshippers. Groups of a maximum of six people for an afternoon cost 160F, while an entire day is 320F, including picnic.

– **The Camargue in a four-wheel-drive**: Gilbert Arnaud, Mas Lou Rayas, route de Sylvéréal. A two-hour trip (book ahead) costs 150F, with children half price. This is an enjoyable way to get up close to the Camargue, although critics say it damages the paths. See parts of the Camargue that other tourists don't reach, the hiding places of wasps' nests and rabbit warrens.

★ **The sea dyke**: built in 1857 and 1858, the dyke is closed to cars but not to mountain bikes. Leave your car in the car park and set off on foot. The dyke is 200 metres (656 feet) in length and leads to the Phare de Gacholle (lighthouse). You can carry on as far as Salin-de-Giraud if you're feeling energetic. All sorts of creatures live between the pools and the sand – sand lizards, purple and grey herons, teal, grass snakes, great bitterns, herring gulls and southern tree frogs.

– **Touring the Camargue**: the Camargue is not a zoo, but a protected natural reserve, which every visitor has a responsibility to safeguard from any form of pollution. Although used to cars, the animals are wild. Drive slowly, using the tracks when it's dry enough (the IGN map of the area is excellent). Don't go off-track, particularly in a four-wheel-drive. To observe the animals, stop your car engine and watch them from inside your vehicle. If you want to get closer, park at a distance of 100–150 metres from the animals and walk, trying to hide behind bushes or grass. Take binoculars (as powerful as possible). Photographers will need at least a 400mm lens.

FESTIVALS

– **Grand Pelèrinage des Gitans** (gypsy pilgrimage): Europe's largest gypsy festival takes place on 24 and 25 May, with hundreds gathering to pay their respects to their patron saint, St Sarah (*see* page 189).

– **La Féria du Cheval**: this three-day festival celebrating the horse takes place in mid-July, with flamenco, *abrivado, novilada, pégoulado, concours* *de doma Vaquera* and all sorts of horse displays can be enjoyed (*see* page 184).

– **La Fiesta Vierginenco**: end July. Frédéric Mistral introduced this festival, in which 15-year-old girls wear traditional costume and head-dresses for the first time. After the Provençal mass, an *abrivado* is followed by the blessing of the bulls and horses in the arena. There's a large procession in the late afternoon and events are held in the amphitheatre.

LEAVING THE CAMARGUE

If you've survived the mosquitoes and your fellow tourists, watch the flamingoes for the last time, before taking time to retrace your tracks on the smaller roads to Arles.

Les Alpilles

You won't always find Les Alpilles marked on a map, but this chain of hills sits between Avignon to the north and Arles to the south, and stretches between Tarascon (to the west of Salon) and the east. Its most famous villages are concentrated around Les Baux-de-Provence and St-Rémy.

A geological extension of the Luberon, the Alpilles owe their name to their rough landscape. Dante sited the gates of Hell in the Vallée des Baux, where, according to legend, witches used to live. If 'hell is other people', then summer, when the Alpilles are plagued by tourists star-spotting in St-Rémy or swarming over the must-see site of Les Baux, is not the time to be here. There are two options to avoid them: either use the little side roads round about or come out of season, when the light has a wonderful quality and the weather can be exceptional. It is worth working out a route that allows you to have the sun at your back.

Visit the area at the end of autumn or in winter, to take advantage of the mild climate and lower prices, and the delights of the olive harvest and the Christmas markets. Summer may not be paradise here, but Christmas Eve is magical, with the sounds of festive song coming from the church of Les Baux, and locals thronging the streets to grab a seat at the most famous of Provençal midnight Masses (*see* page 204).

BOUCHES-DU-RHÔNE

ST-RÉMY-DE-PROVENCE (13210)
Population: 10,007

St-Rémy is a typical Provençal town, with its main avenue shaded by plane trees, encircling old streets baking in the sun. Add the stunning view of the Alpilles and it's easy to see how the charm of this well-preserved town has attracted an invasion of second-home owners and, with them, soaring house prices.

There are different approaches to visiting this much-loved town. You can follow in the footsteps of Nostradamus (1503–66) who was born here, or of

Van Gogh, who spent the last year of his life in the hospice of St-Paul-de-Mausole. You could spend your time lounging on the terraces of the bistrots favoured by the local smart set, or you could visit the Renaissance palaces. Alternatively, you could simply go where your mood takes you, breathing in the scents of Provence – at their most pungent on Wednesday mornings, when the market is in full swing.

USEFUL ADDRESS

🛈 **Tourist office**: place Jean-Jaurès. ☎ 04-90-92-05-22. Fax: 04-90-92-38-52. Open every day in summer, 9am–noon and 2–7pm (Sunday 9am–noon); 9am–noon and 2–6pm in winter (closed Sunday). This welcoming office provides lots of printed information for nature-lovers and walkers. For example, you can take a night walk with an ornithologist to spot archduke owls, of which the Alpilles has the largest population in the world.

WHERE TO STAY

☆☆ Moderate

⬧ **Le Cheval Blanc**: 6 avenue Fauconnet. ☎ 04-90-92-09-28. Fax: 04-90-92-69-05. ♿ Closed November to end January. Renovated double rooms with TV, shower and toilet from 280F to 310F. This hotel is a reliable bet, particularly since it has secure parking, right in the centre of St-Rémy. There's also a pleasant terrace and a veranda.

⬧ **Hôtel de la Caume**: on the road to Cavaillon, 2.5 kilometres (1.5 miles) from St-Rémy. ☎ 04-90-92-43-59. Fax: 04-90-92-06-11. Closed 15 November to 15 March (except for reservations). Double rooms 275F to 335F. The rooms are more or less protected from the noise of the road by a pretty garden and some look right onto it. There's a swimming pool, *pétanque*, games for children, table tennis and mountain bikes. Hotel parking.

⬧ **Le Chalet Fleuri**: 15 avenue Frédéric-Mistral, route de Maillane. ☎ 04-90-92-03-62. Fax: 04-90-92-60-28. Closed from end of November to early March. Restaurant closed on Tuesday from October to mid-March. Double rooms cost from 250F to 290F. Half-board 600F. This peaceful, old-style family *pension* has a small garden with laurels and a pomegranate tree. It's the ideal place for breakfast, or for a stroll as you wait to take your table for an evening meal alongside the local regulars. The rooms are simple, functional and furnished with all sorts of interesting things. Cars can be parked safely at the end of the garden.

☆☆☆ Chic

⬧ **Villa Glanum**: 46 avenue Van-Gogh. ☎ 04-90-92-03-59. Fax: 04-90-92-00-08. Email: villaglanum@wanadoo.fr. Near the Glanum excavations, just 800 metres from the town centre. Closed 15 October to 15 March. Double rooms from 300F to 430F. Both Alphonse Daudet and Vincent Van Gogh stayed in this good two-star hotel, which today has a family atmosphere and offers a friendly welcome. The prices are a little high because there's a swimming pool, a big, shady garden, a terrace and a car park.

⬧ **Hôtel du Soleil**: 35 avenue Pasteur. ☎ 04-90-92-00-63. Fax: 04-90-92-61-07. Email: hotelsoleil@wanadoo.fr. Closed November to March. Double rooms with bath and shower from 306F to 395F. Housed in a former factory, this spacious hotel is arranged round a large courtyard. There's plenty of room to park cars, for free, and there's also a garage (for an extra charge). There's a swimming pool and terrace, and a games room separate from the sitting room. The 15 rooms aren't very big but, as the owner says, 'You don't stay in your room much when you're in St-Rémy'. A deposit will secure a reservation.

🛏 **Hôtel Ville Verte**: place de la République. ☎ 04-90-92-06-14. Fax: 04-90-52-56-54. Located just out of the centre. Closed in January. Rooms range from doubles with shower at 220F, to those with bath and toilet, TV and balcony, up to 280F. Menus at 80F and 100F. In 1863, Charles Gounod lived here, in room No.9, and composed his opera *Mireille*. There's an indoor swimming pool (heated in winter), a pleasant courtyard and terraces. This successful hotel, a maze of corridors, is run exclusively by women.

🛏 **Le Castelet des Alpilles:** 6 place Mireille. 200 metres from the tourist office. ☎ 04-90-92-07-21. Fax: 04-90-92-52-03. Open from April to end of October. Rooms from 255F to 530F (the more expensive ones have a terrace). Buffet breakfast 50F. This cosy hotel has annexe buildings all along its shady garden and a secure garage.

🛏 **Hôtel L'Amandière**: avenue Théodore-Aubanel. ☎ 04-90-92-41-00. Fax: 04-90-92-48-38. 700 metres from the centre of town in the direction of Noves. ⚒ Closed January to mid-March and from the end of October to mid-December. Double rooms from 300F to 330F. It's hard to find a better hotel of this type so close to the centre of St-Rémy. It's green and peaceful, decorated in the colours of Provence, and smelling of the Midi. The atmosphere is young, with a warm welcome, there's a swimming pool and the rooms are spacious and comfortable. Breakfasts are generous in size.

☆☆☆☆ Très Chic

🛏 **L'Hôtel des Ateliers de l'Image**: traverse de Borry, 5 avenue Pasteur. ☎ 04-90-92-51-50. Fax: 04-90-92-43-52. Email: ateliers-images@pacwan.fr. ⚒ 16 contemporary-style rooms from 660F to 750F. Breakfast 70F. Photo buffs will love this hotel, in St-Rémy's old music-hall, which has lots of pictures on the walls and in the bar and is also used as a venue for lectures. In the very heart of the old village, it's very restful.

WHERE TO EAT

🍴 **Le Monocle**: 48 rue Carnot. No telephone. Closed on Thursday evening, on Sunday and from 20 December to end February. Not far from the Bistrot des Alpilles, this restaurant has become rather touristy, but still offers a very friendly welcome. The menus (38F for lunch only, to 98F) are tasty and inventive. À la carte includes mixed salads in a large bowl for around 50F.

🍴 **La Gousse d'Ail**: 25 rue Carnot. ☎ 04-90-92-16-87. Fax: 04-90-92-14-58. Email: gousse.d-ail@wanadoo.fr. Closed in winter. Last orders at 11pm. Menus at 90F (lunch) and 180F. Come here for a warm welcome, pleasant atmosphere and tasty food, with specialities including steak in garlic sauce, *escargots petits-gris à la provençale* (snails) and *bouillabaisse* (on Tuesday). The good-value wine list includes regional wines. On Thursday evenings, Coco Briaval and his band (his brother) play jazz in an intimate setting. Excellent value for money and highly recommended.

✗ **Le Café des Arts:** 30 boulevard Victor-Hugo. ☎ 04-90-92-08-50. Fax: 04-90-92-55-09. ♨ Closed Tuesday and throughout February. Restaurant closed November to February. About 15 rooms at 210–350F for two people. Menus 130F and 160F. This historic café is one of the oldest in the town, its terrace with an awning on the boulevard, the ideal venue for a Provençal aperitif. In the summer, when the restaurant is open, try the dish of the day: aïoli on Friday, or daube de taureau (beef stew) or rouille d'encornets camarguais (queen scallops with spicy mayonnaise). Alternatively, come for a coffee and improve your French by listening to the latest local gossip at the bar, rather than at the outside tables.

✗ **Brasserie Les Variétés:** 32 boulevard Victor-Hugo. ☎ 04-90-92-42-61. Restaurant closed on Tuesday and in January. Menus at 98F and 138F. À la carte around 150F. This sunny, busy brasserie is a popular new meeting place with a terrace. Treat yourself to a generous salad, a plate of tartare à la provençale, one of the chef's excellent terrines or his côte de toro (locally raised beef). The whole world seems to come here on Friday for the aïoli.

✗ **Chez Xa:** 24 boulevard Mirabeau. ☎ and fax: 04-90-92-41-23. Closed Wednesday and from end October to end March. Menu 145F. À la carte starters and main courses around 60–85F. The main room is more like an attractively decorated flat, with its bistrot chairs, mirrors and film projectors, than a dining room, and there's also a terrace. Innovative dishes on the menu might include parfait aux aubergines

(aubergine terrine), sardines à la sicilienne and filets de rougets au fenouil (red mullet).

✗ **Restaurant Alain Assaud:** 13 boulevard Marceau. ☎ 04-90-92-37-11. Closed all day Wednesday, for lunch on Thursday and from 15 November to 15 March. Really tasty meals for around 150F; for example, fresh tomato and basil buckwheat pancake, aïoli with fresh cod, mussels and whelks and a range of other homely dishes, produced by a chef who's passionate about inventing new combinations of Provençal flavours. The decor is zen-à-la-Provençale with beams and exposed stone, and the wine list is good too.

✗ **La Taberna Romana:** Glanum. ☎ 04-90-92-65-97. On the way out of town on the road for Les Baux-de-Provence. Closed from 30 September to 1 April. Same opening hours as the archaeological site (see page 199, 'What to See'), so only open for lunch. Menu at 65F and average à la carte for 90F. If you're worried that this is going to be a tourist trap, you're in for a pleasant surprise. This is a real Roman restaurant, just next to the excavations. Discover flavours from antiquity, including fegatum (liver), sardines with a sauce Alexandrine, and dulcia (sweets). Try a glass of mulsum, a Roman red wine mixed with spices and honey and dangerously easy to drink.

✗ **La Source:** 13 avenue de la Libération. ☎ 04-90-92-44-71. Closed on Wednesday and in January. Menus for 160F and 230F. Just like the young couple who run it, this is a tranquil and discreet restaurant. Book ahead if you want to sit in the garden. The husband is busy in the kitchen preparing traditional and Provençal dishes, while his wife serves the customers with dishes such as rougets au coulis d'olives noires (red mullet with black-olive sauce) or noisettes d'agneau farcies aux truffes (lamb noisettes stuffed with truffles). There's a pool, but no paddling allowed.

☆☆☆☆ Très Chic

✕ **La Maison Jaune**: 15 rue Carnot, in the town centre. ☎ 04-90-92-56-14. Fax: 04-90-92-56-22. Website: www.franceweb.org/lamaison-jaune. Closed in low season on Sunday evening and all day Monday, and in summer all day Monday, and Tuesday lunchtime. Restaurant closed in January and February. Light lunch for 120F (weekdays only), menus ranging in price from 175F to 285F or the menu-dégustation Provençal at 150F. The dining room could easily feature in an interior design magazine. The welcome is lavish, too, but the cooking is original and there are prices to suit all budgets. Specialities include roast pigeon with Baux wine, roast lamb fillet

with tapenade and warm walnut tart. There's a lovely terrace overlooking the gardens of the Hôtel de Sade.

✕ **L'Orangerie Chabert**: 16 boulevard Victor-Hugo. ☎ 04-90-92-05-95. Fax: 04-90-92-66-28. In low season, closed on Sunday evening and all day Monday; in July and August closed on Monday and Tuesday lunchtime. Annual closure over three weeks in November and three in March. Menus at 114F, 162F and 218F. This well-hidden spot welcomes a prime minister or two on holiday, wine-growers and smart local families. The tables in the garden are prettily laid and the service and decor are chic, yet relaxed. Try the goujonette de merlan au jus de pommes vertes (whiting pieces in apple sauce) or marbré de brousse à l'huile d'olive on what is rather inaccurately called the petit (small) menu.

WHAT TO SEE

★ **Old town**: among the grand private mansions in the old town are the Hôtel Mistral de Mondragon (housing the Musée des Alpilles of local arts and culture. ☎ 04-90-92-68-24. Open 10am–noon and 2–5pm, later in summer), with its terrace overlooking the whole of St-Rémy; and the Hôtel de Sade (which displays archaeological artefacts from the excavation at Glanum. ☎ 04-90-92-64-04. Open daily 10am–noon and 2–5pm, 6pm in summer; closed Monday). A combined ticket to both museums and Glanum is available. Equally interesting is the Hôtel de Lagoy, the location for the headquarters of the Maison de l'Amandier.

★ **Musée des Arômes et des Parfums** (scent and perfume museum): 34 cours Mirabeau. ☎ 04-90-92-48-70. Open every day between Easter and mid-September, from 9am (10am at weekends) to 12.30pm and from 2pm (3pm at weekends) to 7pm. Otherwise, open 9am–noon and 2–6pm; closed on Sunday. Entrance free. A completely seductive and original museum showing the paraphernalia of perfumery. Visitors exit via a little shop which sells reasonably priced balms, essential oils and other magical potions.

★ **Les Antiques** (the antiquities): the name refers to the ensemble that includes the Roman arch and the mausoleum. The rich decoration on the well-preserved triumphal arch celebrates the conquest of the Gauls by Caesar. The mausoleum is also in excellent condition, particularly the four allegorical reliefs on the pedestal showing hunting scenes and Amazons fighting. Unfortunately it is not known exactly who it commemorates, but it was probably built for the grandsons of Emperor Augustus, Caesar's successor.

★ **Glanum**: this is the site of a small ancient town, built here in the fourth century BC, to take advantage of a spring that rose in the Alpilles. Open daily 9am–7pm in summer (5pm in winter); from October to March, closed noon–2pm. You can visit two Greek houses, but apart from that this is a Roman site. The town grew from the first century BC but was destroyed at the end of the third century by the Goths. The ruins of the baths, forum, houses and temples give a good idea of what the town must have been like. At the Mas de la Pyramide, 250 metres away, the farmhouse is still lived in and the farm is still active. There is a Musée Rural (country museum) located in Glanum's Roman quarries, offering guided tours led by one of St-Rémy's well-known characters 'Lolo' Mauron. Open every day 9am–noon and 2–5pm (7pm in summer).

★ **Monastery of St-Paul-de-Mausole**: this very pretty Romanesque church has a charming cloister. From 8 May 1889 to 16 May 1890, troubled painter Van Gogh stayed in the mental asylum attached to the monastery. At the beginning of his internment, he was not permitted to go outside the boundary, so he would paint at his easel in the garden. In one year at St-Rémy, he produced more than 150 paintings and numerous drawings, including pictures of the olive groves, with their tortured trunks, and his apocalyptic vision of a starry night. At the end of the year, during which his mental health had deteriorated, he returned to the north, where he took his own life, just two months after getting back to Auvers-sur-Oise.

★ **Centre Art Présence Van Gogh**: 8 rue Estrine, in the town centre. ☎ 04-90-92-34-72. Entrance fee: 20F. Open from end March to end December (except for two weeks in November) 10.30am–12.30pm and 2.30–6.30pm; closed Monday. Housed in a magnificent 18th-century building, this museum has interesting displays and a documentary exhibition on the life and works of Vincent Van Gogh in Provence, including his letters to his brother Theo and paintings of local places. There's also an information centre.

WHAT TO DO

★ **Van Gogh walk**: organized by the tourist office, this walk takes you to the places that inspired the painter. You can go on your own or with a guide from 1 April to 15 October on Tuesday, Thursday or Saturday at 10am.

– There's a guided walk through the streets of St-Rémy every Friday at 10am.

– Ask at the tourist office for information on two new guided visits: 'Discovering the archduke owl' and 'Aromatic herbs and the flora of the Alpilles'.

★ **Walking, cycling or horse riding trails in the Alpilles**:

– The tourist office produces a brochure detailing various cycle trails and five easy walking trails from St-Rémy.

– *Bike hire:* Locations Ferri, 35 avenue de la Libération. ☎ 04-90-92-10-88.

– Organized horse treks around the region: Club Hippique des Antiques. ☎ 04-90-92-30-55.

Note: in July and August, because of the risk of forest fires, some outdoor activities are restricted in wooded areas.

SWEET TREATS

🔒 **Chocolats Joël Durand**: 3 boulevard Victor-Hugo. ☎ 04-90-92-38-25. Closed Sunday afternoon, Monday and public holidays. This talented *chocolatier* serves his customers personally, while overseeing the making of what he sells. He mixes sweets and chocolates with uniquely Provençal flavours – thyme, rosemary, lavender, liquorice and black olives. You can see how they're made and taste them – with clean hands only.

🔒 **Le Petit Duc**: 7 boulevard Victor-Hugo. ☎ 04-90-92-08-31. Anne Daguin and her husband sell jams and preserves made to ancient recipes, as well as sweeties with evocative names: *lunes* (moons), *curs du petit Albert* (little Albert's hearts), all sorts of *calissons*, *pastilles d'amour* (love pastels), *oreilles de la bonne déesse* (ears of the good goddess).

FESTIVALS

– **Fête de la Transhumance** and **flea market**: on Whit Monday, a traditional festival that has remained true to its nature and finishes with a great dinner on the plateau.

– **Festivals of the Route des Peintres** (painters' trail): more than a hundred artists who live in the area gather on the Saturday of Ascension weekend, the first and third Sundays in June, and the first Sunday in September.

– **Féria Provençale**: during the weekend of 15 August. The bulls (which are not killed) are the central attraction of the festival, with Camargue-style racing, among other events.

– **Traditional festival of the *Caretto Ramado***: on the morning of 15 August. A chariot (the *caretto*), painted with flowers, and decorated with fruit and vegetables, is pulled across town by 40 harnessed and garlanded horses.

– **Jazz in Les Alpilles**: this takes place during the second weekend in September.

– **Petit marché du gros souper**: the Christmas market held during the weekend before festivities (the *gros souper* is the traditional family meal) begin.

Check at the tourist office for precise dates, times and locations.

BOUCHES-DU-RHÔNE

LES BAUX-DE-PROVENCE (13520)

Population: 443

At this unique site, impressive rocks jut out of the scrub. A citadel – a vast, ruined eyrie – towers high above. Natural rocks and man-made buildings are practically indistinguishable. By day, the light is clear and bright. When the sun goes down at this magical place, the walls of the natural fortress gleam. From the village, there is a fantastic panorama of the country around Aix and the Ste-Geneviève mountain, as far as the Cévennes.

Les Baux was founded long ago. Legend has it that Balthazar, one of the Magi who followed Christ's star to Bethlehem, met the shepherdess of his dreams here. Whether he did or not, the truth is that the geographical and geological features of the rock made it a place of strategic importance. The Ligurians took possession of it in the fifth century BC. In their Celtic language, *bau* meant 'escarpment', so the town's present-day name owes its origin to them.

Standing on a bare spur surrounded by plunging precipices, the town was home to a 'race of eagles, who would never be slaves', as Mistral called them. You can go back in time to visit their nest (with the help of an audioguide). In the 12th century, 79 towns and boroughs were under the control of the powerful lords, descendants of Balthazar, who reigned here. Fighting and wars were common in the region. In the 13th century, Baux was a place of courtly love. Alix was the last princess of Baux; she was the unfortunate niece of a brute known as the Scourge of Provence. On her death, the domain was given by Good King René to his wife Jeanne de Laval.

Though reunited with the crown of France, the barony rose against Louis XI who countered the revolt and destroyed Baux fortress. It was only as a result of restoration works under Anne de Montmorency that Les Baux recovered its lost vitality. It became a Protestant stronghold and this time it was Richelieu, no tolerator of such heresy, who demolished the chateau and its ramparts. In the end, Les Baux found itself under the control of the Grimaldi family. Although this was not enough to save the town, it at least explains why the streets of St-Rémy are full of visitors from Monaco.

In 1821, the geologist Berthier found a red rock here, which he named 'bauxite'. Since 1945, fashionable travellers have flocked here and, in their wake, millions of tourists every year.

USEFUL ADDRESS

🄱 **Tourist office**: in the village, Îlot Post-Tenebras-Lux. ☎ 04-90-54-34-39. Fax: 04-90-54-51-15. Open in summer 9am–7pm, and 9am–6pm in winter. The competent staff can provide all the necessary information, including a map of walking trails in the region.

BOUCHES-DU-RHÔNE

WHERE TO STAY AND EAT

Les Baux is not short of restaurants or hotels but many fail to understand that their long-term interest is not served by allowing this otherwise pretty village to decline, as it has over the last 15 years. The prices may be lower and the atmosphere relaxing in the nearby towns of Maussane or St-Rémy, but there are one or two worthwhile places closer to Les Baux, as long as you are willing to pay.

☆–☆☆ Budget to Moderate

✗ **Le Variétés**: 29 rue du Trencat. ☎ 04-90-54-55-88. Open from 1 March to 15 October, 11.30am–4.30pm. Open for dinner from 14 July to 15 August. Menu at 75F and mixed salads at 48F. This clean and bright snack bar and *crêperie* serves a variety of light quick dishes, either in the vaulted dining room that opens on to the street, or on the terrace. It has a fun and pleasant atmosphere.

✗ **Café Cinarca**: 26 rue du Trencat. ☎ and fax: 04-90-54-33-94. Closed on Tuesday, between mid-November and 15 December and from 6 January to 6 February. Open in the evening from 15 May to 30 September. Menu at 118F and an *assiette provençale* (platter) at 68F. This pleasant restaurant/tearoom offers refreshment to visitors on their way up to the citadel. It has an open fire in the winter, wooden tables, a pleasant decor, a friendly atmosphere and tasty food, served in the evening in a lovely little courtyard. In short – simple but good.

☆☆☆ Chic

🛏 ✗ **Hostellerie de la Reine Jeanne**: in the village. ☎ 04-90-54-32-06. Fax: 04-90-54-32-33. Open all year. Rooms from 280F to 550F (the most expensive have wonderful views). Menus at 115F and 165F. The main street may be invaded by huge crowds in high season, but safe inside the hotel, and when the crowds have gone home, the lovely rooms and delicious traditional meals are most enjoyable.

🛏 ✗ **Chambres d'hôte Le Mas de L'Esparou** (B&B): on the road to St-Rémy. ☎ and fax: 04-90-54-51-32. Double room for 380F. This house is in a lovely spot among pine and olive trees. The owner is a painter and his wife makes delicious homemade jam. Your job is to enjoy the pool, the wonderful view over the mountains and the friendly atmosphere.

☆☆☆☆ Très Chic

✗ **La Riboto de Taven**: au val d'Enfer, on the D27, below the citadel. ☎ 04-90-54-34-23. Closed on Tuesday evening and Wednesday. À la carte 350–400F, good-value set lunch menu at 220F. There are also troglodyte rooms for 1,300F. If funds don't stretch that far, you can always photograph them from the outside, and enjoy the magnificent terrace. Tucked below the 'witches' rock', this restaurant is a good place to get away from it all. The chef presents simple but flavourful dishes.

WHAT TO SEE

★ **The village**: Les Baux is visited on foot, with cars being left in the car park (20F) at the entrance.

Just through the gate, before the post office, stands the King's House. Turning right you arrive at the town hall, now the home of the **Musée des Santons** (for information on *santons*, *see* page 88). Carry on to the Porte Eyguières for a magnificent view over the Val d'Enfer (Valley of Hell). Re-trace your steps, along the Grand'Rue, then take the rue Neuve to place St-Vincent. On the way, the Fondation Louis-Jou (named after an engraver who died here in 1964) displays several engravings, including work by Dürer and Goya. Take a look at the odd window in the Hôtel de Manville, now the town hall, which has a lintel taken from an old Protestant church. The Hôtel des Porcelet, now the Fondation Yves-Brayer, was named after the painter who made the beautiful frescoes in the nearby chapel of the Pénitents-Blancs.

★ **St-Vincent's church**: on Christmas night, this church is the scene of the famous shepherds' Mass, when the ceremony of the *pastrage* and a living crib are enacted to the sound of Provençal singing. The modern stained-glass windows by Max Ingrand were a gift from Prince Rainier of Monaco, in memory of his ancestors, the last Marquis of Les Baux.

★ **Chateau**: rue du Trencat climbs up to the castle entrance. ☎ 04-90-54-55-56. Fax: 04-90-54-55-00. Website: www.chateau-baux.com. Open 9am–7.30pm from March to May; to 8.30pm in June, July and August; 9am–7pm in September and October; until 5pm the rest of the year. Entrance fee: 37F (adults), 28F (students) and 20F (children). Guided tours for groups available. The ticket office is in the manor of the Tour de Brau (now the Musée Lapidaire, precious stone museum). A free interactive audioguide is available for each visitor.

Once you go through the gate, you get to a promontory where you find the village cemetery, and the Ste-Blaise chapel opposite, by the ruins of the old hospital. The huge terrace overlooks the valley, with the Alpilles below. There's an exhibition in the chateau of full-size medieval war machinery, such as ballistas, trebuchets and battering rams.

WHAT TO SEE OUTSIDE THE VILLAGE

★ **Cathédrale d'Images** ('cathedral of images'): ☎ 04-90-54-38-65. Fax: 04-90-54-42-65. Website: www.cathedrale-images.com. 400 metres from the village. ♿ Open 10am–7pm (6pm from October onwards). Closed from mid-January to mid-February. Entrance fee: 43F (27F for under-18s). The former limestone quarries used in Cocteau's film *Le Testament d'Orphée* are now transformed into huge underground halls, on which are displayed constantly changing images from 50 projectors. The effect is breathtaking. The show lasts 35 minutes and its theme changes every year. It can get quite chilly.

★ Follow the road to St-Rémy and stop in the car park of the **Sarragan quarries** (visits not permitted). The view from here of Les Baux is magnificent. A little further on, wines from the region are on sale in the Caves de Sarragan.

★ The only **working quarry** still using manual labour, almost opposite the Cathédrale d'Images, is a few metres further down the road on the right.

★ For a challenge, climb down into the **Val d'Enfer**. From below, there's a magnificent view of the site and the chance to have a look at some troglodyte houses.

The Aoc of Baux-de-Provence

Wine-producers in Les Baux-de-Provence and the immediate surroundings have long objected to the fact that the name 'Les Baux' was merely an adjunct to 'Coteaux d'Aix-en-Provence' on wine labels. They wanted the name of their village to be taken home in the suitcases of some of the millions of visitors who come here every year. Finally, they have achieved recognition, and the village's wine has been attributed an independent *appellation contrôlée*.

At Mas Cellier, Dominique Hauvette cultivates 5 hectares (12 acres) of vineyards and is responsible for every stage, from grape to glass. Château d'Estoubion is known not only for its wine but also for its olive oils, and for being the setting of a soap opera. The stone and concrete Château Romanin has an almost mythical reputation, treating its vines and nature with respect, as well as concerning itself with the more spiritual aspects of its work. (Some describe it as a 'cathedral'; decide for yourself with a tour and tasting at 40F.) The Mas Ste-Berthe has an unforgettable view of the citadel, while the facade of Mas de la Dame was immortalized in a painting by Van Gogh in 1889. It has sadly now vanished, but remains on the wine label.

They all produce AOC red and rosé wines (the white wine does not have an *appellation*), in some cases using the most sophisticated technology. Twenty-five years ago, Noël Michelin in Les Terres Blanches introduced a wine-producing method, using harmonious biodiversity, assisted by the mistral. In his vineyards, almond, olive and oak trees thrive alongside the vines and around half the wine-producers in the Les Baux area have followed his example.

The properties are not always open for visits but there's also an outlet on the way up to the citadel. Stock up for the winter months with bottles of red and rosé (from 30F to 120F, depending on the year). Back at home, opening the wine will release the sights and sounds of the Alpilles once again.

🔒 **La Maison des Vins**: in the main road of Les Baux. ☎ 04-90-54-34-70. Open every day 10am–7pm. Wine is sold here at the vineyard price plus 5F. A leaflet shows the location of the various vineyards and you can book weekday visits to most of them.

– **Tours of the vineyards**: Mas Ste-Berthe in Les Baux offers tastings. ☎ 04-90-54-39-01. Château Romanin in St-Rémy, on the D99, offers a tour and tastings. ☎ 04-90-92-45-87. Domaines Terres Blanches, near St-Rémy, offers tastings. ☎ 04-90-95-91-66. Mas de Gourgonnier, in Mouriès, offers tastings. ☎ 04-90-47-50-45. Domaine Hauvette, near St-Rémy, is open only by appointment. ☎ 04-90-92-03-90.

BOUCHES-DU-RHÔNE

The Olive Trail

Between the Alpilles to the north and La Crau to the south lies the densest area of olive trees in the south of France, in the valley of Les Baux, with no less than 290,000 olive trees.

In winter, you can combine exploration of the olive groves with visits to the olive oil mills, of which seven remain, grinding 1,400 tonnes of olives between November and January. You can also visit small Romanesque chapels and ancient monasteries, a legacy of the Greeks from the sixth century.

Olive oil is well promoted in the area. Producers, mill owners and hoteliers will all regale you with stories of its power, whether applied externally (either to your body or to your furniture) or consumed in its many forms and in different recipes. Mouriès is the most important olive oil town in France, famous for its green-olive festival, on the third Sunday in September, and its festival celebrating virgin olive oil, in mid-December.

On the olive trail, you'll soon find out that there's a difference between the *salonenque*, the pride of Les Baux from September to November, and December's *grossane*.

A free leaflet showing the roads that are bordered by the most beautiful olive groves and the location of the most important sites is available from all tourist offices.

EYGALIÈRES

Right in the heart of the Alpilles, this village gets its name from the sixth Roman legion that moved here from Arles. Its attractions are obvious: almond trees, olive groves, vines and many other crops, and a peaceful air. In the Middle Ages, a number of jumped-up power-seekers built chateaux for themselves in the town, which then passed into the hands of the counts of Provence. When they fell into debt, one of them sold the town to its inhabitants. To celebrate this momentous event, the locals built a bell-tower and clock, of which the ruins can be seen at the entrance to the village. Remaining as a legacy of the village's turbulent past, some pretty chapels and an old mill are appealing excuses for a short walk, particularly at sunset.

WHERE TO STAY

🛏 **Hôtel Le Mas dou Pastre**: opposite the St-Sixte chapel. ☎ 04-90-95-92-61. Fax: 04-90-90-61-75. Rooms from 480F to 720F. This tastefully decorated hotel has a wonderful location in the olive groves on the way out of the village. Run by two hospitable sisters, the rooms are in their father's converted sheep barn. A lovely breakfast is served under the trees and there's a smart swimming pool, as well as a conservatory with a small jacuzzi. Free parking.

🛏 **Chambres d'hôte** (B&B): Le Contras district. From the village, take the Mollèges road for 3.5 kilometres (2 miles), then follow the signposts to the right. ☎ and fax: 04-90-95-04-89. Closed from 15

October to 15 February. Double rooms from 270F to 300F, including breakfast, served with homemade produce. There's a warm, genuine welcome at this farm, which has simple rooms and serves breakfast on fine days in the shade of an old mulberry tree. There are no other meals but you can make your own picnic.

WHERE TO STAY AND EAT

⚓ **Le Mas de Castellan** (B&B): on the former St-Rémy road, in Verquières, 13670 (7 kilometres/4 miles to the north). Signposted from the centre of the village. ☎ 04-90-95-08-22. Fax: 04-90-95-44-29. Closed in January and February. Rooms for two for around 450F. This unusually designed and decorated house is owned by people who love antiques, and has a conservatory, peaceful grounds and a delightful swimming pool. Credit cards not accepted.

⚓ **La Bergerie de Castellan** (B&B): in Verquières. ☎ 04-90-95-02-07. Two kilometres from the town centre. Closed from 15 December to 31 January. Double rooms for 400F and rooms for three for 500F. This ochre-coloured artists' home is extremely remote, surrounded by fields and orchards and accessed via a dirt track. Simply but attractively decorated, it has a vine-shaded terrace and kitchen facilities for guests. Enjoy a friendly and relaxed welcome, including refreshing drinks.

✕ **Le Croque-Chou**: place de l'église, Verquières. ☎ 04-90-95-18-55. Closed on Monday and Tuesday (except during festivals) and on Sunday evening in winter. ✕ *Formule* menu at 195F, and an alternative menu at 225F. Located in a lovely 18th-century mansion, this restaurant is not cheap, but perfect for an intimate dinner. Credit cards not accepted.

WHAT TO SEE

★ **St-Sixte chapel**: a short walk from the centre of the village, the chapel was built in the 12th century on a little hill where pagan rites used to be celebrated. Every Easter Tuesday, a Mass is celebrated in the Provençal dialect and they also keep an ancient water rite alive. When a couple gets engaged, the future husband must drink springwater from his fiancée's hands; if they do not marry within the year, he will die.

MAUSSANE-LES-ALPILLES

Maussane straggles along the road from Arles to Salon. Its reputation is based on the production of an olive oil that has its own AOC. In 1830, more than half of the land around the town was dedicated to the growing of olive trees. Of the dozen or so oil mills that were still working before the terrible winter of 1956 – which virtually wiped out the olive groves in Provence – there are only two left.

BOUCHES-DU-RHÔNE

USEFUL ADDRESS

🛈 Tourist office: place Joseph-Laugier-de-Monblanc, on the place l'église. ☎ 04-90-54-52-04. Open all year 10am–noon and 3–6.30pm. Closes at 5pm from November to March.

WHERE TO STAY

⌂⌂⌂ Chic

🛏 L'Oustaloun: place de l'église. ☎ 04-90-54-32-19. Fax: 04-90-54-45-57. Closed from 1–10 December and from 4 January to 13 February. Double room with bath or shower from 300F to 400F. Menus from 110F to 220F. The 18th-century facade of this typical little Provençal inn has been restored in keeping with the style of the square on which it stands. Guests sleep under authentic 15th-century beams and can enjoy the local olive oil in all its forms in the restaurant, where specialities include *timbaline d'aubergines au coulis de tomates et poivrons rouges* (aubergine terrine with tomato and red pepper sauce) and rabbit in garlic. In summer, tables are set out in the square. The welcome is warm and there is free parking.

🛏 Le Val Baussenc: 122 avenue de la Vallée-des-Baux. ☎ 04-90-54-38-90. Fax: 04-90-54-33-36. Hotel closed from January to March. Restaurant closed for lunch, on Wednesday and between November and March. This bright and peaceful house is set amid fields and orchards and has rooms for 680F and a menu at 190F. The food is simple, typical of the region and delicious.

WHERE TO EAT

⌂ Budget

✕ La Pitchoune: 21 place de l'église. ☎ 04-90-54-34-84. Closed Monday. Menus at 70F (except for dinner and on Sunday) 94F, 112F and 150F. This relaxed and pleasant town-centre restaurant has two family-style dining rooms with hangings at the windows, a welcoming fireplace, old beams and lovely country furniture. Specialities include bean soup, leg of lamb with *tapenade*, and *pieds et paquets à la marseillaise* (tripe). Portions are generous and there are also tables in the shady garden.

✕ La Cuisine de la Vallée: 15 avenue de la Vallée-des-Baux. ☎ 04-90-54-54-00. Open for lunch every day from Monday to Saturday and for dinner on Friday and Saturday. Menus at 100F (two courses plus a glass of wine) and 150F. Housed in a charming historic house, this restaurant has food at reasonable prices, based on fresh market porduce, with menus that change daily, and an excellent well-priced local wine list. There's even a little shop.

WHAT TO SEE

★ **Musée des Santons Animés** (museum of living *santons*): route de St Rémy, on the D5, 4 kilometres (2.5 miles) from Les Baux-de-Provence. ☎ 04-90-54-39-00. Fax: 04-90-54-52-84. Open every day 10am–8pm in summer and 1.30–7pm in winter. A perfect museum to visit with children.

BOUCHES-DU-RHÔNE

SHOPPING

🔒 **Moulin Jean-Marie Cornille** (oil mill): rue Charloun-Rieu. ☎ 04-90-54-32-37. Open to the public 8.30am–noon and 2–6pm. This mill is now the oil cooperative of the valley of Les Baux. In spite of technological progress, the way the millers work has barely changed since ancient times. After picking, the olives are brought straight to the mill, where they are pounded whole by old millstones. The paste is spread out in pats of 5 to 6 kilograms (about 12 lbs), which are then piled up to go into the water press, where centrifugal force separates the water from the oil. The oil that flows out is described on labels as 'cold-press virgin olive oil'. It is on sale here, alongside locally produced soaps, jams and honey.

🔒 **Confiserie et boutique Jean Martin** (confectionary and fine foods): 10 rue Charloun-Rieu. ☎ 04-90-54-30-04. Open every day 9am–noon and 2–6pm. Closed on Sunday and Monday morning. This business has been passed down from father to son since 1920. There are no sweets on display here, but superb traditional products like *tapenade*, aubergine tart and ratatouille. Confectioners have much work to do on the olive, to take away its bitterness.

🔒 **Mas de Gréoux**: wonderful honey and preserves for sale from keen beekeeper and chef André Camous. ☎ 04-90-54-36-77.

LE PARADOU

This village with the idyllic name is on the small road from Arles to Salon. Provençal poet Charloun Rieu was born here. A modest, humble place, it is an artist's paradise and also seems to appeal to writers.

WHERE TO STAY AND EAT

🛏 ✕ **Du Côté des Olivades**: in the locality of the Bourgeac. Just outside the village. ☎ 04-90-54-56-78. Fax: 04-90-54-56-79. ✕ Closed on Sunday evening and for lunch on Monday. Menus from 180F to 260F, and rooms from 690F to 990F (with a lovely terrace). The smart Belgian *patron* had a glittering career as the boss of a Brussels brewery, before decamping with his wife and daughter to the sunny Alpilles. Waiting for the planning permission to build in an olive grove the hotel of his dreams, he worked at the legendary hotel Baumanière, at Les Baux. He attracted a new clientele with his cooking and his prices and many of them followed him to his charming *mas* in its magical landscape. Today, there are about 12 cosy rooms, and a nice swimming pool. The cooking is very simple, making the best use of fresh produce. Free car park.

WHAT TO SEE

★ **La Petite Provence du Paradou**: 75 avenue de la Vallée-des-Baux. ☎ 04-90-54-35-75. Fax: 04-90-54-35-67. ✕ Open 2–7pm between 1 October and 30 April, and 10am–7pm between 1 May and 30 September. Entrance fee: 25F for adults, 15F for children and groups of 15. This museum, among ancient olive trees, has 300 life-like *santons* in miniature tableaux, recreating scenes of traditional life from the early 20th century. A *santon* craftsman demonstrates all the stages involved in the manufacture of the clay figurines (*see* page 88).

From Paradou take the D78E to Fontvieille.

FONTVIEILLE

USEFUL ADDRESS

🅱 **Tourist office**: 5 rue Marcel-Honorat. ☎ 04-90-54-67-49. Fax: 04-90-54-69-82. Open 9am–noon and 2–6pm. Closed on Sunday and during the first two weeks in January. Office staff provide details of various walks, including access to Daudet's mill, the Daudet museum and, from 1 April to 30 September, to the Château de Montauban.

WHERE TO STAY

☆☆ Moderate

🛌 **Hôtel Le Daudet**: avenue de Montmajour. ☎ 04-90-54-76-06. Fax: 04-90-54-76-95. On the way out of the village towards Arles. Closed between October and Easter. Double rooms from 310F to 370F. This brand-new hotel has 14 rooms, a patio, private terrace, pine grove and swimming pool. It's simple but excellent and has free parking.

🛌 **La Peiriero**: 34 avenue des Baux. ☎ 04-90-54-76-10 and 08-25-09-08-24. Fax: 04-90-54-62-60. 🦽 Closed from All Saints to Easter (except for groups), this good value hotel has rooms from 300F to 560F and has been prettily renovated. The Provençal-style rooms are varied, there's a lovely swimming pool and a nice atmosphere. Free secure parking.

WHERE TO EAT

☆–☆☆ Budget to Moderate

✕ **Le Chat Gourmand**: 14 route du Nord, in the town centre. ☎ and fax 04-90-54-73-17. Closed Tuesday evening and all day Wednesday out of season as well as during February and for All Saints. Menus at 110F and 150F. There's a terrace on the first floor, where you can enjoy dishes such as *pieds-paquets marseillais* (tripe), *soupe de poissons* (fish soup) or *magret et foie gras au vinaigre de framboise* (duck fillet and duck-liver pâté with raspberry vinegar). The welcome is warm and the interior is decorated on a cat theme.

☆☆☆ Chic

✕ **Le Patio**: 117 route du Nord. ☎ 04-90-54-73-10. Fax: 04-90-54-63-52. Closed Wednesday in season, but also Tuesday in winter and during the February school holidays. Menus 98F except for Saturday evening and Sunday lunch, when they cost 138F, 160F and 190F. This pretty Provençal shepherd's house has a patio (of course) and serves a wide choice of good regional dishes, such as cod stew, garlic mayonnaise with fish and vegetables, or *agneau de Provence grillé* (lamb grilled over an open fire). À la carte is a little more expensive. Desserts include lemon tart with apricots and raspberry coulis.

✕ **La Cuisine au Planet**: 144 Grand-Rue. ☎ and fax: 04-90-54-63-97. Closed all day Monday and Tuesday lunchtime in summer as well as for two weeks in February and November. Superb menus at 145F and 190F. This adorable restaurant smothered in Virginia creeper offers a warm atmosphere and regional cooking with an original, light, modern twist. Lovely wine list.

WHAT TO SEE

★ **Alphonse-Daudet Museum**: ☎ 04-90-54-60-78. Open 10am–noon and 2–5pm between October and April; 9am–noon and 1.30–6pm between April and October. Entrance fee: 10F (5F for children). This is one of France's most famous literary landmarks. The restored mill was much loved by writer Alphonse Daudet because of its view of the Alpilles, but, contrary to myth, this is not the place where he wrote his famous book *Lettres de mon moulin* ('Letters from my windmill'). These stories about Provençal life were first published in 1860.

ST-ÉTIENNE-DU-GRÈS

The best way to get to this village is along the early road linking St-Rémy to Arles, a lovely but rather poorly signposted route through amazing countryside. Use a map and drive slowly. You're no longer on the olive trail but a number of other tree species flourish in this tranquil environment.

WHERE TO STAY

🛏 **Le Moulin de la Croix chambres d'hôte** (B&B): 28 avenue Notre-Dame. ☎ 04-90-49-05-78. One room at 300F. You may get lost trying to find this unusual farmhouse, but it's worth it. The welcome is very 'peace and love' and the owners are relaxed artists and hosts. Enjoy breakfast in a large ochre-coloured room, which seems to be sunny even in rainy weather.

SHOPPING

🔒 **Les Olivades factory shop**: chemin des Indienneurs, 13105 St-Étienne-du-Grès. ☎ 04-90-49-19-19. Email: les-olivades@provence-fabrics.com. 8 kilometres (5 miles) from Tarascon along the D99, near the campsite. This is the place to come if you like typically Provençal fabrics. It's a small shop with a fairly large selection of clothes, fabric lengths, scarves, tablecloths and decorative items, all at better prices than you'll find in bigger shops. Come here after visiting the Souleïado museum (*see* page 214).

TARASCON (13150)   Population: 12,991

Tarascon sits between the Alpilles and the small, often forgotten mountain known as Montagnette. It's associated with two key figures, one fictional and one mythological. Tartarin (which means 'braggart' in French) was the teller of tall tales who appeared in three of Alphonse Daudet's comic novels.

BOUCHES-DU-RHÔNE

Tarasque was a man-eating Provençal monster, half-lion, half-armadillo, from which the town derived its name. Both characters seem to be disappearing in the mists of time. Tarascon is rather a sleepy place, with limited nightlife, and desperately in need of renovated hotels and some town planning, with more pedestrianization of the older streets. The **Fête de la Tarasque** at the end of June brings life and colour back to the town as an effigy of the monster that once terrorized the region is paraded through the town.

USEFUL ADDRESS

🛈 Tourist office: 59 rue des Halles. ☎ 04-90-91-03-52, 22-96 (fax) and 00-07 (town hall). Email: tourisme@-tarascon.org. Open Monday to Saturday, 9am–12.30pm and 2–6pm, Sunday 10am–noon. Closed Saturday and Sunday in low season. Pick up the free booklet that describes walks in the surrounding area, including the Parcours des Digues (12 kilometres/7.5 miles) and Boulbon to St-Michel-de-Frigolet (16 kilometres/10 miles).
– **Helicopter flights**: from the base on the route d'Arles. ☎ 04-90-91-43-51-67.

WHERE TO STAY AND EAT

☆ Budget

🛏 Auberge de jeunesse (youth hostel): 31 boulevard Gambetta. A 15-minute walk from the station. ☎ 04-90-91-04-08. Fax: 04-90-91-54-17. Email: tarascon@fuaj.org. Open from March to December. This well-run hostel, with kitchen facilities, charges 48F per night.

☆–☆☆ Budget to Moderate

🛏 ✕ Hôtel des Échevins: 26 boulevard Itam. ☎ 04-90-91-01-70. Fax: 04-90-43-50-44. ✖ Closed from All Saints Day to Easter. **Le Mistral** restaurant closed on Wednesday and lunchtime on Saturday, and on Sunday evening. Rooms in the modern and quite comfortable hotel are reasonably priced, from 300F to 350F, but lack any particular charm. Menus regional and cost from 90F to 150F, including Provençal specialities such as *bourride*, *pieds-paquets* and *daube* as well as *agneau des Alpilles* (Alpilles-style lamb).

✕ Restaurant Terminus: place de la Gare. ☎ 04-90-91-18-95. Fax: 04-90-91-08-00. Closed on Wednesday, for lunch on Saturday and from mid-February to mid-March. The 75F menu is a reminder of the station restaurants of old, with a choice of 16 starters, 10 main courses, and cheese or dessert. There are others at 100F and 130F. Rooms are also available, from 140F to 240F; the owners keep their costs and their prices low. There's secure parking for an extra charge.

✕ Hôtel-Restaurant Le Provençal: 12 cours Aristide-Briand. In the heart of the town, on the main road. ☎ 04-90-91-11-41. Fax: 04-90-91-19-29. Restaurant closed on Sunday evening and all day Monday (except on public holidays). Rooms from 180F to 240F. Menus at 90F and 140F. One brother is busy in the kitchen preparing Provençal dishes while the other runs the dining room and the hotel, and looks after guests. Try the delicious fish in lemon-flavoured olive oil.

✕ Le Bistrot des Anges: place du Marché. ☎ 04-90-91-05-11. Open every day for lunch (except on Sunday) and for two weeks over Christmas. *Formule* menu for 85F, daily specials or salads for 65F and another menu at 100F. In the heart of the town, and integral to the comings and goings of the day, this is a lively and popular spot at lunchtime, serving fresh produce in generous portions. Bright, sunny and spacious, the dining room has lots of feminine touches and there's delightful attention to detail, like the sweets that are served with coffee. Booking advisable, particularly at lunchtime.

☎ **Chambres d'hôte** (B&B): 24 rue du Château. ☎ 04-90-91-09-99. Fax: 04-90-91-10-33. Rooms in this wonderful setting cost 450F, with a reduction after three nights. Behind the heavy wooden door, there's a cool interior courtyard where the hosts offer guests a relaxing drink before taking them up to their room. The bedrooms are tastefully decorated in pastel shades and furnished with fascinating objects. The attic room is particularly lovely.

WHERE TO STAY AND EAT IN THE AREA

Campsite

☎ **St-Gabriel**: on route de Fontvieille, 5 kilometres (3 miles) along the N570 and then left towards St-Rémy. ☎ and fax 04-90-91-19-83. Closed from 1 October to 1 May. 20F per person, 10F for under-10s, and 20F for a pitch. The good facilities include a pool and shade.

☒ Budget

☎ **Tartarin**: route de Vallabrègues, just 300 metres from the town centre. ⚒ ☎ 04-90-91-01-46. Fax: 04-90-91-10-70. Site open from 30 March to 30 October. Similar facilities to the St-Gabriel, plus a snack bar.

☒☒ Moderate

☎ ✕ **Hostellerie St-Michel**: Abbaye de Frigolet, 12 kilometres (7.5 miles) from Tarascon, on the D970 and then the D81. ☎ 04-90-91-52-70. Fax: 04-90-95-75-22. Email: abbayedefrigolet@frigolet.com. Renovated and spacious rooms for 250F, and others for 182–320F. Menus ranging from 90F to 150F.

Housed in a former abbey, this hotel offers a range of comfort, from minimalist to lavish. Meals are served in the former refectory, a real museum piece, with a superb doorway, or in the garden. Finish off with an ice-cream with a dash of Frigolet liqueur.

☎ ✕ **Table et chambres d'hôte de Thécla Fargepallet**: Mas de Gratte Semelle, route d'Avignon, 13150 Tarascon. ☎ 04-90-95-72-48. Fax: 04-90-90-54-87. 6 kilometres (4 miles) from Tarascon. Double room with bath 500F. About 160F for a complete meal. This pretty 18th-century *mas* is right out in the countryside. Napoleon made a stop here when he accompanied Josephine to the Frigolet Abbey, where she prayed to Notre-Dame-de-Bon-Remède for an heir. Today, it's a really nice place to stay or eat, with a friendly welcome. Thécla provides attractive guest rooms and a little swimming pool, as well as cooking full of the savours and flavours of Provence. It's the perfect place for a totally traditional Christmas – as long as you can get a room.

WHAT TO SEE

★ **Château du Roi René:** ☎ 04-90-91-01-93. Fax: 04-90-91-01-93. Open every day, 9am–7pm from 1 April to 30 September. Out of season, open 9am–noon and 2–5pm except Tuesday. Entrance fee: 32Ffor adults, 21F 18 to 25s, free for under-18s. Free first Sunday of the month out of season. This imposing fortress protects a Gothic and Renaissance building, probably one of the most lovely in Provence, with a splendid spiral staircase in the main courtyard and magnificent ceilings with original bosses in all the apartments. Six 17th-century Flemish tapestries hang on the walls, designed by Jules Romain and celebrating the glory of Scipio the African.

There's a superb view from the terrace over Mont Ventoux, and the Frigolet and Montmajour abbeys. The pharmacy of the old hospital has a specialist collection of 210 ceramic pots. Graffitti scratched on the walls includes pictures of galleys, drawn by prisoners, and even a depiction of a bishop.

To get a good view of the chateau, go to Beaucaire over the Rhône bridge and make the long trip round the Bassin Beaucairois. Eventually you'll get to the place for the best view.

★ **Maison de Tartarin** (Tartarin's house): 55 boulevard Itam. ☎ 04-90-91-05-08. Open in winter 10am–noon and 1.30–7pm; in summer, 10am–noon and 2–7pm. Closed on Sunday and from 15 December to 15 March. Entrance fee: 10F (adults) and 5F (children). French novelist Alphonse Daudet is best known for his sketches of Provençal characters. He is said to have based his infamous Tartarin on his cousin Antoine Raynaud, a widower, wine-lover and keen hunter, with whom Daudet had visited Algeria, looking for lions. Originally, the character in the book (first published in series form) was called De Barbarin, but an injunction from the De Barbarin family forced the author to change the name. The annoyed inhabitants of Tarascon eventually forgave Daudet, because in the end he brought their little town such great fame. The Maison de Tartarin was opened in 1985, and visitors can now see the hero in his study.

★ **Ste-Marthe church**: this stunning Provence-Gothic sanctuary houses an interesting collection of 17th- and 18th-century paintings by Carle Van Loo and Mignard, among others.

★ **Old town**: the picturesque winding streets of the old part of town are lined with interesting old buildings, in particular the *ostal del commun*, the 17th-century town hall on the market square.

★ **Musée Souleïado**: 39 rue Proudhon. ☎ 04-90-91-50-11. Open in low season from Tuesday to Saturday, 10am–noon and 2–6pm. Open every day from 10am–6pm from May to September. Entrance fee: 40F. Created in the workshop of this family business, the impressive Charles Demery museum represents a historic record of Provençal fabrics (*see* page 89). It has a fine collection of materials, as well as more than 40,000 woodblocks in different designs. Many of the blocks are still used to produce the Souleïado company's colourful prints (the word *souleïado* means 'the sun passing through the clouds' in Provençal). The museum also tells visitors more about how the fabrics are produced and displays a collection of lovely quilts, together with religious and traditional objects. There are also workshops on certain days, including one on *santons*, given by the curator.

WHAT TO SEE IN THE AREA

– **Abbaye St-Michel-de-Frigolet**: from Tarascon, the abbey is reached via a lovely route through a pine forest. At the top of the Montagnette there is an official picnic site with a trekking centre. ☎ 04-90-95-70-07 (mornings only). One visit a day to the abbey, at 2.30pm; Sundays and public holidays at 4pm. Go to the shop near the entrance. The abbey's name comes from *férigoulo* ('thyme' in Provençal). Notre-Dame-du-Bon-Remède (Our Lady of the Good Remedy) is worshipped here. It's a place the climate has always been health-giving. Around 1,000 AD, the monks from the abbey at Montmajour, suffering from malaria after draining the marshes, used to come here to recuperate. Anne of Austria stopped here in 1632, to pray to her for a son; Louis XIV was born six years later.

The massively built 12th-century cloister is Romanesque, and quite dark because it supports a gallery above. The fascinating guided tour (well worth the charge) compares this with the 12 other Romanesque cloisters in the region. There's also a nativity scene carved in olive wood; 2 tonnes of material were chiselled and planed to make the 15 figures.

On Easter Monday, a big traditional festival takes place, with dances in local costume and games testing the skills of the *gardian* herdsmen. At Christmas, there's a lovely midnight Mass, with a new-born lamb being offered in the *pastrage* ceremony.

Val de Provence

This is typically Provençal countryside, with cypress hedges and marshy farmland. Barbentane is the gateway to the 'Val de Provence', invented by a group of officials to give a clear identity to the villages that lie between Les Alpilles and the valley of the Durance, between Tarascon and Avignon. Fans of Frédéric Mistral will probably want to stop in Maillane to visit the museum (☎ 04-90-95-74-06) and see the tomb of this remarkable local figure. On 14 July each year, Châteaurenard goes back in time to celebrate traditional crafts in an interesting festival.

BARBENTANE

This typical old Provençal village, with its sleepy square shaded by plane trees, lies just off the main road.

USEFUL ADDRESS

🅱 **Syndicat d'Initiative** (information bureau): ☎ 04-90-90-85-85. Open 8.30–11.30am and 1.30–5.30pm (until 4.30pm on Friday).

WHAT TO SEE

★ The beautiful 17th-century **chateau**, standing in a garden, is in classical style. ☎ 04-90-95-51-07. Visits are possible 10am–noon and 2–6pm, daily except Wednesday, between Easter and All Saints. Out of season, open Sunday only. Entrance fee: 30F, children 20F. There are beautiful pieces of Louis XV and Louis XVI furniture in the richly decorated rooms, which have an Italian touch.

★ Also worth seeing: the **town hall** and **Romanesque church** in the town centre, the **Maison des Chevaliers** (Knights' House), and the **Moulins de Mogador**, the museum of old Provençal oil and flour. ☎ 04-90-95-57-90.

GRAVESON

This old village is gradually rediscovering itself, after making its centre more amenable to visitors. As you walk along in the shade of the plane trees, take a look at the fortified door of the Romanesque church. This is a nice place to take it easy.

USEFUL ADDRESS

🅗 **Syndicat d'Initiative** (information bureau): in the town hall. ☎ 04-90-95-71-05. Open 8.30am–noon and 2–6pm.

WHERE TO STAY AND EAT

🛏 **Camping Micocouliers**: route de Cassoulen. ☎ 04-90-95-81-49. One kilometre from Graveson. ✗ Open from 15 March to 15 October. All in price: 75F. Prices are 25F (adults), 12F (children under 7) and 25F for the pitch. This new campsite has no lake or shady area but there's certainly a warm welcome and it's only 12 kilometres (7.5 miles) from Avignon. No credit cards.

🛏 **Chambres d'hotes Le Mas Ferrand** (B&B): 7 avenue Auguste Chabaud. ☎ 04-90-95-85-29. Fax: 04-90-90-55-04. Room for 300F. Photos of grandpa watch over guests in this old family home, with its big old Provençal beds and lovely garden. The welcome is wonderful and the breakfasts memorable.

🛏 ✗ **Le Moulin d'Aure**: in the Cassoulen district. Take the Avignon road from Tarascon and then fork off to Graveson. The restaurant is just outside the village. ☎ 04-90-95-84-05. Fax: 04-90-95-73-84. Email: hotel-moulin-d-aure@wanadoo.fr. Open all year. Pleasant rooms from 320F to 450F. Menus from 130F. This haven of peace stands in a large pine and olive grove, where crickets sing all summer. There's a pleasant family atmosphere, the *patronne* has a winning smile and, in July and August, you can enjoy snacks as you relax by the pool.

🛏 ✗ **Le Mas des Amandiers**: route d'Avignon, in the impasse (cul-de-sac) des Amandiers. 2 kilometres (1 mile) into the countryside via the RN570. ☎ 04-90-95-81-76. Fax: 04-90-95-85-18. ✗ Closed from 15 October to 15 March. Rooms (very popular in summer) for 330F and a small restaurant with menus from 95F. A useful address to remember, this *mas* may not have the most attractive surroundings, but the prices are reasonable, the place itself is pleasant and the swimming pool tempting. The friendly and hospitable owners will point you in the direction of the famous Friday-evening farmers' market, and the perfume museum (*see below*). Free parking.

🏠 **Le Cadran Solaire**: in the village. ☎ 04-90-95-71-79. Fax: 04-90-90-55-04. Double rooms for 310F and 330F. This former staging post, now a delightfully renovated hotel, has colourful and pleasant rooms with contemporary decor, a shady garden and a terrace where you can unpack your purchases from the Friday market. Breakfast is served until noon.

WHAT TO SEE

★ **Musée Auguste-Chabaud**: cours National. ☎ 04-90-90-53-02. Open every day from June to September, 10am–noon and 1.30–6.30pm. Closed in the morning from October to May. Entrance fee: 20F. The collection in this museum includes about 60 works by artists that are little known to the general public. The place also has studios, a programme of conferences and lectures, and offers evening guided tours.

★ **Musée des Arômes et du Parfum** (scent and perfume museum): petite route du Grès. ☎ 04-90-95-81-55. ♿ (for half of the collection). Open all year round 10am–noon and 2–6pm; in July and August 10am–7pm. Housed in a 19th-century *mas*, this museum's collection includes copper stills, oil extractors, bottle labels, and at least 300 bottles. The fascinating guided tour, led by an aromatherapist, celebrates the craftsmen of the past, including the distiller and the glass-blower. There is free access to the Carré des Simples, an experimental garden in which each plant has an explanatory label and, in the summer, a juice bar. Essential oils, flower water, perfumes, and so on, are all on sale here.

★ **Marché paysan** (farmers' market): place du Marché, every Friday 4–8pm from May to the end of October. Dozens of wonderful local producers gathered in one place. Arrive with a big bag to take away a superb picnic – salad leaves, *saucissons d'Arles*, goats' cheeses, organic wines, seasonal fruit, delicious preserves and other sweet treats.

★ **Ciergerie des Prémontrés** (candlemaker): route de Maillane. ☎ 04-90-95-71-14. Candles are made by hand in this amazing workshop, which has barely changed with the years.

MAILLANE

This little Provençal village is charming and quiet, with some really lovely old cafés. For admirers of the great Frédéric Mistral, however, it's unlike any other, since the founder of the Félibrige (*see page 80*) lived here for many years.

USEFUL ADDRESS

🏢 **Syndicat d'Initiative** (tourist information bureau): in the town hall. ☎ 04-90-95-74-06. Fax: 04-90-90-52-84. Open every day 8am–noon and 2–6pm, Saturday 8am–noon. Closed Sunday afternoon.

BOUCHES-DU-RHÔNE

WHERE TO EAT

✕ **Lou Toupin**: cours Guynemer. ☎ 04-90-95-78-11. Open Monday to Friday lunchtime (evenings and weekends by reservation). Closed in August. Menus at 55–120F. A family-run restaurant with a warm atmosphere. Big meals for a few francs.

WHAT TO SEE

★ **Frédéric-Mistral museum:** in the house that the poet had built and where he lived from 1876. ☎ 04-90-95-74-06 (town hall number). Guided visits on request. Open 10–11.30am and 2–4.30pm from October to March, 9.30–11.30am and 2.30–6.30pm from April to September. Entrance fee: 20F. Mistral's widow lived here until the 1940s. The house has been restored, but it retains its original decoration and has a typical 19th-century interior.

The **Chapelle Notre-Dame-Pitié** has 108 works by the painter Mario Prassinos, who settled in the region after being exiled from Turkey.

The Rhône Valley and Haute-Provence

The Vaucluse

AVIGNON (84000) **Population: 85,935**

No trip to Provence is complete without a stop in the city of Avignon. From the first days of spring, the town, and the whole region of the Vaucluse, is invaded by visitors.

Standing at the foot of the Doms rock, and watered by the Rhône, Avignon is sheltered from the maddening mistral by its ancient walls. (Indeed, its original name, Avenio, means either 'the town on the river' or 'the town of strong winds'.) The fascinating history and rich heritage of this ancient papal city (seven pontiffs ruled and resided here between 1309 and 1377, followed by two 'anti-popes') are still much in evidence, with many splendid buildings. On the other side of the tracks, Avignon also has its share of ugly suburban sprawl and high-rise estates, where the local footballing kids have never set foot in the Palais des Papes. Its ramparts, palaces and private townhouses may be breathtaking, but, astonishingly, Avignon is the poorest town in France. The paradox is reflected in the city's internationally famous summer arts festival, which has its respectable main event and its more anarchic 'fringe', known in French as *Le Festival Off*. In the year 2000, Avignon was selected as a European Capital of Culture.

The Festival

During the summer arts festival, in July, the town of Avignon is totally transformed. Thousands of posters are plastered on walls and lamp-posts; the place de l'Horloge is so packed that's it's almost impossible to fight your way through; and the place du Palais looks as it must have done in medieval times, with jugglers, guitar-players and other street performers. Every kind of entertainment is offered. In 1947, when the festival began, fewer than 5,000 visitors attended (and more than 1000 of them were invited guests). In 1999, more than half a million people came to Avignon for the festivities, the vast majority of them buying tickets for fringe events.

In September 1947, Jean Vilar, director of the Théatre National de Paris (TNP) de Chaillot, in collaboration with poet René Char and arts magazine editor Christian Servoz, put on three plays in the main courtyard of Avignon's Palais des Papes. Under the title of Semaine des Arts (Arts Week), the pieces were designed to complement a prestigious exhibition of contemporary art in

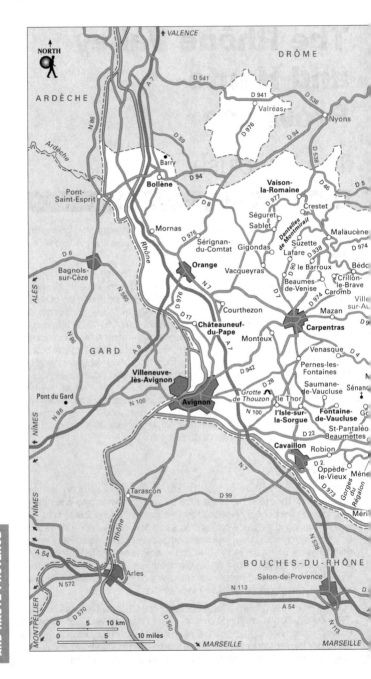

Key to place names

Carpentras	Places covered in guide
Lourmarin	Addresses and places in the area
Manosque	Locator only

THE VAUCLUSE

the great chapel. The following year, the Semaine des Arts became the Festival des Arts.

Vilar was a fervent supporter of public theatre; his aim – somewhat pretentiously expressed, perhaps – was to bring 'the bread and salt of knowledge to the greatest number and, particularly, to the least well served'. From 1951 to 1962, his TNP monopolized the theatre programme of the festival, producing popular classics on almost bare stages. He surrounded himself with a whole new generation of actors, including a very young Jeanne Moreau, who slept on friends' floors and partied on the Île de la Barthelasse. Those early days were captured in pictures taken by Vilar's babysitter Agnès Varda, who was to become a world-famous photographer.

From the 1960s, the festival was opened up to other companies and to other arts, such as dance and cinema. The fringe (*off*) took off in the early 1970s. The 1980s were marked by some exciting theatrical events, from Peter Brook's *Mahôbhôrata*, staged in the Boulbon quarry, to Antoine Vitez's 12-hour *Soulier de satin* (*Satin Shoe*) and Ariane Mnouchkine's Japanese-influenced Shakespearean trilogy.

Having celebrated its half-centenary, the Festival d'Avignon has its critics but it is an institution. Many of the directors and actors are no longer there to bring theatre to the masses, but creativity continues to make its mark. The Avignonnais may be fed up with the July invasion and resentful of the Parisian bias of the festival, but they still go regularly to the shows. Many are quite happy to rent out a courtyard or garage to a young company of actors willing to survive on a diet pasta and sleep under canvas, just to perform at Avignon.

■ **Avignon Festival Office**: 8bis rue de Mons. ☎ 04-90-27-66-50 or ☎ 04-90-14-14-14 (the second number is only for bookings, from the first fortnight in June). Website: www.festival-avignon.com
■ **Avignon public off** (fringe festival): BP 5, 75521 Paris cedex 11. ☎ 01-48-05-01-19. Website: www.avignon-off.org
■ **Maison Jean-Vilar**: 8 rue de Mons. ☎ 04-90-86-59-64. Fax: 04-90-86-00-07. Closed on Sunday, Monday and public holidays. Video library open by appointment 9–noon and 1.30–5.30pm. Information and documentation centre open 1.30–5.30pm. On Saturday, all services operate 10am–5pm. Entrance charge for some of the temporary exhibitions. The information centre holds documents on the history of the festival and its founder, while the video library has an impressive collection of tapes on the performing arts, including films of plays and interviews with directors. Books and reviews can be consulted free of charge.

USEFUL ADDRESSES AND INFORMATION

🄳 **Tourist office** (B3 on the map): 41 cours Jean-Jaurès. ☎ 04-32-74-32-74. Fax: 04-90-82-95-03. Email: information@ot-avignon.fr Website: www.avignon.tourisme.com or www.ot-avignon.fr. Open Monday to Friday 9am–6pm, between April and September. Saturday, Sunday and public holidays, open 9am–1pm and 2–5pm. Between October and March, same opening hours, but closed at the weekend and on public holidays. During the festival, open Monday to Friday 10am–7pm, and at the weekend 10am–5pm. There's another office at Pont St-Bénezet, open every day between 2 May and 30 September, 9am–1pm and 2–5pm. Closed out of season on Monday. Opening hours are sometimes subject to change. An experienced team supplies all kinds of information about Avignon, and organizes guided tours of the town at 10am on Tuesday and Thursday (from April to October).

■ **Comité départemental du tourisme du Vaucluse** (regional tourist office for the Vaucluse): in the former Palais de l'Archevêché, 12 rue Collège-de-la-Croix, BP 147, 84008 Avignon. ☎ 04-90-80-47-00. Fax: 04-90-86-86-08. Website: www.ProvenceGuide.com. Tourist information on the whole region.

✈ **Airport**: Avignon-Caumont, 8 kilometres (5 miles) south of Avignon. ☎ 04-90-81-51-51.

🚆 **SNCF train station** (B3 on the map): ☎ 08-36-35-35-35. The TGV (high-speed train) from Paris to Avignon takes 3 hours 30 minutes.

■ **Car parks**: driving in Avignon is difficult and parking spaces are very limited. There are expensive underground car parks at the Palais des Papes and Les Halles. Even out of season, it is best to park outside the city walls, if possible on the west side of the town, in one of the free car parks. Thefts from cars are frequent, but the following car parks are guarded: Mérindol, Pont-St-Bénézet (in season) and Île Piot (with free shuttle bus to the city walls).

✉ **Post office** (B3 on the map): rue du Blé-de-Lune. ☎ 04-90-13-50-50.

■ *Gîtes ruraux* (country cottages): reservations: ☎ 04-90-85-45-00.

■ **Bike, motorbike or car hire**: Holiday Bikes, 52 boulevard St-Roch, at the coach station: ☎ 04-90-27-92-61.

■ **Useful Addresses**

🛈 Tourist office
✉ Post office
🚆 SNCF train station

🛏 **Where to Stay**

1 Avignon Squash Rackets-Club
2 Hôtel Innova
3 Le Splendid
4 Hôtel du Parc
5 Hôtel Mignon
6 Hôtel Saint-Roch
7 Hôtel Bristol
8 Hôtel de Blauvac
9 Hôtel de Garlande
10 Hôtel-restaurant Le Magnan
11 La Ferme Jamet
12 La Madeleine

✕ **Where to Eat**

21 Tapalocas
22 Cab Vert
23 Le Jujubier
25 L'Épicerie
26 La Ferme
27 La Fourchette
28 Le Woolloomooloo
29 Le Vernet
30 Rose au Petit Bedon
31 Le Bistrot Pierrat
32 Le Caveau du Théâtre
33 Le Grand Café
34 Le Moutardier
36 Le Bain Marie

🍸 **Where to Go for a Drink**

40 Pub Z
41 Utopia Café
42 Mon Bar
43 Le Red Zone

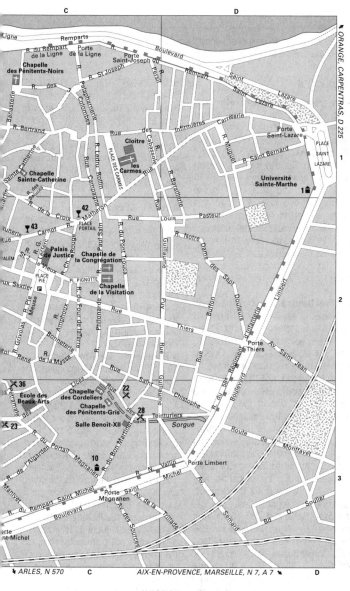

AVIGNON

WHERE TO STAY

Reserve your room well in advance if you're planning to visit Avignon in July, when the arts festival is in full swing.

☆ Budget

♠ Avignon Squash Rackets-Club (D1, **1** on the map): 32 boulevard Limbert, opposite Avignon university. ☎ 04-90-85-27-78. Fax: 04-90-82-90-84. Bus to University. Closed on Sunday out of season and on public holidays (except in June, July and August). Simple rooms for two cost 120F at this hostel (which is not a member of the French youth hostel association); individual rooms with a kitchenette are also available. Bathrooms are shared. Bring your squash racket, too, if you're feeling energetic.

♠ Hôtel Innova (B3, **2** on the map): 100 rue Joseph-Vernet. 3-minute walk from the station and Palais des Papes. ☎ 04-90-82-54-10. Fax: 04-90-82-52-39. ⚒ Rooms from 150F for a double (with washbasin but without TV) to 260F for a four-bed room with shower and toilet. This is one of the cheapest hotels in one of the smartest streets in town. It has simple but comfortable rooms, and those overlooking the small internal courtyard, where there is room to park your bike, are very quiet. The owner is very friendly, and the hotel is often full, so booking is a good idea.

♠ Hôtel Splendid (B3, **3** on the map): 17 rue Agricol-Perdiguier. Between cours Jean-Jaurès and Place des Corps-Saints. ☎ 04-90-86-14-46. Fax: 04-90-85-38-55. ⚒ (in one room). Double rooms 190–260F. This small family-run hotel has simple but well-maintained accommodation.

♠ Hôtel du Parc (B3, **4** on the map): 18 rue Agricol-Perdiguier.

☎ 04-90-82-71-55. Fax: 04-90-85-64-86. Double rooms from 160F (with basin) to 245F (with shower and toilet). This hotel has a good atmosphere and offers a warm welcome. The most peaceful and attractive of the tastefully refurbished rooms overlook the nearby square. It's good value for money for Avignon.

♠ Hôtel Mignon (B2, **5** on the map): 12 rue Joseph-Vernet. ☎ 04-90-82-17-30. Fax: 04-90-85-78-46. Open all year. Double rooms with shower, toilet and (cable) TV cost 230F in this pleasant one-star hotel. The decor may be a bit over the top for some people, but the rooms are tastefully furnished and include extra touches such as double-glazing, soundproofing (for rooms overlooking the street) and 21-channel TV.

♠ Résidence La Madeleine (B3, **12**, off the map): 4 impasse des Abeilles. Close to the train station, in a cul-de-sac near 25 avenue Monclar. ☎ and fax: 04-90-85-20-63. This hotel has rooms for two or four people for 250–350F per night, depending on room size and season. Small studios and family rooms with kitchenette, shower, toilet and TV (and sometimes air-conditioning) are also available. Private car parking costs 30F. The area behind the station isn't particularly pretty, but the cul-de-sac is quiet. The decor is a little dull, but not unpleasant, but the house is bathed in sunlight most of the time and the welcome is friendly.

♠ Hôtel Saint-Roch (A3, **6** on the map): 9 rue Paul-Mérindol. From the station, take boulevard St-Roch, turn left into avenue Eisenhower and then take the first street on the right. ☎ 04-90-16-50-00. Fax: 04-90-82-78-30. ✗ Closed in January and February. All double rooms, equipped with bathroom and TV, are 300F. This hotel is quite a distance from the historic centre, outside the city walls, and is in a rather unattractive area, but it is good. It could easily be in the heart of the Provence countryside, with its handmade floor tiles, bare stone walls and large garden, where you can enjoy breakfast on sunny days. Some rooms have air-conditioning, but there's nothing cool about the welcome. There's a large secure car park next to the hotel.

⚓ **Hôtel-restaurant Le Magnan** (C3, **10** on the map): 63 rue du Portail-Magnanen. Near the ramparts. ☎ 04-90-86-36-51. Fax: 04-90-85-48-90. Email: magnan@wanadoo.fr. Restaurant (booking essential) closed on Saturday, Sunday and during July and August. Menu at 85F. Double rooms with shower or bath and toilet, plus TV, cost 265–365F. The modern building has a fairly unattractive exterior but the hotel is delightful inside, with a refreshing and relaxing patio. The comfortable rooms have a rather sober contemporary decor.

☆☆☆ Chic

⚓ **Hôtel Bristol** (B3, **7** on the map): 44 cours Jean-Jaurès/rue de la République. Close to the train station and virtually opposite the tourist office. ☎ 04-90-16-48-48. Fax: 04-90-86-22-72. ✗ Double rooms with shower and toilet, or bath, plus satellite TV, cost 400–600F. This smart modern hotel has friendly staff (a welcome change from some other hotels in this category) and one great advantage – all rooms are air-conditioned and have efficient double-glazing. Rooms Nos. 205, 225, 301 and 303 are the most spacious and, even better, the most peaceful. You

have to pay to park your car in the (limited) garage spaces under the hotel. No restaurant.

⚓ **Hôtel de Blauvac** (B2, **8** on the map): 11 rue de la Bancasse. ☎ 04-90-86-34-11. Fax: 04-90-86-27-41. Double rooms wth shower and toilet, or bath, plus cable TV cost 310–410F (around 15 per cent less in low season). This excellent hotel stands in a narrow street in Avignon's historic centre, close to the place de l'Horloge. Formerly a 17th-century private townhouse, the property of the Marquis de Blauvac, it still has its elegant wrought-iron banisters and stone arches. The rooms (all different) are lovely, with understated contemporary decor, and the welcome is friendly.

⚓ **Hôtel de Garlande, Citotel** (B2, **9** on the map): 20 rue Galante. ☎ 04-90-80-08-85. Fax: 04-90-27-16-58. Closed on Sunday in low season. Double rooms with shower or bath and toilet, and cable TV, cost 330–450F (around 15 per cent less in low season). Breakfast is 40F. In a lovely building in the town centre, in the shadow of the St-Didier bell-tower, this hotel offers a very warm welcome, together with attractive rooms. It's rather like staying with friends, and very popular as a result.

☆☆☆ Très Chic

⚓ **La Ferme Jamet** (A1, **11**, off the map): chemin de Rhodes, Île de la Barthelasse. Turn right (north) after the bridge, coming from Avignon, then follow the signposts. ☎ 04-90-86-88-35. ✗ Annual holiday from December to 1 March. Double rooms 490–800F including breakfast. Based in and around an authentic 16th-century *mas*, La Ferme has five guest rooms with antique furniture, two very modern apartments with great facilities, three rustic bungalows and a genu-

THE RHÔNE VALLEY AND HAUTE-PROVENCE

ine gypsy caravan for rent, as well as a swimming pool and a tennis court. There are books in every room. It's popular with rich American tourists and inevitably full (of performers) during the festival period, so booking is essential. Private car park.

Campsites

⛺ The campsites are all on the Île de la Barthelasse (A1 on the map). The well-shaded **Camping Municipal Saint-Bénezet** (☎ 04-90-80-63-50; good-size pitches 60–125F for two, depending on season; open from two weeks before Easter until end October) and the **Bagatelle** (☎ 04-90-89-30-39, fax: 04-90-27-96-23, 60F for a pitch for two) both

have a lovely view of the Avignon bridge and the Palais des Papes.

Less smart are the **Deux-Rhônes** (☎ 04-90-85-49-70; 55F for a pitch for two), which is rudimentary but has a swimming pool and tennis courts and is accessible to the disabled, and the **Parc des Libertés** (☎ 04-90-85-17-73; open May to end September; 50F for a pitch for two without electricity).

⛺ During festival time, car drivers will find fewer people at the **Camping du Grand Bois** at Le Pontet, on the way to Vedene (also known as 'la Tapy'; ☎ 04-90-31-37-44). Pitch for two people with tent costs around 70F; open from 1 May to 30 September.

WHERE TO EAT

☆ Budget

✗ **Tapalocas** (B2, **21** on the map): 15 rue Galante. ☎ 04-90-82-56-84. ✗ Open every day throughout the year. Around 50F for a meal. This local institution has grown considerably but its prices have remained virtually unchanged since the late 80s. Customers sit at long wooden tables, and the tequilas add to the warm and lively atmosphere.

✗ **Le Bistrot Pierrat** (off A3, **31** on the map): 4 avenue de la Foire. In the first street at right-angles to avenue Eisenhower, left after the railway bridge opposite the exhibition centre. ☎ 04-90-82-37-41. Closed on Sunday (unless you book). Dish of the day 50F; 75F with a main course and dessert; complete menu 95F. This nice little place, with its half dozen tables in a pretty little dining room, is outside the city walls, so not touristy at all. The sociable owner takes care of everything, from cooking to serving at table. Dishes use market-fresh ingredients and are simple and

tasty, and remarkably good value for money. Reasonably priced wines are available by the glass or carafe.

✗ **Le Caveau du Théôtre** (B3, **32** on the map): 16 rue des Trois-Faucons. ☎ 04-90-82-60-91. Closed Saturday lunchtime and all day Sunday. The lunchtime *formule* menu costs 69F and the *menu-carte* is 110F. A friendly welcome and service, intimate and attractive dining rooms and a list of dishes, most (but not all) of which are infused with the flavours of Provence. The wine list is excellent (the place is also a wine bar).

✗ **Cab Vert** (C3, **22** on the map): 21A rue des Teinturiers. ☎ 04-90-86-81-82. Only open during the festival (in July). Menus at 66F, à la carte around 75F. Daily specials might include *boeuf mode* (beef) or *poulet au whisky* (chicken in whisky), the homemade desserts are tasty and there are huge salads. This is a nice place for lunch with quick service. The owner's father is a farmer and local fresh produce is the order of the day.

☆☆ – ☆☆☆ Moderate to Chic

✕ **Le Jujubier** (C3, **23** on the map): 24 rue des Lices. Close to rue de la République, via rue Fabre. ☎ 04-90-86-64-08. Closed in the evening, on Saturday and on Sunday (except during the festival) and in August. À la carte around 100F. The dining room is pleasant, with farm-house-style decor and a familiar and friendly atmosphere. Enjoy sun-drenched Provençal cuisine, with classic dishes such as *soupe aux orties* (nettle soup) and *agneau à l'épeautre* (lamb). Cards not accepted.

✕ **Le Grand Café** (B1, **33** on the map): cour Maria Casares. Behind the Palais des Papes. ☎ and fax: 04-90-86-86-77. ✕ Closed for Sunday lunch, all day Monday and during January. Menus cost 100F (lunch only) and 175F, and à la carte is around 185F. The decor is 'post-modern', with huge mirrors on shabby walls, bistrot tables, leatherette benches, contemporary pictures and modern sculpture. This unusual spot has a good atmosphere and an interesting mix of customers. Enjoy a coffee, beer or glass of wine, accompanied by a Provençal dish or two, such as *marbré de lapin à la tapenade* (rabbit with olive paste) or *tajine d'agneau aux abricots* (Tunisian-style lamb with apricots). At the weekend it's best to book.

✕ **L'Épicerie** (B2, **25** on the map): 10 place Saint-Pierre. Between the Palais des Papes and the pedestrianized zone. ☎ 04-90-82-74-22. Closed for lunch on Sunday and from November to April. À la carte around 120F. There are tables outside the restaurant on the quiet and unusual place St-Pierre. The Pro-

vençal cooking is tasty, but the welcome can be temperamental.

✕ **La Ferme** (off A1, **26** on the map): chemin des Bois, Île de la Barthelasse. 5 kilometres (3 miles) northwest of the Daladier bridge on the CD228; near Ferme Jamet (signposted). ☎ 04-90-82-57-53. Fax: 04-90-27-15-47. Closed for lunch on Monday and Wednesday, between 1 November to 7 March. Menus at 120F and 240F. Double rooms with shower or bath and toilet, plus TV, 400–450F. Half board (compulsory in July) for 350F per person. Relax by the fireplace in this former farmhouse and enjoy generous portions of dishes such as *sauté d'artichauts et ravioles de champignons* (artichokes with mushroom ravioli) or *filet d'oie à la polenta crémeuse* (goose with creamy polenta). There are 20 comfortable rooms, a pool and a private lock-up garage.

✕ **Restaurant Rose au Petit Bedon** (B3, **30** on the map): 70 rue Joseph-Vernet. ☎ 04-90-82-33-98. Fax: 04-90-85-58-64. ✕ Closed for lunch on Sunday, all day Monday, for three weeks in winter and one week in August. Menus cost 110F (lunch only) and 165F; à la carte around 190F. This place is something of an institution in these parts, run by Rose, a local figure who enjoys life, food and being a hostess. Her flavourful cuisine is traditional and firmly Provençal, with seasonal classic dishes including *ravioles à la crème et aux herbes* (ravioli in cream sauce with herbs), *pieds-paquets marseillais* (tripe) and *crépinette d'agneau crème à l'ail* (lamb with garlic cream), served in the elegant dining room.

✕ **Le Moutardier** (B1, **34** on the map): 15 place du Palais des Papes. ☎ 04-90-85-34-76. Fax: 04-90-14-17-59. Closed between 20 November and 20 December. Menus at 135F and 160F. In an 18th-century building, this restaurant has a superb and unique location, right opposite the Palais des Papes. The friendly owner is more than willing to explain the unusual mural, while pouring you a glass of your choice from his excellent selection of wines. There are two menus, one traditional and the other based on Lyonnais cuisine, created using local produce. In summer, there are tables outside and in the courtyard.

✗ **Le Bercail**: Île de la Barthelasse. Signposted from the bridge. ☎ 04-90-82-20-22. Open every day from Palm Sunday to October. À la carte around 130F. This restaurant has tables on the banks of the Rhône with a view over the town and the Rocher des Doms. Friendly welcome and service and traditional food served in generous portions, including a selection of grilled and regional dishes.

⭐⭐⭐ Chic

✗ **La Fourchette** (B2, **27** on the map): 17 rue Racine. ☎ 04-90-85-20-93. Fax: 04-90-85-57-60. Closed on Saturday, Sunday and from 15–30 August. Menus at 100F (lunchtime only) and 160F. The descendant of Hiely-Lucullus, a top restaurant that served gastronomes in Avignon for many years. Reasonably priced and excellent dishes, such as *sardines marinées* (marinated sardines), *loup grillé sur sel de guérande* (grilled sea bass on rock salt), *meringue glacée au pralin* (meringue with praline) are served in an elegant setting. The wines are well priced, particularly those available by the carafe. Booking essential.

✗ **Le Vernet** (B2, **29** on the map): 58 rue Joseph-Vernet. ☎ 04-90-86-64-53. Fax: 04-90-85-98-14. Open every day (except during annual holidays in December). Menus cost 110F and 210F, with à la carte around 210F. Housed in an 18th-century private mansion, with a leafy garden, it has elegant dining rooms and a menu that changes daily and includes a starter, main course, dessert and a quarter-litre of wine. À la carte includes dishes such as *agnolade d'Avignon* (the chef's lamb special), *nage de lotte crème de crustacés* (monkfish with seafood sauce) and chocolate mousse.

✗ **Le Bain Marie** (C2–C3, **36** on the map): 5 rue Pétramale. ☎ 04-90-85-21-37. Closed Saturday lunch and Sunday. Menus at 140F and 165F. On a winding street, with a courtyard, this restaurant has dining rooms overflowing with plants. The mother and daughter team serve regional and traditional dishes prepared with a personal touch by the son in the kitchen. The food is tasty and full of subtle flavours.

✗ **Le Woolloomooloo** (C3, **28** on the map): 16 rue des Teinturiers. Near door to Les Halles. ☎ 04-90-85-28-44. Fax: 04-90-27-08-67. 🐾 Closed for a week in August. À la carte around 150F. This is one of the most fashionable restaurants in Avignon, housed in a huge space (formerly a printing works) and illuminated by just one light and a huge number of candles. The decor is surprising and the food is fashionable 'fusion' (or 'world food'), including such dishes as 'chicken yassa' and marinated red mullet with cardamom. The service is perhaps a touch over the top.

WHERE TO GO FOR A DRINK

❣ **Pub Z** (C2, **40** on the map): 58 rue Bonneterie. Near Les Halles (the covered market). ☎ 04-90-85-42-84. Open to 1.30am. Closed every Sunday and for the last three weeks in August. 'Happy hour' every day 1.30–9.30pm. 'Z' is for 'zebra', as in the giant model in the entrance. Apart from that, the decor is very 1960s. Bernard, the boss and champion bistrot-owner, has made this pub into a really friendly place that's not flashy or exclusive. In the week, Pub Z is more like a neighbourhood café. At the weekend, DJs liven the place up. The walls are used as a gallery for work by young local artists.

❣ **Bistrot Utopia** (C1, **41** on the map): 4 rue des escaliers Sainte-Anne, La Manutation. ☎ 04-90-27-04-96. Beer around 12F. In the entrance to Utopia, the arthouse and experimental cinema at the centre of Avignon's cultural life. A few tables crowd together under a glass roof along an old counter. Behind the heavy curtains there's a room with a wooden floor, red-velvet sofas and a fireplace. Slightly 'intellectual' crowd and a laid-back welcome. The door beside it is the entrance to the Grand Café (see 'Where to Eat').

❣ **Mon Bar** (C2, **42** on the map): 17 rue Portail-Matheron. ☎ 04-90-85-59-63. A beer costs 12F in this typical local bar. The sign, the decor, the owners and the regulars who prop up the counter seem to have been fixed in a time warp back in the 1940s and 50s.

❣ **Le Red Zone** (C2, **43** on the map): 25 rue Carnot. ☎ 04-90-27-02-44. Open 7pm–3am (from 9pm on Sunday). A beer costs about 14F. At weekends, this very popular bar is a venue for live music, or for DJs mixing salsa, techno and house music.

WHAT TO SEE

The old town of Avignon, covering 14 hectares (35 acres), is the largest listed area in France. Exploring its winding streets, hidden churches, little Italian-style squares, and private mansions to the full can take a number of days, but a whole day will see you through the essentials. Listing sites according to their level of interest is inevitably subjective; instead, the descriptions below follow a walking route that starts and finishes at the station.

If you want to see absolutely everything, the *Carte Pass* (valid for a fortnight for a family of up to five) will save you money. You pay full rate for entrance to the first site you visit, then you get reductions from 20 to 50 per cent for all the other sites in Avignon and Villeneuve-lès-Avignon.

★ **Remparts** (town walls): more than 4 kilometres (2.5 miles) long, with 39 towers and seven main gates, the ramparts are the first view the visitor has of Avignon. The ditches now serve as car parks, and Viollet-le-Duc carried out some rather artificial-looking restorations here and there in the 19th century, but the 11th-century ramparts are still impressive.

★ **Cours Jean-Jaurès** and **rue de la République** (B2–B3 on the map): tourists getting off their tour buses immediately swarm up this right-angled street to get their first view of the Palais des Papes. There are too many fast-food outlets and souvenir shops here, but the narrow side streets hide a few surprises. At the beginning of the cours Jean-Jaurès, turn left before the Le

Cintra brasserie. At the bottom of the rue du Portail-Boquier, you'll find the superb St-Louis cloister, where there is now a smart hotel and an exhibition space (entrance usually free).

★ **Musée Lapidaire** (stone museum) (B3 on the map): 27 rue de la République. ☎ 04-90-86-33-84. Closed Tuesday. Open 10am–1pm and 2–6pm. Entrance fee: 10F. The old chapel of the Jesuit college provides a beautiful setting for part of the archaeological collection of the Musée Calvet (*see* below). The Gallo–Roman period and sculpture dominate. The half-wolf, half-lion *Tarasque de Noves* in the first chapel on the right is a unique piece; experts still don't know whether it dates from Antiquity or medieval times. Also worth seeing is the *Scène de Halage* on the left of the chapel, found at Cabrières-d'Aigue. Used to decorate the mausoleum of a merchant, the frieze shows how wine was transported in Gaul. At the foot of the steps that lead to the choir there's a votive altar to Jupiter-Taranis. There's also a splendid collection of Egyptian, Etruscan and Greek funerary monuments, together with objects from daily life, such as terracotta vases, jewellery, ancient toys, Egyptian and Gallo-Roman bronzes and beautiful stone statues of Gallic warriors.

★ **Rue Joseph-Vernet** (B3–B2 on the map): the smartest street in town, with luxury designer shops side by side with elegant tearooms, housed behind the beautiful facades of 17th- and 18th-century private mansions. The Hôtel de Barbier-Rochefort et de Raousset-Bourbon stands at No. 35, while the Hôtel de Suarez-d'Aula opposite has an old inscription denoting it as a 'modern school for young ladies'. Attached to it is the grimy Oratory chapel, dating from 1747.

★ **Musée Requien** (B2 on the map): 67 rue Joseph Vernet. ☎ 04-90-82-43-51. Closed on Sunday, Monday and public holidays. Open 9am–noon and 2–6pm. Entrance free. This small natural history museum describes how, 6 million years ago, Provence was covered by crystal-clear waters. There's a fine collection of fossils, the petrified trunks of palm trees found at Rustrel, giant gypsum crystals, and stuffed bears from the Ventoux, as well as a display on the production of ochre at Fontaine-de-Vaucluse.

★ **Musée Calvet** (B2 on the map): 65 rue Joseph-Vernet. ☎ 04-90-86-33-84. Closed on Tuesday. Open 10am–1pm and 2–6pm. Entrance fee: 30F, concessions 15F. This superb building from the middle of the 18th century houses a small art museum, displaying works bequeathed in the 19th century, as well as more recent donations. The collection includes French, Spanish and English silver, Chinese and Khmer sculpture and, in the recently opened Victor Martin room, artworks by, among others, Manet, Sisley and Soutine. Even newer rooms display paintings from the 15th to the 19th century (Mignard, Vernet, David and Daumier are all represented), and wrought-iron work.

★ **La Collection Lambert, Musée d'Art Contemporain** (B3 on the map): Hôtel de Caumont, 5 rue Violette-Avignon. ☎ 04-90-16-56-22. Open 11am–7pm (closed on Monday). Entrance fee: 25F (concessions 15F). Yvon Lambert donated this important collection of contemporary art – 450 works, including paintings, installations, videos and photographs – to the town of Avignon. The artists include Christian Boltanski, Nan Goldin, Robert Tyman and Jean-Michel Basquiat. The museum is very well arranged and run, and the building houses an exhibition room, artists' workshops, public seminar rooms, a small restaurant and a bookshop.

★ **Musée Louis Vouland** (A2 on the map): 17 rue Victor-Hugo. ☎ 04-90-86-03-79. Open every day (except Monday and Sunday). Between 2 May and 1 October, open 10am–noon and 2–6pm; during the rest of the year, open 2–6pm only. Entrance fee: 20F (students 10F and children free). This splendid private mansion, built at the end of the 19th century, now houses the prestigious collection of decorative arts amassed by its owner, Louis Vouland. This wealthy Avignonnais made his money in cured meats and in trading with the colonies. From the *salon* to the dining room, practically everything is in perfect condition. It's in an over-the-top Grand Siècle style, but is a real pleasure to visit. Vouland had a particular passion for the 17th and 18th centuries and the collection includes Moustier and Marseilles china, some Delft, delicate statuettes in Saxony porcelain, period chairs from 1720 and 1730 covered in Beauvais tapestries depicting the Fables of La Fontaine (France's answer to Aesop), and a unique (and extremely valuable) travelling tea set belonging to the Countess du Barry. The walls are hung with huge Aubusson and Gobelins tapestries and the Ming vases and porcelain in the Chinese room are exquisite.

★ **Pont St-Bénezet** (B1 on the map): ☎ 04-90-85-60-16. Same opening hours as Palais des Papes (*see below*). Entrance fee: 20F (joint ticket with visit to Palais des Papes, for 56F). This is the bridge of the famous song '*Sur le pont d'Avignon, on y danse, on y danse*'. The song describes people dancing 'on' the bridge but in fact they danced under it, since the traffic crossed over the bridge. It was built in the 12th century and is the oldest construction over the Rhône between Lyon and the Mediterranean. It was destroyed in 1226 and rebuilt in the 13th century with 22 arches. Over time the river swept away the arches and the bridge was finally abandoned in the 17th century. The remains and the two chapels are an essential part of Avignon's history as is the story of the man responsible for the bridge, St Bénezet. It's particularly pretty at sunset when viewed from the Île de la Barthelasse.

★ **Place de l'Horloge** (B2 on the map): on the site of the Roman forum, this square is still the nerve centre of Avignon, with its cafés and outdoor tables. During the festival, it teems with people, who are observed from the facade of the theatre by a statue of Molière. At the corner of the square and the rue de la République, slip into the elegant courtyard of the Palais du Roure (3 rue du Collège-du-Roure, tours possible at 3pm; ☎ 04-90-80-80-88), built in 1469. In the rue de Mons, take a look at the lovely 14th-century Hôtel de Crochans, where you'll find the residence of Jean Vilar, the founder of the Avignon Festival.

★ **Palais des Papes** (Papal Palace) (B1–B2 on the map): ☎ 04-90-27-50-00. Email: rmg@palais-des-papes.com. Open daily 1 April to 1 November 9am–7pm (to 9pm in July, 8pm in August and September). The rest of the year, daily 9.30am–5.45pm. Entrance fee: 46F (56F during summer exhibitions). Last tickets an hour before closing. Guided tours and audio-guides are both included in the price. Some parts of the palace are closed to the public due to renovation work.

Described by Froissart as 'the most beautiful and most heavily fortified house in the world', Avignon's papal palace is a huge Gothic building. Its rooms, chapels and frescoes are very impressive and it's well worth a visit, despite the hype; allow at least an hour.

The Palais des Papes is one of the most significant places in the history of France. A magnificent example of 14th-century Gothic architecture, the building, constructed between 1334 and 1352, is split into two major parts – the 'old' palace and the 'new' one.

First stop on the visit, the *cour d'honneur* (main courtyard), covers 1800 square metres (2150 square yards). At first, theatre director Jean Vilar saw it as *un lieu théâtral impossible* ('an impossible space for theatre'), yet it has acted as a backdrop to the festival for more than half a century now.

The second pope to reside in Avignon, John XXII, was also bishop of the town. He decided to enlarge and improve his episcopal palace, which then became the site for the construction of the first papal palace (Le Palais Vieux), commissioned by the pope who firmly established the papacy in Avignon, Benoît XII. His successor Clement VI built the new palace (Le Palais Neuf) and, in 1348, bought the town from Jeanne, Countess of Provence. Inevitably, the town became one of the most prosperous in Europe. The quality of its architecture improved considerably and the domain was extended as far as Villeneuve, where Innocent VI founded a monastery.

In the portrait gallery, you can put a face to each pope. Or can you? In fact, the portraits were all painted in the same period using the same artist's model!

The palace is rather bare today, but it was incredibly opulent in the time of the popes, as the model in the first room shows. Vast gardens were filled with exotic animals and birds. Grand banquets were held in the 48-metre Salle du Grand Tinel. The pope's table was on a raised dais, reflecting his near-divinity. Guests ate from gold and silver chargers and the cutlery had ivory handles. At the end of a banquet, the doors were closed so the tableware and cutlery could be counted before the guests were allowed to leave. The kitchen workers would prepare amazing feasts. For the coronation of Clement V, for example, they cooked 118 oxen, 1,023 lambs, 60 pigs, 1,195 geese, 1,500 capons, 7,428 chickens and 50,000 tarts. In fact, the illustrious guests apparently tucked into a total of 95,000 dishes.

On the third floor of the Tour des Anges (angels' tower), you find the pope's bed-chamber, where the tiny glazed squares of the floor have been totally restored in the style of the 14th-century original. The beautiful painted decor shows deer hunts, falconry, ferretting and a fascinating 'fish tank', seen from the inside. Interestingly, there are no religious scenes. The larch-wood ceiling is in typical French style. The pontifical chapel, devoid of decoration, frequently hosts exhibitions.

Seven successive popes lived in this palace, until Gregory XI decided to return to Rome in 1376. On his death, in 1378, the Great Schism tore the Catholic Church apart and two popes competed for supremacy – one in the Vatican and one in Avignon (where he and his followers were known as the 'anti-popes'). The conflict was settled politically. Seeing their temporal powers threatened by this war for spiritual dominance, the sovereigns of Europe agreed to throw out the two rivals and install a malleable third in Rome.

★ **Musée du Petit Palais** (B1 on the map): ☎ 04-90-86-44-58. From October to May, open every day (except Tuesday and some public holidays) 9.30am–1pm and 2–5.30pm. Between June and September, open 10am–1pm and 2–6pm. Entrance fee: 30F; free for under-18s every day from 1 September to 30 June. This museum occupies a beautiful 14th-century building, formerly the residence of the town's bishops. It contains works from the Middle Ages and the Renaissance, from the Campana collection, including paintings from the Venice, Florence and Siena schools, the school of the Marches, and by Botticelli.

★ **Cathedral of Notre-Dame-des-Doms** (B1 on the map): the oldest religious building in the town, rebuilt in the middle of the 13th century and topped in the 19th century by a glittering statue of the Virgin (of questionable taste). In the choir, there's a 12th-century seat in white marble where the popes of Avignon sat in session. The tomb of John XXIII (1345) is in the chapel next to the sacristy. Irregular opening hours (closed Sunday morning); a generous donation is invited in lieu of an entrance fee.

★ **Rocher des Doms** (B1 on the map): this landmark rock is a prehistoric site, later a Celto-Ligurian fortified town, and Avignon's birthplace. Today it has been transformed into a park, where there's a lovely walk with a beautiful view of the Rhône and the Île de la Barthelasse (the largest river island in France). On clear days, you can see the Ventoux. There's also a sundial, which uses the observer's shadow to show the time.

★ **Rue Banasterie** (C1–B2 on the map): from the Rocher des Doms, a flight of steps leads to the main road of a peaceful area which used to be the district of the *banastiers* (basket-makers). In the 17th and 18th centuries, the upper-middle class moved in. At the foot of the steps stands the little 17th-century Chapelle des Pénitents Noirs (Chapel of the Black Penitents). Hidden along the rue Banasterie you will find some beautiful private mansions, particularly the 17th-century Maison Gracié-de-Vinay at No. 17, and the Hôtel Madon-de-Château-Blanc at No. 13. At the very end is the church of St-Pierre, where you will have content yourself with admiring the superb 16th-century Gothic facade, the superb portal and the very tall 14th-century belfry; it is usually kept closed.

★ **Chapellerie Mouret** (Mouret hatter's shop) (B2 on the map): 20 rue des Marchands. In the pedestrian district. ☎ 04-90-85-39-38. The first and only hatter's shop in France to be classified by the historic monuments association, the Chapellerie Mouret has kept all its original Louis XVI decor, dating from around 1860.

★ **Church of St-Didier** (B2 on the map): a nice example of a southern Gothic church, built in the 14th century, with a beautifully simple facade. The unique nave is finished with a pentagonal apse. In the first chapel on the right (press the button for illumination), is the 14th-century marble ensemble commissioned by Good King René: the Virgin embodies goodness, while the centurions (particularly the one on the extreme left) really have a look of the gallows about them. Near by, in rue du Laboureur, have a quick look at the facade of the old Livrée Ceccano (cardinal's palace), now the municipal library.

★ **Angladon-Dubrujeaud Foundation** (B3 on the map): 5 rue du Laboureur. ☎ 04-90-82-29-03. Fax: 04-90-85-78-07. Website: www.angladon.

THE RHÔNE VALLEY AND HAUTE-PROVENCE

com. Open all year Wednesday to Sunday 1–6pm. Also open on Tuesday in high season 1–6pm (to 7pm in July and August and from 3pm on public holidays). Guided tours available during the week (must be booked). Entrance fee: 30F (concessions 20F and children 7–14 years old 10F). Jean and Paulette Angladon-Dubrujeaud inherited this collection – which includes works by some of the greatest artists of the 18th, 19th and 20th centuries (from Daumier and Derain to Sisley and Picasso) – from famous collector Jacques Doucet. According to their wishes, it is shown in their own house, an old private mansion.

The rooms of the house are organized around two small courtyards. At garden level, you find a *Nature morte* (Still life) by Cézanne, Sisley's *Paysage sous la neige* (*Countryside in the Snow*) hanging alongside pictures by other masters as well as African masks. On the first floor, where the donors lived, an interior has been re-created to look like the home of an art lover. You go in through a small sitting room, then a large 18th-century *salon*, furnished and hung with pictures, before getting to the Chinese *salon*. In the drawing cabinet, the works have to be presented in rotation, because there are so many of them. Medieval, Renaissance and 17th-century rooms follow, displaying more recent acquisitions. Finally, an artist's studio shows the technique of engraving that was so admired by the Angladon-Dubrujeauds.

★ **Rue du Roi-René** (C2 on the map): this narrow street is lined with the high, dark facades of 17th-century private mansions. Imagine a canal, instead of the road and narrow pavements, and you could be in Venice.

★ **Rue des Teinturiers** (C3–D3 on the map): this charming street, with its river, is quiet out of season, but completely transformed at festival time. Little gangways lead up to the houses. The name (dyers' street), comes from the manufacturers of *indiennes* (traditional printed cotton fabrics), who lived in the district in the 18th century. In the middle of the street stands the Chapelle des Pénitents-Gris (Chapel of the Grey Penitents; open 9am–noon and 2.30–7pm; closed Monday until 3pm and Sunday until noon). It is the headquarters of the last of the seven *confréries* (brotherhoods) that used to exist in Avignon. (Incidentally, if seven is a magic number, then Avignon should be particularly lucky: the name has seven letters, there are seven gates, the town is divided into seven parishes, and it had seven popes . . .)

VILLENEUVE-LÈS-AVIGNON (30400)

Population: 12,078

Even though it definitely smells of and looks like Provence, Villeneuve-lès-Avignon is in fact the most easterly town in the region of Languedoc-Roussillon. Sited on the banks of the Rhône, up against the hills, it has long suffered from being in the shadow of its near neighbour Avignon. However, its own heritage is exceptional and, since its Carthusian monastery became a centre for artistic creativity, this right bank town has developed an independent cultural identity. There's another reason for coming here. The hotels in Avignon are often full in summer, particularly at festival time. It's much easier to find rooms in Villeneuve, or in Les Angles, the little village next door.

History

Separating Villeneuve from Avignon is the River Rhône, a natural and historic border. The country on the Villeneuve side belonged to the Kingdom of France, while Avignon was the domain of the popes and their cardinals. The origins of Villeneuve go back to Casarie, a holy woman and the daughter of a Visigoth king, who died in AD 586. The Abbey of St-André was built on her tomb. It perches today on top of Mount Andaon, looking like a Spanish fortress on this pinnacle of a rock.

French King Philippe le Bel, aware of the strategic importance of French territory so close to Avignon, built a keep at the entrance to the St-Bénezet bridge and fortified the abbey of St-André. In the 14th century, after the popes had set up home over the river, Jean le Bon and Philippe VI de Valois turned the abbey into a symbol of royal power in the sight of the papal palace.

Villeneuve's 'Golden Age' coincided with that of Avignon. Wealthy cardinals settled in sumptuous *livrées cardinalices* (palaces) of which the present-day Musée Pierre de Luxembourg is a fine example. The Carthusian monastery dates from the 14th century and was built around the *livrée* belonging to Étienne Aubert, better known as Pope Innocent VI, who loved Villeneuve.

The splendour of Villeneuve, so closely linked to the power of the Church, was brought to an abrupt end by the Revolution. Since then, the town has returned to a more modest existence as a district of Avignon.

USEFUL ADDRESSES

Tourist office: 1 place Charles-David, near a big car park. ☎ 04-90-25-61-55 (or 61-33). Fax: 04-90-25-91-55. Open daily in July 9.30am–7pm; in August 8.45am–12.30pm and 2–6pm; September to June Monday to Friday 8.45am–12.30pm and 2–6pm. Very helpful staff. Two-hour guided tours, almost essential if you want to understand the Carthusian monastery; leave from the tourist office (ask for times).

■ **Taxis Villeneuvois**: 2 rue de la République (opposite the town hall). ☎ 04-90-25-88-88.

■ **Swimming pool**: chemin St-Honoré. Near the campsite north of the St-André fort.

WHERE TO STAY

☆ Budget

Centre de rencontres internationales du Pont d'Avignon (CRIPA) (YMCA): 7bis chemin de la Justice. ☎ 04-90-25-46-20. Fax: 04-90-25-30-64. ♿ From Villeneuve tourist office, take the Avignon road, turn right by the Royaume bridge (in the direction of Les Angles); chemin de la Justice is 300 metres further on, on the left. The hostel is at the end of this road, on the left again. Closed for one week at Christmas. Rooms for one to three people (no sharing with strangers) for 150–220F, depending on season. There are about 100 beds, and washing facilities; half and full board are also available. The hostel is on the top of a hill, with a fabulous sunset view of Avignon, of the Rhône and Mont Ventoux and, from some rooms, of the Palais des Papes. The group of buildings includes one from the 19th century and there's a swimming pool and a bar. It's a great place to stay, especially when it's buzzing with young people.

☆☆ Moderate

🛏 **Chambres d'hôte** (B&B): with M. Bruno Eyrier, 15 rue de la Foire. Easy to find, in the heart of Villeneuve-lès-Avignon, a minute's walk from the collegiate church and town hall. Ring the bell where you see the sign 'Eyrier'. ☎ and fax: 04-90-25-44-21. Open all year. Double room for 400F. Booking advisable. This rather grand house has a staircase with a wrought-iron banister leading to five rooms and three studios, tastefully arranged with souvenirs and treasures of the Eyrier family. Room No. 1 has a bed with a canopy, a chimney-piece in carved wood, and a French ceiling with period painting. You can make your own breakfast. There are bathrooms in some rooms, and showers on the landing. Cars may be parked in the private courtyard. The owner is warm and friendly, just like his house.

🛏 **Chambres d'hôte Les Jardins de la Livrée** (B&B): 4bis rue Camp-de-Bataille. In the heart of town. ☎ 04-90-26-05-05. Closed on Sunday evening and Monday in low season and in November. Double rooms 300–520F. Menus 110–145F. This relatively new building is attractively decorated, with comfortable rooms, and a lovely swimming pool in the garden. The cuisine is simple but tasty.

🛏 **Hôtel de l'Atelier**: 5 rue de la Foire. Centrally located, at the start of the street. ☎ 04-90-25-01-84. Fax: 04-90-25-80-06. Closed from early November to early December. Double room with shower or bath

275–460F. This 16th-century house has 19 quiet and comfortable rooms furnished in old-fashioned style, with TV and telephone, a pleasant flowery patio for breakfast and a terrace overlooking the rooftops. It's good value for money and essential to book in season. An empty church serves as a garage.

🛏 **Hôtel-restaurant Les Cèdres**: 39 boulevard Pasteur. Two kilometres from the centre of town. ☎ 04-90-25-43-92. Fax: 04-90-25-14-66. Closed from the beginning of November to the end of March. Double rooms with shower (or bath) and toilet 318–450F. Menus 120–175F. In a quiet area, this hotel stands in pleasant grounds with a pool. The rooms, furnished in old-fashioned style, in the steward's house, are pretty smart and reasonably priced. The food is good, with such dishes as *carpaccio de lotte aux senteurs de vanille* (marinated monkfish with vanilla flavouring) and *charlotte d'agneau au basilic* (lamb with basil).

Campsite

🛏 **Camping municipal de la Laune**: chemin St-Honoré, at the base of the northern face of the St-André fort. From the tourist office, take the main road towards Sauveterre. The site is on the right after about 1 kilometre. Bus No. 11 for Avignon stops at the entrance. ☎ 04-90-25-76-06. Fax: 04-90-25-91-88-03. Closed from 16 October to end March. Around 85F per night for two people plus tent and vehicle. This quiet site has good shade and lots of space between the pitches, spotless facilities, a small snack bar and a municipal swimming pool and tennis courts (free for campers) near by. You can also hire bikes.

WHERE TO EAT

✕ **Restaurant La Calèche**: 35 rue de la République. ☎ 04-90-25-02-54. ✕ Closed Thursday evening, all day Sunday and in November. Menus at 79F and 98F. The two communicating rooms of this restaurant, which also has a terrace and patio, are prettily decorated in warm tones with masses of posters and Toulouse-Lautrec reproductions on the walls. The service is friendly and the cooking decent. Specialities include *pieds et paquets marseillais* (tripe) and *confits d'agneau* (preserved lamb).

✕ **Restaurant La Maison**: 1 rue Montée-du-Fort-St-André. ☎ 04-90-25-20-81. Closed Tuesday evening, Wednesday, Saturday lunch and the second fortnight in August. Menu 120F. This restaurant overlooks place Jean-Jaurès, at the back of the town hall. The decor is sophisticated, with lace curtains at the windows and an interesting collection of pottery. The food is simple but well prepared and portions are generous. The prices are fair given the location, and the cooling fans are a godsend on hot days. The service is friendly and good.

WHERE TO EAT AND STAY IN THE AREA

🛏 ✕ **Hôtel-restaurant Le Clément V**: route de Nîmes, Roquemaure. ☎ 04-66-82-67-58. Fax: 04-66-82-84-66. Email: hotel.clement @wanadoo.fr. Closed at the weekend out of season and from 25 October to 15 March. Double rooms 320–340F and half board (compulsory in July and August) 275–295F. Menus at 98F and 125F (restaurant open only to hotel guests). This little-known medieval village in the Côtes du Rhône makes a very pleasant place to stop. The Clément V is run by the very friendly Annie and James. There are 19 rooms, all with well-equipped bathrooms and some with balconies overlooking the swimming pool, as well as a health centre

and a gym. A perfect base for exploring Provence and visiting the summer festivals in Orange and Avignon, and good value for money.

🛏 ✕ **Le Petit Manoir**: 15 avenue Jules-Ferry, 30133 Les Angles (a neighbouring village southwest of Villeneuve). Take the Nîmes road and the follow the signposts to the left. ☎ 04-90-25-03-36. Fax: 04-90-25-49-13. Double rooms 270–360F. The 'manor' is in fact a group of modern buildings arranged around a swimming pool. The comfortable rooms are quiet and clean, and many have terraces. The restaurant, La Tonnelle, serves good menus based on traditional regional fare from 98F to 250F.

WHERE TO HAVE AN ICE CREAM

🍦 **Gelateria Notre-Dame**: 8 rue Fabrigoule (in the old town). ☎ 04-90-26-04-15. Closed on Sunday. This friendly ice-cream parlour makes and sells Italian-style ice-creams and delicious sorbets. Eat on the terrace, inside the shop or take away.

WHAT TO SEE

★ **Chartreuse du Val-de-Bénédiction** (Carthusian monastery, or charter-house, of Val-de-Bénédiction): in the centre of the town, at the foot of the northern slope of Mont Andaon, the site of the St-André fort. Main entrance: rue de la République. ☎ 04-90-15-24-24. Open 9.30am–5.30pm from October to March; 9am–6.30pm from April to September. Closed 1 January, 1 May, 1 and 11 November and 25 December. Entrance fee: 32F (21F for under-25s, free for under-18s, and for all on the first Sunday of the month between October and end May). There is a choice of visits, including a 45-minute self-guided tour, guided tours (book one week ahead) and visits for the visually impaired.

Founded in the 14th century by Pope Innocent VI, and used more recently as a venue for shows during the Avignon Festival, this significant and enthralling place has always been dedicated to spirituality and creativity. In the begin-ning, it was the richest and biggest Carthusian monastery in France, covering 2.5 hectares (6 acres) on one site on the right bank of the Rhône. When the Revolution came, the monks were forced to abandon it. Most of the buildings were sold, while others fell into ruin. The monastery was rediscovered by Mérimée in 1834, classified as a national monument in 1905 and, since 1991, has been the headquarters of the CNES (a national centre for playwriting).

Gradually, the charterhouse is undergoing restoration, while at the same time remaining open both to writers and visitors. Grant-aided, artists writing for the theatre, performance art or the screen may stay here, in the old monks' cells, to work. The programme has brought the old building back to life. The CNES also organizes the Rencontres internationales d'été (international summer encounters), during which shows, seminars, concerts, exhibitions and conferences take place.

While visiting the site, don't miss the tomb of Innocent VI, the small and large cloister, the monks' cells, where the austere contemplative life in the charterhouse is manifest, and the chapel with its frescoes by Matteo Giavannetti.

★ **St-André Fort**: perched atop Mont Andaon, and surrounded by an extraordinary circlet of walls, this fortified castle looks as though it could have been transported from some Castilian desert. Open 10am–noon and 2–5pm (to 5.30pm in summer). Two entrance tickets are available, one for the twin towers (publicly owned), the other for the privately owned abbey gardens. It was built on the orders of King Philippe le Bel of France, between 1362 and 1368, ostensibly to protect the little town of St-André that perched on top of Mont Andaon. But it was there also, and above all, in order to assert the power of the French king, to confront the lands of the papacy and the Holy Roman Empire across the Rhône. The sumptuous Italian-style gardens have admirable views over Avignon and the Rhône valley. Access to the walls is free.

★ **Musée Pierre de Luxembourg**: rue de la République, 50 metres from the collegiate church of Notre-Dame. ♿ Open 10am–noon and 2–5.30pm from October to March; 10am–12.30pm and 3–7pm from April to September. Closed Monday except from mid-June to mid-September, and in February. Entrance fee: 20F (concessions 12F), also gives entry to the cloister of the collegiate church. Housed in the palace of Cardinal Pierre de Luxembourg (first built in the 14th century and reconstructed in 1664), this museum has a number of masterpieces, from the 14th-century *Ivory Virgin*, carved from a single elephant's tusk, to the 15th-century *Coronation of the Virgin*, a superb altarpiece by Enguerrand Quarton.

★ **Tour Philippe-le-Bel**: avenue Gabriel-Péri, on the Avignon road. Same opening times as the Musée Pierre de Luxembourg. ♿ Access to the the ground floor only. Entrance fee: 10F (concessions 6F). Built in 1307 as a watchtower from which to keep an eye on the entrance to Avignon's St-Bénezet bridge, Philippe's tower has a remarkable spiral staircase leading to a top-floor terrace with a wonderful view. The tower is floodlit at night and there's a permanent exhibition room on the ground floor.

★ **Collegiate Church of Notre-Dame**: same opening times as the Musée Pierre de Luxembourg. Entrance fee for the cloister. Built in 1320 by Cardinal Arnaud de Via, the nephew of Pope John XXII, the church has a superb marble altar with a prostrate figure of Christ dating from 1745. The cloister is attached to the northern wall of the church.

★ **Sentier de la plaine de l'abbaye** (path through the abbey garden): this walk takes you along the canal, past plants that provide essential oils, such as bay leaf, hawthorn and sweet rush. If you want to be able to identify them, pick up a free leaflet from the tourist office.

WHAT TO SEE IN THE AREA

★ **Pont du Gard**: this bridge may be a familiar sight from photographs, but it's definitely worth seeing in real life. An aqueduct of impressive dimensions, in a spectacular location, it used to carry water from a spring that rose near Uzès to Nîmes. You can swim in the Gard river below the bridge. Car park 20F (make sure you lock your car securely as a number of thefts have been reported).

FESTIVAL

– **Villeneuve en Scène**: taking its inspiration from the Avignon Festival, Villeneuve now has its own, very different summer event. It does not attempt to rival Avignon, but focuses on musical theatre, with about 20 companies producing shows in the open air or at various indoor venues, such as the Chapelle des Pénitents-Gris (Chapel of the Grey Penitents) and the collegiate church.

LEAVING VILLENEUVE-LÈS-AVIGNON

– **By train**: Avignon SNCF train station. ☎ 08-36-35-35-35. Avignon to Paris by TGV (high-speed train) takes 3 hours 20 minutes.

– **By plane:** Avignon airport is 15 kilometres (9 miles) away.

– **Bus no. 11 for Avignon**: stops outside Villeneuve's collegiate church, near the tourist office, as well as in the rue de la République, just next to the entrance to the monastery. Four buses an hour make the trip, which takes about 15 minutes.

CAVAILLON (84300)　　　Population: 24,563

This town in the middle of a plain between the Durance and the Coulon, at the foot of St-Jacques hill, an outcrop tagged on to the Luberon mountains, is best known for its melons. It's a quiet, very Provençal place, with courtyards that are shaded by plane trees and café terraces along the streets.

Cavaillon Melons

As early as the 15th century, farmers around Cavaillon discovered that their land, combined with the warm, sunny climate, was perfectly adapted to cultivating the melon, originally from India. Today, melons grown in and around Cavaillon have maintained their reputation and still fetch a very high price in the Paris markets. Right from its introduction, this delicious fruit has inspired something of a cult following, from Mazarin, the Duc de Guise, and the Avignon popes (who were very supportive of its cultivation), to writer Alexandre Dumas, who donated his complete works to the library in Cavaillon in exchange for a pension of 12 melons a year.

Cantaloup, Charentais (the best-known variety), Verday and Canari – the Cavaillon melon in all its varieties recalls delightful holidays in the sun. Low in sugar (contrary to some expectations) and rich in vitamins, it's definitely the healthy option – although there is a story that one of the popes died from indigestion after eating too many!

USEFUL ADDRESSES

🛈 **Tourist office** (A2 on the map): place François-Tourel. ☎ 04-90-71-32-01. Fax: 04-90-71-42-99. Open every day (except Sunday afternoon) in summer 9am–12.30pm and 2–7pm. In winter, open from Monday to Saturday 9am–12.30pm and 2–6.30pm. The helpful staff can point you to the use-ful material on Cavaillon and the Luberon.

🚃 **Train station** (B2 on the map): avenue du Maréchal-Joffre. ☎ 08-36-35-35-35.

■ **Bike hire**: Cycles Rieu, 25 avenue du Maréchal-Joffre. ☎ 04-90-71-45-55. Cycles Brignon, 166 cours Gambetta. ☎ 04-90-78-07-06.

WHERE TO STAY

🏠 **Hôtel Bel Air** (B1, **1** on the map): 62 rue Bel-Air. ☎ 04-90-78-11-75. Open all year. Double rooms with washbasin and toilet cost 190F, or 210F with shower and toilet. This small, simple and pleasant hotel with its seven attrac-tive rooms offers a discreet and charming welcome, and plenty of information on Cavaillon and the surrounding area. The breakfast includes seasonal fruit and home-made jam, served at a large com-munal table.

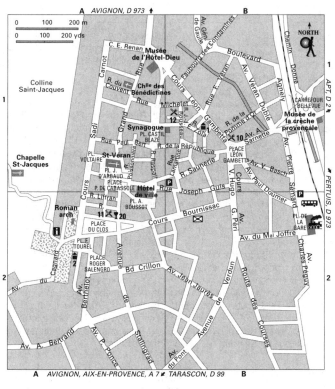

A *AVIGNON, AIX-EN-PROVENCE, A 7 ✈ TARASCON, D 99* **B**

CAVAILLON

- **■ Useful Addresses**

  🛈 Tourist office
  🚆 SNCF train station
  ✉ Post office

- **🏠 Where to Stay**

  1 Hôtel Bel Air
  2 Hôtel du Parc

- **✕ Where to Eat**

  10 La Cuisine du Marché
  11 Le Fin de Siècle
  12 Fleur de thym

- **🍷 Where to Go for a Drink**

  20 Le Fin de Siècle

🏠 Hôtel du Parc (A2, **2** on the map): 183 place François-Tourel. ☎ 04-90-71-57-78. Fax: 04-90-76-10-35. Open all year round. Double rooms with shower and toilet, or with bath, cost 275F and 290F.

This large old house, with a friendly welcome and a family atmosphere, overlooks the Roman arch. The air-conditioned rooms are in classic, even opulent, style and there's a colonnaded sun terrace.

WHERE TO EAT

☆☆ Moderate

✕ **La Cuisine du Marché** (B1, **10** on the map): 13 place Gambetta-l'étoile. ☎ 04-90-71-56-00. Fax: 04-90-38-38-19. Closed on Tuesday evening and on Wednesday. Menus from 80F (weekdays) to 190F. This restaurant is rather let down by its location, on a roundabout and on the first floor of a soulless building, but its decor is simple and the tasty food makes the most of fresh produce from the market. The cooking is Provençal and might include *daurade* (sea bream) or *encornets à la provençale* (squid in tomato and garlic sauce).

✕ **Le Fin de Siècle** (A2, **11** on the map): 42 place du Clos. ☎ 04-90-71-28-85. Brasserie closed on Sunday. The lunch *formule* menu in the brasserie costs 69F. Restaurant menus start at 90F. A staircase leads up to an elegant Louis XIII-style dining room, with a plush atmosphere, silver service, lace napkins and candelabra. The traditional cuisine represents good value for money.

☆☆☆ Chic

✕ **Restaurant Fleur de Thym** (B1, **12** on the map): 91 rue Jean-Jacques-Rousseau (road parallel to cours Gambetta). ☎ and fax: 04-90-71-14-64. Closed on Sunday evening. The lunch *formule* menu (main course and dessert) costs 85F during the week. Other menus at 125F and 180F, and à la carte around 160F. This is another good find in its category. Behind the pale yellow exterior is a lovely vaulted stone cellar with a large fireplace. The chef performs minor miracles with the remarkably fresh produce. His cooking is Provençal in style, but imaginative and innovative too. The pleasant *menu-carte* changes with the seasons.

WHERE TO EAT IN THE AREA

☆☆☆☆ Très Chic

✕ **Nicolet**: route de Pertuis, 84460 Cheval-Blanc. 4 kilometres (2.5 miles) from Cavaillon. ☎ 04-90-78-01-56. Fax: 04-90-71-91-28. ☙ Closed on Sunday evening and on Monday (except in July and August). Menus at 150F, 225F and 360F. This modern, four-star farmhouse in the foothills of the Luberon offers some of the best food in the area around Cavaillon. The floral decor in the dining room matches the waistcoats of the attentive waiters. The pleasant terrace beneath the olive treas has a magnificent view of the Alpilles. Alain Nicolet's cooking evokes natural, mainly Provençal flavours – *pistou de rougets aux petits épeautres du Ventoux* (pesto soup with red mullet and Ventoux spelt), *pigeon rôti sauce Châteauneuf-du-Pape* (roast pigeon in Châteauneuf-du-Pape wine sauce) – and there's a remarkable cheese platter, rye bread with walnuts and a delicious selection of desserts. Everything is perfect, and a little dish of nibbles helps you to forget the bill.

WHERE TO GO FOR A DRINK

⛯ Le Fin de Siècle (A2, **20** on the map): 42 place du Clos. ☎ 04-90-71-28-85. This café-brasserie opened in 1899 and has changed little since. Its vast mirrors have miraculously escaped damage despite a few fights, according to the boss, as have the gilded mouldings and the chandeliers. The whole thing is listed as being of architectural interest, and well worth visiting.

WHAT TO SEE

★ **Arc de Triomphe** (triumphal arch): on the place du Clos, opposite the tourist office. Built by the Romans in the first century in the centre of town, the arch was moved to its present location in the 19th century.

★ **Cathedral of St-Véran**: open 1 October to 31 March, 10am–noon and 2–4pm. Rest of the year 10am–noon and 3–6pm. Closed Sunday and Monday. Consecrated in the 13th century by Pope Innocent IV, the cathedral has retained its Romanesque character. The nave has six bays and broken cradle vaulting. On the right of the entrance, a grimacing skeleton decorates the cenotaph of J.-B. de Sade. In St-Véran chapel, there's a painting by Mignard (1657) of the town's patron saint, restraining the Couloubre, a legendary monster that used to terrorize the region. In the César de Bus chapel there are some wonderful 17th-century gilded carvings. Attached to the cathedral is a charming, cool cloister.

★ **The Synagogue**: rue Hébraïque. ☎ 04-90-76-00-34. Closed on Tuesday throughout the year. From 1 April to 30 September, open 9.30am–12.30pm and 2.30–6.30pm. During the rest of the year, open 9am–noon and 2–5pm but closed on Saturday and Sunday. Entrance fee: 20F (12–15-year-olds 10F, and under-12s, students and the unemployed free). Considered to be one of the jewels of French-Jewish architectural heritage, Cavaillon's synagogue was built in the 18th century and retains its original decoration. The elegant and rich interior is pure Louis XV, with superb bronze light fittings, chandeliers and engraved wooden panelling on the walls. On the pulpit, there's a holy arch surrounded by a metal grill. Inside, in the old baker's shop, there's a small Musée Juif (Jewish museum), recounting the history of the Jewish community in the region and displaying several lovely artefacts, including a 17th-century Torah, a Roman oil lamp, amulets and prayer books.

From 1453, Jews in Cavaillon, as in the rest of the Vaucluse region, were compelled to live in specified districts called *carrières*, symbol of the papal state's attitude of segregation tempered with tolerance. In the 17th century, the community numbered around 200 and operated as a self-ruling republic, with its own rules and leaders. They were forbidden to do business with the Christians. Since the 1950s, there have been no 'Provençal Jews' in Cavaillon.

★ **Musée Hôtel-Dieu**: porte d'Avignon. ☎ 04-90-76-00-34. Signposted from the town centre. ♿ Same opening hours as the Synagogue between 1 June and 30 September. Between 1 October and 31 May, open by appointment for groups and educational tours. Entrance fee: 20F (12–15-year-olds 10F, and under-12s, students and the unemployed free). This museum, housed in the chapel (1775) of the former Hôtel-Dieu, has artefacts from the old hospital pharmacy (pestles and mortars, and vessels for ointments), as well as an interesting archaeological collection (vases, neolithic jewels and weapons found in the Luberon, Gallo-Greek and Gallo-Roman funerary relics, stamped ceramics, statuary, including a beautiful head of Agrippina from the first century AD, Gallo-Roman coins and a medieval altar from the cathedral). Temporary art exhibitions are also held here.

★ **Colline St-Jacques** (St-Jacques hill): from the place du Clos, take the 15th-century steps to the top of the hill (a good 15-minute walk). At the summit stands the Romanesque Chapelle St-Jacques, built in the 12th century. There's a wonderful view, a discovery trail through the Parc du Luberon and a forest track.

★ **Musée de la Crèche Provençale** (museum of Provençal nativity cribs): route des Taillades. ☎ 04-90-71-25-97. ♿ Located 1.5 kilometres from the town centre, signposted from the bypass. Open every day 9am–noon and 2.30–6.30pm, but closed on Sunday morning. Entrance fee: 25F (15F for under-10s). This museum displays the work of an enthusiastic craftsman, who has re-created village scenes from the 19th-century Luberon and Les Alpilles in three different scales. The detail includes hand-carved stones and tiny roof tiles and, inevitably, numerous *santons* (terracotta figurines).

FESTIVALS AND EVENTS

– **Le Corso**: a festive procession of floats that takes place from Ascension Day to the following Saturday.

– **Melon festivals**: in July, the melon is celebrated with public banquets, tastings in the street, enthronements by the Confrérie des Chevaliers de l'Ordre du Melon de Cavaillon (Brotherhood of the Knights of the Order of the Melon of Cavaillon) and exhibitions.

– **International folklore festival**: this celebration of folklore takes place in July and August.

– **Fête de la St-Gilles**: festival over several days at the beginning of September, with events in the streets and a fun fair.

– **Concours de chant**: singing contest held at the beginning of September. Amateurs are welcome, but need to enter before 25 August.

The Luberon

THE RHÔNE VALLEY AND HAUTE-PROVENCE

Located between the superb Roman ruins of Vaison and Aix-en-Provence, with its easy-going atmosphere, this mountain stretches for 65 kilometres (40 miles) west to east, from Cavaillon to Manosque. This natural frontier may only be crossed via the Lourmarin pass, which divides the *petit* and the *grand* Luberon. The locals claim that the air here is the purest in Europe and the Luberon is classified by UNESCO as a biosphere of particular interest. In the north, the mountains fall away towards the valley where the Calavon river snakes down from Apt. It's a landscape of steep slopes, hidden valleys and superb villages facing each other on the outcrops. In the south, the slopes are more undulating and flow along the valley of the Durance. At the top, a narrow and rectangular line of peaks reach 1,125m (3,690 feet) at their highest, at the Mourre-Nègre.

Geographically speaking, this defines the Luberon, but the tourist industry has made it into a micro-region that overlaps the mountains, incorporating Vaucluse mountain villages such as Gordes and Roussillon, while the area of the Parc Naturel Régional, established in 1977, even extends into Haute-Provence.

Looking after the Luberon

Traditionally, farmers left this mountain area to the crickets and troupes of wild boar, choosing instead to work the richer soils of the plain. The area was revived in the 1950s and 60s by artists who came to live in the mountain villages. Tourists and a few jet-setters, bored by St-Tropez, followed, and the Luberon was duly discovered. Gordes, Lourmarin, Ménerbes and Roussillon found themselves on the lists of the 'most beautiful villages in France'. At the end of the 1980s, Peter Mayle's hugely successful book *A Year in Provence* led to an invasion by coach-loads of tourists.

The Luberon's new-found fame has led to some unfortunate results, most obvious in high season. Rich second-home owners live in their superbly restored *mas* and *bastides* for just one month, and close them up behind forbidding security systems for the rest of the year; fashion victims throng the terraces of every village café; town councillors introduce more and more parking charges; hotels and B&Bs automatically assume that every guest is an American tourist; and there has been a staggering increase in hotel and restaurant prices, although service has not necessarily improved in line, especially in establishments with fewer than three stars. Making a hotel booking six months in advance is not uncommon. There are more than 200 *gîtes*, many of which are booked from year to year; indeed, some say that the only *gîtes* available are the ones that have been built that year.

Fortunately, there is more than one Luberon. Beyond the Luberon of writers, painters, show-biz stars and politicians, who live within striking distance of the 'Golden Triangle' of Gordes, Roussillon and Ménerbes, many places have been bypassed by tourism. In the south of the Grand Luberon, in the hills by Apt, it's still possible to find the 'real' Provence. The villages around here may be less spectacular than their more famous neighbours, but they have managed to hold on to their integrity, with games of *pétanque* under the trees, and old men on benches watching the world go by.

When to Go

In summer, the crowds in the Luberon are terrible and the heat can be oppressive; winters, on the other hand, are harsh. Spring is the perfect time to go (although, in the very early months, it can still be fresh and, in spite of the region's 2,800 hours of sun a year, it does rain). As the weather starts to warm up, the countryside is superb. The trees, covered in white and pale pink blossoms, contrast with the pale grey of the rocks and the stone walls,

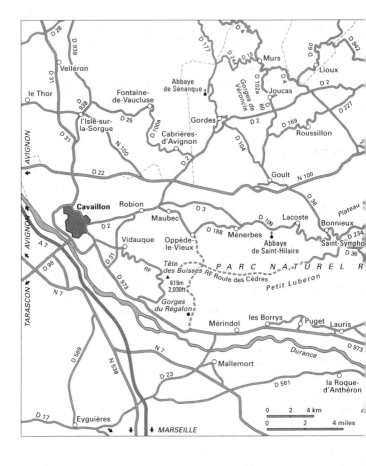

and the many shades of green in the fields. The sun lights the warm stonework of the old villages, and the ochre of the bare hills. Autumn is also a very attractive season (the average temperature in October is 18°C/65°F), when the vineyards and forests are splodged with russet, yellow and scarlet, and there are wild mushrooms to pick (keep an eye out for hunters) in the undergrowth.

Getting Around

– **On foot**: walking is the best way of exploring the Luberon and there are many marked footpaths to follow. Watch out for the scorching sun in summer, because there is very little water; always take a bottle of water with you. A lovely network of trails includes three GRs (long-distance footpaths) (Nos. 4, 6 and 9) and two alternatives, the GR92 and GR97,

TOUR OF THE LUBERON

which allow you either to cross the Luberon or to do a tour of it. Look for the following maps published by IGN: green series No. 67, and *Top 25* series Nos. 3242, 3142, 3243 and 3342.

François Morenas, who lives in the youth hostel above Saignon, is a mine of information. Alternatively, various organizations arrange accompanied hikes:

■ **Détours en Provence**: 104 allée Jean-Jaures, 84200 Carpentras. ☎ 04-90-60-75-37. Fax: 04-90-60-71-96. Email: sandylor.voyages@wanadoo.fr. Hikes from three days to one week in the Luberon (also in the Ventoux, the Baronnies and the mountains of the Vaucluse).

– **By bike**: the quiet little routes (there are still a few left) in the Luberon are excellent for cycling, although many of them are quite steep. For the more energetic there's a marked circuit of about 100 kilometres (60 miles) through the natural park, from Cavaillon to Apt to Forcalquier, avoiding major roads.

USEFUL ADDRESS

🚹 Maison du Parc Naturel Régional du Luberon (centre of the Natural Regional Park of the Luberon): 60 place Jean-Jaurès, 84404 Apt. ☎ 04-90-04-42-00. Fax: 04-90-04-81-15. Email: pnr.luberon@wanadoo.fr. Entrance fee: 10F (free for under-18s). Open every day except Sunday, 8.30am–noon and 1.30–7pm (to 6pm only and closed Saturday afternoon between October and April). Housed in an 18th-century private mansion, the centre provides all sorts of information on the park. In spring, interesting organized walks help visitors discover more about the local flora and fauna, natural history and geology. They are free, but booking is essential. There's also a museum of palaeontology, permanent and temporary exhibitions on the natural history of the Luberon, and a collection of videos.

Around the Petit Luberon

THE RÉGALON GORGES

A dozen kilometres (7 miles) southeast of Cavaillon along the D973, this is one of the most spectacular canyons in the Luberon, with gorges that are less than a metre wide in some places. Fallen blocks of rocks are stuck between the limestone cliffs. To get to the gorges from the car park, follow the red and white GR6 footpath markings for 1.4 kilometres. If you're up to it, you can walk all round the gorges on a five-hour circuit. Beware: the path climbs the river bed, so give it a miss in rainy weather.

🏕 Campsite and walker's shelter, Les Argiles: 84360 Mérindol ☎ 04-90-72-81-02. 🦌 Three kilometres (two miles) from Mérindol along the D973, towards Cavaillon, at the start of the path that leads to the Gorges de Régalon. Annual closure 10 November to 30 March. One night in the comfortable shelter, which has a shower, washing and kitchen facilities, costs 60F. There are 11 beds and a swimming pool. A tent pitch on the campsite at the farm, under the cherry trees, is 22F, plus 22F per person.

MÉRINDOL

Dominated by an abandoned village, this large town in the Durance valley has its place in history, having been the capital of the Vaudois.

The Vaudois in the Luberon

These Vaudois have nothing to do with the citizens of the Swiss canton of Vaud. Theirs is a more tragic story. At the end of the 12th century, Pierre Valdo, a merchant from Lyons, set up a school preaching for a return to the fundamentals of the Christian faith, and spurning many of the rites of the Catholic Church. He and his disciples, known as 'Vaudois', were excommunicated and forced to resettle throughout Europe, notably in Piedmont, in northern Italy. A few noble Piedmontese bought lands in the Luberon and some descendants of the Vaudois settled here. The Provence of the popes found it difficult to accept such heresy and, after the Reformation in 1532, the Vaudois were subjected to the most terrible persecution. The most bloody of the persecutors was Jean Meynier, Baron d'Oppède. In April 1545, in the name of God – and personal gain – the baron and his men razed many towns and villages to the ground, killing about 2,000 people and sending some 600 Vaudois to the galleys. A few survivors managed to reach Piedmont and settle in the Vallées Vaudoises.

The Huguenots also left their traces in the Luberon. In the last quarter of the 14th century, during the wars of the League, they took refuge in the mountain villages and made Ménerbes their centre. Besieged by an army of some 6,000 soldiers, led by the Grand Prior himself, they held out for 15 months before being forced to capitulate.

LAURIS

This large town, perched on a rocky spur between the Durance and the Luberon, is visible from miles away. A few lovely houses, old fountains and a 13th-century tower remain as a legacy of the medieval prosperity of the town. The countryside around is renowned for producing famous asparagus.

WHERE TO STAY AND EAT

⬧ ✕ **Walker's shelter and guest rooms at Le Mas de Recaute**: chemin de Recaute. ☎ 04-90-08-29-58. Fax: 04-90-08-41-37. Email: mas-de-recaute@wanadoo.fr. Open all year. Dormitory beds 80F per night and double rooms with shower and toilet 280F, including breakfast. Double rooms with shower and toilet 290F, including breakfast. The farmhouse is way out in the countryside, with a simple but comfortable dormitory and rooms. The owners organize regular one- to seven-day hikes, bike treks or horse riding in the Luberon. Phone ahead for information and reservations.

☆☆☆ Chic

⬧ ✕ **Guest rooms at the Maison des Sources**: chemin des Fraisses. In the lower part of town. ☎ 04-90-08-22-19 or 06-08-33-06-40. Fax: 04-90-08-22-19. Double rooms 440–450F, including breakfast, and a room for four at 700F. Dinner with the hosts costs 140F, including aperitif, wine and coffee. This solid but elegant 18th-century building on a hillside has four old-fashioned but very comfortable and spacious rooms, as well as a terrace and garden with running water.

CADENET

At the foot of a hill that's pock-marked with troglodyte dwellings, this is a typically Provençal town (try to go on market day). The ghostly ruins of a medieval chateau loom above it.

THE RHÔNE VALLEY AND HAUTE-PROVENCE

WHERE TO STAY AND EAT

🛏 ✕ **Le Mas du Colombier**: route de Pertuis. ☎ 04-90-68-29-00. Fax: 04-90-68-36-77. ✕ Near to the gendarmerie. Closed in February and November. Double rooms with bath, toilet and TV for 350F. Menus from 89F to 159F. This new hotel, built on an old family vineyard, has a pool, terrace and private car park.

WHAT TO SEE

★ **Statue du tambour d'Arcole** (Arcole's drum): on the main square. This statue celebrates a famous son of Cadenet, André Étienne, who helped Bonaparte in November 1796 near Verona in Italy. During a long battle, Étienne swam across the river (carrying his drum) and sounded the charge. The Austrians fled, fooled into thinking that the French were attacking from the rear, and Bonaparte's army was able to cross the bridge.

★ **The church**: the lovely Provençal belfry has an octagonal tower on a square base. Inside, take a look at the baptismal fonts, made from half a marble vat, dating from the third century.

★ **Musée de la Vannerie** (basket-weaving museum): La Glaneuse, avenue Philippe-de-Girard. ☎ 04-90-68-24-44. Open 10am–noon and 2.30–6.30pm between 1 April and 30 October. During the rest of the year, open only to groups with advance bookings. Closed on Tuesday and on Sunday morning. Entrance fee: 20F (10F for students and over-60s, and free for the disabled and under-12s). With the raw materials right at hand (willow is grown on the banks of the Durance), basket-making was one of the main economic activities of the region until the beginning of the 20th century. At that time, there were some 500 basket-weavers in Cadenet, exporting their wares as far as the USA. Since World War II, the Cadenet basket-weavers have found themselves unable to compete with cheap imports of rattan from the Far East, and the last basket-maker stopped work in 1978. The museum has an audiovisual show about the successful pre-war period and records the basket-makers' craftsmanship, with exhibits of tools and a range of products.

IN THE AREA

★ **Abbaye de Silvacane**: 7 kilometres (4.5 miles) southwest of Cadenet on the D943 then the D23. Open daily 1 April to 30 September, 9am–7pm; 1 October to 31 March, daily except Tuesday, 9am–noon and 2–5pm. Standing on the left bank of the Durance, Silvacane (*silva cannae* means 'forest of sweet rushes') was the third Cistercian abbey to be built in the region, after Thoronet and Sénanque (*see* page 279). Founded in 1144, it was built on marshy ground. The buildings seen by visitors today were constructed between 1175 and 1230, apart from the three galleries of the cloister, which date from 1250 to 1300. It is impossible not to be impressed by the cypresses in the cloister garden or the sombre beauty of the Gothic arches in the main room and the monks' room. The dormitory and refectory have recently been restored to their original state.

★ **La Roque-d'Anthéron**: from the abbey, push on to this charming little town to pay respect to César of Cadenet. His motto was *Deus nobis haec otia fecit* ('God made this place of peace for us'). Take a look at the old town hall (try to avoid looking at the siren on the top), the pretty Romanesque-Gothic church (which has a rather ordinary interior) and the lovely Renaissance chateau (note the basket handles above the door).

LOURMARIN

Lourmarin stands at a strategic location at the point where the only route crossing the Luberon comes out, on the Marseille to Apt road. It has three bell-towers (church, temple and belfry) on top of a little hill, opposite its chateau, which is perched on another mound. It was abandoned in the 14th century, then repopulated by the Vaudois (*see* page 250). Today, the village is pretty but the general atmosphere is a bit snobbish and elitist. For literature fans, Henri Bosco and Albert Camus (who owned a house in the village) are buried in the cemetery.

WHERE TO STAY AND EAT

🏠 **Le Four à Chaux**: route d'Apt. ☎ 04-90-68-24-28 or 04-90-68-11-10. Closed in January and February. It costs 60F per night in the dormitory and 150F in the (one) double room. This walker's shelter, which has a garden, was opened by the Reform Church and also serves as a venue for meetings. In principle, it's only open to groups of six.

🏠 ✕ **Hostellerie du Paradou**: 1 kilometre from Lourmarin towards Apt. ☎ 04-90-68-04-05. Fax: 04-90-08-54-94. Closed for lunch on Thursday and Friday (except during school holidays) and between 10 January and 10 February. Double rooms with shower, or bath, and toilet cost 340F and 380F. Half board available in July and August costs 285F per person per day. Menus at 128F and 160F. This hotel is in a lovely setting and has nine peaceful rooms, with bright, sometimes gaudy, interiors. The typically Provençal cuisine includes *pieds-paquets à la marseillaise* (tripe) and *daube provençale* (regio-

nal stew). The local red wine (VDQS) from the Luberon region has won several medals and is excellent. The river, with waterfalls, has a swimming area.

✕ **La Récréation**: ☎ 04-90-68-23-73. Fax: 04-90-68-01-60. Closed from 5 January to 10 February. Menus at 120F and 150F. There's a pretty terrace where you can enjoy grills and tasty regional dishes. Booking strongly advised if you want an outside table.

✕ **L'Antiquaire**: 9 rue du Grand-Pré. ☎ and fax: 04-90-68-17-29. Closed on Sunday evening, and on Monday. Closed annually between 15 November and early December and from 15 January to 2 February. Menus from 95F (weekday lunch) to 120F. There's a pleasant little sitting room on the ground floor and a dining room with air-conditioning on the first floor. The welcome is warm and the cooking, based on fresh produce from the market, is inspired. Remarkable value for money.

WHAT TO SEE

★ **Château de Lourmarin**: ☎ 04-90-68-15-23. Closed January, except weekend afternoons and for groups by appointment. Otherwise guided tours take place every day: July and August, every 30 minutes from 10–11.30am and 3–6pm; May, June and September, at 10am, 11am, 2.30pm, 3.30pm, 4.30pm and 5.30pm; during the rest of the year, at 11am, 2.30pm, 3.30pm and 4.30pm. Entrance fee: 30F (students 20F). François I, Winston Churchill, Albert Camus and Queen Elizabeth II have all been to this chateau, which describes itself as a 'place of significant spirituality'. It has many points of interest, although it does suffer from a shortage of funds.

The chateau was abandoned after the Revolution but was saved from total ruin in 1920 by wealthy heir Robert Laurent-Vibert, who created a foundation for artists. The castle has two main parts: the 'old' 14th-century chateau, which has a tower ornamented with bosses, and the Renaissance-style 'new' chateau, built in the 16th century. The two parts are connected by a tall tower containing an impressive circular staircase. Its 93 steps are hewn from a single piece of stone, from the central cylinder to the outside edge, which is part of the facade.

In the apartments, the beautiful furnishings (some of them rare) include a Provençal Louis XIV wardrobe, a 17th-century Spanish table and porcelain from Apt and Moustiers. There are a few engravings by Piranesi, done in a Romantic, baroque style. On the first floor, the recently restored *Lute Player* is a splendid picture from the school of Leonardo da Vinci. In the music room there are instruments from the Chinese Imperial Palace. Finally, in the State Room, there is a chimneypiece supported by large statues in Aztec style.

An underground passageway, 8 kilometres (5 miles) long, connects the chateau to the Chateau of Ansouis. Unfortunately, it is no longer in use.

★ **La ferme de Gerbaud** (Gerbaud's farm): Campagne Gerbaud. ☎ 04-90-68-11-83. Fax: 04-90-68-37-12. Website: www.lourmarin.com. From 1 April to 1 November, open every day at 5pm; during the rest of the year, open at the weekend and during the holidays at 3.30pm. Entrance fee: 30F (free for under-12s). Explore 25 hectares (62 acres) of aromatic and medicinal herbs and plants for tinctures, and find out about their culinary and medicinal uses, and the myths and legends relating to them.

BONNIEUX

This village, like many others in the area, is perched on a hill. It still has its 13th- and 14th-century ramparts, and old and beautiful houses that seem to envelop the church belfry, which dates from the 13th century. Wandering through the narrow streets is an ideal way to spend an hour or so.

USEFUL ADDRESS

🅱 **Tourist office**: 7 place Carnot. ☎ 04-90-75-91-90. Fax: 04-90-75-92-94. Between 1 April and 31 October, open every day 9.30am–12.30pm and 2.30–7pm. From 1 November to 31 March, open on Monday 2–6pm and from Tuesday to Saturday 9.30am–12.30pm and 2–6pm. Provides information on Bonnieux, Buoux, Lacoste, Ménerbes and Sibergues.

WHERE TO STAY

☒ Budget

⌂ **Municipal Campsite Le Vallon**: route de Ménerbes. About 500 metres from the village. ☎ and fax: 04-90-75-86-14. Open from 15 March to 15 November. A pitch for two people with car and tent costs 48F. This site is decent, shady and very peaceful. Cards not accepted.

⌂ ✕ **Café Clérici – La Flambée**: place du 4-Septembre. ☎ 04-90-75-82-20. Fax: 04-90-74-48-12. Rooms with shower and toilet cost 220F. Menus at 90–130F. This nice little hotel and restaurant in the middle of the village has a convivial host and quite simple rooms that are very good value, given the location. As the name suggests, they offer a number of meals and snacks cooked in their wood-fired oven, such as goat's cheese pizzas. Alternatively, there are regional dishes like *brouillade de truffes* (scrambled eggs with truffles) or *daube* (casserole), and good local wines (try a Côte du Luberon AOC) at attractive prices. The really lovely terrace has a view towards the Ventoux.

☒☒ Moderate

⌂ **Les Trois Sources** (B&B): St-Victor. Two kilometres below the village on the D194 towards Goult, along a small unsurfaced track on the right just beyond the Chateau Luc vineyard. ☎ 04-90-75-95-58. Fax: 04-90-75-89-95. Double rooms with shower or bath and toilet cost 350–500F, including breakfast. This large fortified farmhouse is hidden among vines and cherry trees. The rooms are spacious and attractive with subtle decor, in keeping with the style of the rest of the house, with its thick stone walls, large polished flagstones on the floors, massive beams and tiny windows that keep the house even cooler. It's a lovely spot, with friendly owners.

⌂ ✕ **Hostellerie du Prieuré**: ☎ 04-90-75-80-78. Fax: 04-90-75-96-00. Hotel open every day. Restaurant closed for lunch Tuesday to Friday in July, August and September. Rest of the year, closed for lunch on Tuesday and Thursday and all day Wednesday. Annual holidays from All Saints Day to early March. Double rooms with shower cost 390F, and with bath, toilet and TV (on request) from 560F to 700F. Half board (compulsory for long weekends in spring and in September) costs 400–555F per person. Lunchtime menu for 98F and à la carte around 150F. There is free parking, or you can opt for the secure garage for 40F. This three-star hotel is housed in a superb 17th-century building with a sophisticated rustic decor in the middle of Bonnieux, at the foot of the ramparts. In the bar, there's an unusual collection of models of Paris's great theatres. Most of the rooms have a garden view, and No. 9 has a terrace. In the restaurant, the good local cooking is based on seasonal produce. In summer, meals are served in the garden.

WHERE TO EAT

☒ Budget

✕ **Restaurant de la Gare**: chemin de la gare. 5 kilometres (3 miles) from the centre of the village on the D145 towards Goult. ☎ and fax: 04-90-75-82-00. ✗ Closed all day Monday, Sunday evening, during January and for the first two weeks in February. Weekday lunch menu for 65F (including a quarter-litre of wine). Evening and weekend menus range in price from 120F to 165F. The train station has now become an art gallery, but the station restaurant, opened by the grandmother of the present owner, is still there. In keeping with tradition, the lunch menu, with its selection of *crudités* and daily specials, remains popular with people who work in the area. It's a great spot, although not that well known since it's rather lost in the countryside. The large, old-fashioned dining room is charming and a lovely terrace overlooks the garden. The young owner prepares tasty, fresh and healthy Provençal dishes that change with the seasons. The fish and lamb are both delicious. The welcome is warm and friendly, the service excellent and the dining room peaceful and relaxing – highly recommended.

✕ **Le Pont Julien**: quartier du Pont-Julien. ☎ 04-90-74-48-44. 6 kilometres (4 miles) north of Bonnieux on the D149, then the N100 towards Apt. Menus at 77F (lunch only), 105F and 125F. Increasingly rare in the Luberon, this is a charming stone building with a shady terrace and pretty dining room. It sits on an old branch of the Route Nationale (main road) and serves good, sensibly priced Provençal cuisine with an extra touch of imagination. The small local wine list is very reasonable.

☆☆☆ Chic

✕ **Le Fournil**: 5 place Carnot. In the middle of the village. ☎ 04-90-75-83-62. Fax: 04-90-75-96-19. Closed on Monday all year and on Tuesday out of season. Menus at 98F (lunch) or from 130F to 205F. This restaurant has one of the most unusual terraces in the Luberon, taking up the whole of an adorable little square, with its obligatory fountain. Increasingly popular, it serves food that reflects the roots of the chef (who was born near by), and is prepared with a sure touch, for example, *ravioles à la cervelle d'agneau* (ravioli with lamb's brains), *cabri en deux cuissons* (twice-cooked kid goat), and *agneau de lait rôti* (roast suckling lamb). Given the area, the value for money of the menus is more than fair.

MARKETS AND EVENTS

– **Market**: held every Friday morning.

– **Marché des potiers** (pottery market): on Easter Sunday and Monday, over 50 potters display their work.

– **Festival de musique classique** (classical music festival): concerts every Sunday in July at 9pm, in the old church.

– **Semaine musicale** (music week): in fact more like two weeks, at the beginning of August. Classical music concerts held twice a week at 9pm, in the old church.

WHAT TO SEE

★ **Musée de la Boulangerie** (bakery museum): 12 rue de la République. In an old house, at the top of the village. ☎ 04-90-75-88-34. Open 1 April to 30 September and during All Saints, every day except Tuesday 10am–12.30pm and 2.30–6pm. In October, open Saturday, Sunday and public holidays.

Entrance fee: 20F (students 10F). Based around a Second Empire clay oven (which was in working order until 1920), this museum has a display of implements, including oven paddles and little vessels used to sprinkle water on the bread while it was cooking, to make the crust golden. There are reconstructions of a bake-house and a Provençal kitchen, as well as posters and engravings on the theme of bread, cake tins, ice-cream moulds and biscuit-cutters, and an exhibition on wheat cultivation.

★ **Pont Julien**: about 5 kilometres (3 miles) below the village along the D149. This very attractive Roman bridge spanning the Calavon has three remarkably preserved arches. The open piers control the flow of water when there's a flood.

SWEET TREATS

🔒 **Pâtisserie Henri Tomas**: 7 rue de la République. ☎ 04-90-75-85-52. Closed Tuesday and in February. Next to the bakery museum (*see above*). This shop has a tearoom and an old olive oil press that dates back to before the 12th century. Allow yourself to be tempted by the Provençal waffle, stuffed with hazelnut and almond cream.

In the Area

★ **Cedar forest**: 7 kilometres (4.5 miles) southwest of Bonnieux on the D36. Turn left (follow the signposts) at the pass. The Atlas cedar planted here around 1860 seems to have found the soil of the Petit Luberon to its taste. Since then, this forest has grown into one of the most beautiful cedar groves in Europe. There is a welcome coolness in the undergrowth when the sun is beating down. There's (inevitably) a charge for car parking, and a marked discovery trail, which takes an hour.

LACOSTE

The hill village of Lacoste is overlooked by the ruins (partly restored) of the chateau that once belonged to the notorious Marquis de Sade. When the Marquis wrote his *120 Days of Sodom*, he based his description of the Chateau of Silling upon this, his own. During his stay in the village, from 1771 to 1778, he caused a number of scandals, until his un-Christian conduct led him to be imprisoned in the Bastille prison in Paris. On his death, the chateau was bought by his lodge-keeper. The old owner, André Bouer – unsurpassed expert on the Marquis and his escapades – restored it gradually over some four decades. Sadly, since Bouer's death, restoration work has stopped.

WHERE TO STAY AND EAT

🛏 ✕ **Café de France guest rooms**: Right in the centre of the village. ☎ 04-90-75-82-25. Double rooms with basin cost 190F, with shower and toilet 290F. À la carte about 80F. Cards not accepted. This used to be a coaching inn and it is claimed that American writer Henry Miller stayed and wrote here. It certainly has an old-fashioned charm. Of its eight rooms, three have superb views of the plain, the fortified villages and the Ventoux in the distance. The pleasant terrace is shaded by parasols, and a few simple dishes (salads, omelettes, grilled meats) are on offer.

Café de Sade: rue Basse. In the village. ☎ 04-90-75-82-29. Fax: 04-90-75-95-68. Closed Monday out of season. Annual holidays between 4 January and 15 February. A dormitory bed costs 75F per night. Double rooms range from 260F (with basin) to 300F (with shower and toilet). Weekday lunch menu 75F. Alternative menus range in price from 85F to 135F. This unpretentious old house is a simple place, with dormitories and double rooms. It serves salads and Provençal dishes on the terrace, under the awning, including *daube de toro* (bull-meat casserole), *poulet à la provençale* (chicken with tomato and garlic) and *soupe au pistou* (basil and garlic soup), and has a friendly family atmosphere. The owners can arrange horse riding treks in the 'pays de Sade' (country of de Sade), as they call it.

Restaurant Loofoc: rue Basse. ☎ 04-90-75-89-76. Menus at 110F and 140F. Cards not accepted. Partly in a cave, decorated with Surrealist paintings, this restaurant also has a terrace with an awning and a panoramic view. The cooking marries traditional dishes with Indian specialities, such as king prawns marinated with 13 Indian spices and coconut milk. The welcome is charming.

MÉNERBES

The fortified village of Ménerbes, formerly a Huguenot bastion, perches on an escarpment that reaches out like a promontory, rather like a stone ship on the waves of the Luberon. It has an enormous amount of charm and there's a superb view from the old chateau. There are no cute hotels or trendy restaurants, so evenings are peaceful here. Even so, you can still feel the 'Peter Mayle effect' in the air (he used to live here).

WHERE TO EAT

Le Galoubet: 104 rue Marcellin Poncet. In the centre of the village. ☎ 04-90-72-36-08. Closed on Sunday evening and all day Monday throughout the year. Annual holiday throughout January. Menus from 75F (weekday lunch) to 160F. The cuisine is a successful mix of classic and regional dishes, the welcome is friendly and the dining rooms pleasant, including one housed in a 16th-century vaulted room. On sunny days, meals are served on the terrace.

MARKET

– **Marché aux fromages de chèvre** (goats' cheese market): on the third Sunday in April.

WHAT TO SEE

★ **Musée du Tire-bouchon** (corkscrew museum): domaine de la Citadelle. ☎ 04-90-72-41-58. 1.5 kilometres below the village on the Cavaillon road. Open 1 April to 30 September from Monday to Friday, 9am–noon and 2–

7pm; weekends and public holidays, 10am–noon and 3–7pm. The rest of the year, open Monday to Friday 9am–noon and 2–6pm, Saturday 9am–noon. closed Sunday and public holidays. Entrance fee: 24F (students and over-60s 19F, under-15s free). After discovering the thousand and one ways of uncorking a good bottle, visit the cellar and wine store, and finish with a tasting. The owner of this lovely property is Yves Rousset-Rouard, local official and former film producer (famous for the *Emmanuelle* soft porn series).

OPPÈDE-LE-VIEUX

Among the cluster of Luberon hilltop villages, this hamlet surely has the greatest charm. Its atmosphere is that of an abandoned village at the end of the 17th century. Restored houses stand alongside ruined ones. Tarmac hasn't yet reached Oppède, where the streets are still made of dirt. There isn't much going on, but there is a café (closed Wednesday; prices a bit excessive), with chairs that look out on to the delightful village square.

WHERE TO STAY AND EAT

♠ ✕ **Chambres d'hôte Le Mas des Guillaumets** (B&B): ☎ 04-90-76-82-47. One kilometre from Oppède-le-Vieux on the route de Maubec; sign-posted on the right. Closed 20 October to 20 February. Double rooms with shower and toilet 270–290F, including breakfast. Half board costs 250F and dinner is 100F (booking essential), including aperitif, wine and coffee. Nestled at the foot of the village in the countryside, this house has an authentic Provençal air, with its trellis and cypress trees, and floor tiles worn by generations of feet. The four attractive guest rooms are looked after with care. Highly recommended.

EVENT

– **Semaine musicale** (music week): at the end of July/beginning of August. Performances are held at 9pm on certain days in the Notre-Dame de Dalidon church. Check with the tourist office in Bonnieux for more details.

ROBION

Five kilometres (3.5 miles) from Cavaillon on the D2. Too many people race through this village on the way to Ménerbes or Gordes without stopping. However, the 15th-century church is lovely and the huge square in front has a babbling fountain. The Boulon circus, high above the village, is a beautiful natural site.

WHERE TO STAY AND EAT

♠ **Les Cerisiers campsite**: chemin de la Tour-de-Sabran, route de Lagnes. ☎ 04-90-20-24-25 or 04-90-76-60-57. Two kilometres from the centre. Open April to 31 October. Bank cards are not accepted. You'll pay around 85F for a pitch for two, or you can rent mobile homes by the week. Well-equipped camp-site with swimming pools and paddling pool for children, surrounded by apple orchards. Very friendly welcome.

🛏 **Chambre d'hôte chez Yvette Auzon:** quartier Reynard. Leaving Robion, towards Apt, turn left just before the cemetery, go straight on for 2 kilometres, then turn right onto the unsurfaced road (the chemin de la Marseillaise) that goes between the orchards, it's the second on the right. ☎ 04-90-76-58-27. Annual holiday in August. Double rooms with shower and toilet 300F, including breakfast. In a large and beautiful old house with a big garden.

There's a big and beautiful room at garden level. Really nice welcome. Swimming pool.

✕ **L'Escanson**: avenue Aristide Briand. ☎ 04-90-76-59-61. In the village, on the D2. Closed on Tuesday evening and all day Wednesday as well as every evening (except Saturday) from October to March, the restaurant is also closed for the February holidays. Menus range in price from 70F (weekday lunch) to 190F. The little house stands on the side of the road and doesn't look much but it's a good place. Sort of rustic dining room which is very simple. Nicely prepared Provençal cooking, served with a smile.

WHAT TO SEE AND DO IN THE AREA

★ **Musée de la Lavande** (lavender museum): route de Gordes, 84220 Coustellet. ☎ 04-90-76-91-23. Fax: 04-90-76-85-52. Website: www.guide web.com/provence/musée-lavande. Three kilometres (two miles) northeast of Robion on the D2. Open every day from 1 March to 31 December. In July, August and September 10am–noon and 2–7pm. Out of season until 6pm only. Entrance fee: 15F (free for under-15s). Here in the Vaucluse hills, the skills of growing and distilling fine lavender have been passed on from father to son. This intriguing museum, based around an unusual collection of lavender stills, promotes 'real' lavender, which is protected by an AOC (Appellation d'Origine Contrôlée), and is not to be confused with *lavandin*, a hybrid of French lavender crossed with *Lavandula officinalis* (*see* 'General Information', page 90). The copper stills, most of which have been found in the Alpes de Haute-Provence, date from 1626 to the present day. Guided tours are for groups only, but explanatory panels describe the different distilling techniques – naked flame, *bain-marie*, steaming, and *concrète* (two such stills are left in the world, and one of them is here). A 10-minute documentary film shows the cutting of the flowers and modern distillation, and a little shop sells essential oils, dried lavender and natural cosmetics.

★ **Farmers' market**: in Coustellet, Sunday morning all year round, Wednesday in summer at 6pm. Traditional out of season, in July and August the market attracts the smart set of the Luberon.

The South of the Luberon and the Pays d'Aigues

VAUGINES

This tiny, very pretty village at the foot of the Luberon has its fair share of medieval houses and a superb church, where Claude Berri shot the wedding scene in the successful and evocative French film *Manon des Sources* (*Manon and the Springs*).

WHERE TO STAY AND EAT

♣ ✗ **L'Hostellerie du Luberon**: cours Saint-Louis. ☎ 04-90-77-27-19. Fax: 04-90-77-13-08. Restaurant closed Wednesday lunchtime. Annual holiday from November to early March. Double rooms with bath and toilet cost 350F. Half board (compulsory between April and September) is 320F per person. Menus from 130F to 200F. A modern hotel, in a peaceful spot on the edge of the village, with a large attractive dining room. The Provençal cuisine has its highs and lows, but the garden, swimming pool and sauna are always enjoyable. Private, secure car park.

CUCURON

At the foot of Mourre-Nègre, the highest point (at 1,125 metres/3,691 feet) in the Luberon, this pretty village has a harmonious collection of buildings, from opulent 18th-century residences to a 13th-century church. It, too, has been used as a film set, for Rappeneau's *Un Hussard sur le Toit (The Horseman on the Roof)*. As you're wandering around, don't forget to look up to the rooftops. The interesting Marc Deydier museum (☎ 04-90-77-25-02. Open in theory every day 2–6pm, and sometimes in the morning; free entry) displays an archaeological collection (including a first-century mausoleum), and remarkable daguerrotype plates from the end of the 19th century. Look out for the arts and crafts gallery, which has an oil mill in its back room. (Apparently, a *scourtin* is a basket through which olives are pressed in order to extract their oil.) Two writers liked this village: Alphonse Daudet used it as a model for Cucugnan in his book *Lettres de Mon Moulin*, and Henri Bosco was a frequent visitor.

USEFUL ADDRESS

🚩 **Tourist office**: rue Léonce-Brieugne. ☎ 04-90-77-28-37. Fax: 04-90-77-17-00. Usually open 9am–12.15pm, but opening hours are subject to change.

WHERE TO STAY AND EAT

♣ ✗ **L'Arbre de Mai**: rue de l'église. ☎ and fax: 04-90-77-25-10. Closed on Tuesday out of season and during January and February. All double rooms with shower and toilet cost 340F. Menus at 90F (weekdays only) and 145F. In a large 17th-century house, the simple restaurant has a friendly family atmosphere. Most of the rooms are pretty and have cosy rustic decor with good facilities. Good local cooking and a genuinely warm welcome.

♣ ✗ **Hôtel-restaurant de l'Étang**: place de l'Étang. ☎ 04-90-77-21-25. Fax: 04-90-77-10-98. Closed on Wednesday out of season and from 10 December to 10 January. Double rooms with bath, toilet and TV cost 300F. Menus cost from 110F to 220F and you'll pay around 210F à la carte in this lovely and peaceful spot, opposite a large, rectangular pond surrounded by trees, dug out in the Middle Ages. Peaceful rooms with good facilities. Tasty dishes include *feuilleté de langoustines* (crayfish in pastry) and *agneau du Luberon* (local lamb).

⚓ ✕ **Gîte d'Étape La Resparine** (walkers' shelter): 1 kilometre along the route de la Tour-d'Aigues. ☎ and fax: 04-90-77-21-46. Closed from 1 November to 21 March. Dormitory beds 70F per night, double rooms for 230F, including breakfast. One set menu at 80F (dinner only). This non-smoking shelter has a few double rooms, two dormitories with 12 beds and two with just four. A small campsite, **Lou Badareü**, on the route de l'étang de la Bonde, also belongs to the *gîte*. ☎ and fax: 04-90-77-21-46. ⚒ Open from 20 March to 1 November. It has a garden and a swimming pool.

Campsite

⚓ **Camping Le Moulin à Vent**: ☎ 04-90-77-25-77. Drive along the D182 for 1.3 kilometres, turn left and continue for 1 kilometre. Open from early April to 30 September. A pitch for two costs 56F per day. This site is small, pleasant, shady and restful, and warmly welcomes visitors. Booking is recommended for July and August.

FESTIVALS AND EVENTS

– **L'arbre de mai** (festival of the May tree): held on the Saturday after the third week in May. The May tree is a poplar chosen with great care from the surrounding countryside, then chopped down with an axe. A child, symbolizing youth, straddles the tree like a rider, and is carried on the shoulders of young men through the village streets to the church doors. The child dismounts and the tree is erected before the church. A colourful folk festival, both pagan and Christian, follows, celebrating the arrival of spring and thanking St-Tulle, the patron saint of Cucuron, for her intervention during the plague of 1720.

ANSOUIS

This splendid hill village nestles at the gates of its chateau, which has belonged to the de Sabran family, one of the great families of Provence, since the 12th century. Two family members, Elzéar IV de Sabran and his wife Delphine de Signes, have been beatified by the Church. The current Comte de Sabran is still the mayor of Ansouis. Interestingly, this is one of the very few villages in France that does not celebrate Bastille Day (14 July), France's national holiday.

USEFUL ADDRESS

🏢 **Tourist office**: place du Château. ☎ and fax: 04-90-09-86-98. Open every day 10am–noon and 2–6pm (3–7pm in July and August).

WHERE TO EAT

✕ **L'Olive bleue**: boulevard des Platanes. ☎ 04-90-09-86-84. Closed Wednesday out of season and during January. Around 130F à la carte. Typically Provençal dishes are served in a cosy dining room with ochre walls, in a friendly atmosphere.

WHAT TO SEE

★ **Chateau**: ☎ 04-90-09-82-70. Open every day (except Tuesday during All Saints and at Easter) from 2.30–6pm. Additional tour at 11am between 15 July and 30 August. Group visits to the gardens in June and July. Entrance fee: 30F (20F for students under 25 and 15F for 6- to 18-year-olds). Built in the 10th century purely as a defensive fortress, the chateau was the subject of numerous alterations in the 12th and 13th centuries. The elegant main residential buildings date from the 17th century. The fact that they are still lived in adds to the appeal of the place; sometimes, the owners themselves show visitors around. A monumental staircase is supported by a cradle vault and the apartments have charming 18th-century plasterwork and windows that open on to lovely hanging gardens. Flanders tapestries adorn the dining room, and the kitchen is equipped with shiny copper pans. Children will be thrilled by the dungeon and the suits of armour. In August, the chateau provides a venue for classical concerts and recitals, as part of the summer music festival, Les Musicales.

★ **St-Martin church**: this fortified church, formerly the law court of the chateau, dates from the 12th century, and has statues and altarpieces from the 17th century.

LA TOUR D'AIGUES

On the main square of this peaceful town stand the impressive ruins of a gigantic gateway, looking like a triumphal arch. In fact, they are all that remains of a sumptuous Renaissance building (apparently based on the Louvre palace in Paris) that was destroyed by fire in 1792. Given the magnificence of the gateway, the building must have been quite extraordinary!

There's a small **Musée de la Faïence** (porcelain museum), with pieces from the Aigue area, arranged in the old cellars of the chateau. ☎ 04-90-07-50-33. Open daily in July and August 10am–1pm and 3.30–6.30pm. Rest of the year, open daily (except Tuesday afternoon, Saturday and Sunday morning) 9.30–11.30am and 3–6pm (closes 5pm from October to April).

🛈 **Tourist office of the Vallée d'Aigue**: in the chateau. ☎ 04-90-07-50-29. Open every day in July and August 10am–1pm and 2.30–6.30pm. In April to June and September to October, open 9am–noon and 2–6pm (except on Saturday and Sunday morning and Tuesday afternoon). November to March, open every day 9am–noon and 2–5pm (except on Saturday and Sunday morning and Tuesday afternoon).

WHERE TO EAT

🍴 **Auberge de la Tour**: 51 rue Antoine-de-Très. Opposite the church. ☎ and fax: 04-90-07-34-64. Closed Sunday evening and all day Monday. Menus from 67F (weekday lunch) to 180F. The white-stone vaulted ceiling gives the dining room character, the decor is inspired and the shady terrace is pleasant in summer. The welcome is friendly and the cooking typically Provençal, including *pieds-paquets* (tripe) and *barigoule d'artichauts* (stuffed artichokes). Highly recommended.

GRAMBOIS

The former domain of the counts of Forcalquier, this hill village is much less busy than similar, better-known places in the north of the Luberon. It's not much more than a pretty little central square, with a few old houses and a charming Romanesque church topped by an elegant bell-tower. Make your way through the streets towards the ruined town wall, which provides a superb viewing point.

🏛 Syndicat d'initiative (tourist information centre): rue de la Mairie. ☎ 04-90-77-96-29. Fax: 04-90-77-94-69. Open every day in low season (except Wednesday and Sunday) 10.30am–noon and 2.30–5pm. In high season, open every day (except Sunday) 9.30am–12.30pm and 3–7pm.

WHERE TO STAY

🛏 Chambres d'hôte le Jas de Monsieur (B&B): ☎ 04-90-77-92-08. Take the small cobbled and signposted track, 2 kilometres from Grambois on the D122 towards Beaumont-de-Pertuis. Closed from 15 July to 15 August. Double rooms with shower or bath and toilet 330–350F, including breakfast, depending on the season. This elegant 18th-century country house, in a very rural location, has three rooms with nice family details, such as embroidered sheets and ornaments. Relax in one of the big sitting rooms, sit out on the large south-facing terrace, swim in the pool, or follow one of the little walking trails in the grounds. The owners are extremely kind, provide masses of information about the Luberon, and are committed to offering value for money. Others in the area would do well to follow their example.

WHERE TO EAT IN THE AREA

✕ La Fontaine: place de la Fontaine, 84760 St-Martin-de-la-Brasque. About 10 kilometres (6 miles) west of Grambois on the D27, in the centre of the village. ☎ 04-90-07-72-16. Closed in season on Tuesday and Wednesday (lunchtime only in July and August) and from Sunday evening to Thursday lunchtime in winter. Also closed at Christmas and in February. *Menu-carte* at 155F. The dining room is small and simple but not unattractive, and there are tables outside in the square (which has the obligatory fountain) for sunny days. The welcome is friendly and the cooking is regional and tasty. This is the village's only restaurant – luckily, it's a good one!

The Pays d'Apt

APT (84400)   Population: 11,172

A Roman city, then an episcopal town in the 10th century, Apt may have lost some of its pride but it retains a very particular charm, especially in its old quarter. Many a passing visitor has been seduced by it. Its atmosphere is different from the rest of the Luberon, probably because of the hippies and alternative lifestylists who began to move into the area in the 1970s. Poetry and music festivals used to take place in the old factory and, as in some of the valleys in the Cévennes and the Ariège, there are a few seriously odd folk around here. The Saturday morning market, vibrant with the colours and scents of Provence, brings the whole region together.

USEFUL ADDRESSES

❶ Tourist office (A1 on the map): avenue Philippe-de-Girard. ☎ 04-90-74-03-18. Fax: 04-90-04-64-30. Open Monday to Saturday, 9am–noon and 2–6pm. In July and August, open 9am–1pm and 3–7pm, and 9am–noon on Sunday. Provides useful information about the town and a little Apt tourist guide that details a town walk.

■ **La Maison du Parc Naturel Régional du Luberon**: 1 place Jean-Jaurès, BP 122, 84404 April cedex. ☎ 04-90-04-42-00. Fax: 04-90-04-81-15.

WHERE TO STAY AND EAT

☆ Budget

🛏 ✕ Hôtel-restaurant du Palais (A1, **1** on the map): 24 place Gabriel-Péri. Opposite the town hall. ☎ and fax: 04-90-04-89-32. Restaurant closed on Monday. Annual holidays from 1 October to 1 April. Double rooms with washbasin cost 180F, with shower or bath and toilet from 210F to 280F. Menus from 69F to 129F. Apt lacks any outstanding hotels. This one, in an old house in the town centre, could be described as 'modest', but it's acceptable for a night or so. The cooking is decent, with a Provençal touch: aïoli, soupe au pistou, and so on.

✕ Le Platane (B1, **10** on the map): 13 place Jules-Ferry. ☎ 04-90-04-74-36. Closed on Sunday and Monday from October to June. Between June and September, closed for lunch on Sunday. Annual closure in February. Lunch formule menu for 67F and around 120F à la carte. This tall old townhouse stands on a square that's well off the tourist trail. Climb up a small flight of steps to get to the delightful, shaded terrace. When the weather is cool, there's a nice little dining room inside. The welcome is cool, too, as is the efficient service. The cooking appears simple but it's prepared with a sure hand and some ingenuity. The fresh, tasty dishes have a touch of the exotic: pain de courgettes au basilic (courgette bread with basil) and magret aux zestes d'oranges confites (duck breast with crystallized orange zest). Recommended.

Campsites

🛏 Camping Le Luberon: route de Saignon ☎ 04-90-04-85-40. Fax: 04-90-74-12-19. ⚒ 1.5 kilometres from Apt. Open April to end October. About 70F for a pitch for two. This site, in a rural location, with views of the Monts de Vaucluse and the Ventoux, has a swimming pool and a restaurant.

🛏 Camping La Clef des Champs: quartier du Puits. ☎ 04-90-74-41-41. About 3 kilometres (2 miles) from the town centre. Leave Apt on the Cavaillon road, turn right in the direction of the cité St-Michel, then follow the signs as the road climbs. Open from 31 March to end September. It costs 62F per night with a tent for two. Pitches in the middle of

APT

■ Useful Addresses	✕ Where to Eat
ℹ Tourist office	**10** Le Platane
✉ Post office	
⌂ **Where to Stay**	▼ **Where to Go for a Drink**
1 Hôtel-restaurant du Palais	**20** The Queen Victoria Pub

an orchard, with clean facilities and a friendly welcome.

⌂ **Camping municipal Les Cèdres**: route de Rustrel, 300 metres from the centre of town. ☎ and fax: 04-90-74-14-61. ♿ Open mid-February to mid-November. Around 45F for a pitch for two, with vehicle. The site is well shaded, but too close to the centre of town to be peaceful. Showers cost extra.

WHERE TO STAY AND EAT IN THE AREA

⌂ ✕ **Relais de Roquefure**: ☎ 04-90-04-88-88. Fax: 04-90-74-14-86. On the Cavaillon road, 6 kilometres (about 4 miles) from Apt. Turn left on to the small surfaced road. Restaurant closed for lunch and from 15 December 2001 to 15 February 2002. Double rooms with shower or with shower and toilet from 250F to 380F. Menu costs 110F. Also available, dormitory beds in the walkers' shelter for 65F a night, or 170F for half board. This stone farmhouse is in a really peaceful spot, with reasonably attractive bedrooms, some with a sort of rustic-Provençal decor. Local dishes include *fricassée de pintades à la provençale* (guinea fowl casserole) and *terrine au confit d'oignons* (caramelized onion terrine). There are ten- and four-bed dormitories and a small hut that sleeps six and has kitchen facilities. The swimming pool is reserved for hotel guests, but the garden is nice and there are riding stables just next door.

🛏 ✕ **Bergerie des Millanes**: Les Tourettes. ☎ 04-90-04-63-74. 3.5 kilometres (about 2 miles) southwest of Apt on the D943 towards Lourmarin. Turn left on to the chemin des Endes and follow the signs (the road is unsurfaced at the end). ♿ Open all year. Booking essential. Double rooms with shower and toilet from 200F to 400F, depending on size. Two six-bed rooms available at 450F. Dinner possible, for a minimum of four people (non-residents pay 130F for the menu; daily special 60F; half board residents pay 110F; under-5s free). This lovely house, built by present owners Tobias and Antonia, stands in gloriously wild surroundings on the mountain of the Luberon, near an old sheepfold. It has a *hammam* (steam room) and a pool, a small Moorish-style patio and five lovely rooms, all different and equipped with old-fashioned bathrooms. The view over the countryside around Apt and over Ventoux is spectacular.

The interior is interestingly Gaudíesque, and there's a superb shady terrace where you can indulge in some of the best Mediterranean cooking in the region, including gazpacho, tapas, *gambas* or *melon au pastis* (king prawns or melon in pastis), local cheeses, Tobias' melon chutney and delicious, unusual desserts, such as rosemary or thyme sorbet. There are plenty of activities available, from paragliding to horse riding (book ahead). You can also buy homemade products, with a little notice.

🛏 **Le Massonnet**: route de St-Saturnin, 84400 Apt ☎ and fax: 04-90-04-66-15. Website: www.elansud.fr/ Le Massonnet. Four kilometres (2.5 miles) northwest of Apt. Open all year. Double rooms from 240F to 420F per night for a minimum stay of two or three nights, depending on the season. Apartments for people cost 350–450F per night (minimum stay two or three nights, depending on the time of year; minimum of seven days in July and August). Housed in a former 16th-century flourmill, deep in the countryside, this house has recently been converted into a place to stay. Of the four tastefully furnished apartments, the two at garden level have a well-equipped kitchen, a bedroom with shower and a terrace. The two rooms upstairs share the same bathroom. There's also a pool and substantial breakfasts can be cooked to order. There's a warm atmosphere and real Provençal spirit in the vaulted dining room, where you can see the old quern stone. The hostesses can sort out a tailor-made stay for you, including tickets to the musical week in the spring. No credit cards.

WHERE TO GO FOR A DRINK

🍷 **The Queen Victoria Pub** (A1, **20** on the map): 94 quai de la Liberté, Apt. ☎ 04-90-04-76-30. Annual closure 15 January to 15 February. The decor in this bistrot is rather '70s nightclub', but there's a young, laid-back atmosphere, with amateur philosophers gathering here in winter to exchange views. There's Internet access and, from time to time, rock, jazz and blues concerts (free entry). Breakfast is on offer and the managers are happy to give customers information about local villages.

WHAT TO SEE

★ **Apt old town**: take a walk around the old quarter and see many private mansions that date from the 16th and 17th centuries, and the tower in the ramparts.

★ **Ste-Anne's Cathedral and Basilica**: open Tuesday to Saturday 10am–noon and 3–7pm. Sunday and public holidays, 10am–noon. Built in the 11th and 12th centuries, enlarged in the 14th, then altered in the 17th century, this was the seat of a bishopric until 1801. The elegant semi-circular arches date from the 12th century. The three naves are separated by powerful pillars. There are two crypts under the nave. The upper one (11th century) is like a miniature church, with three small naves, a fifth-century altar and a deambulatory. The lower crypt (first century) is not much more than a narrow corridor, with Carolingian flagstones on the floor, which leads into a chapel. The atmosphere is impressive, and the sacristy of the Royal Chapel of Ste-Anne is stuffed with relics and treasures.

★ **Musée d'Histoire et d'Archéologie** (history and archaeology museum): 27 rue de l'Amphithéâtre. ☎ 04-90-74-00-34. Fax: 04-90-74-28-13. Open 1 June to 30 September 10am–noon and 2–5pm. Rest of the year 2–5pm in the week and 10am–noon and 2–5pm on Saturday. Closed Tuesday and Sunday. Entrance fee: 11F (students, half price, under-16s free). In an 18th-century curate's house, this museum displays around 400 pieces of Apt porcelain, reconstructions of 19th-century porcelain kilns and about 50 ex-voto offerings from the cathedral. The archaeological collection has thousands of pieces (flints, pottery, coins), which date from prehistoric times to the end of the Middle Ages.

SWEET TREATS

Legendary letter-writer Madame de Sévigné (1626–96) compared the region around Apt to a 'huge preserving pan'. It is true that Apt is the world capital of crystallized fruit, even though production has decreased a little since her time.

🔒 **Aptunion**: route d'Avignon. ☎ 04-90-76-31-31. Two kilometres from Apt on the N100. Open Monday to Saturday, 9am–noon and 2–6pm. This friendly shop sells crystallized fruit and chestnuts direct from the factory, as well as nougat and mini-jars of unusual jams (watermelon, fig, melon, banana), all at unbeatable prices. The factory can also be visited (by appointment); the tour includes a free tasting.

🔒 **Confiserie Richaud**: 112 quai de la Liberté. ☎ 04-90-74-43-50. This lovely shop is more expensive than the Aptunion one, but sells excellent crystallized fruit that are handmade using fresh seasonal produce (not all shops do).

FESTIVALS AND EVENTS

– **Jazz in the Pays d'Apt**: this small but imaginative jazz festival takes place in May. Information ☎ 04-90-74-55-98.

SAIGNON

Just 4 kilometres (2.5 miles) southeast of Apt on the D48, Saignon occupies a marvellous position, built against a big rock. There are fabulous views from the village, with panoramas over the Apt valley, the Luberon and the Monts du Vaucluse. It has a pretty Romanesque church and charming little streets.

WHERE TO STAY AND EAT

☆ Budget

♜ ✕ Auberge de jeunesse Regain (youth hostel): ☎ 04-90-74-39-34. Fax: 04-90-74-50-90. Some 2.5 kilometres (1.5 miles) up from the village (poorly signposted). Annual closure from 10 January to 15 February. 80F a night, including breakfast. Communal evening meal 60F, and half board 140F. French youth hostel association card required, but weekend cards are available for 10F. A youth hostel since 1936, this Provençal house clings to a cliff in a dream location. The owner used to be a cinema projectionist and sometimes organizes 'private screenings' of his great collection of old films. He maintains walking trails, writes tra-vel guides and inspires guests to explore the area on foot.

☆☆–☆☆☆ Moderate to Chic

♜ Chambre de séjour avec vue ('room with a view'): in the middle of Saignon village. ☎ and fax: 04-90-04-85-01. Open only at weekends from November to March. Double room with breakfast costs 300F; apartment to rent at 450F. Dinner 140F, including wine. This lovely Provençal house is the domain of a gallery owner and an ex-theatre director. They particularly encourage artists to stay here and work in an intimate setting (there are pictures on all the walls), but the house is open to any guests who want to make the most of the unusual atmosphere. The three rooms and the apartment are decorated in a refined way, with an elegant collection of *objets*, and there are deckchairs in the garden.

♜ ✕ Auberge du Presbytère: place de la Fontaine. In the centre of the village. ☎ 04-90-74-11-50. Fax: 04-90-04-68-51. Email: auberge.presbytere@provence-luberon.com. Restaurant closed Wednesday and Thursday lunch. Annual closure from 15 November to 5 February. Double rooms with shower or bath and toilet 350–700F. Menus from 135F (lunchtime) to 185F. The attractively refurbished rooms of this *auberge* are found in three old village houses. The Lavender Room has a terrace with a magnificent views over the Luberon. Good Provençal cuisine is served in an intimate and charming dining room.

SIVERGUES

Sivergues is 12 kilometres (7.5 miles) south of Apt on the D114. One of the most beautiful hamlets of the Luberon, Sivergues is lucky enough to be at the end of a no-through road and to have no luxurious hotel. It manages to stay well off the tourist trail, which means that it's all the better for those who are prepared to venture this far. It has a delightful 16th-century church.

WHERE TO STAY AND EAT

⚓ ✕ **Ferme-auberge du Castelas**: ☎ 04-90-74-60-89. At the *fin de la route* ('end of the road') signpost, turn left up and carry on for 2 kilometres. Closed for lunch out of season (except on Sunday) and during Christmas. Booking essential. Half board costs 200F per person for a dormitory bed, or 290F in a double room with shower and toilet. The menu costs 150F, including wine and coffee, or you can enjoy a tasting of local ham and cheeses for 120F at lunchtime. This isolated 16th-century Vaudois (see page 250) farm stands all alone on the plateau.

BUOUX

Buoux is 8 kilometres (5 miles) southwest of Apt along the D113. This corner of the Pays d'Apt is less known for the village (which is actually more like a hamlet) than for the neighbouring Vallon de l'Aiguebrun. The gorges of the valley were chiselled out by one of the few rivers in the Luberon that is always full. The precipitous cliffs are heaven for climbers, with a few routes opened up, and it's quite busy when the weather is fine. At the entrance of the valley, it's easy enough to climb up to the ruined Fort de Buoux (entrance fee: 10F, children 7F). The fort was torn down by Louis XIV, who feared that the Huguenots might take refuge here. Little remains, but the site is exceptional.

WHERE TO STAY AND EAT

⚓ ✕ **Auberge des Seguins**: ☎ 04-90-74-16-37. Fax: 04-90-74-03-26. In the hamlet of Les Seguins, 3 kilometres (2 miles) from the village, near the fort. Annual closure from 15 November to 1 March. Double rooms with shower and toilet (half board only available), 260F per person. Menu for 120F. The owner, a Provençal language specialist, built this inn in a wonderful location. Nestled in the hollow of the Vallon du l'Aiguebrun, at the foot of an imposing cliff, it offers accommodation in individual rooms or dormitories, and a swimming pool. Provençal cuisine – *estouffade d'agneau* (lamb casserole) and *aïoli* (Friday lunchtime) – is served in a large dining room with wide bay windows. On warm days, it's extremely popular.

☆☆☆☆ Très Chic

⚓ ✕ **L'Auberge de L'Aiguebrun**: domaine de la Tour. ☎ 04-90-04-47-00. Fax: 04-90-04-47-01. 👃 In the heart of the countryside, signposted from the D943 towards Lourmarin. Restaurant closed Tuesday and Wednesday lunchtime. Annual closure from 15 November to 1 March. Double rooms with bath and toilet plus satellite TV from 650F to 750F. Menu 250F. This marvellous place, run by an energetic and friendly *patronne* from Avignon, stands in the hollow of the Combe de Lourmarin. It's a beautiful stone house with a swimming pool and garden, and pretty, comfortable rooms, with interesting old furniture. The tasty food is heavily influenced by Provençal traditions and makes excellent use of local produce, but it is quite expensive.

LE PLATEAU DES CLAPARÈDES

This little-known but beautiful plateau stretches between Bonnieux and Apt and can be crossed on the D232. A vast expanse of land at altitudes ranging from 500 to 700 metres, it is sparsely populated, but extensively cultivated. Cherry orchards, rows of lavender and cornfields create a patchwork of colour, while the pastures are dotted with flocks of sheep. Little heaps of stones (known locally as *clapas*, hence the name of the plateau) lie throughout the area, picked out of the earth in an effort to make it more fertile. Here and there you'll see *bories* (traditional stone structures).

VIENS

Drive about 15 kilometres (10 miles) northeast of Apt on the N100. Turn left on to the D48 to the pretty, peaceful hill village of St-Martin-de-Castillon, then on to the D190. Viens is a very lovely village, perched like an eyrie, looking out over beautiful views of the Luberon and the Monts de Vaucluse. It has steep streets (though not the crowds you find in Gordes), gatehouses and towers, beautiful old dwellings and a Renaissance chateau (closed to visitors). Follow one of the three little footpaths that start in the village, to see the *bories* on the Caseneuve plateau. A little further afield, there's a lovely walk in the Gorges d'Opédette (*see* 'Haute-Provence', page 383).

RUSTREL AND THE 'COLORADO OF PROVENCE'

About 10 kilometres (6 miles) northeast of Apt on the D22. This small, quiet, typically Provençal village is known mainly for its ochre quarries. In the 1930s, curiously, it was nicknamed the 'Colorado of Provence' by someone who clearly did not know much about the plunging canyons in the US.

🄳 **Tourist information**: contact the town hall in the morning and on Wednesday afternoon: ☎ 04-90-04-91-09. Fax: 04-90-04-78-75.

WHERE TO STAY AND EAT

🛏 **Camping le Colorado**: ☎ and fax: 04-90-04-90-37. One kilometre past Rustrel on the D22 towards Apt; turn left at the signpost. Closed from 15 October to 15 March. From 60F to 70F for a pitch for two with vehicle, depending on the season. Overnight *gîte* accommodation at 60F per person per night. In a lovely spot out in the country, this nice little campsite on a hillside has lots of shade, free hot showers, laundry facilities, a pool and a good family atmosphere. It stands at the starting point of the 'Colorado' discovery trails and the managers are happy to give advice about other walks.

🛏 **Gîte d'Étape le Château**: ☎ 04-90-04-96-77. At the top of the village. Closed from 2 January to 28 February. 70F per night, 110F with breakfast. Half board 180F. The decor – sponged walls and friezes – in this 17th-century chateau is unusually tasteful for *gîte* accommodation. The chateau has a medieval look, with its four turrets. The 10-bed dormitory on the ground floor has a huge chimneypiece and there are small double rooms in the turrets. Laundry facilities are available.

🛏 **Chambres d'hôte Campagne Istrane** (B&B): ☎ 04-90-04-92-86. Signposted on the D22 towards

Apt. Close to Camping le Colorado. Double rooms with shower and toilet for 300F, including breakfast. This old farm, in a peaceful part of the countryside, offers simple rooms and breakfast with homemade jams, cheese and local ham. In good weather, it is served on the terrace under ancient plane trees. There's a little spring in the garden and horses (the owner's passion) in the paddocks around.

WHAT TO SEE AND DO

★ **Le Colorado**: natural erosion and commercial excavation (the ochre has been quarried since the time of the Revolution) have distorted this landscape into a place of weird contours. The palette of colours is remarkable. The Greek word *okhra* means 'yellow earth', but the ochres round here range from pale yellow to vivid red through a whole spectrum of oranges, with odd veins of blue and pine-green. Most of the old quarries are privately owned and there is not access to the whole of the site. You can use the big car park that's signposted on the D22, but there's a charge and the little brochure is not very helpful. Alternatively, follow one of the four marked footpaths (from 1 hour 30 minutes to 4 hours), leaving from the free car park at Bouvène, or from Le Colorado campsite. One important word of advice: don't wear your best clothes, as ochre stains very badly. Local Marseille soap and cold water are recommended if you want to try to remove any marks.

LAGARDE D'APT

About 20 kilometres (12.5 miles) north of Apt. Take the D22, then the winding D34, with panoramic views over the Luberon at every bend. At the top, you come to the smallest *commune* in the Vaucluse, with a charming Romanesque chapel and a few houses at an altitude of 1,000 metres (3,280 feet), scattered in a landscape that feels more Alpine than Provençal. Life here isn't easy, but the location is superb. Unfortunately, a wide road crosses right through the hamlet, because this is on the way to the Albion plateau, where nuclear research was carried out until only recently.

– In summer, **marked footpaths** cross the lavender fields (information from the Lavender Museum, *see* 'Robion', page 260).

WHERE TO STAY AND EAT

🛏 ✕ **Ferme-auberge Les Esfourniaux**: ☎ 04-90-75-01-04. Signposted from Lagarde-d'Apt. Closed Monday. Reservations only. Menus from 90F (weekdays) to 150F. Rooms with washbasin (shower and toilet on the landing) cost 120F. This is the oldest of the farmhouse inns in the Vaucluse and, at 1100 metres (3,608 feet), the highest. An unpretentious, authentically Provençal place, it serves good food that includes *civet de lièvre* (jugged hare), *sanglier* (wild boar) and *coq au vin.* The rooms are basic but ideal for anyone who wants to stay well away from the 'fashionable' Luberon.

ST-SATURNIN-LÈS-APT

This pretty town is 9 kilometres (5.5 miles) northwest of Apt on the D 943 and looks as if it has taken root in the rock. Climb up to the impressive remains of the medieval village and castle, watered by a tiny lake that was dug in the 17th century to provide St-Saturnin with water.

WHERE TO STAY AND EAT

♠ ✕ **Le St-Hubert**: 1 place de la Fraternité. In the middle of the village. ☎ 04-90-75-45-02. Fax: 04-90-75-49-90. ♿ (to the restaurant). Closed on Monday out of season and between 15 January and 15 February. Double rooms with shower or bath and toilet at 280F. Menus for 95F and 145F. This unpretentious spot offers a warm welcome and excellent food, based on fresh produce from the market. The terrace overlooks the Luberon and there's also a wine cellar. Rooms Nos. 3 and 7 have a lovely view.

SHOPPING

🔒 **Huile d'Olive Maurice Jullien**: rue Albert Trouchet. ☎ 04-90-75-45-80. Closed Sunday afternoon. In the centre of town. A charming little shop selling some of the best olive oil in the Vaucluse. Make an appointment to visit the mill where it is pressed according to the rules of the craft.

The Monts de Vaucluse

LIOUX

This tiny little village stands opposite a sheer rock face where birds of prey nest. Climbing is forbidden.

WHERE TO STAY AND EAT

♠ ✕ **Auberge de Lioux**: ☎ 04-90-05-77-52. Fax: 04-90-05-61-09. ♿ Closed in January and February. Double rooms with shower and toilet for 270F. This fairly new hotel lies hidden in beautiful countryside. The restaurant serves a daily special and one set menu, and you can also order ahead for Provençal and Caribbean specialities. There's a small swimming pool and the garden faces the cliff. Best to book.

ROUSSILLON

The houses in this village, poetically nicknamed 'Red Delphi', are identical in colour to the ochre that's extracted from the quarries in the surrounding landscape. The shades and tints are enhanced by the light as it comes and goes. Legend has it that the earth is stained red with the blood of the beautiful Sirmonde, the wife of Raymond d'Avignon, who murdered her young lover. Unable to contemplate life without the handsome troubador, she threw herself to her death from the top of the cliffs here.

THE RHÔNE VALLEY
AND HAUTE-PROVENCE

The village does attract lots of tourists but, if you pick your day carefully, it's worth walking around. Don't miss the view point near the church, the streets that look out over the Val des Fées ('Valley of the Fairies', the red cliffs to the west) and the crumbling cliffs of the Chaussée des Géants ('Giants' Pathway', a few minutes to the east on foot). The car park costs 15F.

USEFUL ADDRESS

🏛 **Tourist office**: ☎ 04-90-05-60-25. Fax: 04-90-05-63-31. Open between 1 April and 1 November, Monday to Saturday, 10am–noon and 2–6.30pm. Closed mornings in winter. Open occasionally on Sunday afternoon in high season.

WHERE TO STAY AND EAT

🏕 **Camping L'Arc-en-ciel**: route de Goult. ☎ 04-90-05-73-96 or 04-90-05-74-93 (out of season). Open 15 March to 30 October. 3 kilometres (2 miles) from the village. About 50F for a pitch for two with a vehicle. A two-star site under the pine trees, offering an excellent welcome and a swimming pool for children.

🏕 ✕ **La Petite Auberge**: Bois de la Cour. ☎ 04-90-05-65-46. Fax: 04-90-05-72-25. Just outside the village, past the Conservatoire des Ocres. Closed on Monday and during February. Double rooms with shower and toilet for 310F. Menus at 70F and 125F. Surrounded by countryside, this nine-room *auberge* was once the headquarters of the tennis club (the four courts are still there). The smallish rooms are comfortable and pleasant and there's a swimming pool. The welcome is warm and the regional home cooking is good, with dishes such as *magret de canard au miel de lavande* (duck breast with lavander honey).

🏕 ✕ **Rooms with Mme Cherel Lie**: ☎ 04-90-05-71-71. On the way out of Roussillon towards St-Pantaléon. Double rooms with shower but shared toilet at 180–220F. Menus from 65F to 100F. The rooms have basic facilities, but some have a lovely view. There's a slightly bohemian air and a friendly welcome, and the prices are low for such a popular village. There's a little area for walkers, with bunk beds, and mountain bikes for hire.

✕ **Restaurant Mincka's**: place de la Mairie. ☎ 04-90-05-66-22. Fax: 04-90-75-53-37. Closed on Thursday and from 15 November to March. Menus at 95F and 105F. This restaurant has two doll's-house dining rooms and a delightful terrace on the village square. The simple and flavoursome food is based on fresh market produce and the menus offer an appealing choice of dishes, such as *daube à la cardamome* (stew with cardamom), *civet de porc au gingembre frais et au miel* (jugged pork with fresh ginger and honey) and *couscous du Luberon*. Warm welcome and relaxed service. Booking advisable.

WHAT TO SEE

★ **Le Conservatoire des Ocres et Pigments Appliqués (Okhra)** (centre for the study of ochre and applied pigments): on the D104. ☎ and fax: 04-90-05-66-69. Email: info@okhra.com. Open every day throughout the year

9am–7pm (from 11am on Monday). Guided tours at 11am, 2pm, 3pm, 4pm and 5pm. Entrance fee: 25F (15F for large families and the disabled, free for accompanied under-10s). All sorts of household items have been dyed using ochre, from the washers round the tops of old-fashioned preserving jars to the inner tubes of bicycle tyres and red elastic bands. The natural pigment is extracted from a sand that has been quarried around Roussillon, Gargas and Rustrel in the Vaucluse since the end of the 18th century. This 'ecomuseum' is housed in an old ochre factory. The guided tour explains all the processes – washing, decanting, shaping and baking – involved in making slabs of ochre, but it also aims to protect the traditional skills. It organizes regular practical workshops for professionals, or interested amateurs, as well as days for children. Apprenticeships are possible in various building techniques (whitewashing, plastering, colour washes and other finishes) and there are also (with the focus on natural pigments) courses on using vegetable dyes, such as indigo and madder. There are annual themed exhibitions and you can also buy natural pigments and pick up a leaflet on their use.

★ **Sentier des Ocres** (ochre path): this 30-minute walk through the old ochre quarries is a good introduction (or complement) to a visit to Okhra (*see above*). From the car park follow the route to the cemetery. Entrance fee: 10F. There are informative panels along the way. It's great fun for children (but be warned that the ochre will certainly stain shoes and clothes, given the chance).

MARKETS, FESTIVALS AND EVENTS

– **Market**: on Thursday mornings.

– **Festival de quatuor à cordes** (festival of string quartets): in conjunction with other towns and villages in the area, including L'Isle-sur-la-Sorgue, this festival takes place between June and September. About five concerts are usually held in Roussillon.

– **Marché potier** (potters' market): one weekend in September.

WHAT TO SEE IN THE AREA

★ **Maison de la Céramique** (pottery museum): place de la Gare, 84220 Les Beaumettes. ☎ 04-90-72-32-61. Fax: 04-90-72-31-66. Open every day 10am–6pm. Free entry. Housed in the former railway inn of Les Beaumettes, this museum tells the story of the craft of pottery, an ancient tradition in the Luberon. A group of 26 potters and ceramic artists works here, and there's also a gallery, a permanent exhibition and an educational area where you can try it out for yourself. Worth a visit.

GOULT

Just above the N100. This characterful village, standing at the foot of a chateau (not open to the public), has a fortified church and some charming old streets.

WHERE TO EAT

✕ **Le Café de la Poste**: place de la Libération. ☎ 04-90-72-23-23. ✕ Closed Wednesday except in July and August. Open lunchtime only. Menu of the day 70F. This country bistrot draws crowds at lunchtime because of its dish of the day and Provençal specialities, which are good value for money. A few tables between the bar and the news-stands are popular with regulars and, in good weather, tables are set up under the elm trees. The atmosphere is good-natured, though it is a bit touristy in summer. The scene may be familiar to aficionados of French film – this is where Adjani and Souchon met in *L'été meurtrier* (*The Fatal Summer*).

☆☆☆ Chic

✕ **Auberge Le Fiacre**: quartier Pied-Rousset ; ☎ 04-90-72-26-31. 5 kilometres (3 miles) from the village on the N100, in the direction of Apt. Closed Wednesday, Sunday evening out of season. Menus cost 110F, 130F and 160F. A good family *auberge* with friendly and welcoming owners and great-value menus. The Provençal dishes are light and inventive, including *ravioles de langoustines* (crayfish ravioli), *tian de morue* (cod flan) or *carré d'agneau*

(rack of lamb). In the autumn, the chef likes to prepare game. In summer, tables are set up under the plane trees. This superb place comes highly recommended.

✕ **Auberge de la Bartavelle**: rue du Cheval-Blanc. ☎ and fax: 04-90-72-33-72. Closed on Wednesday throughout the year and on Tuesday in low season, as well as from end November to early March. Menus from 135F to 175F. It's Provence everywhere you look here: ochre on the walls, bright printed fabrics, and a warm, easy-going atmosphere. The traditional dishes burst with flavour.

✕ **Le Tonneau**: place de l'Ancienne-Mairie. At the top of the village, near the chateau. ☎ and fax: 04-90-72-22-35. Open for dinner from April to December. Restaurant closed on Monday evening in low season and in January and February. Two double rooms with shower or bath and toilet, plus satellite TV, for 530F, including breakfast. Menus from 135F to 198F. The welcome and service are fairly formal in this charming old house. The chef has a passion for cooking, producing delicacies such as *ravioles aux gambas* (prawn ravioli). Excellent value for money.

WHERE TO STAY AND EAT IN THE AREA

Les Beaumettes is a strip of a village just off the N100, and certainly off the tourist track, which is why the prices are among the lowest in the area.

🛌 ✕ **Les Cigales**: on the main road, Les Beaumettes. ☎ 04-90-72-20-61. Double rooms with shower, or shower and toilet, from 220F to 250F. Daily special 49F; à la carte reasonably priced. This tiny hotel has just four very simple rooms, all completely refurbished and really pretty.

Decent family cooking – the house speciality is *jarret grillé* (grilled shin of beef) – and good pastries, served in a reasonably cheery little dining room. The lady owner is English. The welcome is *really* laid-back.

✕ **La Remise**: on the main road, Les Beaumettes. ☎ 04-90-72-23-

05. Closed on Wednesday in high season, on Tuesday and Wednesday in low season and in December and January. Menus from 90F to 180F. The unpretentious 90F menu is one of the cheapest in the Luberon. The house specialities cost a bit more. Try the *filet de loup à l'estragon* (fillet of sea bream with tarragon) or *émincé de boeuf aux cèpes* (sliced beef with mushrooms).

WHAT TO DO

★ **Conservatoire des cultures en terrasses** (centre for the study of terrace cultivation): climb the path up to the left after the church. Entrance free. In the past, the stepped terraces of this region would have looked like vast amphitheatres. They provided Provençal farmers with a solution to the torrential rains that fell in the area, washing the topsoil off the hillsides. This kind of cultivation has practically disappeared from the region, but here the park authorities have sponsored the restoration of the terracing, with its drystone walls. Signs on the beautiful one-hour trail explain how the walls support the terraces, which retain the earth but allow the water to flow away, and the trail also takes you past stone-built reservoirs and traditional *bories* (little buildings constructed in the same stone).

GORDES

The superb village of Gordes perches on top of an escarpment, its colours changing with the light at different times of the day. It was abandoned long ago, but has been brought back to life by painters and 'intellectuals'. Today, some of the old houses look over-restored and Gordes is the most touristy place in the Luberon. Sometimes it's intolerable – you get stung for parking and the streets are packed – but in the middle of winter, it's quite different.

USEFUL ADDRESS

B Tourist office: in the chateau. ☎ 04-90-72-02-75. Fax: 04-90-72-02-26. Open every day 9am–noon and 2–6pm (from 10am on Sunday and until 12.30pm and 6.30pm in summer).

WHERE TO STAY AND EAT

There *is* accommodation in Gordes that doesn't cost a fortune but most of the restaurants are much too expensive (and not sufficiently welcoming) to be recommended.

Campsite

♠ Les Sources: ☎ 04-90-72-12-48. Fax: 04-90-72-09-43. Two kilometres from the village, on the D15 towards Murs. Open from October to March. Restaurant closed Monday and Tuesday in low season. Pitch for two with vehicle around 80F. Set in the countryside, with good shade from an oak tree grove, this site has acceptable washing facilities and a pool.

☆☆ Moderate

🛌 **Chambres d'hôte with Pierrette Lawrence** (B&B): Villa La Lèbre, chemin de la Roque. ☎ and fax: 04-90-72-20-74. Some 5 kilometres (about 3 miles) south of Gordes on the road for St-Pantaléon. Open all year. The comfortable double room with shower and toilet in this small stone house costs 280F, including breakfast. It can accommodate three people with its mezzanine and has air-conditioning and a fantastic view. There's also a garden.

🛌 **Chambre d'hôte with Alain Gaudemard** (B&B): Les Bouilladoires. ☎ 04-90-72-21-59 où 04-90-72-41-90. On the way up to Gordes, 2 kilometres from Les Beaumettes and 3.5 kilometres (2 miles) from St-Pantaléon, at 'Les Martins and Les Bouilladoires'. Open all year round. Double rooms with shower or shower and toilet from 250F to 280F, including breakfast. A studio that sleeps four costs 400F. The house, on a farm, lacks the charm of its neighbours in Gordes, but the countryside is lovely.

🛌 ✕ **Hôtel-restaurant Le Provençal**: place du Château. ☎ 04-90-72-10-01. Fax: 04-90-72-04-20. Double rooms with bath cost 330F. Menu for 120F; à la carte around 130F. Good value for money in the heart of the Luberon. Although not luxurious, the eight rooms are spotless, with new bathroom facilities. Rooms Nos. 1 and 2 have a lovely view of the chateau. The cooking is less interesting, but the à la carte pizzas are acceptable.

🛌 ✕ **Auberge de Carcarille**: Les Gervais. ☎ 04-90-72-02-63. Fax: 04-90-72-05-74. ⚡ 3 kilometres (about 2 miles) below Gordes on the D2. Closed on Friday out of season; Friday evening only between April and September; and from 15 November to 28 December. Double rooms with bath from 370F to 420F. Menus from 95F to 220F. This welcoming *auberge* has an elegant dining room and serves tasty traditional cuisine, including *gibelotte de lapin farcie aux herbes de provence* (rabbit with white wine, bacon, mushrooms and Provençal herbs) and *pieds et paquets* (tripe). The rooms are very pleasant and the prices are good for such an expensive area.

🛌 **Chambres d'hôte with Denise and Claude Peyron** (B&B): 'Les Martins'. ☎ 04-90-72-24-15. Annual closure from mid-November to 1 March. Double rooms with bath and toilet from 300F to 500F, including breakfast. Dinner 100F all-inclusive, but booking is essential. This attractive farmhouse, standing among vineyards, offers four rooms, a garden and sun terraces.

☆☆☆ Chic

🛌 **Le Mas de la Sénancole**: in the hamlet of Les Imberts. ☎ 04-90-76-76-55. Fax: 04-90-76-70-44. Five kilometres (about 3 miles) on the D2. Annual closure from end October to beginning April. Double rooms with shower and toilet plus satellite TV from 550F to 650F. Lovely rooms, with excellent facilities, decorated in typically bright Provençal colours. The apartments, which have covered balconies, outsize bathrooms and wrought-iron furniture, are superb. There's a beautiful garden with a swimming pool, but such luxury comes at a price.

🛌 **Hôtel Le Gordos**: route de Cavaillon. ☎ 04-90-72-00-75. Fax: 04-90-72-07-00. ⚡ One kilometre from Gordes on the D2. Closed from November to March. Double rooms with shower or bath, toilet and TV, from 620F to 930F. This recently built house has lots of local style and charm, comfortable rooms with contemporary Provençal décor, a pretty garden, a patio terrace for breakfast and a swimming pool. Prices can be negotiable out of season. There's no restaurant, but you can ask for sandwiches in the evening.

WHAT TO SEE

★ **The village**: the steep cobbled streets may be hard work, but the village is a pleasant place to walk (except in very high season, when it's unbearably busy). The old houses include the Aumonerie St-Jacques, an ancient hostelry for pilgrims on their way to Santiago de Compostela, in Spain. There are superb views of the Luberon here and there.

★ **Chateau**: open every day from the beginning of May to the end of August 10am–noon and 2–6pm. Closed Tuesday except in July and August. Entrance fee: 20F (under-10s free, concession for under-17s). Gordes' beautiful fortified castle was begun in the 12th century but considerably altered during the Renaissance. Dating from that period are an ingenious spiral staircase, a large reception room with a French-style beamed ceiling, and a superb chimneypiece, the second-largest in France.

The chateau houses the **Musée Pol Mara**, which has a display of around 200 works by the Flemish painter, who lived in the village until his death, in 1988. Open every day throughout the year. Entrance: 25F (10- to 17-year-olds 20F, under-10s free). In the 1960s, he experimented with a range of techniques and materials, including watercolour, collage and plexiglass.

★ **Village des Bories**: 1 kilometre to the west, signposted from Gordes. Open every day throughout the year, 9am–sunset. Information: ☎ 04-90-72-02-08. Entrance fee: 35F (10- to 17-year-olds 20F, under-10s free). Scattered throughout Haute-Provence, the *bories* are little buildings of drystone construction, prehistoric-looking but actually built from the 14th to the 19th century. There are around 3,000 in the Ventoux, the Luberon and on the Lure mountain alone, many practically in ruins. Sometimes they are clustered into little hamlets. The streets, sheepfold, wine store and vat of this village have been the subject of restoration since the 1950s, a labour of love on the part of Pierre Viala, an actor with the Théâtre National de Paris. In a *borie* that used to be a dwelling, there are descriptions of the way the farmers lived, with very simple furniture and with their crockery stacked in cavities in the walls. The village also has archive information on Gordes as it was in days gone by, as well as a photographic exhibition of drystone buildings throughout the world.

WHAT TO SEE AND DO IN THE AREA

★ **Abbaye Notre-Dame de Sénanque**: 3 kilometres (2 miles) north of Gordes, up the escarpment road. Stop at the top for a view of the abbey surrounded by greenery and lavender. ☎ 04-90-72-05-72. Fax: 04-90-72-15-70. Email: abbaye@senanque.fr. Open March to October 10am–noon and 2–6pm, except on Sunday morning and Holy Day mornings. Rest of the year, open 2–5pm. Closed 25 December and Good Friday. Entrance fee:

30F. Last tickets sold 30 minutes before closing time. The abbey was founded in 1148 and is one of the most beautiful buildings belonging to the Cistercian order. There's an impressive dormitory, a wonderful and un-adorned church, a pretty cloister, a large bookshop and a shop selling products made by the monks.

★ **Gorges de la Véroncle**: 4 kilometres (2.5 miles) east of Gordes on the D2. The entrance to the car park is poorly signposted on the left. A path follows these deep gorges that have been hollowed out by the Véroncle between Murs and Gordes. The whole walk takes a good five hours. The location is wonderfully wild, but there are some relics of an industrial past, including a dozen or so abandoned flour mills, some of which have been restored and are now lived in.

★ **Musée du Moulin des Bouillons**: ☎ 04-90-72-22-11. 5 kilometres (3 miles) south on the route de St-Pantaléon (D104). Open every day between 1 February and 30 October 10am–noon and 2–6pm (to 5pm in winter). Entrance fee: 20F (concessions available). Housed in a 16th-century oil mill with an impressive wooden press (which is 10 metres/33 feet long and weighs 7 tonnes), this museum has an exhibition on olive oil and Marseille soap, and a collection of oil lamps, jars and amphorae.

MURS

10 kilometres (6 miles) from Gordes, along a winding road with lovely views. A characterful village that's totally lost in the wilds, Murs was the birthplace of Crillon the Brave, companion-in-arms to Henri IV. The 12th-century chateau is not open to the public.

WHERE TO STAY AND EAT

♠ ✕ **Chambre d'hôte, Les Hauts de Véroncle** (B&B): Les Chalottes. ☎ 04-90-72-60-91. Fax: 04-90-72-62-07. From the centre of the village, take the straight narrow street head-ing downwards. Carry on, following the signposts, until you reach the house at the end of the track. Open all year (reservations necessary from mid-November to mid-March). Dou-ble rooms with shower and toilet cost 295F, including breakfast. Dinner may be booked. This corner of the Parc du Luberon is really close to nature. The little stone house, with three pretty bedrooms at garden level, is totally isolated at the mouth of the Gorges de la Véroncle. There's also a country *gîte* with two rooms that can sometimes be rented by the night. The owners have created a nice family atmosphere and offer a very friendly welcome. Didier is in charge of the kitchen; his inventive cooking is Provençal, although not exclusively. The meals are served as if in a restaurant, at little tables by the fireside or under the awning.

♠ ✕ **Hôtel Le Crillon**: in the village ☎ 04-90-72-60-31. Fax: 04-90-72-63-12. ✖ (to the restaurant). Closed Thursday out of season and during the last two weeks in January. Dou-ble rooms with bath, toilet and TV cost 285F; half board 290F. Menus from 75F (weekday lunch) and 130F. The rooms are smart, and the rest-aurant serves tasty dishes such as *pieds paquets* (tripe), or game and truffle dishes when in season. Re-discover the delights of the country-side here.

The Pays des Sorgues

FONTAINE-DE-VAUCLUSE (84800)

Population: 610

A mysterious spring (hence the fountain in the name) rises here out of an impressive rocky barrier that closes off the valley – *vallis clausa* is the origin of the name of the Vaucluse. It's an exceptional natural site and, consequently, one of the busiest places in the area. Unfortunately, it suffers from all the ills that follow in the wake of mass tourism: unattractive developments, souvenir shops along the road that leads to the spring, no free parking. Petrarch chose this place to lament the death of his beautiful Laura, carried off by the plague. Today, he might look for a less spoiled venue.

USEFUL ADDRESS

🚩 **Tourist office**: chemin de la Fontaine. ☎ 04-90-20-32-22. Fax: 04-90-20-21-37. Email: officetourisme.vaucluse@wanadoo.fr. Open every day (except public holidays) 10am–7pm.

WHERE TO STAY

🛌 **Auberge de jeunesse** (youth hostel): chemin de la Vignasse ☎ 04-90-20-31-65. Fax: 04-90-20-26-20. On the tourist route to Gordes, 800 metres outside the village. Open from 15 February to 15 November. 50 dormitory beds at 48F per night without breakfast. Half board 114F. French youth hostel association card required. This fairly new house has four-, six- and nine-bed dorms, kitchen facilities, places to pitch a tent and bikes for hire.

🛌 **Hostellerie du Château**: quartier Petite-Place. ☎ 04-90-20-31-54. Fax: 04-90-20-28-02. Restaurant closed on Tuesday evening. Double rooms with washbasin cost 220F. Menus from 119F (weekday lunch) to 189F. Three rooms, well maintained, though with limited facilities, in an old house on the banks of the river, with a superb view at dawn. The view from the restaurant's veranda is the same. The regional cooking includes *méli-mélo de poissons* (fish selection) and *ris de veau sauce morilles* (calf sweetbreads with mushroom sauce).

Campsite

🛌 **Camping Municipal Les Prés**: ☎ 04-90-20-32-38. Open all year. This very comfortable site has a swimming pool. Bookings for a minimum of a week.

WHERE TO STAY IN THE AREA

🛌 **Aire naturelle de camping La Folie, Les Grès** (campsite): 84800 Lagnes. ☎ 04-90-20-20-02. Four kilometres (2.5 miles) south of Fontaine, on the D186. Open from April to the beginning of October. This peaceful little campsite on a farm has two showers with hot water.

THE RHÔNE VALLEY AND HAUTE-PROVENCE

WHERE TO EAT

The restaurants around Fontaine, most of which serve the local speciality of trout, are very popular at Sunday lunchtime with local people. They are generally about the same in terms of food and service, but the waterfront places obviously have extra appeal.

SHOPPING

🔒 **Confiserie de la Fontaine**: galerie Vallis-Clausa. ☎ 04-90-20-36-26. Sweet shop dedicated to the treats of Provence, including delicious Ventoux truffles and *caprices d'Offenbach*.

WHAT TO SEE

★ **La source** (the spring): five minutes' walk from the bottom of the village. Free access. The Vaucluse's River Sorgue gushes out of the La Fontaine chasm at an average rate of 630 million cubic metres (824 million cubic yards) a year. Nobody really knows how or why, although the spring has been explored a number of times, first by a Marseillais called Otonelli, who descended to 23 metres (75 feet) in a heavy diving bell. Jacques Cousteau made three dives, in 1946, 1955 and 1967, and in 1983, a German diver went as deep as 205 metres (675 feet). In 1989, the underwater robot Spélénaute reached a depth of 308 metres (1,010 feet, nearly 220 metres/ 720 feet below sea level) and discovered a huge subterranean hall at 174 metres (575 feet). Scientists also know that some of the water from the River Nesque drains into the spring, as well as water from the Vaucluse plateau. In one experiment, they even dyed the Nesque, to follow its course, but they still could not explain why the spring is able to produce a gush that sometimes reaches more than 80 cubic metres (105 cubic yards) of water a second.

Whatever the explanation for its abundance, this spring is one of the most forceful in the world; it has never dried up and gushes constantly, even in the hottest weather. When the spring is at its fullest strength, the water level is about equal with the place where the fig trees grow out of the rocks. Even with around 20 cubic metres (26 cubic yards) per second of water, the spring floods the underwater basin and creates an impressive waterfall.

For a long walk, take the GR6 to the left of the fountain, which leads to the Abbey of Sénanque (*see* page 279) and then to Gordes (*see* page 277).

★ **Musée Petrarch**: rive gauche de la Sorgue (left bank of the river). ☎ 04-90-20-37-20. Open from the beginning of April to the beginning of October, every day except Tuesday 10am–noon and 2–6pm; 10am–12.30pm and 1.30–6pm from July to the end of September. Same times in October, but only open on Saturday and Sunday. Entrance fee: 20F (students half price, under-12s free). This tiny museum tells the story of the poet's stay in the town and his meeting with Laura in Avignon. The collection includes drawings and prints from the 16th to the 19th century, other 18th- and 19th-century works relating to Petrarch and his followers, and a very small collection of modern art, inspired by the writings of René Char, including lithographs by Braque, and drawings by Giacometti and Picasso.

★ **Notre-Dame-St-Véran church**: this delightful 12th-century Provençal Romanesque church is largely overlooked by tourists, as they flock towards the spring. Inside, a carved and moulded 12th-century baptismal font is surmounted by a graceful 18th-century processional crucifix. There's a 15th-century statue of Ste-Anne in polychrome wood and a few relics of old buildings, including Roman columns and fragments of Carolingian friezes.

★ **Musée Norbert-Casteret**: chemin de la Fontaine. ☎ and fax: 04-90-20-34-13. Open 1 February to 11 November 10am–noon and 2–6pm. Entrance fee: 31F (children 21F). Cavers and underground explorers will enjoy this museum's life-size representation of grottoes with rock paintings, its splendid collection of stalactites and other rock crystals collected by a famous speleologist. There's also an exhibition on the site of Fontaine-de-Vaucluse.

★ **Musée de la Résistance**: chemin du Gouffre. ☎ 04-90-20-24-00. Fax: 04-90-20-53-45. From mid-April to mid-October and in the school holidays, open every day except Tuesday 10am–noon and 2–6pm: the rest of the year open weekends only. Entrance: 20F (students half price). This superb museum on the Resistance opened in 1990 and has a collection of around 10,000 pieces relating to life during the Occupation and the activities of the Resistance Movement in the Vaucluse. Records of deportation and other documents are available alongside films, magazines, manuscripts, and artworks by Matisse and Miró.

★ **Musée du Santon et des Traditions de Provence**: galerie Vallis-Clausa. ☎ 04-90-20-20-83. Open every day 10am–noon and 2–6pm in winter, and 10am–7pm in summer. Entrance fee: 25F (children 15F). This museum explains the Provençal tradition of making *santons* (see page 88) and displays a collection of more than 500 pieces.

★ **La vieille papeterie** (old paper mill): galerie Vallis-Clausa. Entrance free. This old mill is all that remains of a paper-making industry that flourished here from the 16th century. The last factory closed in 1968. Visitors can see a working paper press worked by a water-wheel. The rest of the mill has been turned into a (rather touristy) shop.

– **The Sorgue by canoe or kayak**: Kayak-Vert in Fontaine-de-Vaucluse, ☎ 04-90-20-35-44. Fax: 04-90-20-20-28. Website: www.canoefrance.com. Guided trips on the Sorgue river are possible from Fontaine-de-Vaucluse as far L'Isle-sur-la-Sorgue. Other trips are organized by Canoë Évasion: chemin de la Coutelière, on the D24, near Camping de la Coutelière. ☎ and fax: 04-90-38-26-22. It operates between 15 April and 30 September and a trip costs 110F for adults and 70F for children between 7 and 14.

WHAT TO SEE IN THE AREA

★ **Saumane-de-Vaucluse**: 4 kilometres (2.5 miles) north along the D57. This little 15th-century village is dominated by its chateau (not open to the public), beautifully sited on a rocky spur, and formerly the property of Baudet de Sade, a relation of the infamous Marquis.

L'ISLE-SUR-LA-SORGUE (84800)

Population: 16,971

The native town of French poet René Char is delightful, immediately bringing to mind watery Venice. Walk along the banks of the branches of the Sorgue to see gorgeous waterfront houses. There are still a number of working waterwheels; in the past, more than 70 of them would have provided power for local businesses. The old town has a collection of Renaissance houses, private mansions and the superb church of Notre-Dame-des-Anges, with its flamboyant interior, a typical example of Provençal baroque decoration.

L'Isle-sur-la-Sorgue is also a town of antique dealers and junk shops. There are six 'villages' of shops around the station and along the avenue des Quatre-Otages (open on weekends and public holidays). Every Sunday, the huge flea market, an adjunct to the traditional market, is one of the most lively in Provence. Apparently, the best deals are to be had when the stallholders are getting ready to pack up.

USEFUL ADDRESS

B Tourist office: place de l'Église. ☎ 04-90-38-04-78. Fax: 04-90-38-35-43. Open in July and August 9am–1pm and 2.30–6.30pm. In winter open 9.30am–12.30pm and 2.30–6.30pm. Housed in an attractive 18th-century building that was the former municipal granary, the office provides excellent information on the town.

WHERE TO STAY

≜ Hôtel au Vieux-L'Isle: 15 rue Danton. ☎ 04-90-38-00-46. Double rooms with washbasin 130F and 160F with shower (toilet facilities on the landing). This small hotel stands on a pedestrianized street in the old town, near a canal with a chain pump. The eight rooms have seen better days, but they're reasonably well maintained and cheap and the welcome is friendly. There's a shady terrace in the interior courtyard.

≜ La Saladelle: 33 rue Carnot. ☎ and fax: 04-90-20-68-59. Closed on Monday (except in July and August) and Sunday evening. Annual closure from 15 January to 15 February. Rooms by the month around 1,500F. Menus from 85F to 115F. With ultra-simple, but clean rooms, rented out by the month, this typical little family guesthouse on a pedestrianized street is often full. The welcome is polite and a little restaurant on the ground floor serves salads and market-fresh, family-style cooking.

≜ Hôtel-restaurant Le Bassin: avenue Charles-de-Gaulle. Just outside the town centre. ☎ 04-90-38-03-16. Fax: 04-90-38-40-83. Closed Friday in winter. Annual closure during November and December. Double rooms from 230F to 290F. Menu 89F. This appealing pink house with blue shutters, has a waterside terrace and decent rooms looking on to the Sorgue. The restaurant is not so good. Drivers should be aware that several car thefts in the area have been reported.

≜ Camping Municipal La Sorguette (campsite): route d'Apt. ☎ 04-

90-38-05-71. Fax: 04-90-20-84-61. Email: sorguette@wanadoo.fr. 1.5 kilometres from the village on the N100. Open 15 March to the end of October. On the banks of the Sorgue, surrounded by greenery, with a few rather expensive mobile homes and bungalows to rent.

☆☆☆ Chic

🛋 **Mas de Cure-Bourse**: route de Caumont-sur-Durance, at the Velorgues crossroads. ☎ 04-90-38-16-58. Fax: 04-90-38-52-31. Restaurant closed all day Monday and lunchtime on Tuesday as well as for two weeks in January and three weeks in November. Double rooms with bath and toilet plus TV from 450F to 650F. Menus from 170F to 280F. Formerly an 18th-century coaching inn, this *mas*, surrounded by fields and orchards, has been very tastefully renovated. The pretty rooms are furnished in Provençal style and the room at the end has a little balcony overlooking the swimming pool. The dining room has a big fireplace and the restaurant serves regional food that changes with the seasons.

WHERE TO STAY IN THE AREA

🛋 **Chambres d'hôte Lou Mas de Mireio** (B&B): 2739 route des Vignères, 84250 Le Thor. Four kilometres (2.5 miles) from the village on the D98. ☎ 04-90-33-93-64. Double rooms with bath and toilet at 300F (including breakfast); 260F after the third night. Dinner with the hosts is 90F (45F for children under 10). This small working farm, right out in the countryside, offers three reasonably priced new rooms, and Provençal cooking. The farm grows fruit trees and raises chickens, so children enjoy it. The owners organize themed weekends outside school holidays, including visits to the flea market at L'Isle-sur-la-Sorgue.

WHERE TO EAT

✗ **Le Basilic**: 9 quai Rouget de l'Isle. ☎ 04-90-38-39-84. Closed on Monday and from 15 November to 20 March. À la carte about 120F. This restaurant, on the banks of the river, has a tiny dining room and excellent cooking, influenced by both Provence and Italy. Dishes include *terrine de courgettes à la sicilienne* (courgette terrine) and *raviolis maison aux artichauts* (homemade artichoke ravioli), using fresh local produce and unusual flavours.

WHAT TO SEE IN THE AREA

★ **Grotte de Thouzon** (Thouzon cave): ☎ 04-90-33-93-65. Fax: 04-90-33-74-90. 1.5 kilometres from Le Thor (signposted). Closed from beginning December to end February. Open every day in July and August 10am–7pm; rest of the year, open every day 10am–noon and 2–6pm (afternoon only Sunday and public holidays in November and March). Last visit 30 minutes before closing. Entrance fee: 39F (26F for children 5–12 years old, free for under-5s). Discovered in 1902, this is the only natural cave in Provence that is open to the public. The guided tour takes 45 minutes and follows the course of an ancient underground river.

The Comtat Venaissin

CARPENTRAS (84200)   Population: 26,090

There are many delightful places to visit in this area (Ventoux, the Pays de Sault, the Dentelles de Montmirail) and Carpentras, still huddled behind ancient walls, is one of the most appealing. Its ramparts date from the time when it was the fortified capital of the Comtat Venaissin (the domain of the Counts of Venaissin). Founded originally in the fifth century BC, it became the ancient capital of the Mémizien tribe, then, from 1229, it belonged to the papacy. Many beautiful buildings were constructed between the 17th and the 19th century.

Carpentras is best known as the place where the Jews sought refuge, under the tolerance of the popes, when Philippe le Bel threw them out of the kingdom of France. Until the 19th century, Carpentras had a Jewish district with a synagogue, built in the 14th century and enlarged in the 18th. In the ghetto a thousand people lived practically on top of each other along a road just 80 metres (262 feet) long.

USEFUL ADDRESSES

ℹ Tourist office (B2 on the map): 170 allée Jean-Jaurès. ☎ 04-90-63-00-78. Fax: 04-90-60-41-02. Open Monday to Friday 9am–12.30pm and 2–6.30pm; Saturday 9am–noon and 2–6pm. Between June and September, open Monday to Saturday 9am–7pm, Sunday 9.30am–12.30pm. Excellent service.

■ **Bicycle hire**: Terzo Sports, 519 avenue Frédéric-Mistral. ☎ 04-90-67-31-56.

WHERE TO STAY

✩ Budget

🛎 Hôtel du Théâtre (A2, **1** on the map): 7 boulevard Albin-Durand. ☎ 04-90-63-02-90. Closed from 22 December to 4 January. Double rooms 170–210F, with washbasin, or with shower, toilet and TV. Rather old-fashioned little family hotel, with comfortable and well-maintained rooms, a friendly welcome and very reasonable prices. Secure car parking available.

✩✩ – ✩✩✩ Moderate to Chic

🛎 Hôtel du Fiacre (B1–2, **2** on the map): 153 rue Vigne. ☎ 04-90-63-03-15. Fax: 04-90-60-49-73. Open all year. Double room with shower or bath, and toilet, plus TV, 290–390F. This former 17th-century convent, on a quiet town-centre road, has an impressive staircase leading to lovely rooms arranged around a pleasant patio. There are also two superb suites.

🛎 Chambres d'hôte Bastide St-Agnès (B&B) (B1, **3**, off the map): 1043 chemin de la Fourtrousse. 3 kilometres (about 2 miles) north-east of Carpentras. Take the D974 towards Mont-Ventoux-Bédoin, fork left to Caromb (on the D13) and after 300 metres turn left into the chemin de la Fourtrousse. The house is 200 metres along on the right. ☎ 04-90-60-03-01. Fax:

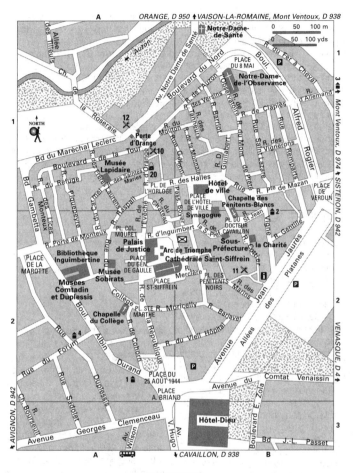

CARPENTRAS

- **Useful Addresses**

  🛈 Tourist office
  ✉ Post office
  🚌 Coach station

- **Where to Stay**

  1 Hôtel du Théâtre

  2 Hôtel du Fiacre
  3 Guest rooms Bastide St-Agnès
  4 Hôtel Forum

✕ **Where to Eat**

  10 Restaurant des Halles
  11 Chez Serge
  12 Les Rives d'Auzon

04-90-60-02-53. Email: gerlinde@ infonie. Website: www.avignon-et-provence.com/saint-agnes. Closed from 1 November to 15 March. Double rooms with shower or bath and toilet from 450F to 520F, including breakfast. This peaceful *bastide* has changed a lot since the 19th century, but it still has a fine Provençal atmosphere, with four rooms (and one suite) with tiled floors and sponge-painted walls. Dinner is not served but you can have a picnic and grill your own provisions at the barbecue. There's a lovely swim-ming pool in the garden and the owners are happy to suggest local restaurants or visits in the region.

Hôtel Forum (A2, **4** on the map): 24 rue du Forum. ☎ 04-90-60-57-00. Fax: 04-90-63-52-65. Double rooms with bath, toilet and TV from 320F to 350F. Car park 30F. A fairly new hotel, built in an attractive neo-Provençal style and colourfully decorated, but rather too standardized. It has 28 modern and well-equipped rooms and a roof terrace that is lovely on sunny days. The welcome is equally warm.

WHERE TO EAT

✗ **Restaurant des Halles** (A1, **10** on the map): 41 rue Galonne. ☎ 04-90-63-24-11. At the back of a courtyard, opposite the town hall. Closed on Sunday. ✗ Lunchtime *formule* menu for 66F, and menus from 75F to 130F. There are fewer and fewer of these small, well-priced eating places in France. The simple dining room, tables decorated with pretty Provençal cloths and lively atmosphere make it very popular, although the welcome can be unpredictable. Tables are set up outside on the square, with its typical bubbling fountain.

✗ **Chez Serge** (B2, **11** on the map): 90 rue Cottier. In the centre, next to the tourist office. ☎ 04-90-63-21-24. ✗ Closed Sunday. Pizzas 70–90F for two people. Menus from 69F (weekday lunch) to 125F. The fashionable decor of this lovely restaurant is somewhere between New York loft and deepest Provence. There's a warm atmosphere, impeccable service and a choice of very good pizzas, an Armenian speciality on Thursday, and delicious desserts.

☆☆☆ Chic

✗ **Les Rives d'Auzon** (A1, **12** on the map): 47 boulevard du Nord. ☎ 04-90-60-62-62. On the ring road outside the city centre, opposite the Porte d'Orange. Closed all day Wednesday and for lunch on Saturday as well as for two weeks in December. Menus from 110F (weekday lunch, including wine and coffee) to 280F. Attractively decorated, and spacious, with a delightful indoor terrace, this restaurant offers a friendly welcome and relaxed but efficient service. Most importantly, the young chef, who surely has a bright future, creates delicious southern dishes using fresh seasonal produce.

SWEET TREATS

Pâtissier-chocolatier Clavel: 30 rue Porte-d'Orange. ☎ 04-90-63-07-59. Closed on Sunday afternoon and for two weeks at the end of January. Mouthwatering sweet temptations including *ardoise de Provence*, *chocolat au café noisette des rocailles* (chocolate with coffee and wild hazelnuts), *divines de Provence*, *truffes du Ventoux* (Ventoux truffles), nougat, *craquelin de Carpentras*, *berlingots* (chocolate bars) and *caprices d'Offenbach*. Clavel has the record for producing the biggest bar of chocolate in the world. It weighed 56.7 kilograms (124lbs), according to the *Guinness Book of Records*, and was quickly eaten up by the children of Carpentras. Clavel has a second shop in Fontaine-de-Vaucluse (Galerie Vallis-Clausa), where the sweets and chocolates are actually made. Unfortunately, nothing in either shop is marked with the price.

WHAT TO SEE

The old quarter of Carpentras has a network of picturesque streets that, as in many other towns in Provence, wind round like a snail shell. Wander around following your nose and in the labyrinth of streets you should come across the 19th-century covered Boyer *passage* and the medieval rue des Halles.

★ **L'hôtel-Dieu**: place Aristide-Briand. Built in the 18th century in luxurious style on the orders of Monsigor d'Inguimbert, the old hospice is unmissable for its spectacular ornamented facade. On Monday, Wednesday and Thursday, 9–11.30am, you can visit the superb old apothecary, which has been preserved as it was in the 18th century, with pottery jars from Montpellier and Moustier, old syringes and glass vessels.

★ **St-Siffrein Cathedral**: Carpentras' splendid cathedral, with its harmonious exterior, took more than a century to build. Above the south door (called the Jews' Door, because it was the entrance to the cathedral for Jewish refugees wishing to convert) is the famous *boule aux rats*, or 'rat ball', a sculpted sphere attacked by rodents – an allusion to the plague that decimated Provence or the world being nibbled away by Time? The interior is typical southern Gothic. Splendid 17th-century wooden carvings ornament the apse and the capitals have carvings of local flora and fauna, including a fable from the Middle Ages about Goupil the Fox.

★ **Palais de justice** (law courts): formerly the bishop's palace, built in a 17th-century Italian style. On the first floor is the bishop's state room, with its impressive, beamed French ceiling. The assizes hall is splendid and the court room contains some interesting scrolls depicting the villages of the Comtat Venaissin.

★ **Synagogue**: place de l'Hôtel-de-Ville. Open Monday to Thursday, 10am–noon and 3–5pm; Friday until 4pm. Built in the 14th century, this is one of the oldest remaining synagogues in France. On the ground floor, there are baths and pools, including a primitive pool fed by springwater, as tradition requires. On the first floor, there is a richly decorated 18th-century prayer room.

★ **Roman arch**: the arch is all that remains of the Roman period in Carpentras, commemorating a Roman victory over the Barbarians without specifying the battle or the date.

Museums

★ **Musée Duplessis**: 234 boulevard Albin-Durand. ☎ 04-90-63-04-92. Open every day except Tuesday and public holidays, 10am–noon and 2–4pm (until 6pm in summer). Entrance fee: 2F (giving access to both museums). On the ground floor, the history of the Comtat Venaissin and its traditions is told through a collection of papal coins and medals, county seals, hunting decoys, head-dresses, *santons* and ex-voto offerings. Upstairs, there are works by local painters, including Joseph-Siffre Duplessis, who was a great portraitist in the 18th century.

★ **Musée Sobirat**: 112 rue du Collège. Same phone number and opening hours as the Musée Duplessis (*see above*). Housed in an 18th-century private mansion, the museum of decorative arts has a sedan chair, Empire and Renaissance furniture, Aubusson tapestries and an 18th-century library.

WHAT TO DO

– **Market**: if you're in Carpentras on a Friday morning, don't miss the traditional market. There's also an **organic market** on Tuesday morning. The **truffle market** takes place on Friday morning on the place Aristide-Briand from the end of November to the beginning of March.

– **Swimming pool**: rue du Mont-de-Piété. ☎ 04-90-60-92-03. Right in the centre. Listed as a historic monument, the indoor swimming pool dates from the 1930s, with a metal and glass roof that's very much in the style of Eiffel.

FESTIVAL

– **Les Estivales** (summer festival): held in July, featuring a wide range of performances, including music, jazz, comedy, theatre, exhibitions. Information and booking: ☎ 04-90-60-46-00.

Around Carpentras

MONTEUX

This large market town, 5 kilometres (3 miles) southwest of Carpentras, is dominated by a tall medieval tower. Take time to wander through its cool, narrow streets.

WHERE TO STAY AND EAT

🛏 ✕ **Sélect Hôtel**: 24 boulevard René-Cassin. ☎ 04-90-66-27-91. Fax: 04-90-66-33-05. Closed on Saturday and Sunday out of season and on Saturday afternoon in high season, as well as from 18 December to 6 January. Double rooms with bath, toilet and cable TV for 340F. Menus from 95F to 170F. A typical old *mas* (farmhouse), with a terrace shaded by plane trees, an olive stone's throw from the pool, run by a friendly Dutch couple. The rooms, decorated in a neo-rustic style, are comfortable and pleasant. The restaurant serves simple, original and light dishes using market-fresh ingredients.

🛏 ✕ **Hostellerie Blason de Provence**: 515 route de Carpentras. ☎ 04-90-66-31-34. Fax: 04-90-66-83-05. One kilometre from the village. Restaurant closed Saturday lunchtime throughout the year and Sunday evening out of season, as well as from 15 December to 31 January. Double rooms with shower or bath, toilet and satellite TV cost 345–450F, depending on season.

Half board compulsory from May to September. Menus from 95F to 280F. Everyone's dream Provençal home, with comfortable rooms in an attractive setting, a swimming pool, garden and tennis court. The restaurant serves local and traditional dishes.

PERNES-LES-FONTAINES

Some 5.5 kilometres (3.5 miles) south of Carpentras on the D938. A short drive from the Carpentras commercial district, the old capital of the Comtat Venaissin looks much as it must have done in the 15th century. It has a good deal of charm, with ancient ramparts and a flowing river, turrets, medieval gates and more than 40 fountains – which explain its name.

USEFUL ADDRESS

🖪 **Tourist office**: place Gabriel-Moutte. ☎ 04-90-61-31-04. Fax: 04-90-61-33-23. From April to October open Monday to Saturday, 9am–noon and 2.30–6.30pm (until 7pm from June to September) and Sunday, 10am–noon. Out of season, open Monday to Saturday 10am–noon and 2–5pm. The office can organize tours of the 13th-century **Tour Ferrande** from April to September (9–11am and 2.30–5.30pm), which has superb medieval frescoes.

WHERE TO STAY AND EAT

🛏 **Chambres d'hôte Domaine de la Petite Cheylude** (B&B): 518 route de la Gasqui. Two kilometres from Pernes on the D38, and then on the D49 towards Carpentras (follow the signposts). ☎ 04-90-61-37-24. Fax: 04-90-61-67-00. Closed from November to end January. Double rooms with shower and toilet from 300F to 340F, depending on size and season, breakfast included. This large 17th-century farmhouse, set in strawberry fields, has four pleasant rooms, a fully-equipped kitchen, a charming vaulted dining room and a lovely swimming pool. Owned by a welcoming Dutch family.

✕ **Dame l'Oie**: 56 rue Troubadour-Durand. ☎ 04-90-61-62-43. Fax: 04-90-61-35-79. Closed on Monday all year and Tuesday lunchtime, and during the month of February. Menus from 70F to 150F. Appropriately for Perne-les-Fontaines, there's a real fountain in the middle of the dining room. The decor is straight out of a Beatrix Potter book, with geese (in papier mâché, porcelain, wood) all over the place (the name means 'Mother Goose'). The welcome and the service are extremely kind, and the southern-style dishes are simple but attractively prepared and flavoursome. The desserts are delicious and the 70F menu represents good value for money. The wine list has some pleasant local bottles on it, and there are even parking spaces for bicycles – a real find.

☆☆ Moderate

🛏 **Hôtel L'Hermitage**: route de Carpentras. Outside the town, on the right of the road towards Carpentras. ☎ 04-90-66-51-41. Fax: 04-90-61-36-41. Closed from 6 January to 1 March. Double rooms with bath and toilet from 350F to 400F, depending on the season. In a lovely bourgeois house surrounded by grounds, the rooms are cosy and charming. The welcome is laid-back and there's also a swimming pool.

WHERE TO EAT IN THE AREA

✘ **L'Autre Côté du Lavoir**: impasse du Lavoir, 134 le Cours, 84210 St-Didier. Three kilometres (2 miles) east of Pernes-les-Fontaines on the D28. ☎ 04-90-66-15-60. ✘ Closed Tuesday and Wednesday lunchtime. Annual closure from November to 31 January. Menus 105F, 111F and 135F. In an old granary surrounded by a garden, right next to the old *lavoir* (public washing place), this restaurant serves fresh regional cuisine, with dishes such as *tarte tatin de tomate* (upside-down tomato tart) and *gratin d'agneau au petit épeautre* (lamb with spelt).

FESTIVALS AND EVENTS

– **Feria des Fontaines**: July festival of traditional events, including Camargue horse races.

– **La Nuit des Légendes** (night of legends): held on the first weekend in August. On Saturday evening legends and stories are told near the key monuments. Live theatrical events take place during the day.

VÉNASQUE

On one of the first hills of the Monts du Vaucluse, 12 kilometres (7.5 miles) south of Carpentras. Another village with a sign claiming that it's 'the most beautiful in France', Vénasque is geographically at the centre of the old Comtat Venaissin and, indeed, gave the county its name. Thanks to a local bye-law in 1967, the village has retained its original architectural style and has great charm. It is protected by a group of towers built to fend off Saracen invaders.

USEFUL ADDRESS

🚹 **Tourist office**: Grand'rue. ☎ and fax: 04-90-66-11-66. Between mid-March and end October, open 10am–noon and 2.30–6.30pm. Closed on Friday morning and Sunday morning. Helpful brochures about the region and small local walking guides for sale.

WHERE TO STAY AND EAT

🛏 ✘ **Chambres d'hôte with Régis Borel** (B&B): Le Camp-Long, route de Murs. Three kilometres (about 2 miles) southwest of Vénasque on the D4. ☎ 04-90-66-03-56. Fax: 04-90-66-60-34. Email: camplong84@aol.com. Closed from 15 December to 15 January. Double rooms with shower or bath, and toilet, from 220F to 310F (depending on size), including breakfast. Way out in the countryside, in the depths of a valley, this old *mas* has five simply decorated bedrooms, a TV and music room, barbecue and kitchen facilities for guests, and a dining room. The welcome is excellent. There's a swimming pool and, for walkers, the long-distance GR91 footpath leaves from the front door.

🛏 ✕ **Hôtel les Remparts**: rue Haute. ☎ 04-90-66-02-79. Fax: 04-90-66-61-67. Annual closure from mid-November to mid-March. Double rooms cost 330F, including breakfast. Menus from 95F to 165F. Half board 260F a day. An old house covered in ivy, sitting in the middle of the village and looking like a real country inn. The interior has been tastefully renovated and the dining room is particularly charming. Dishes served in the restaurant, run by a young and friendly team, include *caillettes vauclusienne* (quail in local style) and *ravioles à la crème de poireaux* (ravioli in a creamy leek sauce).

✕ **Le Bistrot de la Fontaine**: place de la Fontaine. ☎ 04-90-66-02-96. Closed Sunday evening and Monday. Menus from 90F to 190F. The bistrot (not signposted) is an annexe of the more expensive Auberge de la Fontaine. Good, straightforward, fairly priced Provençal dishes and inexpensive local wines are served at a few tables on the ground floor.

WHAT TO SEE

★ **Baptistry**: ☎ 04-90-66-62-01. Open every day except Wednesday and Sunday morning, 10am–noon and 3–7pm from June to September. Out of season 10am–noon and 2–6pm (to 5pm in December and January). Small entrance charge (free for under-12s). Lost among subsequent buildings, the baptistry is almost impossible to see from the outside. It was built in the sixth century (making it one of the oldest Christian buildings in France) and contains architectural elements of an ancient temple. The interior is bathed in a glorious light and has a very special atmosphere. Antique marble columns blend well with elegant Merovingian capitals. In the centre, an eight-sided baptismal font is set in the ground and there is also a marble altar from the sixth century.

★ **Church of Notre-Dame**: most of the building dates from the 12th and 13th centuries. There's a lovely main door and, inside, a crucifix (1498) by an anonymous artist of the Avignon school. It was restored by the Louvre museum in Paris, which would have liked to keep it.

FESTIVALS AND EVENTS

– **Journée artisanale** (arts and crafts day): this is held on 15 August and stalls are set up in the streets.

MAZAN

On the D942, 6 kilometres (3.75 miles) east of Carpentras. The big market town of Mazan is best known for its gypsum quarries (the largest deposits in Europe, apparently), used to make plaster. The Marquis de Sade had a chateau here (now converted into an old people's home), where he used to stage plays (for once, it seems, there was no scandal involved). In the cemetery there's a curious avenue of fifth- and sixth-century sarcophagi.

THE RHÔNE VALLEY AND HAUTE-PROVENCE

USEFUL ADDRESS

🄱 **Tourist office**: 83 place du 8-mai. ☎ 04-90-69-74-24. Fax: 04-90-69-66-31. Email: officetourisme-mazan@wanadoo.fr. In low season, open 9am–noon; mid-season 9.30am–12.30pm and 3–6pm. From 15 June to 15 September, open 9.30am–12.30pm and 3–7pm.

WHERE TO EAT

✕ **L'Oulo**: 239 avenue de l'Europe. ☎ 04-90-69-87-64. Closed Wednesday and Saturday lunchtime (except in season). Daily menu 75F (weekday lunchtime) and other menus from 98F to 210F. The chef takes a number of risks – the menu is written entirely in Provençal and 'surprise' menus (including one for children) are offered – but the regional food is good, based on fresh market produce. The setting is very simple.

The Pays de Sault

This vast limestone plateau, dominated by the round outline of the Ventoux, remains little known, yet its blue skies, golden fields of wheat, green oak groves, rows of purple lavender, and white stone houses all add up to a breathtakingly colourful landscape. Apart from spelt, the wheat of the Gauls, which has been cultivated again in the last few years, the deliciously perfumed Val de Sault produces many delicacies. You can buy the sweet and fattening delicacies of nougat, macaroons and lavender honey in villages all around the area.

THE NESQUE GORGES

The Pays de Sault is reached via the spectacular D942 corniche. The very deep gorges remain a scientific mystery; in theory, the water should have filtered down through the limestone of the plateau instead of gradually wearing away the surface to create this steep canyon. There's a superb panoramic view from the Castelleras bell-tower; apparently, a pair of eagles nests just opposite, in the Rocher du Cire. In summer, you can walk along the gorges on foot, from the hamlet of Veaux to St-Léger-du-Ventoux, but you must be wary of storms, which can cause the water level to rise quickly.

SAULT

Standing on a spur of rock overlooking a wide valley, this big village has a few charming shopfronts from the beginning of the 20th century, a Romanesque church with a 12th century nave and an interesting museum on natural history, archaeology and, somewhat surprisingly, Egypt.

USEFUL ADDRESS

🄱 **Office de tourisme de la région de Sault** (Sault regional tourist office): avenue de la Promenade. ☎ 04-90-64-01-21. Fax: 04-90-64-15-03. Between 1 April and 30 September, open 9am–noon and 2–6pm. Between 1

October and 30 March, open from Tuesday to Saturday. Tourist information is also on offer in the town hall, in the Maison de l'Environnement and at M. Rouchet, the gunsmith. They all provide excellent and comprehensive leaflets about the region and a guide to walks in the area.

WHERE TO STAY AND EAT

⌂ **Camping municipal du Defends** (campsite): ☎ 04-90-64-07-18. 04-90-64-08-59. Three kilometres (nearly 2 miles) from the village. About 45F for a pitch for two. Out in the countryside, surrounded by a cedar forest, this site has free showers and a municipal swimming pool (entrance charge) next door.

✗ **Le Provençal**: rue portes-des-Aires. ☎ 04-90-64-09-09. Closed on Tuesday in low season and from 15 November to 2 February. Menus from 65F to 130F. In the heart of the village, this restaurant has a simple dining room and tables outside, surrounded by picturesque covered *passages*. The delicious, reasonably priced Provençal cooking – including truffles, lamb and local farmhouse goats' cheese, and game in season – is based on fresh ingredients.

☆☆☆☆ Très Chic

⌂ ✗ **Hostellerie du Val de Sault**: ancien-Chemin-d'Aurel. 1.5 kilometres from the village centre on the St-Trinit road (follow the signs). ☎ 04-90-64-01-41. Fax: 04-90-64-12-74. ✗ Restaurant open at lunchtime (except at the weekend and from mid-May to end September). Closed from early November to early April. Double rooms with bath, toilet and satellite TV from 510F to 790F. Half board, compulsory from May to September, from 495F to 620F per person. Menus from 132F (weekday lunch) to 230F, and a 'truffle' menu from 190F to 280F. Private car park. Way out in the colourful Ventoux countryside, this recently built hotel-restaurant is a haven of tranquillity. The 11 spacious rooms are subtly decorated and there's also a small sitting room and terrace, a swimming pool and gym. A few of the more expensive suites have a jacuzzi. Although the rates are quite high, it's still good value for money. The chef skilfully marries traditional produce and innovative mixtures of flavours. Truffle-lovers can order a marvellous special menu for a whole table, but it doesn't come cheap.

WHERE TO STAY IN THE AREA

⌂ **Chambres d'hôte le Moulin** (B&B): 84390 Monieux. ☎ 04-90-64-04-64. Six kilometres (4 miles) southwest of Sault on the D942. Open from March to November. Double rooms for 240F, including breakfast. Just outside a very pretty village, this big old house has very simple rooms. The decor is a little tired, but the welcome is friendly and there's a swimming pool.

SWEET TREATS

⌂ **Confiserie André Boyer:** ☎ 04-90-64-00-23. The Boyers, from father to son, have been making nougat since the end of the 19th century. This lovely shop sells an excellent version made from lavender honey and other delicious specialities, such as stuffed *galettes* made from spelt.

ST-CHRISTOL

Right at the end of the Albion plateau, 11 kilometres (7 miles) southeast of Sault on the D30, where huge military installations have been left behind. At the very top of this quiet village, the beautiful Romanesque church of Notre-Dame has precisely carved columns in its choir. The details on the capitals include foliage and a fantastical bestiary, from birds of paradise to mermaid-birds blowing hunting horns.

WHERE TO STAY AND EAT

🛎 ✕ **Le Lavandin**: in Les Rochers district, route d'Apt. ☎ 04-90-75-09-18. Fax: 04-90-75-09-17. ✗ Double rooms with shower and toilet, TV and mini bar for 310F. Set menu at 110F. In such gorgeous countryside, a modern, functional hotel like this is a bit of a surprise, but the welcome is warm, the rooms are comfortable and the food is tasty, and there's also a pool.

AUREL

5 kilometres (3 miles) north of Sault on the D942. The houses in this beautifully located village, with their tiled roofs and stone walls, seem to be clinging to the slope. Aurel is easily as beautiful as some of the hilltop villages in the Luberon but without the crowds.

WHERE TO STAY AND EAT

🛎 ✕ **Chambres d'hôte Richarnau** (B&B): ☎ and fax: 04-90-64-03.62. 500 metres from Aurel on the Sault road, signposted right on to a little road. Annual closure during January and February. Double rooms with shower or bath and toilet from 390F to 500F for two. *Table d'hôte* menu at 135F. This old farm in the middle of the countryside outside the village has five rooms (including a suite of two rooms accommodating four people). The interior is quite plain but the bathrooms are lovely and there's a very pretty little room with furniture in the style of Louis XV. The lovely dining room has a vast fireplace and on hot summer days, guests may sit in the shade of a huge lime tree on the terrace.

WHAT TO SEE IN THE AREA

★ **Brantes**: this charming village stands in an impressive setting, overlooking the Toulourenc valley, facing the northern slopes of the Ventoux. It is best seen from the road to Montbrun-les-Bains and the Aires pass (the D41). The village has retained a good deal of its authenticity. There's a pottery with a kiln in the old chateau, a dressmaker, a *santon* maker, a little inn-cum-grocery shop and a tea shop. The delightful church is left unlocked as often as possible.

LE MONT VENTOUX

At 1,912 metres (6,271 feet), picturesque Mont Ventoux dominates the region. The winding road up the mountain passes through remarkably varied vegetation, from cedars, green and white oaks and beech via, higher up, pine and larch trees, then scrub and stones, until finally you reach the top, where the landscape is positively lunar. There's an extraordinary, panoramic view from the summit; on a clear day you can see from the Alps to Notre-Dame-de-la-Garde in Marseilles. The walk up the Ventoux at night, in time to get to the top for the sunrise, is a classic.

The climate of Mont Ventoux is harsh. Sometimes the winds reach speeds of more than 200kph (125mph) (*vent* is, of course, French for wind), and it's not uncommon for the pass to be closed by snow until after Easter. There are even two small ski resorts on its slopes. The snow isn't very reliable but it's fascinating to see Swiss-style chalets just a few kilometres from a landscape dotted with Provençal *mas* farmhouses.

BÉDOIN

A market town in a hollow of the southern foothills of the Ventoux, Bédoin is proud of its vast forest, where more than 1,000 types of vegetation grow at a variety of altitudes, from 350 to 1,910 metres (1,150 to 6,265 feet). A large part of it is listed by UNESCO as being of significant environmental interest. Bédoin is popular with bike fiends, who come here to make their assault on the peak of Mont Ventoux, and attack its terrible hills. It's one of the classic stages on the Tour de France and the place where Tommy Simpson expired in 1967 (he was later found to have taken performance-enhancing drugs). Passing amateur cyclists often leave souvenirs by his memorial.

USEFUL ADDRESS

🛈 **Tourist office**: espace Marie-Louis-Gravier, place du Marché. ☎ 04-90-65-63-95. Fax: 04-90-12-81-55. Email: ot-bedoin@axit.fr. Open Monday to Saturday from 1 September to 30 June, 9am–noon and 2–8pm; in July and August, open at lunchtime from Monday to Sunday. Ask for the topological guide to walks in the Ventoux.

WHERE TO STAY AND EAT

🛏 **Hôtel La Garance**: Ste-Colombe. On the road for Mont Ventoux, 3 kilometres (about 2 miles) from the village. ☎ 04-90-12-81-00. Fax: 04-90-65-93-05. ✗ Double rooms with shower or bath and toilet, plus TV, from 260F to 300F. From the terrace, there's a view of Mont Ventoux, its summit sometimes covered in snow, even at the end of spring. The hotel is full of sunny Provence, with its warm colours, charming rooms, low-key but efficient service and a swimming pool. The hotel name refers to the mallow plant, used to dye the red trousers worn by French soldiers in the First World War.

🛏 ✗ **L'Escapade**: place Portail-l'Olivier. In the town centre, next to the tourist office. ☎ and fax 04-90-65-60-21. In winter closed all day Thursday and on Friday morning as well as from 15 November to 15 December and from 10 January to 10 March. Double rooms with shower and toilet from 280F to 320F. Set menu from 80F (weekday lunch) to 150F. This small, classic hotel has been recently renovated. The restaurant serves pizzas cooked over wood fires and traditional Provençal dishes.

Campsites

🏕 **Camping Municipal de la Pinède**: chemin des Sablières. ☎ 04-90-65-61-03 or 06-13-86-31-53. Towards Crillon-le-Brave. Open 1 April to 30 September. Comfortable site with a tennis court and swimming pool.

🏕 **Camping Pastory**: route de Malaucène. ☎ 04-90-65-60-79. Open 15 March to 1 October. Pitch for two with electricity for 59F. A warm welcome and plenty of shade.

CRILLON-LE-BRAVE

This delightful little hilltop village, renamed to commemorate its brave lord, Louis de Balbes de Crillon, has an interesting little **Musée de la Musique mécanique** (museum of mechanical music). ☎ 04-90-65-61-59. Fax: 04-90-12-82-28. Open every day from Easter to 30 September, 3–7pm, in winter Sunday only 3–7pm. Guided tours all the time. Entrance charge reduced for under-12s. There's only one room in the museum, but the guided tour is fascinating. The lovely instruments – including pianolas, barrel organs and steam organs – are as interesting to examine, with their impressive mechanisms, as they are to hear.

WHERE TO STAY

🏠 **Le Clos St-Vincent**: ☎ 04-90-65-93-36. Fax: 04-90-12-81-46. Below the village (signposted). Annual closure from 15 November to 15 February (except for groups). Double rooms with shower and toilet from 470F to 520F, including breakfast. A small separate farmhouse sleeping four people costs 1,020F. Each of the five roooms in this tastefully restored 18th-century farmhouse has different decor. The legendary breakfasts are award-winning. There's a swimming pool, a gym and a little park with a space for *boules*.

CAROMB

The agricultural market town of Caromb sits on one of the last erupting mounds of the Ventoux. The main point of interest is the 14th-century church, one of the biggest in the Vaucluse, and one of the noisiest (the bells can be heard 10 kilometres/6 miles away). Inside, there's a 16th-century tryptich and a marble tomb. Nearby, take a summer swim in the little le Paty artificial lake.

🅸 **Tourist office**: place du Cabaret. ☎ 04-90-62-36-21. In high season, open Tuesday to Friday 9am–noon and 2–6pm, Saturday 9am–noon and 3–6pm.

WHERE TO EAT

✗ **Restaurant Le Four à Chaux**: route de Malaucène. Two kilometres from Caromb along the D938 towards Malaucène. ☎ 04-90-62-40-10. 🍴 Closed Monday and Tuesday as well as in January and from 15 to 30 November. Set menus from 90F (weekday lunch) to 230F. The pleasant decor is pretty smart and there's a lovely terrace by the river and smiling, attentive service. The chef uses simple, fresh produce and the dishes – *noisettes d'agneau à l'ail confit* (lamb noisettes with preserved garlic) and *suprême de pigeonneau au foie gras* (pigeon breast with foie gras) – are prepared with flair.

LE BARROUX

Dominated by a huge, superb fortified chateau (not open to the public), this is another pretty hilltop village (not unusual in these parts). Apparently, Prince Charles sometimes spends a few days here. There's also an inter-denominational abbey near by.

WHERE TO STAY AND EAT

🛏 ✕ **Hôtel-restaurant Les Géraniums**: place de la Croix. ☎ 04-90-62-41-08. Fax: 04-90-62-56-48. ✕ (to the restaurant). Double rooms with shower or bath, and toilet, from 260F to 290F. Set menus from 100F (weekday) to 190F. The facilities are traditional in this 'no-frills' village hotel, which occupies a glorious renovated white stone house. From some of the rooms and the terrace, there's a superb view of the Comtat Venaissin plain. Peace and quiet (apart from the crickets) are guaranteed and the cooking is simple and traditional, Provençal in style. Secure car parking.

MALAUCÈNE

In an attractive location, at the foot of the north face of the Ventoux, the village (or small town) of Malaucène is very typically Provençal, with courtyards shaded by plane trees and winding streets in its historic centre.

🛈 **Tourist office**: place de la Mairie. ☎ and fax: 04-90-65-22-59. Open every day (except Sunday and public holidays) 10am–noon and 2–4pm.

WHERE TO STAY AND EAT

🛏 **Gîte d'Étape la Ferme du Désert**: ☎ 04-90-65-29-54. Two kilometres from Malaucène (signposted) on the D153 towards Beaumont-du-Ventoux. 75F per person per night, 100F with breakfast. Half board available for groups of five or more, at 175F per person. An adorable little stone house, standing among orchards and fields of sunflowers, at the foot of the Ventoux. While away some hours in the garden, but leave enough time to climb the Ventoux. The manager's partner is an enthusiastic walker, who organizes walks in Provence and the Alps, and further afield.

🛏 ✕ **Hôtel-Restaurant L'Origan**: cours des Isnards. ☎ 04-90-65-27-08. Fax: 04-90-65-12-92. ✕ (to the restaurant). Restaurant closed Monday. Annual closure from 1 October to 15 March. In low season, hotel only open at the weekend. Double room with shower and toilet or bathroom, and TV, 230–250F. Set menus from 90F to 125F. This classic hotel is generally comfortable but some of the rooms could do with a facelift. There's a warm atmosphere and straightforward, tasty Provençal cooking. Secure parking for cars and even for bikes (extra charge).

✕ **Le Siècle**: cours des Isnards. ☎ 04-90-65-11-37. ✕ Open all year. Set menus at 70F. Unpretentious little restaurant that's good for its type, with a pleasant setting, a shaded terrace on the avenue and efficient service.

THE RHÔNE VALLEY AND HAUTE-PROVENCE

THE DENTELLES DE MONTMIRAIL

Although *dentelle* means 'lace', this place has nothing to do with traditional crafts. Huge, jagged limestone cliffs erupt between the trees and the moors, creating an amazing natural feature in the landscape. The Dentelles reach an altitude of 734 metres (2,405 feet) and their sheer, silver-grey cliff faces provide superb terrain for climbers. About 580 routes are climbable for 12 months of the year. For walkers, there are 40 kilometres (25 miles) of marked and maintained footpaths (see IGN map No. 3040, in the 'Top 25' series). All around the mountain there are little villages, where wine-producers cultivate grapes that have to ripen in a hellish heat. Gigondas and Beaumes-de-Venise are probably the most familiar names.

BEAUMES-DE-VENISE

A lovely hillside village, Beaumes produces some Côtes-du-Rhône wines of excellent quality. Less well known than the Gigondas wines, they are sold in a special, pretty bottle known as a *vénitienne* ('Venetian'). The dessert wine Muscat de Beaumes is the one of the best in France. It should be drunk chilled and is delicious served in a dish with melon.

USEFUL ADDRESSES

🛈 **Tourist office**: cours Jean-Jaurès. ☎ and fax: 04-90-62-94-39. Information also available at the **Maison des Dentelles-Espace Tourisme**, place du Marché (same telephone number), which has a permanent display of local paintings, crafts and produce. Open in high season on Monday 2–6pm; from Tuesday to Saturday 9am–noon and 2–6pm; and Sunday morning. Closed on Sunday in low season.

VACQUEYRAS

The narrow streets of this charming village wind their way up towards the chateau's retaining wall. There's a lovely Provençal belfry at the top of the 12th-century watchtower.

GIGONDAS

The Roman name for this village was *Jocunditas*, meaning 'joy', and it's certainly still a happy place for wine-lovers. Gigondas is one of the best known of the Côtes-du-Rhône wines. There are more than 40 producers and visitors can buy direct at the Caveau de Gigondas at producers' prices. The village has retained its medieval feel and provides one of the best viewing points for the Dentelles, which belong, in fact, to the same *commune*. Make your way on to the Cayron pass for an impressive view of the whole mountain range, or consider the following walks: the Roche du Midi (50 minutes), the Alsau pass (1 hour) or the Tour Sarazzine (1 hour 30 minutes).

USEFUL ADDRESSES

🛈 Tourist office: rue du Portail. ☎ 04-90-65-85-46. Fax: 04-90-65-88-42. Website: www.beyond.fr/villages/gigondas.html. Open all year 10am–noon and 2–6pm. Ask for a list of wine-producers in the region, and detailed local maps for walkers.

■ Mountain-bike hire: ☎ 04-90-46-83-25.

WHERE TO STAY AND EAT

🛏 Gîte des Dentelles: in the village. ☎ 04-90-65-80-85. Fax: 04-90-65-83-44. 🐾 (one room). Closed in January and February. Between 70F and 80F a night. Two 10-bed dorms and 10 rooms with twin beds plus an equipped kitchenette. Activities include cliff-climbing courses, walks and mountain-bike trails.

✗ Café restaurant de la Poste (with Monique and Jacques): rue Eugène-Raspail. ☎ 04-90-65-89-62. Closed Tuesday out of season and in January. Set menus from 75F to 120F. Tables are squeezed together in the little dining room next to the bar, or you can eat on the sunny terrace. The pizzas and the menu of the day are better than you might expect. Typically Provençal dishes such as *pieds et paquets* (in winter) cost a few francs more and reasonably priced local wines are available by the carafe.

SÉGURET

Go through **Sablet**, a little green town that seems to appeal to writers because of its tranquillity. Séguret, difficult to pick out, is at the bottom of a rocky hill. One of the most beautiful villages in Provence, it has been restored by a local association, who have rebuilt its little streets and covered passageways. On the third weekend in August, there's a wine festival and, at Christmas, a Provençal Mass with an enactment of the nativity, called '*Li Bergié de Séguret*', and the traditional 13 Provençal desserts.

WHERE TO STAY AND EAT

🛏 ✗ Auberge-restaurant la Bastide Bleue: route de Sablet. ☎ and fax: 04-90-46-83-43. 🐾 500 metres before Séguret, coming from Sablet or Vaison. Double rooms with shower and toilet from 280F to 350F, breakfast included. Menus at 70F, 95F and 130F. Generally, the rooms in this very pretty Provençal house are comfortable (although some are less so). There are a few family rooms, a garden and swimming pool among the vines, and Provençal cooking.

✗ Restaurant Le Mesclun: rue des Poternes. On the edge of the village. ☎ 04-90-46-93-43. Fax: 04-90-46-93-48. Closed Monday (except in high season). Annual closure from 1 October to May. Lunch menu 95F and *menu-carte* at 170F. A restaurant that combines olde-worlde charm and modern cuisine, with a very lovely dining room and, in good weather, tables outside on the little square. The *menu-carte* changes several times a week but always offers delicious meals. This is one of the best places around here, so it's best to book.

WALK

– **Séguret and around the Mont Bayon** (8 kilometres/ 5 miles; allow 2 hours for the round trip, plus stops): on this typically Provençal trail between the Ventoux and Montmirail, you'll experience the scent of lavender, thyme and rosemary in the *garrigue*, walk past rows of vines on the Tricastin plain, see mushrooms in the undergrowth and *petit-gris* snails in season, all the time benefiting from the soft air that blows from the Rhône valley.

The walk is a loop, starting at Séguret. The markings are white and red on the long-distance GR4 footpath, then you follow the yellow dots. It is easy, but take care in very hot weather. For details, buy IGN maps (1:25,000 scale) *3140 Ouest* (West) and *3040 Est* (East).

Leave from the car park at the bottom of Séguret (not the one at the beginning of the village). Look out for the white and red signs on the GR4. With your back to the old part of the village, go up between the school and the chapel. The path goes up past young, green oaks and scented plants towards the Vallon de Fournas. Leaving the GR, the path continues, marked with yellow dots. It becomes rocky as you near the summit, which is dominated by the ruined chapel of Notre-Dame-d'Aubusson, and offers a superb view over Mont Ventoux and the Dentelles de Montmirail. Keep going on the marked trail around Mont Bayon until you get to the steep descent going south, through the vineyards. Blue markings lead you back to the GR4 and Séguret, where you can cool off in the Mascarons fountain.

SUZETTE

There are views everywhere you look around here. As you go up towards Suzette, the Dentelles and the Rhône plain appear at every bend in the road. Right at the top, the Ventoux emerges across from the pass, where you find this little village.

WHERE TO STAY AND EAT

⚐ ✕ **Chambres d'hôte Le Dégoutaud** (B&B): Le Barroux, 84340 Malaucène. Two kilometres from Suzette (signposted), on the way to Malaucène. ☎ and fax 04-90-62-99-22. ✕ (1 room). Double rooms with shower and toilet at 310F; *gîte* for four people also available. *Table d'hôte* dinner for 100F. At an altitude of 350 metres (1,150 feet) and surrounded by countryside, this lovely old farmhouse (partly dating from the 16th century) has rooms that are decorated in a mixture of romantic and country styles. Apricot, cherry and olive trees and a few vines grow in the area. The welcome is warm and genuine.

LAFARE

A few kilometres from Beaumes along the D90, Lafare is a pretty little village among the Dentelles and an ideal base camp if you want to walk in the mountains. Oddly, the water of the Salette river here is salty, as its name might indicate.

WHERE TO STAY

♠ **Gîte d'étape** (walkers' shelter): place de la Fontaine. In the village centre. ☎ 04-90-82-20-72. Fax: 04-90-14-96-03. Closed from 8 September to 6 October. Beds at 65F per night, in five-bed dormitories. No meals or breakfast, but there are kitchen facilities. André, a mountain guide who organizes cliff-climbing courses in the Dentelles, offers a warm welcome.

WALK

– **Round the Grand Montmirail** (8 kilometres/5 miles; allow half a day). This walk around the Dentelles has some very steep sections. Leave the car on the edge of the pretty village, near the little chapel beneath the mountain crests and follow the marked track.

The route goes past the de Cassan farm, where you can see their herd of boars and taste their wines. At the end of the tarmac road, follow the sign to Col du Crayon, then, in the vineyards, turn left and follow the brown signs up the track. Take care to follow the path along the bottom of the ridge. The dark blue markings will take you to the end of the *massif*, where you get your reward: a superb view (you are at an altitude of 600 metres/1,968 feet). In season, there will be lots of climbers clinging to the cliffs.

Afterwards, go round the opening then along the Tête-Vieille. The path goes down through the wood, towards the right, but you turn left immediately, in the direction of Col d'Alsau. Take the stairway for the 'Sommet des Dentelles' and an astonishing view.

Follow the yellow markings up to the Crête des Clapis. On the left, you have to go to Vallat-de-l'Aiguille. Cross the ford, then the undergrowth, before going up the other slope to complete the circuit.

VAISON-LA-ROMAINE (84110)
Population: 5,904

Every self-respecting historian knows about Vaison-la-Romaine and its fascinating deep excavations. It was the Celto–Ligurian capital, then an important city allied to Rome, and has some beautiful relics from the period, including the theatre and the baths.

In the fourth century, Vaison became the seat of a bishop and remained as such until 1791. In the fifth and sixth centuries, it was also the seat of two synods. It was at the synod of 529 that the significant decision was taken to sing the *Kyrie* at Sunday Mass. In the 12th century, the counts of Toulouse took possession of Vaison and began construction of the chateau that still dominates the town.

At the end of the 19th century, population growth led to plans for new residential developments on the other bank of the river. The first excavations, in 1907, revealed the ancient importance of the site, where archaeologists have since uncovered an extensive ensemble of first-century architecture.

Today, the busy town stretches along both banks of the Ouvèze river. It may be the third most popular tourist town in the department of the Vaucluse, but it hasn't yet succumbed to the fashion for charging for car parking – a fine surprise.

USEFUL ADDRESSES

⊞ Maison du tourisme (tourist office): place du Chanoine-Sautel, BP 53. ☎ 04-90-36-02-11. Fax: 04-90-28-76-04. Open every day from 1 April to 15 October, 9am–noon and 2–5.45pm (6.45pm in July and August). The rest of the year, same hours, but closed Sunday. Staff can organize 90-minute guided tours. On Friday evening in July and August, there are special Roman meals with a lecturer/guide, for 150F.

■ Bike hire: Mag 2 roues, cours Taulignan. ☎ 04-90-28-80-46. Closed Monday. Around 100F per day for a mountain bike.

WHERE TO STAY

☆–☆☆ Budget to Moderate

🛏 Hôtel Le Théâtre: place de l'Abbé-Sautel, avenue du Général-de-Gaulle. ☎ 04-90-28-71-98. Fax: 04-90-28-86-96. Double rooms from 155F to 280F, depending on facilities. Currently undergoing renovation, this classic hotel, with its attractive rustic decor, is well located, opposite the excavations.

🛏 Hôtel Burrhus: 1 place Montfort. ☎ 04-90-36-00-11. Fax: 04-90-36-39-05. Email: jbgurly@club-internet.com. Closed from 16 November to 20 December. Double rooms with shower or bath and toilet, and TV, from 240F to 320F. Ochre walls, wrought-iron fixtures, a billiard table and a lovely terrace for breakfast, with a view of the morning's activity on the typically Provençal square. The rooms are all different, some in Provençal style, while others are more basic. The welcome is impeccable and the owners, passionate about contemporary art, also organize four exhibitions a year. This is a lovely spot. Secure car parking.

– In an old private mansion, **Hôtel des Lys**, 20 cours Henri-Fabre (across the street), also has rooms, some with a very elaborate decor. Double rooms with shower or bath, even jacuzzi, plus TV, from 350F to 450F.

☆☆☆ Chic

🛏 Hostellerie du Beffroi: rue de l'évêché, Haute-Ville. ☎ 04-90-36-04-71. Fax: 04-90-36-24-78. Email: lebeffroi@wanadoo.fr. Restaurant closed at lunchtime (except at the weekend and from 1 November to 1 April). Annual closure from 1 February to 1 April. Double rooms with shower or bath and toilet from 470F to 700F. Set menus from 98F to 240F. In the upper town, this hotel occupies a pair of houses dating from the 16th and 17th century. It's not cheap, but the charm of the old (stones and woodwork, ornaments and period furniture) combines well with modern facilities. The good, Provençal-influenced cooking – *daube d'agneau à l'avignonnaise* (lamb stew Avignon-style) – is supplemented by salads served in the superb garden in summer, and wines (some available by the glass) at rather steep prices.

🛏 Chambres d'hôte, L'Évêché (B&B): rue de l'évêché, Haute-Ville. In the medieval town, 20 metres further on from the Hostellerie du

Beffroi. ☎ 04-90-36-13-46 and 04-90-36-38-30. Fax: 04-90-36-32-43. Email: eveche@aol.com. Double rooms with shower or bath and toilet from 420F to 470F, breakfast included. Four good rooms in a 17th-century residence, part of the old bishop's house. Family atmosphere, with a library and sitting rooms, a pretty terrace and bicycles for loan. There's a remarkable view of the plain. Booking is essential.

WHERE TO EAT

✕ **Le Brin d'Olivier**: 4 rue du Ventoux. ☎ 04-90-28-74-79. Fax: 04-90-36-13-36. Closed Wednesday all day and Saturday lunch. Annual closure from 25 June to 5 July, and at Christmas. Double rooms with bath, toilet and TV, 400F. Weekday lunch menu 80F and others up to 200F. The few pretty rooms are just a few steps away. The restaurant, with its colourful Provençal decor, has served as a film set. The interior courtyard is the perfect place to enjoy good, enticing food – such as *filet d'agneau aux olives* (lamb fillet with olives) – in an atmosphere that is typical of the south. It definitely makes you want to linger longer.

✕ **La Fête en Provence**: place du Vieux-Marché. ☎ 04-90-36-36-43. Fax: 04-90-36-21-49. Closed Wednesday. Annual closure from 15 November to Easter. Double rooms with shower and toilet 320F; duplex for two to four people from 600F to 700F. Menu for 160F. This pleasant spot in the old stone streets of the upper town serves very rich food, based on quality produce and skilfully prepared by the owner-chef, including *daube de gigot d'agneau* (lamb stew) and *asperges tièdes au foie gras* (warm asparagus with foie gras).

WHAT TO SEE

There is an entrance charge for the excavations, the museum, the cathedral and cloister and the Chapelle St-Quenin. The *billet tous monuments* (museum pass) costs 41F; concessions for students, under-12s free, one 12- to 18-year-old in each family pays 14F. It is valid for several days and allows one entry to each of the sites, not necessarily on the same day. It also entitles the holder to participate in certain guided tours at no extra charge. Opening hours and conditions vary between sites. For more information contact the local tourist office.

★ **La Romaine** (Roman town): two residential districts of the original Roman town have been unearthed, **Puymin** and **La Villasse**. In the Puymin excavations, the remains of villas built by wealthy owners give an idea of the splendour of Roman times. The rooms of the **Villa dei Messii** are described on explanatory panels and, even though some of it is still under the road, you can appreciate how much space the family and their servants must have enjoyed. The **theatre**, on the other side of the hill, is smaller and less well preserved than the one at Orange, but still seats 7,000 people during the town's summer festival. There's a pretty carved cornice in the underground galleries that lead to the tiered seating and, from the top of the seating, a lovely view of the hills. The **Musée Théo-Desplans**, completely refurbished, has a fine collection of imperial statues, including Emperor Hadrian and his wife Sabine, exceptional mosaics that were unearthed in the Villa of the Peacock, as well as more everyday items. In the La Villasse district, near the cathedral, archaeologists have uncovered the **baths** and two houses.

★ **Romanesque buildings**: the former Cathédrale Notre-Dame-de-Nazareth, with its octagonal dome and lovely cloister, is one of the most interesting Romanesque buildings in Provence. The 12th-century Chapelle St-Quenin is 300 metres away. The nave dates from the 17th century.

★ **Medieval city**: cross the old Roman bridge over the Ouvèze; with just a single span, it is 17 metres wide and, remarkably, was the only bridge to survive when the River Ouvèze broke its banks in September 1992. Walk along the stone-paved streets (*calades*) in the old town, where many of the houses, with their superb Renaissance facades, have been restored. Have a look at the fortified gateway, with its belfry, the church and then climb up to the chateau. The place du Vieux-Marché, the rue des Fours and the district de la Juiverie are all interesting.

★ **Wine**: place du Chanoine-Sautel. Open every day (except Sunday out of season) 9am–noon and 2–7pm (6pm in winter). The *Espace Vins* (wine area) in the tourist office offers tastings and sales of wines from local vineyards. There are also grape, apple and apricot juices, and a bilberry liqueur, which is added to rosé wine from the Côtes du Rhône to create a *myro*, the local aperitif.

FESTIVALS AND EVENTS

– **Georges Brassens week**: from the end of April to the beginning of May. Concerts, exhibitions, seminars in memory of the singer-poet, who has become something of a legend in his home country. ☎ 04-90-36-06-68.

– **Les soirées du Théâtre antique** (evenings in the Roman Theatre): a programme of dance performances, plays and concerts from 12 to 25 July. ☎ 04-90-28-84-49.

– **Choir festival**: from the end of July to the beginning of August, Europe's largest gathering of prize-winning choirs takes place in the Romanesque cathedral of Notre-Dame-de-Nazareth.

– **Les Choralies**: the most significant choral festival in Europe, held every three years at the beginning of August (next in 2001). Singers from all over the world gather here for a programme of workshops, rehearsals, recitals and concerts over 10 days.

– Other singing festivals include **Chorijazz** (second week in August) and the **Alto Festival** (second fortnight in August).

– **Les Journées gourmandes** (food festival): at the beginning of November. Programme of events related to eating and drinking, preceded by the Soup Festival (end of October–beginning of November), a competition for the best soup from the villages of the *canton*.

CRESTET

Crestet is 3.5 kilometres (2 miles) southeast of Vaison-la-Romaine on the D938. As its name suggests, charming and picturesque Crestet is a hilltop village perched on a crest. Old stone houses line its tiny streets, where cars are not permitted. At the top of the village, next to the chateau, the old residence of the bishops of Vaison has a splendid view of the Ventoux and the Baronnies. Exhibitions (quite experimental and often very interesting) are held in the summer at the Centre d'Art contemporain (Centre for Contemporary Art), chemin de la Verrière. Open every day from 11am to 6pm or 7pm. ☎ 04-90-36-35-00. The centre also serves as a venue for performances of contemporary dance and music.

⊟ Town hall: ☎ 04-90-36-06-72. Fax: 04-90-28-75-85. Tourist information, also available from the tourist office in Vaison-la-Romaine.

WHERE TO STAY

☎ Chambres d'hôte La Respelido (B&B): ☎ 04-90-36-03-10. Open all year. Double rooms with shower or bath and toilet from 300F to 350F, including a generous breakfast. The owners, great travellers, welcome guests to two pleasant rooms (one spacious, one smaller) in their old oil mill in the heart of the village. Breakfast includes seasonal fruit, farm-fresh eggs and organic bread, served in the little enclosed courtyard or on the terrace. Jacques is happy to organize day trips on a wine or truffle theme.

CHÂTEAUNEUF-DU-PAPE (84230)

Population: 2,078

Close neighbour of the cultural towns of Avignon to the south and Orange to the north, the town of Châteauneuf is world renowned as a wine-growing centre. The town, overlooking extensive vineyards, was once protected by an impressive chateau. Built in the 14th century as the country residence of the Avignon-based popes – and giving the town its name ('new chateau of the popes') – it has since fallen into ruin.

As well as leaving a chateau to Châteauneuf, Pope John XXII was also responsible for the original vineyard. Benefiting from an exceptional situation, climate and soil, its grapes ripen perfectly. Châteauneuf-du-Pape is a unique wine made from 13 different grape varieties. Grenache is the variety that gives the wine its body. Up to 1929, when the Appellation d'Origine Contrôlée was finally obtained, the local wine-makers' product had been used only to improve Burgundies and Bordeaux. Today, this high-quality wine is sold under its own name, in characteristic bottles that carry the papal coat of arms.

USEFUL ADDRESS

⊟ Tourist office: place de la Fontaine. ☎ 04-90-83-71-08. Fax: 04-90-83-50-34. Website: www.perso.wanadoo.fr/ot-chato9-pape. Between July and August, open Monday to Saturday 9am–7pm, Sunday 10am–6pm. During the rest of the year, open from Monday to Saturday 9am–12.30pm and 2–6pm.

THE RHÔNE VALLEY AND HAUTE-PROVENCE

WHERE TO STAY AND EAT

≜ ✕ Hôtel-restaurant La Garbure: 3 rue Joseph-Duclos. ☎ 04-90-83-75-08. Fax: 04-90-83-52-34. Closed Sunday out of season. Double rooms with shower or bath and toilet, and TV, from 320F to 385F. Set menus from 95F to 180F. The atmosphere can be a bit formal, but the rooms are charming and well maintained, and the facilities include a terrace and a garden, a swimming pool and a tennis court near by. The cooking is tasty and seasonal, with the flavours of southwest France. Themed musical evenings are held in the winter. Secure garage parking available.

WHAT TO SEE

★ **Chateau**: just one section of wall from Pope John XII's chateau remains standing, as well as the keep and the lower hall. There's a splendid view of the Rhône valley from the ruins.

★ **Church of Notre-Dame-de-l'Assomption**: the precise date of the building of this church is not known, but it certainly dates back to before the 12th century. It has a lovely Romanesque cradle vault.

★ **Chapel of St-Théodoric**: the oldest building in Châteauneuf, dating from the 10th century, the chapel has a nave ending in an oven-bottomed apse. During recent restorations, painted frescoes from the Middle Ages were uncovered in the choir.

★ **Musée des Vieux Outils de Vigneron, Histoire des Appellations d'Origine Contrôlé** (museum of wine-growing tools and history of AOC): route d'Avignon. ☎ 04-90-83-70-07. Fax: 04-90-83-74-34. Email: brotte@-wanadoo.fr. In low season, open 8am–noon and 2–6pm; non-stop in summer. Significant collection of wine-growers' tools, including barrels, vats, beautiful 16th-century wine presses and medieval tuns.

WHAT TO SEE IN THE AREA

★ **Courthézon**: one of the few Vaucluse villages that still has a large part of its 12th-century ramparts intact.

ORANGE (84100)   Population: 27,989

Orange has been a key stopping-off point since ancient times, and continued to be so until the building of the motorways. The Roman colony was founded in 35 BC by legionnaires, who built a triumphal arch and a remarkable theatre. The rest (including a superb 400 metre by 80 metre gymnasium, temples and ramparts) disappeared under successive waves of Visigoths and other assorted invaders. The city was a vassal to the Holy Roman Empire in the 12th century and then belonged to the domain of Les Baux. In 1530, the principality was willed to the house of Nassau, and this family finally devastated the Roman ruins in the 17th century by using the stones to build a fortress. The chateau of Roman stones was subsequently razed to the ground on the orders of Louis XIV, by Count de Grignan (the son-in-law of Madame de Sévigné), during the wars against William of Orange.

Politics

Since 1995, the town of Orange has been under the control of the extreme right. Democratically elected, yes, but some people think they have acted heavy handedly, interfering with the organization of the Chorégies (*see below*), rearranging the municipal library, outlawing the distribution of political leaflets in the street, for example. The town is still beautiful and full of pleasant people, but there's a danger that officials may not be supporting cultural causes in the right way.

USEFUL ADDRESSES

❚ Tourist office (A–B2 on the map): 5 cours Aristide-Briand. ☎ 04-90-34-70-88. Fax: 04-90-34-99-62. Between 1 April and 30 September, open Monday to Saturday 9am–7pm, Sunday and public holidays 10am–6pm. During the rest the year, open 9am–1pm and 2–5pm. Closed on Sunday.

🚉 SNCF train station (B2 on the map): avenue Frédéric-Mistral. ☎ 08-36-35-35-35. The TGV doesn't stop in Orange. Get off at Valence and take a connecting train.

🚌 Coach station (B2 on the map): cours Pourtoules. One kilometre from the SNCF train station. ☎ 04-90-34-15-59.

▪ Maison de la principauté (principality house), Maison des Vins (house of wine): rue de la République. ☎ 04-90-34-44-44. Open in December for the Christmas market and from time to time in summer.

WHERE TO STAY

☆ Budget

🛏 Hôtel Arcotel (A2, **1** on the map): 8 place aux Herbes. ☎ 04-90-51-09-23. Fax: 04-90-51-61-12. Open all year. Double rooms with washbasin cost 150F and 220F, with shower, toilet and TV. Set menu 50F. This hotel, on a pleasant little square near the Roman theatre, has simple, quiet and well-maintained rooms. Enjoy a warm welcome, light snacks and a small private car park.

🛏 Hôtel de la Gare (B2, **2**, off the map): 60 avenue Frédéric-Mistral. Opposite the station, a 10-minute walk from the centre. ☎ 04-90-34-00-23. Fax: 04-90-34-91-72. Double rooms with shower and toilet for 250F. A former post house, with attractive details, a shady terrace and renovated rooms with air-conditioning, and pretty Provençal fabrics. Good value for money, offering a warm welcome and a (very small) swimming pool on the roof.

☆☆ Moderate

🛏 Le Glacier (A2, **3** on the map): 46 cours Aristide-Briand. In the centre of town. ☎ 04-90-34-02-01. Fax: 04-90-51-13-80. Email: hôtel-gla@aol.com. Double rooms with shower or bath and toilet, plus satellite TV, 320F. This very comfortable hotel has been very well run by the same family for three generations and offers the best value for money in its category in Orange. All the rooms are different, some with Provençal decor and others more

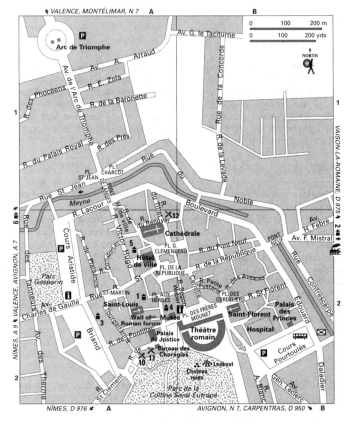

VALENCE, MONTÉLIMAR, N 7

Arc de Triomphe

Av. G. le Taciturne

NORTH

VAISON-LA-ROMAINE, D 975

Av. H. Fabre

Av. F. Mistral

PONT NEUF

Boulevard Noble

Cathédrale

Hôtel de ville

Théâtre romain

Saint-Florent

Palais des Princes

Hospital

Cours Pourtoulès

Château ruins

Lookout

Parc de la Colline Saint-Eutrope

NÎMES, D 976   A

AVIGNON, N 7, CARPENTRAS, D 950   B

ORANGE

■ Useful Addresses

- **Tourist office**
- **SNCF train station**
- **Coach station**
- **Post office**

🏠 Where to Stay

1. Hôtel Arcotel
2. Hôtel de la Gare
3. Le Glacier
4. Hôtel St-Florent
5. Hôtel Arène
6. Camping Le Jonquier

✕ Where to Eat

10. Le Yaca
11. L'Aïgo-Boulido
12. La Roselière

English in style. The musicians who play for the Chorégies often stay here. Free car park or secure parking for an extra charge.

☖ **Hôtel St-Florent** (A2, **4** on the map): 4 rue du Mazeau. ☎ 04-90-34-18-53. Fax: 04-90-51-17-25. Double rooms with shower (or bath) and toilet from 250F to 300F. Some, with shower only, cost 200F. One of the oldest hotels in the town, gradually being brought back to life, with colourful frescoes, friezes, ribbons and brightly-painted panelling. A welcome change from the banal decor found in many other hotels.

☆☆☆ Chic

☖ **Hôtel Arène** (A2, **5** on the map): place de Langes. ☎ 04-90-11-40-40. Fax: 04-90-11-40-45. Annual closure from 8 to 30 November. Double rooms with shower or bath and toilet, and TV, 440–600F. In the heart of the pedestrian district, this hotel is quiet (it's a *Relais du Silence*) and charming, with air-conditioned rooms decorated in a pretty Provençal style.

Campsite

☖ **Camping Le Jonquier** (A2, **6**, off the map): 1321 rue Alexis-Carrel. In the northwest of the town. ☎ 04-90-34-19-83. Fax: 04-90-51-16-17. Open 1 April to 1 October. Pitch for two 150F, including use of a pool, tennis courts, mini-golf, children's games and pony rides.

WHERE TO EAT

☆–☆☆ Budget to Moderate

✗ **Le Yaca** (A2, **10** on the map): 24 place Sylvain. To the right of the theatre. ☎ 04-90-34-70-03. ✗ Closed on Tuesday evening (except in spring) and Wednesday all day. Annual closure for three weeks in November. Menus 65–130F. A nice little place offering reliable, classic cooking that's well prepared, such as *terrine de foies de volaille maison avec sa confiture d'oignons* (house chicken liver terrine with onion conserve) or *cassolette aux fruits de mer* (seafood stew). Intimate, pleasant setting with exposed beams and stonework and pretty pictures on the wall.

✗ **L'Aïgo-Boulido** (A2, **11** on the map): 20 place Sylvain. ☎: 04-90-34-18-19. Fax: 04-90-51-81-46. Closed Thursday evening and Sunday. Annual closure from 1 to 15 October and from Christmas to New Year. Menus at 70F, 95F and 150F.

The very pretty dining room has post-modern decor with a mixture of styles. The atmosphere is laidback but the welcome is elegant and the service well done. The Provençal food is simply but carefully prepared.

✗ **La Roselière** (A2, **12** on the map): 4 rue du Renoyer. ☎ 04-90-34-50-42. Closed on Tuesday and Wednesday. Annual closure in November. Menu 110F, about 170F à la carte. The decor and the music here are rather eclectic. The dishes change every week, depending on the season and what's available at market. On every menu you'll find standards such as *pieds de cochons* (pig's trotters); an exotic dish like *nasi goreng istinewa* (Indonesian rice) and local specialities, for example *rognons de veau au basilic* (veal kidneys with basil). The cellar has a few good, inexpensive bottles. Bank cards not accepted.

THE RHÔNE VALLEY AND HAUTE-PROVENCE

WHERE TO STAY AND EAT IN THE AREA

â ✕ **Auberge L'Orangerie**: 4 rue de l'Ormeau, Piolenc. In the middle of the village, which is 4 kilometres (2.5 miles) north of Orange on the N7. ☎ 04-90-29-59-88. Fax: 04-90-29-67-74. ✖ (restaurant). Website: www.orangerie.net. Closed Monday lunchtime out of season. Annual closure over 10 days in November. Double rooms with shower or bath and toilet, and TV, from 380F to 400F. Half board from 340F to 430F per person. Menus from 100F (weekday lunch) to 210F. This lovely inn, hidden behind a curtain of greenery and run by the same couple for 15 years, has six cosy rooms with rustic furniture. One has a very private terrace. The whole house is decorated with copies of master-pieces, painted by the owner. In the restaurant, exotic ideas such as *crabe farci* (stuffed crab) or *osso-bucco* with fresh noodles are offered alongside Provençal dishes. The cellar has more than 350 wines. The toilets are stuffed with odds and ends and all sorts of sweetly-smelling coloured paper.

– Under the name **La Mandarine** (☎ 04-90-29-69-99. Fax: 04-90-29-67-74), the same couple have a few charming guest rooms in a Proven-çal *mas* on the edge of Piolenc, in the direction of Mornas. In the same style as L'Orangerie, the rooms cost 450F for two (breakfast extra), and there's also a swimming pool and lovely garden.

WHAT TO SEE

★ **Roman theatre**: ☎ 04-90-51-17-60. In summer, open 9am–6.30pm; from 1 October to 31 March, 9am–noon and 1.30–5pm; closed 25 December and 31 January. Entrance fee: 30F for adults (concessions 25F, under-10s free). This extraordinarily well-preserved Roman theatre has excellent acoustics and a practically intact stage backdrop. Louis XIV described the austere but magnificent facade as the 'most beautiful wall in my kingdom'. The corbels, stones sticking out from the top of the facade, were used to tie the masts and ropes that held up the *velum*, an awning that shaded the spectators from the hot sun. Long performances took place in the day time and were, apparently, highly original. The famous mystery plays of the Middle Ages were performed in the theatre and it was then engulfed by houses and little streets, built during the wars of religion. They were only cleared away in the 19th century, when the theatre's magnificence was revealed once again.

★ **Arc de Triomphe**: Orange's arch celebrates Roman imperialist domina-tion of the Gauls, rather than any specific victory. Built in 20 BC, outside the Roman city walls, it is undoubtedly one of the most beautiful of all Gallo–Roman monuments. Its detailed sculpture work has been revealed by two restoration projects. The marine trophies represent the power of Augustus, who triumphed in the naval battle of Actium in 31 BC.

★ **St-Eutrope hill**: overlooking the theatre. The theatre was built up against the St-Eutrope hill in order to minimize construction costs. The hill, with its public park, provides a very lovely view of the Ventoux and the Dentelles de Montmirail, as well as Marcoule (as long as you blank out the nuclear power station).

★ **Museum**: rue Madeleine-Roch. ☎ 04-90-51-18-24. Open every day from October to March, 9am–noon and 1.30–5.30pm. Every day from April to September 9am–7pm. Closed 25 December and 1 January. Entrance fee: 30F (concessions 25F). A surprising little museum in a private 17th-century mansion, with a very beautiful collection of friezes that used to decorate the theatre. The most exceptional document is an official land register of the Orange countryside, drawn up during the first century AD, recording the property of local people.

FESTIVALS AND EVENTS

– **Les Chorégies**: the theatre's acoustics are impressive. In the 19th century, it was decided to take use them again and, in 1869, the Chorégies d'Orange music festival began. It became an annual event in 1902 and in the last few decades has developed a reputation for world-class productions and casts. Detailed information is available from the tourist office or from 18 place Sylvain, BP 205, 84107 Orange. ☎ 04-90-34-24-24. Fax: 04-90-34-87-67.

WHAT TO SEE IN THE AREA

★ **Mornas**: 11 kilometres (7 miles) north of Orange. A fortified village at the foot of a cliff, topped by a ruined fortress. Guided tours from the beginning of March to the end of June, on Sunday and public holidays, at 11am, 2pm, 3.15pm and 4.30pm; in July and August every day (except Saturday) at 11am, 2.15pm, 3.45pm, and 5.30. Entrance fee: 32F (under-10s 23F). Less expensive tours are also available. Information and booking: Amis de Mornas, ☎ 04-90-37-01-26. Fax: 04-90-37-09-88. During the religious wars, Baron des Adrets (a Huguenot captain) made his prisoners jump from the top of the cliff on to the weapons of the soldiers below.

★ **L'Harmas de Jean-Henri Fabre**: route d'Orange, 84830 Sérignat-du-Comtat, 8 kilometres (5 miles) northeast of Orange on the N7 and the D976. ☎ 04-90-70-00-44. Open every day (except Tuesday and Sunday) 9am–11.30am and 2–6pm. Entrance fee: 15F (students 10F, under-8s free). Opening times and prices subject to change in 2001, with the new management. Ring the bell to gain entry. Famous entomologist Fabre lived and worked in this house for 36 years and died here in 1915. Its name 'L'Harmas' means 'fallow land' in Provençal. Nothing much has changed since he departed. His plant box is on the little work table and his hat is just waiting for him to come and put it on for an excursion on the Ventoux. Today, Fabre and his books are very well known in Japan and Japanese tourists crowd into the small, wild, botanical garden. Inside the house, old glass cases contain collections of shells, fossils, birds' nests and bones (including some human remains found near the fire of a tribe of cannibals). The fabulous herborium includes 12,000 plant specimens, in large cardboard files. This multi-talented man also painted (copies of some of his 700 watercolours hang in the house), had correspondence with Charles Darwin and Mistral, and wrote Provençal poetry and music (documents and scores are on display here).

THE RHÔNE VALLEY
AND HAUTE-PROVENCE

BOLLÈNE (84500)   Population: 14,130

This typically Provençal town is often overlooked as visitors rush to see its more famous neighbours. Producing Côte-du-Rhône wines, it stands at the starting point of two wine trails and has a long and rich agricultural and wine-growing tradition. The historic centre is tiny, but it's worth walking through it. At the top of Le Puy hill, the 12th-century collegiate church of St-Martin was destroyed in the wars of religion, but restored in the 16th century. According to legend, the monks were thrown from the top of the tower into the well. Seek out the old Ursuline convent, too, a centuries-old architectural jewel.

Louis Pasteur is remembered in the town. He stayed in Bollène in 1882 to study a pig infection.

In the last few years, Bollène has experienced an economic boom – doubtless something to do with the nearby Pierrelatte nuclear power station.

USEFUL ADDRESSES

🄱 **Tourist office**: place de la Mairie. ☎ and fax: 04-90-40-51-44. Out of season, open 8.30am–noon and 2–5.30pm. In summer, open from Monday to Saturday 8.30am–noon and 2–7.30pm.

■ **Centre de documentation provençale** (centre for Provençal documentation): in the rue du Saint-Sacrement. ☎ 04-90-30-19-54 or 41-39. Open all year. Plenty of archive material on the region and the Provençal character.

WHERE TO STAY AND EAT

🛏 ✕ **Hôtel de Chabrières**: 7 boulevard Gambetta. ☎ 04-90-40-08-08. Fax: 04-90-40-52-88. ✗ Double rooms with shower or bath and toilet, and TV, 360F. Menus at 76F and 99F. This elegant 19th-century house has pleasant rooms and good facilities, and a friendly, family atmosphere. It serves good food and homemade preserves, based on local fresh produce.

WHAT TO SEE AND DO IN THE AREA

★ **Du Barry troglodyte village**: the name is Celtic in origin, from *barros*, meaning 'spur of rock'. The dwellings, abandoned since the end of the 19th century, were originally dug right out of the easily worked sandstone rock. To prevent collapse, the openings were frequently supported by less friable stones. The dwellings were generally a single room with 'cells' leading off it. As there were no windows, light came from oil lamps.

On the top of the hill, the medieval fortifications were built to echo the natural defences of the location. The fortress apparently dates from the 12th century and was partially destroyed in the 16th.

★ **André Blondel lock/power station**: take the D26 in the direction of Valence, and follow the signposts marked 'EDF'. The first French hydro-electric power station was built here in 1952, across a 28-kilometre (17.5-mile) canal, diverted from the Rhône. The lock, the largest in France, is 25 metres (82 feet) high and 185 metres (607 feet) wide, and fills up faster than any other in Europe.

– **Bicycle tour**: Bollène calls itself 'bike town'. Pick up a free leaflet from the tourist office for details of the dozen cycling trails in the area.

FESTIVALS AND EVENTS

– **Les Polymusicales**: in July. Information ☎ 04-90-40-51-17. This festival features all kinds of music, from classical and cabaret, to rock and world music.

The Drôme Provençale

Part of the region of the Rhône-Alpes, the Provençal Drôme is splendidly located in low-lying mountains. In summer, the countryside is bright with colour, from the mauve-blue of lavender to the golden yellow of the wheat, and the air is filled with the intoxicating perfume of box, lime and lavender.

This is not to suggest that nothing happens during the rest of the year. Hard on the heels of the holidays comes the truffle season, when these gourmet items are at their least expensive and most highly flavoured.

USEFUL ADDRESSES

�️ Comité départemental du tourisme de la Drôme (departmental tourist office): 31 avenue du Président-Édouard-Herriot, Valence (26000), ☎ 04-75-82-19-26. Fax: 04-75-56-01-65. Website: www.drometourisme.com

■ Gîtes de France (country cottages): bookings on ☎ 04-75-83-90-20.

MONTÉLIMAR (26200)   Population: 31,344

Before the coming of the motorways, Montélimar was always a traditional stopping-off point for holidaymakers on their way south to the coast. Today, the town has little appeal for drivers hurtling by on the busy A7, except the fact that it is France's nougat capital. Montélimar is only 'Provençal' because of the decision of an official committee. In fact, real Provence starts a little further south, somewhere between Tain and the Tricastin. South of Tain, the vegetation changes. Pendulous oak trees, beech and hornbeam (widely grown in northern climes) give way to copses of green oak, Aleppo pines, gorse and thyme. Around Montélimar, you could almost count the olive trees – one of the symbols of Provence – on the fingers of one hand. Whatever the town has of Provence is mixed with a good helping of the characteristics of the Dauphiné.

THE DRÔME PROVENÇALE

USEFUL ADDRESSES

❶ Tourist office: on the Allées Provençales. ☎ 04-75-01-00-20. In July and August, open Monday to Friday 8.30am–7.30pm, Saturday 9am–7.30pm (6pm in December and January, 6.30pm from September to May, 7pm in June), and 10am–1pm on Sunday (except in winter). The tourist office stands on the *promenade* where most of the smartest bars are found.

■ **Bicycle hire**: Cycles Koustaury, 7 avenue Charles-de-Gaulle. ☎ 04-75-01-26-70. Mountain-bike hire around 80F per day (from 60F per day for a week). Ask for the *La Drôme à Vélo* ('The Drôme by Bike') map at the tourist office.

WHERE TO STAY

Avoid the hotels on the Marseille road if you can. They do not offer value for money and the traffic with huge lorries thundering by outside can be very noisy.

✩ Budget

▲ Hôtel Le Bêtisier: 5 rue des Quatre-Alliances. In the centre of Montélimar. ☎ and fax: 04-75-01-36-12. Closed on Saturday evening and Sunday. This hotel has cheap attic rooms at 160F, particularly No. 5, and offers a straightforward welcome. There's also a restaurant. Credit cards not accepted.

≜ **Hôtel Beausoleil**: 14bis, place d'Armes, not far from the tourist office and the train station. ☎ 04-75-01-19-80. Rooms with washbasin 180F, or 280F with bathroom. The facade is pretty, but the beds would not really do for more than a couple of nights.

☆☆ Moderate

≜ **Hôtel Pierre**: 7 place aux Clercs. ☎ 04-75-01-33-16. Double rooms 160–250F. This attractively renovated 16th-century private mansion on the side of a small square looks like a mini-convent. The porch, the corridor with the candelabra and stone staircase are impressive, but the 12 rooms are fairly dull, although some have been renovated. There's a place to keep your bike, a nice welcome and lots of good information.

≜ **Hôtel Sphinx**: 19 boulevard Marre-Desmarais. ☎ 04-75-01-86-64. Fax: 04-75-52-34-21. Closed from 23 December to 3 January. Double room with shower or bath from 255F to 330F. This 17th-century private mansion is a little cosier than the Pierre (*see above*), with mini bar, air-conditioning and TV in all rooms. There's exposed stonework,

old lace curtains and wooden panelling, but above all, in winter, a fire in the fireplace at breakfast time. Car park is charged extra.

Campsite

≜ **Camping International des Deux-Saisons**: chemin des Deux-Saisons. ☎ 04-75-01-88-99. Open from 1 March to 11 November. Pitch for two 64F. On the right towards Dieulefit. There's no special welcome, but the advantages of this campsite are its prices and its location at the union of the Jabron and the Roubion rivers, just a five-minute walk from the town centre. It's nicely shaded and there's an Olympic pool near by.

– There are other **campsites** virtually every 50 metres.

Bed and Breakfast in the Area

≜ **La Commanderie**: in Montboucher-sur-Jabron, heading east on the D540 (the road for Dieulefit) and the D169. ☎ and fax: 04-75-46-08-91. A double or triple room with shower and toilet costs from 320F to 400F. This little village inn has two spacious rooms, nicely decorated in Provençal style, although a little dull. Breakfast is served on the terrace when the weather's fine. Nice welcome.

WHERE TO EAT

On the Marseille road, there are numerous bars where you can have a drink or a quick sandwich.

☆ Budget

✕ **Le Petit Resto – Chez Titi**: 14 rue Peyrouse. In the town centre, behind the post office. ☎ 04-75-51-02-58. Closed Sunday lunch. One menu only at 70F. Hidden in a little street near the Museum of the Miniature, this

small but interesting eating place has a menu scrawled on a blackboard. Dishes are based on the freshest produce at the market. It's good value for money, but the wine isn't great.

✕ **La Papillote**: 2 place du Temple. ☎ 04-75-01-99-28. Closed

Sunday and Monday. On a little square, just outside the centre, shaded by tall lime trees, including one that's over 100 years old. Menus from 69F to 90F. Specialities include *gâteau de foies blonds sauce écrevisses* (liver cake with crayfish sauce) and *filets de limande sauce Noilly* (fillet of lemon sole with aniseed-flavoured sauce).

☆☆ Moderate

✗ **La Petite France**: 34 impasse Raymond-Daujat. ☎ 04-75-46-07-94. ✗ Closed Saturday lunchtime and Sunday; and from 14 July to 20 August, and 23 to 29 December. Menus at 85F, 118F and 165F. Popular with the locals, this restaurant does not seem to attract many visitors, despite its good specialities of *duo de ris de veau et foie gras chaud au vinaigre de framboise* (duo of veal sweetbreads and warm foie gras with raspberry vinegar) and *noix de St-Jacques à la provençale* (scallops Provençale-style). Limited, regional wine list.

WHERE TO GO FOR A DRINK

♟ **Café de la Bourse**: 7 boulevard Meynot. Near the town centre, opposite the Relais de l'Empereur (Napoleon was here). ☎ 04-75-01-79-68. Fax: 04-75-46-03-54. Menus at 60F, 100F and 140F. A run-of-the-mill café that is enlivened every Friday and Saturday evening by local bands playing jazz or blues, or whatever. Literary evenings and art exhibitions are also planned. The wide selection of whiskies adds to the enjoyment.

WHAT TO SEE AND DO

★ **Nougaterie du Chaudron d'Or**: 7 avenue du 52e-R.I. ☎ 04-75-01-03-95. Website: www.pro.wanadoo.fr/chaudron. Open to visitors every day, 5am–7pm in the week, 8am–7pm on Saturday. Free entrance. The *nougaterie* 'of the golden cauldron' is one of the few places in Montélimar still making nougat in the traditional way. The team is on duty from around 5.30am when the heat is still bearable. You can watch the whole manufacturing process from the first mixing to packaging – the paste is heated in cauldrons over a *bain-marie* and reaches nearly 100°C (212°F). Their most recent creation is *nougat à l'ancienne*, made with chestnut honey, almonds and a touch of caramel.

★ **Nougaterie Arnaud Soubeyran**: ZI Sud (southern industrial zone). From the town centre, take the Marseille road to the McDonald's roundabout. The factory is in the ochre-coloured building on the right. ☎ 04-75-51-01-35. ✗ One of the oldest nougat producers in Montélimar, founded in 1837, the Soubeyrand factory has a little museum about nougat and chocolate (which they also make). This is the only nougat producer that uses almonds from Provence, which it blanches itself. (The almonds in real Montélimar nougat should have had their skins removed.) The Soubeyrand nougat and other products are delicious. In July, go early in the morning, before the huge crowds get there.

★ **Château des Adhémar**: Open 10am–1pm and 3–7pm. ☎ 04-75-01-07-85. Entrance charge modest; no student discount. This was a prison for a long time, but now only the walls remain standing. The architecture is medieval in style and there's a fine view of the Drôme and the Ardèche, especially from what is left of the covered way. There are a few rooms (including one with a loggia), where temporary exhibitions and concerts are held.

WHAT TO SEE AND DO IN THE AREA

★ **Musée de la Soie** (silk museum): on the road to Dieulefit at Montboucher-sur-Jabron. ☎ 04-75-01-47-40. ♿ Open 1 March to 30 November, 9.30–11.30am and 2.30–6.30pm. Entrance fee: 35F (25F for 6- to 12-year-olds). This fascinating museum is well worth a visit, particularly for people travelling with children. The story of how silk is made is told here by enthusiast Pierre Lançon, who has patiently refurbished this old silk-worm house. Silk production was an activity of great significance, providing employment in the whole of the south of the department, after Olivier de Serres persuaded Henri IV to allow him to cultivate silkworms.

– For an extraordinary **panoramic view**, go to **Savasse**, north on the N7, then right on the D165. From the observatory, you can see the towers of Curnas and the Tricastin, Montélimar, Dieulefit, Montboucher, the Vercors and, on a really clear day, the island of Corsica.

✗ While you are in Savasse, try the restaurant **Lou Mas** (☎ 04-75-01-90-83), very close to the cathedral in the Homme d'Armes. ♿ Closed in the second fortnight in August. At lunchtime and on Friday and Saturday nights, this restaurant offers affordable menus at 69F, 149F and 179F, changing daily. There's a lovely, vaulted dining room with faux-rustic wooden furniture. Specialities include *coquilles St-Jacques au beurre d'orange* (scallops with orange butter), *filets de rougets à la niçoise* (red mullet fillets Nice-style). There is a Provençal shop next to the restaurant.

LEAVING MONTÉLIMAR

By train: Trying to travel by train will take longer than the other options, so don't even think about it

By bus:

– In the direction of **Dieulefit** (via Montboucher and Le Poët Laval), five buses a day (except on Sunday) leaving from the SNCF train station; the first leaves at about 8am in summer, the last about 7pm.

– For **Valréas** and **Nyons** (via Valaurie, Grignan), there are three buses a day; the first leaves around 6.30am in school term-time, the last around 7pm. Change at Nyons for Le Buis, La Motte Chalancon et Rémuzat.

CHÂTEAUNEUF-DE-MAZENC (26160)

This dreary little hilltop hamlet doesn't even have a bar! The nearest watering hole is in La Bégude (whose name means 'the place where the cattle drink' in local dialect). However, it's a lovely vantage point for a view over the valley and the road between Souspierre and Eyzahut (a village under the cliffs) is splendid. As you wind up between the terraces, you may well come across a flock of goats, gobbling up everything in their path.

USEFUL ADDRESS

❑ **Tourist office**: next door to the post office in La Bégude-de-Mazenc. ☎ 04-75-46-24-42. Open in high season on Monday 10am–noon and 2–3.30pm, Tuesday to Saturday 10am–12.30pm and 2.30–7pm. Sunday and public holidays, open 10am–1pm.

WHERE TO STAY AND EAT

🛏 **Chambres d'hôte Marjolaine Bergmans** (B&B): 800 metres from the centre in the old village. ☎ 04-75-46-22-49. Allow around 240F. Local artist Marjolaine has beautifully renovated this house, which is opposite her gallery. A wide stone staircase (formerly wood) goes up to two spacious rooms that are well arranged and attractive without being either chintzy or flowery.

✕ **Auberge de la Valdaine**: in the centre of the village of Portes-en-Valdaine. ☎ 04-75-46-22-23. ⅏ Closed Monday evening. The bistrot section of this small, unpretentious place offers dishes and salads for under 50F and a *menu ouvrier* (workers' menu) for 60F. On the newly converted restaurant side, there are *formule* menus at 115F, 135F and 175F and a main dish for less than 100F. There are tables outside and the specialities include *foie gras, choucroute de poisson* (fish choucroute) and other more exotic dishes.

✕ **La Moutardière**: route de Salettes in Eyzahut, on the D183. ☎ 04-75-90-48-07. ⅏ Open every evening but closed in January. Menus from 85F to 100F. Specialities such as steak with *picodon* cheese (*see below*) are served in a pleasant and relaxing setting.

WHAT TO DO

– **La Bellane stables**: ☎ 04-75-90-14-19. The farm stables are at the end of a rutted road, in the middle of a little valley. Experienced riders may join in treks in the area on lovely Arab horses.

WHAT TO SEE IN THE AREA

★ **Château de Rochefort-en-Valdaine**: open every afternoon in high season. Closed October to April. This medieval chateau owes its maintenance to a handful of enthusiasts, who have formed an association called 'Acroch'. Near by, there are a few marked footpaths; one in the old village of Allan (No. 125, yellow markings) will take you to the chateau. You'll need to wear more than flip-flops on all the paths.

SAOU (26400)   Population: 417

Once a year, on the first weekend in July, the sleepy little village of Saou (pronounced *Soo*) wakes up for the Fête du Picodon. About 50 farmers come to the festival to sell their little round *picodon* cheeses from trestle tables, at an impromptu market. According to archaeological finds, these cheeses were already being made in 3,000 BC. In 1983, an AOC was obtained for those made in the Drôme and the Ardèche. The farmers are joined by groups of musicians and street performers. Strictly speaking, it's not exactly in the Drôme Provençale, but it's worth the trip.

This tiny village, at the foot of the Vèbre (the local name for 'beaver'), is equally well known for its Mozart concerts (under the title of *Saoû chante Mozart*, 'Saoû sings Mozart'). Lovely performances take place in early July, the last one in the open air under the plane trees on the place des Cagnards. Concerts are also held in the 11 other *communes* (parishes) of the Drôme Provençale.

USEFUL ADDRESSES AND INFORMATION

🛈 Tourist office: ☎ 04-75-76-01-72. Fax: 04-75-76-05-50. Open Monday, Tuesday and Thursday from September to the end of June, 2–5pm; Friday and Saturday 9am–noon and 2–7pm; Sunday 9am-noon. In summer, Monday to Saturday 9am–noon and 3–6pm, Sunday 9am–noon. Good advice and colourful posters from past Fêtes du Picodon for sale.

■ Saou sings Mozart: programme: ☎ 04-75-76-02-02.

WHERE TO STAY AND EAT

🛏 Clévacances Le Moulin: on the village square. ☎ 04-75-83-01-70. This well-equipped three-roomed house can accommodate up to 10 people and may be rented by the week (from 1,430F to 2,560F, depending on the time of year) or by the weekend (1,030F).

🛏 Aire naturelle de camping La Briance (campsite): ☎ 04-75-76-05-00. Closed from All Saints Day to Easter. 🔧 All-in package deal for 24F per night per person.

✕ L'Oiseau sur sa Branche: in the centre. ☎ 04-75-76-02-03. 🔧 Closed on Monday evening and in January. Daily special for 53F and a menu at 150F. This village restaurant is run by a well-travelled poet, who painted the walls in yellow and blue and plays traditional French music. The dishes are rich in colour, flavour and presentation. In the bistrot, there's a counter offering cheap meals in the week (popular with regulars). Bizarrely, the owner collects canned fish tins; if you bring him one he hasn't got, he'll buy you a drink.

WHERE TO EAT IN THE AREA

✕ Restaurant Chez Denis: at Félines-sur-Rimandoule. ☎ 04-75-90-16-73. Closed Tuesday evening and Wednesday out of season and in January and February. Menus from 100F to 210F. A lovely house way up in the hills, especially popular in fine weather and on Sundays. The atmosphere is very relaxed as guests enjoy a long lazy meal on the cool terrace. The smiling Denis has carried on the good work begun by his father. The dishes are old-style: *escalope de foie gras frais poêlée sauce cassis* (pan-fried slice of fresh foie gras with blackcurrant sauce) *gratinée d'escargots aux nouilles* (snails in a cheese sauce with noodles). Best to book for the weekend.

WHAT TO SEE AND DO

– **Market**: every Saturday morning.

★ **Saou forest**: surrounded by many picturesque peaks, where there are lots of walks – the Roche Colombe (886 metres/2906 feet), the Trois-Becs, the Veyou (1,589 metres/5,213 feet), the Signal (1,559 metres/5,114 feet) and the Roche Courbe (1,545 metres/5,069 feet). Every Wednesday morning, a team of guides leads walks starting from the *mairie* at Tonils (information from Dieulefit tourist office: ☎ 04-75-46-42-49). The Association des Randonneurs du Pays de Bourdeaux (walkers' association for the Bourdeaux area) does the same for a slightly smaller charge (information from the tourist office: ☎ 04-75-53-35-90).

If you want to strike out on your own on a walk of about 4 hours 30 minutes, follow the green signs for Roche Colombe from the centre of the village, next to the church. Go round the Poupoune on the left. From there, there's a splendid view of the region and the forest to the east, and of the Adrans plain to the west. Far off to the northeast you'll see the Glandasse mountain, the Aiguilles de Lus and the Grand Veymont and, to the west, the Rhône valley and the mountains of the Ardèche. Follow the line of the crests to reach the summit (at 886 metres/2,906 feet). Go down again to the Pas de l'Échelette. After the first farm at the bottom, walk along the side of the meadow below the des Blaches farm. From there, returning to the village is easy.

★ **Musée de l'Oeuf de Soyans** (Soyans egg museum): open in the afternoon (not Tuesday) from 1 June to 30 September. Rest of the year, by appointment only. ☎ and fax: 04-75-76-00-15. Free entry. Run by a dynamic retired lady, this unusual museum is housed in a former religious building. It displays all sorts of eggs, from tiny humming birds and stick insects to a Hypsolosaurus dinosaur. Ask for the key to the chapel, too. It's quite a climb but the reward is a splendid view of the sheer cliffs.

LE POËT LAVAL (26160)   Population: 845

This little village has experienced the same old story of being abandoned by inhabitants going to live in the plain, but being re-populated later. Le Poët (from the Latin *podium*, meaning 'little hill') has a hotel that's not very *Routard*, in the old Hospitaller's headquarters, and a museum on the Protestant faith. About 95 per cent of the region's population (from Loriol and Dieulefit to Valdrôme) are Protestant, representing the third-largest Protestant community in France.

As you wander through the narrow cobbled streets of the village, you'll see *soustets*, or covered passageways, running off them here and there. They offer an ideal place to shelter from the rain.

WHAT TO SEE AND DO

★ **Musee du Protestantisme Dauphinois** (Museum of Dauphinois Protestantism): ☎ 04-75-46-46-33. Open 15 April to 15 October. Entrance fee: 25F (concessions for students and free for all on Ascension Day). This informative museum is put together well. The wooden pulpit survives in the church, which used to serve as a village hall. Some of the windows depict the fervour of the Reformation experienced in the village. The endpapers of the rare old psalters are badly damaged. They were hidden in a compost heap, because of the dangers of keeping copies of such scriptures.

✗ **Bouquinerie Dit-elle**: café in the centre of the village, not far from the museum. ☎ 04-75-46-23-05. Open every day from April to September and at the weekend in November, December and January. Closed in February and October. Allow about 70F. A great place to recharge the batteries, with luscious homemade tarts and books for sale. The little terrace upstairs is lovely. Credit cards not accepted.

DIEULEFIT (26220)   Population: 3,096

USEFUL ADDRESSES

🛈 **Tourist office**: 1 place de l'Abbé-Magnet. ☎ 04-75-46-42-49. Fax: 04-75-46-36-48. Email: ot.dieulefit @wanadoo.fr. From 1 April to end September, open 10am–12.30pm and 2.30–6pm. From October to end March, open on Friday morning 10am–noon and on other afternoons 2.30–5.30pm.
✉ **Post office**: cours du Jabron.

WHERE TO STAY

✩ Budget

🛌 **La Source du Jabron campsite**: Comps, 26220 Dieulefit. ☎ and fax: 04-75-90-61-30. ♿ 3 kilometres (about 2 miles) from Dieulefit, towards Bourdeaux alongside the D538. Open 1 May to 15 September. Around 25F per pitch and 17F per person (11F for under-7s). A great campsite with reasonable prices and a pleasant welcome. Ask for a pitch on the terrraces. The bright blue swimming pool contrasts strongly with the brilliant yellow flowering broom. Credit cards not accepted.

✩✩ Moderate

🛌 **Gîte de Fontlargias**: at Roche-St-Secret, 11.5 kilometres (7 miles) north on the D538 and the D545. ☎ 04-75-53-68-10. Closed 15 December to 1 March. Double room for two to four people with shared bathroom, full board 250F, half board 200F. In a five- to eight-bed dormitory, full board 230F, half board 180F. Menu 90F for residents (booking essential). One room has the kind of beds that will bring back memories to old submariners. This is the best and cheapest place around, with a friendly welcome and delicious homemade blackberry pie. The pool is surprisingly large.
🛌 **Château de Comps**: ☎ and fax: 04-75-46-30-00. A good place to stop, despite the two rather ugly modern buildings, 4 kilometres (2 miles) north of Dieulefit. In a separate wing of the chateau, the four brand-new, soberly decorated rooms have very comfortable beds. Room No. 3 up in the eaves, with a bath tub, is 300F a night. The others are cheaper but just as nice. The owner of the chateau allows guests to use her kitchen to make a meal. Credit cards not accepted. Booking absolutely essential.

⌂ **Les Volets Bleus**: in the direction of Bourdeaux on the D538, 9 kilometres (5.5 miles) from Dieulefit, fork left on to the D192 to Truinas. The house is 900 metres further on. ☎ 04-75-53-38-48. Fax: 04-75-53-49-02. Open all year. Double rooms with shower at 330F. Menu 125F including drink. At an altitude of 650 metres (2,132 feet), this restored farmhouse, a mixture of sandstone, ochre and Italian blue, is surrounded by superb valley views all around.

The five en suite rooms are tastefully decorated and comfortable. Pilar and Carlo offer a delightful welcome all year, putting together meals with the flavours of Provence, Spain and Italy. Homemade ravioli, *pintade aux dix parfums* (guinea fowl with ten flavours), *sauté d'agneau au miel et au gingembre* (sautéd lamb with honey and ginger), and homemade jam. There's a children's playground under the oak trees. Credit cards not accepted.

WHERE TO EAT

☆ Budget

– There are a number of **snack bars** and **pubs** across from the church in Dieulefit.

✘ **La Péniche**: 16 quai Roger-Morin. ☎ 04-75-90-62-98. ⌕ Closed from 1 October to 15 April. Menus at 85F (particularly good value for money) and 125F. The restaurant has a small terrace, and cream and terracotta decor in the dining room, inspired by local pottery. It's simple, fresh and delightful. Specialities include *canard aux olives de Nyons* (duck with Nyons olives).

☆☆ Moderate

✘ **Auberge Les Brises**: route de Nyons. One kilometre from the town centre. ☎ 04-75-46-41-49. ⌕ Closed on Tuesday and Wednesday out of season as well as from 15 January to 1 March. Also closed on Tuesday in July and August. Menus at 95F (except Sunday), 125F and 190F. This little corner of Brittany in the heart of the Provençal Drôme serves dishes with Atlantic flavours alongside more local ones, such as *filet de boeuf aux morilles* (fillet of beef with mushrooms). The restaurant has quickly gained a good reputation and guests can enjoy the excellent food in the dining room or, in summer, in the shade on the terrace.

WHAT TO SEE

★ Don't miss the chance to drive route along the D541 and the D191A, between **Dieulefit** and **Bourdeaux**. In the background are the mountains and, in front, a sea of hills with farms clinging to them in determined fashion. There are several good places for a picnic. Stock up on provisions from the market.

★ Dieulefit is a mecca for potters, as is neighbouring Cliousclat. The **Maison de la Terre** (house of clay), in La Baume park, Dieulefit, is worth a look. ☎ 04-75-90-61-80. Entrance fee: 15F. The tour is brisk but informative and there are temporary exhibitions and courses for both adults and children.

Auntie Marguerite

During the Occupation in Dieulefit, a number of local characters came to the fore. Town hall employee Jeanne Barnier falsified identity papers and ration cards, while Marguerite Soubeyrand, a Protestant teacher in Beauvallon, gave refuge to many Spaniards, Jews and German communists. Marguerite's ideas about teaching were revolutionary at the time. She objected to school uniforms, strongly believed in rural schools and promoted group working, freedom of expression and mixed classes.

VALOUSE (26110)   **Population: 36**

The route along the D538 and then the D130 is one of the most beautiful in the area – not recommended for those of a nervous disposition. The views of the deep gorges are magnificent from the top of the Valouse pass (at an altitude of 735 metres/2,410 feet).

WHERE TO STAY AND EAT

≜ ✕ Le Hameau de Valouse: ☎ 04-75-27-72-05. Fax: 04-75-27-75-61. Closed on Monday evening and all day Tuesday as well as from November to February. Menus cost 98F, 135F and 180F. The owner, from Strasbourg, came upon Valouse and rebuilt the ruins of this hamlet with his son. The smart 'Hirondelle' room is full of his grandparents' furniture and also has a private terrace. The attractively coloured 'Mésange' room has a bath tub under a vaulted stone ceiling. 'Cigale' is decorated in warm hues and has two huge beds. There are TVs in all the rooms. The service and welcome are friendly and there's a swimming pool and a lovely terrace on which to sip a *myro* (Côtes-du-Rhône and bilberry liqueur) with a few Nyons olives.

Gîte

≜ Gîtes du Haut Estellon: in Chaudebonne. ☎ and fax: 04-75-27-73-91. Open throughout the year. Accommodation from 1,000F to 3,000F per week, depending on the season, and from 570F to 740F at the weekend. On the slopes of the Montagne de Mielandre in a big garden with a swimming pool. The owner Jacques, who makes a point of eating or having a drink with guests, is gradually reconstructing the hamlet where his parents lived. If he's not up to his eyes in building, in the lavender field or the apricot orchard, he may take you out in his four-wheel-drive to show you the splendid views. Book well in advance.

WHAT TO DO IN THE AREA

– In summer, take the rather difficult road from Valouse to Dieulefit, particularly at the time of year when they 'burn' the *lavandin*, a lime-loving plant that cannot thrive higher than 600 metres (1,968 feet), and lavender, which is hardy and resists the cold up at 1,400 metres (4,593 feet). Stop at the **Distillerie de Teyssières** to find out more.

THE RHÔNE VALLEY AND HAUTE-PROVENCE

– The **Défilé des Trente Pas** (540 metres/1,772 feet), not far from St-Ferréol, jagged heights from which flows the Bentrix (the watercourse that feeds the vine).

– On the D335, between Pradelles and Benoît-en-Diois, you can swim in deep pools formed by the Roanne.

RÉMUZAT (26510)   Population: 283

This little village has an unusual history. In the 17th century, for a reason that remains a mystery, it was torn down and rebuilt stone by stone on its present site at an altitude of 447 metres (1,565 feet). In medieval times, the village was on the other bank of the Oule, at the foot of the St-Auban cliffs, dominating the three watercourses of the Eygues, the Oule and the Rif. Only a few walls and a chapel mark the spot where Rémusat (originally spelt with an 's') used to stand.

USEFUL ADDRESS

🛈 **Tourist information**: on the main village square, near the bridge, next to the Maison aux Vautours. ☎ 04-75-27-85-71. Open 10am–12.30pm and from 3–7pm in July and August. Closed Monday. Good printed information on the region.

WHERE TO STAY

Gîtes

🛏 **Les Curebiasses**: at the end of rue Patouille. ☎ and fax: 04-72-38-07-80 and 04-75-27-84-89. Eight rooms, with between two and eight beds, with shared bathroom, at 70F, or 60F for a minimum of three consecutive nights. Breakfast is optional at 20F. Housed in a 17th-century building near the equestrian centre, with a friendly atmosphere, large kitchen and piano.

🛏 **Gîte de St-May**: ☎ 04-75-27-85-49. Reasonably priced in summer, at 1,500F for a week and 450F for weekends; a little expensive out of season, at 1,200F. Standing at 520 metres (1,700 feet), in the middle of the village, this *gîte* is smaller, but welcoming, and a nice place for a few restful days.

WHERE TO EAT

☆☆ Moderate

✕ **Les Trois Diables**: 47A Grand-Rue, in La Motte-Chalancon. ☎ 04-75-27-21-38. ✕ In the town centre. Closed Tuesday night and Wednesday. Menus 99F, 137F and 179F. 'The Three Devils' is a small, convivial eating place run with energy and purpose by the attentive chef and his two daughters. They serve delicious, well-prepared dishes such as *filet d'agneau grillé aux herbes et sa tapenade* (grilled fillet of lamb with herbs and olive paste). The homemade tarts are also delicious.

WHAT TO SEE

★ **Vultures**: partly because of a law forbidding shepherds to leave sheep carcasses out in the pastures and partly because of campaigns to poison wolves, the carrion-eating vultures had virtually disappeared by the beginning of the 20th century. Through the work of various associations, they have recently been reintroduced, despite the fears of many locals that they would take lambs or even children. In fact, the birds feed only on dead meat. Today, even some of their Spanish relations come here to visit. Keep an eye out for them, particularly in the morning, or take a guided walk with Christian Teissier, who is in charge of the Maison des Vautours (the vulture information centre): ☎ 04-75-27-81-91.

WHAT TO SEE IN THE AREA

★ **St-May** village, on the D94, and its **gorges**: you have to cross a little wooden bridge to get to the pretty road that goes up to the village. From here, there is an impressive view of the gorges, formed by the Eygues. For a bit more excitement, carry on a bit further, for about 3.5 kilometre (2 miles), in the direction of the Rocher au Caire, which has a 777-metre 2,550-foot) peak.

POMMEROL (26470)   Population: 21

About 25 years ago, a Dr Vuillard had the crazy idea of restoring the small hilltop village of Pommerol, way up at 900 metres (2,953 feet) and deserted since the beginning of the 20th century. It was a mammoth project: for a start, he required 25 tonnes of concrete to hold up the body of the chapel, and 45,000 roof tiles, and he had to dig a 1.2 kilometre ditch out of the mountain in order to bring in water. He may have come across as a rather abrasive personality, but he was a real local character. Latterly, he was building a tower from which to observe the columns of eroded rock and digging a 200-metre platform by the chateau.

Dr Vuillard used to make the odd franc out of any lost tourist who happened to stumble across Pommerol. The arbitrarily set fee was 25F, valid for a whole year. Both ticket prices and the style of management are likely to change now, since the doctor has left, to restore the Langoustier fort in Porquerolles. His work at Pommerol was an extraordinary achievement and worth seeing.

🛏 Vuillard used to make reasonably priced accommodation available. Phone to find out the current situation: ☎ 04-75-27-20-05. There was even a swimming pool, heated by solar power, behind the poplar tree.

Les Baronnies

Ste-Jalle, Le Poët, Mévouillon, Pierrelongue and Le Buis all lie in the heart of Les Baronnies, between the mountain tops (the domain of St-Julien, Grimagne and Banne and the passes (where you'll find Ey, Fontaube and Soubeyrand). The eastern part of this little world is hard to get to know, but it's worth the effort. The Ventoux, from its highest point at 1,912 metres (6,273 feet), looks down on it all.

The Baronnies is best known (if it's known at all) for its juicy, sweet apricots, but the land has always been used for all kinds of typically Provençal cultivation, from vines and wheat, to lavender, olives, lemon balm, lime, thyme and rosemary. Some crops are no longer grown. One of these is madder, used to dye the trousers of the soldiers of the Third Republic red.

STE-JALLE (26110)   Population: 269

This little village, at the meeting point of the rivers Rieu Frais and Ennuye, is not particularly interesting, but it is the only Catholic bastion in a Protestant province. In the old part, the church of Notre-Dame-de-Beauver is a mixture of Romanesque and Lombard styles.

WHERE TO STAY AND EAT

☒ Budget

♠ ✕ Auberge de la Vallée: in the centre of the village. ☎ 04-75-27-32-17. Closed on Wednesday out of season and from mid-February to mid-March. Double rooms with shower cost 165F. Simple menu at 75F and a more expensive one at 120F. Half board about 195F per person per day. Brisk service.

✕ Chez Marilou: at Bellecombe Tarendol, 8.5 kilometres (5.5 miles) via the D64 and the D162. Take the little road that descends opposite the church. Everyone in the village knows this friendly old lady, who will serve you with generous portions. Call in the evening before to book.

♠ ✕ Auberge des Garelles: in Tarendol. ☎ and fax: 04-75-27-32-01. Closed in January and February. A few guest rooms available in summer for 220F, including breakfast. Menus at 80F, 100F and 120F. A friendly welcome, good food and comfort in a little riding centre. Dishes, served in generous portions, include chicken and kid with parsley.

SHOPPING

☛ Domaine du Rieu Frais: follow the signs. ☎ 04-75-27-31-54. Fax: 04-75-27-34-47. Wine cellar open every day, all year round, 8am–noon and 2–7pm. Jean-Yves Liotaud is the only wine-grower in the region. His nice little Vins de Pays des Baronnies compete decently with Côtes-du-Rhône and Châteauneuf-du-Pape wines. Try his very affordable Cabernet Sauvignon, matured in oak casks.

WHAT TO SEE

★ Mohair farm: at Arpavon, on the road to Ste-Jalle at Curnier. Follow the blue and white signs. Bring the children to meet this herd of a couple of dozen mohair goats and see the weaving room. The owner also makes a few *picodon* cheeses.

MÉVOUILLON (26560)   Population: 204
AULAN (26570)   Population: 5

What's left of the small hamlet Mévouillon (or Mévouillon-Gresse), hidden on the road from St-Auban-sur-l'Ouvèze to Séderon (D546), is pretty tatty. There are some historic ruins here, but you won't find them on the local tourist map.

In the 11th century, this stretch of land belonged to a powerful woman called Percipia. Her son, Baron Ripert I, built the Mévouillon fortress at 1,200 metres (3,730 feet), and took its name. Despite being the Bishop of Gap, he managed to father two more barons, Ripert II and Reymont I, who went on to found a dynasty. The family remained wealthy in the region – which became known as Les Baronnies – for nearly four centuries, alongside and some-times in conflict with the Montaubans (of Montauban-sur-l'Ouvèze).

There is little left of the fortress, except the stone reservoir, but the walk up to the ruins provides superb views over the mountains and lavender fields; it's especially impressive when the mistral is blowing.

GETTING THERE

Go to the hamlet of Mévouillon-Gresse. Carry on for 300 metres, after the sign marking the pass (at 890 metres/2,920 feet), take the second dirt track on the left before the little chapel. Park at the end. Walk up the sloping path for about 45 minutes to reach the ruins. In summer, go in the late afternoon when a rock slab at the summit provides welcome shade. On the way, dilapidated walls, eaten into by time and grown over by grass, are evidence of an old village.

AULAN

Unlike the Mévouillon fortress, the lovely **Château d'Aulan** is very much alive. On the D546, after Gresse in the direction of St-Auban-sur-l'Ouvèze, turn left on to the D359. Open every day in July and August, 10–11.30am and 2–6.30pm. Out of season, phone ahead to make an appointment: ☎ 04-75-28-80-00. The Comte d'Aulan, who leads tours out of season, is a mine of information about the chateau. In 1915, antique dealers disposed of the furniture and fittings, and the count has had to be most determined in his efforts to open the chateau to visitors. Many of the rooms have busts, pictures, ornaments and furniture belonging to the ancestors of Charles Suarez d'Aulan. One of them, Arthur de Suarez, was equerry to Napoleon III.

The fancy little chapel, outside the chateau walls, is also worth a look.

BUIS-LES-BARONNIES (26170)
Population: 2,226

One of the capitals of the barons' domain, Buis-les-Baronnies (usually referred simply as 'Le Buis') has a number of splendid buildings that are a legacy of its successful commercial history. Walk around the streets and covered passageways, to see the place des Arcades, the ramparts (or what's left of them), and the Dominican and Ursuline convents. On Wednesday mornings, there's a marvellous market.

USEFUL ADDRESS

🏛 **Tourist office**: place du Quinconce. ☎ 04-75-28-04-59. Open in summer 9.15am–noon and 2.30–6.30pm (9.30am–noon on Sunday and 9.15am–noon and 2–5pm between October and April). Friendly staff can find suitable accommodation and supply walking maps and leaflets on the Drôme Provençale.

WHERE TO STAY

☆ Budget

🛏 **Résidence de vacances Escapade Cloître des Dominicains**: in the centre of Buis. ☎ 04-75-28-06-77. Fax: 04-75-28-13-20. Closed from November to March. Open for arrivals 9am–noon and 5–7pm. Double room for 290F and package deals available for weekend and weekly stays, but no student concessions. In a renovated Dominican convent, this is the best option for a cheap room in the town centre. Ask for a room overlooking the cloisters. There are kitchen facilities and showers, and bikes can be left in the courtyard.

☆☆ Moderate

🛏 **Hôtel les Arcades–le Lion d'Or**: on place des Arcades in the centre of the village. ☎ 04-75-28-11-31. Fax: 04-75-28-12-07. Closed from 15 December to 1 February. Double rooms with toilet and TV from 170F to 250F. The hotel is pretty, with art deco touches, but the rooms aren't great, mainly because the bedding is rather old. There's a private, well-maintained garden and you can have breakfast outside. Secure garage.

WHERE TO STAY IN THE AREA

🛏 **Gîte du Lièvre**: at La Roche-sur-le-Buis. ☎ 04-75-28-11-49. Signposted from Poët-en-Percip, 3 kilometres (2 miles) from the centre. Open mid-April to All Saints Day. 30F for a tent pitch; huts and cabins also available. Breakfast 30F. Menus from 65F to 100F. Completely remote and isolated, the site faces due south, towards the Ventoux. There's a swimming pool among the broom bushes and a herd of goats – try their *picoton* cheeses. Good breakfasts with country bread and jam made from Baronnies apricots. Welcoming owners.

🛏 **Gîte le Balcon de Rosine**: route de Propiac, 26170 Mérindol-les-Oli-

viers. ☎ and fax: 04-75-28-71-18. Take the D938 from Vaison-la-Romaine to Nyons, the D46 towards Buis-les-Baronnies, then the D71 to Propiac. From Mérindol-les-Oliviers, carry on to Propiac; the *gîte* is a little further on, on the right. Closed in August. Accommodation is in a separate house with a fabulous view. It costs around 3,000F for two per week, with breakfast available, including homemade jams.

🛏 **Chambres and table d'hôte La Honas**: in La Rochette-du-Buis. ☎ and fax: 04-75-28-55-11. Email: Lahonas@clubinternet.fr. From Buis-les-Baronnies, take the D546 in the direction of Séderon. After Les

Granges, 2 kilometres from La Rochette, turn right on to the D359 in the direction of Aulan and Montbrun-les-Bains. Go on 400 metres, then take the turning to the right. Closed from 15 November to 15 March. Double room with shower from 250F to 300F (breakfast included). Menu at 100F. A beautiful 17th-century farm surrounded by lavender fields, fruit trees, oaks, limes and pines. There are four charmingly furnished rooms, one in an old *pigeonnier*, and all with pretty bathrooms. The dining room is in the vaulted cellar, and there's also a barbecue. Pascal prepares Provençal and Mediterranean specialities, including *aïoli, flan de courgette* and *caviar d'aubergines* using local produce, together with homemade bread and cakes. La Honas is the starting point for many lovely excursions, on foot or mountain bike, trips into the Gorges du Toulourenc, horse riding, hang-gliding and canyoning. There's a friendly atmosphere.

WHERE TO EAT

☆–☆☆ Budget to Moderate

✕ **Bar Grill l'Étoile**: 1 place de Verdun, opposite the tourist office. ☎ 04-75-28-07-68. ✖ Open every day throughout the year. Set menu 35F and around 80F for a meal, including tasty grilled meats (lamb in particular) and pizzas. Relax in the shade of the plane trees.

✕ **Le Grill du Four à Pain**: 24 avenue Boissy-d'Anglas. ☎ 04-75-28-10-34. Closed all day Monday (except on Monday evening in July and August), as well as from 15 November to 15 January. Menus from 88F to 178F. The cooking is delicious and sophisticated, and the service friendly. Tasty dishes include *pavé d'agneau au thym badiane* (lamb steak with thyme), and the wines are very reasonable.

WHERE TO EAT IN THE AREA

✕ **Auberge des Ayguiers**: on the road from Buis to Nyons, in Pierrelongue. ☎ 04-75-28-77-93. Closed on Tuesday evening and Wednesday. Weekday lunch menu 62F and other menus up to 140F. For a relatively modest outlay, treat yourself to some delicious dishes. The family-style cooking is popular with locals. From the terrace there's a view of the strange chapel that overlooks the village.

✕ **Auberge de la Gloriette**: on the D147 in Mérindol-les-Oliviers. ☎ and fax: 04-75-28-71-08. ✖ Closed on Thursday and Sunday evening in low season (on Sunday evening only in summer) as well as in January and February. Double rooms from 200F to 350F. Set menu 100F. This set-up, in the shade of old plane trees, is like a Pagnol film set. On the left is the bakery, producing bread and cakes. On the right is an old-style restaurant dining room and, between the two of then, a gorgeous terrace. There are vineyards as far as the eye can see, olive groves and apricot orchards on the hills and a bubbling fountain. The breakfast is huge. If you want total quiet, ask for the room at the back. If you're still around at lunchtime, try the *saucisson* with olives, or fruit tarts still warm from the oven.

✕ **L'Auberge de la Clue**: at Plaisians. Take the D72 then the D526.

☎ 04-75-28-01-17. Closed during the week out of season and on Monday from April to October. Menus at 135F and 160F. At the weekends this family-run inn, with views of the Ventoux, is invaded by crowds of foodies. Prices are cheap, the portions are generous and the food is very good. The two (very tall) sons of the house are the chefs and their mother runs the dining room. She provides a delicious terrine to keep customers going while they choose from the menu, which might include homemade *pieds-paquets* (lamb tripe and trotters) or *lapin à la tapendade* (rabbit with olive paste).

WHAT TO SEE AND DO

– **Foire au Tilleul** (limeflower fair): dating back to 1808, the limeflower fair of Buis-les-Baronnies takes place on the first Wednesday in July. Such fairs take place throughout the region in July, but the one at Le Buis is the most interesting. This is the capital of the limeflower, responsible for about 90 per cent of the national crop, although production has decreased in recent years. It is difficult to harvest, because the flowers tend to become mixed up with the leaves. Picking is done from June to July, *en famille*, using tall ladders. The flowers are picked into *bourras*, huge jute sacks, which are carried on the pickers' backs and then left on the ground at the end of the day. Early in the morning, the limeflower traders come along to weigh what they want from the sacks, and take it away.

– Herbalist **Bernard Laget**, place aux Herbes (after the place des Arcades, ☎ 04-75-28-16-42) is a mine of information about the limeflower and other medicinal plants.

– **Salon du Livre de Plantes**: this book fair, focusing on aromatic and medicinal plants, is held at the same time as the Foire du Tilleul, but lasts for four days, with exhibitions and seminars.

– **Rock climbing**: Buis-Les-Baronnies is a popular place with climbers. Between Le Rocher-St-Julien, Ubrieux and Beauvoisin, there's plenty to keep them occupied.

To get to the **St-Julien** rock, go to the municipal campsite, then take the small path after the EDF sub-station. There are 100 routes, facing south, in blazing sunshine. The rocks are good and slabbed, but quite variable.

At **Beauvoisin**, the Baume Noire area also faces due south, but the 30 or so routes are protected from the mistral. Pitons could be useful.

Ubrieux isn't hard to find but you need to be careful not to trample the orchards or olive groves. There are 150 southwest-facing routes. It can get very busy, especially in the school holidays, but it's really nice, with the chance to swim in the Ouvèze at the end of the day.

LEAVING BUIS

By bus: there are buses for Avignon, via Nyons, Vaison-la-Romaine, Camaret and Orange – two services a day (7am and 3pm), except Saturday.

NYONS (26110)   Population: 6,723

Surrounded by a circle of hills, and standing beside the Eygues, which sometimes rages like a torrent, the people of Nyons often claim that the mistral doesn't blow in their town. The mountains certainly offer some protection and Nyons enjoys more hours of sunshine per year than the Côte d'Azur. According to the locals, *l'ensouleiado tou l'an* ('the sun shines all year round). They don't tell you about the 'pontias' breeze, which gets up every evening. Cool air comes down the slopes in the valley to replace the hot air from the Tricastin plain, and the pontias blows until the sun is really baking.

Nyons may be best known for its weather, but it also has a fine toll-bridge, evidence of the town's former prosperity. When Les Baronnies lost the town, through their own bad management, Humbert I and Jean I acquired it. In 1352, Nyons fell into the domain of the king of France. The Lombards and Jews arrived, had great success in business and money-lending, and constructed some gorgeous buildings with lovely facades.

Nyons is a pleasant place to stay, with a lively market (albeit more commercial than typically Provençal).

WHERE TO STAY

🛏 **Hôtel Au Petit Nice**: 4 avenue Paul-Laurens. ☎ 04-75-26-09-46. The cheapest option (other than the Nyons campsite). Closed Sunday and Monday evening as well as the first fortnight in July and three weeks in November. Floral-decorated rooms overlooking the road, from 170F to 250F, with or without shower. Straightforward welcome.

🛏 **La Picholine**: promenade de la Perrière. ☎ 04-75-26-06-21. Fax: 04-75-26-40-72. Closed in February and from 15 October to 6 November. Double rooms from 310F to 410F. Half board compulsory in July and August. Excellent restaurant serving a daily regional menu at 135F and other *formule* menus at 165F and 230F. An ideal place to stop in Nyons, run by kind owners, who are particularly attentive towards retired couples. Standing in splendid isolation, high up in the village, it has a garden and a swimming pool set among the olive trees. The rooms are big, bright and pleasant.

Bed and Breakfast

🛏 **L'Ormeraie**: in the Bouchon-Les Blaches district, on the hillside, on the road from Mirabel to Nyons. ☎ 04-75-27-19-49. Closed at the end of January (except at the weekend) and in February. Double rooms from 230F to 380F. The two rooms are pleasant and comfortable, though a bit small. There's a lovely suite (from 350F to 600F, depending on the number of guests), with a terrace overlooking the valley that's the perfect spot for an all-over tan. Facilities include a garden with a swimming pool, laundry and barbecue. The breakfasts are delicious.

Gîte

🛏 **Gîte de la Rouvière**: in Piégon. ☎ 04-75-27-16-38. Panoramic view of the Ventoux. Among the pines and oaks (under which you might find truffles). Three very quiet, well-equipped *gîtes*, with washing machine, dishwasher, oven and fridge), for 2,000F out of season and an extra 500F in season. The welcome is friendly.

WHERE TO EAT

☆ Budget

✕ **Moun Recati**: 13 avenue Paul-Laurens. ☎ 04-75-26-02-03. Closed on Monday and Tuesday in winter; on Monday only in summer. *Formule* menus from 69F to 122F. This is a quite ordinary-looking pizzeria, except for its unusual pink decor. The good pizzas can be eaten in the dining room or at outdoor tables across the road. They also serve more elaborate regional dishes.

☆☆ Moderate

✕ **Le Petit Caveau**: 9 rue Victor-Hugo. ☎ 04-75-26-20-21. Fax: 04-75-26-07-28. Closed Sunday evening and Monday except public holidays and from mid-November to end December. Menus from 110F (including a main course, cheese or dessert) to 240F. Run by a graduate of the wine university of Suze-La-Rousse and an ex-employee of famous chef Robuchon, this is the ideal place for tasting different wines, accompanying excellent food. The *cuisse de lapin confite au thym et à l'huile d'olive* (rabbit leg with thyme and olive oil) is absolutely typical of the region. The prices are quite high.

✕ **La Coloquinte**: avenue de la Résistance, in Mirabel. ☎ 04-75-27-19-89. ✲ Closed on Wednesday, Thursday lunchtime and during the last two weeks in November as well as during All Saints, Christmas and February school holidays. Also closed on Sunday evening out of season. Several *formule* menus from 115F to 205F. Good cooking using only fresh, seasonal produce. The patio is pleasantly shaded. The 145F menu has colourful and flavourful dishes, including *filet de rascasse au beurre d'estragon* (fillet of scorpion fish with tarragon butter) and *crème de basilic* (basil soup). The huge selection of cheeses is impressive. A real find.

✕ **Le Petit Bistrot**: 4 rue Sous-les-Barris (or Place de l'église), in Vinsobres. ☎ and fax 04-75-27-61-90. Closed Wednesday and in January. Menus from 85F to 195F. Double rooms cost 240F, including breakfast, and there's also an apartment for 300F for two. Half board is possible (with lunch only during the winter). Art deco posters add to the atmosphere, and the service is very attentive. Good-quality regional dishes are served with local wines, at unusually good prices. The cheapest menu offers an *assiette de l'auberge* (dish of the day), such as a *daube* (stew), but the crowning glory is the cheese board, and the homemade desserts. The most expensive menu includes a truffle omelette. The rooms and apartment are a good size, charming and quiet. Credit cards not accepted. Free car park.

WHAT TO SEE

★ **Old olive oil mill and Savonnerie Autrand** (soap factory): near the Roman bridge. ☎ 04-75-26-11-00. Open 10am–noon and 2.30–6pm. Closed in January and Sunday and out of season. Guided tours at

10.30am, 11.30am, 3pm, 4pm, 5pm. Entrance fee: 23F (free for under-12s). This private mill is worth a visit to find out about the process of olive oil production. Roughly speaking, the olives are crushed between two mill-stones and turned into a paste. The paste is then laid on *scourtins* (pieces of coconut matting), which are pressed to force the juice to trickle out. About 4–5kg (9–11lbs) of *tanches* (a local olive variety) produce a litre (1.75 pints) of oil. A constant, mild temperature is required, so the system is explained in the basement of the mill.

Recently, the mill's owners discovered a soap factory that had been buried under 80 tonnes of soil deposited by successive floods of the River Eygues. (Incidentally, the name Eygues seems to have little to do with either the Latin or Provençal word for 'water' – *aqua* or *aiguo*. In Gallic, *eger* or *eiger* means 'thunder', which is frequent in the high valleys.)

★ **Scourtins factory**: come here to see the *scourtins* (coconut-matting) being made by hand (except Saturday and Sunday) in an artisan's work-shop. These days, they serve only as decorative objects. Open 9am–noon and 2–5pm from September to June and 9am–noon and 2–6pm in July and August. The shop is open every day except Sunday and public holidays until 6pm in winter and 7pm in summer.

The Tricastin

The domain of the Tricastin covers no more than 30 square kilometres (12 square miles) of the Drôme. Perhaps it would be better described as a *terroir* (a rural area associated with the traditional production of certain foods and wines), because, even though it's not definable geographically, it is based around the Côtes du Rhône. The wine is sanctioned by the chateau of Suze-la-Rousse, which has been the home since 1978 of the very popular university of wine, attended by both amateurs and professionals.

Owing to an administrative anomaly – so common in this area – that goes back to the 14th century, the land around Valréas belongs to the Vaucluse. When the popes bought the lands of the Comtat Venaissin, Valréas was cut off by a strip of land belonging to the Dauphiné. When the departments were drawn up, the Revolutionaries decided to leave the enclave as it was, so the administrative set-up remains as a reminder of the Ancien Régime!

In the 19th century, Valréas was best known for its packaging and printing industries; a visit to its museum is very interesting.

GRIGNAN (26230)   Population: 1,353

The noble chateau here was home to the daughter of the Marquise de Sévigné, one of the famous letter-writing *marquise*'s main correspondents. It faces south, with its back to the mistral, which used regularly to smash the glass in its windows. It wasn't all comfort and luxury for the aristos in those days. Grignan is a bit touristy now, and the chateau draws the crowds, but fewer people know about the interesting typographical museum. Its streets, with their old flowering roses, are lovely.

USEFUL ADDRESS

🛈 Tourist office: on one of the little streets going up around the chateau. ☎ 04-75-46-56-75. Open all year from Tuesday to Saturday (every day in July and August) 10am–noon and 2–6pm.

WHERE TO STAY

🛏 Hôtel Sévigné: in the centre of the village, on the road to Taulignan, next to the post office. ☎ 04-75-46-50-97. Fax: 04-75-46-93-48. Closed Tuesday lunchtime. Double rooms from 180F to 280F. The small reasonably priced rooms are rather old-fashioned but well maintained, and some have small terraces. The hotel may be under new management soon.

WHERE TO STAY IN THE AREA

Gîte

🛏 Domaine de Montine – La Grande Tuilière: on the road to Taulignan, signposted. ☎ 04-75-46-54-21. Fax: 04-75-46-93-26. Open every day throughout the year. Four well-equipped, bright and spacious *gîtes* from 1,400F to 3,200F per week, depending on the season. The pine furniture is practical and functional and there's also a swimming pool. In the season, you can go 'truffling' with the owners, who are farmers.

WHERE TO EAT

☆ Budget

✗ **L'Eau à la Bouche**: rue St-Louis. ☎ and fax: 04-75-46-57-37. ✗ Not far from the typographical museum. Closed Monday all year and Tuesday in winter (Tuesday lunchtime only in spring and autumn); also closed from end September to end October and in January. Menus at 125F, 150F and 180F. The owner is keen on persuading customers to indulge in a glass of wine with their *formule rapide* menu. Vast salads and vegetarian dishes are served on a flower-filled terrace that is very popular on sunny days.

✗ **La Piccolina**: ☎ 04-75-46-59-20. 50 metres from the town hall. Closed Monday and 15 December to 15 January. *à la carte* between 90F and 130F. This adorable and unusual little pizzeria has a wood-fired oven and serves grilled meats, good salads and, of course, tasty pizzas. These days, it seems that many pizzerias are better and more reliable than a lot of 'gastronomic' restaurants.

WHAT TO SEE AND DO

★ **L'atelier-musée du Livre et de la Typographie** (Workshop and museum of the book and typography): Maison du Bailli. ✗ Closed Monday. Open 10am–noon and 2–6pm out of season. In summer, open every day 10am–6pm. ☎ 04-75-46-57-16. Modest entrance fee. Museum manager Philippe Devoghel is the son of a typographer and has worked in printing himself. The temporary exhibitions are good and there's also a print room (where, among other things, they print luncheon vouchers), and a museum with old printing presses, all in working order. Children will enjoy getting their hands dirty.

★ **Château de Grignan**: ☎ 04-75-46-51-56. Open every day from 9.30–11.30am and 2–5.30pm (6pm in July and August). Closed Tuesday from November to March. Entrance fee: 30F (guided tours possible). The chateau, run by the regional council, acts as a venue for a programme of cultural events including classical music and jazz concerts, and exhibitions.

★ **Domaine de Montine**: Grande Tuilière, 26230 Grignan. ☎ 04-75-46-54-21. This local cellar sells 100,000 bottles from here and has tentatively exported a few around the world. Try their astonishing and affordable Terroirs 98 (50 per cent syrah, the main grape variety in the Coteaux-du-Tricastin, and 50 per cent grenache) or the equally good Prestige 1997.

VALAURIE (26230)   Population: 508

The tiny village of Valaurie is the perfect place to experience the good life and indulge in a bit of *farniente*. Foodies will be pleased to hear that it has more than its fair share of good eating places.

WHERE TO STAY AND EAT

– Once a year, the **Fête** gourmande de Valaurie (Valaurie food festival) provides a gargantuan feast for a nominal cost.

☆☆☆ Chic

🛏 ✕ **Le Domaine des Méjeonnes**: Les Méjeonnes, 26230 Valaurie. Take RN7 and then the D133 towards Grignan and Nyons. ☎ 04-75-98-60-60. Fax: 04-75-98-63-44. ✕ Closed on Sunday evening out of season. Double room from 345F to 375F. Menus from 98F to 210F. This former farmhouse has recently been renovated and now offers spacious and comfortable rooms and a superb swimming pool in the garden. Good cooking and a cordial welcome.

WHAT TO SEE IN THE AREA

★ **Le monastère de la Trappe d'Aiguebelle** (monastery): founded in 1137, this was originally a Cistercian monastery dedicated to the Virgin Mary. The monks, who are farmers and craftsmen, strictly respect the rules of prayer, manual work, silence and spiritual contemplation, laid down by St Bernard. They used to make a liqueur called Aiguebelle, but not any more. A little shop sells souvenirs.

LA GARDE-ADHÉMAR (26700)

Population: 1,075

This village, surrounded by beautiful countryside, has a lovely Romanesque church. The chateau, now in ruins, dates from the time of Antoine Escalin, who began his working life as a local shepherd and later became Director General of Prisons.

THE RHÔNE VALLEY AND HAUTE-PROVENCE

USEFUL ADDRESS

B Tourist office: open 9–11.30am and 3.30–7pm (mornings only out of season).

WHERE TO STAY

⊜ Le Logis de l'Escalin: on the route de Donzère. ☎ and fax: 04-75-04-41-32. Closed on Sunday evening, on Monday and during the first week in January. Double rooms 350F (half board possible for 490F, for a minimum of three days). This little hotel stands on a hill overlooking the Rhône valley. The motorway is very close, but the traffic noise doesn't reach here. There are seven totally refurbished rooms, with shower and TV, and a very pleasant shady garden with a children's swing. The prices seem to increase rather often.

Bed and Breakfast

⊜ Gîte du Val des Nymphes: domaine de Magne, 1 kilometre from La Garde-Adhémar. ☎ 04-75-04-44-54. Pleasant rooms for 270F in a house in a quiet garden with almond trees. Dinner is very reasonably priced. There's a menu at 95F based on local and farm produce, and a 'truffle menu' for 135F.

WHERE TO EAT

☒ Budget

✕ L'Absinthe: place G.-Perriot. ☎ 04-75-04-44-38. Open every day. An unpretentious snack bar on the village square offering a selection of grilled dishes, salads and *picodon*, the famous local goats' cheese, served warm.

☆☆–☆☆☆ Moderate to Chic

✕ Le Tisonnier: rue de la Fontaine, a tiny street almost opposite the tourist office. ☎ 04-75-04-44-03. Closed on Monday and Thursday. Two lunch menus, 100F and 180F. Owned by a former antique dealer, this restaurant has a charming atmosphere and decor. A collection of water jugs graces the little room at the back. The cheapest menu offers huge salads, grilled fresh sardines or lamb cutlets, cream cheese and reasaonable wine. It's best to book.

✕ Le Logis de l'Escalin: (*see* 'Where to Stay'). Cheapest weekday menu 120F, with salad fresh from the market, onion and anchovy tart, *millefeuille* with salt cod and other regional dishes, cheese and house dessert (warm tart with dried fruit and pine nuts). Other menus 160F to 305F. The dishes change with the seasons.

WHAT TO SEE

★ Next to the church, there's a little **botanical garden**, on the slopes of the hill.

SUZE-LA-ROUSSE (26790)   Population: 1,564

The village itself is of limited interest, but it's worth stopping for the chateau and the cooperative cellar, which sells the wines of the Coteaux du Tricastin. Leave any prejudices behind. These wines can offer very good value, combining quality with reasonable prices. The chateau stands surrounded by vines, with a lovely view of the neighbouring villages of Grignan, Chamaret, Rousset and Valréas, and of Mont Ventoux and the Dentelles de Montmirail in the distance.

WHERE TO STAY

☆☆ Moderate

☎ **Hôtel du Comte**: route de Bollène. ☎ 04-75-04-85-38. Fax: 04-75-04-85-37. ☟ Double rooms with bath, toilet and TV from 300F to 340F in the mini dungeon. Menus for 75F (lunch), 90F and 198F. This large Provençal farmhouse has luxury bathrooms and wood panelling. Some rooms have a terrace, with a view over the neighbouring vineyards, but the breakfast is rather disappointing.

☆☆☆ Chic

☎ **Ferme St-Michel**: on the D341, at Solérieux. ☎ 04-75-98-10-66. Restaurant closed on Sunday evening, Monday lunchtime, Tuesday lunchtime and from end December to end January. Double room for 360F. Regional menus at 130F and 180F, and a 'truffle discovery' menu for 260F. This little hotel, no longer a farm, is full of romantic charm. Most of the rooms have been tastefully redecorated and the two sitting rooms are just as pleasant. There's a quiet bar where you can relax and linger over a drink. The swimming pool could be better.

Bed and Breakfast

☎ **Domaine des Patras**: in Solérieux. ☎ 04-75-97-22-00. Fax: 04-75-97-22-01. Open from May to November. Double room for 400F, excluding breakfast. Advance booking and a 25 per cent deposit required. A pretty and imposing building with lovely rooms, which are reasonably priced, given their quality. The same is true for the brand-new studios. There's a swimming pool and the welcome is friendly. Horse riding can be arranged. No credit cards.

☎ **Mas de Champelon**: in the hamlet of St-Turquois. ☎ 04-75-98-81-95. Closed from 30 September to 4 April. Double rooms with shower and toilet for 260F, breakfast included. More friendly than the Domaine des Patras, this arc-shaped farmhouse is hidden from the road leading to Beaume-de-Transit. The terrace is lovely; stay and enjoy a dish of grilled meats.

Campsite

☎ **Camping du Lez**: near the bridge, on the road from St-Paul. ☎ and fax 04-75-98-82-83. Open from April to end September. 19F for each person and their vehicle, 20F for a tent and 14–16F for lighting. The view of the chateau, however, comes free of charge. There's a warm welcome and a swimming pool.

THE RHÔNE VALLEY AND HAUTE-PROVENCE

WHERE TO EAT

☆ Budget

✕ **Café du Cours**: in Rochegude, 5 kilometres (about 3 miles) to the south on the D117. Closed Monday and Tuesday evenings. Menus at 65F (weekday lunch) and 85F (dinner and at the weekend). This unpretentious and pleasant café is also a bar, tobacconist, newsagent and lottery ticket outlet, with tables in the shade of imposing plane trees.

☆☆ – ☆☆☆ Moderate to Chic

✕ **Restaurant les Buisses**: in St-Restitut (take the D59 and then the D218). ☎ 04-75-04-96-50. ✕ Closed Saturday lunch and Monday out of season. Just one menu, at 150F, and à la carte lunch for about 100F. This delightful and unpretentious restaurant (housed in a lovely country house surrounded by a pretty Provençal garden) serves good old-fashioned southern-style cooking, which you can enjoy on the terrace.

WHAT TO SEE

★ The **chateau** is the headquarters of the **université du Vin** (university of wine): open every day 9.30–11.30am and 2–5.30pm. Modest entrance fee. Guided tours possible. The building has a medieval-style frontage, while the courtyard is more Renaissance in style. In the past, it belonged to a succession of numerous wealthy families from the region, including the Baux d'Orange and the La Baume Suzes. In 1965, it was bought by the local council, who planned to establish the first wine university in the world. Today, lecturers from the universities of Aix, Grenoble, Besançon and Montpellier run courses here.

The old chapel has been converted into a tasting laboratory. Its air-conditioning system has an ozone diffuser to neutralize the odours and keep the temperature constant from the beginning to the end of the tasting. For the last few years, the Espace Médicis has housed the **Centre de Recherche et de Développement Oenoagronomique** (wine-growing research centre) where professionals attend deeply scientific courses on soil analysis and vine diseases. The extensive library (open to the public) has a collection of precious works and there are also weekend courses on individual *appellations* and other subjects relating to wine production. If your French is up to it, there's more information on ☎ 04-75-97-21-30.

In the garden, the university keeps a selection of grape varieties that are grown in France and elsewhere in the world, including *savagnin, carignan, mourvèdre, colombard, melon-de-bourgogne* and *poulsard*.

WHAT TO SEE IN THE AREA

★ **St-Restitut**: 8 kilometres (5 miles) away, via the D59 then the D218. The village has a pretty view and a lovely Romanesque church. As you come into the village from the south, follow the sign to the 'belvedere'; 3 kilometres (2 miles) further on, on the right, you will see great caverns in the hillside caused by stone quarrying. A little further on there are wine cellars in the quarries.

Board the little electric train (for a fee) to see millions of bottles and to find out more about the Côtes du Rhône.

★ **St-Paul-Trois-Châteaux**: on the D59, this little settlement has a lovely Romanesque church from the 12th century, as well as the Maison de la Truffe et du Tricastin (centre of the truffle and the Tricastin). ☎ 04-75-96-61-29. Open every day except Monday and public holidays.

★ **Clansayes**: take the D59 then the D71 and the D481. Alternatively, coming from St-Paul, it's 5 kilometres (3 miles) on the D133. Come here more for the amazing panoramic view of the Tricastin than for the village itself.

L'ENCLAVE DES PAPES

This administrative oddity ('The Enclave of the Popes') is managed by the Vaucluse but is actually in the department of the Drôme.

VALRÉAS

Perched on a hilltop, and still overlooked by its huge 12th-century keep, this little town has delightful old quarters, the wonderful Romanesque church of Notre-Dame-de-Nazareth, with its Gothic portal, and the Chateau de Simiane, a 17th and 18th-century building that now houses the town hall.

🄱 **Tourist office**: ☎ and fax: 04-90-35-04-71. Open Monday to Saturday 9.15am–12.15pm and 2–6pm.

WHAT TO SEE

★ **Musée du Cartonnage et de l'Imprimerie** (packaging and printing museum): 3 avenue du Maréchal-Foch, Valréas. ☎ 04-90-35-58-75. Fax: 04 90 37 42 60. ♿ to the permanent exhibition room on the ground floor. Between 1 April and 31 October, open every day (except Tuesday and Sunday morning) 10am–noon and 3–6pm. Entrance fee: 20F (concessions for students and over-60s; free for under-12s). The museum has a reconstruction of a workshop of the packaging industry, which was at its height at the beginning of the 20th century. They used to make special boxes with air holes, some attractively decorated, for the safe mailing of silkworm grubs. There's also a shop and a bookshop.

WHERE TO EAT

✗ **La ferme Champ-Rond**: chemin des Anthelmes. ☎ 04-90-37-31-68. Take the Nyons road out of Valréas, turn right towards Orange-Bollène, then turn right at the school, and take the first little road on the left (signposted). Closed on Sunday evening and on Monday out of season and from 15 January to 30 March. Menus from 68F (weekday lunch) to 98F. This substantial building in the middle of the countryside has a dining room that is rather 70s in style, but offers a very friendly welcome, simple but good cooking and wines from neighbouring vineyards.

THE RHÔNE VALLEY AND HAUTE-PROVENCE

FESTIVALS AND EVENTS

– **Night of Petit St-Jean**: the Feast of St-Jean has been celebrated here on 23 June since 1504. A five-year-old boy representing the little St John, the king of the year, is crowned with great pomp and ceremony, and then leads a procession of about 400 people in period costume through the town.

WHAT TO SEE IN THE AREA

ROUSSET-LES-VIGNES

Back in the Drôme, this village nestles on a hillside just off the Valréas-Nyons road. With its small chateau, its delightful church with belfry and its priory, which has a pretty Renaissance facade, the whole settlement is officially listed as being of historic interest.

The friendly *cave* in the main street offers tastings of good local Côtes-du-Rhône wines. Open 15 June to 15 September 9am–noon and 3–7pm. Although this is red-wine country, they also have some surprisingly good whites.

✗ **Au Charbonelon**: rue Principale, 26770 Rousset-les-Vignes (take the Nyons exit). ☎ 04-75-27-91-61. Closed on Monday and Tuesday and from December to February. Menus for 90F (except on Saturday evening and Sunday) and 135F. The owners have renovated this house and opened a restaurant with just one intimate dining room. The menu changes with the seasons and includes delicious tarts. It's good value for money.

GRILLON

Just 4 kilometres (2.5 miles) from Valréas. The Valle *quartier*, a typical feudal settlement, was on the verge of ruin but has been brought back to life by an architect. The mix of resolutely contemporary architecture, using glass and metal, and the old stones works surprisingly well.

RICHERENCHES

Richerenches is 7 kilometres (4.5 miles) from Valréas. The old part of this settlement remains within the walls of a command post of the Knights' Templars, established in 1136 (the first in Provence). Here, they were responsible for equipping the soldier-monks with everything they might need, including their horses, which had to be robust enough to withstand the long journey to Jerusalem. Richerenches is an important truffle centre, with a truffle market every Saturday from 10am to noon, when all sorts of shady deals are done from car boots. There's a truffle Mass on the third Sunday in January, when the collection baskets are filled with truffles, rather than coins.

WHERE TO STAY

♠ ✗ **Chambres d'hôte, Ferme de la Commanderie Hugues de Bourbouton** (B&B): in the Bourbouton district. ☎ 04-90-28-02-29. Fax: 04-90-28-04-45. Open all year. Double rooms with bath and toilet from 420F to 500F, including breakfast. Dinner with the hosts costs 150F, all-inclusive; book ahead. This 15th-century stone house has been transformed from crumbling ruins and now has three charming and spacious bedrooms and a small apartment with a kitchen. The food is Provençal, using fresh produce and the wines come from neighbouring vineyards. Separate from the house, four little wooden huts (more Nordic than Provençal) can be rented by the night or the week.

The Alpes-de-Haute-Provence

Once upon a time, there was a region called the Basses-Alpes, but officialdom decided that the 'lower Alps' would be known by the more evocative name of the 'Alps of Upper Provence'.

According to climatologists working at the observatory on the Plateau de Forcalquier, the skies of the Alpes-de-Haute-Provence are the clearest in Europe. The extraordinary quality of the air has much to do with the winds that blow around the region, before swirling up and around the mountain ranges in their path, but can also be explained by the absence of any large towns. Manosque, with a population of 20,000, is the largest town, while Digne-les-Bains has a population of just 16,000.

The colours of the countryside and the clear light create dazzlingly beautiful scenes, with gold-tinged church belfries, vast green oak forests, and tropically turquoise lakes. The variations in landscape through the region are remarkable. From the high mountains near Barcelonnette, via the deep-cut valleys of the vertiginous Verdon gorges, to the lavender fields on the Valensole plateau towards the Luberon, there's a seemingly limitless selection of photogenic views. And this alpine region is also one of the best places to experience authentic Provençal traditions, which continue to be upheld by its people.

The Alpes-de-Haute-Provence region has long been considered as the poor relation of the Provence-Alpes-Côte d'Azur, but visitors to France are at last beginning to see it for what it is – a hidden corner of paradise for walkers, skiers and foodies.

USEFUL ADDRESSES

◘ Maison des Alpes-de-Haute-Provence (departmental tourist office): 19 rue du Docteur-Honorat, 04005 Digne-les-Bains. ☎ 04-92-31-57-29. Fax: 04-92-32-24-94.

■ Gîtes de France des Alpes-de-Haute-Provence (country cottages): rond-point du 11-Novembre, 04000 Digne. ☎ 04-92-31-52-39. Fax: 04-92-32-32-63.

DIGNE-LES-BAINS (04000)   Population: 16,064

Digne is a spa town surrounded by magnificent mountains. It stands on the route Napoléon, at the confluence of three valleys, and its beneficial waters have always played a large part in the life of the town, drawing rheumatism sufferers for many years.

The first settlement of Dignes grew up in a district of the present-day town. In the 13th century, fortifications were thrown up to protect it from bandits and highwaymen. Far from the main routes of communication, in a remote, enclosed location, Digne only came into its own when Napoleon passed through in 1815 during his attempt to recapture power. Before his arrival, an epidemic of plague that decimated the population was the only event to mark the quiet town's history.

After Napoleon, Digne's most famous visitor was the adventurous Alexandra David-Néel, a *routard* (traveller) before her time, who is remembered today in the museum that bears her name.

USEFUL ADDRESS

🛈 Tourist office: le rond-point, place Tampinet, 04001 Digne. ☎ 04-92-36-62-62. Fax: 04-92-32-27-24. Email: info@ot.dignelesbains.fr. In summer, open Monday to Saturday 8.45am–12.30pm and 2–6.30pm; on Sunday and public holidays 9.30am–12.30pm and 3–6pm. In winter, open from Monday to Saturday 8.45am–noon and 2–6pm; on Sunday and public holidays 10am–noon.

WHERE TO STAY AND EAT

☆☆ Moderate

🛏 ✕ Hôtel du Petit-St-Jean: 14 cours Arès. ☎ 04-92-31-30-04. Fax: 04-92-36-05-80. Closed from 25 December to early January. Single rooms from 150F to 260F. Menus from 60F to 150F. This is like staying with your grandmother, sleeping in a cosy bed in an old-fashioned room, in a warm ambience. The hotel is in a small building on one corner of place Charles-de-Gaulle, and the carefully prepared meals include rabbit with baby onions, pork or beef stew and *aïoli* (on Friday). Private garage.

🛏 ✕ L'Origan: 6 rue Pied-de-Ville. ☎ and fax: 04-92-31-62-13. ♨ Closed on Sunday, for two weeks in February and during the Christmas holidays. Double rooms with shower from 140F. Menus from 118F to 215F. The name means 'oregano'. It may be used in every dish, but like thyme and marjoram, it's one of the quintessential flavours of Provence and an intrinsic part of *aïoli*, *pieds paquets* (tripe and trotters) and *veau farci* (stuffed veal).

🛏 Hôtel de Provence: 17 boulevard Thiers. In the town centre.

☎ 04-92-31-12-19. Fax: 04-92-31-48-39. Open throughout the year. Rooms from 270F to 320F. You wouldn't necessarily spend your whole holidays or your honeymoon at this pleasant provincial establishment (although they do have a honeymoon suite), but it is clean and friendly.

🛏 Hôtel Central: 26 boulevard Gassendi. ☎ 04-92-31-31-91. Fax: 04-92-31-49-78. Closed 2–4pm. Double rooms 150F with wash-basin, 195F with shower, and 260F with shower, toilet and TV. The entrance to this hotel is a bit impersonal – you swipe a card to gain access at night. Choose the rooms overlooking the pedestrianized street rather than the boulevard, which can be noisy early in the morning.

✕ Hôtel de Bourgogne: 3 avenue de Verdun. ☎ 04-92-31-00-19. Fax: 04-92-32-30-59. Closed from mid-December to mid-February. Rooms from 180F to 270F. Menus from 90F to 250F. The rooms are not the best feature of this hotel, but the restaurant is a real highlight. The food is thoughtfully prepared, the tables are stylishly decorated and the view is panoramic. Try the *filets de rouget*

Key to place names

Manosque   Places covered in guide
Valensole   Addresses and places
             in the area
Comps   Locator only

THE ALPES-DE-
HAUTE-PROVENCE

THE ALPES-DE-HAUTE-PROVENCE

fine ratatouille et tapenade (red mullet fillets with ratatouille and olive paste) or *friand d'agneau aux senteurs de Provence* (fried lamb with flavours of Provence). Secure car park.

≜ Chambre d'hôte Les Oliviers: route des Fonts-Gaubert. ☎ 04-92-31-36-04. Closed from early November to end March. Single rooms with shower and toilet cost 230F. This farm just outside Digne also has a *gîte* and a campsite. Rural and quiet except on July evenings, during the local festival.

✕ La Chauvinière: 56 rue de l'Hubac. In the pedestrian zone. ☎ 04-92-31-40-03. Closed Sunday evening, Monday (except in summer) and in January. Menus at 70F (weekday lunch), 95F and 115F. The dining room seems a little gloomy after a day out in the sun, but it's made brighter by pretty Provençal fabrics and a pleasant, cool terrace on which to enjoy the local cuisine. There's a veranda, too.

☆☆☆ Chic

≜ ✕ Hôtel du Grand Paris: 19 bd Thiers. ☎ 04-92-31-11-15. Fax: 04-92-32-32-82. Email: GrandParis@wanadoo.fr. Closed from 1 December to 1 March. Double rooms from 430F to 680F. Menus from 150F at lunchtime. À la carte around 210F. After the last inhabitants of the convent left, this 17th-century building became an excellent hotel. The rooms are lovely, comfortable and very prettily decorated, although the welcome is slightly formal. The chef produces tried and tested classics interpreted with individuality. The cuisine is fresh and flavourful (although rather pricey).

≜ Hôtel et Pension Villa Gaïa: on the route de Nice. ☎ 04-92-31-21-

60. Fax: 04-92-31-20-12. Closed from 1 November to 1 April. Lovely rooms from 490F, with breakfast at 55F and half board (compulsory in July and August) at 440F. Menu for 150F. This quiet hotel is out in the countryside. There's one sitting for dinner, and the one menu features regional dishes based on local and seasonal produce. Guests eat in the library, in the sitting room or on the terrace. Francophile film buffs will be reminded of *Monsieur Hulot's Holiday*. Magnificent breakfasts are served wherever you choose. The luxurious *pension* has 12 rooms on the ground floor, each with a terrace, and there are more upstairs, all tastefully decorated. This is a nice spot for a relaxing stay.

Campsites

≜ Campsite Notre-Dame-du-Bourg: 1.5 kilometres out of town, on the road to Barcelonnette. ☎ and fax: 04-92-31-04-97. Open from April to the end of October. 65F for a pitch for two plus tent. This clean and pleasant site on the banks of the river has 120 pitches, as well as a mobile home for rent and tennis courts.

≜ Campsite des Eaux-Chaudes: 2 kilometres from the centre, on the way to the spa. ☎ 04-92-32-31-04. Fax: 04-92-31-04-87. ⚒ Open from April to the end of October. Fairly new three-star site with 146 pitches and mobile homes. Package price of 75F for two.

Gîte d'étape

≜ Château des Siéyes: avenue Georges-Pompidou. ☎ 04-92-31-20-30 or 04-92-31-42-73. Fax: 04-92-31-27-24. 65F per night in a 22-bed dormitory.

THE ALPES-DE-HAUTE-PROVENCE

WHAT TO SEE

★ **The site**: when you arrive at Digne, you have a beautiful view of the fortified village against a background of rocks and mountains.

★ **Viewpoint**: in the park next to the bridge over the Bléone, a branch of the Durance.

★ **Old town**: the **cathedral** in the old part of the town is one of the most beautiful Romanesque churches in Provence. It features in Victor Hugo's *Les Misérables*, when Jean Valjean steals the bishop's silver after being received by him. The saintly bishop saves him from the police and helps him out. Recent excavations have unearthed the foundations of the first churches, built in the sixth and 11th centuries. Inside, among the remnants of 14th-century mural paintings, you can make out a *Last Judgement*, an *Annunciation* and a *Crucifixion*.

★ **Musée Alexandra David-Néel**: on the road for Nice, 27 avenue du Maréchal-Juin. ☎ 04-92-31-32-38. 90-minute visits every day at 10.30am, 2pm and 4pm; in summer at 10.30am, 2pm, 3.30pm and 7pm. Website: www.alexandra-david-neel.org. Free entry. Some of the tours are led by Madame Peyronnet, who acted as secretary to Alexandra David-Néel during the last 10 years of her life.

The unusual Alexandra was born in 1868 to a Huguenot father and a Catholic mother. Full of curiosity, she left home at a very young age and travelled to Spain by bicycle. After studying Oriental languages and music she went, at the age of 23, to India, which fascinated her. She married an understanding man, who agreed that she could leave on an 18-month trip the day after their wedding. In fact, she stayed away for 14 years; unsurprisingly, he proved to be unfaithful. Alexandra covered thousands of kilometres: she crossed Tibet on foot, became the first European woman to gain access to the forbidden city of Lhasa, where she lived for two months, and met Gandhi and Sri Aurobindo, among other important figures.

Alexandra had fallen in love with Provence and chose Digne as the place to build her retreat, which she called 'Samten Dzong'. At the age of 69, she went again to the Far East and to China, before returning to Digne aged 80 to write numerous books. She renewed her passport at the ripe old age of 100, keen to return to Tibet, but she died in Digne aged 101, on 8 September 1969. Her ashes were scattered on the waters of the Ganges.

★ **Musée municipal**: 64 boulevard Gassendi. ☎ 04-92-31-45-29. Housed in a 16th-century hospice, the municipal museum has some archaeological remains (there are quite a few in the region), as well as a collection of 16th- and 17th-century Italian pictures and others by Provençal painters from the 19th century.

SHOPPING

🔒 **Pâtisserie-confiserie Bardot**: 47 boulevard Gassendi. Bardot's delicious bread is perfect for your picnic and they also make a memorable lavender ice-cream, honey and lavender sweets and 'chocolate ammonites' (the only ones you should bring back from Digne).

WHAT TO DO

★ **Thermes de Digne-les-Bains**: vallon des Sources. ☎ 04-92-32-32-92. Health cures cost around 1,280F and include all sorts of treatments, from mud baths to ice-cold showers to whip up the circulation, offered here by young staff. The trial rate (120F) allows you to try the spa bath and steam room. Aromatherapy treatments are also available; the use of lavender oils seems appropriate in this area.

WHAT TO SEE IN THE AREA

★ **Parc rural de Haute Provence** (country park): in Champtercier, 5 kilometres (3 miles) along the RN85. ☎ 04-92-31-90-80. Open at the weekend in spring and autumn and every day in July and August. Entrance fee: adults 20F (concessions 15F, under-10s free). This privately owned country park has been developed around a *mas*, or old farmhouse, surrounded by abandoned agricultural land. The sheep pen, distillery, chapel, *pigeonnier* and oil mill all give visitors the chance to find out more about the rural culture of the region. The attractive *auberge* offers good, reasonably priced food, and is very quiet in the week, but the welcome is rather starchy. Near by, the **Chocolaterie Darroman** sells sweet treats. ☎ 04-92-31-93-47.

★ **Réserve géologique** (geological reserve): 2 kilometres from the centre of town along the D100. Open Monday to Friday, 9am–noon and 2–5.30pm (4.30pm Friday); same opening hours at the weekend too, from 1 April to 31 October. ☎ 04-92-36-70-70. Entrance fee: 25F (children 15F). There is a wealth of geological and fossil sites in the region and the geological centre, set up in 1979, organizes courses and discovery trails. It also offers the chance to see the famous Stars of St-Vincent. These five-pointed fossils, collected in the past by children, are millions of years old and are the remains of echinoderms (the sea urchin family). Today, they are protected and touching them is forbidden. In the 19th century, the dark little stars, measuring less than a centimetre across, were set in gold or silver jewellery; such pieces may still be found at Turries-Commeiras, the jeweller on the boulevard Cassendi.

Excursions from Digne-les-Bains

FROM DIGNE TO BARLES

★ **Geology**: take the D900 north to Barles, to see the history of the region encrusted in the earth. There are nearly 500 fossils in the stone of the *dalle aux ammonites* (ammonite path), little cephalopods that date back 65 million years. Further along you can see fossilized birds'-claw prints in the sand, where the creatures walked 30 million years ago.

The winding road carries on through a red-earthed landscape before arriving at the Clue du Péroué, then the famous Clue de Barles, with its sheer drop down to the clear-flowing river at the bottom.

★ **Barles**: reached via the D900 then the D900 A, the village of Barles stands at an altitude of 1,000 metres (3,280 feet) and marks the first frontier between Provence and the Alps. The architecture is suddenly more Alpine. The houses are more sturdy, lower and more angular and the roofs are covered in slate tiles, providing protection from the cold.

– Taking the D900 back towards Digne, turn left on to the D107 to get to **Prads**.

WHERE TO EAT

✕ **L'Auberge des Trois Évêchés**: in Prads-Haut-Bléone, 04420. ☎ 04-92-34-92-42. Fax: 04-92-32-21-83. Closed from 1 October to 30 March. Menus at 100F and 120F. This inn stands at the very end of the road in a quiet, contemplative little village. M. Bartolini is in charge in the kitchen and serves excellent food, including *pieds-paquets* (lambs' tripe and trotters), *blanquette de chevreau au vin rouge* (kid with red-wine sauce) and *caille aux pruneaux* (quail with prunes). The tasty, simple dishes are served in a relaxed and friendly atmosphere.

★ **Marcoux**: 6 kilometres (4 miles) north of Digne. A pleasant village with a late Romanesque church and a very fine 17th-century carved wooden altar.

FROM DIGNE TO RIEZ

The road from Digne to Riez is pretty, with beautiful views towards Châteauredon and then of Riez itself. At the fork where the road goes right to Riez, the N85 carries straight on to the Clue de Chabrières, where the scenery is impressively wild. The views from the top of the rise on the way to Riez are really lovely, then the road goes back through lavender fields. Even though you have to double back on yourself, it's worth it, because the scenery is beautiful and completely different in each direction.

WHERE TO STAY AND EAT

🛏 ✕ **Hôtel-restaurant Les Lavandes**: in Châteauredon, RN85, 04270. ☎ 04-92-35-52-80. Open all year (except for Tuesday evening and all day Wednesday out of season and from 1 January to 31 March). Rooms with washbasin for 120F, or 160F with shower. Half board compulsory in July and August. Menus from 50F (lunch) to 128F, offering *pieds-paquets à la provençale* (tripe and trotters) and wood-fired pizzas at the weekend. There's a pretty, flowery terrace.

🛏 ✕ **Le Relais de Chabrières**: RN85 in Chabrières (04270). ☎ 04-92-35-54-04. Closed from end November to 15 January and on Tuesday evening and all day Wednesday between September and May. Rooms from 120F to 250F. Menus from 59F to 120F. This hotel, in a 19th-century posthouse on the route Napoléon in the Vallée de l'Asse, is a real find, with a friendly atmosphere and home cooking.

Campsite

🛏 **La Célestine**: on route de Riez. ☎ 04-92-35-52-54. Open from 15 April to 15 September. Swimming pool.

FROM DIGNE TO ENTREVAUX ON THE TRAIN DES PIGNES

A trip on the 'Pine-Cone Train', which winds at a sedate pace along a tortuous track from Digne to Nice, is a delight. Apparently, it got its name because it used to go so slowly that passengers could get off the train and collect pine cones (*pignes*) and get back on without being left behind. Even if you don't have time to go all the way, the section from Digne to Entrevaux takes you just to the edge of the Var, through amazing landscapes, across rivers, alongside foaming mountain streams, and stops in peaceful villages for a quiet drink.

Alphonse Beau de Rochas from Digne, inventor of the four-speed motor, was the first, in 1861, to dream of connecting Nice (annexed by France in the previous year) to the hinterland by train. The first section of track from Digne to Mézel was opened in 1891 but the Nice to Digne link was not opened until 1911. The first passengers were thrilled as the train passed through 25 tunnels, over 16 viaducts and 15 steel bridges along its 150-kilometre (95-mile) route.

A steam Train des Pignes runs from Puget through Théniers to Annot from May to October. The line is now run by the Société des Chemins de Fer de Provence, which provides four return services a day between Digne and Nice, stopping at about 15 stations along the way. Walkers can get off every three or five kilometres, at points marked by signs alongside the track.

– **Gare des Chemins de Fer de Provence de Digne** (Digne train station): avenue Pierre Sémard. ☎ 04-92-31-01-58.

★ **Barrême**: apparently, this little village gave its name to the Lower Cretaceous – the Barremian period.

WHERE TO EAT

✗ **Domaine d'Aiguines**: in St-Jacques (3km/2 miles from Barrême). 800 metres beyond the village. Follow the signs marked *foie gras*. ☎ 04-92-34-25-72. Open all year, reservations only. Menus from 95F to 155F. This 17th-century farm has been turned into a temple to *foie gras*, but there are plenty of other delights, too, including duck served with delicious potatoes.

WHAT TO SEE IN THE AREA

★ **Cathédral de Senez**: 5 kilometres (3 miles) from Barrême. It's a bit of surprise to find such an imposing cathedral so close to this tiny village. In fact, the village was the seat of a bishop from the sixth to the 17th century. The cathedral, of majestic proportions, is a fine example of unadorned architecture. Inside, there are eight Aubusson tapestries from the end of the 17th century depicting Old Testament scenes, a retable dating from 1679 and some fine, carved choir stalls from the same period.

ST-ANDRÉ-LES-ALPES

Some of the shopfronts in this unspoiled and authentic mountain village haven't been altered for decades.

USEFUL ADDRESS

B Tourist office: place Marcel-Pastorelli. ☎ 04-92-89-02-39. Fax: 04-92-89-19-23. Open in summer from Monday to Saturday, 8.30am–1pm and 2.30–7pm and Sunday morning 9am–noon. In winter, Monday to Friday 9am–noon and 2–5pm. Otherwise, try the town hall (☎ 04-92-89-02-04).

WHERE TO STAY AND EAT

✗ **La Table de Marie**: place Charles Bron. ☎ 04-92-89-16-30. Closed in winter and on Wednesday and Thursday out of season. Daily specials from 55F to 65F. The food is served in the room where the locals used to come to fetch their milk, now redecorated in contemporary colours. Choose from a large selection of salads, fresh pasta, grilled meat and good local *charcuterie*.

â **Camping Municipal Les Iscles**: 1 kilometre along the N202 towards Annot, on the left. ☎ 04-92-89-02-29. Open from 1 May to 30 September. 23F per night for adults. The municipal campsite is well located, close to the River Verdon and to an artificial lake. It's peaceful and shady, with tennis courts and mini-golf near by. Facilities include a laundry and ironing area. Often full in summer.

â **Chambres d'hôte with Raymonde and Georges Neveu** (B&B): in Angles, 8 kilometres (5 miles) from St-André on the N202 and the D33. ☎ 04-92-89-03-39. 236F for two, including breakfast. The last house in this village in the Vallée du Verdon, at an altitude of 1,000 metres (3,280 feet), has two pleasant rooms with private bathrooms and TV. The 'Surcouf' has a raised bed and decor on a marine theme. Food isn't served but each room has an equipped kitchenette.

ANNOT

Annot's finest hour came at the end of the 14th century, when Provence lost control of the county of Nice. Located near the border, the town was chosen as a base for a garrison and became a trading centre between Provence, the county of Nice and Piedmont, with a weekly market and a free trade fair. In the 18th century, the wool industry became very important, but Annot also had factories making roof tiles, millinery firms and distilleries for the extraction of essential oils from lavender. Three mills in the region produced about 30,000 litres (6,600 gallons) of nut oil a year. The decline in oil production began around 1870 and by 1890 it had ceased altogether.

With its considerable attractions, Annot now provides a quiet spot for rural holidays. Standing at an altitude of 705 metres (2,313 feet), the town is part-Provençal and part-Alpine, so it has a cool climate and plenty of walking routes in beautiful mountain scenery. In summer, the valley is full of lavender and limeflower blossom. The town is encircled by the famous *grès d'Annot* (a sandstone), which has been eroded into bizarre shapes. At the entrance of the village, a number of houses are built right into the rock.

The old village has lots of character, with winding streets, vaulted passages, mismatched stones, and 16th- and 17th-century houses with lintels over the doors, engraved with coats of arms. Climb up to the church along the Grand-Rue, passing through the fortified gate. The pillars and paving are made out of *grès d'Annot*. The Romanesque church is flanked by 15th-century buildings and has an apse with a crenellated tower and a pretty Renaissance belfry.

USEFUL ADDRESSES

🛈 **Tourist office**: boulevard St-Pierre. ☎ 04-92-83-23-03. Fax: 04-92-83-32-82. Organizes the renting of rural *gîtes*, and gives information on sports facilities. In summer, open every day except Sunday afternoon, 10am–noon and 3–6pm; out of season, open from Tuesday to Saturday, 9.30am–noon and 3–5.30pm, Sunday 10am–noon.

WHERE TO STAY AND EAT

🛏 ✕ **Hôtel de l'Avenue**: avenue de la Gare. ☎ 04-92-83-22-07. Fax: 04-92-83-33-13. Closed 1 November to 1 April. Rooms from 260F to 400F. Menus at 90 and 150F. Half board compulsory in July and August. The style here tells you that you're halfway between Provence and the Alps – the hotel may have been built to resist the cold but the cooking is definitely Provençal! The 11 lovely rooms have been thoughtfully decorated; some have ceiling fans. In the restaurant the rather impersonal decor contrasts with the delicious food. Try the *tartelette fine de rouget* (red-mullet tart) or *jarret de veau braisé aux épices* (calf's knuckle braised with spices).

🛏 ✕ **Hôtel du Parc**: place du Germe. ☎ 04-92-83-20-03. Fax: 04-92-83-29-84. Open from May to September. Double rooms from 210F to 250F. Delicious menus from 75F to 232F. This old house has a view over the huge place des Platanes and a garden, but somehow lacks that little something to make it really special. Dishes include frogs' legs *à la Provençale* and sea bass with sorrel. Traditional and predictable.

🛏 ✕ **Hôtel-restaurant Beauséjour**: place du Revely. ☎ 04-92-83-21-08. Fax: 04-92-83-39-67. Closed on Friday evening and in December. Rooms with shower and toilet for 220F. Menus from 68F to 118F. A friendly place with a family atmosphere, serving famished walkers with robust mountain dishes, such as local *charcuterie* and pan-fried *andouillette* (chitterlings) with mustard. Very good value for money, with a buffet on Sundays and public holidays. There's a terrace for good weather.

🛏 ✕ **Chalet de Roncharel**: run by Denise and Bernard Audibert. ☎ 04-92-83-35-35. Website: www.annot. com. Reservations preferred. *Nuit rando* (walkers' accommodation) costs 90F per night; half board 195F. The *assiette rando* (walkers' dish of the day) costs 50F. Other meals around 100F. This *gîte* at an altitude of 1,471 metres (4,825 feet) offers three-, four- or five-bed rooms, books, *boules*, a local guide and a donkey to ride.

🛏 ✕ **Gîte St-Pierre**: place de la Mairie, Le Fugeret. ☎ 04-92-83-34-36. Closed on Tuesday in low season. 75F per night. Menu for 69F.

Half board 155F. 5 kilometres (about 3 miles) from Annot, just as you get to the peaceful village of Le Fugeret, typical of the Alpes-de-Haute-Provence. A pleasant place to stay either in winter or summer, with seasonal dishes and a nice view of the village square.

Campsites

⚐ ✕ **Campsite La Ribière**: by the river (hence its name, which means 'river' in local patois) in a rural setting, on the D902 in the direction of La Foux-d'Allos. ☎ 04-92-83-21-44. Open from March to end November. This site, run partly by a private owner and partly by local government, has unbeatable prices and a dynamic and knowledgeable manager, who gives all sorts of advice about places to explore. Free hot water for washing up and laundry, free table tennis (bring your own bat), caravans for hire and farm produce for sale. The friendly little restaurant (around 70F) is open to campers every evening in summer, at lunchtime and in the evening at the weekend, and during the weekend only out of season. It serves omelettes, fresh fish and a house speciality of *pastissoun*, a traditional pâté made from chicken livers marinated in brandy and chestnuts, flavoured with juniper and bay leaves.

⚐ ✕ **Camping à la Ferme** (farm camping): La Rouï, before reaching the village of Le Fugeret, 5 kilometres (3 miles) to the north on the D908, on the road for Argenton. ☎ and fax: 04-92-83-25-90. *Table d'hôte* available at 80F, including drinks, throughout the year (booking essential). Furnished studios for four people also available for rent.

FESTIVALS

– **La St-Fortunat**: from Saturday to the Tuesday of Whit weekend, this village festival involves displays in Empire costume and a brass band.

– **Fête Provençale**: on the last Sunday in June, a traditional festival with a market, a parade and dancing in Provençal costume.

– **National Folklore Festival**: in mid-July.

WALKS

– **Chambre du Roi** ('The King's Room'): take the signposted trail behind the station, which climbs up to 1,000 metres (3,280 feet). At the top, there's a rock formation and, on the right, a vast cavern hollowed out of the rock called the 'Chambre du Roi'. After arriving here, you can retrace your steps straight away. Alternatively, you can carry on for a superb 3-hour walk via the Balcon, a cliff path that offers a fantastic 360 view, the natural sandstone archways known as Les Portettes, the scrub and undergrowth of Les Espaluns, and the chapel of Notre-Dame-de-Vers-la-Ville.

– **Argenton**: take the path from the church, which climbs up to 1,315 metres (4,314 feet). Follow the yellow and red markings. For the whole walk, allow about 5 hours 30 minutes.

– **Le Baou de Parou**: to reach this enormous rock overlooking Annot, take the path that leaves from the church, and turns left after the viaduct.

– **River Vaïre**: to walk along the banks of the river, cross over the water from the place des Platanes, then turn right. The path leads to the very pretty Chapelle de Verimande, built by the Knights Templar.

EXCURSIONS BY CAR

Annot is a good base for many superb excursions by car. The road that runs alongside the River Vaïre goes through the village of **Le Fugeret**, with its old bridge and fountain, offers a fantastic view of the old village of **Méailles**, dominating the bare rocks, and continues up to the cross-country skiing resort of **La Colle St-Michel**. On the way down, it passes through **Thorame-Haute**, where there's a station on the Nice to Digne train line (*see* page 352), in a rather austere but extremely beautiful location.

WHERE TO STAY AND EAT

≜ ✗ **Hôtel-restaurant de la Gare**: route du col d'Allos, 04170 Thorame-Haute. ☎ 04-92-89-02-54. Fax: 04-92-89-11-74. Closed 1 November to 1 May. Rooms from 270F to 300F. Menus at 70F and 148F. If you miss the last train, or your car breaks down, this hotel will be very welcome. It has a view over the valley, a garden and offers good home cooking, including their own ravioli.

≜ ✗ **Auberge L'Oustalet**: 04170 La-Colle-St-Michel. ☎ 04-92-83-23-80. Closed on Wednesday and from 15 November to 15 December. Rooms from 150F to 200F; half board 200–230F per person. Menus from 45F to 100F. Until recently this was a working farm and guests are still greeted by dogs, chickens and geese. The refurbishment isn't great and decoration in the six rooms is dire, but they are quiet. The owners will pick you up at the station. The food is fine, with simple local dishes – *poule au pot* (chicken casserole), *daube* (beef stew with wine), dishes *au gratin* and homemade soups – served in generous portions.

ENTREVAUX

Entrevaux has an extraordinary fortified square, dominated by a citadel perched high above. For quite a time, the town – on the old frontier of the States of the House of Savoy – played a significant strategic role. Legendary military engineer Vauban improved its fortifications in 1692 and 1706. The town is far enough from the big tourist centres of the coast to have escaped aggressive restoration. The cracked stone facades and a certain atmosphere of abandonment contribute to the sense of history.

Wander into the old town across the drawbridge and drift about in the dark streets, admiring the tall, picturesque houses. The place de la Mairie is beautiful. The church, which used to be a cathedral, is oddly integrated into the fortifications and one of its walls serves as a part of the ramparts. The interior is a masterpiece of baroque and Classical decoration. The sumptuous main altar is one of the finest in the region and there are superb choir stalls in carved walnut wood.

Taking the splendid fortified pathway, it will take you about 30 minutes to get up to the citadel. From the top, there is an extremely beautiful view of the town and of the Var valley.

Entrevaux is known for a delicious food speciality called *secca*. One of the muscles from a cow's hindquarters, the *rond de gîte*, is pared, the fat is removed, then the piece of meat is salted. It is dried very slowly, over 90 days, and ends up as a very delicate, low-calorie delicacy. It may be served very finely sliced with a drizzle of olive oil, a squeeze of lemon juice and parmesan shavings, with toasted croutons, with hot goat's cheese, or with a salad of green leaves or tomato and mozzarella slices.

USEFUL ADDRESS

🛈 **Tourist information**: at the entrance to the old town (the tower on the left of the drawbridge). ☎ 04-93-05-46-73. Open 9am–noon and 2–6pm during the week, and every day in high season.

WHERE TO STAY

🛏 **Gîte rural municipal**: Reservations: ☎ 04-93-05-46-73. Check opening times because of continuing renovation work.

🛏 **Chambres d'hôte**: Le Plan (2 kilometres). ☎ 04-93-05-42-92. Open from 1 April to 11 November. Two rooms for 290F. Both are quiet, sunny and located in a separate wing of the house. The owner has plenty of information about local olive oil and truffle oak trees. The breakfasts are huge, with speciality breads, homemade jam and locally made products, including some from Le Pain d'Épices, rue du Marché, Entrevaux.

WHAT TO SEE

★ **Musée de la Moto** (motorbike museum): follow the signs from the place St-Martin.

★ **Ramparts**: visits from 2–5.30pm, leaving from the reception office, just after the drawbridge.

★ **Citadel**: a dozen zig-zagging ramps lead up to the old castle. The path was commissioned by Vauban and took 50 years to build. Inside the citadel there are three barracks, a bakery and the commandant's house. The building is in a poor state of repair but the view from the top is simply fabulous. From a position 150 metres (500 feet) above the Var, you can see the Alpes-de-Haute-Provence, the Var valley, and so on.

WHAT TO SEE IN THE AREA

★ **Gorges du Cians**: the landscape around the gorges is impressive, though the road, dug out of the rock, is pretty poor. On one side are the red rock faces, and on the other pine forests. Waterfalls cascade in torrents from the mountain and sometimes the rocks join together to form a sort of vault. The narrowest passages are called *petites clues* or *grandes clues*. The road rejoins the main road near Touët-sur-Var. Approaching the Côte-d'Azur through the back country behind Nice, either by train or car, is a lovely way to get to the coast.

FESTIVAL

Journées Médiévales (medieval days): every year in early August, the local villagers put on traditional local costume and bring the past back to life, with street performances and stalls, plays and troubadours.

TO THE VAL D'ALLOS AND THROUGH THE HAUT VERDON

If you get off the Train des Pignes at St-André-Les-Alpes and travel on by car, you'll notice how, in just a few kilometres, the temperature drops and the landscape changes. This is the harder and colder world of the mountains. In winter, snowfalls can be very heavy and skiing is possible. The scenery from here to the edge of the Mercantour national park is majestic and memorable.

BEAUVEZER

This agreeable village was completely burned down in 1728. The region's last factory manufacturing bed linen closed down here in 1962.

USEFUL ADDRESSES

🅱 **Maison du Tourisme du Haut Verdon Val d'Allos** (tourist office of the Haut Verdon Val d'Allos): on the edge of Beauvezer. ☎ 04-92-83-43-43. Fax: 04-92-83-59-20. Email: verdon@club-internet. Open Monday to Friday 9am–noon and 2–5pm. On Saturday and Sunday, information is available by telephone only. This efficient office has many useful leaflets on walks, ski resorts and the Mercantour park.

■ **Maison des produits de la Vallée du Haut-Verdon** (local produce centre): next door to the tourist office. ☎ 04-92-83-58-57. Open on Friday, Saturday and Sunday; every day in the school holidays. In summer, 9am–12.30pm and 3–7.30pm (8pm at the weekend); in winter, 9am–12.30pm and 2–6pm (7pm at the weekend). Closed in November. Local craftsmen and producers are represented in this shop, which sells carved wood items, pottery, mohair, lavender or mountain honey, *génépi*, *charcuterie*, mountain cheeses, mead and farm-produced yoghurts. In summer, there's a themed market every Monday.

WHERE TO STAY AND EAT

🛏 ✕ **Hôtel Le Bellevue**: place du Village. ☎ 04-92-83-51-60. Email: lebellevue@wanadoor.fr. Closed from 5 November to 23 December. Double rooms with shower from 250F to 315F. Menus for 85F (lunchtime), 110F and 160F. Behind a lovely ochre facade, there's a haven of peace and tranquillity, run by a friendly Dutch couple. Rooms are tastefully decorated and some have a view to the mountains. Enjoy tasty regional fare on the lovely sunny terrace.

COLMARS-LES-ALPES

Colmars lies among forests and meadows, its remarkable fortifications giving it a fine medieval air. The bastioned, pentagonal towers were added to the ramparts of the Fort de France to the south, which lead to the Fort de Savoie, built in 1693. Vauban was responsible for designing and constructing the whole complex, under orders from Louis XIV, as protection against the Savoyards, who regularly attacked the frontier.

USEFUL ADDRESS

⊞ Tourist office: formerly the Auberge Fleurie. ☎ 04-92-83-41-92. Fax: 04-92-83-52-31. Between September and June, open 9am–12.15pm and from 2–5.45pm (except on Sunday afternoon). Open every day in the summer until 7pm.

WHERE TO STAY

⌂ Gîte Le Gassendi: ☎ 04-92-83-42-25. Fax: 04-92-83-52-31 or 04-92-83-57-75. Open throughout the year. 65F per night, with half board at 150F. This substantial *gîte* provides 155 beds in dormitories that sleep four, six or sixteen, and have washing facilities. Book ahead, because groups of schoolchildren often come on nature holidays.

⌂ Campsite Le Bois Joly: ☎ 04-92-83-40-40. Fax: 04-92-83-50-60. Open from 1 May to 1 October. Pitches cost 25F, plus 18F per person. There are 25 pitches in this simple and inexpensive campsite, set among the trees near the river. Use of the microwave, refrigerator and freezer is free to campers.

MERCANTOUR NATIONAL PARK

Covering 70,000 hectares (270 square miles) between the Alpes-de-Haute-Provence and the Alpes-Maritimes, the Parc National du Mercantour has managed to withstand over-development and damage by tourism. Its protected status goes back to a law of 1860, when the County of Nice was annexed to France and Napoleon III honourably allowed King Victor Emmanuel to continue to enjoy his favourite hunting grounds. The Mercantour did not become part of France in its entirety until 1947 and the region retains its Italian soul. Conditions are challenging, but the people who live in this harsh, unforgiving world are accustomed to it.

In the summer, the Mercantour park offers wonderful walks, with its high mountains, cirques, lakes and glacial valleys. The rich flora is unmatched in Europe; of the 1,500 species that have been located, 200 are rare, including the saxifage which is the emblem of the park. The chamois deer, the ibex and wild sheep all live together in peace, but there are wolves too . . .

USEFUL ADDRESS

⊞ Parc National du Mercantour: ☎ and fax: 04-92-81-21-31. Open from 15 June to 15 September. Guided walks and seminars.

THE ALPES-DE-HAUTE-PROVENCE

VAL D'ALLOS-LA FOUX AND LE SEIGNUS

This pair of mountain resorts in the Alpes-de-Haute-Provence are family oriented and warmly welcoming, enjoyable in winter or summer. The winding road up to them, which can be difficult, depending on the season, takes you over black schist rock. The simple, relaxed resort of **La Foux-d'Allos** is right at the end of the Vallée du Verdon, near the source of the river. The Domaine de l'Espace Lumière links the resort with Pra-Loup. **Le Seignus** (7 kilometres/5 miles away) is a real village resort, with little houses and chalets rather than big apartment blocks. It's a great place to ski with a family – a harmonious mix of traditional mountain life and modern facilities.

In summer, the climate is exceptional, the resorts are uncrowded and you have easy access to breathtaking countryside and endless forests. In a magnificent setting in the village of Allos, the Parc de Loisirs appeals to the young and the not so young.

USEFUL ADDRESS

🚩 **Tourist office**: BP 5, 04260 Allos. ☎ 04-92-83-02-81. Fax: 04-92-83-06-66. Website: www.valdallos.com or www.skifrance.fr. Open daily in summer 8.30am–7pm; during the rest of the year 8.30am–noon and 2–6.30pm.

WHERE TO STAY AND EAT

🛏 ✕ **Gîte-auberge de l'Autapie**: run by Dominique and Jean-Louis Bechet (he is a cross-country skiing instructor). ☎ 04-92-83-06-31. Half board (compulsory) for 180F per person. On the edge of the village, this is a family chalet turned into a friendly stop-over *gîte*, with three little six-bed dormitories. Each has private washing facilities with shower and two basins, and there are two toilets on the landing. Undersheets and quilts are supplied and meals of good traditional, family cooking are served in a communal dining room. The *gîte* is at the foot of the slopes. Walkers with stamina can go as far as the Lac d'Allos, at 2,200 metres (7,220 feet) the highest in Europe.

🛏 ✕ **Hôtel-restaurant Les Gentianes**: Grand'rue. ☎ 04-92-83-03-50. Fax: 04-92-83-02-71. Closed on Tuesday out of season, from 15 April to 5 May, and from 15 to 30 November. Charming little double rooms with shower and toilet for 350F. Menus from 75F to 140F. This small, friendly and family-oriented inn, run by a mother and daughter, is popular with skiers in the winter and with walkers in the summer. The simple food – steak with mushrooms, fish with polenta – is good and filling. This kind of place is rare today.

🛏 ✕ **Hôtel Plein Soleil**: rooms from 280F to 330F. Half board compulsory in winter. Menus from 90F to 120F. Closed from mid-April to mid-June, and mid-September to mid-December. The building is pretty grim but the hotel gets lots of sun and the rooms, even though they are rather old-fashioned, are spacious.

🛏 ✕ **Hôtel-restaurant Le Hameau**: in La Foux. ☎ 04-92-83-82-26. Fax: 04-92-83-87-50. Closed from 15 April to 12 June, and from 15 September to 30 November. Rooms from 465F to 530F, depending on size and number of occupants. Menus from 70F to 250F. This building is typical for the resort. The rooms have modern facilities, and the biggest can sleep up to five people. There's a lovely Norwegian-style chalet for rent next to the hotel, as well as a garden and a swimming pool. Traditional cuisine is served in the dining room with dishes such as *magret au genièvre* (duck breast with juniper) and *ravioles à l'ancienne* (old-style ravioli).

✗ **Restaurant Le Bercail**: Grand'-rue. ☎ 04-92-83-07-53. Lunch menu 69F and others up to 140F. The decor is minimalist, to say the least. There's some lovely stone vaulting, but that's it. As for the food, the chef may not produce marvels but he's efficient and the portions are huge.

WHAT TO DO

– **Skiing**: the Val d'Allos is surrounded by a ring of mountains, with skiing possible on five slopes that each have a different orientation towards the sun. From La Foux-d'Allos, you can get to Pra-Loup, via the Espace Lumière. Overlooked by the Grande Séolane, the Espace is the largest linked ski area of the Alpes du Sud, with 180 kilometres (115 miles) of runs. Après-ski activities include ice-skating, snowshoe treks, driving lessons on ice, snow scooters, paragliding or quad bike circuits.

In summer, the 'Funny Pack' gives discounts of up to 30 per cent on sports and leisure activities. In the village of Allos, you can swim in the artificial lake, and there's also trampolining, tennis, volleyball, archery, a climbing wall, some pedaloes and a mini-golf course.

There are many good **walks** in the area:

– **Lac des Grenouilles**: an easy half-day walk on a circular nature trail, with signs giving information about animals and plants. Departure point at the entrance to the resort, behind the tennis courts.

– **Walk up to the Auriac pass**: this path climbs steeply and the walk lasts 3 hours 30 minutes. Follow the Lac des Grenouilles markings for 45 minutes, then take the left fork that goes up, following the yellow and red markings, heading for the Refuge de l'Estrop. The last 200 metres are quite difficult. After a picnic at the top of the pass, press on up to the summit, if you have the stamina. The round trip will take an extra 1 hour 30 minutes.

– **Lac d'Allos**: the lake is easily accessible by a 45-minute walk from the Laus car park. However, the route to it from Allos, via the GR56 footpath, is for experienced walkers only, and must be guided. The tourist office can provide information. This glacial lake, at an altitude of 2,225 metres (7,300 feet), is 1 kilometre long, 600 metres wide and 42 metres (138 feet) at its deepest, making it the largest high-altitude lake in Europe. At the bottom, there is a stone engraved in the local patois: '*Couvé mi veras, plureras*' ('When you see me, you will weep'). Indeed, if the stone were visible, it would mean that the locals were drastically short of water. The water is incredibly clear and the light is remarkable, soft and intense at the same time.

If you go on foot from Allos, you will need to allow a day, with a night in the mountain hut by the lake.

THE UBAYE VALLEY

Provençal writer Jean Giono loved the Ubaye, describing 'rugged areas are infinitely beautiful and cloaked with lavender fields and forests . . . beneath a sky so constant and so blue'. This is a corner of paradise in high-mountain country – uncrowded, with incredibly pure air, locals who speak with an endearing Provençal accent, and a necklace of summits that easily top 3,000 metres (9,842 feet). As you climb up, you might spot a marmot or two, stop off for a glass of the local tipple *génépi* or bilberry schnapps, or fortify yourself with a plate of succulent lamb with fresh herbs (a welcome change from fondue).

The wild country of the Ubaye is certainly worth visiting, particularly for those who like nature in the raw. Tourism is under-developed, but there are some *gîtes* and mountain huts. Access is cross-country from Barcelonnette, a proud little town on the edge of the valleys of the Ubaye and the Haut Verdon. From the north, you get there via Gap, from the south, via Sisteron.

BARCELONNETTE

Frenchmen who do their military service in Barcelonnette are usually delighted to return to civvy street, as life here is far from easy. It can be cold all year round, and the valley is almost completely cut off from the outside world. The nearest big town is Gap and Barcelonnette itself has just 3,500 inhabitants, or three-quarters of the population of the whole valley. There are some advantages: it hardly ever rains, Nice is only two hours away, there is easily accessible skiing and, at the same time, this is still Provence, with all that that implies. When you hear the people talking, you might imagine yourself in a sort of rural Marseille.

Despite the disadvantages, Barcelonnette – standing at an altitude of 1,132 metres (3,714 feet) – has great Alpine appeal. The people are kind and hospitable, and the town has a genuine, cosy atmosphere. It has a fascinating history, too, and you'll be amazed to see fabulously beautiful Mexican-style villas here. Follow their extraordinary story in the Musée de la Vallée.

USEFUL ADDRESSES

🛈 Tourist office: place Frédéric-Mistral. ☎ 04-92-81-04-71. Fax: 04-92-81-22-67. Email: info@barcelonnette.net. In summer, open daily 9am–8pm; in winter 9am–12.30pm and 2–7pm; mid-season, open Monday to Saturday 9am–noon and 2–6pm. Buy lift passes at Pra-Loup, Le Sauze and Ste-Anne La Condamine. Buying them in advance gives access to the free shuttle buses that serve the ski resorts.

🛈 Services tourisme CCVU (tourism services provided by the association of the villages of the valley): 4 avenue des Trois-Frères-Arnaud. ☎ 04-92-81-03-68. Fax: 04-92-81-51-67. Website: www.ubaye.com. Competent and welcoming staff provide all the information that you are likely to need, including brochures and leaflets with lists of accommodation and *gîtes*.
■ **Honorary Consulate of Mexico**: 7 avenue Porfirio-Diaz. ☎ 04-

92-81-00-27. Fax: 04-92-81-33-70. The Mexican Honorary Consul is one of Barcelonnette's real characters. The consulate has a cultural centre, a tourist office, and information on everything to do with the town's associations with Mexico.

🚌 **Bus station**: place Aimé-Gassier. ☎ 04-92-81-00-20. Three buses a day for Gap, one for Digne. Also an SNCF train ticket office.

Sports

■ **Ubaye Parapente**: Le Pont Long. ☎ 04-92-81-34-93. Fax: 04-92-81-15-17. Website: www. ubaye-parapente.com. Open all year, even in winter. Paragliding for be-ginners, and other courses, including a (time-consuming) pilot's licence. Very well equipped.

■ **Rando Passion**: rue du Commandant-Car. ☎ 04-92-81-43-34. Various excursions, including *marmotte* walks, mountain biking, cross-country skiing and snowshoe treks. **Ubaye Mountains**, rue Manuel. ☎ 04-92-81-42-69, organizes excursions on both sides of the border, including special children's walks, tours of Ubaye fortifications, and so on.

■ **Velo'Loc**: ZA Uvernet. ☎ 04-92-81-36-67. Hire a mountain bike for 100F per day. **Plein Air Sport**: ☎ 04-92-81-23-69. Bicycle and mountain bike hire.

WHERE TO STAY

🛏 ✖ **Hôtel du Cheval Blanc**: 12 rue Grenette. ☎ 04-92-81-00-19. Fax: 04-92-81-15-39. Closed on Sunday lunchtime out of season and in October. Double rooms for 290F, half board 300F per person. Menus from 75F to 100F. The Barneaud family has been running this hotel and restaurant for three generations. Mountain bikes have taken the place of horses and touring cyclists now park their bikes in the old stables. Ask for a packed lunch to put in your panniers or try the special 'sporting' breakfast. The *patron* makes good game pies but no longer produces the long list of dishes on the old menus that he has kept.

🛏 **Azteca Hotel**: 3 rue François-Arnaud. ☎ 04-92-81-46-36. Fax: 04-92-81-43-92. Email: hotel-azteca@wanadoo.fr. Closed 5–30 November. Doubles from 330F to 500F, depending on the season. Substantial breakfast for 50F. This good three-star hotel looks a bit like a smart private clinic from the outside, but the comparison ends there. There are 27 attractively decorated rooms with all facilities, three in a 'Mex-Alpine style' (this old villa was built on wealth made in Mexico in the 19th century). It's a very peaceful place surrounded by a garden that is ideal in summer for breakfast, which is laid out on a buffet in the villa's sitting room. The welcome is convivial and there are shuttle buses to the slopes.

WHERE TO EAT

✖ **Le Poivre d'Ane**: 49 rue Manuel. ☎ 04-92-81-48-67. Closed in January and November; open every day in July and August. Otherwise, closed on Sunday evening, all day Monday and Tuesday lunchtime. Menus from 85F to 160F. Find a relaxing seat on the terrace on a sunny day and enjoy local specialities from the Vallée de l'Ubaye.

✕ **Les Voûtes**: 3 rue Cardinalis. ☎ 04-92-81-34-64. Closed from 1 November to 15 December. Menus from 85F to 230F. This charming restaurant has an internal courtyard for summer eating. Enjoy the cheesey mountain meals of *reblochonnade* or *fondue savoyarde* and large mixed salads, among other dishes.

✕ **Restaurant Adélita**: 19 rue Émile-Donnadieu. ☎ 04-92-81-16-12. Closed on Wednesday and in October. Menu for 70F. À la carte around 120F. A real Mexican restaurant, serving *tacos* with chicken or *mole*, and a host of other dishes. The decor is exactly as you might imagine.

✕ **La Mangeoire Gourmande**: place des Quatre-Vents. ☎ 04-92-81-01-61. Closed on Monday and Tuesday evening and from 11 November to end December. Menus at 98F (lunch), 160F and 210F. The sea meets the mountains in this delightful, 17th-century vaulted dining room. The welcome is warm and sincere, and the meticulously prepared dishes, mixing tradition and innovation, are authentic, unusual and tasty. The kitchen is in a corner just off the dining room, allowing you to see the chef at work. The menu changes every four months and is based exclusively on fresh regional produce.

WHERE TO STAY AND EAT IN THE AREA

🛏 ✕ **Maison d'hôte du Vivier**: Le Vivier, 04400 Enchastrayes. 5 kilometres (about 3 miles) from Barcelonnette on the route du Gaudissard towards La Conchette. ☎ 04-92-81-19-65. Fax: 04-92-81-27-21. Closed at the end of June and in November. Rooms 300F, including breakfast. Meals for around 150F. Meals and guest rooms in a large and lovely farmhouse restored by its *bon vivant* owners M. and Mme Lozach, who cook good regional dishes in front of you. Try the house specialities: *caillettes* (something like haggis), local meats cooked over a wood fire, homemade pasta and pastries. The atmosphere is very enjoyable. Meals and rooms should be booked at least the day before, especially in season. Worth a detour.

✕ **Restaurant Le Passe-Montagne**: at Uvernet-Fours, 4.5 kilometres (3 miles) from Barcelonnette. Take the D902 in the direction of Pra-Loup; turn off before the fork to the Col d'Allos. ☎ 04-92-81-08-58. Closed on Tuesday evening and Wednesday, 15 November to 15 December and during the last week in June. Menus from 98F to 143F. This restaurant has the warm atmosphere of a chalet and a superb view of the Pain de Sucre and the Chapeau de Gendarme peaks. In winter, there's a huge fire in the fireplace. The chef reproduces the Provençal dishes his grandmother used to make but interprets them in his own way.

🛏 **Chambres d'hôte with Annie Sackreuter**: Les Iscles, in Faucon-de-Barcelonnette. Take the D900 towards Jausiers, then the D709 towards Faucon. At the church, follow the road to the convent for 1 kilometre and stop at the first house on the left after the wooden bridge. Open all year round. 270F for two in summer, including breakfast, and 280F in winter. This lovely house is set on the edge of the forest, in attractive grounds full of flowerbeds. There are two lovely rooms on the first floor and breakfast is served in a pleasant red and white kitchen. Evening meals are not provided.

WHAT TO SEE

★ Place Manuel: this square is at the very heart of the citadel. The 14th-century Cardinalis tower, all that's left of a Dominican convent, keeps time for the whole town.

★ Musée de la Vallée: La Sapinière. ☎ 04-92-81-27-15. Open every afternoon during school holidays 3–6pm; the rest of the year, Wednesday, Thursday and Saturday only, 3–6pm. Entrance fee: 20F for adults (10F for 10–21-year-olds). This is just one of five museums in different villages in the Ubaye, each showing different facets of life in the valley. The biggest, Barcelonnette's is housed in a Mexican villa and is a good lesson on the history of the town. Guided tours by appointment only.

History

'For the inhabitants of the Ubaye, Mexico means more than *mariachis* and colourful folklore. It's the very history of their own valley, of their ancestors and of themselves . . . Everyone here has a relative in Mexico . . .'

At the beginning of the 19th century, after 300 years of rule by Spain, Mexico proclaimed independence and threw the Spanish out. The declaration of independence was followed by a wave of immigration, including, in 1821, the three Arnaud brothers from Jausiers. The brothers settled in the country and made their fortune. A stream of people from the Ubaye – or, more precisely, from the cantons of Barcelonnette and St-Paul-sur-Ubaye – followed their example and came back to the valley with their new-found wealth. The phenomenon continued until the end of the World War II.

At the beginning of the 19th century, the economy of the Ubaye still depended largely on agriculture, cattle rearing and forestry. The working and living conditions in the isolated valley were harsh. In slack times, every family in the valley would spin and weave their sheep's wool to make bed linen. All the items produced were sold outside the valley during the winter, to boost the family's income, and the ancient tradition of peddling developed. The winter selling trips took the peddlers of the Ubaye to every part of France, to Belgium, Italy and even Denmark and then further afield, in search of new markets. In 1821, the Arnaud brothers made it to Mexico. It was impossible to get back in time for spring, so they decided to settle there and sell their wares from a permanent outlet. The shop was so successful that some of their old employees from the Ubaye had to be brought out to keep up with demand.

The Arnauds were not the only locals to make their fortune in Mexico. In all, more than 5,000 followed in their footsteps, making money mainly in the textile industry and then in department stores, and in the manufacturing of machinery for the industry. Many of their huge enterprises were quoted on the Mexican stock exchange. This flow of migrants reached its height after two of the Arnauds' employees, after being away 15 years, came back to the valley in 1845 with 250,000 gold francs in their pockets.

Up to 90 per cent of the migrants stayed in Mexico and became Mexican nationals, but a number returned home to Barcelonnette to end their days. They built sumptuous private mansions and family vaults, leaving the town with the tangible evidence of an extraordinary human story.

On the other side of the coin, many of the migrants suffered terrible deprivation and difficulty in their search for success, while others struggled for years, only to die alone and in poverty, on the other side of the world from their families.

WHAT TO SEE IN THE AREA

★ **Fortresses of the Ubaye**: from the middle to the end of the 19th century, 35 kilometres (22 miles) of defences were built in the valley, based around the enormous fortified mountain of Tournoux. The network comprised a system of look-out and signalling posts and strategic routes. It's worth going on the enthusiastically guided tour, which leaves from the tourist office. Tours are possible to the sites at Tournoux, Roche-la-Croix and St-Ours from 22 June to 12 September.

SHOPPING

🔒 **Patisserie Fontaine**: 47 rue Manuel. ☎ 04-92-81-01-46. Their *feuilletine* is excellent. On the other side of the road, there's an interesting little chocolate museum with displays and tastings.

🔒 **Le Pain de Sucre**: 13 rue Manuel. ☎ 04-92-81-01-59. This shop sells lovely cakes and pastries, as well as a delicious ice-cream flav-oured with *génépi* (a local aromatic spice).

🔒 **Ferme de la Salce Basse**: in the Adroit district. ☎ 04-92-81-55-75. Taste sweet and savoury foods among the animals at this 'pick your own' farm. Open throughout the summer, Monday to Saturday, from 1.30pm. Organic produce also for sale.

WHERE TO GO FOR A DRINK

▾ **Le Choucas**: place Manuel. ☎ 04-92-81-15-20. The perfect place to end the evening with a beer, on a charming little square where the whole town walks by.

FESTIVALS

– **Les Enfants du Jazz** ('Jazz Children'): during the third week of July. The three Arnaud brothers, the first emigrants from Barcelonnette, originally went to Louisiana, the cradle of jazz. The concept of this jazz festival is to bring young jazz musicians together with established musicians such as Dee Dee Bridgewater, André Ceccarelli and Sébastien Texier. There's a programme of exhibitions and concerts. Information from the Maison de la Vallée or website: www.lejazz.simplenet.com.

– **Festival of Mexican Folklore**: around 15 August, Barcelonnette celebrates its Mexican connections with a programme of exhibitions and events. The highlight of the event is the performance by the Ballets du Mexique. Information from the tourist office.

PRA-LOUP-LES MOLANES

Pra-Loup (from *pré du loup*, 'the field of the wolf') was built on a flat part of the north side of the Ubaye valley in the 1960s – not an auspicious time in the history of architecture. The centre of the resort , at an altitude of 1,600 metres (5,250 feet) is based around a huge, semi-circular complex, housing rental apartments and many of the restaurants and nightclubs. A natural skating rink and a games area add a little to the ambience, but Pra-Loup is in desperate need of the wooden cladding that is apparently planned. It certainly looks better in winter, when it's disguised by snow. At the end of the afternoon, when the sun illuminates the snowy peaks, the scene is superb.

The skiing is varied and pleasant, particularly good for average skiers and reasonable for the more advanced. For snowboarders, a 250-metre (820-foot) pipe has been added to the half-pipe in the snow park.

The resort has extended to Les Molanes, 1.5 kilometres lower down, at an altitude of 1,500 metres (4,920 feet), where the hotels, *gîtes* and private chalets have more appeal. This is a good place to stay in summer, within walking distance of Pra-Loup, where you can have a drink at Edward's Pub, in the shopping mall, and then go on for a bop at the Loup Garou. At the weekend, party at Les Hauts de Costebelle.

USEFUL ADDRESS

🛈 **Maison de Pra-Loup**: 04400 Pra-Loup. ☎ 04-92-84-10-04. Fax: 04-92-84-02-93. Website: www.praloup.com. Open Monday to Friday 9am–noon and 2–6pm. For lift information, call ☎ 04-92-84-11-54, fax: 04-92-84-18-94.

WHERE TO STAY AND EAT

Les Molanes

🛏 ✕ **Hôtel Le Prieuré**: ☎ 04-92-84-11-43. Fax: 04-92-84-01-88. Email: hotel.leprieure@wanadoo.fr. Closed from 15 April to 1 June and from 15 September to 15 December. Double rooms from 320F to 480F; half board 395F per person. Menus at 110F and 220F. This 18th-century former priory is now a warm rustic hotel that faces due south towards the Pain de Sucre and the Chapeau de Gendarme with a breathtaking view, reasonable prices and a very friendly welcome. The cooking is very tasty and includes lamb with *génépi* (a local aromatic spice). The swimming pool is pleasant in summer.

🛏 ✕ **Auberge du Clos Sorel**: ☎ 04-92-84-10-74. Fax: 04-92-84-09-14. Email: info@seolan.com. Closed from 5 April to 20 June and from 5 September to 15 December. In winter, restaurant only open at lunchtime during school holidays. Rooms from 420F to 900F and half board from 400F to 650F per person. *Menu-carte* at 160F. In summer you can have a good meal for just 90F at lunchtime. Dinner is served by candlelight and tea by the fire in this charming inn, in a lovely setting, where you could happily spend your entire holiday. There's a swimming pool in summer, skiing nearby in winter, and lovely, polished furniture, ancient beams and old stonework in the 11 rooms. The cooking is good, too, with regional and farm fare based on seasonal produce from the market.

♠ ✕ **Chambres d'hôte**: La Ferme du Couvent. ☎ 04-92-84-05-05. Closed during the first two weeks in June. Rooms at 330F and 380F, with half board at 290F. Dinner costs 90F and 140F (reservations required). The rooms in this 600-year-old farm are very simple but it's a nice place to stay in summer and especially in winter. The entrance is built out of logs and there's a warm and convivial atmosphere around the open fire. Traditional cooking prepared by Nathalie, with dishes influenced by her home town of Marseille and using local mountain produce. Husband Jean-Pierre is a ski instructor and lends a hand serving aperitifs. The breakfasts are great.

Pra-Loup

♠ ✕ **Hôtel Le Manon**: ☎ 04-92-84-17-82. Fax: 04-92-84-15-08. Rooms from 280F to 350F in winter. Closed from 1 May to 20 June and in November. A small hotel with a dozen rooms right in the middle of the resort. Superb panoramic view of the mountains and a friendly welcome.

♠ ✕ **Restaurant La Tisane**: in the shopping mall. ☎ 04-92-84-10-55. Closed from 30 April to 1 July and from 10 September to 25 November. Menus from 85F to 245F; à la carte around 180F. The cooking is traditional, with typical Ubaye dishes served in the tastefully decorated restaurant. The service is agreeable and the pastries are so good you'll have to delay your diet.

✕ **Restaurant des Hauts de Costebelle**: ☎ 04-92-81-33-67. Open in summer, and winter season, at lunchtime. Around 100F for lunch. This mountain restaurant, with its vast sun terrace, has been run with good humour for 20 years by the three Akchehirlian brothers. There's a great atmosphere, particularly on Saturday nights from the beginning of December to the end of April, and in July and August. A lift takes people up between 9am and 4pm. The traditional mountain dish of *tartiflette* (melted cheese, potatoes and cured meats) is served, as well as a first-rate *fondue bourgignonne* (meat fondue).

WHAT TO DO

The Espace Lumière, with peaks such as the Pain de Sucre (sugarloaf), is the largest ski area in the southern Alps. It's a favourite with the Marseillais, who come here in the summer as well as for the snow. The many organized activities include rafting, paragliding, canyonning and adventure treks.

– **In winter**: the ski area is large enough to appeal to skiers of all levels, but it is particularly suited to intermediates. It is linked to the resort of La Foux-d'Allos, although it takes the best part of a morning to get there. Lift passes are relatively cheap and the snow is good, well protected from the wind and the sun. The vertical drop is 600m (1,969 feet) and the runs offer moguls, places to schuss, and paths through the trees. It's ideal for snowboarders, especially novices, with a team of good instructors. For off piste and guided skiing, get information from the guides' office. ☎ 04-92-81-04-71.

– **In summer**: a few lovely walks start at the resort itself but there's a much bigger choice further up the Ubaye valley. A classic is the Grande Séolane –

allow a whole day for the round trip and consider doing it with a guide. It is geologically very rich, with a climb over a *klippe* (a huge slab of rock that came loose as the mountains were being formed which seems to have been haphazardly put here upside down on the mountain side). Have a picnic at the top and enjoy the panoramic view over the whole of the Alps.

LE SAUZE

Unlike so many other ski resorts, Le Sauze, lying between 1,400 and 2,400 metres (4,590 and 7,874 feet), is still a proper village. One of the oldest resorts in France, it has kept its genuine mountain ambience and is an ideal place for families. The first brick was laid in 1934 and it has grown gradually since then. There are some good runs – French ski champion Carole Merle came from here – but, generally, the skiing is gentle and the runs are not too taxing. The resort is divided into two: Le Sauze (the original village) and Super-Sauze (with its less attractive concrete buildings). Sauze is inevitably much more appealing. In winter, when the Col d'Allos is closed, people from Nice and Marseille keep away, but in summer, when there are wonderful walks, they come in large numbers.

Try the following walks:

– **Le Chapeau de Gendarme**: start from Super-Sauze, a little higher up. The path has yellow markings, and goes past shepherds' huts and mountain farms.

– **Terre-Plaines lake**: allow 4 hours to go up and 3 to come down the same way. This is an interesting walk, which should introduce you to lots of local flora and fauna.

– There are more than 80 lakes in the area, hidden in valleys, or majestically sited on a pass. Depending on the season, walkers can pick mushrooms, raspberries or wild strawberries.

USEFUL ADDRESSES

🄷 **Sauze–Super-Sauze tourist office**: 04400 Le Sauze–Super-Sauze. ☎ 04-92-81-05-61. Fax: 04-92-81-21-60. Email: info@sauze.com. Open Monday to Friday 9am–noon and 2–6pm.

■ **Motoneiges**: Michel Robert, 16 avenue Ernest-Pellotier, Barcelonn-ette. ☎ 04-92-81-17-76 and 06-81-05-26-27. Snow scooters from 200F for outings leaving at 7.30am, or around 5.30pm to be combined with a meal at night (booking essential). This is a great way of finding out about the mountains, but it's not cheap. Departures are from La Savonnette.

WHERE TO STAY AND EAT

🛏 ✕ **Hôtel-restaurant Le Soleil des Neiges**: Le Sauze. ☎ 04-92-81-05-01. Open from 20 December to 20 April and from 24 June to 15 September. Double rooms from 370F to 400F. Half board from 330F to 375F per person. Menus at 115F and 135F. Located near the ski lifts, this Logis de France is more attractive in winter than in summer. It offers a friendly welcome and Ubaye food specialities such as herb flan and farmhouse chicken with mushrooms.

â **Hôtel Le Pyjama**: Super-Sauze. ☎ 04-92-81-12-00. Fax: 04-92-81-03-16. Closed from 10 September to 15 December and from 15 April to 25 June. Rooms from 260F to 460F. Studios with kitchenettes also available. Run and decorated by the mother of ski champion Carole Merle. The rooms have period furniture and ornaments, and a peaceful view over magnificent larch trees. Some have terraces or mezzanines and lovely bathrooms. There's even a junk shop below and, unusually, animals are made welcome.

✗ **La Cabane à Jo** (mountain restaurant): ☎ 04-92-81-02-86. Open from 10 July to 31 August and from 15 December to 30 April. Around 100F for a meal. This charming mountain chalet, with its friendly atmosphere, is a good skiers' or walkers' pit-stop.

✗ **Restaurant-Bar Le Trappeur**: Super-Sauze. ☎ and fax: 04-92-81-12-13. Closed for a few weeks in May/June, for the month of September and for a few weeks in October/November. Summer menus start at 62F, and in winter you'll pay around 95F. A lovely, sunny terrace at the foot of the ski runs and just the place for something warm at tea time. Regional specialities include a substantial *tartiflette*, with a green salad. Otherwise, you can have pasta, pancakes or grilled meats. The atmosphere is cheery, with live bands playing several times a week.

JAUSIERS

Standing on a hillside, the **Château des Magnans** is a sort of medieval fantasy, recalling some of Ludwig II of Bavaria's more surreal architectural follies. In fact, it was built between 1903 and 1913 and is one of the most extraordinary of the 'Mexican' villas in the valley. It's just one of the reasons to visit this charming mountain village. In both summer and winter, Jausiers is a good departure point for skiing or walking, or any other kind of outdoor sporting activity.

USEFUL ADDRESSES

🖪 **Tourist office**: BP 3, 04850 Jausiers. ☎ 04-92-81-21-45. Fax: 04-92-84-63-42. Open all year.

■ **Maison des produits de pays** (local produce centre): at the entrance to the village. ☎ 04-92-84-63-88. Fax: 04-92-84-67-83. Open 10am–noon and 2.30–6.30pm in mid-season. In summer, open 10am–8pm. Reasonably priced homemade products and local goodies (sweets, honey, *charcuterie*, cheeses and jams) in a large shop with an enticing window display. The *panier-terroir* is a hamper full of local goodies – the perfect souvenir. The staff are very friendly.

WHAT TO SEE

★ **Plan d'eau de Siguret** (Siguret lake): Le Chalet du Lac. ☎ 04-92-84-61-96. Hire pedaloes or canoes, play tennis, climb rocks or enjoy a drink or a meal in the bar-restaurant. There's a reasonable entrance charge.

★ **Musée de la Vallée** (museum of the valley): Grand Rue. In the tourist office. Open in summer 4.30–6.30pm and by appointment (ask at the tourist office). Free entry. Jausiers was built in the 16th century on the bed of the Ubaye and its museum has a permanent exhibition about water in all its guises.

LA HAUTE-UBAYE

The valley of La Haute-Ubaye (the Upper Ubaye), in a privileged position on the edge of the Mercantour National Park, is full of hidden treasures. In summer, a network of long-distance footpaths keeps walkers occupied for days, with overnight stops possible in mountain refuges. In winter, there is cross-country skiing (particularly round Larche or St-Paul), downhill skiing and snow-shoe trekking, often through totally unspoilt, virgin snow. For climbers, Via Ferrata at St-Ours, in the *commune* of Meyronnes, is one of the most famous sites in Europe.

WHERE TO STAY AND EAT

♠ ✕ **Hôtel-restaurant Le Belvédère**: in Ste-Anne-La-Condamine. ☎ 04-92-84-30-16. Fax: 04-92-84-36-48. Closed for a few weeks in April/May and October/November. Rooms with washbasin for 240F. Half board 208F per person. Menus from 85F. This family-run chalet at an altitude of 1,700 metres (5,575 feet), has 12 pleasant rooms, friendly staff and well-prepared food.

♠ ✕ **L'Auberge du Chamois**: place de l'église, in St-Paul-sur-Ubaye. ☎ 04-92-84-31-20. Closed from 15 to 22 June and from 11 November to 26 December. Rooms from 160F to 210F. Menus from 89F. This 16th-century presbytery has been transformed into a homely *auberge*, with unusual decor, simple rooms and good home cooking (dishes include *charcuterie*, local lamb, fresh pasta, and house *raclette* to order). In summer, meals are served in a charming little garden within hearing of the church bells.

♠ ✕ **Auberge du Lauzanier**: in Larche (04530). ☎ 04-92-84-35-93. Closed on Monday outside school terms and from 6 November to 21 December. Open between 1 October and 6 November by reservation only. Menus from 65F to 120F. Half board 195F per person. The atmosphere of a mountain refuge but

with extra comforts. The welcome from the happy trio of owners is remarkably warm and friendly. The decor is somewhat sober but the comfortable rooms (with toilets and showers) are impeccably clean. The food is carefully prepared and over the years both dishes – *charcuterie, fondue savoyarde* or *gigot d'agneau en croûte de morilles* (leg of lamb with mushroom crust) – and guests have become regulars.

♠ ✕ **Gîte-auberge de La Cure** (with Marie-Rose and Michel Longeron): Maurin Maljasset (04530). Take the D900 to St-Paul, then the D25 to Maurin, then follow the signs. ☎ 04-92-84-31-15. Fax: 04-92-84-34-87. Open during school holidays or by prior reservation. Half board 184F per person. Menus from 65F to 100F. Standing at an altitude of 1,900 metres (6,230 feet), this tiny hamlet is just a few kilometres from the Italian border. Out of season, it has only three inhabitants (Marie-Rose, Michel and the postman who lodges with them). This former presbytery has a unique panoramic view of the surrounding mountains. The small vaulted dining room seats 40. A *gîte* provides space for 26 and there are 6- to 18-bed dormitories too. Non-residents are welcome to eat – *baeckeoffe, fondue* and *racl-*

ette need to be ordered in advance. In summer, it's very popular with walkers and in winter there are cross-country skiiers and snow-shoe trekkers. The welcome is friendly and relaxed.

🛌 ✗ **Refuge CAF de Maljasset**: near the Gîte-auberge de La Cure. ☎ 04-92-84-34-04. Fax: 04-92-84-35-28. Closed from 3 May to 10 June, from 3 November to 26 December and from 4 January to 1 February. Half board from 155F to 180F per person (dormitory facilities only). Evening meal 85F. The setting is quite extraordinary and the cooking is wonderful. There's a single dish in the evening, but at lunchtime you can choose from a selection of substantial salads, local dishes and desserts, such as bilberry tart. The welcome is a little unpredictable.

WHAT TO SEE

★ **Ste-Anne la Condamine**: a family resort with a few well-spaced wooden chalets. In the 1960s and 70s a number of new buildings went up, but they are in keeping with their surroundings. The ski area, near the Vallon du Parpaillon, is limited (covering 25 kilometres/16 miles), but it usually has good snow cover and the setting is superb. Information: ☎ 04-92-84-33-01. Fax: 04-92-84-35-98.

★ **St-Paul** and **Larche** are a bit further into the Haute-Ubaye. Before you get to St-Paul, have a look at the Pont du Châtelet, a remarkable listed bridge. St-Paul's **Musée de la Vallée** introduces visitors to the traditions of rural domestic life in the valley. It's housed in the barn belonging to the old Arnaud family house and in the summer there are semi-guided tours between 3 and 7pm. ☎ 04-92-84-36-23.

★ **Hamlet of Maljasset**: this ghostly hamlet, at the end of a no-through road, has just three or four inhabited houses. Its isolated little church has a square tower and a scrap of a cemetery, where there's an inscription recording that in 1531, an avalanche destroyed the 12th-century building. Virtually nothing has changed here, not even the houses but, with Italy very close, the beauty of the French side and the lakes with their amazing colours, there are compensations.

At the Col Marie pass, you'll find the highest letterbox in Europe – the result of a strange practical joke. A letter from Barcelonnette to Italy used to take several days. The French and Italian guides decided to persuade the authorities that there was a letterbox at the Col Marie, at 2,637 metres (8,650 feet), emptied regularly by Maljasset's postman. The mail began to move more quickly between France and Italy. In order to convince the authorities, the box was 'officially' inaugurated with a bizarre fake ceremony and blessed by the priest. Commemorative stamps were issued and wine flowed freely. The postman blanched at the thought of climbing for two and a half hours to empty a letterbox that is hardly ever used.

So the letterbox exists, but it's the mountain guides who pick up the occasional letter, posted by hikers. Nobody expects them to be delivered very quickly.

LA BASSE UBAYE

From Barcelonnette, take the D900 down as far as the Serre-Ponçon lake. This is the Lower Ubaye, with Mediterranean flora on its sunny slopes and deep forest on the northern ones. Crossing these wild hillsides, the Ubaye is virgin territory and a practically unspoilt landscape all the way to the village of Le Lauzet-Ubaye. In 1958, the village of Ubaye was destroyed to make way for the construction of a river dam. All that remains is a 40-metre (130-foot) 'Roman bridge' across the river. Despite its name, it's not Roman at all. It was in fact built in the 12th century, but it's still the oldest bridge in the valley.

WHERE TO STAY AND EAT

â ✕ **Chambres d'hôte** (with Élisabeth and Frédéric Millet): Les Méans, in Méolans-Revel (04340). 12 kilometres (about 7 miles) from Barcelonnette. ☎ and fax: 04-92-81-03-91. Closed from 15 October to 15 June. Around 320F to 380F for two people, breakfast included. Meals for 110F all-inclusive (advance booking essential). This big 16th-century farmhouse has a superb staircase and attractively decorated rooms. Breakfast is served in a huge vaulted room with an American-style kitchen. Two rural *gîtes* are also available. This sporty family (Frédéric is a high-mountain guide and son Vincent is a member of the French ski team) offer walking, canyonning or kayaking, among other activities.

â ✕ **Gîte-auberge Les Terres Blanches**: Méolans-Revel. ☎ 04-92-81-94-37. Fax: 04-92-81-94-38. Closed in November. Double rooms cost 220F. Dinner possible on reservation. Regional menus from 80F to 120F. This little establishment has 10 tastefully renovated rooms that accommodate two, four or six people. Enjoy the friendly welcome and tasty home cooking.

â ✕ **Hôtel-club La Lauzetane**: on the banks of Lake Lauzet. ☎ 04-92-85-55-00. Closed in April and November. Rooms from 300F to 400F. Half board available from 265F to 355F per person. Daily menu (lunchtime) for 60F. Popular with bikers and a great place for kids, too. There's a fabulous terrace, a swimming pool, tennis courts and a children's play room. Carefully prepared food (buffet and regional specialities) and a nice welcome.

✕ **Restaurant Les Séolanes**: aux Thuiles. ☎ 04-82-81-07-37. Closed at the weekend in autumn and during All Saints. Around 100F for a meal. Fresh homemade pasta, stuffed with vegetables, and other excellent local specialities, served in an old vaulted sheep-pen.

WHAT TO SEE

★ **Musée du Lauzet**: in Lauzet (04340). ☎ 04-92-85-51-27 or 04-92-81-27-15. Email: musee.valle@wanadoo.fr. One of the network of museums covering the five areas of the valley, this one has displays on traditional and modern methods of hunting and gathering. Open in the afternoons in summer 5–8pm. The fifth museum is the **Musée de l'Ecole** (school museum) in Pontis (05160), on the banks of the Serre-Ponçon lake. The old school with its one classroom provides the space for the museum and the theme, too. Modern-day schoolchildren will be impressed. From 3–7pm in summer or by appointment. ☎ 04-92-44-26-94. Entrance fee: 10F for adults (5F for children).

WHAT TO DO

– **Sports, including rafting, canoeing and canyonning**: River (Le Four à Chaux) Méolans. ☎ 04-92-85-53-99. Alligator (Le Pont Pont) Barcelonnette ☎ 04-92-81-06-06. Rock'n'Raft (Les Thuiles). ☎ 04-92-81-92-81.

– **Lac du Lauzet**: in the village. ☎ 04-92-85-51-27. There's no charge for swimming in the lake, and fishing is also possible.

WHAT TO SEE IN THE AREA

– **Lac de Serre-Ponçon**: the masterpiece of all the engineering works on the River Durance, built in 1960. The site is majestic. The lake is 20 kilometres (12.5 miles) long and covers 2,900 hectares (11 square miles). It's surrounded by 2,000-metre (6,560-foot) peaks and closed by a dam that is 600 metres (1,968 feet) long and 115 metres (377 feet) high. Its construction dragged this area of the Hautes-Alpes into the 20th century, allowing the development of summer tourism along the banks of the river.

THE BLANCHE VALLEY

Continue along the D900, which forks south, to find yourself in the Vallée de la Blanche. This agricultural area was another that made a contribution to the Mexican exodus, although to a lesser extent. There are a few Mexican-style houses here and there, and a few astonishing tombs in the cemeteries.

SEYNE-LES-ALPES

This little mountain village, perched at an altitude of 1,260 metres (4,134 feet), is officially a *village de caractère des Alpes-de-Haute-Provence*. It looks down on a wide valley that's bordered by mountain peaks, some of which rise above 3,000 metres (9,842 feet). It was highly reputed from the end of the ninth century to the beginning of the 20th for breeding, raising and selling mules. The business has gone into steep decline but you will still see some splendid local specimens around. Seyne-les-Alpes is also a *station verte de vacances et village de neige* (a summer holiday resort and ski village), committed to providing a quality service to its holidaymakers. The village chefs have done their research into local cooking and perfected once again the *fricasse*, based on a recipe that had been lost in the mists of time.

USEFUL ADDRESS

🄱 **Tourist office**: place d'Armes. ☎ 04-92-35-11-00. Fax: 04-92-35-28-84. Email: vallee.de.la.blanche@wanadoo.fr. Open Monday to Friday 9am–12.30pm and 2.30–6pm, and on Saturday 9am–12.30pm.

WHERE TO STAY AND EAT

♙ ✕ **Chambres d'hôte La Ferme des Clots**: 3 kilometres (about 2 miles) to the west in Le Bas Chardavon. ☎ 04-92-35-23-13. Rooms from 250F, including breakfast. Half board 240F per person. This lovely farmhouse is full of character and in a quiet area, perfect whether you want to be active or lazy. The friendly *patronnes* prepare comforting and nourishing meals (no lunch) using only fresh regional produce. Dinner and breakfast are served in the old-fashioned dining room, which has an open fire.

WHAT TO SEE

★ Besides the 11th-century **Grand Tower** and **Vauban's citadel**, this old frontier settlement has fortified towers, gateways with dates carved above them, half-timbered houses, public washing places, small squares, little museums and a permanent exhibition about the mule in the tourist office. In the future, the mule exhibition will be moved to a dedicated farm museum.

★ Make a point of visiting the 12th-century **church of Notre Dame de Nazareth** and its 17th-century Dominican chapel (which has a painting of the Penitents).

WHAT TO DO

– **Reindeer and llama farm**: ☎ 04-92-35-05-57. Entrance fee: 20F.

– **Introduction to hang-gliding**: explore Seyne from the sky as you fly around the highest peaks. ☎ 04-92-35-25-13.

– **Donkey treks**: through the mountain pastures of the Grande Montagne. Donkeys for hire by the hour, the half-day or the day. ☎ 04-92-35-04-08.

FESTIVALS

– **Mule-driving competitions**: second Saturday in August. This is a crucial event in the Seyne calendar, the only competition of its kind that still takes place in France (outlasting the one in the Poitou). The mule breeders show off their animals, foals and mules, the majority of which are brought down from the Alpine meadows the night before.

– **Horse fair**: on the second Saturday in October.

SELONNET

A little village with 300 inhabitants way out in the wilds of nature and overlooked by the Chabanon ski resort.

WHERE TO STAY AND EAT

♙ ✕ **Hôtel-restaurant Chez le Poète**: place du Village. ☎ 04-92-35-06-12. Fax: 04-92-35-29-80. Closed on Sunday evening. Small rooms for 220F. Menus from 70F to 130F. Closed Sunday evening outside the school holidays. Impressive food served in generous portions.

Dishes such as *salade de chèvre chaud* (warm goats' cheese salad) and *entrecôte aux cèpes* (steak with mushrooms) are served in a small and simple dining room with a friendly atmosphere. There are a few rather basic but clean rooms, which are fine if you need somewhere to stay urgently.

🛏 ✕ **Hôtel-restaurant Le Relais de la Forge**: place du Village.

☎ 04-92-35-16-98. Fax: 04-92-35-07-37. ✕ Closed from mid-November to mid-December. Rooms from 195F to 300F. Half board for 250F per person. Menus from 75F to 175F. There are 15 comfortable, well-appointed rooms in this converted forge. The traditional cuisine deserves a mention. Try the *gratin de pied de porc aux truffes* (pig's trotter gratin with truffles).

WHAT TO SEE

★ **La Grosse Pierre** (the big stone): a geological curiosity in the Liberne district, weighing 500 tonnes and standing 5 metres (16 feet) high.

★ **Gorges of the River Blanche**: a narrow gorge with the Blanche snaking through on its way to connect with the Durance.

WHAT TO DO

– **Gourmet outing**: a visit to a number of local producers.

MONTCLAR

St-Jean-Montclar has been officially dubbed a *village de montagne*. A walk lasting a few hours will take you to several of the high-altitude lakes (in summer, you can take the chairlift). Eau de Montclar, springwater from the highest source in Europe, is bottled here, and labelled as 'Eau de Montagne', reflecting the quality of the environment. Try paragliding over the Serre-Ponçon lake, one of the selected locations for the world championships.

WHERE TO STAY AND EAT

🛏 ✕ **L'Espace**: opposite the Dormillouse *massif*. ☎ 04-92-35-37-00. Fax: 04-92-35-31-92. Closed in April and from 15 October to 3 December. Rooms from 255F. Half board from 265F to 280F per person. This Logis de France has an intimate atmosphere but is also very well located, at the foot of the slopes. The chef's specialities in the mountain restaurant include *gigot d'agneau à la provençale* (leg of lamb with tomato and garlic) or ravioli gratin.

WHAT TO SEE IN THE AREA

★ About 20 villages between Rurriers and La Motte are still involved in the breeding of animals, in arable farming and fruit-growing. Summer is the best time to explore the area along the small country roads, as an alternative to taking the main road to Sisteron.

WHERE TO STAY AND EAT IN THE AREA

♠ ✕ **Chambres and table d'hôte Grange Joly**: with Jean-Jacques Leporati, at Bayons (04250). ☎ and fax: 04-92-68-34-32. Closed from All Saints Day to Easter. About 256F for two, including breakfast. 83F for a Provençal (set) meal, including wine. Way out in the country in a grandiose setting, this small house has three guest rooms with simple but pleasant decor. Jean-Jacques loves walking and also cooks for his guests, who eat together in a welcoming room with a fireplace and piano. There's also a small lodge for three or four people. The welcome is convivial and genuine.

The Haute-Provence from Sisteron to Manosque

The route from the Alpine valleys to Sisteron is magical. Detours are possible in a landscape that is extraordinarily beautiful in good weather and rather forbidding when climatic conditions deteriorate. Photographers will love it when the sun shines, as the colours change with the variations in the vegetation and the light. The transition from the mountain country back to the deep south is delightful.

SISTERON (04200)   Population: 6,964

With a patchwork of roofs and labyrinthine streets around a citadel, facing the Rocher de la Baume, Sisteron is the gateway to Provence from the Dauphiné. The town's setting is remarkable, with the Durance river meandering below. Its most famous son is Paul Arène, a writer who has always been over-shadowed by the better-known Alphonse Daudet.

USEFUL ADDRESSES

🛈 **Tourist office**: Hôtel de Ville. ☎ 04-92-61-12-03 and 04-92-61-36-50. Fax: 04-92-61-19-57. Email: office-de-tourisme-sisteron@wanadoo.fr. In July and August open 9am–7pm; Sunday 10am–noon and 2–5pm. During the rest of the year, open Monday to Saturday 9am–noon and 2–6pm (to 5pm in winter).

🚂 **Train station**: avenue de la Libération. ☎ 08-36-35-35-35. Services to Marseille, Gap and Briançon.

🚌 **Buses**: for information on buses ☎ 04-92-61-22-18.

WHERE TO STAY AND EAT

♠ **Grand Hôtel du Cours**: allée de Verdun. ☎ 04-92-61-00-50. Fax: 04-92-61-41-73. Closed from 10 November to 1 March. Double rooms from 320F to 460F with shower or bath, toilet and TV. Menus from 90F to 150F. The smartest hotel in town, with its 50 old-style rooms, is rarely full, although the welcome is cordial and the service attentive. Avoid the rooms overlooking the main road; ask for one with a view of the chateau and cathedral. The pleasant restaurant serves tasty local specialities, such as *gigot d'agneau a l'ail* (leg of lamb with garlic). The staff are young and friendly.

✕ **Les Becs Fins**: 16 rue Saunerie. ☎ 04-92-61-12-04. Closed all day Wednesday and on Sunday evening as well as for a week in June and for ten days in December. Menus from 96F to 286F. This restaurant reflects the town's status as 'lamb capital' of the region – lamb chops take pride of place. The atmosphere is warm and friendly, and the Provençal menus are thoughtful and balanced.

Campsite

🛏 **Le Jas du Moine**: 04290 Salignac. 6 kilometres (about 4 miles) along the D4 between Volonne and Sisteron. ☎ 04-92-61-40-43. Fax: 04-92-61-10-24. ♿ Open all year. Peaceful and shady with a swimming pool and bungalows; mobile homes to rent by the week. Pizzeria and take-away food from July to September.

WHERE TO STAY AND EAT IN THE AREA

🛏 ✕ **L'Iris de Suze**: in Mison-Village. 11 kilometres (about 7 miles) along the N75 towards Grenoble; turn off at Mison-les-Armand, then follow the signs. ☎ 04-92-62-21-69. Menus from 95F to 150F. Named after a book by local writer Jean Giono, this restaurant is in a little house on the edge of the village with a nice awning and whitewashed walls and two mezzanine areas inside. Specialities include *pintadeau aux figues* (guinea fowl with figs) and *feuilleté d'escargots* (snails in pastry).

🛏 ✕ **Le Mas du Figuier**: La Fontaine, in Bevons. ☎ 04-92-62-81-28. Double rooms from 280F to 320F. Half board from 220F to 354F. *Table d'hôte* for 120F including wine. Charming rooms in a relaxing 18th-century *mas*, with huge trees, open spaces, vast terraces and a view due south to the Montagne de Lure. The owner is a mountain guide and organizes day excursions on foot or on donkeys. The home cooking includes organic and healthy dishes with lots of garlic, olive oil and basil alongside mint and cumin; lovely breakfasts are served on the terrace.

🛏 ✕ **Chambres d'hôte Le Jas de Caroline** (with Monique and Henri Morel): Chenebotte, at Noyers-sur-Jabron (04200). 12 kilometres (7.5 miles) from Sisteron along the D946. Go through the village, take the road to the right before the cemetery and follow the signs. ☎ 04-92-62-03-48. Fax: 04-92-62-03-46. 300F for two, 400F for the suite, with a very generous breakfast (with all sorts of jams). Set dinner for 100F, including wine (booking necessary). Standing in this hamlet in the middle of the Jabron valley, this stone-built house has a lovely garden, two rooms and a separate apartment (with a sitting room, TV and kitchen facilities) on the ground floor. In winter, dishes include *daube à la feignasse* (beef stew), *agneau au miel* (lamb with honey). In summer, meals are served on the terrace, which has a lovely view of the Montagne de Lure. There's a pleasant welcome.

🛏 ✕ **Chambres d'hôte L'escapade**: in Noyers-sur-Jabron. ☎ 04-92-62-00-04. Open from 1 April until All Saints. Double rooms for 350F; four-person rooms for 500F and a separate non-smoking *gîte* for three or four, which can be rented by the week. This Italian-style villa, built at the beginning of the 20th century, is superbly appointed, with a huge flower garden. The owners have restored the house to the way it was in their grandparents' time. This is a great place to relax.

WHAT TO SEE AND DO

★ **Church of Notre-Dame-des-Pommiers**: this 12th-century Romanesque cathedral has a surprisingly gloomy interior. There were only a few windows to begin with and some have been blocked up in the course of work on the building. There's a remarkable 17th-century retable.

★ **Old town**: the old part of the town nestles between the Durance and the cliff. There are a few lovely frontages dating from the Middle Ages to the 18th century.

★ **Citadel**: ☎ 04-92-61-27-57. Open from the end of March to 11 November 9am–5pm (until 8pm in July and August). Entrance fee: 20F (10F for 5- to 12-year-olds). Allow an hour to visit this impressive structure, perched on a rock overlooking the Durance. It was built well before the 11th century but was re-thought and entirely rebuilt in the 16th century by a military engineer of Henry IV. Vaubaun obviously admired it greatly because he left it untouched. On the orders of Louis-Philippe, some reinforcing works were carried out in the 19th century.

– Sisteron is the departure point for the **GR6 long-distance footpath**. In three days, walkers can reach Forcalquier, via Notre-Dame-de-Lure, Stétienne and Fontienne.

FESTIVALS AND MARKETS

– **Nuits de la Citadelle** (citadel nights): from mid-July to the beginning of August. Plays, dance and music set against the ramparts of the citadel of the Counts of Provence.

– **Markets**: Wednesday and Saturday morning.

– **Lamb festival**: held on one Sunday during the second half of July.

CHÂTEAU-ARNOUX (04160)   Population: 4,970

A village in a pretty setting on the banks of the Durance, dominated by the tower of its picturesque chateau.

USEFUL ADDRESS

🖪 **Office du tourisme du district de la Moyenne Durance** (tourist office of the Moyenne Durance region): at the Ferme de Font-Robert. ☎ 04-92-64-02-64. Fax: 04-92-64-54-55. Out of season open from Monday to Saturday 9am–noon and 2–6pm; in season until 7pm.

WHERE TO STAY AND EAT

✕ **Au Goût du Jour**: on the RN85. ☎ 04-92-64-48-48. Fax: 04-92-64-37-36. Closed Monday and Tuesday lunchtime (out of season only) and in January. Menus at 90F and 140F. This bistrot belongs to the smart restaurant Bonne Étape, next door. The decor, in tones of ochre and orange, is refined, the atmosphere is relaxed with friendly service and tasty cooking. Specials are listed on a blackboard and change according to what's good at the market. The owners were serving substantial regional dishes in the main restaurant at a time when *nouvelle cuisine* was all the rage. In the bistrot, the comforting food is still a reminder of past times.

✕ **L'oustaou de la Foun**: on the RN85. ☎ 04-92-62-65-30. Fax: 04-92-62-65-32. ✕ Closed Sunday night and Monday (except in July and August). Menus at 95F (weekday lunch), 120F and 208F. The decor here is 'Provençal hacienda' style. The chef, from a family of farmers and sausage-makers, uses fresh produce and is inventive and experimental. The short menu changes regularly, with delicious and flavoursome dishes. The *foun* in the name means 'fountain' in Provençal.

Campsites

⛺ **Les Salettes**: by the lake, 1 kilometre away. ☎ 04-92-64-02-40. Fax: 04-92-64-25-06. 69F for a site for two. Quiet, with a superb view and a swimming pool. Booking advisable in summer.

⛺ **L'Hippocampe**: route Napoléon (D4), 04290 Volonne. ☎ 04-92-33-50-00. Fax: 04-92-33-50-49. Closed from October to the end of March. Quite pricey, from 78F to 124F for a site for two. This site, in a 5-hectare (12- acre) park of cherry and olive trees, has a swimming pool, bar and lots of activities, as well as mobile homes or bungalows for rent.

FESTIVAL

– **Les Festives de Font Robert**: in mid-July. ☎ 04-92-64-02-64. A big gathering for world-music fans, which began 10 years ago. Bands – rock, blues, rap and others – play in a 16th-century arena in a green landscape.

MONTAGNE DE LURE

This part of the Alpes-de-Haute-Provence could be described in shorthand as the Luberon without the snobbery. The countryside has a particular openness and luminosity, because the sky is extraordinarily bright and the air is very pure. Olive trees are replaced by beech, old villages are buried in greenery and churches are tucked away in the valleys. Roof tiles become more rare as many of the houses are roofed in stone. According to local writer Jean Giono, 'This place is the very opposite of the usual. It requires character and a little soul.'

The Montagne de Lure is an unspoiled area of colour and perfume. Even in high summer, it's less busy than the Luberon and prices are much lower. In autumn, the colours are magnificent and more varied than in the regions where pines and conifers grow. Rural traditions, and arts and crafts, are preserved by people who seem to be still in touch with their land.

This area has also been classified as a *site remarquable du goût* (site of special gastronomic interest), largely because of the Banon cheese, Lurs olive oil and the aperitifs made in Forcalquier from aromatic plants.

CRUIS

At the heart of this village, a 14th-century church was built on the site of the 12th-century monastery. In the church choir, you'll find one of the most beautiful retables in Haute-Provence, dating from the 17th century.

WHERE TO STAY AND EAT

♠ ✕ **L'Auberge de l'Abbaye**: ☎ 04-92-77-01-93. Fax: 04-92-77-01-92. Restaurant closed Wednesday, and from December to February. Comfortable double rooms from 295F to 310F. Menus from 100F to 130F. This is a typical Provençal stone house in the middle of the village. Delightfully straightforward food is served on the lovely terrace in the shadow of the church. The rooms are spacious, clean and tastefully furnished in typically Provençal style.

♠ ✕ **Chambres d'hôte Le Moulin d'Anais**: le Moulin de Pologne.

04230 Montlaux. ☎ 04-92-77-07-28. Closed in March. *Table d'hôte* served on Thursday evening. Around 300F for two, including breakfast. This lovely 19th-century stone mill stands up at 550 metres (1,800 feet), in pretty countryside with a river running through it. The five charming rooms all have private facilities. Olive oil, basil, tarragon and rosemary feature strongly in the cuisine, which can be enjoyed in the welcoming dining room or on the terrace in the shade of the plane tree.

ST-ÉTIENNE-LES-ORGUES

At the junction of the D951, the D13 and the D950. The narrow streets in the old part of this village are lined with some beautiful 15th- and 16th-century buildings. In the past, there were many herbalists and shops specializing in natural remedies in the town. Today, on the 14 July, a big fair is held on the theme of herbalism and alternative medicine.

From St-Étienne, you can drive to the Lure Abbey along a winding road lined with cedar trees. Further on, you reach the summit of the mountain, at 1,826 metres (6,000 feet). The views from the top are splendid.

🅱 Tourist office: with a multimedia reference library. ☎ 04-92-73-02-57. Fax: 04-92-73-00-32. Open Tuesday to Saturday 9am–noon and 2–6pm.

FESTIVAL

– **Foire a l'herboristerie**: festival of herbalism, held on 14 July.

WHERE TO STAY AND EAT

♨ ✕ **Hôtel-restaurant St-Clair**: chemin de Serre. ☎ 04-92-73-07-09. Open daily during the week but closed from 15 November to 15 February. Rooms from 195F to 320F. Menus from 80F to 165F. This modern building, in an idyllic and peaceful setting, offers good value for money, with carefully prepared Provençal cooking. There's a swimming pool with a lovely, shady terrace.

LARDIERS

Another charming little village on the hillside, overlooking the Montagne de Lure, where the pale stones of the buildings change colour beautifully with the light. Way back in 1603, Wendelin the astronomer discovered that this area had particularly pure air and established the first observatory in Europe here.

WHERE TO EAT

✕ **Le Café de la Lavande**: ☎ 04-92-73-31-52. Closed on Sunday evening (except in high season), all day Monday, from mid-January to mid-February, and for the second half of November. Menu for 100F. There are so few country cafés like this left in France, where a few locals drop in for a glass of white wine in the morning or a pastis in the evening. The cuisine is simple and fresh. There's a limited number of places, so book ahead.

SAUMANE

Coming from St-étienne-les-Orgues, turn off the D12 on to the D950 just before you get to Banon. The village of Saumane sits at the foot of the Montagne de Lure. The 15th-century church of St-Pierre-aux-Liens is very pretty.

WHERE TO STAY AND EAT

♨ ✕ **Chambres d'hôte** (with Isabelle and Nicolas Barthe): ☎ and fax: 04-92-73-35-56. Around 280F for two, including breakfast. A lovely little place built of stone in the middle of the village, with a garden round it and a splendid view of the mountains. Three charming, old-fashioned rooms with private facilities and two others, also attractive but with shared facilities. Ideal for walkers.

✕ **Chez Marie-Anne**: the mini-auberge. ☎ 04-92-73-20-71. Open every day in July and August. In low season, closed on Tuesday and Wednesday but open during the weekend and weekdays on reservation. Meals for 90F. This simple and unpretentious country café is very friendly. The cooking is not grand but this is a good place to relax between excursions or to have a decent snack, especially if you're staying in the guest rooms.

BANON

At the point where the D950 crosses the D51. This pretty medieval village has loads of charm and a clutch of 15th-century buildings. Banon is famous for producing small goats' cheeses wrapped in oak leaves.

SHOPPING

Charcuterie Melchio Maurice: ☎ 04-92-73-23-05. An impressive number of sausages and goats' cheeses on sale in an old-fashioned grocer's shop that has kept its olde worlde charm. The potted goats' cheese macerated in the strongly alcoholic Marc de Bourgogne is an interesting one – an acquired taste

FESTIVAL

– **Cheese festival**: at the end of May, this festival celebrates the holy trinity of bread, cheese and wine, including a competition to find the best Banon cheese.

SIMIANE-LA-ROTONDE

About 10 kilometres (6 miles) south of Banon on the D51, at the top of the hill. As you approach the village, you see the ruins of La Rotonde itself (the keep) and the chateau of the Lords of Simiane. There are some lovely mansion houses belonging to important families of glassmakers and lawyers, but for 10 months of the year the village is rather ghostly. There's a completely different atmosphere in summer, when the lavender bushes and the wild roses come into flower, and people come for the festival of ancient music, held in the mysterious Rotonde.

Going south towards Opedette, you can take a detour through the gorges (where there is a sheer drop of 150 metres/500 feet), gnawed out of the limestone by the Calavon river.

FESTIVAL

– **Les Riches Heures de la Rotonde**: ancient music festival held in July and August.

WHERE TO STAY

Chambres d'hôte Maison Dumaistre: ☎ 04-92-75-92-08. Fax: 04-92-75-94-96. Rooms from 350F to 500F, and a suite for four people for 1,000F. This delightful house has period Provençal furniture and gardens for breakfast or for a siesta under the awning. It's not cheap, but it offers a nice way of life.

FORCALQUIER (04300)   Population: 4,302

This town, in a pretty position on the slope of a hill, is named for a fountain gushing out of the limestone rock – *font* means 'fountain', *calquier* means 'limestone', hence Font-Calquier, which became Forcalquier. In the 12th century it was a tiny independent state set up by local nobles, who benefited from the rivalries between the counts of Toulouse and Barcelona, the Republic of Genoa and the German emperor. They kept their independence until the end of the 13th century, when plague swept through Provence. This political independence also meant ecclesiastical independence so when it came to an end the bishop of Sisteron found he had a second cathedral in Forcalquier. It's now described as a 'co-cathedral' and is the only one in France.

USEFUL ADDRESS

🛈 Tourist office: 13 place du Bourguet, BP 15. ☎ 04-92-75-10-02. Fax: 04-92-75-26-76. Email: oti@forcalquier.com. Open in summer Monday to Saturday, 9am–12.30pm and 2–7pm; Sunday 10am–1pm. During the rest of the year, open Monday to Saturday 9am–noon and 2–6pm; on Sunday 10am–1pm during holiday periods only.

WHERE TO STAY AND EAT

🛏 ✗ Hostellerie des Deux-Lions: 11 place du Bourguet. ☎ 04-92-75-25-30. Fax: 04-92-75-06-41. Email: hoteldeuxlions@aol.com. Closed on Monday evening and on Tuesday out of season. A few lovely rooms from 280F to 330F. Menus from 82F to 155F. Such solid, stylish places are fewer and further between than they used to be in France. It's easy to imagine how many communion and christening lunches, and wedding breakfasts, have been served here. The food is good – oxtail with *foie gras* and leek jelly or snails in pastry with *aïoli*.

🛏 ✗ Le Charambeau: route de Niozelles. ☎ 04-92-70-91-70. Fax: 04-92-70-91-83. Closed from 15 November to 15 February. Rooms from 305F to 420F. This lovely *auberge* is housed in an 18th-century former farm, a delightful place in any season, overlooking the valley and set in 7 hectares (17 acres) of meadows and hills. There are a dozen fresh, pleasant rooms, some with balconies and others with vast terraces, all comfortably appointed. There's a swimming pool and bicycles available.

WHAT TO SEE

★ **L'Église *Notre-Dame***: the rather forbidding cathedral was built between the 12th and 14th centuries, in both Romanesque and Gothic styles. In a Latin, cruciform shape, it has the tallest nave in Provence and two competing bell-towers: a hefty 14th-century one and a lighter, airy one, built in the 17th century.

★ **Le couvent des Cordeliers:** one of the first Franciscan foundations in Provence.

★ **Cemetery**: north of the town. Very unusual, with clipped yew hedges with arches.

★ **Fountains**: in the place du Bourguet and the place St-Michel.

FESTIVALS AND EVENTS

– **Concerts de carillon** (bell-ringing 'concerts'): every Sunday throughout the year at 11.30am.

– **Fête de la randonnée** (walking festival): held during the last weekend in April. Guided treks on foot, horseback or mountain bikes and thematic walks.

– **Concerts d'orgue** (organ concerts): held every Sunday in July and August, in the cathedral. Free entry.

– **Rencontres du Goût** (food festival): in October. Forcalquier is another *site remarquable du goût*.

– **Ronde des crèches** (tour around the Christmas cribs): in late December/ early January. An itinerary guiding visitors around all the Christmas cribs in the area, with their nativity scenes made with traditional *santons* (terracotta figurines).

From Forcalquier to Manosque

LURS

Make a 12-kilometre (7.5-mile) detour from Forcalquier to find the Ganagobie priory and this agreeable little town. Overlooking the Durance valley, Lurs has delightfully harmonious architecture and lots of character. Unfortunately, it is best known in France for the shocking and mysterious *affaire Dominici*, the trial that took place here in 1952 and fascinated the nation's media for many months.

WHERE TO EAT

🛏 ✕ **Restaurant La Bello Visto**: in the village. Closed on Wednesday and in the evening out of season. ☎ 04-92-79-95-09. Fax: 04-92-79-11-34. Menus from 85F to 200F. À la carte around 250F. Delicious dishes include *pigeon aux truffes* (pigeon with truffles), *lapin rôti sauce poivrade* (roast rabbit with pepper sauce) and *grillade d'agneau au miel de thym* (grilled lamb with thyme honey).

WHAT TO SEE

★ **La Prieuré Ganagobie** (priory): reached via the picturesque little D330. Open every day except Monday 3–5pm (no charge). The priory was built in the middle of the 10th century on an impressive plateau planted with oak trees. You can only visit the existing church, which was built in the 12th century. The apse is paved with remarkable Romanesque mosaics in white, black and red with fabulous monsters representing the eternal struggle between good and evil.

MANE

A large, pleasant town near the Salagon priory. Walk through the streets of the old village, which dates from the 10th century, on the way up to the chateau, to see the richness of its medieval heritage. Fortunately, it has escaped the invasion of fast food outlets catering for the summer visitor.

WHERE TO EAT

✕ **La Reine Rose**: ☎ 04-92-75-35-30. Fax: 04-92-75-43-87. Closed on Wednesday (out of season) and from 20 December to 15 January. Menus from 100F to 160F. This restaurant, rather like a set from a Chabrol film, serves such dishes as *filets de rougets sur poivrons rouges marinés* (red mullet fillets on marinated red peppers).

✕ **La Pie Margot**: rue du Barri, in Dauphin (4 kilometres/2.5 miles). ☎ 04-92-79-51-94. Closed on Wednesday, on Thursday lunchtime out of season, and in December. Menus start at 115F. This delightful place offers *magret miel et pignons* (duck breast with honey and pine nuts) and *St-Jacques aux framboises* (scallops with raspberries), among other delights.

WHAT TO SEE

★ **La Prieuré Salagon** (priory): on the N100, about 4 kilometres (2.5 miles) south of Forcalquier. ☎ 04-92-75-70-50. Open from 1 May to 30 September every day 10am–noon and 2–7pm; rest of the year, open at the weekend, during school holidays and in October, 2–6pm. Entrance fee: 28F (16F concessions and 100F family ticket). The priory retains its double 12th-century church and its prior's house, built in the 15th century adjoining the church. It was closed after the Revolution but opened again in 1981 as a conservation centre. There are annual exhibitions on life in the area and an interesting garden featuring a medieval area, a scented garden, and a contemporary display.

ST-MICHEL L'OBSERVATOIRE

About 3 kilometres (2 miles) south of Forcalquier on the N100. The village of St-Michel has much Provençal charm but the main reason people come here is to visit the Observatory of Haute-Provence, added to the village's name in 1938. The astronomical establishment is open for visits on Wednesday between April and September, from 2pm to 4pm. Between 1 October and 31 March, open on Wednesday at 3pm on the dot. For further information: ☎ 04-92-70-64-00. Entrance fee: 15F.

WHERE TO STAY AND EAT

🛏 ✕ **Chambres d'hôte** (with Pascal and Cathy Depoisson): in Le Farnet. ☎ 04-92-76-65-52. Fax: 04-92-76-65-97. Open from April to end October. Rooms for 280F and *table d'hôte* dinner for 85F. This old sheep farm, overlooking the lavender fields and green oaks of the valley, has been attractively restored, with a lovely swimming pool and appealing rooms. The owners are very welcoming and meals are served on the terrace as soon as the weather is warm enough. Dishes include a number of reliable local specialities.

MANOSQUE (04100)   Population: 19,603

Provençal writer Jean Giono described Manosque in his novel *Jean le Bleu*, in which he wrote, 'at night, the town breathed only through its fountains'. He was, it seems, particularly inspired by the surrounding countryside. The local authority makes the most of the literary connection, promoting books and reading under a programme known as *Manosque, Ville du Livre* ('Manosque, book town'). There are several bookshops and a number of writers live here. Pierre Magnan, for example, who brings the local landscape into his detective stories, can often be seen having coffee on the terrace of the Cigaloun, in the shade of the plane trees on the place de la Mairie.

Manosque has the biggest population of any town in the department. This fact will be come very obvious as you wander down the rue Grande on market day (Saturday).

USEFUL ADDRESS

🛈 **Tourist office**: place du Docteur-P.-Joubert. ☎ 04-92-72-16-00. Fax: 04-92-72-58-98. Open from Monday to Saturday 9am–12.15pm and 1.30–6pm. In summer, the office is also open on Sunday and public holidays 10am–noon and during the week until 6.30pm. Guided tours (20F) round the old part of Manosque from October to May on Thursday at 2.30pm every fortnight and twice a week from June to September.

WHERE TO STAY

☆ Budget

🛏 **Auberge de jeunesse** (youth hostel): parc de la Rochette. 800 metres from the town centre. ☎ 04-92-87-57-44. Fax: 04-92-72-43-91. Closed in January. Double rooms with washbasin for 96F. Half board for 110F per person per day. Meals are 50F. Housed in a modern building, the hostel has kitchen facilities and rooms that accommodate two to six people, with washbasins. There are also 20 beds in communal tents. The swimming pool is 50 metres from the hostel, and there are tennis courts 100 metres away, as well as a lake for sailing and swimming.

☆☆ Moderate

🛏 **Grand Hôtel de Versailles**: 17 avenue Jean-Giono. ☎ 04-92-72-12-10. Fax: 04-92-72-62-57. Rooms from 150F to 280F. Open all year round. Garage extra. Hotels in Manosque are generally not very good – what the Giono's favourite town needs is a simple hotel with books everywhere. This one at least has some atmosphere and attractive handmade floor tiles.

☆☆☆ Chic

🛏 **Hôtel Pré St-Michel**: route de Dauphin. Just outside the town. ☎ 04-92-72-14-27. Fax: 04-92-72-53-04. Hotel open throughout the year. Restaurant closed on Monday all day and Saturday lunchtime. Rooms with shower or bath, toilet and TV from 350F to 500F. Menus from 98F to 178F. Well appointed, simple and pleasant with a swimming pool in the garden for lazy days in the heat of the summer. Some rooms overlook the garden. The restaurant is simple but handy, if you don't feel like driving, and there's a smiling and friendly welcome.

WHERE TO EAT

☆☆ Moderate

✗ **La Barbotine**: 5 place de l'Hôtel-de-Ville. In the old town. ☎ 04-92-72-57-15. Menu at 95F. Closed Sunday and in November. Healthy meals, pancakes and salads, served by a team of women who make customers feel at home. There's a lovely terrace.

✗ **Restaurant Le Luberon**: 21bis place du Terreau. ☎ 04-92-72-03-09. Closed Sunday evening and Monday out of season and from the end of August to early September. Menus for 65F (weekday lunch) and from 100F to 198F. Succulent Provençal dishes – *daube d'agneau à l'ancienne* (old-fashioned lamb stew) – emerge from the kitchen despite the fact that the chef is from the north of France. Olive oil and basil feature prominently. The decor is pleasantly rustic and there's a lovely terrace.

☆☆☆ Chic

✗ **Restaurant Dominique Bucaille**: La Filature, 43 boulevard des Tilleuls. ☎ and fax: 04-92-72-32-28. ✗ Closed Sunday and Wednesday evening, except public holidays; a week in February, and mid-July to mid-August. Menus at 95F and 150F. This is the new smart restaurant in the region, with a very bright modern yet classic decor. Reasonably priced quality cooking, based on intelligently re-vamped traditional dishes. The à la carte dishes, including *l'agneau de lait en cocotte à la fleur de sel de Camargue* (casserole of milk-fed lamb with Camargue salt), are all cooked with care and precision and cleverly flavoured.

WHAT TO SEE

★ **Porte Saunerie**: this gateway protects the entrance to the old town. Built in the 14th century, it owes its name to the salt warehouses that used to be nearby. The battlements above it symbolize the freedom of the town.

★ **In the footsteps of Giono**: at 14 rue Grande you can see the house of 'Jean le Bleu', his mother's ironing workshop and his father's cobbler's shop. Another of his characters, the Hussar Angelo, hid on the roof of the St-Sauveur church. (Look for the 1625 organ and the superb wrought-iron belfry, built in 1725 by Guillaume Bounard de Rians, one of the most intricately worked and one of the oldest in Provence.) Afterwards, go up the Montée des Vraies-Richesses to Giono's house, Lou Paraïs. The Association des Amis de Giono (association of the friends of Giono) organizes tours every Friday 2.30–5pm (his library and his office). Book by phone on Tuesday and Friday afternoons: ☎ 04-92-87-73-03.

The **Centre Jean-Giono** (3 boulevard Élémir-Bourges. ☎ 04-92-70-54-54), housed in a lovely 18th-century Provençal building, hosts exhibitions and organizes literary walks. There's a permanent exhibition on Giono, as well as a book and video library, and a bookshop.

★ **Manosque old town** has a wealth of attractions, starting with its little squares, the perfect place to stop for a drink, and its booksellers. Some of the shops in the **rue Grande** have spoilt their beautiful old doors, but No. 23, the **Hôtel Gassaud** (the presbytery) is still one of the finest private residences in the town. Mirabeau was held here under house arrest in 1774 for non-payment of debts.

★ **L'Église Notre-Dame-de-Romigier**: church of Romanesque origin, but with a Renaissance portal. There's a black Madonna in wood, a palaeo-Christian sarcophagus in Carrara marble dating from the fourth to fifth centuries, a moving, stone cemetery cross from the 16th century, and an organ built in 1850.

★ **Porte Soubeyran**: the vaulting and base of this gateway were built in the 14th century and the belfry was constructed in 1830 by Beauchampt of Apt. Its shape recalls the shape of the town (rather like a pear). On the rue des Martels there's a way on to the old ramparts.

★ **Fondation Carzou**: in the church of the Couvent de la Présentation, 7 boulevard E.-Bourges. ☎ 04-92-87-40-49. Fax: 04-92-87-05-21. Open Friday, Saturday and Sunday 10am–noon and 2.30–6.30pm. Closed for the Christmas holidays. Entrance fee: 25F (children 10F). In 1984, the town council of Manosque restored the convent and created a foundation to Armenian painter Carzou, who took seven years to complete his apocalyptic depiction of the year 2000. Worth seeing.

★ **La Thomassine biodiversity centre**: chemin de la Thomassine. ☎ 04-92-87-74-40. ♿ (to toilets). Open from 1 July to 30 September from Wednesday to Sunday. Self-guided visits from 10.30am to 5pm. One-hour guided tours at 11am and 3pm. Between October and June, they are held on Wednesday only, from 10.30am to 5pm. Entrance fee: 10F. Interesting and instructive, the centre focuses on the extraordinary variety of flora in the world. There's an orchard where 290 varieties of traditional fruit trees are grown and protected, and a kitchen garden growing traditional vegetable varieties. Follow the nature trail through the Mediterranean forest.

★ **Colline du Mont-d'Or** (3-kilometre/2-mile round trip): on the hill to the northeast of the town, you can see the ruined walls of the chateau that belonged to the counts of Forcalquier, to whom Manosque owed allegiance. There's a fabulous view from the top of the pear-shaped old town and its shining rooftops, and the ribbon of canal that runs parallel to the Durance through fields and orchards. The horizon stretches over the Luberon and you can see the peaks of Ste-Victoire, Ste-Baume, the Haut-Var and the Mont d'Aiguines, which looks down on the Gorges du Verdon and the lower peaks of the Alps. The terracing has recently been restored and replanted with olive trees.

On the way back to the town, stop off to taste and buy some Manosque olive oil from the **Moulin de l'Olivette** (place de l'Olivette. ☎ 04-92-72-00-99).

FESTIVALS

– **Medieval festival**: held once every two years over a weekend at the end of June. The old town is decorated for one of the least clichéd and most enjoyable festivals in France.

– **Festival '*Musiks à Manosque*'**: at the end of July, a wide range of music is enjoyed in open-air concerts. This free festival has been running for more than 15 years.

– **Fête de l'Olivier** (olive festival) is generally held on Ascension Thursday in Manosque itself and the villages round about.

– **International Festival of the Luberon**: between 10 and 15 August. Street parades, banquets and performances, and firework displays to confirm that Manosque is still one of the gateways to the Luberon.

– **Les Nuits de la Correspondance** (writing festival): held at the end of September/early October, with creative writing workshops and literary events every evening.

THE VALENSOLE PLATEAU

Between the Durance valley and the Verdon gorges, the Plateau de Valensole is at its perfect best in July, when the lavender is in flower. Come early in the morning or when it's cool so that you can drink in the perfumes and revel in the colours of the earth and the sky.

VALENSOLE

This is the most extensive *commune* in the whole of France. Even though the town itself has old streets and doors, a fountain built in 1734 and lots of chapels, it is less appealing than the plateau and the distilleries, which can be visited in summer. The bee museum on the road to Manosque sells local lavender honey that confirms the plateau as a top spot for flavour and taste.

WHERE TO STAY AND EAT

🏠 ✕ **La Bellencroupe**: La Trinité. 5 kilometres (about 3 miles) on the way to Manosque on the chemin de Riou ☎ 04-92-74-84-06. Closed from November to March. Room at 160F. Half board for 150F per person. There are horses at this old farm and a room for two to four people in the former *pigeonnier*, plus dormitories. Experienced and novice riders will enjoy the horse treks, and tasty Provençal and West Indian dishes are also served.

WHAT TO DO

– **Lavender festival**: mid-July. Distillery visits, products for sale, and helicopter rides over the lavender fields.

GRÉOUX-LES-BAINS

Gréoux is close to the entrance of the Parc Naturel Régional du Verdon (regional natural park of the Verdon), surrounded by the Verdon lakes and the lavender fields of the Valensole plateau. Also a spa resort, the village is interesting because of the architectural unity of its buildings, which cluster around the hill of the Chateau des Templiers.

USEFUL ADDRESS

🛈 **Tourist office**: 5 avenue des Marronniers. ☎ 04-92-78-01-08. Fax: 04-92-78-13-00. Email: tourisme@greoux-les-bains.com. Open every day, except Sunday afternoon, from April to September 9am–noon and 2–6pm. From October to March, open 9am–noon and 2–6pm (except on Sunday and public holidays).

WHERE TO STAY AND EAT

🛏 ✕ **Hôtel-restaurant des Alpes**: 19 avenue des Alpes. ☎ 04-92-74-24-24. Fax: 04-92-74-24-26. Closed from mid-November to end February. Rooms from 275F to 315F. Menus from 90F to 175F. Nothing like a spa hotel, this lovely house is tastefully decorated, has views over the village, the grounds or the swimming pool. The well-appointed restaurant has a range of menus. The welcome is warm.

🛏 ✕ **Hôtel du Grand Jardin**: avenue des Thermes. ☎ 04-92-70-45-45. Fax: 04-92-74-24-79. Closed from 20 November to 10 March. Rooms start at 270F, going up to 340F with bath and toilet. Menus from 100F to 220F. This is a 'grand' hotel in the old sense of the word, practical and pleasant with a lovely swimming pool, good bar and gourmet menu for those in search of something a bit different.

🛏 ✕ **Villa La Castellane**: avenue des Thermes. ☎ 04-92-78-00-31. Fax: 04-92-78-09-77. Closed in January and February. Rooms from 290F to 410F. Menus from 120F to 160F. This former hunting lodge, once owned by the Marquis de Castellane, has kept its aristocratic allure as a small hotel, full of character. The grounds have ancient cedar trees, and the atmosphere is very pleasant. The rooms are full of interesting features, with bright paintings. Enjoy a large selection of buffet starters, followed by Mediterranean dishes. There's a swimming pool and car parking.

✕ **Le Jardin des Lilas**: 7 rue des Lilas. ☎ 04-92-78-11-45. Closed on Tuesday evening (except during school holidays). Around 80F for a meal. This restaurant is a stone's throw from the hubbub of the summer tourists and has a tiny garden. It offers Provençal tarts and pancakes, mixed salads or kebabs.

WHERE TO GO FOR A DRINK

🍷 **La Terrasse**: avenue des Marronniers. ☎ 04-92-74-23-24. Closed from December to February. An ideal spot to savour a cool beer or a cocktail at dusk under the chestnut trees. Snacks include *pan bagnat*, toasted sandwiches and a particularly good *bruschetta* with red peppers, artichokes or basil.

SHOPPING

Calissons Durandeu: 46 rue Grande. ☎ 04-92-78-00-01. Closed Monday and in January and February. This attractive Provençal sweet shop is the only one in the region to make almond-based *calissons*.

Fromages de chevre du Domaine de la Fare (goats' cheeses): on the D82 towards Manosque. ☎ 04-92-74-20-64. Closed in December and January. A good place to buy Banon cheese (*see* page 381).

WHAT TO SEE

★ **L'Église de Notre-Dame-des-Ormeaux**: the name of this 12th-century church comes from the fact that the square used to be planted with elm trees (*ormes*). The nave is Romanesque, the lower part and the chapels were added in the 15th and 16th centuries. There is a square apse and a gilded wooden retable from the 17th century.

★ **Notre-Dame-des-Oeufs**: this little chapel snuggled in the Haut-Var hills is a famous pilgrimage destination for infertile women. There are two pilgrimages a year, on Easter Monday and 8 September.

★ **Château des Templiers**: overlooking the village, the castle of the Knights Templar now houses an exhibition hall and in summer hosts shows in its courtyard. Open every Wednesday for guided tours at 2.30pm (4pm in July and August), leaving from the tourist office.

★ **Musée du Vitrail** (glass museum): rue Grande. ☎ 04-92-74-27-85. Open from Monday to Friday, 8.30am–noon and 1.30–6pm. Entrance fee: 40F (children 30F).

★ **Maison de Pauline**: rue Grande. Open from May to October every day except Sunday. A little museum about local arts and traditions in a 19th-century house, refurnished in 19th-century style.

★ **Crib of Haute Provence**: 36 avenue des Alpes (the road to Vinon). ☎ 04-92-77-61-08. Every day except Monday, 9.30am–noon and 2.30–6pm (7pm in summer). Closed January and February. Call ahead to check opening times. Entrance fee: 25F. An authentic 180-metre (600-foot) Provençal nativity scene, comprising more than 300 *santons* made by Gérard Moine. There's an unusual *son et lumière* show every half an hour.

FESTIVALS

– **Journées gastronomiques**: end of April. 'Gastronomic days', with a market selling all sorts of local produce, street performers and tastings.

– **Festival de tous les Midis and Mercredis du Sourire**: various performances in the courtyard of the chateau, from mid-July to mid-August.

– **Foire aux Santons**: *santon*-makers from the region gather together for a fair during the All Saints holidays (early November).

THE ALPES-DE-HAUTE-PROVENCE

ESPARRON-DE-VERDON

The delightful little road to this hidden, hilltop village passes along the banks of the Esparron lake. The village is very busy in summer, but much quieter out of season. There's a lavender festival on 14 August.

USEFUL ADDRESS

🚹 **Tourist office**: ☎ 04-92-77-15-45. Fax: 04-92-77-12-94. Every Saturday at 9.30am from 1 April to 31 October, there's a guided tour of the village.

WHERE TO STAY AND EAT

🛏 **Chambres d'hôte Le Roumanin**: at the entrance to the village. ☎ 04-92-77-15-91. Closed from 3 November to 1 April. Rooms from 370F to 450F, including breakfast. This quiet romantic hideaway, high up by lake Esparron, is surrounded by flowers. The owners are very respectful of their guests' privacy.

🛏 ✕ **Chambres d'hôte de Castellane**: in the Chateau d'Esparron. ☎ 04-92-77-12-05. Fax: 04-92-77-13-10. Closed from All Saints to Easter. Rooms from 700F to 1,300F. The prices may be a bit of a shock, but the chateau, in the hands of the same family since the 15th century,

is glorious. A tasteful conversion has created luxurious rooms and superb bathrooms. Breakfast is served in the old, attractively refurbished kitchen or on the terrace with a view over the countryside. The ideal place for a romantic weekend of indulgence.

✕ **La Soleillade**: on the village square. ☎ 04-92-77-16-84. Meals for around 70F. Closed on Monday and in the evening out of season and from 15 November to 15 February. This is a lovely peaceful place with a terrace, where you can enjoy local produce, including salads, sweet and savoury tarts, *pan bagnat* or filled rolls.

WHAT TO SEE

★ **Ecomusée 'La Vie d'Antan'** (museum of yesteryear): rue des Fontaines. ☎ 04-92-77-13-70. Open every day (except Tuesday) 2.30–6.30pm between April and October, and 10am–noon and 3–7pm in July and August. Entrance fee: 10F (free for under-12s). This pocket-size museum displays a collection of authentic Provençal costumes and artefacts, including a 19th-century washing machine (made of wood), a black 19th-century wedding dress, a wedding shirt, a wolf-deterrent dog collar, and many other curiosities.

WHAT TO DO

– **Boat trips**: on *La Perle du Verdon*. ☎ 04-92-77-10-74. 45F for adults and 30F for children between six and twelve years. The one-hour tour of the lake includes a commentary on local flora and fauna. Motor boats for up to five people can also be hired, for 160F per hour.

THE ALPES-DE-HAUTE-PROVENCE

ALLEMAGNE-EN-PROVENCE

Some 10 kilometres (6 miles) from Gréoux and 8 kilometres (5 miles) from Riez. A picturesque and appealing village on the road to the gorges, with old stone houses, restaurants, cafés, a grocery, a bakery, and a travelling circus in summer. There is also the 14th- to 16th-century chateau to visit and the lavender distilleries. Wander round the upper part of the village, to get an idea of what Provençal village life used to be like. Choose a little square to sit down and have a drink. Look out for the unusual irrigation system that starts at the old public washing place.

USEFUL ADDRESS

☎ **Maison des Produits du Pays du Verdon** (centre for regional produce): route de Riez. ☎ 04-92-77-40-24. Closed in January, but open every day during the rest of the year. A group of around 30 farmers, craftsmen and artists from the lower Verdon set up this shop on the edge of the Plateau de Valensole to sell their products. You can buy good food for a picnic, or to take home, from cooked Provençal dishes, terrines and pâtés and goats' cheeses, to wine, apple juice, honey, hazelnut jam and any number of products using lavender.

WHERE TO STAY

☎ **Chambres d'hôte** (with Diane and Gérard Angelvin): rue des Jardins. ☎ 04-92-77-42-76. Rooms for 220F for two, including breakfast, or 345F for four people. This 16th-century house, with two pleasant, unpretentious rooms, has lots of character. Animals and children are welcome. There is direct access to the lavender-scented garden from the rooms.

RIEZ

Riez is the oldest town in the Alpes-de-Haute-Provence, a former colony subject to Roman law under Augustus, and a bishopric from the fifth century until the French Revolution. A few granite columns are testament to the existence of a pagan temple dating from the High Empire. An episcopal ensemble – a group of four Corinthian columns with a stone slab on top – remains as a rare example of Provençal architecture from late Antiquity.

The magnificent town is impressive, with medieval houses standing along-side Renaissance buildings. Some of the interiors have *gypseries* (stucco work) of amazing beauty, adding a decorative layer to fireplaces, ceilings or stairwells. Their production was an extremely important industry in Riez.

USEFUL ADDRESS

🄱 **Tourist office**: 4 allée Louis-Gardiol. ☎ 04-92-77-99-09. Fax: 04-92-77-99-07. Open from Tuesday to Saturday 9am–12.30pm and 2–6.30pm.

WHERE TO STAY AND EAT

â Ferme de Vauvenières (with Hélène and Christian Sauvaire): Vauvenières, 04410 St-Jurs. 13 kilometres (8 miles) from Riez on the D953 and then right on to the D108 at Puimoisson. ☎ 04-92-74-72-24. Fax: 04-92-74-44-18. ✗ Open all year. Double rooms for 270F, and an evening meal for 100F. This B&B establishment is very good value for money. There's also a campsite at the farm. Booking essential. Private parking.

✗ **Restaurant Les Abeilles**: chez André Jaubert, 10 allée Louis-Gardiol. ☎ 04-92-77-89-29 or 04-92-77-80-51. Menus from 50F to 120F. Open at lunchtime every day, and in the evening in July and August. The best eating place in the village, with meals served in the dining room or on the terrace, including tasty dishes such as polenta with sausage or egg, Provençal *aïoli* and roast pork, all carefully prepared. Good red wine served by the carafe is included in the price of the menu.

MOUSTIERS-STE-MARIE (04360)

Population: 625

One of the prettiest and most unusual places in the area, Moustiers clings to the mountain. It was founded in AD 433 by monks who came from the Îles des Lérins off Cannes, via Riez. The houses line the fast-moving River Riol, almost as if they're suspended over the water. There's greenery and flowers everywhere, and picturesque hump-back bridges. Above the raging river, a star hangs on a wrought-iron chain, strung between the two cliffs, 227 metres (745 feet) apart. It is said to have been hung there by a crusader in the 13th century as a sign of thanks for his safe return home.

Moustiers is most famous for its china. In the 17th and 18th centuries, there were 700 kilns and more than 30 workshops, employing 400 people. Both Cardinal Richelieu and Madame de Pompadour were customers, but fashions changed and the last Moustiers pottery closed in 1874. In 1927, however, a few enthusiasts fired up the kilns, and the pottery is being made in the village once again.

USEFUL ADDRESS

🛈 Tourist office: BP 1. ☎ 04-92-74-67-84. Fax: 04-92-74-60-65. Email: moustiers@wanadoo.fr. Open in high season every day 10am–noon and 2–6pm (to 7pm in July and August). Out of season, open 2–5pm. Guided tours of the town on Thursday at 10am (booking necessary outside July and August).

WHERE TO STAY AND EAT

â Auberge de la Ferme Rose: chemin Embourgues. ☎ 04-92-74-69-47. Fax: 04-92-74-60-76. At the

foot of the town. Closed from 30 November to mid-March. Double rooms from 390F to 750F. Surrounded by greenery, this lovely Provençal farm has a juke-box, bistrot tables, and lots of bits and pieces in the bar and the rooms. For some, the kitchen where breakfast is prepared might be in questionable taste. The rooms are very quiet and the one on the ground floor has a pretty terrace, ideal for a cosy, romantic stay. The excellent breakfasts are more than substantial and perfect preparation for an energetic day's walk (although you might prefer to take it easy).

≜ **Hôtel Le Clos des Iris**: Pavillon St-Michel. At the foot of the village. ☎ 04-92-74-63-46. Fax: 04-92-74-63-59. ✖ Closed from mid-November to mid-February. Well-maintained rooms with shower or bath and toilet for 390F. A charming pink Provençal *mas* with violet shutters, hidden by chestnut, cherry and fig trees, in a very tranquil setting.

≜ ✖ **Le Relais**: place du Couvert. ☎ 04-92-74-66-10. Fax: 04-92-74-60-47. ✖ Closed Friday and in January and February. Delightful rooms from 285F to 480F. Menus from 135F to 187F. Right in the middle of the village, on the banks of the rushing stream, this is one of the busiest places in Moustiers, so booking is advisable. Some rooms look out over the raging torrent. The restaurant also deserves a mention for its good traditional dishes that change with the seasons.

☆☆☆☆ Très Chic

≜ ✖ **La Bastide de Moustiers**: La Grisolière. ☎ 04-92-70-47-47. Fax: 04-92-70-47-48. Website: www.bastide-moustiers.i2m.fr. Open all year, but closed on Wednesday and Thursday in January and February. Menus at 230F (weekday) and 295F. The peace of this village is often shattered by the arrival of helicopters, bringing guests to enjoy the creations of famous chef Alain Ducasse. He has turned this enchanting 17th-century farmhouse, in a superb 4-hectare (10-acre) park planted with trees, into one of the most beautiful places in the area. The 11 luxuriously decorated rooms and one suite are beyond the reach of mere mortals, but the restaurant prices are just about affordable, particularly for a special occasion. Dishes change every day depending on the produce in the market or the vegetables in the kitchen garden. Ducasse seems to enjoy overseeing the cooking, which shows off the fresh produce to its best advantage. A real success.

WHAT TO SEE

★ **L'Église Notre-Dame-de-Beauvoir**: look up through the yew trees to spot this little church, perched on the hill. The steep climb up is worthwhile, both for the view and for the place itself. There was a chapel here in the fifth century, although the current church building dates from the 13th century. Until the 17th century, it was a place of pilgrimage for the parents of stillborn children. In those days, the Church refused to bury stillborn babies. Parents would bring the tiny corpses here, hoping to see the smallest sign of life, which would allow the baby to be baptised and then buried properly.

★ **Musée de la Faïence**: town hall. ☎ 04-92-74-61-64. Open from 1 April to 31 October every day except Tuesday 9am–noon and 2–6pm, until 7pm in July and August. Entrance fee: 10F (concessions 5F, under-12s free).

This museum covers the history of porcelain from earliest times. The porcelain is made from powdered clay that is dampened and kept in a damp cellar. Individual pieces are thrown on a wheel, shaped, fired for 36 hours and then decorated. To qualify for the Moustiers label, a piece would have to be manufactured entirely in the town itself, according to traditional techniques, then painted by hand.

THE VERDON GORGES

The Gorges du Verdon are the most impressive in Europe, a gash made between the Alps of Haute-Provence and the Var as if by the axe of some great being, creating a 21-kilometre (13-mile) natural frontier. Just a few decades ago, the Verdon at its highest would flow at a rate of 800 cubic metres of water per second. Today, two dams regulate the flow to 30 cubic metres per second and walkers can get down to the canyon floor. The bewilderingly sheer cliffs, 300–600 metres (985–1,968 feet) high, shoot skyward on both sides. Piles of tumbled rocks and untamed riverbanks make it an adventurers' paradise.

Surprisingly, the gorges were a relatively recent discovery and only fully explored at the beginning of the 20th century. In 1997, the site became a *Parc Naturel Régional* (natural regional park) ensuring that any economic development is in tune with environmental protection. The park covers 180,000 hectares (695 square miles) and a number of administrative areas, including 44 *communes*, 25 of which are in the Alpes-de-Haute-Provence. It encompasses the Valensole plateau in the high country of the Var and the Arluby and stretches to the pre-Alpine mountains of Mondenier and Canjuers. Its cultural and ecological management is a challenge and the *communes* are obliged to work together. Most recently, the park authorities waged battle against EDF (the French national electricity company) and prevented the construction of new pylons. For information on the southern gorges, *see* pages [00-00].

USEFUL ADDRESSES

■ **Parc Naturel Régional du Verdon** (regional natural park of the Verdon): 04360 Moustiers, BP 14. ☎ 04-92-74-63-95. Fax: 04-92-74-63-94.

WHAT TO SEE

The Verdon is part of the geological reserve of Haute-Provence and the removal of minerals and fossils from here is forbidden. On the other hand, fishing is open to all, as long as it is done legally. In the Verdon and its tributaries, there are trout, pike, carp and many other freshwater fish. For birdwatchers, swallows, eagles and dozens of other species have been spotted and registered in the area. For plant lovers, information panels along the trails identify trees, bushes and aromatic plants such as sage, fennel and marjoram.

A network of marked footpaths covers a large part of the park. The routes that follow the gorges to the north and south take walkers through breath-

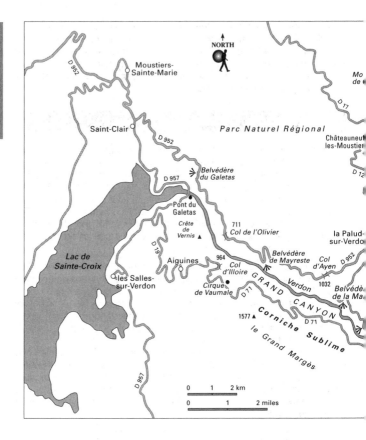

taking scenery. The Verdon also has many delightful hilltop villages, as well as Gallo–Roman ruins, old churches and reminders of local customs that go back centuries.

LA CORNICHE SUBLIME – THE SOUTHERN ROAD ALONG THE GORGES

Before setting off on the Corniche Sublime, the clifftop road on the southern side of the gorge (the D71), try to do a little circuit in the Var.

After Aiguines, you get to the **Col d'Illoire** (pass), where you catch your first superb glimpse of the canyon. A little further on, you reach the **Cirque de Vaumale**, at the highest point on the road (1,200 metres/3,936 feet), from which there's a wide panoramic view. By the **Falaises de Bauchet** (cliffs), the route winds along the narrowest part of the gorges, passing a sequence of lovely views. At the **Falaise des Cavaliers**, there's an impressive sheer

THE VERDON GORGES

drop. At the **Tunnels du Fayet**, there's a superb view (from the second tunnel) along a bend in the canyon (car parking possible here).

The **Artuby bridge** is a splendid single-span construction 180 metres (590 feet) above the Artuby river and a popular place for bungie jumping. From the **Balcons de la Mescla**, 2 kilometres from the bridge, there is an arresting panoramic view of the confluence of the Verdon and the Artuby. The Verdon bends back around a narrow crest of mountain.

When you get to the little hamlet of St-Maymes, turn off the D71 on to the D90, signposted to **Trigance**, a hilltop village dominated by its chateau and its four vast round towers.

Subsequently, the D90 meets the D955 from Comps and you turn left again on to the D925 from Castellane. This is the end of the southern route.

LA ROUTE DU NORD – THE NORTHERN ROAD

The northern route provides a succession of uninterrupted views from Pont-de-Soleils to La Palud-sur-Verdon. In the past, it was possible to take a cliff road that led to the river at the level of the Carejuan bank.

After the Tunnel de Tusset, a road to the left leads to the confluence of the Verdon and the Baou and a viewpoint known as the **Belvédère du Couloir Samson**. It is possible to descend to the bottom here and reach the end of the Sentier Martel, the footpath that begins at the Maline refuge.

Continue on the D952. For a lovely detour, take the D17 up to **Rougon**, an eyrie of a village with a ruined feudal castle on a massive rock and an exceptional panoramic view over the countryside. Return to the Auberge du Point-Sublime along the D952, via the promontory that provides a wonderful glimpse of the beginning of the canyon.

Just before you get to La Palud, turn left on to the D23, along the **Corniche des Crêtes**. The viewpoints all offer magnificent vistas. The first, the **Trescaïre**, is particularly breathtaking, because the cliffs are completely sheer and the view looks over the point where the three valleys connect. The second, the **Belvédère de l'Escalès**, provides views that are much more far-reaching. From the third, the **Dent d'Aires**, you get the widest view of the canyon and the country behind. This is the only place where you can really see the course of the Verdon. At the very bottom is the La Maline refuge.

LA PALUD-SUR-VERDON

This staging-post village is the little 'capital' of the Verdon. The church's lovely Romanesque bell-tower dates from the 12th century and there are a few shops and hotels.

WHERE TO STAY AND EAT

🛋 **L'Immense Botte de Paille** (youth hostel and campsite): La Palud-sur-Verdon. 500 metres from the village on the D23 (route des Crêtes). ☎ and fax: 04-92-77-38-72. Closed from 31 October to 1 March. 68F per night, including breakfast in the hostel, and 28F per pitch in the campsite. This peaceful youth hostel, in a totally isolated location, is well run, with a warm welcome. There are 56 beds in eight-bed dormitories (sheets provided) and a few double rooms. The campsite nearby has washing and kitchen facilities. Youth hostel card required (on sale here).

🛋 ✕ **Hôtel des Gorges du Verdon**: ☎ 04-92-77-38-26. Fax: 04-92-77-35-00. Closed from All Saints Day to end March. Half board compulsory, from 450F to 600F. Menus from 130F to 205F. Standing in the middle of the area of the Verdon gorges, deep in the countryside, on a hill across from La Palud. Rather modern and sombre architecture, but the rooms are well equipped, comfortable and clean and there's a pool and a tennis court. The decent cooking delves deep into the traditions of Provence.

🛋 ✕ **Auberge du Point-Sublime**: in Rougon, at the entrance to the gorges, on the D952. ☎ 04-92-83-60-35. Fax: 04-92-83-74-31. Email: point.sublime@wanadoo.fr. Closed from 24 November to 7 April. Double rooms from 225F to 310F. Half board compulsory at the weekend and during school holidays. Menus from 115F to 210F. Just across from the Point Sublime, this *auberge* has a few pleasant and peaceful rooms plus a terrace with an awning. The food is regionally based. Booking advisable in season.

🛏 ✕ **Hôtel-restaurant Le Provence**: La Palud-sur-Verdon. ☎ 04-92-77-38-88. Fax: 04-92-77-31-05. ⚒ Closed from November to Palm Sunday. Double rooms from 240F to 270F. Menus from 70F to 130F. This pleasant hotel is just 100 metres from the village square and has a clear view of the route des Crêtes. The restaurant serves specialities such as *lapin à la provençale* (rabbit with tomato and garlic) and *saumon à l'oseille* (salmon with sorrel). Have a drink on the peaceful terrace and enjoy the surroundings.

TRANSPORT

🚌 **Bus**: buses leave for Moustiers, Aix-en-Provence and Marseille at 1pm on Monday, Wednesday and Saturday from 1 July to 15 September; Saturday only the rest of the year. From 1 July to 31 August, there are services at 8.05am and 5.40pm every day except Sunday and public holidays.

WALKING

Walking along the bed of the canyon presents no significant difficulties, but it is important to have good equipment and to take a few precautions:

– You will need a pair of good walking shoes, plenty of drinking water, a lightweight anorak, a warm jumper (it can get cold), a reliable torch and a first aid kit.

– Consider buying the 1:50 000 IGN map *Moustiers-Ste-Marie*, and the *topoguide* (topological guide) to the long-distance GR4 footpath *Grasse à Pont-St-Esprit par le Canyon de Verdon*.

– Never leave the marked footpaths. Do not attempt to take short-cuts; some end up in space at the edge of sheer cliffs.

– Do not cross the river unless absolutely necessary. Releases of water through the dams can suddenly cause an unexpected rise in the river's level. There can also be strong currents.

– Pay serious attention to weather forecasts. Storms in the canyon are very violent.

– Do not pick flowers, light a fire or leave any rubbish. More than 100,000 people visit the gorges every year, and the ecosystem could be easily damaged.

EXCURSIONS

– **Pont-du-Galetas**: hire pedaloes, kayaks, canoes, rowing boats or motor boats, for 30 minutes or an hour, to see the breathtaking scenery of the canyon from a different angle.

– **Sentier du Couloir Samson**: for visitors with limited time, this marked footpath presents no major difficulties and provides some good views of the gorges. Take a pocket torch with you (there is a tunnel to pass through). Leave your car at the viewpoint of the Couloir Samson, on the north bank just below the Point Sublime. Allow two hours for the walk, there and back.

– **Sentier Martel**: the classic footpath through the gorges, starting from the Refuge de la Maline, on the north bank, on the D23. Allow about six hours to complete the walk. Marked out with great difficulty by the Touring Club de France in the 1930s, this extremely varied footpath is named after one of the first of the explorers of the gorges. For further information, pick up one of the specialist brochures available. Some sections are quite challenging for sufferers of vertigo, particularly a ravine that is crossed by metal stairs with 240 very narrow treads. However, it's a relatively safe path, because it is not susceptible to the vagaries of the Verdon's water level and it is clearly signposted as GR4.

CASTELLANE (04120)　　　　Population: 1,508

The charming town of Castellane sits at the eastern entrance to the Verdon gorges, surrounded by mountains, on a site that is protected by a sheer drop of 184 metres (600 feet). The chapel perched on the top was a place of refuge for the inhabitants when they were threatened by barbarian invasion.

Today, the town caters for the walkers who come to discover the beautiful countryside and watersports enthusiasts. It's also the home of the sect of the Mandarom. Many of the locals are deeply suspicious of the sect members, but others acknowledge that the area has benefited from their generosity. Officials have recently ordered the demolition of a number of statues and monstrous constructions, built in honour of the 'cosmoplanetary Messiah', so maybe the mountains and their spirits will now have the chance to regain their serenity.

USEFUL ADDRESSES

🏠 Tourist office: rue Nationale, 04120 Castellane. ☎ 04-92-83-61-14. Fax: 04-92-83-76-89. Email: office@castellane.org. Open from Easter to September, Monday to Friday 9am–noon and 2–6pm (on Saturday 10am–noon and 3–6pm). Also open on Sunday morning in July and August. Between October and March, open from Monday to Friday 9am–noon and 2–5pm.

★ A number of organizations in Castellane arrange excursions into the Verdon gorges, including rafting, canyonning and hydrospeed trips: Aqua Verdon (☎ 04-92-83-72-75); Action Aventure Rafting (☎ 04-92-83-79-39); Acti Raft (☎ 04-92-83-76-64); Montagne et Rivière (☎ 04-92-83-67-24); Aboard Rafting (☎ 04-92-83-76-11. Website: www.aboard-rafting.com).

WHERE TO STAY AND EAT

🛏 ✕ Nouvel Hôtel du Commerce: on the main square. ☎ 04-92-83-61-00. Fax: 04-92-83-72-82. Double rooms from 290F to 365F.

Menus from 115F to 260F. Closed from October to March, all day Tuesday and on Wednesday at lunchtime. Choose between a view of the village square or the 184-metre (600-foot) cliff in this large building, nestled between the post office and the town hall. Its decor is a mix of Provençal and kitsch. The flavourful cuisine is based on local produce from Provence and is prepared with care. The atmosphere is mostly friendly, although sometimes a little formal.

â ✕ **Hôtel Restaurant Ma Petite Auberge**: on the main square. ☎ 04-92-83-62-06. Fax: 04-92-83-68-49. Double rooms for 280F. À la carte around 130F. This hotel of the good old days, at the foot of Notre-Dame-du-Roc, has been tastefully renovated. The dining room is in the same sort of style and there's a veranda and a garden, shaded by an ancient lime tree. The menu is also old-fashioned, but not outdated.

â ✕ **Le Moulin de la Salaou**: on the road for the Verdon gorges. ☎ 04-92-83-78-97. Fax: 04-92-83-78-99. Rooms from 210F to 260F, depending on the season. Half board compulsory in July and August. Menus from 60F (weekday lunch) to 140F. This little mill lies deep in the countryside with quiet rooms in an annexe. It's a popular meeting point for bikers and party people, as the owners run a 'folksy' nightclub nearby (open only at weekends out of season). The food is tasty and unpretentious.

✕ **La Main à la Pâte**: rue de la Fontaine. ☎ 04-92-83-61-16. Closed on Wednesday and in January. Meals for around 100F. This simple restaurant has a great atmosphere and serves a selection of pizzas with very Provençal names.

✕ **Le Grilladin**: 26 route de Grasse, on the RN 85. ☎ 04-92-83-72-04. Closed from 1 October to 1 March. Menus at 89F and 139F. A pleasant little eating place on the edge of town, with a shady terrace and a substantial summer buffet of fresh and appetizing food. In low season, good quality meals are served at excellent prices. Vegetarians are catered for with a choice of salads and pizzas.

WHERE TO STAY AND EAT IN THE AREA

â ✕ **Auberge du Teillon**: route Napoléon. At La Garde, 6 kilometres (4 miles) along the Grasse road. ☎ 04-92-83-60-88. Fax: 04-92-83-74-08. Closed on Sunday evening and all day Monday out of season, and from mid-December to mid-March. Rooms from 200F to 290F. Half board from 270F to 300F per person, compulsory in high season. Menus from 110F to 240F. When Napoleon returned in triumph from the island of Elba along this road, he made the mistake of not stopping at this *auberge*. The local people know a good thing when they see one, and throng here at the weekend. The little rustic dining room is a warm and welcoming place in which to try the smoked lamb. There are also a few pleasant rooms, although the ones on the main road can be noisy.

â ✕ **Gîte d'étape des Bayles** (with Bénédicte and Jean-Michel Dufour): rue des Bayles, in Soleihas (04120). Drive along the N85 for 3 kilometres (2 miles) and then take the D102 towards Lake Chaudanne. After passing Demandolx, continue for 8 kilometres (5 miles). ☎ 04-93-60-40-17. Closed 19 to 27 November. Half board for 155F per person (reservation only). This little lodge is at an altitude of 1,100 metres (3,610 feet) in the heart of the valley and can accommodate 15 guests in its three rooms. Traditional family-style cooking is prepared and served by the young and friendly team.

🛏 ✕ **Hôtel-Restaurant 'Lou Jas'**: in Les Bayles district of Soleihas. ☎ and fax: 04-93-60-43-54. Closed from 19 to 30 March and from 19 November to 7 December. Rooms from 210F to 254F. Half board around 250F. Menus from 86F to 150F. This little mountain inn has well-maintained rooms, and a warm and friendly atmosphere. The cuisine is traditional and includes game in season.

WHAT TO SEE AND DO

★ **L'église St-Victor**: church built in the 13th century in a pronounced Provençal style.

★ **Walk through the village streets**: at the end of the rue St-Victor, go by the clock tower with its belfry, which was one of the gates in the old ramparts.

★ **Conservatoire des Arts et Traditions populaires** (centre of folk art and traditions): 34 rue Nationale. ☎ 04-92-83-71-80. Open all summer except for Monday, 9am–noon and 2–6pm. A little museum with a modest entrance fee.

★ **Maison des Sirènes et Siréniens**: on the village square, between the town hall and the post office. ☎ 04-92-83-19-23. Entrance fee: 15F (children 10F). Open 9am–noon and 2–6pm every day from May to September; Monday to Friday between October and April. Geological museum focusing on sea cows or manatees, peaceful plant-eating marine mammals that live near the coastline in warmer regions. Their name in French comes from the sirens of mythology.

★ Visit also the **protected fossil site** 6 kilometres (about 4 miles) from Castellane, at the Col des Léques, where mammal fossils over 40 million years old were found.

★ **La chapelle Notre-Dame-du-Roc**: determination and strong legs are needed to get to this chapel, via the pilgrimage route, because the 30-minute climb is steep, though there are many stopping places on different ledges. There is a huge statue of the Virgin on the top of the chapel. The summit provides a superb view of Castellane and the surrounding countryside.

FESTIVAL

– **Pétardier Festival**: at the end of January. This colourful festival celebrates the end of a siege waged against the town in 1586 by a group of Protestants. Judith Andrau, in particular, is commemorated for her part in warning the inhabitants of Castellane about the Huguenot attack and for slaying their leader.

– **Marathon of the Verdon Gorges**: held at the beginning of October, the marathon is run each year from Moustiers-Ste-Marie to Castellane through the gorges (the road is closed during the event).

Provence-by-the-Sea

Along the road to the Var region from the west, you come across seaside resorts that have grown out of little fishing villages, as well as picturesque hilltop settlements that have held on to their old-fashioned charm. Here, you're in Provence and on the coast at the same time, which is why the marketing executives have started to call the area *La Côte Provençale*, 'Provence-by-the-Sea'.

ST-CYR-SUR-MER (83270)   Population: 9,010

This small, typically Provençal town has a touch of the New World about its main square, where one of the four French replicas of Bartholdi's *Statue of Liberty* stands. A much-reduced scale model of the original *grande dame* was erected in 1913 to commemorate the arrival of running water in St-Cyr. The connection between the two is unclear. St-Cyr is a coastal town and a popular family resort, which extends along to Les Lecques, 2 kilometres to the southwest. There's a lovely beach between Les Lecques and Madrague.

USEFUL ADDRESS

🅱 **Tourist office**: place de l'Appel du 18 Juin, Les Lecques. ☎ 04-94-26-13-46. Fax: 04-94-26-15-44. Website: www.saintcyrsurmer.com. Open between June and September, Monday to Saturday, 9am–6pm (to 7pm in July and August); Sunday and public holidays 10am–1pm and 4–7pm; at the Easter and Pentecost weekends and on Ascension Thursday 10am–noon and 4–6pm; in May and October, open Monday to Friday 9am–6pm and on Saturday 9am–noon and 2–6pm.

WHERE TO STAY AND EAT

🛌 ✗ **Hôtel Le Petit Nice**: 11 allée du Docteur-Seillon, Les Lecques. ☎ 04-94-32-00-64. Fax: 04-94-88-72-39. ✗ Parking charge. Closed from 30 October to 15 March. Double rooms with shower or bath and toilet (and satellite TV), from 280F to 350F. Half board is compulsory in high season, from 280F to 350F per person. Restaurant menu at 130F. This hotel, hidden behind a large park with palm trees, has spacious and pleasant renovated rooms, a welcoming atmosphere and a lovely swimming pool.

☆☆☆ Chic

🛌 ✗ **Grand Hôtel des Lecques**: 24 avenue du Port, Les Lecques. ☎ 04-94-26-23-01. Fax: 04-94-26-10-22. Website: www.lecques-hotel.com. Double rooms with shower or bath, toilet and satellite TV from 380F to 760F, depending on season and view. Half board is compulsory from

1 July to 25 August, between 470F and 695F per person. Menus from 140F to 210F. This old-fashioned hotel is housed in a large Belle Époque villa standing in grounds planted with pines and palm trees. It has a huge foyer with columns and the rooms are all different, with tasteful contemporary decor. The most expensive rooms are near the sea and have a private balcony, the cheaper ones are at garden level and look out over the pine trees. On sunny days, meals can be enjoyed around the lovely pool and there are also tennis courts and a beach just a pebble's throw away. The welcome is friendly and there is still a family atmosphere.

WHAT TO SEE AND DO IN THE AREA

★ **Musée de Tauroentum**: 7 route de la Madrague. ☎ 04-94-26-30-46. Open every day from June to September (except Tuesday) 3–7pm. During the rest of the year, open on Saturday and Sunday 2–5pm. Entrance fee: 15F (10F for over-10s). The Romans built a *villa maritima* here in the second half of the first century BC, with terraced gardens going down to the sea. The museum is arranged around the foundations of the building and protects three sections of first-century mosaic, together with white marble columns from the first and second centuries. Greek and Roman artefacts are kept under glass, including coins, pottery, glassware, jewellery and small statues. Outside there's an unusual two-storey child's tomb. One part, covered in pink marble plaques, contained the body, while the other contained offerings. In its original form, the roof was the only part above ground level.

★ **Centre d'Art Sébastien**: Espace Cauvin, boulevard Jean-Jaurès. ☎ 04-94-26-19-20. Open every day (except Tuesday) from June to October, 10am–noon and 3–7pm; during the rest of the year, open 2.30–5.30pm and on Sunday 10am–noon and 2.30–5.30pm. Entrance fee: 15F. This former caper factory has been attractively converted into a contemporary arts centre. It houses a permanent collection of paintings, watercolours, bronzes and ceramic pieces by the artist Sébastien (1909–90), a friend of Picasso, Cocteau and Gide. Temporary exhibitions of works by the great names of modern art such as Miró and César are held here too.

★ **Calanque de Port d'Alon**: 4–5 kilometres (about 3 miles) south of St-Cyr on the D559, then follow the small signposted route to the right. A series of *calanques*, rocky inlets between vertical white cliffs topped by pine trees, stretch along the coast between Marseille and La Ciotat. In the past, smugglers took advantage of the safe natural harbours, but today you're more likely to see swimmers and sunbathers on the pretty beaches. Parking is expensive but there is also a coastal path for the more energetic (*see* 'Bandol', page 412).

FESTIVALS AND EVENTS

– **Market**: held on Sunday morning.

– **Fête des Vendanges** (autumn wine harvest festival): held in early September in the centre of town, with floats, local dances and processions.

WHAT TO SEE IN THE AREA

Between the Mediterranean and the Massif de Ste-Baume, rounded lime-stone hills rise up in the landscape with ancient *villages perchés* (hilltop villages) clinging to them. This hinterland is a delightful place to visit before the summer crowds arrive. Fruit trees and vegetables flourish here, along with the famous Bandol vine, grown on huge terraces known as *restanques*.

LA CADIÈRE-D'AZUR

This medieval village has an intricate maze of little streets running off the main square and a few vestiges of the ancient ramparts. There's a pretty walk on the D266 from La Cadière across the vineyards to Bandol.

USEFUL ADDRESS

🛈 **Syndicat d'Initiative** (tourist information centre): avenue H. Jansoulin. ☎ 04-94-90-12-56. Fax: 04-94-90-01-94.

WHERE TO STAY AND EAT

Campsite

🛏 ✕ **Camping de la Malissonne**: on the D66 between La Cadière and St-Cyr-sur-Mer. ☎ 04-94-90-10-60. Fax: 04-94-90-14-11. ♿ Closed from 15 November to 1 March. Surrounded by Bandol vine-yards, 4 kilometres (about 2 miles) from the sea, this pleasant site has a grocer's shop, restaurant, laundry facilities, swimming pool and tennis court, and a caravan, chalet or comfortable bungalow for hire. The atmosphere is warm and welcom-ing.

☆☆☆ Plus Chic

🛏 ✕ **Hostellerie Bérard**: rue Gab-riel-Péri. ☎ 04-94-90-11-43. Fax : 04-94-90-01-94. Closed Monday lunch and three weeks in January. Double rooms with shower and toilet from 380F to 510F, with bath and toilet from 760F to 860F. Menus from 160F to 450F. Housed in a former convent at the heart of the medieval village, this *auberge* has comfortable and spacious rooms with air-condi-tioning, a swimming pool and a shady terrace. The regional menu is excellent and well prepared.

LE CASTELLET

This attractive village comes complete with ramparts, a 12th-century church, a chateau, and medieval streets. Marcel Pagnol's film *Femme du Boulanger* ('The Baker's Wife') was shot here, and the place is now home to several artists and craftsmen. Every year, motor-racing fans from all over Europe gather here for the prestigious Ricard-sponsored 'Bol d'Or'.

LE BEAUSSET

This 16th-century agricultural village sits at the foot of the Massif de Ste-Baume. Fans of Provençal-Romanesque style should head along the N8, or the Chemin de Croix (Way of the Cross), to the Chapelle Notre-Dame du Beausset-Vieux (dating from 1164). It has a 'Virgin and Child' from the studio of Pierre Puget, terracotta *santons* over 400 years old, depicting the flight to Egypt, and a moving collection of ex-voto offerings. There's the added bonus of a beautiful panorama of the region.

USEFUL ADDRESS

🛈 Tourist office: place Charles-de-Gaulle. ☎ 04-94-90-55-10. Fax: 04-94-98-51-83. Information on Le Castellet, Le Beausset and Evenos.

WHERE TO EAT IN THE AREA

✗ **Restaurant La Fontaine des Saveurs**: 17 boulevard Chanzy. In the centre of the village. ☎ 04-94-98-50-01. ✗ Closed all day Wednesday, Sunday evening and for three weeks in October and 10 days in February. Menus at 99F (lunch only) and from 139F to 179F. Satisfaction guaranteed with unpretentious but very tasty dishes on a menu that changes regularly.

FESTIVAL

– **La St-Eloi**: this traditional votive festival takes place during the first weekend in July. A procession is held to the sound of fifes and tambourines, with horses in regalia and riders in traditional costume.

EVENOS

Pass through the Ste-Anne district on the N8 and climb up the D462 until you reach Evenos, a village built on an extensive lava flow. One of the most attractive hilltop villages in the area, it is less well known than the other *villages perchés* nearer the motorway. Its streets are cobbled and its basalt houses huddle around a Romanesque church and the dark ruins of a feudal castle. A footpath leads around the ruins and offers a wonderful panorama of the region.

LES GORGES D'OLLIOULES

The N8 crosses the fantastical yellow-tinted Gorges d'Ollioules, where the river has transformed the sheer cliffs into beautiful sculptures. The caves here, inhabited since prehistoric times, more recently sheltered highwaymen and bandits.

OLLIOULES

This large market town on the N8 is the gateway to the famous Gorges d'Ollioules. The old centre is pleasant in a 1950s-cum-medieval way. Attractive porticoes have survived, along with an 11th-century Romanesque church. Fans of ancient stones will enjoy the castle of the lords of Vintimille. The famous Châteauvallon National Theatre of Dance and Image was established here (*see* page 431, 'Toulon').

USEFUL ADDRESS

🛈 Tourist office: 116 rue Philippe de Hautecloque. ☎ and fax: 04-94-63-11-74. Staff offer good advice on attractive walks in the area.

SHOPPING

– **Marché à la brocante** (second-hand market): held every second Sunday in the month.

LE GROS CERVEAU

This wooded mountain ridge may be known as the 'big brain' because of its shape. Others believe that the name may be a corruption of *gros cerf* ('big deer'). Its highest point, reached via the impressive D20 corniche from Ollioules, is at 430 metres (1,410 feet) and provides panoramic views over the coastline from Hyères to Marseille. A young Corsican artillery officer named Bonaparte came here in 1793 to try to work out how to take the fort, which was held by the English.

BANDOL (83150)   **Population: 7,970**

The most famous resort on this part of the coastline, nestling in the hills and protected from the infamous mistral, Bandol has a sizeable marina with a lovely promenade. The old villas above the small coves give the place a certain charm.

USEFUL ADDRESSES

🛈 Tourist office: allée Vivien (on the port), BP 45. ☎ 04-94-29-41-35. Fax: 04-94-32-50-39. Website: www.bandol.org. Opening times: every day in high season, 9am–1pm and 2–7pm; between 15 September and 15 June, 9am–noon and 2–6pm. Closed on Saturday afternoon and on Sunday.

🚃 SNCF train station: on the Marseille to Toulon line. ☎ 08-36-35-35-35.

■ Bus and coach information: ☎ 04-94-74-01-35.

■ Bicycle and mountain-bike hire: Holiday Bikes, 127 route de Marseille. ☎ and fax: 04-94-32-21-89. Reliable equipment at competitive prices, although deposits can be quite high. This company has outlets along the coast from Antibes to Bandol and provides good ideas for routes in the hinterland.

WHERE TO STAY AND EAT

Campsite

▲ Camping Vallongue: 936 avenue des Reganeou. ☎ 04-94-29-49-55. Fax: 04-94-29-49-49-55. Just 2 kilometres from the sea, on the road to Marseille. Open from Easter to end September. *Forfait piéton* (package for travellers on foot, without a vehicle) for 75F in July and August. Outside these months, prices are reduced after three days. Comfortable, shady and the only site in the town, with bungalows for hire and a pool, but they are in need of some maintenance.

☆☆ Moderate

♠ ✕ **L'Oasis**: 15 rue des Écoles. Take rue Gabriel Péri opposite the marina and take the third turn on the left. ☎ 04-94-29-41-69. Fax: 04-94-32-27-85. Website: www.oasisbandol.com. ❄ Closed Sunday evening and in December. Parking charge. Double rooms with shower or bath and toilet, from 300F to 350F. Half board compulsory between 15 June and 15 September, 310F per person. This pleasant hotel is nicely positioned between the port and the beach and has a shady garden and terrace, and rooms with mini-bar, TV and telephone. Avoid rooms overlooking the street. The food served in the restaurant is traditional.

♠ **Hôtel Les Roses Mousses**: 22 rue des Écoles. Virtually opposite L'Oasis. ☎ and fax: 04-94-29-45-14. Closed from 1 October to 1 April. Double rooms with shower, toilet and TV from 240F to 350F. Close to the Renecros beach and the port, this small and simple hotel has an atmospheric interior, an oleander-filled garden and a very homely feel. The rooms are simple but pleasant and regularly renovated, and the welcome is warm.

♠ ✕ **La Brise**: boulevard Victor-Hugo. Above the tourist office, opposite the marina. ☎ 04-94-29-41-70. Closed Wednesday. Double rooms with shower for 250F. Menu at 80F. À la carte between 150F and 180F. This family hotel has four rooms (Nos. 1, 2, 7 and 8) with sea views. The traditional menu features several Provençal specialities.

♠ ✕ **Hôtel Bel Ombra**: rue de la Fontaine. Between the port and the Renecros beach; follow the signposts. ☎ 04-94-29-40-90. Fax :

04-94-25-01-11. Email: belombra@wanadoo.fr. Closed from 15 October to 1 April. Double rooms with shower from 200F to 240F, and from 220F to 340F with shower or bath and toilet. Dinner for 110F. Half board, compulsory from 13 July to 13 September, between 299F and 324F per person. In a quiet spot in a residential area, this hotel offers clean, pleasant rooms, and a warm welcome. Relax in the shade of the trees and plan your next move.

♠ **L'Ermitage**: in the chateau. ☎ 04-94-29-31-60. Fax: 04-94-29-31-99. Website: www.ermitagehotel.com. ❄ Parking charge from early June to end September. Open all year round. Double rooms from 283F to 478F with bath and satellite TV, depending on the season. Air-conditioned studios from 1,426F to 3,075F per week. This hotel (with two well-deserved stars) is in a good location (a stone's throw from the beach), and has a relaxing and peaceful atmosphere.

✕ **L'Oulivo**: 19 rue des Tonneliers. 100 metres from the port, to the left of the church. ☎ 04-94-29-81-79. Closed on Wednesday and in the evening in winter from Sunday to Tuesday. Three-course weekday lunch menu for 75F, including coffee, and dinner menus at 100F and 120F. This small restaurant is a real find, serving simple and delicious meals made from very fresh produce. The owner is friendly and efficient. The authentically Provençal menu includes some very tasty dishes, such as *caillettes* (a cross between faggot and meatloaf using pig's liver, pork fat, spinach and herbs) and *pieds-paquets* (tripe).

☆☆☆ Chic

♠ ✕ **Golf Hôtel**: plage de Renecros. ☎ 04-94-29-45-83. Fax : 04-94-32-42-47. Email: golfhotel@nomade.fr. Free parking. Closed from

November to Easter. Double room with shower and toilet from 350F to 400F, depending on season, and from 450F to 620F with bathroom. Weekday lunch menu for 95F (July and August only). This pleasant and totally revamped hotel is housed in a 1920s neo-Moorish building (the former town casino). The rooms are charming, and Nos. 10 to 15 and 20 to 24 have balconies or a loggia and sea views.

✕ **Auberge du Port**: 9 allée Jean-Moulin. ☎ 04-94-29-42-63. ✠ Open every day. Menus from 128F to 260F. À la carte at least 300F, for classic dishes such as seafood platters, *bouillabaisse*, *bourride* or the catch of the day cooked in a salt crust. The set menus also have a marine theme but include more innovative dishes such as *daube de poissons de roche et de poulpes* (stew of rockfish and octopus) or *risotto de blé* (wheat risotto) and *crêpe de parmesan*. The service is excellent. Keep an eye on the bill.

WHERE TO GO FOR A DRINK

– **Tchin-Tchin Bar**: 11 allée Jean-Moulin. ☎ 04-94-29-41-04. Bars come and go on the seafront, but this one has been more long-lived than most. Its exotic interior has remained unchanged since the 1950s, and its prices are quite appealing too.

WHAT TO SEE AND DO

★ **Île de Bendor**: this little island, just 200 metres from Bandol port, can be reached by a 7-minute crossing (28F return) every 30 minutes. Information: ☎ 04-94-29-44-34. *Pastis* millionaire Paul Ricard bought it in 1950, intending to lead a Robinson Crusoe lifestyle there. It soon became an adult playground, however, with hotels, a business centre and buildings of questionable taste (think kitsch Graeco–Roman statues). There's a concrete path around the island for a 5-minute tour, and a little beach. Look out for the building decorated with frescoes by art students; the Exposition Universelle des Vins et Spiritueux displays 8,000 bottles and glasses from around the world. Open every day (except Wednesday and Saturday morning) 10.15am–noon and 2.15–6pm. Free entry.

Bendor isn't the only island owned by Paul Ricard; the Île des Embiez is probably worth more of a look (*see* page 415, 'Six-Fours-les-Plages').

★ **Jardin exotique de Bandol-Sanary** (exotic garden): 3 kilometres (about 2 miles) from the town. ☎ 04-94-29-40-38. Open every day 8am–noon, 2–7pm (Sunday 10am–noon, 2–7pm). Entrance fee: 40F (25F for children over three years of age). Thousands of plants and tropical flowers grow here in a haven for numerous birds, including toucans, cockatoos, peacocks and macaws.

★ **Beaches**: plage de Renecros is a nicer beach than plage du Lido (to the west towards Sanary). It's in a sheltered spot surrounded by old villas, one of which, Ker Mocotte, used to belong to Provençal actor Raimu. There are a number of tranquil little beaches along the coast, but you have to be prepared to walk to reach them.

WALKS

– The coastal path from **Bandol to St-Cyr-Les Lecques** has yellow markings. For a return trip of 3 hours 30 minutes, start from plage de Renecros. The path first passes through suburbia, but soon becomes much wilder, following the coast, which is punctured with inlets and coves such as Port d'Alon. You can return on foot by the same route or by bus (information from the tourist office).

– The easy 12-kilometre (7.5-mile) walk to the summit of **Le Gros Cerveau** starts at the exotic garden.

– Don't miss the chance to hire a bike (*see above*) and take a **bicycle ride** in the beautiful hinterland.

SHOPPING

🔒 **Maison des Vins de Bandol**: allée Vivien. ☎ 04-94-29-45-03. Wines from more than 20 Bandol vineyards under one roof.

FESTIVALS AND EVENTS

– **Printemps des Potiers** ('Potters' Spring'): during the Easter weekend, potters display and sell their work alongside street workshops by other artists and craftspeople.

– **Fête du Millésime**: in the port, on the first Sunday in December. For this popular event, Bandol wine producers set up stalls on the market square and nearby streets, for tastings and sales.

SANARY-SUR-MER (83110)   Population: 17,200

A busy resort in summer, Sanary-sur-Mer returns to its more usual role of small fishing port in the winter months, when you can sit and wait for the boats to come back from a day at sea. It owes its name to St Nazaire ('San Nary' in Provençal). Not to be confused with the 10 other saints of the same name floating around France, this one was a very 'Atlantic' saint, which makes his arrival on the Mediterranean coast all the more surprising.

Sanary is a charming place, with a harbour lined with palm trees, pink and white houses, ancient streets and a sandy beach. Oddly, it became the capital of German literature in exile between 1933 and 1942. Aldous Huxley already lived here, and was joined by exiled anti-Nazi intelligentsia, including Thomas and Heinrich Mann, Bertolt Brecht and Franz Werfel. A number of the 500 refugees were rounded up under the collaborative Vichy regime and imprisoned in an internment camp near Aix. The luckier ones escaped to the USA in 1942.

USEFUL ADDRESS

⬛ Tourist office: on the port. ☎ 04-94-74-01-04. Fax: 04-94-74-58-04. Website: www.mairie-sanary.fr. Open in high season Monday to Friday 9am–noon, 2–7pm; Sunday 9.30am–12.30pm.

WHERE TO STAY

Campsites

⬛ Les Girelles: 1003 chemin Beaucours. 2.5 kilometres (1.5 miles) from the town centre. ☎ 04-94-74-13-18 (office hours). Fax: 04-94-74-13-18. Open from end March to end September.

⬛ Le Mogador: 166 chemin Beaucours. 2 kilometres from the town centre. ☎ 04-94-74-53-16. Fax: 04-94-74-10-58. Website: www.camping-mogador.com. Open from 5 April to 5 October. Around 115F for a pitch for two with vehicle. Located 400 metres from the sea, this site is shady but noisy; it has a swimming pool.

☆☆ Moderate

⬛ Hôtel-restaurant Bon Abri: 94 avenue des Poilus. ☎ 04-94-74-02-81. Closed on Sunday evening out of season and on Monday. Double rooms with shower from 210F to 265F, depending on season; with shower or bath and toilet from 250F to 325F. Half board compulsory from 1 July and 15 September and during school holidays; from 225F to 255F per person. Menus at 68F (weekday lunch), 110F and 140F. This small and charming hotel, hidden in a dense garden, has a rather fashionable dining room serving interesting cuisine such as *feuilleté de ris de veau* (calves' sweetbreads in pastry) and *émincé de canard au caramel* (duck with caramel). The rooms are simple but pleasant.

⬛ Hôtel-restaurant Le Marina: 4,219 ancien chemin de Toulon. 2 kilometres from the town centre.

☎ 04-94-29-56-48. Fax: 04-94-29-40-14. Closed on Sunday evening and all day Monday as well as from 15 February to 1 March. Double rooms with washbasin or shower for 250F; with bathroom and TV 350F. Half board compulsory in July and August. Menus at 140F and 190F. This rather uninteresting building, hidden behind a few pine trees, has rooms that are pleasant and good value for money. Nos. 11 to 19 are more spacious and nearer the pool. The elegant dining room and its cuisine are worth leaving the port for.

☆☆☆☆ Plus Chic

⬛ Chambres d'hôte Villa Lou Gardian (B&B): 646 route de Bandol. 2 kilometres from the port. ☎ 04-94-88-05-73. Fax: 04-94-88-24-13. Close to the beaches, this establishment has double rooms with shower and toilet for 450F, including breakfast. Dinner (book ahead) from 150F. This peaceful, tastefully furnished house is surrounded by ancient trees, and its characterful owners greet their guests warmly. You can swim in the pool after a game of tennis.

⬛ Hôtel de la Tour: 24 quai du Général-de-Gaulle. ☎ 04-94-74-10-10. Fax: 04-94-74-69-49. E-mail: latour@wanadoo.fr. Restaurant closed on Wednesday in low season and from 1 December to 10 January. Double rooms with shower, toilet and air-conditioning from 350f to 420F; with bathroom from 450f to 540F. Menus from

125F to 250F. This tall building opposite the port is linked to a medieval watchtower. The welcome is friendly, and the rooms comfortable, though the decor is rather old-fashioned. Those facing the port can be noisy in summer. The tasty cuisine is mostly fish-based.

WHERE TO EAT

✗ **L'Océan Jazz**: 74 route de la Gare. ☎ 04-94-07-36-11. Closed Saturday lunchtime and on Sunday evening from November to March. Menus at 80F (weekday lunch) and from 99F to 150F. Slightly outside the town centre, towards the old train station, this is an excellent little spot. The dishes on its great daily menu (100F) wouldn't look out of place in a major restaurant, and wine and coffee are included in the price. The service is good, the welcome friendly, the dining room charming and the terrace a delight. Jazz is played in the background; live on Friday evening.

✗ **La Flambée**: 205 chemin de la Buge. ☎ 04-94-74-17-74. Menus from 75F to 148F. Slightly out of the centre, this traditional restaurant is more 'rustic' than 'seaside' in style, with its large terrace, owner/chef and generous portions of grilled meat and fish. Excellent value for money too.

✗ **L'En K**: 413 rue Louis-Blanc. In the centre, behind the town hall. ☎ 04-94-74-66-57. Fax: 04-94-63-48-41. Closed on Monday (except in July and August) and for the month of November. Menu for 120F. À la carte around 160F. Off the tourist trail, this restaurant is a place where locals meet to enjoy good food in an agreeable atmosphere. Work by local artists is often on display. The food (including the tasty *sandre à la vodka et persil frit*, or fish with vodka and fried parsley) is full of surprises and cooked and served by a young and enthusiastic team.

☆☆☆☆ Plus Chic

✗ **Le Relais de la Poste**: place de la Poste. ☎ 04-94-74-22-20. Closed Sunday evening and Monday. Wide selection of menus from 145F to 265F; allow 250F à la carte. Serious gourmets will appreciate the cuisine and old-fashioned service at this restaurant. The meat and fresh fish are particularly good and specialities include *tartelette de rouget et artichaut* (red mullet and artichoke tart) and *andouillettes de volailles aux gambas* (smoked poultry sausages with prawns).

WHAT TO SEE

★ **Musée de l'histoire de la plongée** (museum of the history of scuba diving): open during the school holidays, at the weekend and on public holidays 10am–noon and 2–6pm. Free entry. Housed in the medieval watchtower, this small museum was established by Frédéric Dumas, one of the three famous French pioneers of scuba diving (along with Cousteau and Taillez). Equipment used from the 1930s to the 1950s is on display, including fins, masks, bottles, underwater guns (Sean Connery's Jaguar among them), the first underwater video and a collection of amphorae and other archaeological finds.

FESTIVALS AND EVENTS

– **Markets**: a typically **Provençal produce market**, one of the largest in the area, is held on Wednesday morning. A **flower market** is held on the port and the wharves every day.

– **Les Floralies** (flower show): held every two years (next in 2003) in May.

– **Procession à la St-Pierre**: this festival celebrating St Peter, the patron saint of fishermen, takes place during the last weekend in June every two years. A giant *bouillabaisse* (mixed fish stew) is enjoyed by the locals.

– **Joutes**: medieval jousting competitions held between June and September.

– **Fête du Nom** (naming festival): held during the first weekend in October. Participants wear traditional costume at several events held in the street, followed by a typically Provençal meal.

SIX-FOURS-LES-PLAGES (83140)

Population: 33,200

The beaches are easy to find in this area (expert windsurfers make a beeline for 'Brutal Beach'), but you could get lost in the *commune* of Six-Fours, an extended parish embracing several hamlets. The centre is not of great interest, so head instead to the pretty fishing village of Le Brusc. The Greeks often sought shelter and rest here from the late third century BC, after sailing round the stormy Cap Sicié. The tiny Île du Gaou (island) has rocky cliffs reminiscent of Brittany and can be reached by a passageway that is open from 8am to 8pm (to 10pm in summer).

USEFUL ADDRESS

fi Tourist office: promenade Charles-de-Gaulle. ☎ 04-94-07-02-21. Fax: 04-94-25-13-36. Website: www.six-fours-les-plages.com. Open between June and September, Monday to Saturday 9am–noon and 2–6.30pm (in July from 9am–7pm and on Sunday 9am–noon). During the rest of the year, open Monday to Friday 8.30am–noon and 2–6.30pm, Saturday 9am–noon and 2–6pm.

WHERE TO STAY AND EAT

â Hôtel du Parc: 112 rue Marius-Bondi, Le Brusc. ☎ 04-94-34-00-15. Fax: 04-94-34-16-94. Closed on Sunday evening out of season and from early October to early April. Double rooms from 230F to 345F. Menus from 75F to 135F. Very close to the port, this small and tranquil hotel has simple but comfortable rooms and a friendly atmosphere.

✕ Lou Figuier: 43 rue Marius-Bondi. Le Brusc. ☎ 04-94-34-00-29. Menus from 75F to 190F. This small eating place has pleasant if eclectic decor and a couple of tables on the terrace. The simple but tasty dishes, including excellent seafood such as *soupe de poissons* (fish soup) or sardines, are based on fresh produce.

✕ **Restaurant Le St-Pierre**: 47 rue de la Citadelle, Le Brusc. ☎ 04-94-34-02-52. Fax: 04-94-34-18-01. Closed on Tuesday evening and all day Wednesday out of season and during January. Menus at 98F (weekdays only), 142F and 198F. Located between the beach and the port, this restaurant serves traditional *bouillabaisse* and *bourride* at around 195F per person, as well as other excellent fish and seafood dishes. The service is good. There are no great culinary surprises, but it's good value for money.

WHAT TO SEE AND DO

★ **Chapelle Notre-Dame-de-Pépiole**: head towards Sanary from Six-Fours and as you enter Sanary, turn right at the roundabout towards Seyne-sur-Mer-Toulon; the chapel is signposted to the right before the level crossing. Open every day 3–6pm. Mass every Sunday 9.30–10.30am. This interesting sixth-century stone-built chapel was modelled on the earliest Syrian churches and looks like a fortress with asymmetric bell-towers, lopsided rooftops and a large porch. Having undergone many changes over the centuries, it is now a unique example of Provençal-Oriental architecture. The interior is refreshingly cool and intimate.

★ **Collégiale de Six-Fours** (St-Pierre collegiate church): leave Six-Fours via avenue du Maréchal Juin (towards Seyne-sur-Mer) and follow the narrow road to the left (signposted). Between June and September, open during the week 3–7pm and on Sunday 9am–noon and 3–7pm. During the rest of the year, visits 2–6pm during the week, and on Sunday 10am–noon and 2–6pm (to 5pm November to March). The only vestige of the former village of Six-Fours, this 11th-century Romanesque church stands on a large hill with a wonderful view of Toulon's seafront, slightly overwhelmed by the huge walls of the nearby military fort. It has two naves, one Romanesque and the other Gothic, built in the 12th century. Finds from an underground sanctuary built by the first Christians are on display in the Romanesque part. The church also houses a number of works of art, including a polyptych of Provence's favourite 16th-century saints and a statue of the Virgin, attributed to Pierre Puget.

WALKS

– **Cap Sicié**: it takes seven hours to walk the entire coastal path from plage de Bonnegrâce to plage des Sablettes (Mar Vivo), but you can just do parts of it. Start at the Île du Gaou for an energetic ramble through unspoilt nature with some memorable views. There are also five **mountain-bike trails** around Cap Sicié. Hire a bike in Six-Fours and contact the tourist office for more information.

FESTIVALS AND EVENTS

– **Les Voix du Gaou** ('Voices of Gaou'): this outdoor festival of funk, African music, gospel sounds and traditional songs is held on the Île du Gaou during the last two weeks of July. For more information: ☎ 04-94-93-55-45.

In the Area

ÎLES DES EMBIEZ

This collection of islands lies close to Le Brusc port. Crossings take place every 40 minutes from 7am to 12.45am in high season. Return trip: 37F (27F for 3- to 12-year-olds). ☎ 04-94-10-65-20 or 04-94-10-65-21. Île des Embiez, the largest of the islands at 95 hectares (235 acres), was purchased by the Paul Ricard trust in 1958. You disembark in the marina, the first to be built in the Mediterranean, in 1963, and the village spreads out around you.

Leave the village with its rather kitsch architecture behind you and head instead for the west coast, where a path hugs the jagged, sea-worn cliffs. The *pastis* baron rests in peace here, overlooking the great expanse of blue. In low season, your walk will be solitary and tranquil, but it's quite the opposite in summer. Climb up to the tower, surrounded by goats, for a wonderful view of the varied landscapes of the island: marshland, pine forests and even vineyards, which produce a pleasant rosé.

WHAT TO SEE

– **Aquarium-Musée Méditerranéen** (aquarium-museum of the Mediterranean): ☎ 04-94-34-02-49. Open every day 10am–12.30pm and 3.30–5.30pm. Closed on Wednesday morning between November and March, and on Saturday until 2pm from September to June. Entrance fee: 25F (12F for under-12s). This small museum, housed in a former marine battery, aims to educate the public about the need to protect the oceans. Cephalopods and fish preserved in formalin can be seen on the ground floor along with amphorae and pieces of pottery found around the Îles des Embiez. Upstairs, you can see a 100 different Mediterranean species in over 30 aquariums. The building also houses the Fondation Océanographique Ricard (Ricard oceanographic foundation), established in 1966 after a pollution incident at Cassis. Researchers at the foundation study ways of combating marine damage; it was here that the method for dealing with the pollution caused by the *Exxon Valdez* was developed after the disastrous oil spill in Alaska.

CAP SICIÉ

Cap Sicié is south of Six-Fours on the D16. In the hamlet of Roche-Blanche, follow the signs to Notre-Dame-Mai. Note: the route is inaccessible between 15 June and 15 September because of the risk of fire.

Enjoy a breath of fresh air before heading to Toulon's busy seafront. This path crosses a section of the thousands of hectares of Mediterranean forest between Le Brusc and Fabregas. Above the rocks, which point out to sea like fingers, sits the pretty Chapelle Notre-Dame-du-Mai, open only during pilgrimages (during the month of May, on Easter Monday, 15 August and 14 September). It houses a collection of ex-voto offerings and affords a wonderful view that stretches from the *calanques* of Marseille to the Îles d'Hyères. The *corniche merveilleuse* ('wonderful clifftop road'), then heads gently back down to Fabregas and Seyne-sur-Mer. You can stop off at several beaches, including the one at Fabregas, where the grey volcanic sand is believed to cure rheumatism. The plage du Jonquet is the only naturist beach on this part of the coast.

SCUBA DIVING

Toulon is an important centre of modern scuba diving. It was here that the aqualung was perfected in the 1940s by eccentric pioneers Jacques-Yves Cousteau, Frédéric Dumas and Philippe Taillez. These passionate scuba-diving professionals caused a revolution at the French school of scuba diving in St-Mandrier, and you can find out about their amazing underwater adventures at the small museum at Sanary-sur-Mer (*see* page 414).

There are some wonderful shallow dive sites in the area, but you should be aware that the mistral can change diving conditions very quickly.

Diving Clubs

■ **Cap Plongée**: 467 chemin de Taurens, 83140 Six-Fours-les-Plages. ☎ 04-94-34-06-64. Website: www.pro.wanadoo.fr/cap.plongée. Open all year. The school meets at the port of La Coudoulière with a small motor boat that takes a maximum of 16 divers. The qualified owner and instructor teaches beginners up to Level III and also organizes exploratory dives. Children over 8 can join classes, and you can hire underwater cameras and professional masks. Bookings essential.

■ **CIP Bendor**: Île de Bendor, 83150 Bandol. ☎ 04-94-29-55-12. Open from 15 February to 15 December. The school has three boats, including a trawler with a compressor on board. The qualified diving instructors (FFESSM, ANMP, PADI) teach beginners, take courses up to instructor level and also arrange exploratory dives. Children over 8 can join classes. All equipment is supplied, and full-board accommodation is available on the island. Booking essential.

■ **Lecques Aquanaut Center**: in the new port of Les Lecques, 83270 St-Cyr-sur-Mer. ☎ 04-94-26-42-18 or 06-09-55-24-26 (mobile). Email: lac diving@csi.com. Open every day from Easter to October. This centre is known for the high standard of its equipment and instruction (FFESSM, ANMP, PADI). A team of qualified instructors teaches beginners, groups up to Level IV and PADI courses. They also lead exploratory dives to the west of Bandol and in the bay of La Ciotat, where the club owner discovered a war plane identical to the one flown by Antoine de St Exupéry, author of *Le Petit Prince*. Equipment is supplied and children over 8 years are accepted. Biology classes are available.

Dive Sites

↩ **Îles des Embiez**: there are some exceptional shallow dive sites off Sanary-sur-Mer, the headquarters of Paul-Ricard Oceanographic Institute. Patient Level II divers can enjoy peaceful moments watching the many beautiful creatures below the **Pierre aux Mérous** (at 35 metres/115 feet maximum). Many are currently endangered by the activity of local fisherman. At 22 metres (72 feet), the **Sèche Guéneaux** faults are home to scorpion fish, sea fans and tube worms. On the plateau of the **Basses Moulinières**

(22 metres/72 feet maximum) Level I divers may be lucky enough to see a school of barracuda and may explore (carefully) a rocky maze covered in yellow sea fans. At **La Merveilleuse** (24–33 metres/78–108 feet), Level II divers can flush out spiny lobsters and might even spot an elegant moon fish going about its business.

⚓ **Île Rousse**: to the west of Bandol. Beautiful flame-red corals grow in the rocks. Take a torch and explore the ridges with their many faults, home to scorpion fish and moray eels. Level I divers can dive (with care) in the very exposed spot of the grotto below the island itself (18 metres/58 feet maximum).

⚓ **L'Arroyo**: to the east of Cap Sicié, this tanker (18–36 metres/58–118 feet) was deliberately sunk by the French navy in 1953, to serve as an instruction site for divers. The wreck is in two sections, one of which is covered in red gorgonian soft coral, and its crew is now made up of conger eel, octopus and scorpion fish. This Level II site is very busy during the summer months.

⚓ **La Pointe Fauconnière**: not far from Port des Lecques, this exceptional site is suitable for divers of all levels and offers an interesting network of caves, tunnels and drops (10–25 metres/32–82 feet). Take a torch to spot scorpion fish and rainbow wrasse, and maybe some mother of pearl.

ST-MANDRIER PENINSULA (83430)

This hilly peninsula protects the southern end of the *grande rade* (large harbour) of Toulon. Formerly an island, it was reconnected to the mainland by movement of the sands in the 17th century. A beach with fine sand sits between Les Sablettes and the port of St-Elme, and the small port and fishing village of St-Mandrier is rather picturesque. The presence of the French navy is very obvious in this area.

USEFUL ADDRESS

🅱 **Tourist office**: place des Résistants in St-Mandrier. ☎ 04-94-63-61-69.

LA SEYNE-SUR-MER (83500) Population: 61,000

The economic boom in La Seyne, a village established in the 16th century by the inhabitants of Six-Fours, was due to the creation in 1855 of shipbuilding yards, where cargo vessels, steamers, battleships and oil platforms have been constructed. Although the yards are now closed, the town is still a dense mass of factories and industry. It takes on a different look when approached from the St-Mandrier peninsula and the fine-sand Les Sablettes beach. The seaside resort is neo-Provençal in style, a product of the 1950s. Nearby, the residential suburb of Tamaris, with its elegant 19th-century villas, overlooks the bay with its mussel beds.

USEFUL ADDRESS

🄸 Tourist office: esplanade des Sablettes. ☎ 04-94-94-73-09. Fax: 04-94-30-84-62. Open in summer every day (except Sunday afternoon) 9am–12.30pm and 2.30–7pm (to 6.30pm in winter, when it's also closed on Monday morning, Saturday afternoon and all day Sunday). The office in the town centre, in place Ledru-Rollin, has the same opening hours.

WHAT TO SEE

★ **Villas de Michel Pacha**: if you spend any time in Sanary, you're bound to come across Michel Pacha. Born Blaise Jean Marius Michel in Sanary in 1819, he was in charge of building lighthouses for the Ottoman Empire before becoming an engineer on the wharves of Istanbul and finally being created pasha by the Sultan. He eventually returned to France and was elected mayor of Sanary. Inspired by what he had seen overseas, he established one of the first seaside resorts on this stretch of coast, as a potential rival to Nice and Cannes. In the 1880s, he purchased most of Tamaris in the hope of turning it into a resort, constructing villas, hotels and public buildings on reclaimed marshland. The architecture was eclectic, with minarets alongside neo-classical columns.

Villa Sylvacane, a concrete 'boathouse' built in the late 1930s, is recognizable by its windmill tower. In 1890, work began on Villa Tamaris Pacha, which was inspired by Tuscan villas. It now houses an elegant art gallery, open every day (except Monday) from 2pm to 6pm. Entry is free.

★ **Fort Balaguier (Musée de la Marine)** (naval museum): 924 corniche Bonaparte. ☎ 04-94-94-84-72. Open 10am–noon and 2–6pm (out of season); in July and August 10am–noon and 3–7pm. Closed Monday. Entrance fee: 10F for adults (children 5F). A tower was first built here in 1636 on the orders of Richelieu, who wanted to secure the defence of the seafront. The small fort dates from the 18th and 19th centuries, and a path around its ramparts provides wonderful views of the Toulon seafront. A small museum is housed in the round rooms of the fort, with its thick walls. Models of boats and memorabilia from the Napoleonic era are on display (Bonaparte distinguished himself in these parts in 1793). The former officers' lodgings now contain a display on the Toulon penal colony with drawings and objects produced by the inmates. An annual exhibition is held on local history.

FESTIVALS AND EVENTS

– **Festival de Jazz**: the oldest jazz festival in the *département* (established in 1985) is held in the Fort Napoléon (built in 1821 by the emperor).

– **Fêtes Calendales**: held in the fort at Christmas.

TOULON (83000)   Population: 166,400

It's all too easy to judge Toulon for its dreadful traffic problems rather than notice its unexpected charm. In fact, despite being France's second-largest port and a naval base, the town is surprisingly interesting and lively, and well worth a visit. When you see the post-war buildings that often obscure the sea view, and the shops that are firmly closed behind iron shutters, you may well be tempted to join some of the locals in maligning the city. However, if you persevere, you should discover that Toulon is a pleasant place to spend some time.

You won't find impressive monuments or innovative architecture here, but there's an enjoyable atmosphere in the city's small streets and charming little squares. Take a seat in one of the cafés on place Puget and enjoy the tranquillity. Then follow the natural slope of the city down to the port, stopping en route to investigate the typically Provençal market stalls.

Take a stroll around the wharves in the company of locals taking time to enjoy life. At dusk, the bars are full of sailors and fisherfolk, but as night falls the atmosphere and the crowds quickly evaporate. Although it's a hive of activity during the day, Toulon is rather lifeless at night. Only a few bars in Le Mourillon or here and there on the wharf stay open, and stories of the notoriously wild nights of the so-called 'Chicago' district belong firmly in the past.

History

In the 15th century, Toulon, along with the whole of Provence, became crown property. Because of its strategic position and its large seafront encompassed by impressive hills, Toulon was soon able to establish itself as a naval and military base. Both Louis XII and Henri IV fortified the town, and the latter created an arsenal from which royal ships sallied forth. Vauban improved Toulon's defence capabilities enormously. In 1748, the ships were replaced by the famous penal colony, from which one of Victor Hugo's characters, Jean Valjean, managed to escape in *Les Misérables*.

In 1793, peace was made with the English, and the then junior officer, Napoleon Bonaparte, made a name for himself by taking the town from the occupying English troops. Toulon became known as the 'town of infamy', and 12,000 workers were ordered to destroy it. The order was rescinded at the eleventh hour and the town ultimately lost no more than its prefectural rights (only recently retrieved from the much smaller town of Draguignan).

■ Useful Addresses

🅸 Tourist office
✉ Post office
🚂 Train station

🛏 Where to Stay

1 Hôtel Le Jaurès
2 Hôtel Molière
5 New Hotel Amirauté
6 Grand Hôtel Dauphiné
7 Hôtel des Allées
8 Hôtel Lamalgue
9 New Hotel Tour Blanche
10 Les Bastidières

✗ Where to Eat

20 Le Cellier
21 La Feuille de Chou
22 Les Bartavelles
23 Le Petit Prince
24 Le Jardin du Sommelier
25 Le Carré du Port
26 Restaurant Herrero

🍸 Where to Go for a Drink

30 Le Bar à Thym
31 Le 113
32 Le B des Cochons

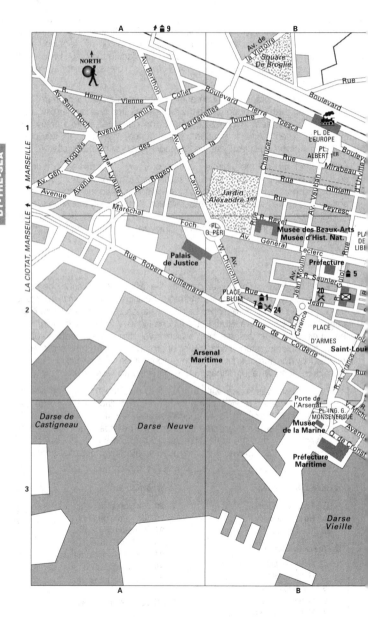

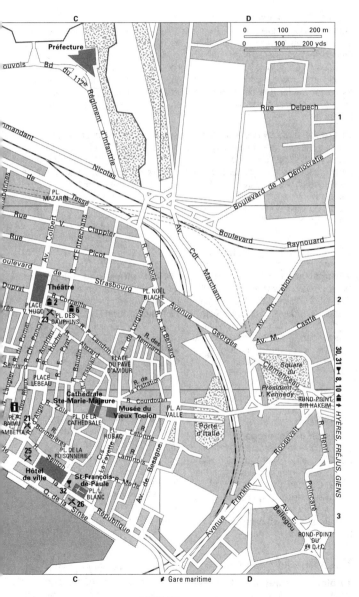

TOULON

For a time, the town became known, rather aptly, as 'Port-la-Montagne' (mountain port). Later, Napoleon made it his key port, and the navy became its principal employer. When the Germans invaded the free zone in 1942, the French fleet scuppered itself rather than falling into their hands. Half the town was destroyed, and its rapid reconstruction left Toulon with little architectural identity. It is now a working port for both leisure and the military. Some of its former character has certainly been lost, partly because French sailors no longer wear the traditional uniform of bellbottoms and hats with red pompoms.

The Toulon of today has a difficult reputation in France, mostly because of the activities of the right wing National Front party. Toulon elected the country's first National Front deputy, and then a mayor from the same party, resulting in some anti-cultural and xenophobic policies. There *is* resistance to this ugly trend and you should not let the minority put you off the place. Most of the locals are friendly enough and enjoy welcoming visitors to their agreeable town, with its interesting contrasts, history and atmosphere.

USEFUL ADDRESSES

◻ Tourist office (C3 on the map): place Raimu. ☎ 04-94-18-53-00. Fax: 04-94-18-53-09. Open in high season Monday to Saturday 9am–6pm; Sunday and public holidays 10am–noon. The staff are efficient and equipped with a range of leaflets on Toulon and the area.

✉ Post office and telephones (B2 on the map): on the corner of rue Ferrero and rue Bertholet.
🚄 Train station (B1 on the map): place Albert-1er. Information: ☎ 08-36-35-35-35.
■ Allô Bus, city transport: ☎ 04-94-03-87-03.

WHERE TO STAY

Campsites

▲ Camping Beauregard: in the Ste-Marguerite district, 83130 La Garde. ☎ 04-94-20-56-35. Between Toulon and Le Pradet on the D559. Open all year, this very pleasant site for tents only is close to the sea, and not too expensive.
▲ There are several campsites in La Seyne-sur-Mer.

☆–☆☆ Budget to Moderate

▲ Hôtel Le Jaurès (B2, **1** on the map): 11 rue Jean-Jaurès. ☎ 04-94-92-83-04. Fax: 04-94-62-16-74. Open all year. Double rooms with shower and toilet for 160F, with bathroom and TV for 180F.

This is one of the most appealing hotels – central, friendly and clean, with reasonable prices. The quietest rooms overlook the courtyard. There's a garage for bicycles (free of charge).
▲ Hôtel Molière (C2, **2** on the map): 12 rue Molière. ☎ 04-94-92-78-35. Fax: 04-94-62-85-82. Closed in January. Double rooms with washbasin for 115F, with shower 155F and with shower, toilet and TV 185F. This hotel in the middle of the pedestrian precinct, not far from the theatre, is small and friendly with unbeatable prices. The owners are always welcoming and do everything possible to make your stay pleasant. The rooms are clean, comfortable

and soundproofed. Room Nos. 18, 19 and 20 have an unrestricted view of the harbour.

⚓ Grand Hôtel Dauphiné (C2, **6** on the map): 10 rue Berthelot. ☎ 04-94-92-20-28. Fax: 04-94-62-16-69. Double room with bathroom, satellite TV, minibar and hairdryer for 240–290F. This popular place has a loyal following because of its reasonable prices, comfortable rooms (air-conditioned and soundproofed) and warm, genuine welcome. A good hotel for its category.

⚓ Hôtel des Allées (B2, **7** on the map): 18 allée Amiral-Courbet. Near place des Armes and the centre. ☎ 04-94-91-10-02. Fax: 04-94-24-15-45. Double rooms from 110F with washbasin to 210F with en suite bathroom (and TV). Small, simple hotel with a friendly female owner, who provides all sorts of information on Toulon. The rooms overlooking the street are noisy, but this is a good place for those on a limited budget.

⚓ Hôtel Lamalgue (D3, **8**, off the map): 124 rue Gubler, Le Mourillon. 2.5 kilometres from the town centre, above the beaches of Le Mourillon. ☎ 04-94-41-36-23. Fax: 04-94-03-56-66. Double rooms from 125F with washbasin to 220F with shower or bath and toilet (and TV). This hotel has a lovely garden and a nostalgic atmosphere. The rooms are furnished simply and tastefully, and those near the balcony have a spectacular view (Nos. 9, 14, 16, 19 and 20). The beach is a stone's throw away.

☆☆☆ Chic

⚓ New Hotel Amirauté (B2, **5** on the map): 4 rue A.-Guiol. ☎ 04-94-22-19-67. Fax: 04-94-09-34-72.

Double rooms with bath, TV, minibar, air-conditioning and hairdryer from 420F to 440F. Housed in a huge building opposite the place de la Liberté, this hotel is new and modern, and what it may lack in atmosphere, it certainly makes up for in comfort. There are 58 pretty and colourful rooms, and the service and welcome are in line with its three-star rating. It offers excellent value for money in its price range.

⚓ Les Bastidières (D3, **10**, off the map): 2371 avenue de la Résistance, Cap Brun. On the corniche. ☎ 04-94-36-14-73. Fax: 03-94-42-49-75. Open all year. Doubles with bathroom, air-conditioning and TV from 500F to 750F, depending on season. No cards accepted. You go through a big 18th-century entrance, along a white-stoned avenue to get to this typically Provençal building, which lies at the heart of a dense, almost exotic, garden. The five spacious rooms in the annexe have a rustic charm, with antique furniture, oak beams and floor tiles, and a private balcony. There's also a swimming pool and the welcome is friendly – it's more like a B&B than a hotel.

⚓ New Hotel Tour Blanche (A1, **9**, off the map): boulevard Amiral-Vence. ☎ 04-94-24-41-57. Fax: 04-94-22-42-25. ⚒ At the foot of Mont Faron. Double rooms with shower or bath and toilet from 440F to 510F. Menus from 100F to 180F. The hotel has a rather faded charm, friendly (sometimes too friendly?) service and rooms with wonderful views of the harbour. Relax in the pool before having a meal on the terrace. The restaurant is improving.

WHERE TO EAT

☆ Budget

Toulon specialities are perfect if you're on the run, or saving your pennies. Try a *cade* (a chickpea pancake served warm – sister of the Niçois *socca*) from the market on **Cours Lafayette**. *Chichi frégi* (a sugar-coated doughnut) is available only from Chez G. Toine, a small and charming kiosk on place Paul Conte, to be found at the top of cours Lafayette.

✕ **La Feuille de Choux** (C3, **21** on the map): 15 rue de la Glacière. ☎ 04-94-62-09-26. Closed every evening (except Saturday). Menu (Saturday evening) for 125F. À la carte 60–100F. The 'Cabbage Leaf' has a bistrot feel and a shady terrace (one of the most attractive in the town) on a quiet square. Customers enjoy Provençal dishes, wine by the carafe and a friendly atmosphere.

✕ **Les Bartavelles** (C1, **22** on the map): 28 rue Gimelli. At the top of the town, behind place de la Liberté heading towards the train station. ☎ 04-94-92-85-00. ♿ Closed Sunday, public holidays and during the first weeks of February and August. Menus at 68F (lunch), 108F (evenings and on Saturday), à la carte around 130F. Two simple and unassuming rooms in an old building (pleasantly cool even at the height of summer) have a village-inn atmosphere. The Provençal menu is good value for money and the owner makes customers feel quite at home.

✕ **Le Cellier** (B2, **10** on the map): 52 rue Jean-Jaurès. ☎ 04-94-92-64-35. Closed Saturday, Sunday, weekends and public holidays as well as during the Easter holidays. Menus from 83F to 160F. This place has rather kitsch decor and a good atmosphere. M. Aujaleu, godson of the former owner and master crafstman, offers an excellent menu with

some delicious Provençal dishes. The restaurant is both charming and tranquil.

✕ **Le Petit Prince** (C2, **23** on the map): 10 rue de l'Humilité. ☎ 04-94-93-03-45. Closed Saturday lunch, Sunday, two weeks in February and three weeks in August. Generous regional dishes for 50F, à la carte around 150F. The small and attractive dining room is decorated in yellows and blues, with model aeroplanes hanging from the ceiling. The atmosphere is relaxed, the welcome warm and the service efficient. The traditional dishes include *escalope de veau cordon bleu* (veal escalope with cheese and ham) and *foie gras maison* (homemade goose-liver pâté).

✕ **Le Carré du Port** (C3, **25** on the map): 219 avenue de la République. ☎ 04-94-09-31-21. Closed on Saturday lunchtime and on Sunday. Main course and dessert for 60F at lunchtime. *Menu-carte* for 148F. This new eating place combines a charmingly elegant dining room with creative Provençal cuisine, based on fresh market produce. The welcome is warm, and no doubt the service will get a little sharper.

✕ **Restaurant Herrero** (C3, **26** on the map): 45 quai de la Sinse. ☎ 04-94-41-00-16. Menus from 110F to 160F. A local institution run by the family of a famous rugby player. The decor is marine in theme, slightly faded by the years, and the terrace gives customers a chance to observe the boats moored on the quay. It's good value for money, with a reliable if not experimental cuisine.

☆☆☆ Chic

✕ **Le Jardin du Sommelier** (B2, **24** on the map): 20 allée Courbet. Next to place d'Armes, behind the arsenal. ☎ 04-94-62-03-27. Email: jsommelier@infonie.fr. ♨ Closed on Saturday lunchtime and on Sunday. Menus from 120F to 220F, à la carte around 220F. Enjoy matching wine with food (or food with wine) against a background of Provençal tastes, colours (blues and yellows) and perfumes. Try the delicious *tartare d'écrevisses moutarde à l'ancienne et basilic* (crayfish with mustard and basil) or *filet de charolais aux girolles* (beef steak with mushrooms), and enjoy the warm welcome.

WHERE TO EAT IN THE AREA

✕ **L'Amourié**: place Jean-Aicard, Sollies-Ville (83210). 15 kilometres (9 miles) northwest of Toulon. ☎ 04-94-33-74-72. Closed on Thursday (except in summer and at New Year). Menus at 90F, 110F and 150F. This restaurant at the heart of a hilltop village has tables outside on a shady terrace. In the cooler months, eat in the cosy and original interior. The menu has a nostalgic and traditional slant, including some specialities from Lyon. A warm reception is guaranteed.

WHERE TO GO FOR A DRINK

♥ **Le Bar à Thym** (D3, **30**, off the map): 32 boulevard Cunéo, Le Mourillon. ☎ 04-94-41-90-10. Open 6pm–1am (6pm–3am Friday and Saturday). Closed Sunday and for three weeks in July. Toulon's only venue for young people, hosting rock, blues, jazz and samba evenings and a 'happy hour' from 6.30pm to 8.30pm. There's a choice of 12 beers on tap.

♥ **Le 113** (D3, **31** on the map): 113 avenue de l'Infanterie de Marine. ☎ 04-94-03-42-41. Open every day from 4pm to midnight. You can come here, to this former hangar, for tapas and little Mexican dishes, as well as a game of pool. There are DJs at the weekend and live performances by local groups during the week.

♥ **Le B des Cochons** (C3, **32** on the map): 503 avenue de la République. ☎ 04-94-03-04-75. Meals in the restaurant section of this colourful bar cost between 45F and 70F. There are just a few tables and the food is predominantly Cuban.

There are a few lively spots on the attractive café-lined place Puget, and **Le Puget**, with its comfy chairs and chess boards, is one of the nicest. On the quay, try out the bars of **Le Soleil** or **Le Navigateur**, particularly animated during the summer or when a foreign vessel is in port. **Grand Café de la Rade** is a smart meeting place for Toulon's trendies.

WHAT TO SEE

Vieille Ville (Old Town)

★ **Fontaine des Trois Dauphins** (fountain of the three dolphins) (C2 on the map): place Puget (also known as place des Dauphins). One of many in Toulon, this fountain dating from 1782 features three sculpted dolphins, which have almost vanished due to foliage growth and sediment. It looks rather like a natural spring and is surrounded by café terraces (*see* 'Where to Go for a Drink').

★ **Rue d'Alger** (C2–3 on the map): this pedestrianized street is the main commerical artery in Toulon's old town. It used to be this quarter's most notorious street but is now a respectable place that is popular with evening promenaders. It hits the quays at square Germain Nouveau, where a bronze statue celebrating the art of navigation stands as a symbol of Toulon.

The ancient streets of the old town lead off rue d'Alger. The maze of narrow alleys – such as **rue St-Vincent**, **rue du Noyer**, **rue des Tombades** and **rue de la Fraternité** – and small squares is full of atmosphere. Newly renovated homes sit shoulder to shoulder with run-down medieval dwellings.

As you head towards place d'Armes you'll find yourself in a popular district, with a mostly North African population, where you can have a plate of couscous for just 3F. People live their life in the street here; children kick footballs around while their parents take time out on their kitchen chairs. **Place d'Armes** (B2 on the map) is one of Colbert's creations and the narrow streets around it, with their unwashed cracked facades, are reminiscent of post-war Toulon. Over-made-up women and sailors' girls hang around dodgy-looking neon-lit bars.

★ **Church of St Louis** (B2 on the map): this neo-classical, late 18th-century edifice looks more like a Greek temple than a church. Corinthian columns in the interior add to the overall impression.

★ **Cathedral of Ste-Marie-Majeure** (C3 on the map): built in the 11th century, restored in the 12th and extended in the 17th and 19th centuries, the cathedral has a classical facade and a tall bell-tower. The interior is rather gloomy, so take a torch to see the baroque altar and the painting of the Annunciation by Puget.

★ **Cours Lafayette** (C3 on the map): this typically Provençal street is the site of a colourful daily market (except on Monday). Famous French singer Gilbert Bécaud sang about it in one of his well-loved lyrics.

★ **Musée du Vieux Toulon** (museum of old Toulon) (C3 on the map): 113 boulevard du Maréchal-Leclerc. ☎ 04-94-93-15-54. Open every day (except on public holidays) 1–7pm in summer and 1–6pm during the rest of the year. Free entry. Models, paintings and old photos of Toulon before the bombings of World War II, together with astonishing objects, such as sculpted coconuts and church interiors in a bottle, made by inmates of the penal colony. Another room houses religious art, including beautiful 16th-century liturgical books from Leyre Abbey in Spain.

★ **Church of St-François-de-Paule** (C3 on the map): badly damaged in 1944 and later restored, this church stands on the corner of avenue de la République and cours La Fayette. It has a baroque facade and a Genoese-style bell-tower. Double columns separate the three naves, and there's a lovely multi-coloured marble altar.

The Port

★ **Les Quais** (wharves): largely hidden by the post-war buildings on rue de la République that have not worn well. The last vestiges of Toulon's past are Pierre Puget's two *Atlantes*, 15th-century sculptures that supported the main balcony of old Hôtel de Ville. Enjoy a stroll around the Darse Vieille, now given over to leisure and pleasure.

★ **Musée de la Marine** (naval museum) (B3 on the map): place Monse-nergue. ☎ 04-94-02-02-01. Open every day from September to June 9.30am–noon and 2–6pm; in July and August, open every day 9.30am–noon and 3–6pm. Closed Tuesday and public holidays. Entrance fee: 29F. Guided tours possible. The museum has a magnificent 18th-century door-way with wooden figures carved by Puget. It displays huge models of 18th-century galleons, used to train novice naval officers. There are some wonderful pieces from the sculpture workshops of the arsenal (*see below*), including a magnificent sculpted figurehead of Neptune, together with photographs, plans and paintings relating to the sea. The unusual items include special smokers' tools (matches were banned on board) and mementoes from colonial battles, including a model junk.

★ **Arsenal Maritime** (A–B2 on the map): to the south of place d'Armes, Toulon's arsenal, created by Colbert, is a town within a town. Covering 268 hectares (660 acres), the arsenal together with the naval base employs nearly 15,000 people, both civilian and military. Don't miss the 18th-century gate with its four Doric columns. Entry is not permitted, but you can find out more from the commentary on the harbour trip (*see* 'What to Do').

La Haute Ville (The Upper Town)

To the north of the Basse Ville (lower town), the Haute Ville (upper town), is rich in monuments. The quarter was redesigned by town planner Baron Haussmann, who more famously completely changed the layout of Paris in the middle of the 19th century, and was prefect of the Var region for a number of years. The renovation was inspired by a visit from Emperor Napoleon III, who felt that the town was too restricted within its old walls.

★ **Theatre** (C2 on the map): the locals continue to call this building 'the opera'. The largest in the province, it can seat 1,800 and has a statue-covered facade.

★ **Place de la Liberté** (B–C2 on the map): in the heart of the Haute Ville, this square has been under renovation for decades.

★ **Museums** (B2 on the map): avenue du Général-Leclerc. Two municipal museums are housed in one Renaissance-style edifice, actually built in the 19th century: **Musée d'histoire naturelle** (natural history museum): ☎ 04-94-36-81-00. Open Monday to Friday 9.30am–noon and 2–7pm, and at the weekend 1–6pm. Free entry. Temporary exhibitions. **Musée des Beaux-Arts** (museum of fine arts): ☎ 04-94-36-81-00. Open every day (except public holidays) 1–7pm. Free entry. Temporary exhibitions focus mainly on local artists.

Mont Faron

Mont Faron means 'lighthouse mountain' in Provençal, and at its summit (584 metres/1,915 feet) you'll be treated to a spectacular view of the harbour, the town and the surrounding area. You can drive up or take the six-minute trip on the little blue *téléphérique* (funicular), ☎ 04-94-92-68-25. It leaves from the secondary train station on boulevard Amiral-Vence. Mid-June to mid-September, open every day (except Monday) 9.30am–7pm. Rest of the year, open 9.30am–noon and 2–6pm. July and August, also

PROVENCE-BY-THE-SEA

open on Monday afternoon. Entrance fee: 38F (26F for 4–10-year-olds; joint zoo and *télépherique* tickets also available). The *télépherique* does not operate in strong winds.

★ **Zoo**: at the summit of Mont Faron. ☎ 04-94-88-07-89. Open in high season 10am–6.30pm. Closed on rainy days. Entrance fee: 40F (30F for 4–10-year-olds). This zoo also calls itself a *centre de reproduction des fauves* (centre for breeding of wild animals). The animals bred and cared for here – big cats such as jaguars, pumas, lions, tigers and snow panthers, and monkeys – are sent to parks and reserves all over France, as well as overseas.

★ **Mémorial du Débarquement en Provence** (memorial to the 1944 landings in Provence): at the summit. ☎ 04-94-88-08-09. Early July to end September, open every day (except Monday) 9.45am–12.45pm and 1.45–6.30pm. In low season, open 9.45am–12.45pm and 2–6pm (to 5.30pm from October to end April). Entrance fee: 25F (10F for 5–16-year-olds and students). This monument commemorates the liberation of southwest France by the Allies in August 1944. A museum tells the story of the operation with a 15-minute diorama and film from the period showing the landings.

Le Mourillon and the Corniche Varoise

One of Toulon's most attractive districts lies to the southeast of the centre, on a point that closes off the *petite rade* (small harbour). There's nothing much more than a few hilly streets, a small port and a popular beach, but the whole ensemble has an authentic village atmosphere.

The Corniche Varoise (coastal road) starts just beyond the plage du Lido. This is one of the town's smartest areas, with lovely villas hidden behind foliage and a botanical garden.

★ **Tour Royale** (royal tower): avenue de la Tour Royale. ☎ 04-94-02-17-99. Between 1 April and 30 September, open every day 10am–6.30pm. During the rest of the year, open during school holidays 1.30–6pm. Free entry. Built in the 16th century to protect the port, the city's oldest fort still has cannon on its platform, but it has served mostly as a prison. The prisoners' graffiti is still visible in the vast guardroom, which is divided into single cells. Temporary exhibitions are held in the summer.

WHAT TO DO

– **Harbour tours**: one-hour boat trips (50F per person) allow you to visit the arsenal, boat 'graves' and the port of La Seyne. Information is available on the wharves or from the tourist office.

– **Boat trips**: head to **plage des Sablettes** and the **St-Mandrier** peninsula. In summer, boats leave for the **îles de Porquerolles**, **Port-Cros** and **Le Levant**, three unspoiled islands off the Var coast. Information is available on the wharves.

– **Sentier des douaniers** (customs officers' path): this is the traditional family walk in Toulon, from the sailing school in Le Mourillon (at the foot of St-Louis fort) to Méjean cove. It's a one-hour return trip with panoramic views, past a number of luxurious villas hidden in wonderful grounds and the large 19th-century fort at Cap Brun. Before you reach Méjean cove, you'll come across other secret inlets where the seawater is beautifully blue.

MARKETS AND FAIRS

– **Marché provençal** (local produce market): takes place every morning (except Monday) on cours La Fayette.

– **Marché bio** (organic market): held on Friday morning on place Dupuy-de-Lôme.

– **Marché aux puces** (flea market): takes place on Saturday, Sunday and public holidays on avenue Ste-Claire. Other venues include La Farlède and Zone Industrielle de Toulon Est (industrial estate of east Toulon), where flea markets are held on Monday and Friday, Wednesday and Sunday.

– **Foire aux vieux papiers de collection**: books and documents are sold on the first Saturday in the month, place Victor-Hugo.

FESTIVALS AND EVENTS

– **Théâtre National de la Danse et de l'Image de Chateauvallon** (national theatre of dance and image): in Ollioules, BP118. ☎ 04-94-92-74-00. This is a wonderful site for cultural events – an open-air amphitheatre with seating for 1,200 people and an ensemble of buildings, including an audition studio and covered theatre, built around a 17th-century tower. The company was established in 1965 and has won an excellent reputation. Between 1972 and 1976, its jazz festivals introduced free jazz to a wider public, while its promotion of contemporary dance is ongoing. During the 1990s, the right-wing local government seriously curtailed the centre's artistic freedom but, despite the setbacks, the site remains magnificent and the programme is still experimental and ambitious.

– **Music concerts** (including rock) take place at **Zénith-Oméga**, ☎ 04-94-22-66-66.

– **Jazz is Toulon**: this is a free festival with street concerts and music workshops. It takes place during July.

– **Festival de musique de Toulon** (music festival of Toulon): in Toulon and the surrounding area from early June to mid-August. The festival features classical music concerts and folk music groups performing in beautiful venues, including the Tour Royale, the Abbaye du Thoronet and the Collégiale de Six-Fours (Six-Fours collegiate church).

Provence d'Azur

The region between Toulon and Le Lavandou has typically Provençal villages and vineyards as well as Côte d'Azur-style seaside resorts. There has been endless debate over the most appropriate name for the area – to be fair, it probably is more Côte d'Azur than Provence, since the name of the former was actually coined in Hyères. The marketing executives have come to the rescue again, with the reasonable and accurate enough compromise of 'Provence d'Azur'.

USEFUL ADDRESS

Maison du Tourisme de la Provence d'Azur: Park Hôtel, 83412 Hyères. ☎ 04-94-35-70-05. Fax: 04-94-35-40-89. Email: www.provence-azur.com

LE PRADET (83220)   Population: 11,160

This typical small seaside resort is much quieter and more restful than its noisy neighbour. Its appeal has not been lost on many key figures, including Winston Churchill, who spent time here. There's no shortage of things to do and see in Le Pradet, where nature can be enjoyed to the full, with pretty walks around the mining museum, in the Courbebaisse woods and along the coastal path. The name of the town derives from *pra* (meaning 'meadow' in the local Provençal dialect), and the town does indeed have wonderful farmland and forests. The Massif de la Colle Noire overlooks Toulon harbour and its botanic richness will fascinate walkers. Vines have been planted here since the Middle Ages, and the area is dotted with interesting old chateaux. Unfortunately, Le Pradet has changed dramatically with the steady influx of tourists.

USEFUL ADDRESS

Tourist office: place du Général-de-Gaulle. ☎ 04-94-21-71-69. Fax: 04-94-08-56-96. Open Monday to Friday 10am–noon and 3–6pm.

WHAT TO DO

★ **Musée de la Mine du Cap Garonne** (Cap Garonne mining museum): chemin du Bau-Rouge. ☎ 04-94-08-32-46. Fax: 04-94-21-95-85. Outside school holidays, open Wednesday, Saturday and Sunday 2–5pm; during school holidays, open every day 2–5pm (to 5.30pm in July and August). Entrance fee: 40F for adults (20F for under-12s, 25F for students). Guided tours last 75 minutes.

Emperor Napoleon III decided to open this mine in 1863, but it fell into disuse after the end of the World War II. It became a museum in 1994 and is one of the most impressive mineralogical sites in the world. It also has magnificent views of the Mediterranean. The life of the 19th-century miners is reconstructed, and you can study tiny crystals through microscopes. The final part of the tour takes you into a unique copper mine. This journey into the centre of the earth is quite fascinating.

★ **Parc Cravero**: in the centre of town, this park has a wide variety of palm trees and rare species as well as a wonderful 17th-century stone pool.

CARQUEIRANNE (83200)   Population: 8,562

The typical market town of Carqueiranne goes quietly about its daily business throughout the year. Eighty per cent of the tulips cultivated in France are grown here, and it's worth visiting in spring when the fields are ablaze with colour. The small and charming fishing port of Les Sablettes is worth seeing, together with several lovely beaches, such as Le Canebas.

USEFUL ADDRESS

🄗 **Point-infos tourisme** (information kiosk): on the ground floor of the town hall, place de la République. ☎ 04-94-01-40-40. Fax: 04-94-01-40-41.

WHERE TO STAY AND EAT

🛏 ✖ **Chambres d'hote L'Aumonerie** (B&B): 620 avenue de Font-Brun. ☎ 04-94-58-53-56. At the exit to Carqueiranne, towards Hyères, take the first turning on the right after the road leading to the campsite. Double rooms with shower or bath and toilet, including breakfast, from 320F to 480F, depending on season. There's also a separate house for two for 500–550F in an idyllic setting and with a fully equipped kitchen – head to the private beach through the garden. There are three charming rooms in a large building, formerly owned by a naval chaplain, with the smallest one housed in what used to be the chapel. The two other rooms are upstairs and have their own shower or bath but share a toilet. Breakfast is served on the terrace, overlooking the sea. You'll receive a warm welcome.

🛏 ✖ **Hôtel Richiardi**: port des Salettes. ☎ 04-94-58-50-13. Fax: 04-94-12-94-64. Restaurant closed on Monday (open Monday lunchtime only in summer), Tuesday lunchtime in summer and on Sunday evening out of season. Also closed from early January to end February. Double rooms with shower or bath and toilet from 220F to 370F with garden view, or from 270F to 470F with sea view. Menus from 100F to 195F. This small family hotel opposite the port offers simple but pleasant rooms, the best of which have a terrace facing the port. The welcome is warm and the fish-based cuisine has lots of flavour.

FESTIVAL

– **Corso**: usually held in mid-April. A pretty procession of flower-filled floats parades through the streets of France's tulip capital.

HYÈRES-LES-PALMIERS (83400)

Population: 53,300

Hyères is the oldest winter resort on the Côte d'Azur and one of the most extended *communes* in France. The parish covers 30 kilometres (nearly 20 miles), from the tip of the Giens peninsula to the Sauvebonne valley, not including its islands.

The town of Hyères was known as 'Olbia' by the Greeks from Marseille, who founded the town, as 'Pomponiana' by the Romans and as 'Castrum Arearum' during the Middle Ages. In this latter period the waterfront was abandoned in favour of the more secure hill near by, where the lords of Fos built their chateau. The salt extracted from the marshlands enabled Hyères to compete economically with Toulon just along the coast. Toulon gained the upper hand when the chateau at Hyères was dismantled on the orders of Louis XIII in 1620, and Hyères had to wait for the advent of tourism before it could return to economic health.

The development of the railway in the 19th century increased the town's popularity and fame, tourism flourished and Empress Josephine, Tolstoy, Victor Hugo and Robert Louis Stevenson were among those who built villas and took tea here. The English, including Queen Victoria, were particularly fond of Hyères. Visitors enjoyed the climate and the scenery, and doctors in London recommended that patients with tuberculosis (one of the most common of 19th-century illnesses) should spend time in the gentle air. Splendid villas were built; a few still stand today, although they are a little less opulent now. As tourism expanded without the necessary infrastructure, the town gradually lost its appeal and faded quietly from fashion. Nice and Cannes soon took over in popularity.

From 1936, the Côte d'Azur changed dramatically, as the first wave of ordinary holidaymakers arrived. Tents began to appear, and today Hyères has a large number of campsites and hotels, and a hugely increased population in the summer months.

USEFUL ADDRESSES

🛈 Tourist office: J.-Salusse rotunda, 83412 Hyères Cedex. ☎ 04-94-65-18-55. Fax: 04-94-35-85-05. In low season, open Monday to Friday 8.30am–6pm, Saturday 9am–noon and 2–6pm; in high season, every day 8.30am–8pm. Group tours (minimum of eight people) organized from 15 June to 15 September, with themes such as medi-eval Hyères and the Cubist-inspired Villa de Noailles.

🚆 Train station: information ☎ 08-36-35-35-35.

■ **Boat trips**: to Port-Cros and Le Levant, ☎ 04-94-57-44-07. To Porquerolles, ☎ 04-94-58-21-81.

■ **Car, bicycle and motorbike hire**: contact the tourist office, ☎ 04-94-65-18-55.

WHERE TO STAY AND EAT

IN HYÈRES-VILLE

⌂ Hôtel du Soleil: rue du Rempart. ☎ 04-94-65-16-26. Fax: 04-94-35-46-00. Website: www.hotel-du-soleil.fr. Double rooms with shower and toilet from 220F to 340F, depending on season, with bath and satellite TV from 250F to 390F. Parking charge. This lovely old stone building, covered in ivy, is in a quiet spot, a stone's throw from the Parc St-Bernard and the Villa Noailles, close to the medieval part of the town. The tastefully renovated rooms are all different. The attic rooms have the best view over the sea, in the distance. The tariff includes discounts on crossings to the Îles d'Hyeres and on bike hire.

⚓ **Hôtel Les Orangers**: 64 avenue des Îles-d'Or. ☎ 04-94-65-07-01. Fax: 04-94-35-25-90. Double rooms with shower, toilet and TV from 225F to 280F, with bath from 250F to 340F. The name of this unpretentious hotel (with motorbike parking) comes from the orange trees on the patio. The absolutely delicious marmalade served at breakfast comes straight from their branches. Try to choose one of the attractive rooms overlooking the courtyard of the pretty building.

⚓ **Hôtel du Portalet**: 4 rue de Limans. ☎ 04-94-65-39-40. Fax: 04-94-35-86-33. Email: damien-v1@wanadoo.fr. Open all year. Double rooms with washbasin from 165F to 180F, with shower and toilet (and TV) from 200F to 240F, with bath from 235F to 300F. Run by a cheerful and friendly couple, this small family hotel has a warm and welcoming atmosphere. The rooms are simple, clean and excellent value for money. You can hire bicycles and cars here. A reduction is available on the Porquerolles boat.

✕ **Restaurant Vanille–Chez Jo**: 22 rue de Limans. ☎ 04-94-65-31-13. Restaurant closed for lunch on Sunday and Monday during the summer, and all day Sunday and Monday in winter. Daily special (*plat du jour*) for 70F, and salads for 40–60F. The tiny dining room is hidden behind a window overgrown with plants. The eclectic interior is mostly baroque in style, kitsch in parts, with garden furniture sitting happily alongside Louis-Philippe, and Christmas decorations. The salads are large and the terrines are tempting, particularly the garlic one. The portions are very generous, the welcome charming and discreet, and the atmosphere relaxed.

✕ **Le Bistrot de Marius**: 1 place Massillon. ☎ 04-94-35-88-38. Closed on Tuesday in low season; also closed from 15 November to 5 December and from 10 January to 5 February. This slightly touristy restaurant, at the foot of the Tour des Templiers (a remnant of a Templar lodge) on a lovely square in the old town, serves pleasant food. There are tables outside on the square in summer.

IN COSTABELLE AND L'ALMANARRE

⚓ ✕ **Hostellerie Provençale La Québécoise**: 20 chemin de l'Amiral-Costebelle. At the motorway exit roundabout, take the turning marked 'Costebelle', then follow the signposts straight on. ☎ 04-94-57-69-24. Fax: 04-94-38-78-27. Open all year. Double rooms with washbasin for 275F, with shower for 290F, and with shower or bath and toilet, from 340F to 412F. Half board compulsory in July and August, between 322F and 392F per person. Menu at 140F for residents. Owned by a Canadian woman, this huge Provençal house is hidden among trees in a residential area. The rooms are charming, not luxurious, but full of character. The cuisine is mostly local in flavour (with a few Canadian dishes), and there's a pleasant pool plus an area for playing *pétanque*.

⚓ ✕ **Hôtel Port-Hélène**: on the N559. ☎ 04-94-57-72-01. Fax: 04-94-57-96-10. Website: www.chez.com/porhelen. Open all year. Double rooms with shower from 180F to 250F, depending on season, and from 225F to 340F with shower or bath and toilet. Studios with kitchenettes are available from 270F to 380F for two. Cross the road to get to the plage de l'Almanarre. The traditional rooms in this 1950s-style house are clean and well maintained, some with their own balcony.

AT PORT DE L'AYGUADE

⚓ **Camping Domaine du Ceinturon**: rue des Saraniers. ☎ 04-94-66-32-65. ✗ Comfortable three-star site, open from end March to 30 September and close to the large beach at L'Ayguade. The second site nearby, with similar facilities, is open from early June to end August. ☎ 04-94-66-39-66. From 1 July to 25 August there's an all-in package price of 88F for a normal pitch.

⚓ ✗ **La Reine Jane**: in Ayguade port. ☎ 04-94-66-32-64. Fax: 04-94-66-34-66. Restaurant closed on Wednesday, at the end of October and in January. Rooms from 150F to 320F, according to facilities. Half board compulsory in summer and during school holidays. Menus from 58F to 180F. This little blue and white house has simple but pleasant rooms with windows opening on to the port. Fish, seafood and meat are all served *à la provençale*, and there's a friendly welcome.

⚓ ✗ **L'Abri Côtier**: 31 place Jean-Pierre-Daviddi. On the promenade that borders the plage de l'Ayguade. ☎ 04-94-66-42-58. Daily special for 50F; à la carte around 100F. Just a few tables in this tiny wooden hut, where you can enjoy tasty dishes of mussels, grilled sardines, octopus and omelette with Corsican *brocciu*. The service and welcome tend to be rather nonchalant.

HYÈRES-PLAGE AND PORT ST-PIERRE

⚓ ✗ **Hôtel-restaurant Les Pins d'Argent**: boulevard de la Marine. Near Port St-Pierre. Follow signs for the airport from Hyères-Ville. ☎ 04-94-57-63-60. Fax: 04-94-38-33-65. Email: pins.d'argent@wanadoo.fr. ✗ Restaurant closed from 1 October to 31 March, and at lunchtime (except on Sunday and public holidays in April, May and September). Double rooms with bathroom and TV from 450F to 540F. Half board compulsory in July and August, from 400F to 460F. Menus from 110F to 190F. Private parking for a charge. This early 20th-century building nestles in a cool green oasis of palm trees and pines. The whole family welcomes guests and makes them feel at home. The characterful rooms are attractively furnished (try No. 205 or 309). The restaurant is near the swimming pool and the chef uses only fresh produce in his tasty and sophisticated dishes.

⚓ **Hôtel Le Calypso**: 36 avenue de la Méditerranée. ☎ and fax: 04-94-58-02-09. Hotel closed between 1 December and 10 January. Double rooms with washbasin from 220F, and with bath up to 280F. In high season, prices rise to between 235F and 310F, including breakfast. Like a charming little doll's house, Le Calypso is in a quiet spot, very close to the sea. Some rooms have windows opening on to the terrace.

⚓ **La Rose des Mers**: 3 allée Émile-Gérard. ☎ 04-94-58-02-73. Fax: 04-94-58-06-16. Email: rosemer@club-internet. Double rooms with shower and toilet from 270F to 470F, depending on season and view. This charming 1950s-style house is virtually on the beach and guests return here regularly. It's run by a couple who do their utmost to make your stay enjoyable and memorable.

ON THE GIENS PENINSULA

Campsites

⌂ L'International: La Réserve, 1737 route de la Madrague. About 1 kilometre from Giens. ☎ 04-94-58-90-16. Fax: 04-94-58-90-50. Open from 1 April to 30 October. Reception open 9am–noon and 3–7pm. The site is clean and close to the sea.

⌂ Le Clair de Lune: 27 avenue du Clair-de-Lune, La Madrague. ☎ 04-94-58-20-19. Fax: 04-94-58-15-90. Email: clair.de.lune@freesbee.fr. Open from 1 February to 15 November. This site is clean and close to the sea, but does not allow camper vans or Kangoo-style vehicles.

☆☆☆☆☆ Plus Chic

⌂ ✕ Hôtel Le Bon Accueil: route du Niel, Giens. Drive past the hospital in Giens then follow signs to Niel and turn left as you leave the village. ☎ 04-94-58-20-48. Fax: 04-94-58-90-46. Closed from early November to March (except during festivals and at New Year). Double rooms with shower or bath, toilet and satellite TV for 350F. Half board compulsory in July and August, from 420F to 450F per person. Menus from 125F to 230F. In the past, it was possible to see the sea, the hills and the lovely little port of Niel from the terrace of this hotel. The view has been slightly obscured by beautiful trees, but at least now you can dine in their shade and breathe in the almost tropical perfumes.

PROVENCE-BY-THE-SEA

WHAT TO SEE AND DO

The Medieval Town

Legendary French film director François Truffaut shot his last film (*Vivement Dimanche*) in the narrow picturesque streets of Hyères' Vieille Ville (old town). Enter the old quarter through the Porte Massillon (gateway), a remnant of early fortifications; a little further along, on the left, is the charming rue couverte des Porches.

★ **Place Massillon**: the square sits at the top of rue Massillon, originally the main street and still commercially active, with a daily market. Look out for Renaissance doorways on the street and the Tour St-Blaise (tower), a remnant from a Templar's lodge.

★ **Collégiale St-Paul** (collegiate church of St Paul): open between April and October 10am–noon (to 12.30pm on Sunday) and 3–6.30pm (to 6pm from November to March). A monumental staircase leads up to a Renaissance doorway with its Romanesque bell. The Renaissance house next door, topped with a round tower, doubles as a city gate. The church has a surprising collection of some 400 ex-voto offerings dating back to the 1600s. An engraved stone marks the final resting place of Robertus, a young child without a burial place, who was entombed in the rock foundation by his father.

★ Climb **rue Ste-Claire** to the Porte des Princes, and at the Cactel Ste-Claire, explore **rue Paradis** with its elegant Romanesque house sporting windows with small columns (No. 6).

★ **Walk up to Parc St-Bernard** (open every day from 8am to 5pm; free entry) and follow the path to the **Vieux Château** (castle) ruins. The view is magnificent.

★ **Villa de Noailles**: montée de Noailles. From place Clemenceau, take cours de Strasbourg to the police station, then follow the signs. Ninety-minute guided group tours (minimum of eight people) possible from 15 June to 15 September; ask at the tourist office. Entrance fee: 30F (10F for students and over-12s). The villa is also open for visits during exhibitions.

The superb Villa de Noailles was built in 1924 by Robert Mallet-Stevens for Charles and Marie-Laure de Noailles, wealthy and aristocratic patrons of modern art. The vast cubist building, with huge bay windows, became one of the great centres of intellectual and creative thought between the two world wars. Man Ray shot his first film here in 1929, and Giacometti, Buòuel and Cocteau often stayed with the de Noailles. The exterior of the building looks like cement but in fact uses traditional Provençal building materials. 'Infinitely practical and simple' (as Viscount de Noailles had requested), the villa covered 2,400 square metres (2,880 square yards). In 1930, it had 600 terraces, a swimming pool, a gymnasium and a squash court, all maintained and run by 20 staff.

This important symbol of modern architecture was more or less abandoned after the death of Marie-Laure de Noailles in 1970, but it is currently undergoing renovation work.

★ **Église St-Louis**: the 13th-century Franciscan church was named in honour of Louis IX, who came here to pray on his return from the Crusades in 1254.

The 19th-Century Town

Below the medieval part of town, wide avenues, villas and elegant public buildings are a legacy of the original 'golden age' of tourism in 19th-century Hyères. During this period a quarter of the town was owned by Alexis Godillot, who made his considerable fortune by supplying shoes to Napoleon II's army during the Crimean War.

★ **Villas**: among the impressive reminders of the Belle Époque are the **Park Hôtel**, on avenue Jean-Jaurès, where Bonaparte left Josephine before embarking on his Egyptian campaign; **Villa Godillot**, at 70 avenue Rondet; in avenue Godillot opposite (an old sign declares it 'forbidden to unsprung vehicles'), the lovely **Maison Mauresque** is a neo-Moorish villa dating from the 1880s; turn left into avenue de Beauregard to find another house of exotic inspiration, the **Villa Tunisienne** (at No. 1).

★ **Parc Olbious-Riquier**: avenue A. Thomas. ☎ 04-94-35-90-65. Open every day in summer from 7.30am to 8pm, and in winter from 8am to 5pm. Free entry. This park is an annexe of the zoological garden in Paris, established in the mid-19th century. Its 6.5 hectares (16 acres) are full of luscious and exotic foliage and plants, including *Ginkgo biloba*, bamboo and palms (inevitably in Hyères-Les-Palmiers, the self-proclaimed French capital of the palm tree). A few birds and animals – monkeys, deer, goats and emus – are kept here, too.

★ **Musée Municipal**: third floor of the municipal building on place Lefebvre. ☎ 04-94-35-90-42. Open Monday to Friday 10am–noon and 2.30–5.30pm;

closed on Tuesday and public holidays (except during temporary exhibitions). The municipal museum houses fragmentary remains of the town's Greek and Roman inhabitants, plus a natural history section.

On the Coast

★ **Archaeological site of Olbia**: towards plage de l'Almanarre. ☎ 04-94-57-98-28. Open every day between 1 April and 30 June 9.30am–12.30pm and 2.30–7pm; between 1 July and 30 September, open 9.30am–12.30pm and 3–7pm. The remains of a Graeco–Roman maritime trading post, including houses and Roman baths, are on display here.

★ **Simone Berriau Plage**: just before you reach Port des Salins. This is a wonderful example of modern architecture, a holiday residence built in 1962 for theatre producer and director Simone Berriau. A number of showbiz personalities have bought apartments in the building.

★ **Beaches**: Hyères has over 20 kilometres (12.5 miles) of beaches. From east to west you'll come across the **plage des Salins** (partly reserved for naturists and the military) and the **plage de l'Ayguade**, a long brown sandy beach that stretches as far as **Port St-Pierre**. The route du sel (salt road) begins at the **plage de l'Almanarre** (the best spot on the coast for funboarding and host to stages of the world championships), and ends at the Giens peninsula. The **plage Capte** and the **plage Bergerie**, sheltered from the wind, are popular with families. For those keen to do a brisk walk before a cool swim, there are some pleasant little beaches on the peninsula, such as **Pointe des Chevaliers** (*see below*).

The Giens Peninsula

Shaped like a boot, the Giens peninsula is a few kilometres south of Hyères-Ville. It's linked to the mainland by two sand-bars that encompass a salt marsh. The Salins de Pesquier (salt marshes) were exploited from the mid-19th century until 1995. Today, the Conservatoire du Littoral, a local conservation organization that works to protect the coastline, is trying to save the area from property developers who want to build villas and hotels on the isthmus. Pink flamingoes from the neighbouring Camargue area visit the peninsula, along with a host of other birds, all visible from the route du sel (salt road), which stretches from plage l'Almanarre to the western edge of the sand-bar. Between 15 November and 15 April the road is closed to traffic. The area is exposed to the mistral and is often flooded. The beaches are reduced in size each year, and the fear is that the pretty hilltop village of Giens may become an island again. Visit it while you can, or head for the little fishing village of Niel, tucked into an inlet.

★ **Écomusée des métiers du sel** (saltworks museum): Salins des Pesquiers, La Capte. ☎ 04-94-58-00-13. Open between 19 June and 9 September 8.30am–noon and 3–6.30pm. Guided 2-kilometre walks across the former salt marshes leave at 9.15am, 9.45am, 11am, 3.45pm, 4.15pm and 5.30pm. Closed on Saturday afternoon and on Sunday. Entrance fee: 20F (10F for 7–12-year-olds). Ornithological tours set off at 9am, 10.45am, 3.30pm and 5.15pm for the same ticket prices.

PROVENCE-BY-THE-SEA

WALKS

★ **Giens peninsula** (8 kilometres/5 miles, 2 hours 30 minutes return, without any stops; IGN 1:25,000 map No. 3446 O): this walk on the peninsula is fairly strenuous and should be undertaken in good weather only. There's a great view of the Îles d'Hyères, but the walk is never crowded. The route is a loop, starting from the far west of the port of La Madrague, to the west of Giens. Follow the yellow markings, watch out for steep sections and do not approach military zones or cliff edges. The wonderful views of the coastline makes the effort worthwhile.

To the right of La Madrague port, walk along the beach (in poor weather, take the Mas de Redouno road) to a set of steps that leads to the inlet (*calanque*) at Le Four-à-Chaux. The path follows the cliff along gulleys and banks. Be careful of the unstable edge. Have a quick look at the Île de la Redonne and continue along the calenque des Chevaliers.

Less energetic walkers can take a shorter route (around 35 minutes) to La Madrague port. The path continues along the coastal ridge to the Pointe des Escaliers and the Pointe Escampobariou (a military zone). Follow the ridge to the Pointe de Rabat and go back down to the plage du Pontillon, keeping to the cliff path. The route takes you to the plage de l'Arbousière, where an old cart track climbs back up northwards to La Madrague.

More energetic walkers can do an 18-kilometre (11-mile) walk around the entire peninsula, which should take about 5 hours.

FESTIVALS AND EVENTS

– **Marché paysan** (farmers' market): on place de la République on Tuesday morning in winter, and on Tuesday and Thursday in summer. Held on avenue Gambetta on Saturday morning.

– **Corso**: carnival procession, held in March.

– **Festival International des Arts de la Mode** (international festival of fashion): held during the first week of May, with young designers showing their work.

– **Les Médiévales**: at the end of June or in early July, St Louis' return from the seventh crusade is recreated in Port de l'Ayguade. There's a procession of locals in period costume, a medieval market, and the blessing of horsemen in front of the collegiate church.

– **Aquaplaning**: end June/early July. This international festival of electronic music is the trendiest of its kind in France. There are DJs on the beach in the late afternoon and evening (free entry) and concerts are held in the Villa de Noailles.

ÎLES D'HYÈRES (83400)

The three famous islands of Porquerolles, Port-Cros and Île du Levant became known collectively as the Îles d'Or (golden islands) during the Renaissance, because of their shining yellow rock. Although they are quite touristy, they are enjoyable and worth seeing.

PORQUEROLLES

The largest of the three islands and the most popular with visitors, Porquerolles is 8 kilometres (5 miles) in length and 3 kilometres (2 miles) wide. It has around 300 permanent residents. Porquerolles has various appropriate nicknames, from Port des Poteries (port of the potteries) and Port de la Bonté-Divine (port of divine bounty), to Port des Rochers (port of the rocks) and Port des Lavandes (port of lavender bushes). It's a wonderful place for family walks, with very few cars and a limited number of real roads. Unsurfaced tracks weave their way through pine trees, and you can hire bicycles by the hour or the day – the best way of getting around. To the north, wonderful sheltered beaches are home to several precious protected species of plant. The dangerous south coast is particularly rugged with a lighthouse run by three people on a rota basis. The pleasant village is centred around the charming place d'Armes.

Outside the months of July and August, you may be lucky enough to enjoy the island without interruption from other visitors.

PROVENCE-BY-THE-SEA

History

The island of Porquerolles was given as a wedding present on two occasions, firstly at the marriage of Henri IV and Marie de Médici in 1600 and secondly at the union of François-Joseph Fournier and his second wife, in 1912.

Fournier was an engineer from a Belgian seafaring family. After some involvement in the construction of the Lesseps canal in Panama, he left for Mexico, where he helped to build the railway. There, he discovered one of the world's richest seams of gold. He was forced to flee during the Mexican Revolution in 1907 and returned to France to marry the daughter of a famous English scholar. Seduced by the beauty of Porquerolles, he purchased the island at auction and went to live there, in a Mexican-style hacienda. He imported Italian families to help with the exploitation of the island's farming potential, planting vines and exotic species. A self-sufficient community was established, with its own school, doctor and electricity supply. Fournier lived on the island until his death, in 1935. In 1971, French President Georges Pompidou ordered Fournier's widow to hand over three-quarters of the land for conservation and tourist purposes. Some of Fournier's vineyards continue to prosper, particularly in the Courtade region.

GETTING THERE

– TLV runs trips from **Port de la Tour-Fondue** to the edge of the Giens peninsula. Information: ☎ 04-94-58-21-81. In low season, there are five departures per day; in July and August, more than 20. The journey takes 20 minutes. Return fare: 80F plus car parking (24F per day). Tours of all three islands take place about twice a week in high season, and the boat departs at 9.15am.

– Boats also leave from **Toulon, Le Lavandou, Cavalaire, La Londe** and Bormes in summer.

– Visits to the island are suspended during bad weather (when the winds are too strong or if there is a high fire risk). An emergency plan is then put into action; check that the suspension is not in force before buying your ticket.

– There are no regular connections between Porquerolles and Port-Cros.

– Seasoned windsurfers can make the crossing from Giens to Porquerolles in just over 10 minutes (with a good wind behind them).

USEFUL ADDRESS

🅑 **Bureau d'information** (information centre): at the port. ☎ 04-94-58-33-76. Fax: 04-94-56-36-39. Website: www.porquerolles.com. Open 9am–1pm, 2.30–5.30pm.

WHERE TO STAY AND EAT

There are seven hotels on the island, all of which are expensive. In high season, you need to book several months in advance, and most places insist on half board.

🛏 ✕ **Les Glycines**: place d'Armes. ☎ 04-94-58-30-36. Fax: 04-94-58-35-22. Email: auberge.glycines@wanadoo.fr. Half board from 390F to 850F per person (depending on season). Menus from 99F to 169F. The hotel has been renovated in Provençal style and has a lovely patio. A night here is a real treat.

🛏 ✕ **Hôtel Sainte-Anne**: place d'Armes. In the heart of the village, near the church. ☎ 04-94-58-30-04. Fax: 04-94-58-32-26. Hotel closed from 5 January to 5 February. Double rooms with shower or bath and toilet from 490F to 1,100F. Half board from 380F to 700F. Menus at 95F and 135F. The rooms are pleasant, but not cheap. The dining room is rustic in style, the atmosphere is friendly and there's a terrace over-looking the place d'Armes.

✕ For lunch there are many tourist restaurants, or alternatively, take a picnic.

✕ **L'Alycastre**: rue de la Ferme. ☎ 04-94-58-30-03. Closed in December. Menus from 120F to 180F. Right at the heart of the village, this restaurant is a pleasant place to eat, with a traditional rustic interior. The menu has a wide choice of fish including an excellent seafood platter.

✕ **Il Pescatore**: at the port. ☎ 04-94-58-30-61. Open every day from 1 March to 1 November. Menus at 78F and 120F. Enjoy tuna or swordfish straight from the Mediterranean at a table looking out over the seafront of Hyères. It can be very touristy at the height of the season.

WHAT TO SEE AND DO

Before setting off to explore, you should be aware of a few regulations. Offsite camping and bivouacking are prohibited. You are not allowed to light fires and you must not smoke outside the village. Underwater fishing is also banned. You are asked to respect the island's environment by leaving all flora in situ, taking rubbish away with you and conserving water wherever possible.

Note: part of the island of Porquerolles is a military zone (not totally cleared of mines), and strictly out of bounds. The zone is marked, in theory, and runs from the Cap des Mèdes to the Pointe de la Galère.

The tourist information office publishes a guide to all the walks you can enjoy, together with details of flora and fauna that might be seen along the way. Other leaflets are also available.

Beaches

– **Plage d'Argent**: to the left of the port, this beach owes its name (silver beach) to its beautiful white quartz sand. Surrounded by trees, it's very sheltered and shady, and you can enjoy a long swim in its clear waters. Not far away, to the west of the island, the **plage du Grand-Langoustier** is overlooked by a fort.

– **Plage de la Courtade**: situated to the right of the port, this is the most popular of the beaches, large, attractive and edged with tamarisk, pine and eucalyptus trees. A series of small sandy coves leads up to **Fort de Lequin**.

– **Plage Notre-Dame**: the largest beach on the island is reached by a lovely 3-kilometre (2-mile) walk. Surrounded by heather and bushes, it's a favourite spot for sun worshippers and featured in one of the films of French New Wave director Jean-Luc Godard.

Walks

The following walks can all be easily completed in a few hours.

– **Lighthouse, Cap d'Armes and Gorge du Loup**: for a more peaceful walk, take the less direct path, past the cemetery. Allow between 1 hour 30 minutes and 2 hours. One of the most powerful lighthouses in the Mediterranean, which has a beam that can be seen from a distance of up to 54 kilometres (34 miles), sits on the highest point of the island. The local inhabitants have resolved the problem of used water with a lagoon sewerage system. The sun, oxygen, algae and bacteria clean the water so successfully that tourists are often tempted to swim in it.

After the Calanque de l'Oustaou-de-Diou and Cap d'Armes, you get to the lovely inlet of the Gorges du Loup, where the sea suddenly rushes in. Swimming here is dangerous. If the mistral is blowing, you'll find it hard enough to stay on your feet.

– **Balade des forts** (walking around the forts): Porquerolles' location means that it has always been of great strategic importance. The islanders apparently understood the art of besieging a town and built their forts to withstand any invasion. The island's network of forts may still be visited on foot.

● The permanent exhibition site at **Fort de Ste-Agathe**, above the village, houses a detailed account of the islands, the national park and the archaeological remains found in Hyères harbour. From May to September, open 10am–12.30pm and 2–5.30pm. In July and August, open 10am–noon and 3.30–5.30pm. There's a beautiful view from the terrace. The fortress was built during the reign of François I on the site of a Roman fortification, and has remarkably thick walls.

• At the most westerly point of the island, on a small islet, the **Fort du Petit-Langoustier** was built by Richelieu. The **Fort du Grand-Langoustier** on the Pointe Ste-Anne is an appealing ruin but its site can be a dangerously windy place.

• Finally, enjoy the short walk to **Fort de la Repentance**, in the northeast, partly buried under mounds of earth.

– **Conservatoire Botanique** (botanical conservatory): sited in the agricultural district at the centre of the island, this academy protects plant varieties threatened with extinction by intensive farming. It promotes biodiversity and its pretty garden is full of aromatic and medicinal plants. There's also an orchard with mandarin, kumquat, fig and grapefruit trees, from which delicious preserves are made.

PORT-CROS

When the last owners of the island of Port-Cros, a couple named Henry, donated the land to the state, they insisted on the entire area being designated a national park. Since 1963, this protected island, with its extensive woodland and important underwater habitats, has been a peaceful, much-loved paradise. For many years, the island was just a fortress, but now a small patch of Mediterranean forest has been preserved, and its endangered marine life and vegetation are also protected. An extensive network of footpaths takes walkers through areas that abound with fascinating plants and flowers.

The most mountainous of the three islands, and almost circular in shape, Port-Cros rises to 195 metres (640 feet) at **Mont Vinaigre**. Just 4.5 kilometres (3 miles) long at its maximum, it can be covered easily in a single day. There are two small beaches along its rocky and jagged shoreline.

Sadly, this ecological paradise is increasingly threatened by its own success. At least 200,000 tourists visit every year, but it is the 2,000 leisure boats that anchor daily in its waters that cause the most serious problems. The island struggles to sustain such a number, and some species of tree on the shore are already dying, damaged by the effluent pumped into the water from boats. The fish seem to be surviving at the moment, but the marine plants are faring less well. The hundreds of anchors dropped and raised daily are tearing at the seabed and pollution from motor boats only makes the situation worse.

To stop the situation becoming worse, radical measures have been put in place. Camping and sleeping out in the wild are now strictly prohibited, as is anchoring in certain zones, where neptune grass in particular needs protection.

Although it is small, the island is home to 114 bird species, some of which are migratory. Alongside bee-eaters, seagulls, warblers, yellowhammers and puffins, you might spot rarer species, such as sparrowhawks, Eleanor's falcon and kestrels. Also living here, standing vertically in the sand, is the world's largest shell, the *pinna nobilis* (mother of pearl), which can reach up to a metre in length.

GETTING THERE

– **From Le Lavandou**: take one of the boats run by **Vedettes Îles d'Or**: 15 quai Gabriel-Péri. ☎ 04-94-71-01-02. Some boats stop at Île du Levant, and the journey takes 45 minutes (with en route stops) or 30 minutes (direct). There are three departures a week in low season, seven a day in summer. Return ticket to Port-Cros or Le Levant: 127F (84F for children). Joint ticket for Port-Cros and Le Levant: 155F (115F for children).

– **From Port d'Hyères**: take one of the trips to Port-Cros and Le Levant, which leave five times a day in July and August only. ☎ 04-94-57-44-07. The journey to Port-Cros takes an hour.

USEFUL ADDRESS

⌷ Bureau d'informations du parc (park information office): ☎ 04-94-01-40-72. Well-informed and friendly staff provide all sorts of information on the island and the national park. Opening hours vary according to season.

WHERE TO STAY AND EAT

Port-Cros has just one hotel, which is charming but very expensive. several restaurants in the port. For a cheaper alternative, stay on Île du Levant, 15 minutes away by boat (one departure a day between March and November, and one departure on Wednesday, Friday, Saturday and Sunday between November and March).

⌷ Maison du Port: ☎ 04-94-05-92-72. Double rooms from 300F to 350F; minimum stay two nights. Apartments for rent by the week for 550F a day for two or 1,000F a day for four.

WHAT TO SEE AND DO

The village of Port-Cros, set on a beautiful harbour with charming houses and swaying palm trees, is the starting point for exploring the island's unique range of Mediterranean flora.

As on Porquerolles, an emergency plan comes into force when there's any risk of fire. The footpaths are closed and visitors may only access the beaches.

– Visitors who are pressed for time should take the **Sentier des Plantes** (botanic footpath); allow 35 minutes one way. The path weaves its way around the **Fort du Moulin** and above the lovely little cemetery planted with cypress trees. (Most cemeteries in Provence are planted these trees which symbolize eternal life and represent the relationship between the sky and the earth.) You'll also see the **Fort de l'Estissac**, built by Richelieu, and open to the public in summer.

The brochure produced by the park information office will help you to identify plants and flowers along the route, such as *ciste de Montpellier* (Montpellier cistus) and *oleaster* (wild olive), various species of pine trees (umbrella, Aleppo, maritime, and so on), stands of holm oak in damp valleys, as well as myrtle and mastic trees. As you walk along, you'll encounter some of the strange workings of the forest. You'll see euphorbia trees that shed all their leaves and twigs in summer and grow new ones in autumn, and catnip, which is said to drive cats mad.

In the *maquis*, or areas of scrubland, the cane-apple is one of a few plants to bear fruit and flowers simultaneously. The heather, which can grow up to 7 metres (25 feet) in height, has pretty white flowers in March. Rosemary, lavender, sage and broom grow in the company of a whole range of salt-loving plants with descriptive names, such as 'witches' claw' and 'stone-piercer'.

After the botany lesson, head to the **plage de la Palud** for a swim. Be prepared for crowds in the summer, and take your own refreshments.

The path comes back via the **Fort de l'Eminence**.

– For a more strenuous, 3-hour walk, try the **Sentier des Crêtes**, which starts in the shade of the thick forest in the Vallon de la Solitude (Valley of Loneliness). Past the **Fortin de la Vigie** (closed to visitors), follow the ridges to the foot of **Mont Vinaigre**, the highest point on the island. The path hugs the impressive craggy cliffs of the south coast to **Pointe de Malalongue**, opposite the reserve of **Île de Bagaud**.

– Take the 10-kilometre (6-mile) **Sentier de Port-Man** for a 4-hour walk via the **Col des Quatre Chemins** (Pass of the Four Ways), the **Fortin de la Vigie**, the former soda factory and **Fort de Port-Man**, from where you can enjoy a pretty view over **Île du Levant**. Head back via Pointe de la Galère and plage de la Palud, through undulating, shady and beautiful scenery. Take a packed lunch with you – the walk can take you most of the day if you make a few stops.

★ Port-Cros offers the unique opportunity for an exploratory dive, from plage de la Palud to the islet of Rascas, with a waterproof leaflet that identifies the underwater flora. Reaching a maximum depth of 5 metres (16 feet), it's perfectly safe. All divers need are fins, a mask and snorkel and the ability to swim more than 300 metres. The marine life is varied and interesting, and you'll see the endangered neptune grass and several species of seaweed. The fish are spectacular and include shoals of red mullet and scorpion fish. The guided tour (every day between 10.30am and 4pm, from 15 June to 15 September, except in bad weather) is free of charge.

Experienced divers can explore the abundant life on the islet of La Gabinière, to the south of the island. Magnificent sea fans, the unusual *trottoir de Lithophyllum tortuosum*, a calcified seaweed that looks like coral, and several large and friendly groupers may be in the welcoming party.

ÎLE DU LEVANT

At 8 kilometres (5 miles) long and 1.5 kilometres wide, Le Levant is the least developed of the three islands. On the side that faces the mainland, sheer cliffs plunge into the sea. Few people live on the island permanently, and it's the least visited of the three, with 20,000 visitors per year compared with 600,000 to Port-Cros. Electricity and running water were installed only in the last couple of decades and there's still no street lighting in the village of Héliopolis (take a torch if you plan to stay over). There are no cars on the island, and the village is reached by boat or on foot.

In the 1930s, doctors André and Gaston Durville, bought 10 per cent of the island with the aim of promoting naturism. Inevitably, Le Levant gained a reputation for naughtiness, but you are likely to be disappointed if you expect any scandalous behaviour today. Minimum cover – a swimming costume or sarong – is recommended around the port or in the village.

People come to Le Levant principally to take time out in the villas or small hotels, hidden among mimosa and laurel trees, or to explore the hilly paths that wind their way through the *garrigue* (scrub). To see a different, rather Asian landscape, climb for 15 minutes up the strenuous Chemin du Val de l'Ayguade. To flex your calf muscles a little more, take the path to the left of the port and then to the right, along the Chemin de la Perspective, for a beautiful view. From the village, you can take a path towards the 25-hectare (62-acre) natural reserve of the Domaine des Arbousiers. But 90 per cent of the island is actually a military zone.

For many decades, the island kept quiet about the most shameful episode in its history. At the end of the 19th century, its owner Comte de Pourtales obtained permission from Napoleon III to create an 'agricultural colony for young delinquents'. It was in fact nothing more than a children's penal colony. Children aged between 5 and 21 years were transferred from the Parisian prison of La Roquette to the island, where they were mistreated, starved and worked to exhaustion. According to the archives, 99 per cent of them perished on the island.

PROVENCE-BY-THE-SEA

GETTING THERE

– Most boats for Port-Cros from **Le Lavandou** stop at Le Levant first (*see* page 445).

– Call the **Hyères** boat company and TLV for information: ☎ 04-94-57-44-07. There are usually five departures per day in high season, but only one in low season. The journey takes an hour. Alternatively, combine your trip to Le Levant with Port-Cros and explore both in one day.

WHERE TO STAY AND EAT

Campsite

🛏 **Camping Colombero**: near to the port. ☎ 04-94-05-90-29. Open from Easter to end September. Well-maintained furnished accommodation from 170F to 230F; basic, but excellent value and with a garden. The owner also has some accommodation with kitchenette on the Chemin de l'Ayguade, between the port and the La Source restaurant.

☆☆ – ☆☆☆ **Moderate to Chic**

Most hotels on Le Levant insist on providing full or half board.

🛏 ✕ **Hôtel Le Ponant**: on the coast, above plage des Pierres Plates. ☎ and fax: 04-94-05-90-41. Closed from 21 September to 1 June. Double rooms with shower available on half board basis only, for 300–450F per person, depending on season. This 1950s-style house rises like a ship from the cliff-top, with its large terraces and great sea views. The unusual *patron* is a talented sculptor and has added a personal touch to all the charming rooms. The cuisine is simple but tasty.

🛏 ✕ **Villa Marie-Jeanne**: between the village and plage des Pierres-Plates. ☎ and fax: 04-94-05-99-95.

Website: www.naturiste.com/ villa-mariejeanne. Closed from end October until Easter. Fully equipped and well-maintained studios from 260F to 440F, for two from 320F to 500F. The accommodation is housed in a seaside villa that has been tastefully renovated. The facilities include a sauna and a gallery. A lovely place with a warm welcome.

La Source: Chemin de l'Ayguade. ☎ 04-94-05-91-36. Fax: 04-94-05-93-47. Closed from 15 October to 1 April. Rooms from 250F to 300F with shower, and from 280F to 320F with shower and toilet. Half board compulsory in July and August, from 300F to 420F. Menus at 110F and 125F. The hotel is located a stone's throw from the sea. After getting off the boat, take the road (not the steps) that climbs up the hill. The restaurant, run by a *patronne* with two fisherman sons, serves deliciously fresh seafood. The very pleasant hotel rooms are located in

buildings surrounded by flowers on the hill. You can eat on the terrace on sunny days.

La Brise-Marine: Héliopolis, near the central square. ☎ 04-94-05-91-15. Fax: 04-94-05-93-21. Closed from mid-January to mid-February. Rooms with shower and toilet for 490F. Menus from 80F to 180F. The pretty rooms are arranged around a patio with a pool, and there's also a sun terrace. Guests receive a friendly welcome at this charming hotel.

Hôtel Gaétan: near the port. ☎ 04-94-05-91-78. Fax: 04-94-36-77-17. Closed from October to April. Double rooms with washbasin for 180F, 220F with shower, or 250F for shower and toilet. Half board compulsory in summer, for 300F to 330F per person. Menus at 90F and 120F. This slightly old-fashioned hotel has just 14 simple rooms and a pretty garden full of exotic flowers and plants.

SCUBA DIVING

According to legend, the daughters of King Olbianus used to swim freely all around this area. One day, they were captured by pirates and the gods intervened and turned the young women into golden islands (the *Îles d'or*). The clear waters around the islands, brimming with fish, are heaven for divers. The national park of Port-Cros is a real sanctuary for marine life, with more than 200 friendly groupers (happy to be touched), living harmoniously alongside bass, octopus, conger and moray eel, amid luxuriant flora. Behind the island of Porquerolles lies the fascinating wreck of the *Donator*, a must for underwater explorers. Remember the cardinal rules of diving: respect the fragile environment, and don't feed the fish; do not remove anything from the wreck or the seabed, and be very careful with your fins; pay attention to the weather at all times, and be aware of the fact that the current can be strong here.

Diving Centres

■ **Porquerolles Plongée**: ZA No. 7, 83400 Île de Porquerolles. ☎ 04-94-58-34-94. Website: www.porquerolles-plongée.com. Open all year. The only dive centre (ANMP, PADI) on the archipelago, this club has been in operation for 15 years now. The owner is a state-qualified instructor, with a stylish catamaran and a trawler with a compressor. The school offers introductory dives, courses up to Level IV and PADI certification, half-day or full-day dives on Porquerolles, Port-Cros, Giens and Cavalaire, as well as wreck dives or Nitrox (mixed gas) dives. Booking essential.

■ **Destination Plongée**: avenue du Dr-Robin, 83400 Hyères. ☎ 04-94-57-02-61. Website: www.destination-plongée.com. Open all year. This school (FFESSM, PADI) on the port at Hyères has a former trawler converted into a dive vessel, with a compressor. Qualified instructors teach beginners, courses to Level IV and PADI certification, and lead exploratory dives around the islands and the Giens peninsula, as well as wreck dives. All equipment is supplied. Booking advised.

■ **CIP Lavandou**: on the quay, 83980 Le Lavandou. ☎ 04-94-71-54-57. Open from 1 April to mid November. This well-equipped school (FFESSM, ANMP) has two large boats and offers introductory dives, courses and exploratory dives. Trips leave daily for Port-Cros and head to other islands several times a week. Book at least two days ahead if possible.

■ **Aqualonde**: place de l'Hélice, in the Nouveau Port, 83250 La Londe-Les Maures. Located opposite the islands. ☎ 04-94-01-20-04. Open from mid-March to mid-November (and on request). This school (FFESSM, ANMP), run by two state-qualified instructors, has a boat called *Idéefixe*, equipped for first and exploratory dives and for instruction to Level III. There are two departures a day to Port-Cros, as well as the possibility of selecting your own site and wreck diving. Booking preferred.

Dive Sites

Port-Cros

La Gabinière: the best diving off Port-Cros is to the south of the island. Descend to a maximum of 40 metres (130 feet) in crystal clear waters to make friends with a shoal of curious and friendly groupers. Sea bass hover in a colourful parade above sea fans, sponges and tube-worms. Beware the strong currents.

Also in the south of the island, just nearby, the **Pointe du Vaisseau** and **Pointe de la Croix** are lovely, often busy Level I sites. Drift and decompression diving are possible here.

Pointe de Montrémian: located to the northeast of the island, this Level I dive site, with a maximum depth of 40 metres (130 feet), features an extraordinary seascape, like an underwater garden. In autumn, impressive rays come to breed among the underwater dunes, which have a drop of 10 metres (35 feet). There's no shortage of flat fish in the area, and stunning red and yellow sea fans form a colourful background for little spiny lobsters and sea bass. The currents can be strong.

La barge aux congres (conger eel ship): this exposed Level III dive site, just next to the Pointe de Montrémian, is known as *Tantine* (auntie) to local regulars. The wreck, at a depth of 48 metres (157 feet), is home to a colony of enormous and impressive grey conger eels, with huge gaping mouths. Use a torch to ferret them out, but do not get too close or feed them. Keep a close eye on the weather.

Porquerolles

Le Donator: located to the southeast of the island, this steamer was torpedoed in 1944 and has rested at a depth of 80 metres (260 feet) under the sea ever since. Wear gloves if you want to take the helm of this wonderfully preserved cargo ship. Surrounded by brightly coloured sea fans, use a torch to explore the bridge, the crow's nest, the propeller and the view from the stern. The spectacular variety of marine life includes moray and conger eels, sea bream and red mullet. A few rules: do not enter the vessel itself; dives should not exceed 15 minutes; and be aware of the potential power of the currents.

The nearby **La Sèche du Sarranier**, lying at a depth of between 15 and 45 metres (50 to 150 feet), is a wonderful spot for Level II divers.

Le Sec du Langoustier: to the west of the island, off a rocky islet, this dive site is at a depth of 18–40 metres (60–130 feet). Take a torch to see conger and moray eels, peaceful groupers and magnificent sea fans, and perhaps a small solitary octopus lurking in the background. Do not touch the red coral. This is a Level I dive, with difficult currents on occasion.

Ville de Grasse: this legendary wreck lies to the northwest of the island at a depth of 50 metres (165 feet). In the 1800s, the *Ville de Grasse* paddle-steamer was cut in two in a collision with the *Ville de Marseille*. The rear section houses the steam engine and two large paddle wheels – a testimony to boat building in days gone by. In the 1950s, Jacques Cousteau showed a lot of interest in the wreck and even now people think there may be treasure aboard. Do not dive for longer than 15 minutes. This is a Level III dive, with strong currents.

Île du Levant

La balise de l'Esquillade: to the east of the island, this site is at a depth of up to 35 metres (115 feet). The fauna includes moray and conger eels, octopus, scorpion fish and timid spiny lobster. Clap your hands at the tube-worms and watch their response. Drift diving and decompression diving are also possible. This is a Level II dive, with unpredictable currents.

LA LONDE-LES-MAURES (83250)

Population: 8,840

This little town half-way between the palm trees of Hyères and the Massif des Maures goes about its business quietly, particularly in low season. The gateway to the *massif*, it offers beaches near by and a wine-growing area for exploration. Around 25 vineyards, many selling high-quality wines, are reached by a delightful little road.

USEFUL ADDRESS

◘ **Tourist office**: avenue Albert-Roux. ☎ 04-94-01-53-10. Fax: 04-94-01-53-19. Open in low season 9am–12.30pm and 2.30–6.30pm; July and August, 9am–12.30pm, 3–8pm.

WHERE TO EAT

✕ **Le Jardin Provençal**: 15–18 avenue Georges-Clemenceau. ☎ 04-94-66-57-34. ✗ In low season, closed on Sunday evening and all day Monday, and from 15 December to 15 January. Menus from 138F to

PROVENCE-BY-THE-SEA

240F. À la carte around 350F. The Provençal-style dining room is straight from the pages of an interior design magazine, and there's a pleasant terrace in the garden. The reception is warm and the service is excellent. The regional food is agreeable and the only missing ingredient is a cheaper fixed-price menu.

✗ **Chez Francis**: in Port-Miramar. ☎ 04-94-36-03-75. Closed on Sunday evening and on Monday (except in July and August) as well as during December and January. Menu at 88F. À la carte around 120F. This popular place – a classic seaside restaurant in a relatively new building – serves simple and tasty dishes, such as *moules frites* (mussels and chips) and grilled fish.

WHAT TO SEE

★ **Jardin d'oiseaux tropicaux** (tropical bird garden): in the St-Honoré district. On the D559. ☎ 04-94-35-02-15. Open every day 9.30am–7.30pm, from June to September, and 2–6pm during the rest of the year. Entrance fee: 35F (25F for children from 3 to 14 years). This unique place has 450 birds and 86 species, from toucans to tropical guinea fowl. The walk around the botanical garden is beautiful and there's a pleasant picnic area.

CABASSON AND CAP DE BRÉGANÇON

Leave the N98 close to Port-de-Miramar and take the lovely Route des Côtes-de-Provence to Cap de Brégançon. This wonderful, undulating road, particularly enjoyable for cyclists, proceeds in a leisurely way through idyllic countryside and past vineyards. Completely undeveloped, this rural area is astonishingly picturesque.

The fine-sand beach at Cabasson is delightful (although parking costs 25F): crowded in summer, and almost deserted out of season, it lines the bay, is flanked by rocks and is backed by greenery. There's a small shop and a play area for children. The silhouette of the Fort de Brégançon is visible in the distance. The French president apparently comes here sometimes to escape the pressures of office.

The village itself is worth a visit. Take the road up the hill overlooking the village for a wonderful view of the whole area.

WHERE TO STAY AND EAT

Campsite

⛺ **Camping de la Griotte**: 2168 route de Cabasson. Between Cabasson and Le Lavandou. ☎ 04-94-15-20-72. Email: lagriotte@free.fr. Open from April to October. Pitch for two with vehicle for 79F. Surrounded by vineyards, this site offers sheltered areas for tents, caravans and mobile-homes.

☆☆☆ Chic

⛺ ✗ **Les Palmiers**: 240 chemin du Petit-Fort, 83230 Cabasson. ☎ 04-94-64-81-94. Fax: 04-94-64-93-61. Email: les.palmiers@wanadoo.fr. Restaurant closed from mid-November to end December, on Sunday evening, and all day Monday in winter (unless you make a reservation). Double rooms with bath from 420F to 675F; three- or four-person rooms also available. Half board compulsory from July to September inclusive, during the Easter holidays and during spring public holiday weekends, from 420F to 557F per person. Menus from 155F to 210F. Peace and quiet are guaranteed at this pretty Provençal house, set in lush gardens. Some rooms have south-facing balconies.

BORMES-LES-MIMOSAS (83230)

Population: 6,400

This is one of the most beautiful villages on the Côte d'Azur and one of the most extensive, with the old village and Cap de Brégançon covering a total of 10,000 hectares (24,700 acres) between them. The old village – thoroughly restored and tarted up – is rather touristy, but it's worth taking time to explore (and parking is free). Out of season, it's easier to identify the undeniable charm of Bormes, which has attracted artists, celebrities and royalty. The ruling families of Luxembourg and Belgium holiday here, and actors relax incognito on the beaches. Bormes added 'Les Mimosas' to its name in 1968, and the yellow mimosa blooms flourish everywhere. The plant was first brought to France by the soldiers of Napoleon III.

USEFUL ADDRESSES

目 Tourist office: 1 place Gambetta. ☎ 04-94-01-38-38. Fax: 04-94-01-38-39. Open from October to March, Monday to Saturday, 8.30am–12.30pm, and 2–6pm. Between April and September, open every day 9am–12.30pm, and 2.30–7pm. Information on the short tour of the old village and a detailed map of the vast *commune* of Bormes.
目 Annexe estivale (summer information point): boulevard du Front-de-Mer. ☎ 04-94-64-82-57. Fax: 04-94-64-79-61. Between June and end September, open Monday to Saturday 9am–12.30pm and 4–7pm.

WHERE TO STAY

Campsite

童 Camp du Domaine: lage de la Favière. From Toulon, take the RN559 and then turn right 500 metres before Le Lavandou. ☎ 04-94-71-03-12. Open from 1 April to end October. Pitch for two plus vehicle for 160F. This site, one of the largest on the Côte d'Azur, benefits from a sandy beach backed by a pine forest. Facilities include a grocer's shop, restaurant and washing machine. The pitches are of a reasonable size, and there are two price categories (with or without an electricity supply). Book ahead for June, July and August. Motorists could take their chance in case a pitch comes free at the last moment. Last book-in time is 7.45pm.

☆ Budget

童 Hôtel Bellevue: 12 place Gambetta. ☎ 04-94-71-15-15. Fax: 04-94-05-96-04. Closed from end November to end January. Double rooms with washbasin for 155F,

195F with shower and toilet, 245F with bath. Menus from 80F to 130F. This small establishment has a peaceful provincial atmosphere, with rooms overlooking village rooftops. The food is unremarkable.

☆☆ Moderate

⌂ Hôtel Paradis: 62 impasse de Castellan. ☎ 04-94-01-32-62. Fax: 04-94-01-32-60. Closed from 1 January to 31 March and from 30 September to 31 December. Double rooms with shower for 260F, with shower for 354F, with bath and toilet from 420F. On the right, coming down from the village, this peaceful hotel is off the beaten track, with a luxurious garden. The rooms are simple, clean and nicely furnished, some with distant sea views.

⌂ Hôtel de la Plage: at the Bienvenue roundabout, La Favière. At the entrance to Bormes, follow signs to the port and then to La Favière. ☎ 04-94-71-02-74. Fax: 04-94-71-77-22. Closed from 1 October to 30 March. Double rooms with shower and toilet from 270F to 300F, and rooms with bath and toilet from 340F to 390F. Half board compulsory in July and August, from 290F to 350F per person. Menus from 80F to 150F. This surprising place has changed little since 1960 (except for a few concessions to modern comfort requirements). The owners and the guests seem to have remained the same, and there's always a game of *pétanque* going on in the garden after meals. Unfortunately, a few concrete blocks obscure the view of the sea.

☆☆☆ Chic

⌂ Le Grand Hôtel: 167 route du Baguier. ☎ 04-94-71-23-72. Fax: 04-94-71-51-20. Website: www.au grandhotel.com. ⚒ Closed in November. Double rooms with shower cost 210F and with shower or bath and toilet from 310F to 400F. Dinner menu at 100F. Parking is free and there's a strict no pets policy. Splendidly located in Bormes itself and very reasonably priced for its category (three-star), this hotel overlooks the entire village. Some rooms are not as up-to-date as they could be, but the atmosphere is pleasant, reminiscent of a turn-of-the-century spa. Breakfast may be taken in the garden, among the palm trees.

⌂ Chambres d'hôte La Bastide Rose (B&B): 358 chemin du Patelin, on the Cabasson road. 2 kilometres from Bormes-Plage. Follow signs to Cabasson from the D559, and turn right after 1 kilometre. ☎ 04-94-71-35-77. Fax: 04-94-71-35-88. Email: bastide.rose@wanadoo.fr. Closed from 1 October to 31 March. Double rooms with shower or bath and toilet from 500F to 700F, depending on season, including breakfast. Suites from 700F to 900F. Bank cards not accepted. Once you walk through the door, you won't want to leave this charming house, where the five beautiful and stylish rooms display touches of Mexico, Italy and Provence. Guests can also enjoy the pool, hot tub and sun terrace. Breakfast on the terrace is an absolute treat. It's not cheap, but it's worth it.

⌂ La Grande Maison: domaine des Campaux, 6987 route du Dom. About 12 kilometres (7 miles) from Bormes on the D41 and then the N98 to La Mole (signposted on the left from the N98). ☎ 04-94-49-55-40. Closed in December and January. Double rooms with shower or bath and toilet between 500F and 600F, excluding breakfast. Two suites at 600F and 800F. Dinner for 160F. This charming former *bastide*, surrounded by vines, has extremely elegant rooms with spacious bathrooms.

WHERE TO EAT

☆☆ – ☆☆☆ Moderate

✕ **Pâtes et . . . Pâtes**: place du Bazar. ☎ 04-94-64-85-75. Closed on Sunday evening and all day Wednesday as well as in November and December. Meals for between 100F and 150F. This rather unusual Italian restaurant is run by a chef from Turin, who serves wonderful pasta dishes in generous portions. The food is simple and delicious and there's a pretty jasmine-scented seating area.

✕ **La Fleur de Thym**: 2 rue P.-Toesca. ☎ and fax: 04-94-71-42-42. Closed on Monday in low season and from 3 to 28 January. Menus at 110F and 185F; à la carte around 250F. Slightly off the tourist map, the atmosphere here is friendly and welcoming. The chef does his cooking in full view of his customers.

☆☆☆ Chic

✕ **Lou Portaou**: 1 rue Cubert-des-Poètes. ☎ 04-94-64-86-37. Closed on Tuesday (except in high season) as well as from 20 November to 20 December. Menu at 98F; à la carte around 180F. Eating here is like sitting on a film set or a stage, surrounded by lovely paintings and furniture that are rather 17th-century in style. The food has a good reputation. In the summer, book a table under the arches of the little street for a rare treat.

✕ **L'Escoundudo**: 2 ruelle du Moulin. ☎ and fax: 04-94-71-15-53. Closed on Monday and Wednesday out of season as well as from October to December. One menu at 170F. À la carte around 200F. The high standards of this little restaurant have been maintained since the day it opened. It serves delicious regional specialities, including marinated sardines with *mesclun* (local salad of green leaves) and *bourride provençale* (white fish soup), as well as good local wines. The service and welcome are excellent and it stays open later than other restaurants. There are tables outside in the little alley.

WHAT TO SEE

Bormes is a pretty medieval village with a maze of narrow streets, lined with flowering plants and attractive houses. It's best explored early in the morning or at sunset.

★ **Chapelle St-François-de-Paule**: the chapel was built in 1560 by the locals, to give thanks to St François for saving the city from the plague. The facade has lovely stained-glass windows.

★ **Église St-Trophyme**: this parish church dates from the 18th century, although its architecture is more Romanesque in style. It houses the modern *Stations of the Cross* by Alain Nonn and three impressive naves, together with some recently uncovered frescoes.

★ **Medieval streets**: lying below the church, medieval Bormes is made up of a labyrinth of steps, flower gardens, vaulted passages known as *cuberts*, cul-de-sacs and alleys with evocative names. Seeing the worn paving stones and precipitous angles of **rue Rompi-Cuou** (literally 'bum breaker'), you can tell how it got its name. The nearby rue des Amoureux (lovers' lane) is close to the square where couples would dance during village festivals.

★ **Musée d'Arts et d'Histoire** (arts and history museum): rue Carnot. ☎ 04-94-71-56-60. Open 10am–noon and 2.30–7pm. Closed on Tuesday, on Sunday afternoon and public holidays. Free entry. Works by local landscape painter Jean-Charles Cazin hang here alongside those of Pissarro and Rivière, and sculptures and sketches by Rodin. The museum also displays amphorae and religious artefacts, and recreates the history of Bormes, Fort du Bregançon and the Carthusian monastery at La Verne. There is also a display on the story of the life of two local 18th-century sailors who took part in the wars of liberation in South and Central America. Incidentally, Bormes celebrates the independence of Argentina annually on 9 July.

★ Last, climb up to the castle ruins to enjoy the view of Bormes, Cap Bénat, and the islands.

★ The little **Chapelle Notre-Dame-de-Constance** was built on the orders of Constance de Provence in the 13th century on the road to Collobrières. Pilgrims still come here and pin their prayers to the walls. It's reached by a 30 minute climb on the former footpath of the Stations of the Cross. There are some very ancient tombstones nearby, together with a wonderful view over the village. From the summit, you can see Toulon in the distance.

WHAT TO DO

– Keen cyclists enjoy this region, but they will need calf muscles of steel. There's a lovely tour in the **Massif des Maures** (*see* page 459), via Bormes-les-Mimosas, Col de Gratteloup and Col de Babaou, Collobrières (an attractive village with quirky fountains), Notre-Dame-des-Anges (the highest point in the Var region), Pignans, Vidaux, and so on. The descent into l'Issemble takes you back to Le Lavandou via La Londe-les-Maures.

FESTIVALS AND EVENTS

– **Marché provençal** (local produce market): on Monday mornings in Le Pin de Bormes and on Wednesdays in place St-François-de-Paule.

– **Mimolasia**: mimosa festival held in the old village over two days in January, with exhibitions and plant sales.

– **Corso Fleuri**: this floral procession, which passes through the old village in January, is Bormes' oldest festival and one of the largest and most beautiful on the Côte d'Azur.

– **Pentecôte** (Pentecost): celebrated in true Provençal style with a procession, dancing, a huge *aïoli* feast and a fairground.

– **Fête des fleurs** (flower festival): in June, dozens of flowersellers set up stalls in the village and flowers are given away at the end of the day.

– **Santo-Coupo**: October wine and vine festival held in Pin de Bormes (below the old village), with tastings of Côtes de Provence wines.

– **Foire aux santons** (*santons* fair): held in December in the old village.

LE LAVANDOU (83980)   Population: 5,510

Somewhat surprisingly, Le Lavandou takes its name not from the lavender fields in the surrounding area, but from the word *lavandou*, which means public wash-house (*lavoir* in French). Today, it's known principally for its lovely sandy beaches and as the main embarkation port for Port-Cros and Le Levant, and the town itself has no particular charm. It's a good base for a combined beach and cycling holiday, with several beautiful routes to choose from in the Massif des Maures.

USEFUL ADDRESSES

◻ **Lavandou Tourism**: Gabriel-Péri quay. ☎ 04-94-00-40-50. Fax: 04-94-00-40-59. Website: www.lela vandou.com. Open from Monday to Saturday 9am–noon and 2.30–6pm (every day in summer).

■ **Holiday Bikes**: avenue du Président-Auriol. ☎ 04-94-15-19-99. Bicycle, motorbike and car hire.

WHERE TO STAY

Campsites

There are no campsites near the sea in Le Lavandou itself. The nearest site to the water is on the beach at Bormes-les-Mimosas.

⌂ **Camping St-Pons**: avenue du Maréchal-Juin, in the St-Pons district; 800 metres from the sea. ☎ 04-94-71-03-93. Open from Easter to end September. Facilities include a snack bar and caravan hire.

⌂ **Parc-camping de Pramousquier**: avenue du Capitaine-Ducournau, 83980 Cavalière. 8 kilometres (5 miles) east of Le Lavandou on the N559. ☎ 04-94-05-83-95. Fax: 04-94-05-75-04. Open from end April to end September. Close to the beach, with fully equipped sites on terraces overlooking the sea, as well as a shop and a bar/restaurant.

☆☆ Moderate

Le Lavandou has a number of hotels that are good value for money. In low season, you're guaranteed to find somewhere to stay, but you should make a reservation in the summer months.

⌂ **Le Rabelais**: 2 rue Rabelais (a small road that runs at right angles to the marina). ☎ 04-94-71-00-56. Fax: 04-94-71-82-55. ♿ Closed from 11 November to 20 January. Free parking. Double rooms with shower and toilet, and TV, from 230F to 380F, depending on the season. This lovely building is close to the town centre and not far from the beach and offers comfortable, recently renovated rooms, some with sea views. Enjoy breakfast on the terrace overlooking the fishing port.

⌂ **Hôtel California**: avenue de Provence. ☎ 04-94-01-59-99. Fax: 04-94-01-59-98. Email: hotel.cali fornia@wanadoo.fr. Free parking. Double rooms with shower, toilet and satellite TV from 240F and 420F, depending on location. This relaxing hotel has been entirely renovated by the young couple who run it. He is an architect and she is an accomplished hostess. The rooms are not huge, but they are well furnished and offer excellent value for money. The less expensive rooms have garden views, while the others look out to sea over the Îles d'Or. It's an 8-minute (brisk) walk to the beaches.

🛌 Hôtel Beau Soleil: Aiguebelle Plage. 5 kilometres (3 miles) from the town centre on the way to Fréjus. ☎ 04-94-05-84-55. Fax: 04-94-05-70-89. 🍴 to the restaurant. Free parking. Closed from early October to Easter. Double rooms with shower and toilet from 280F to 480F, and from 320F to 510F with bathroom. Half board compulsory in July and August, from 325F to 415F per person. Menus from 98F to 165F. This quiet little hotel, far from the noisy summer nightlife of Le Lavandou, is run by young and dynamic owners, who are friendly and thoughtful. There's a wide selection of local specialities on the menu, with *bourride* (white fish soup) as a highlight.

☆☆☆ Chic

🛌 Hôtel L'Escapade: 1 chemin du Vannier. ☎ 04-94-71-11-52. Fax: 04-94-71-22-14. Email: hotelescapade@wanadoo.fr. Closed in December and January. Free private parking. Double rooms with shower and toilet from 250F to 300F, with bathroom from 300F to 350F. Half board compulsory from 15 June to 15 September, between 270F and 380F per person. Menus at 100F and 165F. Small but cosy, standing on a quiet lane that opens on to the Avenue de Provence, this hotel is well maintained, rather British in style and tastefully decorated.

🍴 Les Tamaris: plage St-Clair. 2 kilometres from the town centre, opposite the beach. ☎ 04-94-71-79-19. Fax: 04-94-71-88-64. Website: www.lestamaris.com. Free parking. Closed from 1 November to 1 April. Double rooms with bathroom (and satellite TV) from 350F to 450F, depending on season. A stone's throw from the beach and with a garden, this building is typical of the area and houses quite pleasant modern practical rooms with private balconies. The family-run restaurant (*see* 'Where to Eat') serves tasty cuisine.

WHERE TO STAY AND EAT

🍴 Auberge Provençale: 11 rue du Patron-Ravello. ☎ 04-94-71-00-44. Email: provençale.auberge@wanadoo.fr. Closed on Tuesday and Wednesday lunchtime, and from 3 to 12 January. Simple but pleasant double rooms (some with sea view) from 170F with washbasin to 300F with bathroom. The hotel is in the town centre and can be rather noisy. Menus cost 88F during the week (lunch in summer, both lunch and dinner in winter) with others from 118F to 240F. The lovely dining room is furnished in an unpretentious, rustic style with a huge fireplace. The cuisine is Provençal and tasty.

🍴 Les Tamaris: plage de St-Clair. 2 kilometres from the town centre, opposite the St-Clair beach. ☎ 04-94-71-02-70. Allow around 200F for à la carte. Known to the locals as 'Chez Raymond', this classy but relatively informal restaurant is something of an institution. Just 15 metres from the beach, it is nicely decorated with an old-fashioned charm. It serves sophisticated, high-quality cooking, with seafood specialities and well-sized portions.

WHAT TO SEE AND DO

– **Boat trip to Port-Cros and Île du Levant**: (*see* Îles d'Hyères, page 445). You can combine both destinations in one trip. Information: ☎ 04-94-71-01-02.

– There are a number of very attractive **walks** for those staying in Le Lavandou. The paths are closed in July and August, because of the risk of fire.

– From **plage de la Favière** (on the outskirts of Bormes) to Bormes itself, there is a coastal path divided into two sections. Walkers of all levels of ability can enjoy the first of these, a 1-hour walk that goes to the **Pointe de la Ris** and **plage du Gaou Bénat**. The second part requires a little more effort, with a few steep climbs and steps leading to **Port du Pradet**. The lovely section to the south of **Cap Bénat** rewards the walker with a panoramic view from the castle ruins, across the Massif des Maures and along the coastline.

★ **Seascope**: 15 quai Gabriel-Péri. ☎ 04-94-71-01-02. Fax: 04-94-71-78-95. Departures between 9am and 7pm (every 40 minutes) from the old port. Tickets: 71F (47F for children). Children particularly enjoy this 35-minute underwater journey of discovery in a trimaran with a glass bottom, giving a view of sea bream, bass and neptune grass.

★ **Beaches**: there are 12 beaches and, from west to east, you'll come across: the trendy **plage de l'Anglade**, at the gates of Bormes; **plage du Lavandou**, a central beach popular with families; **plage St-Clair**, best enjoyed in the morning; **plage Fossette** nestling between two rocky cliffs; and **plage Aiguebelle**. Further on, hidden in relatively inaccessible and less busy little coves, you'll find: **plage Jean-Blanc** and **plage Éléphant**; and two naturist beaches, **Le Rossignol** and **Layet**. Further east in a cove is the long and beautiful **plage de Cavalière**, and then **Cap Nègre** on the far point of the peninsula. **Plage Pramousquier** sits between two rocky points before you reach **Le Rayol**.

FESTIVALS AND EVENTS

– **Fête du Romérage**: held on the plage St-Clair at the beginning of September. A procession takes place to commemorate the patron saint of dressmakers, who apparently also had the power to cure blindness.

– **Théâtre de verdure** (theatre of greenery): concerts and shows are held in high season in the open-air theatre.

The Gulf of St-Tropez and the Pays des Maures

This region is famous throughout the world for the seaside resort of St-Tropez, a tourist 'hot spot' once again after a number of years on the fringes of fashion. These days, you will be very lucky to find a room in the resort at the height of summer, even if you're prepared to pay the astronomical prices charged here by exploitative hoteliers. Some of St-Trop's visitors start their day as the sun is setting and go to bed just as it rises. However, those prepared to look further afield, both in the town and in its surrounding area, will be rewarded by attractive, genuine places, beautiful landscapes and charming hotels. Take to the delightful little roads that pass through the Massif des Maures, and promise yourself a return trip in spring or autumn, when the area's traditional way of life really comes into its own.

The regional tourist office (*see below*) is most helpful and can point you in the right direction at any time of year.

USEFUL ADDRESS

🖪 **Gulf of St-Tropez tourist office – Pays des Maures**: La Foux cross-roads, 83580 Gassin. ☎ 04-94-43-42-10. Fax: 04-94-43-42-77. Website: www.franceplus.com/golfe.de.st.tropez. This uniquely efficient establishment deals swiftly with any request for information or reservations. It covers all 14 *communes* in the area.

LES MAURES FOREST

The name 'Les Maures' may sound as if it comes from invading Moors, but it derives in fact from the Provençal word *mauro*, which means 'dark pine forest'. The Massif des Maures, stretching along the coast for 60 kilometres (40 miles) between Hyères and Fréjus, is indeed densely wooded. Its huge numbers of oak and chestnut trees have been the principal source of income for local villagers for many years. The bright orange trunks of the cork oak trees may look like walkers' waymarkings, but they are actually that colour because they have been stripped for their cork. Bottle corks were made in the district, particularly in La Garde-Freinet, until the 19th century and a small-scale industry survives today, with overseas companies (principally Portuguese) now exploiting the raw material. The chestnut trees are still grown today, and Collobrières is proud of its famous and delicious sweet *marrons glacés* (chestnuts preserved in sugar).

For a long time, the Maures district was inhospitable and quite isolated – St-Tropez was accessible by sea alone for many centuries. The coastline remained more or less uninhabited until 1885, when the arrival of the

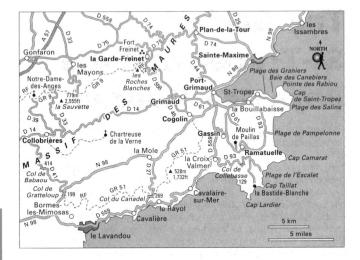

THE MASSIF DES MAURES

Provence railway changed the face of the area for ever, providing a means of transport for the first tourists. Today, beach bunnies and bums head straight for St-Tropez on the N98, via La Môle – not the most attractive route. If you have more time, make your way to St-Tropez and the surrounding area via the small roads that cross the Massif des Maures. The most magical route is the D41 from Bormes-les-Mimosas, which winds its way up to the **Col de Gratteloup** and then crosses the magnificent and impressively hilly Dom forest. After pausing at the **Col de Babaou** (414 metres/1,357 feet), to see the distant view of Hyères and its islands on the horizon, you descend into the valley of Collobrières, the *pays des marrons* (chestnut country). From there, the equally lovely D14 reaches Grimaud via the **Col de Taillude**. A small detour is possible if you want to see the **Chartreuse de la Verne**, a Carthusian complex founded in 1170.

COLLOBRIÈRES (83610)   Population: 1,700

Nestled in the Vallée du Réal Collobrier, at the heart of the *massif*, this quiet and charming old village is the 'capital' of the Maures district. Its 11th-century hump-backed bridge arches over an almost torrential river. It has narrow streets and covered passageways and sits at the foot of the ruins of a 12th-century church. Regular and highly competitive games of *pétanque* are played along the length of the shady tree-lined avenue, where the hotels and restaurants are reasonably priced. It's so peaceful, it seems hardly to have heard of throbbing St-Trop. Try the two specialities of the region – chestnut purée and *marrons glacés*.

USEFUL ADDRESS

🛈 Tourist office: boulevard Charles-Carinat. ☎ 04-94-48-08-00. Fax: 04-94-48-04-10. Website: www.collotour.com. Housed in the former municipal baths – look for the doors marked *Dames* (Ladies) and *Messieurs* (Gentlemen). Open Monday to Saturday 10am–12.30pm and 3–6.30pm (July and August); during school holidays (outside July and August) 10am–noon and 2–6pm; in low season, Tuesday to Saturday 2–6pm.

WHERE TO STAY AND EAT

⛺ Camping municipal St-Roch: just outside the village. ☎ 04-94-28-15-72. Open July and August only; during the rest of the year, call the town hall for information: ☎ 04-94-13-83-83. The entrance to the site is rather narrow, which can make it difficult for caravans.

⛺ ✕ Hôtel-restaurant Notre-Dame: 15 avenue de la Libération. ☎ 04-94-48-07-13. Restaurant closed on Friday, and from 15 December to 15 January. Double rooms with shower for 160F, with shower and toilet up to 200F. Menus from 80F to 150F. This quiet little country hotel is housed in a lovely old building near the river. The rooms are simple but pleasant and the welcome is warm. The cuisine is traditional and tasty, with game on the menu in season.

⛺ ✕ Hôtel-restaurant des Maures: 19 boulevard Lazare-Carnot. ☎ 04-94-48-07-10. Double rooms with shower and toilet for 120F. Menus from 55F to 250F. This is a popular family spot, and its bistrot is packed with locals on football nights. The rooms are simple, very reasonably priced and clean. The cuisine is Provençal and tasty, and you can enjoy meals on a riverside terrace on sunny days. The welcome is authentic and without fuss.

☆☆ Moderate

✕ La Petite Fontaine: 1 place de la République. ☎ 04-94-48-00-12. Closed on Monday, in February during the school holidays, and the last two weeks in September. Menus at 130F (except Sunday) and 160F. This lovely little restaurant serves delicious dishes, including *lapin au vin blanc* (rabbit in white wine) or *fricassée de poulet a l'ail* (chicken in garlic), accompanied by wine from a local co-operative. There are antique tools on the walls. This is one of the best in the area.

☆☆☆ Chic

⛺ ✕ Chambres d'hôte La Bastide de la Cabrière: on the D39. 6 kilometres (4 miles) from Collobrières on the D39 towards Gonfaron. ☎ 04-94-48-04-31. Fax: 04-94-48-09-90. Website: www.provenceweb.fr/83/cabriere. Double rooms with shower or bath and toilet from 390F to 690F, including breakfast. Dinner for 190F, including wine; book ahead. This is a working farm serving meals based on home produced meats, particularly lamb and kid. Guests come here to relax and eat healthily and well, and enjoy the occasional dip in the swimming pool. Bank cards not accepted.

WHERE TO STAY AND EAT IN THE AREA

🛏 ✕ **Gîte d'étape et chambres d'hôte de la Ferme de Capelude**:
Capelude, 83610 Collobrières. 12 kilometres (8 miles) from Collobrières on
the D14 towards Grimaud, below Chartreuse de la Verne. ☎ 04-94-56-80-
35. Website: www.chez.com/capelud. Dormitory beds with shared showers
and toilets, for 90F per person, including breakfast. Double rooms with
shower and toilet for 250F; breakfast 25F extra. *Table d'hôte* dinner for
120F. Two dormitories, ideal for walkers, in a tastefully restored 16th-century
farmhouse in the countryside. There are also five fairly small but pleasant
B&B rooms and a swimming pool. Farm produce such as honey and fig
preserve, chestnut cream, melons and peaches is on sale.

WALKS

There are several fine walks in the area, although some footpaths are closed
in the summer because of the risk of fire. You can explore Plateau de
Lambert, with its two impressive menhirs, and the Pérache valley, or do a
loop around the Verne dam. Leaflets describing the routes are for sale at the
tourist office.

FESTIVAL

– **Fête de la Châtaigne** (chestnut festival): held on the last three Sundays in
October. Sale of local produce, performances by folk groups and other
events held in the streets.

SHOPPING

🔒 **Confiserie Azuréenne**: ☎ 04-94-48-07-20. Open every day 10am–1pm
and 2–6pm. ☎ 04-94-56-80-35. This sweet shop has a small museum
explaining how chestnuts are harvested and transformed into *marrons
glacés*. Of course, it also sells the famous delicacies as well as an unusual
but excellent sweet chestnut ice-cream and a liqueur. Chestnut products are
apparently good for relieving stress and increasing energy levels.

In the Surrounding Area

CHARTREUSE DE LA VERNE

Located 12 kilometres (8 miles) southeast of Collobrières on the D14
towards Grimaud. After 6 kilometres (3.5 miles) on the D14, turn right on to
a small road leading to the site (another 6 kilometres/3.5 miles). The final
kilometre of road is unsurfaced. ☎ 04-94-43-48-28 (call in the afternoon,
preferably). Open every day in summer from 11am to 6pm. Open in winter
from 11am to 5pm (except Tuesday, religious feast days and during the
whole of January). Entrance fee: 30F (8–14-year-olds 10F, students 20F).

Built on a series of terraces on a splendid rocky promontory in a remote
corner of the *massif*, this Carthusian monastery was founded in 1170 by the
bishops of Toulon and Fréjus on the site of an abandoned priory. It has had
an eventful history. The monks may have sought peace and isolation here,

but the outside world refused to leave the monastery alone. It was pillaged by the lords of Bormes in the 15th century, damaged during the religious wars, raided by the Saracens and also the victim of forest fires on several occasions. The building was constantly being rebuilt and expanded by the monks until they were finally forced to flee during the French Revolution. The monastery is currently undergoing restoration, and a community of nuns has lived here since 1984.

The first thing visitors see is a tall boundary wall with an austere white-stone facade that contrasts with the local stone – green with subtle nuances of colour – used around the striking gateway. The entrance opens out on to the courtyard, which is surrounded by functional buildings, including the stables, forge, bakery (with a huge bread oven in which all the community's foods were cooked) and an old olive press. The tour passes by the remains of the small cloister, with its lovely serpentine (green-stone) arcades, the Romanesque church and a church.

There's a reconstruction of typical 17th-century monks' cells. In the four whitewashed rooms, contact with the outside world was kept to a minimum, with frosted-glass windows and a serving hatch through which meals were passed. Each monk would leave his room only twice a day, in order to attend religious services. Otherwise, life was focused around the few square metres of the vegetable garden, a covered walk and the straw mattress of a wooden bed. The large cloister is at the heart of the complex, and the old monks' cells, now subtly restored, open on to it. One of them has recently been occupied again. The high walls surrounding the cemetery symbolize again the reclusive nature of the monks' existence. Behind them lie the tombs of 800 monks buried between the 12th century and the French Revolution.

★ **Chapelle Notre-Dame-des-Anges**: around 20 kilometres (13 miles) from Collobrières on the D14 and then left on to the D39. Turn left at the Col des Fourches and follow the signposts. The 19th-century chapel, of limited architectural interest, replaced a building that had stood on the spot since the sixth century. Pilgrims have been coming here for many years, hence the many ex-voto offerings, including a crocodile suspended from the ceiling! The view from the chapel over the Massif des Maures is superb.

THE CORNICHE DES MAURES

The road to St-Tropez follows the sea, running for the most part along the clifftops, and provides some wonderful views, particularly at Le Rayol. However, the beaches are generally small, and there's rather too much concrete around. For the real charm of Provence, look instead on the St-Tropez peninsula, which has been better protected from unscrupulous developers.

LE RAYOL

Make a pit-stop in this nice little resort to visit the **Domaine du Rayol** (*see below*), the perfect illustration of luxury living on the Corniche des Maures. Dating from the beginning of the 20th century, it has 5 hectares (12 acres) of gardens with flowers and plants from all over the world.

USEFUL NUMBER

🏢 **Tourist office**: ☎ 04-94-05-65-69. Fax: 04-94-05-51-80.

WHERE TO STAY AND EAT

🛏 **Hôtel de la Plage**: on the D559, near the beach. ☎ and fax: 04-94-05-61-22. closed from November to Easter. Double rooms with shower from 270F to 290F, and with shower and toilet from 300F to 340F. Half board compulsory in July and August, from 300F to 340F per person. Menus from 80F to 140F. This pleasant little hotel is charmingly old-fashioned with reasonable prices, a pretty garden and a pool. Unfortunately, it's rather close to the road.

✗ **Maurin des Maures**: avenue du Touring-Club. ☎ 04-94-05-60-11. Fax: 04-94-05-67-70. ✗ Restaurant open from 11 November to 20 December, for dinner only. Menus at 70F (weekday lunch), 119F and 144F. Locals perch on barstools and enjoy serious *pastis* drinking (no ice, no frills) here. The daily menu is unchanging, and the other menus include the speciality *toti du Maurin* (olive bread with tapenade, tomatoes and anchovies), a courgette and goats' cheese flan, and *daube de boeuf à la provençale* (Provençal beef stew). The à la carte menu includes omelettes, mussels, freshly caught fish and *bouillabaisse* (order in advance). Ask for a table by the window for the best view of the bay and enjoy a simple meal far from the madding crowd.

WHAT TO SEE

★ **Domaine du Rayol**: avenue des Belges. ☎ 04-94-05-32-50. Fax: 04-94-05-32-51. ✗ From 3 July to 31 August, open every day 9.30am–12.30pm and 4.30–8pm. Rest of the year, open 9.30am–12.30pm and 2.30–6.30pm. Closed from 24 November to 29 January. Entrance fee: 40F (children 20F). Guided tours available every day at 3pm (and at 10am, 10.30am, 5pm and 5.30pm in July and August). The Le Rayol estate was originally acquired by a banker as a gift for his beautiful, much younger wife. He was ruined in the 1929 crash, and wealthy industrialist Henry Potez moved in. It was he who organized the planting of 400 exotic species. After World War II, the property was bought and sold on a regular basis and the gardens gradually returned to their wild state. Fortunately, the land escaped the attentions of property developers and, in 1989, it was bought by a local preservation society.

The restoration of the gardens is now complete. The designer's plan was to create exotic 'travellers' gardens – Californian, Chilean, South African – reflecting different regions or countries of the world. Marked paths (pick up the leaflet at the entrance) guide visitors around a huge variety of botanical species, collected from places as far apart as Tasmania and the Cape of Good Hope. Alternatively, simply wander at will and take in the atmosphere, pausing on the terrace of the wonderful art-nouveau villa at the entrance (formerly the Hôtel de la Mer) to look out over the Mediterranean.

Surprisingly, the gardens remain relatively peaceful during July and August, since the vast majority of tourists prefer to stay on the beach. In July and August (except on Monday), you can also visit a *jardin marin* (underwater garden). The ticket price (80F, 8–18-year-olds 60F) includes all the necessary equipment. Also in summer, musical evenings take place at 9pm on Mondays (tickets: 100F and 130F). During the interval, you can wander around the illuminated gardens as far as the farm.

In the Area

LA MÔLE

This Provençal village, close to the noisy main road, is reached via the narrow and winding D27. En route, the Col du Canadel provides a wonderful view. To the left of the pass is the starting point of the spectacular Route des Crêtes. If you carry on along the little-used D27, you descend into La Môle through a typically Provençal landscape of *maquis* (scrub). The village has an international aerodrome, no less. Antoine de St-Exupéry, World War II aviator and author of every French child's favourite book *Le Petit Prince* (The Little Prince), spent part of his childhood in the nearby chateau (1 kilometre away).

WHERE TO EAT

✕ **L'Auberge de la Môle**: place de l'Église. ☎ 04-94-49-57-01. Set menus at 150F (lunch) and 310F (dinner). This cosy and intimate restaurant/bar/ *tabac* (and formerly a petrol station – the pumps are still there) is well worth a detour from the coast. It's a great place to come for lunch, but try to take a bit of a walk before – the portions of regional fare are generous! St-Trop trendies sometimes come here for the food.

CAVALAIRE-SUR-MER

Cavalaire-sur-Mer has the longest beach in the bay, and its great expanse of fine sand is much more attractive than the town itself. It's a traditional seaside resort, popular with families because of its still-affordable accommodation. You'll also find the only casino in the gulf here, fully equipped with slot machines, restaurant and nightclubs.

USEFUL ADDRESSES

🄗 **Tourist office**: Maison de la Mer, square Maréchal-de-Lattre-de-Tassigny. On the seafront. ☎ 04-94-01-92-10. Fax: 04-94-05-49-89. Website: www.franceplus.com/cavalaire. Open every day in summer 8.30am–7.30pm; rest of the year 9am –12.30pm and 2–6.30pm.
■ **Bicycle and motorbike hire**: Holiday Bikes, Les Régates, rue du Port. ☎ 04-94-64-18-17. Closed from early December to mid-February.

WHERE TO STAY

Campsites

🛖 ✕ **Camping de la Baie**: boulevard Pasteur. In the town itself, 400 metres from the sea. ☎ 04-94-64-08-15. Fax: 04-94-64-66-10. Email: campbaie@club-internet.fr. Open from 15 March to 15 November. Reservations recommended between 1 June and 15 September (minimum stay of one week). Pitch for two with vehicle from 124F to 175F, depending on season. This comfortable site has 440 sites in a large green park, a swimming pool, provisions shop, bar and restaurant. It gets very busy in the summer months.

🛖 **Camping La Pinède**: chemin des Mannes. At the entrance to the town via the N559. ☎ 04-94-64-11-14. Fax: 04-94-64-19-25. ♿ Open from 15 March to 15 October. Set price for two people 105F (between 15 June and 31 August). Comfortable, sheltered site, close to the sea and equipped with washing machines and a provisions shop. Book ahead in July and August and avoid the left side of the site, which overlooks the busy Toulon road.

☆☆ Moderate

🛖 ✗ **Hôtel Raymond–Restaurant Le Mistral**: avenue des Alliés. ☎ 04-94-64-07-32. Fax: 04-94-64-02-73. Email: raymond.meunier@wanadoo.fr. Closed on Wednesday out of season and from October to March. Double rooms with shower or bath and toilet (plus satellite TV) from 330F to 470F, depending on the season. Half board compulsory in July and August, 380F per person. Menus from 110F to 220F. Close to the beach, this friendly hotel has been passed from father to son for the last three generations and is well maintained and reasonably priced. The architecture is best described as 1960s-style luxury motel, and there's a swimming pool in the garden. The house specialities include *bouillabaisse* and seafood platter.

🛖 **La Bonne Auberge**: 400 avenue des Alliés. ☎ 04-94-64-02-96. Fax: 04-94-64-15-19. Closed on Sunday evening, and during All Saints and Christmas school holidays. Free

parking. Double rooms with washbasin or shower for 200F and 230F; with shower or bath and toilet from 280F to 315F. Half board for 300F per person per day. Dinner for residents at 140F. Another 60s-style motel, with a large terrace at the front. It's quite pleasant and the welcome is warm. Some of the rooms have terraces and picture windows, and are protected from the street by pine trees. Guests can enjoy fresh fish and grilled meat dishes in the garden.

☆☆☆ Chic

🛖 ✗ **La Pergola**: rue du Port. ☎ 04-94-00-42-22. Fax: 04-94-64-60-08. Closed from 5 January to 5 February. Double rooms with shower and toilet for 395F, 685F with bathroom and satellite TV. Free private parking. Half board compulsory in high season, from 850F to 960F for two. Menus at 85F (except on Sunday), 150F (*premier menu*) and from 98F to 185F. Meals are served either in the rustic dining room or on the terrace in the shady garden. The cuisine is traditional Provençal, with such tempting dishes as *pigeonneau confit* (conserve of young pigeon), *chapon de mer farçi* (stuffed capon), *bourride* and *bouillabaisse*. The service can be a little slow (fashionable in these parts), but the rooms are comfortable.

☆☆☆☆ Très Chic

🛖 **Hôtel La Calanque**: rue de la Calanque. ☎ 04-94-64-04-27. Fax: 04-94-64-66-20. Website: www.hotel-la-calanque.com. Closed from end December to 15 March. Free private parking. Double rooms with bathroom, satellite TV and mini-bar cost between 830F and 1,400F, depending on the season and choice of room (some with balcony). Overlooking a little inlet, this hotel has been completely renovated (in rather flashy style) and offers panoramic views from the rooms and from the dining room. Facilities include a swimming pool, jacuzzi, hammam, tennis court, little private beach and bellboy. Treat yourself, if your budget stretches that far.

WHERE TO EAT

✗ **Les Rôtisseurs de la Côte**: promenade du Port. ☎ 04-94-15-46-47. ✗ Closed Sunday lunchtime and from November to February. Daily special for 49F (weekday lunch) and 75F on Sunday. À la carte minimum 100F. This pleasant spot serves grilled meats (as the name suggests) and large salads.

☆☆☆☆ Très Chic

✗ **L'Espadon**: promenade de la Mer. ☎ 04-94-64-66-05. Closed on Tuesday out of season, Wednesday lunchtime and Thursday lunchtime in season. Also closed from 15 November to 15 December. Menus from 108F to 208F. This seafront restaurant is making a name for itself, with excellent cuisine including such dishes as *escabèche de sardines au coulis de tomates au basilic et jeunes olives* (sardines with tomato and basil coulis and green olives) and *blanquette de lotte aux morilles en infusion* (blanquette of monkfish with mushrooms). You can also buy seafood to take away.

FESTIVALS AND EVENTS

– **Rencontres d'art contemporain** (encounters with contemporary art): wide-ranging photographic, sculpture and painting exhibitions held from mid-June to mid-September on the esplanade by the port.

– **Les Estivales** (summer festivals): held from early July to early September on the esplanade by the port, with concerts and performances by folk groups.

DIVING

The bay at Cavalaire, with its long and golden beach, is known as the 'Bay of Wrecks' because of the large number of vessels that lie in its clear waters. The various ships include the *Ramon Membru*, *Torpilleur 178*, *Togo*, *Espingole* and *Prophète*, as well as a few 'ducks', amphibious trucks used by the Americans during the 1944 landings. The bay is partly protected from the mistral by the green hills that have served as a landmark for sailors since antiquity, but is very exposed to the east wind, making diving conditions changeable. Conditions are similar around the magnificent and reasonably well-preserved St-Tropez peninsula, although this area is more at the mercy of the mistral. The *Rubis* submarine wreck lies off Cap Camarat and is a must for more experienced divers.

Dive Schools

■ **Loisirs Méditerranée**: Port-Cavalaire, 83240 Cavalaire. ☎ 04-94-79-60-97. Open from March to mid-November, this school has a very good reputation. The atmosphere on board the *Picantin II*, which has 20 full sets of equipment, is very friendly. State-qualified instructors teach beginners and courses up to Level IV, as well as leading bio and wreck dives, and organizing day trips to Port-Cros and other fascinating sites. Booking essential in summer. Accommodation can also be arranged.

■ **Mio Palmo Plongée**: Port-Cavalaire, 83240 Cavalaire. ☎ 04-94-15-43-10. Open from March to mid-November. The fully equipped *Golfo Paradiso*, a former passenger launch, offers a surprising level of comfort and an on-board compressor. State-qualified instructors (FFESSM, ANMP, PADI) offer rock and wreck diving, trips to Port-Cros, first dives, courses up to Level IV and PADI instructors' courses. Mixed-gas dives are also available. Booking recommended. The boss is also rather knowledgeable about good places to eat.

Dive Sites

⚓ **La Roche Quairolle**: off Cap Lardier. One of the most beautiful dives (Level I) in the area, with colourful marine life. The water at 10 metres (35 feet) is exceptionally clear, giving a good view of bright yellow and flaming red sea fans, and groupers. Shy moray eels and scorpion fish lurk at 40 metres (132 feet) in the numerous faults in the rocks. Take a torch and be careful where you put your hands.

⚓ **Le Prophète**: close to La Roche Quairolle, the *Prophète* steamship sank in 1860 and now lies at 32 metres (105 feet). It's a great place for a wreck dive, with its old engine, two boilers, propeller shaft and unusual screw-propeller. Conger eels, scorpion fish and spiny lobsters now live in and around this museum of old seafaring. Level II.

⚓ **Le Rubis**: the jewel of Mediterranean diving, the submarine *Le Rubis* was scuttled in 1958 at a depth of 40 metres (130 feet), just off Cap Camarat, after an exemplary career. An impressive hulk against a stretch of light-coloured sand, it is now inhabited by large moray and conger eels, and shoals of sea perch and sea bream. Swim above the bridge, but don't feed the fish or enter the wreck itself. The visibility is excellent, but the current can be very strong. Level II.

⚓ **Le Togo**: this wonderful dive is strictly for experienced divers only. This impressive cargo ship lies straight on its keel at a depth of 50–60 metres (165–200 feet) after sinking in 1918. Begin at the huge straight stem for a first-class tour of the gangways inhabited by impressive red sea fans. The galley still exists and you'll probably see conger eels doing a dance in the hold. As you surface, a graceful moon-fish may appear, to give your dive the finishing touch. For your own safety, do not dive at this unusual site for longer than 15 minutes. Confident Level III divers only.

LA CROIX-VALMER

This town harks back to the Côte d'Azur of the 1950s. It has lovely old buildings, including the impressive Hôtel Kensington, a mansion built in 1865, and the Villa Couadan, which was built in 1914 for the actress Sarah Bernhardt. The best way to discover La Croix-Valmer's sandy beaches and coves is on foot. Reach them by the coastal path, or by kayak if you're feeling a little more adventurous.

USEFUL ADDRESS

🔘 **Tourist office**: esplanade de la Gare, BP 56. ☎ 04-94-55-12-12. Fax: 04-94-55-12-10. Email: otac@wanadoo.fr. Open from 1 June to 30 September daily 9am–8pm (to 1pm on Sunday); out of season, every day 9.15am–noon and 2–6pm (Saturday and Sunday mornings only).

WHERE TO STAY

Campsite

🛖 **Sélection Camping**: boulevard de la Mer. ☎ 04-94-55-10-30. Fax: 04-94-55-10-39. Open from 1 April to 15 October. The site is in a 5-hectare (12-acre) park near the sea, with 215 pitches. It has all the modern comforts (mini-market, bar, restaurant, disco) and you should book ahead for the summer months.

☆☆☆☆ Très Chic

🛖 **Parc Hôtel**: avenue Georges-Sellier. 2 kilometres from the town centre. Follow signs for Ramatuelle after the traffic lights. ☎ 04-94-79-64-04. Fax: 04-94-54-38-91. Closed from 1 October to 1 May. Free parking. Double rooms with shower for 380F; with shower or bath and toilet, from 490F to 570F. This authentic and meticulously maintained Belle Époque hotel stands in the middle of a park, with a lovely swimming pool in a palm grove. Most of the rooms are spacious and very comfortable, and all are sunny and furnished with antiques. The prices are reasonable, and the view over the sea and the islands makes the hotel worth every centime. The long-standing owners have vowed not to fall into the 'St-Trop trap', and offer a very warm welcome. Try to make a reservation as early as possible.

WHERE TO EAT

☆☆☆ Chic

✕ **La Petite Auberge de Barbigoua**: avenue des Gabiers. At the Débarquement roundabout, head towards the hill for just over 1 kilometre, take boulevard de la Mer and then avenue Neptune. ☎ 04-94-54-21-82. Fax: 04-94-54-23-38. 🍴 Closed on Sunday evening, on Monday and on Tuesday out of season, as well as from 15 November to 27 December, its 'seasonal' menus cost 175F, 180F and 210F. This unusual restaurant on the top of the hill serves inventive and unpredictable cuisine, which depends upon what's fresh and inviting at the local market. A lovely spot with a peaceful and friendly atmosphere, even at the busiest times.

WHAT TO SEE

★ **La croix de Constantin** (Constantine's cross): this stone monument was put up in honour of the Roman Emperor Constantine, on the spot where he is supposed to have experienced a vision. The story goes that his mother appeared to him to tell him that he would be guided by a cross illuminated in the sky. The cross predicted his victory in his impending battle in Italy against his brother-in-law, and his role as the first Christian emperor.

GULF OF ST-TROPEZ AND PAYS DES MAURES

WALK

– **Cap Lardier**: the coastal path makes a pleasant round trip of between 2 hours 30 minutes and 3 hours. The starting point is the plage de Gigaro, where there is parking and a good beach restaurant. Make sure you have strong comfortable shoes. The markings are yellow (pick up the local walking guide from the tourist office). This is one of the last remaining wild areas on this part of the coast, thanks to the work of the Conservatoire du Littoral (coastline preservation society). At first, the path follows the sea closely along the rocks and then climbs gently between broom and heather before entering a tranquil pine forest. After another climb, it joins the ridge path and heads towards Cap Lardier with its noisy seagulls. The landscape is typical, with *maquis* (scrub), steep cliffs and wonderful views that stretch as far as the islands of Porquerolles and Le Levant on a clear day. In the distance is the impressive silhouette of Cap Taillat, which fitter walkers can reach if they pursue the coastal path (which carries on ultimately to St-Tropez). Otherwise, head back towards Gigaro via an undemanding and shady forest path.

FESTIVALS AND EVENTS

– **Festival des anches d'azur** (wind instrument festival): in July, with competitions and performances.

ST-TROPEZ (83990)   Population: 5,540

It's hard to resist describing St-Tropez in clichés, but they happen to be pretty accurate. This delightful fishing port, with its extraordinary quality of light, attractive harmonious architecture and unusual charm, is fondly known by the French as 'St-Trop'. They pronounce the 'p', to avoid confusion with the French word *trop* (or 'too much'), but in the busy summer months it is often exactly that – too much. The seductive descriptions may be appropriate for 10 months of the year (perhaps 11) but, in August, when everyone tries to squeeze into St-Tropez, it becomes the victim of its own charms. On an average August day, the town is invaded by up to 100,000 people, all, seemingly, showing off to each other. Fancy yachts that have hardly ever sailed anywhere jostle for space in the harbour. Snack bars take over the port. Hotels are full to bursting, prices are sky high, rubbish piles up and the traffic is awful.

You should still visit St-Tropez, but come out of season if you can, when its genuine and inimitable charm is able to shine through. Follow the example of the locals, many of whom go into hiding in July and August. If you do have to visit during the summer, book well ahead in one of the few smaller hotels where prices are more reasonable. Enjoy the town before everyone else gets up. People tend to sleep late in St-Trop and early morning is the time when you'll appreciate what all the fuss is about.

St-Tropez is also home to one of the most fascinating art galleries on the coast, where visitors are treated to an explosion of colour.

History

The natural beauty of the bay at St-Tropez was an irresistible invitation to unwelcome conquerors. In turn the Ligurians, the Celts, the Greeks and the Romans all fell in love with the site.

In AD 68 Torpes, an officer in Nero's army, refused to deny his Christian faith, and was tortured and decapitated. His body was thrown into a boat with a cock and a dog, which were then meant to slowly devour it, but the current returned the boat to the riverbank. Local Christians found the martyr's body and erected a chapel in his name. The legend of St Torpes is still recalled in the names of nearby villages, such as Cogolin (*see* page 484) and Grimaud (which means 'dog' in old French) (*see* page 483).

The region remained one of the last bastions of the Saracens, following their defeat at Poitiers. It was resettled in 1470 by the Genoans and prospered as an autonomous area between the 15th and 17th centuries. Many beautiful houses were built during this period, but Colbert put an end to the town's privileged status with his plan for centralization. During the French Revolution, St-Tropez re-adopted its Roman name of Heraclea Cacabria.

The port was badly damaged during the landings on 15 August 1944, but it was luckier than its neighbouring towns and ports and was reconstructed according to its original design. The way it looks today is very close to how it would have been over 400 years ago.

Artists and Authors

Drawn by the extraordinary quality of light, and the depth and contrast of its natural colours, artists have come to St-Tropez for centuries, closely followed by writers. In the 16th century, painters were inspired by scenes in the town's thriving and picturesque port, where bottles of local rosé wine, Maures chestnuts and cork oak bark were loaded on to cargo ships known as *tartanes*. Exotic plants and trees, such as palms, yuccas and agaves imported from Mexico and eucalyptus from Australia, provided more inspiration.

Colette was one famous French writer who enjoyed the warm, scented evenings here and, in the 1930s, she set up a shop selling cosmetics. Another, Guy de Maupassant, loved the town's simple charm and natural riches; he wrote about being able 'to see, on the pavements, scales from sardines shining like pearls'. One of Napoleon III's ministers fell victim to the seductive charm of St-Trop and bought a castle. The artist Paul Signac also succumbed, producing some of his best work here. Fellow painters Henri Matisse, Pierre Bonnard and Dunoyer de Segonzac all followed in his footsteps.

In the 1920s, St-Tropez became very fashionable, frequently visited by Hollywood actor Errol Flynn and erotic writer Anaïs Nin, among many others. Parisian existentialists and glitterati came in the 1950s and when Brigitte Bardot starred in Roger Vadim's film *Et Dieu crea la femme* (And God Created Woman), shot in St-Trop in 1956, the little fishing village immediately became *the* place for fun, sun and sex.

USEFUL ADDRESSES

⌂ Tourist office: main office on Quai Jean-Jaurès. ☎ 04-94-97-45-21. Fax: 04-94-97-82-66. Website: www.nova.fr/saint-tropez. Open every day in high season 9.30am–1pm and 3–10.30pm; every day in low season 9am–12 noon and 3–7pm.

⌂ Gulf of St-Tropez tourist office: La Foux crossroads, 83580 Gassin. ☎ 04-94-43-42-10. Fax: 04-94-43-42-77. Open in high season Monday to Friday 9am–7.30pm, Saturday and Sunday 10am–6pm. Open in low season Monday to Friday 9am–7pm, Saturday 10am–6pm; closed Sunday.

■ Bicycle and motorbike hire: Holiday Bikes, 14 avenue du Général-Leclerc. ☎ 04-94-97-09-39.

– Établissements Mas Louis, 3 rue Quaranta. Opposite place des Lices. ☎ 04-94-97-00-60. Open every day (except Sunday morning) in summer. Closed from 10 October to Easter. Bicycles, mopeds and motorbikes for hire. Deposits are quite high.

■ Buses: Sodetrav, 47 avenue Alphonse-Denis, Hyères, ☎ 04-94-12-55-00; in summer, at the coach station in St-Tropez: ☎ 04-94-97-88-51.

– In summer, there's also a bus link from **Toulon** airport to **St-Tropez**.

WHERE TO STAY

Campsites

People often talk about camping in St-Tropez, but in fact there are sites only in Ramatuelle (*see* page 478).

☆☆ Moderate

⌂ Lou Cagnard: 18 avenue Paul-Roussel. Near place des Lices and a two-minute walk from the port. ☎ 04-94-97-04-24. Fax: 04-94-97-09-44. Closed from 5 November to 27 December. Double rooms with shower from 280F to 310F, from 340F to 550F with shower and toilet, or bathroom, depending on season. A large Provençal-style house with a lovely terrace. The most peaceful rooms overlook the flower garden. Free private parking.

⌂ Hôtel Le Baron: 23 rue de la Citadelle. ☎ 04-94-97-06-57. Fax: 04-94-97-58-72. Open all year. Double rooms with bathroom between 300F and 650F, depending on season. This stylish little hotel offers rather small but comfortable rooms, just a two-minute walk from the port. It is calm and peaceful except, of course, in July and August. You'll see plenty of Harley Davidsons in and around St-Tropez, but the owner here is a genuine fan. Indeed, a motorbike will be much more practical than a car at Le Baron – it's free to park a bike, but car-parking meters are in operation 24 hours a day around here.

⌂ Lou Troupelen: chemin des Vendanges. ☎ 04-94-97-44-88. Fax: 04-94-97-41-76. Email: troupelen@aol.com. Closed from 15 October to Easter. Double rooms with shower or bath and toilet from 440F and 550F, depending on season. This small hotel, in an old farmhouse close to the centre of the village, has a family atmosphere and quiet rooms at reasonable prices. Free parking. Just five minutes' drive from the beaches, it has a garden where you can enjoy a leisurely outdoor breakfast under the trees.

☆☆☆☆ Très Chic

⌂ La Ponche: Port des Pêcheurs, 3 rue des Remparts. ☎ 04-94-97-02-

53. Fax: 04-94-97-78-61. Website : www.nova.fr/ponche. Closed from early January to March. Double rooms from 1,100F to 2,500F, depending on season. Menus from 130F (lunch) to 190F. À la carte around 250F. In the fishermen's quarter, this charming luxury hotel was one of Picasso's watering holes and home to Bardot during the filming of *Et Dieu créa la femme*. The rooms, in a series of former fishermen's cottages, are furnished with exquisite taste, making it the perfect place for a romantic occasion. The food is excellent.

🛏 **Lou Pinet**: 11 chemin du Pinet. ☎ 04-94-97-04-37. Fax: 04-94-97-04-98. Restaurant closed on Monday out of season and at lunchtime (except in July and August) as well as from 3 October to 20 April. Double rooms with shower and toilet, or bathroom, from 450F to 600F in low season, and from 850F to 1,100F in high season. Menus from 120F (lunch) to 250F. The hotel has a certain charm and a pleasant atmosphere, and offers a refreshingly warm welcome.

🛏 **Mas Bellevue**: route de Tahiti. ☎ 04-94-97-07-21. Fax: 04-94-97-61-07. 🍴 Closed from 5 November to 8 April. Double rooms with shower and toilet, or bathroom, from 380F to 680F in low season, and from 570F to 1,210F in high season. The most expensive rooms have air-conditioning and a large terrace. Menus from 100F to 150F. Overlooking the Pampelonne bay, this farmhouse has been renovated and extended. Standing in a park full of flowers, it's one of the few establishments in the area that offer good value for money. There's a restaurant with terrace near the swimming pool, where you can enjoy a nice plate of grilled meat without going bankrupt. Try the *lapin à l'origan* (rabbit seasoned with oregano) or, every Friday, *le grand aïoli*. One of the most famous feasts in Provence, this consists of a large platter of fish (usually salt cod), vegetables, snails and eggs surrounding a large dollop of traditional garlic mayonnaise.

WHERE TO EAT

On the Beach

✘ **Le Petit Bakoua**: plage de la Bouillabaisse. ☎ 06-60-90-18-99. 🍴 Closed in the evening (except in July and August) and from mid-October to mid-May. Menu at 100F. À la carte around 140F. Watch the sun go down over the beach as you enjoy a simple but tasty meal, served by friendly and welcoming hosts.

✘ **Restaurant Les Graniers**: plage des Graniers. A 10-minute walk from the centre, on the first beach past the fishing port and the naval cemetery. ☎ 04-94-97-38-50. Open every day, for lunch only. Closed from mid-October to mid-April. Daily special 100F; à la carte around 200F. This restaurant, in a lovely spot, with parasol-shaded outdoor tables, enjoys a good reputation. The quality of the food is maintained even during the crazy months of summer. The grilled meat and fish are good value for money and delicious accompanied by wine from the St-Tropez co-operative.

✘ **Les Salins**: plage des Salins. 3 kilometres (2 miles) from the town centre. ☎ 04-94-97-04-40. 🍴 Closed from mid-October to beginning April. Menu at 120F (weekday lunch); allow 150F for à la carte. This is a pleasant spot on a beach, where you can enjoy unpretentious regional dishes, fresh fish or grilled meat.

In Town

✕ **Le Roustidou**: place Grammand. Just around the corner from quai de Suffren. ☎ 04-94-97-01-37. Daily special for 70F, *formule* menus from 75F to 105F and a set menu for 145F. Full of locals at lunchtime, who come here for the warm welcome and tasty food. The service has a touch of St-Tropez about it and can be chaotic.

✕ **La Frégate**: 52–54 rue Allard. ☎ 04-94-97-07-08. Closed on Monday and in January and February. Daily special 68F and menus from 98F to 140F. This small restaurant is off the tourist track. The decor has a very pronounced marine theme, and the menu is good, with the usual Friday *aïoli* and fish specials according to the catch of the day. Rod Stewart has been seen here – although apparently he left without paying!

✕ **La Cascade**: 5 rue de l'église. ☎ 04-94-54-83-46. Closed from November to February. Caribbean-style set menu at 129F, tasty Provençal menu at 98F and a *formule langouste* (lobster menu) at 199F. Good food in a fun atmosphere.

✕ **La Grange**: 9 rue du Petit-St-Jean. ☎ 04-94-97-09-62. Closed from 15 January to 15 March, and from 15 November to 15 December. Open in the evening only. À la carte between 150F and 200F. Pleasant restaurant decorated with red and white tiles, looking rather like a second-hand shop. Homemade and original pasta dishes are served.

✕ **L'Échalote**: 35 rue Allard. ☎ 04-94-54-83-26. ♿ Open for lunch and dinner (until 10pm). Annual vacation from 15 November to 10 December. Closed in low season on Thursday. Menus at 105F and 200F. Hams and dried sausages are presented on a butcher's block at the entrance. The atmosphere is very pleasant, with tables outside in the garden. Although the clientèle tends to be rather trendy, the menu prices remain reasonable.

✕ **La Cantina El Mexicano**: 16 rue des Remparts. Climb up the hill past the town hall, and find the restaurant about 100 metres down on the right. ☎ 04-97-94-97-40-96. À la carte around 160F. This rather eccentric restaurant has kitsch figurines and a statue of the Virgin Mary at its entrance. The atmosphere, decor and food – tacos, quesadillas, tortillas, brownies and a spectacular margarita – are all rather exotic. The food is plentiful, hot and fun. Regulars come back time after time, even out of season.

✕ **Chez Fuchs**: 7 rue des Commerçants. ☎ 04-94-97-01-25. Closed for lunch in high season, Tuesday in low season and from 15 January to 25 February. À la carte from 200F to 250F. Close to the port, this restaurant is full of regulars enjoying authentic dishes such as *artichauts barigoule* (artichokes stuffed with mushrooms and bacon) or *encornets à la provençale* (squid), as well as local wines. In high season, the customers are squeezed in like sardines, but the atmosphere remains genuinely St-Tropezian.

✕ **Le Bistrot du Phare**: 1 quai de l'épi. Near the harbourmaster's office in the marina, next to the large car park. ☎ 04-94-97-46-00. ♿ Closed from 10 January to 12 February and from 15 November to 12 December. À la carte at least 150F. The charismatic and colourful owner is never lost for words, and is a good cook. Unfortunately, set menus are available only for large groups.

✕ **L'Auberge des Maures**: rue du Docteur-Bouttin. ☎ 04-94-97-01-50. Closed from early January to 1 March. Menu at 190F. This restaurant is located in a little street at right angles to the rue Allard, which is so narrow that it allows single file walking only. It offers a shady patio and an authentically Provençal menu right in the heart of St-Tropez. Order ahead for *bouillabaisse*, enjoy grilled fish and meat, and try the fresh local produce. A good place to relax.

☆☆☆ Chic

✕ **Le Café des Arts**: place des Lices. ☎ 04-94-97-02-25. Three-course menu at 160F. À la carte about 200F. This old-fashioned café has everything you could ask for: an old zinc bar, smoke-stained walls, bistrot tables and an ancient coffee machine. Come for lunch and a spot of people-watching.

✕ **Le Relais des Caves du Roy**, **Hôtel Byblos**: avenue Foch. ☎ 04-94-56-68-20. Closed on Monday and Tuesday, and at lunchtime from April to October. À la carte

between 150F and 200F. This venue doesn't appear in many guidebooks, but it's a good place to come to watch St-Tropezians at play. Most of your fellow diners – enjoying Italian or Provençal specialities – will head off later to the latest nightclub, but not everyone is cut out for a night on the town in St-Tropez.

✕ **Le Caprice des Deux**: 40 rue du Portail-Neuf. ☎ 04-94-97-76-78. Open in the evening only. Closed on Wednesday out of season, as well as from 10 January to 2 March, and from 15 November to 20 December. Set menu at 245F. À la carte at least 300F per person. In a charming little street, this is an ideal spot to come with your beloved (potential or existing), but too expensive to bring the whole family. The cuisine is very sophisticated.

WHERE TO GO FOR A DRINK

The sun never sets in St-Trop (at least, in July and August). For dancing, *the* place to be seen is the **Caves du Roy** disco at the Byblos hotel, St-Trop's most celebrated hotel, built in 1967 by a Lebanese millionaire and designed in the style of a hilltop village. If the bouncers won't let you in, try a spot of salsa in the **Bodega du Papagayo** on the Quai d'Épi at the port. The classy and hip **VIP Room**, on the port, is one of the newer additions to the nightclub scene.

❣ **L'Octave-Café**, on the place de la Garonne, is a perennial favourite for music lovers with eclectic taste.

❣ Otherwise, to find the best places to hang out, follow the crowd or ask at the tourist office. In the late afternoon, many head for the **Café des Arts**, for a *pastis* with a view of the *piste de boules* – prepare to be bowled over by the prices! **Sube**, on the port, is more affordable and has a great atmosphere. On the first floor, with a lovely marine-themed interior, it has one of the best terraces in town – a couple of tables on a small balcony.

❣ Early risers should try **Le Sénéquier**, a St-Trop institution on the port, where authors Paul Éluard and Paul Valéry used to come. Lesser writers followed in their footsteps, but today celebrities are rarely seen. True St-Tropezians approach the terrace from the back way (never from the front), and the coolest head for the section of the tables on the far left, known as *Le Paradis*. Those who secure a seat in paradise know they've really arrived.

WHAT TO SEE AND DO

★ **Musée de l'Annonciade**: place Grammont. ☎ 04-94-97-04-01. Open every day (except Tuesday and public holidays) 10am–noon and 3–7pm (2–5pm from October to end May). Closed during November. Entrance fee: 30F (students and 12–16-year-olds 20F).

This innovative museum, with its marvellous paintings, opened in 1955 in the 17th-century former Chapelle de l'Annonciade. This is the personal collection of a wealthy patron of the arts, an adopted local, who donated it to the town. Many of the works were inspired by the wonderful light of St-Tropez and the quality is extraordinary for a museum in what is, after all, simply a small fishing port. On the top floor, you can flop into a comfy chair and feast your eyes on the blaze of colour. The collection includes paintings by Signac, Picabia, Matisse (*Gitane*), Albert Marquet, Dufy (*La Jetée*), Bonnard, Vuillard, Braque (*L'Estaque*), Vlaminck, Rouault, Van Dongen, Derain, Camoin and many others, and there are also interesting temporary exhibitions.

★ **Town walk**: after the tourists have left, St-Tropez reveals its genuine treasures to evening strollers. Wander through its medieval streets, narrow passageways and secret gardens, pausing in tiny squares where ancient and pretty fountains gurgle. The **rue de la Miséricorde** is charming, with its arcades, and you shouldn't miss the **Quartier de la Ponche** with its chic restaurants and bars, its little fishing port and the remains of the town's towers and ramparts.

The **Chapelle de la Miséricorde** on rue Gambetta has a very pretty roof of blue, green and gold glazed tiles. On **rue Allard**, you'll see some appealing details on the houses, particularly on the **Maison du Maure**, with its turbanned Berber's head. The delightful **place aux Herbes**, with its fish, flower, fruit and vegetable markets, has changed very little over the years. On the **place de l'Hôtel-de-Ville**, look out for the elaborately and intricately worked wooden door that was apparently carved by natives of Zanzibar.

★ In the past, the **place des Lices** was the venue for jousting tournaments. Today, the square plays host to a lively market on Tuesday and Saturday morning and, in summer, to fiercely competitive games of *boules* between retired local fishermen and visiting celebs. In season, the **Café des Arts** (*see* 'Where to Go for a Drink') rivals Paris' Aux Deux-Magots café as a place to see and be seen.

★ Climb up to the **Citadelle** to admire the view over the town's glistening roof tiles – and to meet the majestic peacocks. The citadel, built during the 16th and 17th centuries, today houses the **Musée Naval de St-Tropez** (maritime museum): ☎ 04-94-97-06-53 and 59-43. Open 11am–6pm (from 2 May to 30 September) and 10am–noon and 1–5pm during the rest of the year. Closed on Tuesday, on 1 and 17 May, and in November. Entrance fee: 25F (7–15-year-olds 15F). The museum displays models, antique navigational instruments, underwater archaeological finds, and tells the story of the August 1944 landings.

★ **Maison des Papillons** (butterfly house): 9 rue Étienne-Berny. ☎ 04-94-97-63-45. Open every day from 1 April to 30 September 10am–noon and 3–6pm, but closed on Tuesday. In winter, book ahead if you want to visit. Entrance fee: 15F (free for under-12s). Visitors come here to see the thousands of lepidoptera collected by Dany Lartigue and to admire works by his more famous photographer father, Jacques-Henri Lartigue.

★ Head back down towards the sea to visit the picturesque **cemetery**, where some of the direct descendants of the 21 Genoese families that came to the town in the 15th century are buried. One of Liszt's daughters was also laid to rest here.

FESTIVALS AND EVENTS

– **La Bravade**: *bravade* festivals represent one of the oldest of Provençal traditions. Taking place in St-Tropez between 16 and 18 May, this one celebrates the arrival in AD 68 of the body of St Torpes (*see* 'History', page 471). The festival's origins date back to the 13th century, although the earliest descriptions are from 1558. A 'captain' of the town is elected, and the saint's statue is taken through the streets in procession, to the accompaniment of fusillades fired from ancient weapons. The town is completely dressed in red and white, the colours of the costumes of the local *corsairs* (privateers to some, pirates to others). Other events and ceremonies are enthusiastically attended by the local people, who seem to feel the need to reaffirm their cultural identity before the summer invasion.

– **La Petite Bravade**, also known as the **Bravade des Espagnols** (of the Spanish): on 15 June, the town commemorates the 1637 victory of the St-Tropezian navy over a couple of dozen invading Spanish galleys. The *bravade* was established by official decree in that very year. More blunderbusses, smoke, 18th-century uniforms and costumes.

BEACHES

– **Plage des Graniers**: not far from the cemetery, this is the nearest beach to the town centre (within easy walking distance) and inevitably the most crowded.

– **Baie des Canebiers**: a little further away, but just as crowded, though it does have some nice little inlets.

– **Plage des Salins**: 4 kilometres (2.5 miles) to the east, this beach is more or less empty in low season.

– **Plage de la Bouillabaisse**: on the left at the entrance to the village.

– Rather suprisingly, most of St-Tropez's really lovely beaches are at **Ramatuelle**; *see* page 478).

WALKS

– **Peninsula tour**: the 12-kilometre (7.5-mile) tour around the peninsula follows a section of the coastal path. A marked route leaves from the **plage des Graniers**, passes around the northeast side of the peninsula via the **Pointe de Rabiou**, **Cap de Saint-Tropez** and **Pointe de Capon**, and ends up at the **plage de Tahiti**. The walk offers wonderful views of the foothills of the Massif des Maures and the fabulous landscapes of the Éstérel. For an alternative route, after the Baie des Canebiers, take the

Chemin Communal des Salins, which leads on to the **plage des Salins**. A number of clearly marked Conservatoire du Littoral paths wind their way through the umbrella pines. Energetic walkers can press on to **Cap Camarat** after the plage de Pampelonne.

Bicycles and off-site camping are both prohibited.

– For a shorter walk (about 4 kilometres, or 2.5 miles), follow the signs to the little **Chapelle Ste-Anne**, to the south of the town. Built in the 17th century to give thanks to God for sparing the region from the plague, it has lovely ex-voto offerings and a beautiful view over the gulf.

RAMATUELLE (83350)   Population: 2,170

An old village clinging to a hill surrounded by vineyards, Ramatuelle has a collection of medieval houses that actually make up its *enceinte*, or surrounding wall. It has been restored and renovated and can be touristy in high season, but the central square, the place de l'Ormeau, is still charming, with its country policeman directing the traffic and its lovely foliage-draped old bistrot. Wander through the sinuous arcaded alleys of the village, dipping in and out of the numerous antique shops and craftsmen's studios. In the Ramatuelle cemetery, against the wall on the right, you'll find the simple and moving tomb of actor Gérard Philipe, a leading French actor of the 1950s, who died at the age of 37.

USEFUL ADDRESSES

◘ **Tourist office**: place de l'Ormeau. ☎ 04-94-79-26-04. Fax: 04-94-79-12-66. Open in July and August, Monday to Friday 9am–1pm and 3–7.30pm; Saturday 9.30am–1pm and 3–7.30pm; Sunday 10am–1pm and 3–7pm. In low season, Monday to Friday 8am–12.30pm and 2–6pm.

■ **Bicycle** and motorbike hire: *Holiday Bikes*, route de Pampelonne. ☎ 04-94-79-87-75. Open from 1 June to 30 September.

WHERE TO STAY

Campsites

⬗ **Les Tournels**: route de Camarat. ☎ 04-94-55-90-90. Fax: 04-94-55-90-99. Website: www.tournels.com. Closed from mid-January to mid-February. 1,000 pitches with room for a two-person tent and a car for 150F. Bungalows for hire. Despite being further away from St-Tropez than many other sites, Les Tournels is the most attractive, self-contained on a hill and surrounded by pine trees. It's close to the sea and also has a swimming pool.

⬗ **Camping à la Ferme, Biancolini**: Les Tournels. 4 kilometres (3 miles) from the village, in the *commune* of Ramatuelle, near the Les Tournels campsite, on the way back towards the beach road. ☎ 04-94-79-84-59. Usually open mid-April to end September, according to demand. Good value and less congested than its larger counterparts.

⬗ **Camping à la Ferme, Marcel**: chemin des Boutinelles. Le Fond-du-Plan. ☎ 04-94-79-86-07. Open from 15 June to 15 September, the site is 1 kilometre from Plage de Pampelonne and Plage de l'Escalet. It's a shady site in the vineyards.

♠ **La Croix du Sud**: route des Plages. 2 kilometres from the sea. ☎ 04-94-79-80-84. Fax: 04-94-79-89-21. Open from 1 April to end September. Bungalows for hire, guarded by Coco the parrot. The mosquitoes can be annoying and the site can get rather busy in season.

♠ **La Toison d'Or**: on the beach itself, Plage de Pampelonne. ☎ 04-94-79-83-54. Fax: 04-94-79-89-77. Open from Easter to early October. Quite expensive. Caravans and mobile homes for rent. The nearest campsite to St-Tropez and, sadly, rather like an internment camp. Book ahead for July or August.

♠ **Kon Tiki**: plage de Pampelonne. ☎ 04-94-79-80-17. Near La Toison d'Or, Kon Tiki is larger (700 spaces) but equally lacking in atmosphere and charm.

☆☆ – ☆☆☆ Moderate to Chic

♠ **Lou Castellas**: route des Moulins-de-Paillas. ☎ and fax: 04-94-79-20-67. ⚒ Double rooms with shower for 260F, with shower and toilet 280–350F and with bathroom 400–550F. Set menu at 175F. À la carte around 200F. Free private parking. This small provincial hotel just above the village is run by a very friendly owner. The terraces are covered in wisteria and overlook the sea. It's a little haven of peace in a very smart location that charges very reasonable prices. The guaranteed free parking is a great bonus.

♠ **L'Amphore**: route de l'Escalet. ☎ 04-98-12-90-90. Fax: 04-94-79-28-22. Closed from 15 October to 1 April. Double rooms between 390F and 690F, depending on season. This unusual hotel stands close to a pine forest, just a few minutes by car from Ramatuelle and the bay. Reminiscent of an old *pension de famille*, it charges reasonable prices, has a kind and welcoming owner and is always peaceful. There's also a swimming pool.

♠ **Chambres d'hôte Leï Souco** (B&B): Le Plan, plaine de Camarat. 3.5 kilometres (about 2 miles) from the village. Take the route des Plages, then turn right off the D93 at the Total petrol station in the direction of St-Tropez. ☎ 04-94-79-80-22. Fax: 04-94-79-88-27. Website: www.leisouco.com. Closed from November to January. Double rooms with bath and satellite TV 380–520F in low season and 420–610F in high season, including breakfast. Just 7 kilometres (about 4 miles) from St-Tropez and 2 kilometres from the plage de Pampelonne, this old Provençal farmhouse is surrounded by olive trees and mulberry bushes. The rooms are large and attractive. Enjoy the peace and quiet, read a book on the terrace, take a walk in the vineyards or have a game of tennis.

☆☆☆☆ Très Chic

♠ **Motel des Sellettes**: chemin de l'Oumède. 4 kilometres (2.5 miles) from the village. ☎ 04-94-79-88-48. Fax: 04-94-79-82-24. Closed from 12 November to 25 March. Studios for two from 420F to 950F, depending on facilities and season. Apartment for four to six people also available. Delightful little houses nestled among the vineyards at the foot of the hills, each with a fully equipped and very comfortable garden studio, and a small kitchen. There's a swimming pool and the lovely pine forest and the plage de Pampelonne near by.

WHERE TO EAT

Near the Beach

✗ **Le Club 55**: plage de Pampelonne. ☎ 04-94-79-80-14. Open for lunch only. Closed from 11 November to 20 December, and from 10 January to 10 February. À la carte between 200F and 250F. A St-Tropez staple, frequented by wealthy executives and stars on holiday, often lurking behind designer sunglasses. The highlight of the menu, which features a variety of delicious grilled fish, is the *daurade royale* (sea bream). The owner, Patrice de Colmont, is also the creator of the *Nioulargue*, the yacht race that features the oldest and most beautiful yachts in the world. It takes place during the last week of September and the first week of October.

✗ **Plage de L'Orangerie**: boulevard Patch, plage de Pampelonne. ☎ 04-94-79-84-74. ☘ Open for dinner from May to October. À la carte around 120F (without wine). Fresh grilled fish and dishes of the day.

✗ **Key West Beach**: plage de Pampelonne. ☎ 04-94-79-86-58. Open all year round at lunchtime, and for lunch and dinner in July and August. Meals for around 200F. Tasty and exotic food served in a very atmospheric restaurant, with salsa music filling the air in the evening.

✗ **Les Bronzés**: plage de Pampelonne, route de Bonne-Terrasse. ☎ 04-94-79-81-04. Open for lunch only between April and September. Restaurant also open for dinner in July and August. À la carte between 150F and 200F. The restaurant (*bronzé* means 'tanned') sits at the foot of Cap Camarat, and also has a bar and a private beach with parasols and lovely soft sand. The food is simple, local and tasty – giant prawns cooked in *pastis* or *poivrons à l'anchoïade* (sweet peppers in anchovy sauce) and, on Fridays, a delicious *aïoli provençal* (salt cod and garlic mayonnaise feast).

In the Village

✗ **Le Cigalon**: place de l'Ormeau. ☎ 04-94-79-21-08. Closed from October to April. Menus at 70F (weekday lunch) and from 90F to 145F. À la carte between 130F and 150F. This unpretentious restaurant is housed in a pretty Provençal building with a popular terrace, sheltered from the sun and wind. The menu includes tasty pizzas, local specialities and *anchoïades* (anchovy dip served as an appetizer).

☆☆☆ Chic

✗ **Auberge de l'Oumède**: chemin de l'Oumède, route des Plages. 3 kilometres (2 miles) from the centre. ☎ 04-94-79-81-24. Restaurant open in the evening only. One set menu at 295F. Customers at this welcoming farmhouse among the vines enjoy delicious fresh fish, stuffed vegetables and dishes such as *parmentier de queue de buf au foie gras poêlé et jus tranché* (oxtail with fried goose liver and clear sauce). There's a beautiful terrace and the prices are relatively high.

WHAT TO SEE

– **Église Notre-Dame**: this 16th-century church was built on the former ramparts and has a lovely serpentine (green-stone) porch that dates from 1620. The bell-tower was formerly a watchtower. Inside there are two gilded wooden 16th-century statues and a bust of St André, patron saint of Ramatuelle, carved from a fig-tree stump, and two 17th-century retables.

BEACHES

– **Plage de Pampelonne**: 5 kilometres (3 miles) long with soft, fine sand, this is the longest of Ramatuelle's beaches. In summer, the horizon is obscured by luxury yachts and pleasure boats, and the beach is full. There are about 30 restaurants along its stretch (*see* 'Where to Eat'), charging fairly exorbitant prices and providing, as in St-Tropez, a place to see and be seen. They rather spoil the scene – the landscape is officially 'noteworthy' – and plans are afoot to completely redevelop the area and limit the number of people allowed on the beach. One way to escape the crowds is to head further south towards Cap Camarat, where it's less chic but also less choked.

– **Plage de l'Escalet**: further south, between Cap Camarat and Cap Taillat, this beach is harder to reach and much less crowded. Strips of sand alternate with small coves.

– **Plage de la Bastide-Blanche**: furthest south, below Cap Taillat, this beach at the end of a track is a favourite with regulars who want to escape the crowds and parking charges. Take the coastal path from the plage de l'Escalet; about 30 minutes' walk.

FESTIVALS AND EVENTS

– **Les Temps Musicaux** (music festival): classical and folk music concerts held in July.

– **Festival de Ramatuelle**: held during the first two weeks of August. The rather eclectic programme includes works by Molière and others.

– **Jazz festival**: mid-August.

GASSIN (83990) Population: 2,750

The road to Gassin has a series of tricky hairpin bends, but the journey to this lovely hill village is definitely worthwhile. There's a magnificent view over the whole area and a network of vaulted lanes lined with medieval houses to explore. When the weather on the coast is fiercely hot, come here to cool off with a glass of chilled wine.

WHERE TO STAY AND EAT

⌂ ✕ **Hôtel Bello Visto**: place des Barrys, near the panoramic viewpoint. ☎ 04-94-56-17-30. Fax: 04-94-43-45-36. Restaurant closed on Tuesday. Double rooms with shower and toilet from 280F to 420F, depending on season. Evening menu (for residents only) at 120F. À la carte between 200F and 220F. This pleasant hotel at the edge of the village has simple but clean rooms at good prices. Book early – this is a popular spot. The restaurant has a terrace with a good view of the gulf of St-Tropez and serves Provençal cuisine such as *lapin rôti à l'ail* (rabbit roasted with garlic) and *galette de truffes* (truffle pancake).

✕ **Auberge La Verdoyante**: 866 chemin de la Coste-Brigade. 1 kilometre from the village. Take the little road leading off to the right of the cemetery, and follow the signs up the dirt track. ☎ 04-94-56-16-23. ♿ Closed Wednesday lunchtime (except in July and August) and from November to April. The *auberge*, whose name translates literally as 'verdant inn', lies deep in the countryside. There's a lovely big dining room with wooden beams, but from May it's warm enough to eat outside, listening to the churring of the crickets. Try the *daube de boeuf* (beef stew).

WHAT TO SEE

★ **Church**: dating from the 16th century, Gassin's church houses a white-marble holy water basin and a gilded wooden bust of St Laurent, together with a few beautiful paintings that date from the time of its construction. The story goes that, in 1582, in order to avoid paying the costs of the consecration ceremony that had been ordered by the bishop, the parish priest ran away, taking the church keys with him.

PORT-GRIMAUD (83310)

The marina and holiday village of Port-Grimaud, 7 kilometres (4 miles) from St-Tropez on the road for Fréjus, is one of France's most frequently visited 'towns', so be prepared for crowds. It represents one of the few successful modern building projects on this stretch of coastline. The complex was designed by an architect and entrepreneur from Alsace, François Spoerry (1912–98), in the style of a typical and colourful Mediterranean village, arranged around canals reminiscent of Venice. Cars are banned, so visitors park in the paying car park and then explore on foot. Alternatively, you can take a water-taxi along the canals. Climb up to the terrace of the Église St-François, built to resemble a fortified church, and adorned with stained-glass windows by the Hungarian artist Victor Vasarely (1908–97). Your reward is a view of the whole port complex.

– There's a large beach and a campsite near by.

USEFUL ADDRESS

■ **Bicycle and motorbike hire**: Holiday Bikes, RN 98. ☎ 04-94-56-31-28.

WHERE TO EAT

☆☆☆ Chic

✕ **La Table du Mareyeur**: 10 and 11 place des Artisans. ☎ 04-94-56-06-77. Closed on Monday (from March to end June) and from 15 November to 15 December, in January and February. Menus at 150F (lunch), including wine and coffee, and 260F. À la carte much more expensive. All the tables stand at the water's edge, and the team in the kitchen prepares wonderful seafood and fish dishes. Treat yourself to *filets de rouget sur une fondue* *d'artichauts barigoule* (fillets of red mullet with artichokes stuffed with mushrooms and bacon) or *salade de homard tiède au beurre de truffes* (warm lobster salad with truffle butter).

GRIMAUD (83360)　　　　Population: 3,847

This hilltop village is renowned throughout the region. Ancient, fortified and traffic-free, it has a maze of little winding streets to explore, full of flowers and interesting nooks and crannies. Despite its touristy aspect and a tasteful restoration, it has managed to maintain a distinctly Provençal character – interestingly, none of its little streets is named after a historic or famous figure. Head to the superb chateau ruins, and then find a pretty little square and rest your feet.

USEFUL ADDRESSES

◼ Tourist office: 1 boulevard des Aliziers. ☎ 04-94-43-26-98. Fax: 04-94-43-32-40. Open in high season 9am–12.30pm and 3–7pm; in low season 9am–12.30pm and 2.30–6.30pm. Ask for free information on walking routes.

🍴 Sweet-toothed visitors should not miss the cake shop at **Le Pâtissier du Château**, 19 boulevard des Aliziers.

WHERE TO STAY

⚓ Hôtel La Pierrerie: in the Grand-Pont district. 2 kilometres from Port-Grimaud on the D61. ☎ 04-94-43-22-55. Fax: 04-94-43-24-78. Closed from 31 October to 1 April. Double rooms with shower and toilet, or bathroom and TV, from 350F to 640F, depending on season. This popular little hotel feels like a Provençal farmhouse in the heart of the countryside, yet it's right on the St-Tropez gulf. Little stone buildings are hidden among the flowers and vegetation, and the swimming pool is a meeting place for the bronzed and beautiful in the summer months. Peace and quiet guaranteed.

⚓ Hôtel Le Ginestel: chemin des Blaquières. 3 kilometres (2 miles) from Grimaud and 1.5 kilometres from Port-Grimaud. ☎ and fax: 04-94-43-48-45. Website: www.leginestel.hypermart.net. ♿ Closed from October to 1 April. Double rooms with shower or bath and toilet from 350F to 650F. Follow the dirt track to this unpretentious hotel, where the 18 rooms all have a private terrace overlooking the garden and the swimming pool. Boat owners can moor nearby on the River Giscle. The prices are very reasonable.

⚓ Hôtel Athénopolis: in the Mouretti district. 3 kilometres (2 miles) from Grimaud on the road for La Garde-Freinet. ☎ 04-94-43-24-24. Fax: 04-94-43-37-05. Closed from 1 November to 1 April. Double rooms with shower or bath and toilet between 510F and 680F. Dinner (for guests) for 120F. It's easy to relax here. The hotel has pretty rooms, either with a loggia or a terrace, a calm atmosphere, and a lovely swimming pool. There's even a recording studio next door. With its rather high prices, it's the ideal place for a couple to pamper themselves. Breakfasts are big, with plenty of fresh fruit.

WHERE TO EAT

✗ **Restaurant du Café de France**: 5 place Neuve. ☎ and fax: 04-94-43-20-05. Closed from November to February. À la carte between 200F and 250F. Housed in an old, vine-covered stone house, this restaurant has a dining room carved out of the rock itself, providing a cool refuge in the heat of summer. When the outside temperature is more bearable, guests can eat on the terrace. The food is regional, with a few unnecessarily St-Tropezian extras.

WHAT TO SEE

★ **Musée des Arts et traditions populaires** (museum of popular arts and culture): route nationale. ☎ 04-94-43-26-98. Open between Easter and October every day 2.30–6pm. Closed on Tuesday and Sunday. From October to Easter, open on Thursday, Friday and Saturday 2–5.30pm. Free entry. Housed in a former olive mill and in a cork factory, this museum displays old forging tools, harnesses and halters, along with Provençal furniture containing traditional lace hats, clothes and household linen. On the first floor of the mill you can still see the stone niches, called *chapelles*, where the olives were pressed. In summer, there are thematic exhibitions.

★ **Old village**: climb up to the old part of the village via the rue du Porche, where the locals sit and chat on a bench known as the 'bench of the liars'. A bit further on, you'll find the charming little square, place du Cros. The rue des Templiers, lined with basalt arcades, is the most impressive street, with a lovely 18th-century serpentine (green-stone) doorway at No. 10.

★ **Église St-Michel**: this gem of a Romanesque church dates from the 11th and 12th centuries and has a 16th-century bell-tower and a 17th-century sacristy. Its lines are pure, even austere, and inside is a 12th-century baptismal font, in Carrara marble, said to be a gift of the Good King René. The church has modern stained-glass windows by Jacques Gautier (1975) and a contrasting 19th-century fresco portraying St Michael overcoming the dragon.

★ **Chapelle des Pénitents**: another Romanesque edifice, this small and attractive chapel was built in the same era as the church of St Michael, and was then extended in the 16th century and renovated in the 18th. It houses a pretty retable and relics of St Théodore. Surprisingly, it has a slightly Mexican air.

★ **Château**: some vestiges remain of the powerful medieval chateau, which dates from the 11th and 12th centuries and was pillaged during the French Revolution. The three surrounding walls can be made out clearly today and three large round towers still flank the living quarters.

COGOLIN (83310)   Population: 9,180

This charming little village, which enjoys an appealing way of life, sits at the foot of the Massif des Maures. Its old centre has been preserved and is worth a detour but, sadly, the castle built by the Knights of Malta did not survive the religious wars. According to legend, the cock that accompanied the body of

St Torpes (*see* page 471) came from Cogolin. When the boat in which the corpse and the creatures were despatched reached the shore, the cock flew off and landed in a field of flax (*lin*), hence *coq au lin*.

USEFUL ADDRESS

🔳 **Tourist office**: place de la République. ☎ 04-94-55-01-10. Fax: 04-94-55-01-11. Email: office.de.tourisme.cogolin@libertysurf.fr. Open in low season every day (except on Saturday afternoon and on Sunday) 9am–noon and 2.30–6.30pm; in high season, every day (except Sunday afternoon) 9am–12.30pm and 2.30–7pm.

WHERE TO STAY

Campsite

⛺ **Camping L'Argentière**: chemin de l'Argentière. On the D48 towards Collobrières, 4 kilometres (2.5 miles) from the beach. ☎ 04-94-54-63-63. Fax: 04-94-54-06-15. Open from 15 April to 30 September. Caravans and bungalows for hire.

☆☆ Moderate

⛺ **Coq'Hôtel**: place de la Mairie. ☎ 04-94-54-13-71. Fax: 04-94-54-03-06. Open all year. Double rooms with shower or bath and toilet (and satellite TV), from 260F to 410F, depending on season. Menus from 95F to 145F. The rooms in this reasonably priced hotel have been tastefully renovated in Provençal style. It stands in the heart of the village and some rooms have a terrace overlooking the square. They can be noisy.

⛺ **Hôtel du Golfe de St-Tropez**: 13 avenue Georges-Clemenceau. ☎ 04-94-54-40-34. Fax: 04-94-54-14-48. Email: gerald.bitschy@wanadoo.fr. Open all year. Double rooms with shower or bath and toilet for 210–400F. This classic little hotel has well-equipped rooms at reasonable prices. A good choice.

WHERE TO EAT

✕ **La Grange**: 7 rue du 11-Novembre. ☎ 04-94-54-60-97. Closed all day Monday and Saturday afternoon, and in November and January. Lunchtime *formule* menus at 68F and 82F; à la carte around 100F (drinks not included). The dining room is in an old barn and the food is simple, but inexpensive for the area. Try the sweet peppers or the veal liver, or the *aïoli* (salt cod and garlic mayonnaise feast) on Friday.

✕ **La Taverne du Siffleur**: 9 rue Nationale. In the old centre, behind the church. ☎ 04-94-54-67-02. Closed from end September to April. À la carte not more than 100F. The owner of this authentic, unpretentious spot seems to do almost everything herself, including serving flavoursome Provençal cooking. There's a lovely little terrace on which to try an *aïoli* special.

✕ **Pizzeria del Sol**: 34 rue Gambetta. ☎ 04-94-54-47-39. ✕ Open all year. Menus from 68F to 145F. Classic pizzeria with a friendly owner serving large, good-value pizzas to local regulars.

✕ **Le Coq au Lin**: 40 rue Marceau. ☎ 04-94-54-60-50. Closed on Tuesday in low season. Menus at 68F (lunch only), 90F and 145F. Locally owned, this restaurant has a pleasant rustic room, decorated with china from the region. The meat dishes are excellent (the owners have been butchers for generations), but there's also an excellent choice of fresh fish, including sea bream. Homemade couscous is a speciality on Wednesday.

✕ **La Ferme du Magnan**: 5 kilometres (3 miles) from Cogolin on the N98, the road for La Môle. ☎ 04-94- 49-57-54. Closed from November to March. Menus from 155F and 290F. Housed in a 16th-century *bastide* in the foothills of the Massif des Maures, this restaurant is a wonderful place to eat, but not cheap. There's a lovely hillside terrace, not far from the hen-house. Enjoy *coquelet rôti au miel et cinq épices* (roast chicken with honey and five spices) or *lapin à la provençale* (rabbit with tomatoes, onions and garlice), accompanied by a glass of local Cogolin wine.

WHAT TO SEE

★ **Espace Raimu** (Raimu centre): 18 avenue Georges-Clemenceau. ☎ 04-94-54-18-00. Fax: 04-94-54-43-24. Closed on Sunday morning and during the last two weeks in November. Open in low season every day (except Sunday morning) 10am–noon and 3–6pm; from 1 July to 31 August, every day 10am–noon and 4–7pm. Entrance fee: 20F. According to Orson Welles, Provençal-born Raimu was the 'greatest actor in the world'. He certainly became a legend in France and his grand-daughter has kept this museum in his memory since 1989, in the basement of a local cinema. Film buffs will enjoy the letters, documents and photographs. He seems to have had a reputation for being difficult and rather mean, but her recorded memories imply that this was undeserved. From 1912 to 1946, the actor made more than 50 films, among them the Pagnol adaptations, *Fanny* and *César*.

★ **Église St-Sauveur**: Cogolin's Romanesque church dates from the 11th and 16th centuries and houses a fine wooden Florentine triptych from 1540. There's also a lovely portal inspired by the Florentine Renaissance.

★ The **ville haute** (upper town) has maintained its medieval air, with ancient streets and vaulted passageways of lava stone. Some of the houses, particularly along **rue de la Résistance** or **rue du Piquet**, have 12th-century porches made from blocks of serpentine from the Maures.

★ **Maison-musée Sellier**: 46 rue Nationale. ☎ 04-94-54-63-28. Open Monday to Saturday 10.30am–noon and 5–8pm. Entrance fee: 15F (under-15s free). Housed in a pretty 17th-century building, this museum tells the story of the pioneers of wireless telegraphy and the many people involved in the history of the radio.

★ **La manufacture de tapis** (carpet factory): boulevard Louis-Blanc. ☎ 04-94-55-70-65. Open every day (except Saturday and Sunday) 9am–noon and 2–6pm (5pm on Friday). One-off, hand-knotted carpets have been made in this workshop since 1924, when the craft was brought to the area by Armenian immigrants. Today, Cogolin rugs can be seen at all the best addresses, from Paris to Monaco. Visitors can see the work and there's also a salesroom.

★ **La fabrique de pipes Courrieu** (pipe-carving factory): 58 avenue Georges-Clemenceau. ☎ 04-94-54-63-82. Open every day 9am–noon and 2–6pm (5pm on Saturday), except Sunday. In these workshops, the famous Cogolin pipes are carved from the thick roots of briars that grow in the Maures. The art dates back two centuries, and the pipes are considered to be of excellent quality.

LA GARDE-FREINET (83680)   Population: 1,660

This substantial village in the Massif des Maures seems to hang suspended at an altitude of 400 metres (1,300 feet) above a vast forest of chestnut trees. Local legend says that it was the final stronghold of the Saracens in France. Driven out from all other places, they apparently used the strategic position of this site to prolong their stay for another century. However, there is no archaeological evidence to back up the story.

For a long time, the village survived on the local industries of cork production (which employed 700 people in the 19th century) and the cultivation of chestnut trees. The delicious and famous *marrons du Luc* (sweet chestnuts) take their name from the railway station from which they were despatched.

La Garde-Freinet is popular with tourists during the day, but it's set in a lovely natural environment far from the noisy summertime crowds and makes a perfect base from which to explore the area.

USEFUL ADDRESSES

🛈 **Tourist office**: 1 place Neuve. ☎ 04-94-43-67-41. Fax: 04-94-43-08-69. Open every day (except Sunday in low season) 10am–12.30pm and 3–6pm. In high season, closed on Sunday afternoon (from Easter to All Saints).

WHERE TO STAY

Campsites and Walkers' Accommodation

🏠 **Camping municipal Saint-Éloi**: in the St-Éloi district. At the exit to the village towards Grimaud. ☎ and fax: 04-94-43-62-40. Open from 1 June to end September. A pitch for two plus vehicle for around 72F. This site is in large shady grounds, full of cedar trees, cork oaks and pines. Hot showers and free swimming once a day in the council swimming pool. Reservations are possible.

🏠 **Camping La Ferme de Bérard**: on the road for Grimaud, the D558, 5 kilometres (3 miles) from the village. ☎ 04-94-43-21-23. Fax: 04-94-43-32-33. Open from March to November. Swimming pool and caravans for hire.

🏠 **Gîte d'étape** (walkers' accommodation): in the hamlet of La Cour, 6 kilometres (4 miles) from the village on the road for Grimaud. Turn left on to the Plan-de-la-Tour road. ☎ and fax: 04-94-43-64-63. 14 beds in two dormitories at a cost of 70F per night (including breakfast). Half board for 160F. In July and August, it is self-catering and you can only hire the house if there are six people. Bank cards not accepted.

☆☆ Moderate

La Claire Fontaine: place Vieille. ☎ and fax: 04-94-43-63-76. Closed from mid-February to mid-March. Double rooms with washbasin for 190F, and with shower and toilet for 230F. Located in the main square, this establishment has simple but comfortable rooms.

Hôtel Le Suve: 14 rue du Noyer. ☎ 04-94-43-09-86. Fax: 04-94-43-09-89. Closed from 1 October to 31 March. Double rooms with bath from 350F. This traditional house just outside the centre of the village has clean, reasonably priced rooms.

WHERE TO EAT

Le Lézard: 7 place du Marché, opposite the kiosk. ☎ 04-94-43-62-73. Fax: 04-94-43-60-67. Email: lelezard@wanadoo.fr. Closed on Monday and during the month of February. Menus at 105F, 135F and 185F. A great atmosphere, with a patron and chef who is hard to ignore, and outdoor tables in a pleasant setting near a bandstand. Once a month, there are special events with dinner and a concert (reservations possible). Sadly, they are restricted because of complaints about the noise from neighbours.

La Faucado: RN, on the right as you approach from Grimaud. ☎ 04-94-43-60-41. Closed on Tuesday out of season, and from mid-January to mid-March. Set menu at 150F (lunchtime only). À la carte around 200F. This restaurant has a dining room of great rustic charm and a foliage-covered terrace. The traditional food is sophisticated and delicious. Book ahead.

WHAT TO SEE AND DO

★ **The village**: wander around the narrow streets, checking out the evocative names. There's also an old public wash-house, a number of pretty fountains and a Renaissance church with a multi-coloured altar.

★ **Conservatoire du Patrimoine et des Traditions du Freinet** (association for the preservation of the heritage and traditions of Freinet): 1 place Neuve. On the first floor, above the tourist office. ☎ 04-94-43-08-57. Open from Tuesday to Saturday 10am–noon and 3–6pm. Entrance fee: 10F (under-12s free). Guided tours of Fort Freinet and the old village on Thursday at 9am (tickets: 40F). Before climbing up to Fort Freinet (*see below*), pop into this little museum, which clarifies the layout of the site and displays some of the objects found there, including 14th-century thimbles and ceramics from the 12th and 13th century. Thematic exhibitions explain traditional local activities, such as the cork industry.

WALKS

The tourist office has suggestions for a dozen routes for walkers and mountain bikers.

– **Fort Freinet**: the ruins of the Saracen fort are accessed via a good 30-minute walk along the forested route above the village. Walkers are rewarded with a wonderful view, since the legendary eyrie of a fort perches at an altitude of 450 metres (1,475 feet). Evidence suggests that the fortified village was built at the end of the 12th century and the entire complex was hollowed out of the rock. It was then abandoned in the late 14th or early 15th century and the current village, reached via the Col de la Garde, developed further.

– For a shorter walk (20 minutes), head for the **Roches Blanches** (white rocks), which afford similarly panoramic views. From a distance, they look as though they are covered in snow, but they are in fact made of white quartz.

– Alternatively, visit some of the sleepy hamlets around La Garde-Freinet – such as **La Moure**, **Valdegilly** and **Camp de la Suyère** – where time seems to have stood still. Pick up leaflets detailing walks to the surrounding villages from the tourist office.

– Towards the west, the renowned GR9 long-distance footpath reaches **Notre-Dame-des-Anges** (*see* 'Collobrières', page 463).

FESTIVALS AND EVENTS

– **Market**: Wednesday and Sunday morning.

– **Fête de la Transhumance** (transhumance or stock-moving festival): in June, 2,000 sheep come to town and locals enjoy a programme of events including a farmers' market and sheep-dog trials.

– **Bravade de la St-Clément**: held on 1 May, this procession may be less spectacular than the one in St-Tropez (see page 477), but it's still interesting. 'Soldiers' take the ashes of the patron saint from the church to a chapel about 1 kilometre away.

– **Fête de la Châtaigne** (chestnut festival): held at the end of October. A large market with stalls offering tastings and sales of sweet chestnuts.

– **Fête de la Vigne et du Vin** (festival of wine and the vine): at the end of October. Inevitably, tastings and sales of wine, but also performances by traditional folk groups.

– **Foire aux santons** (*santons* fair): held during the last week of December.

In the Area

LES MAYONS

Les Mayons is around 20 kilometres (12.5 miles) from La Garde-Freinet. Take the D558 and then turn left on to the D75 across the attractive plain of Les Maures. The village, clinging to the foothills of the *massif*, was founded in the 16th century by charcoal burners from Italy. It's a peaceful and lovely spot with a church that houses an impressive 17th-century painting of the crucifixion.

WHERE TO STAY AND EAT

🛏 ✕ **Chambres d'hôte et ferme-auberge Domaine de la Fouquette** (B&B on the farm): 83340 Les Mayons. 2 kilometres beyond the village of Les Mayons on the D75 towards Collobrières. ☎ 04-94-43-08-57. Fax: 04-94-60-02-91. Email: domaine.fouquette@wanadoo.fr. Closed from October to March. Double rooms with shower and toilet cost 300F, including breakfast. Dinner available for 100F and *ferme-auberge* menu at 130F; book ahead for both. The three rooms are simply but agreeably decorated. Take a walk in the forest and then enjoy tasty farm food with a glass of home-produced wine. Try the rabbit with saffron or chicken bouillabaisse.

WHAT TO SEE

★ **Village des Tortues** (tortoise village): 83590 Gonfaron. On the D75 between Les Mayons and Gonfaron. ☎ 04-94-78-26-41. Open every day from 9am to 7pm. Closed from early December to end February. Entrance fee: 40F (25F for children between 6 and 16). Some scientists work to reintroduce the bear to the Pyrenees; others work for the preservation in the Massif des Maures of the yellow and black Hermann tortoise, the oldest vertebrate in Europe (the species has been around for over 50 million years). Victim of forest fires and clearing, together with other, more stupid human acts, it survives in just two places – here and on the island of Corsica. It cannot live in captivity and it is bred and cared for in this 'village' only in order to repopulate the Maures. To be sure of seeing the tortoises, visit during the summer around 10–11am, when they are being fed, or around 6–7pm. During the rest of the year, come at the warmest time of the day.

PLAN-DE-LA-TOUR (83120) Population: 2,410

For lovers of long walks in the hills, this place has pretty scented paths that twist and turn as they climb towards and finally reach two lovely villages. The temptation to stay for ever is great.

USEFUL ADDRESS

🆗 **Tourist office**: place du 19-Mars-1962. ☎ 04-94-43-01-50. Fax: 04-94-43-75-08. Open every day in high season 9am–noon and 3–6pm; in low season, 9am–noon and 2–6pm.

WHERE TO STAY AND EAT

🛏 **Mas des Brugassières**: ☎ 04-94-55-50-55. Fax: 04-94-55-50-51. 1 kilometre from the village on the road that meets the N98. Closed from 10 October to 20 March. Double rooms with bathroom between 450F and 560F, according to season. This delightful farmhouse is at the heart of the Massif des Maures, only 5 kilometres (3 miles) from the sea and 12 kilometres (7.5 miles) from St-Tropez. It is run by its friendly and widely travelled owner, with some exotic touches. The atmosphere and the rooms are relaxed and even the swimming pool is relaxed; a large brunch is often served around it, some time between 10am and 1pm. Some of the rooms open on to the peaceful gardens.

🛏 ✕ **La Bergerie**: Le Clos de San Peire. 2 kilometres from the village, on the D44. ☎ 04-94-43-74-74. Fax: 04-94-43-11-22. Double rooms with shower or bath and toilet from 320F to 380F, depending on season, including breakfast. Dinner for 125F. This former sheepfold sits in 6-hectare (15-acre) grounds and has been tastefully renovated with lovely rooms, a pool and a *boules* pitch. Enjoy breakfast with food gathered in the garden. The host is mad about wine and is often to be seen on his tractor, seeing to the vines.

STE-MAXIME (83120)   Population: 12,000

Ste-Maxime is a modern resort town, which is often obliged to accept the overflow of wealthy holidaymakers from St-Tropez. Perhaps less appealing than St-Tropez itself out of season, it's an attractive alternative in July and August. Its beaches are just as lovely as its neighbour's but noticeably less crowded, and there are fewer mobile phones and 'barely-there' bikinis.

USEFUL ADDRESS

🛈 **Tourist office**: promenade Simon-Lorière. ☎ 04-94-96-19-24. Fax: 04-94-49-17-97. Website: www.sainte-maxime.com. Open in high season every day from 9am to 8pm (non-stop); in low season, every day 9am–12.30pm and 2–6pm.

WHERE TO STAY

⌂ **L'Ensoleillée**: 29 avenue Jean-Jaurès. In the centre of town, at the corner of avenue Jean-Jaurès and rue Martin. ☎ 04-94-96-02-27. Closed from October to Easter. Double rooms with shower and toilet, or bathroom, between 250F and 290F, depending on season. Half board compulsory in July and August, from 260F to 340F. *Formule* menu at 70F, and other menus from 99F to 138F. Free parking. The warm welcome and the relaxing decor are balm for the tired soul in this busy, overgrown resort. Travel back in time in the unpretentious rooms, which are clean and comfortable. The restaurant is a lovely surprise too, and all this is just two minutes from the beach.

⌂ **Le Montfleuri**: 3 avenue Montfleuri (at right angles to avenue du Général Leclerc; head towards St-Raphaël from the town centre). ☎ 04-94-55-75-10. Fax: 04-94-49-25-07. Email: montfleuri.ste.maxime @wanadoo.fr. Closed from 7 January to 1 February and from 1 to 20 December. Double rooms with shower and toilet (and satellite TV) from 300F (standard room in low season) to 950F (for large room with terrace and sea view in high season). Menus at 100F (lunchtime) and 150F (evening). From the outside, this looks like any other seaside hotel but, inside, the welcome is warm and charming, the atmosphere relaxed but professional, and the pleasant rooms all different. Tables are arranged around a luxurious swimming pool and the family-style cuisine is tasty.

⌂ **Le Mas des Oliviers**: La Croisette. High up in the town, on the Grimaud side. ☎ 04-94-96-13-31. Fax: 04-94-49-01-46. Closed from 15 January to 15 February. Double rooms with shower and toilet, or bathroom, plus a view over the sun-drenched hills cost between 250F and 570F; rooms with a sea view between 350F and 750F. This farmhouse offers peace, charm and comfort. Pine trees give welcome shade in the hot months, the cicadas serenade you at night and the view over the gulf is magnificent.

☆☆☆ Chic

🛏 **La Croisette**: 2 boulevard des Romarins. High up in the town, on the Grimaud side. ☎ 04-94-96-17-75. Fax: 04-94-96-52-40. Website: www.hotel-la-croisette.com. Closed from 1 November to end February. Double rooms with shower and toilet, or bathroom (and satellite TV) from 390F to 520F in low season, and from 690F to 890F in high season. Housed in a seaside villa, built recently in 19th-century style, this hotel has a rather extravagant foyer but pleasant air-conditioned rooms, some with a small terrace overlooking a garden full of palm and bay trees. The welcome is warm.

🛏 **Hôtel Les Santolines**: La Croisette. High up in the town, on the Grimaud side. ☎ 04-94-96-31-34. Fax: 04-94-49-22-12. ☒ Open all year. Double rooms with shower and toilet, or bathroom (and satellite TV) from 330F in low season (ground floor) to 790F in high season (air-conditioned with sea view). This pleasant place has a friendly atmosphere and a real Provence feel. The prices are reasonable, particularly in low season, and there's also a swimming pool.

WHERE TO EAT

✗ **Restaurant La Maison Bleue**: 48bis rue Paul-Bert. ☎ 04-94-96-51-92. Closed on Tuesday in low season, from 2 November to 26 December, and from 3 January to 30 March. Set menus at 100F and 140F. Every little girl's dream dolls' house, with a dining room painted ochre, yellow and blue. The Provençal 'Arabian Nights' decor is tasteful and the terrace has benches equipped with cushions, where you can relax as you enjoy the excellent food. The service can be slow, but it's worth the wait.

✗ **Auberge Sans Souci**: 34 rue Paul-Bert. ☎ 04-94-96-18-26. Closed from 30 October to 10 February, and on Monday in low season. Menus at 98F and 138F. This unpretentious restaurant, close to the bridge and the church, serves simple, tasty food that is full of Provençal flavours. There's an elegant dining room for the cooler months and a beautiful terrace for the days when the temperature starts to climb. Enjoy *sauté d'agneau minute au basilic* (pan-fried lamb with basil) or *salade tiède de raie aux bulots tripes à la niçoise* (warm skate salad with mushrooms).

WHAT TO SEE AND DO

★ **La tour Carrée**: place des Aliziers. Just behind the marina. ☎ 04-94-96-70-30. Open throughout the year every day (except Monday morning and all day Tuesday) 10am–noon and 3–7pm (to 6pm in winter). Entrance fee: 15F (5–15-year-olds 5F). The appropriately named 'square tower' used to be called the Tour des Dames ('ladies' tower'). The monks of the islands of Lérins (*see* page 557) built the tower in 1520 as a refuge for locals who were under attack from pirates. Before 1935, it served as a granary, prison, school and town hall, and is now a small museum with displays on local traditions and crafts.

– **Beaches**: from east to west, the string of beaches includes the **plage de la Croisette** (a supervised beach with a sailing school for children over 8), the town beaches for urban swimmers and, further on, the **plage la Madrague**, nestled in a cove and very popular with divers. **Plage la Nartelle** comes next, with its private beaches, although the place to (pay and) be seen is still apparently **Pampelonne**. **Plage des Éléphants** is the last of the beaches on this stretch.

FESTIVALS AND EVENTS

– **Marché des vieux quartiers** (old town market): local produce is sold on Thursday morning in the old part of town.

– **Fête de l'huile et de l'olive** (festival of olives and olive oil): held in mid-November.

> ## ROQUEBRUNE-SUR-ARGENS (83520)
> ### Population: 11,540

An enchanting 16th-century village, Roquebrune-sur-Agens marks the end of the Maures range. Its rich historical heritage includes a parish church, chapels, interesting portals and a small museum, open to visitors in high season. The magnificent *massif* of the Rochers de Roquebrune (372 metres/1,220 feet) dominates the valley. The red-sandstone rocks are visible from afar and may be explored following three different routes (information from the tourist office).

The village, medieval at its heart, lies in an area of remarkable contrasts. Mountainous to the north, the extensive *commune* is also home to sea-faring people, in the coastal part, at Les Issambres. The footpath that follows the coastline is beautiful.

USEFUL ADDRESS

🛈 **Tourist office**: 15 rue Grande-André-Cabasse. ☎ 04-94-19-89-89. Open in high season Monday to Saturday 9am–7pm, Sunday 9am–1pm and 3–7pm; in low season, Monday to Friday 9am–noon and 2–6pm, Saturday 9am–noon.

WHERE TO STAY AND EAT

On the Coast

🛏 ✕ **Le Provençal**: on the N98 at Les Issambres. ☎ 04-94-96-90-49. Fax: 04-94-49-62-48. Restaurant closed Tuesday lunchtime, from 7 January to 7 February, and from 1 November to 21 December. Double rooms with shower and toilet, or bathroom (and satellite TV) from 341F to 610F. Set menus at 150F and 210F. Delightfully old-fashioned, this hotel looks as if it has been here forever, although the renovation of the old house took place only a few years ago. It overlooks the gulf of St-Tropez and the beach, and has a shady terrace as well as its own stretch of fine sand.

🛏 **La Caravelle**: N98. Between Les Issambres and St-Aygulf. ☎ 04-94-81-24-03. Closed from October to mid-May. Double rooms with shower, toilet, air-conditioning and sea views from 300F to 600F, depending on season. Four-person rooms also available. This well-maintained hotel overlooks the sea and is reasonably priced.

✕ **Le Chante-Mer**: Les Issambres inlet. ☎ 04-94-96-93-23. Restaurant closed on Sunday evening, on Monday (except in July and August), and from 15 December to 31 January. Set menus at 128F, 175F and 215F. Delicious fish dishes served in the setting of a typically Provençal village.

MARKET

– **Marché à la brocante** (second-hand market): takes place in place Terrin on the second Friday in the month.

The Estérel

This section of coast is a little bit of Africa on the Côte d'Azur. Wrenched from the mainland during the formation of the Mediterranean sea, the Massif de l'Estérel is of volcanic origin. It may not be dramatically high (Mont Vinaigre peaks at no more than 618 metres, or 2,027 feet), but it offers some of the most extraordinary scenery on this coastline – masses of fallen boulders, blood-red cliffs plunging towards the sea and jagged promontories rising up. The distinctive red rock, dotted with vegetation made sparse by the ravages of fire, flashes with occasional yellows, purples and greys.

In the 17th and 18th centuries, the Estérel was a refuge for highwaymen and brigands, including the notorious Gaspard de Besse, as well as convicts escaping from the penal colony in Toulon. Today, it is the domain of walkers and mountain bikers, with an extensive network of footpaths and routes.

Note: walking and biking routes in the Estérel are closed when the fire risk is too high. For more information, call: ☎ 04-98-10-55-41.

FRÉJUS (83600)   Population: 47,900

Fréjus sits in the foothills of the Estérel, seemingly inseparable from its sister town of St-Raphaël. It's difficult to distinguish where one town ends and the other begins, particularly during the hectic summer months. The beach area of Fréjus-Plage is an artificial creation and is of less interest than the town itself, which is built on a small hill.

The appeal of Fréjus is not limited to its Roman remains, but the town was certainly important in Roman times, when its port on the lagoon was one of the most significant on the Mediterranean. It was reached by the Roman galleys via a channel. Julius Caesar founded Forum Julii (Julius' market, which became 'Fréjus') in 49 BC, and Emperor Augustus established a large military base here. After a period of expansion and development, the lagoon began to silt up, until the port's activities came to an end around the second century AD. The port was filled in during 1774, but fragments of Forum Julii can be seen today on the far side of the modern town.

In 1959, the town hit the headlines for tragic reasons, when the Malpasset dam burst, killing 400 people.

USEFUL ADDRESSES

⊞ Municipal tourist office of Fréjus: 325 rue Jean-Jaurès, in Fréjus-Ville. ☎ 04-94-51-83-83. Fax: 04-94-51-00-26. Website: www.ville-frejus.fr. Open all year Monday to Saturday 9.30am–noon and 2–7pm (6pm in winter); Sunday and public holidays during school holidays, 10am–noon and 3–6pm (5.30pm in winter).

⊞ Syndicat d'initiative (tourist information centre): boulevard de la Libération, in Fréjus-Plage. ☎ 04-94-51-48-42. Open from 1 June to 30 September every day 10am–noon and 3–6pm.

■ Bicycle or motorbike hire: Holiday Bikes, 943 avenue de Provence, Fréjus. ☎ 04-94-52-30-65.

WHERE TO STAY

In Fréjus-Ville

♠ Auberge de jeunesse (youth hostel): chemin du Counillier. ☎ 04-94-53-18-75. Fax: 04-94-53-25-86. 2 kilometres from the old town of Fréjus. Take the Fréjus exit from the motorway, and the N7 towards Cannes. By train, get out at St-Raphaël station and take the 6pm bus from platform 7 of the coach station. Open all year (except from 20 December to 31 January), from 6pm. Youth hostel membership card required. Dormitory bed 70F per night, including breakfast. Bed in a four-person room with shower and toilet 85F per person, including breakfast. Camping in the park 33F per night. Dinner costs 52F (no lunch). This pleasant hostel stands in a large park, 4.5 kilometres (about 3 miles) from the beach and a short walk from the historic centre of Fréjus. A bus transports guests every morning to the beach or the train station for just 6F.

☆☆☆☆ Chic

♠ Hôtel Arena: 139 rue du Général-de-Gaulle. In the old centre, next to place Agricola. ☎ 04-94-17-09-40. Fax: 04-94-52-01-52. Website: www.arena-hotel.com. ♿ Double rooms with shower and toilet from 450F to 580F, with bathroom and satellite TV from 480F to 750F. Set menus from 145 to 265F. Parking possible, for a charge. Housed in a former inn (where Napoleon himself is said to have stayed), this hotel has been tastefully renovated in an essentially Provençal style, with warm colours, mosaics and painted furniture. There's a flourishing garden with a lovely pool (unusual right in the town centre) and the rooms are charming, soundproofed (the railway is not far away) and air-conditioned, although not huge. The tasty food has a strong Mediterranean flavour, with a very personal touch.

In Fréjus-Plage and St-Aygulf

Campsites

There are several campsites in Fréjus, but few near the sea. Surcharges are par for the course in the summer.

⛺ **Parc de camping de St-Aygulf**: 270 avenue Salvareli. ☎ 04-94-17-62-49. Fax: 04-94-81-03-16. Open from early April to end October. One of the largest in the area (with 1,600 spaces), this site is in the small parish of St Aygulf, attached to Fréjus. Close to the water, so it is very popular in high season, with English, German, Italian, Danish and Dutch visitors. The facilities have just been renovated, and 75 per cent of the park is shaded.

⛺ **Holiday Green**: on the D4. 7 kilometres (4 miles) from the sea, on the route de Bagnols. ☎ 04-94-19-88-30. Fax: 04-94-19-88-31. ⚒ Open from 1 April to 21 October. The best four-star campsite in the area, with room for 720 tents, pitched on terraces, and for caravans and mobile homes. The restaurant is pretty average, but the site is still a favourite with the Brits, perhaps because of its huge swimming pool.

⛺ Nearby **La Baume** is a similar site.

⛺ **Le Colombier**: 1952 route de Bagnols. ☎ 04-94-51-56-01. Fax: 04-94-51-55-57. Email: colombier@compuserve.com. ⚒ Open from Easter until 30 September. 4 kilometres (2.5 miles) from the sea. Quite comfortable and shady, with a large swimming pool with three water slides.

☆☆ Moderate

⚔ **Hôtel L'Oasis**: impasse Jean-Baptiste Charcot. ☎ 04-94-51-50-44. Fax: 04-94-53-01-04. Website: www.hotel-oasis.net. Closed from 20 October to 15 March. Double rooms with shower or shower and toilet from 200F to 450F, depending on season. Free parking. This small 1950s building at the end of a cul-de-sac is a peaceful spot, run by a very welcoming couple. The rooms are all different, some with old-style wallpaper and others with a Provençal decor. They are not large, but they are quite pleasant. Breakfast can be eaten under the trees on sunny days. It's a 5-minute walk to the beach.

WHERE TO EAT

In Fréjus-Ville

⚔ **Cadet Rousselle**: 25 place Agricola. ☎ 04-94-53-36-92. Closed from 15 December to 15 January, Monday and Thursday lunchtime out of season. Menu at 65F. À la carte between 50F and 80F. This little crêperie is cheap and pleasant, and popular with the locals.

⚔ **L'Arcosolium**: 14 place des Jésuites. ☎ 04-94-40-14-44. Closed all day Sunday (Sunday lunchtime only during July and August) and at the end of December. Set menus between 75F and 140F, and a vegetarian menu at 100F. Housed in a building constructed around the remains of a Roman wall, this restaurant has lovely stone arcades and a Belle Époque interior. The welcome is warm and the food is good, particularly the vegetarian options.

☆☆☆ Chic

✕ **Les Potiers**: 135 rue des Potiers. Near place Agricola. ☎ 04-94-51-33-74. Closed all day Tuesday, Wednesday lunchtime and from 1 to 15 December. Set menus at 130F and 180F. This small restaurant in a quiet little street serves imaginative food, with light and tasty dishes such as *suprême de caille rôti aux petits escargots de Bourgogne* (roast quail with little Burgundy snails) or *saumon rôti a l'ail* (salmon roasted with garlic). Booking essential.

In Fréjus-Plage

✕ **La Romana**: 155 boulevard de la Libération. ☎ 04-94-51-53-36. Closed on Sunday evening and all day Monday out of season. Menus at 99F and 135F. This (slightly kitsch) seafront restaurant looks like a brasserie from around 1900 and serves generous dishes of excellent food at reasonable prices. Enjoy pizzas, fresh pasta, *bourride* (fish stew) or *daube à la provençale* (meat stew). This is a place worth remembering in an area with a number of disappointing tourist traps.

WHERE TO GO FOR A DRINK

♥ **La Maison de la Bière**: 461 boulevard de la Libération, in Fréjus-Plage. ☎ 04-94-51-21-86. Open until 4am in summer and 1am in winter. Almost 200 beers to choose from, with prices starting at 16F.

WHAT TO SEE

★ **Groupe Épiscopale** (episcopal complex): 58 rue de Fleury. ☎ 04-94-51-26-30. Open between 1 October and 31 March every day (except Monday) 9am–noon and 2–7pm; between 1 April and 30 September every day from 9am to 7pm. Entrance fee: 25F (under-25s 15F). This remarkable group of buildings includes the cathedral, baptistry and cloister.

★ **Cathedral**: open every day 8am–noon and 2.30–6pm. The cathedral was built on the site of a Roman temple and signalled the arrival of Gothic architecture in Provence, while retaining several Romanesque features. There's an elegant 13th-century bell-tower and a fine pair of Renaissance doors, carved with sacred scenes, including a gory Saracen massacre. Note the 15th-century choir stalls and their ornate carvings and a painting of St Marguerite of Antioch, by Jacques Durandi (dating from around 1450).

★ **Baptistry**: the oldest baptistry in France, dating from the end of the fourth century. At its centre, it is octagonal in form and in each of the eight corners of the space stands a black granite column with a white capital, salvaged from a Roman building.

★ **Cloister**: the marble-columned cloister is a peaceful and lovely place, its ground floor dating from the 12th century. It originally had two storeys, but only one of the upper galleries remains. Paintings depicting the Apocalypse cover the wooden ceiling. Some of the columns came from the stage of the Roman theatre, and the double staircase was built using stones from the theatre's seating tiers. The little columns of the first floor are delicate and elegant.

★ **Musée archéologique** (archaeological museum): place Calvini. ☎ 04-94-52-15-78. Fax: 04-94-53-85-01. On the first floor of the cloister (joint

GULF OF ST-TROPEZ AND PAYS DES MAURES

ticket). Open between 1 April and 31 October, Monday to Saturday 10am–1pm and 2.30–6.30pm; between 1 November and 31 March, Monday to Friday 10am–noon and 1.30–5.30pm, Saturday 9.30am–12.30pm and 1.30–5.30pm. Closed on Tuesday and Sunday. This museum has a collection of Gallo–Roman finds, a perfectly preserved mosaic, a head of Jupiter and a copy of the wonderful two-faced bust of Hermès, discovered in 1970 and considered to be a world treasure.

★ **Les Arènes** (amphitheatre): rue Henri Vadon. ☎ 04-94-51-34-31. Same opening times as the museum. Fréjus' second-century amphitheatre is less spectacular than the versions at Nîmes and Arles, accommodating 'only' 10,000 spectators. The steps have been restored, but a large section of the vaulted galleries remains intact. Over 100 years ago, the predecessor of the N7 road crossed the amphitheatre through its two great entranceways. Today, the site is reserved for bullfights and sometimes serves as a venue for rock concerts.

★ **Aqueduct**: avenue du 15-ème Corps d'Armée. 2 kilometres from the town centre; follow signs for Cannes on the N7. In ancient times, a 40-kilometre (25-mile) aqueduct stood here. A few of its arches can still be seen in a 22-hectare (54-acre) park, which is also the location for the elegant Villa Aurélienne (☎ 04-94-53-11-30), built in 1880. During its regular photography exhibitions, it is open Tuesday to Saturday 2–7pm (6pm in winter). Free entry.

★ They say that in Fréjus you can't dig a hole without finding something **Roman**. There are fragments of Forum Julii all over the place, including a small Roman theatre, vestiges of the ramparts, the Porte des Gaules (near the amphitheatre), the Roman harbour, the Porte d'Orée (the only remaining arcade from the ancient public baths), and more.

★ **Pagode Hong-Hien**: 13 rue Henri Giraud. 1.5 kilometres from the town centre (follow signs for Cannes on the N7). ☎ 04-94-53-25-29. Open all year, every day 9am–noon, 2–6pm (to 5pm from September to April). Entrance fee: 5F (free for under-7s). This remarkable Buddhist pagoda, based on a traditional Vietnamese design, was built in 1917 by soldiers of the Fourth Regiment of the colonial infantry, as a memorial to their dead. The building is open to Buddhists only, but non-Buddhists may visit the gardens, which are peopled by multi-coloured statues, including a 10-metre (33-foot) Buddha.

★ **Chapelle Notre-Dame-de-Jerusalem**: 5 kilometres (3 miles) from the town centre, on the N7 (follow signs for Cannes). Between 1 April and 31 October, open from Monday to Friday 2.30–6.30pm, Saturday 10am–1pm and 2.30–6.30pm. During the rest of the year, open Monday to Friday 1.30–5.30pm, Saturday 9.30am–12.30pm. Arrive at least 15 minutes before closing time. Free entry. Jean Cocteau designed the interior of this contemporary octagonal chapel, which stands surrounded by pine and olive trees. After his sudden death in 1963, his adopted son Edouard Dermit, also an artist, used his preparatory sketches in order to finish the colouring of the frescoes. The symbolism is rather enigmatic (very Cocteau), mixing the pagan and the sacred. Look out for the figure of Christ pointing to a beetle, symbol of eternal life in ancient Egypt, and the portraits of Jean Marais and of Cocteau himself among the Apostles.

★ **Parc zoologique Safari de Fréjus** (zoo): Le Capitou. 5 kilometres (3 miles) from the town centre on the D4 towards Fayence. ☎ 04-94-40-70-65. Open every day from 10am to 7pm between June and September (to 5.30pm from October to May). Entrance fee: 59F (35F for children between the ages of 3 and 10). Visitors may drive or walk through the park, in the foothills of the Estérel, to see monkeys, parrots and other wild creatures basking in the sun.

FESTIVALS AND MARKETS

– **Bravade de Fréjus**: this traditional town festival takes place on the third Sunday after Easter.

– **Marché à la brocante** (second-hand market): takes place on the second Sunday in January and July. For more information: ☎ 04-94-58-44-29.

– **Les Nuits Auréliennes**: music and drama in the Roman theatre during the last two weeks of July.

– **Fête du Raisin** (festival of the grape): takes place during the first week of August, in the old town.

– **Omelette géante de St-Aygulf**: a huge omelette is made and shared in the village on the second Sunday in September.

– **Noël Provençal**: Christmas celebrations held during the second and third week in December, including a *santons* fair.

LEAVING FRÉJUS

– **To Nice and Marseille**: Cars Phocéens. ☎ 04-93-85-66-61.

– **To St-Tropez and Toulon** (along the coast road): Compagnie Sodetrav. ☎ 04-94-95-24-82.

– **To Bagnols–Fayence–Les Adrets**: Compagnie Gagnard. ☎ 04-93-36-27-97.

ST-RAPHAËL (83700)　　　Population: 31,200

During the period of the Roman Empire, this town was already a residential suburb of Fréjus, known as Epulias (from the Latin for 'feasting', which gives an idea of the town's way of life under the Romans). The little fishing village, which some claim is the birthplace of *bouillabaisse*, the elaborate Provençal fish stew, was originally a quiet little place. In 1864, the arrival of the railway enabled Felix Martin, mayor of the town, to begin St-Raphaël's transformation into a seaside resort.

The town attracted the rich and famous. In the 1930s, F. Scott Fitzgerald wrote *Tender is the Night* here and, later, the British Princess Elizabeth stayed at the home of the Rothschilds. Dating from that era, St-Raphaël still has its casino, a hideous neo-Byzantine church, a seafront walk, the Promenade des Bains, and a number of very chic residential districts, such as Valescure. In the decades that followed, concrete blocks have sprung up in the town, but St-Raphaël none the less retains a certain old-fashioned charm and is the perfect base for discovering the Estérel.

USEFUL ADDRESSES

⊟ St-Raphaël tourist office: Le Stanislas, place de la Gare. ☎ 04-94-19-52-52. Fax: 04-94-83-85-40. Open every day in high season from 9am to 7pm. In low season, open every day (except Sunday) 9am–12.30pm and 2–6.30pm.
– **Hotel reservation centre**: ☎ 04-94-19-10-60. Fax: 04-94-19-10-67. Email: saint-raphael.reservation@wanadoo.fr

– **Train station**: rue Waldeck-Rousseau. ☎ 08-36-35-35-35. The TGV goes to Paris. A regional train goes to Cannes, stopping at the following stations along the Corniche de l'Estérel: Boulouris, Le Dramont, Agay, Anthéor, Cap Roux, Le Trayas Théoule-sur-Mer.
– **Coach station**: behind the train station. ☎ 04-94-83-87-63. Buses go to Fréjus, St-Tropez, Cannes, Draguignan, Fayence, Aix-Marseilles.

WHERE TO STAY AND EAT

☆–☆☆ Budget to Moderate

≜ Centre International du Manoir: chemin de l'Escale, Boulouris. Next to Boulouris station, 5 kilometres (3 miles) from St-Raphaël on the N98. ☎ 04-94-95-20-58. Fax: 04-94-83-85-06. Open from 15 June to 15 September. Double room (some with shower and toilet) 153F per person, including breakfast. Half board 209F per person. This large hostel, run by a private organization (small subscription payable on first visit) is exclusively for 18–35-year-olds (no children). It is by the beach, offers a warm welcome and a cosmopolitan and friendly atmosphere. The manor house and its annexes have rooms accommodating from two to six people, with delightful views of the large, shady park. In the summer, meals can be eaten outside under the palm trees after a spot of windsurfing or tennis, arranged by the hostel. Buses every 30 minutes from St-Raphaël.

≜ Hôtel Le Thimothée: 375 boulevard Christian-Lafon. 1.5 kilometres from the town centre, in the district of Les Plaines. ☎ 04-94-40-49-49. Fax: 04-94-19-41-92. Closed in January. Double rooms with bath from 200F to 450F, depending on season. Free secure parking. This hotel is housed in a 19th-century villa, in a quiet residential area just a few minutes from the sea. The attractive garden has ancient trees and a swimming pool. Every room has satellite TV and a minibar, and some have air-conditioning.

☆☆☆ Chic

✕ Pastorel: 54 rue de la Liberté, in St-Raphaël centre. ☎ 04-94-95-02-36. Fax: 04-94-95-64-07. Restaurant closed on Sunday evening, all day Monday, during the first two weeks in March and November and from 14 to 21 May. Set menus at 100F (lunchtime only), 160F and 210F. Open since 1922, the Pastorel has a rather hushed atmosphere, and serves good Provençal food. There's a pretty ivy-covered terrace and pleasant rooms above the restaurant, in the **Hôtel de Flore**. ☎ 04-94-95-90-00.

✖ **La Bouillabaisse**: 50 place Victor-Hugo, town centre. ☎ 04-94-95-03-57. ⚒ Closed from 27 November to 27 December. À la carte menus from 200F to 250F, and a set menu at 130F. The house speciality is *bouillabaisse*, which can be enjoyed inside in a rather old-fashioned dining room or outside on a terrace under an ivy-covered roof. The market is just around the corner, and there are delicious fishy alternatives on the menu. The prices are reasonable, given the location.

✖ **L'Arbousier**: 6 avenue de Valescure, town centre. ☎ 04-94-95-25-00. Closed all day Monday, Wednesday evening and Sunday out of season, and during the December school holidays. Mid-week lunch menu at 145F and dinner menus from 195F to 320F. The most genial and charming restaurant in town, much frequented by those in the know. Come for the excellent lunch menu during the week, and enjoy it in the scented garden, rather than in the dining room.

WHAT TO SEE AND DO

★ **Musée archéologique** (archaeological museum): in the square of the old church. ☎ 04-94-19-25-75. Open from 1 June to 30 September 10am–noon and 3–6.30pm. During the rest of the year, open 10am–noon and 2–5.30pm. Closed on Sunday and Monday. Entrance fee: 20F. Housed in the former presbytery of the Église St-Pierre, the museum has a courtyard with a strange menhir, engraved with a human figure and a serpent. Inside, are finds from archaeological digs around the bay of St-Raphaël – a fine collection of amphorae and rare Saracen jars, bronze Roman pumps used to empty boats, and a reconstruction of a Roman galley – as well as Bronze Age artefacts such as ceramics, pearl necklaces and a flint dagger.

★ **Église St-Pierre**: the entrance to the 12th-century church is via the museum. The nearby watchtower dates from the 13th and 14th centuries; climb the 129 steps to the summit, for a panoramic view.

EVENT

– **New Orleans-style jazz competition**: held at the beginning of July, with a big procession and competitive concerts.

DIVING

St-Raphaël was the location for the very first French diving club, established in 1935. For centuries it was thought that there might be a sunken city in the local waters, but celebrated diver Jacques Cousteau found a Roman shipwreck full of building materials instead. Some of the artefacts are displayed in the museum (*see above*). The coastal area here has retained its wild beauty, and there are some wonderful dive sites. Beware, however, of the mistral and the wind from the east, which can make diving conditions dangerous.

Diving Clubs

■ **CIP St-Raphaël Odyssée**: Vieux Port, quai Albert Ier, 83700 St-Raphaël. Near the naval station. ☎ 06-03-42-81-60. Operates all year. *La Plongée*, the school's trawler, is equipped with an on-board compressor. State-qualified instructors (FFESSM, PADI) lead first dives and courses up to Level IV. All the necessary equipment is supplied and the school can also help with finding accommodation. Book ahead.

■ **CIP Fréjus**: in the boat maintenance area of Port-Fréjus Est. ☎ 04-94-95-27-18 or 06-09-58-43-52 (mobile). Email: cip@cip-frejus.com. Open all year. This major dive centre (FFESSM, PADI) takes divers to some of the most beautiful sites in the area. A team of state-qualified instructors leads first dives and courses up to Level IV and PADI, as well as night dives and classes for children over 8. The school has a wide range of equipment for hire.

■ **Europlongée**: in the pretty port of Bolouris. ☎ 04-94-19-03-26. Open all year. Small pleasant club (FFESSM) with state-qualified instructors who lead first dives and courses up to Level IV, teach children over 8, and arrange exploratory dives and night dives in summer. The school has a range of equipment for hire. There's a little sandy beach near by.

Dive Sites

Île d'Or: to the southwest of Cap Drammont. This rocky islet is surrounded by clear water 3–30 metres (10–98 feet) deep. Its pretty Byzantine tower is said to have been Hergé's inspiration for Tintin's adventures on the Black Island. Divers will see plateaux, slopes, rockfalls, canyons and arches, inhabited by a parade of groupers, sea bream, moray eels and lobsters. Quite an exposed site, but it can be explored by divers of all levels of ability, with guidance.

Le Lion de Mer: a little rocky islet just outside the port itself. Under the water, divers come across first the 19th-century bronze statue known as *Notre-Dame des Fonds Marins* (Our Lady of the Deep), anchored at a depth of 12 metres (33 feet), then a second statue, of a mermaid, standing at 18 metres (60 feet). Quite a bit deeper, between 22 and 40 metres (72 to 131 feet), there's some stunning red coral. Take a torch. Level I, but exposed to the east wind, so take care.

La Balise de la Chrétienne: this is a rather savage reef off Anthéor, where conger and moray eels and scorpion fish seek shelter among colourful rocks of this stony plateau, at a maximum depth of 25 metres (82 feet). The site is famous in the history of French marine archaeology as a dozen ancient wrecks have been discovered here. It is forbidden to remove any pieces of china and pottery. Level I, but be aware of the currents.

To the southwest is **Dramont**, another site famous for its ancient wrecks, at a maximum depth of 45 metres (145 feet). Graceful groupers flourish in the magnificent underwater meadows. Level II.

Village sous-marin de Silver (underwater village): in front of Cap Dramont. This Lilliputian village, at a maximum depth of 20 metres (66 feet), was built in the 1960s by a team of inspired and artistic divers. Under a rock vault, look for the church and its bell-tower overlooking a series of houses. Level I.

Péniches d'Anthéor (barges): just off Cap Roux, the fascinating remains of two barges that were torpedoed in 1944 and now rest at a depth of 24–36 metres (79–118 feet). It's easy to spot the stern, with its propeller. Swim among conger and moray eels, scorpion fish and groupers, but don't touch the cargo – the vessels were carrying mortar shells when they went down. Keep an eye on the current. Level II.

VIA AURELIA

The Via Aurelia was the inland road that linked St-Raphaël with Cannes. In ancient times, it went from Rome to Arles, and the modern-day N7 more or less follows the same route.

After driving along the 'mountain' road for 11 kilometres (about 7 miles), you'll reach **Col du Testanier** (the pass at 310 metres/1,015 feet). Take the forest road to the right and, when you arrive at the forester's house, the **Maison de Malpey** (which translates as 'house of the evil mountain'), take a left turn then turn left again at the next crossroads. You'll find yourself at the base of the **Mont Vinaigre**. Leave your car here and climb up to the summit, at 618 metres (2,027 feet); the wonderful view from the old look-out tower stretches all the way from the Italian coast to Ste-Baume.

Head back to the N7, then drive up to the Logis de Paris, the highest point of the journey. To the left, the D237 heads to Les Adrets-de-L'Estérel; the road provides lovely views over the sea, the Lérins islands and Cannes.

For information on the Corniche de l'Estérel, *see* page 536 'The Coastline from St-Raphaël to Nice and the Hinterland'.

The Hinterland of the Var Region

For a change of air and some time away from the traffic jams and busy beaches of the coast, head for the hinterland of the Var region, where towns and villages have managed to hold on to their individuality and character. Many have escaped the attentions of the developers, and are largely unknown to tourists, leaving the narrow winding lanes more or less empty. The atmosphere here is genuine. The people who live in the region are authentic locals, or dedicated non-natives who have found out how easy it is to fall completely in love with this part of Provence. Allow yourself to be seduced: step back in time in the Pays de Fayence, explore the dramatic beauty of the Gorges du Verdon and discover the medieval villages of Le Thoronet, La Ste-Baume and Cotignac.

Le Pays de Fayence

This micro-region starts just as you leave Fréjus. The difference is immediately noticeable as you take the D4, which passes by barracks and military training areas, and then climbs up to lovely little villages, perched high in the first foothills of the Alpes de Haute-Provence.

BAGNOLS-EN-FORÊT (83600)   Population: 1,690

This tranquil little village has wonderful walks and spectacular forests, from which it derives its name.

USEFUL ADDRESS

🛈 **Tourist office**: place de la Mairie. ☎ 04-94-40-64-68. Fax: 04-94-40-67-57. Between June and September, open on Monday from 9am to 10am, and on Tuesday to Saturday 9am–12.30pm and 2–6.30pm (to 5.30pm on Saturday).

WHERE TO STAY AND EAT

🛏 **Camping Le Clos**: Les Clos. ☎ 04-94-40-60-69. As you leave the village, 400 metres along the route de Fayence. Open from 1 April to 30 October. Pitch for two around 75F. The site is peaceful and shady, and has a swimming pool and tennis court.

✕ **Le Commerce**: 1 Grand Rue. ☎ 04-94-40-60-05. Open every day. Menus from 90F to 110F. Pizzas from the wood-fired oven cost 40–60F, and they also serve delicious salads. Paëlla and couscous may be ordered ahead.

WHAT TO SEE AND DO

★ **Église St-Antonin**: this church, dating from the 18th century, has some beautiful columned altarpieces.

★ Enjoy the pretty walk to **Chapelle St-Denis**, a Romanesque chapel built on a Roman site 1 kilometre to the east of the village. Cross the vineyard to get to it.

Alternatively, walk to the **Gourbachin waterfall**, first following the Le Muy road, and then turning right after the new bridge.

CALLIAN	**Population: 2,460**
MONTAUROUX and LAC DE ST-CASSIEN	
(83440)	**Population: 4,060**

These attractive villages are 30 kilometres (20 miles) from Fréjus.

CALLIAN

Walk up to the castle through charming narrow streets, past old doors, decorated with sculpted coats of arms, and peer into secret flower gardens before visiting the Chapelle des Pénitents.

MONTAUROUX

Montauroux, known as the 'balcony of the Estérel', owes the restoration of its magnificent chapel to dress designer Christian Dior. There are some lovely old houses in rue de la Rouguière, which still has its original paving stones.

★ **Complexe artisanal** (arts and crafts complex): on the D562, just 2 kilometres from the intersection of the Draguignan and Montauroux roads, with potters, glassblowers, and craftsmen working in olive wood and creating distinctive local fabrics.

★ **Bambous du Mandarin**: is a bamboo workshop in Pont-de-la-Siagne. ☎ 04-93-66-12-94. Between 1 March and 30 November, open on Saturday 8am–6pm and by appointment. Entrance fee: 20F (15F for children over 7).

LAC DE ST-CASSIEN

This huge lake to the south of Montauroux has a circumference of 35 kilometres (22 miles). Visitors can swim in its pure waters, relax in the cool shade of its trees, or take part in one of the exciting watersports on offer.

WHERE TO STAY AND EAT

Campsites

🏕 **Camping Les Floralies**: in Montauroux. 2 kilometres from the village and 2 kilometres from the lake. Leave the motorway at the exit to Les Adrets. ☎ and fax: 04-94-76-44-03. Mobile: 06-15-39-40-96. Open from 1 April to end October. Pitches for two at 70F. Peaceful and shady, with a friendly family atmo-

THE HINTERLAND OF THE VAR REGION

sphere and food or cooked meals for sale from a small on-site shop. Booking advisable in July and August.

🛖 **Camping Les Chaumettes**: in Montauroux. ☎ 04-94-76-43-27. Open from mid-June to mid-October. Quiet and comfortable.

☆–☆☆ Budget to Moderate

🛖 ✕ **Le Relais du Lac**: on the D562, 83440 Montauroux. Between Montauroux and Callian. ☎ 04-94-76-43-65. Fax: 04-94-47-60-13. Email: hotel.relaislac@wanadoo.fr. ♿ Open all year. Double rooms with washbasin for 150F, with shower for 220F, and with shower and toilet, or bathroom from 300F to 340F. Menus between 60F (*routier*) and 205F. Close to the lake, in buildings that are set back slightly from the road. The food is good, but the atmosphere is a little impersonal. The rooms are clean and some overlook a large garden and the countryside beyond. There's also a swimming pool.

🛖 **Résidence de tourisme Le Champ d'Eysson**: Les Chaumettes district, 83440 Montauroux. ☎ 04-94-85-70-00. Fax: 04-94-85-70-01. Email: champleysoon@freesbee.fr. ♿ Closed on Wednesday in low season. Studios for four people for 1,600F a week in low season. Six-person apartment for 5,150F in high season. Just 1.5 kilometres from the Lac de St-Cassien, this quiet establishment charges reasonable prices and has a swimming pool.

✕ **Au Centenaire**: 1 rue Lyle, Callian. ☎ 04-94-47-70-84. ♿ Closed on Tuesday, from 20 to 30 June and from 20 October to 1 November. Menus from 68F to 158F. This little restaurant takes its name from the great-uncle of the owner, who lived to the age of 103. It was opened in

his honour on his birthday. Meat is grilled over a wood fire, and the menus also offer classic *coq au vin* (chicken in red wine), and dishes of duck and wild boar. The owner is in charge of the kitchen, which is always a good sign.

🛖 ✕ **Auberge des Mourgues**: Les Mourgues district, Callian. ☎ 04-94-76-53-99. Fax: 04-94-39-11-32. Email: aubergemourgues@post. club-internet.fr. Closed on Thursday lunchtime in low season and from 12 November to 15 December. Double rooms with shower from 210F to 250F and with shower and toilet, or bathroom, from 250F to 350F. Menus from 90F to 195F. This quiet little *auberge* in the countryside below the village has a family atmosphere. The rooms are simply furnished and clean, and there's also a swimming pool. The food is unpretentious and good, and includes duck and *daube à la Provençale* (traditional meat stew).

☆☆☆☆ Très Chic

🛖 **Chambres d'hôte du Domaine du Riou Blanc** (B&B): Le Grand Chêne, 1345 chemin des Maures, 83440 Callian. 6 kilometres (4 miles) from the village on the D562 towards Draguignan–Grasse. Head for 'Les Coulettes d'Allongue' on chemin des Maures and then follow the signs. ☎ 04-94-47-70-61. Fax: 04-94-47-77-21. Email: dandi@ europost.org. Closed from 15 September to 1 May. Rooms with shower and toilet, or bathroom, from 480F to 580F, including breakfast. Housed in a massive building, this B&B has four rooms and an apartment in a picturesque and peaceful setting. There's a pleasant swimming pool for lazy afternoons. The place is friendly but relatively expensive. Bank cards not accepted.

FAYENCE (83440)   Population: 4,300

The hillside village of Fayence is pretty but inevitably rather touristy. It dominates the entire plain, and its wonderful position makes it a favourite takeoff spot for gliders. There are also several antique dealers, painters, sculptors and potters about town. The 14th-century church has a fortified Saracen gate, and the 18th-century parish church, Eglise St-Jean-Baptiste, has a baroque marble altar and a terrace with a sweeping view. The wrought-iron campanile of the Tour de l'Horloge is also worth seeing, after which you can wander through the picturesque network of narrow streets.

Enjoy the short and pretty walk to the neighbouring village of Tourrettes. To the southeast of the town, take a look at the Romanesque chapel of Notre-Dame-des-Cyprès.

USEFUL ADDRESS

❏ Tourist office: place Léon-Roux. ☎ 04-94-76-20-08. Fax: 04-94-84-71-86. Open Monday to Saturday 8.30am–noon and 2–6pm.

WHERE TO STAY AND EAT

🛏 Chambres d'hôte Mas des Suanes Hautes (B&B): Les Suanes Hautes. 8 kilometres (5 miles) from Fayence on the D562; follow the signposts. ☎ 04-94-76-11-28 or 04-94-84-11-99. Open all year. Double rooms with shower and toilet for 290F, including breakfast. This pretty 17th-century farmhouse has been tastefully restored and now has five stylish rooms and a wonderful view. A perfect base for exploring the region.

🛏 La Sousto: 4 rue du Paty. ☎ 04-94-76-02-16. Double rooms with shower and toilet (and refrigerator, hotplate, sink and shower) for 270F. This hotel at the very heart of the old village, perched above the valley, is a perfect place to stay, offering Provençal hospitality at its best. The rooms are simply but tastefully decorated, each with its own individual character, and guests are immediately made to feel at home. No. 5 has its own sunny terrace overlooking the valley – a great place to relax.

✕ Patin Couffin: placette de l'Olivier. ☎ 04-94-76-29-96. Closed on Monday and from mid-November to January. Set menus at 90F (lunchtime) and 130F. Meals are served on a tiny terrace or in the (equally mini) dining room. Choose from traditional tasty dishes, including *daube provençale* (beef stew) and *bourride aux olives* (white fish stew with olives). You may or may not like the atmosphere, but it certainly won't leave you indifferent.

✕ Le Temps des Cerises: place de la République. ☎ 04-94-76-01-19. Closed all day Tuesday, and from 1 to 15 February, and from 15 to 30 November. Set menu at 120F. À la carte around 195F. On a small square at the heart of the village, tucked in between the church and town hall, this restaurant has new owners and new decor (and prices have gone up a bit). The food is simple but tasty, and meals are served under a pretty creeper-covered pergola on sunny days.

☆☆☆☆ Très Chic

🛏 ✕ Moulin de la Camandoule: chemin Notre-Dame-des-Cyprès.

Five minutes' drive from Fayence, on the road for Seillans. ☎ 04-94-76-00-84. Fax: 04-94-76-10-40. ☘ Restaurant closed on Wednesday lunchtime in low season, and for two weeks in January (but open all year for residents). Double rooms with shower and toilet, or bathroom (and TV), between 470F and 970F, depending on season and facilities.

Menus from 165F to 320F. Half board compulsory from 15 March to 15 October. Housed in a beautifully restored oil mill, its original press and grindstone intact, this hotel is splendidly located in a park near the Camandre river. It has a shady terrace, a swimming pool and excellent food (available to residents and non-residents). Book ahead.

FESTIVALS AND EVENTS

– **Festival Musique en Pays de Fayence**: in October. ☎ 04-94-76-02-03. During the Fayence music festival week, concerts by string quartets are held in a number of the churches within the eight *communes* (parishes) of the district.

SEILLANS (83440)   Population: 2,130

Seillans is a charming hilltop village, 6 kilometres (4 miles) from Fayence, with the remains of its original ramparts, a 13th-century gateway, narrow streets and lovely squares and, in the church, two impressive triptychs. German-born painter Max Ernst chose to spend his last years here.

Just 1 kilometre away, on the road to Fayence, the Romanesque chapel of **Notre-Dame-des-Ormeaux** has a superb altarpiece showing the adoration of the Magi and of the shepherds. Guided tours take place on Thursday from 11am to noon (all year) and on Tuesday in high season. For more details, contact the tourist office.

USEFUL ADDRESS

🛈 Tourist office: Le Valat. ☎ 04-94-76-85-91. Fax: 04-94-76-84-45. Open in summer Monday to Saturday 9am–12.30pm and 2.30–6.30pm; Sunday 10am–1pm and 3–6pm; in low season, Monday to Saturday 9am–12.30pm and 2.30–6.30pm.

WHERE TO STAY AND EAT

🛏 ☘ Hôtel des Deux Rocs: place Font-d'Amont. ☎ 04-94-76-87-32. Fax: 04-94-76-88-68. ☘ Hotel restaurant closed on Tuesday and on Thursday lunchtime between December and April. Hotel closed for a month in winter. Double rooms with shower and toilet from 320F to 600F, and from 500F to 600F with bathroom. Menus at 90F, 160F and 230F. This large Provençal house, full of sophisticated nostalgic charm, stands in a charming spot at the top of the village. The grand, comfortable rooms are hidden behind blue shutters. Meals can be enjoyed on the terrace in summer, in the shade of the plane trees near the old fountain. It would be difficult to imagine a more lovely setting.

⚓ ✖ **Hôtel de France-Restaurant le Clariond**: place du Thouron. ☎ 04-94-76-96-10. Fax: 04-94-76-89-20. Restaurant closed on Wednesday in low season, and from early November to end January (except during the New Year break). Hotel and restaurant closed from 1 November to 15 December. Double rooms with shower and toilet from 350F and 390F, with bathroom from 370F to 400F. Menus at 135F, 175F and 275F. This rather luxurious establishment lacks intimacy but its lovely swimming pool makes up for it and it's a great base for exploring the surrounding area. The rooms in the oldest part of the building are more charming and atmospheric than those in the annexe. The restaurant is rather conventional, but the traditional food is done well. Meals may be enjoyed outside between June and September on tables set up under the plane trees, around the old fountain.

WHAT TO SEE

– **Ernst Collection**: in the village centre (ask for details from the tourist office). Open Tuesday to Saturday 10.30am–12.30pm and 3–7pm (2–6pm out of season). Entrance fee: 10F (free for under-12s). The collection consists of 69 lithographs by Max Ernst, gifted to the parish by his companion, Tanning.

FESTIVALS AND EVENTS

– **Fête des fleurs** (flower festival): at Pentecost every other year (even numbers).

– **Marché potier** (potters' market): on 15 August.

The Pays Dracenois and The Central Var

This was traditionally the major route between Italy and Spain. The A8 motorway is the only part of the area surrounding Draguignan, between the Massif des Maures and the Canjuers plateau, known to tourists flocking to the coast. Knowledgeable visitors take the smaller roads of the Central Var, finding cellars selling Côtes de Provence wines, pretty hilltop villages and one of the most beautiful Cistercian abbeys in Provence.

DRAGUIGNAN (83300)   **Population: 34,800**

Sadly, the charm of Provence has been rather crushed here, perhaps because Baron Haussmann, the planner of modern Paris, was allowed to apply his principles of urbanization in the 19th century. During the French Revolution, Toulon was stripped of its status as local capital of the region, because of its royalist sympathies, and Draguignan assumed the role instead. The administrative anomaly was brought to an end only in 1974.

Try to visit Draguignan on a Wednesday or Saturday, when the colourful morning market is held on the pretty place du Marché, in the historic part of the town.

USEFUL ADDRESSES

■ Tourist office: 2 avenue Carnot. ☎ 04-98-10-51-05. Fax: 04-98-10-51-10. Open in summer, Monday to Friday, from 9am to 7pm; Sunday and public holidays from 10am to 1pm; in low season weekdays from 9am to 7pm; Sunday and public holidays from 9am to noon.

■ CDT du Var (tourist information for the Var region): Conseil Général du Var, 1 boulevard Foch, 83003 Draguignan. ☎ 04-94-50-55-50. Fax: 04-94-50-55-51.

WHERE TO STAY AND EAT

â ✕ Hôtel-restaurant La Pergola: avenue du quatre-Septembre. ☎ 04-94-67-01-12. Closed on Sunday evening and all day Monday. Double rooms with bathroom at 250F. Menus from 60F to 180F. Run by a new team, this pretty yellow house is set back from the road behind a small garden. The rooms are clean and pleasant, but those on the road side can be noisy. Simple local food is served in a friendly atmosphere.

✕ Restaurant Le Baron: 42 Grand-Rue. Near the Église St-Michel. ☎ 04-94-67-31-76. ⚒ Closed on Monday except public holidays. Menus from 67F to 145F. With its white facade, this place may look rather more 'doctor's surgery' than restaurant, but the food is excellent. The menu features great classics from the Mediterranean and from Franche-Comté, including *coq au vin jaune et morilles* (chicken in white wine and morels).

✕ Les Mille Colonnes: place aux Herbes. ☎ 04-94-68-52-58. Closed on Sunday and from 20 to 31 August. Menus from 65F (weekday lunch) to 90F. This lively brasserie at the heart of Draguignan's old town has a very busy terrace on summer concert evenings. The reasonably priced menu is seasonal – *filets de rougets aux herbes et tapenade* (fillets of red mullet with herbs and olive paste) and even apple crumble. The internet café, with its 1830s-style decor, is a meeting place for amateur and professional philosophers in winter.

✕ Restaurant Le Domino: 28 avenue Carnot. ☎ 04-94-67-15-33. Closed on Sunday and Monday, and from 1 to 17 November. À la carte around 150F. This atmospheric restaurant on the main road is full of character, rather like its guests and its menu, which includes salads, spicy meat dishes and Mexican specialities. Relax on the verandah or under the palm trees in the garden. Both the welcome and service are friendly. Interesting art exhibitions are held here from time to time.

WHERE TO STAY AND EAT IN THE AREA

â ✕ Chambres d'hôte Le Mas de l'Hermitage: St-Pons district, 83830 Figanières. A 10-minute drive to the north of Draguignan. ☎ 04-94-67-94-94. Fax: 04-94-67-83-88. Website: www.masdel hermitage.com. Double rooms with shower and toilet, or bathroom, from 300F to 400F, including breakfast. Lunch with your hosts (Michael and Laurence) will cost 100F, and dinner around 130F. Set among the olive and fruit trees, this farmhouse has a warm and welcoming atmosphere. The food is cooked using fresh ingredients from the local markets.

â ✕ Hôtel L'Orée du Bois: Ste-Roseline district, 83490 Le Muy. On the four-lane road linking Draguignan and Le Muy. From the roundabout, take the unsurfaced road to the edge of the forest. ☎ 04-98-11-12-40. Fax: 04-98-11-12-53. **✕** Double rooms with shower and toilet, or bathroom (and satellite TV), from 270F to 325F. Menus between 115F and 160F. A welcome and relaxing pit stop in a lovely natural environment between St-Tropez and the Verdon gorges. Air-conditioned rooms overlook the swimming pool, the service is friendly and the food in the unpretentious restaurant is delicious. The terrace is very attractive.

WHAT TO SEE

★ **Musée Municipal**: 9 rue de la République. ☎ 04-94-47-28-80. Open Monday to Saturday 9am–noon and 2–6pm. Closed on Sunday and public holidays. Entrance fee. This small museum also houses a library. The curator is very friendly and looks after some interesting works of art, from Rembrandt to Renoir. The library has a superbly illuminated 14th-century manuscript (*Roman de la Rose*) and a 15th-century Nuremberg bible. There's also a 16th-century suit of armour, early printed books and collections of china.

★ **Musée des Arts et Traditions Populaires** (museum of popular arts and culture): 15 rue Joseph Roumanille. ☎ 04-94-47-05-72. Open 9am–noon and 2–6pm. Closed on Sunday morning and all day Tuesday. Entrance fee. This museum, housed in a former convent, explains the region's social and economic history. Displays show old trades and crafts, and reconstructed kitchens and farm buildings depict rural life in the region.

★ **Old town**: allow time for a long stroll in the old part of Draguignan, where there are sculpted doors, ancient houses. The atmosphere is pure Provençal, with the sights, smells and sounds of the region and, typically, half-closed shutters on hot afternoons.

★ **Tour de l'Horloge**: the clock tower, on the site of a former keep destroyed by Louis XIV (who ruthlessly ordered much destruction in the area), is adorned with a wrought-iron campanile. Check times of guided tours with the tourist office.

★ **American War Cemetery**: boulevard John-Fitzgerald-Kennedy. War cemeteries may be more closely associated with Normandy, but many American soldiers lost their lives after landing on the coast of Provence in 1944. This cemetery contains the 861 graves of fallen soldiers, and a wall commemorating the 3,000 Americans who were never found.

Around Draguignan

There are a number of attractive routes around Draguignan, but it's a good idea to avoid the busy D555 and its thundering lorries, especially if you're travelling by bike. Instead, work out a route via Flayosc, Lorgues and so on.

This is an area of pretty hinterland villages, lovely abbeys, and impressive chateaux with unusual singsong names. You can also get to the Verdon gorges (*see* page 531) and then return to Draguignan through more appealing villages.

BARGEMON

Clinging to a hillside between Draguignan and Fayence, the medieval hill town of Bargemon was fortified in AD 950. The remains of the four 12th-century gateways in the surrounding walls are still visible. The **Chapelle Notre-Dame-de-Montaigu,** for many years an important place of pilgrimage, contains a 'miraculous' olive-wood carving of the Virgin, brought here by a local monk in 1625, and a beautiful gilded baroque altar. The angels' heads on the high altar of Bargemon's 15th-century church of **St Étienne** are attributed to Pierre Puget. The church also has an unusual portal in Flamboyant style.

USEFUL ADDRESS

🖪 **Syndicat d'initiative** (tourist information centre): ☎ and fax: 04-94-47-81-73. Open Monday to Friday 3–6.30pm; Saturday 10am–noon and 3–6pm; Sunday from 10am to 12.30pm. In low season, Monday to Saturday from 9am to noon.

WHERE TO EAT

✕ **Auberge des Arcades**: 2 avenue Pasteur. ☎ 04-94-76-60-36. Closed on Tuesday. Menus at 98F, 140F and 185F. Pleasant restaurant housed in a venerable early 19th-century building. Try the *morilles* (morels) and *écrevisses* (crayfish) in season, at a table outside on the pretty terrace shaded by plane trees. You could only be in Provence. There are also rooms at the inn, currently being renovated.

✕ **La Taverne**: place Philippe-Chauvier. ☎ 04-94-76-62-19. Closed on Sunday evening and all day Monday in low season. Menus from 110F to 160F. This lovely inn is old-fashioned and charming with service that is as friendly or formal as you wish. The cooking is Provençal with a twist – *ragoût d'escargot de pays en croûte* (snails in pastry) or delicious *brussoles d'agneau confit et tomates séchées* (lamb with sun-dried tomatoes). There's also a pleasant and shady terrace, a favourite Sunday-lunchtime venue for local families.

AMPUS

The agreeable village of Ampus is 25 kilometres (15 miles) northwest of Draguignan. At the top of the settlement, a parish church stands on the site of a former Roman castrum. The greater part of the building is in Romanesque style, dating from the 11th century.

A few kilometres away, the small Chapelle Notre-Dame-de-Spéluque was constructed around the same time. It has an unusual five-footed sculpted altar.

The best way back to Draguignan is via the D49, which offers spectacular viewpoints.

FLAYOSC

The village of Flayosc, 7 kilometres (4 miles) west of Draguignan via the D557, has retained its fortified aspect, with a row of houses that forms a sort of substantial and undulating protective wall. There are several fountains and town gateways, dating from the 14th century. There is a beautiful of the surrounding countryside from the church terrace.

USEFUL ADDRESS

◼ **Tourist office**: place Pied-Barri. ☎ 04-94-70-41-31. Fax: 04-94-70-47-91. Open Monday to Friday 9am–noon and 3–6pm; Saturday from 9am to noon.

WHERE TO EAT

✕ **Restaurant L'Oustaou**: 5 place Brémond. ☎ 04-94-70-42-69. Closed Sunday evening and all day Monday. Menus from 120F to 265F. This is the best place to eat in Flayosc. The menu is creative, and the chef puts new touches to a largely traditional choice of dishes, such as *pieds paquets* (tripe), *daube provençale* (beef stew) and game in season.

LORGUES

To the south of Flayosc, the interesting village of Lorgues is reached by an extremely narrow road. It has a maze of narrow streets with pretty fountains. The majority of its medieval houses have so far escaped renovation, retaining a faded charm that has been rather lost in over-manicured villages such as Tourtour. Many of the little streets have plaques indicating their 'date of birth'.

The stately and massive Collégiale St-Martin, a collegiate church of rather ponderous architecture and with an impressive classical facade, is quite a surprise in such a small village. Inside, it has an attractive high altar in multi-coloured marble.

THE HINTERLAND OF THE VAR REGION

USEFUL ADDRESS

◼ **Syndicat d'initiative** (tourist information centre): place d'Entrechaus. ☎ 04-94-73-92-37. Open 9am–12.30pm and 3–6pm in winter ; 9am–12.30pm and 3.30–7pm in summer.

WHERE TO STAY AND EAT

⬥ ✕ **Hôtel-restaurant du Parc**: 25 boulevard Clemenceau. ☎ 04-94-73-70-01. Fax: 04-94-67-68-46. Closed from 15 November to 5 December and Sunday evening. Double rooms with shower for 170F and from 230F to 280F with shower and toilet, or bathroom (and satellite TV). Menus from 70F to 210F. A stone's throw from the collegiate church, this modest hotel has an old-fashioned charm. Some of the rooms can be noisy, but others overlook the garden; all could do with a bit of upgrading. There are tables in the garden, where guests can eat local dishes such as *daube provençale* (beef stew).

✕ **L'Auberge Josse**: 19 B avenue de Toulon. ☎ 04-94-73-73-55. Ġ Closed on Sunday evening and all day Monday in low season, and during the last fortnights in December and in June. Menus from 80F to 175F. This large inn, a regular venue for the locals' Sunday lunches *en famille*, stands at the edge the village. It has a shady terrace.

✕ **Chez Doumé (Le Bistrot)**: 12 boulevard Clemenceau. ☎ 04-94-67-68-97. Closed from 20 November to 20 January and on Monday. Daily special at 55F (lunch) and set menu at 90F. Around 120F à la carte. A small house with a big personality, pure Provençal in style, and with the warmest of welcomes. Relax by the fountain on the lovely terrace, beneath ancient plane trees. The food is fresh, unpretentious and very varied, including *filet de loup au beurre blanc* (sea bass in butter sauce) and fresh pasta.

✕ **Le Moulin St-Lambert**: 5 rue de Climène. ☎ 04-94-73-98-87. Closed on Sunday evening, all day Monday and from mid-November to mid-Feburary. Menus at 85F (lunchtime) and from 155F to 260F. In the depths of Provence, the decor here is a surprising mix of baroque and Rococo, with wall hangings, velvet-covered chairs and paintings in gilded frames. The terrace is less elaborate and a lovely place to sit on warm days. The food, particularly in the evenings, is highly recommended, and the welcome is friendly. On Saturday evening there's often a show with dinner, creating an entertaining atmosphere.

✕ **Chez Pierrot**: 18 cours de la République. ☎ 04-94-67-67-15. Closed on Wednesday in winter and during January. Menus at 70F (weekday lunch), and from 90F to 230F. Another good place to eat in Lorgues. The interior is not particularly interesting, but the food is. Try the *pieds paquets* (tripe) and tasty meat dishes.

LES ARCS-SUR-ARGENS

A wine-producing village of the Côtes de Provence, Les Arcs-sur-Argens is 12 kilometres (7.5 miles) south of Draguignan, on the edge of the D555. It has a picturesque medieval quarter, with remnants of the surrounding wall and a 12th-century chateau, now a charming hotel. The impressive keep was the look-out from which the return of the Saracens was spotted. Many of the old houses have been beautifully restored and have lovely floral displays in season. Spend a few minutes at dusk wandering round the narrow streets and up and down the vaulted stairways. At the bottom of the village, the parish church (closed from 11.30am to 2pm) contains a screen by Ludovico Bréa (1501) and a mechanical nativity crib.

USEFUL ADDRESSES

▣ **Tourist office**: 21 boulevard Gambetta. ☎ 04-94-73-37-30. Open 9am–noon, 2–6pm.

■ **Maison des vins côtes-de-provence** (wine cellar): on the N7. ☎ 04-94-99-50-10. Wine tastings and sales.

WHERE TO STAY AND EAT

Campsites

☎ **Camping L'Eau Vive**: 800 metres from Les Arcs. ☎ 04-94-47-40-66. Fax: 04-94-47-43-27. Open from 1 March to 1 November. This site is clean and shady, but busy in summer and rather noisy due to its proximity to the main A7 road. There is a swimming pool.

☎ **Camping à la Ferme, Le Préveire**: 300 metres further up the road from the Eau Vive site. ☎ 04-94-45-15-59. Open between 1 June and 15 September. Although close to the main road, it is relatively quiet and quite pleasant.

☆☆☆☆ Très Chic

☎ ✕ **Le Logis du Guetteur**: place du Château. ☎ 04-94-99-51-10. Fax: 04-94-99-51-29. Closed from 15 January to 7 March. Rooms with bathroom for 700F in high season. Menus from 170F to 350F. This hotel ('dwelling of the look-out') is in an unusual 12th-century fortified castle with a rather unusual atmosphere. The staff are so relaxed that you'll have time to wander around the entire place before being approached by anyone. Peace and calm are guaranteed here, and horse riding, tennis or kayaking are also on offer. The restaurant has a good reputation.

The Central Var

To the south, the A8 motorway has had an enormous impact on the landscape. Vidauban, Le Cannet-des-Maures, Le Luc and so on, may not be obvious holiday destinations, but if you do find yourself round this way, there are things to do and places to eat (*see below*). The best route to St-Tropez is via the D74, which winds its way through beautiful countryside and hamlets.

LE VIEUX-CANNET

Just before you reach Le Cannet-des-Maures, a picturesque village clinging to a hill, you'll come to Le Vieux-Cannet, with its wonderful panoramic view of the area. There's a lovely 18th-century campanile on top of the **Église St-Michel** (which is itself more than 600 years old).

LE LUC-EN-PROVENCE

This large agricultural village has little intrinsic charm but attracts philatelists because of its entirely renovated 17th-century **Château de Vintimille**, which houses a **Musée du Timbre-Poste** (stamp museum): place de la Convention, 50 metres from place de la Mairie. ☎ 04-94-47-96-16. The museum covers every aspect of postage stamps, from a complete history to the techniques of design and printing. Albert Decaris was one of the last engravers in France, and there's a reconstruction of his studio.

Between mid-May and mid-October, the **Musée Historique du Centre-Var** (historic museum of the Central Var) is open from Monday to Saturday, 3–6pm. Its exhibits include fossils, weaponry, archival documents and ethnological information.

WHERE TO EAT

✕ **Restaurant Le Gourmandin**: 8 place Louis-Brunet. ☎ 04-94-60-85-92. ✗ Closed on Sunday evening and all day Monday, as well as 20 February to 10 March, and 20 August to 15 September. Menus between 140F and 185F. This nice little establishment, with its regional decor, has a good reputation for its friendly welcome and for its food, which includes *fleurs de courgettes farcies* (stuffed courgette flowers) and *magret de canard braisé au poivre de Séchuan* (duck breast with Sezchuan pepper).

BUYING A GOOD CÔTES-DE-PROVENCE WINE

🍾 **Château St-Martin**: in Taradeau. ☎ 04-94-73-02-01. Fax : 04-94-73-12-36. Open every day in summer from 8am to 8pm. In winter, open every day (except Sunday) from 8am to 7pm. Monks from Lérins started this tradition when they set up a wine-making priory between the 11th and 18th centuries, and not just wine for taking at Mass. At the beginning of the 18th century, the present owner's family took over and built the chateau. They continued with the production of red, white and rosé wines, and introduced different grape varieties. The wine tasting is accompanied by a *son-et-lumière* show in the old wine warehouse, telling the history of the property (except during the grape harvest) with music and lights.

WHAT TO DO IN THE AREA

– Two fairly easy **cycle tours** leave from Le Luc-en-Provence (pick up the leaflet detailing walks and rides from the tourist office: *Promenades et randonnées cyclotouristes*), crossing tranquil countryside and passing by villages that are typical of the Haut-Var region, not over restored and without too many second homes. The *circuit sud* (southerly route) makes its way through Cabasse, Flassans, Besse, Carnoules, Pignans, Gonfaron, Les Mayons (on the D75), Vidauban (on the D48), Entraigues and Le Vieux-Cannet. The *circuit nord* (northerly route) takes you through Cabasse, Le Thoronet, Carcès, Cotignac and Entrecasteaux. Further north, towards Villecroze and Tourtour, it's too hilly for any but the most dedicated cyclists.

ABBAYE DU THORONET

The abbey at Thoronet is one of the most fascinating in the south of France. On the D79, 12 kilometres (7.5 miles) from Lorgues and 4 kilometres (2.5 miles) from the village of Thoronet. ☎ 04-94-60-43-90. Fax: 04-94-60-43-99. ✗ From April to September, open Monday to Friday from 9am to 7pm; Sunday 9am–noon and 2–7pm. In winter, open 10am–1pm and 2–5pm. Interesting tours are led by enthusiastic guides from the Conférenciers des Monuments Historiques (historic monuments association) between April and September at 10.30am, 11.30am, 2pm, 3pm, 4pm, 4.30pm and 5.30pm. Between October and March, tours conclude at 4pm. On Sunday and public holidays, Mass is sung at noon; unusually, the doors are left open for visitors. Festivals are held at the abbey during the summer months.

Like the Abbaye de Sénanque (*see* page 279), built by the Cistercians in 1160, Le Thoronet is sober and austere in style and construction – 'a brittle rock that insists on simple lines, refuses adornment and focuses on its Cistercian vocation', according to one well-known French architect. Although less well known than Sénanque, it's more beautiful and more pure. The simplicity of its architecture harmonizes with the rather inhospitable surroundings of the isolated valley in which it stands. The stone changes colour with the movement and strength of the sun, from white right through to red.

Because of the nature and position of the land, traditional proportions were not respected in the building. The cloister is trapezoidal and the galleries are at a number of levels. The church has clean, harmonious, almost perfect lines, and arched vaults with an early Gothic touch. The monks' Gregorian chant must have sounded marvellous here. Today, an annual festival of music gives audiences the chance to appreciate the superb acoustics. The cloister is substantial yet elegant, with vast arches and fine columns; you can climb up to its terrace. Admire the filleted ribbed vaults and ceilings in the chapterhouse, and then have a look in the monks' dormitory, with its cradle vault.

There are many reminders of the distant past in this moving abbey, where the monks learnt the importance of water, silence and work. It's worth spending a few minutes to absorb the sense of history and atmosphere, and to imagine how life must have been for them.

WHERE TO STAY AND EAT IN THE AREA

🛏 ✖ **Hostellerie de l'Abbaye**: chemin du Château, 83340 Le Thoronet. ☎ 04-94-73-89-24. Fax: 04-94-73-88-24. Email: h.abbaye.var@enfrance. com. ✖ Closed on Sunday evening in low season and for the month of November. Double rooms with bathroom from 300F to 400F. Menus at 120F (weekday), 145F and 195F. This modern concrete hotel, offering clean rooms and efficient service, is gradually shedding its austerity and assuming the warm colours of Provence. The menu is also Provençal in flavour. There's a swimming pool.

'Provence Verte'

If you feel like a little tour in the countryside of 'Green Provence', don't forget your map. This 'no-man's land' used to be part of the Centre-Var (Central Var), with Draguignan as its capital, though it now belongs to the 'Provence Verte' (green Provence) area around Brignoles. Admittedly of limited appeal to tourists, it tends to be quiet for most of the year.

The 'Provence Varoise' area (or whatever you call it), which stretches from Fréjus to St-Maximin, has always offered a peaceful existence, far from busy towns. It lies along the green valley of the Argens river and can be explored by bike or car, on foot or on horseback.

Follow a route east from the Abbaye du Thoronet to Seillons-Source d'Argens, north of St-Maximin and the Massif de la Ste-Baume. From here, you can climb back up to the Haut Var region via Barjols and Cotignac.

BRIGNOLES (83170)   Population: 13,300

Although it sits among a number of villages that are full of character and charm, Brignoles itself is rather lacking in either. Its one point of interest is the **Musée du Pays Brignolais** (regional museum), housed in a delightful 12th-century mansion built for the counts of Provence.

USEFUL ADDRESS

🛈 **Tourist office of Provence Verte**: carrefour de l'Europe (crossroads), 83172 Brignoles. ☎ 04-94-72-04-21. Email: la.provence.verte@wanadoo.fr. Helpful staff and an array of informative brochures, including the indispensable *Chemins de l'Eau*, which details some wonderful routes by the water.

WHAT TO SEE

★ Take a walk around the old part of the town and visit the **Musée du Pays Brignolais**, place des Comtes-de-Provence. ☎ 04-94-69-45-18. Open Monday to Saturday 9am–noon and 2.30–6pm; Sunday and public holidays 9am–noon and 3–6pm. Entrance fee: 20F (children over 8, 10F).

FESTIVAL

– **Festival de jazz**: jazz festival in mid-August.

WHAT TO SEE IN THE AREA

★ **Abbaye Royale de La Celle** (royal abbey of La Celle): 3 kilometres (2 miles) southwest of Brignoles, in the heart of the village. This is one of the oldest monuments in Provence, a 12th-century complex that includes a veritable 'village' of buildings, a Romanesque chapel, dormitories and the lodgings of the prior. One of the other buildings houses the local Maison des Vins (wine centre), and there's also a public washing place, a fountain, old streets and even a miniature village, in the Espace Jean-Giono. Information: ☎ 04-94-59-19-05.

THE MASSIF DE LA STE-BAUME

This is the most extensive *massif* in Provence, straddled between the Var river and the Bouches-du-Rhône (the mouth of the Rhône river). It's a place with a history, chosen by the Druids for celebration of their rites and the location for an important funerary monument erected by the Romans. In the first century, Mary Magdalene was said to have spent the last 30 years of her life as a recluse in a dark and damp Ste-Baume cave, which then became one of the main sites of pilgrimage in France and a stage on the road to Santiago de Compostela. (The local word for 'cave' is *baoumo*, which is obviously the origin of the name of the *massif*.) Mary's cave is also a compulsory rite of passage for the guild of masons known as Les compagnons du Tour de France, being the place where their founder, Master Jacques, was assassinated, around AD 950.

For naturalists, this area is a paradise, with 12 kilometres (7.5 miles) of rocky mountain ridge, vast forests and many springs. There are pretty walks, peaceful villages, old mines and sites of archaeological interest to discover, and the broad-leaved trees of the Massif are ablaze with colour in the autumn.

ST-MAXIMIN-LA-STE-BAUME

This village, known as the 'Gateway to the Var', is surrounded by hills and vineyards and is dominated by its famous basilica.

In the first century, Mary Magdalene and St Maximin came to Provence on an evangelizing mission. After their deaths, the bodies of the two saints were buried by monks in a secret place between Aix-en-Provence and Ste-Baume, so that the remains would not be stolen by the Saracens. In 769, St Mary's body reappeared in Vézelay, after a monk from Burgundy claimed to have discovered it in Aix. The first pilgrimage to the relics was authorized by the Pope, but the count of Provence remained sceptical and commissioned his own search in 1279. Two sarcophagi were uncovered in a crypt. In the jaw of one of the corpses was a sprig of fresh fennel. Even more miraculously, a piece of flesh remained on its forehead, at the same spot where Jesus had touched Mary Magdalene on the morning of his resurrection. There was no doubt in the mind of the archaeologists that this was a 'real' saint. A basilica was built over the crypt and the site became a significant destination for pilgrims.

USEFUL ADDRESS

🛈 Tourist office: place Jean-Salusse. In the Couvent Royal (royal monastery). ☎ 04-94-59-84-59. Fax: 04-94-59-82-92. Open every day 9am–12.30pm and 2.30–6.30pm (2–6pm between September to Easter). Guided tours of the basilica and of the royal monastery itself.

WHERE TO STAY AND EAT

🛏 ✕ Hôtellerie du Couvent Royal: place Jean-Salusse. ☎ 04-94-86-55-66. Fax: 04-94-59-82-82. Website: www.hotelcouventsmaximin.com. Restaurant closed on Sunday evening and all day Monday. Double room with shower and toilet, or bathroom, and TV, from 290F to 480F. *Formule* menu at 95F, market menu at 125F (weekday lunchtime), and others from 185F to 235F. Actually inside the Couvent Royal, this hotel's location is unbeatable. The welcome is professional and the atmosphere is rather formal. There are 30 rooms in the former monks' cells, with their arches and exposed old stones; they are charming rather than austere. The restaurant is in the old chapterhouse and the Provençal cooking is prepared with flair and originality by a chef trained at the best eateries in the area.

WHAT TO SEE

– **Basilique Royale** (royal basilica): open every day 8am–noon and 2–6pm. Built in 1279 by Charles II, count of Provence and king of Sicily (hence the 'royal' in the name), this is the region's finest example of Gothic architecture. Work began in 1296 and dragged on until 1532, but the basilica was still never completed – one facade has no portal or rose window and there is no bell-tower. The interior, however, is very accomplished, with a large nave that is richly furnished – normal for a royal building, but less acceptable, perhaps, for a Dominican order. The superb 18th-century organs are played at free concerts on the first Sunday of every month at 5pm. The wooden pulpits have delicate and intricate carvings. The interesting works of art include a lovely *Descent from the Cross* of the 15th-century Provence School and the splendid wooden retable by François Ronzen (1520) with 22 panels, including the first depiction of the Papal Palace in Avignon.

The **crypt** was constructed in the fourth century and houses four sarcophagi, including the one said to contain the remains of Mary Magdalene. It has been touched by generations of pilgrims. A gilded bronze reliquary holds the death mask of the saint and a glass phial contains the famous strip of flesh. The sarcophagus of St Maximin is adorned with dolphins and mythological creatures.

– **Couvent Royal** (royal monastery): open every day from 9.30am to 6pm. Building work on the monastery began at about the same time as the basilica but the last touches were added only in the mid-19th century. This religious complex housed around 100 monks and has had a colourful history. It was abandoned by the Dominicans on several occasions (finally in 1957), and transformed into a fortress and then a prison during the Revolution. The buildings are impressive and there's an attractive cloister with 30 arcades surrounding a garden. The town hall is in the old hospice, and facilities include a hotel-restaurant (*see above*), a wine bar and a shop selling local Var wines.

– **Medieval district**: to the south of the basilica there are a few very old and beautiful streets, including **rue Colbert** with its arcaded houses from the 13th and 14th centuries, and sculpted doorways. The street leads into the Jewish quarter. At one time, there was a surprising level of tolerance in this devoutly Catholic area, although from the 14th century Jews were used as scapegoats during epidemics of the plague.

ROUGIERS

Just off the N560, between St-Zacharie and Brignoles, this sleepy village has a long main street lined with attractive historic houses. The impressive remains of a chateau and of a fortified medieval village can be seen on a nearby hill. The route is signposted from Rougiers, and the site is reached after a 45-minute walk from the car park.

NANS-LES-PINS

This village, with its medieval castle ruins and its square lined by shady plane trees, is typically Provençal. It's the departure point for several interesting walks into the Massif de la Ste-Baume. The **Chemin des Roys** (royal path) (a walk of 2 hours 30 minutes) has been the traditional pilgrim route to Ste-Baume since the 14th century. The **Chemin de la Glace** (ice path) is so called since ice produced in the glaciers in the 19th century was taken along this route to Marseille or to Aix-en-Provence. Detailed route maps are sold at the tourist office.

USEFUL ADDRESS

🛈 Tourist office: 2 cours du Général-de-Gaulle. ☎ 04-94-78-95-91. Fax: 04-94-78-60-07. Open every day (except Sunday afternoon) 9am–noon and 2–5pm (3–6pm from 1 July to 30 September).

WHERE TO STAY

🛏 Camping municipal la Petite Colle: route de la Ste-Baume. ☎ and fax: 04-94-78-65-98. 5 kilometres (3 miles) from the village on the route de Plan d'Aups. Open all year. Pitch for two with vehicle for 70F. This small site in the woods is ideal for walkers and nature lovers.

PLAN-D'AUPS-STE-BAUME

This little village at an altitude of 700 metres (2,300 feet) has a wonderful natural environment, at the foot of the cliffs of the Ste-Baume *massif*. Near by is the renowned cave of Mary Magdalene.

USEFUL ADDRESS

🛈 Tourist office: place de la Mairie (town hall square). ☎ 04-42-62-57-57.

WHERE TO STAY AND EAT

🛏 ✕ Lou Pèbre d'Aï: in the Ste-Madeleine district, 83640 Plan d'Aups. ☎ 04-42-04-50-42. Fax: 04-42-62-55-52. ✗ Closed on Tuesday evening and on Wednesday out of season, as well as from 2 to 21 January and during February school holidays. Double rooms with shower and toilet from 280F to 310F and with bathroom from 340F to 390F. Menus from 110F to 250F. Half-board compulsory in July and August, 290F per person. Relaxing, comfortable rooms, excellent food served in a huge old-fashioned dining room, and there is a swimming pool for hot afternoons. The food combines traditional and contemporary styles.

🛏 ✕ Hôtellerie de la Ste-Baume: 83640 Plan d'Aups. On the D95, a few kilometres from Plan d'Aups. ☎ 04-42-04-54-84. Fax: 04-42-62-55-56. Open all year. Beds at 50F per person per night in one- to six-bed dorms or a room for four (or more). Double rooms 70F per person per night, single rooms 120F. Meals for 70F. At the foot of the *massif*, at the start of the GR9 footpath, this was formerly an 18th-century hostelry for Benedictine nuns. There's also a *gîte* for groups of seven or more, with cooking facilities.

WHAT TO SEE

★ **Ste-Baume Grotto**: this cave on the cliff, at 950 metres (3,115 feet), is the place where Mary Magdalene is said to have lived, in deep solitude and damp conditions, for 30 years. As a pilgrimage site, it has been visited by no less than 8 popes and 18 sovereigns since the Middle Ages. The cave itself has been closed to visitors since 1998 because of the risk of falling stones, but the 45-minute walk up to it (GR9 red and white waymarkings) is lovely, following the ancient Chemin des Roys. It crosses one of the most beautiful forests in France – 120 sacred hectares (300 acres) of untouched white oaks, beech trees and maples. Energetic walkers can climb on up to the clifftop Chapelle du St-Pilon, for a wonderful view that stretches from the Îles d'Hyères to the summit of Les Écrins.

★ **Écomuséee Ste-Baume**: opposite the hostel. ☎ 04-42-62-56-46. Open every day from 15 April to 30 October, 9am–noon and 2–6pm. During the rest of the year, open every day 2–5pm. Entrance fee: 20F (free for under-14s). This small museum traces the history of pilgrimage and the traditional crafts and industries of the region. There's a recreation of a charcoal burner's hut, an interesting section on working with wool, and videos on the *massif* and on Provençal culture.

To the right of the road leading from the Hôtellerie de la Ste-Baume to Plan d'Aups is an abandoned building, with gaping windows and walls covered in graffiti. It is in fact the work of the architect Le Corbusier, a garage-studio built for Édouard Trouin, whose plan was to dig out a basilica under the *massif*. Le Corbusier was to execute it. This slightly mad project was supported by Picasso, Léger, Matisse and many other key figures in modern art, but was never realized.

MAZAUGUES

This little hilltop village is reached via the pretty and tranquil D95 that hugs the *massif*. A forest road on the right, 10 kilometres (6 miles) before Mazauges, leads to the Glacière de Pivaut (5-minute walk), an impressive stone tower 20 metres (65 feet) in diameter, with thick walls and a tile and earth roof. This 'ice box' was built to hold up to 6,000 tonnes of ice, but was never used. (*See below* for the Musée de la Glace, Mazauges.)

USEFUL ADDRESS

🄱 **Tourist information**: in the town hall. ☎ 04-94-86-95-03.

WHAT TO SEE

★ **Musée de la Glace** (ice museum): ☎ 04-94-86-39-24. Between 1 June to 30 September open every day (except Monday) 9am–noon and 2–6pm. During the rest of the year, open on Sunday 9am–noon and 2–5pm. Entrance fee: 10F (free for under-6s). This unusual museum traces the story of the important commodity of ice, including the construction of huge ice boxes in Provence's hills (17 in the Mazauges district alone, used from 1650 to the early 20th century). The ice was made in layers in the winter and then conserved in vast stone reservoirs. In the summer, it was cut into 'loaves' and transported at night to Toulon or Marseille, to preserve fish or to refresh glasses of coconut milk (the fashionable drink of the 19th century). The process was threatened by the development of the railway, which meant that ice could be brought from much further afield; the invention of the refrigerator was the final nail in the coffin.

From Brignoles to Haut-Var

LE VAL

This charming and lively place has fountains everywhere, an open-air theatre, a belfry and a pleasant atmosphere. In the first week of September, the locals celebrate the **Foire à la Saucisse** (sausage festival), with huge country banquets and a profusion of all things porky. Outside the tourist season, Le Val is a very Provençal village. In December, Christmas traditions are still observed, with exhibitions, midnight Masses and Provençal pastorals. During the season of goodwill, the *santons* workshop is busy making terracotta nativity figurines. There are also several toy museums to visit.

CABASSE

This sleepy little village has narrow streets overlooking the valley, a pretty foaming fountain and a 16th-century church. If you want to see the gilded wooden retable, ask for the key to the church at the *tabac* on the square.

ENTRECASTEAUX

Entrecasteaux is a delightful little medieval village with an intriguing chateau. Wander around its picturesque streets until you come across the 14th-century fortified church, which has an unusual feature – an apse that is lower and narrower than the nave.

WHERE TO EAT

✘ **Lou Picateou**: place du Souvenir. ☎ 04-94-04-47-97. Closed from 15 January to 15 February, and on Thursday except in July and August. Menus at 78F (weekday lunch) and from 98F to 145F. At the foot of the majestic chateau, this restaurant has a tranquil and shady terrace and serves Provençal cuisine. The chef trained at the Epcot Center in the USA.

✘ **La Fourchette**: Le Courtil. Next to the church. ☎ 04-94-04-42-78.

Closed on Sunday evening and on Monday, as well as from December to March. Menus at 90F (lunch), 125F and 165F. In the shadow of the famous chateau, this house is the perfect destination for gastronomic travellers, who will delight in both the food and the view. The *patronne* is an ex-pat from Los Angeles. The prices are reasonable, the quality of the food excellent and the simplicity of the menu appealing.

WHAT TO SEE

★ **Château**: ☎ 04-94-04-43-95. Guided tours every day 4–5pm. Entrance: 30F (children 20F). The chateau at Entrecasteaux is the largest on the Côte d'Azur (although the coast seems far away here). Originally a fortified castle, it became a residence in the 16th century. Following fire, renovation and extension, it's now open to visitors, thanks to its new owner. Like many castles, it has a secret history of crime and intrigue. In 1713, one inhabitant wanted to dispose of his wife in order to avail himself of another. The victim escaped death after slipping down the stairs on carefully positioned cherry stones. She then survived an attempted poisoning but finally succumbed to three razor cuts. The lovely gardens were designed by Le Nôtre; they are best viewed from the terraces.

COTIGNAC

Cotignac is a dream village, with an appealing way of life. Its name comes from the word *coing* (quince), and it was here that the first quince jellies were made. Jars with Cotignac labels even feature in *Marriage at Cana* by 16th-century painter Veronese!

The village has the same sort of shining beauty as its famous fruit. It sits at the bottom of a valley that is cut off by a huge cliff of tufa rock. The cliff is dotted with caves and adorned by a waterfalll, and at the top stand the ruins of a 15th-century castle. For a long time Cotignac was quite isolated (the road wasn't built until the 19th century), and it was the first parish in France to be supplied with electricity generated entirely by its own waterfall.

This little paradise has a main street lined by plane trees. Hollywood actor Robin Williams is one visitor who appreciates its charms; he comes here regularly to stay with friends.

USEFUL ADDRESS

🚩 **Tourist office**: rue Bonaventure. ☎ 04-94-04-61-87. Open in summer Tuesday to Saturday 10am–noon and 3–7pm (5pm in low season).

WHERE TO STAY AND EAT

Campsite

🏕 **Camping Les Pouverels**: route de Sillans. 1 kilometre from the village on the D22. ☎ 04-94-04-71-91. Open from March to October. 42 pitches in a tranquil and natural setting.

☆☆ Moderate

🛏 ✕ **Chambres d'hôte du Domaine de Nestuby** (B&B): Domaine de Nestuby. Take the D22 towards Brignoles. After 4 kilometres (2.5 miles), take the unsurfaced road on the right. ☎ 04-94-04-60-02. Fax: 04-94-04-79-22. Closed from 15 November to end February. Double rooms with shower and toilet, or bathroom, cost 350F. Dinner (not served on Sunday evening) for 110F. Wine lovers have been welcomed at this wonderful home, nestling among the owners' vines, for many years. It's a delightful place to stay, and the hosts are experts not only in wine, but also in welcoming guests and preparing delicious food. The four rooms are all decorated in pastel colours and one has a wrought-iron bed. The cuisine is Provençal in style, and a few bottles of local red, rosé or white make a great souvenir. Bank cards not accepted.

☆☆☆ Chic

✕ **Le Clos des Vignes** (B&B): route de Montfort, opposite the Do-maine de Nestuby. ☎ 04-94-04-72-19. From 1 October to 1 July, closed Sunday evening and on Monday. From 1 July to 1 October, closed for lunch from Monday to Wednes-day. Menus at 145F, 165F and 185F. Good food served on a styl-ish, sheltered veranda, a regularly changing menu (according to what's fresh at the market), and a warm welcome.

WHAT TO SEE

★ **La Roche** (the rock): 80 metres (260 feet) high and 400 metres (1,310 feet) in length, the rock is punctured with caves that served for many years as a place of refuge. Some have stairs and windows, and have been used by generations of soldiers as look-outs.

★ **Old quarter**: the old part of Cotignac has lovely 16th- and 17th-century facades and, on place de la Mairie, one of the most beautiful campaniles in the Var region (1496), and the house of the Prince de Condé. Start your walk from this square and head for the synagogue on the place de la Liberté. The oldest houses of the village, dating back to the Middle Ages, are in the rue Clastre and include a presbytery, a post office and a hospice. As you walk along the Grande-Rue, look up to appreciate three magnificent 17th-century caryatids, erected by middle-class inhabitants to indicate their social status.

★ **Église St-Pierre**: the 13th-century nave in this church is pure Roman-esque, and the beautiful high altar dates from the 16th century. The 19th-century organ is famous for its tone.

★ **Notre-Dame-de-la-Grâce**: this religious complex stands on Mont Verdaille, at the entrance to the village. The sanctuary and chapel, currently occupied by the fathers of the community of St Jean, are worth visiting. This was the site of an apparition in the 16th century, and Notre-Dame-de-la-Grâce is also credited with having provided Louis XIII with an heir. After a revelation, a Parisian deacon advised Anne of Austria to carry out three novenas, one in Cotignac, and the Queen subsequently gave birth to Louis XIV. In 1660, Louis XIV stopped at Notre-Dame-de-la-Grâce on his way to join Maria Theresa of Austria in St-Jean-de-Luz, on the east coast, where they were to marry.

– The family of friendly local character **Gabriel-Henri Blanc** has lived in Cotignac for centuries. If your French is good enough, look him up – he can often be found at the museum-gallery at 3 rue d'Arcole. For the last 30 years he has been transcribing the history of Cotignac and the surrounding area into handwritten books and he now knows more about the town than anyone.

WHAT TO SEE IN THE AREA

★ **Monastère la Font-St-Joseph-du-Bessillon** (monastery): 3 kilometres (2 miles) from Cotignac towards Barjols, at the end of 2 kilometres of dirt track. The monastery of St-Joseph stands in a magnificent location. Inside, 16 nuns sing the service in Gregorian chant to a non-existent congregation. This extraordinary spectacle commands respectful silence from the few who witness it.

The monastery of St-Joseph-du-Bessillon played an important role in the religious life of Provence. It commemorated the saint's appearance on 7 June 1660 to a thirsty shepherd; St Joseph saved the dying man by making a spring (the *font* of the name of the monastery) gush from the ground. The monastery was abandoned after the French Revolution and only rescued from ruin by the Benedictine nuns of Medea, on their return from Algeria. They found the convent in a terrible state, and set about restoring and rebuilding it with the help of architect Fernand Pouillon. After 15 years, 17 cells are now inhabitable and half of the cloister has been finished, and once again the nuns are able to devote themselves to a spiritual existence here. There are 15 cells left to complete, but the nuns now have to rely on occasional gifts of money.

Visitors may attend Mass (every day at 11am) or vespers (at 5pm) celebrated in Latin and sung in Gregorian chant.

BARJOLS

Every year, Barjols' traditional and spectacular **Fête de la St-Marcel** (Festival of St Marcel), held on 17 January, celebrates the arrival in the village of its patron saint. There's dancing in the church during Mass, and an ox is led in a procession through the village. Every four years, there's an ox roast on a public square, shared by all the villagers (next in 2004).

Visit the studio of Marius Fabre, who makes traditional Provençal musical instruments, in the company of several other artisans and craftsmen. The collegiate church is also worth a visit. A walking trail takes you past fountains and public washing places of Barjols, where water has always played an important role.

– The **Maison Régionale de l'Eau**, in the former village hospice (☎ 04-94-77-15-83) has thematic exhibitions on all aspects of water in the region and an aquarium with fish and other creatures from the local rivers. Entrance is free.

WHERE TO STAY AND EAT IN THE AREA

â **Chambres d'hôte Domaine St-Christophe** (B&B): chemin Mareliers. At the exit from Barjols, on the D35 between Brue-Auriac and Varages. ☎ 04-94-77-03-23. Fax: 04-94-77-16-32. Closed from 10 October to Easter. Three lovely double rooms with shower and toilet between 260F and 280F, including breakfast. Large country *bastide* surrounded by vines and olive trees, with a mesmerizing view over the Haut Var countryside. Dinner is not provided, but there are kitchen facilities and you can buy fresh farm produce. Bank cards not accepted.

▲ **Auberge du Montagnier**: chemin du Vieux Village, 83560 St-Julien. 25 kilometres (about 16 miles) northeast of Barjols on the D554 and then the D35. ☎ 04-94-80-06-29. Closed on Monday evening and on Tuesday (except in July and August). Open on Sunday evening by appointment only. Phone ahead in winter. Double rooms with shower and toilet for 250F. Menus at 68F (weekday lunch), 100F and 160F. In the pretty village of St-Julien, the houses jostle together between the remains of the village ramparts and its attractive Romanesque church. This *auberge* has just three rooms, all spacious, sunny and spotlessly clean. The young chef prepares tasty Provençal food from market-fresh ingredients, at very reasonable prices. Worth making the climb.

▲ ✕ **Le Rouge-Gorge**: in the district of Les Costes, 83670 Pontevès. On the D560, between Barjols and Salernes, drive over the bridge and up to Pontevès. ☎ 04-94-77-03-97. Fax: 04-94-77-22-17. ✿ to the restaurant. Closed from 15 November to 15 March. Double rooms with shower and toilet, or bathroom, from 305F to 345F. Half board compulsory in July and August, from 287F to 307F. Menus from 98F to 150F. The attractive village of Pontevès has a rather uninspiring chateau but the atmospheric Rouge-Gorge is much more interesting. The rooms are simple and comfortable, and the menu features local food, using delicious lamb, duck and fresh fish. Everyone eats around the swimming pool in the evening. There are many walks in the area. A delightful place to stay, with friendly owners.

▲ **Chambres d'hôte Domaine de St-Ferréols** (B&B): turn left off the D560, just after the sign announcing Pontevès. ☎ 04-94-77-10-42. Fax: 04-94-77-19-04. Closed from 15 November to 15 March. Double rooms with shower and toilet, or bathroom, from 300F to 350F, including breakfast. Suite for four people for 480F. Simple rooms in a magnificent 18th-century farmhouse, surrounded by vines. The atmosphere is pleasant and there's a lovely swimming pool.

WHAT TO SEE IN THE AREA

★ **Source of the Argens river**: on the D560, before you reach Seillons, along a smaller road, before the St-Estève estate. The source of the river is surrounded by marshy land, and there's also an old olive mill.

LE VALLON SOURN

The name means 'small dark valley' in Provençal dialect. From Barjols, take the Chateauvert road, follow the Argens river and cross the Bagarède gorges. Immediately after, the sinuous gorges of the Vallon Sourn and their jagged rockfaces extend for 5 kilometres (3 miles) as far as Correns. At the entrance to the valley, on the Chemin des Baumes, there are caves and the remains of troglodyte dwellings. Lovely Renaissance houses line the streets of the old village and canoeists and climbers are often seen on and around the river.

Continue on to **Montfort**, a pretty village on the Argens river that used to belong to the Knights Templar.

WHERE TO EAT

✕ **Le Relais des Templiers**: place Gabriel-Péri, 83570 Montfort-sur-Argens. ☎ 04-94-59-55-06. Fax: 04-94-59-58-76. Closed on Tuesday. Double rooms with bathroom cost 200F, excluding breakfast. One menu, between 80F and 120F. This pleasant spot has a vaulted dining room, where the owner serves fresh local produce – cheese or truffle soufflé, terrines or rabbit stew – in lovely terracotta dishes. There are also two rooms.

The Haut Var

FOX-AMPHOUX (83670)　　　Population: 380

This old hilltop village 10 kilometres (6 miles) from Cotignac is perched at an altitude of 515 metres (1,675 feet). Formerly a Roman camp, it was the final staging post of the Knights Templar. It has a 12th-century Romanesque church.

WHERE TO STAY AND EAT

🛏 ✕ **L'Auberge du Vieux Fox**: place de l'église. In the old village ☎ 04-94-80-71-69. Fax: 04-94-80-78-38. ⚘ Open all year. Double rooms with shower and toilet from 390F or with bathroom from 440F to 550F. Menus from 100F to 250F. This historic *auberge* is housed in the former priory of the Romanesque church. Some parts date back to the 11th century. There's also free entrance to a private club with swimming and tennis facilities.

SILLANS-LA-CASCADE (83690)　　Population: 480

This pretty village is typical of the Haut Var region, with around 400 inhabitants, a few ducks and numerous fountains. Totally unrestored, it has retained its authenticity and several of its houses have remained untouched since the departure of their last tenants. This is rural life at its most basic – piles of all sorts of bits and pieces stand in front of some of the houses, and the baker still bakes bread in a wood-fired oven.

On the road between Marseille and Draguignan, you can see the remains of the ramparts of the chateau, some sections of which are almost intact. There's also a little museum with exhibits of old tools, minerals and gems found locally.

It's a delightful walk of about 1 kilometre to the fabulous **Cascade de la Bresque** (waterfall), which is more than 40 metres (about 130 feet) high. Note: there have been some thefts from cars left in the car park.

WHERE TO STAY AND EAT

⚓ ✖ **Hôtel-restaurant Les Pins** (with Luc et Gertrud): in the main street. ☎ 04-94-04-63-26. Fax: 04-94-04-72-71. ✗ Closed on Wednesday evening and all day Thursday, and from mid-January to mid-February. Double rooms with shower and toilet, or bathroom (and TV) from 240F to 280F. Menus between 85F and 210F. This pleasant and reasonably priced hotel is understandably popular. The rustic dining room has a large fireplace and menus with tasty dishes, including the famous *pot-au-feu des mers au pistou* (seafood stew with pesto sauce). Game dishes are available in season, and on sunny days you can eat on the terrace. It's advisable to book a month in advance in summer.

⚓ ✖ **Gîte d'Étape Le Relais de la Bresque**: 15 chemin de la Piscine, 2 kilometres from the village, towards Aups. ☎ 04-94-04-64-89. Closed in January. Comfortable groups-only accommodation at 55F per night. Meals at 65F. For individuals, half board is compulsory, at 155F per person per day. There are two 14-bed dormitories and a swimming pool. In summer there's a pizzeria-grill on the terrace. Booking ahead is advisable.

VILLECROZE (83690)   Population 1,100

Less extensively restored than its neighbour Tourtour, Villecroze has managed to preserve a lively and more traditional atmosphere. Its pretty arcaded streets and the keep of its feudal castle give the place a medieval feel. Walk under the clock tower and follow the picturesque **rue de France**, with its series of arcades and vaults.

The cliffside here is punctured with caves (hence the name of the place, from *ville creuse*, or 'hollowed-out town'). In the 16th century, local lords made dwellings of these caves. Today, the **Grottes Troglodytes** are open to visitors between 9am and noon, and 2–7pm.

WHERE TO STAY AND EAT

⚓ ✖ **Auberge des Lavandes**: place du Général-de-Gaulle. ☎ 04-94-70-76-00. Fax: 04-94-67-56-45. Closed on Tuesday evening, and on Wednesday in low season, as well as from January to March. Double rooms with shower for 280F and with bathroom for 310F. Menus from 90F to 180F. This small but very pleasant house has lovely rooms, with attractive decor and touches of lavender, and an excellent restaurant. Regulars return again and again for the delicious food, which includes *daube à la provençale à l'ancienne* (traditional beef stew) and *coquilles St-Jacques provençale* (scallops).

⚓ ✖ **Au Bien-être**: in the district of Les Cadenières. 3.5 kilometres (2 miles) south of Villecroze, signposted from the D557 (the road for Draguignan). ☎ 04-94-70-67-57. ✗ Closed on Sunday evening and on Monday in low season, as well as during school holidays (except in July and August), and from November to February. Double rooms with shower and toilet from 265F to 345F, and with bathroom from 275F to 365F. Daily special (with a

THE HINTERLAND OF THE VAR REGION

glass of wine or coffee) for 89F, and set menus from 109F to 225F. This large house is set in the countryside at the end of a road leading nowhere in particular. It has a stylish terrace and clean, pretty rooms decorated in pastel tones. The restaurant has a good reputation locally.

BUYING WINE

⌷ Le Château Thuerry: ☎ 04-94-70-63-02. Open all year, this chateau is a good place to buy excellent red wine at reasonable prices. Friendly and helpful staff arrange guided tours and tastings.

TOURTOUR (83690)   **Population: 480**

Pretty Tourtour has been totally restored and is popular with tourists, and consequently is quite expensive. It may lack soul but it does have fine views of the Montagne Ste-Victoire, so often painted by Cézanne. The road leading to the village crosses wide barren hillsides, denuded of trees in recent years by terrible forest fires. There are a few Renaissance-style houses with carved facades and an old chateau. An 11th-century church stands a little apart from the village, providing a superb panorama that reaches as far as the Maures mountains on a clear day.

WHERE TO STAY AND EAT

☆☆ Moderate

⛺ Chambres d'hôte Le Mas de l'Acacia (B&B): route d'Aups. 300 metres from the village centre, at the western entrance to Tourtour. ☎ 04-94-70-53-84. ⚒ Double rooms with shower and toilet, or bathroom (and TV) from 300F to 320F, including breakfast. Four-bed suite for 650F. This attractive Provençal complex comprises several buildings around a lovely pool.

⛺ ✕ La Petite Auberge: 1.5 kilometres from the village, below the little church on the hill (signposted). ☎ 04-94-70-57-16. Fax: 04-94-70-54-52. Closed for lunch on Monday and Thursday, and from 15 November to 15 December. Double rooms with shower and toilet, or bathroom, from 450F (for a standard room in low season) to 810F (for a room with balcony in high season). Menus at 180F and 350F (one entirely truffle-based). Meals are served in a lovely rustic dining room. There's a wonderful view over the countryside, a swimming pool and classes in Provençal cooking can be arranged.

⛺ ✕ Le Mas des Collines: Camp-Fournier. 2 kilometres from Tourtour, on the road for Villecroze. ☎ 04-94-70-59-30. Fax: 04-94-70-57-62. Closed for lunch on Tuesday, except on public holidays. Rooms for two for 540F, including breakfast. Half board is 790F for two (may be obligatory in high season). Menus at 120F, 149F and 164F. This farmhouse, overlooking the valley and facing away from the village of Tourtour, is a lovely place to relax for a few days. The rooms are stylish and freshly decorated, the owners extend a warm welcome and there's also a swimming pool and a sun terrace. The menus offer generous portions of simple and tasty dishes.

AUPS (83630)   Population: 1,930

Aups is a large market town set among undulating wooded hills on the edge of the plateau. Stroll through its narrow medieval streets, particularly the picturesque rue des Aires. To the north of the village you'll find an interesting clock tower and campanile, a sun dial, the remains of the ramparts and the town gateway. Aups has changed little since the early 1900s. The Saracen tower and old washing place can still be seen, together with the 15th-century St-Pancrace collegiate church with its well-restored Renaissance doorway and its inscription reminding onlookers that all churches are the property of the state. Also worth a visit is the Musée Simon Segal, housed in a former Ursuline convent.

WHERE TO STAY AND EAT

Campsites

☎ ✕ **Camping Les Prés**: route de Tourtour. 500 metres from the village. ☎ 04-94-70-00-93. Fax: 04-94-70-14-41. ☒ Open all year. This small site is a quiet spot with a warm welcome, a restaurant and a food shop. Swimming and tennis facilities nearby.

☎ **International Camping**: route de Fox-Amphoux. 500 metres from the village. ☎ 04-94-70-06-80. Fax : 04-94-70-10-51. Open from April to end September. This site has its own swimming pool.

☎ There's a third **campsite** 2 kilometres away, towards Moustiers.

☆☆ Moderate

☎ **L'Escale du Verdon**: route de Sillans. ☎ 04-94-84-00-04. Fax: 04-94-84-00-05. ☒ A studio with shower and toilet or bathrooom plus kitchen facilities will cost you 290F. A good place for peace and quiet, with a chance to relax and soak up the sun by the swimming pool. Good value for money.

☆☆☆ Chic

✕ **L'Aiguière**: place du Maréchal-Joffre. ☎ 04-94-70-12-40. ☒ Closed on Wednesday in low season and during November. Menus at 100F (lunch) and from 135F to 215F. This restaurant stands on a delightful square, between the old washing place and the Saracen tower. There's a terrace for sunny days.

There are a number of restaurants nearby. All are different, but the colours and flavours are all decidedly Mediterranean.

THE HINTERLAND OF THE VAR REGION

THE VERDON GORGES

For general information on the Gorges du Verdon, a map and details on visiting the northern side, Moustiers-Ste-Marie and the highlights of the Corniche Sublime, *see* page 397. For walking on the Var side of the gorges, consider buying the guide to the GR99 footpath, *Collines du Haut-Var de Toulon aux Gorges du Verdon*.

The Southern Gorges

The relatively new roads along the gorges provide spectacular views of the landscape. One of the best routes is via the Lac de Ste-Croix to the D71, heading south, and then joining the D90 to Trigance. On any route in the Verdon, you'll come across hilltop villages, Gallo–Roman ruins and churches steeped in history. This is an area where traditions and customs date back hundreds of years.

LES SALLES-SUR-VERDON

The area around the enormous Lac de Ste-Croix with its azure-blue water is very attractive, although Les Salles itself has the look and feel of a new town. It does actually only date back to 1974 and is a replica of its predecessor, which disappeared under the waters of the lake. It may not be historic, but it makes a delightful holiday resort.

WHERE TO STAY AND EAT

🛏 ✕ **Auberge des Salles**: 18 rue Ste-Catherine. ☎ 04-94-70-20-04. Fax: 04-94-70-21-78. ⚒ Situated at the end of the village, overlooking the lake, this inn is closed from November to March. Double rooms with shower and toilet, or bathroom, from 270F to 390F, depending on season. Menus from 95f to 195F. The Anot family has run an establishment here for five generations – the original house is now under water. The new hotel has the same spirit, with a warm and friendly welcome. The rooms are comfortable and well furnished, and some have a terrace overlooking the lake. The excellent menu features traditional dishes including *cuisses de grenouille* (frog's legs) and *carré d'agneau au miel et au thym* (lamb in honey and thyme).

WHERE TO STAY AND EAT IN THE AREA

🛏 ✕ **L'Auberge du Lac**: rue Grande, 83630 Bauduen. ☎ 04-94-70-08-04 or 04-94-84-39-41. Fax: 04-94-84-39-41. Closed on Wednesday out of season and from 15 November to 15 March. Double rooms with bathroom for 380F. Half board compulsory from early June to end September, 370F per person. Menus from 120F to 220F. This rustic, cosy and friendly house at the heart of the village, on the shores of the lake itself, has a nostalgic feel. The owners are experts at pampering guests. The rooms are attractive and comfortable, particularly those overlooking the deep blue waters of the lake. There's a lovely vine-covered terrace for summer dining, and a dining room for winter guests. The game, fish and homemade cold meats, and local wines, taste equally good in both venues.

WHAT TO SEE

★ **Maison du Lac**: in the tourist office. ☎ 04-94-70-21-84. Open every day in July and August. Limited opening in low season. Explains the history of the village, with a model of the dam and the hydro-electric power station.

AIGUINES

Aiguines stands at 800 metres (2,600 feet) protecting the entry to the gorges. From its magnificent position above the lake, it commands superb views.

The village has been here for almost 1,000 years, clinging to the Montagne de Margès (1,580 metres/5,180 feet). Woodturners have worked the wood of the nearby box-tree forests since the 16th century. The profession has now died out, but in the past a number of factories were built to support the demand for the trade. The village today has 221 inhabitants and is crowned by a beautifully restored 17th-century chateau, with a glazed-tile roof and pepper-pot towers. There's also a parish church, built in 1639.

Aiguines is part mountain and part lakeside resort, with a unique and very special charm. Strolling though its old streets, past houses with pretty terraces and stairways, is rather like walking through a living museum.

USEFUL ADDRESS

⏏ Point d'accueil Verdon (information centre for the Verdon): ☎ 04-94-70-21-64. Fax: 04-94-84-23-59. Open in winter Monday to Friday 10am–noon and 3–5pm; in summer Monday to Saturday 9.30am–noon and 2–5pm. Maps and information on every aspect of the area, including walking routes and advice on accommodation.

WHERE TO STAY AND EAT

⌂ ✕ Auberge-relais Altitude 823: in the village. ☎ and fax: 04-94-70-21-09. Closed on Friday in low season and from All Saints to Palm Sunday. Double rooms with shower and toilet for 320F. Half board compulsory from mid-June to mid-September and at the weekend, from 300F to 330F per person. Menus at 95F to 130F. The dining room is rustic in style and the chef's specialities include *gigot d'agneau aux herbes* (leg of mutton with local herbs). This is a pleasant and unpretentious place to stay.

⌂ ✕ Hôtel du Grand Canyon, Restaurant Les Cavaliers: Falaise des Cavaliers, on the D71. ☎ 04-94-76-91-31. Fax: 04-94-76-92-29. Email: hotel-gd-canyon-verdon@ wanadoo.fr. ✕ Restaurant closed for lunch on Monday in low season, and from 15 October to 30 April. Double rooms with bathroom from 300F to 380F. Half board compulsory at the weekend and on public holidays and in high season, from 320F to 380F per person. Menus from 100F to 250F. From its eyrie-like location 300 metres above the Verdon river, this hotel has comfortable rooms and panoramic views of the gorges. The menu features *estoufade provençale* (meat stew marinated, fried and braised), *soupe au pistou* (vegetable soup with pesto sauce) and *civet de sanglier* (wild boar) in season. It's decent enough, but the view is definitely the highlight.

WHAT TO SEE

★ Musée des Tourneurs sur Bois (woodturning museum): ☎ 04-94-70-20-89. Open every day in summer (except Tuesday). Entrance fee: 10F (concessions 8F). Housed in a very old building in the village, this museum contains pieces turned from various woods in workshops in the 18th and 19th centuries. Snuff boxes, cup-and-ball games, household items are displayed alongside the *boules cloutées* (studded *boules*), for which the area is famous. Widely available in the area, boxwood has long been prized by turners for its fine grain; it is often used to make bowls. There's also a herbarium.

TRIGANCE

This pretty Provençal village is to the east of the Verdon gorges. Its 11th-century chateau has now become a chic hotel and expensive restaurant.

WHERE TO STAY AND EAT

♠ ✕ **Le Vieil Amandier**: montée de St-Roch. ☎ 04-94-76-92-92. Fax: 04-94-85-68-65. ✖ Closed on Wednesday and from December to end February. Double rooms with shower and toilet from 290F to 400F, and with bathroom from 350F to 420F. Half board compulsory in July and August. Menus from 120F to 260F. The architecture may not be very appealing, but this is certainly a pleasant place to stay, with stylish rooms and a swimming pool. The food is excellent and the menu full of variety, with a strong regional influence, including truffles in season.

WHERE TO STAY AND EAT IN THE AREA

♠ ✕ **Grand Hotel Bain**: rue de Praguillem, 83840 Comps-sur-Artuby. About 20 kilometres (13 miles) southeast of Trigance on the D90, and then to the right on to the D955. ☎ 04-94-76-90-06. Fax: 04-94-76-92-24. Closed from 12 November to 26 December. Double rooms with shower and toilet, or bathroom (and TV) from 275f to 295F. Menus from 82F to 198F. This house has been in the Bain family since 1737, and truffle hunters have been coming here for years to enjoy truffle pâté (made with local truffles), omelette with truffles and a selection of goats' cheeses, as well as *daube à la Provençale* (beef stew) or *carré d'agneau* (lamb). The rooms are nice too.

✕ **Le Moulin de Soleils**: Combes de Soleils, 83840 Trigance. 6 kilometres (4 miles) from Trigance and 12 kilometres (7 miles) from Castellane. ☎ 04-94-76-92-62. Fax: 04-94-76-81-89. Closed from 1 November to 1 April. À la carte around 90F. After visiting the last traditional working flourmill in Provence (only open at weekends out of season), make a trip to the baker's to buy your bread. The small restaurant next door, serving pizzas and pancakes made with flour from the mill, is, surprisingly, rather lacking in charm.

After Trigance, the D90 becomes the D955, coming from Comps. Head left to Pont-de-Soleils, where, on the left, you'll join the D952 from Castellane. This marks the end of the route along the southern side of the gorges.

BARGÈME (83840)   Population: 120

Take the D955 from Trigance to Comps-sur-Artuby, and then turn left on to the D21, taking the fork onto the D37, towards Bargème. The village marks the end of the *département*, and it's the highest community in the Var region, at 1,094 metres (3,600 feet). Its surrounding wall is punctuated by two 16th-century gates and dominated by the partially ruined but well-preserved Château des Pontevès. The village and the chateau have been restored, and make a great spot to explore. Guided tours are organized in high season at 4.30pm, 5.30pm and 6.30pm.

There's a panoramic view over the plateau of Canjuers, a military camp, and over the Préalpes, with carpets of lavender between. It is possible to walk through the nearby pine forests along the GR49 footpath, which starts here.

WHERE TO STAY AND EAT

🛏 ✕ **Chambres d'hôte Les Roses Trémières** (B&B): ☎ 04-94-84-20-86. Closed from end October to end March. Double rooms with shower and toilet for 320F, including breakfast. Dinner for 95F, including wine (book ahead). At the foot of the chateau, this establishment has five attractive rooms (non-smoking and no pets) and serves country cuisine that includes homemade soups, flans and pastries.

THE HINTERLAND OF
THE VAR REGION

The Coastline from St-Raphaël to Nice and The Hinterland

The Estérel Coast Road

The road that hugs the coastline from St-Raphaël to Cannes has a series of magnificent viewpoints, tempting secluded coves down below, perfect for swimming, and paths leading up to the clifftops through dense and untouched vegetation. The most striking features of the Estérel section of coast are its promontories, its deep ravines and its *roches rouges*, blood-red boulders that have detached themselves from the cliff-faces and tumbled towards the azure-blue sea.

There are many little seaside resorts along the route, where property developers sell holiday homes 'with unrestricted sea views'. The majority seem to have 'Pine', 'Olive tree' or 'Sun' in their name.

TRANSPORT

– **From St-Raphaël to Cannes**: a bus leaves every hour.

LE DRAMONT

A commemorative monument rises above the shoreline here, where the 36th American Division landed on 15 August 1944. The route of a one-hour waymarked walk starts at the little port.

AGAY

Set under impressive cliffs, this resort is famous for its blue porphyry, from which the Romans cut columns for their monuments. It has a perfect horseshoe-shaped bay with sand and pebble beaches and makes a good base for excursions into the Estérel.

USEFUL ADDRESS

🛈 Tourist office: place Giannetti. ☎ 04-94-82-01-85. Fax: 04-94-82-74-20. Email: agay.tourisme@wanadoo.fr

CAMPSITES

⛺ Camping Agay-Soleil: 1114 boulevard de la Plage, N98. ☎ 04-94-82-00-79. Open from 15 March to 10 November. At the water's edge. Booking advisable.

⛺ Les Rives de l'Agay: avenue du Gratadis. ☎ 04-94-82-02-74. Fax: 04-94-82-74-14. Closed from early November to 1 March. In low season, around 90F for two people.

This pleasant, shady site is on the banks of the river, 400 metres from the sea. Mosquitoes can be a problem. Booking advisable.

WALKS

– **Maison Forestière du Roussiveau**: the lovely three-hour return trip from the Maison Forestière du Roussiveau (forestry house) to the Baisse d'Andoulette (a mountain pass at 245 metres/804 feet) takes walkers into the heart of the Estérel. It is suitable for all levels of walkers. To get to the starting point, head towards St-Raphaël from the bay at Agay. After 4 kilometres (2.5 miles), take an immediate right turn towards the caravan park and park there if the gate is closed. It's a 30-minute walk from here, on a small sealed track through oak, eucalyptus and pine trees, to the Maison Forestière. From here, it's another hour's walk to the mountain pass.

Follow signs first for Le Perthus-Dissate, alongside the fence. At the end of the fence, leave the surfaced road and fork left at the embankment. Cross the smooth rock (take care here – it's slippery) and return to the path that cuts across to the left, through the *maquis* (scrubland), where you might see wild boar.

The path, wide at first, narrows as it climbs north of the Maison Forestière. Then you have to squeeze between bushes and shrubs as it skirts round the mountain on the western side, overlooking the Vallon de l'Apié and then a ravine that ends in a cul-de-sac, until it reaches the Roussiveau ridge at 282 metres (924 feet). Keep an eye on children here.

The route is marked with pebbles from here, on the other side of the mountain, and the view is now out to sea. Cross the plantation of young pine trees, then follow the yellow markings to the Andoulette pass. For the shortest return, go back down the way you came, or take the path to the right, after the pass, to descend via the north side. This route skirts round the Pic du Perthus to the southwest, before arriving back at the Maison Forestière.

– **Cap de Gramont**: from the bay at Agay, turn left into rue Robinson, following the signs for IGESA. Leave your car in the car park under the trees.

After the gate, ignore the path on the right marked 'Le Dramont – Belvédère de la Batterie' and climb the steps to the right near a low building. Follow the blue markings as the path zig-zags along the hillsides, through typically Mediterranean flora, looking down on some pretty inlets. Pass the Belvédère du Camp Long and then turn your back to the sea in order to climb a 30° path, where the vegetation becomes denser. Look for the natural rectangular 'window' in the big rock near by. The red porphyry of the rocks is in sharp contrast with the azure-blue of the sea.

At the intersection, the path to the right leads to the Sémaphore (signal station). It's a 15-minute walk, but this is a military zone and the building is not open to the public. Instead, head to the top, which peaks at an altitude of 136 metres (442 feet), for a superb view over Agay and the plage du Dramont in the distance.

Return to the intersection and take the surfaced path to the right until you reach the footpath that leads to the signal station (blue markings) and goes round the headland. Then take the easy, wide and flat path along the cliff, which is sheltered from the westerly winds and dotted with evidence of climbers. Skirt round the Pointe de l'Esquine de l'Ay to the south of Cap Dramont. At the junction, take the left-hand path to Port du Poussaï. To the right is the way back to plage du Camp Long. The path is lined with pine trees and cork oaks. At the bend, leave the surfaced path and turn left, and then left again, to return to the car park.

ANTHÉOR

The resort of Anthéor is dominated by the peaks of **Cap Roux**. Just before the Pointe de l'Observatoire, there's a stunning view to the left, over the ravine and the red rocks of **St-Barthélemy**, **Saint-Pilon** and **Cap Roux**. Turn left 5 kilometres (3 miles) after Anthéor and join the forest circuit to Cap Roux. The view over Anthéor and the gulf of La Napoule from the **Pointe de l'Observatoire** is wonderful. The coastline around here is very dramatic, with startling red jagged cliffs and a series of inlets.

⌂ Anthéor has two **campsites**.

LE TRAYAS

This is a pleasant resort with coves that are good for swimming, and guaranteed splendid views if you climb up high enough inland.

WALKS

– **Lac des Écureuils**: this loop circuit is quite strenuous. It should take about four hours and there is little shade.

From the train station at Le Trayas, cross the tracks and take the path to the left, on the same side as the mountain. In February the mimosa will be in flower. About 100 metres past the gate take the stony path to the right, following white and red markings, and then blue. The path snakes through the young pine trees, and there is a lovely view of the sea. Turn right at the pile of stones and the blue marker onto a very narrow but well-marked hillside path through scrubland. After about an hour of climbing, the path reaches the Col Notre-Dame, with its view of the summit of Les Petites Grues and, to the south, the antenna of the Pic de l'Ours, at 492 metres (1,613 feet).

At the Notre-Dame pass, cross the small road and follow the path opposite (GR51, red and white markings), which takes you, in about an hour, to the Lac des Écureuils. After the reservoir, cross three areas of scree and carry on to the Couche de l'Ane ravine. At the intersection, take the left-hand path to the lake, where you should see lots of migrating birds in spring and autumn.

Take the GR51 again along the south side of the lake and, after the concrete markers, walk through the corridor of eucalyptus trees. The Mal Infernet biological reserve is at the bottom of the ravine of the same name. The flat and wide path follows the meandering river, surrounded by a striking landscape of blood-red rock formations. The GR51 crosses the river via an iron bridge, past swimming holes in the rocks. At the junction, turn left towards the Col de l'Evêque (pass) on a slightly uphill path overlooking the ravine of Les Lentisques. Allow about an hour of steady climbing to get to the pass, the stony patch of ground before the hairpin turn.

At the car park, head down to the left towards Le Trayas until the second bend. Leave the road and follow signs for the Gare du Trayas (Le Trayas train station), past the base of the Pic d'Aurelle (322 metres/1,056 feet) to the left. There's a wonderful view over the Îles de Lérins and the Théoule bay, and a smell of rosemary. The mimosas mark your return to the station where you started.

– From the train station at Le Trayas, an alternative marked path (after the level crossing) leads to **Pic de l'Ours**. The walk takes about three hours, and offers a great view that stretches from the Maures to the Mercantour.

– Buses from Cannes to St-Raphaël stop at the Maubois inlet, from where you can take a three-hour walk on a marked path to the **Pic du Cap-Roux**.

MIRAMAR

Miramar is a well-to-do resort above La Figueirette bay. In a bend on the left, a path leads in five minutes to the Point de Vue de l'Esquillon, with its panoramic view over the sea, the Îles de Lérins and the Estérel.

WHERE TO STAY AND EAT

🛏 ✖ **Motel Le Patio**: 48 boulevard de Miramar. ☎ 04-93-75-00-23. Fax: 04-93-75-02-87. Closed from the beginning of November to Easter. Rooms from 200F to 400F in high season (with shower and toilet, or bathroom). Menu at 85F. À la carte around 120F. Despite being just off the main road, this motel isn't too noisy at night and has some rooms with sea views and a couple with terraces. There's a swimming pool, a half-sized tennis court and a pizzeria-style restaurant. Parking is free.

– Below the road you'll see the unusual housing development of **La Galère**, created by Jacques Couelle. The facades, in the rocks, look as if they have been sculpted by the sea. It's private, so a close-up view is not possible.

– The wonderful **view** from this point on the road extends over the bay of La Napoule, Cannes, the Îles de Lérins and Cap d'Antibes.

THÉOULE-SUR-MER

This pleasant resort has a main street lined with little villas and kitchen gardens brimming with wisteria. It's not far from Cannes, but is very different from its glamorous neighbour, with small beaches and a restored 18th-century soap factory. The seafront promenade to the right of the beach, with its little benches, is perfect for a romantic evening stroll.

– **Transport**: buses from Cannes or St-Raphaël every hour.

USEFUL ADDRESS

🛈 **Tourist office**: 1 boulevard de la Corniche-d'Or. ☎ 04-93-49-28-28. Fax: 04-93-49-00-04. Website: www.theoule-sur-mer.org. Open every day (except Sunday afternoon) in summer from 9am to 7pm; rest of the year, open Monday to Saturday from 9am to 6.30pm.

Lantosque	Places covered in guide
Bouyon	Addresses and places in the area
Castellane	Locator only

ITALY

le Boréon
Madone *Lac Vert* Valmasque
de Fenestre Casterino *Roya* **Tende**
D 94 *Mont* D 91 la Brigue
St-Martin-Vésubie *Sainte-Marie* Saint-Dalmas-
Venanson Berthemont- Granile de-Tende
Cayre les-Bains
Gros Roquebillière Saorge
Mont *l'Authion* Madone
urnairet *Forêt* 2,082m del Poggio
Lantosque D 70 6,830ft Sainte-Anne
Tour *de* **Col de Turini** Breil-
le Suquet *Turini* sur-Roya
telle Peïra-Cava
Madone Saint-Jean-
d'Utelle la-Rivière Lucéram **Sospel**
Lévens Coaraze
Berre-
lan- les-Alpes l'Escarène Ste-Agnès
u-Var Peille Castellar San Remo
Châteauneuf Contes Gorbio Grottes Grimaldi
Peillon Garavan
arros- A 8 **Menton**
Village **Roquebrune** **Cap Martin**
la Turbie Monte Carlo
int- Cimiez **Eze** **Monaco**
rent- Cap-d'Ail
-Var Beaulieu-sur-Mer
Villefranche-sur-Mer
Nice Saint-Jean-Cap-Ferrat
Cap
Ferrat

d'Antibes
ourmigue,
er de Dante

MEDITERRANEAN

SEA

0 5 10 km
0 5 10 miles

WHERE TO STAY AND EAT

⚑ **Auberge de jeunesse** (youth hostel): Théoule-sur-Mer. Almost 2 kilometres from the SNCF train station up the hill towards Le Trayas (hard work with a rucksack). The last bus leaves from the station around 7pm. ☎ 04-93-75-40-23. Fax: 04-93-75-43-45. Closed in January. Dormitory bed 51F per night, breakfast extra. Book for a stay of more than three nights in summer. Youth hostel card required. Windsurfing lessons can be arranged and camping is also possible. This hostel stands in a wonderful position, with a view over the sea and the Estérel, but it is rather difficult to get to. In the summer it's a sociable place, full of young people.

✗ **Marco Polo Plage**: route de Lérins, halfway along the beach.

☎ 04-93-49-96-59. Dishes from 90F, lunchtime salads at 60F. Dinner around 200F. For more than 50 years, the Marco Polo has been *the* place to eat in Théoule. At dusk, brightly coloured tables cover the beach pontoons and the water-ski jetty, all with a view of the lights of the bay of Nice. The genuinely friendly staff are energetic and efficient, and the menu features fish and seafood dishes, served in generous portions. The local wines are excellent and available in half-bottles. At the end of the evening there's often a singalong with songs from the sixties. In the daytime, the imaginative salads keep the beach crowd going. Booking is strongly recommended in high season.

WALK

– The arch at Pointe de l'Aiguille: this pleasant litte walk leaves from the Promenade Pradayol, at the bottom of the car park in Théoule centre, by the beaches. The route follows the sea along the eastern side of L'Aiguille ('the needle'). The cliffs are sheer, so there's no choice but to stay on the marked paths.

Alongside the path, there's a spring, with lovely ferns and rushes. At the plage de l'Aiguille, climb the concrete steps behind the bar, past eucalyptus trees and a few picnic benches. At the top, turn left (to the right is a dead end), then leave the path about 200 metres further on and head down the steps of the viewpoint above L'Aiguille. The view extends over the Îles de Lérins and Cannes. In the foreground, there are four little inlets with pebble beaches, surrounded by a landscape of red cliffs (formed by a volcanic eruption 300 million years ago). L'Aiguille itself is made of red volcanic rock. The Pointe de l'Aiguille arch is at the bottom of the biggest beach.

Carry on along the original path, then climb the 400 steps for a lovely view towards St-Raphaël. At the intersection, take the right-hand path (straight ahead the path comes to the road), past strawberry trees that are full of fruit in October and November (eat the red ones; the yellow ones aren't ripe), holm oak, heather, small fig trees and broom. On the way back down, you go through a little clearing and the path is scented with rosemary and thyme.

MANDELIEU-LA-NAPOULE

This pleasant summer resort in the gulf of La Napoule has a big marina near an impressive chateau.

USEFUL ADDRESS

◻ Tourist office: 340 rue Jean-Monnet. ☎ 04-92-97-64-66. Fax: 04-92-97-64-66. General information, tickets and hotel reservations. There are also two information bureaux: avenue Henry-Clews, La Napoule, ☎ 04-93-49-95-31, fax: 04-92-94-99-57; and avenue de Cannes (exit 40 from the motorway) ☎ 04-92-97-99-27. Open all year, every day (except Saturday and Sunday in winter).

WHERE TO STAY AND EAT

🏠 Les Pruniers: avenue de la Mer, 118 rue de la Pinea, in the Pinède district. 300 metres from the sea. ☎ 04-92-97-00-44 or 04-93-49-99-23 (bungalows). Fax: 04-93-49-37-45. Closed from 15 November to 15 January. Bungalows for hire from 1,500F per week in low season and 2,800F in summer. Hot showers are free of charge in this shady and tranquil site, as is the welcome drink.

🏠 ✕ La Calanque: boulevard Henry-Clews. ☎ 04-93-49-95-11. Fax: 04-93-49-67-44. Closed from 1 November to 31 March. Rooms from 225F to 370F. Half board compulsory in July and August. Menus from 100F to 150F. Opposite the chateau, with a shady terrace with sea views. The rooms are clean and attractive, some with lovely views. The prices are excellent, and even the cheaper rooms at the back are very acceptable.

✕ Le Boucanier: on the harbour, opposite the chateau of La Napoule. ☎ 04-93-49-80-51. Set menu at 170F. À la carte around 200F. Overlooking the sea, the terrace of this restaurant is particularly enjoyable in the evening, when the chateau is illuminated. Friendly staff serve fresh fish and seafood in a tranquil setting.

WHAT TO SEE

★ **Château-Musée Henry Clews** (Henry Clews chateau and museum): museum closed from November to February. Guided tours at 3pm and 4pm (5pm in July and August). Entrance fee: 25F (concession for students). Only two towers remain of the original 14th-century chateau, converted by American sculptor Henry Clews (1876–1937) into a pseudo-medieval fantasy castle. The site is superb and a patchwork of different architectural styles are represented.

★ **Port de La Rague**: further on towards Théoule, this is a small natural harbour. It is well protected and more appealing than the concrete jetty at La Napoule.

WALKS

– **Sentier Botanique San Peyre** (San Peyre botanical walk): a one-hour easy, well-shaded circuit of 4 kilometres (2.5 miles) in the heart of the Estérel. Branches of cork oak, strawberry trees and juniper protect walkers from the fierce sun and there's a fine view of the Îles de Lérins. The perfumed wood of the local juniper, *Juniperus oxyderus*, is much sought after and polished pebbles of the wood are sold in local shops. Its scent is quite incense-like.

FROM ST-RAPHAËL TO NICE AND THE HINTERLAND

The Greeks and Romans used it for embalming, and the oil is used today in the manufacture of skin products and shampoos, and to deter rabbits from lettuce plants!

Head towards Théoule on the N98, 6 kilometres (3.75 miles) west of Cannes. Park near the Bon-Puits cemetery, 2 kilometres east of Théoule (near the campsite). Follow the wooden signposts. Information is available from the tourist office in Mandelieu-La Napoule, and the relevant map is IGN 1:25, 000 3644 O.

From the car park, a few dozen metres on the right, wooden signposts point towards the Sentier Botanique San Peyre. In autumn, you pass strawberry trees on which white flowers and bright red fruits appear simultaneously. Next, take the slightly uphill path to the left and cross a wood of cork oaks. At the summit of San Peyre (at 133 metres/436 feet) stand the ruins of the St-Pierre chapel, with its magnificent view of La Napoule port, and the Îles Ste-Marguerite and St-Honorat.

CANNES (06400)   Population: 68,200

It's hard to say anything new or original about Cannes, an eccentric town with many different sides to its character. Host to the famous annual Film Festival, it's a resort for the rich and famous. Rolls Royces, Ferraris and Jaguars clog its streets, and its casinos, beach, trade fairs and renowned seafront promenade, La Croisette, are people by a varied and interesting crowd. Despite all its oddities, Cannes remains an exceptional place, a stylish port with numerous hotels and restaurants at surprisingly affordable prices. Off the beaten track, the Îles de Lérins, the avenues of La Californie, hidden under pine trees, and the shady little squares of Le Cannet are all there to be discovered.

Avoid visiting Cannes in July and August. Lunch on the beach in January can be an absolute delight, warmed by a gentle sun, with a view of the mysterious outline of the Estérel against a cloudless blue sky. The Croisette may be relatively empty, but the air outside is clean and crisp.

History

Some say that the name Cannes derives from the *cannes* (canes or reeds), which used to grow in the nearby marshland. It was the Romans who named the site 'Canoïs'. However, it's more likely that the name has Indo-European origins, from the word *kan*, meaning 'summit'.

For many years, the settlement here remained a small fishing town, until the Gallo–Roman Honoratus founded the Lérins monastery, at the end of the fourth century. Cannes was regularly invaded – by barbarians and Saracen pirates, among others – and life for the Cannois until the 18th century was tumultuous. From the 18th century onwards, the construction of the port contributed to the steady development of the little town. In 1815, Napoleon came ashore in Golfe-Juan from Elba, and camped in the dunes outside town. He despatched General Cambronne to seek rations for his troops, but he received a cool reception and was forced to sneak away, to continue his journey on back roads.

In 1834, the destiny of Cannes and of its 3,000 farmers and fisherfolk, was changed for ever by the arrival of Lord Brougham and his ailing daughter. They spent a night in the Auberge Pinchinat, where the *bouillabaisse* was particularly delicious. Trapped in Cannes by a cholera epidemic, the *lord anglais* was so taken with the climate, together with the beauty of the port, the islands, the olive trees and the pine trees, that he decided to stay. He built a lavish home, Château Éléonore, named after his daughter, and spent every subsequent winter in Cannes until his death in 1868. Many of his aristocratic English friends followed suit, and today's Cannes was born.

In 1853, the railway was opened and construction of the fabled boulevard de la Croisette began. By 1870, the town had 35 hotels and 200 new villas, and artists and writers joined the many visitors from overseas. The Rothschilds, Russian aristocrats, French men of power and the Viceroy of India all took up residence in winter, but most left in summer to avoid the sun, which could damage a fashionably lily-white complexion. The most extravagant and sumptuous villas were built, in an extraordinary range of styles, from *faux* Gothic to Oriental, with marble columns, pagodas and minarets.

In 1638, Cannes had a permanent population of 1,430; today, it has reached almost 70,000. Some of the beautiful villas remain, many hidden among the pine trees of La Californie (where Picasso lived for a time), in Super-Cannes or above La Croix des Gardes, but many others have been sold to developers. Modern apartment blocks offer rich retirees 'unique, desirable locations'. Some of the buildings are frankly hideous, concrete adorned with surrealist towers and other medieval features, but providing all mod cons.

■ Useful Addresses

� **1** Tourist office at the Palais des Festivals
� **2** Tourist office at the train station (Gare SNCF)
⌗ Train station
⎁ Bus station
✉ Post office
3 Ferry terminal: boat trips to îles de Lérins

⌂ Where to Stay

8 Appia Hôtel
9 Hôtel de France
10 Centre international de séjour (International Youth Hostel)
11 Le Chanteclair
12 Hôtel National
13 Touring Hôtel
14 Hôtel Albert I
15 Hôtel Molière
16 Hôtel Le Florian
18 Le Splendid
19 AJ Le Chalit (youth hostel)

✕ Where to Eat

20 L'Entracte
21 Aux Bons Enfants
22 Le Lion d'Or
23 Le Bouchon d'Objectif
24 Au Bec Fin
26 Le Bistrot de la Galerie
27 Lou Souléou
28 La Brouette de Grand-Mère
29 Côté Jardin
31 Le Jardin
33 Le Restaurant Arménien
34 Le Montagard
35 Le Comptoir des Vins

⍓ Where to Go for a Drink

40 Le Zanzibar

★ What to See

50 Musée de la Castre
51 Notre-Dame-d'Espérance

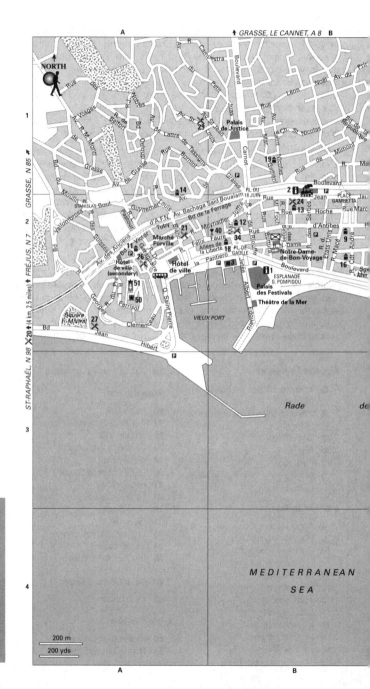

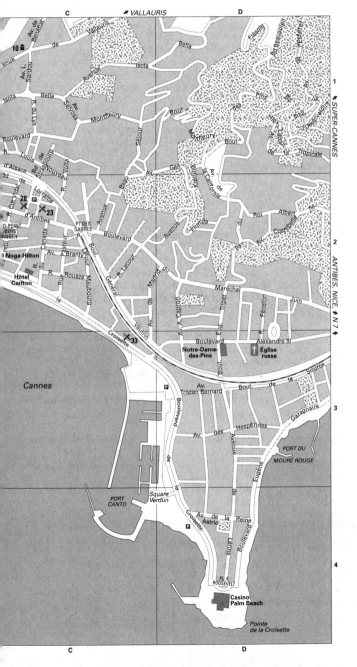

CANNES

The other major change in Cannes is that it is now a year-round convention centre. The Palais des Festivals is hosting some kind of event on 327 days in the year, and this activity is vital to the town's economy. In the past, the casino would close in the summer, but these days Cannes offers events and festivals to attract visitors all year round. In July and August, there are music and fireworks festivals. Every other year, November sees an international puppet festival and in December the town hosts a prestigious international festival of dance.

The Cannes Film Festival takes place around the second week of May every year and is considered by many, including Hollywood, to be the only film festival worth attending. The town is filled with journalists, paparazzi, film stars and fans for the duration, and, amid the publicity and hype, serious business takes place. The chief venue is the Palais des Festivals.

USEFUL ADDRESSES

🄳 **Tourist information** (B2, **1** on the map): at reception in the Palais des Festivals, esplanade du Pré-sident-Georges-Pompidou. ☎ 04-93-39-24-53. Fax: 04-92-99-84-23. Email: semoftou@palais-festival-cannes.fr. Open in winter Monday to Saturday from 9am to 6.30pm; in summer every day from 9am to 8pm. Efficient, well-informed staff equipped with lots of brochures.

🄳 **Accueil Gare SNCF** (train station welcome point) (B2, **2** on the map): ☎ 04-93-99-19-77. Open throughout the year Monday to Friday 9am–noon and 2–6pm (and sometimes non-stop in summer).

🄳 **Tourist office**: in Cannes-La-Bocca, 1 avenue Pierre-Sémard. ☎ 04-93-47-04-12. Fax: 04-93-90-99-85. Open in summer every day from 9am to 9pm; in winter Tuesday to Friday 8.30am–12.30pm and 3.30–6.30pm.

🚆 **Gare SNCF** (train station) (B2 on the map): rue Jean-Jaurès. Information: ☎ 08-36-35-35-35. Very frequent Métrazur trains to all the stations on the coast between St-Raphaël and Menton.

🚌 **Gares routières** (bus stations): there are two bus stations. Next to the train station, Rapides de la Côte d'Azur. ☎ 04-93-39-11-39. Buses to Grasse, Val-de-Mougins and Vallauris. The other station is on place de l'Hôtel-de-Ville (A2 on the map). ☎ 04-93-39-11-39. Buses to Grasse, Nice (via Golfe-Juan) and Nice airport.

■ **Société des transports urbains de Cannes Bus Azur** (urban transport) (A2 on the map): information and departures from place de l'Hôtel-de-Ville. ☎ and fax 04-93-45-20-08.

■ **Cannes Information Jeunesse** (information for young people in Cannes) (A2 on the map): 2 quai St-Pierre. ☎ 04-93-06-31-51. Fax: 04-93-06-31-39. Information on watersports and courses in other sports.

⛴ **Gare maritime** (ferry terminal) (B2, **3** on the map): three companies operate trips to the **Îles de Lérins** from the port at Cannes. Compagnie Estérel Chanteclair: ☎ 04-93-39-11-82. Compagnie Maritime Cannoise: ☎ 04-93-38-66-33. Horizon 4: % 04-92-98-71-36. There is a fourth company on Quai Laubeuf, on the other side of the port: Trans Côte d'Azur. ☎ 04-92-98-71-30.

WHERE TO STAY

Out of season, and when key festivals are not on, there's no problem finding a room to stay in Cannes. All sorts of establishments, from small hotels in Le Suquet to the 'palace' hotels (above ordinary four-star rating) on the Croisette, reduce their prices, making them perfect for a romantic treat. To stay in Cannes in July and August, or during the film festival, you will need to book *well* ahead. Alternatively, look further afield, around Cannes (*see* 'Mougins', 'Valbonne', 'Golfe-Juan' and 'Mandelieu').

☆ Budget

≜ Centre international de séjour (youth hostel) (C1, **10** on the map): 35 avenue de Vallauris. 2 kilometres northeast of the station and town centre, to the left on avenue de Vallauris. ☎ and fax: 04-93-99-26-79. Open all year. Rooms from 50F to 80F per person per night. Between May and August, fixed price deal of 500F per person for seven days. In a large white villa, this hostel has accommodation for 64 people in six-bed dormitories. The rooms and bathrooms are spotless, and there's a well-equipped kitchen and a TV room. Buy your croissants and bread at reduced prices for breakfast and make use of the coffee machine. Young people staying here are spoiled, but the doors do close promptly at 1am. Reservations are essential in summer.

≜ Auberge de jeunesse Le Chalit (youth hostel) (B1, **19** on the map): 27 avenue du Maréchal-Galliéni. 300 metres from the station. ☎ and fax: 04-93-99-22-11. 90F per person per night (no card required). This hostel accommodates a total of 16 guests, in four-person rooms or dormitories with bunk beds. There's a pleasant atmosphere and no curfew.

≜ Le Chanteclair (A2, **11** on the map): 12 rue Forville, Le Suquet. ☎ and fax: 04-93-39-68-88. Closed in November and during the third week in December. Double rooms from 220F to 260F. Ideally located, close to the beach and the liveliest part of town, this hotel has well-equipped rooms (if not absolutely spotless) with white walls and simple furniture in natural wood. Prices are reasonable, and it's quiet and peaceful, particularly in the rooms overlooking the patio, where breakfast can be taken. The *patron* is chatty and friendly. Cards not accepted.

≜ Hôtel National (B2, **12** on the map): 8 rue du Maréchal-Joffre. ☎ 04-93-39-91-92. Fax: 04-92-98-44-06. Email: hotel.national.cannes@wanadoo.fr. Open all year. Double rooms from 250F to 350F. Close to the beaches and the station, this well-maintained hotel is run by an English couple with charm and style. The prices represent good value for money. Book ahead if possible.

☆☆ Moderate

≜ Touring Hôtel (B2, **13** on the map): 11 rue Hoche. Just by the rue d'Antibes. ☎ 04-93-38-34-40. Fax: 04-93-38-73-34. Double rooms with shower and toilet for 300F, with bathroom 400F (both less in low season). Standing in a pedestrianized area, behind a beautiful white Belle Époque exterior, this hotel is reasonably quiet. The rooms (some with balconies) are very pretty, and some even have their own fireplace. Breakfast can be taken on the terrace.

≜ Appia Hôtel (plan B2, **8** on the map): 8 rue de Châteauneuf, on the corner with rue Marceau. ☎ 04-93-06-59-59. Fax: 04-93-39-43-38. Email: appiahotel@wanadoo.fr. Rooms from 300F to 450F. Secure public parking nearby. Pets accepted. Entirely renovated in unpretentious style, this hotel has a calm and relaxing atmosphere. Prices are reasonable, and the friendly managers have been in the business for many years. A good place for a bit of the high life.

☆☆☆ Chic

🛏 **Hôtel Albert I** (A2, **14** on the map): 68 avenue de Grasse. ☎ 04-93-39-24-04. Fax: 04-93-38-83-75. Closed from 20 November to 20 December. Double rooms from 300F to 370F. Not far from the centre of town and a 10-minute walk to the beaches and casino. Rooms have all mod cons (TV, minibar and hairdryer), the atmosphere is friendly and welcoming and there are even frogs croaking outside. Parking is free.

🛏 **Hôtel Molière** (C2, **15** on the map): 5–7 rue Molière. ☎ 04-93-38-16-16. Fax: 04-93-68-29-57. ✗ Closed from 15 November to 25 December. Double rooms from 450F to 700F (less in low season). The rooms in the 19th-century townhouse are very attractive and peaceful, as are those in the modern annexe. It's a five-minute walk to the sea, and close to the centre and the casino. The terrace overlooks a colourful garden and there are three bungalow rooms next to it, with facilities for the disabled. Very popular in high season, so book well in advance, particularly for the film festival.

🛏 **Hôtel Le Florian** (B2, **16** on the map): 8 rue Commandant-André. ☎ 04-93-39-24-82. Fax: 04-92-99-18-30. Closed from 1 November to 15 January. Rooms between 250F and 400F. Owned by the same family for three generations, this well-priced, clean, modern and comfortable hotel is just around the corner from La Croisette. The rooms overlooking the street can be rather noisy in the evenings.

🛏 **Hôtel de France** (B2, **9** on the map): 85 rue d'Antibes. ☎ 04-93-06-54-54. Fax: 04-93-68-53-43. Email: infos@h-de-France.com. Closed from 20 November to 22 December. Double rooms from 470F to 670F. A stone's throw from La Croisette and the Palais des Festivals, this hotel has been totally renovated in its original art deco style. Its 30 modern rooms have air-conditioning, a safe, hairdryer and all other mod cons. Rooms 501 to 508 have a great view.

☆☆☆☆ Très Chic

🛏 **Le Splendid** (B2, **18** on the map): 4–6 rue Félix-Faure. ☎ 04-93-99-53-11. Fax: 04-93-99-55-02. Email: hotel.splendid.cannes@wanadoo.fr. Double rooms from 464F to 900F. This charming family-run hotel, overlooking the Palais des Festivals and the port, survived Cannes' architecturally 'mad' years, and is not one of the fashionable 'palace' hotels of La Croisette. It has a magnificent turn-of-the-century facade and pretty rooms, with antique furniture and brand-new bathrooms. This is the perfect place for a romantic weekend. Reserve ahead to receive a basket of fruit on arrival.

WHERE TO EAT

☆ Budget

✘ **L'Entracte** (A2, **20**, off the map): 106 avenue Francis-Tonner, 06150 Cannes-La Bocca. On the right of the N7, 4 kilometres (2.5 miles) west of the centre of Cannes. ☎ 04-93-48-69-75. Closed from 15 December to 15 January. All-inclusive menu at 63F. The rather unassuming town of La Bocca adjoins Cannes to the west. This little café has been serving family-style cooking for 20 years.

☆☆ Moderate

✘ **Aux Bons Enfants** (A2, **21** on the map): 80 rue Meynadier. No telephone. Closed on Saturday evening (except between May and September), all day Sunday, for the month of August and over New Year. Menu at 96F. Regulars pop in to book their table in person, as vegetables from the nearby Forville market are being peeled. The food is regional and unpretentious, including *terrine de chèvre au confit de tomates* (goat terrine in tomato jam), *sole meunière* (sole with butter, lemon and parsley) and *nougat glacé maison* (homemade nougat ice cream). The service is good and the atmosphere friendly.

✘ **Le Lion d'Or** (B–C1, **22** on the map): 45 boulevard de la République. ☎ 04-93-38-56-57. Closed on Saturday and during November; open lunchtime only in the winter. Menus from 69F to 128F. Daily special 50F (a bargain). This restaurant has been operating for 60 years. During World War II, the menu here cost a mere 5F, and long queues would form daily along the street. The current owners have kept the old traditions alive, and regulars include elderly locals and people who work in nearby offices. The

excellent menu features exclusively homemade dishes, including *baeckeoffe*, a dish from Alsace that is traditionally eaten on Monday evening (wash day).

✘ **Le Jardin** (C1, **31** on the map): 15 avenue Isola Bella. ☎ 04-93-38-17-85. Closed on Sunday evening and on Monday. Menus between 75F and 115F. From April to October, food is grilled outside in the garden at this unassuming little restaurant, far from the madding crowd and the tourist trail. Walk past the buzzing television to the interior courtyard for a peaceful dinner. Try the *daube provençale* (beef stew) or a selection of grilled fish that includes sole, sardines, sea bass or sea bream. The owners are very friendly and the prices reasonable.

✘ **Le Bouchon d'Objectif** (C2, **23** on the map): 10 rue de Constantine. ☎ 04-93-99-21-76. Closed on Sunday evening and on Monday in low season, except during trade fairs. Menus from 92F to 145F. The name of the restaurant translates as 'lens cap', and the walls are decorated with different photographs every month. The food is simple and original, with tasty dishes such as *terrine de lapin aux raisins et pistaches* (rabbit terrine with grapes and pistachio nuts). The service is friendly, and there's a terrace overlooking a modern pedestrianized zone.

✘ **Au Bec Fin** (B2, **24** on the map): 12 rue du 24-Août (near the train station). ☎ 04-93-38-35-86. Closed on Sunday and during the first two weeks of November. Menus from 105F to 125F. Run by the Hugues family since 1955, Au Bec Fin offers an enormous choice of main dishes, mostly regional food. Traditional dishes include *daube de boeuf à la provençale* (beef stew), *soupe au* *pistou* (vegetable soup with a pesto-style sauce) and *filet de rascasse* (scorpion fish). The decor isn't very interesting, but the food, the ambience and the extensive choice are. It can get busy at lunchtime.

☆☆☆☆ Chic

✗ **Le Montagard** (B2, **34** on the map): 6 rue du Maréchal-Joffre. ☎ 04-93-39-98-38. Closed all day Sunday and Monday. *Assiette garnie* at 65F, and set menus from 128F to 225F. This vegetarian restaurant near the market is run by an author and professor. The atmosphere is relaxed, and the setting light and airy. Much thought has been given to the menu, which is based on fresh, healthy food with a few surprises, such as little-known vegetables and organic produce. The organic wine list is also worth sampling.

✗ **Le Comptoir des Vins** (C2, **35** on the map): 13 boulevard de la République. Near the rue d'Antibes. ☎ 04-93-68-13-26. Closed on Sunday and for the month of February; open at lunchtime from Monday to Saturday and for dinner on Thursday, Friday and Saturday. Lunch menus at 89F and dinner at 145F. À la carte around 120F. This 'bistrot-cellar' is a popular spot in the evenings. The entrance to the restaurant is actually in the wine cellar, where you can select a bottle to enjoy with *saucisson pistaché* (dried sausage with pistachio nuts), a wide selection of sandwiches or tasty dishes from the Savoy region. Wine is available by the glass, or by the bottle (at the very reasonable cellar prices plus 40F).

✗ **Le Bistrot de la Galerie** (A2, **26** on the map): 4 rue St-Antoine. ☎ 04-93-39-99-38. Closed Monday lunchtime and in the evening, for eight days in December and from mid-February to mid-March. Menus

at 115F and 149F. This bistrot is actually in a gallery, with an impressive collection of paintings, mostly acrylics. It may be trendy, but it's a good restaurant none the less, with reasonable prices. The atmosphere is young and friendly.

✗ **Lou Souléou** (A2, **27** on the map): 16 boulevard Jean-Hibert. Just behind the old port. ☎ 04-93-39-85-55. Closed all day Monday in low season, for three mornings a week in the summer and closed for the whole of November. Menus at 138F and 218F. The menus represent good value for money, with affordable and delicious seafood, including monkfish stew, sea bass or a traditional *bourride du pêcheur* (a fish stew with monkfish, half a lobster, mussels, garlic croûtons and, of course, spicy *rouille* mayonnaise).

☆☆☆☆ Très Chic

✗ **La Brouette de Grand-Mère** (C2, **28** on the map): 9 rue d'Oran. ☎ 04-93-39-12-10. Open in the evenings only (Monday to Saturday), and closed from 25 June to 12 July, and from 1 November to 15 December. *Formule* menu at 195F, including an aperitif and wine. This pleasant little restaurant is the favourite haunt of rich young Cannois. The early 19th-century interior is rather eclectic in style, but pleasant. The one menu is timeless and delicious, with dishes such as *poulette à la bière brune* (chicken in dark beer), *pot-au-feu aux cinq viandes* (a stew made of five different types of meat) and *cailles rôties à la crème* (roast quail in cream). The name 'Grandmother's Wheelbarrow' apparently derives from a story about the owner's godfather being transported by wheelbarrow – all the way from Cannes to Mougins – for a baptism.

✗ **Le Restaurant Arménien** (C3, **33** on the map): 82 la Croisette.

☎ 04-93-94-00-58. Closed on Monday. One set menu at 250F. The brasserie-style interior has leaded-glass windows. Eating here is like attending an Armenian festival in a private home, with starters, main courses and desserts arriving in rapid succession. Traditional *mezze*, and then no less than 12 main dishes, including beef and lemon kebab and the highlight, a delicious Armenian dish with beef and corn called *kechkek*, cooked for more than 24 hours. Save some room for a fruit sorbet, sesame nougat or *loukoums*. The wine list is impressive with reasonable prices.

✄ **Côté Jardin** (A1, **29** on the map): 12 avenue St-Louis. ☎ 04-93-38-60-28. Closed on Sunday and Monday, and during February. Menus at 125F (lunch) and 205F. Tucked away behind the railway in a small cul-de-sac, far from the tourists, this restaurant is one of the best in Cannes. The interior is light and airy with pastel and floral decor, and there's also a lovely garden terrace. It owes its success to its very high standards. The owner/chef excels in both roles, and changes the menu regularly. Try ginger soup, chicken with coconut, duck with celeriac and orange peel, and fried potatoes in sesame. The dishes are subtle, tasty and balanced, the service is very professional and the whole experience most enjoyable.

WHERE TO GO FOR A DRINK

▼ **Le Zanzibar** (B2, **40** on the map): 85 rue Félix-Faure. ☎ 04-93-39-30-75. Open every day from 5pm to 6am (from 2pm during the festival). Established in 1885, this is one of Cannes' oldest bars, with pictures from the 1960s all over the walls. It is a gay bar, but not overtly so.

▼ **Chez Lucullus** (A2 on the map): 4 place Marché-Forville. ☎ 04-93-39-32-74. This small café is colourful and popular. Wonderful tapas, including courgette fritters, encourage customers to linger and wait patiently for a place to sit. Daily specials and delicious *aïoli* are served at the tables. A great place to people-watch and check out the pulse of Cannes.

WHAT TO SEE

In the Town Centre

★ **Allées de la Liberté** (A2 on the map): plane trees line the streets, where the daily (except Monday) flower market and Sunday flea market take place. The town hall and bus station are at either end.

★ **Vieux port** (old port) (A–B2 on the map): opposite the Allées de la Liberté is the old port, with its fishing boats and luxury pleasure craft. **Le Suquet** and the beautiful pastel exteriors of the charming **quai St-Pierre** form the backdrop. Renovation and displacement are at work in this cramped old quarter of Cannes, but you can still enjoy a stroll along the quay and admire the impressive yachts moored in the port. Hopefully, the concrete carbuncle of the naval station will soon be a thing of the past and the view returned to its former glory. The really luxurious craft are moored on the Albert-Edouard jetty, and at night they are ablaze with lights. There's a lovely old-fashioned merry-go-round on the Esplanade Pompidou, and more than 120 handprints of film celebrities can be seen in the pavement of the Allée des Étoiles. The free public beach here is very pleasant, particularly in low season. As you head back towards the Allées de la Liberté, you'll see the **Square Mérimée**, named in memory of the French Romantic novelist who died here in 1870.

★ **Palais des Festivals** (B2 on the map): built in 1982, this modern slab of concrete and glass, known as 'The Bunker', is next to the old port at the western end of the seafront promenade. Although attempts have been made to soften its exterior with greenery, its interior is much more impressive, extensively equipped for conventions and for the film festival. It also has a casino, a nightclub and an extension that has caused a stir in the courts and the cafés of Cannes.

★ **Rue d'Antibes** (B–C2 on the map): this street is the commercial heart of Cannes, the town with the French record for the most shops per capita. Locals somewhat optimistically compare the rue d'Antibes with the prestigious Faubourg-St-Honoré in Paris. Well, the prices are similar

★ **Rue Meynadier** (A–B2 on the map): this attractive street links the new town with Le Suquet. Formerly the main street, it's still very lively today and has some lovely food shops. Buy cheese at Ferme Savoyarde, bread at Jacky Carletto, and fresh pasta at Maison des Ravioli or Aux Bons Ravioli. Lovers of Tunisian-style couscous should head to Taty Danièle at No. 82. ☎ 04-93-38-94-95.

★ **Marché Forville** (A2 on the map): Cannes' sumptuous covered market has succulent regional produce, and sells to all the top restaurants as well as to the locals doing their everyday shopping. The fish is super-fresh, and the fruit and vegetables are wonderful. Follow the Cannois to the best stalls and then have a relaxing drink in a nearby café.

Cannes Old Town

Take the picturesque **rue St-Antoine** and climb up past its numerous restaurants. The low houses have green or pale blue shutters, old plaques and vaulted entrances. The **place de la Castre** retains its ancient surrounding wall. From one side you can see La Californie and the Observatory, and from the other there's an equally impressive view over the Estérel.

★ **Notre-Dame-d'Espérance** (A2, 51 on the map): this Gothic Provençal church was built in 1627, when Cannes had just 1,000 inhabitants. For years, pilgrims came to the church, which houses classical altarpieces and a multi-coloured wooden statue of St Anne, dating from the end of the 15th century. There's a statue of the Virgin above the outer door, where you'll also spot two tibias and a corpse's head (strange symbols of hope).

★ **Tour du Suquet** (Le Suquet tower): this former watchtower, sitting above a vault, was completed in 1385. Walk under the old bell-tower and relax on the pleasant terrace, with its view over the port and the Allées de la Liberté. Also on this agreeable site are the small Cistercian **Chapelle Ste-Anne**, the square **Tour du Mont Chevalier** (watchtower) and the remains of the chateau built by the abbots of Lérins.

★ **Musée de la Castre** (A2, 50 on the map): in the Château de la Castre, Le Suquet. ☎ 04-93-38-55-26. Between 1 October and 31 March, open every day (except Tuesday) 10am–noon and 2–5pm (to 6pm from 1 April to 30 June); from 1 July to 30 September, open 10am–noon and 3–7pm.

Closed in January. Entrance fee: 10F (free for students and schoolchildren). Housed in the former chateau of the abbots of Lérins monks, built in the 11th and 12th centuries, this museum houses archaeological and ethnographical collections from the five continents, donated by a Dutch baron in 1873. Study the history of Cannes through a series of paintings by local artists, including many works by the 19th-century Orientalist, Ernest Buttura. An impressive collection of musical instruments includes more than 200 contemporary and antique pieces from Asia, Africa and the South Pacific, many brought back by forgotten 19th-century explorer, Ginou de La Coche.

★ Explore the rest of the seven or eight streets of **Le Suquet** – **rue de la Suisse**, **rue Coste-au-Corail**, **rue de la Boucherie**, and its steps, **rue du Château-Vert**, **rue de la Bergerie**, and **rue du Moulin** – as well as the quarter's small alleys and vaulted passageways.

La Croisette

This is millionaires' row, with palace hotels, luxury shops and other exclusive venues, but you don't have to be part of this elite to enjoy the splendour of the seafront promenade, with its views over the Estérel. Lined with palm trees and adorned with flowers, La Croisette is a must for every visitor. In winter, rich ladies in pearl necklaces walk (or carry) their pampered pooches up and down. The population in summer is much younger, and the few public stretches of beach are very crowded. The kiosks sell papers in dozens of different languages.

Of the palace hotels along the boulevard de la Croisette, the Belle Époque **Carlton Hotel** is probably the most famous. It has an enormous Rococo-style dining room and a wedding-cake exterior with tiny balconies.

At the **Port Canto**, there are immaculate gardens, and a merry-go-round and other entertainments for children. The lovely view over the old part of town is best at night, when the Le Suquet tower and the road to the Estérel are lit up.

At the very end of the promenade is the Pointe de la Croisette. The boulevard got its name from a simple cross that used to stand here at the point, where penitents and pilgrims would meet to set off for the monastery of St Honorat. The **Palm Beach** casino at the point has been used as a film set, but is now better known as a place of political and financial intrigue.

Around Cannes

★ **Chapelle Bellini**: parc Fiorentina, 67bis avenue de Vallauris. ☎ 04-93-39-15-55. Open every day (except Saturday and Sunday) from 2pm to 5pm (to 6pm in summer). Built in 1880 in a Florentine-baroque style by Count Vitali, the chapel was bought later by local artist Emmanuel Bellini, who established his studio in the building. The interior is calm and serene and the surrounding gardens are full of cedars of Lebanon, ancient cypresses, palm, olive and orange trees. A haven of peace, it must have been a wonderful source of inspiration for Bellini.

★ **La Croix des Gardes**: this rocky hill to the northwest of Cannes offers one of the most beautiful walks in the area, with superb views of Cannes and the Estérel. Take the avenue du Docteur-Picaud and then turn right on to boulevard Leader. Walk along the footpath under the pine trees, to the summit at 163 metres (535 feet), where there's a large iron cross attached to a rock. Return along the avenue J.-de-Noailles or walk a bit more in the many avenues, past a series of luxury hillside villas.

★ **Le Cannet**: 2.5 kilometres (1.5 miles) to the north of Cannes; take bus No. 4 or 5 from the place de l'Hôtel-de-Ville, or drive along the boulevard Carnot and carry straight on. Quieter and calmer than Cannes, the fashionable suburb of Le Cannet is known for its gentle climate. Impressionist artist Pierre Bonnard (1867–1947) spent the last years of his life in a villa here, producing colour-saturated landscapes and domestic scenes. The old streets have 18th-century houses, and the town's little shady squares offer unexpected and delightful sea views. Place Bellevue has a panoramic view over the bay of Cannes.

DIVING

There are over 30 beautiful dive sites around Golfe-Juan, which can be enjoyed by both novices and experienced divers. Some sites are more exposed than others, but you can always find a sheltered spot somewhere.

Dive School

■ **Plongée Club de Cannes**: quai St-Pierre, on the Vieux Port. ☎ 04-93-38-67-57 or ☎ 06-11-81-76-17 (mobile). Website: www.sylpa.com. Open every day between April and October (except Sunday afternoon). One of the longest-standing dive schools (FFESSM, ANMP and PADI), with a friendly atmosphere aboard its spacious dive vessel. The instructors teach novices, children over eight, courses up to Level III and PADI certificates, as well as leading exploratory dives to the best local sites, and night dives. They supply all necessary equipment, including an on-board compressor.

Dive Sites

⚓ **Le Tombant de la Tradelière**: to the east of Île Ste-Marguerite, with sea bream, octopus and saupe, around a rock at a depth of 6–40 metres (20–197 feet). At around 20 metres (66 feet), use a torch to illuminate the flaming red coral of the little cave. A sensational Level I dive.

⚓ **L'Enfer de Dante**: 'Dante's Inferno' is near La Fourmigue. Its peaks (at a depth of 20–40 metres/66–197 feet) are spectacular. There are meadows of sea fans and clouds of fish. Level II and rather exposed.

⚓ **Le Vengeur**: to the northeast of Île Ste-Marguerite. Underwater riches, including conger eels, at a colourful site at 40 metres (131 feet). Watch out for the current. Level II.

⚓ **La Fourmigue**: this renowned site in the middle of the Golfe-Juan offers six different dives, between 5 and 50 metres (16 and 164 feet), with shelves, canyons and promontories carpeted in sea fans and inhabited by rainbow wrasse. Near by, a miniature town was built in the 1960s at a depth of 15 metres (50 feet), with a stadium, post office and a few conger eels at the windows of the houses. The **Grotte de Miro** (at 18 metres/59 feet) shelters a statue of Le Prieur, a great pioneer of submarine exploration. For all levels of ability.

THE ÎLES DE LÉRINS

These two green and wooded islands lie just a short boat trip away from Cannes, but are far removed from the hustle and bustle of the mainland. Known in ancient times as Lero and Lérina, they are now called Ste-Marguerite and St-Honorat, after two fourth-century saints. They are little oases of sunshine, tranquillity and vegetation, and a wonderful refuge from the holiday crowds.

GETTING THERE

⚓ **Gare maritime** (ferry terminal to the Îles de Lérins): in the Vieux-Port (old port). ☎ 04-93-39-11-82. Ferries depart every 30 minutes from 9am (between June and September). Between October and May, every hour from 10am. Return ticket: 40F to Ste-Marguerite, 45F to St-Honorat, 60F to both islands (half price for children).

ÎLE STE-MARGUERITE

The larger of the two islands, Île Ste-Marguerite has a vast forest and nicer beaches than St-Honorat. You can walk around the island in approximately two hours or wander through the forest on a network of paths. Boats drop anchor to the north and south of the island, and you can swim off the rocks and from a few of the sandy and shingle beaches.

History

In 1685, the fort on Ste-Marguerite became a state prison. One of its most famous and mysterious prisoners was the Man in the Iron Mask, who came here in 1687 and stayed until 1698, when he was removed to the Bastille in Paris. Speculation about his identity has always intrigued historians and film-makers. Voltaire thought he was the twin brother of Louis XIV, and others have suggested he might have been the gossiping son-in-law of the doctor who performed the autopsy on Louis XIII. He is thought to have read the document suggesting the king was incapable of producing children. Some believe he might have been Count Mattioli, an Italian diplomat said to have cheated Louis XIV, or Eustache Dauger, one of Fouquet's servants involved in a poisoning plot. In any case, his real identity remains a mystery.

Another famous inmate of the prison was Marshal Bazaine, who surrendered without a fight during the 1870 war. He managed to escape the prison after only a few months.

WHAT TO SEE

★ **Fort Royal**: built under Richelieu as a defence against the Spaniards and strengthened by Vauban in 1712, the island's fort now houses a museum on its ground floor. Former barracks line the central Allée des Officiers, and the prisons (where the Man in the Iron Mask was held) are found to the northeast, overlooked by a tower. The place has a chilling and gloomy atmosphere, even at the height of summer, and you can imagine the misery of the prisoners, locked away in silence. The warders were not allowed to speak to them, and many are known to have lost their minds. Marshal Bazaine, on the other hand, had the run of a separate building, with a terrace with a superb view. He doesn't seem to have suffered unduly during his short detention. Visitors may also see the cells of Huguenot pastors, imprisoned after the revocation of the Edict of Nantes. The northwest corner has Roman ruins that have only recently been uncovered.

The ticket (10F) gives entry to the prisons and to the **Musée de la Mer** (museum of the sea), which is open every day (except on Tuesday, public holidays and in January) 10.30am–12.15pm and 2–5.30pm. It houses archaeological finds made near the island, including relics from the only Saracen wreck in Europe. The fine Romanesque vaulted rooms remain intact.

★ **Sentier botanique** (botanical route): a well-maintained and signed path indicates different species, from umbrella, maritime and Aleppo pines to holm oak, eucalyptus and strawberry trees, and a wide variety of flowers and plants, including some poisonous ones.

ÎLE ST-HONORAT

The smaller island, Île St-Honorat is the private property of the monastery, but visitors are allowed to walk around through the undergrowth, enjoying the ever-present sea views. There are no real beaches but you can still find spots to go swimming.

History

The monastery of St-Honorat is one of the most renowned in the Christian world, with 20 saints among its alumni, including St Patrick, who trained here before going to Ireland, St Hilaire, St Cézaire, St Salvien and St Vincent de Lérins. In AD 660, St Aygulph introduced the rule of St Benedict. By the seventh century, the monastery had 700 monks, and its influence extended far beyond Provence. Gradually, as the island suffered regular attacks by Saracen pirates, then by the Genoese and the Spanish, its power diminished. In 1788, it was secularized by the pope.

In 1791, French actress St-Val, a contemporary and colleague of Voltaire, acquired the island and moved her household here. Apparently, her former lover, the painter Fragonard, came to stay and decorated her boudoir with frescoes that were rather inappropriate for a former monastery chapter-house.

In 1859, the bishop of Fréjus bought back the island, and in 1869, Cistercians from Sénanque began to rebuild the abbey. Today, 36 monks live here, cultivating part of the island, and producing and selling honey, lavender, wine and a delicious golden liqueur called Lérina (after the Greek name for the island). They also offer simple accommodation for visitors and even have a website, at www.abbayedelerins.cica.fr.

WHAT TO SEE AND DO

★ **Monastère-forteresse** (fortified monastery): open in high season. Built in 1073 by Abbot Aldebert, to protect the monks from Saracen pirates, this 'keep' is surrounded by sea on three sides. Vauban considered this fine building to be a masterpiece, in need of neither extensions nor alterations.

The cloister on the first floor has 14th- and 15th-century vaults and a column made partly from a Roman milestone. A huge Roman water tank sits in the middle, and above it is a gallery with white marble columns brought by the Genoese. The 72 steps leading to the **Chapelle de la Ste-Croix** from the gallery represent the 72 rules of St Benedict. Precious relics were formerly housed in the chapel.

On the top floor, a terrace provides panoramic views over the Estérel, the bay of Cannes and the old Le Suquet fortress, as well as the endless sea and, on a clear day, the snow-covered Alps.

★ **Monastery**: the buildings of the modern monastery date from the end of the 19th century. Visitors may only see the church. All that remains of the former Romanesque church is the moving **Chapelle des Morts**, in the left transept, dating from the 11th century.

– To tour the island, take the pretty and shady path, past the many chapels that bear witness to the earlier religious life of the island. You'll also see the oven installed by Napoleon, where cannonballs were heated to very high temperatures.

MOUGINS (06250)　　　　　**Population: 16,300**

Mougins was an important staging post for the Romans on the Via Aurelia (*see* page 503). In the Middle Ages, it was more important than Cannes, and today it is Cannes' luxurious front garden. The old hilltop town nestles around its medieval bell-tower inside the remains of its 15th-century ramparts, and it has a lovely atmosphere. The olive groves and fields of roses may have been built over, but this idyllic spot still worked its charm on some of the key artistic figures of the 20th century. Francis Picabia fell under its spell in 1924, building a beautiful house here and inviting some of the stars of his generation to stay. Picasso spent the final years of his life in a house opposite the Chapelle de Notre-Dame-de-Vie, and Jean Cocteau, Paul Éluard, Man Ray, Fernand Léger and Isadora Duncan were frequently seen in Mougins' narrow streets. Many artists are still based here, inspired by the charm of the surrounding countryside and by the nearby seascape.

USEFUL ADDRESS

🄱 **Tourist office**: 15 avenue Jean-Charles-Mallet. Situated at the entrance to the village, near the washhouse *(lavoir)*, which now houses exhibitions. ☎ 04-93-75-87-67. Fax: 04-92-92-04-03. Website: www.mougins-cote azur.org. Open in winter Tuesday to Saturday from 10am to 5.30pm; in summer every day from 10am to 7pm. Ask for the *Agenda des Manifestations*, which lists events in the theatre, on the golf course and in the villages, and festivals such as St-Jean (end June) and St-Barthelmy (22 August). The major event at the end of July is **Les Arts dans la Rue** ('Art in the Streets').

WHERE TO STAY AND EAT

🛏 ✕ **Les Liserons de Mougins**: 608 avenue St-Martin (towards Mouans-Sartoux). ☎ 04-93-75-50-31. Fax: 04-93-75-56-13. Rooms between 280F and 650F. Half board reasonably priced. This hotel is outside the old town and is reached via the dual carriageway from Cannes. The recently renovated rooms are comfortable and there's also a large swimming pool and free parking. The rooms facing the road can be noisy.

☆☆☆ Chic

🛏 ✕ **Le Manoir de l'Étang**: Les-Bois-de-Fontmerle, route d'Antibes. ☎ 04-92-28-36-00. Fax: 04-92-28-36-10. Closed between November and January, and on Monday (restaurant only) out of season. Small but very expensive rooms for between 600F and 900F. Menus at 150F (weekday lunch) and 190F. This lovely building sits in splendid isolation on a little rise. The hotel has pleasant spacious rooms, a huge garden, a large pond (hence the name) and a swimming pool. The menu features simple, fresh and well-prepared dishes, such as warm red mullet tart with onions and anchovies, sea bass in thyme and lobster cannelloni.

WHERE TO EAT

Mougins, renowned for its ability to attract film stars and millionaires, is one of the smartest (and most expensive) places to eat in France. Some of its high-class restaurants continue to trade on the slightly faded glory of Roger Vergé's very successful Moulin de Mougins.

✕ **Resto des Arts**: rue du Maréchal-Foch. ☎ 04-93-75-60-03. Closed on Monday throughout the year, on Tuesday lunchtime in low season, and from mid-November to mid-December. Menus at 65F (weekday lunch) and 100F. Untypical of Mougins, this place is good value, with traditional and tasty food based on recipes inherited from the cook's grandmother. She buys all her produce at the market in the morning and makes delicious *daubes provençales* (beef stew), *aïoli*, fish casserole and lamb with polenta and stuffed vegetables. Front of house, Grégory is relaxed and entertaining.

✕ **Aux Trois Étages**: 10 place du Commandant-Lamy. ☎ 04-93-90-01-46. Closed on Wednesday. Menus between 98F and 198F. Of the three floors (hence the name) of this fashionable eating place, choose the terrace, for its wonderful view over the old village. Enjoy lobster ravioli or lamb braised in cumin. The staff are pleasant and efficient.

✕ **L'Amandier**: place des Patriotes. ☎ 04-93-90-00-91. Menus at 155F and 195F. Owned by legendary restaurateur Roger Vergé, this establishment is housed in a 14th-century olive mill in the heart of the old village. The menu draws its inspiration from the region, with such dishes as fillets of red mullet, courgette flowers, breast of duck and little *gnocchi* with miniature beans. The welcome is friendly and discreet.

✗ **L'Estaminet des Remparts**: 24 rue Honoré-Henry. ☎ 04-93-90-05-36. Closed on Monday and Tuesday, during January, and for a week at the beginning of June. Menu at 120F. Delightful in summer, this authentic little village bistrot has thick stone walls which keep its customers cool. The atmosphere is warm and friendly, and the owner cooks the food herself. The room is decorated with interesting finds from the flea markets, and there's a pretty terrace.

✗ **Les Pins de Mougins**: 2308 avenue Maréchal-Juin, in the Val-de-Mougins district. ☎ 04-93-45-25-96. Closed on Sunday evening (except 1 July and August) and all day Monday. Menus at 100F (lunch), 135F and 155F. On the edge of Mougins, towards Le Cannet and

away from the tourists, this pretty yellow and green restaurant offers delicious dishes, such as scallops on avocado and fresh tomatoes, aïoli and lavender *crème brûlée*. There's a pretty terrace and garden behind, for quiet moments under the pine trees.

✗ **Le Rendez-vous de Mougins**: place du Vieux-Village. ☎ 04-93-75-87-47. Closed on Sunday evening and from November to March. Menu at 100F on weekdays, including a drink (except between June and September), and 238F for the truffle menu. A favourite with locals, serving aromatic dishes such as beef in wild mushroom sauce and sea bass with truffles. If the main truffle menu is beyond your budget, treat yourself to an affordable Rosevald potato salad with truffles, which lingers on the palate and in the memory.

WHAT TO SEE

★ **Old village**: sited at 260 metres (855 feet) above sea level, there are wonderful panoramic views over Cannes, the Îles de Lérins, Mandelieu, Grasse and the Préalpes from the old town of Mougins. The narrow streets are arranged snailshell-style around the bell-tower and the symmetry of the village derives from its fortifications, of which you can still see a few vestiges. Only one of the medieval gateways remains intact, **Porte Sarrazine**. The central square, with its beautiful late 19th-century fountain, is almost *too* picturesque! The **rue des Orfèvres**, with its painted doors, is one of the prettiest streets. The **rue de la Glissade** slopes steeply.

★ Visit the **Église St-Jacques-le-Majeur**, a mixture of Romanesque and 19th-century styles. The view from the top of the tower is superb, as long as you ignore the more recent buildings. Open every day in summer 2–7pm, and out of season Wednesday to Sunday 2–5pm. Collect the keys from the Musée de la Photographie opposite.

★ **Musée de la Photographie** (photography museum): ☎ 04-93-75-85-67. Open Wednesday to Sunday 2–6pm (to 11pm in July and August). Entrance fee: 5F. Next to the Porte Sarrazine, this museum houses a collection of old photographic equipment and hosts temporary exhibitions. On the second floor, there are photographs of Picasso signed by Doisneau and Lartigue, among others, that used to belong to the artist.

★ **Musée municipal**: place du Commandant-Lamy. ☎ 04-92-92-50-42. Open all year (except November) from Monday to Friday, 10am–noon and 2–6pm. Free entry. Local history in the former Chapelle St-Bernardin des Pénitents Blancs (1618).

★ **Notre-Dame-de-Vie**: 2.5 kilometres (1.5 miles) southeast of Mougins via the D35 and D3. This 12th-century priory was founded on a beautiful site by monks from the island of St-Honorat. Picasso lived next door in a villa called 'L'Antre du Minotaure' from 1961 until his death, in 1973. The view over Mougins and the countryside is magnificent. A beautiful avenue of cypress trees leads to the priory, which is preceded by a porch with three arcades. The chapel is named 'Our Lady of Life' because it was one of those places where parents would bring stillborn babies, to be revived just long enough to be baptized. The practice was banned in 1730.

★ **Musée de l'Automobiliste** (motor museum): on the A8 between Antibes and Cannes, at the aire des Bréguières, 5 kilometres (3 miles) south of Mougins. ☎ 04-93-69-27-80. Open every day from 10am to 7pm in the summer months, and from 10am to 6pm during the rest of the year. Closes in November. Entrance fee: 40F. Founded in 1984 by Adrien Maeght and housed in an ultra-modern radiator-shaped building, this is a 20th-century temple to the car. Its collection, one of the most impressive in Europe, ranges from the very first motorized vehicles to Formula 1 cars, all in working order. A thematic exhibition is organized each summer.

WHAT TO SEE IN THE AREA

★ **Valmasque forest park**: the 427-hectare (1055-acre) protected park offers 20 kilometres (12.5 miles) of footpaths under the pine trees, picnic sites, bridleways and several marked botanical paths. The natural lake in the park, the Étang de Fontmerle (*see* 'Walks'), is home to an important collection of giant Asian waterlilies, unique in Europe. Between early July and mid-September, beautiful pink flowers blossom on large pads up to a metre in diameter. Migratory birds also gather here, some endangered species.

This natural body of water is overlooked by a hill and the Manoir de l'étang, now a hotel (*see* 'Where to Stay'). After World War II, Maurice Gridaine, the architect of the first Palais des Festivals in Cannes, fell in love with the ruined manor and the typical Provençal countryside around it. In 1949, Gridaine, Jean Cocteau and Jean Marais planned the creation of a 'cinema city' based at the manor. However, with the crisis in French cinema, the building of Cinecitta in Italy and the modernization of the Victorine studios in Nice, the project had to be abandoned and Gridaine was left with his beloved property as his sole consolation.

WALKS

– **Canal de la Siagne, Étang de Fontmerle and Chapelle Notre-Dame-de-Vie**: this is a pretty 90-minute walk on flat ground and ideal for jogging. Leave Mougins towards Valbonne and park on the left after the Russian St-Pétersbourg restaurant. Cross the road and look for the canal gate, in the bend.

The canal winds its way along, below some of the finest properties of Mougins, and is crossed from time to time by small bridges. Go under a bouganvillea-covered archway, then under the main road and follow the viaduct. Cross the little road leading to the Chapelle Notre-Dame-de-Vie and then follow the canal.

Beyond a meadow on the right, leave the canal and take a small path before rejoining the canal 50 metres further on, below Picasso's old house. There's a lovely view over Cannes. The canal changes direction in the forest and when it reaches a surfaced road, come back on yourself for 300 metres. Climb back up the path to the right, alongside a small stone house, to the Étang de Fontmerle, with the mountains in the background. For guided tours of the lake, contact the tourist office in Mougins. ☎ 04-93-75-87-67.

Head back to the canal path and take a right turn onto a narrow and winding path, past the lovely 17th-century Chapelle Notre-Dame-de-Vie, with its pretty avenue of cypress trees. The house next door was Picasso's. Continue down the path for 20 metres and then take an immediate left turn on to a stretch of concrete that leads back to the canal. Follow this to the right to get back to your car.

GRASSE (06130)   Population: 44,800

Grasse, 17 kilometres (11 miles) from Cannes, has been the capital of perfume since the 16th century. The picturesque town dates originally from the seventh century, when entire families fled the coast and its invaders to seek refuge in the hills. Several decades ago, the inhabitants started to decamp to the surrounding countryside and many of the town buildings now have a somewhat abandoned air. In some ways, Grasse resembles a lethargic sleeping beauty. There are plans to breathe new life into its centre, but the work demands a great deal of money.

The soil and climate of Grasse present the perfect conditions for the cultivation of flowers, which have been used for centuries in the manufacture of perfume. The perfume industry is the main attraction, but visitors also come for the gentle and healing climate, which is supposed to be good for asthma sufferers, and for the wonderful walks in the hinterland.

The traffic system in Grasse seems to send drivers round and round in circles. The best solution is to go straight to an underground car park (*parking souterrain*). Alternatively, there are regular buses to the town from the bus station in Cannes.

USEFUL ADDRESS

❚ **Tourist office**: Palais des Congrès. ☎ 04-93-36-66-66. Fax: 04-93-36-86-36. Website: www.ville-grasse.fr. Open from 1 July to 15 September, Monday to Saturday 9am–7pm, Sunday 9am–12.30pm and 1.30–6pm; from 15 September every day (except Sunday) 9am–12.30pm and 1.30–6pm. Their historic map of the town is very useful. Audioguides for a town tour can be hired for 20F.

WHERE TO STAY

⌂ Hôtel Panorama: 2 place du Cours. ☎ 04-93-36-80-80. Fax: 04-93-36-92-04. Double rooms between 300F and 420F. Centrally located modern hotel, with rather uninteresting architecture. The rooms are equipped with TV, telephone, minibar and balconies with views over the town and the surrounding countryside. The rooms overlooking the garden have a shower and toilet. Those that face south have a bathroom. The welcome is friendly.

⌂ Hôtel-pension Ste-Thérèse: 39 avenue Y.-E.-Baudoin (on the Route Napoléon). From the bus station, take the boulevard du Jeu-de-Ballon, then turn right towards Digne and St-Vallier. It's a 15-minute walk along avenue Baudoin. ☎ 04-93-36-10-29. Fax: 04-93-36-11-73. Closed from 15 October to 15 November. Double rooms for 245F with shower and toilet; 260F with bathroom. This establishment, run by nuns, has a good position with a wonderful view of Grasse, the gulf of La Napoule and, in the distance, the Îles de Lérins. The rooms are simple, but spacious and spotless, and facilities include a sitting room, a library, a pretty garden, a magnificent terrace, and even your own chapel. The guests tend to be older, but it's a reliable and good-value place to stay.

⌂ Hôtel des Parfums: boulevard Eugène-Charabot. ☎ 04-92-42-35-35. Fax: 04-93-36-35-48. Closed between November and end January. Double rooms from 450F to 675F. Menus at 88F and 130F. A charming location above the town, but the hotel itself is merely functional, with 70 rooms and a dining room. It's fine for one night in town, with lovely views and a restaurant serving typical regional dishes such as *fassum* (stuffed cabbage) or rabbit cooked Provençal style.

WHERE TO EAT

☆ Budget

✗ Le Gazan: 3 rue Gazan. ☎ 04-93-36-22-88. Closed on Sunday and from 15 December to 1 May. Menus from 90F to 195F. Eat under the parasols on the terrace or in the pleasant dining room, with its friendly and relaxing atmosphere. The food is simple and tasty, with dishes such as fresh sardines, leg of lamb and delicious homemade pastries.

WHERE TO EAT IN THE AREA

✗ Le Relais de la Pinède: route de la Roquette-sur-Siagne (D409), 06370 Mouans-Sartoux. ☎ 04-93-75-28-29. Closed on Wednesday (in low season) and on Sunday evening, as well as between 5 January to 5 February. Menus from 99F to 169F. This is a real find in the area, with its subtle decor, professional service, prices to suit all budgets and menus to suit all tastes. The wine list is rather expensive.

WHAT TO SEE

★ **Old town**: first, pick up the town map from the tourist office. Start your tour on the 15th-century **place aux Aires**, near the top of the town, the scene of the morning produce and flower market. Have a quick coffee before embarking on an exploration of the network of streets with their attractive old houses and private mansions, some of which are not very well maintained. The 18th-century **Hôtel Isnard** on the place aux Aires is worth a look and there's also a superb medieval house in rue de l'Oratoire.

★ **Ancienne Cathédrale Notre-Dame-du-Puy**: open Monday to Saturday, 8.30–11.45am and 2.30–5pm (Sunday from 8am). The 12th-century former cathedral, restored in the 17th century, was built in Provençal Romanesque style in white limestone with a very spartan exterior. It has an equally bare nave, but houses some interesting works by Rubens (*Crown of Thorns* and a *Crucifixion*) and Fragonard (*The Washing of the Feet*, one of his finest religious works) together with a triptych by Ludovico Bréa.

★ **Villa-Musée Fragonard** (Fragonard villa and museum): 23 boulevard Fragonard. At the entrance to the town from Cannes, near the cours H.-Cresp car park. ☎ 04-93-40-02-71. Open 10am–noon and 2–5pm from 1 October to 31 May and 10am–7pm in summer. Closed on Monday and Tuesday, and from 8 November to 8 December. Entrance fee: 20F for permanent exhibitions and 25F for temporary ones. The artist Jean-Honoré Fragonard (1732–1806) was born in Grasse and lived in this opulent villa during the French Revolution, following a noticeable decline in commissions for royal and noble portraits in Paris. The walls are covered with paintings, drawings, sketches and engravings of the great master and his family.

★ **Musée International de la Parfumerie** (international perfumery museum): 8 place du Cours. ☎ 04-93-36-80-20. Open 10am–noon and 2–5pm from 1 October to 31 May, and 10am–7pm in summer. Closed on Monday and Tuesday, and from 8 November to 8 December. Entrance fee: 20F. The perfumery museum tells the history of the perfume industry, which began with Italian immigrant *gantiers parfumeurs*, manufacturers of perfumed gloves. Among its displays are precious little bottles dating from Roman times to the present day, and Marie Antoinette's exquisite vanity case.

The rise of the perfume industry in Grasse dates back to the 16th century, when the inimitable scent of the *Rosa centifolia*, which flowers only in Grasse, began to be exploited. Almost all the perfumes of the great fashion houses are created in Grasse. Today, they are manufactured mainly from imported flowers and the production of essential oils for aromatherapy is a growing industry.

★ Whichever Grasse **perfumery** you visit, you won't be allowed into the inner sanctum where the perfumes are created, partly because the recipes are trade secrets but also because the essential oils can be almost noxious to the untrained nose. The three major perfumeries in Grasse are Fragonard, Molinard and Galimard. They all offer free visits, but there's inevitably a shop at the end of the guided tour. These three are essentially museums and very much aimed at the tourist market. The factories for the big perfume companies are outside the town and don't allow visits by tourists.

– **Ateliers de création** (perfume workshops): the major perfume houses run courses to allow amateurs to create a perfume themselves. Becoming a *nez* ('nose') can take more a dozen years, but these workshops aim to sharpen the senses. You can take your recipe with you if you're happy with the result.

★ **Musée d'Art et d'Histoire de la Provence** (museum of Provençal art and history): 2 rue Mirabeau. ☎ 04-93-36-01-61. Open 10am–noon and 2–5pm from 1 October to 31 May, and 10am–7pm in summer. Closed on Monday and Tuesday, and from 8 November to 8 December. Entrance fee: 20F. Housed in a magnificent 18th-century building that belonged to the frisky sister of Count Mirabeau of Aix, this museum has a rich collection of china, furniture in all the Louis styles, costumes, utensils and terracotta *santons* figurines.

★ **Musée de la Marine** (museum of the sea): 2 boulevard du Jeu-de-Ballon. ☎ 04-93-09-10-71. Open every day in summer from 10am to 7pm. In winter, open Monday to Saturday 10am–noon and 2–6pm. Closed during the first two weeks of November. Entrance fee: 20F. The museum is dedicated to the life and career of the intrepid Admiral of Grasse, hero of the American War of Independence. There are 30 ship models in the vaulted rooms.

★ **Musée du Costume et du Bijou** (museum of costume and jewellery): Hôtel de Clapiers-Cabris, 2 rue Jean-Ossola. ☎ 04-93-36-44-65. Open every day 10am–1pm and 2–6pm. Free entry. The former home of the Marquise de Cabris, sister of French statesman Mirabeau, now houses a wonderful collection of costumes and jewellery from the 18th and 19th centuries. There's also a souvenir shop.

SHOPPING

There's no lack of perfume, soap and associated bits and pieces to buy in Grasse, but you can also take advantage of the variety of markets in the town.

🔒 **Marché aux fleurs**: the flower market takes place each morning (except Monday) on the place aux Aires.

🔒 **Marché provençal**: the local produce market takes place every morning on the place aux Aires, selling the usual fruit and veg as well as interesting spices and crystallized fruits. In summer, a market is also held once a week on place du Cours.

🔒 At 7 rue Marcel-Journet, there's a wonderful bakery and pastry shop, where you can buy a croissant for breakfast or something savoury for lunch.

🔒 **Grasse Bonbon**: rue Marcel-Journet. This shop is renowned for its crystallized fruits, particularly violets.

🔒 **Huilerie Autran**: rue Mougins-Roquefort. ☎ 04-93-36-03-23. The best local produce, including special olive oils and soaps.

FESTIVALS

Grasse holds two flower festivals every year:

– **Expo Rose**: during the first weekend in May, 30,000 roses from France and Italy may be viewed in the gardens of the Villa Fragonard.

– **Fête du Jasmin**: the jasmine festival takes place during the first weekend in August.

WHAT TO SEE IN THE AREA

★ **Espace de l'Art Concret**: Château de Mouans-Sartoux, 13 place Suzanne-de-Villeneuve. ☎ 04-93-75-71-50. From 1 June to 30 September open every day from 11am to 7pm (to 6pm from 1 October to 31 May). Entrance fee: 15F. This interesting cultural and exhibition space is housed in a beautifully restored 500-year-old chateau. It has an unusual triangular shape, and hosts temporary exhibitions of modern art, with engaging guided tours.

CABRIS (06530)   Population: 1,510

Cabris, 6 kilometres (4 miles) from Grasse on the road towards St-Cézaire, 'basks in the sun like a lizard on an old wall'. This ancient hilltop village offers a magnificent view over the surrounding countryside, a green landscape punctuated by splodges of ochre villa and the geometric shapes of bright blue swimming pools. From the castle ruins, the panorama stretches all the way from Nice to the foothills of Toulon. The spectacular view from the village church, which, unusually, has no transept, takes in the Lac de St-Cassien.

Once favoured by artists and authors, including Camus, Gide and St-Exupéry, the village is now very touristy. Today, coast dwellers come here for weekends in the hills, and the meadow is often used for cricket matches between English employees from the nearby Sophia-Antipolis technology centre – a rather surreal sight in the heart of Provence. The mother of the legendary aviator and author of *Le Petit Prince* (1943), Antoine de St-Exupéry, lived in this area, which explains why many sites have his name.

USEFUL ADDRESS

🅱 **Syndicat d'initiative** (tourist information centre): ☎ 04-93-60-55-63.

WHERE TO STAY AND EAT

🛏 ✕ **L'Auberge Le Vieux Château**: place Mirabeau. ☎ and fax: 04-93-60-50-12. 🍴 Restaurant closed on Tuesday evening and on Wednesday from October to March and on Tuesday evening from April to June. Open every day from July to September. Double rooms from 380F to 650F with shower and toilet. Menus from 145 (weekday lunch) to 240F. This charming establishment is built among the ruins of the old chateau. It has four rooms, all tastefully furnished and decorated, and there's a large dining room, in which you can try delicious specialities such as *agneau des Alpes cuit en croûte* *d'herbes fraîches au fumet de thym sauvage* (Alpine lamb cooked in a fresh herb crust with wild thyme) or *pigeon farci aux noisettes et aux* choux (roast pigeon stuffed with nuts and cabbage).

WHAT TO SEE IN THE AREA

★ **Domaine des grottes des Audides** (Les Audides cave site): on the route de Cabris (D4), a few kilometres to the north of Cabris. ☎ 04-93-42-64-15. Open every day in July and August. Guided tours every hour from 10am to 7pm. During the rest of the year, open from 2pm to 5pm but closed on Monday and Tuesday. These caves – the Grotte du Grand Dôme and the remains of a neolithic dwelling – were first discovered by one Herbert Reich, who was looking for a source of water for his sheep. The site has since been developed, and a little open-air museum displays scenes from prehistoric life.

ST-VALLIER-DE-THIEY (06460)

Population: 2,280

This medieval town, 12 kilometres (7.5 miles) northeast of Grasse, makes a pleasant pit-stop for foodies. It's also a starting point for many fine walks, particularly the route to the Pas de la Faye, with its wonderful view. The old church is Provençal-Romanesque in style.

USEFUL ADDRESS

🖪 **Tourist office**: place du Tour. ☎ and fax: 04-93-42-78-00. Open Monday to Saturday 9am–noon and 3–5pm (to 6pm in summer), Sunday from 10am to noon. A wide selection of leaflets, including one detailing local walks.

WHERE TO STAY AND EAT

🛏 **Camping du parc des Arboins**: on the N85, 1.5 kilometres towards Grasse. ☎ 04-93-42-63-89. Fax: 04-93-09-61-54. 90F for two people, including tent and car (or caravan). This site is shady and has a heated swimming pool. Deserves its three stars.

🛏 ✕ **Hostellerie Le Préjoly**: place Rouguière ☎ 04-93-42-60-86. Fax: 04-93-42-67-80. Closed on Sunday evening, all day Monday (except in July and August), and during December and January. Rooms, most with little terraces, and all with shower and toilet or bathroom, from 250F to 350F. Half board compulsory in summer, between 340F and 380F. Menus from 100F (weekdays) and 195F. This charming hotel has 17 rooms, a large garden behind, a sauna and a sun terrace, and an excellent restaurant frequented by celebrities such as Charles Bronson, William Holden and French actress Mireille Darc. Enjoy fine and classic food, such as scallops, breast of duck in honey or entrecôte steak in truffle juice. The house aperitif is known as the *péché mignon* (meaning 'little sin').

WHAT TO SEE

★ **Souterroscope de Baume-Obscure** (subterranean lake): from St-Vallier, follow the signs to St-Cézaire, turn right on to the route du cimetière, then take the unsurfaced road for 2 kilometres. ☎ 04-93-42-61-63. Fax: 04-93-42-69-19. Site open every day from 10am to 5pm during the week, and from 10am to 7pm at weekends and on public holidays. Entrance fee: 50F (children 25F). Allow an hour to visit. The temperature remains constant, at 12C (50F), and there are underground pools and waterfalls and a high-tech sound and light show.

WHAT TO SEE IN THE AREA

★ **Grottes de St-Cézaire**: 9 boulevard du Puits-d'Amon, in St-Cézaire. ☎ 04-93-60-22-35. From June to September open 10.30am–6pm, and all day in July and August. In low season, open 2.30–5pm. Entrance fee: 30F (half price for children between 5 and 11). These caves are famous for their extraordinary red colour, and iron-rich stalactites that make unusual music when struck by the guide.

★ **Plateau de Caussols**: (*see* 'Routes around Vence', page 612). To return to the coast without going through Grasse again, take the superb route across the Caussols plateau, which takes you up to Gourdon, in the direction of Opio and Valbonne. This will give a foretaste of the hinterland around Vence.

WALKS

Two pleasant and undemanding walks in the area lead to sites of cultural interest.

– **From Col Ferrier to the oppidum**: this easy two-hour return trip is well-marked, first in yellow and then in orange. Leave St-Vallier-de-Thiey on the Route Napoléon and turn right immediately towards Caussols. Park at the Col du Ferrier (at the pass).

Take the footpath that climbs at right angles to the road and turn immediately before the very steep incline. The mountainside path passes through a landscape of lavender and broom bushes, and pine trees, and has a view over the St-Vallier plateau. It's surfaced on the bend and on the sloping section. Leave the main path, go round the padlocked gate to the left and climb up towards the mountain for a short distance. There's an old *borie* (a round, conical dry-stone shepherd's hut) on the right. Go through the second metal gate and leave the electricity poles on your right, to find them again on your left after crossing a small ford. Walk past a modern sheepfold, with aluminium shutters, on a lovely wide, grassy path, lined with huge juniper trees (with black berries), a fine Montpellier maple and high walls to the left. Stop for a picnic lunch (or a snooze) in the first clearing, between two maple trees, or further along, in the clearing after the restored sheepfold. After this, the path enters private land via a gate.

Don't go through the gate. Instead, follow the big stone arrow at ground level, which directs you off the path and on to a smaller one. Cross the old pasture and climb the hill through a copse and along a well-marked, stony route, to arrive at two rocks topped by the oppidum. This impressive elliptical wall, built by a Celtic-Ligurian tribe around 300 BC, overlooks the St-Vallier mountain range on one side and the Château de Malle perched above a beautiful plain on the other. The sea, Nice and Cap Ferrat can be seen in the background. Descend via the same path.

– **To the** *pierre druidique* (druid's stone): this agreeable and relatively easy round trip should take about an hour. Having left St-Vallier, pass the petrol station and take the road towards St-Cézaire to the left. After about 1 kilometre, leave the main road just before the garage and turn left to the Collet d'Assou. Carry on until you cross avenue Séverine. Park at the crossroads, marked by a black iron cross.

Take the furthest path on the right, following the yellow markers, to enter a lovely landscape of dry-stone walls and cork oaks. At the junction of paths, turn left; on your right, you'll see a wooden house. At the next intersection, take the path to the right, lined with maples and holm oaks, and you'll come across the stunning smoke tree which has red leaves in autumn and white cotton buds in winter. Walk between the two large fields (the one on the left has a cairn). Leave the right-hand path, which goes between two pillars towards a private property, and carry on for about 30 metres. The path to the left leads to the *pierre druidique* (druid's stone), a large limestone monolith. Erosion over the centuries has formed it into a large 'T'-shape and it is now reinforced with concrete to prevent any dangerous collapse. Retrace your steps to get back to your car.

VALBONNE (06560)　　　　Population: 11,200

The checkerboard layout of the lovely village of Valbonne was inspired by Roman town plans and reconstructed by the monks of Lérins. This 'town in the country' is popular with English employees based at the Sophia-Antipolis technology park.

USEFUL ADDRESS

🛈 **Tourist office**: 11 avenue St-Roch. Slightly out of the centre, on the road to Cannes. ☎ 04-93-12-34-50. Fax: 04-93-12-34-57. Open in summer Monday to Friday 9am–6pm; Saturday 9am–12.30pm and 3–6pm; Sunday 9am–12.30pm. From mid-September to mid-June, open Monday to Friday 9am–5pm; Saturday 9am–12.30pm. Closed on Sunday. Lots of leaflets and information on the area.

WHERE TO EAT

✕ **La Fontaine aux Vins**: 3 rue Grande. ☎ 04-93-12-93-20. Closed on Wednesday, except in high season. À la carte around 80F. This lively wine bar in the old part of Valbonne serves imaginative sandwiches and small dishes such as Provençal tapas (an unusual cultural combination). There's a good selection of reasonably priced wines, including local Coteaux du Bellet bottles, and light beer from Nice. Buy them next door, too, at the friendly and efficient 'Olivier and Co' shop. On Saturday musical evenings, live bands entertain customers while they eat.

✕ **L'Auberge Fleurie**: 1016 route de Cannes. ☎ 04-93-12-02-80. Closed on Sunday evening (in low season), on Monday and from mid-December to end January. Menus at 128F and 165F. Appealing decor, friendly service and simple, tasty and enjoyable food. Regulars return here again and again, which is always a good sign.

WHERE TO STAY AND EAT IN THE AREA

✕ **Le Mas des Géraniums**: in the San Peyre district in Opio. ☎ 04-93-77-23-23. Closed all day Wednesday, and on Thursday lunchtime in July and August; on Tuesday evening and all day Wednesday in low season; from mid-November to mid-January. Menus at 150F and 195F. This blue-shuttered farmhouse is surrounded by olive trees and has a pretty terrace and garden. The owners, from Burgundy, have established a popular spot where locals enjoy high-class (but not very local) food, such as *escargots en coquille* (snails in their shells) and *marengo de poulet aux écrevisses* (chicken with crayfish). The quality is good, but prices are relatively high.

WHAT TO SEE

★ **Place des Arcades**: the street around this square passes under the arcades of its houses.

★ **Romanesque church**: at the bottom of the village, on the riverbank, with a terrace in front. The church belongs to the former abbey (a rare example of chalaisian architecture), and both buildings may be visited by arrangement: ☎ 04-93-12-15-72.

– Part of the church houses the **Musée des Arts et Traditions Populaires** (museum of popular arts and culture): ☎ 04-93-12-96-54. Open from 1 May to end September, every day (except Monday) 3–7pm. Out of season, open at the weekend only, 2–6pm. Entrance fee: 10F. Old postcards and various tools illustrate the way of life in the town and the parish in days gone by.

★ **Old fountain and drinking trough**: in front of the town hall.

★ **Hôtel de Ville** (19th century) and the **Moulin des Artisans** (craftsmen's mill).

FESTIVALS AND EVENTS

– **Fête de la St-Blaise, du Raisin et des Produits du Terroir** (festival of the grape and of local produce): during the last weekend in January and the first weekend of February. This festival celebrates the late golden Servan grape, which has the particular distinction of staying fresh for months. Since ancient times, it has been kept carefully at a temperature of 5°C (40°F), its stem plunged into a jar with the bunch of grapes outside, to be eaten at Christmas time as one of the traditional 13 desserts. The *terroir* of the festival comprises Valbonne, Plascassier, Opio and Biot.

– **Brocante**: the second-hand market takes place the first Sunday in every month.

WHAT TO SEE IN THE AREA

OPIO

This little village specializes in the cultivation of flowers for perfume, and also has an old olive mill. Much-loved French comedian Coluche died here. Despite his efforts in fighting poverty – he set up the Restos du Coeur (Restaurants of the Heart), which feed those in need in France – local politicians refused to allow a statue to be built in his memory. He is commemorated instead by a cross that is always covered in flowers. French photographer Lartigue also spent his final years here.

Visitors can spend a day or two (from 10am to 8pm) at the Club Med all-inclusive village at Opio. Information: ☎ 04-93-09-71-53 or 04-93-09-71-00. Booking: ☎ 0801-802-803. There's a gym, sauna, hammam, outdoor and indoor swimming pools, and a whole range of sporting activities, amid ancient olive trees.

SOPHIA-ANTIPOLIS

The technology park in the woods to the southwest of Valbonne has been described as the 'silicon valley of France'. The inspiration for the complex came from IBM's installation near Cagnes and, later, from the Texas Instruments research centre at Villeneuve-Loubet. The proximity of an international airport and the beautiful countryside were just two of the attractions of the area. In 1972, 2,400 hectares (5,928 acres) of forest were purchased and the Sophia-Antipolis technology park was established. Today, 18,000 people work at the steadily expanding site, many in the fields of telecommunications and biotechnology. Its highly advanced communications centre is unique in Europe.

GOLFE-JUAN (06220)
Population: 25,900 (including Vallauris)

The small Côte d'Azur town of Golfe-Juan, often bypassed on the N7 or the coastal road, is worth a detour for its pretty little beaches, two ports and a view over the Îles de Lérins on one side and Cap d'Antibes on the other.

Many celebrities have spent time in Golfe-Juan. The most famous is surely Napoleon I, 'The Eagle', who disembarked here on 1 March 1815. At that time, the harbour was a natural anchorage, with a few fishermen's huts and warehouses storing pottery. An obelisk and a column commemorate the landing. The column, topped by a Napoleonic bust, is on the RN7, at the junction with the CD135, heading towards Vallauris. It marks the departure point of the Route Napoléon (the first tourist attraction named after an historic figure). On his return from exile in Elba, Napoleon travelled with his troops from Golfe-Juan to Digne in six days; today, the Route Napoléon follows the route he took, with enough plaques and monuments to satisfy even his enormous ego. The party managed to avoid the troops in Marseille and the town of Antibes, which were royalist at the time, and overthrew the monarchy of Louis XVIII. The route culminates in the city of Grenoble, where The Eagle was welcomed on 7 March 1815.

Each year over a weekend in March, visitors can relive the glorious times of 1815 alongside costumed locals from Vallauris and Golfe-Juan. There are exhibitions and events, and even special dishes (chicken Marengo, Frascatti cake) commemorating Napoleon's battles. Find out more at the tourist office.

Many writers, including Chateaubriand, Victor Hugo and George Sand, as well as high-profile 19th-century politicians, have followed in Napoleon's footsteps and visited the town.

USEFUL ADDRESSES

🅱 Tourist office: 84 avenue de la Liberté. ☎ 04-93-63-73-12. Fax: 04-93-63-95-01. Open in summer every day from 9am to 7pm; rest of the year Monday to Friday 9am–noon and 2–6pm, Saturday from 9am to noon.

🚌 Buses: buses leave for Cannes and Nice every 20 minutes. Buses leave for Vallauris every 15 minutes.

WHERE TO STAY

🛏 Hôtel California: 222 avenue de la Liberté. 800 metres from the train station, on the N7 near the sea. ☎ 04-93-63-78-63. Closed during All Saints public holiday. Double rooms from 250F to 280F in high season and from 150F to 200F in low season. This 1930s building has been transformed into a hotel with pretty rooms and a relaxing atmosphere.

🛏 Le Palm-Hôtel: 17 avenue de la Palmeraie. ☎ 04-93-63-72-14.

Restaurant closed from 15 October to 1 March. Double rooms between 380F and 480F. Menus at 100F and 149F. Half board from 280F. The busy N7 does pass near by, but this old house, shaded by palm trees, has lots of charm. It has a pleasant terrace and exotic plants in the garden, and its owners extend a warm welcome. There are two car parks just 200 metres from the sea.

WHERE TO EAT

✕ Restaurant Bruno: 27 avenue Roustan (on the harbour). ☎ 04-93-63-72-12. Closed on Sunday evening and on Monday in low season, and from mid-November to mid-December. Menus at 88F and 145F. À la carte around 180F. This classic restaurant is in a lovely setting, with a fountain in the garden. The excellent Provençal food includes *bouillabaisse* and *petits rougets du pays flambés au pastis* (local red mullet in pastis). It's good value for money and the atmosphere is at its best in the evening.

✕ La Taverne: 45 boulevard des Frères-Roustan, in the port. ☎ 04-93-63-72-14. Closed in December and January and on Wednesday out of season. Menus at 100F and 130F. This unassuming but excellent fish restaurant charges reasonable prices. The *menu du port* features a selection of fish and seafood dishes, including fried fish, *grosse raviole aux fruits de mer dans son bouillon de légumes au pistou* (ravioli with seafood in a pesto and vegetable stock) and baked sea bream 'Golfe-Juan' style. The dining room is less than memorable, but there are tables outside.

DIVING

Dive School

■ **Golfe Plongée Club**: in the Golfe-Juan port, on quai Napoléon. ☎ 06-09-55-73-36 or 04-93-64-22-67. Email: golfplonge@aol.com. Website: www.members.aol.com/golfeplong. Open between March and December, and every day between April and October. The dive boat, the *Souvenez-vous*, has an on-board compressor and the school's state-qualified instructors (FFESSM, ANMP) teach novices, courses up to Level IV, and lead bio dives and exploratory dives to the best local sites (*see* 'Cannes', 'Dive Sites'). All necessary equipment is supplied and prices come down for 6 or 12 dives. The atmosphere on board is friendly. Book ahead if possible.

VALLAURIS (06220)
Population: 25,900 (including Golfe-Juan)

Vallauris, 2 kilometres northwest of its twin sister Golfe-Juan, has been equally well protected from development by its position in the valley of the Issourdadou. Surrounded by seven hills, this pottery town owes its reputation today to Picasso, who lived here for a couple of years, developing a passion for ceramics. The artist was instrumental in turning a traditional industry producing domestic ware into a respected decorative art. In summer, Vallauris is very touristy, with large crowds of visitors gazing at works in gallery and shop windows, unaware of whether the creator is dead or alive!

For serious art lovers, Vallauris is the venue for the Biennale Internationale de Céramique d'Art, a biennial celebration of ceramic art. Around 200 master potters still work in the town, using traditional methods. In a welcome commercial initiative, the best are allowed to display a 'quality-assurance' sticker. Many of the most famous decorative artists are represented in the important Musée de la Céramique (ceramics museum) in Sèvres – look out for Roger Collet, Gilbert Portanier, Roger Capron, Jean Derval, Yvan Koenig (Mosaïques Gerbino), Sassi-Milici and Gilbert Valentin – but theirs are inevitably the most expensive pieces.

Picasso and Vallauris

The inhabitants of Vallauris have been working in clay since Roman times. In 1501, following the decimation of the area by the plague, 70 Genoese families were brought in to repopulate the town, many of which were skilled potters. They contributed to the rebuilding of Vallauris and gave it the checkerboard street layout that is still partly evident.

In 1946, Picasso, living in Golfe-Juan with his family, was invited to visit the workshop of the Madoura Pottery, in Vallauris. He was impressed by the work of the potters and soon became passionate about ceramics, sometimes producing up to 25 pieces a day. He moved into La Galloise, a simple Vallauris villa where he lived, according to his friend Cocteau, 'like a splendid pauper'.

From 1949, Picasso concentrated on ceramics rather than painting. In 1951, the town asked him to decorate the deconsecrated chapel of the Vallauris priory. Some say that he completed the huge fresco, *Guerre et Paix*, in less time than it would have taken a decorator to slap paint on the wall.

Picasso was given honorary citizenship of Vallauris. He left for Cannes in 1955, and then moved to Mougins, but he remained very attached to the town. Vallauris arranged a big party for his 90th birthday, but Picasso declined the invitation, saying that he would like to attend the show but not *be* the show. He watched the celebrations at home on television.

Local Festivals

In mid-July, Vallauris is decked out for its Picasso festival in Spanish colours, and echoes to the sounds of Spanish music. The Fête des Potiers (potters' festival) takes place on the second Sunday in August, with *It's a Knockout*-style games, including a potters' version of *roumpa-pignata*, in which blindfolded players have to smash terracotta cooking pots suspended in front of them. The pots contain either a prize, or flour and water. All over the town, artists set up stalls, making little souvenirs for visitors out of local clay.

USEFUL ADDRESS

🛈 Tourist office: square du 8-Mai-1945. In the south car park. ☎ 04-93-63-82-58. Try to make a stop here before going into Vallauris, particularly in the summer, for a wide range of information and leaflets.

WHERE TO STAY

🛌 Hôtel Val d'Aurea: 11bis boulevard Maurice-Rouvier. ☎ 04-93-64-64-29. Closed from mid-September to April. Double room with bathroom around 280F in July and August, or 260F during the rest of the year. There are 26 simple, pleasant and peaceful rooms in this central and atmospheric hotel, regularly redecorated by the owner. His wife is friendly and charming, and guests can pop across the road to Au Temps Jadis for breakfast.

WHERE TO EAT

☆ Budget

✗ **Restaurant La Tonnelle**: rue Hoche (at right-angles to the main street). ☎ 04-93-64-34-01. Closed on Sunday and on Monday evening (except in July and August). One set menu at 100F, with a daily special at 45F and à la carte around 120F. Choose from a huge variety of pizzas and plates of fresh pasta as well as a selection of Provençal dishes. A great place to have lunch, either under the arbour or in the cool dining room. The mezzanine is quieter. The staff are very pleasant.

✗ **Lou Pichinet**: 16bis place Jules-Lisnard. Opposite the Espace Jean Marais. ☎ 04-93-64-63-70. Opens early in the day and closes in the evening. Menu at 100F. This bistrot serves delicious simple but tasty regional food. Daily specials include *daube* (beef stew), ravioli bolognaise, tripe and *petits farcis* (stuffed vegetables). The pretty terrace is far from the hordes.

|☆☆ – ☆☆☆| Moderate to Chic

✕ **Le Manuscrit**: 224 chemin Lintier, off boulevard du Tapis-Vert, in the centre of town; 50 metres on the right. ☎ 04-93-64-56-56. Closed on Monday in high season, on Sunday evening, all day Monday and Tuesday in low season. Closed from 15 November to 3 December each year. Menus at 105F (weekday lunch) and between 140F and 185F. This lovely grey stone house, a former perfume distillery, was a favourite of artist Jean Marais, whose works can be viewed in the garden and on the walls. It has a peaceful location, a delicious menu, offering local fish and regional food (from snails in garlic cream to a delicious fish stew), good wines and attractive prices. It's not unusual to see respectable ladies leaving their table from time to time to pick cherries and other ripe fruit from the nearby orchard.

WHAT TO SEE AND DO

★ **Place Paul-Isnard**: Picasso's bronze statue of a man with a sheep (*L'Homme au Mouton*, 1943) stands in this square, a rare example of a publicly displayed sculpture by the master. It was his gift to the town. Sadly, the commercial surroundings no longer provide an absolutely fitting environment. There's also a baroque church with a Romanesque tower.

★ **Château**: the former priory of Lérins, rebuilt in the 16th century. The square chateau is flanked by towers and houses two museums:

★ **Musée National Picasso**: ☎ 04-93-64-16-05. Open in July and August from 10am to 6.30pm; rest of the year, 10am–noon and 2–6pm. Closed on Tuesday and public holidays. Entrance fee: 17F. Picasso's *Guerre et Paix* (*War and Peace*, 1951) hangs in the crypt of the Romanesque chapel. War, on the left, is represented by a hearse and is painted in shades of grey, black and green. Horses drag the cart over the bloody earth, treading on books, symbolizing civilization. The soldier carries a shield bearing the image of a white dove and a spear shaped like a set of scales, symbolizing justice. On the opposing panel, painted in serene blue and white, figures dance and play under a flowering tree and a sun. An ideal society of fraternity without bigotry is shown in a simple mosaic of four differently coloured figures holding up a globe marked with a dove.

★ **Musée Magnelli, Musée de la Céramique** (ceramics museum): paintings and collages by the Italian abstract master Alberto Magnelli (1888–1971) hang here alongside pieces by the winners of the Biennale Internationale de Céramique d'Art (*see* page 574).

★ **Musée de la Poterie** (pottery museum): rue Sicard. ☎ 04-93-64-66-51. Open every day (except Sunday morning) 9am–noon and 2–6pm (afternoons only in winter). Entrance fee: 10F. This museum displays a faithful reproduction of a potter's studio from the beginning of the 20th century.

★ **Vallauris streets**: there are many ceramic shops in Vallauris, some selling beautiful pieces and others offering rather less attractive things. Two of the galleries deal in the work of two of the most famous artists in France: **Galerie Madoura**, just off rue du Mars 1962, sells copies of works by Picasso as well as pieces by contemporary artists. **Galerie Jean Marais**, in avenue des Martyrs-de-la-Résistance, is run by a friend of Marais, who produced a huge number of works and now attracts equally huge numbers of visitors to Vallauris.

★ **Maison de la Pétanque** (*pétanque* centre): 1193 chemin de St-Bernard. ☎ 04-93-64-11-36. Open Monday to Friday 9am–noon and 2–6.30pm (and Saturday in summer). Entrance fee: 20F. Housed in a cleverly converted factory, which has ceased actual manufacture of the *boules*, but continues to tell the story of the local game. Enthusiasts will love it and there's even the chance to order a set of *boules* engraved with your own name.

SHOPPING

🔒 **Nérolium**: access via avenue Georges-Clemenceau or avenue des Deux-Vallons. ☎ 04-93-64-27-54. The town's farmers' cooperative, whose name comes from neroli, or orangeflower essence. The shelves are full of bottles of olive oil, and jars of honey and marmalade.

🔒 **Gerbino mosaïque Koenig**: 8 avenue du Stade, to the right at the lower end of avenue Georges-Clemenceau). ☎ 04-93-63-77-18. Vases, plates and decorative items in mixed clay.

🔒 **Galerie Sassi-Milici**: 65 avenue Georges-Clemenceau. ☎ 04-93-64-65-71. Fine gallery with an interesting atmosphere, displaying ceramic pieces by Boncompain and a permanent exhibition of work by Roger Capron.

🔒 **Roger Collet**: montée Ste-Anne. ☎ 04-93-64-65-84. Tucked in beside the church, this is the studio of a talented and modest ceramic artist, skilled in working with enamel.

JUAN-LES-PINS (06160)
Population: 72,310 (with Antibes)

In 1881, a banker, realizing the potential of the stretch of coastline that was to become the Côte d'Azur, created the 'land association of Cannes and the coast', and this resort was born – the Duke of Albany, son of Queen Victoria, quickly registered his interest – the town could have been called Albany-les-Pins – and the society purchased large tracts of land in the splendid pine forest. However, at the beginning of the 20th century, the speculative company went bankrupt, having built just eight hotels and two villas. The casino was built in 1908, but World War I put paid to any more development for a while.

In 1924, Édouard Baudouin, owner of a casino in Deauville on France's northern coast, saw Florida's Miami Beach in a film at the cinema and was inspired to recreate it on the warm Côte d'Azur. He bought the casino in Juan-les-Pins, added a restaurant and saw his investment flourish. American railroad heir Frank Jay Gould fell in love with the area while on honeymoon with his third wife, Florence, and teamed up with Baudouin in 1927 to build Le Provençal, a huge luxury hotel. The construction took less than 12 months.

About the time of the launch of Le Provençal, the tradition of the summer season began; before, visitors had come only in winter. These were Juan's glory days, often tainted by scandal. A tan suddenly became fashionable and young women would go swimming in revealing costumes. Celebrities poured into the resort, including Scott Fitzgerald, Rudolf Valentino, the Warner brothers, Ernest Hemingway, and a selection of kings, queens and maharajahs. The visitors had two things in common: money and a desire to spend it on themselves. Jazz hit Europe in Juan, where Louis Armstrong, Count Basie and Errol Garner were frequent visitors. Today, a major jazz festival still takes place in July.

After World War II, it all got going once again, when the children of the rich Americans who had helped to launch Juan originally returned to fill its coffers again. In the 1950s, sailors of the Sixth Fleet would stop over for R and R, the resort partied just as it had between the wars and Juan flourished again.

Jazz in Juan

Juan's world-renowned jazz festival is held during the last two weeks of July. Book tickets in writing through the tourist office of Antibes–Juan-les-Pins, or for more information call: ☎ 04-92-90-53-00. The festival grew out of the regular visits of the American clarinettist and saxophonist Sidney Bechet, who loved Juan and its ambience. He died in 1959, but since 1960, Europe's first jazz festival has been held in the Gould pine forest (named after Frank Jay). All the greats of jazz have played at the festival, including Ella Fitzgerald, Al Jarreau, Fats Domino and Lionel Hampton, under the ancient pine trees, with the Mediterranean Sea, the Îles de Lérins and the Estérel as a backdrop.

USEFUL ADDRESSES

🛈 **Tourist office**: 51 boulevard Guill-aumont. ☎ 04-92-90-53-05. Open from September to end June Monday to Friday 9am–noon and 2–6pm, Saturday 9am–noon; in summer Monday to Saturday 8.45am–7.30pm, Sunday 9.30am–12.30pm. Website: www.guide-azur.com.

🚆 **Train station**: place de la Gare (avenue de l'Estérel). ☎ 08-36-35-35-35.

■ **Bicycle and motorbike hire**: Thrifty Elite, 122 boulevard Wilson. ☎ 04-93-67-66-94.

WHERE TO STAY

The streets in Juan town centre buzz until the early hours, with shops staying open late, and cafés and nightclubs catering for night owls. However, there are a few very pleasant spots where hotel guests can find peace and quiet.

☆☆ – ☆☆☆☆ Moderate to Chic

🛏 **La Marjolaine**: 15 avenue du Docteur-Fabre. ☎ 04-93-61-06-60. Fax: 04-93-61-02-75. Closed in November and at the end of March. Double rooms with shower and toilet from 210F to 310F, with bathroom from 240F to 360F (less for a stay of three nights or more between October and June). Secure parking. This charming hotel is in a quiet street and has a pretty garden with oleanders. The pleasant rooms are decorated and furnished with taste, and identified not by numbers but by interesting names, such as 'La Loggia', 'Le Manoir' and 'L'Églantine'.

⌂ **Hôtel Christie**: rue de l'Oratoire. ☎ 04-93-61-01-98. Fax: 04-93-61-47-52. Email: hotelchristie@wanadoo.fr. Rooms between 400F and 450F. Agatha Christie would certainly have appreciated this nostalgic establishment. Regulars recommend it wholeheartedly as the perfect place for a short stay.

⌂ **Hôtel Ste-Valérie**: rue de l'Oratoire. ☎ 04-93-61-07-15. Fax: 04-93-61-47-52. Email: sainte-valerie @wanadoo.fr. Closed from 30 September to 15 April. Double rooms with shower and toilet from 580F to 700F, and with bathroom from 640F to 960F. Menu at 135F. À la carte around 150F. This is a discreet and smart hotel in a quiet part of Juan-les-Pins, a stone's throw from the Gould pine forest and the sea. It has modern but pleasantly decorated rooms, a cool shady garden, with magnolia trees, and a glamorous swimming pool. All in all, the perfect place for a romantic break.

WHERE TO EAT

✗ **Le Capitole**: 26 avenue Amiral-Courbet. ☎ 04-93-61-22-44. Closed on Tuesday, and for two weeks in November. Menus from 70F (until 8pm only) to 105F. Not far from the town centre, Le Capitole has been offering good value for money since 1956, serving scallops, *confit de canard* (duck terrine), nougat ice-cream and grapefruit soufflé.

☆☆☆ Chic

✗ **Restaurant Le Perroquet**: avenue G.-Gallice. ☎ 04-93-61-02-20. Menus at 145F and 175F. À la carte around 200F. This pretty restaurant, decorated in pink and pastel blue, is a relaxing venue, Provençal in style. A pleasant terrace overlooks the Pinède garden and fish features strongly on the menu. There are reduced-price dishes for children.

WHERE TO GO FOR A DRINK

❢ **Le Pam Pam**: 137 boulevard Wilson. ☎ 04-93-61-11-05. Le Pam Pam stays open until the early hours, but is closed between November and the end of March. Brazilian bands and excellent exotic cocktails attract people from all along the coast, and it's difficult to find somewhere to sit after 9pm in the summer. The salt cod is expensive but excellent.

WHAT TO SEE

★ **Exflora Gardens**: avenue de Cannes. Open every day from 9.30am to 7pm. Within 5 hectares (12 acres), visitors can walk through different examples of Mediterranean gardens, from ancient Rome to the exuberant style of the Riviera of the 19th century.

CAP D'ANTIBES

Among the superb villas and luxurious palaces set among the pines on the splendid peninsula that separates Antibes from Juan-les-Pins, the most famous is the Hôtel du Cap. It was here that the legend of the Cap and of

Juan-les-Pins began. In 1914, Italian hotelier André Sella bought the Villa Soleil, abandoned for nearly 50 years, restored it and turned it into a hotel for the rich bourgeoisie. It was the first hotel to remain open throughout the summer and is still in operation today. In the past, its glamorous guests included Marlene Dietrich, Douglas Fairbanks, Mary Pickford and Gloria Swanson, while in more recent times Madonna, Claudia Cardinale, Alain Delon, Robert de Niro and Arnold Schwarzenegger have all stayed here.

On the Antibes side the Cap starts at the small **Port de la Salis**, which has a lovely (free) beach. Swimmers have a wonderful view of the mimosas and pines on the Cap. On the other side is the grey mass of the ramparts of Antibes and its chateau, with the Baie des Anges and the Alps in the background.

As soon as the beach resort at Juan was properly set up, it became a success. Oddly, speculation on the Cap d'Antibes failed equally rapidly, which explains why the headland remains relatively unscathed. The local council later passed a law governing the protection of the area, and building in concrete was limited in a way that was not possible on other parts of the coast.

At the end of the 19th century, artists drawn to the area included Anatole France, Jules Verne (author of *20,000 Leagues Under the Sea*) and the writer Guy de Maupassant. Later, celebrity figures moved in, buying up large properties surrounded by countryside, seeking peace and privacy. The Duke of Windsor and Wallis Simpson spent time in the Château de la Croë, which was bought in 1952 by Greek shipowner Stavros Niarchos, and then destroyed in a fire in 1980. The nearby Villa Eilenroc was designed in 1867 by Charles Garnier (architect of the Paris opera house) for the governor of the Dutch East Indies). Its name was an anagram of Cornélie, his wife's name. The singer Hélène Beaumont bought it in 1927 and spent 180,000F on an antique bathroom, or more than an entire villa would have cost at the time. The villa sat in magnificent grounds, and Léopold II of Belgium, ex-King Farouk of Egypt, Aristotle Onassis and Greta Garbo were among the guests.

Today, the extraordinary splendour and fierce security systems of the villas hint at the fact that very important – and fortunate – people still live here, if only for a few months of the year.

Cap d'Antibes also has retirement homes, childrens' holiday camps and huge greenhouses. The world's most productive grower of carnations is from Antibes, but the region is more famous for its roses: it now claims that one rose in three was created here.

Some of the most surprising buildings on the Cap are the lovely *cabanons* (chalets), with their little gardens, which sit next to the millionaires' properties. From the plage de la Garoupe, the Sentier du Tir-Poil footpath follows the sea. It's a lovely walk for people of all ages and in almost all weathers, with partial views of huge properties, well hidden behind the pines.

WHERE TO STAY

☆ Budget

☗ **Relais International de la Jeunesse** (youth hostel): 60 avenue de l'Antiquité, at the corner of boulevard de la Garoupe. ☎ 04-93-61-63-54. Fax: 04-93-80-65-33. Open from mid-March to November. 75F per night, with breakfast included, and 145F for half board. A wonderful position among the pines on the Cap d'Antibes. The pretty four-person room, with balcony and a direct sea view, is perfect for a family or a group of friends. There's a small camping area for a dozen tents.

☆☆ Moderate

☗ **La Jabotte**: 13 avenue Max-Maurey, at right-angles to boulevard James-Wyllie, on the edge of Cap d'Antibes. ☎ 04-93-61-45-89. Fax: 04-93-61-07-04. Closed from 15 November to 15 December. Double rooms with shower and toilet between 290F and 410F. Half board 250F to 370F per person. This hotel offers excellent value for money, particularly in the bungalows that overlook the terrace. The welcome is friendly and the atmosphere relaxing. Try to avoid arriving on a Sunday between 1pm and 6pm, the only time when the owners take a few hours off.

☆☆☆ Chic

☗ **Villa Panko**: 17 chemin du Parc-Saramartel. ☎ 04-93-67-92-49. Fax: 04-93-61-29-32. Double rooms between 500F and 730F. Just a 10-minute walk from the sandy beaches, this villa is a dream place, with two prettily decorated, comfortable rooms. Gourmet breakfasts can be taken in the floral garden and picnics on the terrace.

WHAT TO SEE

★ **Plateau de la Garoupe**: the plateau is on the highest point of the headland, and has a lighthouse, a grand view from St-Tropez to the Italian Alps and an ancient seamen's chapel. **Notre-Dame-de-Bon-Port** has two naves, one dating from the 13th century and one from the 16th century, and wrought-iron gates. It also has a collection of interesting ex-voto offerings, which include paintings, models of ships, family photos, paintings and simple messages on scraps of paper. The oldest commemorates a surprise attack on Antibes by Saracen pirates. There are two wooden statues, one of Notre-Dame-de-la-Garde and the other Notre-Dame-de-Bon-Port (Our Lady of Safe Haven), protectress of seafarers.

You can get to the plateau on the chemin du Calvaire, from the end of plage de la Salis. If you have the energy after the walk, climb the 116 steps of the **lighthouse**, which was built in 1837. The view from the top is magnificent, as far as Corsica on a good day. The lens of the lighthouse is supported by 25 litres of mercury. Unfortunately, visits are not possible.

★ **Jardin Thuret** (gardens): 1 boulevard du Cap. Open every day (except Saturday and Sunday) from 8am to 6pm. Entry is free. The gardens were laid out in 1866 by botanist Gustave Adolphe Thuret, and visited two years later by George Sand who was most impressed 'by this Eden'. Today, under the guardianship of l'Institute National de la recherche Agronomique (the national institute for agronomic research), there are around 140 different botanical specimens, a dozen of which are very rare.

★ **Musée Naval et Napoléonien** (naval and Napoleonic museum): avenue J.-F.-Kennedy. ☎ 04-93-61-45-32. Open 9.30am–noon and 2.15–6pm. Closed on Saturday afternoon, Sunday, and in October. Entrance fee: 20F. At the tip of the Cap, the Tour Grillon (the tower also known as the Tour Sella) rises above the remains of a former battery, built facing the Îles de Lérins. It houses a museum with ships' models and items relating to Napoleon's connections with Antibes. From the summit of the tower, there's a view over the extreme tip of the headland, covered in trees and inaccessible to walkers because the land is all private, as well as the Pointe de La Croisette and the Îles de Lérins.

ANTIBES (06600)
Population: 72,400 (with Juan-les Pins)

Antibes benefits from a beautiful site, between two coves. Its city walls reach into the ocean, and it has a lovely harbour, and a charming old town with narrow winding lanes and tall, ivy-covered houses. Unlike Juan-les-Pins, Antibes is not just a summer resort and doesn't rely on tourism alone. It has the second-largest population in the *département*, after Nice. Stroll along the quay at the Port Vauban, explore the ramparts, wander through the pleasant lanes of the old town or simply relax on a café terrace on the place Nationale, shaded by plane trees. Sometimes, the sea seems far away, but the seamen at the nearby table are a reminder that the port is just around the corner.

History

Towards the fourth century BC, the Greeks established a trading colony here and called it *Antipolis*, 'the city opposite' – in this case, opposite Nice. In the Middle Ages, it became known as *Antiboul*. The pope established a bishopric here and the religious influence of the city grew alongside that of the monastery in Lérins. In the middle of the eighth century, repeated invasions by the Visigoths and the Saracens almost destroyed the city, and any prosperity that survived fell victim to the plague. The bishop left for Grasse in 1236, and Antibes remained anonymous for more than two centuries.

In the 14th century, the kings of France turned their attention to Antibes' strategic position, on the frontier between France and the kingdom of Savoy. Henri IV began a process of fortification, which was pursued by Vauban (1707). When Napoleon landed in Golfe-Juan in 1815, royalist Antibes refused to welcome him. His 40 envoys were imprisoned, but Napoleon himself was not attacked by the local leader; if he had been, history may well have taken a different course. Louis XVIII later formally acknowledged the loyalty shown by the town.

In 1894, the fortifications were almost totally destroyed in order to allow the expansion of the town. Up to this point, Antibes had managed to resist the influx of foreigners, who went instead to Cannes or Nice. After 1920, tourists began to be welcomed in Antibes, in moderation, and creative stars such as Max Ernst, Picasso, Prévert, Sidney Bechet and Nicolas de Staël came too.

USEFUL ADDRESSES

🏛 Tourist office: 11 place du Général-de-Gaulle. ☎ 04-92-90-53-00. Fax: 04-92-90-53-01. Open from Easter to end June, and in September, from Monday to Friday 9am–12.30pm and 2–7pm; Saturday 9am–noon and 2–6pm. In July and August, Monday to Saturday 8.45am–7.30pm; Sunday 9.30am–12.30pm. During the rest of the year Monday to Friday 9am–12.30pm and 2–6.30pm; Saturday 9am–noon and 2–6pm. The office has a good range of brochures and information.

🚆 Train station: avenue Robert-Soleau, behind Port Vauban, at the exit from Antibes towards Nice. ☎ 08-36-35-35-35. There are several Métrazur trains a day to Cannes and Nice. The station is about a 10-minute walk from the centre.

🚌 Bus station: from place du Général-de-Gaulle, walk down the rue la République. The building is immediately on the right. Buses for Nice, Cannes and Cagnes leave place du Général-de-Gaulle.

■ Buses to Nice airport: the bus to Nice goes via the airport.

■ Bicycle and motorbike hire: several hire companies; ask at the tourist office for a list.

WHERE TO STAY

☆☆ Moderate

🛏 Le Ponteil (B&B): 11 impasse J.-Mensier. ☎ 04-93-34-67-92. Fax: 04-93-34-49-47. Closed from 22 November until early February, except for festivals. Rooms between 370F and 420F. Half board compulsory from June to end September, for 310F to 410F. A quiet and friendly spot, surrounded by vegetation, with a good host and pretty and clean rooms (either in the villa itself or the bungalow). The food is traditional – savoury tarts, *gratins* – cooked by the owner himself for half-board guests.

🛏 L'Étoile: 2 avenue Gambetta. A five-minute walk from the train station. ☎ 04-93-34-26-30. Fax: 04-93-34-41-48. Email: info@hotel etoile.com. Double rooms from 280F to 310F, with shower and toilet, and from 320F to 350F with bathroom. The only hotel in its price category right in the centre of Antibes. Modern and comfortable, it has spacious, soundproofed rooms. The welcome is warm and friendly but, rather unusually, you are asked to settle your account on arrival.

☆☆☆☆ Très Chic

🛏 L'Auberge Provençale: 61 place Nationale. ☎ 04-93-34-13-24. Fax: 04-93-34-89-88. Closed on Monday, Tuesday lunch and in January. Double rooms with bathroom for 450F. Excellent menus at 85F, 145F and 240F. A cosy house under the plane trees, with just six rooms, all spotless and well furnished in Provençal style. The small garden has tables under the trees, and the menu offers some delightful fish dishes, including scorpion fish and salmon in tasty sauces.

🛏 Chambres d'hôte La Bastide du Bosquet (B&B): with Christian and Sylvie Aussel, 14 chemin des Sables. ☎ and fax: 04-93-67-32-29. Closed in November. Rooms between 420F and 480F (depending on season), including breakfast.

Half-way between the beaches in Antibes and Juan-les-Pins, this hotel is housed in a 12th-century building, with three spacious, charming, en suite rooms, furnished in old Provençal style and well kept. The welcome is warm, and the place is very peaceful. French author Guy de Maupassant spent a winter here.

🛏 **Mas Djoliba**: 29 avenue de Provence. ☎ 04-93-34-02-48. Fax: 04-93-34-05-81. Email: info@pcastel-djoliba.com. Closed in November, December and January. Double rooms between 450F and 490F with shower and toilet and from 540F to 640F with bathroom. Half board preferred (but not compulsory), 400F to 505F per person in high season. This pretty Provençal *mas* stands in a small park and has comfortable pleasant rooms and a nice pool. A good place to relax if you don't fancy the beach. The prices represent good value for money and the welcome is warm.

WHERE TO EAT

☒ Budget

✕ **La Socca, Chez Jo**: 1 rue James-Close. ☎ 04-93-34-15-00. Closed on Monday, and from mid-December to mid-January. Eat on the hop here for between 40F and 80F, or try *socca*, a Nice speciality, at just 12F. The pizzas are among the best in Antibes, and there's often a queue at this smallish venue, particularly at Sunday lunchtime.

✕ **Adieu Berth**: 26 rue Vauban. Between the port and the post office. ☎ 04-93-34-78-84. Closed on Tuesday in low season and during the first two weeks in January. Meals for around 70F. Good crêpes served until 1am, with all kinds of fillings, in an unpretentious Provençal-style restaurant.

✕ **Comic Strips Café**: 4 rue James-Close. ☎ 04-93-34-91-40. Meals for around 50F in this pleasant restaurant, also a bookshop, and very popular with lovers of comic books.

✕ **Key-West**: 30 boulevard de l'Aiguillon. ☎ 04-93-34-58-20. Closed on Tuesday (except in July and August) and from December to end February. Open from 8.30am. Quick meals (from full English breakfast to chilli con carne), for around 50F. The prices are low, the welcome warm and the food is perfect for a quick snack as you stroll through the narrow streets or along the port. Popular with locals, which is always a good sign.

☒☒ Moderate

✕ **Le Latino**: 24 boulevard de L'Aiguillon. ☎ 04-93-34-44-22. Closed for lunch on Saturday, Sunday and Monday. Meals around 100F. This young and hip venue serves tapas and cocktails. The service can be slow, but the atmosphere is friendly and the food is good value for money.

✕ **Le Safranier**: 1 place du Safranier. ☎ 04-93-34-80-50. Closed on Sunday evening and all day Monday in winter; Monday and Tuesday lunchtime in high season, and from 15 December to 15 January. Menu at 62F. À la carte 120–160F. Enjoy grilled fish on the terrace under the arbour. The service and welcome are friendly and the atmosphere is more like a small village bistrot. Order ahead for *bouillabaisse*. Bank cards not accepted.

✕ **L'Oiseau Qui Chante**: 3 boulevard du Général-Vautrin. ☎ 04-93-74-88-75 or 04-93-74-87-78. À la carte around 70F. This unassuming restaurant is tucked away between a bridge, a bypass and busy traffic, but regulars come back again and again. The pizzas are excellent, and the ravioli delicious. The fish might be frozen (*poisson congelé*), but it is specified on the menu.

✗ **Chez Juliette**: 18 rue Sade, a pedestrianized street in the old quarter of Antibes. ☎ 04-93-34-67-37. Closed for lunch on Monday and Tuesday. Menus between 80F and 160F. This restaurant, in a vaulted cellar, serves food cooked in a wood-fired oven, including *daube provençale* (beef stew) with polenta and *lapin façon Juliette* (rabbit in house style). The service is friendly and efficient and the atmosphere is perfect for a cosy evening with friends.

☆☆☆☆ Très Chic

✗ **L'Oursin**: 16 rue de la République. ☎ 04-93-34-13-46. Closed on Sunday evening and on Monday in winter, as well as at the end of May, the end of November and the end of February. Set menu 195F. À la carte around 180F. L'Oursin is famous for its fresh fish and inventive seafood dishes. Locals come here for the attractive marine decor, the warm welcome and the good service.

✗ **La Bonne Auberge**: on the RN7 towards Nice, just before Villeneuve-Loubet. ☎ 04-93-33-36-65. Closed on Monday (except 1 July and August) and from 20 November to 10 December. *Menu-carte* at 220F (changes each month). The chef's key dish is *salade de homard aux ravioles de Romans* (salad of lobster and ravioli), but the *daube aux olives* (stew with olives) is also delicious, and the lunch menu is good value. There's a lovely wine list but you should stick to local wines if you're on a budget. Booking recommended.

NIGHTLIFE

❢ **Legend Café**: place Audiberti. Open until 2.30am. The atmosphere is young, trendy and lively, and there's a good choice of beers in this upturned ship's hull.

– **La Siesta**: on the seafront (towards Nice). ☎ 04-93-33-31-31. Thousands of people come to this famous club on summer evenings. There are seven dance floors, all with exotic decor, but it's not cheap.

WHAT TO SEE

★ From the Porte Marine, take a left turn to reach the **seafront promenade** on avenue Amiral-de-Grasse. The walk goes along the only remaining section of the ramparts of Antibes, which has survived revolution, war and the commercial expansion of the town. At the beginning is the house in which the artist Nicolas de Staël is said to have committed suicide. From one side of the ramparts, the view is over Cap d'Antibes; the other side looks out over the magnificent coastline, stretching as far as Nice and Le Mercantour. Half-way along the avenue Amiral-de-Grasse, take a right turn into the old town, by the Château Grimaldi, formerly a residence of the Grimaldi family, a Roman castrum and an episcopal building. Today, it houses the Musée Picasso.

★ **Musée Picasso**: Château Grimaldi (behind the town hall). ☎ 04-92-90-54-20. Fax: 04-92-90-54-21. Open from 1 June to 30 September every day (except Monday) from 10am to 6pm; during the rest of the year, every day (except Monday) 10am–noon and 2–6pm. Closed on public holidays. Entrance fee: 30F.

In the summer of 1946, Picasso, on holiday in Golfe-Juan, was invited to create a work for the Musée d'Antibes. The legendary artist had been looking to paint on large surfaces and was quickly offered a substantial space in the museum. He took a part of the building as his studio, with windows overlooking the tiled roofs of the old town, the port, the bay and the distant mountains. Inspired by his surroundings, he worked night and day during the autumn of 1946. The exhilarating works that he produced, and gave to the museum, reflect an exuberant mood. Alongside the paintings, the museum displays black and white photos of Picasso at work, taken by such luminaries as Brassaï, Capa and Villers. They clearly show the raw energy and dynamism of the artist.

Three themes dominate Picasso's work from his time in Antibes: mythology, local activity painted in naturalist style, and nudes. Mythological figures such as nymphs, centaurs and fauns appear in *Triptyques au Centaure*, *Ulysse et les Sirènes* and *Faunes musiciens*. Local people going about their daily business are captured on canvas. *Le Gobeur d'oursins*, the best example of this naturalist style, was painted over a portrait of an Antibes general – it seems that canvases were in short supply after the war, and stocks could not keep up with such a level of productivity. His nudes – particularly *Nus couchés: au lit blanc, au lit bleu* and *sur fond vert* – have direct links with cubism.

As well as a number of paintings on wood, completed in 1946, the collection has been added to with the bequeathing of nearly 80 ceramic pieces made by Picasso in Vallauris and other works such as *Buste d'homme au chapeau*. The ensemble is dominated by Picasso's famous and monumental *Joie de Vivre*, which glorifies everything that Antibes meant to the artist.

The museum also houses a collection of works by Léger, Hartung, Ernst, Miró, Calder, Magnelli and Nicolas de Staël. De Staël completed 350 striking paintings in just six months alone in his studio in Antibes, before his death (suicide, or an accidental fall from his window), in 1955. *Grand Concert* was his final work, but it is *Nature morte sur fond bleu* that really reflects the coldness and terrible solitude of the artist's life. His work is displayed on the second floor.

On the terrace, facing the sea, the bronze and stone sculptures by Germaine Richier are reminiscent of the work of Giacometti. Also in the collection are Miró's *Sea Goddess*, *Hommage à Picasso* by Arman, and *Jupiter et Encelade* by Patrick and Anne Poirier, created from 10 tons of white marble and Roman remains.

★ **Musée Peynet**: place Nationale. ☎ 04-92-90-54-30. Open Tuesday to Sunday, 10am–noon and 2–6pm. Closed on public holidays. Entrance fee: 20F. Set in a 19th-century school, this exhibition takes you on a journey back to the 1960s with its love postcards, penned by Raymond Peynet, father of the genre, who lived in Antibes from 1978. Works in gouache are on display together with sketches that combine humour and poetry. A collection of Peynet's famous dolls can also be seen, together with some of his stage sets.

ANTIBES | WHAT TO SEE | 587

★ **Les Bains Douches**: boulevard de L'Aiguillon. Open every day. Free entry. This art and exhibition space is housed in the former municipal baths and artists' studios have been created in the renovated ramparts.

★ **Église de L'Immaculée Conception**: just across the street from the Musée Picasso, this church was built over a Greek temple. The frontier town of Antibes was heavily bombarded by marauders from the sea, particularly during the period when the county of Nice did not belong to France, and this church was in the firing line. It also suffered a fire under the reign of Louis XV. It has a lovely classical facade, with sculpted wooden doors dating back to 1710. Only the chevet is Romanesque. Inside, there's a wooden crucifix from 1147, a 16th-century *Christ* and, in the right-hand chapel, a fine altarpiece by Bréa (1515), depicting the Virgin Mary.

★ **Market**: daily (except Monday) from 6am to noon, in the Cours Masséna, the main street of Greek Antipolis. Antibes' market is one of the most interesting in the region, selling a cornucopia of the best produce that Provence has to offer. A second-hand market takes place on the nearby place Audiberti on a Thursday from 6am to 6pm.

★ **Old streets**: in the old streets in Antibes, on either side of the market square, particularly in the **rue de l'Horloge, rue du Révely, rue des Arceaux** and **rue du Bari**, there's a refreshing tranquillity. The narrow alleys are lined with small homes, many of which have been renovated, and there are pretty fountains on the squares.

★ **Commune libre du Safranier** (free parish of Le Safranier). Paris has Montmartre and, since 1966, Antibes has had Le Safranier, an independent community of 2,000 parishioners, with its own mayor, festival committee and policeman. Legend has it that there was a small port on place du Safranier in days gone by. Today, it's the venue for parish festivals; the mayor officiates at weddings. The name Le Safranier may have come from the French for 'saffron', to describe the colour of the soil, or from the same word meaning 'rudder blade', referring to the boat parts that were made in the region.

The streets, particularly **rue du Haut** and **rue du Bas-Castelet**, are pretty, with scented flowers. Towards the end of his life, Nikos Kazantzakis, the author of *Zorba the Greek*, would pass the time of day on the bench in the little square that now bears his name. For him, being in Antibes was like being back in Greece.

★ **Musée de la Tour** (tower museum): Portail de l'Orme (next to Cours Masséna). ☎ 04-93-34-50-91. Open on Wednesday, Thursday and Saturday 4pm to 7pm in summer, and from 3pm to 5pm in winter. Entrance fee: 10F. This old-fashioned and nostalgic museum has costumes, furniture, photographs, household items and tools belonging to the fisher-folk of Antibes. A display on the third floor tells the story of water-skiing, invented in 1931 in Juans-Pins. There's also a lovely 16th-century limewood statue of St Sebastian, the town's patron saint.

★ **Musée d'Histoire et d'Archéologie** (history and archaeology museum): in the Bastion St-André. ☎ 04-92-90-54-35. Open 10am–noon and 2–6pm. Closed on Monday , public holidays and during November. Entrance fee: 10F. The museum, housed in an impressive part of the remains of Vauban's fortifications, takes visitors through the entire history of

FROM ST-RAPHAËL TO NICE AND THE HINTERLAND

Antipolis, with Greek and Etruscan amphorae, coins and jewels dredged up from the sea in 1970. Some fragments date as far back as the fourth century.

★ **Port Vauban**: the large harbour is overlooked by the well-armed 16th-century Fort Carré, which was never conquered. Visits to the fort are in guided groups only. Open from Tuesday to Sunday in high season (Wednesday, Saturday, Sunday and public holidays in winter) 10am–12.30pm and 1.30–4pm. You have to leave by 6pm in summer, and tickets cost 30F for adults.

Unlike the artificial marinas elsewhere along the coast, the port at Antibes is a beautiful natural site, totally integrated into the Anse St-Roch (cove), with the fortress in the background and overlooked by the old ramparts. The new pre-port section can accommodate vessels up to 150 metres (490 feet) long. Antibes also has the biggest marina in Europe, for ships of more than 165 metres (540 feet). The famous Quai des Mille-et-Une-Nuit (1001 Nights Quay), near the harbourmaster's office, is the spot for the really luxurious yachts. Along the other wharves and through the old port, hidden behind the old town fortifications, you might well see a film being shot.

WHAT TO DO

– **Marineland**: at the junction of the N7 and route de Biot. By train, get off at Biot station. ☎ 04-93-33-49-49. Open every day from 10am to 8pm (until midnight in July and August). Around 150F for adults and 100F for children. Special deals allow entry to the Parc de la Mer (marine park), the Petite Ferme (little farm) and the Jungle des Papillons (butterfly house). Refreshments available. Allow at least half a day, or more. The sea-life show has dolphins, killer whales, sea-lions and seals, and there's also a museum and a number of aquaria, as well as domestic animals and tropical insects. Sharks swim around the 30-metre (100-foot) tunnel.

– **Aquasplash**: next to Marineland. ☎ 04-93-33-49-49. Open every day in summer. Entrance fee: 98F (children 82F). Water park with a pool with a wave machine, and 12 water slides.

– **Adventure Golf**: 46F. Mini golf at an exotic site.

DIVING

There are over 50 lovely dive sites around Antibes, suitable for divers of all levels, although some are rather exposed. Although there are few wrecks, there is a wealth of natural riches. The importance of the sport in this region is reflected in the prestigious Festival Mondial de l'Image Sous-marine (international festival of underwater photography), which has been held in Antibes and Juan-les-Pins for 30 years.

Dive School

■ **Fabulite**: Hôtel Fabulite, 150 traverse des Nielles (small street at the top of the Port de l'Olivette). ☎ 04-93-61-47-45. Email: fabulite@wanadoo.fr. Open from April to All Saints public holiday. Small dive club (FFESSM, ANMP, PADI) with state-qualified instructors who lead first dives and courses up to

Level III as well as PADI courses, and classes for children over 8. Their vessel, *Fabulite*, is moored in Port des Croûtons and exploratory dives take place in the best spots in the area. Equipment is supplied and educational bio dives and mixed gas diving (Nitrox and Trimix) are also offered.

Dive Sites

Cap Gros: moray and conger eels inhabit this flat rock (at 10 metres/33 feet), followed by a 25-metre (82-foot) drop covered in anenomes and sea fans. All levels.

La Love: near Cap d'Antibes. The plateau is covered in Neptune grass and then there are four canyons in a star shape (at 25 metres/82 feet), with angler fish and rays. The rocks are covered in sea fans, and there are often conger eels and scorpion fish. Tranquil site that is ideal for beginners.

Le Boule: not far from Cap d'Antibes. An attractive canyon (10–35 metres/33–115 feet), followed by an abrupt drop, full of holes. Look out for sea bream. For divers of all levels, but be careful of passing boats and keep an eye on the current.

Le Raventurier: out to sea. Isolated rocky plateau (at 35–45 metres/115–148 feet) with clear waters and luxurious aquatic life, including groupers and moray eel, and possibly a barracuda or two. Magnificent Level III dive.

BIOT (06410)   Population: 7,490

The picturesque village of Biot (pronounced to rhyme with 'yacht'), just a few kilometres from the sea, is famous first for its traditional crafts of pottery and bubble-flecked, mouth-blown glassware, and then for the Musée Fernand-Léger. The old village, with its sloping streets and its arcaded square, has loads of charm.

Biot has long been known for its pottery industry. The Romans used the fine clay of the region to make huge wine and oil jars. At the end of the 19th century, metal tanks began to be used to carry wine and oil, and the industry declined. However, in the 1950s, it began to be reborn, as second-homers demanded traditional decorative vessels for their gardens.

USEFUL ADDRESSES

Tourist office: place de la Chapelle. ☎ 04-93-65-05-85. Fax: 04-93-65-70-96. Open every day (except Saturday and Sunday morning) 10am–noon and 2.30–7pm; in winter, 9am–noon and 2–6pm.

Buses: nine return buses run each day from Antibes train station to Biot. The Biot bus stop is by the sea at La Brague, a steep 4-kilometre (2.5-mile) walk up to the village itself.

WHERE TO STAY AND EAT

Auberge de la Vallée Verte: 3400 route de Valbonne. ☎ 04-93-65-10-93. Fax: 04-92-94-04-91.

Closed on Wednesday. No dinner served between 31 October and 1 February. Double rooms from 250F to 320F, with bathroom. Half board around 320F per person. Menus at 120F and 160F. This attractive farmhouse, stands in a garden slightly out of the centre of town and almost lost in the hills. There's a pleasant pool, surrounded by lounge chairs, and the restaurant offers traditional cooking, including delicious mussels and kidneys.

Campsites

There are several sites around Biot, rather spoiling the landscape.

☗ **Les Oliviers**: 274 chemin des Routes-Vignasses. From the seafront, drive past the Biot glassworks and take the road that climbs up to the right. Turn right at chemin des Hautes-Vignasses, and follow the signposts. ☎ 04-93-65-02-79 (in low season: ☎ 04-93-65-11-12). Open from June to September.

120F for two. Principally for campers with their own transport, but the site can be reached by bus. It's exclusively for tents, and highly recommended, with its terraces and ancient olive trees, a lovely view of Biot and a swimming pool.

☗ **Le Mistral**: 1780 route de la Mer. 800 metres from the sea. ☎ 04-93-65-61-48. Fax: 04-93-65-75-64. Open from 25 March to 27 October. Clean camping site offering sites for mobile homes. Dogs not allowed.

Rural Gîte

☗ **Villa des Roses**, with M and Mme R Dalmasso: 14 chemin Neuf. ☎ 04-93-65-02-03. Fax: 04-93-65-62-85. Open all year. From 1,485F per week to 2,314F in high season. Four comfortable self-catering units in a beautiful building, just 200 metres from the village. Book ahead.

WHERE TO GO FOR A DRINK

♟ **Café Brun**: 44 impasse St-Sébastien, terrace level. ☎ 04-93-65-04-83. Closed at lunchtime on both Saturday and Sunday (and Sunday evening in low season). The atmosphere in this temple of beer, rather like a Dutch pub inside, is young and relaxed. You can nibble on a few unremarkable snacks.

WHAT TO SEE

★ **Medieval village**: start your stroll early in the morning or in the evening, in order to avoid the tourists. Follow the signposts for the best route around the village, which has retained much of its character despite a number of renovations. The impressive Porte des Tines and Porte des Migraniers (gateways) are substantial vestiges of the 16th-century surrounding wall. Five centuries ago, Italian accents would have been heard in the central place des Arcades (dating from the 14th and 15th century), a particularly picturesque square. When Biot's population was decimated by the plague, the bishop of Grasse invited Genoese families to resettle the village, in 1460. The square was also the place where travelling artists would try to pay their way by selling their work.

★ **Église Ste-Madeleine**: tucked in among the arcades, this church lost its frescoes in 1700, scrubbed out on the orders of the bishop of Grasse, on the grounds of indecency. The church interior is below ground level and has two superb altarpieces from the 15th century: the *Vierge au rosaire*, attributed to Bréa, and the recently restored *Christ aux plaies* by Giovanni Canavesio, who married a local girl.

★ **Musée d'Histoire et de Céramique Biotoises** (museum of Biot history and ceramics): 9 rue St-Sébastien. ☎ 04-93-65-54-54. Fax: 04-93-65-51-73. Between July and end September, open every day (except Monday and Tuesday) 10am–6pm, and between October and end June 2–6pm. Guided tours available. Entrance fee: 10F (children free). Housed in the remains of the Chapelle des Pénitents-Blancs, this museum tells the history of Biot through various documents and items donated by old families in the village, including wonderful old costumes. There's a reconstruction of a typical 19th-century Biot kitchen, and an attractive collection of glazed terracotta fountains.

★ **Bonsai Arboretum**: 299 chemin du Val-de-Pôme. ☎ 04-93-65-63-99. Fax: 04-93-65-10-78. Open every day (except Tuesday) from October to April, 10am–noon, and 2–5.30pm. From May to September, open 10am–noon and 3–6.30pm. Entrance fee: 25F. More than 5,000 bonsai examples in this large nursery, which also organizes courses for enthusiasts. The trees are for sale, but they are time-consuming and difficult to look after.

★ **Verrerie de Biot** (Biot glassworks): chemin des Combes, at the foot of the village, near the D4. ☎ 04-93-65-03-00. Open every day from 9am to 6pm in winter, and until 8pm in summer. Guided tour: 20F. Follow the process of creating traditional Biot mouth-blown glassware, and see some wonderful pieces in the gallery and the little museum.

– There are seven glassworks in Biot, all open to visitors. To get away from the tourist trail, try the **Vieux Moulin**, 9 chemin du Plan, on the corner of the sea road. ☎ 04-93-65-01-14.

★ **Musée Fernand Léger**: chemin du Val-de-Pome, 3 kilometres (2 miles) from the seafront, on the right before the village. ☎ 04-92-91-50-30. ♿ Open July to September from 11am to 6pm; October to June 10am–12.30pm and 2–5.30pm. Closed on Tuesday. Entrance fee: 30F.

This superb, well-run museum is housed in a rather sober building, constructed to provide the optimum environment for two Léger pieces: a huge ceramic mosaic on the facade and the lovely stained-glass window that illuminates the hallway on the first floor. Another, more recent mosaic captures the setting sun, and is reflected in the pond in the interior courtyard.

Born in 1881, Léger was discovered at the age of 30 by Kahnweiler, the art patron who also launched the careers of Braque and Picasso. Gassed in World War I, the artist was influenced by the imagery of war as much as by Cézanne and the Impressionists. In the 1930s he painted mostly figures before embarking upon a series of larger subjects. His stay in the USA during World War II was a source of inspiration, and he returned to France keen to create art for the working classes and to use geometric forms and new colours to depict workers and factories.

On the ground floor of the museum, an exhibition of photographs and documents recounts the life of the painter. The displays on the first floor trace the evolution of his painting, from the study for *La Femme en bleu*, which marked his break with Impressionism, through the introduction of pure colour, to his great work of 'social realism' *Les Constructeurs* (1950), a huge canvas that reveals the artist's sentiments of equality with the people.

The newer wing houses the artist's less well-known mural art, mosaics, tapestries, ceramics and glass pieces. The tapestry *La Création du Monde* (1922) hangs here, near Léger's mural *Liberté*, which illustrates the poem of the same name by his friend Paul Éluard. Léger was also interested in theatre and cinema design; he collaborated with a number of architects, including Le Corbusier; illustrated books; decorated churches and other buildings with his colourful mosaics; and produced interesting garden sculptures.

FESTIVALS AND EVENTS

– **Heures musicales** (musical events): concerts in the church from mid-May to mid-October.

– **Fête des Métiers d'Art** (festival of trades): in June.

– **Fête de la St-Julien**: four-day festival in the third week of August.

– **Fête des Vendanges** (harvest festival): around 21 September, with the opportunity to taste local produce.

VILLENEUVE-LOUBET (06270)

Population: 13,100

This superb village on the left bank of the River Loup sits on a hill dominated by a medieval chateau. François I was one of a number of famous people who lived in the chateau; in 1538, he signed a peace treaty with Charles V there. Villeneuve-Plage, the built-up area near the sea, is made up of a series of campsites, motels and restaurants in all shapes and sizes. Drive on for a while to look for a more attractive place to stay.

USEFUL ADDRESSES

◼ **Tourist office**: rue de l'Hôtel-de-Ville. ☎ 04-93-20-20-09. Open Monday to Friday 9.30am–12.30pm and 3–7pm; Saturday from 9.30am to 12.30pm.

◼ **Tourist office annexe**: 16 avenue de la Mer. Open Monday to Friday from 9am to 9.30pm; Saturday from 9.30am to 12.30pm; Sunday from 10am to noon. Opening hours change in winter.

◼ **Bicycle and motorbike hire**: Holiday Bikes, Port de Marina-Baie des Anges. ☎ 04-93-22-55-85.

WHERE TO STAY AND EAT

⌂ **Motel-camping de l'Hippodrome**: 'Bouches-du-Loup', 5 avenue des Rives. 250 metres (272 yards) from the beach, behind the big Casino supermarket. ☎ 04-93-20-02-00. Fax : 04-92-13-20-07. Studios between 185F and 300F per night. Studios with bathroom and fully equipped kitchen for hire by the week. Tent pitch from 69F. This shady site has a pool and sun terrace that are covered in winter.

✕ **Le Mail Post**: 12 avenue de la Libération. ☎ 04-93-20-89-53. Closed on Tuesday and in January. Menus from 75F to 145F. This 17th-century coaching inn is now a charming rustic restaurant. The delicious dishes include fondues (meat, fish or chocolate) and *tartiflette paysanne* (oven-baked potatoes with cream and ham).

✗ **La Vieille Auberge**: 11–13 rue des Mesures. ☎ 04-93-73-90-92. Closed on Wednesday and on Sunday evening out of season. Menus at 108F (weekday lunch) and 188F. Excellent traditional food, served in agreeable rustic surroundings. The flavours are lively in dishes such as beef marinaded in olive oil and fresh thyme, and *crème brûlée à la lavande* (lavender *crème brûlée*), and there are also 30 different brands of whisky on offer. A real find.

WHAT TO SEE

★ **Musée de l'Art culinaire (Fondation Auguste Escoffier)** (museum of culinary art): 3 rue Auguste Escoffier. ☎ 04-93-20-80-51. Open every day (except Monday and public holidays as well as during October and November) from 2pm to 6pm (to 7pm in summer). Closed in November. Entrance fee: 10F. The birthplace of Auguste Escoffier, 'the chef of kings and the king of chefs', now houses memorabilia of the celebrated chef. His culinary inventions included *pêche Melba* (a dessert created in honour of the Australian soprano Dame Nellie Melba). There are menus dating from the end of the 19th century, including a New Year's Eve 1870 menu from the Voisin restaurant, which included meat from zoo animals, sacrifced because of the war. Many Côte d'Azur restaurants claim that their chef is a 'disciple of Escoffier'.

★ **Marina-baie des Anges** (Bay of Angels marina): on the seafront, of course, and visible from a great distance. On the way out of Antibes, at the end of the day, there's a lovely view of the marina, with the mountains in the background. The buildings around the marina represent an amazing range of architectural styles, and arouse much comment, not all of it flattering. Some of the luxury apartments have terraced gardens that go right down to the sea. One resident lost hundreds of thousands of francs-worth of paintings in a burglary, including a Renoir, no less.

CAGNES-SUR-MER (06800)　　Population: 44,200

Cagnes-sur-Mer has three distinct parts: Haut-de-Cagnes, the medieval upper town and the most picturesque part, Cagnes-Centre, the modern, commercial and rather ordinary centre, and Cros-de-Cagnes, the seafront town around the fishing village and beach. The N98 runs alongside, with its restaurants, pizzerias and *crêperies*, which vary enormously in quality.

Traffic is a serious problem in lower Cagnes, particularly in the summer, and this part of town is in urgent need of a new system, one-way streets, and car parks. If you're driving, make sure you know where you're heading. The three parts of Cagnes-sur-Mer are separated by several unpleasant kilometres of road, crossed here and there by the motorway and the N7.

FROM ST-RAPHAËL TO NICE AND THE HINTERLAND

USEFUL ADDRESSES

🛈 Tourist office: 6 boulevard du Maréchal-Juin, Cagnes-Centre. ☎ 04-93-20-61-64 or 04-93-73-66-66. Fax: 04-93-20-52-63. Open in summer every day (except Sunday) from 9am to 7pm; rest of the year, open every day (except Sunday) 8.30am–12.15pm and 2–6pm. Plenty of brochures and information.
🛈 Tourist office: 20 avenue des Oliviers, Cros-de-Cagnes. ☎ 04-93-07-67-08.

🚄 Train station: avenue de la Gare. ☎ 08-36-35-35-35. Nice is easily reached by train in just a few minutes. Tourist information desk in summer.

✉ Post offices: Cagnes Renoir, avenue de l'Hôtel-des-Postes (in the town centre); Cagnes le Cros, avenue des Oliviers, in Cros-de-Cagnes; Cagnes Principal, avenue de la Serre, in Cros-de-Cagnes.

WHERE TO STAY

Campsites

⛺ Camping Panoramer: chemin des Gros-Buaux, to the north of Cros-de-Cagnes. Take chemin du Val-Fleuri and then chemin des Gros-Buaux. ☎ 04-93-31-16-15. Open 1 March to 31 October. Quite expensive but very comfortable, shady and well located, with a view over the entire bay. Very busy in July and August.
⛺ La Rivière: 168 chemin des Salles. 4 kilometres (2.5 miles) from the sea. ☎ 04-93-20-62-27. Open all year. Reasonably priced, less in low season. Peaceful and shady, with a pool and food available on site between 1 April and 15 September. Accessible by bus.
⛺ Camping Le Colombier: 35 chemin Ste-Colombe. Head towards Vence from the centre of Cagnes. ☎ 04-93-73-12-77. Open from April to September. Set prices for two to four people, from 59F to 127F, depending on the position of pitch and season. Weekly hire between 1,000F and 3,050F. This small family campsite is shady, comfortable and quiet, with hot showers in low season, washing, drying and ironing facilities, and a swimming pool. In pleasant surroundings, it's just a few minutes by

foot from Cagnes' old town, 1.5 kilometres from the station and 2 kilometres from the beach, and possibly the best spot to camp on the Côte. Prices are reasonable, too.

☆–☆☆ Budget to Moderate

⛺ Turf Hôtel: 9 rue des Capucines, Cros-de-Cagnes. ☎ 04-93-20-64-00. Fax: 04-93-73-23-84. Open all year. Rooms from 240F to 270F. This hotel looks rather like an American motel from the outside. Its location, just 100 metres from the beach, is its only real advantage; the construction of a tall building between it and the road does not augur well for the future. The double rooms are painted entirely white, and some of them have TVs. The rooms on the ground floor are cooler in summer. There's car parking in front of the hotel.
⛺ Le Val Duchesse: 11 rue de Paris, Cros-de-Cagnes. ☎ 04-92-13-40-00. Fax: 04-92-13-40-29. Studios between 250F and 370F, and apartments from 350F to 510F. Less for stays of a week or more. Just 50 metres from the beach, this peaceful hotel has well-decorated rooms, and a nice garden with palm trees, a swimming pool, table

tennis and children's games. The welcome is warm and the prices reasonable. Private parking.

🛏 **Le Mas d'Azur**: 42 avenue de Nice, Cros-de-Cagnes. ☎ 04-93-20-19-19. Just 15 rooms, with TV, telephone, shower and toilet, at between 310F and 335F. Cros-de-Cagnes may not be the nicest part of town, but this old Provençal home, which dates from 1751, is run by a very welcoming couple, with peaceful rooms and a relaxing garden. It's just a three-minute walk from the beach, with free car parking.

WHERE TO EAT

In the Town Centre

✗ **Le Renoir**: 10 rue J.-R.-Giacosa. ☎ 04-93-22-59-58. Closed on Sunday evening, on Monday and on Friday evening. Also closed between Christmas and New Year, and for three weeks in July. Menus at 80F and 140F. Behind an unassuming entrance, the smart yellow dining room is on the first floor. It's a warm and friendly place, and the food is good, with dishes such as *lapin à la purée d'olives* (rabbit in olive purée), *daube aux cèpes* (beef stew with cep mushrooms) and *fricassée de poissons* (fish fricassee).

In Haut-de-Cagnes

✗ **Les Baux**: 2 place du Château. ☎ 04-93-73-14-00. Closed in the evening between May and September, and from 15 to 31 December. Menu at cost 68F (lunch). À la carte around 150F. This restaurant has a pretty terrace in the shade of the chateau, and a cosy dining room. The menu might include mixed salads or grilled pink sea bream and the air seems cleaner than in the town centre.

✗ **Entre Cour et Jardin**: 102 montée de la Bourgade, in the old part of Cagnes. ☎ 04-93-20-72-27. Closed all day Tuesday, Wednesday lunchtime and for the month of January. Menus between 150F and 240F. The attractive green dining room has wicker chairs and an attention to detail. Of the two rooms, one is in a 13th-century vaulted cellar. The menu is well balanced, the food well prepared and full of subtle flavours. Try the *petits feuilletés d'escargots à l'anis* (snails with pastis in pastry), *charlotte de homard aux jeunes pousses d'épinards* (lobster with baby spinach leaves) and *risotto de St-Jacques* (risotto with scallops).

✗ **La Table d'Yves**: 85 montée de la Bourgade. ☎ 04-93-20-33-33. Closed all day Wednesday, and at lunchtime on Tuesday and Thursday, as well as during the school holidays in February and at All Saints. Menus at 135F and 170F, and a brilliant one at 230F. The chef spent 20 years in the kitchens of the great hotels and now prepares excellent food at reasonable prices here. His wife reigns supreme in the blue and ochre dining room, with its brightly coloured curtains and whitewashed beams. The three menus change frequently, but the food is always imaginative, with such dishes as *tian d'agneau aux senteurs de romarin* (casserole of lamb with rosemary).

At the Port

✗ **Restaurant La Villa du Cros**: port de Cros-de-Cagnes. ☎ 04-93-07-57-83. Closed in the evening on Sunday and Monday. Menus between 90F to 210F. Opposite the fishing port, an ideal choice for a romantic evening meal, with tables in a lovely flower garden. The welcome and service are attentive. Try the grilled sea bass, grilled calamari and fresh fish of the day, all from the Port de Cros.

WHAT TO SEE

The Old Town

The pedestrianized historic centre of Cagnes is a maze of steep streets, stairways, vaulted passageways and eye-catching dwellings. The most interesting buildings include the 14th-century Logis de la Goulette, the 17th-century *maison commune*, and the numerous 15th- and 17th-century houses.

(To visit the village, park in the underground car park.)

★ **Église St-Pierre**: the church has two naves, one archaic-Gothic in style with its characteristic square-ribbed vaults, and the other dating from the 17th century.

★ **Château-Musée Grimaldi**: ☎ 04-93-20-85-57. The Grimaldi chateau dominates the old part of Haut-de-Cagnes, with its dour feudal exterior and its crenellated tower. Its interior courtyard is less austere, with tiers of galleries providing light and air, and a 200-year-old capsicum tree in the entrance. Unusually, the chateau is triangular in shape. It was built in 1310 by the first Rainier Grimaldi as a fortress-prison, and remained under the ownership of the influential Grimaldi family until the French Revolution. One of the Grimaldis forged coins in a workshop in one of the cellars of the former citadel, until an individual known as d'Artagnan scuppered the illegal activity in 1710.

Today, the fortress is reached by an impressive double ramped stairway and houses two museums. Open every day (except Tuesday and public holidays), 10am–noon and 2–5pm in winter (to 6pm in summer). Closed for three weeks in November. Entrance fee: 20F.

– **Musée de l'Olivier** (olive tree museum): in the vaulted halls on the ground floor, the first museum in the chateau celebrates the symbolic tree of Provence. The *salle des fêtes* on the first floor, decorated with a trompe l'il ceiling painting by Carlone and Benso in the 18th century, is reserved for receptions. The Donation Suzy-Solidor (gift of Suzy Solidor) is a collection of 40 paintings of the 1930s *chanteuse* and star of the Parisian cabaret, by some of the most famous artists of the 20th century. She spent the last 25 years of her life in Haut-de-Cagnes, and was painted by 244 artists during her lifetime.

– **Musée d'Art Moderne Méditerranéen**: on the second floor, the second museum in the chateau has canvases by many of the great artists who loved the Côte d'Azur, including Chagall, Dufy, Brayer, Foujita, Carzou and Cocteau. There's a beautiful view from the top of the tower.

★ **Chapelle Notre-Dame-de-la-Protection**: visits only as part of the guided tour of Haut-de-Cagnes organized by the tourist office. Every Sunday afternoon, at 3pm in winter and 4pm in summer, leaving from place Grimaldi. Tickets: 25F per person, including entrance to the chateau. There's a magnificent sea view from the porch of this chapel, which is said to have inspired Renoir. Inside, there are frescoes from 1530, and a 17th-century altarpiece (the donkey and the cow are smaller than the baby Jesus).

★ **Musée Renoir**: Les Collettes (Renoir's last home). Take the Nice–Cannes bus, and get off at the Beal-les Collettes stop. By car, follow the signs from the N7. ☎ 04-93-20-61-07. Open every day (except Tuesday and public holidays) 10am–noon and 2–6pm (to 5pm in winter). Arrive an hour before closing time. Closed in November. Guided tours on Sunday at 10.30pm. Entrance fee: 20F.

Suffering badly from rheumatism, Pierre Auguste Renoir was advised by doctors to head south to a warmer climate. He tried Magagnosc, Le Cannet, Villefranche, Cap-d'Ail, Vence, La Turbie, Biot, Antibes and Nice, but settled finally in Cagnes, where he lived from 1903 to 1919, and first experimented with sculpture. He felt inspired and rejuvenated by the light and felt himself at a perfect distance from the mountains, able to admire them but without having to be dominated by them. He often told his son that he had never seen anything so beautiful as the valley of the little River Cagne, with the view of the Baou de St-Jeannet seen through the reeds.

From 1903, Renoir rented the Maison de la Poste (currently the town hall). He bought the ancient olive grove of Les Collettes in 1907, had a house built and spent the last 12 years of his life there. In 1960, the property was acquired by the town of Cagnes and now looks almost exactly as it did when Renoir died. On the ground floor are the drawing room and dining room, and the bedrooms used by visiting friends, including Durand-Ruel, the first art dealer to have real faith in Renoir.

It was at Les Collettes that Renoir painted *Les Grandes Baigneuses*, which he considered to be his life's greatest achievement. When his heirs offered the work to the Paris Louvre, it was at first rejected, because of its 'garish' colours.

On the first floor is the artist's studio, a moving sight, together with Renoir's own room, and those of his wife and his three children, Claude, Jean and Pierre. The view from the balcony stretches over Cap d'Antibes, the old village of Cagnes and the sea. The museum also has ten original canvases by the master.

The garden is huge, with silver-leafed olive trees, orange and lemon trees and roses, Renoir's favourite flower. The garden was specially arranged so that the artist, crippled from 1912, could still enjoy it in his wheelchair (which is displayed today in his workshop).

Cros-de-Cagnes

The tourist office arranges guided tours of the fishing village every Thursday, with a walk around the port, an explanation of the local traditions and festivals (including Fête de la St-Pierre) and an introduction to local specialities, including the popular *poutine*, a young fish harvested between 1 February and 30 April by dragging a net along the seaweedy bottom of the sea.

★ **Église des pêcheurs** (fishermen's church): painted in yellow ochre and a little lost in the traffic on the main road along the seafront, this charming fishermen's church has featured in films on a number of occasions. Cagnes is one of the few towns in the Alpes-Maritimes where fishing still exists as a way of life.

FESTIVALS AND EVENTS

– **Exposition Internationale de la Fleur** (international flower show): over 10 days at the beginning of April, the flower festival in the Côte d'Azur Hippodrome celebrates spring on the coast. For 40 years, exhibitors from all over the world have come to Cagnes-sur-Mer for the event.

– **La Nuit des Contes** (storytelling night): at the end of July and in early August, in the gardens of the Musée Renoir. Free entry. Take a rug and some anti-mosquito cream and settle down for an interesting event.

– **Fête médiévale** (medieval festival): in August in Cagnes old town. Tournaments, shows, flag-twirling and a medieval market. Restaurants in the town offer medieval menus for the two days of the festival

– **Pedestrianization of the seafront**: on the evening of 15 August (or thereabouts), the seafront is closed to traffic. The event is very popular with the people of Cagnes-sur-Mer, who can sit on the terraces of the cafés and restaurants and dream about how things could be.

– **Championnat de Boules carrées** (square *boules* championship): this unusual event takes place during the penultimate weekend in August in the montée de la Bourgade, the street that climbs up to the chateau.

– **Festival international de la Peinture** (international festival of painting): in autumn, with artists from more than 40 countries. ☎ 04-93-20-87-29.

– **Fête de l'Olivier** (olive festival): in the olive grove of Renoir's house, a celebration of the olive tree in November, with traditional dancing and other events.

– **Salon du Palais gourmand**: food festival in November, with local produce and excellent wines on display.

WHAT TO SEE IN THE AREA

ST-LAURENT-DU-VAR

After just a short walk from the port at Cagnes you'll find yourself in Port de St-Laurent-du-Var, a favourite evening gathering place for young people and boat lovers.

WHERE TO EAT

✗ **L'Aigue Marine**: 167 promenade des Flots-Bleus. ☎ 04-93-07-84-55. Closed on Saturday for lunch in summer and on Sunday evening out of season. *Menu-astuce* ('smart' menu) at 128F. À la carte 200F. To the east of the port, this is the best place on the seafront and very popular at the weekend. The delicious selection of fish dishes includes salmon, prawn and fish risotto and the *menu-astuce* is a good one, with a selection of starters and a delicious main dish.

✕ **Madame Nature**: promenade des Flots-Bleus. On the seafront. ☎ 04-92-27-15-45. Closed on Sunday evening and all day Monday. Menu at 140F. This small meat-free restaurant looks like a cosy tearoom and serves tasty vegetable tarts and quiches, and fish dishes. The sweet tarts are also excellent, the wine is organic and the atmosphere is lively.

LA COLLE-SUR-LOUP

After Cagnes, the road is pretty uninteresting until you reach the village of La Colle-sur-Loup, founded in 1540 when François I decided to reinforce the defences of St-Paul-de-Vence. Many houses were destroyed to make room for the ramparts, and those families forced to leave set up house in the hamlets further down and on the neighbouring slopes or *colles* (hence the name of the new village). The new settlement had a good supply of water, and grew vines and wheat for many years. Later, it turned its hand to growing scented plants, producing around 500 tons of roses a year at the beginning of the 19th century. The economic focus changed once again, when it embarked on fruit farming and market gardening. Finally, when the price of land increased, some market gardeners sold their properties to developers for holiday homes, of which there are now sadly too many.

There's a pretty footpath along the River Loup (*see* 'Les Gorges du Loup'). Towads Bar-sur-Loup, take the chemin de la Canière to the river, which is a good spot for swimming.

The road from La Colle takes you first to St-Paul-de-Vence and then to Vence.

WHERE TO STAY AND EAT

Campsite

⛺ **Camping Les Pinèdes**: route du Pont-de-Pierre, 1.5 kilometres to the west on the road for Grasse. ☎ 04-93-32-98-94. Fax: 04-93-32-50-20. Closed between 15 October and 1 March. From 73F to 88F for two, with a tent. Mobile homes and chalets for hire too. This pleasant and relaxing site has a pool, TV room and children's games. Booking in high season is recommended.

☆☆☆ Chic

⛺ **Hôtel Marc-Hély**: 535 route de Cagnes, 800 metres from the village. ☎ 04-93-22-64-10. Fax: 04-93-22-93-84. Email: marc-hely@accesinter.com. Double rooms from 390F to 480F. A comfortable hotel with Provençal decor, a pleasant garden and a pool. The ideal place for a quiet retreat, with a view of St-Paul.

⛺ ✕ **La Vieille Ferme**: 660 route de Cagnes. ☎ 04-93-22-62-42. Fax: 04-93-22-47-98. Closed on Saturday in winter and during December. Rooms between 280F and 300F. Menus between 85F and 145F. Attractive decor and good, family-style cuisine, with tasty fish, chicken and meat dishes. There's a lovely view from the terrace, and a pool for hot afternoons.

⛺ **Le Clos de St-Paul**: 71 chemin de la Rouguière. ☎ and fax: 04-93-32-56-81. Three comfortable double rooms for between 300F to 400F, at this B&B, including breakfast on the verandah. Large Provençal building at the foot of St-Paul-de-Vence, in a pretty garden with a large pool. Chic and charming.

ST-PAUL-DE-VENCE (06570)

Population: 2,890

For centuries, St-Paul was a little-known hilltop village, no different from the many others on the old frontier of the Var region. In the 1930s, artists began to be drawn to the village by the extraordinary quality of the light. Often penniless, they sought refuge at the *auberge* in the square, where the owner would extend a welcome to the talented ones, accepting paintings in return for meals and lodging. The inn was turned into the legendary Colombe d'Or hotel (*see* page 601), and St-Paul found itself on the world map. Hotels and restaurants sprang up, and tourists began to add St-Paul to their route, particularly in summer.

The village has lived with its tourist hordes for more than a quarter of a century, and now seems to have decided to take control of them. In the height of the season, non-residents are banned from driving through the village streets and parking is difficult and expensive. Try to arrive early in the morning. Enjoy a quiet breakfast, and then head to the Fondation Maeght (*see* page 603) to be first in the queue. Do a little tour by car in the hills and come back in the late afternoon to enjoy St-Paul. Enter the village via the south rampart, go down the rue Grande – look at the departing crowds – and watch the sun set from a pretty terrace, waiting for the ramparts to be lit up.

USEFUL ADDRESS

⚓ **Tourist office**: 2 rue Grande. ☎ 04-93-32-86-95. Fax: 04-93-32-60-27. Email: artdevivre@wanadoo.fr. Open every day from early June to end September from 10am to 7pm; rest of the year, every day 10am–noon and 2–6pm.

WHERE TO STAY

⚓ **Auberge Le Hameau**: 528 route de La Colle. ☎ 04-93-32-80-24. Fax: 04-93-32-55-75. Closed from mid-November to mid-February, except over New Year. Double rooms from 580F to 830F. Three apartments for hire. This inn stands in pretty countryside, with a terrace, a pool and a wonderful view over St-Paul. The air-conditioned rooms are comfortable and well furnished. The rooms in the main building are more charming than those in the annexe. This is a perfect place for a romantic break.

☆☆☆☆ Très Chic

⚓ **La Grande Bastide**: route de La Colle. ☎ 04-93-32-50-30. Fax: 04-93-32-50-59. Closed from 15 November to 15 March (except during festivals). Rooms from 750F to 950F. Housed in an 18th-century building that has been entirely restored and transformed, with lovely rooms painted in subtle pastel colours. It offers a warm and professional welcome, delicious breakfasts and a swimming pool. The garden has a view over St-Paul and the sea in the distance. There's no restaurant.

🛏 **Le Mas des Gardettes**: 139 chemin de la Vieille-Bergerie. At the entrance to the village. ☎ 04-93-32-33-90. Rooms for between 1,500F and 3,300F per week (depending on season and size). Slightly more ex-pensive, but ideal for those in search of comfort, peace and a really lovely environment. The tasteful rooms and apartments are clean and well maintained, and there's a terrace, pergola and garden.

WHERE TO EAT

✗ **Café de la Place**: place du Général-de-Gaulle. ☎ 04-93-32-80-03. Open every day, but only for lunch. Daily special around 60F. Popular spot, both with Japanese tourists and with locals, some of whom knew Simone Signoret and Yves Montand, and the other celebrities who used to come here. The café has its own *boules* area, a covered terrace and a Parisian-style mirrored interior. Sustain yourself with a tasty *daube aux raviolis* (stew) as you engage in some serious people-watching.

✗ **Chez Andréas**: remparts ouest (western ramparts). ☎ 04-93-32-98-32. Open every day from noon to midnight. Menus from 50F to 80F. This small wine bar, slightly out of the village centre, has warm ochre-coloured walls and a good selection of wines. Enjoy a lentil salad, or potato and bacon salad, with a glass of wine, on the terrace. Finish off your evening in **La Cocarde,** in rue Grande, owned by the same characterful young man.

✗ **La Voûte**: remparts ouest (western ramparts). ☎ 04-93-32-09-47. Closed on Wednesday and for lunch on Thursday, except in high season, and during January. Menu at 160F. À la carte around 200F. A nice surprise, particularly in the evening, when the hordes have left and peace descends on the village again. The welcome is warm and the food delicious, including *carré d'agneau de Provence tout simple au romarin* (local lamb with rosemary).

✗ **La Fontaine**: place de la Fontaine. In the heart of the village. ☎ 04-93-32-74-12. Closed on Tuesday. Daily special at 90F and meals for 150F to 200F. People don't really come here for the food, but to sit at a table on the terrace, with a decent enough *plat du jour*, and watch the crowds go by.

☆☆☆☆ Très Chic

✗ **La Colombe d'Or**: place du Général-de-Gaulle. ☎ 04-93-32-80-02. Closed from 2 November to 20 December. Meals for around 400F. St-Paul's most famous hotel-restaurant, housed in an old farmhouse. In the 1920s, La Colombe d'Or was a modest inn called à Robinson on the way in to St-Paul-de-Vence. The village began to be patronized by as yet unknown (and often impoverished) artists from the coast. The son of the owner, Paul Roux, recognized their talent and, in exchange for hospitality, would accept paintings from such artists as Signac, Soutine, Derain, Utrillo, Vlaminck and Matisse. He also recognized the potential of the property. He converted à Robinson into a hotel, called it La Colombe d'Or (or The Golden Dove) and launched it with a party for journalists and celebrities.

The Colombe d'Or became increasingly popular in creative circles and more wealthy guests followed in the footsteps of the poor painters. Belgian poet Maurice Maeterlinck, Rudyard Kipling, and French singer and actor Maurice Chevalier all passed through its doors. In the 1940s, film stars began to come to La Colombe. French screen legends Simone Signoret and Yves Montand had their wedding reception at the hotel. Paul Roux renovated the exterior of the hotel with stones from a chateau in the Pyrénées and commissioned a ceramic mural for the terrace from Fernand Léger.

After Paul Roux died, in 1953, his family kept the place largely unchanged, and the wonderful paintings that he collected are still on display. Customers come here for the visual delights as much as for the culinary ones, but the food is sophisticated, well prepared and full of flavour. The whole experience is most enjoyable.

WHAT TO SEE

St-Paul suffers a serious influx of tourists in high season and it's easy to understand why local people may seem impatient at times. Outside the main visiting hours, however, it's a vibrant village, with inhabitants who are happy to welcome guests, but prefer to guard against invasions of their own privacy.

★ **Rue Grande**: the main street of the village, with the tourist office on the right, is lined with pretty 16th- and 17th-century houses, now converted into studios, workshops, souvenir shops and (not always tasteful) tourist traps. The old and noble homes are reminders of St-Paul's former status as a prosperous royal town. Visit **place de la Grande-Fontaine**, with its elegant urn-shaped fountain and an arcaded *lavoir* (public washing place). At the far end of the village is the former hospital, now converted into a school. The **Porte du Sud** (southern town gate), or **Porte de Vence**, stands near the cemetery, where Chagall is buried, a touching chapel with 100-year-old cypress trees.

Walk around the ramparts, which have remained unchanged since François I financed their construction. The 'ace of spades' layout of the bastions is characteristic of the 16th century, and the view over the countryside, which bears a strong resemblance to that of Tuscany, is magnificent. Close to the surrounding wall there are some superb renovated houses, with mullioned windows and ivy-covered walls.

★ **Musée d'Histoire locale** (museum of local history): place de l'église. ☎ 04-93-32-41-13. Open all year from 10am to 5.30pm (to 7pm in summer). Closed for two weeks in November/December. Entrance fee: 20F. Among the displays in this medieval residence is a collection of old photos showing film stars enjoying the delights of La Colombe d'Or.

★ **Église collégiale** (collegiate church): keen to rival the nearby town of Vence, St-Paul asked for its own church to be promoted to collegiate status, making it a sort of under-cathedral. The request was granted, but the privilege was withdrawn during the French Revolution. The church dates back to the 13th century but was extended and restored at the end of the 1700s. The steeple was built in 1740, and to the left of the entrance, near the baptismal fonts, there's a 15th-century Virgin. The painting of St Catherine of Alexandria is attributed to Tintoretto. To the right, there's a chapel decorated with plasterwork. The front of the altar depicts the martyred St Clement, and above there's an Italian 17th-century painting of St Charles Borromée offering his works to the Virgin in the presence of St Clement.

★ **Fondation Maeght**: ☎ 04-93-32-81-63. Open every day in summer from 10am to 7pm. Open in winter 10am–12.30pm, and 2.30–6pm. Entrance fee: 45F in summer, 40F in winter (concessions available). Permit required for photography; otherwise, cameras may be left in a locker. Small café at the entrance. This is one of the best attractions of the Côte, and France's second most popular museum of modern art, with over 200,000 visitors a year, half from outside France.

Impressed by the studio in Palma, Majorca of Spanish artist Miró, Aimé Maeght came up with the project for a foundation in the 1960s. He wanted to provide an ideal environment for contemporary art, while at the same time respecting the environment. His success was to create, not a pseudo-Provençal setting, but instead a wonderful art space.

There's a real sense of harmony between the environment, the architecture of the building and the works of art. The materials used in the construction are simple – concrete and pink brick. The foundation stands on a steep slope, and little stone walls prevent any soil erosion. Striking white concrete structures collect rainwater for the fountains and pools. The garden is a multi-level maze of trees and sculpture, including a number by Miró.

Many artists contributed to the decoration of the building, which now has Chagall mosaics, ceramic tiles by Miró, a stained-glass window by Braque in the pretty chapel, and fountains designed by Pol Bury.

The foundation was opened in 1964 and today houses an important collection of paintings and sculpture by great 20th-century artists, including Bonnard, Matisse, Léger, Tal-Coat, Pol Bury, Riopelle and Tapiés. The lighting is subtle and effective, and each year major exhibitions are held here. In the past, there have been retrospectives of Dubuffet, Max Ernst, Fernand Léger and Nicolas de Staël, among others. The foundation is more than simply a museum, and offers a vibrant place for artists to work and exchange ideas. It receives no state aid, and this gives it total artistic and bureaucratic freedom.

★ **Artists' studios**: there are around 25 artists living and working in St-Paul, many of whom open their studios to visitors. A list is available from the tourist office. Painter and sculptor Sultan, in place de la Mairie, regales visitors with his views on fellow artists. The paintings of Geneviève Turtaut, in rue Grande, are as exuberant as the artist herself. The unusual and expressive sculptures in rue de la Boucherie were created by Marie Orsoni, who works with industrial packaging and polyester.

SHOPPING

🔒 **Un Cur en Provence**: 3 montée de l'église. ☎ 04-93-32-87-81. This lovely shop is full of fascinating books, original stationery, pretty fabrics and a tempting selection of teas, perfumes and sweets.

🔒 **Les Trois Étoiles de St-Paul**: place de la Mairie. ☎ 04-93-32-79-68. Like a modern-day alchemist's laboratory, with stills full of quince, raspberry, cherry or peach essences, lovely bottles of olive oil flavoured with ceps, truffles or garlic, and inventive vinegars, including a lavender-flavoured version.

VENCE (06140)   Population: 17,200

'Vence' rhymes with 'Provence' – appropriately enough, since this is much more a town of the region of Provence than a Riviera hotspot. The house facades are weathered by time, you can buy real *herbes de Provence* in the markets and it's a great base for some wonderful trips into the hinterland. The coast feels a long way away.

The population of Vence increased after World War I, when people were drawn to the lovely old town and its gorgeous countryside. Authors and artists staying in Vence included André Gide, Paul Valéry, Chaim Soutine, and Raoul Dufy, who set up home in the route du Var, opposite the old town, in 1919. Gradually, hotels and rest homes began to be built.

After the end of World War II, Vence was fortunate enough to develop more slowly than the towns on the coast. In 1955, the town's population was no more than 6,000, the public *lavoirs* were still used for washing and the olive mills still functioned. Artists continued to be drawn to Vence, for its authentic ambience. Cocteau and Matisse both spent time here, and Chagall moved here in 1949, and turned his hand to designing the new ceiling for the Opéra de Paris.

Vence couldn't withstand the onslaught for ever, and in the 1960s, villas with pools and designer gardens began to take over from the fields and olive groves. In just 10 years, the town doubled in size, and car parks and a bypass were built. Happily, the old town managed to survive the expansion almost untouched, but urbanization continued its relentless march, with the construction of large buildings that changed the contours of the landscape. Chagall was one artist who suddenly departed for St-Paul.

Today, a number of organizations fight to save a square here, a listed building there, but what Vence really needs is a proper traffic system to deal with the tourist invasion.

GETTING THERE

– **From Cagnes-sur-Mer**: regular buses for Vence and St-Paul between 7.25am and 8pm.

– **From Nice**: buses almost every hour. Last departure from Nice at 7.30pm and last return from Vence at 6.30pm. Return ticket: 18F.

USEFUL ADDRESS

❶ **Tourist office**: 8 place du Grand-Jardin. ☎ 04-93-58-06-38. Fax: 04-93-58-91-81. Open in summer Monday to Saturday 9am–1pm and 2–7pm; rest of the year Monday to Friday 9am–12.30pm and 2–6pm.

WHERE TO STAY

Campsite

⛺ **Camping-caravanning Domaine de la Bergerie**: on route de la Sine, 3 kilometres (2 miles) to the southwest of Vence, towards Tourrettes and Grasse. Follow the signs to the left at the roundabout. ☎ 04-93-58-09-36. Closed between mid-October and end March. Between 73.50F and 119.50F in low season. This three-star site is quiet and pleasant, nestled at the foot of the *baou*, the sheer rock that dominates the countryside, and the Col de Vence, in a wooded and relaxing location. There are children's games, a pool and tennis courts.

☆☆ Moderate

⛺ **La Maison du Rosaire**: 466 avenue Henri-Matisse. ☎ 04-93-58-03-26. Fax: 04-93-58-21-10. Half board at 160F and full board at 220F (for a minimum stay of three days). Remarkable accommodation, with comfortable rooms, in two villas near the famous Chapelle du Rosaire (*see* page 607). Ideal for a couple hoping to discover the quieter side of Vence, with a magnificent view and beautiful terraced gardens. There's no obligation to join the sisters for dinner at the communal table, or to attend Mass, but it is a wonderful experience in the serene chapel, which is filled with a beautiful light.

⛺ **Villa Le Rêve**: 261 avenue Henri-Matisse. ☎ 04-93-58-01-43. Fax: 04-93-58-91-81. Double rooms for 280F. Closed in February. Matisse lived in this villa and painted in the garden, which is overlooked by the guest rooms. Particularly recommended as a place to stay for amateur artists, who are given priority by the owners and come from all over the world in search of inspiration. The level of comfort is quite basic, but the view is magnificent and the welcome warm.

⛺ **La Closerie des Genêts**: 4 impasse Maurel. In the heart of Vence. ☎ 04-93-58-33-25. Fax: 04-93-58-97-01. Open all year. Double rooms between 220F and 360F. This little hotel at the end of a quiet cul-de-sac has rather tricky access, but the spacious rooms have been renovated in different decors, and are reasonably priced. The garden is a nice place to relax after a busy day exploring the region.

☆☆☆ Chic

⛺ **Auberge des Seigneurs**: place du Frêne. ☎ 04-93-58-04-24. Fax: 04-93-24-08-01. Restaurant closed all day Monday, at lunchtime on Tuesday and Wednesday. Annual closure between 1 November and 15 March. Rooms between 374F and 394F. Menus from 170F. Housed in a beautiful 15th-century building at the entrance to Vence's old town, the rooms in this *auberge* are named after famous painters. Modigliani and Soutine have lovely views of the mountain and are reasonably priced. Half board is not available, but the food in the restaurant is sophisticated and inventive. The welcome is warm.

WHERE TO EAT

☆☆ Moderate

✕ **Le Troquet**: 13 place du Grand-Jardin. ☎ 04-93-58-64-31. Meals from 50F to 100F. This small restaurant is popular with regulars, who come as much for the hospitality of the owners as for the daily specials. The food is simple and excellent, and you can enjoy the famous *bruschetta* on the sunny terrace on the square. The service is relaxed, and the menu includes *salade niçoise*, *cuisse de canette aux olives* (duckling with olives) and *raviolis maison* (homemade ravioli).

✗ **Le P'tit Provençal**: 4 place Clemenceau. In the centre of the old town. ☎ 04-93-58-50-64. Closed on Sunday evening; on Monday in low season; for three weeks in November/December, and two in Januuary. Menus from 75F (weekday lunch) to 155F. This place has a young, relaxed atmosphere, an imaginative cuisine and a very Provençal feel. The terrace opens onto the heart of the historic centre, and the regularly changing menu includes *daube de joue de porcelet* (traditional stew), *raviolis à la bouillabaisse* (ravioli with fish stew), *cuisse et épaule de lapereau au jus de tapenade* (young rabbit in olive paste sauce) and *petits farcis niçois*.

✗ **Le Pigeonnier**: 3–7 place du Peyra. ☎ 04-93-58-03-00. Closed on Friday, Saturday lunchtime, and from November to end March. *Formule rapide* at 82F and set menus at 110F and 150F. On the most beautiful square in the town centre, this slightly touristy restaurant is housed in a three-storey 16th-century building. The terrace on the square is a good place to people-watch, and the kitchen makes its own pasta and ravioli and serves up good fish dishes.

✗ **Le Pêcheur de Soleil**: 1 place Godeau. ☎ 04-93-58-32-56. Open every day, except Monday in low season, on All Saints Day and at Christmas. This place, on one of the most beautiful squares in Vence, is fine as long as you aren't intimidated by the choice of over 600 pizzas. They cost between 40F and 130F.

✗ **Chez Jordi**: 8 rue de l'Hôtel-de-Ville. ☎ 04-93-58-83-45. Closed on Sunday and Monday, as well as from mid-December to mid-January and from mid-July to mid-August. Menus at 110F and 145F. Small restaurant in the old town serving delicious, flavoursome dishes from Spain and Provence, including *morue pil-pil*, *zarzuela*, *paella*, *poêlée de gambas au beurre citronné* and *aïoli*.

✩✩✩ Chic

✗ La Farigoule: 15 avenue Henri-Isnard. ☎ 04-93-58-01-27. Closed on Tuesday and Wednesday in winter, and on Wednesday and Thursday lunchtime in high season. Menus at 135F and 160F. À la carte 250F. The sometimes slow service doesn't really matter, because customers come here for the ambience, the excellent regional cuisine and good fresh fish on seasonal menus. The talented chef is famous for his dessert of *figues rôties* (roast figs). Save some room for them after trying the delicious *lapin sauté aux olives* (rabbit pan-fried with olives) or fresh sardine tart with coriander and preserved lemons. The lovely patio is a delightful place to dine.

✗ **Le Vieux Couvent**: 37 avenue Alphonse-Toreille. ☎ 04-93-58-78-58. Closed on Wednesday, and from 15 January to 15 March. Menus from 165F to 205F. Housed in a former 17th-century seminary, this restaurant serves excellent locally produced food. The regional dishes, fresh and subtle in flavour, include *fleurs de courgettes farcies d'une mousseline de rascasse* (courgette flowers stuffed with fish mousse), *roulade de lapin rôti* (roast rabbit) and *galette aux olives* (olive pancakes). The setting is lovely, and the atmosphere relaxed.

WHAT TO SEE

Start your walk from the paying car park at place du Grand-Jardin, in the centre of the modern town. Head for **place du Frêne**, named in honour of a majestic ash tree planted here in 1538 to commemorate visits by François I and Pope Paul III. The tree is a botanical enigma, since ash trees rarely grow at any altitude (Vence stands at 325 metres/1,065 feet). The square is bordered by the impressive walls of the *château seigneurial* (castle of the lords of Villeneuve), with its square tower. From **place Thiers**, which continues on from Place du Frêne, there's a lovely view of the rocky *baous* and the small valley of La Lubiane.

★ **Old town:** this part of Vence, hidden behind its medieval walls, has retained much of its original character. Get to it via the pretty place du Peyra, which has no fewer than three fountains, one of which is urn-shaped and dates from 1822. The square was the site of the Roman forum, and is still the venue for the daily market. Here too was the large flat stone (*peyra*), where, after a public trial, the condemned would kneel before being beheaded.

Take the rue du marché and turn left towards the place Clemenceau.

– **Place Clemenceau** is an attractive square on which sits the town hall, built in 1908 on the site of the former bishop's palace.

– **Ancienne cathédrale**: the facade of the old cathedral dates from the end of the 19th century, but the nave and aisles are much earlier, dating from the 11th century. The cathedral has been extended and renovated many times. The interior, rather small for a cathedral, houses gilded wooden altarpieces. The tomb of St Lambert is in a chapel to the right, and there's a Roman sarcophagus, said to belong to St Véran, who died in AD 492, as well as the unmissable mosaic by Chagall, *Moïse sauvé des eaux* (*Moses in the bullrushes*).

The most impressive part of the cathedral is the tribune, with its oak and pearwood stalls carved by a native of Grasse, Jacotin Bellot, who worked in Vence for five years in the 1450s. They satirize Renaissance customs and mores, and were restored in the 19th century.

– **Place Surian**: a picturesque square near place Clemenceau is the venue for a tiny morning market selling the best regional products. Make your way to the **Porte de Signadour** via a small alley, and then turn left to the **Porte de l'Orient**. Continue your walk along the boulevard Paul-André, which has wonderful views of the rocky *baous*. Take rue du Portail-Lévis, lined with beautiful old facades, to get back to place du Peyra.

★ **Chapelle des Pénitents-Blancs**: place Frédéric-Mistral. Open between April and December 10am–12.30pm and 2.30–6pm. Free entry. This pretty chapel – with touches of Provence, Italy and the Orient in its architecture – has an Italianate pinnacle and a multi-coloured tiled dome. It houses art exhibitions.

★ **Chapelle Matisse** (or Chapelle du Rosaire): on the route de St-Jeannet. Follow the signs carefully. To the east of Vence, cross the bridge and follow the D2210 towards St-Jeannet. After 200 metres, take avenue Henri-Matisse, and look for the chapel on the right, past the former convalescent home. ☎ 04-93-58-03-26. Open to visitors on Tuesday and Thursday from

10am to 11.30am, and every day (except Friday, Sunday and public holidays) from 2pm to 5.30pm. Also open on Friday afternoon during school holidays. Annual closure from 1 November to mid-December. Mass is held at 10am on Sunday. Entrance fee: 15F.

In 1942, Matisse advertised in Nice for a 'young and pretty night nurse' to help him recover from a serious operation. Monique Bourgeois was taken on for the job and also became the artist's model for a while. Between 1943 and 1948, Matisse came to Vence for some rest, and renewed his friendship with Monique, now Sister Jacques-Marie, based in a convent just 100 metres from the Villa Le Rêve, where Matisse was living.

The sisters at the convent had long been considering the building of a proper chapel, and Sister Jacques-Marie had even drawn preliminary design sketches. Through a happy set of circumstances, Matisse was able to be involved in the project.

The Chapelle du Rosaire overlooks the small Lubiane valley, facing Vence. From the road, it looks quite ordinary, but from the garden side, the beautiful white facade makes a fine picture against the mountain backdrop. Matisse designed every aspect of this religious space and decorated every part of its simple and harmonious interior. Everything is painted white, and the bright blue, lemon yellow and glorious green of the geometrically patterned stained-glass windows, on three walls, light up the interior with colour and vitality. On the white-tiled walls, Matisse made sweeping black line drawings of the 14 Stations of the Cross, St Dominic, the Crucifixion, and the Virgin and Child.

Two rooms in the Musée Matisse in Nice are dedicated to Matisse's prelimary sketches for the chapel interior.

★ **Château des Villeneuve – Fondation Émile Hughes**: 3 place du Frêne. ☎ 04-93-58-15-78. Open from 10am to 6pm between June and October; during the rest of the year 10am–noon and 2–6pm. Closed on Monday. Entrance fee: 25F. The former castle of the lords of Villeneuve, *seigneurs* of Vence, is now an interesting museum, the venue for many temporary exhibitions. It was tastefully renovated in 1992, and its thematic exhibitions showcase the work of artists connected with Vence, including Dufy, Matisse and Chagall. It also exhibits the work of other contemporary painters.

★ **Galerie Beaubourg**: Château Notre-Dame-des-Fleurs, 2618 route de Grasse. On the way to Tourrettes-sur-Loup. ☎ 04-93-24-52-00. Between 15 March and 15 January, open every day (except Sunday) from 11am to 7pm. Entrance fee: 40F. Paris gallery owners Marianne and Pierre Nahon bought this old chateau and filled it with sculptures by Niki de St-Phalle, together with several works by other contemporary artists, including Schnabel, César and Keith Haring. The works are exhibited both inside and outside the building.

FESTIVALS AND EVENTS

– **Jardins dans la cité** (gardens of Vence): in mid-April, Vence is transformed into a huge garden, with flower and plant markets, walking trails, and exhibitions.

– **Marché des Potiers** (potters' market): end May/beginning of June, in the place du Grand-Jardin.

– **Fête de l'Ail et de l'Aïoli** (garlic festival): in June, in place Clemenceau and place Mars.

– **Les Nuits du Sud** (festival of music from the south): between mid-July and mid-August, with concerts on place du Grand-Jardin and in the wild outdoor setting of the Col de Vence, the pass at an altitude of 1,000 metres (3,280 feet).

– **Fête de Ste-Elisabeth**: end July/early August. Festival of the patron saint, held in Vence since the 19th century.

– **Fête du Moyen et du Haut-Pays**: festival celebrating the traditions, trades, music and dances of the Middle Ages, held at the end of summer.

WALK

– **To Village Nègre**: this easy walk, suitable for all ages and levels of fitness, should take two hours from the village of St-Barnabé. Take the D2 from the centre of Vence and head towards the Col de Vence-Coursegoules. Just after you reach the pass, turn left on to the D302, passing the ranch. Park on the left, just before St-Barnabé, where cars are banned. Walk through the village to the locksmith's, then turn immediately left on to the GR51. The landscape of the karstic plateau is very attractive, with strangely sculpted rocks and arid scrub dotted with thyme, thistles and hawthorn. Small paddocks enclosed by oak hedges surround the village.

The footpath starts under a leafy arch. Cross a clearing and then go past two drystone buildings. After a few fields, veer right under the electricity lines to follow the red and white markers of the GR51. At the edge of the plateau, leave the path that leads to the village of Courmes (after admiring the view), and take the left path as if you were heading back to the village of St-Barnabé. You'll see the ruins of a sheepfold in the middle of the loop you have just made. To the right is a pretty house. Leave the path to skirt the house between the ruins and the windmill, and carry on in the same direction. After a circular depression full of broad-leaved trees, head towards the mound. White monoliths, some 2 metres (6.5 feet) high, indicate your arrival at Village Nègre, also known as Village des Idoles (village of the idols). Rainwater has traced patterns in the stones.

Retrace your steps to the house and the electricity lines. After rejoining the GR51, a path heading off to the right will take you back to the car park, bypassing St-Barnabé. Climb the hill and go around the gate on the path to get there.

LES GORGES DU LOUP

Vence is a fine base for two magnificent excursions: one to the Gorges du Loup and the other to Les Clues (*see* page 614). Close to the coast, yet offering superb mountainous landscapes, both locations can be very busy in high season.

The Loup river rises in Andon, and reaches the Mediterranean at Cagnes-sur-Mer. It supplies Cannes, Grasse and Villeneuve-Loubet.

The D2210 from Vence towards Tourrettes-sur-Loup is lined with luxury villas hidden behind immaculate, very tall hedges.

TOURRETTES-SUR-LOUP

The village of Tourrettes is one of the most beautiful in the region, and a target for many unwanted visitors over the years, from the Franks and the Huns, to the Visigoths and the Lombards. Rebuilt in the 15th century, it sits on a rocky outcrop, surrounded by ravines, and its houses huddle together to form a surrounding wall defended by three towers (hence the name of *tourrettes*).

The **Puy de Tourrettes** mountain looms over the village. A fit climber should be able to reach its summit (at 1,267 metres/4,155 feet) in a couple of hours, to be rewarded by a predictably splendid view.

WHERE TO STAY AND EAT

Campsite

☎ **La Camassade**: 523 route de Pie-Lombard. Drive along the D2210 for 500 metres, and then to the left for around 1.5 kilometres. ☎ 04-93-59-31-54. Fax: 04-93-59-31-81. Email: camassade@aol.com. Open all year. 94F for a site for two people with a car. There's a swimming pool, and the environment is relaxing and shady. Book ahead.

In Camassade

☎ **Le Mas des Cigales**: 1673 route des Quenières, in Camassade. ☎ 04-93-59-25-73. Closed between 1 October and 25 December. Double rooms from 450F to 500F, including breakfast. There are four pretty rooms (two communicating) at this farmhouse, which also has a pool, a tennis court, a patio and a lovely view over the Baie des Anges.

In the Old Town

✗ **Le Médiéval**: 6 Grande-Rue. ☎ 04-93-59-31-63. Closed on Thursday and from 15 December to 15 January. Menus at 95F and 130F. The regional food includes such dishes as *lapin en gelée de légumes* (rabbit in a vegetable jelly), *caille rôtie dur canapés aux morilles* (roast quail with mushrooms), *noisettes d'agneau au basilic* (lamb noisettes with basil) and *crème caramel à l'orange confite* (crème caramel with caramelized oranges). Enjoy your meal as you admire the view from the terrace.

✗ **Le Petit Manoir**: 21 Grande-Rue. ☎ 04-93-24-19-19. Closed on Wednesday and on Sunday evening, as well as from mid-November to mid-December and during the February holidays. Menus from 98F to 260F. An intimate atmosphere and a menu that includes *foie gras chaud au miel d'acacia* (warm foie gras with Acacia honey) and *risotto aux légumes* (vegetable risotto).

WHAT TO SEE

★ **Church**: on the Grand-Place, shaded by elm trees, the church was built around 1400 and houses works by the schools of Bréa and Leonardo da Vinci together with a third-century altar dedicated to the Roman god Mercury.

★ **Chapelle St-Jean**: near the main road overlooking the village, this chapel was decorated in 1959 with naive frescoes by Ralph Soupault.

★ **Old village**: the medieval ensemble of the old quarter is superb and very well preserved. Enter it via a gate topped by a belfry, and follow the main street to the square on the other side, past workshops producing decorated furniture and painted silk items. The village turns into a veritable souk in the summer months, but stays cool even on the hottest days, with its plane trees and pretty fountains. Out of season, visitors can enjoy the authentic old village at its best.

FESTIVAL

– **Fête des Violettes** (violet festival): at the beginning of March, there's a procession of floats decorated with violets and mimosa. Violets were grown in Tourettes to be eaten in crystallized form, for the perfumeries in Grasse, or to be sold as little posies.

From Tourettes to Gourdon

After Tourettes, the road overlooks the Loup valley. **Pont-du-Loup** marks the start of the gorge.

The **Confiserie Florian** (sweet-making factory) organizes free guided tours every day from 9am to noon and from 2pm to 6pm. See fresh fruits being crystallized and turned into sweets, then taste and buy. There are some beautiful pieces of antique furniture from the 17th and 18th century.

– There was a railway viaduct here until 1944, but only three arches remain after it was mined in World War II.

– At **Saut-du-Loup**, take the D6, which follows the Gorges du Loup, where the steep limestone cliffs are cooled by waterfalls. The glacial potholes are called *marmites*.

– From **Pont de Bramafan**, further on, you can reach **Courmes**, a small village with an excellent restaurant for those who are hungry after an energetic exploration of the area. The GR51 goes through the village, and those still keen to exert themselves can reach the summit of the **Puy de Tourettes** in around two hours and look smugly down on the distant tourists.

WHERE TO STAY AND EAT

🛏 ✖ **L'Auberge de Courmes**: 3 rue des Platanes. At the entrance to the village. ☎ 04-93-77-64-70. Closed on Sunday evening and on Monday, as well as in January. This much talked about *auberge* has five rooms at 260F and serves excellent traditional and regional fare with menus at 120F and 140F. It has a relaxing terrace.

To continue your journey through the gorges, take the D3 from Pont de Bramafan, towards Gourdon. As the road goes up into the gorge, the views over the valley become more and more stunning, and the vegetation gradually diminishes. You're not far from **Plan de Caussols**.

– The panorama from the **viewing point** (at an altitude of 700 metres/2,300 feet) is spectacular.

GOURDON

Gourdon is a typical *village perché*, an eyrie best visited out of season if you're not fond of crowds, souvenir shops and pretty boutiques selling regional produce and local art. There's quite a different atmosphere out of season in this village with its great views and impressive rectangular chateau.

WHERE TO EAT

✕ **Au Vieux Four**: rue Basse. ☎ 04-93-09-68-60. Closed in the evening, all day Saturday, during the first two weeks in June, and from mid-November to end December. Set menu at 98F. À la carte around 120F. Make a pitstop here for a tasty lunch. Try the local *assiette de charcuterie* or *salade du berger* ('shepherd's salad') before enjoying *lapin au thym de la garrigue* and a delicious *clafoutis* (berry tart). The welcome is warm and friendly.

WHAT TO SEE AND DO

★ **Château de Gordon**: open from June to October, 11am–1pm and 2–7pm; afternoon only out of season. Closed on Tuesday. Guided tours available. Entrance fee: 25F. Built in the 13th century, the chateau was extensively restored in 1610, and now has an interesting collection of antique arms and armour, torture instruments (in the dungeon), a Rembrandt self-portrait and a strange 'salt chair'. The highlight is an extremely rare sculpture of St Sebastien, attributed to El Greco. There's a panoramic view from the three-tiered gardens, which were laid out by Le Nôtre and are now dominated by alpine plants.

– You can also take a picturesque 45-minute walk on the lovely but rather demanding **Sentier du Paradis** (paradise walk) from Gourdon to Pont-du-Loup. The return journey is steep and may take 1 hour 30 minutes to 2 hours. The spectacular views stretch to Nice. In days gone by, the postman would take this route every day!

PLATEAU DE CAUSSOLS

Drive up the D12 to the Plateau de Caussols, with its arid almost lunar landscape, punctuated by grottoes and crevices, and often used in films for desert scenes. You're on a different planet.

★ You can take a small road to the **Plaine de Rochers**, with its magnificent stony landscape dotted with wild flowers. It looks rather like the Syrian desert and has strange rock sculptures with a lunar background. The air is extremely dry and clear, making it a perfect site for an observatory. You'll spot the remnants of shepherds' huts.

– The GR4, with its red and white markers, crosses the **Plateau de Caussols** from north to south. You can reach **Col de Clapier** (1,257 metres/4,122 feet) or the summit of **Colle du Maçon** (1,417 metres/4,825 feet). If you head out from Caussols village on the small path to the right past the restaurant and head to the T-junction, you can park and enjoy a two-hour round trip (with a small and undemanding slope) to the ridge (1,260 metres/4,132 feet). The path leaves from opposite the road (GR4, marked 124).

LE BAR-SUR-LOUP

From the D3, which goes to Pré-du-Lac, take a left turn onto the D2210 towards Le Bar-sur-Loup. The village has narrow streets lined with tightly packed tall buildings, overlooked by the **Château des Comtes de Grasse**. Its most famous inhabitant was the Admiral of Grasse, who took part in the War of American Independence. He was born in Le Bar-sur-Loup in 1722.

Don't miss the fountain on the square. Those of you interested in industrial archaeology will be interested in the buildings belonging to the former papermaking factory to the east, on the river Loup. It's a perfect place to use as a base for exploring Grasse and the surrounding area.

USEFUL ADDRESS

🚹 **Tourist office**: place Francis-Paulet. ☎ 04-93-42-72-21. Fax: 04-93-42-92-60. Open Monday to Sunday from 9am to 6.30pm (closed at lunchtime in winter).

WHERE TO STAY

🛏 **Hôtel de la Thébaïde**: 54 chemin de la Santoline. Just 2 kilometres from Le Bar-sur-Loup and 7 kilometres (4 miles) from Grasse. ☎ 04-93-42-41-19. Open all year. Rooms between 210F and 275F. A simple and well-maintained hotel.

Campsite

🛏 **Camping des Gorges du Loup**: 965 chemin des Vergers. To the northeast, take the D221 and after 1 kilometre make a right turn on to chemin des Vergers. The site is about 1 kilometre down this road. ☎ and fax: 04-93-42-45-06. Open between April and September. Set price for two people from 110F to 155F. This is a lovely campsite, with a pretty view over the valley and mountains and a swimming pool. It's very quiet and makes a great base for exploring the area. You can also try out a variety of different sports.

WHERE TO EAT

🍴 **L'École des Filles**: 380 avenue Amiral-de-Grasse. ☎ 04-93-09-40-20. This restaurant is closed on Sunday evening and Monday lunchtime (and for dinner in low season), and menus cost from 68F (weekday lunch) to 195F. The decor is more of a talking point than the food (wood-fired pizzas), but those of you nostalgic for your youth will enjoy the setting. Housed in a former classroom, it offers unpretentious but sun-drenched cuisine and a chance to relive your childhood.

✗ **La Jarrerie**: at the foot of the village. ☎ 04-93-42-92-92. The restaurant is closed in January, on Monday evening and all day Tuesday from mid-September to mid-June, and all day Tuesday and Wednesday lunchtime in summer. It closes annually from 2 to 31 January. Set menus range in price from 110F (weekday lunch) to 250F, and the dining room has lovely rustic decor. Try the quail salad with raspberry vinegar or scallops with fresh pasta.

WHAT TO SEE

★ **Église St-Jacques-le-Majeur**: enter the church on the right through a splendid Gothic door with a panel representing St Jacques carved by Jacotin Bellot (*see* 'Vence cathedral', page 607). It has a 13th-century nave and a retable depicting St-Jacques le Majeur, attributed to Bréa. The most curious painting is the 15th-century *Danse macabre*, under the gallery, which depicts the Comte du Bar's ball, held during Lent. Legend has it that all the party guests perished when the ground opened up in punishment for their sacrilege. The count begged St Arnoux for forgiveness and promised to build a chapel in the saint's name. The St Arnoux hermitage was duly constructed and still stands today, beyond Pont-du-Loup. The artist (an itinerant painter from Nice) portrays elegant noble folk dancing to the sound of a drum, unaware of the tiny demons of doom on their heads. Death is gradually taking its victims, and souls are weighed on scales held by St Michael at the foot of Christ, while a demon tries to tip the balance in his favour. The condemned souls are thrown into the gaping mouth of Hell.

From the **church square**, there's a glimpse of the view over the cliffs of the Gorges du Loup.

– To continue the **Gorges du Loup Circuit**, make your way back to the D2085, and turn left on to the D7 after Pons and Le Collet to return to the Loup valley. After a superb viewing point and a clifftop section, the road descends into the valley and crosses the River Loup to arrive at La Colle-sur-Loup. The road then returns to St-Paul and Vence.

LES CLUES DE HAUTE-PROVENCE

From Vence to Coursegoules

Leave Vence to the north on the D2. The road climbs quickly up into the hills, with some spectacular views. The landscape changes equally rapidly, becoming more austere, with large expanses of scrub. The view opens up as the road continues to climb, and before the Col de Vence, or pass, there's a breathtaking view of the coast from the Estérel to Cap Ferrat. The contrast between the mountain, desert and coastal landscapes is striking.

– The **walk** from here to St-Jeannet takes about four hours. Alternatively, there's a two-hour route that starts further along (before the yellow house) and goes to Vence via Les Salles. The third alternative is a route to Coursegoules via La Combe Moutonne, which takes about 2 hours 30 minutes.

✕ At the Col de Vence, the **snack-bar El Bronco**, which is open all year. ☎ 04-93-58-09-83. They also organize horse-riding treks in the beautiful countryside.

The road continues through a dramatic and arid landscape, overlooking the Cagne. Turn right to get to Coursegoules.

COURSEGOULES

Just off the D2, the tiny village of Coursegoules teeters on the brink of a ravine on the side of the Cheiron range. It seems to belong to a different time. In the 17th century, it was a royalist town, with 1,000 inhabitants. In 1900, it still had its own lawyer, doctor and justice of the peace, but poor communications and difficulties in cultivation led to a massive exodus. Today, many of its historic houses have been converted into holiday homes, but the village has kept much of its character and is a peaceful refuge from the busy coast. The architecture of the village is attractive, with vaulted streets and remnants of former defences. The tiny church (often closed) used to house a retable by Ludovico Bréa, dedicated to St John the Baptist, but this was recently stolen.

Take a walk along the path along the valley of the Cagne, amid cypress trees, to the door of the beautiful restored St-Michel chapel, which used to belong to a community of monks attached to the Lérins monastery. Climb on up to the pass above Boyon for a magnificent view.

WHERE TO STAY AND EAT

⌂ **Camping St-Antoine**: ☎ 04-93-59-12-36. This site is open from May to October, but it doesn't take advance bookings. Quiet, friendly and quite comfortable, it also has showers, but its best feature is its wonderful location. No food facilities.

⌂ **Gîtes communaux** (walkers' accommodation): in the town hall behind the church. ☎ 04-93-59-11-28. Well-equipped accommodation for around 1,150F per week (more in summer).

⌂ ✕ **Auberge de l'Escaou**: in the heart of the village. ☎ 04-93-59-11-28. Fax: 04-93-59-13-70. Closed on Sunday evening and on Monday out of season. Rooms for 390F, including breakfast. Menus at 76F (weekday lunch), 100F and 168F. The restaurant serves rustic Provençal cuisine. There are a dozen clean rooms, all with views of the valley or the mountain.

⌂ **Chambre d'hôte** (B&B): L'Hébergerie, with Guy and Martine Durand, 350 chemin du Brec. ☎ 04-93-59-10-53. Around 290F for two people (including breakfast). This non-smoking B&B has a room for two (or possibly three) people and a wonderful view over the valley.

From Coursegoules to Thorenc

Head back to the D2. After Coursegoules, the landscape becomes much greener and the road carries on the high valley of the Loup.

GRÉOLIÈRES

This village in the foothills of the Cheiron is overlooked by the ruins of the ancient village of Les Hautes-Gréolières. Stroll through its picturesque narrow streets and stop to admire the facade of the church, renovated in the 12th century and extended in the 16th. The building houses a retable of St Etienne, painted in 1480 by a monk from the school of Bréa. There's also a processional cross in gold and silver.

The ruins of the chateau stand opposite the church.

USEFUL ADDRESSES

☐ Syndicat d'initiative (tourist information centre): ☎ 04-93-59-97-94.

🚌 Bus from Grasse: there are two buses a day in summer, on Tuesday and Friday.

WHERE TO STAY AND EAT

🛏 Gîte de France: above the studio of Juliette Derel, place Pierre-Merle, in the village. ☎ 04-93-59-98-32. 100F per person per night, or an apartment for 2,400F per week (Saturday to Saturday), including sheets and kitchen facilities. This studio, above the owner's shop, can sleep five to seven people. Guests are given coffee in the morning.

✕ La Barricade: in the village. ☎ 04-93-59-98-68. Restaurant is closed on Monday and Tuesday (except during school holidays in the summer). Menus at 69F and 99F. Tasty terrines, warm goat's cheese, meat and game grilled in a wood-fired oven, served in a pleasant setting and charged at reasonable prices.

GRÉOLIÈRES-LES-NEIGES

This ski resort is the furthest south in France and is reached easily by the D802. It has 11 lifts, serving 30 kilometres (18 miles) of downhill runs and 20 kilometres (12.5 miles) of cross-country trails. Snow-making machines ensure good conditions.

USEFUL ADDRESS

☐ Syndicat d'initiative (tourist information centre): call the Gréolières tourist office. ☎ 04-93-59-97-94.

THORENC

Pronounced 'Toron' and known today as 'Switzerland in Provençe', this cross-country ski resort was created at the beginning of the 20th century by English and Russian entrepreneurs. It stands at 1,250 metres (4,100 feet), and its architecture is unusual. The road up to the resort is dramatic and rather wild, passing through rock at some points.

WHERE TO STAY AND EAT

The resort's two pleasant hotels stand facing each other:

♠ ✗ **Hôtel des Voyageurs**: avenue du Belvédère. ☎ 04-93-60-00-18. Fax: 04-93-60-03-51. Closed on Thursday in low season and from 15 November to 1 February. Spotless rooms from 280F to 300F. Half board compulsory in season, at 280F per person per day. Menus from 95F (weekday) to 155F, including *tête de veau* or young rabbit. There's a terrace and gardens, a view of the village, and a free garage.

♠ ✗ **Auberge Les Merisiers**: ☎ 04-93-60-00-23. Fax: 04-93-60-02-17. Closed on Tuesday out of season and in March. Rooms with shower and toilet at 200F. Half board compulsory in August, at 250F per person. Menus between 100F and 170F. Rooms have been entirely renovated, and some have a balcony. Specialities include duck, rabbit and guinea fowl, all of which can be enjoyed near the open fire.

WHERE TO EAT IN THE AREA

✗ **Restaurant Le Christiania**: L'Audibergue. Accessible from St-Vallier. ☎ 04-93-60-45-41. Closed in the evening and from 1 to 26 December. Daily special at 65F, and set menu at 120F. This mountain chalet at the bottom of the ski slopes in L'Audibergue welcomes many visitors from Cannes, who come for the food and for the clean summer air. The menu has a wide selection of traditional dishes, including ham, tripe, wild boar and leg of lamb. Book ahead for weekends or public holidays.

From Coursegoules to Bouyon

Head back on the D2 to the Quatre-Chemins junction, where you take the road to the **Col de Bleine**, the pass at an altitude of 1,440 metres (4,723 feet). The road descends through pine trees towards **Le Mas** and **Pont-d'Aiglun**. The rocky cleft of the Clue d'Aiglun is spectacular – just a few metres wide, but 200–400 metres (656–1,312 feet) high. Stop a little further on at the **Pont du Riolan**, where a torrent of water tumbles between enormous rocks below the bridge.

The road carries on and crosses **Roquestéron**. As you leave the village, take the D1 on the right, towards Bouyon, which goes via the **Clue de la Bouisse**. After Conségudes, you can see the **Clue de la Péguière** to the left. The clifftop road above the Estéron is very beautiful and provides some breathtaking views.

BÉZAUDUN-LES-ALPES

This village is even more isolated than Coursegoules. Its ochre-coloured walls, matching roofs, cobbled main street and vaulted passages make it a picturesque spot. It also has a rectangular tower, a small and simple church and a cemetery.

WHERE TO EAT

✗ **Auberge des Lavandes**: ☎ 04-93-59-11-08. Open for lunch only, and closed on Thursday. Menus at 120F and 140F. The cheapest menu at this excellent restaurant includes *crudités*, ham and *saucisson*, fresh trout, rabbit in herbs, salad, cheese *and* bilberry tart! For just a few more francs, you can treat yourself to delicious freshwater crayfish.

– **Walks**: a quiet path across Le Chiers mountain leads through woods of oak and nut trees, to the wine-making village of St-Jeannet.

ROUTE DES CRÊTES

The 'road of the ridges' is so called because it links the hilltop villages above the valleys of the Estéron and the Var. It offers an unhurried route back from Vence or a pleasant way of getting to the Haut Pays (high country, *see below*).

BOUYON

The frontier village of Bouyon stands at the crossroads between the Var and the Estéron. The views are spectacular and it's a great base for a number of excursions in the area. Although it was half destroyed by an earthquake in 1884, it has suffered to a lesser extent from the sort of rural exodus that afflicted neighbouring Coursegoules. Opposite the town hall, a narrow passageway on the left leads to a terrace, from which there's a dizzying view over the forests.

GETTING THERE

– **Bus**: daily buses from and to Nice.

WHERE TO STAY AND EAT

🛏 ✗ **Hôtel La Catounière**: place de la Mairie. ☎ and fax: 04-93-59-07-15. Open lunchtime and evening from 1 March to 30 October and at the weekend from early November to early March. Double rooms from 220F to 240F. Half board 200F per person. Menus at 80F and 120F. The rooms in this charming rustic hotel, with its exposed stonework and fireplace, are very pleasant, some with mountain views. The regional cuisine includes *lapin chasseur aux champignons* (wild rabbit with mushrooms), *daube provençale* (traditional stew), *épaule d'agneau au four* (roast shoulder of lamb) and *poulet aux écrevisses* (chicken with crayfish, depending on seasonal availability).

FESTIVALS

– **Procession des Limaces**: this festival dates back to the 16th century and takes place on the second Sunday after Corpus Christi. The streets are lit with little lamps made of snail shells (*limassa* in the Provençal dialect) filled with olive oil with a small cotton wick burning in them.

LE BROC

The name of the lovely hilltop village of Le Broc comes from the Provençal *broco*, which means 'edge' or 'embankment'. It stood sentry over the frontier until the 1860s. In the 17th century it had as many inhabitants as Vence, together with its own hospital, customs offices and a bishops' rest home. Today, there's still a pretty arcaded square with a fountain dating from 1812, plane trees, a café and the obligatory benches. In one of the neighbouring streets, two houses are linked up on first-floor level, forming a bridge. The church houses a painting by **Canavesio** and a modern stations of the cross. The **Ste-Marguerite** chapel and its tiny cemetery stand surrounded by oak trees.

Along the road to Carros (*see below*) there are some wonderful views over the valley of the River Var, its banks lined with greenhouses, and of more hilltop villages.

WHERE TO EAT

✕ **Restaurant L'Estragon**: on the side of the road, to the left towards Carros. ☎ 04-93-29-08-91. Open only at lunchtime and closed on Friday, as well as from 1 December to 1 February. Two excellent menus (at 83F and 165F). Pleasant terrace overlooking the Var and the mountains, and specialities including cheese soufflé, salt cod, and chicken with cream and tarragon, not forgetting delicious *crêpes Suzette*.

CARROS-VILLAGE

Carros gets its name from the word for 'rock', and the village does indeed perch on a 300-metre (985-foot) rocky outcrop, overlooking the Var. It is crowned by a 13th- and 14th-century chateau, currently being restored, with a fine tower at each corner. The old part of the village, with its stepped stone streets, has been renovated, and is rather like a living museum. Find the viewing platform, just below the old village, for a staggering panorama of the Var, the hilltop villages and the Alps.

With the damming of the Var and the creation of a new industrial estate, a new, frankly uninteresting Carros town has been developed, opposite Pont de la Manda.

GATTIÈRES

This lovely village, surrounded by olive groves, has typically Provençal small squares, fountains and arcaded houses. It has some pretty shopfronts, including the bakery, and many streets with Italian names. To visit the church, ask at the presbytery.

GETTING THERE

– **From Nice**: the bus leaves from the coach station every day at 7.40am, 8.30am (except Tuesday and Friday), 5.30pm (except Sunday and public holidays) and 6.20pm.

– **Return to Gattières**: buses leave every day at 6.45am, 7am, 1.30pm and 4.55pm.

USEFUL ADDRESS

🛈 **Syndicat d'initiative** (tourist information centre): in the town hall. ☎ 04-92-08-45-70.

WHERE TO STAY AND EAT

🛏 ✕ **Hôtel Beau Site**: route de Vence. ☎ 04-92-08-21-00. Fax: 04-92-08-21-11. Restaurant closed on Sunday. Hotel closed for part of November. Rooms from 300F to 350F. Menu including dessert at 250F. Main courses between 60F and 70F. The hotel has panoramic views of the Var, and as far as the sea, and a pleasant garden. It recently changed hands but is still a good place to stay.

✕ **L'Hostellerie Provençale**: just before the old town, near the car park. ☎ 04-93-08-60-40. Closed on Tuesday and Wednesday as well as from mid-September to mid-October. Menus between 98F and 160F. Meals can be taken outside under the cypress trees. Start with Parma ham, homemade terrine and then a huge platter of *hors-d'œuvres*, including seafood, sweet peppers and rice salad. Ravioli follows, with rabbit or excellent beef stew in hot pursuit, and cheese and dessert (including delicious raspberry mousse) yet to come. Phew!

ST-JEANNET (06640)   Population: 3,650

From the road back to Vence, there's a good view of the distinctive Baou de St-Jeannet, a sheer rock with a flat summit that dominates the surrounding countryside. A small road to the right leads to the village of St-Jeannet, so close to the coast, yet so rural in character. It balances on a terrace beneath the famous rock and has inspired many artists, including Chagall and Poussin, as well as film director Alfred Hitchcock, who shot some scenes from *To Catch a Thief* here. Take the one-hour path from the village to the summit of the rock, for views stretching to the Alps.

St-Jeannet was famous for a long time for its wine; its delicious whites are said to make the drinker hear angels singing. At one point, there were 4,000 parcels of land given over to wine production. It's a village of artists, too. One of the founders of dadaism and surrealism, Ribemont-Dessaignes, appreciated the peaceful way of life here.

GETTING THERE

– **From Nice**: there are two daily buses.

USEFUL ADDRESS

🄱 Syndicat d'initiative (tourist information centre): in summer only. ☎ 04-93-24-73-83. Open every day (except Tuesday and Wednesday) 9.30am–12.30pm and 3–7pm.

WHERE TO STAY AND EAT

🛏 ✕ Hôtel-restaurant Le Ste-Barbe: at the entrance to the village, on the left just before the square. ☎ and fax: 04-93-24-94-38. Closed on Tuesday evening. Rooms from 175F to 240F. Half board at 260F. Restaurant menu at 95F. Some of the rooms at this small and unpretentious hotel have balconies and they don't charge much more for a lovely sea view. Local people eat in the restaurant, which is always a good sign, or you can just have a drink.

🛏 Gîte d'Étape La Ferrage: in the village itself; follow the signposts. ☎ 04-93-24-87-11. Fax: 04-93-24-73-07. From 65F per person per night. Half board 110F. The decor at this walker's accommodation is rustic, and there's a lovely fireplace, a fully equipped kitchen and a shared bathroom. Bring your own sleeping bag, but don't worry about wine – the father of the affable manager sells his own excellent vintages.

✕ Restaurant Au Vieux Four: opposite the town hall. ☎ 04-93-24-97-41. Open every evening in summer, but closed on Tuesday in low season, as well as from 20 to 27 November and from 15 to 23 January. Menu at 95F. À la carte around 120F. Customers eat fondue, pizza or chilli con carne in a sweet little dining room. The restaurant is also a meeting place and information point for walkers.

WHAT TO SEE

★ Behind the church in St-Jeannet, down the little street, there's a wonderful **panoramic view** stretching out to sea. Sadly, the area has been rather built up, with an incredible number of new *mas*-style houses, complete with pools, as well as a series of greenhouses.

★ **Fortified church**: the simple church with its square clocktower is certainly worth a look. On the church square, a plaque commemorates Joseph-Rolalinde Ranchier (1785–1843), of the Félibrige movement (*see* page 80).

★ As you stroll through the evocatively named streets, look out for the pretty fountain and the wonderful old public washing place. Among the moving inscriptions on a building at the corner of rue de la Mairie and rue du Château is one to Mayor Clary-Louis, who brought electric light to the 'eternally grateful' town of St-Jeannet in 1902.

WHAT TO DO

– A lovely **walk** passes through the gorges, along the river. Follow the signs to 'Col de Vence' and then take the 'Chemin du Riou', 1 kilometre further on, on the right. Follow the track for 5 kilometres (3 miles), then take the next path for about 30 minutes, for a fabulous view and a nice spot for swimming.

The Azur Alps

The hills and valleys of the *haut pays* (high country) of the Alpes-Maritime region, recently renamed the 'Alpes d'Azur', are dotted with little villages – an ideal place to escape from the crowds and recharge the batteries before heading back towards the coast. Nice and Menton are good starting points for trips into the *haut pays*.

THE VALLÉE DU VAR BY THE TRAIN DES PIGNES

The delightful train journey between Nice and Digne is a wonderful way to discover the Var valley. Going north, there are four return trips a day, leaving from Nice's Gare des Chemins de Fer de Provence. The station is in the northern part of the city, also known as Nice Nord, at rue Alfred-Binet.

For more information on the Train des Pignes, and on journeys in the other direction, *see* page 352.

MALAUSSÈNE

Passengers should get off the Train des Pignes 45 kilometres (28 miles) from Nice, at the request stop, for a walk to Malaussène. This typical hilltop village, perched on its rocky outcrop, can be reached on foot in about 30 minutes. It is supplied with water from a 17th-century viaduct and there's a lovely stroll along the canal.

VILLARS-SUR-VAR

Villars-sur-Var is just an hour by train from Nice (less by car if the roads are clear), and yet you could be hundreds of miles from the Côte d'Azur. Vines have flourished here since the Middle Ages, and the wine produced is the only one in the *haut pays* that has been granted an Appellation Côtes-de-Provence. In summer, walkers come here to enjoy the fresh air and peaceful atmosphere.

WHERE TO EAT

✕ **Chez Simone**: on the village square. ☎ 04-93-05-76-14. A great place to meet up for a plate of ravioli, rabbit or a tasty roquefort flan.

WHAT TO SEE

★ Cars are not allowed in the old streets of the village, so it's a fine place for a stroll. The **Église St-Jean-Baptiste** has been beautifully restored and houses trompe-l'il frescoes and, to the left of the choir, an impressive altarpiece of *The Annunciation*, from the 16th-century Nice school.

★ A fine street lined with columns leads to a platform, which provides a panorama of the Var valley.

TOUËT-SUR-VAR

This amazing old village is reached via a picturesque path from the Touët train station (a 10-minute walk). With its dramatic vertical backdrop and steep, tangled streets, it is sometimes nicknamed the 'Tibetan village'. The church was constructed in the 12th century over a torrent of water, which can be seen through a grille in the floor of the nave. There's a viewpoint behind the square and almost all the tall houses have a *soleillaire*, an open space used for (among other things) drying figs in the sun.

WHERE TO EAT

✗ **L'Auberge des Chasseurs**: on the side of the road, on the right as you approach from Nice. ☎ 04-93-05-71-11. Closed on Tuesday. Menus at 100F (weekday) and 195F. This adorable little restaurant in the woods of the Var, covered in climbing vines, has pretty wooden balconies overlooking the valley. It serves appetizing dishes at reasonable prices, including *magret de canard au miel* (duck breast in honey) or locally caught game, including hare, wild boar, pheasant and trout.

WALKS

– **Mont Rourebel** (1,210 metres/3,968 feet): allow three hours to reach the summit. The path crosses the Var river and climbs to the right, and then the left, before reaching the mountain pass, Col de Rourebel, followed by the summit.

– **Thiéry**: the two-hour walk to this isolated village follows a very pretty path. The village sits in a rather wild *cirque*, a round natural depression created by erosion at the loop of the river.

PUGET-THÉNIERS

At the foot of a rocky peak, this attractive village – typically Provençal, yet at the same time with the feel of a mountain settlement – nestles at the confluence of the Roudole and the Var rivers, on the right bank of the Roudole. In the 13th century, it was a domain of the Knights Templar. Its houses are very old, including some fine manorial dwellings with overhanging roofs. Rue Gisclette used to be at the heart of the Jewish ghetto; you can still see the rings used to hold the chains that barred access to the street at night.

From place A.-Conil, at the foot of the old town, cross the Roudoule to get to the 13th-century parish church of Notre-Dame-de-l'Assomption, built by the Knights Templar and restored in the 17th century. It has a lovely altarpiece by Antoine Ronzen and a 17th-century square tower with an attractive campanile. Look for the old-fashioned shops with unusual names, such as *Au Pied Mignon* ('pretty foot').

Beside the main road, in a pretty square, stands a statue of a woman with her hands tied. *L'Action enchaînée*, by Aristide Maillot (1861–1944) symbolizes the life of the revolutionary Louis-Auguste Blanqui, who was born in

Puget-Théniers. One of the socialist heroes of the 1871 Paris Commune, he spent 36 years of his life in prison.

After Puget-Théniers, the D16 climbs up the Gorges de la Roudoule, to the north. After 2.5 kilometres on this road, you arrive at the pretty villages of Puget-Théran, right at the top, and Auvare, lost in the foothills of the Dôme de Barrot. Both are starting points for some excellent footpaths.

USEFUL ADDRESS

🏢 **Syndicat d'initiative** (tourist information centre): ☎ 04-93-05-05-05. Information on various activities, including walking, kayaking, the steam Train des Pignes, and so on.

WHERE TO STAY AND EAT

✕ **Les Acacias**: at the entrance to Puget, on the right, 1 kilometre from the village. ☎ 04-93-05-05-25. Closed on Monday and in January. Menus at 80F (weekday lunch), 115F and 195F. A Provençal-style setting on the edge of the Var, with a shady terrace, and cooking based on excellent local produce. Try the home-made ravioli or traditional tripe dish.

Campsite

🛏 ✕ **Camping Lou Gourdan**: ☎ 04-93-05-10-53. Open from April to October. At the water's edge, this comfortable site has a pool and tennis court 150 metres away, and a small snack bar.

WHERE TO STAY AND EAT IN THE AREA

🛏 ✕ **Auberge de La Penne**: in La Penne. 10 kilometres (6 miles) from Puget-Théniers. ☎ 04-93-05-60-26. Double rooms for 195F out of season. Menus at 100F and 130F. This *auberge communale* has a dozen rooms overlooking the Chéron. Rise early to explore the surrounding area, then come back for the well-prepared local food, which includes duck, home-made ravioli and gnocchi.

WHAT TO SEE IN THE AREA

★ **Écomusée du Pays de la Roudoule**: place des Tilleuls, in Puget-Rostang. ☎ 04-93-05-07-38. Fax: 04-93-05-13-25. Open every day (between April and November) 9am–noon and 2–6pm. Weekends only during the rest of the year. This museum describes life in the villages of the Roudoule area through reconstructed workshops and everyday scenes, together with exhibitions and photographs.

– The **Train des Pignes** (*see* page 352) continues its leisurely journey to Digne via Entrevaux and Annot through scenery – gorges, precipitous edges and fast-flowing rivers – that is sometimes breathtaking. A wonderful way to discover the Alpes de Haute-Provence.

GORGES DE DALIUS AND GORGES DU CIANS

The route around and through these two gorges, linked by the road to Valberg, is spectacular. The countryside is some of the most beautiful in the region.

Start your journey to the Gorges de Daluis on the N202, half-way between Annot and Entrevaux. From Daluis, the winding road follows the right bank of the River Var. Going up, towards Guillaumes, it is *en corniche* (clinging to the clifftops), with breathtaking views – not for those who suffer badly from vertigo. Coming down, it's so narrow that cars have to pass through tunnels carved right out of the rock itself. The gorges are hewn from deep red slate, and the landscape is strewn with strangely shaped rocks, with green splodges, and crashing waterfalls.

GUILLAUMES

This charming, isolated village, between the low country and the high country, is dominated by the ruins of a fortified chateau.

USEFUL ADDRESS

🚪 **Syndicat d'initiative** (tourist information centre) in the town hall: ☎ 04-93-05-57-76. Fax: 04-93-05-54-75.

WHERE TO STAY AND EAT

🛏 ✕ **Hôtel-restaurant Les Chaudrons**: ☎ 04-93-05-50-01. Closed on Sunday evening and on Monday in low season, as well as in January. Double rooms for 230F. Half board available at 240F per person. Menus at 80F and 110F. This simple, unpretentious hotel is clean and well run, with a restaurant terrace that is delightful in summer. Enjoy fresh trout from the Cians river or *civet de porcelet* (pork stew, marinated in wine).

✕ **Restaurant La Diligence**: on the main village street of Guil-laumes. ☎ 04-93-05-50-33. Closed annually from the day after the local agricultural fair (10 October) until early December. Daily special at 68F. À la carte around 120F (for pasta or pizza) or 180F (with a meat dish). Tasty pizzas named after villages in the area, very good fresh pasta and excellent meat dishes, particularly the delicious *tartare*. The welcome is warm, but the dining room can be rather charmless, so head for the terrace in summer.

WHERE TO STAY AND EAT IN THE AREA

🛏 ✕ **Hébergement à la Ferme** (with Gérard et Christine Kieffer): Villeplane, 06470 Guillaumes. ☎ 04-93-05-56-01. Email: itinerance@ wanadoo.fr. Farmhouse accommodation with meals that are generous and full of flavour. There are lovely walks in the hinterland, accompanied by friendly donkeys.

🛏 ✕ **Ferme-auberge Le Trauc**: in Bantes, 06470 Guillaumes. About 13 kilometres (8 miles) from the village, at an altitude of 1,300 metres (4,265 feet). ☎ 04-93-05-54-64.

Open every day (on reservation) from Easter to November. Around 100F per person. In splendid rural isolation, this farm offers *gîte* accommodation in its outhouses and flavoursome Mediterranean fare.

VALBERG

From Guillaumes, take the tree-lined D28 to Valberg, a summer and ski resort surrounded by meadows at an altitude of 1,670 metres (5,477 feet), just a two-hour drive from Nice. In winter, there are special ski schools for children. The Oroski lift pass allows holders to ski a limited number of hours and can be more economical than a day pass (more information from the tourist office). In summer, the Multi-Loisirs pass allows holders to participate in the many different activities offered by the resort.

USEFUL ADDRESSES

🛈 **Tourist office**: ☎ 04-93-23-24-25. Open every day 9am–noon and 2–6pm. Accommodation lists.
■ **Bureau des guides** (guide office): avenue de Valberg. ☎ 04-93-02-32-15.

■ **Bureau de l'École du ski français** (French ski school office): at the bottom of the slopes. ☎ 04-93-02-51-20.

WHERE TO STAY AND EAT

🛏 **Hôtel Le Chastellan**: rue St-Jean. ☎ 04-93-02-57-41. Fax: 04-93-02-61-65. Open all year. Double rooms for 380F, including breakfast. Five family rooms at 580F. Half board 335F per person per day. This family-run hotel, with its pretty stone facade, is a favourite with those travelling with children. Most of the rooms (some with balcony) have lovely views. They are spotlessly clean, the dining room is large and attractive, and the welcome in the hotel is warm. There's also a secure garage, a TV corner and a playroom for children.

🛏 **La Clé des Champs**: 20 avenue de Valberg. ☎ 04-93-02-51-45. Fax: 04-93-02-62-52. Closed from 10 April to 8 July, and from 20 September to 20 December. Half board and double rooms from 300F to 360F. Menus between 96F and 120F. This big, chalet-like hotel-restaurant has a number of lovely rooms with balconies that face the rising sun. The owner is also in charge, which makes it a good place to stay. The cuisine is family-style and the atmosphere is relaxed.

✕ **Côté Jardin**: behind the main square. ☎ 04-93-02-64-70. Open every day in high season. Closed on Thursday in low season, as well as in June and October. Menus range from 85F to 185F. Generally, ski resorts aren't known for their gastronomic achievements, but this restaurant is a rare exception. It serves the usual mountain dishes of fondue and *raclette*, but there are also delicious Provençal menus, with scallops, delicate *foie gras* terrine or lamb with *tapenade*. The food is beautifully presented and may be enjoyed in the pretty flower garden in summer. The service is friendly and the food excellent.

WHERE TO STAY AND EAT IN THE AREA

★ ✕ **Hôtel-restaurant Le Col de Crous**: in the middle of the village of Péone, 8 kilometres (5 miles) north of Valberg. ☎ 04-93-02-58-37. Closed on Sunday evening, on Monday, and during the last two weeks of November and early December. Rooms from 240F to 340F. Half board compulsory between October and April, 225F per person. Set menus at 80F and 120F. This good-value hotel-restaurant is a peaceful place to stay, nestled in the mountains some distance from Valberg and the ski slopes. The family-style cooking is reliable, with homemade ravioli, tripe and marinaded pork on the menu.

WHAT TO SEE AND DO

Valberg's ski season goes on right into April, as in Auron and Isola 2000, but Valberg is different in that it aims to provide a lively atmosphere all year round.

★ The attractive **Chapelle Notre-Dame-des-Neiges** is dedicated to the patron saint of skiers. Despite appearing rather unassuming, its interior has been decorated by modern artists.

– **Walk to Croix de Valberg**: leave from the Col du Sapet mountain pass and climb up the well-kept path for a magnificent panorama over the surrounding mountains. The round trip should take 45 minutes.

– **Toboggans**: the toboggan run is used even in summer. To get to it, take the Garibeuil chairlift (free for accompanied children under 6).

– **Snow scooters**: snow scooter trips leave late in the afternoon and include dinner, followed by a trip home in the dark. More information from the tourist office.

– **La Valbergane**: this annual cycling race, held during the last week of August, crosses the three valleys of the Var, Tinée and Ubaye, and takes in the four mountain passes of Couillole, La Bonette-Restefond (the highest point, at 2,802 metres/9,190 feet), Cayolle and Valberg.

BEUIL

The road carries on down to the relaxing winter and summer resort of Beuil (at 1,480 metres/4,854 feet).

USEFUL ADDRESS

🅱 **Tourist office**: in the Pissai-Re quarter. ☎ 04-93-02-32-58. Fax: 04-93-02-35-72.

WHERE TO STAY AND EAT

★ ✕ **Hôtel L'Escapade**: ☎ 04-93-02-31-27. Open every day for lunch and dinner, but closed annually from 1 November to 24 December. Double rooms from 220F to 310F, with shower or bathroom. Half board at 320F per day per person. Menus from 100F to 150F. Some rooms have balconies with magnificent views. The cheapest menu offers terrine, cold meats and bacon salad, followed by a substantial dish such as *daube à l'ancienne* (beef stew) and then *fromage du pays* (local cheese). The more expensive one will fill you up so much, you'll have to roll back down the mountain.

🛏 ✕ **Restaurant La Chaumière–Chez Max**: 06470 Les Launes de Beuil. 2 kilometres before Beuil (coming from Valberg), on the right-

hand side. ☎ 04-93-02-30-09. Closed for two weeks in May and for two weeks in October. Studios cost 330F. Menu at 105F (lunchtime). This restaurant, with a view over the Olympic ski jump, is famous for its delicious homemade pasta. It also has clean, spacious studios (for three or four, with kitchen, bathroom and TV) for rent for a night or for a week. The welcome is very friendly.

WHAT TO SEE AND DO

★ The village has an adorable little square with a church and a pretty chapel. The 18th-century church has retained its 15th-century Romanesque steeple, and on its facade, to the left, an attractive statue. The interior is richly decorated and houses a recently restored painting of *The Adoration of the Magi* by the school of Veronese.

★ **Granges du Scrouis** (goat cheese tasting): on the route de la Couillole. Opposite the tourist office, take the road to the left that climbs slightly and then look for signposts on the left. ☎ 04-93-02-31-66. Visit this goat farm to find out how goat cheese is made, then taste and buy some. The countryside is lovely and children will love the goats.

– Mont Mounier (2,800 metres/9,185 feet): the walk to the top and back down takes about six hours, so pack a picnic and find out the weather forecast before setting off. There's an extraordinary view over the Alps from the summit.

ST-ÉTIENNE-DE-TINÉE (06660)
Population: 1,680

This large village, at an altitude of 1,140 metres (3,739 feet), marks the junction between Nice and Barcelonnette, between Provence and Piedmont. The mountains around it form a natural amphitheatre, making it a popular summer resort and base for tours in the area.

St-Étienne-de-Tinée voted to join France in a local referendum in 1860. The western part of the village was destroyed by fire in 1929. Until the beginning of the 20th century, the village was an active commercial centre for the manufacture of sheets in the high country of the Tinée.

USEFUL ADDRESS

🏠 **Tourist office**: 1 rue des Communes-de-France. ☎ 04-93-02-41-96. Fax: 04-93-02-48-50. Open on Wednesday and Saturday 9am–noon and 2–6pm; Sunday, open from 9am to noon only.

WHERE TO STAY AND EAT

⬧ There are several rural *gîtes* in the area. Information is available from the Centrale des Gîtes Ruraux in Nice: ☎ 04-92-15-21-30.

⬧ ✕ **Hôtel-restaurant Le Régalivou**: 8 boulevard d'Auron. ☎ 04-93-02-49-00. Fax: 04-93-23-00-40. Double rooms from 300F, in low season. In high season, half board from 280F per person. Daily special around 50F. Menus from 90F to 120F. This simple establishment has comfortable renovated rooms, without any particular charm. The welcome is warm and the family-style cooking is good.

WHAT TO SEE

To visit these chapels in summer, ask at the tourist office:

★ **Église St-Étienne**: restored in the 19th century, the church has a pretty Romanesque belfry and a four-storey tower. Inside is a gilded wooden high altar from 1669, quite Spanish in its design.

★ **Chapelle des Trinitaires**: the chapel has frescoes dating from 1685 showing Notre-Dame-du-Bon-Remède, the patroness of naval combat. The battle of Lépante, which involved many men from Nice, is depicted on the vault. The *Trinitaires* were charged with rescuing Christians captured by the Barbarians.

★ **Chapelle St-Sebastien**: at the entrance to the village, this chapel has remarkable frescoes dating from the end of the 15th century, painted by Baleisoni.

★ **Chapelle des Pénitents-Noirs** (also known as **Chapelle St-Michel**): now a museum of religious art, featuring a 16th-century altarpiece.

★ **Musée des Traditions**: museum founded by the Association des Stéphanois, as a venue for cultural evenings and traditional festivals.

WALKS

– Follow the path alongside the River Ardon, past the Ste-Anne chapel and on to the **Col de Pal** mountain pass at 2,208 metres (7,242 feet). At the place known as La Vacherie, another route leads to the **Col de Bouchiet**, and then on to Auron.

– You can also walk to the **Col de la Bonette** mountain pass, at 2,750 metres (9,020 feet), on the highest surfaced track in Europe. From the pass, the view over the Alps is amazing. At the **Cime de la Bonette** (at 2,862 metres/9,387 feet) there's an explanatory chart. This is the mountain link between the Tinée and Ubaye valleys.

WHAT TO SEE IN THE AREA

★ **St-Dalmas-le-Selvage**: 7 kilometres (4 miles) from St-Étienne-de-Tinée, towards Barcelonnette and Col de la Bonette. This village has retained an unpretentious and picturesque charm, and some of the buildings still have their original larch-shingle roofs.

– The highest hamlet (not village) in Europe, **Bousieyas**, sits above the *commune* at 1,950 metres (6,396 feet), along with the highest mountain pass, La Bonette-Restefond, at an altitude of 2,860 metres (9,380 feet). Two-thirds of the parish are in the Mercantour national park. This is the starting point for cross-country skiing trails and snow-shoe treks. More information is available from the town hall. ☎ 04-93-02-41-01. Fax: 04-93-02-48-82.

WHERE TO EAT

✕ **L'Auberge de l'Étoile**: at the heart of the hamlet. ☎ 04-93-02-44-97 (bookings). Closed from October to mid-December, and from May to mid-June. Menu at 88F. This charming *auberge* has a terrace and a rustic dining room full of mountain atmosphere and interesting paintings. Enjoy *côtelettes d'agneau aux herbes* (lamb cutlets with herbs), *daube* (traditional beef stew) or the *assiette du randonneur* ('walker's platter'), with omelette, mixed salad, mushrooms, ham and terrine. Dinner by candlelight is a good way to escape the crowds.

AURON (06660)   Population: 1,530

Auron, on a lovely sunny plateau at an altitude of 1,600 metres (5,248 feet), is encircled by mountains. Originally a small hamlet, it first became a renowned resort after hosting the French skiing championships in 1938. In 1982, the world championships took place here, but the resort has retained a family feel and its streets are less lively in the evening than in Isola 2000. With 130 kilometres (80 miles) of runs, it's the only resort in the region to have a cable car.

GETTING THERE

– **From Nice**: buses leave daily from the coach station, train station and airport. Booking is necessary. Santa Azur: ☎ 04-93-85-92-60.

USEFUL ADDRESSES

🄷 **Tourist office**: in the Annapurna building. ☎ 04-93-23-02-66. Open all year.

■ **École du ski français** (French ski school): ☎ 04-93-23-02-53.

■ **Services des remontées mécaniques** (ski lifts): ☎ 04-93-23-00-02.

WHERE TO STAY AND EAT

🛏 ✕ **Las Donnas**: Grand-Place. ☎ 04-93-23-00-03. Fax: 04-93-23-07-37. Website: www.lasonnas. com. Closed from end April to mid-July and from end August to mid-December. Rooms from 250F to 500F. Menus at 110F and 140F. Half board compulsory during school holidays, between 220F and 400F. À la carte around 160F. Half of the rooms in this pleasant and quiet hotel, overlooking the centre of the village, have balconies with mountain views. The home cooking includes tasty fondue and delicious *raclette* in winter; in summer, the menu is more likely to include *mousseline de poisson* (fish mousse) and *rillettes de lapereau* (rabbit pâté).

♨ Maison familiale Le Collet: boulevard Georges-Pompidou. ☎ 04-93-23-01-06. Fax: 04-93-23-03-85. Open from end December to April and in July and August. Full board 1,700F per person for a week in the winter; less in summer. Full board from 200F to 305F per day, depending on season. Clean and well run, with a discount on ski and boot hire.

☆☆☆ Chic

♨ ✕ Le Savoie: boulevard Georges-Pompidou. ☎ 04-93-23-02-51. Fax: 04-93-23-04-04. Open in July and August, and from mid-December to Easter. Double rooms for 400F. Menus available in winter at 130F and 190F. Slightly ageing hotel, with three-star facilities and comfort. The terrace has wonderful views of the mountain, and there's a pleasant bar.

✕ Restaurant La Grange d'Aur: Belvedere run. ☎ 04-93-23-18-20. Open for lunch and dinner every day from mid-December to mid-April, and from end June to mid-September. Menus at 100F and 120F. À la carte (including a drink) around 200F. This attractive little barn reminds visitors that Auron was formerly the grain warehouse for St-Étienne-de-Tinée. Today, the owners serve tasty mountain fare, such as fondues and different flavoured *raclettes*, or salads such as *salade aux sanguins et aux noix* (with mushrooms and nuts). The decor is tasteful, the service good and the welcome warm.

WHAT TO SEE AND DO

★ **Chapelle St-Érige**: St Érige protected the stillborn and untied the tongues of the mute. This Romanesque alpine church, with its Lombard-style steeple, dates from the 13th century and has some exceptional religious frescoes dating back as far as 1451. The paintings portray the life of St Érige, the bishop of Gap in the sixth century. There are moving depictions of St Mary Magdalen in the central chapel and St Denis in the left apse. Ask for the keys (in return for a credit card as security) at the tourist office. Commentaries are available in several languages.

– **Téléphérique de Las Donnas**: in winter and summer, the cable car takes passengers up to an altitude of 2,256 metres (7,400 feet), for a panoramic view of the high country of the Tinée and of the Alps.

– **Ski runs**: Auron has more than 130 kilometres (65 miles) of runs in a ski area that extends over two valleys (more than in Isola). As the resort is very sunny, its snow is not always good, and it tends to suit more experienced skiers as a result.

– **Summer sports**: summer activities available range from climbing, walking and riding to golf and tennis.

ISOLA 2000 (06420)   Population: 540

Created in 1972, just 90 minutes' drive from Nice, the ski resort of Isola 2000 claims to offer 'guaranteed sun and snow'. To a large extent, it manages to fulfil its promise. All its hotels, restaurants and shops are built around a large commercial centre and it is now a year-round resort, with skiing in winter and a wide variety of sports in summer, including tennis, swimming, horse-riding, mountain-biking and climbing.

GETTING THERE

– **Buses from Nice**: booking necessary. ☎ 04-93-85-92-60. Buses leave from Nice bus station every day at 9am and 4.30pm, on Friday at 5.20pm and on Saturday at 1.15pm. In high season, buses leave from 8.30am to 7pm. The *skibus* (the ticket price includes lift pass) operates on Wednesday, Saturday and Sunday at 7.30am.

USEFUL ADDRESSES

◗ **Tourist office**: ☎ 04-93-23-15-15. Fax: 04-93-23-14-25. Open 9am–noon and 2–6pm every day (except during weekends between seasons).

■ **Accommodation**: Ask at the tourist office for information on accommodation. Prices in low and high season vary dramatically (the Christmas holidays, February and Easter are very expensive). Try Isola Locations for apartment rentals: ☎ 04-93-23-14-07.

■ **École du ski français** (French ski school): Isola has 80 permanent instructors. ☎ 04-93-23-28-00.

SKIING

Isola is the highest resort in the Alpes du Sud and has one of the best snow records in France, despite being just 50 kilometres (around 30 miles) as the crow flies from the sea. Its microclimate provides it with an abundance of excellent snow, much of it powder, for its 120 kilometres (75 miles) of runs. The nightlife is livelier than in Auron.

WALKS

Located in the centre of the Mercantour national park, Isola is the ideal departure point for a number of walks and excursions. The area around the village once belonged to Italy and provided King Victor-Emmanuel II with his private hunting grounds. Today, a network of superb footpaths is a legacy of those times. Many of the delightful walks lead to one or more of the 30 lakes that surround the ski resort.

The relevant map is IGN Haute Tinée 2 Isola 2000.

– **Traversée du Pas-du-Loup – Cime de la Lombarde**: this is a really enjoyable six-hour round trip, which climbs 1,000 metres (3,300 feet), and skirts the summits of the Franco-Italian border. Take a picnic lunch. From the Maison d'Isola, climb up the path from the bottom of the ski slopes for 100 metres, then turn left and take the little road that leads to the start of the 'Lacs de Terre Rouge' and 'Pas du Loup' footpaths. Rest and eat your lunch near one of the beautiful lakes before carrying on to the Cime de la Lombarde. The view from the summit is magnificent. On one side is the resort of Isola , and on the other, the valleys descend towards Piedmont and the Po plain.

Detailed walking maps are available from the tourist office. This walk, for example, can be shortened or even made longer.

WHAT TO SEE IN THE AREA

As you leave Isola 2000, the landscape changes as you get back to the Vallée de la Tinée.

★ **Isola**: this alpine town belonged in succession to the counts of Provence, the duchy of Savoy and the kingdom of Sardinia, before becoming part of France once again in 1861. It is surrounded by forests of chestnut trees, and stands at the convergence of the Tinée river and the fast-flowing Chastillon. It looks out on to two vast rock faces and the superb **Cascade de la Louch** (waterfall). At the entrance to Isola there's a Romanesque square tower belonging to the church of St-Pierre. The village itself has lovely old schist buildings and a pretty fountain in the church square.

Drive back down the D2205 and the road through the Valabres gorges to reach St-Sauveur-de-Tinée, 14 kilometres (about 9 miles) further on.

USEFUL ADDRESS

🛏 **Chalet d'Accueil** (welcome centre): Isola. ☎ 04-93-02-18-97. Office in charge of the area's eight *gîtes* (walkers' shelters).

VALLÉE DE LA TINÉE

The D2205 proceeds along the Tinée gorges, from Auron to the point where the Tinée river meets the Var.

From Auron to Pont de La Mescla

ST-SAUVEUR-SUR-TINÉE

This is the commercial centre of the valley, on the route to the ski resorts, and a good base for exploration of the area. Its pretty medieval church has a 14th-century square belfry and a retable of *Notre-Dame* by Guillaume Planeta (1483). The tall buildings of the village are architecturally rather severe, some with carved lintels.

USEFUL ADDRESS

🛈 **Syndicat d'initiative** (tourist information centre): in the town hall. ☎ 04-93-02-00-22. Fax: 04-93-02-05-20. Ask for information about walkers' accommodation.

WHERE TO STAY

🛏 **Camping municipal**: at the edge of the river. ☎ 04-93-02-03-20. Clean and pleasant site open from 15 June to 15 September.

🛏 **Gîte d'étape** (walkers' accommodation): 7 rue du Mortis. Open from May to November (ask at the town hall for details).

WHAT TO SEE IN THE AREA

★ **Roure**: this archetypal old mountain village is 4 kilometres (2.5 miles) from St-Sauveur-sur-Tinée, after a left turn on to the road to Beuil. Perched on a promontory overlooking St-Sauveur and the Vallée de la Violène, it has houses with beautiful slate or larch-shingle roofs, and barns dating from the 17th and 18th centuries. The church houses an altarpiece depicting the *Assumption*, attributed to François Brea.

MARIE

The charming village of Marie sits on a plateau above the valley, engulfed in olive trees. It's full of character, with shuttered windows and some slate-roofed houses, and has a real mountain feel. A century ago, Marie had 238 inhabitants, but today, despite its obvious appeal, it has a population of around 50. Wander through its narrow stepped streets and look out for the interesting public washing place, surrounded by pillars, the restored olive mill and the bread oven.

WHERE TO STAY AND EAT

🛏 ✕ **Le Panoramique**: ☎ and fax 04-93-02-03-01. Closed on Thursday in low season. Five rustic and spotless rooms from 190F to 250F (shared facilities). Half board for 260F. Menus between 90F and 180F. This little rural *auberge* serves very tasty regional fare, with dishes such as homemade ravioli, *lapin chasseur* (rabbit) and *agneau frotté de piments de Nice et de romarin* (lamb rubbed with fresh local spices and rosemary).

WALK

– **Mont Tournairet**: the summit (at 2,085 metres/6,838 feet) is reached via the path that goes up the Vallon d'Oglione and then by joining the GR5 long-distance footpath.

CLANS

This isolated hilltop village is surrounded by a beautiful forest, which was, for a long time, its main natural resource.

WHAT TO SEE

★ On the church square, there is an interesting collection of medieval houses and an old public washing place. The 13th-century (formerly collegiate) church has been restored and transformed; the frescoes that were uncovered behind the altar are considered to be the oldest in the Nice area. Unusually for church paintings, they are based on the theme of hunting.

★ **Chapelle St-Antoine**: this simple chapel is 500 metres from the village. To visit, check at the village grocery. It houses amusing frescoes showing the life of St Antoine, and the themes of 'virtue' and 'vice'.

WALKS

– **Cayre Cros** (2,088 metres/6,848 feet): this high point is reached after climbing Mont Casteo (1,159 metres/3,801 feet), and then going up to the Pointe de Serenton (at 1,839 metres/6,031 feet).

– **Mont Tournairet** (2,085 metres/6,838 feet): follow the path up the Clans valley and after passing Chapelle Ste-Anne, carry on up to the Col de Monigas pass. From here, the path leads to Mont Tournairet or, alternatively, walkers can head for the Granges de la Brasque via the Col du Fort mountain pass.

LA TOUR

After about 3 kilometres (2 miles), a small winding road to the right takes you to the hamlet of La Tour. With its pretty square and fountain surrounded by arcaded houses, it feels much more like a Provençal village than an alpine one.

WHAT TO SEE

– The **church** has two baptismal fonts and a Renaissance-style altarpiece (for information about visits, call the town hall: ☎ 04-93-02-05-27).

– You should also visit the **Chapelle des Pénitents-Blancs** (again, call the town hall for more details), which has murals painted in 1491 and attributed to Bevesi and Nadale. They feature *Vice* and *Virtue*; the figures representing the former are chained at the neck, heading for the mouth of Hell.

– The 19th-century town hall is decorated with Italian-style trompe-l'il paintings.

WALKS

A pretty path climbs up to the **Chapelle St-Jean** and then continues on to the **Col de Gratteloup** mountain pass (at 1,411 metres/4,628 feet).

Leaving the hamlet of La Tour, you can rejoin the D2205 on the left, towards Nice. The D2565, 8.5 kilometres (about 5 miles) past Pont de la Mescla, again to the left, then goes along the length of the Vallée de la Vésubie.

VALLÉE DE LA VÉSUBIE

One of the most beautiful valleys in the region, the Vallée de la Vésubie can be reached by one of two roads. The quickest is the N202 from Nice to Digne, turning off at Plan-du-Var. The alternative is to take the D19 and approach the valley via the hinterland behind Nice, through Levens (*see* page 694). The D2565 makes its way into the valley, where deep and winding gorges suddenly open up.

At **St-Jean-la-Rivière**, take the road to the left, which winds its way up Utelle. The view soon becomes quite amazing. A network of little walls supports the terraces, known as *restanques*, an arrangement that makes the cultivation of vines and olive trees possible.

UTELLE

Once upon a time, when donkeys were the only means of transport, Utelle was a very important village, dominating the entire valley from its altitude of 800 metres (2,625 feet). Today, rather isolated from the mainstream, it has retained its appeal, with fortifications, medieval houses, pretty stepped streets and some old sundials.

WHERE TO STAY AND EAT

🛏 ✕ **Hôtel-restaurant Le Belle-vue**: route de La Madone. ☎ 04-93-03-17-19. Fax: 04-93-03-19-17. Open in July and August only. Restaurant closed in January and February, as well as on Wednesday in low season. Rooms with shower and toilet for 300F. Half board compulsory in August, 290F per person. Menus from 80F to 160F. This hotel is unpretentious but excellent, with clean and comfortable rooms. The wallpaper may not be to everyone's taste, but the view is indisputably lovely, as is the swimming pool. The restaurant has a good reputation, serving homemade ravioli, *daube provençale* (beef stew) and tasty rabbit with herbs in a rustic dining room. Book a table with a view.

✕ **Aubergerie Del Campo**: route d'Utelle. ☎ 04-93-03-13-12. Restaurant open all year for lunch.

Book ahead for dinner. Lunch *formule* menu at 80F, and other menus at 110F and 190F. As the road climbs steadily up to Utelle, you may be surprised suddenly to see a number of cars parked under a tree on the edge of the road. Just below, a sheep barn dating from 1785 has been lovingly restored and now has rustic decor with a beautiful fireplace and olivewood flooring. The owner serves classic dishes using local produce, such as *raviolis de canard aux cèpes* (duck ravioli with mushrooms) or *fricassée de St-Jacques au vinaigre de framboise* (scallops in raspberry vinegar). There's an attractive terrace with a magnificent view of the gorges and the atmosphere is friendly. The place is often reserved for parties and customers also come for a range of different breakfasts.

WHAT TO SEE

★ **Église St-Véran**: the church has a Gothic porch with a sculpted door tracing the legend of St Véran (449–81). Romanesque and pre-Romanesque columns stand in fascinating contrast alongside baroque-style arches. A 17th-century sculpted wooden altarpiece depicts the *Passion*.

★ **Chapelle des Pénitents-Blancs**: near the church, the chapel houses a 17th-century wooden gilded *Descent from the Cross*.

WHAT TO SEE AND DO IN THE AREA

★ **La Madone d'Utelle**: a tough 6-kilometre (4-mile) walk, with a steep ascent and descent, requiring stamina. The reward is an unforgettable view over the Var valley, the coastline and Cap d'Antibes on one side, and the snow-capped Alps (on clear mornings), and the Vésubie and Tinée valleys on the other. This wild and windy spot, which manages to be tranquil and evocative too, has been a sanctuary for visitors and pilgrims since as early as AD 850.

– Notre-Dame-des-Miracles: the sanctuary has been rebuilt and restored several times over the centuries, but it retains an atmosphere of mystery. Its origins go back to the sinking of a Spanish ship, whose sailors were saved by prayer. The Virgin appeared before them and showed them the mountain, bathed in light. The sailors climbed to the top to build a monument to the miracle of their rescue. Later, a chapel was erected and became a place of miracles – dozens of sick people were cured after praying to the Virgin here. Evidence of the miracles, sometimes amusing and often moving, adorns the walls of the tiny chapel.

– Pèlerinages (pilgrim processions): Easter Monday, Ascension Thursday, Pentecost, 15 August and 8 September.

– Étoiles mystérieuses (mysterious stars): the Madone-d'Utelle plateau is littered with unusual star-shaped pieces of rock, often picked up on the mountain by pilgrims and walkers. Some say that they were sent from Heaven by Our Lady as a sign of love but they are actually fossils of creatures similar to sea urchins, which lived in the area when it was submerged 140 million years ago. Their decomposition produced a star-shaped fragment of limestone. On 14 August, the Marche aux Étoiles (walk to the stars) takes place.

★ **Belvédère du Saut des Français**: the D19 ascends to the viewpoint known as Le Saut des Français (the leap of the French), a very beautiful spot 300 metres (985 feet) above the river. In 1793, Republican soldiers were hurled to their deaths from this point by rebels from Nice, supported and armed by Sardinians.

★ Not far from here is the village of **Duranus**, surrounded by orchards, with its public washing place built into the rock. A path leads up to **Col St-Michel** mountain pass at 953 metres (3,125 feet) and the summit of **Rocca Seira**, at an altitude of 1,504 metres (3,457 feet). From Duranus, a spectacular *corniche* road overlooking the gorges leads to **Levens** and the hinterland behind Nice, through some of the most beautiful hilltop villages of the region.

LANTOSQUE

Although Lantosque, overlooking the Vésubie valley, suffered earthquakes in 1494, 1564, 1566 and 1644, it has nevertheless managed to retain its old feudal homes, stepped streets and intrinsic character. The grocery opposite the post office sometimes sells the most delicious sausages, flavoured with nuts, as well as water from the Vallée des Merveilles.

WHERE TO STAY AND EAT

Campsite

🛏 **Camping des Merveilles**: Le Suquet, 5 kilometres (3 miles) south of the village. At the junction of the D2565 and the D373. ☎ 04-93-03-15-73. Open from 1 July to 15 September. From 70F per person for a large tent, caravan or campervan. This well-maintained site is close to the Vésubie river, with a lovely view of the mountain. Booking advised for July and August.

☆☆–☆☆☆ Moderate to Chic

🛏 ✕ **L'Auberge du Bon Puits**: Le Suquet, 5 kilometres (3 miles) from Lantosque. ☎ 04-93-03-17-65. Fax: 04-93-03-10-48. Closed on Tuesday (except in July and August) and from December to Easter. Double rooms from 310F to 350F. Menus from 100F to 160F. Ask for a room overlooking the garden to avoid the rather noisy road. The restaurant at this *auberge* is very good and offers delicious duck and trout dishes as well as tasty tripe and *raviolis à la niçoise*, served in the huge dining room. There's a children's play area opposite.

🛏 ✕ **Hostellerie de l'Ancienne Gendarmerie**: Le Rivet, on the D2565, the main road through the valley. ☎ 04-93-03-00-65. Fax: 04-93-03-06-31. Closed on Monday in low season, and from 1 October to 1 April. Rooms at 500F and 710F. Half board around 500F. Excellent menus from 165F to 210F. A Danish couple has completely transformed this building near the river into a lovely home, its pretty facade covered in geraniums. The sunniest rooms overlook the garden, with a view over the village to the mountain beyond. Some have Scandinavian furniture and Nos. 2 and 9 have private jacuzzis. There's also a swimming pool. Specialities in the restaurant include smoked salmon, trout and monkfish. The welcome is warm and friendly, but it's a little more expensive here than elsewhere.

ROQUEBILLIÈRE

There are three parts to this *commune*: the old village, the new village and Berthemont-les-Bains. The old village is made up of little houses huddled together, on the left bank of the Vésubie. A landslide in 1926, which resulted in 17 deaths, forced the villagers to build new dwellings on the other side of the river. The **St-Michel-de-Gast** church is particularly remarkable, having been destroyed several times. It assumed its final form in 1533, after intervention by the Knights of Malta, and today Romanesque and Gothic styles stand side by side. There's a 16th-century altarpiece depicting St Anthony and a baptismal font of volcanic rock, adorned with a Maltese cross. To visit the church, ask for the key at Mme Madeleine Périchon's house opposite. According to Roquebillière tradition, someone is always on hand to give visitors a guided tour.

USEFUL ADDRESS

🛈 **Tourist office**: 26 avenue Corniglion-Molinier. ☎ 04-93-03-51-60.

WHERE TO STAY

☎ **Camping Les Templiers**: 500 metres from the historic village. Take the D69 and then the road to the left at the edge of the Vésubie river. ☎ 04-93-03-40-28. Open all year (unusual in this area). 55F per day. Caravans also for hire. This site is tranquil and pleasant, run by an affable owner, who is full of information on walks in the Vallée des Merveilles. There's a tennis court nearby and a bicycle hire shop at the entrance to the new village, a little further up the valley. Booking recommended for July and August.

EXCURSIONS FROM ROQUEBILLIÈRE

★ **Vallon de la Gordolasque**: from route de St-Martin turn right on to the winding road that climbs back up the Gordolasque valley. The picturesque village of **Belvédère** lives up to its name, with a splendid view over the valleys of the Gordolasque and Vésubie rivers. A footpath leads up to the **Granges du Colonel** and **Cime de Rans** summit (at 2,160 metres/7,084 feet). From the top, walkers can rejoin the **Roya valley** via the smaller Cayros valley.

The little road carries on past waterfalls and spectacular rock formations until it reaches the **Cascade du Ray**, and then the **Cascade de l'Estrech** (waterfalls). Around here, there are a number of superb footpaths, taking walkers to the **Madone de Fenestre**, to the **Vallée des Merveilles** or to the **Lac Long**. This area is a walkers' paradise.

★ **Berthemont-les-Bains**: this invigorating little spa town is 4 kilometres (2.5 miles) to the right of the road to St-Martin. It sits in a valley under the shade of chestnut trees and was known even in Roman times. The **Grotte St-Julien** is a cave with a 20-person bathing pool that dates back to Roman times. It will take two hours to get from Berthemont to St-Martin-Vésubie along a pretty footpath through the chestnut trees.

★ **Vallée des Merveilles** (for more information on the valley, *see* page 654). For a two-day walking tour in the valley, park at one of the passes and simply set off. There are mountain huts for overnight stays. Before leaving, check the map carefully at **Les Templiers** campsite (*see above*).

ST-MARTIN-VÉSUBIE (06450) Population: 1,100

This pretty mountain village stands at the point where the two rivers, the Boréon and the Madone de Fenestre, converge to form the Vésubie river. The air is pure and invigorating, and the village is a popular summer activity centre. Climbers and walkers gather here, many referring fondly to the region as 'Nice's Switzerland'. The village's most famous sons were the Hugo brothers, who were both 2.30 metres tall (well over 7 feet) and weighed in at 200 kilos (about 30 stone). It was also home to Joseph Mottet, who saw to it that St-Martin became the second town in France to enjoy the luxury and benefits of electric light, in 1893.

GETTING THERE

– **From Nice**: TRAM buses leave from the bus station on promenade du Paillon. ☎ 04-93-85-61-81 and 04-93-85-92-22. In summer, departures are at 8am, 9am, 5.30pm (Monday to Saturday) and 8am, 9am and 6pm (Sunday). In winter, departures are at 9am and 5.30pm during the week, and at 9am on Sunday and public holidays. The journey takes 1 hour 50 minutes.

– **Return from St-Martin**: in summer, departures are at 7am, 1pm and 5pm (at 7am, 4pm and 6pm on Sunday and public holidays). In winter, departures are at 7am and 1pm (at 5pm only on Sunday and public holidays). For more information call: ☎ 04-93-03-20-23.

USEFUL ADDRESSES

🚪 **Tourist office**: place Félix-Faure. ☎ 04-93-03-21-28. Open Monday to Saturday 10am–noon and 2.30–5.30pm, Sunday from 10am to noon; in summer every day 9am–12.30pm and 3–7pm.
■ **Bureau des guides de la haute Vésubie** (guides to the high Vésubie): rue Gagnoli. ☎ 04-93-03-26-60. Guided mountain walks for groups or individuals, and photographic outings.

■ **Bureau des guides du Mercantour** (guides to the Mercantour national park): rue Gagnoli. ☎ 04-93-03-31-32. Guided walks and climbing tours, plus canoe trips.
■ **École française de vol libre** (gliding school): J.-J. Davillier, la Colmiane. ☎ 04-93-02-83-88.
■ **Randonnées à cheval** (horse-riding treks): ☎ 04-93-03-30-23.

WHERE TO STAY AND EAT

In St-Martin-Vésubie

🛏 ✕ **La Bonne Auberge**: allée de Verdun. On the left, on the way from St-Martin to La Colmiane. ☎ 04-93-03-20-49. Fax: 04-93-03-20-69. Closed from mid-November to mid-February. Double rooms with shower and toilet at 270F, and at 300F with bathroom. Half board for 280F per person. Menus at 99F and 150F. This attractive stone *auberge* is comfortable and well maintained, but the rooms overlooking the road can be noisy. The food is traditional and includes trout, duck, lamb and quail, all of which can be enjoyed on the terrace, bordered by hedges.

🛏 **Hôtel La Châtaigneraie**: allée de Verdun. ☎ 04-93-03-21-22. Fax: 04-93-03-33-99. Closed from October to June. Rooms from 355F to 445F, with shower or bathroom. Half board between 290F and 325F per person. This pretty and tranquil hotel, with its large garden and meadow, is hidden behind a curtain of trees. It's like an upmarket spa resort *pension*. Marcel Pagnol slept in room No. 207.

Campsite

🛏 **Le Champouns**: route de Venanson, 1.5 kilometres from St-Martin-Vésubie. ☎ 04-93-03-23-72. 65F per person per night. Caravans and three- or four-person apartments, with bathroom, kitchen and balcony, for hire. The agreeable rustic *gîte d'étape* (walkers' shelter) sleeps 16. There's a splendid view of the valley.

In Boréon

Some 8 kilometres (5 miles) from St-Martin, at 1,500 metres/4,920 feet.

🛏 ✕ **Hôtel du Cavalet**: ☎ 04-93-03-21-46. Fax: 04-93-03-34-34. Open all year. Rooms with shower and toilet at 350F. Half board for 300F per person. Set menus from 89F to 139F. Standing on the edge of a lake, opposite the forest, this hotel is unsurprisingly rather touristy. Specialities include home-made ravioli, leg of lamb and bilberry tart. Booking recommended in summer.

In La Madone de Fenestre

About 12 kilometres (7.5 miles) from St-Martin

🛏 ✕ **Refuge du CAF**: ☎ 04-93-02-83-19 and 04-93-02-20-73. In low season, check opening times at the Club Alpin de Nice (☎ 04-93-62-59-99). Shelter offering half board for 195F per person.

WHAT TO SEE

★ **Rue droite**: this narrow sloping street crossing the village has a central channel that allows rainwater and melted snow to drain away. It's lined with alpine-style houses with high balconies; the house with the arcades (No. 25) belonged to the lords of Gubernati.

★ **Chapelle des Pénitents-Blancs** (or Ste-Croix): the bell-tower has a white-metal dome that gives it a rather Oriental air. Inside, the walls are decorated with eight huge paintings from the 18th century, depicting the *Passion* and the *Death of Christ*. Each face is in fact a portrait of a key figure of the period. There's a sculpted high altar showing the *Descent from the Cross*, and the facade has three works by Parini from 1848: a *Pietà* in the centre, *St Helen* to the left and *Emperor Constantine I* to the right.

★ **Church**: the first chapel was built by the Benedictine monks on the site of a pagan sanctuary dedicated to the god Jupiter. In 1136, the Knights Templar took over from the Benedictines, and the sanctuary became attached once more to St-Martin. Today, it houses the 12th-century statue of Notre-Dame de Fenestre, which has miraculously survived intact despite the church being destroyed more than once by fire or pillage. On 15 August, she is carried in procession to the craggy alpine setting of the Chapelle de la Madone de Fenestre, where she remains until September. On the left are two retables attributed to Bréa. The terrace in front of the church has a view over the Boréon valley.

WALKS FROM ST-MARTIN

– **Chemin de Berthemont**: from allée de Verdun, take the path leading up to the school and carry on straight ahead to the junction, where you turn right. Cross the fast-flowing Madone river and walk on for 8 kilometres (5 miles) among chestnut trees and across alpine pastures.

– **Venanson**: it's a 4-kilometre (2.5-mile) walk to this village overlooking the valley of St-Martin. Follow the road to the left after the bridge at the end of allée de Verdun. From the square in Venanson, there's a nice view over St-Martin, in its mountain setting.

– **Sentier de la Palu**: after about 1 kilometre on the Chemin de Berthemont (*see above*), a path on the left crosses the Toron valley, a pine forest and then the Peyra-de-Villars valley, before finally reaching the Baisse de la Palu (2,093 metres/6,865 feet) and the **Cime du Palu** summit (2,132 metres/6,992 feet). The view is well worth the effort.

IN THE AREA

The area around Le Boréon and La Madone de Fenestre is high mountain country and you must be properly equipped for walking here: wear suitable footwear and clothing, carry a rucksack with provisions and take enough water with you. Some of the climbs may look easy but the summits reached are actually quite high (Gélas, Ponset), so do take care.

★ **Le Boréon**: this little mountain resort, with chalets and huts, a lovely waterfall and a little reservoir lake, at an altitude of 1,500 metres (4,920 feet), is 8 kilometres (5 miles) from St-Martin. A haven for ecologists, Le Boréon is the starting point for a number of walks into the forest and hikes up to the summits in the Mercantour national park.

The hike up to the **Cime du Mercantour** summit is just one of the excellent routes in the area. Follow the path to the Lac de Cerise (two hours), then it's a five-minute climb towards the Col de Cerise, where a terrace on the right gives access to the Lac du Mercantour. Sometimes, flocks of chamois may be seen in this fairly wild area.

From Le Boréon, a route (2.5 kilometres/1.5 miles) leads to the cowsheds, from which a three-hour path leads to the **Refuge de la Maïris** (mountain hut) and the **Pas des Roubines** (2,130 metres/6,986 feet). More energetic walkers can carry on to La Madone de Fenestre.

★ **La Madone de Fenestre**: take the D94 from St-Martin and head up the Madone de Fenestre valley along rather steep and barren slopes before crossing a beautiful forest. After 13 kilometres (8 miles) you'll reach La Madone de Fenestre, a favourite, rather wild and austere spot for climbers. Behind the snow-covered **Mont Gélas** (3,143 metres/10,309 feet) is the Italian border.

The chapel at the summit is a destination for many pilgrims. In the summer it houses the famous 12th-century statue of Notre-Dame-de-Fenestre, from the church in St-Martin.

COL DE TURINI

From the Vallée de la Vésubie, the D70 and its hairpin bends lead to the Col de Turini mountain pass. It sits at the junction of several routes and is the starting point for a variety of excursions. The road from Sospel is lined with olive trees and follows the river Bévéra in a valley that gradually becomes steeper and steeper. The river becomes increasingly fast-flowing and then transforms itself into waterfalls that tumble down the mountain, eventually arriving at the wild and jagged Gorges du Piaon.

Take a breather at the **Chapelle Notre-Dame-de-la-Menour**, reached by a path to the left that crosses a bridge above the road. A monumental stairway leads to the chapel's Renaissance facade. There's a superb view over the gorges, and signs of the age-old cultivation of vines and olive trees, on terraces supported by little walls known as *restanques*.

The road crosses the pretty village of **Moulinet**, with its pink houses and shady square lined with plane trees, and carries on, through more hairpin bends until it reaches the Col de Turini. The Monte-Carlo rally climbs up to the pass at night every year, and the Turini section is one of the most demanding challenges on the course.

The Turini pass is the starting point for a number of different excursions.

WHERE TO STAY AND EAT

♙ ✕ **Le Ranch**: 06440 La Bollène-Vésubie, Col de Turini. ☎ 04-93-91-57-23. Closed on Sunday evening and on Monday (except in July and August), and from 15 November to 28 December. Double rooms with shower and toilet for 240F. Half board 250F. Menus at 85F, 98F and 148F. Unpretentious but agreeable hotel. Rooms Nos. 7 and 8 have balconies with pretty mountain views. The restaurant's smallest menu features *charcuterie* (cold meats), *daube provençale* (beef stew), cheese and dessert. The larger menu is altogether more satisfying, offering cured meats such as *jambon cru* and *saucisson de montagne*, *raviolis farcis aux blettes ou aux épinards sauvages* (ravioli stuffed with Swiss chard or wild spinach) and *tarte aux myrtilles* (bilberry tart) to finish.

L'AUTHION

The D68 from the Col de Turini climbs up to the **Baisse de Tueis**, where there's a monument commemorating French soldiers who lost their lives fighting in 1793 and 1945. The views become increasingly spectacular as the road ascends to the mountains.

The road to the left heads up to the **Pointe des Trois-Communes** (2,082 metres/6,830 feet), the highest point of the Authion mountain, topped by the ruins of a castle. It offers superb views of the hills around Nice and the peaks of the Mercantour national park. For a different perspective, make your way back along the equally lovely route that passes the **Camp de Cabanes-Vieilles**, an old barracks damaged in the fighting in 1945.

From the Col de Turini to Peïra-Cava

The D2566 comes down from the Col de Turini to Peïra-Cava through the Turini forest, with its beech, maple, sweet chestnut and huge pine trees.

WHERE TO EAT

✕ **Auberge L'Haïga Blanca**: ☎ 04-93-91-57-19. Double rooms with shower and toilet or bathroom for 220F. Half board 250F. Menus from 75F to 115F. Dishes including *daube de sanglier ou de buf avec raviolis maison* (beef or wild boar stew with homemade ravioli), *civet de porcelet* (suckling

THE AZUR ALPS

pig) or *coq au vin*, can be enjoyed on the veranda or terrace between June and October. The view is quite something. The friendly hosts sometimes offer free pony rides.

PEÏRA-CAVA

Peïra-Cava is a popular resort for both summer and winter activities. Climb to the Cime de Peïra-Cava summit (on the left as you approach the village), for a wonderful view over the valley of the Bévéra and the Mercantour national park on one side, and the mountains and the Vallée de la Vésubie on the other. On a clear day, you may be able to see as far as Corsica.

The location of the village of Peïra-Cava, on a narrow ridge between the valleys of the Vésubie and Bévéra rivers, is extraordinary and impressive.

After leaving Peïra-Cava, make your way back to Lucéram on a winding road, to make a tour of the hilltop villages of the Nice hinterland. The views are fantastic. The alternative route passes via the Col de Braus and Sospel to Vallée de la Roya.

From the Col de Turini to Sospel

The winding descent from the pass to the village of Sospel re-crosses the refreshing pine-scented forest, around 30 kilometres (20 miles) from the coast.

SOSPEL (06380)   Population: 2,940

The little town of Sospel lies in a lovely setting in a green hollow on the Bévéra river, at the crossroads of various routes. It has a charming old town and a shady square, and is also a good base for a number of lovely walks.

GETTING THERE

– **By bus**: for more information call the tourist office or Transports Rey (☎ 04-93-04-01-24).

From Menton (bus station): buses from Menton to Sospel at 9.30am, 2pm and 6pm.

Buses leaving Menton at 2pm and Sospel at 1pm operate on Tuesday, Wednesday, Thursday and Saturday *only*. The 6pm bus from Menton, and the 12.45pm bus from Sospel, connect with train services to Breil, Saorge, St-Dalmas, Tende, and so on.

To Menton: buses leave from the market square at 7am, 1pm and 4.30pm. The journey takes 50 minutes.

– **By train**: six trains a day from Nice (central station), on the Nice-Tende-Cuneo line.

USEFUL ADDRESS

⊞ Tourist office: at Pont Vieux. ☎ 04-93-04-15-80. Fax: 04-93-04-19-96. Open during the week 10am–noon and 2–6pm (to 4.30pm in winter). A good range of leaflets and information on climbing and paragliding (*parapente*).

■ **Sospel VTT/FFC** (cycling and mountain biking): information at the tourist office. There are over 130 kilometres (80 miles) of marked bike trails around Sospel. Hire a bike and join a guided tour, but be prepared to use your calf muscles – this is not the flattest area of France.

WHERE TO STAY

Campsite

⚑ Camping Le Mas Fleuri: La Vasta district. 2 kilometres from Sospel on the D2566. Follow the road up to the Col de Turini and turn left. ☎ 04-93-04-03-48. Fax: 04-93-04-11-27. Open from Easter to end September. This site has a lovely view, and facilities include hot showers and a swimming pool. There are mobile homes and bungalows for hire, and a restaurant serving Italian food.

⚑ Camping St-Sébastien: 06380 Moulinet. At the exit from the village of Moulinet. ☎ 04-93-04-80-37 and 04-93-04-81-47. On a farm in a splendid spot at the foot of Le Mercantour. The facilities are clean and the prices reasonable, but large vehicles may find access difficult.

☆ – ☆☆ Budget to Moderate

⚑ Domaine Ste-Madeleine (B&B): route de Moulinet. 4.5 kilometres (about 3 miles) north of Sospel, on the road towards the Col de Turini. ☎ 04-93-04-10-48. Closed from 1 October to 1 April. Rooms for 250F, including breakfast. Guests can prepare their own meals in a communal kitchen and then eat with their hosts in a large dining room. There's also a swimming pool.

⚑ Hôtel des Étrangers: 7 boulevard de Verdun. ☎ 04-93-04-00-09. Fax: 04-93-04-12-31. Closed from 28 November to 15 February. Rooms from 300F to 400F. Menus from 120F to 240F. The hotel has 35 comfortable rooms, overlooking the river, and terraces with sea views. Facilities include a garden, heated pool, sauna, gym, jacuzzi, tennis and bike hire (free for guests). There's also walkers' accommodation behind the hotel. The delicious food, prepared by the fifth generation of the Domerego family, includes *raviolis maison à la bourrache* (ravioli flavoured with borage), *marmite d'écrevisses* (crayfish casserole) and *carré d'agneau rôti au thym frais* (roast lamb with fresh thyme).

⚑ Chambres d'hôte Marie Mayer (B&B): Domaine du Paraïs. 3 kilometres (2 miles) from Sospel, on route de Moulinet towards Col de Turini. ☎ 04-93-04-15-78. Rooms between 290F and 400F, including breakfast. This rather grand Italianate house stands in grounds of 4 hectares (10 acres), surrounded by woods and olive groves. The rooms are sophisticated and authentic in style – it's the perfect spot for a romantic stay.

WHERE TO EAT

✕ **L'Escargot d'Or**: 3 boulevard de Verdun. Next door to the Hôtel des Étrangers. ☎ 04-93-04-00-43. Fax: 04-93-04-04-69. Closed in the evening in winter, and for two weeks in December. Menus between 70F and 160F. Ask for a table on the pleasant terrace, with its mountain and sea views, and enjoy regional dishes such as *crottin de chèvre de Moulinet* (goat's cheese cooked in olive oil), rabbit in mustard, *daube provençale* (beef stew) and *pétoncles au beurre de basilic* (scallops in basil butter).

✕ **Auberge du Pont Vieux**: opposite the bridge. ☎ 04-93-04-00-73. Closed on Sunday evening (in low season), for the school holidays at Christmas, in February and at All Saints. Menus at 69F, 88F and 120F. Unpretentious and popular with locals, this *auberge* serves excellent traditional dishes, such as *daube de boeuf aux pâtes fraîches* (beef stew with fresh pasta), *tripes à la provençale* (regional-style tripe) and *raviolis au saumon* (salmon ravioli). Rooms are also available.

✕ **La Lavina**: route du Col de Braus. ☎ 04-93-04-04-72. Fax: 04-93-04-12-25. Rooms from 250F to 300F. Menu at 110F; *menu gastronomique* at 170F, including aperitif, wine and coffee. Customers come to this farm-*auberge* for the spectacular view over Sospel and Le Mercantour as much as for the food, which is none the less exclusively homemade and includes such dishes as *terrine de lapin* (rabbit terrine), *pintade à l'estragon* (guinea fowl with tarragon) and *canette braisée* (braised duckling).

WHAT TO SEE

On the Left Bank

★ To visit Sospel, cross the delightful old **bridge**, which dates from the 17th century. It was originally on the 'salt route' and is the only toll bridge in the Alpes-Maritimes. Badly damaged in World War II, it has been rebuilt. **Place St**-Nicolas has arcaded houses and a former parish hall, where all local decisions were made. There's also a 15th-century fountain on the square.

★ The **rue de la République** is lined with historic houses, which all look the same and are linked by wide vaults. This district was once full of inns, which provided hospitality for merchants waiting to cross the toll bridge.

★ **Rue Longue**, also lined with ancient houses, leads to the Chapelle des Pénitents-Blancs, once called the Église Ste-Croix.

On the Right Bank

★ **Place de la Cathédrale**: the architecture in the square is particularly attractive, with its houses built over arcades and with lovely facades. The ensemble is dominated by the imposing **Cathédrale St-Michel**, which was built in the 17th century, restored in 1888 and still retains its Romanesque belfry. In the chapel to the left of the chancel is one of Ludovico Bréa's masterpieces, a 15th-century altarpiece of the *Virgin*, painted on wood. It came from the Chapelle des Pénitents-Noirs.

To the right of the church is the **Palais Ricci**, where Pope Pius VII lodged in 1809, on the orders of Napoleon.

★ Lose yourself in the historic, narrow winding streets. Along **rue St-Pierre**, with its arcades and its fountain, you'll find the Maison du Viguier and place des Pastoris. Head back along the promenade that runs alongside the river, past houses with trompe-l'œil facades, green shutters, balustrades and windows strewn with washing.

★ **Fort St-Roch**: on the N2204. En route to Col de Braus, behind the cemetery. ☎ 04-93-04-00-70. Between June and end September, open every day (except Monday) from 2pm to 6pm. In October, April and May, open only at weekends and on public holidays (same hours). The fort was part of Sospel's Maginot Line, built in 1932 to protect the region against potential Italian invasion. It's a small town in itself, 50 metres (164 feet) underground, with 2,000 metres (6,560 feet) of passageways. Huge quantities of concrete and steel were used in its construction, and it was designed to be self-sufficient for more than three months, with living quarters, kitchens, ventilation shafts and artillery blocks. There's also a museum.

★ **Barbonnet Fort**: Col St-Jean. Open in July and August for one guided tour on Sunday afternoon. Check opening hours: ☎ 04-93-04-15-80 or 04-93-04-14-29. This historic, panoramic site takes visitors back to the events of the Bataille des Alpes, in June 1940.

WALKS

– **Le calvaire** (calvary): round trip of around 20 minutes. Head west to the D2204 and then take the D2566 towards Moulinet, under the railway track. Follow signs for the Resseraya district and Col de Braus. After 200 metres, rejoin the footpath to the right, waymarked in yellow and signposted 'Les Cyprès – Le Calvaire'. To return, retrace your steps.

– **Mont Agaisen**: two to three hours of walking. After 1.2 kilometres on the road that climbs the left bank of the River Bévéra, turn right and climb up to the Chapelle St-Joseph and the Bérins greenhouses. At the first fork in the road after Bérins, head back south to Mont Agaisen (745 metres/2,440 feet). About 600 metres from the summit, turn left towards Sospel.

– **Le Merlanson**: three hours of walking there and back. Leave Sospel from the Hôtel de la Gare, walk under the railway track and take the path that hugs the right bank of the Merlanson river. After Erch, climb up the Vallon de Valescure and then leave the valley straight away, taking the path to the left to Col de Castillon instead. Head back from the mountain pass to Sospel on the D2566.

– **Le Mangiabo**: allow six hours for the round trip. Follow the GR52 from Sospel to the Baisse de La Linière and then Mangiabo (1,820 metres/6,000 feet). Continue 200 metres to the north of the Mangiabo and take a right turn, retracing your steps. At the summit, Cime du Ters, turn left and take the path to the Col de Brouis mountain pass. Make your way back along the D2204.

– **Clues de la Bévéra**: set off on the D2204 and follow the *sentier botanique* (botanical path) along the left bank of the Bévéra river. After about two hours, the path reaches **Olivetta**, in Italy. Carry on to San Michele on the same path and head back on the road.

VALLÉE DE LA ROYA

In the extreme east of the Alpes du Sud, this valley is one of the most beautiful areas in the hinterland that stretches as far as the Italian border. It was the private hunting ground of King Victor-Emmanuel II, who liked to chase chamois here. The Italian aristocrats spent their summers here; many are reputed to have lived into their hundreds because of the quality and purity of the air.

Today, the air is still invigorating, but the hunters have been superseded by walkers and conservationists. The Didier & Richard IGN map No. 9 has details of all the walks that can be enjoyed in the Mercantour national park.

BREIL-SUR-ROYA

This little town is equidistant from the sea and the high mountains, nestled between the left bank of the Roya river and the foot of a peak topped by a tower. The land around is dedicated to the cultivation of olive trees, which produce a delicious oil that was served at the Russian court and has been exported to Scandinavia.

USEFUL ADDRESSES

🖪 **Tourist office**: on the ground floor of the town hall, place Biancheri. ☎ 04-93-04-99-76. Email: tourismebreilsurroya@wanadoo.fr. In summer, open Monday to Saturday 9am–noon, and 1.30–5.30pm; on Sunday, open from 9am to noon. In winter, open Monday to Friday at the same times.

🖪 **Association pour le développement touristique de la vallée de la Roya** (tourist development association): boulevard Rouvier. ☎ 04-93-04-92-05. Fax: 04-93-04-99-91.
– The French-language magazine *Le Haut Pays*, on sale at the Maison de la Presse, has lots of information.

WHERE TO STAY AND EAT

Campsite

🛖 **Camping municipal**: ☎ 04-93-04-46-66. Open all year. Two-room bungalows (sleeping four plus two), with kitchen, shower and toilet for rent at 2,400F a week. This riverside site has a swimming pool, but you have to pay to use it.

☆☆ Moderate

🛖 ✕ **Restaurant Le Roya**: 2 place Brançion ☎ 04-93-04-47-38.

Closed on Monday. *Formule menu* at 70F with coffee and a carafe of wine. Menus at 98F (except public holidays) and 128F. The first menu includes appetizers, dish of the day, cheese, dessert and wine. The more expensive version gives customers the chance to taste Franco-Italian cuisine, with such dishes as *épaule d'agneau en croûte* (shoulder of lamb in pastry), *escargots façon Roya* (snails, local style) and fresh trout prepared in a variety of ways.

WHAT TO SEE

★ **Old village**: with its arcaded squares, brightly coloured houses and trompe-l'il facades, there's an obvious Italian influence in the old part of the village. The remains of the former ramparts include the **Porte de Gênes**.

★ **Église Sancta-Maria-in-Albis**: open every day 8am–noon and 2.30–7pm (to 6pm in winter). This restored church is impressive in size and has an attractive three-storey belfry. The church houses the most beautiful organ-chest in the area, in gilded sculpted wood, together with an altarpiece of *St Peter* from 1500.

★ **Écomusée du Haut-Pays** (regional museum): at the exit from the town on the road towards Tende. For opening times: ☎ 04-93-04-99-76. This original and informative museum covers the area thematically, with displays on local farming traditions, history, communications, arts and crafts, and flora and fauna.

FESTIVALS AND EVENTS

– **A Stacada**: this unusual festival, held every four years in Breil (next in 2002), commemorates the revolt of the locals against the 'droit de cuissage', a barbaric custom which gave a feudal landlord the right to sleep with the bride of a vassal on her wedding night. A hundred costumed actors re-create the famous rebellion and the re-enactment is followed by 'reconcilia-tory' folk dancing and a grand ball.

– **Les Baroquiales**: impressive baroque festival at the beginning of July, organized by the tourist development association (*see above*, 'Useful Addresses'). Art exhibitions, film shows, tastings, church Masses, guided tours, Venetian jousts, operas, plays and concerts take place in Breil, Sospel, Fontan, Saorge, La Brigue and Tende.

WALKS

– **Baignoires chaudes** (hot baths): on the road for Tende, past the Gorges de Saorge. Take a right turn into the no-entry road. Climb up the Vallon de la Bendola, to see bathing areas dug out of the rocks, containing delightfully soft spring water. The area is also known as **Bain du Sémite** (the Semite's bath), because of an inscription left by a Jewish soldier.

– **Notre-Dame-du-Mont**: allow around one hour. Cross the Breil lake over the Pont Charabot bridge, walk under the railway track and turn left to climb back up it. A path branches off to the right into countryside dotted with medlar trees. Follow the Lavina river before crossing it on an iron bridge and negotiating three short bends. The country house known as Notre-Dame-du-Mont (Our Lady of the Mount of Olives) stands in an olive grove. Originally constructed in the 11th century, it was rebuilt in the 13th century. Head back towards Breil along a small road and then a paved, stepped path before rejoining the avenue de l'Authion, with its pretty fountain.

– **Chapelle Ste-Anne**: a four-hour walk. After walking for 2 kilometres on the D2204 towards Col de Brouis, turn right onto the road that leads to Gavas, La Tour, La Maglia and Chapelle Ste-Anne.

– From Breil, the road follows the valley that becomes increasingly narrow beyond the hamlet of La Giandola, until it forms a series of spectacular **gorges**. There's a wonderful view over the *village empilé* (stacked village) of Saorge, built in semi-circular tiers halfway up a hill covered in olive trees.

SAORGE

Set in a natural amphitheatre, the well-preserved village of Saorge is one of the prettiest spots in the Roya valley. The slate-roofed houses stand in tiers against the slopes, their foundations clinging to the steep rockfaces that overlook a slight widening in the riverbed. The locals have an open and friendly disposition, and the town counts a surprising number of young people among its population. It's a most agreeable place to stay for a few days, wandering through the maze of narrow sreets and enjoying the views over the gorges.

Because of its particular geographic position, Saorge has always played an important strategic role, protecting the high valley of the Roya. A stronghold in the 15th century, it was finally taken by the French under Masséna in 1794. Today, it remains an exceptional example of a medieval village, with tall houses from the 15th, 16th and 17th centuries in narrow, sometimes stepped streets.

WHERE TO STAY AND EAT

Campsite

⛺ **Camping municipal**: 06540 Fontan. ☎ 04-93-04-50-01. Open from 15 June to 15 September. The site is located among the trees near the river.

⛺ ✕ **Gîte d'Étape de Bergiron** (walkers' accommodation): a 20-minute walk behind the convent. ☎ 04-93-04-55-49. 80F per night in the dormiory, including breakfast. Half board 160F per person. The house has a lovely rustic feel.

✕ **Lou Pountin**: rue Revelli. In the village, on the way up to the monastery. ☎ 04-93-04-54-90. Open until 11pm, but closed on Wednesday. Meals around 80F. Choose between the cool dining room or the sunny terrace and enjoy the fresh pasta and the view.

✕ **Le Bellevue**: 5 rue Louis-Péris-sol. ☎ 04-93-04-51-37. Closed on Tuesday evening, and Wednesday (except in high season), as well as during the last week in June, and the first week in September. Also closed from 1 to 15 December. Menus at 98F, 128F and 145F. This restaurant and tearoom has a wonderful panorama of the Gorges de la Roya. The simple and tasty dishes include a Parma ham salad, fresh trout, *pavé de boeuf* (beef steak), roast quail with thyme, pigeon in port and prawns with ginger. *Tapenade* is served with aperitifs and you can finish off with a homemade tart.

WHAT TO SEE

★ **Église St-Sauveur**: the church was built in the 15th century and renovated in the 18th century, and houses a lovely *Madonna and Child* from 1708. There are also 15th-century baptismal fonts.

★ **Église de la Madone-del-Poggio**: a privately owned church with a seven-storey octagonal Romanesque tower.

THE AZUR ALPS

★ **Former monastery of Notre-Dame-des-Miracles**: at the top of the village. ☎ 04-93-04-55-55. Between May and October, open every day (except Tuesday) from 2pm to 6pm; between November and April, open Saturday and Sunday afternoon from 2pm to 5pm. The attractive 17th-century former monastery has frescoes with rustic themes and sundials in the cloister.

WALKS

– **Chapelle Ste-Anne**: 2 kilometres to the east.

– **Chapelle Ste-Croix**: 2 kilometres, more to the north.

– **Ruins of the A Malamorte fortress**: a strenuous 5-kilometre (3-mile) walk to the other side of the valley.

ST-DALMAS-DE-TENDE

This pleasant summer resort was very popular in the 1930s, when it was the border station for the Nice to Cuneo railway line. The large stone station building with its balustrades still stands at the exit from the village.

St-Dalmas is the starting point for several excursions into the Vallée des Merveilles.

WHERE TO STAY AND EAT

♠ ✕ **Hôtel Terminus**: rue des Martyrs-de-la-Résistance. On the road to the Vallée des Merveilles, near the station. ☎ 04-93-04-96-96. Fax: 04-93-04-96-97. Closed at lunchtime from 15 September to 15 June, and in November. Rooms between 248F and 314F. Half board for 255F. Menus between 95F and 170F. Guests are made to feel at home straight away in this relaxing hotel, where the nights are cool (it is in the mountains, after all) and birds provide a wake-up call. The double rooms are simple but charming, and there's also a pleasant garden. The dining room has a fireplace and is decorated with copper pans and antique plates. The *patronne* does all the cooking and her ravioli is particularly memorable.

LA BRIGUE

Delightful La Brigue, which only became part of France in 1947, is well located in the valley of the Levenza and has retained its medieval character. The ruins of the chateau and of the Lascaris tower overlook the village, which has buildings constructed out of green schist from the High Roya valley, arcaded houses and trompe-l'œil decoration.

GETTING THERE

To get to La Brigue, take the D43 to the left as you leave St-Dalmas and head through the lush Levenza valley.

USEFUL ADDRESS

ℹ Tourist office: place St-Martin (the church square). ☎ 04-93-04-36-07. Fax: 04-93-04-36-09. Open all year; in summer 8.30am–noon and 2–6.30pm, and in winter 9am–noon and 2–6pm.

WHERE TO STAY AND EAT

🛏 ✕ Auberge St-Martin: on the church square, at the entrance to the village. ☎ and fax: 04-93-04-62-17. Closed on Monday evening and on Tuesday out of season, as well as from the end of November to end February. Rustic rooms from 200F to 250F. Generous menus from 90F (weekday lunch) to 140F. The rooms are clean, relaxing and peaceful with mountain views, and some have small terraces. Specialities include *tourte brigasque* (a local flan with leeks, courgettes and potatoes) and *truite aux amandes* (trout with almonds), served in the vaulted dining room or on the shady terrace.

🛏 ✕ Hôtel-restaurant Fleur des Alpes: in the church square. ☎ 04-93-04-61-05. Fax: 04-93-04-69-58. Closed from 15 December to 15 February as well as on Wednesday in low season. Double rooms from 200F to 235F. Menus at 80F (weekday), 110F and 150F. The small hotel is unassuming and charming, with a dining room that overlooks the river. Treat yourself to a lunch of delicious gnocchi or *sugeli*, the local fresh pasta, followed by succulent rabbit or local trout with almonds, and then apple soufflé.

🛏 Chambres d'hôte (B&B): in Le Pra Reound. ☎ 04-93-04-65-67. Closed from 1 December to 15 March. Double rooms with bath, toilet and TV for 220F, without breakfast. A haven of peace, with facilities for *boules* or table tennis, a children's play area, a fully equipped kitchen and a barbecue.

✕ La Cassolette: in the street near the river. ☎ 04-93-04-63-82. Restaurant closed on Sunday evening and all day Monday (except public holidays), as well as for two weeks at the end of March. Daily special for 55F and menus between 80F and 160F. The charming, non-smoking dining room is full of chickens (yes, really) and the owner is a real character. Sometimes, he pops out to the butcher's to buy extra meat and occasionally, apparently, he doesn't come back. The cheapest menu includes *tourte brigasque* (local flan with leeks, courgettes and potatoes), *lapin à la provençale* (rabbit with tomatoes and onions), cheese and dessert. Alternatively, try the ravioli or the duck with *foie gras*.

☆☆☆ Chic

🛏 ✕ Hôtel-restaurant Le Mirval: 3 rue Vincent-Ferrier. ☎ 04-93-04-63-71. Fax: 04-93-04-79-81. Closed from 1 November to 1 April. Double rooms with shower and toilet from 250F to 270F, and with bath from 295F to 350F. Half board compulsory in summer, for 270F per person. Menus from 100F to 150F. This agreeable establishment was built at the end of the 19th century, with a garden overlooking the fast-flowing river. At the weekend, the restaurant is full of local people enjoying the local speciality *tourte brigasque*, cannelloni and lasagne.

WHAT TO SEE

★ **Église Collégiale St-Martin**: the collegiate church has a Lombard belfry with an observation tower, and loopholes on its northern facade. The church apparently also served as a fortress. Inside is a lovely collection of primitive paintings, a *Crucifixion* by the school of Bréa, an altarpiece *of St Martha* from the Italian Renaissance and another featuring *St Elma*, martyred in AD 303. The nativity scene is also attributed to Bréa, and the painting of *Notre-Dame des Neiges* (Our Lady of the Snows) is by Fuseri (1507). Visit the church in the evening – the lights are operated by an automatic timer.

★ **Musée des Traditions Apicoles** (beekeeping museum): beekeeping and the life of bees. Ask at the tourist office for information about opening hours and entry charges.

★ **Place du Rattachement**: the houses on this unusual square are built on both sides of the dry watercourse and all have arcaded galleries on the ground floor.

WALKS

– **Cime de Maria**: from La Brigue, drive towards the Vallée des Prés, turning right to Baisse de Géréon. Park the car here and continue on foot along the path to the Cime de Maria (summit), for a lovely panoramic view over the Massif du Mercantour and the Mediterranean.

– **Mont Bertrand**: drive to Baisse d'Ugail from Morignole and then continue on foot towards Baisse de la Crouscia and then to the summit of Mont Bertrand. As long as there's no mist, the magnificent view can stretch from the Alps to Corsica.

– **Pas du Tanarel**: head towards the Chapelle Notre-Dame-des-Fontaines (Our Lady of the Fountains). Just before you reach it, turn left towards the Vallée de Bens. Leave the car and continue on foot towards the Pas du Tanarel.

WHAT TO DO IN THE AREA

★ **Sanctuaire Notre-Dame-des-Fontaines**: take the D43 and then turn right onto the D143. Go past the Pont du Coq bridge, and the old brick oven a little further on to the right. Following a theft, the chapel is now under close surveillance. Ask for the key in one of the village restaurants. Open from 3pm to 5.30pm in summer, and from 2.30pm to 4.20pm from October to May. (For more information, ask at La Brigue tourist office.)

The sanctuary of Our Lady of the Fountains was built in a rugged gorge above seven intermittent springs, overlooking the fast-flowing river. Its sumptuous interior houses several wonderfully preserved and very moving frescoes. The oldest, in the chancel, are by Jean Balaison and portray the Virgin and the Evangelists. The others are the work of Jean Giovanni, dating back to 1492 and tracing the important events in Christ's life. They are vigorously painted, with rich colours and surrealist touches. The haunting portrayal of Judas Iscariot is particularly striking.

GRANILE

From St-Dalmas-de-Tende, follow signs to Castérino and Lac des Mesches. After 1.5 kilometres, take the road to the right and drive up the rather steep hill for another 5 kilometres (3 miles). Granile lies at the end of the road, which comes to a sudden halt.

This charming little village basks in the sunshine, surrounded by mountains. Its 30 wood and stone dwellings, roofed with uneven slate tiles, house just ten inhabitants. There are miraculously suspended gardens, mountain paths and stone steps, but no shops. The tiny church has a bell-tower and the place Ste-Anne is a marvel of engineering, constructed on an artificial terrace on the slope.

VALLÉE DES MERVEILLES

Located to the west of St-Dalmas, the Vallée des Merveilles national park is the most spectacular part of the Mercantour. With clear high-mountain lakes and undulating terrain interspersed with pink- and grey-tinted rocks, the landscape is impressive, wild and mysterious. The national park is also famous for its remarkable prehistoric carvings.

Climbing one of the peaks of the Vallée des Merveilles will take at least a day or, preferably, two days, with a night in a *refuge* or mountain hut. It's vital to have the correct equipment, particularly for two-day excursions. Ensure you have proper walking shoes, waterproofs and warm clothing. The IGN maps 3741 Ouest (west) and 3841 Ouest (west) cover the area. Pedestrian access is possible only between June and October.

The prehistoric carvings may only be seen in the company of a guide (*see* 'Useful Addresses' for details of the *bureau des guides*). The guides also help walkers to spot the protected wildlife, which includes marmots, ibex, deer and, if you're lucky, chamois.

USEFUL ADDRESSES

■ **Bureau des guides** (guide centre): the tourist office in Tende can advise on walking and hiking.
■ **Maison de la montagne** (mountain centre): avenue du 16-Septembre-1947, 06437 Tende. ☎ and fax: 04-93-04-77-73.

■ Further information is available from the **Parc National de la Vallée des** Merveilles (national park of the Vallée des Merveilles), avenue du 16-Septembre-1947, 06437 Tende. ☎ 04-93-04-67-00 or 04-93-04-68-66.

WHERE TO STAY AND EAT

To stay in one of the *refuges* (mountain huts), book ahead in writing. There are a few good hotels in Castérino.

⌂ ✕ **Hôtel Les Mélèzes**: ☎ 04-93-04-95-95. Fax: 04-93-04-77-49. Closed between 15 November and 28 December. Rooms with shower and toilet for 270F. Half board for 300F. Excellent menus at 100F and 120F. The rooms are rather small, but spotless, and those at the front have a balcony and a view of the mountain. Mouth-watering specialities in the restaurant include *fondue savoyarde aux cèpes* (cheese fondue with mushrooms), *truite au basilic* (trout with basil), *filet de buf aux morilles* (fillet of beef with mushrooms), *raviolis maison à la ricotta* (ricotta-stuffed homemade ravioli) and *soufflé chaud aux myrtilles*

(warm soufflé with bilberries). The hotel also arranges four-wheel-drive guided tours.

✕ **Auberge Santa Maria Maddalena**: ☎ 04-93-04-65-93. Fax: 04-93-04-77-65. Meals for around 80F. This *auberge* at the foot of the Vallée des Merveilles has a friendly atmosphere and serves unpretentious local specialities.

WALKS

Drive up the Vallon de la Minière on the D91 to the **Lac des Mesches**, surrounded by mountains at the confluence of two fast-flowing rivers. Park the car here.

– Take the winding path to the left past the **Lac de la Minière** and follow signs to the Val d'Enfer (Valley of Hell). It's a three-hour walk to the **Refuge des Merveilles** mountain hut.

– The *refuge* is the starting point for several excursions, including the two-hour climb to the summit of **Mont Bégo** (2,873 metres/9,400 feet), the two-to three-hour climb up to **Grand Capelet** (2,935 metres/9,600 feet) or the two-hour ascent to the **Cime du Diable** (Devil's Summit) (2,686 metres/8,800 feet).

WHAT TO SEE AND DO

The Vallée des Merveilles opens up to the north of the Refuge des Merveilles between the steep slopes of Mont Bégo and the Rocher des Merveilles (rock).

★ Over the 12 kilometres (7.5 miles) of the valley, many thousands of **engravings** have been discovered. Attributed to the Ligurian people of the Bronze Age or the early Iron Age (around 1,800 bc), most portray agricultural scenes, including horned animals, ploughs and sickles. There are human figures, too, and attempts have been made to identify a sorcerer, a tribal chief or even Christ. It seems also that an ancient cult was followed around Mont Bégo, where rites and rituals were practised.

Sadly, vandals have repeatedly struck here, plundering the site. As a result, the engravings may only be visited in the company of an official guide. The most precious originals have been transferred to a museum in Tende and replaced by plaster reconstructions.

– At the far end of the valley, cross the Baisse de la Valmasque and head towards the Lac du Basto (on the GR52 long-distance footpath). The route passes by the Lac Noir and the Lac Vert until it reaches the **Refuge de Valmasque**, nestled in an idyllic mountain setting.

Follow the **Vallon de Valmasque** until you reach the Vacherie de Valmasque, where a path leads off to the left to the frontier ridge. Keep going until you arrive at the hamlet of **Castérino**.

Alternatively, Castérino can also be reached by car from St-Dalmas. From the hamlet, continue on foot to the Refuge de Fontanalbe, then on to the **Lac Vert de Fontanalbe**.

TENDE (06430)   Population: 1,890

Like La Brigue, Tende has only been part of France since 1947. The village, nestling in an amphitheatre above the Roya river, is quite striking. Its tall green-grey schist buildings seem to be piled on top of each other, and suspended between the sky and the earth.

In the Middle Ages, Tende played a vital role as guardian of the mountain pass between Piedmont and Provence. In 1691, during the struggle with the House of Savoy, the French destroyed the fortified castle of the Lascaris; just one section wall still stands above the town, seemingly defying the laws of gravity. One of the castle towers was adapted as a belfry in the 19th century and is now known as the **Tour de l'Horloge**. An unusual tiered cemetery overlooks the town.

In the narrow, picturesque streets of Tende, look out for the alpine-style balconies, the overhanging roofs, which protect the houses from heavy snowfall, and the door lintels of green schist bearing the coats of arms of the Lascaris feudal lords and of the House of Savoy. The church has an attractive Renaissance facade and sculpted doorway. Lions symbolizing power and strength support the pillars around it.

USEFUL ADDRESS

🄸 **Tourist office**: avenue du 16-Septembre-1947. ☎ 04-93-04-73-71. Fax: 04-93-04-35-09. Open in winter every day (except Thursday and Sunday) 9am–noon and 1–5pm; in high season, open every day 9am–noon and 2–6pm (to 5pm on Sunday).

WHERE TO STAY AND EAT

Campsite

🛖 **Camping municipal**: ☎ 04-93-04-78-06 or 04-93-04-60-90 (town hall). Fax: 04-93-04-74-54. Basic site, open from 1 April to 31 October.

🛖 ✕ **Gîte d'Étape Les Carlines**: chemin Ste-Catherine (1 kilometre). ☎ 04-93-04-62-74. This old slate-tiled house in the village offers walkers accommodation non-stop from mid-April to end September. During the rest of the year, it's open only at weekends and during school holidays. One night's stay costs 73F.

Meals are 74F and half board is 170F. It's advisable to phone ahead.

✕ **Auberge Tendasque**: 65 avenue du 16-Septembre-1947. ☎ 04-93-04-62-26. Closed on Tuesday from June to October. Menus at 75F and 130F. The food at this simple rustic *auberge* is excellent and full of surprises. Try the trout mousse, veal escalope, omelette with ceps or duck, also served with tasty ceps. A good stroll after a delicious meal is a fine way to spend the afternoon in Tende.

WALK

Tende is the starting point for a number of walks, including the following:

– **Vallon du Refrei**: take the road from the Refrei valley to the barns at La Pré (4 kilometres/2.5 miles). Several further footpaths leave from this point.

THE AZUR ALPS

The Coast from Nice to Menton

As you drive back towards Nice and the coast, you leave behind the small, uncluttered winding roads, the hilltop villages, the flower- or snow-covered mountains and the welcome isolation of the hinterland.

The first 'tourists' came to Nice as early as the 18th century. Aristocrats in all shapes and sizes – Russian princes and dukes, monocled English lords and their ladies with tiaras – transformed the town and the charming nearby villages with luxurious villas and elaborate palaces. The French Riviera became a place to party, day and night. In 1887, guidebook-writer Stephen Liégeard (1830–1925) christened the stretch of coastline between Nice and Menton 'La Côte d'Azur'. In those heady days, the Riviera was a delightful place for the privileged few. Some of the magic remains, but you have to look hard amongst the concrete.

For your stay in the city, leave the car in a garage; it may be horribly expensive, but it's the best option if you want it to remain in one piece for the rest of your journey along the French Riviera, from Nice to Menton.

NICE (06000) Population: 345,900

> Other places may be fun,
> But when all is said and done,
> It's so much nicer in Nice.
> Sandy Wilson, *The Boyfriend*

History

The area around Nice has been settled for many, many years – there is evidence that man lived here, in the so-called *Terra Amata*, 400,000 years ago, and discovered how to make fire here. In the fourth century BC, the Greeks from Marseille founded a commercial colony that they named *Nikaia* (victory). Later, the Romans founded *Cemenelum* (modern-day Cimiez), on a nearby hilltop, and made it the capital of their maritime-alpine province. It became one of the most important and civilized Western towns of the third century, boasting its own amphitheatre, swimming pools and even a system of central heating.

The turning point in Nice's more recent history came in 1388, when the citizens voted not to recognize the governance of Louis d'Anjou, Count of Provence. They indicated instead their allegiance to Amadeus VII, count of Savoy, who had profited from the difficulties within the town. He marched triumphantly into Nice and created a new province or county, the Comté de Nice. The town remained loyal to the house of Savoy until 1860 (with a few minor interruptions). For over three centuries, it had been the most important fortified town in the area.

Commercial Development

Work began in 1748 on the excavation of the port of Lympia, which was to form the basis of Nice's commercial development. In 1750, place Garibaldi was opened up and the first seafront terrace was built. Napoleon stayed in the town on two occasions, once in 1794, when he almost married the daughter of his host, at 6 rue de la Bonaparte. After the fall of the Empire, the 1814 Treaty of Paris handed Nice over to the kingdom of Sardinia and the House of Savoy. Nice found itself in fierce competition with the port of Genoa, attached to the kingdom of Piedmont-Sardinia.

Nice's relationship with France remained tricky but the House of Savoy was friendly with the English, who began to discover and enjoy the Riviera winters in increasing numbers. Many came to recover from tuberculosis, but the climate is not in fact ideal for this kind of affliction, and the majority of them were never able to return home again. One Brit, the Reverend Lewis Way, built the first section of the Promenade des Anglais, now one of the most famous seafront promenades in the world. Russian visitors began to make their presence felt from about 1850, with artists, princes (real and fake) and tsars coming to enjoy the weather and the social life.

Return to France and La Belle Époque

Following the war in Italy, the treaty of 24 March 1860 and the subsequent plebiscite of 15 and 16 April, the county of Nice became part of France once again. Tourism developed and the town flourished. In 1890, around 22,000 people came to Nice to enjoy the mild winter weather. By 1910, the number of visitors had risen to 150,000.

Many of the tourists would stay for a number of months and it became clear that they were worth investing in. Capital was invested in the construction and tourism industries, and sumptuous buildings began to appear to house the wintering English and Russians. Royal visitors included Queen Victoria, who liked the smart suburb of Cimiez, the Queen of Portugal and the Russian imperial family. The demand for manual workers increased and Italians came to fill the jobs, taking over entire districts, such as Riquier and La Madeleine.

In the 19th century, Nice's reputation eclipsed that of Cannes, Monaco and Menton (which were all destined to develop later, during the 20th century). By the 1930s, the Promenade des Anglais had assumed its current appearance, with an uninterrupted line of buildings overlooking the stony beaches.

Nice Today

Known as the Queen of the Riviera, Nice gradually began to lose its particular charm and provincial customs. The town appeared, on the face of it, to be happy with the way it had developed, but it was hiding problems of decay and corruption. For many years, it was run as a sort of personal fiefdom by the Médecin family. Jacques Médecin, the city's right-wing mayor, was eventually imprisoned for corruption and died in exile.

Today, Nice has escaped the clutches of the Médecins and its way of life is attracting huge numbers of visitors once again. It has 7.5 kilometres (4.5 miles) of beaches, 150 pools and fountains, and basks in a total of 2,640 hours of sunshine per year. Despite the traffic problems, it still feels very much like a Mediterranean town, fronted by the celebrated Promenade des

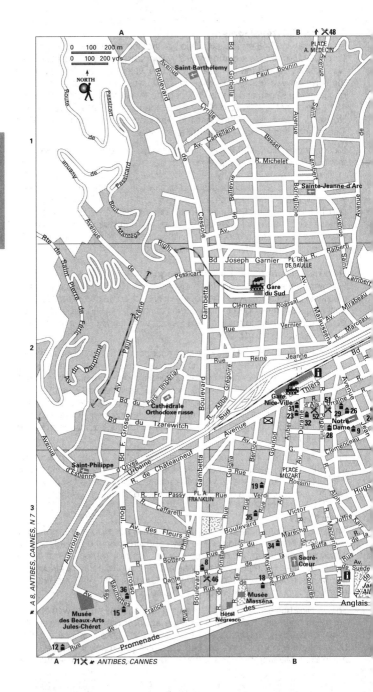

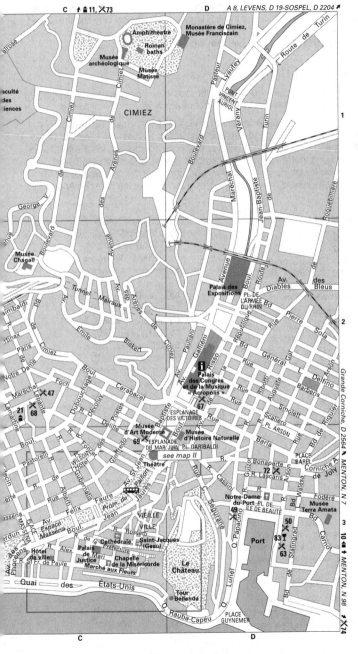

NICE (MAP I)

Anglais with its big hotels. These days, many of the hotel guests are from within France itself. Nice is the fifth-biggest city in the country and the largest tourist resort. Its population of nearly 350,000 comprises artists, writers, musicians and young people, with around 25,000 students.

Eating and Drinking

Nice has a rich, varied cuisine. Its food has strong links with the city's Provençal and Italian neighbours, but retains a very individual flavour.

Just a stone's throw from the Promenade des Anglais, the stallholders of Nice's daily market go about their business in line with the seasons. **Cours Saleya** in the old town overflows every day (except Monday) with flowers and wonderful displays of vegetables, herbs and crystallized fruits – a paradise for shoppers and gourmands, and a must on any tour of the town. *Nissart* life is lived between the 17th-century palace, the Baie des Anges and

■ **Useful Addresses**

- 🚹 Tourist office (map I)
- 🚆 Train station (map I)
- 🚌 Coach station (map I)
- ✉ Post office (map I)

🛏 **Where to Stay**

- **8** Hôtel de la Buffa (map I)
- **9** Hôtel Notre-Dame (map I)
- **10** AJ (youth hostel) (map I)
- **11** Relais International de la Jeunesse Clairvallon (map I)
- **12** Espace Magnan (map I)
- **15** Hôtel du Danemark (map I)
- **17** Au Picardy (map II)
- **18** Hôtel de la Fontaine (map I)
- **19** Hôtel Oasis (map I)
- **21** Hôtel Les Camélias (map I)
- **23** La Belle Meunière (map I)
- **24** Hôtel du Petit Louvre (map I)
- **26** Hôtel des Alizés (map I)
- **28** Hôtel Clair Meublé (map I)
- **29** Hôtel Amaryllis (map I)
- **31** Hôtel Excelsior (map I)
- **32** Hôtel Durante (map I)
- **34** Hôtel Windsor (map I)
- **35** Hôtel Gounod (map I)
- **36** Hôtel Locarno (map I)

✕ **Where to Eat**

- **44** L'Adresse (map II)
- **46** La Petite Marmite (map I)
- **47** The Jungle Arts (map I)
- **48** L'Olympic (map I)
- **49** La Zucca Magica (map I)
- **50** L'Âne rouge (map I)
- **51** La Petite Biche (map I)
- **52** Restaurant Voyageur Nissart (map I)
- **53** Café-Restaurant de la Bourse (map II)
- **55** Nissa la Bella (map II)
- **56** La Cave (map II)
- **57** L'Escalinada (map II)
- **59** Acchiardo (map II)
- **60** Le 22 Septembre (map II)
- **62** La Merenda (map II)
- **63** Les Pêcheurs (map II)
- **65** Le Grand Café de Turin (map II)
- **67** Le Lydo (map I)
- **68** Lou Mourelec (map I)
- **69** Le Rive Droite (map I)
- **71** Restaurant de l'École hôtelière (map I)
- **72** Chez Pipo (map I)
- **73** L'Auberge de Théo (map I)
- **74** Le Sextant (map I)
- **75** Restaurant du Gesù (map II)
- **76** Don Camillo (map II)
- **77** L'Auberge des Arts (map II)

🍷 **Where to Go for a Drink**

- **80** Wayne's (map II)
- **81** Le Bar des Oiseaux (map II)
- **82** Fenocchio (map II)
- **83** Iguane Café (map I)

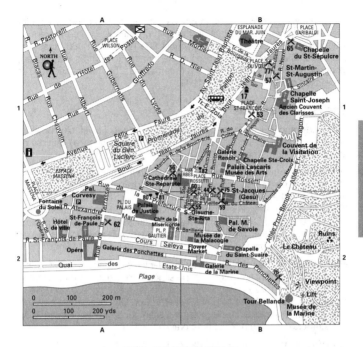

NICE – OLD TOWN (MAP II)

the chateau on the hill. Take a break on the terrace of a restaurant to enjoy an authentic *salade niçoise*, with quartered tomatoes, capers, black olives, spring onions, anchovies or tuna, green beans, with or without hard-boiled eggs and potatoes, with olive oil and without vinegar. There are as many 'genuine' ways of preparing this classic Niçois dish as there are of making *bouillabaisse*. Properly prepared, it also forms the basis of the *pan-bagnat* (soaked bread), the on-the-run version, with the ingredients squeezed and pressed into a bread roll.

As you explore the little streets near the Cathédrale Ste-Réparate, look for places to try other Niçois specialities such as *pissaladière* (onion tart with anchovies and black olives), *socca* (a pancake made of chickpea flour, sprinkled with olive oil and served in hot, crisp slices) and *tourte de blettes* (a sweet-savoury Swiss chard pie). Watching the *socca* street vendors prepare their portable machinery is an event in itself.

If you're very hungry, take a seat inside (or outside) a restaurant in Nice's old town and try *farcis* (stuffed vegetables), ravioli, *estocaficada* (salt cod stewed with tomatoes, olives, garlic and *eau-de-vie*), tripe or *bagna cauda* (raw vegetables dipped in a hot fondue of garlic, anchovies and olive oil).

The perfect accompaniment to all these dishes is a glass of **vin de Bellet**, Nice's own rather costly wine, produced on the sun-drenched hills nearby. There are still around a dozen wine producers in the region, which is one of the oldest wine-growing areas in France – it has been producing wine for over 2,000 years. At its height, in the 19th century, it covered more than 1,000 hectares (2,470 acres); today, just 600 hectares (1,480 acres) are cultivated. The vines are grown on stone terraces (known as *restanques*), alongside olive trees and fields of carnations. The wine secured its *appellation d'origine contrôlée* in 1941.

The School of Nice

Artists past and present have been drawn to Nice in considerable numbers, perhaps because of its particular quality of light, described by Matisse as 'clear, precise and limpid'.

The most important artistic movement to come out of the city was the School of Nice, which developed *nouveau réalism* (new realism). Born at the end of the 1950s, it was officially dissolved in 1970. Yves Klein was one of the founders, and key figures included Arman, César, Martial Raysse, Jean Tinguely and, later, Niki de St-Phalle and Christo (famous for 'wrapping' buildings and bridges). Many of the artists are less well known in France than elsewhere in the world.

Klein believed in the expressive, poetic potential of pure colour and space, conceiving his paintings as living presences. His monochrome work is famous – artists today refer to 'Yves Klein blue' – and he also used fire to make his pieces, with the help of a flamethrower. One of his most powerful works, *Anthropométrie* (1960), can be seen today in the Musée d'Art Contemporain (museum of contemporary art) in Nice.

Following in the footsteps of Marcel Duchamp, France's godfather of contemporary art, the neo-realists worked with the detritus of everyday life. Art critic Pierre Restany described their torn posters and junk as the 'poetry of urban civilization'. Some of the work began to come close to American pop art. For Martial Raysse, another founder member of the school, the theory behind the movement was that 'life is more beautiful than anything else'.

At the end of the 1960s, another movement was flourishing under the Niçois sun, and in Montpellier, known as '*Supports-Surfaces*'. Its members chose to focus on the components or 'hardware' of painting, including the canvas, its reverse side and the texture of the paint. Alongside them, Daniel Buren and his companions complemented Klein's concepts, showing a preoccupation with the colour, composition and structure of their art. Buren particularly is concerned with space and its dynamics.

In more recent years, two of Nice's most famous artists have been 'Ben', creator of 'graffiti-paintings' and 'happenings', and sculptor Bernar (without a 'd') Venet, who is more famous on the other side of the Atlantic than in his native country. Ben lives in St-Pancrace, one of Nice's hill districts, while Venet is represented in Nice by his unmissable *Arc* sculpture, in place Masséna.

Carnival

Nice's legendary carnival was first mentioned in the 13th century, when the lords of Provence and of Savoy used to take part. The church tried to curb the excesses of the carnival-goers, but it had a hard time persuading its own abbots to stop donning disguises and dancing.

In the late 1530s, four different carnival balls would take place on four different squares in the town, separated according to social class – nobles, merchants, craftsmen and fishermen could only mix by using appropriate and clever disguises. In the 18th century, the narrow streets of the old town became too small for the growing population and festivities moved indoors. The battles of confetti and other projectiles, such as sweets and flowers, only began under the Second Empire.

In 1873, an official festival committee was set up and painters Alexis and Gustav-Adolf Mossa took over the show. They initiated a burlesque royal parade to escort the figure of 'King Carnival' down avenue Jean-Médecin. The town was making a great effort to entertain its winter visitors, so masquerades and fireworks became part of the parade, with King Carnival reigning from place Masséna and being set alight on the night of Mardi Gras to the sound of exploding fireworks.

The carnival takes place during the second two weeks of February and festivities have only been suspended in recent times during World Wars I and II.

– **Information and reservations**: 5 promenade des Anglais. ☎ 04-92-14-48-00.

USEFUL ADDRESSES

🅱 Tourist information for Riviera-Côte d'Azur: 55 promenade des Anglais, 06011 Nice. ☎ 04-93-37-78-78. Fax: 04-93-86-01-06. Open Monday to Friday 8.30am–noon and 2–6pm. A wide range of brochures and **Gîtes de France** information (☎ 04-92-15-21-30).

There are a number of other **information points**:

• At the **train station**, avenue Thiers (B2 on map I). ☎ 04-93-87-07-07. The office is open in summer every day from 8am to 8pm. During the rest of the year it's open from 8am to 7pm, and you can get maps, leaflets and advice on hotel reservations. It's usually very busy.

• 5 Promenade des Anglais (B3 on map I). ☎ 04-92-14-48-00. Fax: 04-92-14-48-03. Open Monday to Friday from 9am to 6pm; open in summer from 8am to 8pm (from 9am on Sunday).

• Airport Terminal 1. ☎ 04-93-21-

44-11. Open every day from 8am to 10pm.

✉ Main post office (B2 on map I): 23 avenue Thiers. ☎ 04-93-82-65-00.

■ **Regional office for information for young people** (C3 on map I): 19 rue Gioffredo. ☎ 04-93-80-93-93. Open Monday to Friday from 10am to 7pm. Information on courses and a place for posting small ads.

🚂 **Train station** (B2 on map I): avenue Thiers. ☎ 08-36-35-35-35. A full timetable of Métrazur trains serves all the stations along the coast between St-Raphaël and Menton. The delightful line between Nice and Tende operates several trains daily. The showers on the lower ground floor of the station are open from 6am to 7pm.

🚌 **Bus station** (C3 on map I): Promenade du Paillon, near Place St-François du Vieux-Nice. ☎ 04-93-85-61-81 or 04-93-80-08-70. Information available from 8am to

6.30pm, and a left-luggage area. Buy tickets on the bus.

■ **Public transport in Nice (ST2N)**: for information ☎ 04-93-62-67-20. Central station at 10 avenue Félix-Faure. A *pass touristique* (visitor's pass), available from place Masséna, allows limitless bus travel. Seven days 110F; five days 85F; one day 22F. Displays at bus stops show passengers where their bus has got to.

✈ **Airport Nice-Côte d'Azur**: ☎ 04-93-21-30-30 or 04-93-21-30-12.

■ **SNCM (Société Nationale Maritime Corse-Méditerranée)**: quai du Commerce, 06303 Nice. ☎ 04-93-13-66-66. Information: ☎ 08-36-67-95-00. Reservations: ☎ 04-93-13-66-99. For sailings to Corsica.

■ **Nicea Location Rent** (B2 on map I): 9 avenue Thiers. Opposite the train station (and down a bit). ☎ 04-93-82-42-71. Open every day. Bikes, mopeds and scooters for hire.

■ **Grande Pharmacie Élysée** (chemist) (C3 on map I): 45 avenue Jean-Médecin. ☎ 04-93-88-20-66.

■ **Club alpin français** (French Climbing Club): ☎ 04-93-62-59-99.

■ **Taxis**: ☎ 04-93-13-78-78.

■ **Météo** (weather): ☎ 08-36-68-02-06.

■ **Météo montagne** (mountain weather): ☎ 08-36-68-04-04.

■ **Météo plaisance** (coastal weather): ☎ 08-36-68-08-06.

WHERE TO STAY

Out of the Centre

☆ Budget

🛏 **Auberge de jeunesse de Nice** (youth hostel) (D3, **10**, off map I): Route forestière du Mont-Alban. A 45-minute walk from the train station, or take bus No. 17 to the Sun Bus station and then bus No. 14 to the hostel, in Mont-Boron park. ☎ 04-93-89-23-64. Fax: 04-92-04-03-10. Open all year (staffed 7am–10am, and 5–11pm). 70F per night, including breakfast. Kitchen facilities also available. This hostel, with its fabulous hilltop view over Nice, the port and the Baie des Anges, is very popular. Booking is not possible, so try to turn up before 10am to secure a bed. There's a good atmosphere and a warm welcome is guaranteed. From the hostel, a 30-minute walk brings you to the fort that overlooks the seafront at Villefranche-sur-Mer and St-Jean-Cap-Ferrat.

🛏 **Clairvallon Relais International de la Jeunesse** (youth hostel) (C1, **11**, off map I): 26 avenue Scuderi, in Cimiez. Bus No. 15 from the train station to the Scuderi stop. ☎ 04-93-81-27-63. Fax: 04-93-53-35-88. Open all year. 72F per night in dormitories, including breakfast and sheets. Menu at lunch or dinner for 60F. Half board for 140F. Space often available. This accommodation for young people is in a wonderful location, in large grounds with a swimming pool, in the residential area of Cimiez. The Matisse and Chagall museums are just around the corner. For summer eating, there's a shady terrace. Morning arrivals may leave luggage in a locker and there's a warm welcome at 5pm.

🛏 **Espace Magnan** (youth hostel) (A3, **12** on map I): 31 rue Louis-de-Coppet. Near Florida beach. Hop on one of the frequent airport buses from the town centre, getting off at the Rosa-Bonheur stop. ☎ 04-93-86-28-75. Fax: 04-93-44-93-22. Open to individual visitors from 15 June to 15 September. 50F per night, sheets included, in a six-bed dormitory. This is a friendly spot with free showers and a cafeteria serving breakfast and pizzas.

Near the Centre

☆–☆☆ Budget to Moderate

â **Hôtel Au Picardy** (B1, **17** on map II): 10 boulevard Jean-Jaurès. Near the bus station, at the entrance to Nice old town. ☎ 04-93-85-75-51. Double room with shower and toilet for 199F, including breakfast. This is the only hotel in the old part of Nice and it's a good one, with a pretty floral balcony, enclosed courtyard and friendly family atmosphere. The rooms overlooking the road, which can be noisy, are soundproofed.

â **Hôtel du Petit Louvre** (B2, **24** on map I): 10 rue Emma-Tiranty. Close to the Nice-Étoile centre. ☎ 04-93-80-15-54. Fax: 04-93-62-45-08. Closed in November, December and January. Double room for 210F with shower, and 240F with shower and toilet. A hotel with rather old-fashioned charm, and walls covered in the owner's paintings. Microwave and fridge at the guests' disposal. Book ahead.

â **Hôtel de la Buffa** (A3, **8** on map I): 56 rue de la Buffa (on the corner with rue Gambetta). ☎ 04-93-88-77-35. Fax: 04-93-88-83-39. Email: buffa.3soleils@informa.fr. Double rooms between 320F and 380F. This attractive little hotel is in a part of Nice that you wouldn't otherwise necessarily visit. Its air-conditioned rooms are small and simple; peace and quiet are guaranteed in the rooms overlooking the courtyard. There's a mini tourist office in the foyer and the welcome is warm and friendly.

☆☆☆ Chic

â **Hôtel Oasis** (B3, **19** on map I): 23 rue Gounod. In the town centre, half-way between the train station and the Promenade des Anglais. ☎ 04-93-88-12-29. Fax: 04-93-16-14-40. Open all year. Double rooms with TV from 410F to 470F. Set back from the road, L'Oasis stands in shady grounds and is as quiet and relaxing as its name suggests. Some of the comfortable rooms overlook the garden. Famous guests have included Chekhov and Vladimir Ilitch Oulianov (aka Lenin). The rooms in the annexe cost the same as the others, but are less appealing. Parking is possible, for a charge.

â **Hôtel Gounod** (B3, **35** on map I): 3 rue Gounod. ☎ 04-93-16-42-00. Fax: 04-93-88-23-84. Closed from 15 November to 20 December. Double rooms for 520F (in low season) and 750F (from 1 April to 31 October). This large Belle Époque building still looks rather like a seafront 'palace' hotel. The rooms are chic, well equipped and air-conditioned, and a few even have terraces. The atmosphere is old-fashioned in an agreeable kind of way, but be prepared for a slightly frosty reception. You can use the car park and swimming pool at the Hôtel Splendid next door.

â **Hôtel Les Camélias** (C2, **21** on map I): 3 rue Spitalieri. ☎ 04-93-62-15-54. Fax: 04-93-80-42-96. Closed in November. Rooms with shower and toilet at 300F, or 400F with bathroom, including breakfast. Half board 250F. Menu at 70F. Mme Vimont-Beuve has run this establishment in the heart of Nice for more than 50 years and is now ably assisted by her son. With its exotic garden, it's a haven of peace. Guests can order drinks at the bar or read in the lounge. The simple menu is enjoyed by regulars. Private parking is available, for a charge.

Near the Train Station

⊡ Budget

♠ La Belle Meunière (B2, **23** on map I): 21 avenue Durante. ☎ 04-93-88-66-15. Closed in December and January. Double rooms cost 285F with shower and toilet, including breakfast. One room is big enough for three or four, complete with balcony, at 448F. This popular and friendly hotel, just a stone's throw from the train station, is a favourite with budget travellers from all over the world. Breakfasts and picnics can be eaten in the garden. The patron is friendly and there's a private car park.

♠ Hôtel des Alizés (B2, **26** on map I): 10 rue de Suisse, on the second floor. ☎ 04-93-88-85-08. Rooms between 170F and 240F. Clean, unpretentious hotel, popular with travellers seeking a young, cosmopolitan atmosphere rather than luxury or charming decor. The area is up-and-coming. Students enjoy breakfast on the house.

♠ Hôtel Notre-Dame (B2, **9** on map I): 22 rue de Russie. ☎ 04-93-88-70-44. Fax: 04-93-82-20-38. Pleasant rooms between 200F and 240F. Entirely renovated, this hotel in a quiet street offers a warm welcome, and attractive prices. Not to be confused with the restaurant downstairs.

♠ Hôtel Clair Meublé (B2, **28** on map I): 6 rue d'Italie. ☎ 04-93-87-87-61. Fax: 04-93-16-85-28. Double rooms with shower and toilet from 180F to 230F (minimum two-night stay). Just 14 simple rooms, and a kitchen. Rather unassuming from the outside, this hotel is a pleasant surprise inside, with a relaxed and youthful atmosphere. Book ahead in summer.

♠ Hôtel Amaryllis (B2, **29** on map I): 3 rue Alsace-Lorraine. ☎ 04-93-88-20-24. Fax: 04-93-87-13-25. Double rooms with shower, toilet and TV at 360F. The decor is a bit 'Downtown Manhattan' but, fortunately, the prices are still French. Some of the rooms look on to a small and peaceful courtyard.

☆☆☆ Chic

♠ Hôtel Excelsior (B2, **31** on map I): 19 avenue Durante. ☎ 04-93-88-18-05. Fax: 04-93-88-38-69. Open all year. Double rooms between 330F and 550F. Set menu at 100F for half-board guests. Pleasant turn-of-the-century hotel with wrought-iron balconies and a sweet little garden with palm trees, flowers, fountain and pond. The rooms are pretty and tastefully furnished in a rustic style. The restaurant, once requisitioned by the Gestapo, now offers classic cuisine. The owner, well-known French comedian Tristan Bernard, managed to escape the clutches of the Nazis.

♠ Hôtel Durante (B2, **32** on map I): 16 avenue Durante. ☎ 04-93-88-84-40. Fax: 04-93-87-77-76. Double rooms at 420F (with shower and toilet) and 480F (with bathroom). This part of town isn't the first place you'd come for a holiday, but the hotel is at the end of a private road. The very helpful owner is always on hand to make your stay more enjoyable, offering secret tips on sightseeing off the tourist trail. There's a pleasant garden, and the rooms are clean and quiet. Parking is free, on a 'first come first served' basis.

Near the Promenade des Anglais

⊡ Budget

♠ Hôtel du Danemark (A3, **15** on map I): 3 avenue des Baumettes. In the heart of Nice, a stone's throw from the Promenade des Anglais. ☎ 04-93-62-48-46. Double rooms for 220F, with shower or bath and toilet. This lovely ochre-coloured building is located in a peaceful and pretty spot among the pine trees. The area has been rather taken over by big blocks of flats, but the hotel owners are so friendly and the rooms so clean and tasteful that it really doesn't matter too much.

☆☆☆ Chic

⌂ **Hôtel Locarno** (A3, **36** on map I): 4 avenue des Baumettes. ☎ 04-93-96-28-00. Fax: 04-93-86-18-81. Rooms between 280F and 420F with shower and toilet, and 380F and 580F with bathroom. A quick walk from the Promenade des Anglais, this hotel has all the modern comforts, including lounges and a billiard room. The recently redecorated rooms are comfortable and some have air-conditioning. Popular with business folk because of its friendly, efficient service. Garage parking available (book ahead).

⌂ **Hôtel de la Fontaine** (B3, **18** on map I): 49 rue de France. ☎ 04-93-88-30-38. Fax: 04-93-88-98-11. Email: hotel-fontaine@webster.fr. Rooms between 550F and 590F, depending on season. Buffet breakfast for 50F. Right in the heart of

Nice, within walking distance of the sea and the pedestrianized area. The rooms at this charming hotel are pretty, clean and very pleasant, especially those overlooking the courtyard. Enjoy the tasty breakfast on the patio, serenaded by the fountain. The owners are friendly and helpful, and they will do anything to make your stay a happy one.

☆☆☆☆ Très Chic

⌂ **Hôtel Windsor** (B3, **34** on map I): 11 rue Dalpozzo, at the corner of Maréchal-Joffre. ☎ 04-93-88-59-35. Fax: 04-93-88-94-57. Email: windsor@webstore.fr. Double rooms with shower and toilet for 550F, 750F with bathroom. Menu around 150F (no meals on Sunday). Behind its tall facade, this is a wonderful place, with Oriental furniture in the reception area, a tropical garden full of bougainvillea and bamboo, and a small palm-fringed pool. Even more surprising are the Turkish hammam, the Thai-style sitting room and the English-style pub. The rooms have frescoes by contemporary artists. The whole ensemble has masses of exotic charm.

WHERE TO EAT

On the Run

There are plenty of gastronomic delights in Nice's old town. Head straight for the Cours Saleya and join the queue for your **socca** or your **pissaladière** (see page 91 for descriptions). Don't leave without trying an authentic **pan-bagnat**, best enjoyed with a view over the sea. Wait until the market is about to close before you select your dessert. Just before noon, the fruit and veg is sold for a song – it doesn't last long in the heat.

Near the Train Station

☆ Budget

✕ **La Petite Biche** (B2, **51** on map I): 9 rue d'Alsace-Lorraine. ☎ 04-93-87-30-70. Menus from 67F to 87F. A nostalgic spot where the clientele has changed over the years. Elderly regulars still come to enjoy the traditional roast lamb on Sunday lunchtime, but now they find themselves surrounded by tourists in search of authenticity and atmosphere.

✕ **Restaurant Voyageur Nissart** (B2, **52** on map I): 19 rue d'Alsace-

Lorraine. ☎ 04-93-82-19-60. Open 11.30am–2pm and 6.45–10pm. Closed on Monday and for two weeks at the end of July/beginning of August. Two wide-ranging menus, at 67F and 109F. Simple and well-prepared Niçois cuisine, including specialities such as osso bucco, ravioli, courgette tart, stuffed vegetables and *soupe au pistou*. The daily special changes every day.

In Nice Old Town

✕ **Restaurant du Gesù** (B2, **75** on map II): 1 place de Jésus. ☎ 04-93-62-26-46. Closed on Sunday. Meals for between 100F and 120F. This restaurant is typical of the area, very 'Vieux Nice', with an Italian influence, good atmosphere and excellent food. The pizzas are delicious, as are the fresh pasta and the stuffed vegetables. The atmosphere is relaxed and friendly, but it can get very busy.

✕ **Le café-restaurant de la Bourse** (B1, **53** on map II): 15 place St-François. ☎ 04-93-62-38-39. Open for lunch only and closed on Sunday and Monday. Menu at 70F. Unassuming restaurant in the Old Town, at the entrance to rue Pairolière. The food is tasty and plentiful, served in a straightforward but friendly manner. The bar and restaurant are popular with locals, which is always a good sign.

✕ **Nissa La Bella** (B2, **55** on map II): 6 rue Ste-Réparate. ☎ 04-93-62-10-20. Closed in summer at lunchtime on Tuesday, Wednesday and Thursday, and out of season all day Tuesday and at lunchtime on Wednesday, and from 1 to 15 June. À la carte around 130F. Tasty Provençal food with a distinct Niçois flavour, served in a large ochre-coloured dining room that opens on to the street. The second room at the back of the restaurant is nice and cool in summer.

✕ **La Cave** (A1, **56** on map II): rue Francis-Gallo, in the Old Town. ☎ 04-93-62-48-46. Open in the evening every night of the week (except Monday). Menus from 130F to 220F. Despite the name, the restaurant entrance is not underground. Its terrace and small dining room are both visible from the street. It's often busy, and the food is Provençal in style, with tasty dishes such as *fricassée de scampis à la provençale* (scampi) and *pot-au-feu de poisson à la marseillaise* (fish stew). Finish off with a delicious lemon tart.

✕ **L'Adresse** (B1, **44** on map II): 27 rue Benoît-Bunico. ☎ 04-93-80-15-66. Closed at lunchtime and on Sunday. À la carte 120F. This popular spot serves excellent 'southern' cuisine, with influences from Greece, Spain, Africa and South America (via Italy). It has eclectic decor, ochre and red walls, and a good atmosphere.

✕ **L'Escalinada** (B1, **57** on map II): 22 rue Pairolière. At the foot of the steps to the Old Town, as the name suggests. ☎ 04-93-62-11-71. Open every day. Set menu at 125F. The patrons here have been serving Niçois specialities for 45 years, including *cochon de lait farci* (stuffed pork), *testicules de mouton panés* (sheeps' testicles), homemade ravioli and gnocchi and the unusually named *merda de can* (don't ask).

✕ **Acchiardo** (B2, **59** on map II): 38 rue Droite. ☎ 04-93-85-51-16. Closed on Saturday evening, Sunday and for the month of August. À la carte between 120F and 150F. Delicious ravioli flavoured with *pistou*, gorgonzola or Bolognaise sauce, served at tables covered in wax cloths, right in the heart of Nice. House wines straight from the cask. Cards not accepted.

✕ **Le 22 Septembre** (B1–2, **60** on map II): 3 rue Centrale. ☎ 04-93-80-87-90. Closed at lunchtime but open every evening (except Sunday).

Menus at 78F and 96F. This favourite student haunt has a good atmosphere in its small dining room. Try fresh *salade de mesclun* (mixture of green salad leaves, including rocket, lamb's lettuce, chervil and endive) served with camembert fritters or a tasty dish of sea bass with basil.

☆☆☆ Chic

✗ **La Merenda** (A2, **62** on map II): 4 rue de la Terrasse (near Cours Saleya). No telephone. Closed on Saturday, Sunday, public holidays, during the Christmas, Easter and February holidays, and for the first three weeks in August. À la carte menu around 160F. This tiny, rather idiosyncratic bistrot is celebrated for its Niçois cuisine. The dining room holds only 24 people and is always bursting at the seams. You have to come in person to book a table, but it's worth it for the tantalizing menu, which includes tripe, stuffed sardines, *daube provençale, stockfish* (wind-dried cod), pizza and *ratatouille*. Cards not accepted.

✗ **Le Grand Café de Turin** (B1, **65** on map II): 5 place Garibaldi. ☎ 04-93-62-29-52. Open from 8am to 8pm in July and August, and 5–11pm in July and August. À la carte between 150F and 200F. This restaurant specializes in seafood, including delicious (and very fresh) oysters all day (except in summer, when they are served in the evening only). The seafood platters include oysters, prawns and sea urchins (*oursins*) in season.

✗ **Don Camillo** (B2, **76** on map II): 5 rue des Ponchettes. Between the Cours Saleya and the seafront. ☎ 04-93-85-67-95. Closed on Sunday and for lunch on Monday. 'Market' menu at 185F. À la carte around 250F. This is a foodie's paradise, a central and peaceful venue where you can enjoy wonderful cuisine in a spacious and tasteful dining room.

The unpretentious menu is based on fresh local and regional ingredients, with a wonderful blend of farm and sea produce. The service is professional and friendly.

✗ **L'Auberge des Arts** (B1, **77** on map II): 9 rue Pairolière. Close to the bus station. ☎ 04-93-85-63-53. Closed on Sunday, and for lunch on Monday and Tuesday. Menus at 138F (for lunch) and from 196F to 325F (until 9pm). An entertaining *patron* serving tasty Niçois cuisine under a 17th-century vaulted ceiling brings locals back here again and again. Try the *St-Pierre au four servi avec artichauts* (baked fish with artichokes), or the excellent 'Autour du Comté de Nice' menu, which offers a starter and a choice of main dish based on local ingredients. Quite smart and not the cheapest of choices.

Near the Centre

✗ **La Petite Marmite** (B3, **46** on map I): 1bis rue René-Sainson. Behind the Hotel Négresco. ☎ 04-93-16-28-16. Closed for lunch on Saturday. Menus from 69F to 109F. Little restaurant specializing in fresh and flavoursome Egyptian dishes, based on market-fresh ingredients bought just around the corner. The prices are very reasonable, and stuffed aubergines are the speciality on Tuesday nights.

✗ **The Jungle Arts** (C2, **47** on map I): 6 rue Lépante. ☎ 04-93-93-00-18. Closed on Sunday and during August. Lunchtime *formule* menu at 65F and evening menu at 95F. Culinary traditions from around the world join forces in the kitchen here. The menu has ranged from kangaroo meat to goose, via a few African dishes. The decor is imaginative and exotic, with yellows, oranges and ochres, and animal skins on the walls.

✗ **Le Lydo** (D2, **67** on map I): 44 boulevard Risso. On a main road at the edge of Old Nice. ☎ 04-93-89-62-19. Closed on Sunday, and for two weeks in August. Menus at 85F and 120F. The view isn't wonderful but the food makes up for it. Try the gnocchi with mushrooms or the scallops with apple. The service can be a bit temperamental.

✗ **Lou Mourelec** (C2, **68** on map I): 15 rue Biscarra. ☎ 04-93-80-80-11. Closed all day Sunday and on Monday evening. Menus at 130F and 180F. Daily specials (lunchtime only) at 60F. Unpretentious Niçois bistrot serving simple daily specials such as *raviolis à la daube* (meat ravioli), stuffed sardines and octopus, and smarter evening meals, such as delicious rock-fish soup, ravioli with foie gras and squid marinated in olive oil, among other lovely dishes.

✗ **Le Rive Droite** (C3, **69** on map I): 22 avenue St-Jean-Baptiste. Just behind the Musée d'Art Moderne. ☎ 04-93-62-16-72. Closed on Sunday. One menu at 180F. This appealing restaurant has big wooden tables, pretty decor and a lively atmosphere. The food, worth making a detour for, includes such specialities as stuffed fried courgette flowers, *raviolis aux cèpes* (mushroom ravioli) and flambéed fig tart to finish.

Further Afield

✗ **Restaurant de l'École Hôtelière** (A3, **71**, off map I): 163 boulevard René-Cassin. Near the airport in the modern Arenas district; take bus No. 23. ☎ 04-93-72-77-79. Open for lunch from Monday to Friday. Closed at the weekend and during school holidays. Arrive before 12.30pm, having booked in advance. Menus from 60F to 130F. The school of hospitality offers excellent value for money and is conveniently close to the Musée des Arts Asiatiques. The prices are unbeatable.

✗ **L'Olympic** (B1, **48**, off map I): 1 avenue Ernest-Lairolle. Opposite the Ray stadium in the Parc Chambrun district. ☎ 04-93-52-41-61. Open every day from 8am to midnight. À la carte between 50F and 100F. Pictures of sporting heroes adorn the walls, but couch potatoes are also welcome to enjoy the friendly and lively atmosphere, and the pizzas, *carpaccios* and other dishes cooked in a wood-fired oven, as well as lasagne at the weekend.

✗ **L'Auberge de Théo** (C1, **73**, off map I): 52 avenue Cap-de-Croix, in Cimiez. ☎ 04-93-81-26-19. Closed on Monday and from 20 August to 10 September. Dinner served until 11pm. Menus at 105F (weekday lunch), 160F and 250F. This *auberge* at the top of the town has an adorable patio and is more reminiscent of Florence than France. Try the genuine Italian pizzas, fresh pasta with king prawns or grilled fish with balsamic vinegar.

Around the Port

✗ **La Zucca Magica** (D3, **49** on map I): 4bis quai Papacino. ☎ 04-93-56-25-27. Closed on Monday and sometimes on Sunday. Lunch for 90F. Dinner for around 140F. This unusual and fascinating vegetarian restaurant ('The Magic Pumpkin'), on the port's west quay, has to turn people away every day. There's no official menu – the owner (a cousin of Luciano Pavarotti) is in charge of everything. In the evening, the atmospheric room is candlelit and specialities include peppers stuffed with pasta, tasty lasagne, and a pumpkin and gorgonzola tart, all cooked with local fresh produce straight from the market. The portions are generous and the prices are reasonable.

✗ **Chez Pipo** (D3, **72** on map I): 13 rue Bavastro. Behind the port. ☎ 04-93-55-88-82. Open only in the evening during the week (from 5.30pm) and for lunch on Saturday and Sunday. Closed on Monday, for two weeks in January, and from 15 to 25 March. Meals around 50F. Customers are seated elbow to elbow at long wooden tables in the rather dark dining room. The *socca* is said to be the most delicious in the whole of Nice (if not the world). The *pissaladière* and the *tourte aux blettes sucrée* are equally delicious.

✕ **Le Sextant** (D3, **74**, off map I): 60 boulevard Franck-Pilatte. Take the No. 32 bus to the La Réserve. ☎ 04-93-55-82-77. Open for lunch every day. Closed in January. Menus at 82F (weekday) and 100F on Sunday and public holidays. Unusually for Nice, this little restaurant below the boulevard has a clear view of the sea. The menus offer a choice of starter, a daily Niçois special, a delicious dessert, and a *pichet* (small jug) of wine.

☆☆☆☆ Très Chic

✕ **Les Pêcheurs** (D3, **63** on map I): 18 quai des Docks. In the old port, past Quai des Deux-Emmanuel. ☎ 04-93-89-59-61. Closed on

Tuesday evening and on Wednesday from December to April; on Wednesday, and at lunchtime on Thursday, from May to October; and for the month of November. One menu at 160F. A 10-minute walk from the harbour, with its yachts, this air-conditioned restaurant overlooks the wooded hill of the magnificent chateau, illuminated in the evening. The decor includes fishing nets and brass cooking pots. People come here mainly to enjoy the delicious fresh *bouillabaisse*, but there's also a selection of other fish dishes to choose from, including *bourride* (white fish stew) and *meunière de turbot à la crème de poivrons* (fillet of turbot with pepper sauce).

✕ **L'Âne Rouge** (D3, **50** on map I): 7 quai des Deux-Emmanuel. ☎ 04-93-89-49-63. Closed on Wednesday. Menus at 158F and 208F, and a gourmet *dégustation menu* at 258F. This restaurant's current chef works miracles with fish. The cuisine is traditional Niçois and is enjoyed regularly by well-dressed locals.

WHERE TO GO FOR A DRINK OR AN ICE-CREAM

♈ **Wayne's** (A2, **80** on map II): 15 rue de la Préfecture. At the entrance to the Old Town. ☎ 04-93-13-46-99. Open every day from 9am to midnight. Entrance charge on Friday and Saturday nights. This British-owned bar has loads of atmosphere (and beer), and a live band playing sixties and seventies music most nights. The customers eating the hamburgers and Tex-Mex food are mostly American.

♈ **Le Bar des Oiseaux** (A2, **81** on map II): 5 rue St-Vincent. ☎ 04-93-80-27-33. Open from 11am to 3pm and then from 7pm until 2.30am. Closed on Sunday. Sandwiches and light meals around

40F. This bar in the Old Town looks rather unassuming from the outside, but inside there's a lively atmosphere. It's a popular meeting place for local artists, and budgies fly around freely, old advertising posters adorn the walls, and the music is just at the right volume for conversation. In November to December and May to June the owner, Noëlle, puts on an entertaining one-woman show about life in Nice. She uses old Provençal or *Nissart* expressions to teach you how to eat a *pan-bagnat* properly. Local drinks include liqueurs flavoured with gentian, peach and even thyme.

✝ **Fenocchio** (B1, **82** on map II): 2 place Rossetti. ☎ 04-93-80-72-52. Open every day, but closed from November to January. This ice-cream parlour is a Niçois institution. It offers more than 70 flavours, including lavender, jasmine, tomato and basil, prune, ginger and even chewing gum.

❢ **Iguane Café** (D3, **83** on map I): 5 quai Deux-Emmanuel, along the port. ☎ 04-93-56-83-83. Open every day from 10pm to 4am. Dancing until midnight to the latest sounds as well as to Afro-Cuban, Brazilian and reggae music. Just smile cheerily, and you'll get in.

WHAT TO SEE

Nice's Old Town (Map II)

The 'Vielle Ville' (Old Town) sits between the Château hill, the boulevard Jean-Jaurès and Cours Saleya. The hill was the ancient acropolis of Nikaia and the site of the 10th- to 12th-century town. From the end of the 13th century, the inhabitants began to move downhill and westwards and, by the 16th century, when the fortifications were built, the high part of town had been completely abandoned. In the 18th century, the rue Pré-aux-Oies (now François-de-Paule) and place Victor (now Garibaldi) were laid out.

The streets around the boulevard Jean-Jaurès are lively, but some of the narrow alleys and passageways of the old part of town are more or less deserted. There's a strong Italian influence around here. The network of streets will entertain you for hours, with its dark churches, the plaques on the facades, and shops and stalls where T-shirts being next to dried sausages, and chickens turn on roasting spits alongside handbags for sale.

★ **Le Château** (B2 on map II): this hill is named after the castle which once stood here. In the 12th century, the town and its fortified chateau occupied the whole summit, but in 1705, when the town handed itself over to Louis XIV, a 41-day siege left only the ruins of the chateau. The Sun King subsequently ordered the total demolition of the garrison.

To get up to the summit, take the lift at the eastern end of the Quai des États-Unis (for a few francs), climb the steep path that starts on the attractive rue Rossetti, or take the Montée Monica-Rondelluy (steps) from rue Pairolière near place St-François and rue Dufour. Alternatively, there's a romantic route up the gentle slope from rue Catherine-Ségurane, with a wonderful view over the old port and Mont Boron.

The **Parc du Château** (open every day from 7am to 7pm), with its green oaks, is rarely busy and seems miles away from the noisy city. Some stones of the chateau and of the Cathédrale Ste-Marie, which met the same fate, can still be found if you look hard enough. From the site of the former castle keep, there's a lovely view over the Baie des Anges, the Old Town, with its sparkling glazed tiles and church towers, and, in the distance, Cap d'Antibes.

Every day at noon a cannon blast from the lower terrace of the chateau is heard right across Nice. The old Scottish custom was introduced in 1862 by wealthy Englishman Sir Thomas Coventry, who wanted to ensure that his lunch was never served late. From 1881, all the clocks in the town were set by the midday cannon.

★ **Cemetery** (B1 on map II): head down towards the old town and then take Allée François-Aragon. On Sunday morning, the bells in all the churches will be ringing merrily. The white-marble tombs add to the serenity of the environment, and there's also a wonderful view of the surrounding mountains. The cemetery was built here on the site of the ancient citadel in 1783, for reasons of hygiene. Up until then, the Niçois had been buried around their churches, but the space ran out.

Immediately opposite the entrance, a monument remembers the victims of the fire at the town theatre, which used to stand on the site currently occupied by the opera house. The statuary is very elaborate and sometimes ostentatious, reminiscent of Italian cemeteries. The most impressive monument is dedicated to the François Grosso family, and shows the father of the family, hat in hand, sculpted alongside his wife and moving busts of his two young children. It's even visible from place Masséna.

To the right is the tomb of Robert Hudson, the first Baron Hamshead, Count of Lancaster. It's guarded by two lions and shows a woman with her hand to her forehead in a gesture of despair. Other famous figures buried here include the Jellinek Mercedes family. A commemorative plaque explains that, in 1902, Émile Jellinek gave his daughter's name, Mercedes, to cars produced by the Daimler Motor Company. Overlooking the bay of Nice is the monument erected by the town in honour of French Republican statesman Léon Gambetta. The lovely little chapel in the cemetery has a multi-coloured glazed-tile dome.

Finish off your tour of this quiet place at the tomb of the 'most famous Niçois', Giuseppe Garibaldi, born near the port in 1807. It's in a little alley to the left, past the monument to the theatre fire victims.

★ **Jewish cemetery** (B1 on map II): near by, with ancient tombs.

★ **Chapelle St-Martin-St-Augustin** (B1 on map II): rue Sincaire, near the foot of the chateau, as you head back down to rue Catherine-Ségurane. The chapel, one of the most impressive baroque buildings in the area, is one of the oldest parish churches in Nice. A monk named Martin Luther said a mass here during his momentous pilgrimage to Rome in 1514. Among its treasures, the building has an altarpiece showing *St Augustine ascending to Heaven*, a fine *Pietà* (1489) and a painting *of St Anthony* (1530) by Ludovico Bréa. To the right of the entrance lies a cannonball fired by Barbarossa on 15 August 1543. To the left is a copy of Garibaldi's baptismal certificate, dated 19 July 1807.

★ **Place Garibaldi** (B1 on map II): this wide square, with its handsome ochre-coloured arcaded buildings, was built in the second half of the 18th century on the orders of the Count of Savoy, who wanted to mark the point of departure for the road to Turin. It was later dedicated to the Count himself, then to the Republic and afterwards to the two Napoleons. In 1870, it was named after local boy Garibaldi, the hero of Italy's unification. He stands at its centre, surrounded by jets of water and lush greenery. To the southwest of the square sits the **Chapelle du St-Sépulcre** (or des Pénitents-Bleus), with its neoclassical facade and triangular tower.

★ **Port** (D3 on map I): from place Garibaldi, take rue Cassini. The place de l'Île-de-Beauté, with its lovely Église Notre-Dame-du-Port, the Quai Emmanuel-II and the Quai Papacino make up an impressive architectural ensemble with their early 19th-century warm ochre facades. It's a lovely place for a walk.

If you fancy a trip out to sea, **Trans-Côte-d'Azur** (☎ 04-92-00-42-30) organizes tours of the Iles de Lérins. Office open from July to September.

★ **Place St-François** (B1 on map II): the very busy rue Pairolière (formerly rue des Chaudronniers) leads to this small charming square, with its arcades and yellow walls. A thriving fish market is held here each morning around a pretty fountain of entwined fish. The baroque building in the northeast corner was once the Palais Communal and is now a job centre. Take rue Droite (straight street), which isn't actually straight but is so called, as in all medieval towns, because it was the shortest route from one rampart to another. At the junction with place du Jésus, the **Boulangerie Espuno** is a bakery selling a huge range of different breads, including loaves flavoured with olives, fennel, roquefort or aniseed, as well as a special bread for eating with *bouillabaisse*. Closed on Monday, Tuesday and at the end of June.

★ **Palais Lascaris** (B1 on map II): 15 rue Droite. ☎ 04-93-62-05-54. Open every day (except Monday and some public holidays) 10am–noon and 2–6pm. Entrance fee: 25F. The Visite du Vieux Nice Baroque (tour of baroque Nice) meets at the Palais Lascaris, and takes in the palace, the Eglise du Gesù and the Chapelle de la Miséricorde. Every Tuesday and Sunday at 3pm. Tickets: 45F.

– This grand mansion was originally built in 1643 for Jean-Baptiste de Castellar and remained in his family until the French Revolution. The Genoese-style palace then fell into the hands of a variety of owners and was, inevitably, converted into flats. In 1922, the town of Nice bought and restored it.

Strong local traditions are evident in the construction of the mansion. To the right as you enter the ground floor is a recreation of a 1738 pharmacy, with a lovely collection of pots, Delftware fittings and wooden cabinets full of small drawers. An opulent staircase, decorated with 17th-century frescoes and 18th-century statues of *Mars* and *Venus*, leads up to the *étage noble*, where guests would be received in elegant salons with ornate ceilings, beautiful Flemish tapestries, elaborate woodwork and a 1578 Italian precursor of the pianoforte, decorated with paintings of skaters. An ornamental stucco wall divides off the ceremonial chamber.

On the third floor is the **Musée des Arts et Traditions Populaires** (museum of popular arts and culture), where traditional activities and crafts, such as the preparation of butter and bread, are explained in recreated rooms.

As you leave, you'll see a cannonball lodged in the plaster of a house at the corner of rue de la Loge and rue Droite. It was fired in 1545 by the Turks, allies of François I.

★ **Église St-Jacques** (B2 on map II): cross rue Rossetti with its pretty pastel-coloured facades, and then carry on along rue Droite. On the left is the Église St-Jacques, once owned by the Jesuits, with a baroque interior full of marble and ornate stucco. The life of the saint is portrayed in the frescoes of the nave.

★ Retrace your steps and go down the pleasantly cool rue Rossetti, which crosses rue Benoît-Benico, formerly Nice's **Jewish ghetto**. Leading all the way to the sea, the street was once called rue Giudaria (street of the Jews). A law in 1430 decreed that there should be an enclosed place for Jewish people in the town, and at dusk this street was closed off at either end by gates. However, they forgot that it might be possible to escape via the cellars. In the 18th century, the king of Sardinia decreed that members of the Jewish community must wear a yellow star, and this continued until the French Revolution.

As you descend rue Rossetti, you'll come to the place Rossetti, with its cafés overlooked by the 17th-century cathedral.

★ **Cathédrale Ste-Réparate** (A–B1 on map II): the cathedral has a handsome lantern dome of glazed tiles in emerald bands, visible from a distance. Its heavy classical facade and adjoining 18th-century tower are bare of any decorative features, but the interior is adorned with plasterwork, original panelling and marbling. In the fourth chapel on the left is a fine 17th-century wooden statue of Notre-Dame de l'Assomption. There are numerous relics, including the bones of St Alexander, to whom worshippers pray for rain. Sadly, several artworks in the building were damaged in a fire.

★ **Chapelle St-Giaume** (B2 on map II): also known as Chapelle de l'Annonciation, but the locals call it the 'Église de Ste Rita', after the Italian saint whose name comes from 'Margarita', the Latin for 'pearl'. She is immensely popular with the locals, and is found in the first chapel on the left, surrounded by huge floral tributes and lit candles. The interior of the church is decorated in Italian baroque style with a plethora of marble and stucco.

★ **Rue de la Préfecture**: runs parallel with Cours Saleya. Virtuoso violinist Paganini died in 1840 at No. 23, at the home of the Comte de Cessole. The musician drove the neighbours mad with his playing which they thought sounded like the howling of cats. The bishop of Ste-Réparate believed him to be possessed by the devil and would not allow him a Christian burial. He would have preferred to toss Paganini's body into the waters of the Paillon, but the Comte de Cessole took the body first to Villefranche, then to the Îles de Lérins, then, two years later, to the cemetery at Genoa. Paganini's remains were subsequently moved to the family estate near Parma, and finally buried in the new cemetery there in 1896.

At 22 rue de la Préfecture, climb up to see some interesting sculptures on the first floor.

★ **Cours Saleya** (A–B2 on map II): according to Louis Nucera, 'All roads lead to Rome; in Nice Old Town, they all lead to Cours Saleya.' The *cours*, or long square, is a lovely place to walk, lined to the south with a double row of low, one-storey dwellings. The colourful **outdoor market** (every morning except Monday) is a must, but out of hours there are shops, cafés and restaurants to enjoy. On Monday morning there's a second-hand market, selling everything from old records and books, to toys and 1930s silver. The area has been tastefully restored and the car parks are hidden behind a series of clever trompe l'oeil facades. Sadly, many splendid elm trees had to be cut down when the market was built in 1900.

At the back of the square half-way down Cours Saleya, the palace of the Préfecture has an 18th-century facade and alternating Doric and Corinthian columns. It's the former residence of the governors of the region.

The highlight of the area is the **Chapelle de la Miséricorde** or des Pénitents-Noirs, a baroque masterpiece built in 1736. It's open only on Sunday for one mass, at 10.30am, but there are special guided tours; ask at the tourist office. The opulent interior displays an extraordinary architectural virtuosity, with a perfect juxtaposition of stucco and gold, a retable of *La Vierge de Miséricorde* by Jean Miralhet (1420) in the sacristy, and a second *Vierge de Miséricorde*, attributed to Bréa, with a strong Italian Renaissance influence.

★ **Palais du Sénat** (senate palace): this Genoese-style building at the far end of Cours Saleya was extended in the 18th century. Nearby is the Chapelle de la Trinité, now the **Chapelle des Pénitents-Rouges**.

★ **Rue St-François-de-Paule** (A2 on map II): this street is at the other end of Cours Saleya from the senate palace. Bonaparte moved into No.2 in 1796, and No. 8 was home to the brother of Robespierre.

★ **Opéra** (A2 on map II): the ornate and sumptuous Belle Époque opera house was built in 1855, based on Garnier's opera house in Paris. It replaced the former municipal theatre, which was destroyed by fire in 1881. Great stars have performed here and tickets are often in great demand.

★ **Église St-François-de-Paule**: sober, almost austere church marking the transition between the baroque and neoclassical periods. In the first chapel to the right is the *Communion de St Benoît*, attributed to the painter Van Loo, who was born in Nice.

★ **Auer**: a landmark in Nice, owned by the same family since 1820, and housed in a stunning rococo building, this shop sells fabulous confectionery, jams and chocolates, and legendary *fruits confits*, and you can visit the workshops to watch them being made. Rather unusually, they even produce and sell crystallized strawberries.

– Buy your olive oil in aluminium containers with attractive labels at *Alziari*, 14 rue St-François-de-Paule. Closed on Sunday and Monday.

On the Seafront

★ **Place Masséna** (A1–2 on map II): the centre of Nice, this vast square has interesting arcaded buildings from 1815 and a lovely fountain on its south side, decorated with bronze statues representing the planets. The municipal casino that stood here was destroyed and replaced with gardens and water features, giving the *place* a sense of space and perspective. The adjacent Jardin Albert I is linked to the place by a wide, well-arranged promenade. To the north is avenue Jean-Médecin, the main shopping street. To the west is the pedestrianized zone, which looks no different from any other pedestrian precinct in any other town, except possibly for the number of tourists. The huge *Arc* sculpture is by Bernar Venet.

★ **Jardin Albert-I** (A2, off map II): the garden between place Masséna and the sea, above the mouth of the Paillon. Its exotic trees and palms look beautiful against the sky at dusk, and concerts are held often in its open-air theatre.

★ **Promenade des Anglais**: the fabled palm-lined seafront street starts at the Jardin Albert I and stretches westwards for several kilometres. The British, tourists in Nice since the 17th century, preferred the seafront to the Old Town. In 1822, Lewis Way organized a collection among his fellow Brits for the construction of a seafront promenade, which gave work to many unemployed local people during a particularly harsh winter. The Promenade des Anglais is still a proud and impressive walkway, enjoyed by strolling tourists, local youngsters on rollerblades and the not-so-young with their little dogs. The beach below is pebbled but this doesn't deter Nice's many sun-worshippers.

There are some impressive buildings along the promenade, including the **Palais de la Méditerranée** casino, a masterpiece of French art deco by Frank Jay Gould, opened in 1929. It closed in 1978 and its facade was rescued from impending demolition by an eleventh-hour historic monument listing. There are various projects afoot, but at the moment the facade hides nothing more than a gaping hole.

The famous and splendid **Hôtel Négresco**, further on, is another fine example of Belle Époque architecture. It was built in 1906 by Niermans for Henri Négresco, who saw the enormous economical potential offered by the promenade, but failed to profit from it. The hotel was requisitioned during World War I and became a convalescence home, and Négresco was bankrupted.

Further west, lovely turn-of-the-century villas have remained miraculously intact. No. 139 was built in 1910 and is worth a look.

To the east is the appropriately named Pointe de Rauba Capeu (which means 'flying hat point' in the local Nissart dialect). It's certainly very windy here sometimes. Tell the time with your own shadow on the human sundial.

In Cimiez

For details on the Roman ruins at Cimiez, *see* 'Musée Archéologique', page 684).

★ **Monastery** (D1 on map I): in the 16th century, the Franciscans installed themselves in Cimiez in the former Benedictine priory, which they extended and restored. A sculpture of the crucified seraphim that appeared before St Francis of Assisi features on a column. The church facade was built in 1850 in the *troubadour* style, and the porch dates from the 17th century. Inside, there are three important works from the School of Nice. The *Vierge de Pitié*, one of Bréa's earliest works, is in the first chapel on the right. The *Crucifixion* in the third chapel on the left, again by Bréa, is painted on a gold background. Finally, you'll see the *Déposition*, attributed to Antoine Brea. At the back is a large baroque sculpted wooden altarpiece.

The traditional buildings to the south of the church are quite moving in their simplicity. The two **cloisters**, one small and one large, have ornate vaults featuring remarkable paintings. The large cloister opens on to the garden with its lemon trees, flower beds and fine views over the valley of the Paillon and the Colline du Château.

★ In the **Cimiez cemetery**, old Niçois families lie buried, along with Raoul Dufy (1877–1953) and Henri Matisse (1869–1954).

★ **Cimiez**: the large and luxurious residential district of Cimiez was built in the second half of the 19th century, with the wide boulevard de Cimiez (1881) as its main focal point. A statue of Queen Victoria stands in front of her favourite lodging, the Hotel Excelsior Regina Palace, where she spent several winters.

Matisse lived in Nice for 20 years, staying first at the **Hôtel Beau-Rivage** on the seafront. He is honoured in a trompe-l'il by Fabio Rieti on the building's facade. Later, he set up home in the **Hôtel Régina**, in Cimiez, until his death, in 1954.

Many of the buildings in Cimiez still have their original features, particularly the **Palace Régina**, with its veranda, loggias and third-floor bow window, the **Winter Palace**, **Alhambra**, the vast **Majestic** and the **Hermitage**. For some buildings, however, time has not stood still. **Il Paradiso** has become a music conservatory set in beautiful gardens and the **Château de Valrose** is now part of Nice university. Today, many of the villas have been replaced by genteel apartment buildings, but Cimiez is still the city's most luxurious suburb.

MUSEUMS

★ **Musée Matisse** (C1 on map I): 164 avenue des Arènes-de-Cimiez. ☎ 04-93-81-08-08. From 1 April to 30 September, open from 10am to 6pm. From 1 October to 31 March, open from 10am to 5pm. Closed on Tuesday. Entrance fee: 25F. Take bus No. 15, 17, 20 or 22 from Promenade des Anglais or avenue Jean-Médecin to Arènes.

Henri Matisse was devoted to Nice and its beautiful light. The artist came to Nice in 1917, after a bout of bronchitis, drawn by the healing climate and the reputation of the hotels. From Nice, he visited Renoir at Les Collettes (*see* 'Cagnes-sur-Mer', page 597) and became a friend of Picasso. He died here in 1954 and is buried in the cemetery close by. Just before his death, a collection of his works was bequeathed to the city. They now form the core of the display at the Musée Matisse, housed in a beautiful 17th-century Genoese-style villa with a trompe-l'oeil facade. The entire ensemble, now complete with new extension, celebrates every facet of the life and work of Matisse.

The museum's vast collection comprises works from all periods of Matisse's career, from his first paintings in 1890 to the cut-paper pictures – including *La Vague* (1952), *Fleurs et Fruits* (1952–53) and the famous *Nu Bleu IV* (1952) – created by the bedridden artist towards the end of his life. The rooms are arranged thematically – two rooms are devoted to his decoration of the Chapelle du Rosaire in Vence, with 60 studies made between 1948 and 1950, while another displays his studies for *La Danse* (1930–32). Lovely portraits of the artist's models and friends include *Portrait de Madame Matisse* (1915) and *Aragon* (1942) (of writer Louis Aragon). The wonderful painting *Nature Morte aux Grenades* (Still Life with Pomegranates, 1947) is a masterpiece of his later period. The museum's collection of drawings is one of the finest in the world, covering all genres, including landscape, portrait and nudes.

There are many personal belongings on display in the museum. Matisse himself is represented, in Nice and on his travels, in signed photographs by Man Ray, Henri Cartier-Bresson and Pierre Boucher. Other pieces include a gilded rococo armchair, painted by Matisse in 1946, Chinese ceramics and Moroccan textiles.

There's a relaxed atmosphere at this museum and a noticeable lack of signposting and security guards. Temporary exhibitions are held from time to time, and there's also a shop selling books, posters and postcards, and an information centre.

★ **Musée d'Art Moderne et d'Art Contemporain** (MAMAC) (museum of modern and contemporary art) (C2–3 on map I): Promenade des Arts. ☎ 04-93-62-61-62. Open every day (except Tuesday) from 10am to 6pm. Also closed on 25 December, 1 January, Easter Sunday and 1 May. Entrance fee: 25F. Take bus No. 5 or 17 from the train station. Car parking for a charge.

In the 1980s, after the phenomenal success of the Pompidou Centre in Paris, many French provincial towns decided to build their own museum of contemporary art. Generally, they were disappointing, with poor collections and no convincing aesthetic policy. Nice's MAMAC was different. The town, home to such artists as Matisse, Picasso, Chagall, Renoir, Klein, Raysse, Arman, Malaval and Ben, had already played a key role in the development of 20th-century art. And the MAMAC was housed in a striking building, designed by Yves Brayard, with four towers covered in Carrara marble linked by glass passageways.

The collection reflects the history of art from 1960 to the present day. Temporary exhibitions (around four per year) are mounted on the first floor. On the second floor works from the Second School of Nice and its affiliates are displayed, including Alain Jacquet's version of Manet's *Déjeuner sur l'herbe* (1964), Jean Tinguely's *Relief Bleu* and Daniel Spoerri's delicate assemblages. The work of new realists César and Arman is also displayed along with that of Malaval.

Don't miss the wonderful Yves Klein room, which shows the artist's famous blue monochromes (and his yellow and gold ones). Christo contributed to his representation of his marriage in 1962, just a few months before his death. Other artists from the Second School of Nice include Mimmo Rotella and Jacques Villeglé, who worked with torn posters from the streets.

On the third floor, Pop Art is vividly represented by Andy Warhol, James Rosenquist, Tom Wesselman, Roy Lichtenstein and Claes Oldenburg. The work of Keith Haring is displayed as well as that of the British artists Gilbert and George. Dan Flavin's neon installations illuminate the subject of trans-Atlantic art. *Boutique de Ben* (Ben's Hut) by Benjamin Vautier is a humorous and educational vision of society and contemporary art. His push-button fun-house is quite something.

Climb up to the terrace for unforgettable views of the town and to see two works by Klein: *Mur du feu* (Wall of Fire) and *Jardin d'Éden* (Garden of Eden). The former is in action every Friday at 9.30pm.

MAMAC also has an auditorium, a contemporary art studio for scholars of the period and a shop. Socks signed by Ben are on sale alongside Di Rosa watches and other objects by today's greatest designers.

✕ The **Café Sud** below the museum stays open until midnight. The museum bar, with its lovely terrace, is on the first floor.

★ **Musée National Message Biblique Marc-Chagall** (national museum of the biblical message of Marc Chagall) (C2 on map I): avenue du Dr-Ménard, Cimiez. Take bus No. 15. ☎ 04-93-53-87-21. Open from 10am to 6pm between 1 July and 30 September. During the rest of the year, open from 10am to 5pm but closed on Tuesday. Entrance fee: 30F (concessions 20F).

This superb museum displays the world's most important collection of Marc Chagall's work, with most of the pieces having been donated by the artist himself. The complex is a pleasant and relaxing one. The building, designed by the architect André Hermant in 1972, specifically to house the works, stands in a biblical garden of olives and cypresses. Big picture windows allow the light to stream in and show the vivid paintings to their best effect.

For Chagall, the Bible was the greatest source of poetry. The 17 canvases from his *Message Biblique* series hang here, including *Noah's Ark*, the stories of *Abraham*, *Jacob* and *Moses*, *The Creation of Man* and five versions of *The Song of Songs*. The latter, a rapturous red series, was dedicated to his wife Vava.

There's a beautiful tapestry in the foyer, as well as sculpture, engravings, lithographs and an exterior mosaic, reflected in the pool. Three stained-glass windows depict the *Creation of the World*.

❢ Finish off your visit with a drink in the outdoor **café** among the cypress trees.

★ **Musée des Beaux-Arts Jules-Chéret** (Jules Chéret fine arts museum) (A3 on map I): 33 avenue des Baumettes. Take bus No. 38 from Masséna. ☎ 04-92-15-28-28. Open 10am–noon and 2–6pm. Closed on Monday. Entrance fee: 25F.

The fine arts museum is in a sumptuous 1876 villa built in the Italian Renaissance style for Ukrainian Princess Kotschoubey. One of the last examples of the excesses of the Belle Époque, it was saved from demolition in 1973 and subsequently renovated in 1987.

Climb the ceremonial staircase to the room devoted to Jules Chéret (1836–1932), the inventor of modern colour posters, and decorator of the Hôtel-de-Ville in Paris, the theatre at the Musée Grévin and several other buildings in the area. A room on the first floor is dedicated to the Impressionists: works by Sisley include *Allée des Peupliers* and *Rue de Louveciennes*. Other rooms display the work of Pierre Bonnard and Édouard Vuillard. There are sculptures and paintings by Jean-Baptiste Carpeaux (1827–75) and works by Carle Van Loo, a native of Nice. All the major artistic movements of the 20th century are represented too.

Nice's Musée des Ponchettes used to be dedicated entirely to Raoul Dufy (1877–1953). After it closed, many of the artist's canvases came here. Dufy was strongly influenced by Cézanne, fauvism and cubism, and his works hang alongside those of some of his friends and contemporaries, such as Kees Van Dongen, Henri Lebasque or Charles Camoin. Dufy also designed ceramics and tapestries, and fabrics for the couturier Paul Poiret.

★ **Musée des Arts Asiatiques** (museum of Asiatic arts) (A3, off map I): 405 Promenade des Anglais, in the Arenas district. Take bus No. 9, 10 or 23. ☎ 04-92-29-37-00. Fax: 04-92-29-37-01. From 2 May to 15 October, open from 10am to 6pm. From 16 October to 30 April, open from 10am to 5pm. Closed on Tuesday, 1 January, 1 May and 25 December. Entrance fee: 35F for adults (students 15F, under-6s free).

The austere white marble building of this museum was designed by Japanese architect Kenzô Tange as a 'swan that floats on the water of a peaceful lake'. The central building is based on the geometrical forms of the square and circle, symbolizing the earth and the sky, reflected in a pool. Four cube buildings, spread out over the lake, house the permanent collection of Japanese lacquer and ceramics, Chinese jade and bronze, Cambodian sculpture and Indian textiles.

Many of the objects are on loan, while others are gifts. The emphasis is on presentation rather than accumulation, and the museum has a really original collection of both decorative and fine art, with wonderful ancient and stunning contemporary pieces. It's possible for visitors to journey through neolithic South China to contemporary Japan, navigating their way with an audioguide.

A small footbridge leads to the tea pavilion, where tea ceremonies take place several times a month, with limited numbers. There are up-to-the-minute multimedia displays inside the rotunda.

★ **Musée International d'Art Naïf Anatole Jakovsky** (Anatole Jakovsky international museum of naïve art) (A3, off map I): avenue Val-Marie, in the Château de Ste-Hélène. Take bus No. 9, 10 or 12, connecting to 34. ☎ 04-93-71-78-33. Open 10am–noon and 2–6pm. Closed on Tuesday and on certain public holidays. Entrance fee: 25F (under-18s free). In 1882, the founder of the Monte-Carlo casino built the Château de Ste-Hélène, standing in beautiful grounds. Perfume manufacturer Coty was the last person to live in this lovely residence. Supported by donations from art critic Anatole Jakovsky, a keen promoter of naïve art, this museum opened in 1982.

Some 600 canvases (half of which are on display) trace the history of naïve art from the 18th century to the present day. The movement really came into its own after the French Revolution. The Croatians, including Ivan Lackovic, are especially well represented, alongside French, Swiss, Belgian, Italian, American (René Rimbert, André Bauchant, Gertrude O'Brady) and South American artists. Some paintings resemble the work of Balinese artists exhibited in the Neka Museum in Ubud, Bali. Jean Klissak's *Congés payés* ('paid days off') is a critical vision of the holiday season.

★ **Musée du Prieuré du Vieux-Logis** (B1, off map I): 59 avenue St-Barthélemy. Take bus No. 5 to Gorbella. ☎ 04-93-84-44-74. Open from 3pm to 5pm on Wednesday, Thursday, Saturday and the first Sunday in the month. Guided visits only. This museum is the work of a Dominican monk, Alfred Lemerre, who was passionate about objects and furniture from the 14th, 15th and 16th centuries. The superb collection is housed on an old farm, converted into a priory, with a lovely little garden. The pride of the collection is a 15th-century Flemish *pietà*.

★ **Musée de la Marine** (B2 on map II): in the Bellanda tower, in the Parc du Château. ☎ 04-93-80-47-61. Open every day (except Monday and Tuesday) 10am–noon and 2–7pm (until 5pm from October to May). Closed from 15 November to 15 December. Nice's maritime history told through models of boats and displays of all things naval and maritime. Berlioz lived in the tower in 1844 and composed *King Lear* there.

★ **Musée Terra Amata** (D3 on map I): 25 boulevard Carnot. Take bus no. 1, 2, 7, 9, 10 or 14 on the Villefranche–Menton route. By car, take the first road on the left, on a bend, on the Basse Corniche as you approach from Nice. ☎ 04-93-55-59-93. Open every day (except Monday) 10am–noon and 2–6pm. Closed 1 May, at Christmas and on New Year's Day, and during the first two weeks of September. Entrance fee: 25F. In 1966, preparations for the building of a block of flats uncovered evidence of the life of the Archanthropians, who often sheltered here at the foot of Mont Boron. The dwellings at the Terra Amata site are some of the oldest in the world. The museum displays a reconstruction of a prehistoric pebble-walled wind-shelter, which would have been used by elephant-hunters 400 millennia ago. Fascinating tools and bones evoke life in Nice at the dawn of time.

★ **Musée Archéologique** (archaeological museum) (C1 on map I): 160 avenue des Arènes-de-Cimiez. Next to Musée Matisse; the entrance is through the excavations on avenue Monte-Croce. ☎ 04-93-81-59-57. Closed on Monday and some public holidays, as well as for three weeks in November and December. Between 1 April and 30 September, open 10am–noon and 2–6pm. On Sunday and in low season, open 10am–1pm and 2–5pm. Entrance fee: 25F. The archaeological museum displays finds from the excavations in Cimiez and the surrounding area, including ceramics, jewellery and coins.

Adjoining the museum is the site of the **Roman ruins**, with hot, medium and cold baths, vestiges of the heating apparatus, a marble summer pool and Nice's **amphitheatre**. It is relatively small, but it none the less had seating for 4,000 spectators. It now provides a venue for the July jazz festival.

★ **Musée Masséna** (B3 on map I): 65 rue de France. Next to the Hotel Négresco, but accessed via rue de France. Take bus No. 3, 7, 8, 9, 10, 12, 14 or 22. ☎ 04-93-88-11-34. Open every day (except Monday) 10am–noon and 2–6pm. Closed in January. Entrance fee: 25F. This 19th-century Italianate villa was built for the grandson of Napoleon's Marshal Masséna, Victor. Prince Victor's own son subsequently handed it over to the town after World War I, on the condition that it be transformed into a museum of local history. The museum duly opened in 1921.

On the ground floor there's an impressive collection of Empire-style salons and there are four Thomire torch-holders in the gallery. The sculpted wooden doors came from a chateau owned by Lucien Bonaparte, one of Napoleon's brothers. On the first floor, the collection includes paintings by Niçois primitives, a 15th-century marriage casket, decorative liturgical items featuring fish and hearts made of silver, and armour.

A copy of the 1860 plebiscite is on display here. In 1859, Napoleon III had helped Vittorio Emanuele II of Savoy to chase the Austrians from the northern provinces in Italy, and his reward was the secession of Nice and Savoy to

France. Under the Treaty of Turin, the return of Nice had to be supported by the citizens. The final result in the plebiscite was 25,743 votes in favour of France and 260 against.

The second floor is devoted to traditional life in the region. There are several watercolours by local artists, including a painting of the Niçois coast and bay, and a deserted beach – a rare sight a century and a half later.

WHAT ELSE TO SEE

★ **Cathédrale Orthodoxe Russe** (Russian Orthodox Church) (A2 on map I): avenue Nicolas-II, at the beginning of boulevard du Tzarewitch. ☎ 04-93-96-88-02. In summer, visits possible 9am–noon, and 2.30–6pm. Open in winter 9.30am–noon and 2.30–5pm. Entrance fee (except for orthodox worshippers). Services are held on Saturday at 6pm (in summer) and 5.30pm (in winter) and on Sunday at 10am throughout the year. No shorts or sleeveless shirts allowed.

This tranquil place is quite a surprise in modern Nice. It stands on the spot where Prince Nicolas Alexandrovitch, heir to the throne of Russia, died in 1864. Forty years later, his former fiancée, subsequently the wife of Tsar Alexander III, ordered a chapel to be constructed here. Of impressive dimensions, it's the largest Russian church outside Russia, with five magnificent domes. The layout is based on St Basil's basilica in Moscow's Red Square. Its opulent interior is in the shape of a Greek cross and has gilded frescoes, woodwork and icons, including that of Notre-Dame-de-Kazan, on the right of the choir.

★ **Église Ste-Jeanne-d'Arc** (B1 on map I): at the corner of avenue St-Lambert and rue Charles-Péguy. This church is interesting for its 1930s architecture.

★ **Parc de Valrose**: 128 avenue de Valrose, in north Nice. Set in Mediterranean countryside, where olive and orange trees grow side by side with palms, eucalyptus and magnolia trees, you'll find an authentic Russian *isba* (country cabin). It was brought here piece by piece from a large estate near Kiev, belonging to the fabulously wealthy Von Derwies family, builders and owners of the legendary Trans-Siberian railway. In 1865, Baron Von Derwies, a celebrated engineer to the Tsars, bought land in the Vallon des Roses district, on the hill in Cimiez. He built the impressive Château Valrose, moved in with his family and transplanted the *isba* to a spot opposite, with a magnificent view over Baie des Anges. His parties were legendary, attracting major performers, until a change in fortunes and the advent of war put an end to his dream. Today, the chateau and the *isba* belong to the university and you can eat there for just a few francs.

★ **Ben Vautier's house**: 103 route de St-Pancrace, on one of Nice's hills. This large white building belongs to contemporary artist Ben, born in Naples to a Swiss father and Irish mother. His house has been described as 'a metaphor for his own ego', and he has collected some unusual pieces, including a pile of bidets! Unfortunately, the house is not open to the public.

★ **Acropolis** (D2 on map I): Esplanade Kennedy-et-de-Lattre-de-Tassigny. ☎ 04-93-92-83-00. This vast congress and arts centre, built of concrete slabs and smoked glass, can accommodate 4,500 delegates a day. It provides all the latest technology, and its auditorium (Apollon) can seat 2,500. There's also a *cinémathèque*, with an excellent programme of films, and space for temporary exhibitions. The artwork in the entrance is *Music Power* by Arman.

★ **Villa Arson**: 20 rue Stephen-Liégeard, on Cessole hill. Take bus No. 4 or 7 (to Fanny), 20 (to Fontaine du Temple), 1 or 18 (to boulevard Gorbella). ☎ 04-92-07-73-73. Open every day between July and September from 1pm to 7pm. From October open every day (except Monday) from 1pm to 6pm. Free entry. French foreign minister Talleyrand came to this superb 17th-century Niçois building for some rest and relaxation after the Congress of Vienna. Today, it houses the **École Nationale d'Art Décoratif** (national school for decorative arts) and is a centre for the study of contemporary art, with research facilities for students, a library, a café and accommodation. Around 15 exhibitions are held here each year.

★ **Château du Mont Boron**: also known as the Château de l'Anglais, this eccentric residence was built in 1858 by Colonel Robert Smith, a military engineer in India. With its pink exterior and turrets, it's quite startling, combining various styles with a touch of 'Mogul palace'.

★ **Parc Floral Phnix**: 405 Promenade des Anglais. By car, follow signs for the airport, turn right at the huge greenhouse and follow the signposts. ☎ 04-93-18-03-33. Open every day from 9am to 7pm (to 5pm between October and March). Entrance fee: 40F (12–18-year-olds 30F, 6–12-year-olds 25F, under-6s free).

Nice's botanical gardens, opened in 1991, nurture more than 2,000 species of plants from five different tropical climates. Each zone echoes to the appropriate birdsong, piped through well-hidden speakers, and butterflies and birds live in the vegetation. The giant greenhouse is one of the largest in the world, and an upturned pyramid provides a fascinating journey through the world of flora and fauna.

FESTIVALS AND EVENTS

– **Festin des Cougourdons**: this popular festival in May celebrates the strangely shaped gourds known as *cougourdons*, with folk dancing and picnics.

– **Jazz festival**: taking place over eight days in the second half of July, Nice's jazz festival has attracted big names such as Louis Armstrong, Bechet, Miles Davis and Dizzy Gillespie, and it is still one of the best in France. For around 150F you can listen to performances on three separate stages between 6pm and midnight.

DIVING

There are over 30 lovely dive sites suitable for all levels around Nice's Baie des Anges, near the Villefranche-sur-Mer harbour and in the Baie de Beaulieu.

Dive Schools

■ **CIP Nice**: 2 ruelle des Mouline, behind the quays from where ships leave for Corsica. ☎ 04-93-55-59-50 or 06-09-52-55-57. Email: cip-nice@web store.fr. Open from mid-March to mid-November (except on Sunday). This club (FFESM and PADI) is renowned for the excellence of its state-qualified instructors, who lead first dives and teach up to instructor level and PADI courses. Night dives are available and children over 8 are welcome.

Dive Sites

↜ **La grotte à corail**: a red coral cave at 15–20 metres (50–65 feet). Take a torch to see the blaze of colour, but be careful with your fins, which can damage the coral. Suitable for all levels.

↜ **Pointe de la Cuisse**: not far from Cap Ferrat, an underwater cliff inhabited by moray eels, scorpion fish and lobsters at around 20 metres (65 feet). There's an interesting tunnel – for experienced divers only. Suitable for all levels.

↜ **Vallée des Gorgones**: beneath Cap de Nice, close to the port. Be aware of the boats. There's a lovely canyon at 20–30 metres (65–100 feet) between two rocks covered with huge scarlet sea fans. On the branches, you may spot dogfish eggs, small translucents sacks in which the baby creatures are already visible. Level II.

↜ **Le Sec à Merlot**: to the east of Cap Ferrat. After a vertiginous descent, shine your torch on this wonderful rock at around 40 metres (130 feet). There's a mass of colour, with scorpion fish and moray eels joining you on the tour. The current can be very strong at times. Level II divers only.

THE HILLTOP VILLAGES AROUND NICE

Make your way out of Nice along boulevard Jean-Jaurès, boulevard Risso and route de Turin. At Pont-de-Peille, the D21 climbs back up the Le Paillon river. After St-Thècle, turn right along the D21 to Peillon.

PEILLON

Peillon is one of the most beautiful villages on the Côte d'Azur. The narrow road up to it winds its way through olive trees and pines, with beautiful views of the village itself. Like many other *villages perchés*, clifftop Peillon seems to blend organically into its mountainous landscape and it has been perfectly restored. Many artists are based in the village, and Peillon also has one of the best hotels on the Côte, although it is predictably expensive.

GETTING THERE

– **By train**: take the Nice–Sospel–Breil line to the station at Peillon-Ste-Thècle. The walk along the small path to the old village of Peille will take you around two hours.

WHERE TO STAY AND EAT

☆☆☆ Chic

🛌 ✕ **Auberge de la Madone**: just outside the walled village. ☎ 04-93-79-91-17. Fax: 04-93-79-99-36. Email: cmillo@club-internet.fr. Closed on Wednesday, from 20 October to 20 December, and between 7 and 31 January. Double rooms from 480F to 960F. Half board between 580F and 800F. Menus at 150F (weekday lunch), 220F and 260F. The comfortable rooms in this *auberge* have Provençal furnishings, and balconies with astonishing views over the valley and Peillon itself. You can dine on the terraces among the mimosa and olive trees. For three generations, the Millo family has warmly welcomed customers to its excellent restaurant, serving fresh, authentic and seasonal Provençal cuisine. Try the *poulette fermière farcie aux figues et pignons de pins* (chicken stuffed with figs and pine nuts). The food is inventive and infused with sunshine.

WHAT TO SEE AND DO

★ **Village**: as you enter the village, you'll see a beautiful fountain from the 1800s on the cobbled square. The magnificently preserved village has so far escaped the arrival of souvenir sellers and arty-crafty workshops. Its steep, narrow streets snake past rows of arcades and through vaulted passage-ways. The rather austere exteriors of the houses have scarcely changed since the Middle Ages. The church in the little square at the highest point of the village, built on the spot where there used to be a chateau, is baroque in style and has an octagonal lantern.

★ **Chapelle des Pénitents-Blancs**: open on Saturday and Sunday only; during the week, ask for the key at the town hall. ☎ 04-93-79-91-04. Built around 1495 and restored in the 17th century, the chapel houses stunning frescoes by Giovanni Canavesio, which depict the *Passion of Christ* with emotion and beautiful detail.

– Walkers can enjoy a lovely **footpath** that follows the route of an ancient Roman road, linking Peillon with Peille in around two hours.

PEILLE

Head back by car to the D21 and you'll soon see Peille on the right, clinging to the side of the mountain. At the La Grave cement works, take the D53, a winding road that leads to the hilltop village, overlooked by the ruins of a feudal chateau and set against the backdrop of the Pic de Baudon (1,264 metres/4,160 feet high). Usually free of tourists during the week, Peille is a lovely place to visit. Little old ladies sit in the sun on benches along the main street, often talking in *Pelhasc*, Peille's own dialect. Similar to the language spoken in Nice, it has very distinctive pronunciation.

Peille has been through some turbulent times. In the Middle Ages, it was governed by an elected council and was the county town of a bailiwick. On two occasions, the inhabitants chose to be ex-communicated rather than pay taxes to the bishop of Nice.

GETTING THERE

– **From Nice by bus**: two departures each morning (via La Turbie) and one late afternoon (via the Grande Corniche) every day except Sundays and public holidays. The trip takes a good hour.

– **From Nice by train**: take the Nice–Sospel–Breil line to the station at Peillon-Ste-Thècle. The walk to the old village will take between two and three hours.

– **From Nice by car**: follow the signs for Monte-Carlo, and leave the motorway at La Turbie.

USEFUL ADDRESS

🛈 **Town hall**: ☎ 04-93-91-71-71.

WHERE TO STAY AND EAT

🛌 ✕ **Belvédère Hôtel**: 3 place Jean-Miol, as you enter the village. ☎ 04-93-79-90-45. Closed on Monday and from 20 November to 29 December. Double rooms with wash-basin for 250F. Half board 250F per person. Menus from 100F to 170F. Five simple but clean rooms, all with lovely mountain views. The restaurant has a bay window overlooking the valley and serves delicious rabbit, ravioli, gnocchi and other local dishes. The owner is very friendly.

🛌 ✕ **Auberge du Seuillet**: Le Buon Pin, 2 kilometres along the road from Peille to La Turbie, at the foot of the Col de la Madone pass. ☎ and fax: 04-93-41-17-39. Closed on Tuesday and Wednesday, and in October, November and December. Double rooms with shower and toilet for 260F. Menus at 75F (lunchtime *express*) and 115F. This *auberge* offers a refuge from the modern world. There's a garden and a lovely view of the hills, and the restaurant serves *foie gras* or *saumon fumé maison* (home-smoked salmon), *pavé au poivre* (steak with pepper sauce) or *lapin aux champignons* (rabbit with mushrooms).

WHAT TO SEE

★ The **old village** has beautiful Gothic houses, vaulted passageways and stepped streets. The house at the corner of place Mont-Agel was the seat of the counts of Provence, lords of the castle. From the arcaded square, with its pretty Gothic fountain, take the arcade on the right to **ruelle Lascaris** and then **rue Mary-Gorden** to get to the war memorial. There's a spectacular view from here over the olive groves and walled gardens of Peille, with Nice beyond. The 12th-century church of St-Marie has a Romanesque nave and a medieval depiction of Peille. A path behind the church leads to the ruins of the 14th-century chateau.

★ **Musée du Terroir** (museum of the region): in summer, open on Wednesday, Saturday and Sunday from 2pm to 6pm. In winter, visits on Saturday and Sunday only. Free entry. Housed in a small and pretty house, this museum displays objects from daily life in the 19th century and explains the traditions and language of the village.

WALKS

– **Mont Baudon**: a two-hour walk to the northeast, along a pine forest to the St Bernard mountain pass, and then on to the summit for a pretty view.

– **Peillon**: to walk to the neighbouring village of Peillon, take the ancient Roman road, now a mule path.

– **Col de la Madone**: the walk up to the pass takes about an hour.

FESTIVAL

– **Fête des Baguettes** (bread festival): on the first Sunday in September, young women present their loved ones with decorated *baguettes* (French bread sticks). The festival commemorates an event from the Middle Ages when the town was in drought. Peille asked for help from a sorcerer-cum-shepherd, and he made it rain on condition that the lord of the castle gave him his daughter as a wife.

L'ESCARÈNE

Return to the D21, which follows the Gorges de Paillon; the road is sometimes closed when explosives are being used in the nearby quarry. L'Escarène is a former strategic pit-stop on the road from Nice to Turin, where the torrents of the rivers Braus and Lucéram meet to form the Paillon de L'Escarène. From the bridge, there's a picturesque view of the houses overhanging the river. The large church of St-Pierre-aux-Liens, with its pretty baroque facade, is an exceptionally beautiful building. Its Italianate interior houses a lovely organ by the Grindo brothers (1791), famous organ-builders from Nice. In the central chapel there's an 18th-century *Vierge de l'Assomption* in sculpted wood. The village has an attractive tree-lined square.

LUCÉRAM

This is a typical fortified hilltop village in the Niçois hinterland. Its tall houses cling to the rock on which it perches, piled on top of one another. It's also an excellent departure point for various excursions and one way of reaching the hinterland behind Menton or the Vallée de la Roya via the Turini and Sospel mountain pass (*see* page 642).

GETTING THERE

– **From Nice**: buses leave the bus station during the week from bays 29 or 31 at 8am, 9am, 5.30pm and 6pm. On Sunday and public holidays, buses leave at 9am and return at 5.30pm.

WHAT TO SEE

Lucéram occupied a strategic position on the 'salt route', when salt from the marshes of Hyères and Toulon was loaded on to mules in Nice and taken across the mountains. The village received certain privileges, and, in 1272, was given administrative independence.

★ The **old village** retains its medieval fortified aspect, with lovely restored Gothic houses, bread ovens, narrow winding streets and arcades. *Pontis* (little bridges) were built above the street to link the houses and make more space.

★ **Église Ste-Marguerite**: the 15th-century church was renovated in Italian rococo style in the 18th century. Its pink and white exterior hides several art treasures from the School of Nice (*see* page 664). If the church is locked, ask for the key at the presbytery to the right of the porch. There's a 10-panelled altarpiece of *St Marguerite* by Bréa (1500), a retable of *St Anthony* by Canavesio, and of *St Peter and St Paul* (1500), *St Bernard* (1500) and *St Lawrence*. Other treasures include a silver reliquary of the Tarascon dragon and a statue of *St Rosalie*, patron saint of Palermo, introduced into the area with the arrival of the Barralis family from Sicily in the 17th century.

The church square is very picturesque with its fountain and public washing place, and its pretty view over Lucéram, the hills and the coast.

FESTIVAL

– **Noël des Bergers** (shepherds' Christmas): every year, the shepherds come down from the mountains and come into the church with their sheep. Mass is held and the shepherds make an offering of fruits (usually dried figs) and bread.

COARAZE

The first written record of Coaraze dates back to 1108, when it was known as *Cauda Rasa*. In fact, it's likely to be much older than that, even pre-Roman. The charming circular medieval village is set against a mountain backdrop and is famous for its sunny aspect – more like Tuscany than France. When the sun is hot, take a walk through the quiet stepped streets and shady vaulted passageways and relax in the small squares with their attractive cooling fountains. There are wonderful views over the valley and Rocca Seira from the terraced garden among the cypress trees.

Climb up to the church through the unusual cemetery that looks out over the valley. The baroque church dates from the 14th century and was destroyed and rebuilt on three occasions. There's a pretty marble statue of the *Virgin* (1600) above the altar.

In the 1950s, several artists came to live in the village, including Jean Cocteau, to whom the town owes its sundial on the wall of the town hall. Less well-known painters have also made their mark in Coaraze.

GETTING THERE

– **From Nice**: buses leave every day (except Sunday and public holidays) at 10.30am and 5.30pm. Returning from Coaraze, there's a bus at 7.20am (via Contes) and a direct bus at 1.20pm.

USEFUL ADDRESS

🛈 Tourist office: at the entrance to the village. Open every day in summer from 3pm to 6pm. Ask for opening times in winter: ☎ 04-93-79-37-47. Information on accommodation.

WHERE TO STAY AND EAT

🛏 ✕ Auberge du Soleil: ☎ 04-93-79-08-11. Fax: 04-93-79-37-79. Closed from 1 November to 15 February. Rooms for 380F. Half board compulsory in July and August, for 380F. Menus at 120F and 145F. Dining possible for non-residents. This well-restored 19th-century house has pretty rooms at reasonable prices, given the location. The airy terrace looks out over an idyllic landscape and the food is good, even if the service is sometimes a bit too relaxed. There's a pool in the garden. Guests have to reach the building on foot, but the owners will help carry luggage from the car.

FESTIVALS

– **Fête médiévale** (medieval festival): during the first weekend of June.

– **Fête de l'Olivier** (olive festival): on 15 August.

– **Festin de la Ste-Catherine**: on the first Sunday in September or the last Sunday in August, the locals celebrate the local saint's day by bringing a dish and sharing it with their neighbours.

– **Fête de la Châtaigne** (chestnut festival): in October.

WALKS

Walks around the village are well marked in yellow and blue, maintained by a local organization, which has also produced a 20F leaflet describing around 25 routes. Buy it from the information centre, at the town hall or at the Auberge du Soleil.

– **Mont Férion** (1,410 metres/4,625 feet): this walk takes two hours.

– **L'Escarène**: a three-hour walk to the neighbouring village via Baisse de la Croix and Berre-les-Alpes.

– **Rocca Seira summit** (1,500 metres/4,920 feet): take the path from the exit to the village and climb north to the St-Michel mountain pass (950 metres/3,115 feet), overlooked by the ruins of the Château de Rocca-Sparviera. From there, you can climb to the Autaret summit (1,300 metres/ 4,265 feet) and Rocca Seira in two hours.

– **The 'route to paradise'**: 7 kilometres (4 miles) north of Coaraze on the D15, just past the village of L'Engavin, you'll reach a bridge over the Paillon river. Follow the signposted path to a series of pools and waterfalls; although it's tempting to paddle, proper swimming is *forbidden* and *dangerous*. Content yourself with enjoying the lovely spot, where the sun filters through arching branches. The locals call it 'paradise' and it's a favourite meeting place for young lovers on a Sunday.

CONTES

The late 16th-century church at the top of the village has a multi-panel painting of *St Mary Magdalene*, attributed to François Brea, with over a dozen depictions of biblical scenes. There's a two-tiered Renaissance fountain (1587) and a lovely view over the valley from the nearby terrace.

The village is associated with a strange legend. In 1508, the locals appealed to the bishop of Nice to protect them from an imminent plague of caterpillars. The bishop decreed that the tiny creatures should be exiled and they were sentenced with eviction. That very day, the offenders left town in a long line.

This village is less interesting than Lucéram and has a rather unattractive industrial zone at its foot, dominated by a cement works.

GETTING THERE

– **From Nice**: buses leave bay 25 almost every hour until 7.45pm on weekdays, for the 40-minute journey. On Sunday and on public holidays departures are at 9am, 10am, 12.15pm, 2pm, 3pm, 4pm, 6.05pm and 7pm. Buses return from Contes during the week from 6.15am to the last one at 8.15pm.

USEFUL ADDRESS

🖪 Syndicat d'initiative (tourist information centre): place Albert-Ollivier. ☎ 04-93-79-13-99. Open from 2pm to 6pm.

WHERE TO STAY

🛖 Camping de la Ferme Riola: in Sclos-de-Contes. ☎ 04-93-79-03-02. Closed between end October and April. Daily set price at 35F. Set in a large wooded park, this site provides a pool, a space for volleyball, and showers. Campers can buy produce such as olive oil and poultry direct from the farm. There's also a *gîte* for rent by the week from 1,000F to 2,400F, throughout the year. Booking advisable.

CHÂTEAUNEUF-VILLE-VIEILLE

This hilltop village is reached from Contes by a winding road of hairpin bends. Surrounded by olive trees and orchards, it has a colourful glazed-tile bell-tower.

Just 2 kilometres further on, a path on the left leads to the ruins of the old medieval village. In the Middle Ages, the locals took refuge on the high ground from a range of aggressors. From the summit, there's a magnificent view over the hinterland. You have to walk the final 200 metres and it can be dangerous, so stick closely to the path.

Note: from 1 May to 30 September, the road up to the village ruins is open only on Saturday, Sunday and public holidays between 9am and 8pm. From 1 October to 30 April, it's open from 9am to 6pm. The best course of action is to ask for information in the village of Contes.

If you come down the other side of the hill, you can rejoin the D19 to Nice, via Tourrette-Levens.

LEVENS

Before returning to the Côte d'Azur, take a little detour to Levens. This characterful medieval hilltop town was under the control of the Riquiers in the 13th century and was then ruled by the Grimaldi family. In 1621, the locals rebelled against their feudal masters and became independent. The feudal chateau was destroyed, and a *boutau* (stone) was fixed in its place. During the village festival, all the villagers meet at the site and everyone puts one foot on the stone, the symbol of release from oppression.

The village has ancient streets, vaulted passageways and old doorways. Look out for the house belonging to the Napoleon family's Marshal Masséna. Climb to the top of the village to enjoy a splendid view over the Vésubie and the Var, which meet at the Férion ridge.

USEFUL ADDRESS

🛈 Tourist office: ☎ 04-93-79-11-00. Open in summer Monday to Saturday 9.30am–12.30pm (except Monday morning) and 2.30–5.30pm (reduced hours in winter).

WHERE TO STAY AND EAT

🛏 ✗ Le Mas Fleuri: in Les Prés district. 2 kilometres from Levens, to the left, on the D19. ☎ 04-93-79-70-35. Double rooms for 250F and half board 240F. Menus at 105F and 155F. This charming hotel is well maintained and pleasant, peaceful and relaxing, with a pretty exterior and a huge lawn behind. Good food is served in the large dining room and diners can watch it being prepared.

🛏 ✗ La Vigneraie: 82 route de St-Blaise. 1.5 kilometres to the southeast. ☎ 04-93-79-70-46. Open for lunch only, and closed between mid-October and the end of January. Comfortable rooms from 180F, with shower or bath and toilet. Menus between 110F and 150F. The cuisine is good but not particularly inventive. There's a relaxing garden.

✗ Les Santons: 3 rue de l'Escalada. ☎ 04-93-79-72-47. Open for lunch only (except Wednesday), and Saturday evening. Closed from 7–13 February, 24 June to 3 July and from 30 September to 9 October. Menus at 110F (except on Sunday and public holidays) and from 145F to 195F. À la carte around 250F. A pleasant spot, serving traditional food, such as rabbit with pinenuts, on a peaceful garden terrace. Leave room for the delicious desserts. The welcome is warm and friendly and the service good.

🛏 ✗ Le Malausséna: 9 place de la République, in the village. ☎ 04-93-79-70-04. Fax: 04-93-79-85-89. Closed on Monday in low season, and for the month of November. Menus between 95F and 165F. This restaurant is famous throughout the area for its excellent and well-priced food, such as ravioli, and duck in strawberry vinegar. Ring ahead out of season, as they don't always serve dinner.

WALK

– **To the chapel** (1,258 metres/4,126 feet): two-hour walk from Les Grands-Prés, 1 kilometre from the village, towards Tourrette. This walk along a superb avenue of cedars makes a lovely excursion before heading back to Nice.

The Corniches

The corniches comprise three coastal roads which run parallel along the Côte D'Azur from Nice to Menton via Monaco.

Built by the Prince of Monaco in the 19th century, the Basse Corniche (also known as the Corniche Inférieure or the Corniche du Littoral), is the lowest of the three roads and closely follows the geography of the coast. Above lies the Moyenne Corniche, constructed at the start of the 20th century to help alleviate traffic congestion along the French Riviera – already a popular spot with the rich and famous at this time. The Grande or Haute Corniche, built by Napoléon along the old Roman route of the Via Augusta, is the highest of the three and offers splendid views over Monaco at a height of 450 metres (1,476 feet).

THE COAST FROM NICE TO MENTON

THE BASSE CORNICHE

VILLEFRANCHE-SUR-MER

The well-preserved town of Villefranche, overlooking its lovely natural harbour, makes a welcome change from busy, built-up Nice. It's in a wonderful and unique location, with a spectacular waterfront, a small sheltered port and a beautiful view of Cap Ferrat. The Niçois often come to Villefranche for lunch or in the evening, to enjoy the peace and tranquillity. The old part of the town has an interesting history too.

History

The town was founded in the 13th century by Charles II, who gave it a commercial franchise (hence its name of 'free town'). In 1388, Villefranche handed itself over to the House of Savoy at the same time as Nice and became the official port of the counts and dukes of Savoy.

In the 16th century, Holy Roman Emperor Charles V, an ally of the Duke of Savoy, came to Villefranche to meet François I. The imperial galley was connected to the quay by a wooden footbridge. When Charles Quint's sister and the Queen of France approached on the bridge, it cracked and everyone, Charles Quint, the Queen, the Duke of Savoy and the ladies-in-waiting included, took a surprise and unwelcome bath. In 1543, it was the pirate Barbarossa, at the head of the Turkish fleet, who dropped his anchor in the harbour at Villefranche. The locals did not entirely benefit from the alliance between François I and the Turks.

In 1557, the Duke of Savoy fortified Villefranche, erecting a stronghold and digging out the Darse port. However, after the port was constructed in Nice,

Villefranche began to decline in importance and its harbour was rented out to the Russian fleet. After the town returned to France, Napoleon III turned Villefranche into the fifth most important military port in the country. An American naval base was established here after the end of World War II, until France left NATO.

USEFUL ADDRESSES

❂ Tourist office: Jardin François-Binon, near the Basse Corniche. ☎ 04-93-01-73-68. Fax: 04-93-76-63-65. Website: www.villefranche-sur-mer.com. Open every day in July and August from 9am to 7pm. Open in winter Monday to Saturday 9.30am–noon and 2–6pm (to 6.30pm in June and September).

✉ Post office: avenue Albert-I (on the Basse Corniche) and Sadi-Carnot.

Buses: services to Nice, Monte-Carlo and Menton leave from Jardin François-Binon every 15 minutes during the week (every 20 minutes on Sunday).

WHERE TO STAY AND EAT

♠ ✕ Le Provençal: 4 avenue du Maréchal-Joffre. ☎ 04-93-76-53-53. Fax: 04-93-76-96-00. Closed from end October to Christmas. Air-conditioned double rooms from 380F to 590F. Menus at 105F and 125F. Housed in a pretty building with blue shutters and three towers, this hotel has some rooms overlooking the garden or the sea. Book well ahead to secure these, as they are very popular. Meals are served on a lovely patio, and dishes include *terrine de porcelet aux pistaches* (suckling pig terrine with pistachio nuts), *ragoût de morue en stofficada* (fish stew) or delicious *sardines farcies* (stuffed sardines).

✕ Restaurant Michel's: Place Amélie-Pollonnais. ☎ 04-93-76-73-24. Closed on Tuesday. Meals around 160F. There's no set menu but instead a wonderful selection of fresh seasonal, and mainly seafood-based dishes (around 80F). This popular and rather laid-back place is well worth a detour on a summer evening. Try the *terrine de lotte en gelée de bouillabaisse* (monkfish terrine in fish jelly) or *scampis au Noilly prat beurre de crustacé* (scampi in

vermouth with seafood sauce). The service is friendly and attentive.

✕ La Grignotière: 3 rue du Poilu, in Villefranche's Old Town. ☎ 04-93-76-79-83. Open every evening from 7pm. Closed on Wednesday between November and April. Menus at 109F and 149F. Nibble on light dishes, try the Provençal menu, or plump for the gourmet menu, after which you'll need a long walk around the port. It offers *soupe de poisson de roche* (rockfish soup), *salade de pousses d'épinards au foie de volailles* (baby spinach salad with chicken livers), ravioli, lasagne, snails, duck, cheese and dessert. The dining room is small and tastefully decorated in pink tones.

☆☆☆ Chic

✕ La Mère Germaine: on the port, Gustave-Courbet quay. ☎ 04-93-01-71-39. Open every day in high season. Menu at 225F. À la carte from 300F to 400F. This lovely spot on the harbour, one of the best restaurants between Nice and Monaco, has a magnificent view of the seafront, a lovely dining room and terrace, elegant tables and an army of waiters and waitresses. The food is fresh and well prepared, and the fish dishes are excellent. The *escabèche de sardines* and *filets de sole* are cooked to perfection.

WHERE TO GO FOR A DRINK

Le Britt In Bar: 14 rue du Poilu. ☎ 04-93-01-70-38. This cosy British-style pub has a selection of 30 international beers at reasonable prices. It's all about darts rather than *boules* here . . .

WHAT TO SEE

THE COAST FROM NICE TO MENTON

★ **Old town**: set off from the charming fishing port with its brightly coloured buildings and head for rue du Poilu, the main street. The unusual rue Obscure (dark street) is so overhung with houses that it's almost a tunnel. Indeed, it provided shelter from bombardment as recently as World War II. Stroll through ancient streets, up steep lanes and flights of steps into small squares, which offer glimpses of the sea. The 15th-century church (reshaped in the 18th century) houses altarpieces from the 17th century, and a recumbent Christ carved from a fig tree by a slave.

★ **Port**: on the harbourside there are ancient red and ochre Italianate houses, and several cafés and restaurants with lovely views of the water and of Cap Ferrat.

★ **Chapelle Cocteau**: Chapelle St-Pierre, quai Courbet. On the right as you head towards the port. Usually open 9.30am–noon and 2–6pm (later according to season). Information on exact opening hours: ☎ 04-93-76-90-70. Closed on Monday. Entrance fee: 12F.

Between the wars, Jean Cocteau, poet and surrealist film director, lived in Villefranche and wrote his film *Orphée* (*The Temptation of Orpheus*) here. He was fascinated by the small abandoned Romanesque chapel on the port (used by local fishermen for storing their nets) and, after a long battle with the local municipal authorities, finally won the permission, in 1957, to restore and renovate it. He decorated it with lavish and symbolic frescoes, including a candelabra with human faces, topped by *fouanes* (a Provençal tool used for night fishing), scenes from the life of St Peter, patron saint of fishermen, and images of the fishergirls of Villefranche.

For the **Festival of St Peter**, at the beginning of July, a decorated boat is set alight in the harbour at Villefranche.

★ Walk from the **port to the citadel**, to see fishermen at work. The building on the other quay is a bit of an anomaly in the landscape.

★ **Citadel**: built by the duke of Savoy at the end of the 16th century, Villefranche's citadel managed to escape Louis XIV's destruction orders. The impressive ditches that surround it were dug right out of the rock. To the left there's the wreck of a 16th-century ship, discovered in 1919 by a local diver. A little museum shows some of the contents found on the wreck, which included 16th-century almonds and peach kernels. There's a lovely view from the open-air theatre.

The beautiful **Hôtel de Ville** (town hall) at the centre of the citadel is a hacienda-style building. Paintings by Jean Cocteau hang on the first floor and temporary exhibitions are held on the ground floor.

Three other museums may be visited free of charge. The exhibits at the **Musée Volti** (closed on Sunday morning, Tuesday and in November) include bronze, copper and terracotta female figures, sculpted by Antoniucci Volti. The **Musée Goetz-Boumeester** (closed on Sunday, Tuesday and in November) has paintings and engravings by the American artists and collectors Henri Goetz and his wife Christine Boumeester, along with a few drawings by masters such as Picasso, Picabia, Miró and Hartung. The **Collection Roux** displays ceramic figurines inspired by medieval and Renaissance manuscripts.

CAP FERRAT AND ST-JEAN-CAP-FERRAT

One of the most beautiful and well-preserved spots on the Côte d'Azur, the peninsula of Cap Ferrat and St-Jean have both been spared to a significant extent from the ravages of 'progress'. Exclusive villas hide behind lush greenery and the peninsula has protected its lovely pine forest well. It has provided (and continues to provide) a haven for celebrities and intellectuals. Nietzsche, King Léopold II of Belgium (long-time owner of half the land on Cap Ferrat), Somerset Maugham, American film director Otto Preminger, Marc Chagall and Jean Cocteau were all residents. Today, French writer Raymond Barre and Jean-Paul Belmondo both have houses on the peninsula.

GETTING THERE

– **From Nice**: there are a dozen buses a day, from Monday to Saturday. Some go to Beaulieu and do the tour of Cap Ferrat. The last bus to Nice from St Jean leaves at 7.35pm.

USEFUL ADDRESS

🛈 **Tourist office**: 59 avenue Séméria. ☎ 04-93-76-08-90. Fax: 04-93-76-16-67. Open in winter Monday to Friday 8.30am–noon and 1–5pm. Open in summer every day from 8.30am to 6pm.

WHERE TO STAY AND EAT

Surprisingly, there are some charming hotels at reasonable prices in this very exclusive and expensive town.

🛏 ✗ **La Bastide**: 3 avenue Albert-I. ☎ 04-93-76-06-78. Fax: 04-93-76-19-10. Closed at lunchtime on Monday, and from November to mid-December. Double rooms with shower and toilet between 300F and 400F. Half board compulsory in summer. Menus at 120F and 170F. Some may find the welcome a little restrained but the rooms are reasonably priced and some have nice sea views, particularly those upstairs. There's a small garden, and the owner prepares the Provençal-style food, which can be eaten on the terrace in the summer.

✗ **La Goélette**: in the port. ☎ 04-93-76-14-38. Closed on Tuesday (except in July and August) and in November and February. Menus at 99F and 159F. Tasty fish dishes, Spanish specialities such as *zarzuela* and paella, a selection of Provençal delicacies, including *aïoli* and *bouillabaisse*, and pizzas too. The choice is rather eclectic but it's well priced and well prepared.

☆☆☆☆ Très Chic

☎ **Le Clair Logis**: 12 avenue Centrale, on the corner with allée des Brises. Near the centre of the peninsula. ☎ 04-93-76-04-57. Fax: 04-93-76-11-85. Website: www.hôtel-clair-logis.fr. Closed between 15 November and 15 December and from mid-January to early March. Book at least three weeks ahead in summer. Double rooms with shower and toilet for 450F, with bath for 650F; 700F in high season. This villa, set in a lush enclosed garden in a peaceful residential area, extended its hospitality to General de Gaulle in 1952. The 18 rooms all have a balcony or a small terrace. The prices are quite high but reasonable, given the location. The perfect choice for a romantic weekend.

✕ **Le Sloop**: in the new port. ☎ 04-93-01-48-63. Closed on Tuesday evening, and all day Wednesday out of season; at lunchtime on Tuesday and Wednesday in summer; and from mid-November to mid-December. Set menu at 160F. This restaurant has a pleasant terrace facing the port. The welcome is warm and the food – *quenelles de sole à la pomme de terre* (sole quenelles with potatoes), *loup rôti entier à la niçoise* (roast bass niçois-style) or *côte de veau pignée de truffes dans son jus* (veal cutlet with truffles) – is sophisticated and good value for money. A great place to eat, although the service can be slow at times.

✕ **Le Skipper**: in the marina. ☎ and fax: 04-93-76-01-00. Closed Monday and Thursday morning between June and September and on Thursday evening out of season. Set menus at 100F (served until 2pm and 10pm) and 160F. This brasserie-style fish restaurant has a terrace overlooking the boats, and swift and friendly service.

WHAT TO SEE

★ **Villa Ephrussi de Rothschild**: high up in St-Jean, avenue Ephrussi de Rothschild. A 10-minute walk from the Corniche Inférieure, or take the St-Jean bus, which passes by the entrance. ☎ 04-93-01-45-90 Fax: 04-93-01-31-10. Open every day from 10am to 6pm (to 7pm in July and August). Closed at Christmas and New Year). Entrance fee: 50F. Visitors are free to wander around the villa and gardens, otherwise, there are 45-minute guided tours in season.

The magical pink and white Villa Île-de-France stands surrounded by seven wonderful gardens, based on different themes – Florentine, Spanish, Exotic, Japanese, French, English and Provençal. There's also a lapidary garden decorated with Romanesque capitals, arches and gargoyles, and the views from the grounds are spectacular. The villa combines both Venetian and Moorish architectural styles and is surrounded by magnolias and bougainvillea. The sea is visible from all sides of the patio, and the gardens appear to tumble into the deep blue water.

The villa was originally built for Béatrice de Rothschild, wife of wealthy banker Baron Ephrussi. She was a flamboyant and eccentric woman, who had a

THE COAST FROM NICE TO MENTON

collection of 50 wigs and was accustomed to dressing in pink from head to toe. She amused herself for seven years building the house and laying out the gardens, employing and dismissing dozens of architects and designers. Part of the house is supposed to resemble a ocean liner, to remind Baroness Ephrussi of a memorable journey aboard the *Île-de-France*. In 1934, she bequeathed the villa to the Académie des Beaux-Arts (the academy of fine arts); on her insistence, it has been kept more like a lived-in house than a museum.

The villa was built to house the Rothschilds' art treasures, acquired by experts despatched all over Europe by the fantastically rich family. Visitors enter via a covered patio, with several salons opening off it, adorned with works of art from different periods: splendid Louis XV and Louis XVI furniture, Beauvais and Aubusson carpets, ceilings painted by Pellegrin, Sèvres and Meissen porcelain, and paintings by Boucher and Fragonard. The Far East room is particularly impressive. The collection includes a laquered screen from Coromandel and other precious objects brought back from travels to China.

Outside, the French garden has a copy of the *Amour* (love) fountain in the Petit Trianon at Versailles, the Spanish garden features papyrus, dates and pomegranates. There are benches dotted around the grounds, and a *salon de thé* (tearoom) with a wonderful view over the sea, where you can enjoy a snack or a cup of tea in delightful surroundings. In the summer, the gardens provide a venue for cultural events and concerts.

Baroness Ephrussi lived in the completed villa for just three years, preferring to stay instead in one of her two residences in Monaco or in her suite of rooms at the Hôtel de Paris in Monte-Carlo, which she rented by the year.

★ **St-Jean-Cap-Ferrat**: this former fishing village is now an agreeable seaside and winter resort. Some of the original houses around the port remain, along with the small church. The Salle des Mariages (the room in the town hall where weddings are conducted) features a painting by Jean Cocteau, who was very fond of St-Jean. It gives a rather original view of the institution of marriage.

WALKS

– **Footpath to Pointe St-Hospice**: this path provides wonderful views of Beaulieu, Èze and Monaco, on the way to Pointe St-Hospice and Pointe du Colombier, before rejoining avenue Jean-Mermoz. The luxury villas are barely visible behind their high hedges.

– **Promenade Maurice-Rouvier**: footpath from the beach at St-Jean to Beaulieu.

– **Chemin des Contrebandiers** (smugglers' path): this path follows the coastline, so take care if the sea is rough. Leaving from the lighthouse, you can either take a 50-minute path towards Villefranche (to the right) and the Plage du Lido, or turn left towards La Carrière to join the route around Pointe St-Hospice via Port de St-Jean. Come back to the coastal path to Plage du Lido and make your way back towards the lighthouse. The longer route should take about four hours.

WHAT ELSE TO SEE

Stroll or drive around the quiet avenues of the peninsula, past well-manicured hedges hiding the villas, with their evocative names, 'Beware of the Dog' signs and security arrangements. Listen out for the sound of tennis ball on racket or the splash of swimmers in the pools behind the walls. Some of the villas are quite remarkable architecturally, with columns, balustrades and fountains, and superb views over the pine trees to the sea.

BEAULIEU-SUR-MER

Beaulieu derives its name from Napoleon, who is reputed to have exclaimed 'Qual bel luogo!' ('What a beautiful place!') on discovering the place. This is the 'pearl of the Côte d'Azur', and the last bastion of the Belle Époque, with a number of glamorous buildings from that era. Well sheltered by the belt of mountains that surrounds it, the town is one of the Riviera's warmest winter resorts – its palm-lined promenade quarter overlooking the Baie des Anges is even known as 'La Petite Afrique' (Little Africa).

Some interesting personalities have lived in Beaulieu. Gustave Eiffel, engineer of the Eiffel Tower, enjoyed the climate at the age of 90. Gordon Bennett, owner of the *New York Herald Tribune*, wanted to build a marina here at his own expense, but was refused permission. The port was not created until 1968. The **Baie des Fourmis**, surrounded by palms and immaculate gardens, has a charmingly old-fashioned atmosphere.

USEFUL ADDRESS

⊟ Tourist office: place Georges-Clemenceau. ☎ 04-93-01-02-21. Fax: 04-93-01-44-04. Website: www.ot-beaulieu-sur-mer. Open Monday to Saturday 9am–noon and 2–6pm (to 7pm and on Sunday morning in high season).

WHERE TO STAY AND EAT

⍨ Hôtel Riviera: 6 rue Paul-Doumer. In the port district. ☎ 04-93-01-04-92. Fax: 04-93-01-19-31. Email: m.hannoteaux@wanadoo.fr. Closed for All Saints. Double rooms between 170F and 280F, depending on level of comfort and season. This clean and peaceful hotel is run by friendly and helpful owners. It's good value for money, given its location, but don't expect four-star service. If you stay a few nights, the daily rate is reduced.

⍨ Hôtel Select: 1 place du Général-de-Gaulle. ☎ 04-93-01-05-42. Fax: 04-93-01-34-30. Closed in November. Double rooms from 280F to 320F, with shower or bath and

toilet. In the town centre, this cosy and friendly place is good value for money, although some of the rooms overlooking the square can be rather noisy. The owner is very friendly and loves the area. Enjoy breakfast on the terrace on the square. Stay six nights to get the seventh free.

⍨ Le Havre Bleu: 29 boulevard du Maréchal-Joffre. ☎ 04-93-01-01-40. Fax: 04-93-01-29-92. Email: hotel.lehavrebleu@wanadoo.fr. Open all year. Double rooms from 300F to 320F, with shower or bath and toilet. The décor is marine in theme and the 19th-century building has a white exterior with Matisse

THE COAST FROM NICE TO MENTON

blue shutters. There's a friendly and peaceful atmosphere, and some rooms have a pleasant, sunny terrace.

☆☆☆ Chic

☎ **Hôtel Comté de Nice**: 25 boulevard Marinoni. Five minutes from the beach and the port. Coming from Nice, carry straight on towards the market square. ☎ 04-93-01-19-70. Fax: 04-93-01-23-09. Double rooms from 395F to 580F, depending on season. Delicious breakfast for 48F. Garage parking. This pleasant, unassuming hotel has well-equipped rooms (with air-conditioning, TV, telephone, mini-safe, bathroom, toilet and hairdryer), a sauna and a gym. The welcome is friendly and warm.

✕ **L'African Queen**: in the marina. ☎ 04-93-01-10-85. Daily specials between 60F and 110F. Set menu on Sunday at 175F. This Beaulieu institution is an interesting and amusing restaurant, with a tropical theme. Huge salads and simple but tasty dishes are served by waiters in white shorts and a tie. The name of the restaurant stems from the owner's passion for the Bogart and Hepburn film, and the bill arrives in a video case of the film. Regulars and sometimes local celebrities enjoy it here.

WHAT TO SEE AND DO

★ **Villa Kerylos**: ☎ 04-93-01-01-44 or 04-93-01-61-70. Between 15 February and 11 November, open from 10.30am to 6pm; during July and August, open from 10.30am to 7pm. Between mid-December and 14 February, open 2–6pm; at the weekend and during the Christmas holidays, open from 10.30am to 6pm. Entrance fee: 40F (children and students 25F).

Archaeologist Théodore Reinach commissioned the building of Villa Kerylos on the Pointe de la Baie des Fourmis, in the style of a residence of Ancient Greece. The villa derives its name from *kerylos*, the Greek word for 'halcyon', a mythical bird of the sea considered to bring good luck. Authentic techniques and precious materials, including marble, ivory and bronze, were used to build the house and to create the mosaics and frescoes. All the details were copied faithfully from archaeological documents.

The villa is now a museum, with a collection of pieces from the sixth to first centuries BC. The garden reproduces the kind of setting that a Greek nobleman would have aspired to, with Mediterranean flowers, oleanders, olive and palm trees. There's a splendid view of Cap Ferrat, Baie des Fourmis and Cap-d'Ail. Gustave Eiffel was a neighbour of Reinach and a frequent visitor to his home.

★ On the left as you enter the town, the **Rotonde** is a legacy of the Belle Époque. A commemorative plaque describes how it was formerly the dining room of a large hotel, which was converted into a hospital during World War II. Today, it's the town's conference venue and, sadly, not open to visitors.

– **Promenade Maurice-Rouvier**: this path follows the shoreline to St-Jean-Cap-Ferrat. The views are spectacular and walking is easier in the cool of the afternoon.

– **Plateau St-Michel**: this path is rather steep so you'll need good calf muscles. Take the path that leaves from the boulevard Édouard-VII, below the Moyenne Corniche, and 45 minutes' walking should bring you to the Plateau St-Michel and its orientation chart.

MONACO (98000)   Population 30,000

The principality of Monaco is a small country with a big reputation. The old part of the town sits proudly on an impressive rock and is visited by hordes of tourists every year, many of whom come to see the traditional changing of the guard in front of the imposing palace. It also has a wonderful aquarium, a bijou opera-theatre, lots of souvenir shops, and a family of princes and princesses who are often in the pages of *Hello* magazine.

The best-known area of Monaco, **Monte-Carlo** is the 'Hong Kong of Europe', with a cosmopolitan population, Belle Époque palaces, a world-famous casino and highly prized (and highly priced) apartment blocks.

This tiny principality is an impossible dream for some, a contemporary fairytale for others and a dreadful soap opera for many.

History

Monaco's rock is a finger of land extending 792 metres (2,600 feet) into the sea and has always been on the wanted list, with its easily defended site and small sheltered port in a natural harbour. The Phoenicians first occupied it and constructed a temple to Melkart, which was then used by the Greeks for the worship of Heracles or Mono-ikos ('only god'), hence the name.

Monaco was invaded by the Goths, Lombards and Saracens before passing into the hands of the Genoese. The town's two key political parties were the Guelfs, allies of the Pope and the counts of Provence, and the Ghibellines, supporters of the German Empire. In 1297, a member of Genoa's Guelf party, Francesco Grimaldi the Spiteful, disguised himself as a friar and took over the Monaco fortress through his clever ruse. The Grimaldi crest (showing two sword-waving monks) has presided over the principality ever since. Charles I Grimaldi also acquired Menton in 1346 and Roquebrune in 1355. The Grimaldis found that ruling over Monaco wasn't always easy. Jean II was killed in 1505 by his brother Lucien, who later suffered a similar fate at the hands of his own nephew. In 1604, Honoré I was cast into the sea by his disgruntled subjects. Within the space of six centuries, Monaco changed allegiance several times, finding itself under the protection of Genoa, Savoy, Spain and France in turn.

In 1848, when Menton and Roquebrune declared themselves free towns. the principality was reduced to Monaco alone. Its economy was in trouble, so the ruling prince gave permission for a money-spinning gaming house to be opened. Monaco really took off – in 1861, the Société des Bains de Mer (the society of sea bathing) was created, the railway was extended to the principality, the magnificent Hôtel de Paris was constructed and wealthy high-rollers poured in. The prince was able to lift taxes, providing even more incentive to the super-rich. In 1872, the famous casino received 160,000 visitors.

In 1933, France and Italy both legalized gambling, putting an abrupt end to Monaco's monopoly. The principality continued to offer financial privileges to

THE COAST FROM NICE TO MENTON

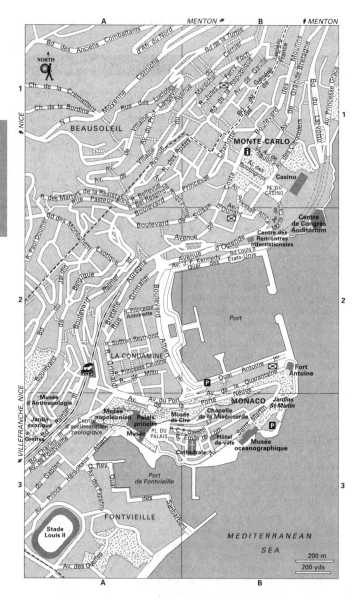

MONACO

overseas companies, however, who kept coming, until almost every scrap of land had been used up. After World War II, skyscrapers sprang up and new apartment blocks were built on land reclaimed from the sea. The current ruler Prince Rainier was the main architect of this extensive urban development, which has had its fair share of critics. According to some, it was wholly appropriate that his lovely wife – Hollywood actress Grace Kelly, whom he married in 1956 – happened to be the daughter of a bricklayer.

Monaco Today

Monaco tends to be associated with the social life of its princes and princesses, with Formula 1 racing and, in France, with its football team. However, the principality is about much more than that. The proportion of its revenue from gambling has declined from 95 per cent in 1890 to only 4 per cent today, but other industries have taken over to compensate for the decline. Every day, 15,000 people living over the border in France and Italy come to Monaco to work, and 83 per cent of its residents are from other countries (40 per cent from France).

The hereditary and constitutional monarchy operates with a national council that is renewed every five years, and a communal council, elected every four years. Only the 5,000 Monegasque subjects are eligible to vote, and they are exempt from both tax and from military service. Monaco is a country where the head of state is usually pretty popular!

Every year, millions of tourists come to Monaco, and its hotels are almost always full. A large number of visitors come here on business; with its new Palais des Congrès under the Hôtel de Paris, which hosts around 100 conferences a year, the principality now rivals Nice and Cannes as a congress town. The low crime level plays an important role in Monaco's success; the law courts are busier with divorce cases than with juvenile criminals. Police officers and surveillance cameras are very visible on the streets, and true Monegasques respect law and order. It's noticeable how local pedestrians never cross the road on a red light, and local drivers often give way to other cars and pedestrians.

The official language is French and the currency is the French franc (soon to be the euro). Postage stamps are Monegasque, and popular with collectors. Avoid visiting during the Grand Prix, when the streets are closed to traffic and only spectators in possession of a (very expensive) ticket may enter the town.

USEFUL ADDRESSES

Monaco tourist office (B1 on the map): 2A boulevard des Moulins, Monte-Carlo, 98030 Principality of Monaco. ☎ 00-377-92-16-61-16. Open Monday to Saturday from 9am to 7pm, and Sunday and public holidays from 10am to noon. There are six smaller annexes in the port and in town, which operate all day every day from 15 June to 30 September.

Beausoleil tourist office: 32 boulevard de la République. Opposite the town hall square. ☎ 04-93-78-01-55. Open Monday to Friday 9am–noon and 2–6pm. Underground parking in the Libération car park (first hour free).

Train station (A3 on the map): several trains a day to Nice or Menton. ☎ 08-36-35-35-35.

WHERE TO STAY

There are a few affordable places to stay in the principality, but it's much cheaper and nicer to stay in the surrounding area (Menton, Roquebrune and Cap-d'Ail) and come to Monaco for the day.

In Monte-Carlo

🛏 **Centre de la Jeunesse Princesse-Stéphanie** (youth hostel): 24 avenue Prince-Pierre. Near the train station. ☎ 00-377-93-50-83-20. Fax: 00-377-93-25-29-82. Open from 7am. Closed for two weeks in winter. Hostel beds at 80F per night, including breakfast and sheets; maximum stay of five nights in summer. This hostel is for 16–26-year-olds only (and for students up to the age of 31). The rooms are very clean and sleep four or ten. It fills up early each day in summer, but bookings are possible. There's a safe and a left luggage facility, as well as a pretty garden where you can enjoy a picnic.

In Monaco

🛏 **Hôtel de France**: 6 rue de La Turbie, near to the station. ☎ 00-377-93-30-24-64. Fax: 00-377-92-16-13-34. Room with shower and cable TV around 420F. Several rooms have been entirely renovated in a modern style, with bathrooms that look like boat cabins. Car park nearby. The restaurant next door, **Restaurant-pension de Tende**, serves tasty home-style cooking. ☎ 00-377-93-30-37-72.

🛏 **Hôtel Helvetica**: 1bis rue Grimaldi. ☎ 00-377-93-30-21-71. Fax: 00-377-92-16-70-51. Rooms from 290F to 410F (depending on facilities and season). Slightly old-fashioned but well-positioned hotel (upstairs), close to the port and place d'Armes. Nearly all 25 well-maintained rooms have shower or bathroom. Excellent value for money and a warm welcome.

In Beausoleil

In this unusual suburb, those living in houses with even numbers do not pay tax, but those at uneven numbers are in France and are subjected to French tax laws.

🛏 **Hôtel Villa Boeri**: 29 boulevard du Général-Leclerc. ☎ 04-93-78-38-10. Fax: 04-93-41-90-95. Open all year. Double rooms with shower from 250F, and from 325F with a bathroom. This nice little place, with its palm trees and its window-boxes full of geraniums, nestles among the tower blocks on the edge of the principality. The double rooms are air-conditioned and spacious, and there are glimpses of the sea from room Nos. 201, 202, 301 and 302.

🛏 **Hôtel Diana**: 17 avenue du Général-Leclerc, near the casino. ☎ 04-93-78-47-58. Fax: 04-93-41-88-94. Double rooms with shower for 290F, and 340F with bathroom. The green Belle Époque exterior of this hotel makes a welcome change from the concrete structures around it. All the rooms are air-conditioned and there's also a TV and a rather wobbly lift.

In the Surrounding Area

🛏 **Relais International de la Jeunesse** (youth hostel): Thalassa, boulevard de la Mer, 06320 Cap d'Ail. Take the pedestrian tunnel from the train station and follow signs until you reach the seafront. ☎ 04-93-78-18-58. Fax: 04-93-53-

35-88. Open between May and October. 75F per night, including breakfast and sheets in six- or eleven-bed dormitories. Half board for 140F. This hostel is in a wonderful position, at the very edge of the sea and next to the former home of Greta Garbo. There's a lively family atmosphere and you can book ahead on ☎ 04-93-81-27-63.

WHERE TO EAT

Monaco certainly has its gourmet restaurants, but it also has plenty of little places, particularly in the old part of town, with affordable menus and a great atmosphere.

✕ **La Cigale**: 18 rue de Millo. ☎ 00-377-93-30-16-14. Closed on Sunday and from mid-July to end August. Menus from 75F to 130F. This restaurant, just a stone's throw from the port and off the tourist trail, serves good food, particularly grilled fish.

✕ **Tony**: 6 rue Comte-Félix-Gastaldi. Close to the palace and overlooking two streets of the old town. ☎ 00-377-93-30-81-37. Closed on Saturday in low season and from 1 November to 27 December. Menus at 85F and 125F. Rather like a provincial bistrot. The proprietor is quite a character and the food is tasty and plentiful, including the *moules frites* (mussels and chips). The wine list is good, too.

✕ **Le Huit et Demi**: 4 rue Langlé, in Monaco. ☎ 00-377-93-50-97-02. Closed for lunch on Saturday and all day Sunday. Meals around 100F. Eat in the company of fishermen, traders and insurance brokers, in a friendly atmosphere. Tasty desserts.

☆☆ Moderate

✕ **Le Périgordin**: 5 rue des Oliviers, in Monte-Carlo. ☎ 00-377-93-30-06-02. Closed at lunchtime on Saturday, all day Sunday, and from 15 to 25 August. Dinner served until 10.30pm. Menus at 60F (week-day lunch) and from 100f to 180F. This restaurant is popular with young people, for its rich flavourful food at affordable prices. The *patron* is from the Périgord region and so fond of duck that he serves it in a whole range of delicious dishes, from terrine and *confit*, to escalope and *magret* (duck breast). There are also some excellent fish dishes on the menu. The often-packed dining room is decorated in pink.

☆☆☆ Chic

✕ **Café de Paris**: place du Casino, in Monte-Carlo. ☎ 00-377-92-16-20-20. Open until 2am. Around 250F (unless you get carried away). Edward VII was a frequent visitor at this very famous brasserie. It's just next door to the casino, so prices can be high, but a good risotto or some grilled fish may be affordable.

✕ **Polpetta**: 2 rue du Paradis, in Monte-Carlo. ☎ 00-377-93-50-67-84. Closed for lunch on Saturday and all day Tuesday, as well as for three weeks in June and October. Set menu at 150F. À la carte around 250F. Menus may include delicious pasta with truffles, scampi and other traditional Italian dishes. The Italian wines are excellent and affordable, and the atmosphere is very pleasant.

WHERE TO GO FOR A DRINK

❢ **Stars'n'Bars – Sports Bar and Club**: 6 Quai Antoine-I, on the port, facing Monte-Carlo. ☎ 00-377-93-50-95-95. Between 120F and 150F, with drinks. Known simply as 'Le Stars', this museum-restaurant-nightclub is popular with young people from all along the coast. An impressive collection of sports memorabilia includes items belonging to such great figures as André Agassi, David Coulthard, Michael Schumacher and Ayrton Senna, and even the bobsleigh of Monaco's own Prince Albert. Jetsetters enjoy it and Stevie Wonder, Julian Lennon, Peter Gabriel and Magic Johnson have apparently all been spotted here.

GETTING THERE

– **By car**: be aware that traffic jams start at the entrance to the principality in summer, particularly on the way in from the motorway. Leave the car in one of the many car parks provided. 'Des Pêcheurs' gives relatively easy access on foot to the old town.

– **By bus**: Line 1 goes to the casino from Monaco-Ville, Line 2 goes to the Jardin Exotique, and Line 4 from the train station in Monaco goes to the various beaches. Tickets valid for four or eight trips will save you money. More information: ☎ 00-377-93-50-62-41.

– **By train**: regular trains along the coast from Nice and Menton. ☎ 08-36-35-35-35.

WHAT TO SEE

The principality comprises **Monaco-Ville**, the old town on its rock, and **Monte-Carlo**, the quarter around the casino, linked by the harbour area and commercial district of **La Condamine**. To the west is the **Fontvieille** district. Some parts of Monaco are steep, but escalators and lifts operate free of charge between the different street levels.

Monaco's Old Town

Monaco is the capital of the principality, built on a rock promontory just 300 metres (985 feet) wide, which juts 800 metres (2,630 feet) out into the sea. The setting is superb and there's plenty to explore.

Start your walk from the pretty **place d'Armes**, with its arcades and colourful fish, fruit and flower market. Under cover, you'll find delicious cake shops and stalls selling cured meats, and a sort of bar selling sandwiches. From the square, you can see the wall surrounding the late 16th-century chateau, on the western tip of the rock.

The Rampe Major, built in 1714, gives access to the **place du Palais** (*see below*), via three town gateways, dating from the 16th and 17th centuries. The **Monte-Carlo Story** at the exit from the car parks is a 30-minute spectacle on the life of the royal family (best avoided). Visit instead the **Musée de Cire** (wax museum) (*see* page 710).

★ **Musée Océanographique** (oceanographic museum) (map B3): avenue

St-Martin. ☎ 00-377-93-15-36-00. Open every day (except during the Grand Prix) from 9.30am to 7pm (from 9am to 8pm in July and August). Entrance fee: 60F (half price for children and students). Allow three hours for the full tour. Monaco's fascinating clifftop oceanographic museum is one of the most famous and best of its genre in the world. It was founded in 1910 by Prince Albert I to house treasures collected during his many voyages. Marine explorer Jacques Cousteau was director here for 30 years, until 1988.

The museum's aquarium, in the basement, is home to rare marine plants and animals, and a collection of shells, coral and pearls. Ninety seawater-fed tanks hold some amazing fish, including a hairy-nosed sturgeon, a clawless crab and an 'invisible' plaice, as well as sharks, of course. A coral reef imported from the African Republic of Djibouti has continued to thrive in the aquarium in its own ecosytem.

The museum on the ground floor has a 20-metre (65-foot) whale, together with an explanation of how this giant creature functions and how baby whales grow by a gram per second. On the first floor, there's a life-sized model of a giant squid. The view from the second floor is spectacular.

★ **Jardins St-Martin** (B3 on the map): the restful gardens, with their amazing tropical vegetation, were laid out in the 1830s, looking out to sea and with their back to the cathedral.

★ **Place du Palais** (A3 on the map): impeccably clean, the square is full of people at 11.55am, when the changing of the Monegasque guard takes place. Their uniforms are black in winter and white in summer. There's a wonderful view from the square over the port, with Monte-Carlo and Italy on one side, and Fontvieille and the coastline to Cap d'Ail on the other. The cannons were given by Louis XIV to the Prince of Monaco. The barracks opposite the palace are Genoese in style.

★ **Palais Princier** (palace) (A3 on the map): open from June to end September from 9.30am to 6.30pm. Between 1 and 31 October, open from 10am to 5pm. Entrance fee: 30F. Photography prohibited. The palace stands on the site of a 13th-century fortress. All that remains is the isolated Serravale tower and part of the surrounding wall, built into the rock and enlarged under Vauban. The palace is entered by the impressive *cour d'honneur* (court of honour), surrounded by an arcaded gallery and paved with white and coloured pebbles. The splendid stairway leads to the Galerie d'Hercule (Hercules Gallery), decorated with 17th-century frescoes. The Salle du Trône (throne room) was the venue for the civil marriage ceremony of Prince Rainier and Grace Kelly. The sumptuous salons have lovely furniture and carpets, and paintings by such masters as Rigaud, Van Loo and Largillierre. A standard is raised on the main tower when the ruling prince is at home. The royal family's private rooms are not open to the public.

★ **Musée des Souvenirs Napoléoniens** (museum of Napoleonic memorabilia) (A3 on the map): place du Palais. Open every day in summer from 9.30am to 6.30pm. From 17 December to 31 May, open 10.30am–12.30pm and 2–5pm. From 1 October to 11 November, open from 10am to 5pm. Closed from 11 November to 16 December, and on Monday from December to end May. Entrance fee: 20F.

Installed in one of the wings of the palace, this museum was founded by Prince Rainier and combines local history with Napoleonic memorabilia – the Grimaldi and Bonaparte families share a family tree. There are hundreds of items belonging to Napoleon, together with busts of the emperor and his empress.

★ **Musée de Cire** (wax museum) (B3 on the map): 27 rue Basse. Between April and October, open every day from 9.30am to 6pm; in low season, open from 11am to 4pm. Entrance fee: 26F. Forty wax figures retracing the history of the Grimaldi family, displayed in 14th-century vaulted rooms.

★ The streets of the old town have had rather too much cosmetic surgery, although **rue Basse** retains much of its original appearance. There's certainly no shortage of shops; money is important here.

★ **Cathédrale** (B3 on the map): the neo-Romanesque church, built using white stone from La Turbie at the end of the 19th century, is unremarkable. What's more, the 13th-century church of St-Nicolas was destroyed to make way for it. Inside, however, there's an altarpiece by Bréa near the ambulatory, and a *Pietà* above the door of the sacristy. The majority of visitors come to see the tomb of Grace Kelly, which is often adorned with little bunches of flowers brought by locals.

LA CONDAMINE

The natural amphitheatre of La Condamine lies in the valley between the rock of Monaco and Monte-Carlo, beneath the rocky wall that dominates the principality. Sadly, property speculators have moved in here in force.

★ **The port**: constructed in 1901, the port of La Condamine harbours many splendid yachts. There's an Olympic pool nearby and a selection of snack bars selling affordable food.

★ **Église Ste-Dévote** (A2 on the map): dedicated to Monaco's patron saint, St Dévote, who was martyred in Corsica in AD 305. Her body was put in a boat that sailed by itself to Monaco, guided by a dove. In the 11th century the relics of the saint were stolen and taken away by ship. However, the culprits were caught and their vessel was set on fire. This event is re-enacted every 26 January, when a boat is burned in front of the church. The following day, there's a procession to the place du Palais. The church was built on the site of an 11th-century votive chapel and has an 18th-century marble altar.

MONTE-CARLO

★ **Casino** (B1 on the map): place du Casino. Entrance to gaming rooms: 50F. In its heyday, Monte-Carlo's casino was described as the 'cathedral of hell', and its twin towers were seen as representing the horns of the devil. The building is made up of a number of sections, the oldest one designed in 1878 by Charles Garnier, architect of the Paris Opéra. The decor is pretty sumptuous.

Access to the front of the central foyer is free, but you have to pay to see the gaming rooms, to the left, with their remarkable ceilings. There are slot machines, but gamblers can also indulge in games where the stakes are much higher. Fortunes are made and lost daily. In a three-day gambling spree in 1891, Charles Deville Wells turned $400 into $40,000, inspiring the song *The Man Who Broke the Bank at Monte-Carlo*.

The terrace of the casino has superb views of Monaco, the manmade beaches, swimming pools, palace hotels and, below, the vast conference centre. Wander through the casino's gardens and admire the wonderful facade of the **Hôtel de Paris**, which has played host to many celebrities, including Sarah Bernhardt, Queen Victoria, Winston Churchill (and his disappearing parrot) and Michael Jackson. In the past, rich families would take a suite of rooms in the hotel for a year. Today, high-rollers and other personalities stay just a few nights in this splendid establishment, where the prices are as opulent as the furnishings.

★ **Musée National** (Poupées et Automates d'Autrefois) (museum of antique dolls and automata) (B1, off the map): 17 avenue Princesse-Grace. In low season, open 10am–12.15pm and 2.30–6.30pm; in summer, open from 10am to 6.30pm non-stop. Entrance fee: 30F.

This museum is housed in Garnier-designed Villa Sauber, which stands in a pretty rose garden adorned with sculptures. The extraordinary collection of 19th-century automata and dolls used to belong to Mme de Galéa, a friend of Prince Rainier. There's also an enormous Neapolitan Christmas crib, large enough to hold 250 figurines.

★ **Opéra**: Charles Garnier designed the tiny opera-theatre in record time (five months), inspired by the new concepts in set design on show in Bayreuth. It became one of the most unusual in Europe, with its rectangular stalls and no balcony. The royal box looks as if it's suspended in mid-air. The red and gold interior of the building is quite charming.

Inaugurated on 25 January 1879 by Sarah Bernhardt, the opera saw the creation of many works, including Berlioz's *Faust* (1893) and *L'Enfant et les Sortilèges* by Maurice Ravel, in 1925. The greatest singers in the world have performed in the Salle Garnier, along with Diaghilev's innovative Ballets Russes, which first performed in 1909. Diaghilev was to be the key source of inspiration for the avant-garde movement over the next 20 years (interrupted only by war and revolution).

If you manage to buy one of the 600 sought-after tickets, do observe the dress code (to hire a dinner jacket, try **Ets Bourdin** at 5 rue Princesse-Caroline), and remember to stand up if the royal family arrives.

★ **Jardin Japonais** (Japanese garden): avenue Princesse-Grace. Open all year from 9am to sunset. Free entry. Relax in this wonderful natural world, with its waterfall (*taki*), ponds, cedar-wood tea house, and red curved footbridge, its colour symbolizing good luck and happiness. Emerge with a new sense of harmony.

WHAT ELSE TO SEE

★ **Jardin Exotique** (exotic garden) (A3, off the map): near the Moyenne Corniche. Bus No. 2 from the palace or the town centre. Open from 9am to 7pm (to 6pm in low season). Entrance fee: 39.50, also gives access to the Grottes de l'Observatoire and the Musée d'Anthropologie Préhistorique in season (*see below*). The view of the principality from the gardens is splendid.

Fragile tropical and sub-tropical plants flourish here and the extraordinary collection also includes 7,000 succulents, planted in the rock face.

★ **Grottes de l'Observatoire** (observatory caves): the caves are in the exotic garden, a little further down. Last visit at 6.10pm in summer; allow 40 minutes. One of the few places in Provence inhabited in the Palaeolithic era, you'll see a parade of stalactites and stalagmites here. This is the only cave in Europe where you get warmer instead of cooler as you descend.

★ **Musée d'Anthropologie Préhistorique** (museum of prehistoric anthropology): reached via the garden. This museum houses a collection of prehistoric tools, figurines and bones of prehistoric reindeer, mammoths, hippopotami and early humans.

THE MOYENNE CORNICHE

The Moyenne Corniche (middle coast road) from Nice to Menton (look for the signposts in front of Notre-Dame-du-Port in Nice), provides wonderful views. Its main attraction is the splendid village of Èze, one of the most dramatic of all the *villages perchés*.

ÈZE

Èze is the highest hilltop village in France, clinging to a rock at an altitude of 427 metres (1,400 feet) above sea level. It is said to derive its name from Isis, the Egyptian goddess to whom the Phoenicians built a temple. In fact, its history goes back to a time when the Ligurians settled a little further to the west, and their descendants in the Middle Ages sought refuge higher up on the rock, on the existing site. The village passed into the hands of the Romans and then the Saracens (and so on), but rarely by force. In the 12th century, the ramparts were built, only to be dismantled by Louis XIV. In the past, the villagers fought off the Ottomans and the French army – its attackers were often confused by the tight maze of flights of steps and alleys; today, the inhabitants simply close their shutters against the invading tourist crowds. Try to arrive early in the morning, to get the best out of Èze.

USEFUL ADDRESS

🅱 **Tourist office**: place du Général-de-Gaulle, at the entrance to the village, near the first car park. ☎ 04-93-41-26-00. Fax: 04-93-41-04-80. In summer, there's also an office in Èze-Bord-de-Mer. ☎ 04-93-01-52-00. Email: eze@webstore.fr. Daily guided tours of the village and of the Jardin Exotique (on request).

WHERE TO STAY

Campsite and *Gîte*

🏕 **Les Romarins**: Grande Corniche. As you leave Èze, take the D46 and then the Grande Corniche or the D2564 to the left; the site is 2 kilometres away. ☎ 04-93-01-81-64. Open from Easter to end September. 100F for two people with tent. The view over the sea from this tents-only site is wonderful. There's little shade, but the facilities are new and it's the only site in the area.

La Bergerie: at Col d'Èze, 2607 avenue des Diables-Bleus. ☎ 04-92-15-21-30. A unique *gîte*, set in splendid grounds and with wonderful views – and just 5 minutes from Monaco.

☆☆ Moderate

Hermitage du Col d'Èze: 2.5 kilometres from Èze via the D46 and the Grande Corniche. ☎ 04-93-41-00-68. Fax: 04-93-41-24-05. Hotel closed from 1 December to 31 January. Restaurant closed on Monday, and at lunchtime on Thursday and Friday; annual closure between 15 October and 15 February. Double rooms between 170F and 310F. Half board from 230F to 275F. Menus at 95F (weekday) and 190F. Breathtaking views over the Alps and down to the Mediterranean, a swimming pool, excellent food (using ingredients straight from the kitchen garden) and a well-priced wine list.

Hôtel du Golf: place de la Colette, in Èze-Village. ☎ 04-93-41-18-50. Fax: 04-93-41-29-93. Hotel open all year. Rooms from 230F to 260F. Menus at 90F and 125F. This little hotel at the edge of the Moyenne Corniche is easily recognizable by its pink exterior. The rooms are simple but spotless, and some have terraces. They can be a little noisy since they all overlook the road.

Auberge des Deux-Corniches: in Èze-Village, on the D46, 1 kilometre from the centre. ☎ 04-93-41-19-54. Fax: 04-92-10-86-26. Closed at lunchtime on Thursday and from early November to Easter. Pleasant double rooms, some with a balcony, cost 340F. This *auberge* just above Èze-Village has lovely sea views and guaranteed peace and quiet. The *patronne* welcomes guests warmly. Book ahead, especially in summer.

WHERE TO EAT

In Èze-Village

✕ **Le Nid d'Aigle**: 1 rue du Château. ☎ 04-93-41-19-08. Closed on Wednesday, and from 10 January to 10 February, this restaurant has menus at 140F and 190F. Next door to the Jardin Exotique on the summit of the rock, overlooking the rooftops of Èze. Its terraces are surrounded by vines and trees, one of which (a mulberry) is over 300 years old. The food is Provençal, including such dishes as *daurade au pistou* (traditional beef stew).

☆☆☆ Chic

✕ **Le Troubadour**: 4 rue du Brec, as you climb up into the old village. ☎ 04-93-41-19-03. Closed all day Sunday and for lunch on Monday, as well as from 24 November to 20 December, during the February holidays, and from 1 to 10 July. Menus at 125F (lunch), 175F and 250F. Highlights include *fricassée de homard aux asperges* (lobster with asparagus), *filet d'agneau pané aux truffes* (lamb fillets with truffles), and honey and nougat ice-cream to finish. The atmosphere is friendly and the decor an interesting combination of rustic and luxury.

☆☆☆☆ Très Chic

✕ **Château Eza**: at the top of the village. ☎ 04-93-41-12-24. Closed on Tuesday and Wednesday in winter, and from All Saints to Christmas. Set menu at lunchtime at 250F, with wine and coffee. This former royal residence used to belong to King William of Sweden and is a collection of medieval houses linked together. A double room here costs a king's ransom, but the beds are enormous, the balconies overlook the sea and the breakfast is fit for both a king and queen. Alternatively, enjoy an unforgettable lunch on the terrace, with its magnificent panorama. The interesting menu includes *carpaccio de thon* (marinated tuna steak), *fricassée de lapin* (rabbit stew), *râble farci aux champignons des bois* (saddle of hare stuffed with wild mushrooms) and homemade *tiramisu*. Or you can plump for a more popular (and cheaper) alternative: a tomato and mozzarella salad with a glass of wine. The service is rather more relaxed than you might expect from an establishment of this calibre.

WHAT TO DO

★ **Old streets**: the old village is entered via an impressive fortified double gateway, which leads to a cluster of ancient and restored buildings in a maze of narrow, sometimes vaulted, sometimes stepped streets. The layout of the village is circular. Window-boxes and small gardens add splashes of colour to the old stonework.

In the evening, after all the tourists have gone, the village regains a quiet and peaceful atmosphere, enjoyed only by those lucky visitors who have a room at the Château Eza or La Chèvre d'Or.

★ **Église Notre-Dame-de-l'Assomption**: the attractive classical facade of the church, rebuilt in the 18th century, contrasts with the magnificence of its nave. It's a fine example of Niçois baroque architecture. Inside, an arm brandishing a crucifix emerges from the pulpit. The church itself seems to be strangely cut off from the village itself, and the houses are hidden from view by the rock. On the other side of the church square is the cemetery, with its view of the mountains. The tomb of French actor Francis Blanche bears the epitaph: 'Let me sleep, it's what I was born for!'

★ **Fragonard** and **Galimard**: the two perfume factories on the Moyenne Corniche can be visited free of charge, together with the Galimard museum, soap factory and outlet. Guides explain the different processes involved in the manufacture of perfumes and soap before letting visitors loose in the shop where products are sold at factory prices.

★ **Chapelle des Pénitents-Blancs**: the Chapelle de la Ste-Croix (its real name) dates from 1306 and is probably the oldest building in the parish. It houses a *Crucifixion* by the school of Bréa and an *Adoration of the Magi* by the Italian school. In the 14th-century *Madone des Forêts*, the baby Jesus holds, unusually, a pine cone.

★ **Jardin Exotique** (exotic gardens): open in winter 9am–noon and 2–6.30pm, and in summer, from 8.30am to 8pm. Entrance fee: 15F. These gardens contain an impressive collection of exotic plants, including some huge cacti. But they are worth visiting above all for the panoramic view, from the castle ruins at the top, over the Riviera and on a good day as far as the island of Corsica.

★ **Sentier Frédéric-Nietzsche** (footpath): this one-hour scenic route (formerly a mule path) links Èze-Bord-de Mer (or, to be more precise, the beach) with Èze-Village, through olive trees and pine woods. It's named after the philosopher, because he was inspired when following the path to write the third part of his *Thus Spake Zarathustra* – he described it as the 'painful climb up to the marvellous village of Èze, built in the middle of the rocks'. Alternatively, a number of buses run between Èze-Plage and Èze-Village from mid-May to mid-September.

★ **Astrorama**: observatory on the crest of the Grande Corniche (*see below*). The permanent museum holds *ciel ouvert* ('open sky') evenings, when visitors can observe the sky through telescopes. They take place between October and April on Tuesday and Friday from 6.30pm. Between May and September, the evenings are held every day (except Sunday) from 5.30pm. In high season, they happen every day. The site is spectacular.

★ **Parc de la Revère**: carry on along the Grande Corniche. The national park of La Revère is an ideal place for a day out. Take a one-hour walk along the *sentier botanique* (botanical path) to find out more about typically Mediterranean flora and the geology of the plateau. The **Maison de la Nature** (nature centre) is open on Wednesday (☎ 04-93-41-24-36). There's a 360 panorama of the Mediterranean, and of the hinterland as far as the Parc du Mercantour. The Fort de la Revère was the site of two of the most important escapes of World War II, including one involving around 60 British prisoners in 1942.

The **museum** (opposite the buildings) is the starting point for two pleasant walks. To the left, the path skirts the fort to the north and heads back to the car park or continues to the Astrorama (*see above*). The other path (to the right) leads to the Massif de la Forna in around 90 minutes, with magnificent views.

★ At **Èze-Bord-de-Mer** there's a pebbled and rocky beach, sometimes used by naturists. Park on the road.

FESTIVALS

– **Èze d'Antan** (Èze of yesteryear): a weekend of turning back the clock, every year at the end of July, with a programme of events and costumes.

– **Tremplin du Rire**: festival of comedy held every year at the beginning of August.

THE GRANDE CORNICHE

The Grande Corniche partly follows the route of the ancient Via Julia Augusta. The views are spectacular and occasionally precipitous.

LA TURBIE

The small town of La Turbie is famous for its 'Trophée des Alpes' (Trophy of the Alps), a commemorative monument that is a masterpiece of Roman art. The Romans' name for it was *Tropea Augusti* (Augustus' Trophy), which eventually became 'La Turbie'. The duke of Savoy used the high vantage point of La Turbie for surveillance over Monaco. Unfortunately, these days, houses are springing up here, as everywhere else along the coast.

GETTING THERE

– **From Nice**: buses depart at 10.45am, 2.15pm, 5.30pm and 6.30pm druing the week. The journey takes 40 minutes. No buses on Sunday. Return from La Turbie at 7.10am, 8am, 1.20pm and 5.20pm.

– **From Monaco**: buses leave at 7.40am, 10.30am, 12.05pm, 5pm and 6.20pm during the week. On Saturday, buses only leave in the morning, and there are no buses on Sunday.

USEFUL ADDRESS

■ **Town Hall**: ☎ 04-93-41-10-10.

WHERE TO STAY AND EAT

🛏 ✕ **Hôtel-restaurant Le Napoléon**: 7 avenue de la Victoire. ☎ 04-93-41-00-54. Fax: 04-93-41-28-93. ♿ Closed from 20 November to 20 December, and on Sunday evening in low season. Double rooms with bath and toilet between 400F and 450F. Menus between 70F and 155F. This building has an attractive pink facade with green shutters. Some of the very comfortable, spotless rooms overlook the garden and others have a terrace. There's a view of the Roman monument from the second floor.

WHAT TO SEE

★ **Old town**: access to the old part of town is through the western gateway and the rue Comte-de-Cessole, the former Via Julia Augusta, which climbs up towards the monument. Some verses from Dante's *Divine Comedy* describing the village are inscribed on a plaque on one of the towers. In the narrow vaulted alleys, medieval, classical and baroque styles stand side by side. There are many well-restored old houses, such as the one at the corner of rue de l'Empereur-Auguste and rue Droite, and along the rue Dominique-Durandy. Some vestiges of the medieval surrounding wall remain.

★ **Trophée des Alpes**: walk to the monument across the old village. ☎ 04-93-41-10-11. From 1 June to 30 September, open from 9am to 7pm; from 1 April to 31 May, open from 9am to 6pm and from 1 October to 31 March, open from 9.30am to 5pm. Closed on Monday in winter. This is the finest Roman monument in the region, built out of local white stone to commemorate the victory by Augustus in 13 BC over 44 fractious Ligurian tribes. In 6 BC, the Senate ordered the construction of a temple on the highest point of the route that had been created during the military operations, a strategic site on the Aurelian Way. It was completed in 5 BC.

After the Romans left, the monument was used first as a fortress, then as a quarry, and a number of its stones provided material for the construction of the church of St-Michel. In the Middle Ages, apparently, anxious husbands came from far and wide to consult the trophy, which was reputed to contain an oracle that could enlighten them about their wife's fidelity, or otherwise.

Restoration did not begin until 1920, with the intervention of a philanthropic American called Edward Tuck. What visitors see today are not ruins, but a reconstruction. The original trophy was 50 metres (165 feet) high, but the reconstruction measures only 35 metres (115 feet), and a large part of the monument has been left incomplete.

It is possible to climb to the top of the monument, if enough visitors want to. Alternatively, visit the museum that retraces the history of the trophy and houses a reconstructed model, together with drawings. There's a lovely garden, too; picnickers are encouraged to take care of the environment.

★ **Raised terraces**: follow the small path from the far side of the grounds in which the trophy stands for a huge panoramic view over the entire Riviera. It's a 400-metre (1,312-foot) drop down to Monaco and the skyscrapers of Monte-Carlo.

★ **Église St-Michel**: the lovely elliptical 18th-century church has a sumptuous baroque interior. The altar is made from 17 different types of marble, there are two 17th-century triptychs in the choir, and a glittering onyx and agate communion table. The window shows the head of the martyred St Vincent and the paintings housed in the church are attributed to, or are by the schools of, Raphaël (*St Mark writing the Gospel*), Veronese and Rembrandt. There's also a painting by Van Loo.

ROQUEBRUNE-CAP-MARTIN

This hilltop village above the Grande Corniche is dominated by a Carolingian fortress at its summit, the only example of its kind in France to remain practically intact. Ancient streets redolent with history lead up to the feudal chateau. The tall houses, many beautifully restored, peaceful squares, vaulted alleys and pretty fountains of the village have been joined in recent years by the inevitable array of souvenir shops.

Picturesque rue Moncollet, tunnelled out of the rock, is particularly interesting, with its long vaulted passageways and steps, and medieval houses with barred windows. The pretty place des Deux-Frères (two brothers square) owes its name to the two rocks that frame it; the view from the square is a dizzying one across the rooftops and over the bay.

In Roquebrune, as in most of the Côte d'Azur, arrive as early as possible to avoid the tourist groups, have a nap in the afternoon and then come back when the streets are deserted.

USEFUL ADDRESS

🄱 **Tourist office**: 218 avenue Aristide Bruant (next to the market square). ☎ 04-93-35-62-87. Fax: 04-93-28-57-00. Open Monday to Saturday 9am–12.30pm and 2–6pm. Between June and September, open until 6.30pm and on Sunday morning. In summer, open every day 9am–1pm and 3–7pm.

WHERE TO STAY AND EAT

🛦 ✗ **Les Deux Frères**: in the village. ☎ 04-93-28-99-00. Fax: 04-93-28-99-10. Closed at lunchtime in high season, on Sunday evening and all day Monday out of season, and from mid-November to mid-December. Rooms for 595F. Menus from 120F (lunch) to 245F. Located at the entrance to the village on an imposing belvedere, this recently re-novated hotel-restaurant offers its customers the good life. The views are wonderful and the regional cuisine combines top-quality produce with imagination.

✘ **Les Tables du Berger**: 4 rue Victor-Hugo-Cannolès. ☎ 04-93-57-40-60. Closed on Sunday evening and all day Monday, as well as from mid-July to mid-August. *Rapide* menus from 65F to 95F (week-day lunch), and other menus at 145F and 180F. This romantic rest-aurant specializes in cheese dishes, but there's plenty to tempt non-cheese lovers, including *foie gras poêlé aux pommes* (pan-fried foie gras with apples). The wine list is impressive, too.

✘ **La Roquebrunoise**: 12 avenue Raymond-Poincaré. At the entrance to the old part of the village, oppo-site the car park. ☎ and fax: 04-93-35-02-19. Closed on Monday and Tuesday lunchtime, as well as from November to January (except during New Year festivities). Set menu at 115F. À la carte between 150F and 200F. This restaurant is on the first floor of a pink building and its tables

on the large terrace have a specta-cular view over the sea and the village. Dishes from the interesting and well-priced menu include *terrine aux raisins secs* (terrine with raisins), *daube façon bonne maman* (tradi-tional beef stew) and *soufflé glacé au Grand Marnier* (iced soufflé with Grand Marnier).

☆☆☆☆ Très Chic

⬧ **Hôtel Diodato**: Pointe de Cabbé. ☎ 04-92-10-52-52. Fax: 04-92-10-52-53. Closed from November to mid-December. Double rooms from 650F to 880F. Half board between 450F and 660F. Menus at 140F and 190F. At the foot of the medieval village, on a rocky promontory over-looking the sea, this is a charming venue. Housed in a former holiday home, which used to belong to Russian aristocrats, 30 very com-fortable rooms have TV and air-conditioning. There's also a swim-ming pool and private access to the sea. The simple and excellent cuisine is based on fresh seasonal market produce, and can be en-joyed on the perfect terrace.

WHAT TO SEE AND DO

★ **Chateau**: open 10am–12.30pm and 2–5pm (to 7.30pm in summer). Entrance fee: 20F (children and students half price).

The castle at Roquebrune has had a turbulent history. Built in 970 by Conrad I, Count of Ventimiglia, to ward off a Saracen attack, it belonged in the 14th century (along with the rest of the village) to the Grimaldis. It was confiscated in 1793, but in 1808 five citizens of Roquebrune procured it at auction for the princely sum of 490F. Wealthy Englishman Sir William Ingram became one of the first tourist residents in the village when he bought the property in 1911; he subsequently donated the building to the town in 1926.

On the first floor of the *donjon* (keep) is the ceremonial hall and, below, a storeroom carved out of the rock. On the second floor is the small guardroom with a prison on the right (used only during the time of the Grimaldi – before, there was a minuscule prisoner's cell right underneath the keep) and the archers' dormitory. The third floor houses the baronial apartments, including the reception hall, the simply furnished living room, and the kitchen with its olivewood chimney hood and its bread oven. The fourth floor affords a wonderful view over the picturesque rooftops in the foreground, and Cap Martin and Monaco from the upper artillery platform.

★ **Église Ste-Marguerite**: open from 3pm to 6pm. This pink and orange church was originally built in the 13th century but was extended in the 16th century and 'baroqued' in the next. It houses two interesting paintings, a *Resurrection* and a *Pietà* by the 17th-century Roquebrune artist Marc-Antoine Otto. There's a copy of the *Last Judgement* by Michelangelo, 54 times smaller than the original in the Sistine Chapel.

★ **Le Corbusier's tomb**: before heading to the *olivier millénaire*, one of the oldest olive trees in the world (*see below*), take the steps to the left leading to the cemetery. The view over Cap Martin is worth seeing (*see below*). In avenue 'H' on the right is the tomb of the architect Le Corbusier and his wife, designed by Le Corbusier himself. He lived in Roquebrune for many years before drowning in the sea in 1965.

★ **L'olivier millénaire** (ancient olive tree): chemin de St-Roch, just after you leave the village. The tree is 10 metres (35 feet) in circumference and is thought to be over 1,000 years old.

★ **Cap Martin**: with luxury homes hidden among the pines, olive trees and mimosas, Cap Martin is a rich, almost miraculously well-preserved suburb of Menton. One of the first of the illustrious figures to live here was Empress Elisabeth of Austria, or Sissi, who installed herself in the Grand Hôtel in Roquebrune-Cap-Martin just after it was built. There were no villas in the area at the time and the empress enjoyed frolicking unnoticed in the countryside and getting lost on the old mule paths. Napoleon's wife, Empress Eugénie, often accompanied Sissi on her walks; she lived to the ripe old age of 94, so all that fresh air obviously did her some good. Other famous tourists who followed in their footsteps included Winston Churchill and Le Corbusier.

The eastern side of the Cap has a very pretty road with wonderful views over Menton and Italy. Ask at the tourist office for walking maps.

★ **Promenade Le Corbusier and his cabin**: this is a lovely walk around the cape along a former customs officers' path that hugs the sea and passes through some fascinating and typically Mediterranean flora. Le Corbusier built a cabin here on the side of the rock; it was a sort of minimalist holiday unit or an early version of a Club Med hut! It measured 3.66 metres (12 feet) on each side and its furnishings were strictly limited – functionality was all-important. It is open to visitors; meet at the tourist office on Tuesday at 10am or on Friday at 2.30pm. ☎ 04-93-35-62-87. Guided tours: 30F.

FESTIVALS AND EVENTS

Roquebrune is famous for its traditional annual processions.

– **Procession de la Passion**: every 5 August, 500 locals take part in staging Christ's Passion, to honour a promise made to the Virgin, who saved the town from plague in 1467. The procession attracts huge numbers of pilgrims and tourists.

– **Procession des Limaces**: dating from 1315, this procession is held on the Thursday of Fête-Dieu (Corpus Christi) in June. The streets are lit with little lamps made of snail shells (*limassa* in the Provençal dialect) filled with olive oil, with a small cotton wick burning in them. Locals dressed as disciples and legionnaires take part in a procession and then recreate the entombment of Christ.

– **Festival de Théâtre**: at the end of June, plays are held on the square of the chateau as part of the theatre festival.

A **dance festival** takes place in July, and **musical evenings** are held throughout July and August.

MENTON (06500)   Population: 29,300

The sedate town of Menton is literally at the end of France, but it sometimes feels like another world altogether, with its extraordinarily mild climate – lunch may often be eaten outdoors in December – and its mountains which seem to tumble into the sea. The most Italianate of French resorts, it has great charm, with its old town and cemetery, its squares lined with plane trees, its bars serving *pastis*, its colourful market and its elegant seafront promenade. Lemon and mandarin trees grow all over town; in season, they are laden with the fruits that thrive so well in this climate. There's even a lemon festival in February.

It may be a long time since the grand seafront residences – the Orient, the Winter Palace and the Riviera – were first converted into apartment buildings, but there's still a fine whiff of nostalgia in Menton's fine gardens. You could easily spend a whole day doing a tour of them all. The grounds of the Villa Fontana Rosa and the greenhouse of La Madone are particularly impressive.

Beach lovers should remember two important tips about Menton. First, rise and shine early, and head to the beach as soon as possible to secure a good spot, and second, bring a mattress and plastic sandals, because the pebbles are rather uncomfortable for walking!

History

In 1346, Charles Grimaldi of Monaco bought the town of Menton, 10 years before acquiring Roquebrune. As early as 1466, the first revolt occurred in Menton and the locals allied themselves with the Duke of Savoy. Two years later, the Duke of Milan, Galeazzo Maria Sforza, took over the town, only to return it to Lambert Grimaldi in 1477. In 1524, the Treaty of Burgos placed the area under Spanish protectorship, since Grimaldi had embraced the cause of Charles V. In 1641, the Treaty of Péronne returned Menton to French rule because of 'turncoat' Honoré II Grimaldi.

The seemingly constant changes in allegiance didn't prevent the development of the town. New roads were built and local noble families (including de Brea, Massa and de Monléon) put their money into lovely private mansions. The St-Michel church was built between 1640 and 1653.

During the French Revolution, the principality was re-appropriated. In 1793, it became part of the department of Alpes-Maritimes but in 1814 the Treaty of Paris returned it once again to the Grimaldis!

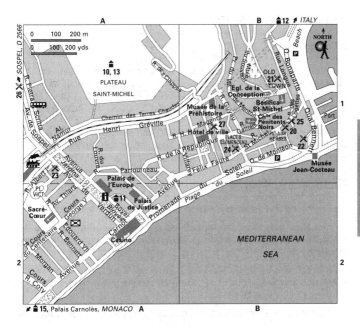

MENTON

■ Useful Addresses		13	Camping municipal
ℹ	Tourist office	15	Hôtel Prince de Galles
🚂	Train station		
🚌	Coach station	✕ **Where to Eat**	
✉	Post office	20	Le Chaudron
		21	A Braïjade Meridiounale
⌂ **Where to Stay**		22	Le Pistou
		23	Le Terminus
10	Auberge de Jeunesse (youth hostel)	24	Ou Pastré
11	Hôtel Chambord	26	Le Midi
12	Hôtel Napoléon	27	Oh! Matelot

In 1848, Menton and its neighbour Roquebrune declared their independence, under the protection of the Sardinian government. This status endured until 1860, when the people voted to unite with France, and Prince Charles III of Monaco sold his claims on the towns to Emperor Napoleon.

Today, the town is still a popular resort with a number of prestigious visitors, such as Gustav V of Sweden, Queen Astrid of Belgium and the King of Wurtemberg.

USEFUL ADDRESSES

🅱 **Tourist office** (A2 on the map): Palais de l'Europe, 8 avenue Boyer, BP 239, 06506 Menton Cedex. ☎ 04-92-41-76-50 or 04-92-41-76-76. Fax: 04-92-41-76-78. In winter, open Monday to Saturday 8.30am–12.30pm and 1.30–6pm; in summer, open Monday to Saturday from 8.30am to 6.30pm and on Sunday from 10am to noon. Provides maps of the town and lists of hotels.

🚌 **Coach station** (A1 on the map): avenue de Sospel. ☎ 04-93-28-43-27. Rapides Côte d'Azur: ☎ 04-93-85-64-44. Autocars Breuleux: ☎ 04-93-35-73-51.

🚆 **Train station** (A1 on the map): near the coach station. ☎ 08-36-35-35-35.

GETTING AROUND

Several buses and trains link Menton to all the towns on the Côte d'Azur.

– **From Nice**: buses depart every 20 minutes. Rapides Côte-d'Azur: ☎ 04-93-55-24-00. Buses depart from the coach station into the hinterland regularly.

– **To Èze**: buses to Nice leave every 15 minutes. Alight in front of the casino in Monaco and take a bus from there (they run every two hours but not on Sunday or public holidays).

– **To Sospel**: buses leave from the coach station at 9.30am, 2pm and 6pm.

From Sospel: buses leave the market square at 7am, 1pm and 4.30pm. The journey takes 50 minutes. Note: departures from Menton at 2pm and from Sospel at 1pm take place only on Tuesday, Wednesday, Thursday and Saturday.

The 6pm bus from Menton and the 12.45pm bus from Sospel meet the trains to Breil, Saorge, Saint-Dalmas, Tende, etc.

– **To Ste-Agnès**: one bus leaves in the morning and there are two in the afternoon. The last bus from Ste-Agnès departs at 5.05pm.

– **To Roquebrune-Cap-Martin**: there are four daily departures from the coach station. For Roquebrune-Village, take the TUM bus No. 3, Pont de l'Union. Alight at the BP petrol station. There are four buses every day (except Sunday and public holidays).

WHERE TO STAY

Campsites

⛺ **Camping municipal St-Michel** (A1, **13** on the map): Plateau St-Michel. ☎ 04-93-35-81-23. Open from 1 April to mid-October. In high season, a small tent for two people costs 70F. Take the minibus from the coach station. If you're driving, take the route des Ciappes et de Castellar from the town hall in Menton (in the centre). If you're coming by foot from the coach station, follow the route des Terres-Chaudes to the left of the avenue de la Gare and then take the steps, from where you'll enjoy a wonderful view. There are 130 pitches, but you can't make a booking. Arrive as early as possible to secure a site, and enjoy sleeping under the eucalyptus and olive trees. There's not a great deal of shade but the smell is glorious! There's also an outdoor laundry, you can buy food, enjoy a snack, and the bar is very friendly.

▲ If it's full try **Campings de Gorbio.** It's not luxurious but it does have a view to Italy.

✩ Budget

▲ **Auberge de jeunesse** (youth hostel) (A1, **10** on the map): Plateau St-Michel. By car, take the route des Ciappes et de Castellar near the town hall (or follow the signposts for the campsite). A minibus runs from the bus station, or take bus No. 6 from the train station. ☎ 04-93-35-93-14. Fax: 04-93-35-93-07. Closed from noon to 7pm, and from 15 November to 1 February. Around 70F a night in an eight-bed dormitory, including breakfast and shower. Over-26s need to join the association, for 100F. Dinner for just 50F. There are 80 beds. Booking is not possible by phone, so arrive early in the morning to secure a place. The hostel has a great view.

✩✩✩ Chic

▲ **Hôtel Chambord** (A2, **11** on the map): 6 avenue Boyer. In the heart of the town, next to the casino. ☎ 04-93-35-94-19. Fax: 04-93-41-30-55. Rooms from 500F to 680F,

depending on season. A friendly, family-run establishment, popular with its regulars. The twin-bed rooms have the best view over the gardens. All rooms are spacious and very comfortable with bathrooms, toilet and TV. The hotel is a stone's throw from the sea and near the tennis club. Parking available for a charge.

▲ **Hôtel Napoléon** (B1, **12**, off the map): 29 porte de France, in Garavan bay. ☎ 04-93-35-89-50. Fax: 04-93-35-49-22. Closed from mid-November to mid-December. Double rooms between 400F (mountain view) and 680F (sea view). À la carte meals from 180F to 200F. The hotel has unassuming 1960s–70s exterior, but inside there are several references to its namesake (the Emperor). The rooms are spacious and comfortable, most have a sea view and some have a terrace. Breakfast is served either in your room or by the pool. The staff are friendly and obliging. Private beach open between April and October.

▲ **Hôtel Prince de Galles** (A2, **15**, off the map): 4 avenue du Général-de-Gaulle. ☎ 04-93-28-21-21. Fax: 04-93-35-92-91. Single rooms from 250F and doubles from 360F to 510F (mountain view) and from 420F to 590F (sea view). Menus from 105F to 150F. This hotel is by the sea, towards Roquebrune, and is charming, friendly and comfortable.

WHERE TO EAT

✕ **Le Chaudron** (B1, **20** on the map): 28 rue St-Michel. ☎ 04-93-35-90-25. Closed on Tuesday in summer; on Tuesday evening and all day Wednesday for the rest of the year; for the first two weeks in July; and from 28 October to 28 December. Menus between 95F (weekday) and 145F. In the heart of Menton,

this small restaurant serves fresh and pleasant Provençal cuisine in an air-conditioned room or at tables outside in the pedestrianized street. Regulars enjoy *mousse de courgettes glacée et son coulis de tomates* (iced courgette mousse with tomato coulis), or *filet de St-Pierre aux petits légumes* (John Dory with vegetables). Warm welcome guaranteed.

⊁ **A Braïjade Meridiounale** (B1, **21** on the map): 66 rue Longue. ☎ 04-93-35-65-65. Open every evening in summer and at lunchtime every day (except Wednesday) in low season. Closed from mid-November to mid-December. Huge choice of menus from 115F (weekday lunch) to 265F. The rustic dining room has exposed stonework and an open fire where marinated meats are grilled. Provençal cuisine includes *daube de boeuf niçoise aux ravioles* (beef stew) and *aïoli niçois* (garlic mayonnaise feast). The service is extremely friendly.

⊁ **Le Pistou** (B1, **22** on the map): 9 quai Gordon-Bennett, in the old port. ☎ 04-93-57-45-89. Closed on Monday. Set menu at 88F. À la carte around 170F. This stylish place promotes local produce and cuisine, serving delicious Provençal dishes at reasonable prices, including *fleurs de courgettes farcies* (stuffed courgette flowers), *soupe au pistou* (basil and garlic flavoured soup) or *lapin à la provençale* (rabbit cooked local style). The homemade ravioli is excellent.

⊁ **Le Terminus** (A1, **23** on the map): place de la Gare. ☎ 04-92-10-49-80. Closed on Saturday and on Sunday evening. Menus from 55F to 160F. Customers can eat either on the pleasant terrace or in the dining room, which is decorated with turn-of-the-century posters. Try the *beignets de fleurs de courgettes* (deep-fried courgette flowers), *tripes à la génoise* (Genose-style tripe), *buf à la provençale* (beef Provençal style) and *tarte au citron* (lemon tart). The restaurant is full of atmosphere, and the food is typical of Menton, but the hotel lacks any particular charm.

⊁ **Ou Pastré** (B1, **24** on the map): 9 rue Trenca and 9 rue St-Michel. ☎ 04-93-57-29-58. Open almost all hours. Closed on Thursday in low season (except during school holidays). Menus at 95F and 115F. The pizza oven at this rustic-style eating place keeps going for hours and they carry on serving their fresh pasta, in little skillets, into the small hours. The prices are very reasonable and the staff are characterful.

⊁ **Le Midi** (B1, **26**, off the map): 103 avenue de Sospel. Out of the centre, towards Sospel and the motorway. ☎ 04-93-57-55-96. Closed on Sunday and Wednesday evenings. Menus at 75F (weekday lunch) and 140F. À la carte around 200F. Traditional Mentonnais cooking, with such dishes as *pan d'anchoue braija, frichaïa de sucan, barba juan, pichade, picate* (medallions of veal with ceps or lemon). The *Assiette du Midi* invites customers to taste local specialities. The *formule* menu is excellent, too, featuring lots of small dishes and a delicious homemade tart. A family-run restaurant that is certainly worth a detour.

⊁ **Oh! Matelot** (B1, **27** on the map): place Lorédan-Larchey. ☎ 04-93-28-45-40. Open every day (except on Sunday in winter). Closed in January. Speedy lunches for around 50F or an all-inclusive *formule buffet* at 100F, on summer evenings. A breath of fresh air in Menton, with its all-wood terrace, looking like the bridge of a cruise ship. The self-service buffet is Club Med-style, the *matelot* menu includes *bruschetta*, and there's also a choice of sandwiches and other snacks.

WHERE TO STAY AND EAT IN THE AREA

🛏 ✕ **Auberge Pierrot et Pierrette**: place de l'Église. At the entrance to the village of Monti, about 5 kilometres (3 miles) from Menton via the route de Sospel. ☎ 04-93-35-79-76. Closed on Monday and from 1 December to 15 January. Rooms between 360F and 410F. Half board compulsory in summer, for 360F and 410F per person. Menus from 150F to 200F. This *auberge* has panoramic views over the sea and interesting menus with dishes such as delicious fresh blue trout, rabbit with rosemary or chicken with prawns. Enjoy the garden and pool, or a little post-prandial siesta.

WHAT TO SEE

Menton Old Town

First, head for the jetty beside the old port, for a lovely view of the **old town**, built on a series of arches, against the picturesque backdrop of mountains. The harmony of the architecture is beautifully offset by the tall cypress trees in the cemetery. Take rue des Logettes to the right of rue St-Michel, to get to the small and serene place des Logettes. Carry on along the narrow former main street, rue Longue, under the porch; the street follows the route of the ancient Roman Via Julia Augusta.

★ Climb the cobbled steps of the Rampes du Chanoine-Ortmans or du Chanoine-Gouget (from rue Longue) to get up to the attractive *parvis* (square) in front of the basilica of **St-Michel**. Paved with a black-and-white pebble mosaic of the Grimaldi coats of arms, and with two ornate baroque churches and a dramatic sea view, this is one of the most delightful Italianate squares in France. It provides a charming venue for Menton's chamber music festival in August.

★ **Basilica St-Michel-Archange** (B1 on the map): open 10am–noon and 3–5pm. Closed on Saturday morning. The church has a multi-coloured baroque façade, two storeys and twin towers. Its interior was inspired by the church of the Annunziata in Genoa, and houses a main altarpiece by Manchello (1565), showing *St Michael*, *St Peter* and *St John the Baptist*. The frescoes under the arches recount the life of St Michael, and there's a splendid 17th-century organ in the chancel. The church owns some superb damask wall hangings from 1757, donated by Honoré III of Monaco, after his marriage in the church; they are occasionally – *very* rarely – hung over all the columns to form a gorgeous canopy. They are brought out only every five years or on the grandest of occasions.

★ **Eglise de l'Immaculée Conception ou des Pénitents-Blancs** (B1 on the map): at the back of place St-Michel, this little church has a Renaissance facade, elaborate festooning and stucco work, and ornamented vaulting. It can be visited between 3pm and 5pm; ask at the basilica St-Michel for the door to be opened. There's an interesting trompe-l'oeil under the dome of the altar, and a number of lanterns used in town processions.

★ Keep climbing and head for **rue Mattoni**, with its covered passageways, and then to rue de la Côte, which leads to the quiet **rue du Vieux-Château**, where washing is hung out to dry between ancient houses.

★ **Cimetière du Vieux Château**: open from 7am to 6pm in winter and from 7am to 8pm in summer. The ancient citadel was replaced in the 19th century by this romantic cemetery, which has four terraces and magnificent views to France on one side, and Italy on the other. Cypress trees add to the atmosphere.

The inscriptions on the tombs give a good idea of what was happening in Menton at the end of the 19th century. Wealthy foreigners were coming here, sometimes from very far afield, in search of the sun and the healing climate. Many were suffering from tuberculosis. Evelyn, wife of William Rosamond, came from Toronto, Canada, and died at the age of just 19. Next to her lies Veronica Christine, daughter of General Genkin Jones, who died aged 15. Not far away are the Russian-inscribed tombs of some grand princes and the last resting place of Henry Taylor of Dundee, who died aged 25 in 1888. William Webb-Ellis, credited with inventing the game of rugby, is buried here, as is eccentric British illustrator Aubrey Beardsley, a consumptive who came to Menton to end his days. The view from the cemetery looks out over Menton's old town and the tower of the basilica of St-Michel.

★ Head back down to **place St-Michel** via the very steep rue des Écoles-Pie, then take rue de Brea to the **Chapelle des Pénitents-Noirs**, at the bottom. Continue along rue du Général-Gallieni. All that remains of the former fortified surrounding wall are the gateways of St-Julien and St-Antoine, and the hexagonal tower.

★ **Rue St-Michel** is the commercial heart of the town, lined with shops and orange trees. Immediately on the left is the charming **place aux Herbes** with its tempting café terraces and plane trees. A second-hand market takes place here every Friday. Nearby are the covered market, flower market and the market square, all lively in the mornings, and a good place to try local specialities such as *pichade* (tomato and onions) and *barba juan*. Inside the market, buy a *fougasse Mentonnaise* (local pastry flavoured with orange, almond or aniseed), at Au Baiser du Mitron.

★ **Rue de Brea**, below the basilica of St-Michel, dates back to 1618. the ubiquitous Napoleon Bonaparte spent time at No. 3 in 1796, and General de Brea was born at No. 3; he was shot in 1848 by Parisian rebels.

Elsewhere in Menton

★ **Promenade du Soleil** (A–B2 on the map): Menton's 'sunny promenade' is well named and its benches are busy with retirees almost all year long. Almost 30 per cent of Menton's residents are past retirement age, more than in any other town in France, although young people are coming to the area in increasing numbers.

★ **Palais Carnolès**: avenue de la Madone, to the west of the town. ☎ 04-93-35-49-71. Open every day (except Tuesday) 10am–noon and 2–6pm. Free entry. The former summer residence, in 1715, of Antoine I, Prince of Monaco, was subsequently a casino and then a private home. In 1961, it became an art museum. Europe's biggest collection of citrus fruit trees is cultivated in its pretty gardens.

The art museum houses the Charles Wakefield Mori collection, bequeathed in 1959. Among the important works are Bréa's luminous *Madonna and*

Child with St Francis and pieces from the European schools of the 17th and 18th centuries. The School of Paris (1920–40) features, with works by André Derain and Raoul Dufy, among others. On the ground floor, modern and contemporary works by Paul Delvaux, Gromaire and Tal Coat are displayed, alongside previous winners from Menton's own arts festival.

★ **Jardins Biovès** (A1–2 on the map): in the town centre. The exotic and immaculate town gardens have palm trees, citrus trees, flowers and fountains, as well as splendid views over the surrounding mountains. A monument commemorates the return of Menton to French ownership. The gardens provide the venue for the **Fête du Citron** (lemon festival, *see below*), which takes place from just before Shrove Tuesday to the following Sunday. It dates back to the 1930s, when Menton was still the major producer of lemons on the Continent. In 1895, a flower and citrus fruit exhibition in the gardens of the Hôtel Riviera was proposed. It was so successful that it soon became a street festival with a procession of beauty queens in wooden floats, planted with orange and lemon trees, being added to the festivities. In 1936, the exhibition was held for the first time in the Jardins Biovès. Today, a walkway is built over the gardens for a bird's-eye view of the exhibits and the festival attracts huge numbers of visitors.

★ **Palais de l'Europe** (A1 on the map): avenue Boyer. The former casino, built in 1909, now houses a tourism and cultural centre, as well as a gallery of contemporary art.

★ **Hôtel de Ville** (1860) and **Cocteau's Salle des Mariages** (B1 on the map): town hall open 9am–12.30pm and 2–5pm. Closed on Saturday, Sunday and public holidays. Entrance fee: 10F.

The room in the town hall where marriages are celebrated was decorated by Cocteau in 1957–58. The colourful images include a fisherman and his bride, and the less cheerful tale of *Orpheus and Eurydice*. The fisherman's eye is represented by the Provencal motif of a fish. Marianne, symbol of the French Republic, makes her appearance in Cocteau's *Les Deux Mariannes*; according to French law, she must be present at every marriage.

★ **Musée Jean-Cocteau** (B1 on the map): in the 17th-century harbour bastion. ☎ 04-93-57-72-30. Open every day (except Tuesday and on public holidays). Entrance fee: 20F.

The three pebble mosaics outside the building are based on designs by Cocteau. Inside, the ground has been covered in a huge mosaic of a salamander, *La Salamandre*, in grey and white pebbles. The museum also houses Cocteau's first tapestry, *Judith et Holopherne*, examples of his set designs, and a collection of drawings. On the upper floor is Cocteau's *Les Innamorati* (*The Lovers*), splendid pastels portraying the love affairs of Mentonnais fisherfolk, the stunning ceramic *Animaux Fantastiques*, and a portrait of Cocteau by Picasso, displayed on an easel.

★ **Quai Napoléon-III**: the quay protects the old port with a 600-metre long sea wall. There's a wonderful view from here of Menton and the mountains.

★ **Musée Municipal de Préhistoire Régionale** (municipal museum of local prehistory) (B1 on the map): rue Lorédan-Larchey. In the town centre, not far from the town hall. ☎ 04-93-35-84-64. Open every day (except Tuesday) 10am–noon and 2–6pm. Free entry.

THE COAST FROM NICE TO MENTON

Run by friendly and well-informed staff, this museum has reconstructions of cave interiors found in the area, with bones, shaped stones and elephants' jaws. The highlight is the 30,000-year-old skeleton of 'Menton Man', discovered in one of the Grimaldi caves, now in Italian territory (*see* page 730). Seashells and deer's teeth have been calcified into the bone of its skull.

★ **Garavan**: this fabulous area benefits from the mildest temperatures on the Côte d'Azur. Near the frontier, the hills of Menton form an arch that faces the sea, sheltered from the northerly winds. A number of visitors from overseas moved in at the end of the 19th century, building elegant villas among the olive trees. A few of the villas remain, with a somewhat abandoned and nostalgic air.

WHAT TO DO

– **Bateaux de la French Riviera**: quai Napoléon-III, in the old port. ☎ 04-93-35-51-72. Daily boat trips from mid-April to end October. From 70F per adult (half price for under-10s), depending on destination. This rather touristy boat trip gives an unusual view of Monaco, St-Jean-Cap-Ferrat and the French Riviera from the sea.

– **Base nautique de l'office du tourisme** (watersports tourist office): ☎ 04-93-35-49-70. Office open all year. Menton is the perfect place for watersports, with 216 cloudless days per year, or so they say. This office organizes equipment rental and lessons.

SHOPPING

🔒 **Confitures Herbin**: 2 rue du Vieux-Collège. ☎ 04-93-57-20-29. This shop has specialized for many years in the manufacture of delicious preserves, including orange marmalade, as well as more unusual combinations and flavours, such as vegetable jams. Tours of the factory every Wednesday morning at 10.30am.

– **Ventimiglia market**: the town of Ventimiglia, over the border in Italy, has an extraordinary market every Friday, which completely takes over the town. The usual fake accessories (Vuitton, Chanel, Rolex, Lacoste, etc) are on offer – you're strongly advised not to indulge – but there are some real bargains to be had, too.

FESTIVALS

– **Fête du Citron**: the main theme of Menton's two-week lemon festival changes each year. There are exhibitions of orange and lemon trees, and orchids; lemons are used to make huge sculptures. According to Menton legend, Eve, chased out of the Garden of Eden with a lemon in her hand, decided to plant it in the best place she could find on earth – that place just happened to be Menton.

Parking is a serious problem during the lemon festival; hundreds of cars are towed away every year, and their drivers fined almost 1,000F. Don't risk it.

– **Fête des Bazaïs**: during this August festival, locals gather around a cauldron of bean soup in a tradition that goes back to the Middle Ages.

– **Festival de Musique** (chamber music festival): held on the square in front of the basilica of St-Michel during August. Music lovers have been coming to Menton for this highly-reputed festival for over 50 years.

– **Journées Méditerranéennes du Jardin** (Mediterranean garden open days): many of the private gardens of Menton (whose motto is 'My town is a garden') are opened to the public for several days in June and September. Find out more at the tourist office.

GARDENS

Some of the following sites may only be visited as part of a guided tour, except on open days in June and September (*see above*). For more information: Maison du Patrimoine (heritage office), rue Ciapetta. ☎ 04-92-10-33-66.

★ **Jardin Botanique Exotique de Val Rahmeh** (exotic botanic gardens in the grounds of the Villa Val Rameh): avenue St-Jacques. ☎ 04-93-35-86-72. Open to visitors between 1 May and 30 September, 10am–12.30pm and 3–6pm; rest of the year, open 10am–12.30pm and 2–5pm.

These gardens were planted by English botanists in the early 1900s, and since 1966 they have played a key role in the work of the Paris natural history museum. Waterlily ponds and fountains sit among the exotic plants, some of which bear edible fruits such as kiwis, avocados and bananas. The plants are grouped thematically, and the collection includes the only known example of the *Sophora toromiro*, the legendary tree of Easter Island. In all, there are more than 700 tropical and subtropical species. The garden has a fine view over the bay of Garavan, and a lovely avenue of palm trees leads to the villa.

★ **Jardin du Pian**: next door to the Jardin Botanique Exotique. This agreeable, rather sleepy garden has a fine grove of olive trees, some of which are more than 1,000 years old. Cultural events are held here in the summer.

★ **Villa Fontana Rosa**: avenue Blasco-Ibáñez. Bus No. 3 to Blasco-Ibáñez. Vicente Blasco Ibáñez lived in the Villa Fontana Rosa from 1922 until his death in 1928. The Spanish novelist, who wrote *The Horsemen of the Apocalypse*, brought in colourful tiles from his native Valencia, and there are tiled columns and wide fountains in his garden. The house is private and the gardens may only be visited on open days.

★ **Jardin des Colombières**: route des Colombières, in Garavan. The French artist and writer Ferdinand Bac (1859–1952) designed and built this garden between 1918 and 1927. Closed for a long time for restoration, it now takes visitors on a journey around the globe. There are cypress and olive trees, statues, ponds and fountains, as well as splendid views of the historic town and the bay. One of the trees is reputed to be the oldest carob in France.

★ **Serre de la Madone**: 74 route de Gorbio. ☎ 04-93-28-29-17. Bus No. 7 to Mer et Monts. Visits possible every day from 10am, or as part of a guided tour. The views are beautiful, but the emphasis is more on the rare species brought back by the garden's creator, Major Lawrence Johnston, from his many travels in Asia. It's a botanical paradise of acclimatized plants. The whole ensemble is a fine example of garden design, with ponds and fountains lending a nostalgic air, and the kind of intimacy that is found in many English gardens of the early 20th century.

★ **Jardin de Maria Serena**: promenade Reine-Astrid, near the frontier. This garden belongs to the town of Menton and may be visited as part of a guided tour. There's a superb view over Menton as you stand surrounded by subtropical plants and palm trees. The most surprising species flourish in the microclimate of this lemon town, which is sheltered from the cold north winds by the huge rocks that surround it.

Dip a toe into Italy and visit another botanical paradise, **Hanbury Gardens**, founded in 1867 by Sir Thomas Hanbury and his brother Daniel.

On the Italian Border

★ **Grimaldi caves**: cross the Garavan district and follow the seafront until you reach the customs point. Just over the border, behind a restaurant and to the right, you'll find the caves. Open every day (except Monday) from 9am to 1pm and from 2.30pm to 7.30pm. Entry fee.

It was in these caves that archaeologists found the bones of 'Menton Man', as the French call him (or 'Grimaldi Man', as he's known by the Italians). There's a small museum, although it is less interesting than the one in Menton, which displays the man himself. Follow the guide across the railway track to the **Caviglione Cave**, which is very tall but shallow, and contains cave drawings of a horse. The blackness of the rock is due not to fires lit by our ancient ancestors, but to steam from the trains. Not far away, the **Florestano cave** is more beautiful, but shows no evidence of life.

AROUND MENTON

See 'Menton: Getting Around', page 722 for details of bus services to the villages around Menton.

STE-AGNÈS

Take the D22 to the north, via avenue des Alliés. Clinging to a peak at a dizzying height of 780 metres (2,560 feet), the village seems to be a part of the rock of the cliff. It has all the typical features of a hilltop village of the Côte d'Azur, with a maze of vaulted passageways, narrow cobbled streets and ancient doorways. There are little shops selling all sorts of artefacts and craft pieces, and rue Longue, paved with pebbles, leads to a wonderful belvedere with a view of the Riviera and, on a good day, as far as Corsica.

The energetic can walk down to the **Collet de St-Sébastien**, where there's a chapel. From there, it's possible to follow a path to Menton or Gorbio.

WHERE TO EAT

✕ **Le Logis Sarrasin**: ☎ 04-93-35-86-89. Closed on Monday, and from 19 October to 19 November. Menus at 85F and 105F during the week. The *menu traditionnel* at 125F is served on Sunday. This friendly eating place offers excellent value for money, with generous portions of simple family cooking (rabbit with herbs, chicken with mushrooms, or hake with capers).

GORBIO

After driving along the walls of the Palais Carnolès, take the rue A.-Reglion to the right, and then the D23, which follows the fast-flowing Gorbio river. The road is lined with luxury villas hidden among olive trees. Gorbio, a hilltop village with sea views, is best known for its Corpus Christi festival, the **Procession aux Limaces**. As in Roquebrune (*see* page 719), the locals fill snail shells, called *limassa* in the Provençal dialect, with olive oil and light them with a small wick. Thousands of these tiny lamps line the streets and decorate the windowsills. The procession dates from the nocturnal arrival of a pope in the area and many pilgrims attend the annual event, which has its own individual character in Gorbio.

The twisting cobbled streets of the village, linked by arcades, show evidence of considerable age and usage. There's an impressive elm tree, planted in 1713, and an ancient fountain at the entrance to the village.

– **Walks**: walking paths with splendid sea views lead to Roquebrune (a 90-minute walk from the main square) and to Ste-Agnès.

WHERE TO EAT

✕ **Restaurant Beau Séjour**: on the village square. ☎ 04-93-41-46-15. Closed on Wednesday (from September to June), and in November. Menus from 125F to 185F. Tasty, sunshine-filled dishes such as *fleurs de courgettes en beignets* (deep-fried courgette flowers) or *lapin sauté à la marjolaine* (rabbit pan-fried with marjoram) served at tables right on the village square.

CASTELLAR

Two routes lead to Castellar from Menton – either follow the D24 via the Promenade du Val de Menton or take the route des Ciappes. They join up again at the place known as La Pinède.

The hilltop village of Castellar is the departure point for several walks along marked paths linked to the long-distance GR52 footpath. There's a lovely view of the sea from the terrace of the **Hôtel des Alpes**. The rue de la République goes right through the former **Palais des Lascaris**, and there's a moving chapel in the cemetery further down.

– **Footpaths**: there are paths to **Le Restaud** (1,145 metres/3,755 feet) taking around two hours; **Le Grammont** (1,380 metres/4,526 feet), about three hours; and to the **ruins of old Castellar**, about one hour.

WHERE TO STAY AND EAT

Campsite

🛏 ✕ **Ferme St-Bernard**: with Daniel and Evelyne Bovis. ☎ 04-93-28-28-31. A pitch costs 25F. Meals for 90F or 130F, without wine. Tucked into the mountainside, the farm is accessible via four-wheel-drive vehicles only. The owner will come to collect you. You're in the heart of the countryside here, and the difficult camping terrain is made up for by the very warm welcome. You can hire a caravan if you prefer. Dogs, ducks and deer all live together in rural harmony. The food is straight from the farm and therefore even more delicious.

☆☆ Moderate

🛏 ✕ **Hôtel des Alpes**: 1 place Clemenceau. ☎ 04-93-35-82-83. Fax: 04-93-28-24-95. The hotel is closed on Friday, as well as in November and December. The restaurant is open every day in summer. Double rooms with shower cost from 250F, and half board in summer cost 250F. Menus cost 90F and 110F. The rooms are small and clean, and some have grand views. It's a peaceful spot and the food is regional and tasty. Try the home-made terrine, prawns *à la provençale,* rabbit with herbs and game in season.

Understanding the Menu

During your stay you are sure to have a few meals out in a restaurant – after all, what would a trip to France be without sampling the cuisine? This list has been compiled to help you understand the menu and enjoy your meal. Bon appétit!

À point medium rare
Abats offal
Abricot apricot
Acarne sea-bream
Affiné(e) improve, ripen, mature (common term with cheese)
Africaine (à l') african style: with aubergines, tomatoes, ceps
Agneau lamb
Agrumes citrus fruits
Aigre-doux sweet-sour
Aiguillette thin slice
Ail garlic
Aile (Aileron) wing (winglet)
Aïoli mayonnaise, garlic, olive oil
Algues seaweed
Aligot purée of potatoes, cream, garlic, butter and fresh Tomme de Cantal (or Laguiole) cheese
Allemande (à l') German style: with sauerkraut and sausages
Alsacienne (à l') Alsace style: with sauerkraut, sausages and sometimes foie gras
Amande almond
Amandine almond-flavoured
Amer bitter
Américaine (à l') Armoricaine (à l') sauce with dry white wine, cognac, tomatoes, shallots
Amuse-gueule appetizer
Ananas pineapple
Anchoiade anchovy crust
Anchois anchovy
Ancienne (à l') in the old style
Andouille smoked tripe sausage
Andouillette small chitterling (tripe) sausage
Aneth dill
Anglaise (à l') plain boiled
Anguille eel
Anis aniseed

Arachide peanut
Arc-en-ciel rainbow trout
Artichaud artichoke
Asperge asparagus
Assaisonné flavoured or seasoned with; to dress a salad
Assiette (de) plate (of)
Aubergine aubergine, eggplant
Aumônière pancake drawn up into shape of beggar's purse
Auvergnate (à l') Auvergne style: with cabbage, sausage and bacon
Avocat avocado pear
Baba au rhum sponge dessert with rum syrup
Baguette long bread loaf
Baie berry
Baigné bathed or lying in
Banane banana
Bar sea-bass
Barbeau de mer red mullet
Barbue brill
Basilic basil
Basquaise (à la) Basque style: Bayonne ham, rice and peppers
Baudroie monkfish, anglerfish
Bavette skirt of beef
Béarnaise thick sauce with egg yolks, shallots, butter, white wine and tarragon vinegar
Béchamel creamy white sauce
Beignet fritter
Belle Hélène poached pear with ice cream and chocolate sauce
Berrichonne bordelaise sauce
Betterave beetroot
Beurre (Échiré) butter (finest butter from Poitou-Charentes)
Beurre blanc sauce with butter, shallots, wine vinegar and sometimes dry white wine

Beurre noir sauce with brown butter, vinegar, parsley
Bière à la pression beer on tap
Bière en bouteille bottled beer
Bifteck steak
Bigarade (à la) orange sauce
Bisque shellfish soup
Blanc (de volaille) white breast (of chicken); can also describe white fish fillet or white vegetables
Blanchaille whitebait
Blanquette white stew
Blé corn or wheat
Blettes swiss chard
Blinis small, thick pancakes
Boeuf à la mode beef braised in red wine
Boeuf Stroganoff beef, sour cream, onions, mushrooms
Bombe ice-cream
Bonne femme (à la) white wine sauce, shallots, mushrooms
Bordelaise (à la) Bordeaux style: brown sauce with shallots, red wine, beef bone marrow
Boudin sausage-shaped mixture
Boudin blanc white coloured mixture; pork and sometimes chicken
Boudin noir black pudding
Bouillabaisse Mediterranean fish stew and soup
Bouillon broth, light consommé
Bouquet garni bunch of herbs used for flavouring
Bourguignonne (à la) Burgundy style: red wine, onions, bacon and mushrooms
Bourride creamy fish soup with aioli
Brandade de morue salt cod
Bretonne sauce with celery, leeks, beans and mushrooms
Brioche sweet yeast bread
Brioche sweet yeast bread
Brochet pike
Brochette (de) meat or fish on a skewer
Brouillé scrambled
Brûlé(e) toasted
Bruxelloise sauce with asparagus, butter and eggs

Cabillaud cod
Cacahouète roasted peanut
Cacao cocoa
Café coffee
Caille quail
Cajou cashew nut
Calmar (Calamar) inkfish, squid
Campagne country style
Canard duck
Caneton (Canette) duckling
Cannelle cinnamon
Carbonnade braised beef in beer, onions and bacon
Carré chop
Casse-croûte snack
Cassis blackcurrant
Cassolette small pan
Cassoulet casserole of beans, sausage and/or pork, goose, duck
Cèpe fine, delicate mushroom
Cerise (noire) cherry (black)
Cerneau walnut
Cervelas pork garlic sausage
Cervelle brains
Champignons (des bois) mushrooms (from the woods)
Chanterelle apricot coloured mushroom
Chantilly whipped cream sugar
Charcuterie cold meat cuts
Charcutière sauce with onions, white wine, gherkins
Chasseur sauce with white wine, mushrooms, shallots
Chateaubriand thick fillet steak
Chaussons pastry turnover
Chemise (en) pastry covering
Chicon chicory
Chicorée curly endive
Chipiron see Calmar
Choix (au) a choice of
Chou (vert) cabbage
Choucroute souring of vegetables, usually with cabbage (sauerkraut), peppercorns, boiled ham, potatoes and Strasbourg sausages
Chou-fleur cauliflower
Chou rouge red cabbage
Choux (pâte à) pastry

Ciboule spring onions
Cidre cider
Ciboulette chive
Citron (vert) lemon (lime)
Citronelle lemon grass
Civet stew
Clafoutis cherries in pancake batter
Clou de girofle clove (spice)
Cochon pig
Cochonailles pork products
Cocotte (en) cooking pot
Coeur (de) heart (of)
Coing quince
Colin hake
Compote stewed fruit
Concassé(e) coarsely chopped
Concombre cucumber
Confit(e) preserved or candied
Confiture jam
Confiture d'orange marmalade
Consommé clear soup
Coq (au vin) chicken in red wine sauce (or name of wine)
Coque (à la) soft-boiled or served in shell
Coquillage shellfish
Coquille St-Jacques scallop
Coriandre coriander
Cornichon gherkin
Côte d'agneau lamb chop
Côte de boeuf side of beef
Côte de veau veal chop
Côtelette chop
Coulis de thick sauce (of)
Courge pumpkin
Couscous crushed semolina
Crabe crab
Crécy with carrots and rice
Crème cream
Crème anglaise light custard sauce
Crème brûlée same, less sugar and cream, with praline (*see* Brûlée)
Crème pâtissière custard filling
Crêpe thin pancake
Crêpe Suzette sweet pancake with orange liqueur sauce
Cresson watercress
Crevette grise shrimp
Crevette rose prawn

Croque Monsieur toasted cheese or ham sandwich
Croustade small pastry mould with various fillings
Croûte (en) pastry crust (in)
Cru raw
Crudité raw vegetable
Crustacés shell fish
Cuisse (de) leg (of)
Cuissot (de) haunch (of)
Cuit cooked
Datte date
Daube stew (various types)
Daurade sea-bream
Décaféiné decaffeinated coffee
Dégustation tasting
Diane (á la) pepper cream sauce
Dieppoise (à la) Dieppe style: white wine, cream, mussels, shrimps
Dijonaise (à la) with mustard sauce
Dinde young hen turkey
Dindon turkey
Dorade sea-bream
Doux (douce) sweet
Échalotte shallot
Écrevisse freshwater crayfish
Émincé thinly sliced
Encre squid ink, used in sauces
Endive chicory
Entrecôte entrecôte, rib steak
Entremets sweets
Épaule shoulder
Épice spice
Épinard spinach
Escabèche fish (or poultry) marinated in court-bouillon; cold
Escalope thinly cut (meat or fish)
Escargot snail
Espadon swordfish
Estouffade stew with onions, herbs, mushrooms, red or white wine (perhaps garlic)
Estragon tarragon flavoured
Farci(e) stuffed
Farine flour
Faux-filet sirloin steak
Fenouil fennel
Fermière mixture of onions, carrots, turnips, celery, etc.
Feuille de vigne vine leaf

Feuilleté light flaky pastry
Fève broad bean
Ficelle (à la) tied in a string
Ficelles thin loaves of bread
Figue fig
Filet fillet
Financière (à la) Madeira sauce with truffles
Fine de claire oyster (*see* Huîtres)
Fines herbes mixture of parsley, chives, tarragon, etc.
Flageolet kidney bean
Flamande (à la) Flemish style: bacon, carrots, cabbage, potatoes and turnips
Flambée flamed
Flamiche puff pastry tart
Foie liver
Foie de veau calves liver
Foie gras goose liver
Fond d'artichaut artichoke heart
Fondu(e) (de fromage) melted cheese with wine
Forestière bacon and mushrooms
Four (au) baked in oven
Fourré stuffed
Frais fresh or cool
Fraise strawberry
Fraise des bois wild strawberry
Framboise raspberry
Frappé frozen or ice cold
Friandise sweets (petits fours)
Fricassée braised in sauce or butter, egg yolks and cream
Frisé(e) curly
Frit fried
Frites chips/french fries
Friture small fried fish
Fromage cheese
Fromage de tête brawn
Fruit de la passion passion fruit
Fruits confits crystallised fruit
Fruits de mer seafood
Fumé smoked
Galette pastry, pancake or cake
Gamba large prawn
Ganache chocolate and crème fraîche mixture used to fill cakes
Garbure (Garbue) vegetable soup
Gâteau cake
Gauffre waffle
Gelée aspic jelly

Genièvre juniper
Gésier gizzard
Gibelotte *see* Fricassée
Gibier game
Gigot (de) leg of lamb; can describe other meat or fish
Gingembre ginger
Girofle clove
Glacé(e) iced, crystallized, glazed
Glace ice-cream
Gougère round-shaped, egg and cheese choux pastry
Goujon gudgeon
Goujonnettes (de) small fried pieces (of)
Gourmandises sweetmeats; can describe fruits de mer
Graisse fat
Gratin browned
Gratin Dauphinois potato dish with cheese, cream and garlic
Gratin Savoyard potato dish with cheese and butter
Gratiné(e) sauced dish browned with butter, cheese, breadcrumbs, etc.
Gravette oyster (*see* Huîtres)
Grenouille (cuisses de grenouilles) frog (frogs' legs)
Gribiche mayonnaise sauce with gherkins, capers, hardboiled egg yolks and herbs
Grillade grilled meat
Grillé(e) grilled
Griotte (Griottine) bitter red cherry
Gros sel coarse rock or sea salt
Groseille à maquereau gooseberry
Groseille noire blackcurrant
Groseille rouge redcurrant
Gruyère hard, mild cheese
Hachis minced or chopped-up
Hareng herring
  à l'huile cured in oil
  fumé kippered
  salé bloater
  saur smoked
Haricot bean
Haricot blanc dried white bean
Haricot vert green/French bean

Hollandaise sauce with butter, egg yolk and lemon juice
Homard lobster
Hongroise (à la) Hungarian style: sauce with tomato and paprika
Huile oil
Huîtres oysters
Les claires: the oyster-fattening beds in Marennes terrain (part of the Charente Estuary, between Royan and Rochefort, in Poitou-Charentes).
Flat-shelled oysters: *Belons* (from the River Belon in Brittany); *Gravettes:* from Arcachon in the South West);
both the above are cultivated in their home oyster beds.
Marennes are those transferred from Brittany and Arcachon to les claires, where they finish their growth.
Dished oysters (sometimes called *portuguaises*):
these breed mainly in the Gironde and Charentes estuaries; they mature at Marennes.
Fines de claires and *spéciales* are the largest; *huîtres de parc* are standard sized.
All this lavish care covers a time span of two to four years.
Hure (de) head (of); brawn, jellied
Île flottante unmoulded soufflé of beaten egg with white sugar
Imam bayeldi aubergine with rice, onions, and sautéed tomatoes
Infusion herb tea
Italienne (à l') Italian style: artichokes, mushrooms, pasta
Jalousie latticed fruit or jam tart
Jambon ham
Jambonneau knuckle of pork
Jambonnette boned and stuffed (knuckle of ham or poultry)
Jarret de veau stew of shin of veal
Jarreton cooked pork knuckle
Jerez sherry
Joue (de) cheek (of)
Julienne thinly-cut vegetables: also ling (cod family)
Jus juice

Lait milk
Laitue lettuce
Lamproie eel-like fish
Langouste spiny lobster or crawfish
Langoustine Dublin Bay prawn
Langue tongue
Lapereau young rabbit
Lapin rabbit
Lard bacon
Lardons strips of bacon
Laurier bay-laurel, sweet bay leaf
Léger (Légère) light
Légume vegetable
Lièvre hare
Limaçon snail
Limande lemon sole
Limon lime
Lit bed
Lotte de mer monkfish, anglerfish
Loup de mer sea-bass
Louvine (Loubine) grey mullet, like a sea-bass (Basque name)
Lyonnaise (à la) Lyonnais style: sauce with wine, onions, vinegar
Mâche lamb's lettuce; small dark green leaf
Madeleine tiny sponge cake
Madère sauce *demi-glace* and Madeira wine
Magret (de canard) breast (of duck); now used for other poultry
Maïs maize flour
Maison (de) of the restaurant
Maître d'hôtel sauce with butter, parsley and lemon
Manchons *see* Goujonnettes
Mangetout edible peas and pods
Mangue mango
Manière (de) style (of)
Maquereau mackerel
Maraîchère (à la) market-gardener style; velouté sauce with vegetables
Marais marsh or market garden
Marbré marbled
Marc pure spirit
Marcassin young wild boar
Marché market
Marchand de vin sauce with red wine, chopped shallots

Marengo tomatoes, mushrooms, olive oil, white wine, garlic, herbs
Marennes (blanches) flat-shelled oysters (*see* Huîtres)
Marennes (vertes) green shell oysters
Marinières *see* Moules
Marmite stewpot
Marrons chestnuts
Médaillon (de) round piece (of)
Mélange mixture or blend
Ménagère (à la) housewife style: onions, potatoes, peas, turnips and carrots
Mendiant (fruits de) mixture of figs, almonds and raisins
Menthe mint
Merguez spicy grilled sausage
Merlan whiting (in Provence the word is used for hake)
Merlu hake
Merluche dried cod
Mesclum mixture of salad leaves
Meunière sauce with butter, parsley, lemon (sometimes oil)
Meurette red wine sauce
Miel honey
Mignon (de) small round piece
Mignonette coarsely ground white pepper
Mijoté(e) cooked slowly in water
Milanaise (à la) Milan style: dipped in breadcrumbs, egg, cheese
Mille-feuille puff pastry with numerous thin layers
Mirabeau anchovies, olives
Mirabelle golden plums
Mitonée (de) soup (of)
Mode (à la) in the manner of
Moelle beef marrow
Moelleux au chocolat chocolate dessert (cake)
Montmorency with cherries
Morilles edible, dark brown, honeycombed fungi
Mornay cheese sauce
Morue cod
Moules mussels
Moules marinières mussels cooked in white wine and shallots
Mousseline hollandaise sauce with whipped cream

Moutarde mustard
Mouton mutton
Mûre mulberry
Mûre sauvage (de ronce) blackberry
Muscade nutmeg
Museau de porc (de boeuf) sliced muzzle of pork (beef) with shallots and parsley with vinaigrette
Myrtille bilberry (blueberry)
Mystère a meringue dessert with ice cream and chocolate; also cone-shaped ice cream
Nature plain
Navarin stew (usually lamb)
Navets turnips
Nid nest
Noilly sauce based on vermouth
Noisette hazelnut
Noisette sauce of lightly browned butter
Noisette (de) round piece (of)
Noix nuts
Noix de veau topside of leg (veal)
Normande (à la) Normandy style: fish sauce with mussels, shrimps, mushrooms, eggs and cream
Nouille noodle
Nouveau (Nouvelle) new or young
Noyau sweet liqueur from crushed stones (usually cherries)
Oeufs à la coque soft-boiled eggs
Oeufs à la neige *see* Île flottante
Oeufs à la poêle fried eggs
Oeufs brouillés scrambled eggs
Oeufs en cocotte eggs cooked in individual dishes in a bain-marie
Oeufs durs hard-boiled eggs
Oeufs moulés poached eggs
Oie goose
Oignon onion
Ombrine fish, like sea-bass
Onglet flank of beef
Oreille (de porc) ear (pig's)
Oreillette sweet fritter, flavoured with orange flower water
Origan oregano (herb)
Orléannaise Orléans style: chicory and potatoes
Ortie nettle

Os bone
Osso bucco à la niçoise veal braised with orange zest, tomatoes, onions and garlic
Pain bread
Pain de campagne round white loaf
Pain d'épice spiced honey cake
Pain de mie square white loaf
Pain de seigle rye bread
Pain complet/entier wholemeal
Pain grillé toast
Pain doré/Pain perdu bread soaked in milk and eggs and fried
Paleron shoulder
Palmier palm-shaped sweet puff pastry
Palmier (coeur de) palm (heart)
Palombe wood pigeon
Palomête fish, like sea-bass
Palourde clam
Pamplemousse grapefruit
Panaché mixed
Pané(e) breadcrumbed
Papillote (en) cooked in oiled paper or foil
Paquets (en) parcels
Parfait (de) mousse (of)
Paris-Brest cake of *choux* pastry, filled with butter cream and almonds
Parisienne (à la) leeks, potatoes
Parmentier potatoes
Pastèque watermelon
Pastis (sauce au) aniseed based
Pâte pastry, dough or batter
Pâte à choux cream puff pastry
Pâte brisée short crust pastry
Pâté en croûte baked in pastry crust
Pâtes fraîches fresh pasta
Pâtisserie pastry
Paupiettes thin slices of meat or fish, used to wrap fillings
Pavé (de) thick slice (of)
Pavot (graines de) poppy seeds
Paysan(ne) (à la) country style
Peau (de) skin (of)
Pêche peach
Pêcheur fisherman
Pèlerine scallop

Perche perch
Perdreau young partridge
Perdrix partridge
Périgourdine (à la) goose liver and sauce *Périgueux*
Périgueux sauce with truffles and Madeira
Persil parsley
Persillade mixture of chopped parsley and garlic
Petit gris small snail
Pétoncle small scallop
Picholine large green table olives
Pied de cheval large oyster
Pied de mouton blanc cream coloured mushroom
Pied de porc pig's trotter
Pigeonneau young pigeon
Pignon pine nut
Piment (doux) pepper (sweet)
Pintade (pintadeau) guinea fowl (young guinea fowl)
Piperade omelette or scrambled eggs with tomatoes, peppers, onions and sometimes ham
Piquante (sauce) sharp tasting sauce with shallots, capers and wine
Pissenlit dandelion leaf
Pistache green pistachio nut
Pistou vegetable soup bound with *pommade* (thick smooth paste)
Plateau (de) plate (of)
Pleurote mushroom
Poché(e), pochade poached
Poêlé fried
Poire pear
Poireau leek
Pois pea
Poisson fish
Poitrine breast
Poitrine fumée smoked bacon
Poitrine salée unsmoked bacon
Poivre noir black pepper
Poivron (doux) pepper (sweet)
Polonaise Polish style: with buttered breadcrumbs, parsley, hard-boiled eggs
Pomme apple
Pommes de terre potatoes
  dauphine croquettes
  château roast

frites chips
gratinées browned with cheese
Lyonnaise sautéed with onions
vapeur boiled
Porc (carré de) loin of pork
Porc (côte de) loin of pork
Porcelet suckling pig
Porto (au) port
Portugaise (à la) Portuguese style: fried onions and tomatoes
Portugaises oysters with long, deep shells (*see* Huîtres)
Potage thick soup
Pot-au-feu clear meat broth served with the meat
Potimarron pumpkin
Poularde large hen
Poulet chicken
Poulet à la broche spit-roasted chicken
Poulpe octopus
Poussin small baby chicken
Pré-salé (agneau de) lamb raised on salt marshes
Primeur young vegetable
Profiterole puffs of *choux* pastry, filled with custard
Provençale (à la) Provençal style: tomatoes, garlic, olive oil, etc.
Prune plum
Pruneau prune
Quenelle light dumpling of fish or poultry
Queue tail
Queue de boeuf oxtail
Quiche lorraine open flan of cheese, ham or bacon
Raclette scrapings from specially-made and heated cheese
Radis radish
Ragoût stew, usually meat but can describe other ingredients
Raie (bouclée) skate (type of)
Raifort horseradish
Raisin grape
Ramier wood pigeon
Rapé(e) grated or shredded
Rascasse scorpion fish
Ratatouille aubergines, onions, courgettes, garlic, red peppers and tomatoes in olive oil
Réglisse liquorice

Reine-Claude greengage
Rémoulade sauce of mayonnaise, mustard, capers, herbs, anchovy
Rillettes (d'oie) potted pork (goose)
Ris d'agneau lamb sweetbreads
Ris de veau veal sweetbreads
Riz rice
Robe de chambre jacket potato
Rognon kidney
Romarin rosemary
Rôti roast
Rouget red mullet
Rouget barbet red mullet
Rouille orange-coloured sauce with peppers, garlic and saffron
Roulade (de) roll (of)
Roulé(e) rolled (usually crêpe)
Sabayon sauce of egg yolks, wine
Sablé shortbread
Safran saffron
Saignant(e) underdone, rare
St-Jaques (coquille) scallop
St-Pierre John Dory
Salade niçoise tomatoes, beans, potatoes, black olives, anchovy, lettuce, olive oil, perhaps tuna
Salade panachée mixed salad
Salade verte green salad
Salé salted
Salmis red wine sauce
Salsifis salsify (vegetable)
Sandre freshwater fish, like perch
Sang blood
Sanglier wild boar
Saucisse freshly-made sausage
Saucisson large, dry sausage
Saucisson cervelas saveloy
Sauge sage
Saumon salmon
Saumon fumé smoked salmon
Sauvage wild
Scipion cuttlefish
Sel salt
Soja (pousse de) soy bean (soy bean sprout)
Soja (sauce de) soy sauce
Soubise onion sauce
Sucre sugar
Tapenade olive spread
Tartare raw minced beef

Tartare (sauce) sauce with mayonnaise, onions, capers, herbs

Tarte open flan

Tarte Tatin upside down tart of caramelized apples and pastry

Terrine container in which mixed meats/fish are baked; served cold

Tête de veau vinaigrette calf's head vinaigrette

Thé tea

Thermidor grilled lobster with browned béchamel sauce

Thon tuna fish

Thym thyme

Tiède mild or lukewarm

Tilleul lime tree

Tomate tomato

Topinambour Jerusalem artichoke

Torte sweet-filled flan

Tortue turtle

Tournedos fillet steak (small end)

Touron a cake, pastry or loaf made from almond paste and filled with candied fruits and nuts

Tourte (Tourtière) covered savoury tart

Tourteau large crab

Tranche slice

Tranche de boeuf steak

Traver de porc spare rib of pork

Tripoux stuffed mutton tripe

Truffade a huge sautéed pancake or galette with bacon, garlic and Cantal cheese

Truffe truffle; black, exotic, tuber

Truite trout

Truite saumonée salmon trout

Turbot (turbotin) turbot

Vacherin ice-cream, meringue, cream

Vapeur (à la) steamed

Veau veal

Veau pané (escalope de) thin slice of veal in flour, eggs and breadcrumbs

Venaison venison

Verveine verbena

Viande meat

Vichyssoise creamy potato and leek soup, served cold

Viennoise coated with egg and breadcrumbs, fried (usually veal)

Vierge literally virgin (best olive oil, the first pressing)

Vierge (sauce) olive oil sauce

Vinaigre (de) wine vinegar or vinegar of named fruit

Vinaigrette (à la) French dressing with wine vinegar, oil, etc.

Volaille poultry

Yaourt yogurt

© *Richard Binns*

Index